The Sporting News

T4-AFX-835

PRO FOOTBALL GUIDE

1997 EDITION

Editors/Pro Football Guide
CRAIG CARTER
DAVE SLOAN

The Sporting News

━━━PUBLISHING CO.━━━

Efrem Zimbalist III, President and Chief Executive Officer, Times Mirror Magazines; **James H. Nuckols,** President, The Sporting News; **Francis X. Farrell,** Senior Vice President, Publisher; **John D. Rawlings,** Senior Vice President, Editorial Director; **John Kastberg,** Vice President, General Manager; **Kathy Kinkeade,** Vice President, Operations; **Steve Meyerhoff,** Executive Editor; **Mike Huguenin,** Assistant Managing Editor; **Joe Hoppel,** Senior Editor; **Mark Bonavita and Sean Stewart,** Assistant Editors; **Marilyn Kasal,** Production Director; **Bob Parajon,** Prepress Director; **Chris Placzek,** Database Analyst; **Michael Behrens and Christen Webster,** Macintosh Production Artists.

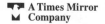

A Times Mirror
Company

CONTENTS

ON THE COVER: Brett Favre led the Packers to a Super Bowl victory and was named THE SPORTING NEWS Player of the Year. (Photo by Albert Dickson/THE SPORTING NEWS.)

Spine photo of Steve Young by Albert Dickson/THE SPORTING NEWS.

NFL week-by-week and postseason highlights written by Mark Bonavita, Dennis Dillon, Joe Hoppel, Leslie Gibson McCarthy, Carl Moritz, Dave Sloan, Ray Slover, Sean Stewart, Larry Wigge and George Winkler of THE SPORTING NEWS.

NFL statistics compiled by STATS, Inc., Lincolnwood, Ill.

ISBN: 0-89204-577-9

10 9 8 7 6 5 4 3 2 1

1997 SEASON

NFL directory
Team information
Schedule
College draft
Playoff plan

NFL DIRECTORY

COMMISSIONER'S OFFICE

Address
280 Park Avenue
New York, NY 10017
Phone
212-450-2000
212-681-7573 (FAX)
Commissioner
Paul Tagliabue
President
Neil Austrian
Sr. v.p. of comm. and gov't affairs
Joe Browne
Sr. v.p. of business development
Roger Goodell
Sr. v.p. of broadcasting and productions
Val Pinchbeck Jr.
Chief financial officer
Tom Spock
Executive director of special events
Jim Steeg
Vice president-internal audit
Tom Sullivan
V.p.-law/enterprises, broadcast & finance
Frank Hawkins

Exec. v.p. for labor rel./chairman NFLMC
Harold Henderson
Vice president/general counsel
Dennis Curran
V.p. for operations and compliance
Peter Ruocco
Dir. of player personnel/football op.
Joel Bussert
Director of player programs
Lem Burnham
Director of communications
Greg Aiello
Director of international public relations
Pete Abitante
Director of information, AFC
Leslie Hammond
Director of information, NFC
Reggie Roberts
Director of broadcasting services
Dick Maxwell
Director of broadcasting research
Joe Ferreira
Asst. dir. of broadcasting/productions
Nancy Behar

Exec. director club relations & stadium management
Joe Ellis
League secretary
Jan Van Duser
Director of football development
Gene Washington
Assistant director of game operations
Tim Davey
Director of administration
John Buzzeo
Treasurer
Joe Siclare
Director of officiating
Jerry Seeman
Supervisors of officials
Al Hynes
Ron DeSouza
Director of security
Milt Ahlrich

OTHER ORGANIZATIONS

NFL MANAGEMENT COUNCIL
Address
280 Park Avenue
New York, NY 10017
Phone
212-450-2000
212-681-7590 (FAX)
Exec. v.p. for labor rel./chairman NFLMC
Harold Henderson
Sr. vice president and general counsel
Dennis Curran
Director of labor relations
Lal Heneghan
Assistant general counsel
Buckley Briggs
Labor relations counsel
Belinda Lerner
Rapheal Prevot
Ed Tighe
Sr. v.p. of operations and compliance
Peter Ruocco
Director of compliance
Michael Keenan
V.p. of player & employee development
Lem Burnham
Director of player personnel
Joel Bussert

PRO FOOTBALL HALL OF FAME
Address
2121 George Halas Drive, N.W.
Canton, OH 44708
Phone
330-456-8207
330-456-8175 (FAX)
Executive director
John W. Bankert
V.p./communications & exhibits
Joe Horrigan
V.p./operations and marketing
Dave Motts
V.p./merchandising & licensing
Judy Kuntz

PRO FOOTBALL WRITERS OF AMERICA
President
Steve Schoenfeld, Arizona Republic
First vice president
John Clayton, Tacoma Morning News Tribune
Second vice president
Adam Schefter, Rocky Mountain News
Secretary/treasurer
Howard Balzer

NFL FILMS, INC.
Address
330 Fellowship Road
Mt. Laurel, NJ 08054
Phone
609-778-1600
609-722-6779 (FAX)
President
Steve Sabol

NFL PLAYERS ASSOCIATION
Address
2021 L Street, N.W.
Washington, DC 20036
Phone
202-463-2200
202-835-9775 (FAX)
Executive director
Gene Upshaw
Assistant executive director
Doug Allen
Dir. P.R. and NFLPA retired players org.
Frank Woschitz
General counsel
Richard Berthelsen
Director of communications
Carl Francis
Director of player development
Stacey Robinson

NFL PROPERTIES
Address
280 Park Avenue
New York, NY 10017
Phone
212-450-2000
212-758-4239 (FAX)
Interim chief operating officer
Sara Levinson
V.p., world wide retail licensing
Jim Connelly
V.p., development/special events
Don Garber
V.p., corporate sponsorship
Jim Schwebel
V.p., marketing
Howard Handler
V.p., club marketing
Mark Holtzman
V.p., advertising and design
Bruce Burke
V.p., legal and business affairs
Gary Gertzog

NFL ALUMNI ASSOCIATION
Address
6550 N. Federal Highway
Suite 400
Ft. Lauderdale, FL 33308-1400
Phone
954-492-1220
954-492-8297 (FAX)
Executive director/CEO
Frank Krauser
Vice president/alumni relations
Tim Williams
Chairman of the board
Randy Minniear
Director of public relations
Remy Mackowski

ARIZONA CARDINALS
NFC EASTERN DIVISION

1996 REVIEW
RESULTS

Sept. 1—at Indianapolis	L	13 -20
Sept. 8—MIAMI	L	10-38
Sept.15—at New England	L	0-31
Sept.22—at New Orleans	W	28-14
Sept.29—ST. LOUIS (OT)	W	31-28
Oct. 6—Open date		
Oct. 13—at Dallas	L	3-17
Oct. 20—TAMPA BAY	W	13-9
Oct. 27—N.Y. JETS	L	21-31
Nov. 3—at N.Y. Giants	L	8-16
Nov. 10—at Washington (OT)	W	37-34
Nov. 17—N.Y. GIANTS	W	31-23
Nov. 24—PHILADELPHIA	W	36-30
Dec. 1—at Minnesota	L	17-41
Dec. 8—DALLAS	L	6-10
Dec. 15—WASHINGTON	W	27-26
Dec. 22—at Philadelphia	L	19-29

RECORDS/RANKINGS

1996 regular-season record: 7-9 (4th in NFC East); 4-4 in division; 7-5 in conference; 5-3 at home; 2-6 on road.
Team record last five years: 30-50 (.375, ranks 22nd in league in that span).

1996 team rankings:	No.	NFC	NFL
Total offense	*324.4	6	13
Rushing offense	*93.9	13	25
Passing offense	*230.5	3	6
Scoring offense	300	9	22
Total defense	*335.1	12	21
Rushing defense	*116.4	9	21
Passing defense	*218.7	13	21
Scoring defense	397	13	26
Takeaways	25	12	25
Giveaways	35	12	25
Turnover differential	-10	13	26
Sacks	28	15	T29
Sacks allowed	36	T7	T13

*Yards per game.

TEAM LEADERS

Scoring (kicking): Kevin Butler, 59 pts. (17/19 PATs, 14/17 FGs).
Scoring (touchdowns): Larry Centers, 54 pts. (2 rushing, 7 receiving).
Passing: Boomer Esiason, 2,293 yds. (339 att., 190 comp., 56.0%, 11 TDs, 14 int.).
Rushing: LeShon Johnson, 634 yds. (141 att., 4.5 avg., 3 TDs).
Receptions: Rob Moore, 58 (1,016 yds., 17.5 avg., 4 TDs).
Interceptions: Aeneas Williams, 6 (89 yds., 1 TD).
Sacks: Simeon Rice, 12.5.
Punting: Jeff Feagles, 43.8 avg. (76 punts, 3,328 yds., 1 blocked).
Punt returns: Marcus Dowdell, 8.7 avg. (34 att., 297 yds., 0 TDs).
Kickoff returns: Leeland McElroy, 21.3 avg. (54 att., 1,148 yds., 0 TDs).

1997 SEASON
CLUB DIRECTORY

President
William V. Bidwill
Vice president
William Bidwill Jr.
Vice president, general counsel
Michael Bidwill
Secretary and general counsel
Thomas J. Guilfoil
Vice president
Larry Wilson
Vice president/player personnel
Bob Ferguson
Treasurer/chief financial officer
Charley Schlegel
Assistant to the president
Joe Woolley
Vice president, sales
John Shean
Director/marketing
Joe Castor
Ticket manager
Steve Bomar
Director/community affairs
Adele Harris
Director/public relations
Paul Jensen
Media coordinator
Greg Gladysiewski
Player program/community outreach
Garth Jax
Director/college scouting
Bo Bolinger
Director/pro scouting
Keith Kidd
Scouts
Jim Carmody
Jerry Hardaway
Bob Mazie
Cole Proctor
Jim Stanley

Head coach
Vince Tobin

Assistant coaches
George "Geep" Chryst (tight ends/ quality control)
Alan Everest (special teams)
Joe Greene (defensive line)
Dick Jamieson (offensive coord.)
David Marmie (defensive backs)
Carl Mauck (offensive line)
Dave McGinnis (defensive coordinator)
Glenn Pires (linebackers)
Vic Rapp (wide receivers)
Johnny Roland (running backs)

Head trainer
John Omohundro
Assistant trainers
Jim Shearer
Jeff Herndon
Orthopedist
Russell Chick
Internist
Wayne Kuhl
Equipment manager
Mark Ahlemeier
Assistant equipment manager
Steve Christensen
Video director
Benny Greenberg

SCHEDULE

Aug. 31— at Cincinnati	1:00
Sept. 7— DALLAS	5:00
Sept. 14— at Washington	1:00
Sept. 21— Open date	
Sept. 28— at Tampa Bay	1:00
Oct. 5— MINNESOTA	1:00
Oct. 12— N.Y. GIANTS	1:00
Oct. 19— at Philadelphia	1:00
Oct. 26— TENNESSEE	2:00
Nov. 2— PHILADELPHIA	2:00
Nov. 9— at Dallas	12:00
Nov. 16— at N.Y. Giants	1:00
Nov. 23— at Baltimore	1:00
Nov. 30— PITTSBURGH	2:00
Dec. 7— WASHINGTON	2:00
Dec. 14— at New Orleans	3:00
Dec. 21— ATLANTA	2:00

All times are for home team.
All games Sunday unless noted.

DRAFT CHOICES

Tom Knight, DB, Iowa (first round/ninth pick overall).
Jake Plummer, QB, Arizona State (2/42).
Ty Howard, DB, Ohio State (3/84).
Chris Dishman, G, Nebraska (4/106).
Chad Carpenter, WR, Washington State (5/139).
Rod Brown, RB, North Carolina State (6/175).
Tony McCombs, LB, Eastern Kentucky (6/188).
Mark Smith, DE, Auburn (7/212).

1997 SEASON
TRAINING CAMP ROSTER

No.	QUARTERBACKS	Ht./Wt.	Born	NFL Exp.	College	How acq.	'96 Games GP/GS
15	Case, Stoney	6-3/203	7-7-72	3	New Mexico	D3/95	0/0
11	Graham, Kent	6-5/242	11-1-68	6	Ohio State	FA/96	10/8
5	May, Chad	6-1/220	9-28-71	3	Kansas State	FA/96	0/0
16	Plummer, Jake	6-2/195	12-19-74	R	Arizona State	D2/97	—

No.	RUNNING BACKS	Ht./Wt.	Born	NFL Exp.	College	How acq.	'96 Games GP/GS
31	Brown, Rod	5-11/245	2-28-74	R	North Carolina State	D6b/97	—
37	Centers, Larry	6-0/220	6-1-68	8	Stephen F. Austin State	D5/90	16/14
36	Christopherson, Ryan (FB)	5-11/246	7-26-72	3	Wyoming	FA/96	6/0
26	Dunson, Walter (KR)	5-8/173	10-24-70	2	Middle Tennessee State	FA/95	0/0
32	Johnson, LeShon	6-0/201	1-15-71	4	Northern Illinois	W-GB/95	15/8
30	McElroy, Leeland	5-10/200	6-25-74	2	Texas A&M	D2/96	16/6
40	Moore, Derrick	6-1/227	10-13-67	4	Northeastern Oklahoma State	T-Det/95	0/0
45	Smith, Cedric (FB)	5-11/238	5-27-68	6	Florida	FA/96	15/2

No.	RECEIVERS	Ht./Wt.	Born	NFL Exp.	College	How acq.	'96 Games GP/GS
82	Anderson, Stevie	6-6/216	5-12-70	4	Grambling State	W-NYJ/95	8/0
12	Carpenter, Chad	5-11/197	7-17-73	R	Washington State	D5/97	—
84	Gedney, Chris (TE)	6-5/255	8-9-70	5	Syracuse	FA/97	0/0
89	Hayes, Jarius (TE)	6-3/260	3-27-73	2	North Alabama	D7/96	4/0
87	McWilliams, Johnny (TE)	6-4/270	12-14-72	2	Southern California	D3/96	12/0
85	Moore, Rob	6-3/200	9-27-68	8	Syracuse	T-NYJ/95	16/16
81	Sanders, Frank	6-3/205	2-17-73	3	Auburn	D2/95	16/16

No.	OFFENSIVE LINEMEN	Ht./Wt.	Born	NFL Exp.	College	How acq.	'96 Games GP/GS
75	Brown, Lomas (T)	6-4/272	3-30-63	13	Florida	FA/96	16/16
62	Devlin, Mike	6-2/300	11-16-69	5	Iowa	FA/96	11/11
64	Dexter, James (T)	6-5/303	3-3-73	2	South Carolina	D5/96	6/1
67	Dishman, Chris (G)	6-3/322	2-27-74	R	Nebraska	D4/97	—
54	Graham, Aaron (C)	6-4/275	5-22-73	2	Nebraska	D4/96	16/7
66	Jonassen, Eric (T)	6-5/310	8-16-68	4	Bloomsburg (Pa.)	FA/96	0/0
73	Joyce, Matt (G)	6-7/316	3-30-72	3	Richmond	FA/96	2/0
60	Redmon, Anthony (G)	6-5/284	4-9-71	4	Auburn	D5b/94	16/16
70	Scott, Lance	6-3/285	2-15-72	2	Utah	D5/95	0/0

No.	DEFENSIVE LINEMEN	Ht./Wt.	Born	NFL Exp.	College	How acq.	'96 Games GP/GS
63	Bankston, Michael	6-3/274	3-12-70	6	Sam Houston State	D4/92	16/16
76	Drake, Jerry	6-3/293	7-9-69	3	Hastings (Neb.) College	FA/95	0/0
92	England, Eric (E)	6-3/273	3-25-71	4	Texas A&M	D3b/94	11/1
96	Ottis, Brad (E)	6-4/280	8-2-72	4	Wayne State (Neb.)	FA/96	11/1
97	Rice, Simeon (E)	6-5/265	2-24-74	2	Illinois	D1/96	16/15
93	Smith, Mark (E)	6-4/273	8-28-74	R	Auburn	D7/97	—
98	Swann, Eric (T)	6-5/295	8-16-70	7	Wake Technical (N.C.)	D1/91	16/15
94	Wilson, Bernard (T)	6-4/297	8-17-70	5	Tennessee State	W-TB/94	16/16

No.	LINEBACKERS	Ht./Wt.	Born	NFL Exp.	College	How acq.	'96 Games GP/GS
58	Hill, Eric	6-2/253	11-14-66	9	Louisiana State	D1a/89	16/16
56	Irving, Terry	6-0/237	7-3-71	4	McNeese State	D4c/94	16/0
59	Joyner, Seth	6-2/244	11-18-64	12	Texas-El Paso	FA/94	16/16
52	Leasy, Wesley	6-3/235	9-7-71	3	Mississippi State	D7/95	16/0
50	McCombs, Tony	6-2/240	8-24-74	R	Eastern Kentucky	D6/97	—
57	McKinnon, Ronald	6-0/238	9-20-73	2	North Alabama	FA/96	16/0
95	Miller, Jamir	6-4/250	11-19-73	4	UCLA	D1/94	16/16

No.	DEFENSIVE BACKS	Ht./Wt.	Born	NFL Exp.	College	How acq.	'96 Games GP/GS
46	Alexander, Brent	5-10/184	7-10-70	4	Tennessee State	FA/94	16/15
28	Bennett, Tommy (S)	6-2/209	2-19-73	2	UCLA	FA/96	16/1
43	Darby, Matt (S)	6-2/203	11-19-68	6	UCLA	FA/96	15/15
29	Howard, Ty	5-9/177	11-30-73	R	Ohio State	D3/97	—
	Jackson, Kevin (S)	6-2/200	10-27-73	R	Alabama	FA/96	—
22	Knight, Tom	5-11/195	12-29-74	R	Iowa	D1/97	—
42	Lassiter, Kwamie	5-11/180	12-3-69	3	Kansas	FA/95	14/0
44	McCleskey, J.J. (CB)	5-7/177	4-10-70	4	Tennessee	W-NO/96	*10/0
24	McGee, Dell (CB)	5-8/180	9-7-73	1	Auburn	D5/96	0/0
27	Paul, Tito	6-0/200	5-24-72	3	Ohio State	D5c/95	16/3
35	Williams, Aeneas (CB)	5-10/197	1-29-68	7	Southern (La.)	D3/90	16/16

No.	SPECIALISTS	Ht./Wt.	Born	NFL Exp.	College	How acq.	'96 Games GP/GS
3	Butler, Kevin (K)	6-1/200	7-24-62	13	Georgia	FA/97	7/0
10	Feagles, Jeff (P)	6-1/204	3-7-66	10	Miami (Fla.)	FA/94	16/0

*McCleskey played 5 games with Saints and 5 games with Cardinals in '96.
Abbreviations: D1—draft pick, first round; SupD2—supplemental draft pick second round; W-Den—waivers acquisition from Denver; T-Sea—trade acquisition from Seattle; PlanB—Plan B free-agent acquisition; FA—free-agent acquisition (other than Plan B).

MISCELLANEOUS TEAM DATA

Stadium (capacity, surface):
Sun Devil Stadium (73,243, grass)
Business address:
P.O. Box 888
Phoenix, AZ 85001-0888
Business phone:
602-379-0101
Ticket information:
602-379-0102
Team colors:
Cardinal red, black and white
Flagship radio station:
KHTC, 96.9 FM
Training site:
Northern Arizona University
Flagstaff, Ariz.
520-523-1818

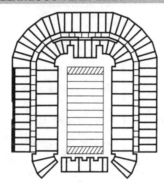

TSN REPORT CARD

Coaching staff   **B +**   Vince Tobin walked into a cesspool and came out smelling like a rose. He assembled an impressive staff on short notice in 1996 that included offensive coordinator Jim Fassel. Then, Tobin took a team that hadn't won during its existence in Arizona to wins in seven of its final 13 games.

Offensive backfield   **B -**   The club would be better off if quarterbacks Kent Graham and Boomer Esiason could have coexisted peacefully. Now, Esiason is gone and they'll have a rookie backup, Jake Plummer. The ball carriers are small. There isn't an established every-down running back, not even Pro Bowler Larry Centers. But he can catch.

Receivers   **B -**   They generally catch everything thrown to them in short possession routes, but there isn't a blazing deep threat who can give a secondary pause. There isn't a great deal of depth among the wideouts, either. That might be minimized by an overabundance of tight ends and the coaches' desire to run more.

Offensive line   **C**   Maybe the grade should be incomplete. The Cardinals were effective as pass protectors but generally average at best opening holes for backs. But the test was somewhat unfair because the Cardinals often trailed early and had to pass. With the entire group back, potentially, the task of five working as one should become easier.

Defensive line   **C +**   It would have been worse if rookie end Simeon Rice had not shone with 12½ sacks, earning NFL defensive rookie of the year honors. There was not an overabundance of heat placed on the quarterback, nor a great deal of fear stricken in the hearts of opposing running backs.

Linebackers   **C**   It was as if average students suddenly found themselves in an advanced-placement class. The linebackers struggled to learn the new system. The zone coverages were especially troublesome after they'd been groomed on man-to-man. They're a year older, and perhaps smarter. There still is not a great deal of depth, and things will get worse if Seth Joyner is let go.

Secondary   **C -**   Anyone who missed breakfast might enjoy the toast here. Even Pro Bowl left cornerback Aeneas Williams wasn't immune. There is help coming at right corner from rookies Tom Knight, the projected starter, and Ty Howard. The safeties remain a big concern. They had to help on run support, often leaving the corners with no help.

Special teams   **C -**   Punter Jeff Feagles often had rushers in his face. Kicker Kevin Butler set a club record for field-goal accuracy but his kickoffs rarely got inside the 5. The Cardinals are looking for a punt returner to replace Marcus Dowdell. Kickoff returner Leeland McElroy should be more confident than he was as a rookie.

ATLANTA FALCONS
NFC WESTERN DIVISION

1996 REVIEW

RESULTS

Sept. 1—at Carolina	L	6-29
Sept. 8—MINNESOTA	L	17-23
Sept.15—Open date		
Sept.22—PHILADELPHIA	L	18-33
Sept.29—at San Francisco	L	17-39
Oct. 6—at Detroit	L	24-28
Oct. 13—HOUSTON	L	13-23
Oct. 20—at Dallas	L	28-32
Oct. 27—PITTSBURGH	L	17-20
Nov. 3—CAROLINA	W	20-17
Nov. 10—at St. Louis	L	16-59
Nov. 17—NEW ORLEANS	W	17-15
Nov. 24—at Cincinnati	L	31-41
Dec. 2—SAN FRANCISCO	L	10-34
Dec. 8—at New Orleans	W	31-15
Dec. 15—ST. LOUIS	L	27-34
Dec. 22—at Jacksonville	L	17-19

RECORDS/RANKINGS

1996 regular-season record: 3-13 (T4th in NFC West); 3-5 in division; 3-9 in conference; 2-6 at home; 1-7 on road.

Team record last five years: 31-49 (.388), ranks T20th in league in that span).

1996 team rankings:	No.	NFC	NFL
Total offense	*319.8	7	17
Rushing offense	*91.3	14	27
Passing offense	*228.4	6	9
Scoring offense	309	6	19
Total defense	*361.6	15	29
Rushing defense	*127.6	13	26
Passing defense	*234.1	15	27
Scoring defense	461	15	30
Takeaways	23	13	T26
Giveaways	41	14	28
Turnover differential	-18	15	29
Sacks	36	8	14
Sacks allowed	42	T11	T21

*Yards per game.

TEAM LEADERS

Scoring (kicking): Morten Andersen, 97 pts. (31/31 PATs, 22/29 FGs).

Scoring (touchdowns): Terance Mathis, 44 pts. (7 receiving, 1 2-pt. conv.).

Passing: Bobby Hebert, 3,152 yds. (488 att., 294 comp., 60.2%, 22 TDs, 25 int.).

Rushing: Jamal Anderson, 1,055 yds. (232 att., 4.5 avg., 5 TDs).

Receptions: Bert Emanuel, 75 (921 yds., 12.3 avg., 6 TDs).

Interceptions: Brad Edwards, 2 (15 yds., 0 TDs).

Sacks: Clay Matthews, 6.5.

Punting: Dan Stryzinski, 42.0 avg. (75 punts, 3,152 yds., 0 blocked).

Punt returns: Eric Metcalf, 11.0 avg. (27 att., 296 yds., 0 TDs).

Kickoff returns: Roell Preston, 21.3 avg. (32 att., 681 yds., 0 TDs).

1997 SEASON

CLUB DIRECTORY

Chairman of the board
Rankin M. Smith Sr.

President
Taylor Smith

Special assistant to president
Jerry Rhea

Vice president and chief financial officer
Jim Hay

Administrative assistants
Kevin Anthony
John O. Knox

Director of administration
Rob Jackson

Marketing representatives
Chris Demos   Trisha Williamson
Todd Marble

Director of public relations
Charlie Taylor

Assistant director of public relations
Frank Kleha

Public relations assistant
Gary Glenn

Director of community relations
Carol Breeding

Coordinator of player programs
Billy "White Shoes" Johnson

Director of ticket operations
Jack Ragsdale

Asst. director of ticket operations
Mike Jennings

Controller
Wallace Norman

Accounting
Carolyn Cathey

Admin. assistants/player personnel
Danny Mock   LaDonna Jones

Scouts
Bill Baker   Scott Campbell
Dick Corrick   Elbert Dubenion
Bill Groman

Director of pro personnel
Chuck Connor

Head coach/ executive v.p. for football operations
Dan Reeves

Assistant coaches
Rich Brooks (assistant head coach/defensive coordinator)
Harold Richardson (asst. head coach/football operations)
George Sefcik (offensive coordinator/running backs)
Don Blackmon (linebackers)
Jack Burns (quarterbacks)
James Daniel (tight ends)
Joe DeCamillis (special teams)
Tim Jorgensen (assistant strength & conditioning)
Bill Kollar (defensive line)
Pete Mangurian (offensive quality control)
Ron Meeks (secondary)
Al Miller (strength & conditioning)
Rod Rust (def. quality control)
Art Shell (offensive line)
Rennie Simmons (wide receivers)

Director of player development
Tommy Nobis

Trainers
Arnold Gamber   Matt Smith
Ron Medlin

Equipment manager
Brian Boigner

Sr. equip. dir./gameday op. coord.
Horace Daniel

Video director
Tom Atcheson

SCHEDULE

Aug. 31— at Detroit		1:00
Sept. 7— CAROLINA		1:00
Sept. 14— OAKLAND		1:00
Sept. 21— at San Francisco		1:00
Sept. 28— DENVER		1:00
Oct. 5— Open date		
Oct. 12— at New Orleans		12:00
Oct. 19— SAN FRANCISCO		1:00
Oct. 26— at Carolina		8:00
Nov. 2— ST. LOUIS		1:00
Nov. 9— TAMPA BAY		1:00
Nov. 16— at St. Louis		12:00
Nov. 23— NEW ORLEANS		1:00
Nov. 30— at Seattle		1:00
Dec. 7— at San Diego		1:00
Dec. 14— PHILADELPHIA		1:00
Dec. 21— at Arizona		2:00

All times are for home team.
All games Sunday unless noted.

DRAFT CHOICES

Michael Booker, DB, Nebraska (first round/11th pick overall).
Nathan Davis, DE, Indiana (2/32).
Byron Hanspard, RB, Texas Tech (2/41).
O.J. Santiago, TE, Kent (3/70).
Henri Crockett, LB, Florida State (4/100).
Marcus Wimberly, DB, Miami, Fla. (5/133).
Calvin Collins, C, Texas A&M (6/180).
Tony Graziani, QB, Oregon (7/204).
Chris Bayne, DB, Fresno State (7/222).

Atlanta Falcons

1997 SEASON

No.	QUARTERBACKS	Ht./Wt.	Born	NFL Exp.	College	How acq.	'96 Games GP/GS
12	Chandler, Chris	6-4/225	10-12-65	10	Washington	FA/95	*12/12
13	Graziani, Tony	6-2/195	12-23-73	R	Oregon	D7/97	—
8	Maddox, Tommy	6-4/218	9-2-71	6	UCLA	FA/97	0/0
11	Tolliver, Billy Joe	6-1/217	2-7-66	7	Texas Tech	FA/96	0/0
	RUNNING BACKS						
32	Anderson, Jamal	5-11/234	9-30-72	4	Utah	D7/94	16/12
44	Christian, Bob	5-11/230	11-14-68	4	Northwestern	FA/97	0/0
45	Downs, Gary	6-1/212	6-7-72	3	North Carolina State	FA/97	*6/1
24	Hanspard, Byron	5-10/198	1-23-76	R	Texas Tech	D2b/97	—
33	Huntley, Richard	5-11/224	9-18-72	2	Winston-Salem (N.C.) State	D4a/96	1/0
	RECEIVERS						
80	Brown, Tyrone	5-11/168	1-3-73	3	Toledo	FA/95	9/4
87	Emanuel, Bert	5-10/180	10-27-70	4	Rice	D2/94	14/13
89	Kinchen, Todd (KR)	5-11/187	1-7-69	6	Louisiana State	FA/97	*7/0
49	Kozlowski, Brian (TE)	6-3/255	10-4-70	4	Connecticut	FA/97	*5/0
81	Mathis, Terance	5-10/180	6-7-67	8	New Mexico	FA/94	16/16
85	Preston, Roell	5-10/185	6-23-72	3	Mississippi	D5/95	15/2
88	Santiago, O.J. (TE)	6-7/267	4-4-74	R	Kent	D3/97	—
84	Scott, Freddie	5-10/189	8-26-74	2	Penn State	FA/96	10/0
83	West, Ed (TE)	6-1/250	8-2-61	14	Auburn	FA/97	*16/4
	OFFENSIVE LINEMEN						
73	Brooks, Ethan (T)	6-6/290	4-27-72	2	Williams (Conn.)	D7/96	2/0
74	Collins, Calvin (C)	6-2/307	1-5-74	R	Texas A&M	D6/97	—
76	Davis, Antone (T)	6-4/330	2-28-67	7	Tennessee	FA/96	16/10
65	Fortin, Roman (C)	6-5/297	2-26-67	7	San Diego State	PlanB/92	16/16
64	Loneker, Keith (G)	6-3/330	6-21-71	4	Kansas	FA/93	0/0
64	Pahukoa, Jeff (G/T)	6-2/298	2-9-69	6	Washington	FA/95	14/3
61	Tobeck, Robbie (C)	6-4/295	3-6-70	3	Washington State	FA/93	16/16
70	Whitfield, Bob (T)	6-5/310	10-18-71	6	Stanford	D1a/92	16/16
69	Williams, Gene (T/G)	6-2/306	10-14-68	7	Iowa State	T-Clev/95	10/0
77	Willig, Matt (T)	6-8/317	1-21-69	5	Southern California	T-NYJ/96	12/0
	DEFENSIVE LINEMEN						
92	Archambeau, Lester (E)	6-5/275	6-27-67	8	Stanford	T-GB/93	15/15
75	Brown, Shannon (T)	6-5/290	5-23-72	1	Alabama	D3/96	0/0
91	Burrough, John	6-5/275	5-17-72	3	Wyoming	D7/95	16/1
99	Davis, Nathan (E)	6-5/312	2-6-74	R	Indiana	D2a/97	—
98	Hall, Travis	6-5/278	8-3-72	3	Brigham Young	D6/95	14/13
96	Kelly, Todd (E)	6-2/259	11-27-70	5	Tennessee	FA/96	2/0
93	Owens, Dan (E)	6-3/280	3-16-67	8	Southern California	FA/96	16/9
	LINEBACKERS						
97	Bennett, Cornelius	6-2/238	8-25-66	11	Alabama	FA/96	13/13
51	Brandon, David	6-4/240	2-9-65	9	Memphis State	FA/93	16/2
94	Crockett, Henri	6-2/249	10-28-74	R	Florida State	D4/97	—
	Croel, Mike	6-3/235	6-6-69	6	Nebraska	FA/97	*16/16
95	Davis, Paschall	6-2/225	7-5-69	3	Texas A&I	FA/97	*10/0
56	Fields, Scott	6-2/220	4-22-73	2	Southern California	FA/96	6/0
52	Sauer, Craig	6-1/232	12-13-72	2	Minnesota	D6/96	16/1
90	Smith, Chuck (E)	6-2/282	12-21-69	6	Tennessee	D2/92	15/15
59	Styles, Lorenzo	6-1/245	1-31-74	3	Ohio State	D3/95	16/0
58	Tuggle, Jessie	5-11/230	2-14-65	11	Valdosta (Ga.) State	FA/87	16/16
	DEFENSIVE BACKS						
47	Bayne, Chris	6-1/205	3-22-75	R	Fresno State	D7/97	—
43	Bolden, Juran (CB)	6-2/201	6-27-74	2	Miss. Delta CC	D4b/96	9/0
20	Booker, Michael	6-2/203	4-27-75	R	Nebraska	D1/97	—
38	Boyd, Sean (S)	6-2/206	12-19-72	1	North Carolina	FA/96	2/0
23	Bradford, Ronnie (CB)	5-10/188	10-1-70	5	Colorado	FA/97	*15/11
34	Buchanan, Ray	5-9/195	9-29-71	5	Louisville	FA/97	0/0
25	Bush, Devin (S)	5-11/210	7-3-73	3	Florida State	D1/95	16/15
28	McGill, Lenny (CB)	6-1/198	5-31-71	4	Arizona State	T-GB/96	16/8
26	Phillips, Anthony (CB)	6-1/205	10-5-70	4	Texas A&M-Kingsville	D3/94	7/5
35	White, William (S)	5-10/205	2-19-66	10	Ohio State	FA/97	*12/2
48	Wimberly, Marcus	5-11/192	7-8-74	R	Miami (Fla.)	D5/97	—

No.	SPECIALISTS	Ht./Wt.	Born	NFL Exp.	College	How acq.	'96 Games GP/GS
5	Andersen, Morten (K)...................	6-2/225	8-19-60	16	Michigan State	FA/95	16/0
4	Stryzinski, Dan (P)	6-2/200	5-15-65	8	Indiana	FA/95	16/0

*Bradford played 15 games with Cardinals in '96; Croel played 16 games with Ravens; P. Davis played 10 games with Rams; Downs played 6 games with Giants; Kinchen played 7 games with Broncos; Kozlowski played 5 games with Giants; West played 16 games with Eagles; White played 12 games with Chiefs.

Abbreviations: D1—draft pick, first round; SupD2—supplemental draft pick second round; W-Den—waivers acquisition from Denver; T-Sea—trade acquisition from Seattle; PlanB—Plan B free-agent acquisition; FA—free-agent acquisition (other than Plan B).

MISCELLANEOUS TEAM DATA

Stadium (capacity, surface):
Georgia Dome
(71,280, artificial)
Business address:
Atlanta Falcons Complex
One Falcon Place
Suwanee, Ga. 30174
Business phone:
770-945-1111
Ticket information:
404-223-8000
Team colors:
Black, red, silver and white
Flagship radio station:
WZGC, 92.9 FM
Training site:
Atlanta Falcons Complex
Suwanee, Ga.
770-945-1111

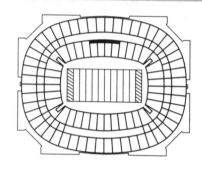

TSN REPORT CARD

Category	Grade	Comments
Coaching staff	B	Dan Reeves ranks 10th all-time in NFL victories, and his staff includes two former NFL head coaches in Rich Brooks and Art Shell. But Reeves failed in his attempt to land a creative offensive coordinator. Eventually, he'll need one.
Offensive backfield	C +	Quarterback Chris Chandler won't do anything electrifying, but he's better than most of the journeyman-types and will do as a temporary fix. Running back Jamal Anderson, a star in the run-and-shoot, should make the transition to a conventional offense. Rookie running back Byron Hanspard is an intriguing prospect.
Receivers	C	Bert Emanuel and Terance Mathis were acquired specifically for the run-and-shoot offense, which has been canned. They're talented and smart, but each lacks size. A player or two could be added to the group this summer. Tight end Ed West is 36.
Offensive line	C	Bob Whitfield has been a mild underachiever who has the potential to become an All-Pro. There are no other stars on the line, but no glaring weaknesses, either. Center Roman Fortin, tackle Antone Davis and guards Gene Williams and Robbie Tobeck figure to be the other starters.
Defensive line	D	Right end Chuck Smith's motor always runs, but he's undersized. The rest of the line is pretty pedestrian. Shannon Brown, a '96 draft pick who missed last season with a knee injury, could add bulk in the middle. Rookie Nathan Davis, a high second-round pick, also has size.
Linebackers	C	Cornelius Bennett still can cover and he loves the game. Middle man Jessie Tuggle plays the run as well as anybody, but he's average against the pass and is getting long in the tooth. There's no telling who will line up at the other outside spot.
Secondary	C	The cornerback position should be better than it's been in years, with the additions of free agent Ray Buchanan and rookie Michael Booker. Safety remains a trouble spot. Devin Bush probably will switch from strong to free safety, and former Chiefs backup William White may start at strong safety.
Special teams	B	Kicker Morten Andersen still has a strong leg, though he struggled with his long-distance accuracy last year. Dan Stryzinski is one of the better "hang-time" punters. Hanspard, Roell Preston and Todd Kinchen should make the return game respectable.

BALTIMORE RAVENS
AFC CENTRAL DIVISION

1996 REVIEW
RESULTS

Sept. 1—OAKLAND	W	19-14
Sept. 8—at Pittsburgh	L	17-31
Sept.15—at Houston	L	13-29
Sept.22—Open date		
Sept.29—NEW ORLEANS	W	17-10
Oct. 6—NEW ENGLAND	L	38-46
Oct. 13—at Indianapolis	L	21-26
Oct. 20—at Denver	L	34-45
Oct. 27—ST. LOUIS (OT)	W	37-31
Nov. 3—CINCINNATI	L	21-24
Nov. 10—at Jacksonville	L	27-30
Nov. 17—at San Francisco	L	20-38
Nov. 24—JACKSONVILLE (OT)	L	25-28
Dec. 1—PITTSBURGH	W	31-17
Dec. 8—at Cincinnati	L	14-21
Dec. 15—at Carolina	L	16-27
Dec. 22—HOUSTON	L	21-24

RECORDS/RANKINGS

1996 regular-season record: 4-12 (5th in AFC Central); 1-7 in division; 2-10 in conference; 4-4 at home; 0-8 on road.

1996 team rankings:	No.	AFC	NFL
Total offense	*357.7	3	3
Rushing offense	*109.1	9	14
Passing offense	*248.6	2	2
Scoring offense	371	4	6
Total defense	*368.1	15	30
Rushing defense	*120	13	23
Passing defense	*248.1	15	30
Scoring defense	441	14	28
Takeaways	22	15	T28
Giveaways	33	T12	T21
Turnover differential	-11	14	27
Sacks	30	13	T25
Sacks allowed	38	T8	T16

*Yards per game.

TEAM LEADERS

Scoring (kicking): Matt Stover, 91 pts. (34/35 PATs, 19/25 FGs).

Scoring (touchdowns): Michael Jackson, 88 pts. (14 receiving, 2 2-pt. conv.).

Passing: Vinny Testaverde, 4,177 yds. (549 att., 325 comp., 59.2%, 33 TDs, 19 int.).

Rushing: Bam Morris, 737 yds. (172 att., 4.3 avg., 4 TDs).

Receptions: Michael Jackson, 76 (1,201 yds., 15.8 avg., 14 TDs).

Interceptions: Antonio Langham, 5 (59 yds., 0 TDs); Eric Turner, 5 (1 yd., 0 TDs).

Sacks: Mike Caldwell, 4.5.

Punting: Greg Montgomery, 43.8 avg. (68 punts, 2,980 yds., 1 blocked).

Punt returns: Jermaine Lewis, 9.4 avg. (36 att., 339 yds., 0 TDs).

Kickoff returns: Jermaine Lewis, 21.5 avg. (41 att., 883 yds., 0 TDs).

1997 SEASON
CLUB DIRECTORY

Owner/president
Arthur B. Modell
Executive V.P./legal and administration
Jim Bailey
Executive V.P./assistant to the president
David O. Modell
V.P. of player personnel
Ozzie Newsome
Vice president/public relations
Kevin Byrne
Vice president of marketing and sales
David Cope
Chief financial officer
Pat Moriarty
Treasurer
Steven Costa
Director of operations and information
Bob Eller
Director of publications
Francine Lubera
Director of broadcast operations
Lisa Bercu
Director of tickets
Roy Sommerhof
Director of pro personnel
James Harris
Director of college scouting
Phil Savage
Scouting/pro personnel
George Kokinis
Ron Marciniak
Terry McDonough
Ernie Plank
Ellis Rainsberger
Bill Shunkwiler
Lionel Vital
Facilities manager
Charlie Cusick
Head trainer
Bill Tessendorf

SCHEDULE

Aug. 31— JACKSONVILLE	4:00
Sept. 7— CINCINNATI	1:00
Sept. 14— at N.Y. Giants	1:00
Sept. 21— at Tennessee	12:00
Sept. 28— at San Diego	1:00
Oct. 5— PITTSBURGH	1:00
Oct. 12— Open date	
Oct. 19— MIAMI	4:00
Oct. 26— at Washington	1:00
Nov. 2— at N.Y. Jets	1:00
Nov. 9— at Pittsburgh	8:00
Nov. 16— PHILADELPHIA	1:00
Nov. 23— ARIZONA	1:00
Nov. 30— at Jacksonville	1:00
Dec. 7— SEATTLE	1:00
Dec. 14— TENNESSEE	1:00
Dec. 21— at Cincinnati	1:00

All times are for home team.
All games Sunday unless noted.

Head coach
Ted Marchibroda

Assistant coaches
Maxie Baughan (linebackers)
Jacob Burney (defensive line)
Kirk Ferentz (assistant head coach/offense)
Ken Whisenhunt (tight ends)
Al Lavan (running backs)
Marvin Lewis (defensive coordinator)
Lester Erb (quality control-offense)
Scott O'Brien (special teams)
Alvin Reynolds (secondary)
Jim Schwartz (quality control-defense)
John Settle (strength & cond./quality control-special teams)
Richard Mann (receivers)
Jerry Simmons (strength & conditioning)
Don Strock (quarterbacks)

Assistant trainer
Mark Smith
Team physicians
Dr. John Bergfeld
Dr. Claude T. Moorman III
Dr. Andrew Pollak
Dr. Andrew M. Tucker
Equipment manager
Ed Carroll

DRAFT CHOICES

Peter Boulware, DE, Florida State (first round/fourth pick overall).
Jamie Sharper, LB, Virginia (2/34).
Kim Herring, DB, Penn State (2/58).
Jay Graham, RB, Tennessee (3/64).
Tyrus McCloud, LB, Louisville (4/118).
Jeff Mitchell, C, Florida (5/134).
Steve Lee, RB, Indiana (6/167).
Cornell Brown, LB, Virginia Tech (6/194).
Chris Ward, DE, Kentucky (7/205).
Wally Richardson, QB, Penn State (7/234).
Ralph Staten, DB, Alabama (7/236).
Leland Taylor, DT, Louisville (7/238).

1997 SEASON
TRAINING CAMP ROSTER

No.	QUARTERBACKS	Ht./Wt.	Born	NFL Exp.	College	How acq.	'96 Games GP/GS
14	Richardson, Wally	6-4/225	2-11-74	R	Penn State	D7b/97	—
11	Stark, Jon	6-4/222	2-22-73	R	Trinity International (Ill.)	D7/96	—
12	Testaverde, Vinny	6-5/227	11-13-63	11	Miami (Fla.)	FA/93	16/16
10	Zeier, Eric	6-0/205	9-6-72	3	Georgia	D3a/95	1/0
	RUNNING BACKS						
21	Byner, Earnest	5-10/225	9-15-62	14	East Carolina	FA/94	16/8
34	Graham, Jay	5-11/220	7-14-75	R	Tennessee	D3/97	—
39	Lee, Steve (FB)	6-0/265	4-16-74	R	Indiana	D6a/97	—
33	Morris, Bam	6-0/245	1-13-72	4	Texas Tech	FA/96	11/7
	RECEIVERS						
82	Alexander, Derrick	6-2/195	11-6-71	4	Michigan	D1b/94	15/14
85	Ethridge, Ray	5-10/180	9-11-68	2	Pasadena (Calif.) City College	FA/95	14/1
88	Kinchen, Brian (TE)	6-2/240	8-6-65	10	Louisiana State	FA/91	16/16
84	Lewis, Jermaine	5-7/172	10-16-74	2	Maryland	D5/96	16/1
83	Roe, James	6-1/187	8-23-73	2	Norfolk State	D6b/96	1/0
	OFFENSIVE LINEMEN						
69	Blackshear, Jeff (G)	6-6/323	3-29-69	4	Northeast Louisiana	T-Sea/96	16/12
77	Brown, Orlando (T)	6-7/340	12-12-70	5	South Carolina State	FA/93	16/16
62	Goeas, Leo (G/T)	6-4/300	8-15-66	8	Hawaii	FA/97	*16/13
64	Isaia, Sale (G)	6-5/315	6-13-72	3	UCLA	FA/95	9/0
60	Mitchell, Jeff (C)	6-4/300	1-29-74	R	Florida	D5/97	—
67	Neujahr, Quentin (C)	6-4/285	1-30-71	3	Kansas State	FA/95	5/0
75	Ogden, Jonathan (T)	6-8/318	7-31-74	2	UCLA	D1a/96	16/16
63	Williams, Wally (C)	6-2/305	2-19-71	5	Florida A&M	FA/93	15/13
	DEFENSIVE LINEMEN						
58	Boulware, Peter (E)	6-4/255	12-18-74	R	Florida State	D1/97	—
78	Footman, Dan (E)	6-5/290	1-13-69	5	Florida State	D2/93	10/8
94	Frederick, Mike (E)	6-5/280	8-6-72	3	Virginia	D3b/95	16/11
73	Goad, Tim (NT)	6-3/280	2-28-66	10	North Carolina	FA/95	16/5
97	Jones, James (T)	6-2/290	2-6-69	7	Northern Iowa	FA/96	16/11
99	McCrary, Michael (E)	6-4/267	7-7-70	5	Wake Forest	FA/97	*16/13
96	Siragusa, Tony (NT)	6-3/320	5-14-67	8	Pittsburgh	FA/97	*10/10
92	Taylor, Leland (T)	6-3/305	10-25-72	R	Louisville	D7d/97	—
95	Ward, Chris (E)	6-3/275	2-4-74	R	Kentucky	D7a/97	—
	LINEBACKERS						
51	Brown, Cornell	6-0/240	3-15-75	R	Virginia Tech	D6b/97	—
52	Lewis, Ray	6-1/235	5-15-75	2	Miami (Fla.)	D1b/96	14/13
54	McCloud, Tyrus	6-1/250	11-23-74	R	Louisville	D4/97	—
59	Powell, Craig	6-4/235	11-13-71	3	Ohio State	D1/95	9/0
55	Sharper, Jamie	6-3/240	11-23-74	R	Virginia	D2a/97	—
	DEFENSIVE BACKS						
24	Brady, Donny	6-2/195	11-24-73	3	Wisconsin	FA/95	16/13
29	Brew, Dorian (CB)	5-10/182	7-19-74	2	Kansas	D3a/96	7/0
20	Herring, Kim	5-11/210	10-10-75	R	Penn State	D2b/97	—
25	Jenkins, DeRon (CB)	5-11/186	11-14-73	2	Tennessee	D2/96	15/2
31	Jones, Rondell (S)	6-2/210	5-7-71	5	North Carolina	FA/97	*16/0
38	Langham, Antonio (CB)	6-0/180	7-31-72	4	Alabama	D1a/94	15/14
27	Moore, Stevon (S)	5-11/210	2-9-67	9	Mississippi	PlanB/92	16/16
41	Staten, Ralph	6-3/205	12-3-74	R	Alabama	D7c/97	—
37	Thompson, Bennie (S)	6-0/214	2-10-63	8	Grambling State	FA/94	16/0
	SPECIALISTS						
9	Montgomery, Greg (P)	6-4/215	10-29-64	9	Michigan State	FA/96	16/0
3	Stover, Matt (K)	5-11/178	1-27-68	8	Louisiana Tech	PlanB/91	16/0

*Goeas played 16 games with Rams in '96; R. Jones played 16 games with Broncos; McCrary played 16 games with Seahawks; Siragusa played 10 games with Colts.

Abbreviations: D1—draft pick, first round; SupD2—supplemental draft pick second round; W-Den—waivers acquisition from Denver; T-Sea—trade acquisition from Seattle; PlanB—Plan B free-agent acquisition; FA—free-agent acquisition (other than Plan B).

Stadium (capacity, surface):
Memorial Stadium
(64,522, grass)
Business address:
11001 Owings Mills Blvd.
Owings Mills, MD 21117
Business phone:
410-654-6200
Ticket information:
410-261-RAVE
Team colors:
Purple, black and metallic gold
Flagship radio stations:
WJFK/WLIF
Training site:
Western Maryland College
Westminster, Md.
401-654-6200

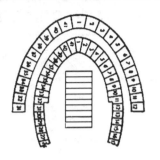

1997 SEASON Baltimore Ravens

TSN REPORT CARD

Coaching staff	C +	The offensive staff seems to be in good hands, but defensive coordinator Marvin Lewis and his staff have something to prove after last year's dismal effort that saw Baltimore lead the NFL in yards allowed.
Offensive backfield	B	If Bam Morris comes to camp in shape, this group should roll. Watch out for rookie runners Priest Holmes and Jay Graham. Vinny Testaverde is making up for lost time.
Receivers	B +	This corps, headed by wide receivers Michael Jackson and Derrick Alexander, has the potential to be one of the best in the NFL. If tight end Eric Green completes rehabilitation from a knee injury, the Ravens have the total passing package.
Offensive line	C +	Before center Wally Williams got hurt in the offseason, this group looked to be almost as good as last year's strong edition. With Williams out for the first six to seven games, the unit drops a notch. Tackles Jonathan Ogden and Orlando Brown are anchors.
Defensive line	C	There's good potential. Tackle Tony Siragusa, a free agent from the Colts, and end Rob Burnett are coming off major knee injuries. End Michael McCrary, a free agent from the Seahawks, should boost the rush.
Linebackers	C	The Ravens will start rookies Peter Boulware, a first-round pick who played end in college, and Jamie Sharper, a second-rounder, outside, and a second-year player (Ray Lewis) in the middle. Don't look for quick results.
Secondary	C -	The right cornerback position is shaky for the second consecutive year and the Ravens might start rookie Kim Herring, a second-round selection, at free safety. This unit would be helped by an improved pass rush.
Special teams	C -	Greg Montgomery is a great punter, but kicker Matt Stover has to rebound from an uneven 1996. Jermaine Lewis and Graham could make the return game formidable.

BUFFALO BILLS
AFC EASTERN DIVISION

1996 REVIEW

RESULTS

Sept. 1—at N.Y. Giants (OT)	W	23-20
Sept. 8—NEW ENGLAND	W	17-10
Sept.16—at Pittsburgh	L	6-24
Sept.22—DALLAS	W	10-7
Sept.29—Open date		
Oct. 6—INDIANAPOLIS (OT)	W	16-13
Oct. 13—MIAMI	L	7-21
Oct. 20—at N.Y. Jets	W	25-22
Oct. 27—at New England	L	25-28
Nov. 3—WASHINGTON	W	38-13
Nov. 10—at Philadelphia	W	24-17
Nov. 17—CINCINNATI	W	31-17
Nov. 24—N.Y. JETS	W	35-10
Dec. 1—at Indianapolis (OT)	L	10-13
Dec. 8—at Seattle	L	18-26
Dec. 16—at Miami	L	14-16
Dec. 22—KANSAS CITY	W	20-9
Dec. 28—JACKSONVILLE*	L	27-30

*AFC wild-card game.

RECORDS/RANKINGS

1996 regular-season record: 10-6 (2nd in AFC East); 4-4 in division; 6-6 in conference; 7-1 at home; 3-5 on road.
Team record last five years: 50-30 (.625), ranks 6th in league in that span).

1996 team rankings:	No.	AFC	NFL
Total offense	*319.9	10	16
Rushing offense	*118.8	10	8
Passing offense	*201.1	10	17
Scoring offense	319	10	15
Total defense	*296.1	5	9
Rushing defense	*104.3	8	14
Passing defense	*191.8	3	8
Scoring defense	266	2	6
Takeaways	28	8	T18
Giveaways	37	14	T26
Turnover differential	-9	13	25
Sacks	48	T2	T3
Sacks allowed	48	14	27

*Yards per game.

TEAM LEADERS

Scoring (kicking): Steve Christie, 105 pts. (33/33 PATs, 24/29 FGs).
Scoring (touchdowns): Thurman Thomas, 48 pts. (8 rushing).
Passing: Jim Kelly, 2,810 yds. (379 att., 222 comp., 58.6%, 14 TDs, 19 int.).
Rushing: Thurman Thomas, 1,033 yds. (281 att., 3.7 avg., 8 TDs).
Receptions: Andre Reed, 66 (1,036 yds., 15.7 avg., 6 TDs).
Interceptions: Kurt Schulz, 4 (24 yds., 0 TDs).
Sacks: Bruce Smith, 13.5.
Punting: Chris Mohr, 41.5 avg. (101 punts, 4,194 yds., 0 blocked).
Punt returns: Jeff Burris, 10.6 avg. (27 att., 286 yds., 0 TDs).
Kickoff returns: Eric Moulds, 23.2 avg. (52 att., 1,205 yds., 1 TD).

1997 SEASON

CLUB DIRECTORY

President
Ralph C. Wilson Jr.
Exec. vice president/general manager
John Butler
Vice president/administration
Jim Miller
Corporate vice president
Linda Bogdan
Treasurer
Jeffrey C. Littmann
Director of administration/ticket sales
Jerry Foran
Asst. g.m./business operations
Bill Munson
Director of business operations
Jim Overdorf
Controller
Frank Wojnicki
Director of merchandising
Christy Wilson Hofmann
Director of player/alumni relations
Jerry Butler
Director of marketing and sales
John Livsey
Dir. of public/community relations
Denny Lynch
Director of media relations
Scott Berchtold
Ticket director
June Foran
Video director
Henry Kunttu
Director of stadium operations
George Koch
Director of security
Bill Bambach
Engineering and operations manager
Joe Frandina
Director of pro personnel
A.J. Smith
Director of player personnel
Dwight Adams

Vice president/ head coach
Marv Levy

Assistant coaches
Elijah Pitts (assistant head coach/running backs)
Tom Bresnahan (offensive line)
Ted Cottrell (linebackers)
Bruce DeHaven (special teams)
Dan Henning (offensive coordinator/quarterbacks)
Charlie Joiner (receivers)
Rusty Jones (strength & cond.)
Don Lawrence (offensive quality control/tight ends)
Chuck Lester (def. quality control/ admin. asst. to head coach)
Wade Phillips (def. coordinator)
Dick Roach (defensive backs)
Dan Sekanovich (defensive line)

Scouts

Tom Beck	Doug Majeski
Buddy Nix	Bob Ryan
Chink Sengel	Dave G. Smith
Dave W. Smith	

Head trainer
Bud Carpenter
Assistant trainer
Melvin Lewis
Greg McMillen
Equipment manager
Dave Hojnowski
Assistant equipment manager
Woody Ribbeck

SCHEDULE

Aug. 31— MINNESOTA	1:00
Sept. 7— at N.Y. Jets	1:00
Sept. 14— at Kansas City	12:00
Sept. 21— INDIANAPOLIS	4:00
Sept. 28— Open date	
Oct. 5— DETROIT	1:00
Oct. 12— at New England	1:00
Oct. 20— at Indianapolis (Mon.)	8:00
Oct. 26— DENVER	1:00
Nov. 2— MIAMI	1:00
Nov. 9— NEW ENGLAND	4:00
Nov. 17— at Miami (Mon.)	9:00
Nov. 23— at Tennessee	12:00
Nov. 30— N.Y. JETS	1:00
Dec. 7— at Chicago	12:00
Dec. 14— JACKSONVILLE	1:00
Dec. 20— at Green Bay (Sat.)	11:30

All times are for home team.
All games Sunday unless noted.

DRAFT CHOICES

Antowain Smith, RB, Houston (first round/23rd pick overall).
Marcellus Wiley, DE, Columbia (2/52).
Jamie Nails, T, Florida A&M (4/120).
Sean Woodson, DB, Jackson State (5/153).
Marcus Spriggs, T, Houston (6/185).
Pat Fitzgerald, TE, Texas (7/226).

No.	QUARTERBACKS	Ht./Wt.	Born	NFL Exp.	College	How acq.	'96 Games GP/GS
15	Collins, Todd	6-4/224	11-5-71	3	Michigan	D2/95	7/3
8	Hobert, Billy Joe	6-3/230	1-8-71	3	Washington	T-Oak/97	*8/3
10	Van Pelt, Alex	6-0/220	5-1-70	2	Pittsburgh	FA/94	1/0
	RUNNING BACKS						
45	Bender, Carey	5-8/185	1-28-72	1	Coe College	FA/95	1/0
29	Bratton, Jason	6-1/252	10-19-72	1	Grambling	FA/96	2/0
44	Holmes, Darick	6-0/226	7-1-71	3	Portland State	D7b/95	16/1
26	Smith, Antowain	6-2/224	3-14-72	R	Houston	D1/97	—
34	Thomas, Thurman	5-10/198	5-16-66	10	Oklahoma State	D2/88	15/15
33	Tindale, Tim (FB)	5-10/220	4-15-71	3	Western Ontario	FA/94	14/3
	RECEIVERS						
81	Armour, Justin	6-4/209	1-1-73	2	Stanford	D4b/95	0/0
82	Brantley, Chris (KR)	5-10/180	12-12-70	3	Rutgers	FA/96	10/0
86	Cline, Tony (TE)	6-4/247	11-24-71	3	Stanford	D4c/95	16/7
87	Coons, Robert (TE)	6-5/249	9-18-69	3	Pittsburgh	FA/95	16/0
88	Early, Quinn	6-0/190	4-13-65	10	Iowa	FA/96	16/13
48	Fitzgerald, Pat (TE)	6-2/228	12-4-74	R	Texas	D7/97	—
84	Johnson, Lonnie (TE)	6-3/240	2-14-71	4	Florida State	D2b/94	16/15
80	Moulds, Eric	6-0/204	7-17-73	2	Mississippi State	D1/96	16/5
83	Reed, Andre	6-2/190	1-29-64	13	Kutztown (Pa.) State	D4a/85	16/16
49	Riemersma, Jay (TE)	6-5/254	5-17-73	R	Michigan	D7b/96	—
89	Tasker, Steve	5-9/183	4-10-62	13	Northwestern	W-Hou/86	8/5
	OFFENSIVE LINEMEN						
76	Albright, Ethan	6-5/283	5-1-71	3	North Carolina	FA/96	16/0
79	Brown, Ruben (T)	6-3/304	2-13-72	3	Pittsburgh	D1/95	14/14
70	Fina, John (T)	6-4/285	3-11-69	6	Arizona	D1/92	15/15
68	Lacina, Corbin (G)	6-4/297	11-2-70	4	Augustana (S.D.)	D6/93	12/2
72	Louchiey, Corey (T)	6-8/305	10-10-71	3	South Carolina	D3b/94	16/4
65	Nails, Jamie (T)	6-6/354	6-3-75	R	Florida A&M	D4/97	—
60	Ostroski, Jerry (G)	6-4/310	7-12-70	4	Tulsa	FA/93	16/16
74	Parker, Glenn (G/T)	6-5/305	4-22-66	8	Arizona	D3/90	14/13
69	Spriggs, Marcus (T)	6-3/295	5-17-74	R	Houston	D6/97	—
61	Zeigler, Dusty (C/G)	6-5/298	9-27-73	1	Notre Dame	D6b/96	2/0
	DEFENSIVE LINEMEN						
90	Hansen, Phil (E)	6-5/278	5-20-68	7	North Dakota State	D2/91	16/16
77	Jeffcoat, Jim (E)	6-5/280	4-1-61	15	Arizona State	FA/95	16/0
98	Moran, Sean (E)	6-3/255	6-5-73	2	Colorado State	D4/96	16/0
94	Pike, Mark (E)	6-4/272	12-27-63	11	Georgia Tech	D7b/86	16/0
91	Price, Shawn (E)	6-5/260	3-28-70	5	Pacific	FA/96	15/0
78	Smith, Bruce (E)	6-4/273	6-18-63	13	Virginia Tech	D1a/85	16/16
92	Washington, Ted (NT)	6-4/325	4-13-68	7	Louisville	FA/95	16/16
75	Wiley, Marcellus (E)	6-5/271	11-30-74	R	Columbia	D2/97	—
	LINEBACKERS						
96	Brandenburg, Dan	6-2/255	2-2-73	1	Indiana State	D7a/96	0/0
57	Covington, Damien	5-11/236	12-4-72	3	North Carolina State	D3b/95	9/2
52	Holecek, John	6-2/238	5-7-72	1	Illinois	D5/95	0/0
55	Maddox, Mark	6-1/233	3-23-68	6	Northern Michigan	D9/91	14/14
99	Northern, Gabe (E)	6-2/240	6-8-74	2	Louisiana State	D2/96	16/2
95	Paup, Bryce	6-5/247	2-29-68	8	Northern Iowa	FA/95	12/11
58	Perry, Marlo	6-4/250	8-25-72	4	Jackson State	D3/94	13/0
59	Rogers, Sam	6-3/245	5-30-70	4	Colorado	D2c/94	14/14
54	Spielman, Chris	6-0/247	10-11-65	10	Ohio State	FA/96	16/16
51	White, David	6-2/235	2-27-70	4	Nebraska	FA/95	16/5
	DEFENSIVE BACKS						
22	Burris, Jeff (CB)	6-0/204	6-7-72	4	Notre Dame	D1/94	15/15
27	Irvin, Ken (CB)	5-10/182	7-11-72	3	Memphis	D4a/95	16/1
31	Jackson, Raymond	5-10/189	2-17-73	2	Colorado State	D5/96	12/0
20	Jones, Henry (S)	5-11/197	12-29-67	7	Illinois	D1/91	5/5
46	Kerner, Marlon (CB)	5-10/187	3-18-73	3	Ohio State	D3a/95	15/0
20	Martin, Emanuel (CB)	5-11/184	7-31-69	2	Alabama State	FA/96	16/1
24	Schulz, Kurt (S)	6-1/208	12-28-68	6	Eastern Washington	D7/92	15/15
40	Smedley, Eric (S/CB)	5-11/199	7-23-73	2	Indiana	D7c/96	6/0
28	Smith, Thomas (CB)	5-11/188	12-5-70	5	North Carolina	D1/93	16/16

No.	DEFENSIVE BACKS	Ht./Wt.	Born	NFL Exp.	College	How acq.	'96 Games GP/GS
23	Stevens, Matt (CB)	6-0/206	6-15-73	2	Appalachian State	D3/96	13/11
37	Woodson, Sean	6-1/214	8-27-74	R	Jackson State	D5/97	—
	SPECIALISTS						
2	Christie, Steve (K)	6-0/185	11-13-67	8	William & Mary	PlanB/92	16/0
3	Huerta, Carlos (K)	5-7/185	6-29-69	2	Miami (Fla.)	FA/96	*4/0
9	Mohr, Chris (P)	6-5/215	5-11-66	8	Alabama	FA/91	16/0

*Hobert played 8 games with Raiders in '96; Huerta played 3 games with Bears and 1 game with Rams.

Abbreviations: D1—draft pick, first round; SupD2—supplemental draft pick second round; W-Den—waivers acquisition from Denver; T-Sea—trade acquisition from Seattle; PlanB—Plan B free-agent acquisition; FA—free-agent acquisition (other than Plan B).

MISCELLANEOUS TEAM DATA

Stadium (capacity, surface):
Rich Stadium (80,091, artificial)
Business address:
One Bills Drive
Orchard Park, N.Y. 14127
Business phone:
716-648-1800
Ticket information:
716-649-0015
Team colors:
Royal blue, scarlet and white
Flagship radio station:
WBEN, 930 AM
Training site:
Fredonia State University
Fredonia, N.Y.
716-648-1800

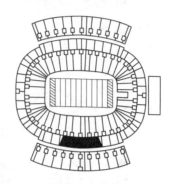

TSN REPORT CARD

Coaching staff	C	The rebuilding chore might be more than Marv Levy can or even wants to handle at age 72 and with two years left on his contract. Levy likes to let his players lead themselves, though that approach might not be as effective with a younger team. The jury is out on whether Dan Henning can upgrade the offense. The defensive coaching remains outstanding.
Offensive backfield	D	An unproven quarterback is the biggest problem. Opponents will load up to stop the run, and force Todd Collins or Billy Joe Hobert to try to beat them throwing. If Thurman Thomas is still the featured runner, that could spell trouble. Rookie Antowain Smith should take over and Thomas should be a specialist.
Receivers	C	Given the offense's new power-oriented philosophy, one of the Bills' top three receivers figures to spend more time watching than catching. Andre Reed made a remarkable comeback last year from leg-muscle problems in 1995, but might not be as productive without Jim Kelly throwing to him. Quinn Early needs to step up to be the home-run threat the club was looking for. Eric Moulds must overcome off-field problems to take advantage of his considerable talent.
Offensive line	F	Kent Hull's retirement leaves a gaping hole in the middle that second-year man Dusty Zeigler or converted guard Jerry Ostroski will be hard-pressed to fill. Corey Louchiey probably will become the new right tackle, while Glenn Parker replaces Ostroski at right guard. The line must overcome all that disruption and still get much better play from left tackle John Fina and left guard Ruben Brown.
Defensive line	A	Right end Bruce Smith is, by far, the best player on the team and the only reason the Bills have any hope of making a playoff run. The next-most critical player is nose tackle Ted Washington, who consistently dominates the middle better than anyone else in the league at that position. Left end Phil Hansen is quietly effective as a pass-rusher and run-stopper. Rookie Marcellus Wiley could significantly upgrade the depth here.
Linebackers	B	With Washington in front of him, Chris Spielman lived up to his reputation as one of the foremost run-stuffing inside linebackers in the NFL. Left outside linebacker Bryce Paup is looking to rebound from groin-muscle problems that slowed him for most of last year. The other inside spot is a question mark, which could be filled by undersized Damien Covington or perhaps John Holecek, whose body has yet to survive an NFL training camp since '95.
Secondary	B	There are plenty of talented athletes in this group, and they do a wonderful job of covering receivers. What they don't do enough of, however, is intercept passes. The biggest question mark is at strong safety, where Henry Jones is trying to battle back from a shattered left tibia that he suffered last season. Matt Stevens struggled badly in his place, and a better replacement has yet to be found.
Special teams	A	The Bills continue to have arguably the best overall kicking game in the NFL. They have a reliable place-kicker in Steve Christie and a punter whose towering kicks enhance coverage and off-set the often difficult weather conditions of Rich Stadium. Moulds is a deadly kickoff-return threat, and cornerback Jeff Burris and Steve Tasker are outstanding on punt returns.

CAROLINA PANTHERS
NFC WESTERN DIVISION

1996 REVIEW
RESULTS

Sept. 1—ATLANTA	W	29-6	
Sept. 8—at New Orleans	W	22-20	
Sept.15—Open date			
Sept.22—SAN FRANCISCO	W	23-7	
Sept.29—at Jacksonville	L	14-24	
Oct. 6—at Minnesota	L	12-14	
Oct. 13—ST. LOUIS	W	45-13	
Oct. 20—NEW ORLEANS	W	19-7	
Oct. 27—at Philadelphia	L	9-20	
Nov. 3—at Atlanta	L	17-20	
Nov. 10—N.Y. GIANTS	W	27-17	
Nov. 17—at St. Louis	W	20-10	
Nov. 24—at Houston	W	31-6	
Dec. 1—TAMPA BAY	W	24-0	
Dec. 8—at San Francisco	W	30-24	
Dec. 15—BALTIMORE	W	27-16	
Dec. 22—PITTSBURGH	W	18-14	
Jan. 5—DALLAS*	W	26-17	
Jan. 12—at Green Bay†	L	13-30	

*NFC divisional playoff game.
†NFC championship game.

RECORDS/RANKINGS

1996 regular-season record: 12-4 (1st in NFC West); 7-1 in division; 9-3 in conference; 8-0 at home; 4-4 on road.

1996 team rankings:

	No.	NFC	NFL
Total offense	*300.8	10	23
Rushing offense	*108.1	6	15
Passing offense	*192.7	11	22
Scoring offense	367	3	7
Total defense	*298.5	5	10
Rushing defense	*97.6	3	8
Passing defense	*200.9	8	12
Scoring defense	218	2	2
Takeaways	38	3	5
Giveaways	25	4	T7
Turnover differential	13	2	3
Sacks	60	1	1
Sacks allowed	36	T7	T13

*Yards per game.

TEAM LEADERS

Scoring (kicking): John Kasay, 145 pts. (34/35 PATs, 37/45 FGs).
Scoring (touchdowns): Wesley Walls, 60 pts. (10 receiving).
Passing: Kerry Collins, 2,454 yds. (364 att., 204 comp., 56.0%, 14 TDs, 9 int.).
Rushing: Anthony Johnson, 1,120 yds. (300 att., 3.7 avg., 6 TDs).
Receptions: Mark Carrier, 58 (808 yds., 13.9 avg., 6 TDs).
Interceptions: Chad Cota, 5 (63 yds., 0 TDs); Eric Davis, 5 (57 yds., 0 TDs).
Sacks: Kevin Greene, 14.5.
Punting: Rohn Stark, 40.6 avg. (77 punts, 3,128 yds., 0 blocked).
Punt returns: Winslow Oliver, 11.5 avg. (52 att., 598 yds., 1 TD).
Kickoff returns: Michael Bates, 30.2 avg. (33 att., 998 yds., 1 TD).

1997 SEASON
CLUB DIRECTORY

Owner & founder
Jerry Richardson
President of Carolina Panthers
Mark Richardson
General manager
Bill Polian
Assistant general manager
Joe Mack
President of Carolinas Stadium Corp.
Jon Richardson
Chief financial officer
Dave Olsen
General counsel
Richard Thigpen Jr.
Asst. dir. of business operations
Charles Waddell
Director of sales
Phil Youtsey
Director of communications
Charlie Dayton
Director of player relations
Donnie Shell
Director of football security
Ed Stillwell
Director of facilities
Tom Fellows
Director of player personnel
Dom Anile
Pro scout
Hal Hunter
Chris Polian
Regional scouts
Jack Bushofsky
Ralph Hawkins
Scouting assistant
Tom Telesco
Area scouts

Hal Athon	Joe Bushofsky
Bob Guarini	Tony Softli
Todd Vasvari	

SCHEDULE

Aug. 31—	WASHINGTON	8:00
Sept. 7—	at Atlanta	1:00
Sept. 14—	at San Diego	1:00
Sept. 21—	KANSAS CITY	1:00
Sept. 29—	SAN FRANCISCO (Mon.)	9:00
Oct. 5—	Open date	
Oct. 12—	at Minnesota	3:00
Oct. 19—	at New Orleans	12:00
Oct. 26—	ATLANTA	8:00
Nov. 2—	OAKLAND	1:00
Nov. 9—	at Denver	2:00
Nov. 16—	at San Francisco	1:00
Nov. 23—	at St. Louis	3:00
Nov. 30—	NEW ORLEANS	1:00
Dec. 8—	at Dallas (Mon.)	8:00
Dec. 14—	GREEN BAY	4:00
Dec. 20—	ST. LOUIS (Sat.)	4:00

All times are for home team.
All games Sunday unless noted.

Head coach
Dom Capers

Assistant coaches
Don Breaux (tight ends)
George Catavolos (def. backs)
Billy Davis (outside linebackers)
Vic Fangio (defensive coordinator)
Ted Gill (defensive line)
Chick Harris (running backs)
Jim McNally (offensive line)
Chip Morton (strength & cond.)
Joe Pendry (offensive coordinator)
Brad Seely (special teams)
John Shoop (quality control/offense)
Kevin Steele (linebackers)
Richard Williamson (wide receivers)

Head groundskeeper
Michal Martin
Equipment manager
Jackie Miles
Video director
Dave Sutherby
Head trainer
John Kasik
Assistant trainer
Al Shuford
Orthopedist
Dr. Don D'Alessandro

DRAFT CHOICES

Rae Carruth, WR, Colorado (first round/27th pick overall).
Mike Minter, DB, Nebraska (2/56).
Kinnon Tatum, LB, Notre Dame (3/87).
Tarek Saleh, LB, Wisconsin (4/122).
Matt Finkes, DE, Ohio State (6/189).
Kris Mangum, TE, Mississippi (7/228).

1997 SEASON
TRAINING CAMP ROSTER

No.	QUARTERBACKS	Ht./Wt.	Born	NFL Exp.	College	How acq.	'96 Games GP/GS
11	Barker, Jay	6-3/215	7-20-72	1	Alabama	D5/95	0/0
7	Beuerlein, Steve	6-3/220	3-7-65	9	Notre Dame	FA/96	8/4
12	Collins, Kerry	6-5/240	12-30-72	3	Penn State	D1a/95	13/12

RUNNING BACKS

No.	RUNNING BACKS	Ht./Wt.	Born	NFL Exp.	College	How acq.	'96 Games GP/GS
21	Biakabutuka, Tim	6-0/210	1-24-74	2	Michigan	D1/96	4/4
43	Greene, Scott (FB)	5-11/225	6-1-72	2	Michigan State	D6/96	8/0
23	Johnson, Anthony	6-0/225	10-25-67	8	Notre Dame	W-Chi/95	16/11
26	O'Neal, Brian (FB)	6-0/233	2-25-70	3	Penn State	FA/95	0/0
20	Oliver, Winslow	5-7/180	3-3-73	2	New Mexico	D3a/96	16/0
22	Smith, Marquette	5-7/190	7-14-72	2	Central Florida	D5/96	0/0

RECEIVERS

No.	RECEIVERS	Ht./Wt.	Born	NFL Exp.	College	How acq.	'96 Games GP/GS
86	Carruth, Rae	5-11/194	1-20-74	R	Colorado	D1/97	—
81	Ismail, Rocket (KR)	5-11/175	11-18-69	5	Notre Dame	T-Oak/96	13/5
48	Mangum, Kris (TE)	6-4/249	5-15-73	R	Mississippi	D7/97	—
89	Mills, Ernie	5-11/192	10-28-68	7	Florida	FA/97	*9/3
87	Muhammad, Muhsin	6-2/217	5-5-73	2	Michigan State	D2/96	9/5
88	Rasby, Walter (TE)	6-3/247	9-7-72	3	Wake Forest	FA/95	16/1
49	Tucker, Syii (TE)	6-4/236	7-31-73	1	Miami (Fla.)	FA/96	0/0
85	Walls, Wesley (TE)	6-5/250	2-26-66	9	Mississippi	FA/96	16/15
84	Wiggins, Brian	5-11/187	6-14-68	2	Texas Southern	FA/95	0/0

OFFENSIVE LINEMEN

No.	OFFENSIVE LINEMEN	Ht./Wt.	Born	NFL Exp.	College	How acq.	'96 Games GP/GS
78	Brockermeyer, Blake (T)	6-4/300	4-11-73	3	Texas	D1c/95	12/12
66	Campbell, Mathew (T)	6-4/270	7-14-72	3	South Carolina	FA/95	9/8
76	Davidds-Garrido, Norberto (T)	6-6/313	10-4-72	2	Southern California	D4a/96	12/8
52	Elliott, Matt (C/G)	6-3/295	10-1-68	4	Michigan	FA/95	16/12
65	Garcia, Frank (C)	6-1/295	1-28-72	3	Washington	D4/95	14/8
67	Hayes, Brandon (G)	6-4/305	3-11-73	2	Central State (Ohio)	FA/95	7/0
63	Rodenhauser, Mark (C)	6-5/280	6-1-61	10	Illinois State	ED/95	16/0
75	Skrepenak, Greg (T)	6-7/325	1-31-70	6	Michigan	FA/96	16/16
64	Whitley, Curtis (C)	6-1/295	5-10-69	6	Clemson	ED/95	11/8

DEFENSIVE LINEMEN

No.	DEFENSIVE LINEMEN	Ht./Wt.	Born	NFL Exp.	College	How acq.	'96 Games GP/GS
59	Finkes, Matt (E)	6-3/272	2-12-75	R	Ohio State	D6/97	—
93	Fox, Mike (E)	6-8/295	8-5-67	8	West Virginia	FA/95	11/11
96	King, Shawn (E)	6-3/278	6-24-72	3	Northeast Louisiana	D2/95	16/0
71	Kragen, Greg (NT)	6-3/267	3-4-62	13	Utah State	ED/95	16/16
90	Philion, Ed (T)	6-2/277	3-27-70	3	Ferris State (Mich.)	W-Buf/96	0/0
99	Seals, Ray (E)	6-3/306	6-17-65	9	None	FA/97	0/0
98	Williams, Gerald (E)	6-3/290	9-8-63	12	Auburn	FA/95	16/14

LINEBACKERS

No.	LINEBACKERS	Ht./Wt.	Born	NFL Exp.	College	How acq.	'96 Games GP/GS
56	Barrow, Micheal	6-2/236	4-19-70	5	Miami, Fla.	FA/97	*16/16
91	Greene, Kevin	6-3/247	7-31-62	13	Auburn	FA/96	16/16
	Herrin, Errick	6-1/235	4-3-69	1	Southern California	FA/97	0/0
50	Jacobs, Ray	6-2/244	8-18-72	3	North Carolina	FA/97	0/0
57	Lathon, Lamar	6-3/260	12-23-67	8	Houston	FA/95	16/16
51	Mills, Sam	5-9/232	6-3-59	11	Montclair (N.J.) State	FA/95	16/16
58	Royal, Andre	6-2/238	12-1-72	3	Alabama	FA/95	16/0
94	Saleh, Tarek	6-1/240	11-7-74	R	Wisconsin	D4/97	—
50	Tatum, Kinnon	6-0/222	7-19-75	R	Notre Dame	D3/97	—

DEFENSIVE BACKS

No.	DEFENSIVE BACKS	Ht./Wt.	Born	NFL Exp.	College	How acq.	'96 Games GP/GS
24	Abraham, Clifton (CB)	5-9/185	12-9-71	2	Florida State	W-Chi/97	*2/0
37	Cota, Chad (S)	6-1/195	8-13-71	3	Oregon	D7a/95	16/2
25	Davis, Eric (CB)	5-11/185	1-26-68	8	Jacksonville (Ala.) State	FA/96	16/16
26	McDaniel, Emmanuel	5-9/178	7-27-72	2	East Carolina	D4b/96	2/0
30	Minter, Mike	5-10/188	1-15-74	R	Nebraska	D2/97	—
27	Pieri, Damon (S)	6-0/186	9-25-70	3	San Diego State	FA/95	16/1
38	Poole, Tyrone (CB/KR)	5-8/188	2-3-72	3	Fort Valley (Ga.) State	D1b/95	15/15
45	Reed, Michael (CB)	5-9/182	8-16-72	2	Boston College	D7b/95	2/0
31	Smith, Rod (CB)	5-11/187	3-12-70	6	Notre Dame	FA/96	8/1
40	Terrell, Pat (S)	6-2/210	3-18-68	8	Notre Dame	FA/95	16/16

No.	SPECIALISTS	Ht./Wt.	Born	NFL Exp.	College	How acq.	'96 Games GP/GS
82	Bates, Michael (KR)	5-10/189	12-19-69	5	Arizona	FA/96	14/0
14	Gragert, Brian (P)........................	6-1/228	8-14-72	1	Wyoming	FA/97	0/0
4	Kasay, John (K)...........................	5-10/198	10-27-69	7	Georgia	FA/95	16/0

*Abraham played 2 games with Bears in '96; Barrow played 16 games with Oilers; Mills played 9 games with Steelers.
Abbreviations: D1—draft pick, first round; SupD2—supplemental draft pick second round; W-Den—waivers acquisition from Denver; T-Sea—trade acquisition from Seattle; PlanB—Plan B free-agent acquisition; FA—free-agent acquisition (other than Plan B).

MISCELLANEOUS TEAM DATA

Stadium (capacity, surface):
Ericsson Stadium
(72,520, grass)
Business address:
800 S. Mint St.
Charlotte, NC 28202-1502
Business phone:
704-358-7000
Ticket information:
704-358-7800
Team colors:
Blue, black and silver
Flagship radio station:
WBT-1110 AM
Training site:
Wofford College
Spartanburg, S.C.
704-358-7000

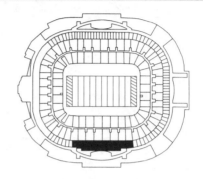

TSN REPORT CARD

Coaching staff	A	In two years, Dom Capers and his staff took a group of players largely comprised of other clubs' rejects and transformed them into a team that won a division championship and came within a victory of the Super Bowl. The staff is intact, for now, but defensive coordinator Vic Fangio is a future NFL head coach.
Offensive backfield	B	Much of this season's success hinges on the left knee of Tim Biakabutuka, who missed most of his rookie year after surgery to repair a torn anterior cruciate ligament. But Anthony Johnson, a 1,000-yard rusher last season, provides solid insurance in case Biakabutuka falters, and Winslow Oliver is an exciting threat as a runner and receiver on third down.
Receivers	C	This group has been transformed from one of the slowest in the league to one of the swiftest. But what the older, departed receivers lacked in speed, they made up for in savvy and production. The new group, which includes first-round pick Rae Carruth, is inexperienced and basically unproven.
Offensive line	C +	Assistant Jim McNally deserves a gold star for keeping this unit together through an injury-riddled '96 season. But the overall consistency would improve if he could find five guys who could stay relatively healthy, which would enable him to cut back on the shuffling.
Defensive line	C -	One of the offseason priorities was to get younger. It didn't happen, which could hamper the plan to put a faster defensive unit on the field. One free agent was signed, but Ray Seals is 32 and missed last season with a rotator-cuff injury. As for the other top three linemen, Greg Kragen and Gerald Williams are older than Seals and Mike Fox turns 30 in August.
Linebackers	A	This group has no peer. Outside backers Kevin Greene and Lamar Lathon are pass-rushing forces who combined to collect 28 sacks last season. Inside, the Panthers have Sam Mills, 37, who continues to age gracefully, and Micheal Barrow, the former Oiler signed as a free agent. Mills, Greene and Lathon were Pro Bowl starters, and Barrow's presence should improve this group, if that's possible.
Secondary	C	Tyrone Poole enters his third season needing to prove himself at cornerback, and Chad Cota will have to step up as the starter at strong safety in place of the departed Brett Maxie. The other starters, cornerback Eric Davis and free safety Pat Terrell, are proven and solid. Second-round pick Mike Minter, a safety, adds speed and depth.
Special teams	A	Capers stresses special teams, and it shows. John Kasay was the top kicker in the league in production last year and Michael Bates was one of the best kick returners. Both made the Pro Bowl. In addition, Oliver is a quality punt returner. But what makes Capers most proud is the consistently superb performance of his coverage units.

CHICAGO BEARS
NFC CENTRAL DIVISION

1996 REVIEW
RESULTS

Sept. 2—DALLAS	W	22-6
Sept. 8—at Washington	L	3-10
Sept.15—MINNESOTA	L	14-20
Sept.22—at Detroit	L	16-35
Sept.29—OAKLAND	W	19-17
Oct. 6—GREEN BAY	L	6-37
Oct. 13—at New Orleans	L	24-27
Oct. 20—Open date		
Oct. 28—at Minnesota	W	15-13
Nov. 3—TAMPA BAY	W	13-10
Nov. 10—at Denver	L	12-17
Nov. 17—at Kansas City	L	10-14
Nov. 24—DETROIT	W	31-14
Dec. 1—at Green Bay	L	17-28
Dec. 8—ST. LOUIS	W	35-9
Dec. 14—SAN DIEGO	W	27-14
Dec. 22—at Tampa Bay	L	19-34

RECORDS/RANKINGS

1996 regular-season record: 7-9 (3rd in NFC Central); 3-5 in division; 5-7 in conference; 6-2 at home; 1-7 on road.
Team record last five years: 37-43 (.463), ranks T16th in league in that span).

1996 team rankings:	No.	NFC	NFL
Total offense	*306.6	9	21
Rushing offense	*107.5	7	16
Passing offense	*199.1	9	19
Scoring offense	283	12	26
Total defense	*305.3	7	12
Rushing defense	*101.1	6	11
Passing defense	*204.2	9	14
Scoring defense	305	7	12
Takeaways	28	11	T18
Giveaways	27	6	T10
Turnover differential	1	T7	T14
Sacks	30	T13	T25
Sacks allowed	23	4	5

*Yards per game.

TEAM LEADERS

Scoring (kicking): Jeff Jaeger, 80 pts. (23/23 PATs, 19/23 FGs).
Scoring (touchdowns): Curtis Conway, 42 pts. (7 receiving).
Passing: Dave Krieg, 2,278 yds. (377 att., 226 comp., 59.9%, 14 TDs, 12 int.).
Rushing: Raymont Harris, 748 yds. (194 att., 3.9 avg., 4 TDs.).
Receptions: Curtis Conway, 81 (1,049 yds., 13.0 avg., 7 TDs.).
Interceptions: Donnell Woolford, 6 (37 yds., 1 TD).
Sacks: Alonzo Spellman, 8.0.
Punting: Todd Sauerbrun, 44.8 avg. (78 punts, 3,491 yds., 0 blocked).
Punt returns: Bobby Engram, 9.1 avg. (31 att., 282 yds., 0 TDs).
Kickoff returns: Bobby Engram, 23.2 avg. (25 att., 580 yds., 0 TDs).

1997 SEASON
CLUB DIRECTORY

Chairman of the board
Edward W. McCaskey
President and chief executive officer
Michael B. McCaskey
Vice president
Timothy E. McCaskey
Secretary
Virginia H. McCaskey
Vice president of operations
Ted Phillips
Director/administration
Tim LeFevour
Director/marketing and communications
Ken Valdiserri
Mgr. of promotions and special events
John Bostrom
Manager of sales
Jack Trompeter
Director/public relations
Bryan Harlan
Assistant directors/public relations
Scott Hagel
Phil Handler
Ticket manager
George McCaskey
Pro scout
Mike McCartney
Regional scouts
Charles Garcia
Jeff Shiver
Charlie Mackey
Gary Smith
Bobby Riggle
Head trainer
Tim Bream
Assistant trainers
Jeff Hay
Eric Sugerman

Head coach
Dave Wannstedt

Assistant coaches
Keith Armstrong (special teams)
Clarence Brooks (defensive line)
Matt Cavanaugh (offensive coordinator/quarterbacks)
Ivan Fears (wide receivers)
Carlos Mainord (defensive backs)
Willie Peete (running backs)
Ted Plumb (tight ends)
Greg Schiano (def. assistant)
Bob Slowik (defensive coordinator/linebackers)
Tony Wise (assistant head coach/offensive line)

Physical development coordinator
Russ Riederer
Asst. physical development coordinator
Steve Little
Equipment manager
Tony Medlin
Assistant equipment managers
Randy Knowles
Carl Piekarski
Director of video services
Dean Pope
Assistant video director
Dave Hendrickson

SCHEDULE

Sept. 1— at Green Bay (Mon.)	8:00
Sept. 7— MINNESOTA	12:00
Sept. 14— DETROIT	12:00
Sept. 21— at New England	1:00
Sept. 28— at Dallas	3:00
Oct. 5— NEW ORLEANS	7:00
Oct. 12— GREEN BAY	12:00
Oct. 19— Open date	
Oct. 26— at Miami	4:00
Nov. 2— WASHINGTON	12:00
Nov. 9— at Minnesota	12:00
Nov. 16— N.Y. JETS	3:00
Nov. 23— TAMPA BAY	12:00
Nov. 27— at Detroit (Thanks.)	12:30
Dec. 7— BUFFALO	12:00
Dec. 14— at St. Louis	7:00
Dec. 21— at Tampa Bay	1:00

All times are for home team.
All games Sunday unless noted.

DRAFT CHOICES

John Allred, TE, Southern California (second round/38th pick overall).
Bob Sapp, G, Washington (3/69).
Darnell Autry, RB, Northwestern (4/105).
Marcus Robinson, WR, South Carolina (4/108).
Van Hiles, DB, Kentucky (5/141).
Shawn Swayda, DE, Arizona State (6/196).
Richard Hogans, LB, Memphis (6/200).
Ricky Parker, DB, San Diego State (6/201).
Mike Miano, DT, Southwest Missouri State (7/210).
Marvin Thomas, DE, Memphis (7/233).

TRAINING CAMP ROSTER

No.	QUARTERBACKS	Ht./Wt.	Born	NFL Exp.	College	How acq.	'96 Games GP/GS
12	Kramer, Erik	6-1/200	11-6-64	8	North Carolina State	FA/94	4/4
13	Mirer, Rick	6-2/214	3-19-70	5	Notre Dame	T-Sea/97	*11/9
18	Stenstrom, Steve	6-1/202	12-23-71	3	Stanford	W-KC/95	1/0
	RUNNING BACKS						
21	Autry, Darnell	5-10/210	6-19-76	R	Northwestern	D4a/97	—
30	Carter, Tony (FB)	5-11/232	8-23-72	4	Minnesota	FA/95	16/11
38	Dulaney, Mike (FB)	6-0/245	9-9-70	3	North Carolina	FA/95	16/0
29	Harris, Raymont	6-0/225	12-23-70	4	Ohio State	D4/94	12/10
44	Hicks, Michael	6-0/194	2-1-73	2	South Carolina State	D7b/96	4/0
31	Salaam, Rashaan	6-1/224	10-8-74	3	Colorado	D1/95	12/6
	RECEIVERS						
84	Allred, John (TE)	6-4/246	9-9-74	R	Southern California	D2/97	—
82	Bownes, Fabien	5-11/180	2-29-72	1	Western Illinois	FA/95	0/0
86	Coleman, Mill	5-9/175	6-19-72	1	Michigan State	FA/95	0/0
80	Conway, Curtis (KR)	6-0/194	3-13-71	5	Southern California	D1/93	16/16
81	Engram, Bobby	5-10/192	1-7-73	2	Penn State	D2/96	16/2
88	Jackson, Jack	5-8/174	11-11-72	3	Florida	D4/95	12/0
85	Jennings, Keith (TE)	6-4/275	5-19-66	8	Clemson	FA/91	6/5
87	Neely, Bobby (TE)	6-3/255	3-22-74	2	Virginia	FA/96	11/5
83	Proehl, Ricky	6-0/190	3-7-68	8	Wake Forest	FA/97	*16/7
19	Robinson, Marcus	6-3/213	2-27-75	R	South Carolina	D4b/97	—
89	Wetnight, Ryan (TE)	6-2/235	11-5-70	5	Stanford	FA/93	11/5
	OFFENSIVE LINEMEN						
63	Burger, Todd (G)	6-3/303	3-20-70	4	Penn State	FA/93	11/8
72	Clark, Jon (T)	6-6/345	4-11-73	2	Temple	D6/96	1/0
64	Heck, Andy (T)	6-6/298	1-1-67	9	Notre Dame	FA/94	16/16
79	Parrish, James (T)	6-5/292	5-19-68	4	Temple	FA/96	*1/0
75	Perry, Todd (G)	6-5/312	11-28-70	4	Kentucky	D4a/93	16/16
65	Pilgrim, Evan (G)	6-4/304	8-14-72	3	Brigham Young	D3/95	6/0
62	Sapp, Bob (G)	6-4/303	9-22-73	R	Washington	D3/97	—
58	Villarrial, Chris (C/G)	6-4/305	6-9-73	2	Indiana (Pa.)	D5/96	14/8
71	Williams, James (T)	6-7/340	3-29-68	7	Cheyney (Pa.)	FA/91	16/16
	DEFENSIVE LINEMEN						
60	Davis, Robert (T)	6-3/271	12-10-68	2	Shippensburg (Pa.)	FA/96	16/0
99	Flanigan, Jim (T)	6-2/286	8-27-71	4	Notre Dame	D3/94	14/14
93	Grasmanis, Paul (T)	6-2/298	8-2-74	2	Notre Dame	D4/96	14/3
	Keyes, Marcus (T)	6-3/303	10-20-73	2	North Alabama	D7a/96	2/0
96	Miano, Mike (T)	6-3/303	12-17-73	R	Southwest Missouri State	D7a/97	—
68	Reeves, Carl (E)	6-4/265	12-17-71	2	North Carolina State	D6b/95	5/0
98	Simpson, Carl (T)	6-2/292	4-18-70	5	Florida State	D2/93	16/16
90	Spellman, Alonzo (E)	6-4/292	9-27-71	6	Ohio State	D1/92	16/15
78	Swayda, Shawn (E)	6-5/279	9-4-74	R	Arizona State	D6a/97	—
94	Thierry, John (E)	6-4/265	9-4-71	4	Alcorn State	D1/94	16/2
95	Thomas, Mark (E)	6-5/273	5-6-69	5	North Carolina State	FA/97	*12/0
73	Thomas, Marvin (E)	6-5/264	10-19-73	R	Memphis	D7b/97	—
97	Zorich, Chris (T)	6-1/282	3-13-69	7	Notre Dame	D2/91	0/0
	LINEBACKERS						
52	Cox, Bryan	6-4/250	2-17-68	7	Western Illinois	FA/96	9/9
57	Harris, Sean	6-3/245	2-25-72	3	Arizona	D3/95	15/0
94	Hogans, Richard	6-2/249	7-8-75	R	Memphis	D6b/97	—
95	Howard, Dana	6-1/244	2-25-72	3	Illinois	FA/96	3/0
53	Lowery, Michael	6-0/224	2-14-74	2	Mississippi	FA/96	16/0
92	Minter, Barry	6-2/242	1-28-70	5	Tulsa	T-Dal/93	16/7
54	Peterson, Tony	6-0/223	1-23-72	4	Notre Dame	FA/97	*13/0
	DEFENSIVE BACKS						
35	Burton, James (CB)	5-9/184	4-22-71	4	Fresno State	FA/94	16/3
23	Carter, Marty (S)	6-1/212	12-17-69	7	Middle Tennessee State	FA/95	16/16
30	Carter, Tom (CB)	6-0/187	9-5-72	4	Notre Dame	FA/97	*16/16
46	Forbes, Marlon (S)	6-1/205	12-25-71	3	Penn State	FA/95	15/0
27	Harris, Walt (CB)	5-11/194	8-10-74	2	Mississippi State	D1/96	15/13

1997 SEASON Chicago Bears

No.	DEFENSIVE BACKS	Ht./Wt.	Born	NFL Exp.	College	How acq.	'96 Games GP/GS
48	Hiles, Van	6-0/195	11-1-75	R	Kentucky	D5b/97	—
33	Hughes, Tyrone (CB/KR)	5-9/175	1-14-70	5	Nebraska	FA/97	*16/1
32	Joseph, Dwayne (CB)	5-9/186	6-2-72	3	Syracuse	FA/94	0/0
26	Mangum, John (S)	5-10/190	3-16-67	8	Alabama	FA/90	16/2
36	Marshall, Anthony (S)	6-1/212	9-16-70	4	Louisiana State	FA/94	13/3
22	Martin, Chris (CB)	5-9/181	9-1-74	1	Northwestern	FA/96	1/0
24	Miniefield, Kevin	5-9/180	3-2-70	4	Arizona State	FA/93	13/3
37	Parker, Ricky	6-1/205	12-4-74	R	San Diego State	D6c/97	—
	SPECIALISTS						
1	Jaeger, Jeff (K)	5-11/190	11-26-64	11	Washington	FA/96	13/0
16	Sauerbrun, Todd (P)	5-10/209	1-20-71	3	West Virginia	D2/95	16/0

*T. Carter played 16 games with Redskins in '96; Hughes played 16 games with Saints; Mirer played 11 games with Seahawks; Parrish played 1 game with Jets; Peterson played 13 games with 49ers; Proehl played 16 games with Seahawks; Mark Thomas played 12 games with Panthers.

Abbreviations: D1—draft pick, first round; SupD2—supplemental draft pick second round; W-Den—waivers acquisition from Denver; T-Sea—trade acquisition from Seattle; PlanB—Plan B free-agent acquisition; FA—free-agent acquisition (other than Plan B).

MISCELLANEOUS TEAM DATA

Stadium (capacity, surface):
Soldier Field (66,944, grass)
Business address:
Halas Hall
250 N. Washington Road
Lake Forest, IL 60045
Business phone:
847-295-6600
Ticket information:
847-615-2327
Team colors:
Navy blue, orange and white
Flagship radio station:
WGN, 720 AM
Training site:
University of Wisconsin-Platteville
Platteville, Wis.
608-342-1201

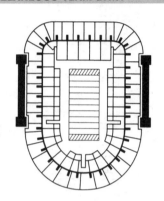

TSN REPORT CARD

Coaching staff	C	The Bears tend to be too predictable as games and the season progress. Play-calling on both sides of the ball has created some uncertainty at times. The staff needs to get young players on the field and producing faster.
Offensive backfield	B	There's excellent depth, but injuries have retarded development the past two years. The problem may be that there are a lot of good backs but no great one to establish a dominant running game. All eyes will be on new starting quarterback Rick Mirer this season.
Receivers	B	Curtis Conway is top-echelon and Bobby Engram showed rookie flashes. Ricky Proehl, who arrives from the Seahawks, is a quality No. 3 man, but there is no depth beyond that trio.
Offensive line	A	This underrated group is as good as there is at pass protection. Moving Chris Villarrial from guard to center muscles up the interior, but he needs to master the Bears' zone-blocking schemes the way former center Jerry Fontenot, a free agent not expected to return, did.
Defensive line	C -	If left end John Thierry can break through the way right tackle Carl Simpson did in '96, this group could become a force. Speed is not a problem; size is. The staff's schemes have not helped the pass rush.
Linebackers	C -	The changing of the guard makes '97 a pivotal year. Sean Harris finally starts after sitting two years and must provide impact to upgrade a solid, if unspectacular, unit.
Secondary	C	Tom Carter, signed from the Redskins, is not the tackler that Donnell Woolford, now with the Steelers, was. But if coaches allow Carter and Walt Harris to press and take advantage of their size and speed, the cornerbacks could be a factor.
Special teams	C -	The kicking has been above average, but the return and coverage units were adequate—at best. Tyrone Hughes, signed from the Saints, adds a home-run hitter to the kickoff return team.

CINCINNATI BENGALS
AFC CENTRAL DIVISION

1996 REVIEW
RESULTS

Sept. 1—at St. Louis	L	16-26
Sept. 8—at San Diego	L	14-27
Sept.15—NEW ORLEANS	W	30-15
Sept.22—Open date		
Sept.29—DENVER	L	10-14
Oct. 6—HOUSTON (OT)	L	27-30
Oct. 13—at Pittsburgh	L	10-20
Oct. 20—at San Francisco	L	21-28
Oct. 27—JACKSONVILLE	W	28-21
Nov. 3—at Baltimore	W	24-21
Nov. 10—PITTSBURGH	W	34-24
Nov. 17—at Buffalo	L	17-31
Nov. 24—ATLANTA	W	41-31
Dec. 1—at Jacksonville	L	27-30
Dec. 8—BALTIMORE	W	21-14
Dec. 15—at Houston	W	21-13
Dec. 22—INDIANAPOLIS	W	31-24

RECORDS/RANKINGS

1996 regular-season record: 8-8 (T3rd in AFC Central); 5-3 in division; 6-6 in conference; 6-2 at home; 2-6 on road.
Team record last five years: 26-54 (.325, ranks 26th in league in that span).

1996 team rankings:	No.	AFC	NFL
Total offense	*326.6	6	10
Rushing offense	*112.1	8	13
Passing offense	*214.5	6	12
Scoring offense	372	3	5
Total defense	*341.8	13	25
Rushing defense	*102.7	6	12
Passing defense	*239.1	14	29
Scoring defense	369	11	23
Takeaways	44	1	1
Giveaways	25	4	T1
Turnover differential	19	1	1
Sacks	32	11	T21
Sacks allowed	47	13	26
*Yards per game.			

TEAM LEADERS

Scoring (kicking): Doug Pelfrey, 110 pts. (41/41 PATs, 23/28 FGs).
Scoring (touchdowns): Carl Pickens, 74 pts. (12 receiving, 1 2-pt. conv.).
Passing: Jeff Blake, 3,624 yds. (549 att., 308 comp., 56.1%, 24 TDs, 14 int.).
Rushing: Garrison Hearst, 847 yds. (225 att., 3.8 avg., 0 TDs).
Receptions: Carl Pickens, 100 (1,180 yds., 11.8 avg., 12 TDs).
Interceptions: Ashley Ambrose, 8 (63 yds., 1 TD).
Sacks: Dan Wilkinson, 6.5.
Punting: Lee Johnson, 45.4 avg. (80 punts, 3,630 yds., 1 blocked).
Punt returns: Corey Sawyer, 7.8 avg. (15 att., 117 yds., 0 TDs).
Kickoff returns: David Dunn, 22.3 avg. (35 att., 782 yds., 1 TD).

1997 SEASON
CLUB DIRECTORY

Chairman of the board
Austin E. Knowlton
President/general manager
Mike Brown
Vice president
John Sawyer
Asst. g.m./director of player personnel
Pete Brown
General counsel/corporate secretary
Katherine Blackburn
Asst. sec./treasurer; scouting/personnel
Paul Brown
Business manager
Bill Connelly
Director of stadium development
Troy Blackburn
Director of community affairs
Jeff Berding
Stadium sales/marketing
Jennifer L. McNally
Scouting/personnel
Jim Lippincott
Scouts
Kale Ane
Earl Biederman
Frank Smouse
Frank Uible
Public relations director
Jack Brennan
Assistant public relations director
Patrick J. Combs
Comptroller
Jay Reis
Financial director
Bill Scanlon
Director of marketing
Mike Hoffbauer
Asst. dir. of marketing/entertainment dir.
Dave Slyby
Ticket manager
Paul Kelly

Head coach
Bruce Coslet

Assistant coaches
Paul Alexander (offensive line)
Jim Anderson (running backs)
Ken Anderson (offensive coord.)
Louie Cioffi (def. staff assistant)
Mark Duffner (linebackers)
John Garrett (off. staff assistant)
Ray Horton (defensive backs)
Tim Krumrie (defensive line)
Dick LeBeau (defensive coord./
    assistant head coach)
Al Roberts (special teams)
Kim Wood (strength & cond.)
Bob Wylie (tight ends)

Team physicians
Robert Heidt Jr.   Doug Logan
Walter Timperman   Michael Welch
Trainer
Paul Sparling
Assistant trainers
Billy Brooks
Rob Recker
Equipment manager
Tom Gray
Video director
Al Davis
Assistant video director
Travis Brammer

SCHEDULE

Aug. 31— ARIZONA		1:00
Sept. 7— at Baltimore		1:00
Sept. 14— Open date		
Sept. 21— at Denver		2:00
Sept. 28— N.Y. JETS		4:00
Oct. 5— at Jacksonville		1:00
Oct. 12— at Tennessee		12:00
Oct. 19— PITTSBURGH		4:00
Oct. 26— at N.Y. Giants		1:00
Nov. 2— SAN DIEGO		1:00
Nov. 9— at Indianapolis		1:00
Nov. 16— at Pittsburgh		1:00
Nov. 23— JACKSONVILLE		4:00
Nov. 30— at Philadelphia		1:00
Dec. 4— TENNESSEE (Thur.)		8:00
Dec. 14— DALLAS		1:00
Dec. 21— BALTIMORE		1:00

All times are for home team.
All games Sunday unless noted.

DRAFT CHOICES

Reinard Wilson, LB, Florida State (first round/14th pick overall).
Corey Dillon, RB, Washington (2/43).
Rod Payne, C, Michigan (3/76).
Tremain Mack, DB, Miami, Fla. (4/111).
Andre Purvis, DT, North Carolina (5/144).
Canute Curtis, LB, West Virginia (6/176).
William Carr, DT, Michigan (7/217).

TRAINING CAMP ROSTER

No.	QUARTERBACKS	Ht./Wt.	Born	NFL Exp.	College	How acq.	'96 Games GP/GS
8	Blake, Jeff	6-0/202	12-4-70	6	East Carolina	W-NYJ/94	16/16
7	Esiason, Boomer	6-5/224	4-17-61	14	Maryland	FA/97	*10/8
4	Wilhelm, Erik	6-3/217	11-16-65	8	Oregon State	FA/96	3/0
	RUNNING BACKS						
21	Bieniemy, Eric	5-7/198	8-15-69	7	Colorado	FA/95	16/0
32	Carter, Ki-Jana	5-10/227	9-12-73	3	Penn State	D1/95	16/4
29	Cothran, Jeff (FB)	6-1/249	6-28-71	4	Ohio State	D3/94	11/11
28	Dillon, Corey	6-2/220	10-24-75	R	Washington	D2/97	—
41	Graham, Scottie	5-9/222	3-28-69	5	Ohio State	FA/97	*11/0
44	Milne, Brian (FB)	6-3/254	1-7-73	2	Penn State	D4/96	6/5
	RECEIVERS						
89	Battaglia, Marco (TE)	6-3/250	1-25-73	2	Rutgers	D2/96	16/0
80	Dunn, David (KR)	6-3/210	6-10-72	3	Fresno State	D5/95	16/0
84	Hill, Jeff (KR)	5-11/178	9-24-72	3	Purdue	FA/94	10/0
85	Hundon, James	6-1/195	4-9-71	2	Portland State	FA/96	5/0
83	Jordan, Kevin	6-1/188	12-14-72	1	UCLA	W-Ari/96	0/0
82	McGee, Tony (TE)	6-3/246	4-21-71	5	Michigan	D2/93	16/16
81	Pickens, Carl	6-2/206	3-23-70	6	Tennessee	D2/92	16/16
87	Sadowski, Troy (TE)	6-5/250	12-8-65	8	Georgia	FA/94	16/0
86	Scott, Darnay (KR)	6-1/180	7-7-72	4	San Diego State	D2/94	16/16
	OFFENSIVE LINEMEN						
71	Anderson, Willie (T)	6-5/325	7-11-75	2	Auburn	D1/96	16/10
66	Blackman, Ken (G)	6-6/315	11-8-72	2	Illinois	D3/96	14/10
74	Braham, Rich (C/G)	6-4/290	11-6-70	4	West Virginia	W-Ari/94	16/16
65	Brilz, Darrick (C)	6-3/287	2-14-64	11	Oregon State	FA/94	13/13
75	Brown, Anthony (T/G)	6-5/310	11-6-72	3	Utah	FA/95	7/0
72	Brumfield, Scott (G)	6-8/320	8-19-70	4	Brigham Young	FA/93	9/8
60	Jones, Rod (G/T)	6-4/315	1-11-74	2	Kansas	D7/96	6/1
64	Payne, Rod (C)	6-4/305	6-14-74	R	Michigan	D3/97	—
77	Sargent, Kevin (G)	6-6/284	3-31-69	6	Eastern Washington	FA/92	0/0
59	Truitt, Greg (C)	6-0/235	12-8-65	4	Penn State	FA/94	16/0
61	Tuten, Melvin (T)	6-6/305	11-11-71	3	Syracuse	D3/95	16/7
63	Walter, Joe (T)	6-7/292	6-18-63	13	Texas Tech	D7a/85	15/15
	DEFENSIVE LINEMEN						
96	Carr, William (T)	6-0/269	1-13-75	R	Michigan	D7/97	—
92	Copeland, John (E)	6-3/286	9-20-70	5	Alabama	D1/93	13/13
90	Johnson, Tim (T)	6-3/286	1-29-65	11	Penn State	FA/96	14/13
94	Langford, Jevon (E)	6-3/275	2-16-74	2	Oklahoma State	D4/96	12/3
93	Morabito, Tim (T)	6-3/288	10-12-73	2	Boston College	FA/96	7/1
97	Purvis, Andre (T)	6-5/290	7-14-73	R	North Carolina	D5/97	—
70	Smith, Artie (E)	6-4/285	5-15-70	5	Louisiana Tech	W-SF/94	16/14
79	Stallings, Ramondo (E)	6-7/285	11-21-71	4	San Diego State	D7/94	13/3
99	Wilkinson, Dan (T)	6-5/313	3-13-73	4	Ohio State	D1/94	16/16
67	von Oelhoffen, Kimo (T)	6-4/300	1-30-71	4	Boise State	D6/94	11/1
	LINEBACKERS						
55	Collins, Andre	6-1/231	5-4-68	8	Penn State	FA/95	14/0
98	Curtis, Canute	6-2/250	8-4-74	4	West Virginia	D6/97	0/0
51	Dixon, Gerald	6-3/250	6-20-69	6	South Carolina	FA/96	16/1
50	Francis, James	6-5/252	8-4-68	8	Baylor	D1/90	16/15
56	McDonald, Ricardo	6-2/240	11-8-69	6	Pittsburgh	D4/92	16/15
52	Neal, Randy	6-3/236	12-29-72	3	Virginia	FA/96	1/0
57	Sutter, Eddie	6-3/235	10-3-69	5	Northwestern	FA/97	*16/4
58	Tovar, Steve	6-3/244	4-25-70	5	Ohio State	D3/93	13/13
53	Tumulty, Tom	6-2/242	2-11-73	2	Pittsburgh	D6/96	16/3
91	Wilson, Reinard	6-2/259	12-12-73	R	Florida State	D1/97	—
	DEFENSIVE BACKS						
33	Ambrose, Ashley	5-10/182	9-17-70	6	Mississippi Valley State	FA/96	16/16
38	Borgella, Jocelyn (CB)	5-10/180	8-26-71	4	Cincinnati	FA/97	*11/0
24	Jones, Roger (CB)	5-9/175	4-22-69	7	Tennessee State	W-TB/94	14/1
34	Mack, Tremain	6-0/195	11-21-74	R	Miami (Fla.)	D4/97	—
31	Myers, Greg (S)	6-1/197	9-30-72	2	Colorado State	D5/96	14/0
26	Orlando, Bo (S)	5-10/180	4-3-66	8	West Virginia	FA/96	16/16

No.	DEFENSIVE BACKS	Ht./Wt.	Born	NFL Exp.	College	How acq.	'96 Games GP/GS
23	Sawyer, Corey (CB)	5-11/171	10-4-71	4	Florida State	D4/94	15/2
35	Shade, Sam (S)	6-1/191	6-14-73	3	Alabama	D4/95	12/0
22	Spencer, Jimmy (CB)	5-9/180	3-29-69	6	Florida	FA/96	15/14
27	Walker, Bracey (S)	6-0/200	10-28-70	4	North Carolina	W-KC/94	16/16
37	Wheeler, Leonard (CB)	5-11/189	1-15-69	6	Troy (Ala.) State	D3/92	13/0
	Wright, Lawrence (S)	6-1/209	9-6-73	R	Florida	FA/97	—
	SPECIALISTS						
11	Johnson, Lee (P)	6-2/200	11-27-61	13	Brigham Young	W-Cle/88	16/0
9	Pelfrey, Doug (K)	5-11/185	9-25-70	5	Kentucky	D8/93	16/0

*Borgella played 11 games with Lions in '96; Esiason played 10 games with Cardinals; Graham played 11 games with Vikings; Sutter played 16 games with Ravens.

Abbreviations: D1—draft pick, first round; SupD2—supplemental draft pick second round; W-Den—waivers acquisition from Denver; T-Sea—trade acquisition from Seattle; PlanB—Plan B free-agent acquisition; FA—free-agent acquisition (other than Plan B).

MISCELLANEOUS TEAM DATA

Stadium (capacity, surface):
Cinergy Field
(60,389, artificial)
Business address:
One Bengals Drive
Cincinnati, OH 45204
Business phone:
513-621-3550
Ticket information:
513-621-3550
Team colors:
Black, orange and white
Flagship radio stations:
WBOB 1160 AM; WUBE 105.1 FM
Training site:
Georgetown College
Georgetown, Ky.
502-863-7088

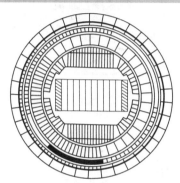

TSN REPORT CARD

Coaching staff	B	Players believe in Bruce Coslet, and they seem to be behind Dick LeBeau. Coslet, Jeff Blake and offensive coordinator Ken Anderson all seem to be on the same wavelength. Last year's second half went so smoothly; how will Coslet react to adversity?
Offensive backfield	C	Ki-Jana Carter really hasn't proven a thing, except that he can score on 1- or 2-yard runs and find his way to the edge of the stands to give the ball to his mom. Eric Bieniemy is a superior third-down back but too small to handle a greater role. Corey Dillon has potential but also must prove himself.
Receivers	B +	Carl Pickens is one of the best around, and Darnay Scott may yet develop into Pro Bowl material. Every team would like to have somebody like David Dunn to make the tough catches at crucial times. All this group lacks is a little overall speed.
Offensive line	C	Their problems appear to be solved, but like the running backs, they'll have to prove it first. At least depth shouldn't be a problem; four of the projected backups have started before, and the fifth, center Rod Payne, is a highly regarded third-round draft choice.
Defensive line	C	Lack of an experienced nose tackle hurts. In fairness, few of these animals exist. But it'll be a long year for the Bengals if Kimo von Oelhoffen or somebody doesn't emerge. John Copeland is certainly talented, but can he stay healthy? The move to end should only help Dan Wilkinson.
Linebackers	C	This grade will rise dramatically if Reinard Wilson handles the transition from end. Otherwise, the Bengals may wish they were still playing a 4-3. The new scheme could help James Francis have a career year. Steve Tovar has been dependable, but he's trying to overcome a major injury.
Secondary	B	Tremain Mack may have been the steal of the draft. He should make an immediate impact. Ashley Ambrose is excellent and improving. Deep balls occasionally give Jimmy Spencer trouble, but he's definitely capable. Still, depth at cornerback is a problem.
Special teams	B -	They were awful last year, but they appear on the road to recovery with new coach Al Roberts. Mack could lend some dash to the return teams and some big plays on coverage units. Kicker Doug Pelfrey and punter Lee Johnson are steady and solid.

DALLAS COWBOYS
NFC EASTERN DIVISION

1996 REVIEW
RESULTS

Sept. 2—at Chicago	L	6-22
Sept. 8—N.Y. GIANTS	W	27-0
Sept.15—INDIANAPOLIS	L	24-25
Sept.22—at Buffalo	L	7-10
Sept.30—at Philadelphia	W	23-19
Oct. 6—Open date		
Oct. 13—ARIZONA	W	17-3
Oct. 20—ATLANTA	W	32-28
Oct. 27—at Miami	W	29-10
Nov. 3—PHILADELPHIA	L	21-31
Nov. 10—at San Fran. (OT)	W	20-17
Nov. 18—GREEN BAY	W	21-6
Nov. 24—at N.Y. Giants	L	6-20
Nov. 28—WASHINGTON	W	21-10
Dec. 8—at Arizona	W	10-6
Dec. 15—NEW ENGLAND	W	12-6
Dec. 22—at Washington	L	10-37
Dec. 28—MINNESOTA*	W	40-15
Jan. 5—at Carolina†	L	17-26

*NFC wild-card game.
†NFC divisional playoff game.

RECORDS/RANKINGS

1996 regular-season record: 10-6 (1st in NFC East); 5-3 in division; 8-4 in conference; 6-2 at home; 4-4 on road.
Team record last five years: 59-21 (.738, ranks 2nd in league in that span).
1996 team rankings:

	No.	NFC	NFL
Total offense	*297.7	11	24
Rushing offense	*102.6	8	18
Passing offense	*195.1	10	20
Scoring offense	286	11	25
Total defense	*273.9	2	3
Rushing defense	*98.5	4	9
Passing defense	*175.4	2	2
Scoring defense	250	3	3
Takeaways	33	7	12
Giveaways	29	7	T12
Turnover differential	4	5	T9
Sacks	37	T6	T10
Sacks allowed	19	1	1

*Yards per game.

TEAM LEADERS

Scoring (kicking): Chris Boniol, 120 pts. (24/25 PATs, 32/36 FGs).
Scoring (touchdowns): Emmitt Smith, 90 pts. (12 rushing, 6 receiving).
Passing: Troy Aikman, 3,126 yds. (465 att., 296 comp., 63.7%, 12 TDs, 13 int.).
Rushing: Emmitt Smith, 1,204 yds. (327 att., 3.7 avg., 12 TDs).
Receptions: Michael Irvin, 64 (962 yds., 15.0 avg., 2 TDs).
Interceptions: Kevin Smith, 5 (45 yds., 0 TDs); Darren Woodson, 5 (43 yds., 0 TDs).
Sacks: Tony Tolbert, 12.0.
Punting: John Jett, 42.6 avg. (74 punts, 3,150 yds., 0 blocked).
Punt returns: Kelvin Martin, 9.1 avg. (41 att., 373 yds., 0 TDs).
Kickoff returns: Herschel Walker, 28.9 avg. (27 att., 779 yds., 0 TDs).

1997 SEASON
CLUB DIRECTORY

President/general manager
  Jerry Jones
Vice presidents
  Charlotte Anderson
  George Hays
  Jerry Jones Jr.
  Stephen Jones
Treasurer
  Robert Nunez
Director of public relations
  Rich Dalrymple
Assistant director of public relations
  Brett Daniels
Ticket manager
  Carol Padgett
Director of college and pro scouting
  Larry Lacewell
Scouts
  Tom Ciskowski
  Jim Garrett
  Walter Juliff
  Bobby Marks
  Walt Yowarsky
Head trainer
  Jim Maurer
Assistant trainers
  Britt Brown
  Bob Haas
Physicians
  Robert Vandermeer
  John Baker
  J.R. Zamorano
Equipment/practice fields manager
  Mike McCord

SCHEDULE

Aug. 31— at Pittsburgh	1:00	
Sept. 7— at Arizona	5:00	
Sept. 15— PHILADELPHIA (Mon.)	8:00	
Sept. 21— Open date		
Sept. 28— CHICAGO	3:00	
Oct. 5— at N.Y. Giants	1:00	
Oct. 13— at Washington (Mon.)	9:00	
Oct. 19— JACKSONVILLE	12:00	
Oct. 26— at Philadelphia	1:00	
Nov. 2— at San Francisco	1:00	
Nov. 9— ARIZONA	12:00	
Nov. 16— WASHINGTON	12:00	
Nov. 23— at Green Bay	12:00	
Nov. 27— TENNESSEE (Thanks.)	3:00	
Dec. 8— CAROLINA (Mon.)	8:00	
Dec. 14— at Cincinnati	1:00	
Dec. 21— N.Y. GIANTS	12:00	

All times are for home team.
All games Sunday unless noted.

Head coach
Barry Switzer

Assistant coaches
Hubbard Alexander (wide receivers)
Joe Avezzano (special teams)
Jim Bates (linebackers)
Craig Boller (defensive tackles)
Joe Brodsky (running backs)
Dave Campo (def. coordinator)
Robert Ford (tight ends)
Tommy Hart (defensive ends)
Steve Hoffman (kickers/quality control)
Hudson Houck (assistant head coach/offensive line)
Joe Juraszek (strength & cond.)
Clancy Pendergrast (defensive assistant)
Jack Reilly (quarterbacks)
Mike Zimmer (defensive backs)

Video director
Robert Blackwell
Director of operations
Bruce Mays

DRAFT CHOICES

David LaFleur, TE, Louisiana State (first round/22 pick overall).
Dexter Coakley, LB, Appalachian State (3/65).
Steve Scifres, T, Wyoming (3/83).
Kenny Wheaton, DB, Oregon (3/94).
Antonio Anderson, DT, Syracuse (4/101).
Macey Brooks, WR, James Madison (4/127).
Nicky Sualua, RB, Ohio State (4/129).
Lee Vaughn, DB, Wyoming (6/187).
Omar Stoutmire, DB, Fresno State (7/224).

No.	QUARTERBACKS	Ht./Wt.	Born	NFL Exp.	College	How acq.	'96 Games GP/GS
8	Aikman, Troy	6-4/219	11-21-66	9	UCLA	D1/89	15/15
17	Garrett, Jason	6-2/195	3-28-66	5	Princeton	FA/93	1/0
18	Wilson, Wade	6-3/208	2-1-59	17	East Texas State	FA/95	3/1
	RUNNING BACKS						
48	Johnston, Daryl (FB)	6-2/242	2-10-66	9	Syracuse	D2/89	16/15
22	Smith, Emmitt	5-9/209	5-15-69	8	Florida	D1/90	15/15
45	Sualua, Nicky (FB)	5-11/257	4-16-75	R	Ohio State	D4c/97	—
	Walker, Herschel	6-1/225	3-3-62	11	Georgia	FA/96	16/1
20	Williams, Sherman	5-8/202	8-13-73	3	Alabama	D2/95	16/1
	RECEIVERS						
86	Bjornson, Eric (TE)	6-4/236	12-15-71	3	Washington	D4/95	14/10
19	Brooks, Macey	6-5/220	2-2-75	R	James Madison	D4b/97	—
87	Davis, Billy	6-1/205	7-6-72	3	Pittsburgh	FA/95	13/0
88	Irvin, Michael	6-2/207	3-5-66	10	Miami, Fla.	D1/88	11/11
89	LaFleur, David (TE)	6-7/280	1-29-74	R	Louisiana State	D1/97	—
	Martin, Kelvin (KR)	5-9/162	5-14-65	10	Boston College	FA/96	16/1
	Miller, Anthony	5-11/190	4-15-65	10	Tennessee	FA/94	*16/16
84	Novacek, Jay (TE)	6-4/234	10-24-62	12	Wyoming	PlanB/90	0/0
83	Watkins, Kendell (TE)	6-1/282	3-8-73	3	Mississippi State	D2/95	0/0
80	Williams, Stepfret	6-/170	6-14-73	2	Northeast Louisiana	D3b/96	5/0
	OFFENSIVE LINEMEN						
73	Allen, Larry (G/T)	6-3/326	11-27-71	4	Sonoma State (Calif.)	D2/94	16/16
63	Flannery, John (G/C)	6-3/304	1-13-69	7	Syracuse	FA/96	1/0
69	Hegamin, George (T)	6-7/331	2-14-73	4	North Carolina State	D3/94	16/1
70	Hellestrae, Dale (G/C)	6-5/291	7-11-62	13	Southern Methodist	T-Rai/90	16/0
61	Newton, Nate (G)	6-3/320	12-20-61	12	Florida A&M	FA/86	0/0
77	Scifres, Steve (G/T)	6-4/300	1-22-72	R	Wyoming	D3a/97	—
50	Shiver, Clay (C)	6-2/294	12-7-72	2	Florida State	D3a/96	14/0
71	Tuinei, Mark (T)	6-5/314	3-31-60	15	Hawaii	FA/83	15/15
79	Williams, Erik (T)	6-6/328	9-7-68	7	Central State (Ohio)	D3/91	16/16
	DEFENSIVE LINEMEN						
96	Anderson, Antonio (T)	6-6/318	6-4-73	R	Syracuse	D4a/97	—
91	Benson, Darren (T)	6-7/308	8-25-74	3	None	FA/95	0/0
98	Carver, Shante (E)	6-5/253	2-12-71	4	Arizona State	D1/94	10/7
75	Casillas, Tony (T)	6-3/278	10-26-63	12	Oklahoma	FA/96	16/3
94	Haley, Charles (E)	6-5/260	1-6-64	12	James Madison	T-SF/92	5/5
95	Hennings, Chad (T)	6-6/291	10-20-65	6	Air Force	D11/88	15/15
78	Lett, Leon	6-6/295	10-12-68	7	Emporia (Kan.) State	D7/91	13/13
97	Pittman, Kavika (E)	6-6/267	10-9-74	2	McNeese State	D2a/96	15/0
62	Renfro, Leonard (T)	6-3/308	6-29-70	3	Colorado	FA/96	0/0
51	Thomas, Broderick (E)	6-4/254	2-20-67	9	Nebraska	FA/96	16/9
92	Tolbert, Tony (E)	6-6/263	12-29-67	9	Texas-El Paso	D4/89	16/16
93	Ulufale, Mike (E)	6-4/284	2-1-72	2	Brigham Young	D3c/96	3/0
	LINEBACKERS						
59	Campos, Alan	6-3/236	3-3-73	2	Louisville	D5b/96	15/0
52	Coakley, Dexter	5-10/215	10-20-72	R	Appalachian State	D3/97	—
56	Godfrey, Randall	6-2/237	4-6-73	2	Georgia	D2b/96	16/6
90	Mack, Rico	6-4/248	2-22-71	4	Appalachian State	FA/97	0/0
55	Strickland, Fred	6-2/251	8-15-66	10	Purdue	FA/96	16/16
	DEFENSIVE BACKS						
29	Brice, Alundis (CB)	5-10/178	5-1-70	3	Mississippi	D4b/95	14/1
35	Davis, Wendell (CB)	5-10/183	6-27-73	2	Oklahoma	D6/96	13/0
24	Harper, Roger (S)	6-2/223	10-26-70	5	Ohio State	T-Atl/96	14/0
31	Marion, Brock (S)	5-11/197	6-11-70	5	Nevada	D7/93	10/10
21	Sanders, Deion (CB)	6-1/185	8-9-67	9	Florida State	FA/95	16/15
26	Smith, Kevin (CB)	5-11/190	4-7-70	6	Texas A&M	D1/92	16/16
43	Stoutmire, Omar (S)	5-11/198	7-9-74	R	Fresno State	D7/97	—
37	Vaughn, Lee (CB)	5-11/184	11-27-74	R	Wyoming	D6/97	—
30	Wheaton, Kenny (CB)	5-10/190	3-8-75	R	Oregon	D3b/97	—
42	Williams, Charlie (S)	6-0/189	2-2-72	3	Bowling Green State	D3/95	7/0
28	Woodson, Darren (S)	6-1/219	4-25-69	6	Arizona State	D2/92	16/16

No.	SPECIALISTS	Ht./Wt.	Born	NFL Exp.	College	How acq.	'96 Games GP/GS
	Calicchio, Lonnie (P)	6-3/230	10-24-72	1	Mississippi	FA/97	0/0
	Cunningham, Richie (K)	5-10/170	8-18-70	1	S.W. Louisiana	FA/97	0/0

*Miller played 16 games with Broncos in '96.

Abbreviations: D1—draft pick, first round; SupD2—supplemental draft pick second round; W-Den—waivers acquisition from Denver; T-Sea—trade acquisition from Seattle; PlanB—Plan B free-agent acquisition; FA—free-agent acquisition (other than Plan B).

MISCELLANEOUS TEAM DATA

Stadium (capacity, surface):
Texas Stadium
(65,812, artificial)
Business address:
One Cowboys Parkway
Irving, TX 75063
Business phone:
972-556-9900
Ticket information:
972-579-5000
Team colors:
Blue, metallic silver blue and white
Flagship radio station:
KVIL, 103.7 FM
Training site:
St. Edward's University
Austin, Tex.
214-556-9900

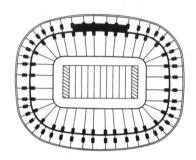

TSN REPORT CARD

Coaching staff	B	Judging from last year's effort, not a bad group, considering this club was one game away from its fourth consecutive NFC title game after all the injuries and suspensions. Addition of Jack Reilly should take some of the load off offensive coordinator Ernie Zampese.
Offensive backfield	A	When healthy, one of the best, if not the best, in football. What other team has a quarterback and running back the quality of Troy Aikman and Emmitt Smith? A healthy Smith will put the Cowboys running game back on its steam-rolling track.
Receivers	C	Michael Irvin can't do it all, exemplified by the team's offensive woes in the playoff loss to Carolina when he was injured the first series of the game. The Cowboys must solve second receiver dilemma and hope the Eric Bjornson-David LaFleur combo does the job at tight end. Watch for Stepfret Williams to make a contribution.
Offensive line	B +	If the Cowboys find a center to their liking, this offensive line still can be one of the league's best at both run blocking and pass protection. But once you get past the starters, the talent drastically drops off. Guard Larry Allen has a chance to be the best in the league.
Defensive line	C +	This is one of those unknowns: If unproven youngsters come through, the Cowboys might be able to hold the fort until Leon Lett returns from suspension. If not, an inability to stop the run could be the Cowboys' downfall this year, as it was in the second round of last season's playoffs. Making up for Charles Haley's impending retirement also looms large.
Linebackers	B -	Two out of three isn't bad, and if you remember, the Cowboys got by with inexperience on the weakside in 1993 when rookie Darrin Smith was forced into the starting lineup, and fill-in Godfrey Myles in 1995 when Smith was a contract holdout. The other two starters, Fred Strickland and Randall Godfrey, will be strong. But again, no depth, especially after the losses of Jim Schwantz and Myles.
Secondary	A	This is one of the best in the league with Deion Sanders manning the right corner spot. But if baseball gets in the way in the first month of the season, the Cowboys will scramble to cover themselves on Sanders' side, and likely do the same if injuries occur.
Special teams	D	Totally incomplete. The Cowboys will go into training camp grading competition at both kicker and punter, and possibly even searching for kickoff and punt returners, depending on what happens in free agency. The coverage units, as usual, will be retooled again.

DENVER BRONCOS
AFC WESTERN DIVISION

1996 REVIEW

RESULTS

Sept. 1—N.Y. JETS	W	31-6	
Sept. 8—at Seattle	W	30-20	
Sept.15—TAMPA BAY	W	27-23	
Sept.22—at Kansas City	L	14-17	
Sept.29—at Cincinnati	W	14-10	
Oct. 6—SAN DIEGO	W	28-17	
Oct. 13—Open date			
Oct. 20—BALTIMORE	W	45-34	
Oct. 27—KANSAS CITY	W	34-7	
Nov. 4—at Oakland	W	22-21	
Nov. 10—CHICAGO	W	17-12	
Nov. 17—at New England	W	34-8	
Nov. 24—at Minnesota	W	21-17	
Dec. 1—SEATTLE	W	34-7	
Dec. 8—at Green Bay	L	6-41	
Dec. 15—OAKLAND	W	24-19	
Dec. 22—at San Diego	L	10-16	
Jan. 4—JACKSONVILLE*	L	27-30	

*AFC divisional playoff game.

RECORDS/RANKINGS

1996 regular-season record: 13-3 (1st in AFC West); 6-2 in division; 10-2 in conference; 8-0 at home; 5-3 on road.
Team record last five years: 45-35 (.563), ranks 11th in league in that span).

1996 team rankings:

	No.	AFC	NFL
Total offense	*361.9	1	1
Rushing offense	*147.6	1	1
Passing offense	*214.3	7	13
Scoring offense	391	2	4
Total defense	*279.4	2	4
Rushing defense	*83.2	1	1
Passing defense	*196.2	4	10
Scoring defense	275	3	7
Takeaways	32	T6	T13
Giveaways	32	T10	T17
Turnover differential	0	8	16
Sacks	40	4	T8
Sacks allowed	31	4	9

*Yards per game.

TEAM LEADERS

Scoring (kicking): Jason Elam, 109 pts. (46/46 PATs, 21/23 FGs).
Scoring (touchdowns): Terrell Davis, 90 pts. (13 rushing, 2 receiving).
Passing: John Elway, 3,328 yds. (466 att., 287 comp., 61.6%, 26 TDs, 14 int.).
Rushing: Terrell Davis, 1,538 yds. (345 att., 4.5 avg., 13 TDs).
Receptions: Shannon Sharpe, 80 (1,062 yds., 13.3 avg., 10 TDs).
Interceptions: Tyrone Braxton, 9 (128 yds., 1 TD).
Sacks: Alfred Williams, 13.0.
Punting: Tom Rouen, 41.8 avg. (65 punts, 2,714 yds., 0 blocked).
Punt returns: Rod Smith, 12.3 avg. (23 att., 283 yds., 0 TDs).
Kickoff returns: Vaughn Hebron, 24.4 avg. (45 att., 1,099 yds., 0 TDs).

1997 SEASON

CLUB DIRECTORY

President/chief executive officer
  Pat Bowlen
General manager
  John Beake
Vice president of business operations
  David Wass
Director of player personnel
  Neal Dahlen
Controller
  Alex Rohr
Dir. of ticket operations/business dev.
  Rick Nichols
Stadium operations manager
  Gail Stuckey
Director of operations
  Bill Harpole
Director of media relations
  Jim Saccomano
Asst. to the g.m./community relations
  Fred Fleming
Director of player relations
  Bill Thompson
Community relations coordinator
  Steve Sewell
Director of pro personnel
  Jack Elway
Director of college scouting
  Ted Sundquist
Scouts
  Bob Beers
  Marv Braden
  Scott DiStefano
  Dave Gettleman
  Cornell Green
  Charlie Lee
Head trainer
  Steve Antonopulos
Assistant trainers
  Ulysses Byas
  Jim Keller

Head coach
Mike Shanahan

Assistant coaches
  Frank Bush (linebackers)
  Alex Gibbs (assistant head coach/ offensive line)
  Barney Chavous (defensive assistant)
  Rick Dennison (special teams)
  Ed Donatell (defensive backs)
  George Dyer (defensive line)
  Mike Heimerdinger (wide receivers)
  Gary Kubiak (offensive coordinator/ quarterbacks)
  Brian Pariani (tight ends)
  Ricky Porter (offense assistant)
  Greg Robinson (defensive coordinator)
  Greg Saporta (assistant strength & conditioning)
  Rick Smith (defensive assistant)
  John Teerlinck (pass rush specialist)
  Bobby Turner (running backs)
  Rich Tuten (strength & cond.)

Physician
  Richard Hawkins
Equipment manager
  Doug West
Director/video operations
  Kent Erickson

SCHEDULE

Aug. 31—	KANSAS CITY	2:00
Sept. 7—	at Seattle	1:00
Sept. 14—	ST. LOUIS	2:00
Sept. 21—	CINCINNATI	2:00
Sept. 28—	at Atlanta	1:00
Oct. 6—	NEW ENGLAND (Mon.)	7:00
Oct. 12—	Open date	
Oct. 19—	at Oakland	1:00
Oct. 26—	at Buffalo	1:00
Nov. 2—	SEATTLE	2:00
Nov. 9—	CAROLINA	2:00
Nov. 16—	at Kansas City	12:00
Nov. 24—	OAKLAND (Mon.)	7:00
Nov. 30—	at San Diego	5:00
Dec. 7—	at Pittsburgh	1:00
Dec. 15—	at San Francisco (Mon.)	6:00
Dec. 21—	SAN DIEGO	2:00

All times are for home team.
All games Sunday unless noted.

DRAFT CHOICES

Trevor Pryce, DT, Clemson (first round/ 28th round).
Dan Neil, C, Texas (3/67).
Corey Gilliard, DB, Ball State (4/124).

TRAINING CAMP ROSTER

No.	QUARTERBACKS	Ht./Wt.	Born	NFL Exp.	College	How acq.	'96 Games GP/GS
7	Elway, John	6-3/215	6-28-60	15	Stanford	T-Bal/83	15/15
8	Lewis, Jeff	6-2/217	4-17-73	2	Northern Arizona	D4a/96	2/0
	RUNNING BACKS						
30	Davis, Terrell	5-11/200	10-28-72	3	Georgia	D6b/95	16/16
29	Griffith, Howard (FB)	6-0/240	11-17-67	5	Illinois	FA/97	*16/14
22	Hebron, Vaughn	5-8/195	10-7-70	5	Virginia Tech	FA/96	16/0
45	Loville, Derek (KR)	5-10/205	7-4-68	7	Oregon	FA/97	*12/6
37	Lynn, Anthony	6-3/230	12-21-68	4	Texas Tech	FA/97	*16/1
42	Smith, Detron (FB)	5-9/231	2-25-74	2	Texas A&M	D3/96	13/0
24	Willis, Jamal	6-2/218	12-12-72	2	Brigham Young	FA/95	0/0
	RECEIVERS						
19	Branch, Darrick	6-0/196	2-10-70	1	Hawaii	FA/94	0/0
89	Carswell, Dwayne (TE)	6-3/261	1-18-72	4	Liberty (Va.)	FA/94	16/2
86	Chamberlain, Byron	6-1/240	10-17-71	2	Wayne (Neb.) State	D7/95	11/0
85	Green, Willie	6-4/188	4-2-66	8	Mississippi	FA/97	*15/10
81	Jeffers, Patrick	6-3/217	2-2-73	2	Virginia	D5/96	4/0
87	McCaffrey, Ed	6-5/215	8-17-68	7	Stanford	FA/95	15/15
84	Sharpe, Shannon (TE)	6-2/230	6-26-68	8	Savannah (Ga.) State	D7/90	15/15
80	Smith, Rod	6-0/190	5-15-70	3	Missouri Southern	FA/95	10/1
	OFFENSIVE LINEMEN						
63	Alex, Keith (G)	6-4/307	6-9-69	2	Texas A&M	FA/94	0/0
60	Banks, Chris (G)	6-1/286	4-4-73	R	Kansas	D7b/96	—
70	Brown, Jamie (T)	6-8/320	4-24-72	3	Florida A&M	D4/95	12/2
63	Diaz-Infante, David	6-3/292	3-31-64	2	San Jose State	FA/95	9/2
62	Green, Reggie (G)	6-5/310	11-23-73	R	Florida	D6a/96	—
75	Habib, Brian (G)	6-7/299	12-2-64	9	Washington	FA/93	16/16
77	Jones, Tony (T)	6-5/295	5-24-66	10	Western Carolina	T-Bal/97	*15/15
66	Nalen, Tom	6-2/280	5-13-71	4	Boston College	D7c/94	16/16
62	Neil, Dan (G/C)	6-2/291	10-21-73	R	Texas	D3/97	—
64	Nutten, Tom (C)	6-4/295	6-8-71	1	Western Michigan	D7a/96	0/0
69	Schlereth, Mark (G)	6-3/278	1-25-66	9	Idaho	FA/95	14/14
74	Swayne, Harry (T)	6-5/295	2-2-65	11	Rutgers	FA/97	*16/3
	DEFENSIVE LINEMEN						
67	Campbell, Mark (E)	6-1/290	9-12-72	1	Florida	D3/96	0/0
97	Geathers, Jumpy (T)	6-7/300	6-26-60	14	Wichita State	FA/93	16/0
96	Hasselbach, Harald	6-6/280	9-22-67	4	Washington	FA/94	16/1
72	Jones, Ernest (E)	6-2/255	4-1-71	3	Oregon	FA/96	6/0
95	Perry, Michael Dean (T)	6-1/285	8-27-65	10	Clemson	FA/95	15/15
93	Pryce, Trevor (T)	6-5/285	8-3-75	R	Clemson	D1/97	—
99	Smith, Neil (E)	6-4/273	4-10-66	10	Nebraska	FA/97	*16/16
98	Tanuvasa, Maa (T)	6-2/277	11-6-70	3	Hawaii	FA/95	16/1
94	Traylor, Keith (T)	6-2/295	9-3-69	3	Central Oklahoma	FA/95	*15/2
91	Williams, Alfred (E)	6-6/265	11-6-68	7	Colorado	FA/96	16/16
90	Williams, Dan (E)	6-4/290	12-15-69	5	Toledo	D1/93	15/15
	LINEBACKERS						
57	Aldridge, Allen	6-1/245	5-30-72	4	Houston	D2/94	16/16
49	Ale, Arnold	6-2/235	6-17-70	3	UCLA	FA/96	*7/0
56	Burns, Keith	6-2/245	5-16-72	4	Oklahoma State	D7a/94	16/0
59	Cadrez, Glenn	6-3/245	1-2-70	6	Houston	FA/95	16/0
96	Carter, Bernard	6-3/238	8-22-71	2	East Carolina	FA/95	0/0
51	Mobley, John	6-1/230	10-10-73	2	Kutztown (Pa.) University	D1/96	16/16
52	Myles, Godfrey	6-1/240	9-22-68	7	Florida	FA/97	*16/0
53	Romanowski, Bill	6-4/241	4-2-66	10	Boston College	FA/96	16/16
53	Russ, Steve	6-4/237	9-16-72	R	Air Force	D7a/95	—
	DEFENSIVE BACKS						
27	Atwater, Steve (S)	6-3/217	10-28-66	9	Arkansas	D1/89	16/16
34	Braxton, Tyrone (CB)	5-11/185	12-17-64	11	North Dakota State	FA/95	16/16
39	Crockett, Ray (CB)	5-10/185	1-5-67	9	Baylor	FA/94	15/15
33	Dodge, Dedrick (S)	6-2/184	6-14-67	6	Florida State	FA/97	*16/3
	Ellis, Jamal (CB)	5-11/190	6-21-72	1	Duke	FA/96	0/0
40	Gilliard, Cory	6-0/210	10-10-74	R	Ball State	D4/97	—
23	Gordon, Darrien (CB)	5-11/182	11-14-70	4	Stanford	FA/97	*16/6

No.	DEFENSIVE BACKS	Ht./Wt.	Born	NFL Exp.	College	How acq.	'96 Games GP/GS
21	Hilliard, Randy (CB)	5-11/165	2-6-67	8	Northwestern (La.) State	FA/94	13/3
20	James, Tory (CB)	6-1/188	5-18-73	2	Louisiana State	D2/96	16/2
25	Johnson, Darrius (CB)	5-9/175	9-17-72	2	Oklahoma	D4b/96	13/0
43	Joseph, Vance	6-0/202	9-20-72	3	Colorado	FA/97	*4/0
32	Veland, Tony (S)	6-0/205	3-11-73	R	Nebraska	D6/96	—
	SPECIALISTS						
1	Elam, Jason (K)	5-11/192	3-8-70	5	Hawaii	D3/93	16/0
16	Rouen, Tom (P)	6-3/215	6-9-68	5	Colorado	FA/93	16/0

*Ale played 7 games with Chargers in '96; Dodge played 16 games with 49ers; Gordon played 16 games with Chargers; Green played 15 games with Panthers; Griffith played 16 games with Panthers; T. Jones played 15 games with Ravens; Joseph played 4 games with Colts; Loville played 12 games with 49ers; Lynn played 16 games with 49ers; Lynn played 16 games with 49ers; Myles played 16 games with Cowboys; N. Smith played 16 games with Chiefs; Swayne played 16 games with Chargers; Traylor played 15 games with Chiefs.

Abbreviations: D1—draft pick, first round; SupD2—supplemental draft pick second round; W-Den—waivers acquisition from Denver; T-Sea—trade acquisition from Seattle; PlanB—Plan B free-agent acquisition; FA—free-agent acquisition (other than Plan B).

MISCELLANEOUS TEAM DATA

Stadium (capacity, surface):
  Mile High Stadium
  (76,078, grass)
Business address:
  13655 Broncos Parkway
  Englewood, CO 80112
Business phone:
  303-649-9000
Ticket information:
  303-433-7466
Team colors:
  Orange, navy blue and white
Flagship radio station:
  KOA, 850 AM
Training site:
  University of Northern Colorado
  Greeley, Colo.
  303-623-5212

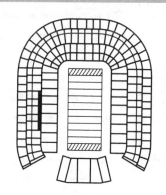

TSN REPORT CARD

Coaching staff — B + — Mike Shanahan is an offensive whiz, and there was no better proof than last season, when Denver finished first in the league in total offense. Shanahan's schemes are complicated—and also hard to defend. Offensive coordinator Gary Kubiak will be an NFL coach someday. Greg Robinson is entering his fourth season as the defensive coordinator.

Offensive backfield — A — John Elway alone makes any group worthy of top-grade consideration, but Terrell Davis clinches it. Davis is the best running back Elway has played alongside and may be the best in team history. The Broncos don't expect any dropoff at fullback, where Howard Griffith replaces Aaron Craver.

Receivers — B — Willie Green and Ed McCaffrey are reliable possession-type receivers, but the gem of the group is tight end Shannon Sharpe. Sharpe has caught at least 80 passes in three of the past four seasons, and Elway loves throwing to him. Shanahan has high hopes for Rod Smith, a backup wide receiver/punt returner last season who figures to start in '97. Smith compensates for his lack of size with speed and good hands.

Offensive line — B — This unit is aging but still productive. Center Tom Nalen is considered one of the game's rising stars, and right guard Brian Habib is dependable. Left guard Mark Schlereth had five knee operations last season alone, but he's a gritty veteran. A big key for this season is how well Tony Jones—acquired from Baltimore in an offseason trade—can replace former Pro Bowler Gary Zimmerman at left tackle.

Defensive line — A — The Broncos think Neil Smith has a lot left. He will start at left end, with Alfred Williams starting at right end. Although Williams and tackle Michael Dean Perry made the Pro Bowl last season, the Broncos seldom dominated the line of scrimmage. The additions of Smith, tackle Keith Traylor and first-round pick Trevor Pryce will help.

Linebackers — B — The starting trio of Bill Romanowski, Allen Aldridge and John Mobley is better than most. Romanowski, signed as a free agent before last season, became a defensive leader and was a good mentor for Mobley, a '96 rookie who was making the difficult leap from Division II to the NFL.

Secondary — B — With right cornerback Lionel Washington, 36, expected to retire, the Broncos will get much younger fast. The new starter will be either Tory James, 24, or free-agent signee Darrien Gordon, 26. The other three starters all are over 30, and strong safety Tyrone Braxton are solid. Braxton tied for the league lead with nine interceptions last season.

Special teams — C + — The Broncos have no worries about kicker Jason Elam, but they do about punter Tom Rouen, who didn't finish in the top 10 in the AFC in net average. Gordon led the AFC in punt returns last year, and Vaughn Hebron finished third in kickoff returns. The coverage teams need work.

DETROIT LIONS
NFC CENTRAL DIVISION

1996 REVIEW
RESULTS

Sept. 1—at Minnesota	L	13-17
Sept. 8—TAMPA BAY	W	21-6
Sept.15—at Philadelphia	L	17-24
Sept.22—CHICAGO	W	35-16
Sept.29—at Tampa Bay	W	27-0
Oct. 6—ATLANTA	W	28-24
Oct. 13—at Oakland	L	21-37
Oct. 20—Open date		
Oct. 27—N.Y. GIANTS	L	7-35
Nov. 3—at Green Bay	L	18-28
Nov. 11—at San Diego	L	21-27
Nov. 17—SEATTLE	W	17-16
Nov. 24—at Chicago	L	14-31
Nov. 28—KANSAS CITY	L	24-28
Dec. 8—MINNESOTA	L	22-24
Dec. 15—GREEN BAY	L	3-31
Dec. 23—at San Francisco	L	14-24

RECORDS/RANKINGS

1996 regular-season record: 5-11 (5th in NFC Central); 3-5 in division; 4-8 in conference; 4-4 at home; 1-7 on road.
Team record last five years: 39-41 (.488, ranks T13th in league in that span).

1996 team rankings:	No.	NFC	NFL
Total offense	*313.3	8	20
Rushing offense	*113.1	5	12
Passing offense	*200.2	8	18
Scoring offense	302	8	21
Total defense	*334.4	11	20
Rushing defense	*125.4	12	25
Passing defense	*209	11	18
Scoring defense	368	12	22
Takeaways	19	15	30
Giveaways	26	5	9
Turnover differential	-7	12	24
Sacks	32	T11	T21
Sacks allowed	46	13	25

*Yards per game.

TEAM LEADERS

Scoring (kicking): Jason Hanson, 72 pts. (36/36 PATs, 12/17 FGs).
Scoring (touchdowns): Barry Sanders, 66 pts. (11 rushing).
Passing: Scott Mitchell, 2,917 yds. (437 att., 253 comp., 57.9%, 17 TDs, 17 int.).
Rushing: Barry Sanders, 1,553 yds. (307 att., 5.1 avg., 11 TDs).
Receptions: Herman Moore, 106 (1,296 yds., 12.2 avg., 9 TDs).
Interceptions: Ryan McNeil, 5 (14 yds., 0 TDs).
Sacks: Robert Porcher, 10.0.
Punting: Mark Royals, 43.8 avg. (69 punts, 3,020 yds., 1 blocked).
Punt returns: Glyn Milburn, 8.4 avg. (34 att., 284 yds., 0 TDs).
Kickoff returns: Glyn Milburn, 25.4 avg. (64 att., 1,627 yds., 0 TDs).

1997 SEASON
CLUB DIRECTORY

Chairman & president
William Clay Ford
Vice-chairman
William Clay Ford Jr.
Exec. V.P./chief operating officer
Chuck Schmidt
Vice president/player personnel
Ron Hughes
V.P. of communications, sales and mktg.
Bill Keenist
V.P. of football administration
Larry Lee
V.P. of finance and chief financial officer
Tom Lesnau
Vice president-general counsel
David Potts
Secretary
David Hempstead
Director/salary cap & stadium dev.
Tom Leward
Executive director/marketing
Steve Harms
Dir./community relations and charities
Tim Pendell
Director of media relations
Mike Murray
Media relations assistant
James Petrylka
Exec. director/ticket sales & cust. serv.
Duane McLean
Box officemanager
Mark Graham
Director/pro scouting
Kevin Colbert

Scouts

Russ Bolinger	Dirk Dierking
Tom Dimitroff	Scott McEwen
Jim Owens	Rick Spielman

Head athletic trainer
Kent Falb
Assistant athletic trainers

Bill Ford	Joe Recknagel

SCHEDULE

Aug. 31— ATLANTA	1:00
Sept. 7— TAMPA BAY	1:00
Sept. 14— at Chicago	12:00
Sept. 21— at New Orleans	12:00
Sept. 28— GREEN BAY	1:00
Oct. 5— at Buffalo	1:00
Oct. 12— at Tampa Bay	1:00
Oct. 19— N.Y. GIANTS	4:00
Oct. 26— Open date	
Nov. 2— at Green Bay	7:00
Nov. 9— at Washington	1:00
Nov. 16— MINNESOTA	1:00
Nov. 23— INDIANAPOLIS	1:00
Nov. 27— CHICAGO (Thanks.)	12:30
Dec. 7— at Miami	8:00
Dec. 14— at Minnesota	12:00
Dec. 21— N.Y. JETS	4:00

All times are for home team.
All games Sunday unless noted.

Head coach
Bobby Ross

Assistant coaches
Brian Baker (defensive line)
Sylvester Croom (offensive coord.)
Frank Falks (running backs)
Jack Henry (offensive line)
Bert Hill (strength & conditioning)
John Misciagna (quality control/
offense/admin. asst.)
Gary Moeller (linebackers)
Dennis Murphy (quality control/
defense)
Bob Palcic (tight ends)
Larry Peccatiello (defensive coord.)
Chuck Priefer (special teams)
Dick Selcer (defensive backs)
Jerry Sullivan (wide receivers)
Marc Trestman (quarterbacks)
Don Clemons (defensive asst./
asst. strength coach)
Stan Kwan (offense/special teams
assistant)

Physicians

Keith Burch	David Collon

Groundskeeper
George Karas
Equipment manager
Dan Jaroshewich
Assistant equipment manager
Mark Glenn
Video director
Steve Hermans

DRAFT CHOICES

Bryant Westbrook, DB, Texas (first round/fifth pick overall).
Kevin Abrams, DB, Syracuse (2/54).
Matt Russell, LB, Colorado (4/130).
Pete Chryplewicz, TE, Notre Dame (5/135).
Duane Ashman, DE, Virginia (5/161).
Tony Ramirez, T, Northern Colorado (6/168).
Terry Battle, RB, Arizona State (7/206).
Marcus Harris, WR, Wyoming (7/232).
Richard Jordan, LB, Missouri Southern (7/239).

1997 SEASON *Detroit Lions*

No.	QUARTERBACKS	Ht./Wt.	Born	NFL Exp.	College	How acq.	'96 Games GP/GS
12	Blundin, Matt	6-6/233	3-7-69	5	Virginia	FA/97	0/0
19	Mitchell, Scott	6-6/230	1-2-68	8	Utah	FA/94	14/14
14	Reich, Frank	6-4/210	12-4-61	13	Maryland	FA/97	*10/7
	RUNNING BACKS						
23	Battle, Terry	5-11/197	2-7-76	R	Arizona State	D7b/97	—
42	Baxter, Brad	6-1/235	5-5-67	7	Alabama State	FA/97	0/0
26	Lynch, Eric	5-10/224	5-16-70	5	Grand Valley State (Mich.)	FA/92	16/0
34	Rivers, Ron	5-8/205	11-13-71	3	Fresno State	FA/94	15/0
20	Sanders, Barry	5-8/203	7-16-68	9	Oklahoma State	D1/89	16/16
30	Schlesinger, Corey (FB)	6-0/230	6-23-72	3	Nebraska	D6/95	16/1
44	Vardell, Tommy (FB)	6-2/230	2-20-69	6	Stanford	FA/97	*11/7
21	Williams, Allen (KR)	5-10/205	9-17-72	2	Georgia	FA/95	0/0
	RECEIVERS						
	Bronson, Ben	5-9/159	9-9-72	1	Baylor	FA/95	0/0
48	Chryplewicz, Pete (TE)	6-5/253	4-27-74	R	Notre Dame	D5a/97	—
11	Harris, Marcus	6-2/213	10-11-74	R	Wyoming	D7b/97	—
81	Hickman, Kevin (TE)	6-4/258	8-20-71	2	Navy	D6/95	0/0
10	McCorvey, Kez	6-0/180	1-23-72	3	Florida State	D5/95	1/0
89	Metzelaars, Pete (TE)	6-7/254	5-24-60	16	Wabash, Ind.	FA/96	15/11
33	Milburn, Glyn	5-8/177	2-19-71	5	Stanford	T-Den/96	16/0
84	Moore, Herman	6-4/217	10-20-69	7	Virginia	D1/91	16/16
87	Morton, Johnnie (KR)	6-0/190	10-7-71	4	Southern California	D1/94	16/15
82	Price, Derek (TE)	6-3/240	8-12-72	2	Iowa	FA/96	13/1
86	Sloan, David (TE)	6-6/254	6-8-72	3	New Mexico	D3/95	4/4
49	Stocz, Eric (TE)	6-4/278	5-25-74	1	Westminster (Pa.)	FA/96	1/0
	OFFENSIVE LINEMEN						
77	Compton, Mike (C/G)	6-6/297	9-18-70	5	West Virginia	D3/93	15/15
76	Conover, Scott (T)	6-4/285	9-27-68	7	Purdue	D5/91	10/7
53	Glover, Kevin (C)	6-2/282	6-17-63	13	Maryland	D2/85	16/16
64	Hartings, Jeff (G)	6-3/283	9-7-72	2	Penn State	D1b/96	11/10
66	Hempstead, Hessley (G)	6-1/295	1-29-72	3	Kansas	D7/95	13/0
70	Jones, Jeff (T)	6-6/310	5-30-72	3	Texas A&M	FA/95	7/0
75	Ramirez, Tony (T)	6-6/296	1-26-73	R	Northern Colorado	D6/97	—
72	Roberts, Ray (T)	6-6/308	6-3-69	6	Virginia	FA/96	16/16
73	Roque, Juan (T)	6-8/333	1-6-74	R	Arizona State	D2a/97	—
62	Semple, Tony (G)	6-4/286	12-20-70	4	Memphis State	D5/94	15/1
61	Smothers, Howard	6-3/278	11-16-73	1	Bethune-Cookman	FA/96	0/0
69	Solomon, Ariel (C/G)	6-5/295	7-16-68	7	Colorado	FA/97	*16/0
71	Tharpe, Larry (T)	6-4/300	11-19-70	6	Tennessee State	FA/97	0/0
	DEFENSIVE LINEMEN						
68	Ashman, Duane (E)	6-4/274	12-29-73	R	Virginia	D5b/97	—
96	Bonham, Shane	6-2/275	10-18-70	4	Tennessee	D3/94	15/2
92	Dronett, Shane (E)	6-6/275	1-12-71	6	Texas	FA/96	*12/0
94	Elliss, Luther (E)	6-5/291	3-22-73	3	Utah	D1/95	14/14
91	Porcher, Robert (E)	6-3/270	7-30-69	6	South Carolina State	D1/92	16/16
93	Waldroup, Kerwin	6-3/260	8-1-74	2	Central State (O.)	D5/96	16/10
90	Washington, Keith (E)	6-4/268	12-18-73	2	UNLV	FA/96	12/0
95	Wells, Mike (E)	6-3/287	1-6-71	6	Iowa	FA/94	16/1
	LINEBACKERS						
51	Beer, Thomas	6-1/237	3-27-69	4	Wayne State (Neb.)	D7/94	16/1
57	Boyd, Stephen	6-0/247	8-22-72	3	Boston College	D5/95	8/5
59	Brown, Reggie	6-2/241	9-28-74	2	Texas A&M	D1a/96	10/10
50	Hamilton, Rick	6-2/241	4-19-70	4	Central Florida	FA/97	*15/4
58	Jamison, George	6-1/235	9-30-62	12	Cincinnati	FA/97	*5/0
99	Jordan, Richard	6-1/265	12-1-74	R	Missouri Southern	D7c/97	—
	Kowalkowski, Scott	6-2/228	8-23-68	5	Notre Dame	FA/94	0/0
55	London, Antonio	6-2/234	4-14-71	5	Alabama	D3/93	14/12
54	Russell, Matt	6-2/245	7-5-73	R	Colorado	D4/97	—
97	Scroggins, Tracy	6-2/255	9-11-69	6	Tulsa	D2/92	6/6
	DEFENSIVE BACKS						
24	Abrams, Kevin	5-8/175	2-28-74	R	Syracuse	D2b/97	—
23	Bailey, Robert (CB)	5-9/174	9-3-68	7	Miami (Fla.)	FA/97	*14/0
29	Colon, Harry (S)	6-0/203	2-14-69	6	Missouri	FA/97	0/0
27	Ford, Brad (CB)	5-10/170	1-11-74	2	Alabama	D4/96	14/0

No.	DEFENSIVE BACKS	Ht./Wt.	Born	NFL Exp.	College	How acq.	'96 Games GP/GS
25	Jeffries, Greg (CB)	5-9/184	10-16-71	5	Virginia	D6/93	16/4
39	Malone, Van (S)	5-11/195	7-1-70	4	Texas	D2/94	15/15
28	Rice, Ron (S)	6-1/206	11-9-72	2	Eastern Michigan	FA/96	13/2
38	Stewart, Ryan (S)	6-1/207	9-30-73	2	Georgia Tech	D3/96	14/2
32	Westbrook, Bryant	6-0/199	12-19-74	R	Texas	D1/97	—
	SPECIALISTS						
4	Hanson, Jason (K)	5-11/183	6-17-70	6	Washington State	D2/92	16/0
18	Jett, John (P)	6-0/199	11-11-68	5	East Carolina	FA/97	*16/0

*Bailey played 14 games for Dolphins in '96; Dronett played 5 games with Falcons and 7 games with Lions; Hamilton played 15 games with Jets; Jamison played 5 games with Chiefs; Jett played 16 games with Cowboys; Reich played 10 games with Jets; Solomon played 16 games with Vikings; Vardell played 11 games with 49ers.

Abbreviations: D1—draft pick, first round; SupD2—supplemental draft pick second round; W-Den—waivers acquisition from Denver; T-Sea—trade acquisition from Seattle; PlanB—Plan B free-agent acquisition; FA—free-agent acquisition (other than Plan B).

MISCELLANEOUS TEAM DATA

Stadium (capacity, surface):
Pontiac Silverdome
(80,368, artificial)
Business address:
1200 Featherstone Road
Pontiac, MI 48342
Business phone:
810-335-4131
Ticket information:
810-335-4151
Team colors:
Honolulu blue and silver
Flagship radio station:
WXYT, 1270 AM
Training site:
Pontiac Silverdome
Pontiac, Mich.
810-335-4131

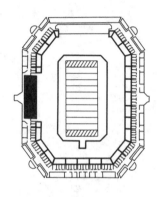

TSN REPORT CARD

Coaching staff	B	Bobby Ross provides the stability and direction that was lacking in the former regime, but he has yet to prove he can do it with a first-place schedule. But that question will have to wait because the Lions are coming off a fifth-place finish and will have the league's softest schedule.
Offensive backfield	B	Barry Sanders is the best in the business and Tommy Vardell will add some versatility at fullback, but Scott Mitchell is the wild card. While Sanders will be more involved in the passing game, Detroit's success will be predicated on Mitchell's downfield accuracy.
Receivers	A	Herman Moore is one of the top receivers in the league and can be effective even against double teams. Johnnie Morton finally gets a chance to shine on the outside and tight end David Sloan will emerge as one of the league's best. This could be Glyn Milburn's last chance to prove himself in the slot.
Offensive line	C +	The potential is here for great things, but the present day reality makes them just slightly above average. Center Kevin Glover must return to Pro Bowl form and rookie second round pick Juan Roque must quickly become a force at right tackle. Ray Roberts is solid on the left side.
Defensive line	C	Continuity has always been the biggest problem here and it continues. After two years of playing the aggressive one-gap style, they're reverting to a two-gap approach and they'll do it without Henry Thomas. Robert Porcher must have another big year and it's time for Luther Elliss to hit the big time.
Linebackers	D	There is a critical lack of experience at this position. Reggie Brown is entering his second year, but only has 10 starts. The middle linebacker position will be contested between a fourth-round rookie draft choice (Matt Russell) and a veteran who only has five career starts (Stephen Boyd). Antonio London is still learning the strong side position and will be backed up by 12-year veteran George Jamison.
Secondary	D	Another area with an alarming lack of playing experience. Rookie Bryant Westbrook will start at left cornerback with rookie Kevin Abrams the heir apparent on the right side. Free safety Van Malone switches to the strong side to replace Bennie Blades and that's a good move, but he's never had a start at that spot. Ron Rice is the No. 1 free safety, but has only two career starts.
Special teams	C	These units should be better across the board because an improved offense will give kicker Jason Hanson more chances, punter John Jett (signed from Dallas) is more accurate than his predecessor and Ross is paying more than lip service to improving the overall speed. With a little help, Milburn will become one of the league's most dangerous return specialists again.

GREEN BAY PACKERS
NFC CENTRAL DIVISION

1996 REVIEW

RESULTS

Sept. 1—at Tampa Bay	W	34-3
Sept. 9—PHILADELPHIA	W	39-13
Sept.15—SAN DIEGO	W	42-10
Sept.22—at Minnesota	L	21-30
Sept.29—at Seattle	W	31-10
Oct. 6—at Chicago	W	37-6
Oct. 14—SAN FRAN. (OT)	W	23-20
Oct. 20—Open date		
Oct. 27—TAMPA BAY	W	13-7
Nov. 3—DETROIT	W	28-18
Nov. 10—at Kansas City	L	20-27
Nov. 18—at Dallas	L	6 -21
Nov. 24—at St. Louis	W	24-9
Dec. 1—CHICAGO	W	28-17
Dec. 8—DENVER	W	41-6
Dec. 15—at Detroit	W	31-3
Dec. 22—MINNESOTA	W	38-10
Jan. 4—SAN FRANCISCO*	W	35-14
Jan. 12—CAROLINA†	W	30-13
Jan. 26—New England‡	W	35-21

*NFC divisional playoff game.
†NFC championship game.
‡Super Bowl XXXI.

RECORDS/RANKINGS

1996 regular-season record: 13-3 (1st in NFC Central); 7-1 in division; 10-2 in conference; 8-0 at home; 5-3 on road.
Team record last five years: 51-29 (.638, ranks 5th in league in that span).

1996 team rankings:	No.	NFC	NFL
Total offense	*345.9	2	5
Rushing offense	*114.9	4	11
Passing offense	*231.1	2	5
Scoring offense	456	1	1
Total defense	*259.8	1	1
Rushing defense	*88.5	1	4
Passing defense	*171.3	1	1
Scoring defense	210	1	1
Takeaways	39	T1	T3
Giveaways	24	T2	T2
Turnover differential	15	1	2
Sacks	37	T6	T10
Sacks allowed	40	10	19

*Yards per game.

TEAM LEADERS

Scoring (kicking): Chris Jacke, 114 pts. (51/53 PATs, 21/27 FGs).
Scoring (touchdowns): Keith Jackson, 60 pts. (10 receiving); Dorsey Levens, 60 pts. (5 rushing, 5 receiving).
Passing: Brett Favre, 3,899 yds. (543 att., 325 comp., 59.9%, 39 TDs, 13 int.).
Rushing: Edgar Bennett, 899 yds. (222 att., 4.0 avg., 2 TDs).
Receptions: Antonio Freeman, 56 (933 yds., 16.7 avg., 9 TDs).
Interceptions: Eugene Robinson, 6 (107 yds., 0 TDs).
Sacks: Reggie White, 8.5.
Punting: Craig Hentrich, 42.4 avg. (68 punts, 2,886 yds., 0 blocked).
Punt returns: Desmond Howard, 15.1 avg. (58 att., 875 yds., 3 TDs).
Kickoff returns: Desmond Howard, 20.9 avg. (22 att., 460 yds., 0 TDs).

1997 SEASON

CLUB DIRECTORY

President/chief executive officer
Robert E. Harlan
Vice president
John Fabry
Secretary
Peter M. Platten III
Treasurer
John R. Underwood
Executive V.P./general manager
Ron Wolf
Executive assistant to president
Phil Pionek
Chief financial officer
Mike Reinfeldt
General counsel
Lance Lopes
Corporate security officer
Jerry Parins
Accountants
Duke Copp
Vicki Vannieuwenhoven
Executive director/public relations
Lee Remmel
Director/marketing
Jeff Cieply
Asst. directors/public relations
Jeff Blumb
Mark Schiefelbein
Ticket director
Mark Wagner
Director of family programs
Sherry Schuldes
Director/pro personnel
Ted Thompson
Director/college scouting
John Dorsey
College scouts
John "Red" Cochran   Will Lewis
Shaun Herock   Scot McLoughan
Sam Seale   Johnny Meads
Head trainer
Pepper Burruss

Head coach
Mike Holmgren

Assistant coaches
Larry Brooks (defensive line)
Nolan Cromwell (special teams)
Gil Haskell (wide receivers)
Johnny Holland (defensive assist./ quality control)
Kent Johnston (strength & cond.)
Sherman Lewis (offensive coord.)
Jim Lind (linebackers)
Tom Lovat (offensive line)
Andy Reid (quarterbacks)
Mike Sherman (tight ends)
Fritz Shurmur (defensive coord.)
Harry Sydney (running backs)
Bob Valesente (secondary)

Assistant trainers
Kurt Fielding   Sam Ramsden
Physicians
Patrick McKenzie
John Gray
Buildings supervisor
Ted Eisenreich
Fields supervisor
Todd Edlebeck
Equipment manager
Gordon Batty
Assistant equipment managers
Bryan Nehring   Tom Bakken
Video director
Al Treml

SCHEDULE

Sept. 1— CHICAGO (Mon.)	8:00
Sept. 7— at Philadelphia	4:00
Sept. 14— MIAMI	12:00
Sept. 21— MINNESOTA	12:00
Sept. 28— at Detroit	1:00
Oct. 5— TAMPA BAY	12:00
Oct. 12— at Chicago	12:00
Oct. 19— Open date	
Oct. 27— at New England (Mon.)	9:00
Nov. 2— DETROIT	7:00
Nov. 9— ST. LOUIS	12:00
Nov. 16— at Indianapolis	1:00
Nov. 23— DALLAS	12:00
Dec. 1— at Minnesota (Mon.)	8:00
Dec. 7— at Tampa Bay	1:00
Dec. 14— at Carolina	4:00
Dec. 20— BUFFALO (Sat.)	11:30

All times are for home team.
All games Sunday unless noted.

DRAFT CHOICES

Ross Verba, T, Iowa (first round/30th pick overall).
Darren Sharper, DB, William & Mary (2/60).
Brett Conway, K, Penn State (3/90).
Jermaine Smith, DT, Georgia (4/126).
Anthony Hicks, LB, Arkansas (5/160).
Chris Miller, WR, Southern California (7/213).
Jerald Sowell, RB, Tulane (7/231).
Ronnie McAda, QB, Army (7/240).

TRAINING CAMP ROSTER

No.	QUARTERBACKS	Ht./Wt.	Born	NFL Exp.	College	How acq.	'96 Games GP/GS
	Bono, Steve	6-4/215	5-11-62	13	UCLA	FA/97	*13/13
4	Favre, Brett	6-2/225	10-10-69	7	Southern Mississippi	T-Atl/92	16/16
7	McAda, Ronnie	6-3/205	3-6-74	R	Army	D7b/97	—
18	Pederson, Doug	6-3/215	1-31-68	5	Northeast Louisiana	FA/95	1/0
	RUNNING BACKS						
34	Bennett, Edgar (FB)	6-0/217	2-15-69	6	Florida State	D4/92	16/15
44	Darkins, Chris	6-0/215	4-30-74	1	Minnesota	D4/96	0/0
30	Henderson, William (FB)	6-1/248	2-19-71	3	North Carolina	D3b/95	16/11
32	Jervey, Travis	6-0/225	5-5-72	3	The Citadel	D5/95	16/0
25	Levens, Dorsey	6-1/235	5-21-70	4	Georgia Tech	D5b/94	16/1
35	Sowell, Jerald	6-0/248	1-21-74	R	Tulane	D7a/97	—
	RECEIVERS						
82	Beebe, Don	5-11/183	12-18-64	9	Chadron (Neb.) State	FA/96	16/6
87	Brooks, Robert (KR)	6-0/180	6-23-70	6	South Carolina	D3/92	7/7
89	Chmura, Mark (TE)	6-5/250	2-22-69	6	Boston College	D6/92	13/13
86	Freeman, Antonio	6-1/190	5-27-72	3	Virginia Tech	D3d/95	12/12
88	LeBel, Harper (TE)	6-4/250	7-14-63	9	Colorado State	FA/97	*16/0
80	Mayes, Derrick	6-0/200	1-28-74	2	Notre Dame	D2/96	7/0
85	Mickens, Terry	6-0/198	2-21-71	4	Florida A&M	D5/94	8/5
81	Miller, Chris	5-10/192	7-10-73	R	Southern California	D7/97	—
46	Pinkney, Lovell (TE)	6-4/248	8-18-72	2	Texas	FA/97	0/0
83	Thomason, Jeff (TE)	6-5/250	12-30-69	5	Oregon	FA/95	16/1
47	Wachholtz, Kyle (TE)	6-4/235	5-17-72	1	Southern California	D7a/96	0/0
20	Yarborough, Ryan	6-2/195	4-26-71	3	Wyoming	T-NYJ/96	0/0
	OFFENSIVE LINEMEN						
68	Brown, Gary (T/G)	6-4/315	6-25-71	4	Georgia Tech	W-Pit/96	8/5
60	Chung, Eugene (G/T)	6-5/311	6-14-69	5	Virginia Tech	FA/97	0/0
72	Dotson, Earl (T)	6-4/315	12-17-70	5	Texas A&I	D3/93	15/15
58	Flanagan, Mike (C)	6-5/290	11-10-73	1	UCLA	D3/96	0/0
65	Knapp, Lindsay (G/T)	6-6/300	2-25-70	5	Notre Dame	T-KC/95	9/0
77	Michels, John (T)	6-7/290	3-19-73	2	Southern California	D1/96	15/9
60	Peterson, Andrew (T)	6-5/300	6-11-72	2	Washington.	FA/97	0/0
62	Rivera, Marco (G)	6-5/295	4-26-72	1	Penn State	D6/96	0/0
76	Spears, Marcus (G/T)	6-4/302	9-28-71	4	Northwestern (La.) State	FA/97	*9/0
73	Taylor, Aaron (G)	6-4/305	11-14-72	4	Notre Dame	D1/94	16/16
63	Timmerman, Adam (G)	6-4/295	8-14-71	3	South Dakota State	D7/95	16/16
78	Verba, Ross (T)	6-4/299	10-31-73	R	Iowa	D1/97	—
64	Wilkerson, Bruce (T/G)	6-5/305	7-28-64	11	Tennessee	FA/96	14/2
52	Winters, Frank (C)	6-3/295	1-23-64	11	Western Illinois	PlanB/92	16/16
	DEFENSIVE LINEMEN						
93	Brown, Gilbert (T)	6-2/325	2-22-71	5	Kansas	W-Min/93	16/16
91	Clavelle, Shannon (E)	6-2/287	12-12-73	3	Colorado	FA/95	8/0
71	Dotson, Santana (T)	6-5/282	12-19-69	6	Baylor	FA/96	16/15
90	Holland, Darius (T)	6-5/310	11-10-73	3	Colorado	D3/95	16/0
	Johnson, Eric (E)	6-5/261	3-31-73	1	Texas Southern	FA/97	0/0
94	Kuberski, Bob (T)	6-4/295	4-5-71	3	Navy	D7/93	1/0
74	Scott, Walter (E)	6-3/285	5-18-73	2	East Carolina	FA/97	*1/0
99	Smith, Jermaine (T)	6-3/289	2-3-72	R	Georgia	D4/97	—
97	Thompson, Mike (T)	6-3/279	12-22-72	1	Wisconsin	FA/97	0/0
92	White, Reggie (E)	6-5/300	12-19-61	13	Tennessee	FA/93	16/16
98	Wilkins, Gabe (E)	6-5/305	9-1-71	4	Gardner-Webb (N.C.)	D4/94	16/1
	LINEBACKERS						
48	Clark, Reggie	6-2/240	10-17-67	4	North Carolina	FA/97	*5/0
54	Cox, Ron	6-2/235	2-27-68	8	Fresno State	FA/96	16/1
55	Harris, Bernardo	6-2/243	10-15-71	3	North Carolina	FA/95	16/0
50	Hicks, Anthony	6-1/242	3-31-74	R	Arkansas	D5/97	—
56	Hollinquest, Lamont	6-3/243	10-24-70	4	Southern California	FA/96	16/0
53	Koonce, George	6-1/243	10-15-68	6	East Carolina	FA/92	16/16
95	McKenzie, Keith	6-3/242	10-17-73	2	Ball State	D7b/96	10/0
59	Simmons, Wayne	6-2/248	12-15-69	5	Clemson	D1/93	16/16
51	Williams, Brian	6-1/235	12-17-72	3	Southern California	D3c/95	16/16
	DEFENSIVE BACKS						
36	Butler, LeRoy (S)	6-0/200	7-19-68	8	Florida State	D2/90	16/16
23	Dorsett, Matthew (CB)	5-11/190	8-23-73	2	Southern	FA/95	0/0
27	Edwards, Brad (S)	6-2/208	3-22-66	9	South Carolina	FA/97	*16/7
33	Evans, Doug (CB)	6-1/190	5-13-70	5	Louisiana Tech	D6a/93	16/16
40	Hayes, Chris	6-0/200	5-7-72	1	Washington State	D7/96	2/0

No.	DEFENSIVE BACKS	Ht./Wt.	Born	NFL Exp.	College	How acq.	'96 Games GP/GS
28	Mullen, Roderick	6-1/204	12-5-72	3	Grambling State	D5/95	14/0
21	Newsome, Craig (CB)	6-0/190	8-10-71	3	Arizona State	D1/95	16/16
39	Prior, Mike (S)	6-0/208	11-14-63	12	Illinois State	FA/93	16/0
41	Robinson, Eugene (S)	6-0/195	5-28-63	13	Colgate	T-Sea/96	16/16
42	Sharper, Darren	6-2/206	11-3-75	R	William & Mary	D2/97	—
37	Williams, Tyrone (CB)	5-11/195	5-31-73	2	Nebraska	D3b/96	16/0
	SPECIALISTS						
10	Conway, Brett (K)	6-2/191	3-8-75	R	Penn State	D3/97	—
17	Hentrich, Craig (P)	6-3/200	5-18-71	4	Notre Dame	FA/93	16/0

*Bono played 13 games with Chiefs in '96; Clark played 5 games with Jaguars; Edwards played 16 games with Falcons; LeBel played 16 games with Falcons; Scott played 1 game with Patriots; Spears played 9 games with Bears.

Abbreviations: D1—draft pick, first round; SupD2—supplemental draft pick second round; W-Den—waivers acquisition from Denver; T-Sea—trade acquisition from Seattle; PlanB—Plan B free-agent acquisition; FA—free-agent acquisition (other than Plan B).

MISCELLANEOUS TEAM DATA

Stadium (capacity, surface):
Lambeau Field
(60,790, grass)
Business address:
P.O. Box 10628
Green Bay, WI 54307-0628
Business phone:
920-496-5700
Ticket information:
920-496-5719
Team colors:
Dark green, gold and white
Flagship radio station:
WTMJ, 620 AM
Training site:
St. Norbert College
West De Pere, Wis.
920-496-5700

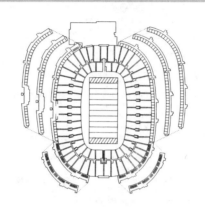

TSN REPORT CARD

Coaching staff	A -	Mike Holmgren and offensive coordinator Sherman Lewis are master strategists who embrace the West Coast philosophy and then structure it to fit their talent. Defensive coordinator Fritz Shurmur has been given a wealth of talent and makes it work as a unit.
Offensive backfield	A -	Any group that has Brett Favre in it can't possibly go wrong. Provided he has the longevity of guys like Dan Marino and John Elway, he'll be in the Hall of Fame someday. The backfield isn't overly talented, but Dorsey Levens has a chance to be a legitimate 1,000-yard rusher.
Receivers	B	The only question mark with the receivers is whether Robert Brooks will be 100% again. He was never the fastest receiver, so he can't afford to lose a step. Antonio Freeman has greatness written all over him; the only concern is his consistency. If Derrick Mayes reaches his potential this may be the best group Holmgren and Lewis have ever worked with.
Offensive line	B -	Without any stars on the line, the Packers rely on functioning as a unit. Early last season they struggled and Favre spent a good deal of the time running for his life. It just so happened he made a lot of plays doing so. Late in the year, however, the group jelled and especially excelled at opening running holes for Edgar Bennett and Levens. The addition of John Michels and Ross Verba gives the Packers three first-round picks among their top six linemen.
Defensive line	A	As long as Reggie White keeps getting double-teamed, the Packers are going to dominate up front. No team can double White and then expect to handle Gilbert Brown and Santana Dotson inside. If Gabe Wilkins can make plays on a consistent basis the way he did in spot duty he could wind up with double-digit sacks.
Linebackers	C	Re-signing Wayne Simmons would provide a lift for the defense, even if it meant having to deal with his volatile personality. Simmons adds some nastiness to a unit that is sometimes not aggressive enough. The absence of George Koonce in the early part of the season will hurt if Bernardo Harris doesn't come through. Depth will be a problem if the Packers don't add some veteran help.
Secondary	B +	The Packers were lucky they didn't sustain any injuries at cornerback last year, otherwise they might have been in trouble. They need Ron Davis and Darren Sharper to contribute at corner. With Leroy Butler and Eugene Robinson at safety and Craig Newsome and Doug Evans at corner, the Packers have a solid if unspectacular foursome.
Special teams	B -	The key to the Packers' great returns last year was the blocking. It just so happened that Desmond Howard turned big holes into touchdowns. This year they might have to settle for 20-yard returns instead of six points. Rookie Brett Conway will be under tremendous pressure to replace Chris Jacke, let alone kick for a defending Super Bowl champion.

INDIANAPOLIS COLTS
AFC EASTERN DIVISION

1996 REVIEW
RESULTS

Sept. 1—ARIZONA	W	20-13	
Sept. 8—at N.Y. Jets	W	21-7	
Sept.15—at Dallas	W	25-24	
Sept.23—MIAMI	W	10-6	
Sept.30—Open date			
Oct. 6—at Buffalo (OT)	L	13-16	
Oct. 13—BALTIMORE	W	26-21	
Oct. 20—NEW ENGLAND	L	9-27	
Oct. 27—at Washington	L	16-31	
Nov. 3—SAN DIEGO	L	19-26	
Nov. 10—at Miami	L	13-37	
Nov. 17—N.Y. JETS	W	34-29	
Nov. 24—at New England	L	13-27	
Dec. 1—BUFFALO (OT)	W	13-10	
Dec. 5—PHILADELPHIA	W	37-10	
Dec. 15—at Kansas City	W	24-19	
Dec. 22—at Cincinnati	L	24-31	
Dec. 29—at Pittsburgh*	L	14-42	

*AFC wild-card game.

RECORDS/RANKINGS

1996 regular-season record: 9-7 (3rd in AFC East); 4-4 in division; 6-6 in conference; 6-2 at home; 3-5 on road.
Team record last five years: 39-41 (.488), ranks T13th in league in that span).

1996 team rankings:	No.	AFC	NFL
Total offense	*296.5	14	25
Rushing offense	*90.5	14	28
Passing offense	*206	9	16
Scoring offense	317	T11	T16
Total defense	*337.7	10	22
Rushing defense	*110	11	18
Passing defense	*227.7	10	23
Scoring defense	334	9	18
Takeaways	23	14	T26
Giveaways	24	T1	T2
Turnover differential	-1	9	T17
Sacks	29	14	28
Sacks allowed	43	11	23

*Yards per game.

TEAM LEADERS

Scoring (kicking): Cary Blanchard, 135 pts. (27/27 PATs, 36/40 FGs).
Scoring (touchdowns): Marvin Harrison, 48 pts. (8 receiving).
Passing: Jim Harbaugh, 2,630 yds. (405 att., 232 comp., 57.3%, 13 TDs, 11 int.).
Rushing: Marshall Faulk, 587 yds. (198 att., 3.0 avg., 7 TDs).
Receptions: Marvin Harrison, 64 (836 yds., 13.1 avg., 8 TDs).
Interceptions: Jason Belser, 4 (81 yds., 2 TDs).
Sacks: Richard Dent, 6.5.
Punting: Chris Gardocki, 45.7 avg. (68 punts, 3,105 yds., 0 blocked).
Punt returns: Ray Buchanan, 16.8 avg. (12 att., 201 yds., 0 TDs).
Kickoff returns: Aaron Bailey, 24.2 avg. (43 att., 1,041 yds., 1 TD).

1997 SEASON
CLUB DIRECTORY

Owner and CEO
James Irsay
V.p. and director of football operations
Bill Tobin
Exec. vice president and general counsel
Michael G. Chernoff
Vice president
Bob Terpening
Controller
Kurt Humphrey
Executive director/operations
Pete Ward
Director/public relations
Craig Kelley
Assistant director/public relations
Todd Stewart
Director of ticket operations & sales
Larry Hall
Purchasing administrator
David Filar
Administrative assistant
Nicole Kucharski
Director of pro player personnel
Clyde Powers
Director of college player personnel
George Boone
College scouts
Mike Butler
John Goeller
Paul Roell
William Scherer
Duke Tobin
Ron Toman
Head trainer
Hunter Smith
Assistant trainers
Dave Hammer
Dave Walston

SCHEDULE

Aug. 31— at Miami	1:00	
Sept. 7— NEW ENGLAND	12:00	
Sept. 14— SEATTLE	3:00	
Sept. 21— at Buffalo	4:00	
Sept. 28— Open date		
Oct. 5— N.Y. JETS	3:00	
Oct. 12— at Pittsburgh	8:00	
Oct. 20— BUFFALO (Mon.)	8:00	
Oct. 26— at San Diego	1:00	
Nov. 2— TAMPA BAY	1:00	
Nov. 9— CINCINNATI	1:00	
Nov. 16— GREEN BAY	1:00	
Nov. 23— at Detroit	1:00	
Nov. 30— at New England	1:00	
Dec. 7— at N.Y. Jets	4:00	
Dec. 14— MIAMI	1:00	
Dec. 21— at Minnesota	12:00	

All times are for home team.
All games Sunday unless noted.

Head coach
Lindy Infante

Assistant coaches
Tom Batta (tight ends/quality control)
Greg Blache (defensive line)
Ron Blackledge (offensive line)
Chuck Bresnahan (linebackers)
Fred Bruney (defensive assistant)
Charlie Davis (asst. offensive line)
Buddy Geis (asst. quarterbacks)
Gene Huey (running backs)
Jim Johnson (def. coordinator)
Hank Kuhlmann (special teams)
Jay Robertson (def. assistant)
Jimmy Robinson (receivers)
Pat Thomas (secondary)
Tom Zupancic (strength & cond.)

Team physician/orthopedic surgeon
K. Donald Shelbourne
Orthopedic surgeon
Arthur C. Rettig
Equipment manager
Jon Scott
Assistant equipment manager
Mike Mays
Video director
Marty Heckscher

DRAFT CHOICES

Tarik Glenn, T, California (first round/19th pick overall).
Adam Meadows, T, Georgia (2/48).
Bert Berry, LB, Notre Dame (3/86).
Delmonico Montgomery, DB, Houston (4/117).
Nate Jacquet, WR, San Diego State (5/150).
Carl Powell, DE, Louisville (5/156).
Scott Von Der Ahe, LB, Arizona State (6/182).
Clarence Thompson, DB, Knoxville (7/219).

TRAINING CAMP ROSTER

No.	QUARTERBACKS	Ht./Wt.	Born	NFL Exp.	College	How acq.	'96 Games GP/GS
12	Bell, Kerwin	6-3/210	6-15-65	1	Florida	FA/96	1/0
4	Harbaugh, Jim	6-3/215	12-23-63	11	Michigan	FA/94	14/14
	Holcomb, Kelly	6-3/170	7-9-73	1	Middle Tennessee State	FA/97	0/0
11	Justin, Paul	6-4/211	5-19-68	3	Arizona State	FA/94	8/2
	RUNNING BACKS						
32	Crockett, Zack (FB)	6-2/246	12-2-72	3	Florida State	D3/95	5/5
28	Faulk, Marshall	5-10/211	2-26-73	4	San Diego State	D1a/94	13/13
33	Groce, Clif	5-11/245	7-30-72	2	Texas A&M	FA/95	15/8
44	Hetherington, Chris	6-2/233	11-27-72	2	Yale	FA/96	6/0
27	Mickens, Arnold	5-11/217	10-12-72	2	Butler	FA/96	3/0
20	Neal, Leon	5-9/185	9-11-72	1	Washington	D6a/96	0/0
42	Potts, Roosevelt	6-0/250	1-8-71	4	Northeast Louisiana	D2/93	0/0
21	Warren, Lamont	5-11/214	1-4-73	4	Colorado	D6/94	13/3
	RECEIVERS						
80	Bailey, Aaron	5-10/185	10-24-71	4	Louisville	FA/94	14/2
83	Banta, Brad (TE)	6-6/260	12-14-70	4	Southern California	D4/94	13/0
87	Dawkins, Sean	6-4/215	2-3-71	5	California	D1/93	15/14
85	Dilger, Ken (TE)	6-5/259	2-2-71	3	Illinois	D2/95	16/16
15	Doering, Chris	6-4/195	5-19-73	1	Florida	FA/96	1/0
88	Harrison, Marvin	6-0/181	8-25-72	2	Syracuse	D1/96	16/15
18	Jacquet, Nate	6-0/173	9-2-75	R	San Diego State	D5a/97	—
81	Pollard, Marcus (TE)	6-4/257	2-8-72	3	Bradley	FA/95	16/4
84	Slutzker, Scott (TE)	6-4/250	12-20-72	2	Iowa	D3/96	15/0
86	Stablein, Brian	6-1/193	4-14-70	4	Ohio State	FA/93	16/0
10	Stock, Mark	5-11/184	4-27-66	5	Virginia Military Institute	FA/96	14/0
	OFFENSIVE LINEMEN						
75	Auzenne, Troy (T)	6-7/305	6-26-69	6	California	FA/96	12/5
78	Glenn, Tarik (T)	6-5/335	5-25-76	R	California	D1/97	—
66	Hardin, Steve (G)	6-7/338	12-30-71	1	Oregon	FA/95	0/0
58	Leeuwenburg, Jay (G/C)	6-3/290	6-18-69	6	Colorado	FA/96	15/7
63	Lowdermilk, Kirk (C)	6-4/284	4-10-63	12	Ohio State	FA/93	16/16
65	Mahlum, Eric (G)	6-4/302	12-6-70	4	California	D2/94	13/9
79	Mandarich, Tony	6-5/324	9-23-66	5	Michigan State	FA/96	15/6
67	Mathews, Jason (T)	6-5/304	2-9-71	4	Texas A&M	D3/94	16/15
73	Meadows, Adam (T)	6-5/292	1-25-74	R	Georgia	D2/97	—
71	Vickers, Kipp	6-2/303	8-27-69	3	Miami (Fla.)	FA/93	10/6
72	West, Derek (T)	6-8/312	3-28-72	3	Colorado	D5/95	1/0
64	Widell, Doug (G)	6-4/296	9-23-66	9	Boston College	FA/96	16/16
	DEFENSIVE LINEMEN						
99	Fontenot, Albert (E)	6-4/287	9-17-70	5	Baylor	FA/97	*16/15
62	Johnson, Ellis (T)	6-2/292	10-30-73	3	Florida	D1/95	12/6
90	Martin, Steve (T)	6-4/303	5-31-74	2	Missouri	D5/96	14/5
61	McCoy, Tony (NT)	6-0/282	6-10-69	6	Florida	D4b/92	15/15
92	Powell, Carl (E)	6-3/265	1-4-74	R	Louisville	D5b/97	—
97	Shello, Kendell (T)	6-3/301	11-24-73	1	Southern	FA/96	0/0
95	Whittington, Bernard (E)	6-6/280	7-20-71	4	Indiana	FA/94	16/14
	LINEBACKERS						
51	Alberts, Trev	6-4/245	8-8-70	4	Nebraska	D1b/94	9/4
50	Alexander, Elijah	6-2/237	8-8-70	6	Kansas State	FA/96	14/3
56	Bennett, Tony	6-2/250	7-1-67	8	Mississippi	FA/94	14/13
57	Berry, Bert	6-2/248	8-15-75	R	Notre Dame	D3/97	—
55	Coryatt, Quentin	6-3/250	8-1-70	6	Texas A&M	D1b/92	8/7
59	Grant, Stephen	6-0/244	12-23-69	6	West Virginia	D10/92	11/11
54	Herrod, Jeff	6-0/249	7-29-66	10	Mississippi	D9/88	14/14
52	Morrison, Steve	6-3/246	12-28-71	3	Michigan	FA/95	16/8
93	Von Der Ahe, Scott	5-11/242	10-12-75	R	Arizona State	D6/97	—
	DEFENSIVE BACKS						
29	Belser, Jason	5-9/188	5-28-70	6	Oklahoma	D8a/92	16/16
38	Daniel, Eugene	5-11/178	5-4-61	14	Louisiana State	D8/84	16/9
26	Gray, Carlton (CB)	6-0/200	6-26-71	5	UCLA	FA/97	*16/16
30	Gray, Derwin	5-11/210	4-9-71	5	Brigham Young	D4/93	10/1

1997 SEASON Indianapolis Colts

No.	DEFENSIVE BACKS	Ht./Wt.	Born	NFL Exp.	College	How acq.	'96 Games GP/GS
35	Hall, Steven (S)	6-0/212	4-15-73	2	Kentucky	FA/96	0/0
39	Jones, Richard (S)	5-9/183	8-4-73	2	Texas A&M-Kingsville	FA/96	4/0
23	Mathis, Dedric (CB)	5-10/188	9-26-73	2	Houston	D2/96	16/6
40	McElroy, Ray (CB/KR)	5-11/207	7-31-72	3	Eastern Illinois	D4/95	16/5
34	Montgomery, Delmonico	5-11/183	12-8-73	R	Houston	D4/97	—
49	Tate, David	6-1/209	11-22-64	10	Colorado	FA/94	10/10
31	Thompson, Clarence	6-1/192	1-5-75	R	Knoxville	D7/97	—
36	Watts, Damon	5-10/190	4-8-72	4	Indiana	FA/94	10/0
	SPECIALISTS						
14	Blanchard, Cary (K)	6-1/227	11-5-68	5	Oklahoma State	FA/95	16/0
17	Gardocki, Chris (P)	6-1/200	2-7-70	7	Clemson	FA/95	16/0

*Fontenot played 16 games with Bears in '96; C. Gray played 16 games with Seahawks.

Abbreviations: D1—draft pick, first round; SupD2—supplemental draft pick second round; W-Den—waivers acquisition from Denver; T-Sea—trade acquisition from Seattle; PlanB—Plan B free-agent acquisition; FA—free-agent acquisition (other than Plan B).

MISCELLANEOUS TEAM DATA

Stadium (capacity, surface):
RCA Dome (60,599, artificial)
Business address:
P.O. Box 535000
Indianapolis, IN 46253
Business phone:
317-297-2658
Ticket information:
317-297-7000
Team colors:
Royal blue and white
Flagship radio stations:
WIBC, 1070 AM
WNAP, 93.1 FM
Training site:
Anderson University
Anderson, Ind.
317-649-2200

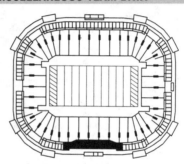

TSN REPORT CARD

Coaching staff	B	Lindy Infante did an outstanding job getting an injury-plagued team to the playoffs a year ago, and his delegation-of-authority approach seems to be working.
Offensive backfield	B	Forget last year's No. 25 offensive ranking. Injuries and an ineffective line were the primary culprits. Jim Harbaugh can deliver the goods, and Marshall Faulk, Lamont Warren and Zack Crockett are a solid group. The probable return of Roosevelt Potts only strengthens the unit.
Receivers	B	Good a year ago, better this year if for no other reason than experience. Marvin Harrison, Sean Dawkins and Ken Dilger are proven talents, but the key to a breakout season could be the long-awaited emergence of Aaron Bailey.
Offensive line	D	Ever-changing and ever-criticized, this group will remain a sore spot until it quiets its skeptics with improved play. Rookie tackle Tarik Glenn isn't expected to be a savior, but he's an immediate upgrade.
Defensive line	C	The unit must prove it will remain a force against the run without anchor Tony Siragusa. And one of these days someone other than right end Tony Bennett must be a pass-rush presence. Maybe newcomer Al Fontenot is the answer.
Linebackers	B	The unit is strong enough to absorb the retirement of Trev Alberts. Jeff Herrod and Stephen Grant are the blue-collar guys, but it's time for Quentin Coryatt to elevate himself to Junior Seau's level as an impact player.
Secondary	C	The key to success will hinge upon how quickly newcomer Carlton Gray and second-year pro Dedric Mathis gel as the starting corners. And while no one ever has questioned the safeties' ability to hit, they need to pick up their coverage game.
Special teams	A	Chris Gardocki and Cary Blanchard were just the third kicking tandem in league history to earn Pro Bowl spots in the same year. Blanchard arrived in town with a reputation for possessing modest range, but he has hit his last 10 attempts from at least 43 yards and nailed all five of his 50-yarders last year.

JACKSONVILLE JAGUARS
AFC CENTRAL DIVISION

1996 REVIEW

RESULTS

Sept. 1—PITTSBURGH	W	24-9
Sept. 8—HOUSTON	L	27-34
Sept.15—at Oakland	L	3-17
Sept.22—at New England (OT)	L	25-28
Sept.29—CAROLINA	W	24-14
Oct. 6—at New Orleans	L	13-17
Oct. 13—N.Y. JETS	W	21-17
Oct. 20—at St. Louis	L	14-17
Oct. 27—at Cincinnati	L	21-28
Nov. 3—Open date		
Nov. 10—BALTIMORE	W	30-27
Nov. 17—at Pittsburgh	L	3-28
Nov. 24—at Baltimore (OT)	W	28-25
Dec. 1—CINCINNATI	W	30-27
Dec. 8—at Houston	W	23-17
Dec. 15—SEATTLE	W	20-13
Dec. 22—ATLANTA	W	19-17
Dec. 28—at Buffalo*	W	30-27
Jan. 4—at Denver†	W	30-27
Jan. 12—at New England‡	L	6-20

*AFC wild-card game.
†AFC divisional playoff game.
‡AFC championship game.

RECORDS/RANKINGS

1996 regular-season record: 9-7 (2nd in AFC Central); 5-3 in division; 7-1 at home; 2-6 on road.

1996 team rankings:	No.	AFC	NFL
Total offense	*360	2	2
Rushing offense	*103.1	10	17
Passing offense	*256.9	1	1
Scoring offense	325	9	14
Total defense	*317.8	6	15
Rushing defense	*111.3	12	19
Passing defense	*206.5	6	16
Scoring defense	335	10	19
Takeaways	27	T9	T20
Giveaways	30	T7	T14
Turnover differential	-3	10	19
Sacks	37	T5	T10
Sacks allowed	50	15	28

*Yards per game.

TEAM LEADERS

Scoring (kicking): Mike Hollis, 117 pts. (27/27 PATs, 30/36 FGs).
Scoring (touchdowns): James Stewart, 60 pts. (8 rushing, 2 receiving).
Passing: Mark Brunell, 4,367 yds. (557 att., 353 comp., 63.4%, 19 TDs, 20 int.).
Rushing: James Stewart, 723 yds. (190 att., 3.8 avg., 8 TDs).
Receptions: Jimmy Smith, 83 (1,244 yds., 15.0 avg., 7 TDs).
Interceptions: Chris Hudson, 2 (25 yds., 0 TDs); Kevin Hardy, 2 (19 yds., 0 TDs); Dave Thomas, 2 (7 yds., 0 TDs); Travis Davis, 2 (0 yds., 0 TDs).
Sacks: Clyde Simmons, 7.5.
Punting: Bryan Barker, 43.7 avg. (69 punts, 3,016 yds., 0 blocked).
Punt returns: Chris Hudson, 10.9 avg. (32 att., 348 yds., 0 TDs).
Kickoff returns: Randy Jordan, 21.3 avg. (26 att., 553 yds., 0 TDs).

1997 SEASON

CLUB DIRECTORY

Chairman, president & CEO
  Wayne Weaver
Senior vice president/football operations
  Michael Huyghue
Senior v.p./marketing
  Dan Connell
Chief financial officer/vice president
  Bill Prescott
General counsel/vice president, admin.
  Paul Vance
Vice President/ticket operations
  Judy Seldin
Exec. director of communications
  Dan Edwards
Director of pro personnel
  Ron Hill
Director of college scouting
  Rick Reiprish
Director of finance
  Kim Dodson
Director of facilities
  Jeff Cannon
Director of security
  Skip Richardson
Director of information services
  Bruce Swindell
Director of team operations
  Daren Anderson
Director of broadcasting
  Jennifer Kumik
Head athletic trainer
  Mike Ryan
Video director
  Mike Perkins

SCHEDULE

Aug. 31—	at Baltimore	4:00
Sept. 7—	N.Y. GIANTS	4:00
Sept. 14—	Open date	
Sept. 22—	PITTSBURGH (Mon.)	9:00
Sept. 28—	at Washington	1:00
Oct. 5—	CINCINNATI	1:00
Oct. 12—	PHILADELPHIA	1:00
Oct. 19—	at Dallas	12:00
Oct. 26—	at Pittsburgh	4:00
Nov. 2—	at Tennessee	3:00
Nov. 9—	KANSAS CITY	1:00
Nov. 16—	TENNESSEE	1:00
Nov. 23—	at Cincinnati	4:00
Nov. 30—	BALTIMORE	1:00
Dec. 7—	NEW ENGLAND	1:00
Dec. 14—	at Buffalo	1:00
Dec. 21—	at Oakland	1:00

All times are for home team.
All games Sunday unless noted.

Head coach
Tom Coughlin

Assistant coaches
  Joe Baker (asst. special teams)
  Pete Carmichael (wide receivers)
  Randy Edsall (secondary)
  Fred Hoaglin (tight ends)
  Jerald Ingram (running backs)
  Dick Jauron (defensive coordinator)
  Mike Maser (offensive line)
  Chris Palmer (offensive coordinator)
  Jerry Palmieri (strength & conditioning)
  Larry Pasquale (special teams coordinator)
  John Pease (defensive line)
  Lucious Selmon (outside linebackers)
  Steve Szabo (inside linebackers)

Equipment manager
  Bob Monica

DRAFT CHOICES

Renaldo Wynn, DT, Notre Dame (first round/21st pick overall).
Mike Logan, DB, West Virginia (2/50).
James Hamilton, LB, North Carolina (3/79).
Seth Payne, DT, Cornell (4/114).
Damon Jones, TE, Southern Illinois (5/147).
Daimon Shelton, RB, Cal State Sacramento (6/184).
Jon Hesse, LB, Nebraska (7/221).

1997 SEASON *Jacksonville Jaguars*

No.	QUARTERBACKS	Ht./Wt.	Born	NFL Exp.	College	How acq.	'96 Games GP/GS
8	Brunell, Mark	6-1/216	9-17-70	4	Washington	T-GB/95	16/16
11	Johnson, Rob	6-3/212	3-18-73	3	Southern California	D4a/95	2/0
5	Philcox, Todd	6-4/225	9-25-66	5	Syracuse	FA/96	0/0
	RUNNING BACKS						
49	Hallock, Ty (FB)	6-3/256	4-30-71	4	Michigan State	T-Det/95	7/0
23	Jordan, Randy (KR)	5-10/213	6-6-70	4	North Carolina	FA/94	15/0
35	Maston, Le'Shai	6-0/237	10-7-70	5	Baylor	ED/95	15/7
20	Means, Natrone	5-10/240	4-26-72	5	North Carolina	W-SD/96	14/4
31	Shelton, Daimon	6-0/250	9-15-72	R	Cal State Sacramento	D6/97	—
33	Stewart, James	6-1/224	12-27-71	3	Tennessee	D1b/95	13/11
	RECEIVERS						
84	Barlow, Reggie	5-11/186	1-22-73	2	Alabama State	D4/96	7/0
86	Brown, Derek (TE)	6-6/267	3-31-70	6	Notre Dame	ED/95	16/14
88	Bullard, Kendricke	6-2/190	4-30-72	2	Arkansas State	FA/96	12/0
49	Griffin, Chris (TE)	6-4/257	7-26-74	R	New Mexico	D6a/96	—
85	Griffith, Rich (TE)	6-5/256	7-31-69	4	Arizona	FA/95	16/2
80	Jackson, Willie (KR)	6-1/208	8-16-71	3	Florida	ED/95	16/2
81	Jones, Damon (TE)	6-5/282	9-18-74	R	Southern Illinois	D5/97	—
89	Marsh, Curtis (KR)	6-2/201	11-24-70	3	Utah	D7/95	1/0
87	McCardell, Keenan	6-1/186	1-6-70	6	UNLV	FA/96	16/15
83	Mitchell, Pete (TE)	6-2/238	10-9-71	3	Boston College	D4/95	16/7
3	Moore, Will	6-2/180	2-21-70	3	Texas Southern	FA/97	*2/1
82	Smith, Jimmy (/KR)	6-1/204	2-9-69	5	Jackson State	FA/95	16/9
	OFFENSIVE LINEMEN						
71	Boselli, Tony (T)	6-7/322	4-17-72	3	Southern California	D1a/95	16/16
63	Cheever, Michael (C)	6-3/298	6-24-73	2	Georgia Tech	D2b/96	11/2
62	Coleman, Ben (G/T)	6-6/326	5-18-71	5	Wake Forest	W-Ari/95	16/16
73	DeMarco, Brian (G)	6-7/325	4-9-72	3	Michigan State	D2a/95	10/9
	Dukes, Jamie (C)	6-1/285	6-14-64	10	Florida State	FA/96	0/0
74	Herndon, Jimmy (T)	6-8/316	8-30-73	2	Houston	D5/96	0/0
66	Huntington, Greg (G)	6-4/302	9-22-70	4	Penn State	FA/96	2/0
67	Novak, Jeff (G/T)	6-5/298	7-27-67	4	Southwest Texas State	ED/95	5/0
75	Price, Marcus (T)	6-6/318	3-3-72	1	Louisiana State	D6/95	0/0
72	Searcy, Leon (T)	6-3/315	12-21-69	6	Miami, Fla.	FA/96	16/16
76	Tylski, Rich (G/C)	6-4/304	2-27-71	2	Utah State	W-NE/95	16/7
79	Widell, Dave (C)	6-7/312	5-14-65	10	Boston College	FA/95	15/14
	DEFENSIVE LINEMEN						
90	Brackens, Tony (E)	6-4/266	12-26-74	2	Texas	D2a/96	16/1
92	Davey, Don (E/T)	6-4/270	4-8-68	7	Wisconsin	FA/95	16/12
77	Davis, Andre (T)	6-3/330	10-7-75	1	Southern	FA/96	2/0
91	Frase, Paul (E/T)	6-5/271	5-5-65	9	Syracuse	ED/95	14/0
64	Jurkovic, John (NT)	6-2/295	8-18-67	6	Eastern Illinois	FA/96	16/14
56	Lageman, Jeff (E)	6-6/267	7-18-67	9	Virginia	FA/95	12/9
70	Payne, Seth (T)	6-4/306	2-12-75	R	Cornell	D4/97	—
94	Pritchett, Kelvin (T)	6-3/296	10-24-69	7	Mississippi	FA/95	13/4
96	Simmons, Clyde (E)	6-6/281	8-4-64	12	Western Carolina	FA/96	16/14
99	Smeenge, Joel (E)	6-6/270	4-1-68	8	Western Michigan	FA/95	10/10
97	Wynn, Renaldo (T)	6-2/296	9-3-74	R	Notre Dame	D1/97	—
	LINEBACKERS						
52	Boyer, Brant	6-1/231	6-27-71	4	Arizona	ED/95	12/0
54	Hamilton, James	6-4/237	4-17-74	R	North Carolina	D3/97	—
51	Hardy, Kevin	6-4/246	7-24-73	2	Illinois	D1/96	16/15
44	Hesse, Jon	6-3/250	6-6-73	R	Nebraska	D7/97	—
57	Kopp, Jeff	6-3/243	7-8-71	3	Southern California	FA/96	12/0
55	McManus, Tom	6-2/247	7-30-70	3	Boston College	FA/95	16/11
50	Robinson, Eddie	6-1/238	4-13-70	6	Alabama State	FA/96	16/15
58	Schwartz, Bryan	6-4/253	12-5-71	3	Augustana (S.D.)	D2b/95	4/3
97	White, Jose	6-3/274	2-2-73	1	Howard	D7a/95	0/0
	DEFENSIVE BACKS						
21	Beasley, Aaron	5-11/206	7-7-73	2	West Virginia	D3/96	9/7
42	Bell, Ricky (CB)	5-10/186	10-2-74	2	North Carolina State	W-Pit/96	12/0
22	Brooks, Bucky (CB)	6-0/195	1-22-71	3	North Carolina	W-GB/96	*8/1
45	Davis, Travis (S)	6-0/203	1-10-73	4	Notre Dame	FA/95	16/7
27	Figures, Deon (CB)	6-0/192	1-10-70	5	Colorado	FA/97	*16/3
24	Fisher, John (S)	5-10/204	7-28-73	2	Missouri Western	D6a/96	0/0
28	Hall, Dana (S)	6-2/209	7-8-69	6	Washington	FA/96	16/10
37	Hudson, Chris (S)	5-10/200	10-6-71	3	Colorado	D3/95	16/16
32	Logan, Mike	6-0/203	9-15-74	R	West Virginia	D2/97	—

No.	DEFENSIVE BACKS	Ht./Wt.	Born	NFL Exp.	College	How acq.	'96 Games GP/GS
40	Massey, Robert (CB)	5-11/200	2-17-67	9	North Carolina Central	FA/96	16/2
30	Studstill, Darren (S)	6-1/190	8-9-70	3	West Virginia	D6/94	0/0
41	Thomas, Dave (CB)	6-3/215	8-25-68	5	Tennessee	ED/95	9/5
	SPECIALISTS						
4	Barker, Bryan (P)........................	6-2/191	6-28-64	8	Santa Clara	FA/95	16/0
1	Hollis, Mike (K)	5-7/178	5-22-72	3	Idaho	FA/95	16/0
7	O'Neill, Pat (P)	6-1/200	2-9-71	3	Syracuse	FA/97	0/0

*Brooks played in 2 games with Packers and 6 games with Jaguars in '96; Figures played 16 games with Steelers; Moore played 2 games with Patriots.

Abbreviations: D1—draft pick, first round; SupD2—supplemental draft pick second round; W-Den—waivers acquisition from Denver; T-Sea—trade acquisition from Seattle; PlanB—Plan B free-agent acquisition; FA—free-agent acquisition (other than Plan B).

MISCELLANEOUS TEAM DATA

Stadium (capacity, surface):
Alltel Stadium (73,000, grass)
Business address:
One Alltel Stadium Place
Jacksonville, FL 32202
Business phone:
904-633-6000
Ticket information:
904-633-2000
Team colors:
Teal, black and gold
Flagship radio station:
WOKV, 690 AM
Training site:
Alltel Stadium
Jacksonville, Fla.
904-633-6000

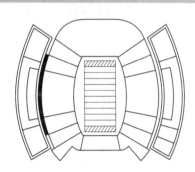

TSN REPORT CARD

Coaching staff	B	Tom Coughlin proved to his doubters that his way can work in the NFL. A workaholic, Coughlin appears to have adjusted to the NFL player, which should make him a better coach. The big question will be how Chris Palmer takes over for Kevin Gilbride, but he is respected. Defensive coordinator Dick Jauron is one of the more underrated coaches in the league.
Offensive backfield	A	Mark Brunell has developed into the best young quarterback in the league. In the final half of the 1996 season, he became a much better pocket passer, his feel for the game much better. He still has great athletic ability, but now he's more of a quarterback. Natrone Means will carry most of the time, and a 1,500-yard season is possible. Backup James Stewart is a capable reserve who is solid catching the football.
Receivers	B	In Jimmy Smith and Keenan McCardell, the Jaguars have a solid tandem. Smith, the deep threat, has quietly developed into one of the best receivers in the AFC. McCardell, the precision route runner, does most of his damage in the middle of the field. Third receiver Willie Jackson doesn't always run the right route, but he is tough after the catch. Curtis Marsh and Reggie Barlow need to have breakout seasons. Tight end is still a concern with Derek Brown and Pete Mitchell, but the team has high hopes for rookie Damon Jones.
Offensive line	B	The tackles, Tony Boselli and Leon Searcy, are as good a pair as there is in the league. Boselli is the best pass-blocking tackle in the league, while his run-blocking has made big strides. Searcy is a solid run blocker, who has improved as a pass protector. Guards Ben Coleman and Brian DeMarco are huge, but they need to be more consistent. Look for Michael Cheever to beat out veteran Dave Widell at center.
Defensive line	B -	There is a lot of depth, and the team likes to rotate players on a regular basis. The ends, with veterans Clyde Simmons and Jeff Lageman the likely starters, are solid. Second-year man Tony Brackens is a future pass-rush star. Joel Smeenge is undersized, but he is a capable pass rusher. Inside, John Jurkovic and Don Davey are scrappers who make up for physical deficiencies with hard play. Kelvin Pritchett has been a free-agent bust, but the team thinks he can bounce back for a big 1997.
Linebackers	B	It wasn't long ago that this was a team weakness. Now it's a strength. Outside linebackers Kevin Hardy and Eddie Robinson are both coming off solid seasons, with Robinson leading the team in tackles after a slow start. Hardy is an all-purpose linebacker who is adept at coverage and attacking the quarterback. The return of 260-pound linebacker Bryan Schwartz from knee surgery will help the run defense. Tom McManus is a solid reserve.
Secondary	C	The cornerbacks have been a major concern the first two seasons, but the team feels better about that position than at any other time. Dave Thomas and Aaron Beasley will be the starters, and both are physical players. Free-agent signee Deon Figures will be the nickel back. Free safety Chris Hudson needs to play better than he did a year ago, while Dana Hall is a veteran leader at strong safety.
Special teams	C	The coverage teams were of major concern last season, but the team feels it has improved there by adding team speed. Punter Bryan Barker had an off year last season, but he is still a top-flight punter. Kicker Mike Hollis is solid, but his kickoffs were poor. The return game isn't much, although Bucky Brooks has potential as a kickoff returner. Look for rookie Mike Logan to take over the punt-return duties.

KANSAS CITY CHIEFS
AFC WESTERN DIVISION

1996 REVIEW
RESULTS

Sept. 1—at Houston	W	20-19
Sept. 8—OAKLAND	W	19-3
Sept.15—at Seattle	W	35-17
Sept.22—DENVER	W	17-14
Sept.29—at San Diego	L	19-22
Oct. 7—PITTSBURGH	L	7-17
Oct. 13—Open date		
Oct. 17—SEATTLE	W	34-16
Oct. 27—at Denver	L	7-34
Nov. 3—at Minnesota	W	21-6
Nov. 10—GREEN BAY	W	27-20
Nov. 17—CHICAGO	W	14-10
Nov. 24—SAN DIEGO	L	14-28
Nov. 28—at Detroit	W	28-24
Dec. 9—at Oakland	L	7-26
Dec. 15—INDIANAPOLIS	L	19-24
Dec. 22—at Buffalo	L	9-20

RECORDS/RANKINGS

1996 regular-season record: 9-7 (2nd in AFC West); 4-4 in division; 5-7 in conference; 5-3 at home; 4-4 on road.
Team record last five years: 52-28 (.650), ranks 4th in league in that span).

1996 team rankings:	No.	AFC	NFL
Total offense	*306.2	13	22
Rushing offense	*125.6	4	4
Passing offense	*180.6	14	26
Scoring offense	297	14	24
Total defense	*325.3	8	18
Rushing defense	*104.1	7	13
Passing defense	*221.1	9	22
Scoring defense	300	5	11
Takeaways	27	T9	T20
Giveaways	24	T1	T2
Turnover differential	3	T6	T11
Sacks	31	12	24
Sacks allowed	27	2	6

*Yards per game.

TEAM LEADERS

Scoring (kicking): Pete Stoyanovich, 85 pts. (34/34 PATs, 17/24 FGs).
Scoring (touchdowns): Marcus Allen, 54 pts. (9 rushing).
Passing: Steve Bono, 2,572 yds. (438 att., 235 comp., 53.7%, 12 TDs, 13 int.).
Rushing: Marcus Allen, 830 yds. (206 att., 4.0 avg., 9 TDs).
Receptions: Chris Penn, 49 (628 yds., 12.8 avg., 5 TDs).
Interceptions: Mark Collins, 6 (45 yds., 0 TDs).
Sacks: Derrick Thomas, 13.0.
Punting: Louis Aguiar, 41.7 avg. (88 punts, 3,667 yds., 0 blocked).
Punt returns: Chris Penn, 10.6 avg. (14 att., 148 yds., 0 TDs).
Kickoff returns: Tamarick Vanover, 25.9 avg. (33 att., 854 yds., 1 TD).

1997 SEASON
CLUB DIRECTORY

Founder
Lamar Hunt
Chairman of the board
Jack Steadman
President/g.m./chief executive officer
Carl Peterson
Vice president/administration
Dennis Watley
Executive vice president/assistant g.m.
Dennis Thum
Secretary/legal
Jim Seigfreid
Treasurer and director/finance
Dale Young
Director/sales and marketing
Wallace Bennett
Director/operations
Steve Schneider
Director/development
Ken Blume
Director/corporate sponsorships
Anita McDonald
Director/public relations
Bob Moore
Assistant director/public relations
Jim Carr
Community relations manager
Brenda Sniezek
Director of pro scouting
Mark Hatley
Director of college scouting
Terry Bradway
Scouts
Bill Baker
Chuck Cook
Roger Jackson
Fred Schubach
Trainer
Dave Kendall
Assistant trainer
Bud Epps

Head coach
Marty Schottenheimer

Assistant coaches
Russ Ball (administrative assistant to the head coach)
Gunther Cunningham (def. coord.)
Jim Erkenbeck (tight ends)
Paul Hackett (off. coordinator)
Bob Karmelowicz (defensive line)
Woodrow Lowe (defensive & special teams assistant)
Michael McCarthy (quarterbacks)
Jimmy Raye (running backs)
Dave Redding (strength & conditioning)
Al Saunders (assistant head coach/receivers)
Kurt Schottenheimer (def. backs)
Mike Solari (offensive line)
Mike Stock (special teams)
Darvin Wallis (quality control/defense)
Roberto Parker (assistant strength & conditioning)

Physicians
Jon Browne
Ray Baker
Chris Barnthouse
Equipment manager
Mike Davidson

SCHEDULE

Aug. 31— at Denver	2:00
Sept. 8— at Oakland (Mon.)	6:00
Sept. 14— BUFFALO	12:00
Sept. 21— at Carolina	1:00
Sept. 28— SEATTLE	3:00
Oct. 5— at Miami	1:00
Oct. 12— Open date	
Oct. 16— SAN DIEGO (Thur.)	7:00
Oct. 26— at St. Louis	12:00
Nov. 3— PITTSBURGH (Mon.)	8:00
Nov. 9— at Jacksonville	1:00
Nov. 16— DENVER	12:00
Nov. 23— at Seattle	1:00
Nov. 30— SAN FRANCISCO	12:00
Dec. 7— OAKLAND	12:00
Dec. 14— at San Diego	1:00
Dec. 21— NEW ORLEANS	12:00

All times are for home team.
All games Sunday unless noted.

DRAFT CHOICES

Tony Gonzalez, TE, California (first round/13th pick overall).
Kevin Lockett, WR, Kansas State (2/47).
Pat Barnes, QB, California (4/110).
June Henley, RB, Kansas (5/163).
Isaac Byrd, WR, Kansas (6/195).
Nathan Parks, T, Stanford (7/214).

TRAINING CAMP ROSTER

No.	QUARTERBACKS	Ht./Wt.	Born	NFL Exp.	College	How acq.	'96 Games GP/GS
17	Barnes, Pat	6-3/215	2-23-75	R	California	D4/97	—
12	Gannon, Rich	6-3/210	12-20-65	10	Delaware	FA/95	4/3
11	Grbac, Elvis	6-5/232	8-13-70	5	Michigan	FA/97	*15/4
15	Matthews, Steve	6-3/209	10-13-70	1	Memphis State	D7a/94	0/0
	RUNNING BACKS						
32	Allen, Marcus	6-2/210	3-26-60	16	Southern California	FA/93	16/15
30	Bennett, Donnell (FB)	6-0/248	9-14-72	4	Miami (Fla.)	D2/94	16/0
21	Henley, June	5-10/226	9-4-75	R	Kansas	D5/97	—
27	Hill, Greg	5-11/214	2-23-72	4	Texas A&M	D1/94	15/1
49	Richardson, Tony	6-1/237	12-17-71	3	Auburn	FA/95	13/0
22	Smith, J.J.	6-0/203	10-14-72	1	Kansas State	FA/95	0/0
	RECEIVERS						
88	Bailey, Victor	6-2/203	7-3-70	4	Missouri	T-Phi/95	2/0
1	Byrd, Isaac	6-0/173	11-11-74	R	Kansas	D6/97	—
80	Dawson, Lake	6-1/200	1-2-72	4	Notre Dame	D3a/94	4/0
88	Gonzalez, Tony (TE)	6-4/244	2-27-76	R	California	D1/97	—
84	Horn, Joe	6-1/199	1-16-72	2	Itawamba JC (Miss.)	D5/96	9/0
83	Hughes, Danan (KR)	6-2/211	12-11-70	5	Iowa	D7/93	15/2
9	Jones, Reggie	6-0/191	5-5-71	2	Louisiana State	FA/97	0/0
18	LaChapelle, Sean	6-3/217	7-29-70	3	UCLA	FA/96	12/8
89	Lockett, Kevin	6-0/177	9-8-74	R	Kansas State	D2/97	—
91	McBride, Oscar (TE)	6-5/266	7-23-72	3	Notre Dame	FA/97	*2/1
81	Penn, Chris (KR)	6-0/200	4-20-71	4	Tulsa	D3b/94	16/16
47	Senters, Michael	5-11/186	12-14-71	1	Northwestern.	FA/96	0/0
87	Vanover, Tamarick (KR)	5-11/218	2-25-74	3	Florida State	D3a/95	13/6
82	Walker, Derrick (TE)	6-0/250	6-23-67	8	Michigan	FA/94	11/9
6	Winans, Tydus	5-11/185	7-26-72	4	Fresno State	FA/97	*2/0
	OFFENSIVE LINEMEN						
76	Alt, John (T)	6-8/307	5-30-62	14	Iowa	D1b/84	12/11
71	Barndt, Tom (C/G)	6-3/285	3-14-72	2	Pittsburgh	D6b/95	13/0
69	Criswell, Jeff (T)	6-7/294	3-7-64	11	Graceland College (Ia.)	FA/95	15/5
61	Grunhard, Tim (C)	6-2/307	5-17-68	8	Notre Dame	D2/90	16/16
67	Hernandez, Jesus (T/G)	6-2/300	10-16-71	1	Florida State	FA/97	0/0
74	Jenkins, Trezelle (T)	6-7/317	3-13-73	3	Michigan	D1/95	6/0
72	Parks, Nathan (T)	6-5/303	10-25-74	R	Stanford	D7/97	—
68	Shields, Will (G)	6-3/305	9-15-71	5	Nebraska	D3/93	16/16
65	Smith, Jeff (C)	6-3/322	5-25-73	2	Tennessee	D7b/96	0/0
79	Szott, David (G)	6-4/290	12-12-67	8	Penn State	D7/90	16/16
	DEFENSIVE LINEMEN						
62	Barnard, David (T)	6-2/302	11-26-74	1	Florida	FA/96	0/0
99	Booker, Vaughn (E)	6-5/295	2-24-68	4	Cincinnati	FA/94	14/12
93	Browning, John (T)	6-4/290	9-30-73	2	West Virginia	D3/96	13/2
94	Buckner, Brentson (E)	6-2/315	9-30-71	4	Clemson	T-Pit/97	*15/14
64	Gaines, Wendall (E)	6-4/293	1-17-72	3	Oklahoma State	FA/96	0/0
96	Hicks, Kerry	6-6/283	12-29-72	2	Colorado	D7b/96	0/0
98	Maumalanga, Chris (T)	6-3/300	12-15-71	3	Kansas	FA/97	*1/0
77	McDaniels, Pellom (E)	6-3/285	2-21-68	5	Oregon State	FA/92	9/1
75	Phillips, Joe (T)	6-5/310	7-15-63	12	Southern Methodist	FA/92	16/16
67	Proby, Bryan (T)	6-5/285	11-30-71	2	Arizona State	D6a/95	0/0
97	Saleaumua, Dan (T)	6-0/300	11-25-64	11	Arizona State	PlanB/89	15/14
	LINEBACKERS						
50	Davis, Anthony	6-0/235	3-7-69	5	Utah	FA/94	16/15
55	Dumas, Troy	6-3/242	9-30-72	3	Nebraska	D3b/95	6/0
59	Edwards, Donnie	6-2/236	4-6-73	2	UCLA	D4/96	15/1
54	Simien, Tracy	6-1/255	5-21-67	7	Texas Christian	FA/90	16/13
58	Thomas, Derrick	6-3/247	1-1-67	9	Alabama	D1/89	16/13
90	Wooden, Terry	6-3/239	1-14-67	8	Syracuse	FA/97	*9/9
	DEFENSIVE BACKS						
44	Anderson, Darren (CB)	5-10/189	1-11-69	5	Toledo	T-TB/94	11/3
41	Cade, Eddie (S)	6-1/206	8-4-73	2	Arizona State	FA/97	0/0
34	Carter, Dale (CB)	6-1/188	11-28-69	6	Tennessee	D1/92	14/14
40	Hasty, James (CB)	6-0/208	5-23-65	10	Washington State	FA/95	15/14
45	Stargell, Tony (CB)	5-11/192	8-7-66	8	Tennessee State	FA/96	8/4

No.	DEFENSIVE BACKS	Ht./Wt.	Born	NFL Exp.	College	How acq.	'96 Games GP/GS
41	Tongue, Reggie (CB/S)	6-0/201	4-11-73	2	Oregon State	D2/96	16/0
29	Washington, Brian (S)	6-1/210	9-10-65	9	Nebraska	FA/95	16/16
42	Williams, Darrell (KR)	5-11/196	6-29-73	R	Tennessee State	D7c/96	—
31	Woods, Jerome (CB/S)	6-2/200	3-17-73	2	Memphis	D1/96	16/0
	SPECIALISTS						
5	Aguiar, Louie (P)	6-2/219	6-30-66	6	Utah State	FA/94	16/0
10	Stoyanovich, Pete (K)	5-11/195	4-28-67	9	Indiana	FA/96	16/0

*Buckner played 15 games with Steelers in '96; Grbac played 15 games with 49ers; Maumalanga played 1 game with Cardinals; McBride played 2 games with Cardinals; Winans played 2 games with Bengals.

Abbreviations: D1—draft pick, first round; SupD2—supplemental draft pick second round; W-Den—waivers acquisition from Denver; T-Sea—trade acquisition from Seattle; PlanB—Plan B free-agent acquisition; FA—free-agent acquisition (other than Plan B).

MISCELLANEOUS TEAM DATA

Stadium (capacity, surface):
Arrowhead Stadium
(79,101, grass)
Business address:
One Arrowhead Drive
Kansas City, MO 64129
Business phone:
816-924-9300
Ticket information:
816-924-9400
Team colors:
Red, gold and white
Flagship radio station:
KCFX, 101.1 FM
Training site:
U. of Wisconsin-River Falls
River Falls, Wis.
715-425-4580

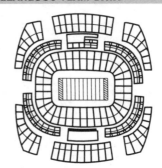

TSN REPORT CARD

Coaching staff	B -	The Chiefs faltered miserably last season, failing to make the playoffs after a 4-0 start. This underachievement is rare, however. Six straight playoff appearances from 1990 through 1995 attest to that. Still, Marty Schottenheimer and his staff haven't found a way to get the Chiefs over the hump and into the Super Bowl.
Offensive backfield	B	The Chiefs gambled to an extent by making largely unproven Elvis Grbac their starting quarterback. He seems to have the proper talent to fit their offense. Behind him, the club has a versatile collection of backs. Greg Hill, newly installed as the featured back, has tremendous speed and game-breaking ability.
Receivers	C	The lack of a receiving tight end crippled the passing game for several years. If first-round tight end Tony Gonzalez is the real deal, the Chiefs have a bargain. He should help take pressure off the wide receivers, a collection of good possession players. But that group lacks a dangerous downfield threat.
Offensive line	B -	The Chiefs have one of the best cores in the NFL in guards Dave Szott and Will Shields and center Tim Grunhard. Trouble looms at tackle, where veteran John Alt was pondering retirement and Ricky Siglar was available in the free-agent market. Jeff Criswell and Trezelle Jenkins, their probable replacements, have done little to inspire confidence.
Defensive line	C	This unit needs to rebound from a subpar 1996 season. Losing a major talent like Neil Smith isn't a great start. Moving Derrick Thomas to end should help improve the pass rush, which turned timid last season. Inexperienced end John Browning needs to have a big season.
Linebackers	B	The signing of veteran free agent Terry Wooden should be a good one. His speed will fit nicely into the Chiefs' defensive scheme. The other outside linebacker, Anthony Davis, also runs well. If young Donnie Edwards succeeds in ousting veteran Tracy Simien on the inside, the Chiefs will have one of the fastest trios in the NFL.
Secondary	B +	This is a veteran unit that has yet to show its age. The club MVP award won by since-released free safety Mark Collins last season was well-earned. Brian Washington plays the run as well as most strong safeties. One cornerback, Dale Carter, is spectacular. The other, James Hasty, is well-suited to play the Chiefs' aggressive bump-and-run style.
Special teams	C -	Kicker Pete Stoyanovich and punter Louie Aguiar need to bounce back from subpar seasons. Coverage units need to patch some leaks that popped up last season. Tamarick Vanover, if healthy, remains one of the NFL's most dangerous returners.

MIAMI DOLPHINS
AFC EASTERN DIVISION

1996 REVIEW
RESULTS

Sept. 1—NEW ENGLAND	W	24-10
Sept. 8—at Arizona	W	38-10
Sept.15—N.Y. JETS	W	36-27
Sept.23—at Indianapolis	L	6-10
Sept.30—Open date		
Oct. 6—SEATTLE	L	15-22
Oct. 13—at Buffalo	W	21-7
Oct. 20—at Philadelphia	L	28-35
Oct. 27—DALLAS	L	10-29
Nov. 3—at New England	L	23-42
Nov. 10—INDIANAPOLIS	W	37-13
Nov. 17—at Houston	W	23-20
Nov. 25—PITTSBURGH	L	17-24
Dec. 1—at Oakland	L	7-17
Dec. 8—N.Y. GIANTS	L	7-17
Dec. 16—BUFFALO	W	16-14
Dec. 22—at N.Y. Jets	W	31-28

RECORDS/RANKINGS

1996 regular-season record: 8-8 (4th in AFC East); 6-2 in division; 7-5 in conference; 4-4 at home; 4-4 on road.
Team record last five years: 47-33 (.588, ranks T7th in league in that span).

1996 team rankings:	No.	AFC	NFL
Total offense	*322.8	8	14
Rushing offense	*101.4	11	19
Passing offense	*221.4	5	11
Scoring offense	339	8	13
Total defense	*324.4	7	17
Rushing defense	*96	5	7
Passing defense	*228.4	11	24
Scoring defense	325	8	17
Takeaways	36	T3	T6
Giveaways	24	T1	T2
Turnover differential	12	2	T4
Sacks	37	T5	T10
Sacks allowed	36	7	T13

*Yards per game.

TEAM LEADERS

Scoring (kicking): Joe Nedney, 89 pts. (35/36 PATs, 18/29 FGs).
Scoring (touchdowns): Karim Abdul-Jabbar, 66 pts. (11 rushing).
Passing: Dan Marino, 2,795 yds. (373 att., 221 comp., 59.2%, 17 TDs, 9 int.).
Rushing: Karim Abdul-Jabbar, 1,116 yds. (307 att., 3.6 avg., 11 TDs).
Receptions: O.J. McDuffie, 74 (918 yds., 12.4 avg., 8 TDs).
Interceptions: Terrell Buckley, 6 (164 yds., 1 TD).
Sacks: Trace Armstrong, 12.0.
Punting: John Kidd, 46.3 avg. (78 punts, 3,611 yds., 0 blocked).
Punt returns: O.J. McDuffie, 9.6 avg. (22 att., 212 yds., 0 TDs).
Kickoff returns: Irving Spikes, 24.3 avg. (28 att., 681 yds., 0 TDs).

1997 SEASON
CLUB DIRECTORY

Owner/chairman of the board
 H. Wayne Huizenga
Vice chairman
 Don Shula
President/chief operating officer
 Eddie J. Jones
Vice president/administration
 Bryan Wiedmeier
Vice president/finance
 Jill R. Strafaci
Director of football operations
 Bob Ackles
Director/Pro Player stadium personnel
 Tom Heckert
Director of college scouting
 Tom Braatz
Director of media relations
 Harvey Greene
Media relations coordinator
 Neal Gulkis
Director of publications
 Scott Stone
Community relations director
 Fudge Browne
Ticket director
 Bill Galante
Scouts
 Mike Cartwright
 Tom Heckert, Jr.
 Ron Labadie
 Jeff Smith
 Jere Stripling
Head trainer
 Kevin O'Neill
Trainers
 Troy Mauer
 Ryan Vermillion
Physician
 Daniel Kanell
 John Uribe

SCHEDULE

Aug. 31— INDIANAPOLIS	1:00
Sept. 7— TENNESSEE	1:00
Sept. 14— at Green Bay	12:00
Sept. 21— at Tampa Bay	8:00
Sept. 28— Open date	
Oct. 5— KANSAS CITY	1:00
Oct. 12— at N.Y. Jets	1:00
Oct. 19— at Baltimore	4:00
Oct. 26— CHICAGO	4:00
Nov. 2— at Buffalo	1:00
Nov. 9— N.Y. JETS	1:00
Nov. 17— BUFFALO (Mon.)	9:00
Nov. 23— at New England	1:00
Nov. 30— at Oakland	1:00
Dec. 7— DETROIT	8:00
Dec. 14— at Indianapolis	1:00
Dec. 22— NEW ENGLAND (Mon.)	9:00

All times are for home team.
All games Sunday unless noted.

Head coach
Jimmy Johnson

Assistant coaches
Larry Beightol (assistant head coach/offensive line)
Kippy Brown (running backs)
Joel Collier (defensive staff assistant)
John Gamble (strength & conditioning)
Cary Godette (defensive line)
George Hill (defensive coordinator/ linebackers)
Pat Jones (tight ends)
Les Koenning (offensive staff assistant)
Bill Lewis (defensive nickel package)
Rich McGeorge (assistant offensive line)
Mel Phillips (secondary)
Larry Seiple (wide receivers)
Gary Stevens (offensive coordinator)
Mike Westhoff (special teams)

Equipment manager
 Tony Egues
Video manager
 Dave Hack

DRAFT CHOICES

Yatil Green, WR, Miami, Fla. (first round/ 15th pick overall).
Sam Madison, DB, Louisville (2/44).
Jason Taylor, DE, Akron (3/73).
Derrick Rodgers, LB, Arizona State (3/92).
Ronnie Ward, LB, Kansas (3/93).
Brent Smith, T, Mississippi State (3/96).
Jerome Daniels, T, Northeastern (4/121).
Barron Tanner, DT, Oklahoma (5/149).
Nicholas Lopez, DE, Texas Southern (5/157).
John Fiala, LB, Washington (6/166).
Brian Manning, WR, Stanford (6/170).
Mike Crawford, LB, Nevada (6/173).
Ed Perry, TE, James Madison (6/177).
Hudhaifa Ismaeli, DB, Northwestern (7/203).

1997 SEASON — Miami Dolphins

No.	QUARTERBACKS	Ht./Wt.	Born	NFL Exp.	College	How acq.	'96 Games GP/GS
7	Erickson, Craig	6-2/205	5-17-69	6	Miami (Fla.)	FA/96	7/3
14	Fischer, Spence	6-3/221	11-30-72	1	Duke	D6b/96	0/0
11	Huard, Damon	6-3/220	7-9-73	1	Washington	FA/97	0/0
13	Marino, Dan	6-4/224	9-15-61	15	Pittsburgh	D1/83	13/13
	RUNNING BACKS						
33	Abdul-Jabbar, Karim	5-10/194	6-28-74	2	UCLA	D3b/96	16/14
48	McClinton, Lee (FB)	5-10/252	8-2-72	1	New Hampshire	FA/96	0/0
32	McPhail, Jerris	5-11/201	6-26-72	2	East Carolina	D5a/96	9/1
30	Parmalee, Bernie	5-11/196	9-16-67	6	Ball State	FA/92	16/0
36	Pritchett, Stanley (FB)	6-1/245	12-12-73	2	South Carolina	D4b/96	16/16
35	Spikes, Irving	5-8/206	12-21-70	4	Northeast Louisiana	FA/94	15/1
20	Wilson, Robert (FB)	6-0/255	1-13-69	5	Texas A&M	FA/94	15/0
	RECEIVERS						
80	Barnett, Fred	6-0/199	6-17-66	8	Arkansas State	FA/96	9/7
89	Dar Dar, Kirby	5-9/183	3-27-72	2	Syracuse	FA/95	11/0
86	Dawsey, Lawrence	6-0/192	11-16-67	7	Florida State	FA/97	*16/4
84	Drayton, Troy (TE)	6-3/270	6-29-70	5	Penn State	T-STL/96	10/10
87	Green, Yatil	6-2/205	11-25-73	R	Miami (Fla.)	D1/97	—
88	Jordan, Charles (KR)	5-11/183	10-9-69	5	Long Beach (Calif.) City Col.	FA/96	6/0
18	Manning, Brian	5-11/180	4-22-75	1	Stanford	D6b/97	0/0
81	McDuffie, O.J. (KR)	5-10/188	12-2-69	5	Penn State	D1/93	16/16
83	Miller, Scott	5-11/185	10-20-68	6	UCLA	D9/91	12/1
44	Perry, Ed (TE)	6-4/245	9-1-74	R	James Madison	D6c/97	—
83	Reeves, Walter (TE)	6-3/275	12-16-65	9	Auburn	FA/97	*9/2
85	Thomas, Lamar	6-1/175	2-12-70	5	Miami, Fla.	FA/96	9/3
82	Wainright, Frank (TE)	6-3/245	10-10-67	7	Northern Colorado	FA/95	16/0
	OFFENSIVE LINEMEN						
60	Bock, John (G)	6-3/290	2-11-71	3	Indiana State	FA/96	2/0
76	Brown, James (T)	6-6/329	1-3-70	5	Virginia State	T-NYJ/96	16/16
77	Buckey, Jeff (G)	6-5/300	8-7-74	2	Stanford	D7a/96	15/1
73	Daniels, Jerome (T)	6-5/355	9-13-74	R	Northeastern	D4/97	—
63	Dixon, Cal (C/G)	6-4/285	10-11-69	6	Florida	FA/96	11/0
67	Elmore, John (G)	6-3/320	3-2-73	1	Texas	FA/96	0/0
62	Gray, Chris (G)	6-4/296	6-19-70	5	Auburn	D5/93	11/11
66	McIver, Everett (G)	6-5/315	8-5-70	4	Elizabeth (N.C.) City State	FA/96	7/5
64	Patrick, Garin	6-3/269	8-31-71	2	Louisville	FA/97	0/0
61	Ruddy, Tim (C)	6-3/290	4-27-72	4	Notre Dame	D2/94	16/16
69	Sims, Keith (G)	6-3/315	6-17-67	8	Iowa State	D2/90	15/15
	Smith, Gary (T)	6-5/303	11-21-73	R	Mississippi State	D3d/97	0/0
78	Webb, Richmond (T)	6-6/310	1-11-67	8	Texas A&M	D1/90	16/16
65	Young, Donnie (G)	6-4/315	11-17-73	1	Florida	FA/97	0/0
	DEFENSIVE LINEMEN						
56	Armstrong, Antonio (E)	6-1/234	10-15-73	2	Texas A&M	FA/95	0/0
93	Armstrong, Trace (E)	6-4/260	10-5-65	9	Florida	T-Chi/95	16/9
95	Bowens, Tim (T)	6-4/310	2-7-73	4	Mississippi	D1/94	16/16
75	Burton, Shane (T)	6-6/300	1-18-74	2	Tennessee	D5b/96	16/8
92	Gardener, Daryl (T)	6-6/310	2-25-73	2	Baylor	D1/96	16/12
98	Hand, Norman (T)	6-3/325	9-4-72	3	Mississippi	D5/95	9/0
90	Lopez, Nicholas (E)	6-4/250	8-17-72	R	Texas Southern	D5/97	—
96	Stubbs, Daniel (E)	6-4/272	1-3-65	9	Miami (Fla.)	FA/96	16/15
97	Sturgis, Oscar (E)	6-5/291	1-12-71	2	North Carolina	FA/96	0/0
72	Tanner, Barron (T)	6-3/318	9-14-73	R	Oklahoma	D5/97	—
99	Taylor, Jason (E)	6-6/243	9-1-74	R	Akron	D3a/97	—
	LINEBACKERS						
57	Brigance, O.J.	6-0/223	9-29-69	2	Rice	FA/96	12/0
56	Crawford, Mike	6-1/230	10-29-74	R	Nevada	D6c/97	—
58	Fiala, John	6-1/230	11-25-73	R	Washington	D6a/97	—
51	Harris, Anthony	6-1/224	1-25-73	2	Auburn	FA/96	7/3
50	Hollier, Dwight	6-2/250	4-21-69	5	North Carolina	D4/92	16/15
53	Izzo, Larry	5-10/220	9-26-74	2	Rice	FA/96	16/0
59	Rodgers, Derrick	6-1/223	10-14-71	R	Arizona State	D3b/97	—
54	Thomas, Zach	5-11/231	9-1-73	2	Texas Tech	D5c/96	16/16
55	Ward, Ronnie	6-0/225	2-11-74	R	Kansas	D3c/97	—
	DEFENSIVE BACKS						
27	Buckley, Terrell (CB)	5-9/176	6-7-71	6	Florida State	T-GB/95	16/16
26	Davis, Cedric (CB)	5-9/172	9-7-72	2	Tennessee State	FA/97	0/0
25	Harris, Corey (CB)	5-11/201	10-25-69	6	Vanderbilt	FA/97	*16/16

No.	DEFENSIVE BACKS	Ht./Wt.	Born	NFL Exp.	College	How acq.	'96 Games GP/GS
31	Hill, Sean (S)	5-10/182	8-14-71	4	Montana State	D7/94	12/5
47	Holmes, Clayton (CB)	5-10/174	8-23-69	5	Carson-Newman (Tenn.)	FA/97	0/0
37	Ismaeli, Hudhaifa (CB)	5-11/197	7-30-75	R	Northwestern	D7/97	—
38	Jackson, Calvin (CB)	5-9/185	10-28-72	3	Auburn	FA/95	16/15
34	Jacobs, Tim (CB)	5-10/185	4-5-70	5	Delaware	FA/96	12/0
29	Madison, Sam (CB)	5-11/180	4-23-74	R	Louisville	D2/97	—
23	Teague, George (S)	6-0/196	2-18-71	5	Alabama	FA/97	*16/8
24	Wilson, Jerry (CB)	5-10/187	7-17-73	3	Southern	D4/95	2/0
22	Wooden, Shawn	5-11/186	10-23-73	2	Notre Dame	D6/96	16/11
	SPECIALISTS						
17	Kidd, John (P)	6-3/214	8-22-61	14	Northwestern	FA/94	16/0
10	Mare, Olindo (K)	5-10/178	6-6-73	1	Syracuse	FA/97	0/0
6	Nedney, Joe (K)	6-4/205	3-22-73	2	San Jose State	FA/96	16/0

*Dawsey played 16 games with Giants in '96; C. Harris played 16 games with Seahawks; Reeves played 9 games with Chargers; Teague played 16 games with Cowboys.

Abbreviations: D1—draft pick, first round; SupD2—supplemental draft pick second round; W-Den—waivers acquisition from Denver; T-Sea—trade acquisition from Seattle; PlanB—Plan B free-agent acquisition; FA—free-agent acquisition (other than Plan B).

MISCELLANEOUS TEAM DATA

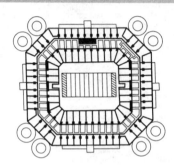

Stadium (capacity, surface):
Pro Player Stadium
(74,916, grass)
Business address:
7500 S.W. 30th St.
Davie, FL 33314
Business phone:
954-452-7000
Ticket information:
305-620-2578
Team colors:
Aqua, coral, blue and white
Flagship radio station:
WQAM, 560 AM
Training site:
Nova University
Davie, Fla.
954-452-7000

TSN REPORT CARD

Coaching staff	A	How do you argue with a coach who has won two Super Bowls in six seasons? Perhaps the most impressive thing about Jimmy Johnson in his year-plus with the Dolphins is that he has avoided the temptations of big-money free agency and stayed true to his principles of building through the draft.
Offensive backfield	B +	If this were four years ago, Dan Marino would merit an A all by himself. But three injuries later, the questions about Marino's reliability make it tough. Even an improved cast of running backs to help him and an emphasis on the running game don't make up for the questions.
Receivers	B	The explosiveness is so much better now with the addition of first-round pick Yatil Green and the overall depth should be excellent. A full, healthy season by Fred Barnett is needed. A real deep threat could help open the running game by getting safeties to back off.
Offensive line	C	The talent rates a B, but the attitude is just not there yet. Richmond Webb, Keith Sims and Tim Ruddy just aren't the nastiness guys in the world. Somehow, the coaching staff has to whip this group into a frenzy.
Defensive line	B -	If tackles Daryl Gardener and Tim Bowens play up to their potential, this grade should go way up. They are every bit as talented as any pair of tackles in the league. The depth is good, but this group, like its offensive counterpart, is just not consistent enough.
Linebackers	B -	Zach Thomas is a marvel and fun guy for fans to cheer for. He also has great instincts and makes people around him better. But he isn't a game-changing player just yet and he can be accounted for, as opponents showed late last season. In addition, the outside linebackers are average at best.
Secondary	C +	The improved depth could have this grade shoot way up by the end of the season. But that's supposition. Until then, the Dolphins are an inconsistent coverage team that doesn't have a true playmaker in the secondary. This also isn't a great tackling group, particularly at cornerback.
Special teams	B +	This may sound high for a team that doesn't have a proven kicker, but Joe Nedney has huge potential and the rest of the special teams are so technically sound and create so many plays that this could be the best part of the team. Johnson and assistant Mike Westhoff certainly emphasize it enough.

MINNESOTA VIKINGS
NFC CENTRAL DIVISION

1996 REVIEW
RESULTS

Sept. 1—DETROIT	W	17-13
Sept. 8—at Atlanta	W	23-17
Sept.15—at Chicago	W	20-14
Sept.22—GREEN BAY	W	30-21
Sept.29—at N.Y. Giants	L	10-15
Oct. 6—CAROLINA	W	14-12
Oct. 13—at Tampa Bay	L	13-24
Oct. 20—Open date		
Oct. 28—CHICAGO	L	13-15
Nov. 3—KANSAS CITY	L	6-21
Nov. 10—at Seattle	L	23-42
Nov. 17—at Oakland (OT)	W	16-13
Nov. 24—DENVER	L	17-21
Dec. 1—ARIZONA	W	41-17
Dec. 8—at Detroit	W	24-22
Dec. 15—TAMPA BAY	W	21-10
Dec. 22—at Green Bay	L	10-38
Dec. 28—at Dallas*	L	15-40

*NFC wild-card game.

RECORDS/RANKINGS

1996 regular-season record: 9-7 (2nd in AFC Central); 5-3 in division; 8-4 in conference; 5-3 at home; 4-4 on road.
Team record last five years: 47-33 (.588, ranks T7th in league in that span).

1996 team rankings:	No.	NFC	NFL
Total offense	*325.3	5	12
Rushing offense	*96.6	12	24
Passing offense	*228.6	5	8
Scoring offense	298	10	23
Total defense	*317.9	10	16
Rushing defense	*122.9	11	24
Passing defense	*195.1	6	9
Scoring defense	315	9	15
Takeaways	35	T4	T8
Giveaways	32	T8	T17
Turnover differential	3	6	T11
Sacks	43	3	6
Sacks allowed	34	6	T11

*Yards per game.

TEAM LEADERS

Scoring (kicking): Scott Sisson, 96 pts. (30/30 PATs, 22/29 FGs).
Scoring (touchdowns): Cris Carter, 60 pts. (10 receiving).
Passing: Brad Johnson, 2,258 yds. (311 att., 195 comp., 62.7%, 17 TDs, 10 int.).
Rushing: Robert Smith, 692 yds. (162 att., 4.3 avg., 3 TDs).
Receptions: Jake Reed, 72 (1,320 yds., 18.3 avg., 7 TDs).
Interceptions: Orlando Thomas, 5 (57 yds., 0 TDs).
Sacks: John Randle, 11.5.
Punting: Mitch Berger, 41.1 avg. (88 punts, 3,616 yds., 2 blocked).
Punt returns: David Palmer, 9.8 avg. (22 att., 216 yds., 1 TD).
Kickoff returns: Qadry Ismail, 18.8 avg. (28 att., 527 yds., 0 TDs).

1997 SEASON
CLUB DIRECTORY

Chairman of the board
John C. Skoglund
President/chief executive officer
Roger Headrick
V.P., administration/team operations
Jeff Diamond
V.P., player personnel
Frank Gilliam
V.P., marketing/business development
Stew Widdess
Assistant general manager, college scouting
Jerry Reichow
Assistant general manager, pro personnel
Paul Wiggin
Director of finance
Nick Valentine
Director of research and development
Mike Eayrs
Director of marketing
Kernal Buhler
Director of public relations
David Pelletier
Public relations assistants
Debra Jones
Bob Hagan
Director of security
Steve Rollins
Player personnel coordinator
Scott Studwell
Head scout
Don Deisch
Assistant head scout
Conrad Cardano
Regional scouts
Roger Jackson
John Fitzpatrick
Director of team operations
Breck Spinner

SCHEDULE

Aug. 31— at Buffalo	1:00
Sept. 7— at Chicago	12:00
Sept. 14— TAMPA BAY	12:00
Sept. 21— at Green Bay	12:00
Sept. 28— PHILADELPHIA	7:00
Oct. 5— at Arizona	1:00
Oct. 12— CAROLINA	3:00
Oct. 19— Open date	
Oct. 26— at Tampa Bay	1:00
Nov. 2— NEW ENGLAND	12:00
Nov. 9— CHICAGO	12:00
Nov. 16— at Detroit	1:00
Nov. 23— at N.Y. Jets	1:00
Dec. 1— GREEN BAY (Mon.)	8:00
Dec. 7— at San Francisco	1:00
Dec. 14— DETROIT	12:00
Dec. 21— INDIANAPOLIS	12:00

All times are for home team.
All games Sunday unless noted.

Head coach
Dennis Green

Assistant coaches
Dave Atkins (tight ends)
Brian Billick (offensive coord.)
Foge Fazio (defensive coordinator)
Jeff Friday (assistant strength & conditioning)
Carl Hargrave (running backs)
John Levra (defensive line)
Chip Myers (receivers)
Tom Olivadotti (inside linebackers)
Ray Sherman (quarterbacks)
Richard Solomon (secondary)
Mike Tice (offensive line)
Trent Walters (outside linebackers)
Steve Wetzel (strength & conditioning)
Gary Zauner (special teams)

Equipment manager
Dennis Ryan
Medical director
Dr. David Fischer
Trainer
Fred Zamberletti
Assistant trainer
Chuck Barta

DRAFT CHOICES

Dwayne Rudd, LB, Alabama (first round/20th pick overall).
Torrian Gray, DB, Virginia Tech (2/49).
Stalin Colinet, DE, Boston College (3/78).
Antonio Banks, DB, Virginia Tech (4/113).
Tony Williams, DT, Memphis (5/151).
Robert Tate, WR, Cincinnati (6/183).
Artie Ulmer, LB, Valdosta State (7/220).
Matthew Hatchette, WR, Langston (Okla.) (7/235).

1997 SEASON *Minnesota Vikings*

No.	QUARTERBACKS	Ht./Wt.	Born	NFL Exp.	College	How acq.	'96 Games GP/GS
7	Cunningham, Randall	6-4/205	3-27-63	11	UNLV	FA/97	0/0
14	Johnson, Brad	6-5/219	9-13-68	6	Florida State	D9/92	12/8
6	Walker, Jay	6-3/229	1-24-72	1	Howard	FA/96	1/0
	RUNNING BACKS						
29	Evans, Chuck (FB)	6-1/244	4-16-67	5	Clark Atlanta (Ga.)	D11/92	16/6
44	Hoard, Leroy	5-11/225	5-15-68	8	Michigan	FA/96	6/6
33	Morrow, Harold	5-11/210	2-24-73	2	Auburn	W-Dal/96	8/0
26	Smith, Robert (KR)	6-2/212	3-4-72	5	Ohio State	D1/93	8/7
28	Stewart, James	6-2/246	12-8-71	2	Miami (Fla.)	D5/95	0/0
21	Williams, Moe	6-1/196	7-26-74	2	Kentucky	D3/96	9/0
	RECEIVERS						
80	Carter, Cris	6-3/208	11-25-65	11	Ohio State	W-Phi/90	16/16
85	DeLong, Greg (TE)	6-4/251	4-3-73	3	North Carolina	FA/95	16/8
87	Goodwin, Hunter (TE)	6-5/274	10-10-72	2	Texas A&M	D4/96	9/6
19	Hatchette, Matthew	6-2/195	5-1-74	R	Langston	D7b/97	—
89	Jordan, Andrew (TE)	6-4/254	6-21-72	4	Western Carolina	D6/94	13/9
22	Palmer, David	5-8/169	11-19-72	4	Alabama	D2/94	11/1
86	Reed, Jake	6-3/216	9-28-67	7	Grambling State	D3/91	16/15
12	Tate, Robert	5-10/185	10-19-73	R	Cincinnati	D6/97	—
81	Walsh, Chris	6-1/198	12-12-68	6	Stanford	FA/94	15/0
	OFFENSIVE LINEMEN						
62	Christy, Jeff (C)	6-3/282	2-3-69	5	Pittsburgh	FA/93	16/16
76	Dill, Scott (T/G)	6-5/294	4-5-66	10	Memphis State	FA/96	9/1
71	Dixon, David (G/T)	6-5/348	1-5-69	4	Arizona State	FA/94	13/6
61	Lindsay, Everett (G/C)	6-4/290	9-18-70	3	Mississippi	D5/93	0/0
76	McDaniel, Kenneth (G)	6-5/310	12-20-73	1	Norfolk State	D5a/96	0/0
64	McDaniel, Randall (G)	6-3/278	12-19-64	10	Arizona State	D1/88	16/16
68	Morris, Mike (C)	6-5/276	2-22-61	11	Northeast Missouri State	FA/91	16/0
65	Ruether, Mike (C)	6-4/286	9-20-62	10	Texas	FA/94	0/0
73	Steussie, Todd (T)	6-6/309	12-1-70	4	California	D1b/94	16/16
77	Stringer, Korey (T)	6-4/353	5-8-74	3	Ohio State	D1/95	16/15
	DEFENSIVE LINEMEN						
90	Alexander, Derrick (E)	6-4/271	11-3-73	3	Florida State	D1a/95	12/9
92	Clemons, Duane (E)	6-5/263	5-23-74	2	California	D1/96	13/0
99	Colinet, Stalin (E)	6-6/288	7-19-74	R	Boston College	D3/97	—
72	Fisk, Jason (T)	6-3/291	9-4-72	3	Stanford	D7b/95	16/6
75	Manley, James (T)	6-2/302	7-11-74	1	Vanderbilt	D2/96	0/0
93	Randle, John (T)	6-1/282	12-12-67	8	Texas A&I	FA/90	16/16
95	Smith, Fernando (E)	6-6/277	8-2-71	4	Jackson State	D2b/94	16/16
94	Williams, Tony (T)	6-5/292	7-9-75	R	Memphis	D5/97	—
	LINEBACKERS						
56	Bercich, Peter	6-1/238	12-23-71	3	Notre Dame	D7/94	15/1
50	Brady, Jeff	6-1/243	11-9-68	7	Kentucky	FA/95	16/16
59	Edwards, Dixon	6-1/228	3-25-68	7	Michigan State	FA/96	14/13
	Hanks, Ben	6-2/221	7-31-72	2	Florida	FA/96	12/0
58	McDaniel, Ed	5-11/230	2-23-69	5	Clemson	D5/92	0/0
57	Rudd, Dwayne	6-2/241	2-3-76	R	Alabama	D1/97	—
53	Ulmer, Artie	6-2/239	7-30-73	R	Valdosta State	D7a/97	—
	DEFENSIVE BACKS						
30	Banks, Antonio	5-10/195	3-12-73	R	Virginia Tech	D4/97	—
54	Briggs, Greg (S)	6-3/212	10-1-68	3	Texas Southern	FA/97	*14/0
38	Ellis, Kwame (CB)	5-10/188	2-27-74	2	Stanford	FA/96	*8/0
27	Fuller, Corey (CB)	5-10/205	5-11-71	3	Florida State	D2/95	16/14
23	Gray, Torrian	6-0/200	3-18-74	R	Virginia Tech	D2/97	—
24	Griffith, Robert (S)	5-11/189	11-30-70	3	San Diego State	FA/94	14/14
35	Johnson, Chris (S)	6-0/199	8-7-71	2	San Diego State	FA/96	5/0
43	Thomas, Orlando (S)	6-1/211	10-21-72	3	Southwestern Louisiana	D2/95	16/16
20	Washington, Dewayne (CB)	5-11/186	12-27-72	4	North Carolina State	D1a/94	16/16
	SPECIALISTS						
17	Berger, Mitch (P)	6-2/220	6-24-72	3	Colorado	FA/96	16/0
5	Davis, Greg (K)	6-0/205	10-29-65	11	The Citadel	FA/97	*9/0
9	Sisson, Scott (K)	6-0/197	7-21-71	3	Georgia Tech	FA/95	16/0

*Briggs played 14 games with Bears in '96; G. Davis played 9 games with Cardinals; Ellis played 8 games with Jets.
Abbreviations: D1—draft pick, first round; SupD2—supplemental draft pick second round; W-Den—waivers acquisition from Denver; T-Sea—trade acquisition from Seattle; PlanB—Plan B free-agent acquisition; FA—free-agent acquisition (other than Plan B).

MISCELLANEOUS TEAM DATA

Stadium (capacity, surface):
Metrodome (64,035, artificial)
Business address:
9520 Viking Drive
Eden Prairie, MN 55344
Business phone:
612-828-6500
Ticket information:
612-333-8828
Team colors:
Purple, gold and white
Flagship radio station:
WCCO, 830 AM
Training site:
Mankato State University
Mankato, Minn.
612-828-6500

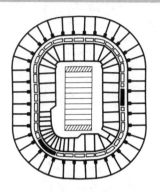

TSN REPORT CARD

Coaching staff	B	If Dennis Green were able to win in the post-season, the Vikings would have themselves A material. But Green has the respect of his players and is a sharpe judge of personnel. Defensive coordinator Foge Fazio motivates and did wonders with virtually no depth and no nose tackle last year.
Offensive backfield	B	QB Brad Johnson has yet to prove it for 16 games, but showed more than flashes of potential in 1996. Randall Cunningham provides an intriguing but risky backup option. Lead runner Robert Smith hasn't stayed healthy long enough to become a star, thus Leroy Hoard will come in handy.
Receivers	A -	With Cris Carter and Jake Reed on hand, the Vikings can't rate anything but the upper percentile. Carter remains a ballet artist in pads, and Reed was second in receiving yardage in '96. A third, speed receiver must emerge, and tight end remains a position the Vikings get little pass-catching from.
Offensive line	B +	Only right guard is a question mark. With perennial Pro Bowler Randall McDaniel at left guard, and book-end first-round picks Korey Stringer and Todd Steussie at the tackles, the line is above average. Center Jeff Christy is a solid fourth and oversized guard David Dixon is serviceable.
Defensive line	B	The unit is a nose tackle away from being a force. With Pro Bowl regular John Randle leading the way, and left end Fernando Smith emerging, the pass rush made strides. The run-stopping, especially at the nose, needs work. Right end Derrick Alexander and nickle-end Duane Clemons should get better.
Linebackers	B -	The Vikings prefer light, quicker linebackers, but that caused problems last year when power running teams steamrolled the defensive front. Ed McDaniel, the Vikings' leading tackler in 1995, returns from knee surgery, but depth could again be a problem. No. 1 pick Dwayne Rudd should help.
Secondary	B -	The Vikings improved at two of the secondary spots in '96, but still lack the strong coverage they were once known for. Cornerback Dewayne Washington rebounded, but Corey Fuller is better suited to a third corner role. Safety Orlando Thomas is coming off knee surgery and depth is not a strength.
Special teams	C -	The team's punting, kick returns and coverage units need improvement. Scott Sisson made some big kicks, but missed some makeable ones. Punter Mitch Berger also kicks off and may not be able to do both. Punt returner David Palmer is solid, and rookie Robert Tate will return kickoffs.

NEW ENGLAND PATRIOTS
AFC EASTERN DIVISION

1996 REVIEW

RESULTS

Sept. 1—at Miami	L	10-24
Sept. 8—at Buffalo	L	10-17
Sept.15—ARIZONA	W	31-0
Sept.22—JACKSONVILLE (OT)	W	28-25
Sept.29—Open date		
Oct. 6—at Baltimore	W	46-38
Oct. 13—WASHINGTON	L	22-27
Oct. 20—at Indianapolis	W	27-9
Oct. 27—BUFFALO	W	28-25
Nov. 3—MIAMI	W	42-23
Nov. 10—at N.Y. Jets	W	31-27
Nov. 17—DENVER	L	8-34
Nov. 24—INDIANAPOLIS	W	27-13
Dec. 1—at San Diego	W	45-7
Dec. 8—N.Y. JETS	W	34-10
Dec. 15—at Dallas	L	6-12
Dec. 21—at N.Y. Giants	W	23-22
Jan. 5—PITTSBURGH*	W	28-3
Jan. 12—JACKSONVILLE†	W	20-6
Jan. 26—Green Bay‡	L	21-35

*AFC divisional playoff game.
†AFC championship game.
‡Super Bowl XXXI.

RECORDS/RANKINGS

1996 regular-season record: 11-5 (1st in AFC East); 6-2 in division; 9-3 in conference; 6-2 at home; 5-3 on road.
Team record last five years: 34-46 (.425, ranks 19th in league in that span).

1996 team rankings:

	No.	AFC	NFL
Total offense	*335.6	4	7
Rushing offense	*91.8	13	26
Passing offense	*243.8	3	3
Scoring offense	418	1	2
Total defense	*331.6	9	19
Rushing defense	*93.9	4	6
Passing defense	*237.7	13	28
Scoring defense	313	6	14
Takeaways	34	5	T10
Giveaways	27	5	T10
Turnover differential	7	T3	T7
Sacks	33	T9	T19
Sacks allowed	30	3	T7

*Yards per game.

TEAM LEADERS

Scoring (kicking): Adam Vinatieri, 120 pts. (39/42 PATs, 27/35 FGs).
Scoring (touchdowns): Curtis Martin, 104 pts. (14 rushing, 3 receiving, 1 2-pt. conv.).
Passing: Drew Bledsoe, 4,086 yds. (623 att., 373 comp., 59.9%, 27 TDs, 15 int.).
Rushing: Curtis Martin, 1,152 yds. (316 att., 3.6 avg., 14 TDs).
Receptions: Terry Glenn, 90 (1,132 yds., 12.6 avg., 6 TDs).
Interceptions: Willie Clay, 4 (50 yds., 0 TDs).
Sacks: Willie McGinest, 9.5.
Punting: Tom Tupa, 43.5 avg. (63 punts, 2,739 yds., 0 blocked).
Punt returns: David Meggett, 11.3 avg. (52 att., 588 yds., 1 TD).
Kickoff returns: David Meggett, 23.0 avg. (34 att., 781 yds., 0 TDs).

1997 SEASON

CLUB DIRECTORY

President and chief executive officer
  Robert K. Kraft
Vice president/owner's representative
  Jonathan A. Kraft
Vice president, business operations
  Andrew Wasynczuk
Vice president, finance
  James Hausmann
Vice president, marketing
  Daniel A. Kraft
V.p., public and community relations
  Donald Lowery
Vice president, player personnel
  Bobby Grier
Director of media relations
  Stacey James
Director of player resources
  Andre Tippett
Director of football operations
  Ken Deininger
Controller
  Jim Nolan
Director of ticketing
  Mike Nichols
Corporate sales executive
  Jon Levy
Director of stadium operations
  Dan Murphy
Building services superintendent
  Bernie Reinhart
Head trainer
  Ron O'Neil

Head coach
Pete Carroll

Assistant coaches
  Paul Boudreau (offensive line)
  Jeff Davidson (tight ends)
  Ray Hamilton (defensive line)
  Larry Kennan (offensive coord.)
  Ron Lynn (secondary)
  Johnny Parker (strength & conditioning)
  Andre Patterson (defensive assistant)
  Bo Pelini (linebackers)
  Dante Scarnecchia (special teams)
  Steve Sidwell (defensive coord.)
  Carl Smith (assistant head coach/quarterbacks)
  Steve Walters (wide receivers)
  Kirby Wilson (running backs)

Equipment manager
  Don Brocher

SCHEDULE

Aug. 31—	SAN DIEGO	1:00
Sept. 7—	at Indianapolis	12:00
Sept. 14—	N.Y. JETS	8:00
Sept. 21—	CHICAGO	1:00
Sept. 28—	Open date	
Oct. 6—	at Denver (Mon.)	7:00
Oct. 12—	BUFFALO	1:00
Oct. 19—	at N.Y. Jets	1:00
Oct. 27—	GREEN BAY (Mon.)	9:00
Nov. 2—	at Minnesota	12:00
Nov. 9—	at Buffalo	4:00
Nov. 16—	at Tampa Bay	1:00
Nov. 23—	MIAMI	1:00
Nov. 30—	INDIANAPOLIS	1:00
Dec. 7—	at Jacksonville	1:00
Dec. 13—	PITTSBURGH (Sat.)	4:00
Dec. 22—	at Miami (Mon.)	9:00

All times are for home team.
All games Sunday unless noted.

DRAFT CHOICES

Chris Canty, DB, Kansas State (first round/29th pick overall).
Brandon Mitchell, DT, Texas A&M (2/59).
Sedrick Shaw, RB, Iowa (3/61).
Chris Carter, DB, Texas (3/89).
Damon Denson, G, Michigan (4/97).
Ed Ellis, T, Buffalo (4/125).
Vernon Crawford, LB, Florida State (5/159).
Tony Gaiter, WR, Miami, Fla. (6/192).
Scott Rehberg, T, Central Michigan (7/230).

1997 SEASON
TRAINING CAMP ROSTER

No.	QUARTERBACKS	Ht./Wt.	Born	NFL Exp.	College	How acq.	'96 Games GP/GS
11	Bledsoe, Drew	6-5/233	2-14-72	5	Washington State	D1/93	16/16
16	Zolak, Scott	6-5/235	12-13-67	7	Maryland	D4/91	3/0

	RUNNING BACKS						
46	Barber, Kantroy (FB)	6-1/243	10-4-73	2	West Virginia	D4b/96	0/0
41	Byars, Keith (FB)	6-1/255	10-14-63	12	Ohio State	FA/96	*14/10
33	Gash, Sam (FB)	6-1/235	3-7-69	6	Penn State	D8/92	14/9
34	Grant, Rupert	6-1/233	11-5-73	3	Howard	FA/95	0/0
35	Grier, Marrio	5-10/225	12-5-71	2	Tennessee-Chattanooga	D6b/96	16/0
28	Martin, Curtis	5-11/203	5-1-73	3	Pittsburgh	D3/95	16/15
22	Meggett, Dave (KR)	5-7/195	4-30-66	9	Towson State	FA/95	16/1
44	Shaw, Sedrick	6-0/214	11-16-73	R	Iowa	D3a/97	—

	RECEIVERS						
86	Bartrum, Michael (TE)	6-5/245	6-23-70	4	Marshall	T-GB/96	16/0
82	Brisby, Vincent	6-2/188	1-25-71	5	Northeast Louisiana	D2c/93	3/0
80	Brown, Troy (KR)	5-9/190	7-2-71	5	Marshall	D8/93	16/0
85	Burke, John (TE)	6-3/248	9-7-71	4	Virginia Tech	D4/94	11/2
87	Coates, Ben (TE)	6-5/245	8-16-69	7	Livingstone College (N.C.)	D5/91	16/15
17	Gaiter, Tony	5-8/169	7-15-74	R	Miami (Fla.)	D6/97	—
2	Glenn, Terry	5-10/184	7-23-74	1	Ohio State	D1/96	0/0
81	Graham, Hason	5-10/176	3-21-71	3	Georgia	FA/95	9/0
84	Jefferson, Shawn	5-11/180	2-22-69	7	Central Florida	FA/96	15/15
83	Jells, Dietrich	5-10/186	4-11-72	2	Pittsburgh	D6/96	7/1
15	Lucas, Ray	6-2/201	8-6-72	1	Rutgers	FA/96	2/0
48	Purnell, Lovett (TE)	6-2/250	4-7-72	2	West Virginia	D7a/96	2/0
18	Ryans, Larry	5-11/182	7-28-71	2	Clemson	FA/97	*3/0

	OFFENSIVE LINEMEN						
78	Armstrong, Bruce (T)	6-4/295	9-7-65	11	Louisville	D1/87	16/16
	Bivins, Marquin (G/T)	6-2/317	7-24-72	1		FA/97	0/0
70	Conrad, J.R. (T)	6-3/300	2-2-74	1	Oklahoma	D7b/96	0/0
61	Denson, Damon (G)	6-3/304	2-8-75	R	Michigan	D4/97	—
66	Ellis, Ed (T)	6-7/340	10-13-75	R	Buffalo	D4/97	—
67	Gisler, Mike (G/C)	6-4/300	8-26-69	5	Houston	FA/93	14/0
63	Irwin, Heath (G)	6-4/300	6-27-73	2	Colorado	D4a/96	0/0
68	Lane, Max (T)	6-6/305	2-22-71	4	Navy	D6/94	16/16
62	Moss, Zefross (T)	6-6/324	8-17-66	9	Alabama State	FA/97	*15/15
60	Rehberg, Scott (T)	6-8/336	11-17-73	R	Central Michigan	D7/97	—
71	Rucci, Todd (G)	6-5/291	7-14-70	5	Penn State	D2b/93	16/12
64	Wohlabaugh, Dave (C)	6-3/292	4-13-72	3	Syracuse	D4/95	16/16

	DEFENSIVE LINEMEN						
92	Collons, Ferric (E)	6-6/285	12-4-69	3	California	T-GB/95	15/5
90	Eaton, Chad (T)	6-5/292	4-6-72	2	Washington State	D7/95	4/0
96	Jones, Mike (E)	6-4/295	8-25-69	7	North Carolina State	FA/94	16/12
98	Mitchell, Brandon (T)	6-3/289	6-19-75	R	Texas A&M	D2/97	—
75	Sagapolutele, Pio	6-6/297	11-28-69	7	San Diego State	FA/96	15/10
74	Sullivan, Chris (E)	6-4/279	3-14-73	2	Boston College	D4b/96	16/0
97	Wheeler, Mark (T)	6-3/285	4-1-70	6	Texas A&M	FA/96	16/15
72	Wyman, Devin (T)	6-7/307	8-29-73	2	Kentucky State	D6c/96	9/4

	LINEBACKERS						
93	Brown, Monty	6-1/240	4-13-70	5	Ferris State (Mich.)	FA/96	11/7
54	Bruschi, Tedy	6-1/245	6-9-73	2	Arizona	D3/96	16/0
59	Collins, Todd	6-2/242	5-27-70	5	Carson-Newman (Tenn.)	D3a/92	16/9
99	Crawford, Vernon	6-3/250	6-25-74	R	Florida State	D5/97	—
52	Johnson, Ted	6-3/240	12-4-72	3	Colorado	D2/95	16/16
55	McGinest, Willie	6-5/255	12-11-71	4	Southern California	D1/94	16/16
58	Moore, Marty	6-1/244	3-19-71	4	Kentucky	D7/94	16/0
53	Slade, Chris	6-5/245	1-30-71	5	Virginia	D2/93	16/9
90	Williams, James	6-0/230	10-10-68	6	Mississippi State	FA/97	0/0

	DEFENSIVE BACKS						
30	Brown, Corwin (S)	6-1/200	4-25-70	5	Michigan	D4b/93	14/0
26	Canty, Chris (CB)	5-9/194	3-30-76	R	Kansas State	D1/97	—
42	Carter, Chris	6-1/201	9-27-74	R	Texas	D3b/97	—
32	Clay, Willie (S)	5-10/198	9-5-70	6	Georgia Tech	FA/96	16/16
31	Hitchcock, Jimmy (CB)	5-10/188	11-9-71	3	North Carolina	D3b/95	13/5
37	Israel, Steve (CB)	5-11/188	3-16-69	6	Pittsburgh	FA/97	*14/2
24	Law, Ty (CB)	5-11/196	2-10-74	3	Michigan	D1/95	13/12

No.	DEFENSIVE BACKS	Ht./Wt.	Born	NFL Exp.	College	How acq.	'96 Games GP/GS
27	McGruder, Mike (CB)	5-11/184	5-6-64	8	Kent	FA/96	14/0
36	Milloy, Lawyer (S)	6-1/208	11-11-73	2	Washington	D2/96	16/10
25	Whigham, Larry (S)	6-2/205	6-23-72	4	Northeast Louisiana	FA/94	16/1
	SPECIALISTS						
19	Tupa, Tom (P)	6-4/220	2-6-66	9	Ohio State	FA/96	16/0
4	Vinatieri, Adam (K)	6-1/200	12-28-72	2	South Dakota State	FA/96	16/0

*Byars played 4 games with Dolphins and 10 games with Patriots in '96; Israel played 14 games with 49ers; Moss played 15 games with Lions; Ryans played 3 games with Buccaneers.

Abbreviations: D1—draft pick, first round; SupD2—supplemental draft pick second round; W-Den—waivers acquisition from Denver; T-Sea—trade acquisition from Seattle; PlanB—Plan B free-agent acquisition; FA—free-agent acquisition (other than Plan B).

MISCELLANEOUS TEAM DATA

Stadium (capacity, surface):
Foxboro Stadium
(60,292, grass)
Business address:
60 Washington St.
Foxboro, MA 02035
Business phone:
508-543-8200
Ticket information:
508-543-1776
Team colors:
Silver, red, white and blue
Flagship radio station:
WBCN, 104.1 FM
Training site:
Bryant College
Smithfield, R.I.
508-543-8200

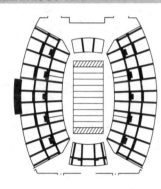

TSN REPORT CARD

Coaching staff	C	Pete Carroll has a limited resume as a coach, with one season and six wins to his credit. Defensive coordinator Steve Sidwell had consistent success in New Orleans and Houston, and his aggressive, blitzing style fits Carroll's philosophy. Offensive coordinator Larry Kennan is a respected veteran. But this is the first year this staff has been together. Chemistry could take time.
Offensive backfield	A	Drew Bledsoe and Curtis Martin went to the Pro Bowl last season. If he hadn't been hurt late in the year, fullback Sam Gash might have joined them. This is one of the best groups in the league. Bledsoe and Martin have to stay healthy, though, because there is no depth.
Receivers	A	With Terry Glenn and Shawn Jefferson outside and Ben Coates inside, the Patriots had a formidable 1-2-3 punch. They should be better this year, their second together as a group. If Vincent Brisby can stay healthy (he didn't have a catch last season because of a chronic hamstring problem), this will be A-1 material, as good as any in the league.
Offensive line	C	There are plenty of question marks here. Bruce Armstrong had a Pro Bowl year in 1996 and should be at that level again. Armstrong and center Dave Wohlabaugh, who went through a sophomore slump, may be the only starters back in the same spots. Zefross Moss could have problems at right tackle, and Max Lane hasn't played left guard before. The Patriots have to improve their run blocking.
Defensive line	C	Carroll thinks end Willie McGinest can be an all-star and will use him like the 49ers and Cowboys used Charles Haley. If rookie Brandon Mitchell can develop consistency to go with his quickness, he can help the interior pass rush. The same is true for Ferric Collons. Pio Sagapolutele and Mark Wheeler are OK against the run but aren't factors in the pass rush.
Linebackers	B	As long as Chris Slade keeps his intensity level up, he is the team's best pass rusher. By the end of last season, Ted Johnson was peerless as a run stopper at inside linebacker. Todd Collins is the best athlete among the linebackers and can make things happen. There isn't much depth, though.
Secondary	B -	Rookie Chris Canty and free-agent pickup Steve Israel, a former 49er, are the keys. They're going to be asked to play a lot of man coverage in Carroll's aggressive system. If they develop like Ty Law did, the Pats are in good shape. Free safety Willie Clay should be more of a playmaker in this system, and strong safety Lawyer Milloy has the potential to be a high-impact player.
Special teams	B	David Meggett was a Pro Bowl selection last year, and the coverage units were generally solid, providing a consistent advantage in field position. Punter Tom Tupa is dependable, and if Adam Vinatieri can sustain his strong rookie performance, the Pats should again have quality special teams.

NEW ORLEANS SAINTS
NFC WESTERN DIVISION

1996 REVIEW
RESULTS

Sept. 1—at San Francisco	L	11 -27
Sept. 8—CAROLINA	L	20-22
Sept.15—at Cincinnati	L	15-30
Sept.22—ARIZONA	L	14-28
Sept.29—at Baltimore	L	10-17
Oct. 6—JACKSONVILLE	W	17-13
Oct. 13—CHICAGO	W	27-24
Oct. 20—at Carolina	L	7-19
Oct. 27—Open date		
Nov. 3—SAN FRANCISCO	L	17-24
Nov. 10—HOUSTON	L	14-31
Nov. 17—at Atlanta	L	15-17
Nov. 24—at Tampa Bay	L	7-13
Dec. 1—ST. LOUIS	L	10-26
Dec. 8—ATLANTA	L	15-31
Dec. 15—at N.Y. Giants	W	17-3
Dec. 21—at St. Louis	L	13-14

RECORDS/RANKINGS

1996 regular-season record: 3-13 (T4th in NFC West); 0-8 in division; 2-10 in conference; 2-6 at home; 1-7 on road.
Team record last five years: 37-43 (.463, ranks T16th in league in that span).

1996 team rankings:	No.	NFC	NFL
Total offense	*262.9	14	29
Rushing offense	*81.8	15	30
Passing offense	*181.1	12	25
Scoring offense	229	14	29
Total defense	*306.9	8	14
Rushing defense	*129.8	14	27
Passing defense	*177.1	3	3
Scoring defense	339	10	20
Takeaways	22	14	T28
Giveaways	37	13	T26
Turnover differential	-15	14	28
Sacks	41	4	7
Sacks allowed	22	T2	T3

*Yards per game.

TEAM LEADERS

Scoring (kicking): Doug Brien, 81 pts. (18/18 PATs, 21/25 FGs).
Scoring (touchdowns): Michael Haynes, 26 pts. (4 receiving, 1 2-pt. conv.).
Passing: Jim Everett, 2,797 yds. (464 att., 267 comp., 57.5%, 12 TDs, 16 int.).
Rushing: Mario Bates, 584 yds. (164 att., 3.6 avg., 4 TDs).
Receptions: Michael Haynes, 44 (786 yds., 17.9 avg., 4 TDs).
Interceptions: Anthony Newman, 3 (40 yds., 0 TDs); Greg Jackson, 3 (24 yds., 0 TDs).
Sacks: Wayne Martin, 11.0.
Punting: Klaus Wilmsmeyer, 40.8 avg. (87 punts, 3,551 yds., 0 blocked).
Punt returns: Tyrone Hughes, 5.1 avg. (30 att., 152 yds., 0 TDs).
Kickoff returns: Tyrone Hughes, 25.6 avg. (70 att., 1,791 yds., 0 TDs).

1997 SEASON
CLUB DIRECTORY

Owner
Tom Benson
President/g.m./COO
Bill Kuharich
Sr. v.p. of marketing and administration
Greg Suit
Asst. g.m./v.p. of football operations
Chet Franklin
Treasurer
Bruce Broussard
Comptroller
Charleen Sharpe
NFL salary cap consultant
Terry O'Neil
Director of corporate sales
Bill Ferrante
Director of ticket sales
Greg Seeling
Director of media and public relations
Greg Bensel
Assistant director of media and public relations/publications coordinator
Robert Gunn
Assistant director/media relations
Neal Gulkis
Dir. travel/entertainment/special projects
Barra Birrcher
Player programs
Austin Dejan
Director of college scouting
Bruce Lemmerman
Scouts
Marty Barrett   Hamp Cook
Hokie Gajan   Tom Marino
Steve Sabo
Trainer
Dean Kleinschmidt
Asst. trainer/director of rehabilitation
Kevin Mangum
Assistant trainer
Buck Oubre
Physicians
Charles L. Brown   Terry Habig
Tim Finney

SCHEDULE

Aug. 31— at St. Louis	12:00	
Sept. 7— SAN DIEGO	12:00	
Sept. 14— at San Francisco	1:00	
Sept. 21— DETROIT	12:00	
Sept. 28— at N.Y. Giants	1:00	
Oct. 5— at Chicago	7:00	
Oct. 12— ATLANTA	12:00	
Oct. 19— CAROLINA	12:00	
Oct. 26— SAN FRANCISCO	12:00	
Nov. 2— Open date		
Nov. 9— at Oakland	1:00	
Nov. 16— SEATTLE	12:00	
Nov. 23— at Atlanta	1:00	
Nov. 30— at Carolina	1:00	
Dec. 7— ST. LOUIS	12:00	
Dec. 14— ARIZONA	3:00	
Dec. 21— at Kansas City	12:00	

All times are for home team.
All games Sunday unless noted.

Vice president/ head coach
Mike Ditka

Assistant coaches
Bobby April (special teams)
Bruce Arians (tight ends)
Dave Atkins (running backs)
Jeff Davidson (offensive assistant)
Jim Haslett (def. coordinator)
John Matsko (offensive line)
Jim L. Mora (defensive backs)
Wayne Nunnely (defensive line)
John Pagano (defensive assistant)
Russell Paternostro (strength & conditioning)
Carl Smith (offensive coordinator/ quarterbacks)
Rick Venturi (linebackers)
Steve Walters (wide receivers)

Facilities manager
Luke Jenkins
Grounds superintendent
Lester Vallet
Equipment manager
Dan Simmons
Assistant equipment manager
Glennon "Silky" Powell
Video director
Joe Malota
Assistant video director
Dan Whisenhunt

DRAFT CHOICES

Chris Naeole, G, Colorado (first round/ 10th pick overall).
Rob Kelly, DB, Ohio State (2/33).
Jared Tomich, DE, Nebraska (2/39).
Troy Davis, RB, Iowa State (3/62).
Danny Wuerffel, QB, Florida (4/99).
Keith Poole, WR, Arizona State (4/116).
Nicky Savoie, TE, Louisiana State (6/165).

1997 SEASON New Orleans Saints

No.	QUARTERBACKS	Ht./Wt.	Born	NFL Exp.	College	How acq.	'96 Games GP/GS
13	Nussmeier, Doug	6-3/211	12-11-70	4	Idaho	D4/94	2/1
5	Shuler, Heath	6-2/216	12-31-71	4	Tennessee	T-Was/97	*1/0
7	Wuerffel, Danny	6-1/212	5-27-74	R	Florida	D4a/97	—

RUNNING BACKS

No.		Ht./Wt.	Born	NFL Exp.	College	How acq.	GP/GS
24	Bates, Mario	6-1/217	1-16-73	4	Arizona State	D2/94	14/10
40	Bender, Wes	5-10/230	8-2-70	2	Southern California	FA/97	0/0
22	Brown, Derek	5-9/205	4-15-71	5	Nebraska	D4b/93	11/0
28	Davis, Troy	5-7/191	9-14-75	R	Iowa State	D3/97	—
32	Hunter, Earnest (KR)	5-8/201	12-21-70	3	Southeastern Oklahoma State	FA/96	6/0
44	McCrary, Fred (FB)	6-/218	9-19-72	2	Mississippi State	FA/97	0/0
23	Whittle, Ricky	5-9/200	12-21-71	2	Oregon	D4/96	10/0
34	Zellars, Ray	5-11/233	3-25-73	3	Notre Dame	D2/95	9/6

RECEIVERS

No.		Ht./Wt.	Born	NFL Exp.	College	How acq.	GP/GS
15	Baker, Shannon	5-9/195	7-20-71	3	Florida State	FA/97	0/0
80	Barnes, Johnnie	6-1/185	7-21-68	4	Hampton (Va.)	FA/95	0/0
87	DeRamus, Lee	6-0/205	8-24-72	3	Wisconsin	D6/95	15/4
85	Green, Paul (TE)	6-3/253	10-8-66	5	Southern California	FA/96	14/5
18	Guess, Terry	6-0/200	9-22-74	2	Gardner-Webb (N.C.)	D5c/96	3/2
	Hastings, Andre	6-1/190	11-7-70	5	Georgia	FA/97	*16/10
89	Hayes, Mercury	5-11/195	1-1-73	2	Michigan	D5a/96	7/0
	Hill, Randal	5-10/180	9-21-69	6	Miami (Fla.)	FA/97	*14/5
80	Hobbs, Daryl	6-2/175	5-23-68	5	Pacific	T-Oak/97	*16/1
84	Jeffires, Haywood	6-2/210	12-12-64	11	North Carolina State	FA/96	9/1
86	Johnson, Tony (TE)	6-5/255	2-5-72	2	Alabama	D6b/96	9/7
88	Lusk, Henry (TE)	6-1/240	5-8-72	2	Utah	D7/96	16/3
16	Poole, Keith	6-0/188	6-18-74	R	Arizona State	D4b/97	—
48	Savoie, Nicky (TE)	6-5/253	9-21-73	R	Louisiana State	D6/97	—
82	Smith, Irv (TE)	6-3/246	10-13-71	4	Notre Dame	D1b/93	7/7

OFFENSIVE LINEMEN

No.		Ht./Wt.	Born	NFL Exp.	College	How acq.	GP/GS
69	Ackerman, Tom (C)	6-3/290	9-6-72	2	Eastern Washington	D5b/96	2/0
70	Age, Louis (T)	6-7/350	2-1-70	2	Southwestern Louisiana	FA/97	0/0
	Fontenot, Jerry (C)	6-3/285	11-21-66	9	Texas A&M	FA/97	*16/16
62	Gammon, Kendall (C)	6-4/288	10-23-68	6	Pittsburg (Kan.) State	FA/96	16/0
76	Hills, Keno (T)	6-6/305	6-13-73	2	Southwestern Louisiana	D6a/95	1/0
74	Jones, Clarence (T)	6-6/280	5-6-68	7	Maryland	FA/96	16/16
61	King, Ed (G)	6-4/300	12-3-69	5	Auburn	FA/95	16/16
67	McCollum, Andy (C/G)	6-5/295	6-2-70	4	Toledo	FA/94	16/16
65	Naeole, Chris (G)	6-3/313	12-25-74	R	Colorado	D1/97	—
77	Roaf, Willie (T)	6-5/300	4-18-70	5	Louisiana Tech	D1/93	13/13
66	Verstegen, Mike (G/T)	6-6/311	10-24-71	3	Wisconsin	D3/95	8/4
63	Willis, Donald (G)	6-3/330	7-15-73	3	North Carolina A&T	FA/96	4/0

DEFENSIVE LINEMEN

No.		Ht./Wt.	Born	NFL Exp.	College	How acq.	GP/GS
99	Broughton, Willie (T)	6-5/285	9-9-64	11	Miami (Fla.)	T-Oak/95	14/5
94	Johnson, Joe (T)	6-4/270	7-11-72	4	Louisville	D1/94	13/13
93	Martin, Wayne (T)	6-5/275	10-26-65	9	Arkansas	D1/89	16/16
92	Mickell, Darren (E)	6-4/291	8-3-70	6	Florida	FA/96	12/12
75	Palmer, Emile (T)	6-3/320	4-5-73	1	Syracuse	FA/96	1/0
95	Robbins, Austin (T)	6-6/290	3-1-71	4	North Carolina	T-Oak/96	15/7
91	Smith, Brady (E)	6-5/260	6-5-73	2	Colorado State	D3/96	16/4
71	Stokes, Fred (E)	6-3/274	3-14-64	11	Georgia Southern	FA/96	9/0
90	Tomich, Jared (E)	6-2/258	4-24-74	R	Nebraska	D2b/97	—
97	Turnbull, Renaldo (E)	6-4/250	1-5-66	8	West Virginia	D1/90	12/7

LINEBACKERS

No.		Ht./Wt.	Born	NFL Exp.	College	How acq.	GP/GS
53	Davis, Don	6-1/240	12-17-72	2	Kansas	FA/96	11/0
55	Fields, Mark	6-2/244	11-9-72	3	Washington State	D1/95	16/15
52	Harvey, Richard	6-1/242	9-11-66	8	Tulane	FA/95	14/7
58	Jones, Brian	6-1/250	1-22-68	4	Texas	FA/95	16/1
59	Mitchell, Keith	6-2/240	7-24-74	1	Texas A&M	FA/97	0/0
51	Sims, William	6-3/271	12-30-70	2	Southwestern Louisiana	FA/97	0/0
54	Tubbs, Winfred	6-4/250	9-24-70	4	Texas	D3/94	16/13

DEFENSIVE BACKS

No.		Ht./Wt.	Born	NFL Exp.	College	How acq.	GP/GS
27	Adams, Vashone (S)	5-10/198	9-12-73	2	Eastern Michigan	FA/97	*16/2
21	Allen, Eric (CB)	5-10/180	11-22-65	10	Arizona State	FA/95	16/16
37	Cherry, Je'Rod (S)	6-0/196	5-30-73	2	California	D2/96	13/0
43	Duckett, Forey (CB)	6-3/195	2-5-70	3	Nevada	FA/97	0/0

No.	DEFENSIVE BACKS	Ht./Wt.	Born	NFL Exp.	College	How acq.	'96 Games GP/GS
20	Hoskins, Derrick (S)	6-2/200	11-14-70	5	Southern Mississippi	FA/96	1/0
33	Kelly, Rob (S)	6-0/199	6-21-74	R	Ohio State	D2a/97	—
46	Lumpkin, Sean (S)	6-0/206	1-4-70	5	Minnesota	D4b/92	7/1
25	Molden, Alex (CB)	5-10/190	8-4-73	2	Oregon	D1/96	14/2
30	Newman, Anthony (S)	6-0/200	11-21-65	10	Oregon	FA/95	16/16
41	Strong, William (CB)	5-10/191	11-3-71	2	North Carolina State	D5/95	9/0
	Washington, Mickey (CB)	5-10/191	7-8-68	7	Texas A&M	FA/97	*16/16
	SPECIALISTS						
10	Brien, Doug (K)	6-0/180	11-24-70	4	California	FA/95	16/0
6	Edge, Shayne (P)	5-11/174	8-21-71	1	Florida	FA/97	*4/0
9	Royals, Mark (P)	6-5/215	6-22-64	8	Appalachian State	FA/97	*16/0

*Adams played 16 games with Ravens in '96; Edge played 4 games with Steelers; Fontenot played 16 games with Bears; Hastings played 16 games with Steelers; Hill played 14 games with Dolphins; Hobbs played 16 games with Raiders; Royals played 16 games with Lions; Shuler played 1 game with Redskins; Washington played 16 games with Jaguars.

Abbreviations: D1—draft pick, first round; SupD2—supplemental draft pick second round; W-Den—waivers acquisition from Denver; T-Sea—trade acquisition from Seattle; PlanB—Plan B free-agent acquisition; FA—free-agent acquisition (other than Plan B).

MISCELLANEOUS TEAM DATA

Stadium (capacity, surface):
Louisiana Superdome
(69,729, artificial)
Business address:
5800 Airline Highway
Metairie, LA 70003
Business phone:
504-733-0255
Ticket information:
504-731-1700
Team colors:
Old gold, black and white
Flagship radio station:
WWL, 870 AM
Training site:
University of Wisconsin-La Crosse
La Crosse, Wis.
608-789-4550

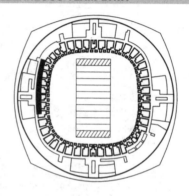

TSN REPORT CARD

Coaching staff	B -	Mike Ditka has assembled a knowledgeable, veteran staff featuring seven assistants—Walt Corey, Tom Moore, Dick Stanfel, Willie Shaw, Harold Jackson, Bobby April and Mike Woicik—who collectively own 13 Super Bowl rings. Stanfel, Corey and Moore have 29, 24 and 20 years coaching in the NFL. But, interestingly, Ditka chose two first-time NFL coordinators in Danny Abramowicz (offense) and Zaven Yaralian (defense).
Offensive backfield	C -	Heath Shuler is unproven and Heisman Trophy winner Danny Wuerffel is, well, an NFL rookie. Regardless of who the quarterback is, he will need play-makers surrounding him, as last season proved. Mario Bates and Ray Zellars are unproven commodities as running backs. Third-round pick Troy Davis could surprise.
Receivers	D	This was the least productive area on the team in 1996, and changes have been virtually negligible. Six individual NFL players caught as many or more passes (94) as starters Michael Haynes and Torrance Small. Ex-Raider Daryl Hobbs may make Haynes expendable. The healthy return of tight end Irv Smith is a big positive.
Offensive line	C +	This could end up as the offense's strongest position, but to do so this group finally must prove it can run block. All-Pro left tackle Willie Roaf, center Andy McCollum and right guard Chris Naeole, the club's No. 1 pick, are potential anchors. The probable loss of left guard Jim Dombrowski hurts a lot.
Defensive line	B -	Depth appears to be better, and if Darren Mickell, who is moving inside from end to left tackle, supplies the run support that's anticipated, this unit should be solid. Right tackle Wayne Martin and right end Joe Johnson are quality players. Left end is a question mark.
Linebackers	C -	Mark Fields and Winfred Tubbs are entering their third and fourth seasons as inside 'backers in the 4-3 and they finally should be ready to take off. Fields has star-power ability. How well they play will go a long way in determining the defense's improvement from No. 27 in the league in defending the run.
Secondary	B -	This group was the defense's strongest unit in 1996, but two new starters have been inserted in left corner Alex Molden and free safety Je'Rod Cherry. They own two career starts and both belong to Molden as a nickel back. Right cornerback Eric Allen's leadership will be needed.
Special teams	D -	Coach Bobby April lost one of the NFL's top return men in Tyrone Hughes, who joined the Bears via free agency. But Doug Brien returns as kicker and the loss of Hughes was offset by the addition of several rookies who should improve the coverage teams. Terry Guess was an electrifying returner in college, but must prove he can consistently field punts. Mark Royals is the new punter.

NEW YORK GIANTS
NFC EASTERN DIVISION

1996 REVIEW
RESULTS

Sept. 1—BUFFALO (OT)	L	20-23
Sept. 8—at Dallas	L	0-27
Sept.15—WASHINGTON	L	10-31
Sept.22—at N.Y. Jets	W	13-6
Sept.29—MINNESOTA	W	15-10
Oct. 6—Open date		
Oct. 13—PHILADELPHIA	L	10-19
Oct. 20—at Washington	L	21-31
Oct. 27—at Detroit	W	35-7
Nov. 3—ARIZONA	W	16-8
Nov. 10—at Carolina	L	17-27
Nov. 17—at Arizona	L	23-31
Nov. 24—DALLAS	W	20-6
Dec. 1—at Philadelphia	L	0-24
Dec. 8—at Miami	W	17-7
Dec. 15—NEW ORLEANS	L	3-17
Dec. 21—NEW ENGLAND	L	22-23

RECORDS/RANKINGS

1996 regular-season record: 6-10 (5th in NFC East); 2-6 in division; 4-8 in conference; 3-5 at home; 3-5 on road.
Team record last five years: 37-43 (.463, ranks T16th in league in that span).

1996 team rankings:

	No.	NFC	NFL
Total offense	*246.4	15	30
Rushing offense	*100.2	10	21
Passing offense	*146.2	15	30
Scoring offense	242	13	28
Total defense	*315.4	9	14
Rushing defense	*109.3	7	16
Passing defense	*206.2	10	15
Scoring defense	297	6	10
Takeaways	35	T4	T8
Giveaways	34	T10	T23
Turnover differential	1	T7	T14
Sacks	30	T13	T25
Sacks allowed	56	14	29

*Yards per game.

TEAM LEADERS

Scoring (kicking): Brad Daluiso, 94 pts. (22/22 PATs, 24/27 FGs).
Scoring (touchdowns): Chris Calloway, 24 pts. (4 receiving); Thomas Lewis, 24 pts. (4 receiving).
Passing: Dave Brown, 2,412 yds. (398 att., 214 comp., 53.8%, 12 TDs, 20 int.).
Rushing: Rodney Hampton, 827 yds. (254 att., 3.3 avg., 1 TD).
Receptions: Chris Calloway, 53 (739 yds., 13.9 avg., 4 TDs).
Interceptions: Jason Sehorn, 5 (61 yds., 1 TD).
Sacks: Michael Strahan, 5.0; Chad Bratzke, 5.0.
Punting: Mike Horan, 42.0 avg. (102 punts, 4,289 yds., 0 blocked).
Punt returns: Amani Toomer, 16.6 avg. (18 att., 298 yds., 2 TDs).
Kickoff returns: Tyrone Wheatley, 21.9 avg. (23 att., 503 yds., 0 TDs).

1997 SEASON
CLUB DIRECTORY

President/co-CEO
Wellington T. Mara
Chairman/co-CEO
Preston Robert Tisch
Exec. v.p./general counsel
John K. Mara
Senior vice president/general manager
George Young
Treasurer
Jonathan Tisch
Assistant general manager
Ernie Accorsi
Assistant to the general manager
Harry Hulmes
V.P. and chief financial officer
John Pasquali
Controller
Christine Procops
Director/player personnel
Tom Boisture
Director/administration
Tom Power
Vice president, marketing
Rusty Hawley
Director/promotion
Francis X. Mara
Ticket manager
John Gorman
Director/pro personnel
Tim Rooney
Assistant director/player personnel
Rick Donohue
Director/research and development
Raymond J. Walsh Jr.
Director/college scouting
Jerry Shay
Vice president/public relations
Pat Hanlon
Assistant director/public relations
Aaron Salkin
Assistant director/marketing
Bill Smith
Director of player development
Greg Gabriel

SCHEDULE

Aug. 31— PHILADELPHIA	1:00
Sept. 7— at Jacksonville	4:00
Sept. 14— BALTIMORE	1:00
Sept. 21— at St. Louis	3:00
Sept. 28— NEW ORLEANS	1:00
Oct. 5— DALLAS	1:00
Oct. 12— at Arizona	1:00
Oct. 19— at Detroit	4:00
Oct. 26— CINCINNATI	1:00
Nov. 2— Open date	
Nov. 9— at Tennessee	3:00
Nov. 16— ARIZONA	1:00
Nov. 23— at Washington	8:00
Nov. 30— TAMPA BAY	4:00
Dec. 7— at Philadelphia	1:00
Dec. 13— WASHINGTON (Sat.)	12:30
Dec. 21— at Dallas	12:00

All times are for home team.
All games Sunday unless noted.

Head coach
Jim Fassel

Assistant coaches
Dave Brazil (def. quality control)
Rod Dowhower (quarterbacks)
John Dunn (strength & conditioning)
John Fox (defensive coordinator)
Mike Gillhamer (off. quality control)
Mike Haluchak (linebackers)
Milt Jackson (wide receivers)
Johnnie Lynn (defensive backs)
Larry Mac Duff (special teams)
Denny Marcin (defensive line)
John Matsko (offensive line)
Dick Rehbein (tight ends)
Jim Skipper (offensive coord./ running backs)
Craig Stoddard (assistant strength & conditioning)

Scouts

Rosey Brown	John Crea
Jeremiah Davis	Ken Kavanaugh
Jerry Reese	Steve Verderosa

Head trainer
Ronnie Barnes
Assistant trainers

Michael Colello	Steve Kennelly

Team physician
Russell Warren
Locker room manager
Ed Wagner
Equipment manager
Ed Wagner Jr.
Video director
John Mancuso

DRAFT CHOICES

Ike Hilliard, WR, Florida (first round/ seventh pick overall).
Tiki Barber, RB, Virginia (2/36).
Ryan Phillips, LB, Idaho (3/68).
Brad Maynard, P, Ball State (3/95).
Pete Monty, LB, Wisconsin (4/103).
Sam Garnes, DB, Cincinnati (5/136).
Mike Cherry, QB, Murray State (6/171).
Matt Keneley, DT, Southern California (7/208).

1997 SEASON — New York Giants

No.	QUARTERBACKS	Ht./Wt.	Born	NFL Exp.	College	How acq.	'96 Games GP/GS
17	Brown, Dave	6-5/223	2-25-70	6	Duke	SupD1/92	16/16
18	Cherry, Mike	6-3/222	12-15-73	R	Murray State	D6/97	—
13	Kanell, Danny	6-3/222	11-21-73	2	Florida State	D4/96	4/0
8	White, Stan	6-2/218	8-14-71	2	Auburn	FA/94	0/0
	RUNNING BACKS						
21	Barber, Tiki	5-10/200	4-7-75	R	Virginia	D2/97	—
27	Hampton, Rodney	5-11/230	4-3-69	8	Georgia	D1/90	15/15
33	Walker, Robert	5-10/197	6-26-72	1	West Virginia	FA/96	1/0
30	Way, Charles (FB)	6-0/245	12-27-72	3	Virginia	D6b/95	16/12
28	Wheatley, Tyrone	6-0/228	1-19-72	3	Michigan	D1/95	14/0
	RECEIVERS						
86	Alexander, Kevin	5-9/184	1-23-75	2	Utah State	FA/96	4/0
80	Calloway, Chris	5-10/191	3-29-68	8	Michigan	PlanB/92	16/15
87	Cross, Howard (TE)	6-5/265	8-8-67	9	Alabama	D6/89	16/16
82	Douglas, Omar	5-10/182	6-3-72	4	Minnesota	FA/94	4/0
89	Hilliard, Ike	5-11/189	4-5-76	R	Florida	D1/97	—
4	Lewis, Thomas	6-1/195	1-10-72	3	Indiana	D1/94	13/11
84	Pierce, Aaron (TE)	6-5/250	9-6-69	6	Washington	D3/92	10/3
83	Saxton, Brian (TE)	6-6/256	3-13-72	2	Boston College	FA/95	16/2
89	Toomer, Amani	6-3/202	9-8-74	2	Michigan	D2/96	7/1
	OFFENSIVE LINEMEN						
78	Bishop, Greg (T)	6-5/300	5-2-71	5	Pacific	D4/93	16/16
74	Gragg, Scott (T)	6-8/325	2-28-72	2	Montana	D2/95	16/16
68	Kline, Alan (T)	6-5/290	5-25-71	2	Ohio State	FA/94	0/0
72	Oben, Roman (T)	6-4/297	10-9-72	1	Louisville	D3/96	2/0
66	Reynolds, Jerry (T)	6-6/315	4-2-70	4	UNLV	FA/95	8/0
65	Stone, Ron (T/G)	6-5/325	7-20-71	5	Boston College	FA/96	16/16
59	Williams, Brian (C)	6-5/300	6-8-66	9	Minnesota	D1/89	14/14
73	Zatechka, Rob	6-4/315	12-1-71	3	Nebraska	D4/95	15/6
	DEFENSIVE LINEMEN						
93	Agnew, Ray (T)	6-3/285	12-9-67	8	North Carolina State	FA/95	13/2
77	Bratzke, Chad (E)	6-4/273	9-15-71	4	Eastern Kentucky	D5/94	16/16
96	Duff, Jamal (E)	6-7/271	3-11-72	3	San Diego State	D6a/95	0/0
75	Hamilton, Keith (T)	6-6/285	5-25-71	6	Pittsburgh	D4/92	14/14
97	Harris, Robert (E)	6-4/295	6-13-69	6	Southern (La.)	FA/95	16/16
79	Holsey, Bernard (T)	6-2/284	12-10-73	2	Duke	FA/96	16/0
94	Jones, Cedric (E)	6-4/275	4-30-74	2	Oklahoma	D1/96	16/0
76	Keneley, Matt (T)	6-4/286	12-1-73	R	Southern California	D7/97	—
99	Peter, Christian (T)	6-3/304	10-5-72	1	Nebraska	FA/96	0/0
92	Strahan, Michael (E)	6-4/268	11-21-71	5	Texas Southern	D2/93	16/16
	LINEBACKERS						
98	Armstead, Jessie	6-1/232	10-26-70	5	Miami, Fla.	D8/93	16/16
55	Buckley, Marcus	6-3/240	2-3-71	5	Texas A&M	D3/93	15/2
58	Colman, Doug	6-2/252	6-4-73	2	Nebraska	D6a/96	13/0
52	Galyon, Scott	6-2/237	3-23-74	2	Tennessee	D6b/96	16/0
57	Miller, Corey	6-2/245	10-25-68	7	South Carolina	D6/91	14/13
51	Monty, Pete	6-2/253	7-13-74	R	Wisconsin	D4/97	—
91	Phillips, Ryan	6-4/250	2-7-74	R	Idaho	D3a/97	—
54	Talley, Ben	6-3/245	7-14-72	2	Tennessee	D4/95	0/0
90	Widmer, Corey	6-3/250	12-25-68	6	Montana State	D7/92	16/16
	DEFENSIVE BACKS						
43	Ellsworth, Percy (S)	6-2/199	10-19-74	2	Virginia	FA/96	14/4
20	Garnes, Sam (S)	6-3/225	7-12-74	R	Cincinnati	D5/97	—
41	Hamilton, Conrad (S)	5-10/184	11-5-74	2	Eastern New Mexico	D7/96	15/1
	Nelson, Picasso (S)	5-11/208	5-1-73	1	Jackson State	FA/97	0/0
23	Randolph, Thomas (CB)	5-9/178	10-5-70	4	Kansas State	D2a/94	16/2
31	Sehorn, Jason (CB)	6-2/210	4-15-71	4	Southern California	D2b/94	16/15
22	Sparks, Phillippi (CB)	5-11/190	4-15-69	6	Arizona State	D2/92	14/14
29	Wooten, Tito (S)	6-0/195	12-12-71	4	Northeast Louisiana	SupD4/94	13/12
47	Young, Rodney (S)	6-1/212	1-25-73	3	Louisiana State	D3/95	12/0

No.	SPECIALISTS	Ht./Wt.	Born	NFL Exp.	College	How acq.	'96 Games GP/GS
3	Daluiso, Brad (K)...............	6-2/210	12-31-67	7	UCLA	FA/93	16/0
9	Maynard, Brad (P).............	6-1/184	2-9-74	R	Ball State	D3b/97	—

*Abbreviations: D1—draft pick, first round; SupD2—supplemental draft pick second round; W-Den—waivers acquisition from Denver; T-Sea—trade acquisition from Seattle; PlanB—Plan B free-agent acquisition; FA—free-agent acquisition (other than Plan B).

MISCELLANEOUS TEAM DATA

Stadium (capacity, surface):
Giants Stadium
(78,148, artificial)
Business address:
East Rutherford, NJ 07073
Business phone:
201-935-8111
Ticket information:
201-935-8222
Team colors:
Blue, white and red
Flagship radio station:
WNEW, 102.7 FM
Training site:
University at Albany
Albany, N.Y.
201-935-8111

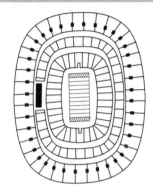

TSN REPORT CARD

Coaching staff	B +	Coach Jim Fassel has taken charge and won the respect of the players with his knowledge and organization. He is being trusted to change the offense because of his track record. Fassel also will be able to get along with the conservative front office and deal with the New York media. His staff is versatile and experienced.
Offensive backfield	C +	The biggest question of the season is whether quarterback Dave Brown will enjoy his breakout year. The key among the backs is Tyrone Wheatley, who has been unpredictable and injury-prone. Rodney Hampton is aging, so he can't be counted on, and rookie Tiki Barber is unproven. Charles Way is one of the league's best young fullbacks.
Receivers	B -	The competition for jobs should be interesting among a group that includes No. 7 overall draft pick Ike Hilliard, along with Amani Toomer, Thomas Lewis and Chris Calloway. The tight ends are led by Aaron Pierce, who should catch a lot of passes in Fassel's scheme.
Offensive line	C -	Other than center Brian Williams, there are plenty of questions. They begin at left tackle, where lumbering Greg Bishop apparently will remain the starter. The line will be OK if the mammoth right side of tackle Scott Gragg and guard Ron Stone develops into a force.
Defensive line	C	The four starters—Michael Strahan, Keith Hamilton, Robert Harris, Chad Bratzke—are back, but a key might be the contribution of reserves like Cedric Jones, Jamal Duff and Christian Peter. No one on the team had more than five sacks in 1996.
Linebackers	B -	Jessie Armstead, Corey Widmer and Corey Miller were better than expected last season, but the team still lacks star power. The big news this season is the depth at linebacker, featuring Ben Talley and rookies Ryan Phillips and Pete Monty.
Secondary	A -	There is plenty of uncertainty at safety beyond Percy Ellsworth, but that is made up for by one of the best groups of cornerbacks in the NFL. Starters Phillippi Sparks and Jason Sehorn are as good as any. They are backed up by former starter Thomas Randolph and Conrad Hamilton.
Special teams	B	This grade rises if rookie punter Brad Maynard is as good as advertised. Already proven is kicker Brad Daluiso, who always has had a strong leg but in '96 showed finesse. Toomer has proven to be a top-notch return man. Barber is expected to supplement the kick-return game.

NEW YORK JETS
AFC EASTERN DIVISION

1996 REVIEW
RESULTS

Sept. 1—at Denver	L	6-31
Sept. 8—INDIANAPOLIS	L	7-21
Sept.15—at Miami	L	27-36
Sept.22—N.Y. GIANTS	L	6-13
Sept.29—at Washington	L	16-31
Oct. 6—OAKLAND	L	13-34
Oct. 13—at Jacksonville	L	17-21
Oct. 20—BUFFALO	L	22-25
Oct. 27—at Arizona	W	31-21
Nov. 3—Open date		
Nov. 10—NEW ENGLAND	L	27-31
Nov. 17—at Indianapolis	L	29-34
Nov. 24—at Buffalo	L	10-35
Dec. 1—HOUSTON	L	10-35
Dec. 8—at New England	L	10-34
Dec. 14—PHILADELPHIA	L	20-21
Dec. 22—MIAMI	L	28-31

RECORDS/RANKINGS

1996 regular-season record: 1-15 (5th in AFC East); 0-8 in division; 0-12 in conference; 0-8 at home; 1-7 on road.
Team record last five years: 22-58 (.275, ranks 27th in league in that span).

1996 team rankings:	No.	AFC	NFL
Total offense	*325.5	7	11
Rushing offense	*98.9	12	23
Passing offense	*226.6	4	10
Scoring offense	279	15	27
Total defense	*347.8	14	27
Rushing defense	*137.5	15	29
Passing defense	*210.3	8	19
Scoring defense	454	15	29
Takeaways	26	T11	T22
Giveaways	46	15	30
Turnover differential	-20	15	30
Sacks	28	15	T29
Sacks allowed	41	10	20

*Yards per game.

TEAM LEADERS

Scoring (kicking): Nick Lowery, 77 pts. (26/27 PATs, 17/24 FGs).
Scoring (touchdowns): Keyshawn Johnson, 50 pts. (8 receiving, 1 2-pt. conv.).
Passing: Frank Reich, 2,205 yds. (331 att., 175 comp., 52.9%, 15 TDs, 16 int.).
Rushing: Adrian Murrell, 1,249 yds. (301 att., 4.1 avg., 6 TDs).
Receptions: Wayne Chrebet, 84 (909 yds., 10.8 avg., 3 TDs).
Interceptions: Aaron Glenn, 4 (113 yds., 2 TDs).
Sacks: Hugh Douglas, 8.0.
Punting: Brian Hansen, 44.5 avg. (74 punts, 3,293 yds., 0 blocked).
Punt returns: Wayne Chrebet, 5.0 avg. (28 att., 139 yds., 0 TDs).
Kickoff returns: Reggie Cobb, 21.2 avg. (23 att., 488 yds., 0 TDs).

1997 SEASON
CLUB DIRECTORY

Chairman of the board
Leon Hess
President
Steve Gutman
Treasurer & chief financial officer
Mike Gerstle
Controller
Mike Minarczyk
Director/public relations
Frank Ramos
Assistant director/public relations
Doug Miller
Public relations assistants
Berj Najarian
Sharon Czark
Coordinator of special projects
Ken Ilchuk
Exec. director of business operations
Bob Parente
Senior marketing manager
Marc Riccio
Marketing manager
Beth Conroy
Director of ticket operations
John Buschhorn
Director/operations
Mike Kensil
Travel coordinator
Kevin Coyle
Director/player personnel
Dick Haley
Assistant general manager
James Harris
Director of player administration
Pat Kirwan
Scouts

Joey Clinkscales	Jesse Kay
Bob Schmitz	Lionel Vitale
Marv Sunderland	

Head trainer
David Price

**Head coach/
chief football
operations
officer**
Bill Parcells

Assistant coaches
Bill Belichick (assistant head coach/defensive backs)
Maurice Carthon (running backs)
Romeo Crennel (defensive line)
Ron Erhardt (quarterbacks/special assistant coach)
Al Groh (linebackers)
Todd Haley (offensive assistant/quality control)
Pat Hodgson (tight ends)
John Lott (strength & conditioning)
Eric Mangini (defensive assistant/quality control)
Bill Muir (offensive line)
Mike Sweatman (special teams)
Charlie Weis (wide receivers)
Josh Zitomer (strength & conditioning assistant)

Assistant trainer
John Mellody
Equipment manager
Bill Hampton
Equipment director
Clay Hampton
Groundskeeper
Bob Hansen
Video director
Jim Pons

SCHEDULE

Aug. 31— at Seattle	1:00
Sept. 7— BUFFALO	1:00
Sept. 14— at New England	8:00
Sept. 21— OAKLAND	1:00
Sept. 28— at Cincinnati	4:00
Oct. 5— at Indianapolis	3:00
Oct. 12— MIAMI	1:00
Oct. 19— NEW ENGLAND	1:00
Oct. 26— Open date	
Nov. 2— BALTIMORE	1:00
Nov. 9— at Miami	1:00
Nov. 16— at Chicago	3:00
Nov. 23— MINNESOTA	1:00
Nov. 30— at Buffalo	1:00
Dec. 7— INDIANAPOLIS	4:00
Dec. 14— TAMPA BAY	1:00
Dec. 21— at Detroit	4:00

All times are for home team.
All games Sunday unless noted.

DRAFT CHOICES

James Farrior, LB, Virginia (first round/eighth pick overall).
Rick Terry, DT, North Carolina (2/31).
Dedric Ward, WR, Northern Iowa (3/88).
Terry Day, DE, Mississippi State (4/102).
Leon Johnson, RB, North Carolina (4/104).
Lamont Burns, G, East Carolina (5/131).
Raymond Austin, DB, Tennessee (5/145).
Tim Scharf, LB, Northwestern (6/164).
Chuck Clements, QB, Houston (6/191).
Steve Rosga, DB, Colorado (7/202).
Jason Ferguson, DT, Georgia (7/229).

No.	QUARTERBACKS	Ht./Wt.	Born	NFL Exp.	College	How acq.	'96 Games GP/GS
7	Clements, Chuck	6-3/214	9-29-73	R	Houston	D6b/97	—
4	Foley, Glenn	6-2/210	10-10-70	4	Boston College	D7/94	5/3
4	O'Donnell, Neil	6-3/228	7-3-66	8	Maryland	FA/96	6/6

RUNNING BACKS

No.		Ht./Wt.	Born	NFL Exp.	College	How acq.	'96 Games GP/GS
0	Anderson, Richie	6-2/225	9-13-71	5	Penn State	D6/93	16/13
8	Cobb, Reggie	6-1/212	7-7-68	7	Tennessee	FA/96	15/0
7	D'Agostino, Lou (FB)	6-0/235	12-12-73	2	Rhode Island	FA/96	9/0
2	Johnson, Leon	6-0/209	7-13-74	R	North Carolina	D4b/97	—
9	Murrell, Adrian	5-11/214	10-16-70	5	West Virginia	D5b/93	16/16
2	Neal, Lorenzo (FB)	5-11/240	12-27-70	5	Fresno State	FA/97	*16/11
4	Rasheed, Kenyon (FB)	5-10/235	8-23-70	4	Oklahoma	FA/95	0/0

RECEIVERS

No.		Ht./Wt.	Born	NFL Exp.	College	How acq.	'96 Games GP/GS
4	Baxter, Fred (TE)	6-3/260	6-14-71	5	Auburn	D5a/93	16/4
8	Brady, Kyle (TE)	6-6/260	1-14-72	3	Penn State	D1a/95	16/16
0	Chrebet, Wayne	5-10/180	8-14-73	3	Hofstra	FA/95	16/9
3	Davis, Tyrone (TE)	6-4/255	6-30-72	3	Virginia	D4b/95	2/0
1	Graham, Jeff	6-2/200	2-14-69	7	Ohio State	FA/96	11/9
9	Johnson, Keyshawn	6-3/215	7-22-72	2	Southern California	D1/96	14/11
3	Jones, Clarence	6-0/184	3-12-73	1	Tennessee State	FA/96	0/0
6	Van Dyke, Alex	6-0/200	7-24-74	2	Nevada	D2/96	15/1
9	Ward, Dedric	5-9/180	9-29-74	R	Northern Iowa	D3/97	—

OFFENSIVE LINEMEN

No.		Ht./Wt.	Born	NFL Exp.	College	How acq.	'96 Games GP/GS
3	Burns, Lamont (G)	6-4/300	3-16-74	R	East Carolina	D5a/97	—
2	Duffy, Roger (G/C)	6-3/305	7-16-67	8	Penn State	D8/90	16/16
6	Elliott, Jumbo (T)	6-7/308	4-1-65	10	Michigan	FA/96	14/14
4	Galbreath, Harry (G)	6-1/295	1-1-65	10	Tennessee	FA/97	15/8
5	Hudson, John (C/G)	6-2/276	1-29-68	8	Auburn	FA/96	16/0
5	Malamala, Siupeli (G/T)	6-5/305	1-15-69	6	Washington	D3/92	4/1
0	O'Dwyer, Matt (G)	6-5/294	9-1-72	3	Northwestern	D2/95	16/16
6	Palelei, Lonnie (G)	6-3/320	10-15-70	2	UNLV	FA/96	0/0
0	Wiegmann, Casey (C)	6-3/290	7-20-73	1	Iowa	W-Ind/96	0/0
3	Williams, David (T)	6-5/300	6-21-66	9	Florida	FA/96	14/14

DEFENSIVE LINEMEN

No.		Ht./Wt.	Born	NFL Exp.	College	How acq.	'96 Games GP/GS
8	Day, Terry (E)	6-4/280	9-18-74	R	Mississippi State	D4a/97	—
0	Dixon, Ronnie	6-3/310	5-10-71	4	Cincinnati	T-Phi/97	*16/4
9	Douglas, Hugh (E)	6-2/270	8-23-71	3	Central State (O.)	D1b/95	10/10
2	Ferguson, Jason (T)	6-3/305	11-28-74	R	Georgia	D7b/97	—
2	Hamilton, Bobby (E)	6-5/280	1-7-71	2	Southern Mississippi	FA/96	15/11
8	Logan, Ernie (E)	6-3/290	5-18-68	6	East Carolina	FA/97	*4/0
5	Lyle, Rick	6-5/280	2-26-71	3	Missouri	FA/97	*11/3
4	Terry, Rick (T)	6-4/309	4-5-74	R	North Carolina	D2/97	—
7	Washington, Marvin (E)	6-6/280	10-22-65	9	Idaho	D6a/89	14/14
5	White, Reggie (T)	6-5/310	3-22-70	5	North Carolina A&T	FA/97	0/0

LINEBACKERS

No.		Ht./Wt.	Born	NFL Exp.	College	How acq.	'96 Games GP/GS
3	Cascadden, Chad	6-1/235	5-14-72	3	Wisconsin	FA/95	16/8
5	DuBose, Demetrius	6-2/230	3-23-71	5	Notre Dame	FA/97	*14/0
3	Farrior, James	6-2/240	1-6-75	R	Virginia	D1/97	—
5	Houston, Bobby	6-2/245	10-26-67	7	North Carolina State	PlanB/91	15/15
2	Johnson, Pepper	6-3/248	7-29-64	12	Ohio State	FA/97	*15/12
4	Jones, Marvin	6-2/250	6-28-72	5	Florida State	D1/93	12/12
7	Lewis, Mo	6-3/255	10-21-69	7	Georgia	D3/91	9/9
4	Scharf, Tim	6-1/244	3-20-75	R	Northwestern	D6a/97	—

DEFENSIVE BACKS

No.		Ht./Wt.	Born	NFL Exp.	College	How acq.	'96 Games GP/GS
6	Austin, Raymond	5-11/190	12-21-74	R	Tennessee	D5b/97	—
8	Brown, Lance	6-0/200	2-2-72	3	Indiana	FA/96	*1/0
0	Coleman, Marcus (S)	6-2/205	5-24-74	2	Texas Tech	D5/96	13/4
6	Glenn, Aaron (CB/KR)	5-9/185	7-16-72	4	Texas A&M	D1/94	16/16
6	Green, Victor (S)	5-9/195	12-8-69	5	Akron	FA/93	16/16
2	Greenwood, Carl (CB)	5-11/186	3-11-72	3	UCLA	D5/95	14/2
6	Henderson, Jerome (CB)	5-10/188	8-8-69	7	Clemson	FA/97	*7/0
6	Jones, Gary (S)	6-1/217	11-30-67	8	Texas A&M	FA/95	15/15
6	Mickens, Ray (CB)	5-8/180	1-4-73	2	Texas A&M	D3/96	15/10
6	Rosga, Steve (S)	6-1/215	7-10-74	R	Colorado	D7a/97	—

No.	SPECIALISTS	Ht./Wt.	Born	NFL Exp.	College	How acq.	'96 Games GP/GS
11	Hansen, Brian (P)	6-4/215	10-26-60	13	Sioux Falls (S.D.) College	FA/94	16/0
5	Silvestri, Don (K)	6-4/220	12-25-68	3	Pittsburgh	FA/95	12/0

*Brown played 1 game with Cardinals in '96; Dixon played 16 games with Eagles; DuBose played 14 games with Buccaneers; Henderson played 7 games with Patriots; P. Johnson played 15 games with Lions; Logan played 4 games with Jaguars; Lyle played 11 games with Ravens; Neal played 16 games with Saints.

Abbreviations: D1—draft pick, first round; SupD2—supplemental draft pick second round; W-Den—waivers acquisition from Denver; T-Sea—trade acquisition from Seattle; PlanB—Plan B free-agent acquisition; FA—free-agent acquisition (other than Plan B).

MISCELLANEOUS TEAM DATA

Stadium (capacity, surface):
Giants Stadium
(77,716, artificial)
Business address:
1000 Fulton Avenue
Hempstead, NY 11550
Business phone:
516-560-8100
Ticket information:
516-560-8200
Team colors:
Kelly green, white with black trim
Flagship radio station:
WFAN, 660 AM
Training site:
Hofstra University
Hempstead, N.Y.
516-560-8100

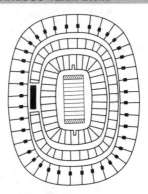

TSN REPORT CARD

Coaching staff	A	Bill Parcells is one of the premier coaches in the NFL. He has won two Super Bowls and one AFC title. Sure he's a stubborn control freak, but he knows how to drive a team to its potential. Parcells has an experienced, top-shelf staff, most of whom have been with him since the early 1980s.
Offensive backfield	B	One of the strengths of the team. QB Neil O'Donnell is coming off a poor season, but he has proven he capable of winning. Adrian Murrell is one of the top five backs in the AFC. FB Lorenzo Neal is strictly blocker, but a good one.
Receivers	B +	Terrific depth. The Jets have three potential starters in Jeff Graham, Keyshawn Johnson and Wayne Chrebe The X factor is Johnson. If he reaches his potential, watch out. The Jets must get more production out o the tight ends, who had only 23 catches last season.
Offensive line	C	Same group that finished last season. It can be a very good line, but only if tackles Jumbo Elliott and Davi Williams avoid their usual back problems. The interior—Roger Duffy, Matt O'Dwyer and Harry Galbreath— won't dominate, but they're not bad.
Defensive line	D	One rising star (DE Hugh Douglas) and a lot of question marks. The two tackle spots are up for grabs, wit journeyman Ronnie Dixon and rookie Rick Terry the leading candidates to start. Marvin Washington star at left end. Otherwise, there's not much here.
Linebackers	C +	Parcells revamped the unit, signing one of his old warhorses, Pepper Johnson, to start in the middle ar moving Mo Lewis from the weak side to the strong side. Injury-plagued Marvin Jones, booted out of th middle, will battle top pick James Farrior for the weak-side job.
Secondary	C -	CB Aaron Glenn is a terrific player who improves every year, but the unit suffers a big dropoff after him. Th safeties, Victor Green and Gary Jones, are ordinary. The other cornerback job is unsettled, with Ray Micker and Jerome Henderson the best of the candidates.
Special teams	D +	Parcells is gambling that rookie specialists Dedric Ward and Leon Johnson can improve the woeful retur units. Better coaching should help, too. Punter Brian Hansen is solid. Is there a kicker in the house?

OAKLAND RAIDERS
AFC WESTERN DIVISION

1996 REVIEW
RESULTS

Sept. 1—at Baltimore	L	14-19	
Sept. 8—at Kansas City	L	3-19	
Sept.15—JACKSONVILLE	W	17-3	
Sept.22—SAN DIEGO	L	34-40	
Sept.29—at Chicago	L	17-19	
Oct. 6—at N.Y. Jets	W	34-13	
Oct. 13—DETROIT	W	37-21	
Oct. 21—at San Diego	W	23-14	
Oct. 27—Open date			
Nov. 4—DENVER	L	21-22	
Nov. 10—at Tampa Bay (OT)	L	17-20	
Nov. 17—MINNESOTA (OT)	L	13-16	
Nov. 24—at Seattle	W	27-21	
Dec. 1—MIAMI	W	17-7	
Dec. 9—KANSAS CITY	W	26-7	
Dec. 15—at Denver	L	19-24	
Dec. 22—SEATTLE	L	21-28	

RECORDS/RANKINGS

1996 regular-season record: 7-9 (T4th in AFC West); 3-5 in division; 6-6 in conference; 4-4 at home; 3-5 on road.
Team record last five years: 41-39 (.513, ranks 12th in league in that span).
1996 team rankings:

	No.	AFC	NFL
Total offense	*328.3	5	8
Rushing offense	*135.9	3	3
Passing offense	*192.4	12	23
Scoring offense	340	7	12
Total defense	*293.6	4	8
Rushing defense	*104.8	9	15
Passing defense	*188.8	2	7
Scoring defense	293	4	T8
Takeaways	26	T11	T22
Giveaways	31	9	16
Turnover differential	-5	12	T21
Sacks	34	8	T17
Sacks allowed	45	12	24

*Yards per game.

TEAM LEADERS

Scoring (kicking): Cole Ford, 108 pts. (36/36 PATs, 24/31 FGs).
Scoring (touchdowns): Tim Brown, 54 pts. (9 receiving).
Passing: Jeff Hostetler, 2,548 yds. (402 att., 242 comp., 60.2%, 23 TDs, 14 int.).
Rushing: Napoleon Kaufman, 874 yds. (150 att., 5.8 avg., 1 TD).
Receptions: Tim Brown, 90 (1,104 yds., 12.3 avg., 9 TDs).
Interceptions: Terry McDaniel, 5 (150 yds., 1 TD).
Sacks: Chester McGlockton, 8.0.
Punting: Jeff Gossett, 39.7 avg. (57 punts, 2,264 yds., 0 blocked).
Punt returns: Tim Brown, 8.5 avg. (32 att., 272 yds., 0 TDs).
Kickoff returns: Napoleon Kaufman, 21.9 avg. (25 att., 548 yds., 0 TDs).

1997 SEASON
CLUB DIRECTORY

President of the general partner
Al Davis
Executive assistant
Al LoCasale
Pro personnel
George Karras
Senior assistant
Bruce Allen
Senior administrator
Morris Bradshaw
Public relations director
Mike Taylor
Administrative assistants
Mario Perez
Marc McKinney
Finance
Tom Blanda
Marc Badain
Mark Fletcher
Legal affairs
Jeff Birren
Amy Trask
Senior executive
John Herrera
Ticket manager
Peter Eiges
Administrative assistant to head coach
Mark Arteaga
Head trainer
Rod Martin
Trainers
Jonathan Jones
Scott Touchet
Strength and conditioning
Garrett Giemont
Player personnel
Angelo Coia
Dan Conners
Ken Herock
Bruce Kebric
Jon Kingdon

Head coach
Joe Bugel

Assistant coaches
Dave Adolph (linebackers)
Fred Biletnikoff (wide receivers)
Willie Brown (def. backs/squad dev.)
Garrett Giemont (strength & cond.)
John Guy (defensive assistant)
Bishop Harris (running backs)
Bill Meyers (tight ends)
Ray Perkins (offensive coordinator)
Keith Rowen (offensive line/asst. head coach)
Steve Shafer (defensive backs)
Kevin Spencer (qual. control/def.)
Rusty Tillman (special teams)
Bill Urbanik (defensive line)
Fred Whittingham (def. coord.)

Mickey Marvin
David McCloughan
Kent McCloughan
Building and grounds
Ken Irons
Equipment manager
Bob Romanski
Equipment assistant
Richard Romanski
Video coordinators
Dave Nash
Jim Otten
John Otten

SCHEDULE

Aug. 31— at Tennessee	12:00	
Sept. 8— KANSAS CITY (Mon.)	6:00	
Sept. 14— at Atlanta	1:00	
Sept. 21— at N.Y. Jets	1:00	
Sept. 28— ST. LOUIS	1:00	
Oct. 5— SAN DIEGO	1:00	
Oct. 12— Open date		
Oct. 19— DENVER	1:00	
Oct. 26— at Seattle	1:00	
Nov. 2— at Carolina	1:00	
Nov. 9— NEW ORLEANS	1:00	
Nov. 16— at San Diego	5:00	
Nov. 24— at Denver (Mon.)	7:00	
Nov. 30— MIAMI	1:00	
Dec. 7— at Kansas City	12:00	
Dec. 14— SEATTLE	1:00	
Dec. 21— JACKSONVILLE	1:00	

All times are for home team.
All games Sunday unless noted.

DRAFT CHOICES

Darrell Russell, DT, Southern California (first round/second pick overall).
Adam Treu, G, Nebraska (3/72).
Tim Kohn, T, Iowa State (3/85).
Chad Levitt, RB, Cornell (4/123).
Calvin Branch, RB, Colorado State (6/172).
Grady Jackson, DE, Knoxville (6/193).

1997 SEASON Oakland Raiders

No.	QUARTERBACKS	Ht./Wt.	Born	NFL Exp.	College	How acq.	'96 Games GP/GS
3	George, Jeff	6-4/215	12-8-67	8	Illinois	FA/97	*3/3
16	Hollas, Donald	6-3/215	11-22-67	4	Rice	FA/95	0/0
15	Hostetler, Jeff	6-3/215	4-22-61	13	West Virginia	FA/93	13/13
7	Klingler, David	6-2/205	2-17-69	6	Houston	FA/96	1/0
	RUNNING BACKS						
35	Aska, Joe	5-11/230	7-14-72	2	Central Oklahoma	D3/95	15/2
	Branch, Calvin	5-11/200	5-8-74	R	Colorado State	D6/97	—
24	Davison, Jerone	6-1/225	9-16-70	1	Arizona State	FA/96	2/0
45	Hall, Tim	5-11/218	2-15-74	1	Robert Morris	D6/96	2/0
26	Kaufman, Napoleon	5-9/185	6-7-73	3	Washington	D1/95	16/9
	Levitt, Chad	6-1/233	11-21-75	R	Cornell	D4/97	—
22	Williams, Harvey	6-2/215	4-22-67	7	Louisiana State	FA/94	13/5
	RECEIVERS						
81	Brown, Tim	6-0/195	7-22-66	9	Notre Dame	D1/88	16/16
83	Dudley, Rickey (TE)	6-6/250	7-15-72	2	Ohio State	D1/96	16/15
	Foster, Sean	6-1/190	12-22-67	1	Long Beach State	FA/96	0/0
81	Hervey, Edward	6-3/179	5-4-73	1	Southern California	FA/96	0/0
85	Hinton, Marcus (TE)	6-4/260	12-27-71	1	Alcorn State	FA/96	2/0
21	Howard, Desmond	5-10/180	5-15-70	6	Michigan	FA/97	*16/0
82	Jett, James	5-10/165	12-28-70	5	West Virginia	FA/93	16/16
	Junkin, Trey (TE)	6-2/241	1-23-61	13	Louisiana Tech	FA/90	6/0
84	Shedd, Kenny	5-9/171	2-14-71	2	Northern Iowa	FA/94	0/0
83	Smith, Kevin (TE)	6-4/265	7-25-69	3	UCLA	FA/97	*1/0
88	Truitt, Olanda	6-0/195	1-4-71	5	Mississippi State	FA/96	10/0
	OFFENSIVE LINEMEN						
68	Cunningham, Rick (T)	6-6/307	1-4-67	5	Texas A&M	FA/95	13/0
68	Freeman, Russell (T)	6-7/290	9-2-69	3	Georgia Tech	FA/92	0/0
75	Harlow, Pat (T)	6-6/290	3-16-69	7	Southern California	T-NE/96	10/9
73	Holmes, Lester (G)	6-3/305	9-27-69	4	Jackson State	D1/93	*16/14
	Jenkins, Robert (T)	6-5/285	12-30-63	10	UCLA	FA/94	10/6
72	Kennedy, Lincoln (G/T)	6-6/325	2-12-71	5	Washington	T-Atl/96	16/16
	Kohn, Tim (T)	6-5/313	12-6-73	R	Iowa State	D3/97	—
79	Kysar, Jeff (T)	6-7/320	6-14-72	1	Arizona State	D5/95	0/0
70	McRae, Charles (T/G)	6-7/306	9-16-68	6	Tennessee	FA/96	13/1
63	Robbins, Barret (C)	6-3/305	8-26-73	3	Texas Christian	D2/95	14/14
	Treu, Adam (C)	6-5/302	6-24-74	R	Nebraska	D3/97	—
72	Villa, Danny (G)	6-5/308	9-21-64	11	Arizona State	FA/97	*16/0
76	Wisniewski, Steve (G)	6-4/285	4-7-67	9	Penn State	D2/89	16/16
65	Wylie, Joey (G)	6-2/298	4-25-74	1	Stephen F. Austin State	D7/96	0/0
	DEFENSIVE LINEMEN						
99	Bruce, Aundray (E)	6-5/265	4-30-66	10	Auburn	PlanB/92	16/0
55	Folston, James (E)	6-3/235	8-14-71	3	Northeast Louisiana	D2/94	12/0
92	Glover, La'Roi (T)	6-0/280	7-4-74	2	San Diego State	D5/96	2/0
	Jackson, Grady (E)	6-2/320	1-23-73	R	Knoxville	D6b/97	—
94	Johnson, Kevin (NT)	6-1/310	10-30-70	3	Texas Southern	FA/97	*12/0
51	Johnstone, Lance (E)	6-4/252	6-11-73	2	Temple	D2/96	16/10
97	Maryland, Russell (T)	6-1/279	3-22-69	7	Miami (Fla.)	FA/96	16/16
91	McGlockton, Chester (T)	6-4/315	9-16-69	6	Clemson	D1/92	16/16
	Russell, Darrell (T)	6-4/321	5-27-76	R	Southern California	D1/97	—
94	Smith, Anthony (E)	6-3/265	6-28-67	7	Arizona	D1/90	6/4
56	Swilling, Pat (E)	6-3/245	10-25-64	12	Georgia Tech	FA/95	16/16
	LINEBACKERS						
54	Biekert, Greg	6-2/240	3-14-69	5	Colorado	D7/93	16/15
	Franklin, Keith	6-2/230	3-4-70	2	South Carolina	FA/95	0/0
53	Fredrickson, Rob	6-4/240	5-13-71	4	Michigan State	D1/94	10/10
57	Holmberg, Rob	6-3/230	5-6-71	4	Penn State	D7/94	13/1
50	Morton, Mike	6-4/235	3-28-72	3	North Carolina	D4/95	16/6
	DEFENSIVE BACKS						
33	Anderson, Eddie (S)	6-1/210	7-22-63	12	Fort Valley (Ga.) State	FA/87	7/5
24	Brown, Larry (CB)	5-11/186	11-30-69	7	Texas Christian	FA/96	8/1
22	Carter, Perry (CB)	5-11/206	8-15-71	3	Southern Mississippi	FA/96	4/0
78	Faumui, Ta'ase	6-3/278	3-19-71	3	Hawaii	FA/97	0/0
	Kidd, Carl (CB)	6-1/205	6-14-73	2	Arkansas	FA/95	16/0
29	Lewis, Albert (CB)	6-2/195	10-6-60	15	Grambling State	FA/94	16/13
43	Lynch, Lorenzo (S)	5-11/200	4-6-63	10	Sacramento State	FA/96	16/16

No.	DEFENSIVE BACKS	Ht./Wt.	Born	NFL Exp.	College	How acq.	'96 Games GP/GS
23	Lyons, Lamar (S)	6-3/213	3-25-73	2	Washington	FA/96	6/0
36	McDaniel, Terry (CB)	5-10/180	2-8-65	9	Tennessee	D1/88	16/15
48	Mustafaa, Najee (CB)	6-1/190	6-20-64	9	Georgia Tech	FA/95	0/0
37	Trapp, James (CB)	6-0/185	12-28-69	5	Clemson	D3/93	12/4
29	Turner, Eric (S)	6-1/207	9-20-68	7	UCLA	FA/97	*14/14
	SPECIALISTS						
	Araguz, Leo (P)	6-0/185	1-18-70	2	Stephen F. Austin	FA/96	3/0
	Ford, Cole (K)	6-2/195	12-31-72	1	Southern California	FA/95	16/0

*George played 3 games with Falcons in '96; Holmes played 16 games with Eagles; Howard played 16 games with Packers; K. Johnson played 12 games with Eagles; K. Smith played 1 game with Packers; Turner played 14 games with Ravens; Villa played 16 games with Chiefs.

Abbreviations: D1—draft pick, first round; SupD2—supplemental draft pick second round; W-Den—waivers acquisition from Denver; T-Sea—trade acquisition from Seattle; PlanB—Plan B free-agent acquisition; FA—free-agent acquisition (other than Plan B).

MISCELLANEOUS TEAM DATA

Stadium (capacity, surface):
Oakland-Alameda County Coliseum
(62,500, grass)
Business address:
1220 Harbor Bay Parkway
Alameda, CA 94502
Business phone:
510-864-5000
Ticket information:
800-949-2626
Team colors:
Silver and black
Flagship radio station:
The Ticket, 1050 AM
Training site:
Napa, Calif.
707-256-1000

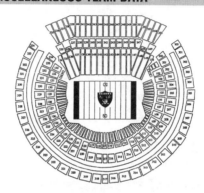

TSN REPORT CARD

Coaching staff — C
Joe Bugel climbs into the top job, hoping to bely his 20-44 record with Arizona. Bugel was an accomplished assistant, but he still must prove he can run the show. Ray Perkins and Fred Whittingham are solid coordinators. The staff includes several assistants (such as Fred Biletnikoff and Willie Brown) with connections to the team's long-ago glory days.

Offensive backfield — B
Jeff George gets his third chance to lift an ordinary team to new heights. George should find plenty of help in the backfield, where Napoleon Kaufman has become one of the league's most explosive backs. Joe Aska is promising and Harvey Williams must adjust to a reduced role. Fullback remained unresolved heading into training camp.

Receivers — B -
Tim Brown deserves his own grade (A, absolutely), given his superb play the last four seasons. James Jett took a sizable step forward last season, but he still needs to become more consistent. Jett and Desmond Howard must blossom, or defenses will continue to devote extra attention to Brown. This is also an important year for tight end Rickey Dudley.

Offensive line — C
Kevin Gogan departed via free agency and Orlando Pace never materialized. So the Raiders begin the season with one huge question at guard and two tackles (Pat Harlow and Lincoln Kennedy) who excel as run blockers but struggle in pass protection. This line should create space for Kaufman; can it keep George healthy?

Defensive line — B +
The line brims with talent, from big Chester McGlockton to quick Lance Johnstone. The Raiders also added top draft choice Darrell Russell to the equation. Now they need to finish the job, sacking the quarterback more often and eliminating the games in which opponents run wild.

Linebackers — B -
This group requires a wait-and-see approach. Much hinges on the comeback of Rob Fredrickson, who missed the final six games last season because of shoulder surgery. Mike Morton replaces Mike Jones, a strikingly athletic linebacker who led the team in tackles. Greg Biekert supplies stout defense against the run.

Secondary — C +
Terry McDaniel and Albert Lewis are hardly getting younger, but they play aggressive, man-to-man coverage. McDaniel's zest for interceptions occasionally costs him, but the Raiders need him to play boldly. Eric Turner created havoc at free safety, given his speed and penchant for causing turnovers. The Raiders thirst for more turnovers.

Special teams — B
Desmond Howard and Napoleon Kaufman form the league's most explosive kick-return tandem. Opponents often avoided Kaufman last year, but now the alternative is equally dangerous. Kicker Cole Ford must prove himself in pressure situations; punter Leo Araguz, like Ford, shows promise but remains unproven at this level.

PHILADELPHIA EAGLES
NFC EASTERN DIVISION

1996 REVIEW
RESULTS

Sept. 1	—at Washington	W	17-14
Sept. 9	—at Green Bay	L	13-39
Sept.15	—DETROIT	W	24-17
Sept.22	—at Atlanta	W	33-18
Sept.30	—DALLAS	L	19-23
Oct. 6	—Open date		
Oct. 13	—at N.Y. Giants	W	19-10
Oct. 20	—MIAMI	W	35-28
Oct. 27	—CAROLINA	W	20-9
Nov. 3	—at Dallas	W	31-21
Nov. 10	—BUFFALO	L	17-24
Nov. 17	—WASHINGTON	L	21-26
Nov. 24	—at Arizona	L	30-36
Dec. 1	—N.Y. GIANTS	W	24-0
Dec. 5	—at Indianapolis	L	10-37
Dec. 14	—at N.Y. Jets	W	21-20
Dec. 22	—ARIZONA	W	29-19
Dec. 29	—at San Francisco*	L	0-14

*NFC wild-card game.

RECORDS/RANKINGS

1996 regular-season record: 10-6 (2nd in NFC East); 5-3 in division; 8-4 in conference; 5-3 at home; 5-3 on road.
Team record last five years: 46-34 (.575), ranks 10th in league in that span.

1996 team rankings:	No.	NFC	NFL
Total offense	*351.7	1	4
Rushing offense	*117.6	2	9
Passing offense	*234.1	1	4
Scoring offense	363	5	9
Total defense	*285.1	3	5
Rushing defense	*98.9	5	10
Passing defense	*186.2	5	6
Scoring defense	341	11	21
Takeaways	31	8	15
Giveaways	32	T8	T17
Turnover differential	-1	9	T17
Sacks	40	5	T8
Sacks allowed	39	9	18

*Yards per game.

TEAM LEADERS

Scoring (kicking): Gary Anderson, 115 pts. (40/40 PATs, 25/29 FGs).
Scoring (touchdowns): Ricky Watters, 78 pts. (13 rushing).
Passing: Ty Detmer, 2,911 yds. (401 att., 238 comp., 59.4%, 15 TDs, 13 int.).
Rushing: Ricky Watters, 1,411 yds. (353 att., 4.0 avg., 13 TDs).
Receptions: Irving Fryar, 88 (1,195 yds., 13.6 avg., 11 TDs).
Interceptions: Michael Zordich, 4 (54 yds., 0 TDs).
Sacks: William Fuller, 13.0.
Punting: Tom Hutton, 42.6 avg. (73 punts, 3,107 yds., 1 blocked).
Punt returns: Mark Seay, 8.7 avg. (35 att., 305 yds., 0 TDs).
Kickoff returns: Derrick Witherspoon, 24.0 avg. (53 att., 1,271 yds., 2 TDs).

1997 SEASON
CLUB DIRECTORY

Owner/chief executive officer
Jeffrey Lurie
Senior vice president
Joe Banner
Sr. vice president/chief financial officer
Mimi Box
Vice president/sales
Vic Gregovits
Vice president/sales & marketing
Len Komoroski
Exec. dir. of Eagles Youth Partnership
Sarah Helfman
Director of football operations
Dick Daniels
Director of college scouting
John Wooten
Director of corporate sales
Dave Rowan
Director of business development
David Perry
Director of public relations
Ron Howard
Assistant director of public relations
Derek Boyko
Director of administration
Vicki Chatley
Director of merchandising
Steve Strawbridge
Director of advertising & promotions
Kim Babiak
Ticket manager
Leo Carlin
Director of penthouse operations
Christiana Noyalas
Trainer
James Collins

SCHEDULE

Aug. 31	— at N.Y. Giants	1:00
Sept. 7	— GREEN BAY	4:00
Sept. 15	— at Dallas (Mon.)	8:00
Sept. 21	— Open date	
Sept. 28	— at Minnesota	7:00
Oct. 5	— WASHINGTON	1:00
Oct. 12	— at Jacksonville	1:00
Oct. 19	— at ARIZONA	1:00
Oct. 26	— DALLAS	1:00
Nov. 2	— at Arizona	2:00
Nov. 10	— SAN FRANCISCO (Mon.)	9:00
Nov. 16	— at Baltimore	1:00
Nov. 23	— PITTSBURGH	1:00
Nov. 30	— CINCINNATI	1:00
Dec. 7	— N.Y. GIANTS	1:00
Dec. 14	— at Atlanta	1:00
Dec. 21	— at Washington	1:00

All times are for home team.
All games Sunday unless noted.

Head coach
Ray Rhodes

Assistant coaches
Bill Callahan (offensive line)
Gerald Carr (wide receivers)
Juan Castillo (tight ends)
Jon Gruden (offensive coordinator)
Chuck Knox Jr. (def. assistant)
Sean Payton (quarterbacks)
David Shaw (offensive assistant)
Danny Smith (defensive backs)
Emmitt Thomas (def. coordinator)
Mike Trgovac (defensive line)
Joe Vitt (linebackers)
Joe Wessel (special teams)
Ted Williams (running backs)
Mike Wolf (strength & conditioning)

Assistant trainers
Scottie Patton
Scott Trulock
Peak performance specialist
Baron Baptiste
Equipment manager
Rusty Sweeney
Video director
Mike Dougherty

DRAFT CHOICES

Jon Harris, DE, Virginia (first round/25th pick overall).
James Darling, LB, Washington State (2/57).
Duce Staley, RB, South Carolina (3/71).
Damien Robinson, DB, Iowa (4/119).
Ndukwe Kalu, DE, Rice (5/152).
Luther Broughton, TE, Furman (5/155).
Antwuan Wyatt, WR, Bethune-Cookman (6/190).
Edward Jasper, DT, Texas A&M (6/198).
Koy Detmer, QB, Colorado (7/207).
Byron Capers, DB, Florida State (7/225).
Deauntae Brown, DB, Central State (Ohio) (7/227).

1997 SEASON
TRAINING CAMP ROSTER

No.	QUARTERBACKS	Ht./Wt.	Born	NFL Exp.	College	How acq.	'96 Games GP/GS
10	Detmer, Koy	6-0/180	7-5-73	R	Colorado	D7a/97	—
14	Detmer, Ty	6-0/194	10-30-67	6	Brigham Young	FA/96	13/11
7	Hoying, Bobby	6-3/221	9-20-72	1	Ohio State	D3/96	1/0
9	Peete, Rodney	6-0/225	3-16-66	9	Southern California	FA/95	5/5
	RUNNING BACKS						
29	Croom, Corey (KR)	5-11/208	5-22-71	4	Ball State	FA/97	0/0
30	Garner, Charlie	5-9/187	2-13-72	4	Tennessee	D2/94	15/1
42	Harris, Rudy (FB)	6-2/257	9-18-70	3	Clemson	FA/97	0/0
37	Jones, Larry (FB)	6-0/232	2-16-71	1	Miami (Fla.)	FA/97	0/0
26	Jourdain, Yonel	5-11/204	4-20-71	3	Southern Illinois	FA/97	0/0
41	Staley, Duce	5-11/220	2-27-75	R	South Carolina	D3/97	—
34	Turner, Kevin (FB)	6-1/231	6-12-69	6	Alabama	FA/95	16/12
32	Watters, Ricky	6-1/217	4-7-69	7	Notre Dame	FA/95	16/16
31	Witherspoon, Derrick	5-10/196	2-14-71	3	Clemson	FA/95	16/0
	RECEIVERS						
49	Broughton, Luther (TE)	6-2/248	11-30-74	R	Furman	D5b/97	—
85	Caldwell, Mike	6-2/200	3-28-71	3	California	FA/97	*1/0
87	Dunn, Jason (TE)	6-4/257	11-15-73	2	Eastern Kentucky	D2a/96	16/12
80	Fryar, Irving	6-0/200	9-28-62	14	Nebraska	FA/96	16/16
82	Jones, Chris T.	6-3/209	8-7-71	3	Miami (Fla.)	D3/95	16/16
17	Knox, Kevin	6-2/199	1-30-71	1	Florida State	FA/97	0/0
83	President, Andre (TE)	6-3/255	6-16-71	2	Angelo State (Tex.)	FA/97	0/0
16	Rhem, Steve	6-2/212	11-9-71	4	Rowan (N.J.)	FA/97	0/0
89	Singleton, Nate	5-11/190	7-5-68	5	Grambling State	FA/97	*2/0
84	Solomon, Freddie	5-10/180	8-15-72	2	South Carolina State	FA/95	12/0
1	Wyatt, Antwuan	5-10/199	7-18-75	R	Bethune-Cookman	D6a/97	—
	OFFENSIVE LINEMEN						
69	Boatswain, Harry (T)	6-4/310	6-26-69	6	New Haven, Conn.	FA/97	*16/4
76	Brooks, Barrett (T)	6-4/309	5-5-72	3	Kansas State	D2b/95	16/15
77	Cooper, Richard (T)	6-5/290	11-1-64	8	Tennessee	FA/96	16/16
74	Devries, Jed (T)	6-6/300	1-6-71	1	Utah State	FA/94	0/0
75	Drake, Troy (T)	6-6/305	5-15-72	3	Indiana	FA/95	11/0
61	Everitt, Steve (C)	6-5/290	8-21-70	5	Michigan	FA/97	*8/7
71	Mayberry, Jermane (G/T)	6-4/325	8-29-73	2	Texas A&M-Kingsville	D1/96	3/1
72	Panos, Joe (G/C)	6-2/293	1-24-71	4	Wisconsin	D3/94	16/16
68	Unutoa, Morris (C)	6-1/284	3-10-71	2	Brigham Young	FA/96	16/0
66	Zandofsky, Mike (G)	6-2/308	11-30-65	9	Washington	FA/97	*14/14
	DEFENSIVE LINEMEN						
96	Dillard, Stacey (T)	6-5/290	9-17-68	5	Oklahoma	FA/97	0/0
94	Duff, John (E)	6-8/282	7-31-67	3	New Mexico	FA/97	0/0
91	Hall, Rhett (T)	6-2/276	12-5-68	7	California	FA/95	16/16
91	Harmon, Andy (T)	6-4/278	4-6-69	7	Kent	D6/91	2/2
90	Harris, Jon (E)	6-7/280	6-9-74	R	Virginia	D1/97	—
74	Jasper, Edward (T)	6-2/295	1-18-73	R	Texas A&M	D6b/97	—
79	Jefferson, Greg (E)	6-3/257	8-31-71	3	Central Florida	D3/95	11/0
75	Kalu, Ndukwe (E)	6-3/246	8-3-75	R	Rice	D5a/97	—
98	Samson, Michael (T)	6-3/294	2-17-73	1	Grambling	FA/96	2/0
78	Thomas, Hollis (T)	6-0/306	1-10-74	2	Northern Illinois	FA/96	16/5
52	Wright, Sylvester (E)	6-2/258	12-30-71	3	Kansas	FA/95	16/0
	LINEBACKERS						
57	Darling, James	6-0/250	12-29-74	R	Washington State	D2/97	—
55	Farmer, Ray	6-3/225	7-1-72	2	Duke	D4/96	16/11
59	Mamula, Mike (E)	6-4/252	8-14-73	3	Boston College	D1/95	16/16
58	Marshall, Whit	6-2/247	1-6-73	2	Georgia	D5/96	1/0
56	Smith, Darrin	6-1/230	4-15-70	5	Miami, Fla.	FA/97	*16/16
51	Thomas, William	6-2/223	8-13-68	7	Texas A&M	D4/91	16/16
50	Willis, James	6-2/237	9-2-72	5	Auburn	D5/93	16/13
	DEFENSIVE BACKS						
25	Boykin, Deral (S)	5-11/198	9-2-70	5	Louisville	FA/96	10/0
35	Brown, Deauntae (CB)	5-10/195	4-28-74	R	Central State (O.)	D7a/97	—
43	Capers, Byron (CB)	6-1/194	3-21-74	R	Florida State	D7b/97	—
20	Dawkins, Brian (S)	5-11/190	10-13-73	2	Clemson	D2b/96	14/13
46	Ford, Frederic (CB)	6-3/196	1-2-73	1	Mississippi Valley State	FA/96	0/0
22	Fuller, James (S)	5-11/208	8-5-69	4	Portland State	FA/96	13/2
28	Robinson, Damien (S)	6-2/210	12-22-73	R	Iowa	D4/97	—
27	Sutton, Eric (CB)	5-10/169	10-24-72	2	San Diego State	FA/97	*4/0
21	Taylor, Bobby (CB)	6-3/216	12-28-73	3	Notre Dame	D2/95	16/16

No.	DEFENSIVE BACKS	Ht./Wt.	Born	NFL Exp.	College	How acq.	'96 Games GP/GS
23	Vincent, Troy (CB)	6-0/194	6-8-70	6	Wisconsin	FA/96	16/16
33	Watson, Tim (S)	6-2/221	8-13-70	4	Howard	FA/97	0/0
36	Zordich, Michael (S)	6-1/212	10-12-63	11	Penn State	FA/94	16/16
	SPECIALISTS						
18	Boniol, Chris (K)	5-11/167	12-9-71	4	Louisiana Tech	FA/97	*16/0
4	Hutton, Tom (P/K)	6-1/193	7-8-72	2	Tennessee	FA/95	16/0

*Boatswain played 16 games with Jets in '96; Boniol played 16 games with Cowboys; Caldwell played 1 game with 49ers; Everitt played 8 games with Ravens; Singleton played 2 games with 49ers; Smith played 16 games with Cowboys; Sutton played 4 games with Redskins; Zandofsky played 14 games with Falcons.

Abbreviations: D1—draft pick, first round; SupD2—supplemental draft pick second round; W-Den—waivers acquisition from Denver; T-Sea—trade acquisition from Seattle; PlanB—Plan B free-agent acquisition; FA—free-agent acquisition (other than Plan B).

MISCELLANEOUS TEAM DATA

Stadium (capacity, surface):
Veterans Stadium
(65,352, artificial)
Business address:
3501 South Broad Street
Philadelphia, PA 19148
Business phone:
215-463-2500
Ticket information:
215-463-5500
Team colors:
Midnight green, silver and white
Flagship radio station:
WYSP, 94.1 FM
Training site:
Lehigh University
Bethlehem, Pa.
610-758-6868

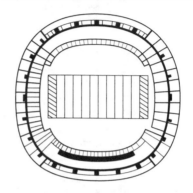

TSN REPORT CARD

Coaching staff	B	Head coach Ray Rhodes has turned the Eagles back into a playoff team after the Rich Kotite debacle. Rhodes' strength is his relationship with players and his ability to get them ready to play. His talent evaluation has been suspect. Offensive coordinator Jon Gruden is among the best and will be a head coach very soon. Line coaches Bill Callahan (offense) and Mike Trgovac (defense) are excellent position coaches.
Offensive backfield	B	Give the running backs an A, and the quarterbacks a C. Ricky Watters causes as many problems on the field for defenses as he does off the field for the Eagles. And that's a lot. Fullback Kevin Turner is among the top three blocking backs in the league and will be utilized more this season as a runner and receiver. Rookie Duce Staley could also be a factor. Ty Detmer and Rodney Peete are both very good backups, and very average starters.
Receivers	B -	The starters, 35-year-old Irving Fryar and third-year man Chris T. Jones and second-year man Jason Dunn at tight end, are fine. The problem comes with depth. Unless someone emerges, or is signed late, the No. 3 receiver will be either former practice squadder Dialleo Burks, oft-injured Nate Singleton, or sixth-round draft pick Antuwan Wyatt. Someone needs to be groomed to eventually take over for Fryar.
Offensive line	C	If center Steve Everitt is over the injuries that caused him to miss half the season in Baltimore last year, the Eagles have a legitimate All-Pro up front for the first time in years. After that it's spotty. Left tackle is being handed to second-year man Jermane Mayberry, who did basically nothing as a rookie. The right tackle is Richard Cooper, who did not play up to his $2.5 million average salary last season. The guards, Mike Zandofsky and Joe Panos are average.
Defensive line	C -	The Eagles are counting on Andy Harmon, after a year of knee injuries that limited him to two games, to bounce back to his near All-Pro form; on Mike Mamula to break out with a big sack number year; on unheralded and undrafted Hollis Thomas to continue his progress and on rookie first-round pick Jon Harris to make an immediate impact. That's a lot to ask. Rhett Hall provides a decent inside rush as a backup.
Linebackers	B -	William Thomas is an All-Pro on the right side, and Darrin Smith is an excellent cover guy on the left. Neither, however, is a big run-stuffer type and the team could be vulnerable against the run. Key backup Ray Farmer is out of the same mold as the starters. Rookie James Darling is being asked to replace James Willis in the middle, and the training camp battle should be interesting.
Secondary	B	Cornerbacks Troy Vincent and Bobby Taylor were both hurt last year by the lack of an effective pass rush. Both are expected to bounce back with big years. The nickel cornerback job is wide open, although a veteran should be signed late. Brian Dawkins did a decent job as a rookie at free safety. He should only get better. The Eagles hope savvy veteran Mike Zordich can give them one more year at strong safety.
Special teams	C	New kicker Chris Boniol helps this unit get a passing grade. Derrick Witherspoon is a good kick returner but the team for some reason may replace him. Punter Tom Hutton is average. There are no experienced punt returners on the team, and coverage teams were among the worst in the league a year ago.

PITTSBURGH STEELERS
AFC CENTRAL DIVISION

1996 REVIEW

RESULTS

Sept. 1—at Jacksonville	L	9-24
Sept. 8—BALTIMORE	W	31-17
Sept.16—BUFFALO	W	24-6
Sept.22—Open date		
Sept.29—HOUSTON	W	30-16
Oct. 7—at Kansas City	W	17-7
Oct. 13—CINCINNATI	W	20-10
Oct. 20—at Houston	L	13-23
Oct. 27—at Atlanta	W	20-17
Nov. 3—ST. LOUIS	W	42-6
Nov. 10—at Cincinnati	L	24-34
Nov. 17—JACKSONVILLE	W	28-3
Nov. 25—at Miami	W	24-17
Dec. 1—at Baltimore	L	17-31
Dec. 8—SAN DIEGO	W	16-3
Dec. 15—SAN FRANCISCO	L	15-25
Dec. 22—at Carolina	L	14-18
Dec. 29—INDIANAPOLIS*	W	42-14
Jan. 5—at New England†	L	3-28

*AFC wild-card game.
†AFC divisional playoff game.

RECORDS/RANKINGS

1996 regular-season record: 10-6 (1st in AFC Central); 4-4 in division; 8-4 in conference; 7-1 at home; 3-5 on road.
Team record last five years: 53-27 (.663), ranks 3rd in league in that span).
1996 team rankings:

	No.	AFC	NFL
Total offense	*321.3	9	15
Rushing offense	*143.7	2	2
Passing offense	*177.6	15	27
Scoring offense	344	6	11
Total defense	*272.6	1	2
Rushing defense	*88.4	3	3
Passing defense	*184.2	1	5
Scoring defense	257	1	T4
Takeaways	40	2	2
Giveaways	33	T12	T21
Turnover differential	7	T3	T7
Sacks	51	1	2
Sacks allowed	21	1	2

*Yards per game.

TEAM LEADERS

Scoring (kicking): Norm Johnson, 106 pts. (37/37 PATs, 23/30 FGs).
Scoring (touchdowns): Jerome Bettis, 66 pts. (11 rushing).
Passing: Mike Tomczak, 2,767 yds. (401 att., 222 comp., 55.4%, 15 TDs, 17 int.).
Rushing: Jerome Bettis, 1,431 yds. (320 att., 4.5 avg., 11 TDs).
Receptions: Charles Johnson, 60 (1,008 yds., 16.8 avg., 3 TDs).
Interceptions: Rod Woodson, 6 (121 yds., 1 TD).
Sacks: Chad Brown, 13.0.
Punting: Josh Miller, 41.0 avg. (55 punts, 2,256 yds., 0 blocked).
Punt returns: Andre Hastings, 6.5 avg. (37 att., 242 yds., 0 TDs).
Kickoff returns: Andre Hastings, 42.0 avg. (1 att., 42 yds., 0 TDs).

1997 SEASON

CLUB DIRECTORY

President
Daniel M. Rooney
Vice presidents
John R. McGinley
Arthur J. Rooney Jr.
Vice president/general counsel
Arthur J. Rooney II
Administration advisor
Charles H. Noll
Director of marketing
Mark Fuhrman
Director of business
Mark Hart
Business coordinator
Dan Ferens
Accounts coordinator
Jim Ellenberger
Ticket sales manager
Geraldine Glenn
Director of football operations
Tom Donahoe
Player relations
Anthony Griggs
Media relations director
Rob Boulware
Director of pro personnel
Tom Modrak
College scouting coordinator
Charles Bailey
College scouts
Mark Gorscak
Phil Kriedler
Bob Lane
Max McCartney
Trainers
John Norwig
Rick Burkholder
Physicians
James P. Bradley

Head coach
Bill Cowher

Assistant coaches
Mike Archer (linebackers)
David Culley (wide receivers)
Chan Gailey (offensive coordinator)
Dick Hoak (running backs)
Dick LeBeau (defensive coordinator)
Tim Lewis (defensive backs)
John Mitchell (defensive line)
Mike Mularkey (tight ends)
Kent Stephenson (offensive line)
Ron Zook (special teams)

Richard Rydze
Abraham J. Twerski
Anthony P. Yates
Equipment manager
Rodgers Freyvogel
Field manager
Rich Baker
Video director
Bob McCartney
Video assistant
Pat Dolan
Photographer
Mike Fabus

SCHEDULE

Aug. 31—	DALLAS	1:00
Sept. 7—	WASHINGTON	1:00
Sept. 14—	Open date	
Sept. 22—	at Jacksonville (Mon.)	9:00
Sept. 28—	TENNESSEE	1:00
Oct. 5—	at Baltimore	1:00
Oct. 12—	INDIANAPOLIS	8:00
Oct. 19—	at Cincinnati	4:00
Oct. 26—	JACKSONVILLE	4:00
Nov. 3—	at Kansas City (Mon.)	8:00
Nov. 9—	BALTIMORE	8:00
Nov. 16—	CINCINNATI	1:00
Nov. 23—	at Philadelphia	1:00
Nov. 30—	at Arizona	2:00
Dec. 7—	DENVER	1:00
Dec. 13—	at New England (Sat.)	4:00
Dec. 21—	at Tennessee	12:00

All times are for home team.
All games Sunday unless noted.

DRAFT CHOICES

Chad Scott, DB, Maryland (first round/24th pick overall).
Will Blackwell, WR, San Diego State (2/53).
Paul Wiggins, T, Oregon (3/82).
Mike Vrabel, DE, Ohio State (3/91).
George Jones, RB, San Diego State (5/154).
Daryl Porter, DB, Boston College (6/186).
Rod Manuel, DE, Oklahoma (6/199).
Mike Adams, WR, Texas (7/223).

1997 SEASON

TRAINING CAMP ROSTER

No.	QUARTERBACKS	Ht./Wt.	Born	NFL Exp.	College	How acq.	'96 Games GP/GS
16	Miller, Jim	6-2/216	2-9-71	3	Michigan State	D6a/94	2/1
10	Stewart, Kordell	6-1/212	10-16-72	3	Colorado	D2/95	16/2
18	Tomczak, Mike	6-1/201	10-23-62	13	Ohio State	FA/93	16/15
	RUNNING BACKS						
36	Bettis, Jerome	5-11/243	2-16-72	5	Notre Dame	T-STL/96	16/12
43	Jones, George	5-9/204	12-31-73	R	San Diego State	D5/97	—
34	Lester, Tim (FB)	5-10/233	6-15-68	6	Eastern Kentucky	FA/95	16/13
25	McAfee, Fred	5-10/193	6-20-68	7	Mississippi College	FA/94	14/0
20	Pegram, Erric	5-10/195	1-7-69	7	North Texas	FA/95	12/4
33	Phillips, Bobby	5-9/187	12-8-69	2	Virginia Union	FA/96	0/0
44	Richardson, Terry	6-0/204	10-8-71	1	Syracuse	FA/96	1/0
38	Witman, Jon (FB)	6-1/240	6-1-72	2	Penn State	D3b/96	16/4
	RECEIVERS						
15	Adams, Mike	5-11/184	3-25-74	R	Texas	D7/97	—
80	Arnold, Jahine	6-0/187	6-19-73	2	Fresno State	D4b/96	9/0
14	Bailey, Henry (KR)	5-8/176	2-28-73	2	UNLV	D7/95	*8/0
89	Blackwell, Will	6-0/184	7-9-75	R	San Diego State	D2/97	—
84	Botkin, Kirk (TE)	6-3/245	3-19-71	3	Arkansas	W-NO/96	16/0
87	Bruener, Mark (TE)	6-4/258	9-16-72	3	Washington	D1/95	12/12
86	Farquhar, John (TE)	6-6/278	3-22-72	2	Duke	FA/96	4/0
	Hawkins, Courtney	5-9/183	12-12-69	6	Michigan State	FA/97	*16/16
83	Holliday, Corey	6-2/208	1-31-71	3	North Carolina	FA/95	11/0
81	Johnson, Charles	6-0/193	1-3-72	4	Colorado	D1/94	16/12
17	Kearney, Jay	6-1/195	9-29-71	1	West Virginia	FA/94	0/0
85	Lyons, Mitch (TE)	6-4/265	5-13-70	5	Michigan State	FA/97	*14/4
82	Thigpen, Yancey	6-1/202	8-15-69	6	Winston-Salem (N.C.) State	FA/92	6/2
	OFFENSIVE LINEMEN						
72	Dafney, Bernard	6-5/335	11-1-68	6	Tennessee	FA/96	14/1
63	Dawson, Dermontti (C)	6-2/288	6-17-65	10	Kentucky	D2/88	16/16
65	Jackson, John (T)	6-6/297	1-4-65	10	Eastern Kentucky	D10/88	16/16
74	Martin, Emerson (G)	6-3/302	5-6-70	1	Hampton (Va.)	FA/96	0/0
62	Myslinski, Tom	6-3/287	12-7-68	6	Tennessee	FA/96	8/6
68	Stai, Brenden (G)	6-4/305	3-30-72	3	Nebraska	D3/95	9/9
67	Stephens, Jamain (T)	6-6/330	1-9-74	1	North Carolina A&T	D1/96	0/0
73	Strzelczyk, Justin (G/T)	6-6/302	8-18-68	8	Maine	D11/90	16/16
66	Sweeney, Jim (C)	6-4/295	8-8-62	14	Pittsburgh	FA/96	16/0
79	Wiggins, Paul (T)	6-3/303	8-17-73	R	Oregon	D3/97	—
77	Wolford, Will (T)	6-5/300	5-18-64	13	Vanderbilt	FA/96	—
	DEFENSIVE LINEMEN						
98	Gibson, Oliver (T)	6-2/298	3-15-72	3	Notre Dame	D4a/95	16/0
74	Harrison, Nolan (E)	6-5/285	1-25-69	6	Indiana	D6/91	*15/2
76	Henry, Kevin (E)	6-4/282	10-23-68	5	Mississippi State	D4/93	12/10
97	Manuel, Rod (E)	6-5/281	10-8-74	R	Oklahoma	D6b/97	—
91	Raybon, Israel (E)	6-6/293	2-5-73	2	North Alabama	D5/96	3/0
71	Roye, Orpheus (E/T)	6-4/290	1-21-74	2	Florida State	D6a/96	13/1
93	Steed, Joel (NT)	6-2/300	2-17-69	6	Colorado	D3/92	16/14
96	Vrabel, Mike (E)	6-4/270	8-14-75	R	Ohio State	D3b/97	—
	LINEBACKERS						
53	Conley, Steven	6-5/235	1-18-72	2	Arkansas	D3a/96	2/0
51	Emmons, Carlos	6-5/246	9-3-73	2	Arkansas State	D7/96	15/0
92	Gildon, Jason	6-3/245	7-31-72	4	Oklahoma State	D3a/94	14/13
50	Holmes, Earl	6-2/246	4-28-73	2	Florida A&M	D4a/96	3/1
54	Jones, Donta	6-2/226	8-27-72	3	Nebraska	D4b/95	15/2
99	Kirkland, Levon	6-1/264	2-17-69	6	Clemson	D2/92	16/16
95	Lloyd, Greg	6-2/228	5-26-65	11	Fort Valley (Ga.) State College	D6b/87	1/1
55	Olsavsky, Jerry	6-1/224	3-29-67	9	Pittsburgh	D10/89	15/13
57	Ravotti, Eric	6-2/250	3-16-71	4	Penn State	D6b/94	15/2
	DEFENSIVE BACKS						
40	Bell, Myron (S)	5-11/203	9-15-71	4	Michigan State	D5a/94	16/4
27	Brown, J.B. (CB)	6-0/191	1-5-67	9	Maryland	FA/97	*14/1
41	Flowers, Lethon (CB)	6-0/213	1-14-73	3	Georgia Tech	D5a/95	16/0
29	Fuller, Randy (CB)	5-10/185	6-2-70	4	Tennessee State	FA/95	14/1
37	Lake, Carnell (S)	6-1/210	7-15-67	9	UCLA	D2/89	13/13
28	Mays, Alvoid (CB)	5-9/180	7-10-66	7	West Virginia	FA/97	0/0
49	Miles, Barron (CB)	5-8/165	1-1-72	1	Nebraska	D6/95	0/0
24	Oldham, Chris (CB)	5-9/193	10-26-68	7	Oregon	FA/95	16/0
39	Perry, Darren (S)	5-11/196	12-29-68	6	Penn State	D8a/92	16/16

No.	DEFENSIVE BACKS	Ht./Wt.	Born	NFL Exp.	College	How acq.	'96 Games GP/GS
23	Pointer, Kirk	5-11/178	2-13-74	1	Austin Peay	D4a/96	0/0
45	Porter, Daryl (CB)	5-8/188	1-16-74	R	Boston College	D6/97	—
30	Scott, Chad	6-1/203	9-6-54	R	Maryland	D1/97	—
21	Woolford, Donnell (CB)	5-9/188	1-6-66	8	Clemson	D1a/89	*15/15
	SPECIALISTS						
9	Johnson, Norm (K)	6-2/202	5-31-60	16	UCLA	FA/95	16/0
4	Miller, Josh (P)	6-3/215	7-14-70	2	Arizona	FA/96	12/0

*Bailey played 8 games with Jets in '96; Brown played 14 games with Dolphins; Harrison played 15 games with Raiders; Hawkins played 16 games with Buccaneers; Lyons played 14 games with Falcons; Woolford played 15 games with Bears.

Abbreviations: D1—draft pick, first round; SupD2—supplemental draft pick second round; W-Den—waivers acquisition from Denver; T-Sea—trade acquisition from Seattle; PlanB—Plan B free-agent acquisition; FA—free-agent acquisition (other than Plan B).

MISCELLANEOUS TEAM DATA

Stadium (capacity, surface):
Three Rivers Stadium
(59,600, artificial)
Business address:
300 Stadium Circle
Pittsburgh, PA 15212
Business phone:
412-323-0300
Ticket information:
412-323-1200
Team colors:
Black and gold
Flagship radio station:
WTAE, 1250 AM
Training site:
St. Vincent College
Latrobe, Pa.
412-539-8515

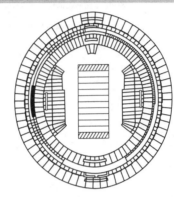

TSN REPORT CARD

Coaching staff	B +	Bill Cowher is one of the best, if not the best, young coaches in the game. He is intense, loves his players and is a great motivator. But the team is on its third defensive coordinator in four years, and this one—Jim Haslett—worked with a 4-3, not a 3-4, scheme last year.
Offensive backfield	B -	Jerome Bettis is one of the best backs in the league, combining power with tremendous leg strength and agility. He has a quality backup in Erric Pegram. But the Steelers will have an untested quarterback, whether it's Kordell Stewart or Jim Miller.
Receivers	B -	When healthy, the combination of Yancey Thigpen and Charles Johnson is outstanding. Mark Bruener is a promising tight end who may blossom. But too many losses at this position have turned what was a strength into a question mark.
Offensive line	B	Center Dermontti Dawson is the best in the NFL, but the left side of the line might be starting to show age with tackle John Jackson and guard Will Wolford, each of whom remains among the best in the game. Depth is the biggest problem, especially if Jackson or right tackle Justin Strzelczyk gets hurt.
Defensive line	D	Joel Steed might be the most underrated nose tackle in the NFL, but the loss of ends Ray Seals and Brentson Buckner will hurt the Steelers more than they think. Their replacements, Kevin Henry and Nolan Harrison, won't cause opponents any sleepless nights. Buckner and Seals were 300-plus pounders who could stuff the line. Henry and Harrison are considerably lighter.
Linebackers	A -	Even with the loss of Pro Bowler Chad Brown, this remains the strongest position on the team. Five-time Pro Bowler Greg Lloyd returns to join one of the best inside linebackers in the league in Levon Kirkland. Outside linebacker Jason Gildon came on strong at the end of the season, and inside linebacker Earl Holmes is waiting to shine.
Secondary	C	This is a big question mark because of the loss of Rod Woodson, Deon Figures and Willie Williams. Woodson will be replaced by Donnell Woolford, who is a very good corner. But he's not Woodson. Rookie No. 1 pick Chad Scott will have to step in and start at the other corner spot. Strong safety Carnell Lake is one of the best in the league, while free safety Darren Perry is steady and smart.
Special teams	C	The biggest question will be how well kicker Norm Johnson's 37-year-old leg holds up. He is pretty reliable inside 40 yards. Punter Josh Miller has a strong leg but has to realize his potential. The loss of Ernie Mills, Andre Hastings and Jahine Arnold will hurt the return units, but rookie receiver Mike Adams could step in and provide a spark.

ST. LOUIS RAMS
NFC WESTERN DIVISION

1996 REVIEW
RESULTS

Sept. 1—CINCINNATI	W	26-16
Sept. 8—at San Francisco	L	0-34
Sept.15—Open date		
Sept.22—WASHINGTON	L	10-17
Sept.29—at Arizona (OT)	L	28-31
Oct. 6—SAN FRANCISCO	L	11-28
Oct. 13—at Carolina	L	13-45
Oct. 20—JACKSONVILLE	W	17-14
Oct. 27—at Baltimore (OT)	L	31-37
Nov. 3—at Pittsburgh	L	6-42
Nov. 10—ATLANTA	W	59-16
Nov. 17—CAROLINA	L	10-20
Nov. 24—GREEN BAY	L	9-24
Dec. 1—at New Orleans	W	26-10
Dec. 8—at Chicago	L	9-35
Dec. 15—at Atlanta	W	34-27
Dec. 21—NEW ORLEANS	W	14-13

RECORDS/RANKINGS

1996 regular-season record: 6-10 (3rd in NFC West); 4-4 in division; 4-8 in conference; 4-4 at home; 2-6 on road.
Team record last five years: 28-52 (.350, ranks 25th in league in that span).

1996 team rankings:	No.	NFC	NFL
Total offense	*273.3	12	27
Rushing offense	*100.4	9	20
Passing offense	*172.8	13	28
Scoring offense	303	7	20
Total defense	*345.6	13	26
Rushing defense	*115.9	8	20
Passing defense	*229.7	14	26
Scoring defense	409	14	27
Takeaways	39	T1	T3
Giveaways	44	15	29
Turnover differential	-5	T10	T21
Sacks	32	T11	T21
Sacks allowed	57	15	30

*Yards per game.

TEAM LEADERS

Scoring (kicking): Chip Lohmiller, 91 pts. (28/29 PATs, 21/25 FGs).
Scoring (touchdowns): Eddie Kennison, 66 pts. (9 receiving, 2 punt returns).
Passing: Tony Banks, 2,544 yds. (368 att., 192 comp., 52.2%, 15 TDs, 15 int.).
Rushing: Lawrence Phillips, 632 yds. (193 att., 3.3 avg., 4 TDs).
Receptions: Isaac Bruce, 84 (1,338 yds., 15.9 avg., 7 TDs).
Interceptions: Keith Lyle, 9 (152 yds., 0 TDs).
Sacks: Kevin Carter, 9.5.
Punting: Sean Landeta, 44.8 avg. (78 punts, 3,491 yds., 0 blocked).
Punt returns: Eddie Kennison, 14.6 avg. (29 att., 423 yds., 2 TDs).
Kickoff returns: J.T. Thomas, 21.4 avg. (30 att., 643 yds., 0 TDs).

1997 SEASON
CLUB DIRECTORY

Owner/chairman
Georgia Frontiere
Vice chairman
Stan Kroenke
President
John Shaw
Senior vice president
Jay Zygmunt
Vice president/football operations
Lynn Stiles
Vice president/administration
Bob Wallace
Vice president/media and community relations
Marshall Klein
Vice president/marketing
Phil Thomas
Ticket manager
Mike Naughton
Director of operations
John Oswald
Director/public relations
Rick Smith
Asst. director/public relations
Tony Wyllie
Director/player personnel
John Becker
Entertainment coordinator
Tom Guthrie
Scouts
Greg Gaines
Lawrence McCutcheon
David Razzano
Pete Russell
Harley Sewell
Trainers
Jim Anderson
Assistant trainers
Ron DuBuque
Dake Walden

Head coach
Dick Vermeil

Assistant coaches
Nick Aliotti (defensive assistant)
Steve Brown (defensive assistant)
John Bunting (linebackers)
Bud Carson (defensive coordinator)
Chris Clausen (strength & conditioning)
Dick Coury (wide receivers)
Frank Gansz (special teams/ offensive assistant)
Peter Giunta (defensive backs)
Kerry Goode (strength & conditioning)
Carl Hairston (defensive line)
Jim Hanifan (offensive line)
Wilbert Montgomery (running backs)
John Ramsdell (offensive assistant)
Jerry Rhome (offensive coordinator/ quarterbacks)
George Warhop (offensive line)
Mike White (assistant head coach/tight ends)

Physician
To be announced
Equipment manager
Todd Hewitt
Video director
Larry Clerico

SCHEDULE

Aug. 31— NEW ORLEANS	12:00
Sept. 7— SAN FRANCISCO	12:00
Sept. 14— at Denver	2:00
Sept. 21— N.Y. GIANTS	3:00
Sept. 28— at Oakland	1:00
Oct. 5— Open date	
Oct. 12— at San Francisco	1:00
Oct. 19— SEATTLE	12:00
Oct. 26— KANSAS CITY	12:00
Nov. 2— at Atlanta	1:00
Nov. 9— at Green Bay	12:00
Nov. 16— ATLANTA	12:00
Nov. 23— CAROLINA	3:00
Nov. 30— at Washington	1:00
Dec. 7— at New Orleans	12:00
Dec. 14— CHICAGO	7:00
Dec. 20— at Carolina (Sat.)	4:00

All times are for home team.
All games Sunday unless noted.

DRAFT CHOICES

Orlando Pace, T, Ohio State (first round/ first pick overall).
Dexter McCleon, DB, Clemson (2/40).
Ryan Tucker, C, Texas Christian (4/112).
Taje Allen, DB, Texas (5/158).
Muadianvita Kazadi, LB, Tulsa (6/179).
Cedric White, DE, North Carolina A&T (7/215).

TRAINING CAMP ROSTER

St. Louis Rams

1997 SEASON

No.	QUARTERBACKS	Ht./Wt.	Born	NFL Exp.	College	How acq.	'96 Games GP/GS
12	Banks, Tony	6-4/225	4-5-73	2	Michigan State	D2a/96	14/13
2	Furrer, Will	6-3/210	2-5-68	3	Virginia Tech	W-Chi/93	0/0
10	Martin, Jamie	6-2/210	2-8-70	2	Weber State	FA/93	6/0
11	Rypien, Mark	6-4/231	10-2-62	11	Washington State	FA/97	*1/0
	RUNNING BACKS						
34	Harris, Derrick	6-0/250	9-18-72	2	Miami (Fla.)	D6a/96	11/6
34	Heyward, Craig (FB)	5-11/250	9-26-66	10	Pittsburgh	FA/97	*15/5
44	Moore, Jerald (FB)	5-9/229	11-20-74	2	Oklahoma	D3/96	11/4
29	Moore, Ronald (KR)	5-10/225	11-26-70	5	Pittsburg (Kan.) State	FA/97	*16/0
21	Phillips, Lawrence	6-0/212	5-12-75	2	Nebraska	D1a/96	15/11
28	Philyaw, Dino	5-10/203	10-30-70	3	Oregon	FA/97	*9/0
	RECEIVERS						
80	Bruce, Isaac	6-0/186	11-10-72	4	Memphis State	D2/94	16/16
89	Clay, Hayward (TE)	6-4/256	7-25-73	2	Texas	D6b/96	11/4
84	Conwell, Ernie (TE)	6-1/255	8-17-72	2	Washington	D2b/96	10/8
81	Crawford, Keith	6-2/185	11-21-70	4	Howard Payne (Tex.)	W-GB/96	16/0
88	Kennison, Eddie	6-0/195	1-20-73	2	Louisiana State	D1b/96	15/14
86	Laing, Aaron (TE)	6-3/255	7-19-71	3	New Mexico State	W-SD/95	12/8
17	Lee, Kevin	6-1/190	1-1-71	3	Alabama	FA/97	*2/0
82	Ross, Jermaine	6-0/196	4-27-71	3	Purdue	FA/94	15/0
16	Tellison, A.C.	6-2/208	9-5-71	1	Miami (Fla.)	FA/96	0/0
87	Thomas, J.T.	5-10/182	7-11-71	3	Arizona State	D7/95	16/1
19	Williams, Billy (KR)	5-11/175	6-7-71	1	Tennessee	FA/95	1/0
	OFFENSIVE LINEMEN						
61	Brostek, Bern (C)	6-3/300	9-11-66	8	Washington	D1/90	16/16
	Dye, Ernest (G)	6-6/325	7-15-71	5	South Carolina	FA/97	*8/0
70	Gandy, Wayne (T)	6-4/300	2-10-71	4	Auburn	D1/94	16/16
66	Gerak, John (G)	6-3/295	1-6-70	5	Penn State	FA/97	*14/10
50	Gruttadauria, Mike (C)	6-4/290	12-6-72	1	Central Florida	FA/96	9/3
68	James, Jesse (C)	6-4/311	9-16-71	3	Mississippi State	D2/95	1/0
65	Kirksey, Jon	6-4/345	2-21-70	2	Cal State-Sacramento	FA/95	11/1
73	Miller, Fred (T)	6-7/306	2-6-73	2	Baylor	D5/96	14/0
79	Milner, Billy (T)	6-4/304	6-21-72	3	Houston	T-Mia/96	*14/0
76	Pace, Orlando (T)	6-7/334	11-4-75	R	Ohio State	D1/97	—
	Pollard, Trent (G/T)	6-4/330	11-20-72	4	Eastern Washington	FA/97	0/0
	Smith, Vernice (G)	6-3/300	10-24-65	6	Florida A&M	FA/97	0/0
50	Tucker, Ryan (C)	6-5/285	6-12-75	R	Texas Christian	D4/97	—
67	White, Dwayne (G)	6-2/315	2-10-67	8	Alcorn State	FA/95	16/16
72	Wiegert, Zach (T)	6-4/305	8-16-72	3	Nebraska	D2a/95	16/16
	DEFENSIVE LINEMEN						
93	Carter, Kevin (E)	6-5/280	9-21-73	3	Florida	D1/96	16/16
75	Farr, D'Marco (T)	6-1/280	6-9-71	4	Washington	FA/94	16/16
99	Harris, James (E)	6-6/285	5-13-68	5	Temple	FA/96	16/0
91	O'Neal, Leslie (E)	6-4/270	5-7-64	11	Oklahoma State	FA/96	16/16
97	Osborne, Chuck (T)	6-2/295	11-2-73	2	Arizona	D7/96	15/1
98	Parten, Ty (E)	6-4/272	10-13-69	3	Arizona	FA/97	0/0
94	Robinson, Jeff (E)	6-4/265	2-20-70	5	Idaho	FA/97	*16/0
63	White, Cedric (E)	6-2/298	10-22-74	R	North Carolina A&T	D7/97	—
96	Williams, Jay (E)	6-3/280	10-13-71	3	Wake Forest	FA/94	2/0
90	Zgonina, Jeff (T)	6-2/285	5-24-70	5	Purdue	FA/97	*8/0
	LINEBACKERS						
53	Dingle, Nate	6-2/242	7-23-71	3	Cincinnati	FA/97	*2/0
54	Gaskins, Percell	6-0/226	4-25-72	2	Kansas State	D4/96	15/1
51	Jenkins, Carlos	6-3/230	7-12-68	7	Michigan State	FA/95	13/10
52	Jones, Mike	6-1/230	4-15-69	6	Missouri	FA/97	*15/15
55	Jones, Robert	6-3/242	9-27-69	6	East Carolina	FA/96	16/13
59	Kazadi, Muadianvita	6-2/236	12-20-73	R	Tulsa	D6/97	—
58	Phifer, Roman	6-2/239	3-5-68	7	UCLA	D2/91	15/15
	DEFENSIVE BACKS						
20	Allen, Taje	5-10/180	11-6-73	R	Texas	D5/97	—
41	Lyght, Todd (CB)	6-0/189	2-9-69	7	Notre Dame	D1/91	16/16
35	Lyle, Keith (S)	6-2/209	4-17-72	4	Virginia	D3/94	16/16
23	McBurrows, Gerald (S)	5-11/206	10-7-73	3	Kansas	D7/95	16/7

No.	DEFENSIVE BACKS	Ht./Wt.	Born	NFL Exp.	College	How acq.	'96 Games GP/GS
24	McCleon, Dexter	5-10/198	10-9-73	R	Clemson	D2/97	—
27	Parker, Anthony (CB)	5-10/185	2-11-66	8	Arizona State	FA/95	14/14
22	Scurlock, Mike (CB)	5-10/199	2-26-72	3	Arizona	D5/95	16/0
38	Walker, Marquis (CB)	5-10/173	7-6-72	2	Southeast Missouri State	FA/96	*9/4
32	Wright, Toby (S)	5-11/215	11-19-70	4	Nebraska	D2/94	12/12
	SPECIALISTS						
14	Wilkins, Jeff (K)	6-2/192	4-19-72	4	Youngstown State	FA/97	*16/0

*Dingle played 2 games for Jaguars in '96; Dye played 8 games for Cardinals; Gerak played 14 games for Vikings; Heyward played 15 games for Falcons; M. Jones played 15 games for Raiders; Lee played 2 games for 49ers; Milner played 4 games for Dolphins and 10 games for Rams; R. Moore played 16 games for Jets; Philyaw played 9 games for Panthers; Robinson played 16 games for Broncos; Rypien played 1 game for Eagles; Walker played 8 games for Rams and 1 game for Redskins; Wilkins played 16 games for 49ers; Zgonina played 8 games for Falcons.

Abbreviations: D1—draft pick, first round; SupD2—supplemental draft pick second round; W-Den—waivers acquisition from Denver; T-Sea—trade acquisition from Seattle; PlanB—Plan B free-agent acquisition; FA—free-agent acquisition (other than Plan B).

MISCELLANEOUS TEAM DATA

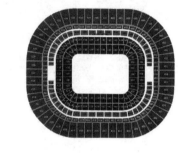

Stadium (capacity, surface):
  Trans World Dome (66,000, artificial)
Business address:
  1 Rams Way
  St. Louis, MO 63045
Business phone:
  314-982-7267
Ticket information:
  314-425-8830
Team colors:
  Royal blue, gold and white
Flagship radio station:
  KSD, 550 AM
Training site:
  Western Illinois University
  Macomb, Ill.
  314-982-7267

TSN REPORT CARD

Coaching staff	A-	There are five former NFL head coaches among the assistants, more than any staff in the league. During free agency, the draft and minicamps, Dick Vermeil proved to be a quick study. He has leaned on the likes of Mike White, Bud Carson, Jerry Rhome, Frank Gansz and Jim Hanifan to bridge the gap from the early '80s to the late '90s.
Offensive backfield	C	Even if Lawrence Phillips had been a boy scout in the offseason —and he wasn't—the continued problems with his left knee would be a concern. Craig "Ironhead" Heyward adds versatility and leadership. Jets castoff Ron Moore could surprise. Tony Banks must cut way down on fumbles to become a first-rate quarterback.
Receivers	B	Isaac Bruce proved last season that he deserves to be ranked among the league's elite. Only the Patriots' Terry Glenn had a better rookie season than Eddie Kennison. But there is no proven third receiver. Second-year man Ernie Conwell has promise but still must earn his spurs at tight end.
Offensive line	C	The arrival of left tackle Orlando Pace and line coach Hanifan should be enough to pull this group up to respectability. Pace will struggle some with his pass blocking but should be an immediate force as a run blocker. Hanifan's coaching can improve any group. Gerald Perry's return after a year out of football will help.
Defensive line	D	Leslie O'Neal, 33, slipped to seven sacks last season, the second-lowest total of his career, and could be sliding. At the other end, Kevin Carter is proving to be a solid performer against the run and pass. Starting at tackle are untested Jon Kirksey and D'Marco Farr, who slumped to 4½ sacks in '96.
Linebackers	C +	A year ago, the Rams were easy pickings for runs up the middle and passes to running backs. The addition of free agent Michael Jones should help the coverage. But Robert Jones needs to play more consistently in the middle against the run. Roman Phifer is durable and underrated.
Secondary	B -	If hard-hitting Toby Wright can stay healthy, the Rams could have one of the league's better safety tandems. Keith Lyle shared the NFL lead in interceptions (nine) in '96. Todd Lyght has developed into a steady, dependable cornerback. But will rookie Dexter McCleon be ready to step in at the other corner?
Special teams	C	The team's most curious offseason move was releasing punter Sean Landeta without a clear replacement lined up. Free-agent pickup Jeff Wilkins is one of the top young kickers in the league. Kennison returned two punts for touchdowns last year; Kennison and Johnny Thomas will handle kickoff returns.

SAN DIEGO CHARGERS
AFC WESTERN DIVISION

1996 REVIEW
RESULTS

Sept. 1—SEATTLE	W	29-7
Sept. 8—CINCINNATI	W	27-14
Sept.15—at Green Bay	L	10-42
Sept.22—at Oakland	W	40-34
Sept.29—KANSAS CITY	W	22-19
Oct. 6—at Denver	L	17-28
Oct. 13—Open date		
Oct. 21—OAKLAND	L	14-23
Oct. 27—at Seattle	L	13-32
Nov. 3—at Indianapolis	W	26-19
Nov. 11—DETROIT	W	27-21
Nov. 17—TAMPA BAY	L	17-25
Nov. 24—at Kansas City	W	28-14
Dec. 1—NEW ENGLAND	L	7-45
Dec. 8—at Pittsburgh	L	3-16
Dec. 14—at Chicago	L	14-27
Dec. 22—DENVER	W	16-10

RECORDS/RANKINGS

1996 regular-season record: 8-8 (3rd in AFC West); 5-3 in division; 7-5 in conference; 5-3 at home; 3-5 on road.
Team record last five years: 47-33 (.588, ranks T7th in league in that span).
1996 team rankings:

	No.	AFC	NFL
Total offense	*291.9	15	26
Rushing offense	*82	15	29
Passing offense	*209.9	8	14
Scoring offense	310	13	18
Total defense	*338.8	11	23
Rushing defense	*109.7	10	17
Passing defense	*229.1	12	25
Scoring defense	376	T12	T24
Takeaways	36	T3	T6
Giveaways	32	T10	T17
Turnover differential	4	5	T9
Sacks	33	T9	T19
Sacks allowed	33	5	10

*Yards per game.

TEAM LEADERS

Scoring (kicking): John Carney, 118 pts. (31/31 PATs, 29/36 FGs).
Scoring (touchdowns): Tony Martin, 84 pts. (14 receiving).
Passing: Stan Humphries, 2,670 yds. (416 att., 232 comp., 55.8%, 18 TDs, 13 int.).
Rushing: Leonard Russell, 713 yds. (219 att., 3.3 avg., 7 TDs).
Receptions: Tony Martin, 85 (1,171 yds., 13.8 avg., 14 TDs).
Interceptions: Rodney Harrison, 5 (56 yds., 0 TDs).
Sacks: Junior Seau, 7.0.
Punting: Darren Bennett, 45.6 avg. (87 punts, 3,967 yds., 0 blocked).
Punt returns: Darrien Gordon, 14.9 avg. (36 att., 537 yds., 1 TD).
Kickoff returns: Andre Coleman, 22.0 avg. (55 att., 1,210 yds., 0 TDs).

1997 SEASON
CLUB DIRECTORY

Chairman of the board
Alex G. Spanos
President/vice chairman
Dean A. Spanos
Executive vice president
Michael A. Spanos
General manager
Bobby Beathard
Vice president/finance
Jeremiah T. Murphy
Chief financial & administrative officer
Jeanne Bonk
Director/player personnel
Billy Devaney
Director/pro personnel
Rudy Feldman
Coordinator/football operations
Marty Hurney
Business manager
John Hinek
Director/marketing
Richard V. Israel
Director/ticket operations
Ron Tuck
Director/public relations
Bill Johnston
Director/premium seating
Lynn Abramson
Director/security
Dick Lewis
Trainer
Keoki Kamau
Equipment manager
Sid Brooks

Head coach
Kevin Gilbride

Assistant coaches
Mike Cavanaugh (quality control/offense)
George DeLeone (offensive line)
Tyrone Dixon (wide receivers)
John Hastings (strength & conditioning)
Kevin Lempa (administrative assistant/defense)
Bill MacDermott (tight ends)
Nick Nicolau (asst. head coach)
Frank Novak (special teams)
Wayne Nunnely (defensive line)
Joe Pascale (defensive coordinator)
Derrell Pasquale (quality control/special teams)
Rod Perry (defensive backs)
Mike Sheppard (offensive coordinator)
Jim Vechiarella (linebackers)
Ollie Wilson (running backs)

Director/video operations
Dusty Alves

SCHEDULE

Aug. 31—	at New England	1:00
Sept. 7—	at New Orleans	12:00
Sept. 14—	CAROLINA	1:00
Sept. 21—	at Seattle	1:00
Sept. 28—	BALTIMORE	1:00
Oct. 5—	at Oakland	1:00
Oct. 12—	Open date	
Oct. 16—	at Kansas City (Thur.)	7:00
Oct. 26—	INDIANAPOLIS	1:00
Nov. 2—	at Cincinnati	1:00
Nov. 9—	SEATTLE	1:00
Nov. 16—	OAKLAND	5:00
Nov. 23—	at San Francisco	1:00
Nov. 30—	DENVER	5:00
Dec. 7—	ATLANTA	1:00
Dec. 14—	KANSAS CITY	1:00
Dec. 21—	at Denver	2:00

All times are for home team.
All games Sunday unless noted.

DRAFT CHOICES

Freddie Jones, TE, North Carolina (second round/45th pick overall).
Michael Hamilton, LB, North Carolina A&T (3/74).
Raleigh Roundtree, T, South Carolina State (4/109).
Kenny Bynum, RB, South Carolina State (5/138).
Paul Bradford, DB, Portland State (5/146).
Daniel Palmer, C, Air Force (6/178).
Toran James, LB, North Carolina A&T (7/218).
Tony Corbin, QB, Cal State Sacramento (7/237).

1997 SEASON
TRAINING CAMP ROSTER

No.	QUARTERBACKS	Ht./Wt.	Born	NFL Exp.	College	How acq.	'96 Games GP/GS
7	Corbin, Tony	6-4/215	3-21-74	R	Cal State Sacramento	D7/97	—
12	Humphries, Stan	6-2/223	4-14-65	10	Northeast Louisiana	T-Was/92	13/13
8	Salisbury, Sean	6-5/225	3-9-63	9	Southern California	FA/96	16/3
5	Whelihan, Craig	6-5/220	4-15-71	1	Pacific	D6c/95	0/0

No.	RUNNING BACKS	Ht./Wt.	Born	NFL Exp.	College	How acq.	'96 Games GP/GS
33	Bouie, Kevin	6-1/230	8-18-71	3	Mississippi State	D7/95	1/0
22	Bradley, Freddie	5-10/208	6-12-70	2	Sonoma State (Calif.)	D7/96	10/1
32	Brown, Gary	5-11/228	7-1-69	6	Penn State	FA/97	0/0
43	Bynum, Kenny	5-11/191	5-29-74	R	South Carolina State	D5a/97	—
39	Craver, Aaron	6-0/220	12-18-68	7	Fresno State	FA/95	*15/15
41	Fletcher, Terrell	5-8/196	9-14-73	3	Wisconsin	D2b/95	16/0
35	Gardner, Carwell (FB)	6-2/240	11-27-66	8	Louisville	FA/97	*13/3
24	Hayden, Aaron	6-0/218	4-13-73	3	Tennessee	D4b/95	11/0

No.	RECEIVERS	Ht./Wt.	Born	NFL Exp.	College	How acq.	'96 Games GP/GS
83	Coleman, Andre (KR)	5-9/165	1-18-71	4	Kansas State	D3a/94	16/10
84	Ellison, 'OMar	6-0/200	10-8-71	3	Florida State	D5/95	10/1
82	Jones, Charlie	5-8/175	12-1-72	2	Fresno State	D6c/96	14/4
98	Jones, Freddie (TE)	6-5/260	9-16-74	R	North Carolina	D2/97	—
81	Martin, Tony	6-0/181	9-5-65	8	Mesa State (Colo.)	T-Mia/94	16/16
21	Metcalf, Eric (KR)	5-10/190	1-23-68	9	Texas	FA/97	*16/11
89	Mitchell, Shannon (TE)	6-2/245	3-28-72	4	Georgia	FA/94	16/11
85	Oliver, Jimmy	5-10/173	1-30-73	1	Texas Christian	D2c/95	0/0
86	Pupunu, Alfred (TE)	6-2/265	10-17-69	6	Weber State	W-KC/92	9/8
87	Roche, Brian (TE)	6-4/255	5-5-73	2	San Jose State	D3/96	13/0
80	Still, Bryan	5-11/174	6-3-74	2	Virginia Tech	D2a/96	16/0

No.	OFFENSIVE LINEMEN	Ht./Wt.	Born	NFL Exp.	College	How acq.	'96 Games GP/GS
75	Berti, Tony (T)	6-6/300	6-21-72	3	Colorado	D6b/96	16/14
50	Binn, Dave (C)	6-3/240	2-6-72	4	California	FA/94	16/0
68	Cocozzo, Joe (G)	6-4/300	8-7-70	5	Michigan	D3/93	16/11
76	Davis, Isaac (G)	6-3/320	4-8-72	4	Arkansas	D2a/94	14/5
60	Engel, Greg (C)	6-3/285	1-18-71	4	Illinois	FA/94	12/9
63	McKenzie, Raleigh (C)	6-2/283	2-8-63	13	Tennessee	FA/97	*16/16
66	Mills, Jim (T)	6-4/290	3-30-73	1	Idaho	D6a/96	1/0
73	Palmer, Dan (C)	6-4/290	8-24-73	R	Air Force	D6/97	—
70	Parker, Vaughn (G/T)	6-3/296	6-5-71	4	UCLA	D2b/94	16/16
74	Roundtree, Raleigh (T)	6-5/295	8-31-75	R	South Carolina State	D4/97	—
65	Sienkiewicz, Troy (T)	6-5/310	5-27-72	2	New Mexico State	D6a/95	7/0
64	Stoltenberg, Bryan (C)	6-1/293	8-25-72	2	Colorado	D6b/96	9/0

No.	DEFENSIVE LINEMEN	Ht./Wt.	Born	NFL Exp.	College	How acq.	'96 Games GP/GS
90	Coleman, Marco (E)	6-3/267	12-18-69	6	Georgia Tech	FA/96	16/15
93	Davis, Reuben (T)	6-5/320	5-7-65	10	North Carolina	FA/94	15/15
94	Edwards, Vernon (E)	6-4/255	6-23-72	2	Southern Methodist	FA/95	5/1
95	Fuller, William (E)	6-3/280	3-8-62	12	North Carolina	FA/94	*16/16
99	Johnson, Raylee (E)	6-3/265	6-1-70	5	Arkansas	D4a/93	16/1
98	Lee, Shawn (T)	6-2/300	10-24-66	10	North Alabama	FA/92	15/7
97	Parrella, John (T)	6-3/290	11-22-69	5	Nebraska	FA/94	16/9
96	Sasa, Don (T)	6-3/286	9-16-72	3	Washington State	D3a/95	4/1

No.	LINEBACKERS	Ht./Wt.	Born	NFL Exp.	College	How acq.	'96 Games GP/GS
58	Bush, Lewis	6-2/245	12-2-69	4	Washington State	D4b/93	16/16
51	Cummings, Joe	6-3/240	6-8-72	2	Wyoming	FA/96	3/0
54	Gouveia, Kurt	6-1/240	9-14-64	12	Brigham Young	FA/96	16/16
92	Griggs, David	6-3/250	2-5-67	7	Virginia	FA/94	0/0
53	Hamilton, Michael	6-2/243	12-3-73	R	North Carolina A&T	D3/97	—
59	James, Toran	6-4/247	3-8-74	R	North Carolina A&T	D7/97	—
56	Sapp, Patrick	6-4/258	5-11-73	2	Clemson	D2b/96	16/0
55	Seau, Junior	6-3/250	1-19-69	8	Southern California	D1/90	15/15

No.	DEFENSIVE BACKS	Ht./Wt.	Born	NFL Exp.	College	How acq.	'96 Games GP/GS
25	Bradford, Paul	5-11/185	4-20-74	R	Portland State	D5b/97	—
44	Castle, Eric (S)	6-3/212	3-15-70	5	Oregon	D6/93	16/0
31	Clark, Willie (CB)	5-10/186	1-6-72	4	Notre Dame	D3b/94	16/4
28	Harper, Dwayne (CB)	5-11/175	3-29-66	10	South Carolina State	FA/94	6/6
37	Harrison, Rodney (S)	6-0/201	12-15-72	4	Western Illinois	D5b/94	16/16
38	Hendrix, David (S)	6-1/213	5-29-72	3	Georgia Tech	FA/95	14/0
40	Montreuil, Mark (CB)	6-2/200	12-29-71	3	Concordia (Canada)	D7/95	13/0
29	Shaw, Terrance (CB)	5-11/190	11-11-73	3	Stephen F. Austin State	D2a/95	16/16
47	Thomas, Johnny (CB)	5-9/191	8-3-64	9	Baylor	FA/97	*9/0

No.	SPECIALISTS	Ht./Wt.	Born	NFL Exp.	College	How acq.	'96 Games GP/GS
2	Bennett, Darren (P)	6-5/235	1-9-65	3	None	FA/94	16/0
3	Carney, John (K)	5-11/170	4-20-64	9	Notre Dame	FA/90	16/0

*Craver played 15 games for Broncos in '96; Fuller played 16 games for Eagles; Gardner played 13 games for Ravens; McKenzie played 16 games for Eagles; Metcalf played 16 games for Falcons; Thomas played 9 games for Eagles.

Abbreviations: D1—draft pick, first round; SupD2—supplemental draft pick second round; W-Den—waivers acquisition from Denver; T-Sea—trade acquisition from Seattle; PlanB—Plan B free-agent acquisition; FA—free-agent acquisition (other than Plan B).

MISCELLANEOUS TEAM DATA

Stadium (capacity, surface):
Qualcomm Stadium, Jack Murphy Field
(71,000, grass)
Business address:
P.O. Box 609609
San Diego, CA 92160-9609
Business phone:
619-874-4500
Ticket information:
619-280-2121
Team colors:
Navy blue, white and gold
Flagship radio station:
XTRA, 690 AM
Training site:
UC San Diego
La Jolla, Calif.
619-874-4500

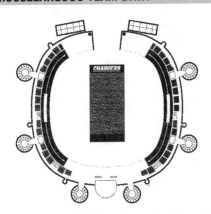

TSN REPORT CARD

Coaching staff — C
Kevin Gilbride, an offensive genius as an assistant coach, gets his first chance as an NFL head coach. He'll be hard-pressed to match the Chargers' last rookie coach, Bobby Ross, who won the AFC West title in his debut. Gilbride appears to be a hit with the players, and he was smart to select two veterans to lead his staff—Nick Nicolau as assistant head coach and Joe Pascale as defensive coordinator.

Offensive backfield — C -
This unit is a mystery. There is some potential here with Gary Brown and Aaron Hayden. But Brown was out of work last year and Hayden was out of sync. Eric Metcalf can't be expected to help much here; Terrell Fletcher will continue to contribute, although he is far from an every-down back. Sixth-round pick Kenny Bynum from South Carolina State has awesome speed, but making the jump from Division I-AA to the NFL will be the ultimate challenge.

Receivers — B
The M & M men should make the passing game exciting to watch. Tony Martin, the team's MVP in '96, has earned his stripes and Metcalf gives defenses fits when he's cradling the ball in the open field. If Charlie Jones can build on his productive rookie year and Bryan Still snaps from his rookie funk, the receivers will be a secondary's nightmare.

Offensive line — C -
This unit has been completely overhauled. Starting guard Eric Moten and center Courtney Hall were waived; they're replaced by Troy Sienkiewicz and Raleigh McKenzie. The tackles will switch sides, with Tony Berti moving to left tackle and Vaughn Parker to the right. The Chargers like Ike Davis at the other guard, but he has to be more consistent.

Defensive line — B
In with the old, out with the fairly new. The Chargers brought in veteran William Fuller and gave Chris Mims the boot. That's a huge upgrade. Fuller, even at 35, remains a force. Mims' work ethic and pride were non-existent. Marco Coleman hopes opposing lines will be so worried about Fuller, he'll shine. Coleman's six sacks hardly made the Chargers' brass do backflips, but he is steady. In the middle, the Chargers resigned Reuben Davis (wise-move) and kept Shawn Lee (questionable).

Linebackers — B -
With All-Pro Junior Seau, some wonder why this unit doesn't get an automatic A. There's no denying Seau is one of the NFL's best, but his supporting staff isn't that special. MLB Kurt Gouveia is on the downside of his career and Lew Bush is adequate, although improving.

Secondary — B -
If CB Dwayne Harper can stay healthy—he couldn't last year—the defensive backfield is a team strength. Opposite Harper—the team's best cover man—is Terrance Shaw. The third-year pro rebounded from a shaky rookie year last season and made his mark with his aggressive style. SS Rodney Harrison has corralled his undisciplined play and isn't far from a Pro Bowl invitation. The biggest question mark is at free safety, where injury-prone veteran Mike Dumas will likely start.

Special teams — A
The addition of the shifty Metcalf to return punts solidifies an impressive special teams unit. The kicking combination of John Carney and Darren Bennett is one of the NFL's best. Carney is the league's fourth-most accurate kicker of all-time; Bennett has set team marks in punting in each of the last two years and Andre Coleman complements Metcalf on kick returns.

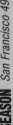

SAN FRANCISCO 49ERS
NFC WESTERN DIVISION

1996 REVIEW

RESULTS

Sept. 1—NEW ORLEANS	W	27-11
Sept. 8—ST. LOUIS	W	34-0
Sept.15—Open date		
Sept.22—at Carolina	L	7-23
Sept.29—ATLANTA	W	39-17
Oct. 6—at St. Louis	W	28-11
Oct. 14—at Green Bay (OT)	L	20-23
Oct. 20—CINCINNATI	W	28-21
Oct. 27—at Houston	W	10-9
Nov. 3—at New Orleans	W	24-17
Nov. 10—DALLAS (OT)	L	17-20
Nov. 17—BALTIMORE	W	38-20
Nov. 24—at Washington (OT)	W	19-16
Dec. 2—at Atlanta	W	34-10
Dec. 8—CAROLINA	L	24-30
Dec. 15—at Pittsburgh	W	25-15
Dec. 23—DETROIT	W	24-14
Dec. 29—PHILADELPHIA*	W	14-0
Jan. 4—at Green Bay†	L	14-35

*NFC wild-card game.
†NFC divisional playoff game.

RECORDS/RANKINGS

1996 regular-season record: 12-4 (2nd in NFC West); 6-2 in division; 8-4 in conference; 6-2 at home; 6-2 on road.
Team record last five years: 60-20 (.750), ranks 1st in league in that span).

1996 team rankings:

	No.	NFC	NFL
Total offense	*344.1	3	6
Rushing offense	*115.4	3	10
Passing offense	*228.7	4	7
Scoring offense	398	2	3
Total defense	*291.3	4	7
Rushing defense	*93.6	2	5
Passing defense	*197.8	7	11
Scoring defense	257	4	T4
Takeaways	34	6	T10
Giveaways	24	T2	T2
Turnover differential	10	4	6
Sacks	45	2	5
Sacks allowed	42	T11	T21

*Yards per game.

TEAM LEADERS

Scoring (kicking): Jeff Wilkins, 130 pts. (40/40 PATs, 30/34 FGs).
Scoring (touchdowns): Jerry Rice, 54 pts. (1 rushing, 8 receiving).
Passing: Steve Young, 2,410 yds. (316 att., 214 comp., 67.7%, 14 TDs, 6 int.).
Rushing: Terry Kirby, 559 yds. (134 att., 4.2 avg., 3 TDs).
Receptions: Jerry Rice, 108 (1,254 yds., 11.6 avg., 8 TDs).
Interceptions: Marquez Pope, 6 (98 yds., 1 TD).
Sacks: Roy Barker, 12.5.
Punting: Tommy Thompson, 44.1 avg. (73 punts, 3,217 yds., 2 blocked).
Punt returns: Dexter Carter, 8.8 avg. (36 att., 317 yds., 0 TDs).
Kickoff returns: Dexter Carter, 22.2 avg. (41 att., 909 yds., 0 TDs).

1997 SEASON

CLUB DIRECTORY

Owner
Edward J. DeBartolo Jr.
President
Carmen Policy
V.P./director of football operations
Dwight Clark
V.P./business operations and CFO
Bill Duffy
Director of player personnel
Vinny Cerrato
Ticket manager
Lynn Carrozzi
Pro personnel/AFC
George Streeter
Pro personnel/NFC
Joe Collins
Controller
Melrene Frear
Director of public/community relations
Rodney Knox
Manager of media relations
Kirk Reynolds
Public relations assistants
Darla Maeda
Kimberly McIntyre
Pro personnel administration
Joe Collins
George Streeter
Scouts
Jim Abrams
John Brunner
Mike Faulkiner
Brian Gardner
Jim Gruden
Oscar Lofton
Head trainer
Lindsy McLean
Assistant trainers
Jasen Powell
Ray Tufts
Physicians
Michael Dillingham, M.D.
James B. Klint, M.D.

Head coach
Steve Mariucci

Assistant coaches
Jerry Attaway (physical development coordinator)
Mike Barnes (strength development coordinator)
Dwaine Board (defensive line)
Jaime Hill (def. quality control)
Larry Kirksey (wide receivers)
Johnny Lynn (defensive backs)
Greg Knapp (offensive quality control)
John Marshall (defensive coordinator)
Bobb McKittrick (offensive line)
Bill McPherson (defensive assistant)
Jim Mora Jr. (defensive backs)
Marty Mornhinweg (offensive coordinator/quarterbacks)
Patrick Morris (tight ends)
Tom Rathman (running backs)
Richard Smith (linebackers)
George Stewart (special teams coordinator)

Stadium operations director
Mo Fowell
Equipment manager
Bronco Hinek
Equipment assistants
Jason Fery
Tony Fery
Director/video operations
Robert Yanagi

SCHEDULE

Aug. 31— at Tampa Bay	4:00
Sept. 7— at St. Louis	12:00
Sept. 14— NEW ORLEANS	1:00
Sept. 21— ATLANTA	1:00
Sept. 29— at Carolina (Mon.)	9:00
Oct. 5— Open date	
Oct. 12— ST. LOUIS	1:00
Oct. 19— at Atlanta	1:00
Oct. 26— at New Orleans	12:00
Nov. 2— DALLAS	1:00
Nov. 10— at Philadelphia (Mon.)	9:00
Nov. 16— CAROLINA	1:00
Nov. 23— SAN DIEGO	1:00
Nov. 30— at Kansas City	12:00
Dec. 7— MINNESOTA	1:00
Dec. 15— DENVER (Mon.)	6:00
Dec. 21— at Seattle	5:00

All times are for home team.
All games Sunday unless noted.

DRAFT CHOICES

Jim Druckenmiller, QB, Virginia Tech (first round/26th pick overall).
Marc Edwards, FB, Notre Dame (2/55).
Greg Clark, TE, Stanford (3/77).

San Francisco 49ers

1997 SEASON

No.	QUARTERBACKS	Ht./Wt.	Born	NFL Exp.	College	How acq.	'96 Games GP/GS
	Barr, Dave	6-3/210	5-9-72	1	California	D4/94	0/0
11	Brohm, Jeff	6-1/205	4-24-71	2	Louisville	FA/96	3/0
14	Druckenmiller, Jim	6-4/234	9-19-72	R	Virginia Tech	D1/97	—
8	Young, Steve	6-2/205	10-11-61	13	Brigham Young	T-TB/87	12/12
	RUNNING BACKS						
44	Edwards, Marc (FB)	6-0/236	11-17-74	R	Notre Dame	D2/97	—
40	Floyd, William (FB)	6-1/242	2-17-72	4	Florida State	D1b/94	9/8
20	Hearst, Garrison	5-11/215	1-4-71	5	Georgia	FA/97	*16/12
41	Kirby, Terry	6-1/223	1-20-70	5	Virginia	T-Mia/96	14/10
	RECEIVERS						
88	Clark, Greg (TE)	6-4/262	4-7-72	R	Stanford	D3/97	—
86	Cooper, Adrian (TE)	6-5/255	4-27-68	7	Oklahoma	FA/96	6/0
43	Fann, Chad (TE)	6-3/250	6-7-70	5	Florida A&M	FA/97	0/0
19	Harris, Mark	6-4/197	4-28-70	1	Stanford	FA/97	0/0
84	Jones, Brent (TE)	6-4/230	2-12-63	12	Santa Clara	FA/87	11/10
32	Levy, Chuck (KR)	6-0/197	1-7-72	3	Arizona	FA/96	0/0
82	Manuel, Sean (TE)	6-2/245	12-1-73	2	New Mexico State	D7a/96	11/0
81	Owens, Terrell	6-3/213	12-7-73	2	Tennessee-Chattanooga	D3/96	16/10
80	Rice, Jerry	6-2/200	10-13-62	13	Mississippi Valley State	D1/85	16/16
83	Stokes, J.J.	6-4/217	10-6-72	3	UCLA	D1/95	6/6
89	Uwaezuoke, Iheanyi	6-2/195	7-24-73	2	California	D5/96	14/0
	OFFENSIVE LINEMEN						
79	Barton, Harris (T)	6-4/286	4-19-64	11	North Carolina	D1/87	13/13
65	Brown, Ray (G)	6-5/315	12-12-62	12	Arkansas State	FA/96	16/16
67	Dalman, Chris (G/C)	6-3/285	3-15-70	5	Stanford	D6/93	16/16
63	Deese, Derrick (G)	6-3/275	5-17-70	6	Southern California	FA/92	16/0
66	Gogan, Kevin (G/T)	6-7/325	11-2-64	11	Washington	FA/97	*16/16
59	Gordon, Steve (C)	6-3/288	4-15-69	1	California	FA/95	0/0
77	Hanshaw, Tim (G)	6-5/300	4-27-70	3	Brigham Young	D4/95	0/0
69	Milstead, Rod (G)	6-2/290	11-10-69	6	Delaware State	FA/94	11/0
75	Pollack, Frank (G/T)	6-5/285	11-5-67	6	Northern Arizona	FA/94	16/2
60	Rudolph, Joe (G)	6-2/290	7-21-72	2	Wisconsin	FA/97	0/0
76	Scrafford, Kirk (T)	6-6/275	3-15-67	8	Montana	FA/95	7/1
93	Swinson, Corey (T)	6-5/355	12-15-69	1	Hampton (Va.) Institute	FA/97	0/0
	DEFENSIVE LINEMEN						
92	Barker, Roy (E)	6-5/290	2-14-69	6	North Carolina	FA/96	16/16
78	Brandon, Michael (E)	6-4/290	7-30-68	4	Florida	FA/95	4/0
90	Bryant, Junior (E)	6-4/275	1-16-71	3	Notre Dame	FA/93	16/1
95	Coleman, Herb (E)	6-4/285	9-4-71	1	Trinity College (Ill.)	FA/97	0/0
56	Doleman, Chris (E)	6-5/275	10-16-61	13	Pittsburgh	FA/96	16/16
64	Ifeanyi, Israel (E)	6-3/246	11-21-70	2	Southern California	D2/96	3/0
91	Price, Daryl (E)	6-3/274	10-23-72	2	Colorado	D4/96	14/0
94	Stubblefield, Dana (T)	6-2/290	11-14-70	4	Kansas	D1a/93	15/15
97	Young, Bryant (T)	6-0/280	1-27-72	4	Notre Dame	D1/94	16/16
	LINEBACKERS						
57	Kirk, Randy	6-2/231	12-27-64	10	San Diego State	FA/96	16/0
59	Manuel, Sam	6-2/235	12-1-73	1	New Mexico State	D7b/96	0/0
55	Mitchell, Kevin	6-1/250	1-1-71	4	Syracuse	D2a/94	12/3
51	Norton, Ken	6-2/241	9-29-66	10	UCLA	FA/94	16/16
50	Plummer, Gary	6-2/247	1-26-60	12	California	FA/94	13/11
58	Sander, Mark	6-3/238	3-21-68	3	Louisville	FA/96	0/0
52	Schwantz, Jim	6-2/240	1-23-70	4	Purdue	FA/97	*16/0
54	Woodall, Lee	6-0/220	10-31-69	4	West Chester (Pa.)	D6/94	16/13
	DEFENSIVE BACKS						
28	Buckley, Curtis (S)	6-1/191	9-25-70	5	East Texas State	FA/96	15/0
29	Covington, John	6-0/206	4-22-72	2	Notre Dame	FA/97	0/0
25	Dowden, Corey	5-11/190	10-18-68	2	Tulane	FA/97	*12/0
22	Drakeford, Tyronne (CB)	5-9/185	6-21-71	4	Virginia Tech	D2b/94	16/16
36	Hanks, Merton (S)	6-2/185	3-12-68	7	Iowa	D5/91	16/16
46	McDonald, Tim (S)	6-2/215	1-6-65	11	Southern California	FA/93	16/16
23	Pope, Marquez (S/CB)	5-11/193	10-29-70	6	Fresno State	FA/95	16/16
27	Smith, Frankie (CB)	5-9/182	10-8-68	5	Baylor	FA/96	14/0

No.	DEFENSIVE BACKS	Ht./Wt.	Born	NFL Exp.	College	How acq.	'96 Games GP/GS
38	Walker, Darnell (CB)	5-8/168	1-17-70	5	Oklahoma	FA/97	*15/9
45	Williams, Michael	5-10/193	5-28-70	1	UCLA	FA/95	0/0
	SPECIALISTS						
7	Baker, Jon (K)	6-1/170	8-13-72	1	Arizona State	FA/96	0/0
3	Thompson, Tommy (P)	5-10/192	4-27-72	3	Oregon	FA/94	16/0

*Dowden played 9 games with Packers and 3 games with Ravens in '96; Gogan played 16 games with Raiders; Hearst played 16 games with Bengals; Schwantz played 16 games with Cowboys; Walker played 15 games with Falcons.

Abbreviations: D1—draft pick, first round; SupD2—supplemental draft pick second round; W-Den—waivers acquisition from Denver; T-Sea—trade acquisition from Seattle; PlanB—Plan B free-agent acquisition; FA—free-agent acquisition (other than Plan B).

MISCELLANEOUS TEAM DATA

Stadium (capacity, surface):
3Com Park at Candlestick Point
(70,270, grass)
Business address:
4949 Centennial Blvd.
Santa Clara, CA 95054-1229
Business phone:
408-562-4949
Ticket information:
415-468-2249
Team colors:
Forty Niners gold and cardinal
Flagship radio station:
KGO, 810 AM
Training site:
Sierra Community College
Rocklin, Calif.
916-624-8241

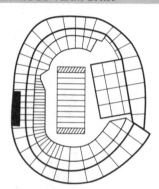

TSN REPORT CARD

Coaching staff	C	While prized veteran coaches such as offensive line mentor Bobb McKittrick and defensive line coach Dwaine Board remain from George Seifert's staff, the club has major question marks surrounding head man Steve Mariucci, new offensive coordinator Marty Mornhinweg and new defensive coordinator John Marshall. The jury is definitely out.
Offensive backfield	B	Steve Young is an "A", but must remain healthy. If he doesn't, backup Jeff Brohm and rookie Jim Druckenmiller have virtually no experience between them. The halfbacks are strong, with a Garrison Hearst-Terry Kirby combination filling both running and pass-catching needs. If fullback William Floyd gets back to his promised 1994 condition, he's one of the best around.
Receivers	A -	Any group with Jerry Rice probably deserves an A plus, but the 49ers must coax big years out of second-year man Terrell Owens, who had a promising rookie season, and out of J.J. Stokes, who has been injured in each of his first two seasons. Tight end Brent Jones shows no signs of slowing at age 34.
Offensive line	C -	The team is dangerously thin at tackle, where 33-year-old Harris Barton is new at left tackle and Kirk Scrafford is coming off a foot injury. Beyond Scrafford and Barton, depth is an issue at that position. The guards are big and beefy—Ray Brown and Kevin Gogan go over 320 pounds—but must show they can get out on the sweep.
Defensive line	A -	The tackles, Dana Stubblefield and Bryant Young, might be the best tandem in the game. Young has turned into one of the NFL's most fearsome wrecking balls in the middle. The ends are consistent, too: Chris Doleman and Roy Barker play through injuries and produce ($23\frac{1}{2}$ combined sacks a year ago). Like the offensive line, depth is a concern.
Linebackers	B	Fourth-year man Kevin Mitchell slides into the starting lineup to replace 37-year-old Gary Plummer. Mitchell has impressed coaches with his tackling and athletic ability. Ken Norton and Lee Woodall fill out the other two slots and are proven Pro Bowlers. A solid group.
Secondary	B -	Free safety Merton Hanks must climb his way back into the big play realm he occupied in 1994 and 1995. Strong safety Tim McDonald must prove he's not getting too old to help out in pass defense. Left cornerback Tyronne Drakeford must silence critics again after an uneven first year starting. Right corner Marquez Pope, meanwhile, must continue his surprisingly physical and effective play.
Special teams	D +	The grade is no knock on special teams coach George Stewart, who did a good job last year. But losing kicker Jeff Wilkins to free agency was a big mistake. A proven, tough field goal kicker must be found for what should be several close games in an evening NFC West. Punter Tommy Thompson is solid, but coverage units must rally behind Pro Bowl free agent Jim Schwantz.

SEATTLE SEAHAWKS
AFC WESTERN DIVISION

1996 REVIEW
RESULTS

Sept. 1—at San Diego	L	7-29
Sept. 8—DENVER	L	20-30
Sept.15—KANSAS CITY	L	17-35
Sept.22—at Tampa Bay	W	17-13
Sept.29—GREEN BAY	L	10-31
Oct. 6—at Miami	W	22-15
Oct. 13—Open date		
Oct. 17—at Kansas City	L	16-34
Oct. 27—SAN DIEGO	W	32-13
Nov. 3—HOUSTON	W	23-16
Nov. 10—MINNESOTA	W	42-23
Nov. 17—at Detroit	L	16-17
Nov. 24—OAKLAND	L	21-27
Dec. 1—at Denver	L	7-34
Dec. 8—BUFFALO	W	26-18
Dec. 15—at Jacksonville	L	13-20
Dec. 22—at Oakland	W	28-21

RECORDS/RANKINGS

1996 regular-season record: 7-9 (T4th in AFC West); 2-6 in division; 5-7 in conference; 4-4 at home; 3-5 on road.
Team record last five years: 29-51 (.363, ranks T23rd in league in that span).
1996 team rankings:

	No.	AFC	NFL
Total offense	*314	12	19
Rushing offense	*124.8	5	5
Passing offense	*189.2	13	24
Scoring offense	317	T11	T16
Total defense	*339.8	12	24
Rushing defense	*131.1	14	28
Passing defense	*208.7	7	17
Scoring defense	376	T12	T24
Takeaways	32	T6	T13
Giveaways	29	6	T12
Turnover differential	3	T6	T11
Sacks	48	T2	T3
Sacks allowed	38	T8	T16

*Yards per game.

TEAM LEADERS

Scoring (kicking): Todd Peterson, 111 pts. (27/27 PATs, 28/34 FGs).
Scoring (touchdowns): Lamar Smith, 54 pts. (8 rushing, 3 2-pt. conv.).
Passing: John Friesz, 1,629 yds. (211 att., 120 comp., 56.9%, 8 TDs, 4 int.).
Rushing: Chris Warren, 855 yds. (203 att., 4.2 avg., 5 TDs).
Receptions: Joey Galloway, 57 (987 yds., 17.3 avg., 7 TDs).
Interceptions: Darryl Williams, 5 (148 yds., 1 TD).
Sacks: Michael McCrary, 13.5.
Punting: Rick Tuten, 44.1 avg. (85 punts, 3,746 yds., 1 blocked).
Punt returns: Ronnie Harris, 10.2 avg. (19 att., 194 yds., 0 TDs).
Kickoff returns: Steve Broussard, 22.8 avg. (43 att., 979 yds., 0 TDs).

1997 SEASON
CLUB DIRECTORY

Owner
Ken Behring
President
David Behring
Executive vice president
Mickey Loomis
Vice president/football operations
Randy Mueller
V.P./public relations/administration
Gary Wright
Public relations director
Dave Neubert
Community services director
Sandy Gregory
Player programs director
Reggie McKenzie
Administrative assistant
Charlotte Kores
Co-player personnel directors
Mike Allman
Phil Neri
Assistant player personnel director
Rick Thompson
Eastern supervisor
Pat Mondock
Scouts
Warren Harper
Derrick Jensen
Doug Kretz
Dave Nusz
Ticket director
James Nagaoka
Head trainer
Jim Whitesel
Assistant trainer
Todd Sperber
Physicians
Kevin Auld
Pierce Scranton
James Trombold

Head coach
Dennis Erickson

Assistant coaches
Dave Arnold (special teams)
Tommy Brasher (defensive line)
Bob Bratkowski (offensive coordinator/wide receivers)
Dave Brown (defensive coach)
Keith Gilbertson (tight ends)
Ned James (defensive assistant)
Darren Krein (assistant strength & conditioning)
Dana LeDuc (strength & conditioning)
Greg McMackin (defensive coordinator)
Howard Mudd (offensive line)
Mike Murphy (linebackers)
Rich Olson (quarterbacks)
Willy Robinson (defensive backs)
Clarence Shelmon (running backs)
Gregg Smith (assistant head coach/offensive line)

Equipment manager
Terry Sinclair
Assistant equipment manager
Howard Baus
Video director
Thom Fermstad
Assistant video director
Craig Givens

SCHEDULE

Aug. 31— N.Y. JETS	1:00
Sept. 7— DENVER	1:00
Sept. 14— at Indianapolis	3:00
Sept. 21— SAN DIEGO	1:00
Sept. 28— at Kansas City	3:00
Oct. 5— TENNESSEE	1:00
Oct. 12— Open date	
Oct. 19— at St. Louis	12:00
Oct. 26— OAKLAND	1:00
Nov. 2— at Denver	2:00
Nov. 9— at San Diego	1:00
Nov. 16— at New Orleans	12:00
Nov. 23— KANSAS CITY	1:00
Nov. 30— ATLANTA	1:00
Dec. 7— at Baltimore	1:00
Dec. 14— at Oakland	1:00
Dec. 21— SAN FRANCISCO	5:00

All times are for home team.
All games Sunday unless noted.

DRAFT CHOICES

Shawn Springs, CB, Ohio State (first round/third pick overall).
Walter Jones, T, Florida State (1/6).
Eric Stokes, DB, Nebraska (5/142).
Itula Mili, TE, Brigham Young (6/174).
Carlos Jones, DB, Miami, Fla. (7/211).

– 83 –

TRAINING CAMP ROSTER

Seattle Seahawks

1997 SEASON

No.	QUARTERBACKS	Ht./Wt.	Born	NFL Exp.	College	How acq.	'96 Games GP/GS
17	Friesz, John	6-4/219	5-19-67	8	Idaho	FA/95	8/6
1	Moon, Warren	6-3/213	11-18-56	14	Washington	FA/97	*8/8
13	Torretta, Gino	6-3/215	8-10-70	4	Miami (Fla.)	FA/94	1/0
	RUNNING BACKS						
31	Broussard, Steve	5-7/201	2-22-67	8	Washington State	FA/95	12/0
34	Brown, Reggie (FB)	6-0/244	6-26-73	2	Fresno State	D3b/96	7/0
32	Gray, Oscar (FB)	6-1/255	8-7-72	2	Arkansas		9/0
28	Innocent, Dou	5-11/212	7-9-72	2	Mississippi	FA/96	4/0
25	Smith, Lamar	5-11/218	11-29-70	4	Houston	D3/94	16/2
38	Strong, Mack (FB)	6-0/235	9-11-71	4	Georgia	FA/93	14/8
42	Warren, Chris	6-2/228	1-24-68	8	Ferrum (Va.)	D4/90	14/14
	RECEIVERS						
89	Blades, Brian	5-11/190	7-24-65	10	Miami (Fla.)	D2/88	11/9
87	Crumpler, Carlester (TE)	6-6/260	9-5-71	4	East Carolina	D7/94	16/7
86	Fauria, Christian (TE)	6-4/245	9-22-71	3	Colorado	D2/95	10/9
84	Galloway, Joey	5-11/188	11-20-71	3	Ohio State	D1/95	16/16
88	Goines, Eddie	6-0/186	8-16-72	3	North Carolina State	D6b/95	0/0
81	Harris, Ronnie	5-11/179	6-4-70	4	Oregon	FA/94	15/0
88	May, Deems (TE)	6-4/263	3-6-69	5	North Carolina	D7/92	*16/12
82	McKnight, James	6-/194	6-17-72	3	Liberty (Va.)	FA/94	16/0
49	Mili, Itula (TE)	6-4/265	4-2-73	R	Brigham Young	D6/97	—
85	Pritchard, Mike	5-10/193	10-26-69	7	Colorado	FA/96	16/5
83	Williams, Ronnie (TE)	6-3/258	1-19-66	6	Oklahoma State	FA/96	14/3
	OFFENSIVE LINEMEN						
74	Atkins, James (G)	6-6/306	1-28-70	4	Southwestern Louisiana	FA/93	16/16
75	Ballard, Howard (T)	6-6/325	11-3-63	10	Alabama A&M	FA/94	16/16
64	Barr, Robert (T)	6-4/316	6-7-73	2	Rutgers	D3a/96	0/0
63	Beede, Frank (G)	6-4/296	5-1-73	2	Panhandle State	FA/96	14/2
77	Graham, Derrick (G)	6-4/315	3-18-67	8	Appalachian State	FA/96	16/16
68	Greene, Andrew (G)	6-3/304	9-24-69	2	Indiana	FA/97	0/0
71	Jones, Walter (T)	6-5/300	1-19-74	R	Florida State	D1b/97	—
66	Kendall, Pete (G)	6-5/292	7-9-73	2	Boston College	D1/96	12/11
52	Mawae, Kevin (C)	6-4/296	1-23-71	4	Louisiana State	D2/94	16/16
69	Williams, Grant (T)	6-7/323	5-10-74	2	Louisiana Tech	FA/96	8/0
	DEFENSIVE LINEMEN						
98	Adams, Sam (T)	6-3/297	6-13-73	4	Texas A&M	D1/94	16/15
91	Bryant, Keif (E)	6-4/287	3-12-73	2	Rutgers	D7/95	0/0
93	Daniels, Phillip (E)	6-5/263	3-4-73	2	Georgia	D4a/96	15/0
94	Edwards, Antonio (E)	6-3/271	3-10-70	5	Valdosta (Ga.) State	D8b/93	12/3
	Harrison, Martin (E)	6-5/251	9-20-67	6	Washington	FA/97	*16/8
96	Kennedy, Cortez (T)	6-3/306	8-23-68	8	Miami, Fla.	D1/90	16/16
67	LaBounty, Matt (E)	6-4/278	1-3-69	5	Oregon	T-GB/96	3/0
92	McMillian, Henry (T)	6-3/290	10-17-71	3	Florida	D6/95	3/0
78	Riley, Patrick (E)	6-5/290	3-8-72	2	Miami (Fla.)	FA/96	0/0
70	Sinclair, Michael (E)	6-4/267	1-31-68	7	Eastern New Mexico	D6/91	16/16
	LINEBACKERS						
54	Barber, Michael	6-1/246	11-9-71	3	Auburn	FA/95	13/7
99	Brown, Chad	6-2/240	7-12-70	5	Colorado	FA/97	*14/14
59	Cain, Joe	6-1/239	6-11-65	8	Oregon Tech	FA/93	*16/15
57	Kyle, Jason	6-3/242	5-12-72	3	Arizona State	D4b/95	16/0
56	Logan, James	6-2/225	12-6-72	3	Memphis	W-Cin/95	6/0
55	Moss, Winston	6-3/245	12-24-65	11	Miami (Fla.)	FA/95	16/16
53	Unverzagt, Eric	6-1/241	12-18-72	2	Wisconsin	D4c/96	8/0
95	Wells, Dean	6-3/248	7-20-70	5	Kentucky	D4/93	16/15
	DEFENSIVE BACKS						
20	Bellamy, Jay (S)	5-11/199	7-8-72	4	Rutgers	FA/94	16/0
36	Blades, Bennie (S)	6-1/221	9-3-66	10	Miami (Fla.)	FA/97	*15/15
21	Cunningham, T.J. (S)	6-/197	10-24-72	2	Colorado	D6b/96	9/0
30	Jones, Carlos (CB)	5-10/180	8-31-73	R	Miami (Fla.)	D7/97	—
29	Richardson, C.J. (S)	5-10/209	6-10-72	4	Miami (Fla.)	FA/97	0/0
23	Seigler, Dexter (CB)	5-9/178	1-11-72	2	Miami (Fla.)	FA/95	12/0
26	Springs, Shawn (CB)	5-11/200	3-11-75	R	Ohio State	D1a/97	—

No.	DEFENSIVE BACKS	Ht./Wt.	Born	NFL Exp.	College	How acq.	'96 Games GP/GS
37	Stokes, Eric (S)	5-11/200	12-18-73	R	Nebraska	D5/97	—
22	Thomas, Fred (CB)	5-9/172	9-11-73	2	Tennessee-Martin	D2/96	15/0
33	Williams, Darryl (S)	6-0/202	1-7-70	6	Miami (Fla.)	FA/96	16/16
27	Williams, Willie (CB)	5-9/180	12-26-70	5	Western Carolina	FA/97	*15/14
	SPECIALISTS						
2	Peterson, Todd (K)	5-10/171	2-4-70	3	Georgia	FA/95	16/0
14	Tuten, Rick (P)	6-2/221	1-5-65	9	Florida State	FA/91	16/0

*Blades played 15 games with Lions in '96; C. Brown played 14 games with Steelers; Cain played 16 games with Bears; Harrison played 16 games with Redskins; May played 16 games with Chargers; Moon played 8 games with Vikings; W. Williams played 15 games with Steelers.

Abbreviations: D1—draft pick, first round; SupD2—supplemental draft pick second round; W-Den—waivers acquisition from Denver; T-Sea—trade acquisition from Seattle; PlanB—Plan B free-agent acquisition; FA—free-agent acquisition (other than Plan B).

MISCELLANEOUS TEAM DATA

Stadium (capacity, surface):
Kingdome (66,400, artificial)
Business address:
11220 N.E. 53rd Street
Kirkland, WA 98033
Business phone:
206-827-9777
Ticket information:
206-827-9766
Team colors:
Blue, green and silver
Flagship radio station:
KIRO, 710 AM
Training site:
Eastern Washington University
Cheney, Wash.
206-827-9777

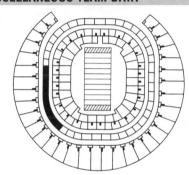

TSN REPORT CARD

Coaching staff — B
Dennis Erickson guided the Seahawks through two of the toughest years in franchise history. With the threat of a franchise move behind him, Erickson can make his third year a charm thanks to the backing of billionaire Paul Allen.

Offensive backfield — A
The Seahawks have the best one-two halfback punch in the NFL in Chris Warren and Lamar Smith. Because of their unselfish approach to the position, the Seahawks plan on being in the top five of rushing statistics even if Warren doesn't get enough carries to take him back to the Pro Bowl.

Receivers — B +
Last year, the Seahawks had too many slot receivers and not enough outside threats. The Seahawks shuffled the unit a bit by moving speedy Joey Galloway to flanker for big plays and letting Mike Pritchard and Brian Blades work their way to open short routes.

Offensive line — B -
They are young, talented and feisty. Potentially, Walter Jones is the most talented lineman this franchise has ever had. Left guard Pete Kendall and Kevin Mawae are fighters who don't back down to anyone. Balancing everything else out is Howard Ballard's experience at right tackle, which makes James Atkins' transition to right guard so easy.

Defensive line — A -
On passing downs, the Seahawks line up four players — Chad Brown, Cortez Kennedy, Sam Adams and Michael Sinclair — who can each have 10-sack seasons. The key to the unit is how well Antonio Edwards and Phillip Daniels handle the running plays.

Linebackers — B
The Seahawks will look to $24 million linebacker Chad Brown for sacks and interceptions but the key to the unit is keeping Winston Moss and Dean Wells healthy. This trio has great speed in chasing down just about any type of play.

Secondary — A -
This is the most overhauled unit on the team with at least five new players. It should be better. The trio of Shawn Springs, Willie Williams and Fred Thomas is the fastest in the division, which is necessary because of the number of speedy receivers in the AFC West. Safeties Bennie Blades and Darryl Williams will provide leadership and smarts.

Special teams — C -
The concern is the coverage teams. The Seahawks allowed too many big plays on kickoff and punt returns even though they have Pro Bowl talent in safety Jay Bellamy, kicker Todd Peterson and punter Rick Tuten.

TAMPA BAY BUCCANEERS
NFC CENTRAL DIVISION

1996 REVIEW
RESULTS

Sept. 1—GREEN BAY	L	3-34
Sept. 8—at Detroit	L	6-21
Sept.15—at Denver	L	23-27
Sept.22—SEATTLE	L	13-17
Sept.29—DETROIT	L	0-27
Oct. 6—Open date		
Oct. 13—MINNESOTA	W	24-13
Oct. 20—at Arizona	L	9-13
Oct. 27—at Green Bay	L	7-13
Nov. 3—at Chicago	L	10-13
Nov. 10—OAKLAND (OT)	W	20-17
Nov. 17—at San Diego	W	25-17
Nov. 24—NEW ORLEANS	W	13-7
Dec. 1—at Carolina	L	0-24
Dec. 8—WASHINGTON	W	24-10
Dec. 15—at Minnesota	L	10-21
Dec. 22—CHICAGO	W	34-19

RECORDS/RANKINGS

1996 regular-season record: 6-10 (4th in NFC Central); 2-6 in division; 4-8 in conference; 5-3 at home; 1-7 on road.
Team record last five years: 29-51 (.363, ranks T23rd in league in that span).

1996 team rankings:	No.	NFC	NFL
Total offense	*269.8	13	28
Rushing offense	*99.3	11	22
Passing offense	*170.4	14	29
Scoring offense	221	15	30
Total defense	*300.9	6	11
Rushing defense	*118.1	10	22
Passing defense	*182.8	4	4
Scoring defense	293	5	T8
Takeaways	29	10	17
Giveaways	34	T10	T23
Turnover differential	-5	T10	T21
Sacks	35	9	T15
Sacks allowed	30	5	T7

*Yards per game.

TEAM LEADERS

Scoring (kicking): Michael Husted, 93 pts. (18/19 PATs, 25/32 FGs).
Scoring (touchdowns): Mike Alstott, 36 pts. (3 rushing, 3 receiving).
Passing: Trent Dilfer, 2,859 yds. (482 att., 267 comp., 55.4%, 12 TDs, 19 int.).
Rushing: Errict Rhett, 539 yds. (176 att., 3.1 avg., 3 TDs).
Receptions: Mike Alstott, 65 (557 yds., 8.6 avg., 3 TDs).
Interceptions: Donnie Abraham, 5 (27 yds., 0 TDs).
Sacks: Warren Sapp, 9.0.
Punting: Tommy Barnhardt, 43.1 avg. (70 punts, 3,015 yds., 1 blocked).
Punt returns: Karl Williams, 21.1 avg. (13 att., 274 yds., 1 TD).
Kickoff returns: Nilo Silvan, 22.4 avg. (28 att., 626 yds., 0 TDs).

1997 SEASON
CLUB DIRECTORY

Owner
  Malcolm Glazer
Executive vice president
  Bryan Glazer
Executive vice president
  Joel Glazer
General manager
  Richard McKay
V.p., marketing and communications
  Rick McNerney
Vice president, sales administration
  Roni Costello
Communications managers
  Scott Smith
  Nelson Luis
Communications assistant
  Jenny Egger
Dir./corporate sales and broadcasting
  Jim Overton
Controller
  Patrick Smith
Director/sales and advertising
  Paul Sickmon
Assistant director/sales and advertising
  Jayne Portnoy
Assistant director/sales and fundraising
  Sherry Gruden
Director/player personnel
  Jerry Angelo
Director/college scouting
  Tim Ruskell
College personnel scouts
  Mike Ackerley
  Dave Boller
  Ruston Webster
  Mike Yowarsky
Pro personnel assistants
  Mark Dominik
  Dennis Hickey

Head coach
Tony Dungy

Assistant coaches
  Mark Asanovich (strength & conditioning)
  Clyde Christensen (tight ends)
  Herman Edwards (assistant head coach/defensive backs)
  Chris Foerster (offensive line)
  Monte Kiffin (def. coordinator)
  Joe Marciano (special teams)
  Rod Marinelli (defensive line)
  Tony Nathan (running backs)
  Kevin O'Dea (defensive assistant)
  Mike Shula (off. coordinator)
  Lovie Smith (linebackers)
  Ricky Thomas (offensive asst.)
  Charlie Williams (wide receivers)

Coordinator of football administration
  John Idzik
Trainer
  Todd Toriscelli
Assistant trainer
  Mark Shermansky
Team physicians
  Joseph Diaco
  William Carson
Equipment manager
  Darin Kerns
Video director
  Dave Levy
Assistant video director
  Pat Brazil

SCHEDULE

Aug. 31— SAN FRANCISCO	4:00
Sept. 7— at Detroit	1:00
Sept. 14— at Minnesota	12:00
Sept. 21— MIAMI	8:00
Sept. 28— ARIZONA	1:00
Oct. 5— at Green Bay	12:00
Oct. 12— DETROIT	1:00
Oct. 19— Open date	
Oct. 26— MINNESOTA	1:00
Nov. 2— at Indianapolis	1:00
Nov. 9— at Atlanta	1:00
Nov. 16— NEW ENGLAND	1:00
Nov. 23— at Chicago	12:00
Nov. 30— at N.Y. Giants	4:00
Dec. 7— GREEN BAY	1:00
Dec. 14— at N.Y. Jets	1:00
Dec. 21— CHICAGO	1:00

All times are for home team.
All games Sunday unless noted.

DRAFT CHOICES

Warrick Dunn, RB, Florida State (first round/12th pick overall).
Reidel Anthony, WR, Florida (1/16).
Jerry Wunsch, T, Wisconsin (2/37).
Frank Middleton, G, Arizona (3/63).
Ronde Barber, DB, Virginia (3/66).
Alshermond Singleton, LB, Temple (4/128).
Patrick Hape, TE, Alabama (5/137).
Al Harris, DB, Texas A&M-Kingsville (6/169).
Nigea Carter, WR, Michigan State (6/197).
Anthony DeGrate, DT, Stephen F. Austin (7/209).

TRAINING CAMP ROSTER

No.	QUARTERBACKS	Ht./Wt.	Born	NFL Exp.	College	How acq.	'96 Games GP/GS
2	Dilfer, Trent	6-4/235	3-13-72	4	Fresno State	D1/94	16/16
3	Milanovich, Scott (P)	6-3/212	1-25-73	1	Maryland	FA/96	1/0
4	Walsh, Steve	6-3/205	12-1-66	9	Miami (Fla.)	FA/97	*3/3
	RUNNING BACKS						
40	Alstott, Mike (FB)	6-1/244	12-21-73	2	Purdue	D2/96	16/16
31	Brooks, Reggie	5-8/211	1-19-71	5	Notre Dame	W-Was/96	11/4
28	Dunn, Warrick	5-8/176	1-5-75	R	Florida State	D1/97	—
37	Ellison, Jerry	5-10/204	12-20-71	3	UT-Chattanooga	FA/94	16/2
42	Rhett, Errict	5-11/211	12-11-70	4	Florida	D2/94	9/7
46	Ross, Dominique	6-0/203	1-12-72	1	Valdosta (Ga.) State	FA/97	*2/0
33	Staten, Robert (FB)	5-11/240	11-23-69	2	Jackson State	FA/96	6/0
36	Thompson, Leroy	5-11/216	2-3-68	5	Penn State	T-Pit/94	5/0
	RECEIVERS						
5	Anthony, Reidel	5-11/183	10-20-76	R	Florida	D1/97	—
8	Carter, Nigea	6-1/176	9-1-74	R	Michigan State	D6/97	—
88	Copeland, Horace	6-3/202	1-2-71	5	Miami (Fla.)	D4b/93	0/0
83	Greene, Tracy (TE)	6-5/270	11-5-72	3	Grambling State	FA/96	0/0
8	Hape, Patrick (TE)	6-4/253	6-6-74	R	Alabama	D5/97	—
80	Harper, Alvin	6-4/218	7-6-68	7	Tennessee	FA/95	12/7
81	Harris, Jackie (TE)	6-4/246	1-4-68	8	Northeast Louisiana	FA/94	13/12
2	Hunter, Brice	6-0/211	4-4-74	1	Georgia	FA/96	0/0
89	Marshall, Marvin (KR)	5-10/162	6-21-72	2	South Carolina State	FA/95	5/0
83	Moore, Dave (TE)	6-2/248	11-11-69	5	Pittsburgh	FA/92	16/8
87	Silvan, Nilo (KR)	5-9/184	10-2-73	2	Tennessee	D6/96	7/0
9	Spann, Gregory	6-0/215	4-16-73	1	Jackson State	FA/97	0/0
82	Tate, Willy (TE)	6-3/243	9-7-72	2	Oregon	FA/96	13/0
6	Thomas, Robb	5-11/175	3-29-66	9	Oregon State	FA/92	12/8
86	Williams, Karl	5-10/163	4-10-71	2	Texas A&M-Kingsville	FA/96	16/0
	OFFENSIVE LINEMEN						
1	Adams, Scott (T)	6-5/305	9-28-66	5	Georgia	FA/96	7/2
4	Diaz, Jorge (G)	6-4/295	11-15-73	2	Texas A&M-Kingsville	FA/96	11/6
5	Dogins, Kevin (C)	6-1/290	12-7-72	1	Texas A&M-Kingsville	FA/96	1/0
4	Gruber, Paul (T)	6-5/296	2-24-65	10	Wisconsin	D1/88	13/13
7	Ingram, Stephen (T/G)	6-4/320	5-8-71	3	Maryland	D7a/95	0/0
6	Love, Sean (G)	6-3/304	9-6-68	4	Penn State	FA/97	0/0
61	Mayberry, Tony (C)	6-4/292	12-8-67	8	Wake Forest	D4/90	16/16
3	Middleton, Frank (G)	6-3/324	10-25-74	R	Arizona	D3a/97	—
9	Miller, Jeff (T)	6-4/305	11-23-72	3	Mississippi	FA/96	0/0
70	Odom, Jason (T)	6-5/296	3-31-74	2	Florida	D4a/96	12/7
9	Pierson, Pete (T)	6-5/295	2-4-71	3	Washington	D5/94	11/2
0	Pyne, Jim (C)	6-2/290	11-23-71	4	Virginia Tech	D7/94	12/11
1	Wunsch, Jerry (T)	6-6/327	1-21-74	R	Wisconsin	D2/97	—
	DEFENSIVE LINEMEN						
2	Ahanotu, Chidi (E)	6-2/283	10-11-70	5	California	D6/93	13/13
7	Culpepper, Brad (T)	6-1/275	5-8-69	6	Florida	W-Min/94	13/13
5	Curry, Eric (E)	6-5/270	2-3-70	5	Alabama	D1/93	12/3
6	DeGrate, Anthony (T)	6-2/333	5-24-74	R	Stephen F. Austin	D7a/97	—
7	Jackson, Tyoka (E/T)	6-2/266	11-22-71	3	Penn State	FA/95	13/2
8	Jones, Marcus (E)	6-6/282	8-15-73	2	North Carolina	D1b/96	16/3
0	Maniecki, Jason (T)	6-4/295	8-15-72	2	Wisconsin	D5/96	5/0
5	McKenzie, Rich (E)	6-2/265	4-15-71	2	Penn State	FA/97	0/0
9	Sapp, Warren (T)	6-2/288	12-19-72	3	Miami (Fla.)	D1/95	15/14
1	Upshaw, Regan (E)	6-4/264	8-12-75	2	California	D1a/96	16/16
	LINEBACKERS						
5	Brooks, Derrick	6-0/231	4-18-73	3	Florida State	D1b/95	16/16
7	Jones, LaCurtis	6-0/200	6-23-72	2	Baylor	FA/96	10/0
4	Mason, Eddie	6-0/245	1-9-72	3	North Carolina	FA/97	0/0
6	Nickerson, Hardy	6-2/233	9-1-65	11	California	FA/93	16/16
9	Porter, Rufus	6-1/230	5-18-65	10	Southern (La.)	FA/97	*13/9
2	Rouse, Wardell	6-2/235	6-9-72	3	Clemson	D6/95	0/0
1	Singleton, Alshermond	6-2/224	8-7-75	R	Temple	D4/97	—
4	White, Steve	6-2/232	10-25-73	2	Tennessee	FA/96	4/0
8	Williams, Mark	6-4/240	5-17-71	3	Ohio State	FA/96	0/0
	DEFENSIVE BACKS						
1	Abraham, Donnie (CB)	5-10/181	10-8-73	2	East Tennessee State	D3/96	16/12
7	Austin, Eric (S)	5-11/217	6-7-73	2	Jackson State	D4b/96	2/0
0	Barber, Ronde (CB)	5-10/185	4-7-75	R	Virginia	D3b/97	—
3	Bouie, Tony (S)	5-10/193	8-7-72	3	Arizona	FA/95	16/0

No.	DEFENSIVE BACKS	Ht./Wt.	Born	NFL Exp.	College	How acq.	'96 Games GP/GS
39	Dimry, Charles (CB)	6-0/176	1-31-66	10	UNLV	FA/94	16/7
29	Gant, Kenneth (S)	5-11/203	4-18-67	8	Albany (Ga.) State	FA/95	16/0
24	Gayle, Rashid (CB)	5-9/185	4-16-74	1	Boise State	FA/96	*2/0
50	Gooch, Jeff (S)	5-11/218	10-31-74	2	Austin Peay State	FA/96	15/0
30	Harris, Al (CB)	6-0/178	12-7-74	R	Texas A&M-Kingsville	D6/97	—
25	Johnson, Melvin (S)	6-0/198	4-15-72	3	Kentucky	D2/95	16/16
45	Legette, Tyrone (CB)	5-9/177	2-15-70	6	Nebraska	FA/96	15/0
47	Lynch, John (S)	6-2/210	9-25-71	5	Stanford	D3b/93	16/14
22	Mincy, Charles (S)	5-11/198	12-16-69	7	Washington	FA/96	2/0
26	Rusk, Reggie (CB)	5-10/182	10-19-72	1	Kentucky	D7/96	1/0
38	Scott, Todd (S)	5-11/205	1-23-68	7	Southwestern Louisiana	W-NYJ/95	2/2
	SPECIALISTS						
6	Barnhardt, Tommy (P)	6-2/207	6-11-63	11	North Carolina	FA/96	16/0
5	Husted, Michael (K)	6-0/195	6-16-70	5	Virginia	FA/93	16/0
9	Nittmo, Bjorn (K)	5-11/179	7-26-66	2	Appalachian State	FA/97	0/0

*Gayle played 2 games with Jaguars in '96; Porter played 13 games with Saints; Ross played 2 games with Cowboys; Walsh played 3 games with Rams.

Abbreviations: D1—draft pick, first round; SupD2—supplemental draft pick second round; W-Den—waivers acquisition from Denver; T-Sea—trade acquisition from Seattle; PlanB—Plan B free-agent acquisition; FA—free-agent acquisition (other than Plan B).

MISCELLANEOUS TEAM DATA

Stadium (capacity, surface):
Houlihan's Stadium (74,301, grass)

Business address:
One Buccaneer Place
Tampa, FL 33607

Business phone:
813-870-2700

Ticket information:
813-879-2827

Team colors:
Buccaneer red, pewter, black and orange

Flagship radio station:
WQYK, 99.5 FM

Training site:
University of Tampa
Tampa, Fla.
813-253-6215

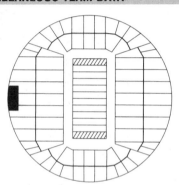

TSN REPORT CARD

Coaching staff	B +	Tony Dungy truly is a players' coach, as long as the player is his type of guy. Dungy has done a wonderful job of weeding out the bad apples from Sam Wyche's regime and he's left with a young roster that believe in his system. He showed remarkable patience last year and quietly assembled a very good defense. The heat will be on offensive coordinator Mike Shula and his players to match the defense's productivity.
Offensive backfield	B	Everything starts with QB Trent Dilfer, and he showed signs at the end of last year that he's finally comfortable with the NFL game. His job should get easier with Warrick Dunn in the backfield. The Bucs envision Dunn as a Dave Meggett-type back, but they plan to use him in more than third-down situations. Mike Alstott developed into one of the league's best FBs as a rookie and earned more carries. Errict Rhett's playing time will depend on how the slender Dunn holds up against NFL defenses.
Receivers	C	The team still is recovering from the damage done by free-agent flop Alvin Harper. His inability to be a go-to receiver hurt Dilfer's development. Horace Copeland returns from knee surgery and the Bucs are hoping he can fill the role Harper never could. Rookie Reidel Anthony will get the first shot at the other starting job.
Offensive line	C -	The left side is solid with T Paul Gruber and dependable G Jim Pyne. C Tony Mayberry is steady. After that, though, it gets pretty scary, unless a couple of rookies come through. T Jerry Wunsch and G Frank Middleton could end up as starters on the right side.
Defensive line	C +	DT Warren Sapp is on the verge of becoming a superstar. Dungy's defense seems to be tailor-made for the athletic Sapp, who could be the team's best lineman since Hall of Famer LeRoy Selmon. Sapp's statistics could go through the roof if second-year players Regan Upshaw and Marcus Jones show improvement.
Linebackers	B -	Hardy Nickerson went to the Pro Bowl and a case could have been made for Derrick Brooks. But the loss of Lonnie Marts will hurt. Rufus Porter is a strong hitter, but lacks Marts' athleticism, which was a huge advantage in the zone blitz. Porter has had some injury problems in the past.
Secondary	C +	John Lynch and Melvin Johnson aren't the quickest safeties around, but both can hit and have great instincts. With Donnie Abraham on one corner, 75 percent of the defensive backfield is in very good hands. But the other corner could be a problem. Veterans Martin Mayhew and Charles Dimry aren't as fast as they used to be and rookie Ronde Barber can't be counted on to have the sudden impact Abraham did last year.
Special teams	B	This was a strength last year and should be even better with Dunn helping out Karl Williams on punt and kickoff returns. Williams will handle most of the punts and he and Dunn will share the kickoffs. Tommy Barnhardt is one of the game's most consistent punters. Kicker Michael Husted is productive, but inconsistent.

TENNESSEE OILERS
AFC CENTRAL DIVISION

1996 REVIEW
RESULTS

ept. 1—KANSAS CITY	L	19-20
ept. 8—at Jacksonville	W	34-27
ept.15—BALTIMORE	W	29-13
ept.22—Open date		
ept.29—at Pittsburgh	L	16-30
ct. 6—at Cincinnati (OT)	W	30-27
ct. 13—at Atlanta	W	23-13
ct. 20—PITTSBURGH	W	23-13
ct. 27—SAN FRANCISCO	L	9-10
ov. 3—at Seattle	L	16-23
ov. 10—at New Orleans	W	31-14
ov. 17—MIAMI	L	20-23
ov. 24—CAROLINA	L	6-31
ec. 1—at N.Y. Jets	W	35-10
ec. 8—JACKSONVILLE	L	17-23
ec. 15—CINCINNATI	L	13-21
ec. 22—at Baltimore	W	24-21

RECORDS/RANKINGS

996 regular-season record: 8-8 (T3rd in
FC Central); 5-3 in division; 6-6 in con-
erence; 2-6 at home; 6-2 on road.
eam record last five years: 39-41 (.488,
anks T13th in league in that span).

996 team rankings:

	No.	AFC	NFL
otal offense	*315.5	11	18
ushing offense	*121.9	6	6
assing offense	*193.6	11	21
coring offense	345	5	10
otal defense	*288.1	3	6
ushing defense	*86.6	2	2
assing defense	*201.6	5	13
coring defense	319	7	16
akeaways	26	T11	T22
iveaways	30	T7	T14
urnover differential	-4	11	20
acks	35	7	T15
acks allowed	34	6	T11

*Yards per game.

TEAM LEADERS

coring (kicking): Al Del Greco, 131 pts.
35/35 PATs, 32/38 FGs).
coring (touchdowns): Eddie George, 48
ts. (8 rushing).
assing: Chris Chandler, 2,099 yds. (320
tt., 184 comp., 57.5%, 16 TDs, 11 int.).
ushing: Eddie George, 1,368 yds. (335
tt., 4.1 avg., 8 TDs).
eceptions: Chris Sanders, 48 (882 yds.,
8.4 avg., 4 TDs).
nterceptions: Darryll Lewis, 5 (103 yds.,
TD).
acks: Anthony Cook, 7.5.
unting: Reggie Roby, 44.4 avg. (67 punts,
,973 yds., 1 blocked).
unt returns: Mel Gray, 9.3 avg. (22 att.,
05 yds., 0 TDs).
ickoff returns: Mel Gray, 24.5 avg. (50
tt., 1,224 yds., 0 TDs).

1997 SEASON
CLUB DIRECTORY

Owner/president
K.S. "Bud" Adams Jr.
Executive vice president/general manager
Floyd Reese
Executive vice president/administration
Mike McClure
Executive assistant to president
Thomas S. Smith
V.P./player personnel and scouting
Mike Holovak
Vice president/legal counsel
Steve Underwood
Vice president/finance
Jackie Curley
Sr. v.p./broadcasting and marketing
Don MacLachlan
Director of player personnel
Rich Snead
Director/business operations
Lewis Mangum
Dir. of media relations and services
Dave Pearson
Dir. of public and community relations
Rod St. Clair
Director of accounting services
Marilan Logan
Director/ticket admin. and services
Mike Mullis
Director/security
Grady Sessums
Director/player relations
Willie Alexander
Asst. dir. of media relations and services
Bob Schranz
Head trainer
Brad Brown
Scouts
Ray Biggs
C.O. Brocato
Glenn Cumbee
Dub Fesperman

SCHEDULE

Aug. 31— OAKLAND	12:00
Sept. 7— at Miami	1:00
Sept. 14— Open date	
Sept. 21— BALTIMORE	12:00
Sept. 28— at Pittsburgh	1:00
Oct. 5— at Seattle	1:00
Oct. 12— CINCINNATI	12:00
Oct. 19— WASHINGTON	12:00
Oct. 26— at Arizona	2:00
Nov. 2— JACKSONVILLE	3:00
Nov. 9— N.Y. GIANTS	3:00
Nov. 16— at Jacksonville	1:00
Nov. 23— BUFFALO	12:00
Nov. 27— at Dallas (Thanks.)	3:00
Dec. 4— at Cincinnati (Thur.)	8:00
Dec. 14— at Baltimore	1:00
Dec. 21— PITTSBURGH	12:00

All times are for home team.
All games Sunday unless noted.

Head coach
Jeff Fisher

Assistant coaches
Les Steckel (offensive coordina-
tor/quarterbacks)
Gregg Williams (defensive
coordinator)
Bart Andrus (offensive assistant/
quality control)
Greg Brown (defensive backs)
O'Neill Gilbert (linebackers)
Jerry Gray (defensive assistant/
quality control)
George Henshaw (offensive line/
tight ends)
Alan Lowry (wide receivers)
Mike Munchak (offensive line)
Rex Norris (defensive line)
Russ Purnell (special teams)
Sherman Smith (running backs)
Steve Watterson (strength &
rehabilitation)

Equipment manager
Paul Noska
Videotape coordinator
Ken Sparacino
Physicians
James Bocell
Walter Lowe
James Muntz

DRAFT CHOICES

Kenny Holmes, DE, Miami, Fla. (first round/
18th pick overall).
Joey Kent, WR, Tennessee (2/46).
Denard Walker, DB, Louisiana State (3/75).
Scott Sanderson, T, Washington State
(3/81).
Derrick Mason, WR, Michigan State (4/98).
Pratt Lyons, DE, Troy State (4/107).
George McCullough, DB, Baylor (5/143).
Dennis Stallings, LB, Illinois (6/181).
Armon Williams, DB, Arizona (7/216).

No.	QUARTERBACKS	Ht./Wt.	Born	NFL Exp.	College	How acq.	'96 Games GP/GS
17	Krieg, Dave	6-1/202	10-20-58	18	Milton College, Wis.	FA/97	*13/1
9	McNair, Steve	6-2/224	2-14-73	3	Alcorn State	D1/95	9/

No.	RUNNING BACKS	Ht./Wt.	Born	NFL Exp.	College	How acq.	'96 Games GP/GS
22	Archie, Mike	5-8/205	10-14-72	2	Penn State	D7/96	2/0
27	George, Eddie	6-3/232	9-24-73	2	Ohio State	D1/96	16/1
33	Harmon, Ronnie	5-11/200	5-7-64	12	Iowa	FA/96	16/6
20	Thomas, Rodney	5-10/213	3-30-73	3	Texas A&M	D3b/95	16/

No.	RECEIVERS	Ht./Wt.	Born	NFL Exp.	College	How acq.	'96 Games GP/GS
84	Davis, Willie	6-0/181	10-10-67	6	Central Arkansas	FA/96	16/1
83	Floyd, Malcolm	6-0/194	12-29-72	4	Fresno State	D3/94	16/
86	Kent, Joey	6-1/186	4-23-74	R	Tennessee	D2/97	—
88	Lewis, Rod (TE)	6-5/254	6-9-71	4	Arizona	D5a/94	16/7
13	Mason, Derrick	5-11/193	1-17-74	R	Michigan State	D4a/97	—
87	McKeehan, James (TE)	6-3/251	8-9-73	2	Texas A&M	FA/95	14/0
80	Roan, Michael (TE)	6-3/251	8-29-72	3	Wisconsin	D4/95	15/1
85	Russell, Derek (KR)	6-0/195	6-22-69	7	Arkansas	FA/95	16/5
81	Sanders, Chris	6-0/184	5-8-72	3	Ohio State	D3a/95	16/1
82	Wilson, Sheddrick	6-2/210	11-23-73	2	Louisiana State	FA/96	11/
89	Wycheck, Frank (TE)	6-3/247	10-14-71	5	Maryland	W-Was/95	16/16

No.	OFFENSIVE LINEMEN	Ht./Wt.	Born	NFL Exp.	College	How acq.	'96 Games GP/GS
77	Donnalley, Kevin (T/G)	6-5/305	6-10-68	7	North Carolina	D3b/91	16/1
75	Eatman, Irv (T)	6-7/305	1-1-61	12	UCLA	FA/95	16/1
60	El-Mashtoub, Hicham (C/G)	6-2/288	5-11-72	3	Arizona	D6/95	1/
71	Hayes, Melvin (T)	6-6/325	4-28-73	3	Mississippi State	D4a/95	*1/
72	Hopkins, Brad (T)	6-3/306	9-5-70	5	Illinois	D1/93	16/1
66	Layman, Jason (T/G)	6-5/306	7-29-73	2	Tennessee	D2b/96	16/
74	Matthews, Bruce (G/C)	6-5/298	8-8-61	15	Southern California	D1/83	16/16
64	Norgard, Erik (G/C)	6-1/282	11-4-65	9	Colorado	FA/90	13/
69	Runyan, Jon (T/G)	6-7/308	11-27-73	2	Michigan	D4b/96	10/
73	Sanderson, Scott (T)	6-6/290	7-25-74	R	Washington State	D3b/97	—
53	Stepnoski, Mark (C)	6-2/269	1-20-67	9	Pittsburgh	FA/95	16/1

No.	DEFENSIVE LINEMEN	Ht./Wt.	Born	NFL Exp.	College	How acq.	'96 Games GP/GS
94	Burton, Kendrick (E)	6-5/288	9-7-73	2	Alabama	D4a/96	4/2
78	Cook, Anthony	6-3/293	5-30-72	3	South Carolina State	D2/95	12/1
91	Evans, Josh	6-0/280	9-6-72	3	Alabama-Birmingham	FA/95	8/
92	Ford, Henry (E)	6-3/284	10-30-71	4	Arkansas	D1/94	15/1
93	Halapin, Mike (T)	6-4/294	7-1-73	2	Pittsburgh	FA/96	9/0
99	Holmes, Kenny (E)	6-4/270	10-24-73	R	Miami (Fla.)	D1/97	—
98	Lyons, Pratt (E)	6-5/278	9-17-74	R	Troy State	D4b/97	—
97	Mix, Bryant (E)	6-3/301	7-28-72	2	Alcorn State	D2a/96	6/2
90	Roberson, James (E)	6-3/275	5-3-71	2	Florida State	FA/96	15/5
96	Walker, Gary (E)	6-2/285	2-28-73	3	Auburn	D5/95	16/16
76	Young, Robert (E)	6-6/273	1-29-69	6	Mississippi State	D5/91	15/1

No.	LINEBACKERS	Ht./Wt.	Born	NFL Exp.	College	How acq.	'96 Games GP/GS
58	Bowden, Joe	5-11/230	2-25-70	6	Oklahoma	D5a/92	16/1
51	Hall, Lemanski	6-0/229	11-24-70	3	Alabama	D7/94	3/
57	Jones, Lenoy	6-1/232	9-25-74	2	Texas Christian	FA/96	11/0
50	Killens, Terry	6-1/232	3-24-74	2	Penn State	D3/96	14/
56	Marts, Lonnie	6-2/240	11-10-68	8	Tulane	FA/97	*16/1
59	Stallings, Dennis	6-0/234	5-25-74	R	Illinois	D6/97	—
52	Wortham, Barron	5-11/244	11-1-69	4	Texas-El Paso	D6b/94	15/1

No.	DEFENSIVE BACKS	Ht./Wt.	Born	NFL Exp.	College	How acq.	'96 Games GP/GS
23	Bishop, Blaine (S)	5-9/197	7-24-70	5	Ball State	D8/93	15/1
39	Cole, Lee (CB)	5-11/188	6-25-74	2	Arizona State	FA/96	0/
30	Dorsett, Anthony (CB)	5-11/203	9-14-73	2	Pittsburgh	D6/96	8/
24	Jackson, Steve (CB)	5-8/182	4-8-69	7	Purdue	D3a/91	16/
29	Lewis, Darryll (CB)	5-9/183	12-16-68	7	Arizona	D2b/91	16/1
28	McCullough, George	5-10/187	2-18-75	R	Baylor	D5/97	—
31	Robertson, Marcus (S)	5-11/197	10-2-69	7	Iowa State	D4b/91	16/1
37	Robinson, Rafael (S)	5-11/200	6-19-69	6	Wisconsin	FA/96	16/2
26	Stewart, Rayna (CB)	5-10/192	6-18-73	2	Northern Arizona	D5/96	15/
25	Walker, Denard	6-1/186	8-9-73	R	Louisiana State	D3a/97	—
42	Williams, Armon	6-1/223	8-13-73	R	Arizona	D7/97	—

No.	SPECIALISTS	Ht./Wt.	Born	NFL Exp.	College	How acq.	'96 Games GP/GS
3	Del Greco, Al (K)	5-10/200	3-2-62	14	Auburn	FA/91	16/0
21	Gray, Mel (KR)	5-9/171	3-16-61	12	Purdue	FA/95	14/0
7	Roby, Reggie (P)	6-2/258	7-30-61	15	Iowa	FA/96	16/0

*Hayes played 1 game for Jets in '96; Krieg played 13 games for Bears; Marts played 16 games for Buccaneers.

Abbreviations: D1—draft pick, first round; SupD2—supplemental draft pick second round; W-Den—waivers acquisition from Denver; T-Sea—trade acquisition from Seattle; PlanB—Plan B free-agent acquisition; FA—free-agent acquisition (other than Plan B).

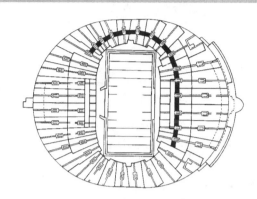

MISCELLANEOUS TEAM DATA

Stadium (capacity, surface):
Liberty Bowl
(62,420, grass)
Business address:
Baptist Sports Park
7640 Highway 70 S.
Nashville, TN 37221
Business phone:
615-673-1500
Ticket information:
615-673-1500
Team colors:
Columbia blue, scarlet and white
Flagship radio station:
WGFX, 104.5 FM
Training site:
Tennessee State University
Nashville, Tenn.
615-673-1500

TSN REPORT CARD

Coaching staff   A

This staff has done a remarkable job keeping the team from imploding with over two years' worth of franchise relocation talk, unfriendly Astrodome crowds and a continuing rebuilding effort from the 2-14 debate of 1994. The coaches' only flaw was they didn't always communicate with each other, and Jeff Fisher has addressed that, too.

Offensive backfield   B +

Simply because he has not played much, Steve McNair is difficult to grade. But in the few games he played McNair showed poise, intelligence, leadership and playmaking. He has a rocket arm and brims with confidence; if he does his homework, he could be a star. Dave Krieg at backup is a tremendous help and could step in if needed. Eddie George earns the bulk of the grade for running backs—over 1,300 yards as a rookie gets you an A. The Oilers could use more production from Ronnie Harmon, especially in the third-down situations where he has made a career.

Receivers   C -

Overall this group is better than the numbers they put up last season. Chris Sanders is an exceptional talent who needs to step to the forefront, while Willie Davis needs to have more than the 39 catches he had last season. There's room for rookie Joey Kent to step in if he wants it badly enough.

Offensive line   C +

Another group that is better than it showed last season. They did pave the way for George, but were just 11-of-20 on third-and-1 and just 12-of-18 on third-and-2. Kept sacks to a minimum—35—but were slightly worse than the 32 sacks they surrendered in 1995.

Defensive line   D

The Oilers need more production here, especially in the pass rush, especially in the middle of the field. They did not collapse the pocket, did not intimidate many quarterbacks. Play the run well, but suffer in passing downs. Most sacks were the result of coverage in the secondary.

Linebackers   B

If Lonnie Marts can play more consistently than the occasionally superb, occasionally invisible Micheal Barrow, this is a solid group that won't make many mistakes. Joe Bowden is a significantly underrated player.

Secondary   B +

Effective group last season, but faded in the interception department—six in the first four games compared to six in the last 12 games. Play the run superbly, hold coverages for extended periods of time. Surrendered big play late at times to tip the game away.

Special teams   C

This group is probably closer to an A in the kicking game with Al Del Greco and Reggie Roby, but the Oilers were decidedly unspectacular in the return game in a year when the Super Bowl was decided by a kick returner. They had no touchdowns on returns all season. Improvement is needed. Coverage units were solid with only occasional lapses.

WASHINGTON REDSKINS
NFC EASTERN DIVISION

1996 REVIEW
RESULTS

Sept. 1—PHILADELPHIA	L	14-17
Sept. 8—CHICAGO	W	10-3
Sept.15—at N.Y. Giants	W	31-10
Sept.22—at St. Louis	W	17-10
Sept.29—N.Y. JETS	W	31-16
Oct. 13—at New England	W	27-22
Oct. 20—N.Y. GIANTS	W	31-21
Oct. 27—INDIANAPOLIS	W	31-16
Nov. 3—at Buffalo	L	13-38
Nov. 10—ARIZONA (OT)	L	34-37
Nov. 17—at Philadelphia	W	26-21
Nov. 24—SAN FRAN. (OT)	L	16-19
Nov. 28—at Dallas	L	10-21
Dec. 8—at Tampa Bay	L	10-24
Dec. 15—at Arizona	L	26-27
Dec. 22—DALLAS	W	37-10

RECORDS/RANKINGS

1996 regular-season record: 9-7 (3rd in NFC East); 4-4 in division; 6-6 in conference; 5-3 at home; 4-4 on road.
Team record last five years: 31-49 (.388, ranks T20th in league in that span).

1996 team rankings:	No.	NFC	NFL
Total offense	*326.8	4	9
Rushing offense	*119.4	1	7
Passing offense	*207.4	7	15
Scoring offense	364	4	8
Total defense	*357.7	14	28
Rushing defense	*142.2	15	30
Passing defense	*215.5	12	20
Scoring defense	312	8	13
Takeaways	30	9	16
Giveaways	18	1	1
Turnover differential	12	3	T4
Sacks	34	10	T17
Sacks allowed	22	T2	T3

*Yards per game.

TEAM LEADERS

Scoring (kicking): Scott Blanton, 118 pts. (40/40 PATs, 26/32 FGs).
Scoring (touchdowns): Terry Allen, 126 pts. (21 rushing).
Passing: Gus Frerotte, 3,453 yds. (470 att., 270 comp., 57.4%, 12 TDs, 11 int.).
Rushing: Terry Allen, 1,353 yds. (347 att., 3.9 avg., 21 TDs).
Receptions: Henry Ellard, 52 (1,014 yds., 19.5 avg., 2 TDs).
Interceptions: Tom Carter, 5 (24 yds., 0 TDs).
Sacks: Rich Owens, 11.0.
Punting: Matt Turk, 45.1 avg. (75 punts, 3,386 yds., 0 blocked).
Punt returns: Brian Mitchell, 11.2 avg. (23 att., 258 yds., 0 TDs).
Kickoff returns: Brian Mitchell, 22.5 avg. (56 att., 1,258 yds., 0 TDs).

1997 SEASON
CLUB DIRECTORY

Chairman of the board/CEO
John Kent Cooke Sr.
House counsel
Stuart Haney
Vice president of finance
Greg Dillon
Vice president of marketing
John Kent Cooke Jr.
General manager
Charley Casserly
Assistant general manager
Bobby Mitchell
Director of public relations
Mike McCall
Director of media relations
Chris Helein
Public relations assistants
Scott McKeen
Reggie Saunders
Asst. promotions/advertising director
John Wagner
Ticket manager
Jeff Ritter
Director of stadium operations
Jeff Klein
Director of player development
Joe Mendes
Director of administration
Barry Asimos
Director of college scouting
George Saimes
Scouts
Gene Bates
Larry Bryan
Scott Cohen
Mike Hagen
Mike MacCagnan
Miller McCalmon
Head trainer
Bubba Tyer

Head coach
Norv Turner

Assistant coaches
Jason Arapoff (conditioning director)
Russ Grimm (offensive line)
Tom Hayes (def. backs)
Bobby Jackson (running backs)
Earl Leggett (defensive line)
Dale Lindsey (linebackers)
Mike Martz (quarterbacks)
LeCharls McDaniel (defensive asst. coach/admin. asst.)
Mike Nolan (defensive coach)
Michael Pope (tight ends)
Dan Riley (strength)
Terry Robiskie (wide receivers)
Pete Rodriguez (special teams)

Assistant trainers
Al Bellamy
Kevin Bastin
Equipment manager
Jay Brunetti
Assistant equipment manager
Jeff Parsons
Director of video
Donnie Schoenmann
Asst. director of video —
Hugh McPhillps
Video analyst
Mike Bean

SCHEDULE

Aug. 31— at Carolina	8:00
Sept. 7— at Pittsburgh	1:00
Sept. 14— ARIZONA	1:00
Sept. 21— Open date	
Sept. 28— JACKSONVILLE	1:00
Oct. 5— at Philadelphia	1:00
Oct. 13— DALLAS (Mon.)	9:00
Oct. 19— at Tennessee	12:00
Oct. 26— BALTIMORE	1:00
Nov. 2— at Chicago	12:00
Nov. 9— DETROIT	1:00
Nov. 16— at Dallas	12:00
Nov. 23— N.Y. GIANTS	8:00
Nov. 30— ST. LOUIS	1:00
Dec. 7— at Arizona	2:00
Dec. 13— at N.Y. Giants (Sat.)	12:30
Dec. 21— PHILADELPHIA	1:00

All times are for home team.
All games Sunday unless noted.

DRAFT CHOICES

Kenard Lang, DE, Miami, Fla. (first round/17th pick overall).
Greg Jones, LB, Colorado (2/51).
Derek Smith, LB, Arizona State (3/80).
Albert Connell, WR, Texas A&M (4/115).
Jamel Williams, DB, Nebraska (5/132).
Keith Thibodeaux, DB, Northwestern (La.) State (5/140).
Twan Russell, LB, Miami, Fla. (5/148).
Brad Badger, G, Stanford (5/162).

1997 SEASON Washington Redskins

No.	QUARTERBACKS	Ht./Wt.	Born	NFL Exp.	College	How acq.	'96 Games GP/GS
12	Frerotte, Gus	6-2/240	7-31-71	4	Tulsa	D7/94	16/16
10	Green, Trent	6-3/212	7-9-70	2	Indiana	FA/95	0/0
	RUNNING BACKS						
21	Allen, Terry	5-10/208	2-21-68	8	Clemson	FA/95	16/16
36	Bell, William	5-11/216	7-22-71	4	Georgia Tech	FA/94	16/0
47	Bowie, Larry	6-0/249	3-21-73	2	Georgia	FA/96	3/0
48	Davis, Stephen	6-0/234	3-1-74	2	Auburn	D4/96	12/0
20	Logan, Marc (FB)	6-0/228	5-9-65	10	Kentucky	FA/95	14/9
30	Mitchell, Brian (FB/KR)	5-10/221	8-18-68	8	Southwestern Louisiana	D5/90	16/2
	RECEIVERS						
84	Asher, Jamie (TE)	6-3/245	10-31-72	3	Louisville	D5a/95	16/12
41	Connell, Albert	6-0/179	5-13-74	R	Texas A&M	D4/97	—
85	Ellard, Henry	5-11/188	7-21-61	15	Fresno State	FA/94	16/16
89	Galbraith, Scott (TE)	6-2/254	1-7-67	8	Southern California	FA/95	16/6
80	Malone, Toderick	5-10/177	11-11-74	1	Alabama	D6b/96	0/0
13	Maxwell, DeAndre	6-1/209	4-6-73	1	San Diego State	D7b/96	0/0
19	Olive, Bobby	6-1/168	4-22-69	3	Ohio State	FA/97	*1/0
86	Shepherd, Leslie	5-11/186	11-3-69	4	Temple	FA/94	12/6
82	Westbrook, Michael	6-3/220	7-7-72	3	Colorado	D1/95	11/6
	OFFENSIVE LINEMEN						
77	Ashmore, Darryl (T)	6-7/310	11-1-69	5	Northwestern	D7/92	5/0
74	Badger, Brad (G)	6-4/298	1-11-75	R	Stanford	D5d/97	—
61	Batiste, Michael (G)	6-3/325	12-24-70	3	Tulane	FA/97	0/0
75	Dahl, Bob (G)	6-5/319	11-5-68	6	Notre Dame	FA/96	15/15
69	Johnson, Andre (T)	6-5/314	8-25-73	2	Penn State	D1/96	0/0
77	Johnson, Tre' (T)	6-2/326	8-30-71	4	Temple	D2/94	15/15
68	Patton, Joe (G)	6-5/306	1-5-72	3	Alabama A&M	D3b/94	16/16
62	Pourdanesh, Shar (T)	6-6/312	7-19-70	2	Nevada	FA/96	16/8
62	Raymer, Cory (C)	6-2/289	3-3-73	3	Wisconsin	D2/95	6/5
69	Sedoris, Chris (C)	6-3/289	4-25-73	2	Purdue	FA/96	9/0
76	Simmons, Ed (T)	6-5/334	12-31-63	11	Eastern Washington	D6/87	11/11
	Uhlenhake, Jeff (C)	6-3/284	1-28-66	8	Ohio State	FA/94	12/11
	DEFENSIVE LINEMEN						
72	Bandison, Romeo (T)	6-5/303	2-12-71	4	Oregon	FA/95	10/0
93	Boutte, Marc (T)	6-4/307	7-25-69	6	Louisiana State	W-RAM/94	10/10
91	Foley, Mike (T)	6-3/290	11-12-71	1	New Hampshire	D6/95	0/0
95	Gaines, William (T)	6-5/318	6-20-71	4	Florida	FA/95	16/6
94	Gilbert, Sean (T)	6-5/303	4-10-70	6	Pittsburgh	T-StL/96	16/16
70	Kinney, Kelvin (E)	6-6/264	12-31-72	1	Virginia State	D6/96	0/0
78	Kuehl, Ryan (T)	6-4/289	1-18-72	1	Virginia	FA/96	2/0
90	Lang, Kenard (E)	6-4/277	1-31-75	R	Miami (Fla.)	D1/97	—
92	Nottage, Dexter (E)	6-4/274	11-14-70	4	Florida A&M	D6/94	16/4
96	Owens, Rich (E)	6-6/281	5-22-72	3	Lehigh	D5b/95	16/16
97	Palmer, Sterling (E)	6-5/273	2-4-71	5	Florida State	D4/93	6/5
99	Rucker, Keith (T)	6-3/331	11-20-68	5	Ohio Wesleyan	FA/97	0/0
	LINEBACKERS						
58	Alexander, Patrise	6-1/244	10-23-72	2	Southwestern Louisiana	FA/96	16/1
54	Asher, Jeremy	6-0/235	10-5-72	1	Oregon	D7a/96	0/0
57	Harvey, Ken	6-2/237	5-6-65	10	California	FA/94	16/16
54	Jones, Greg	6-4/238	5-22-74	R	Colorado	D2/97	—
53	Patton, Marvcus	6-2/236	5-1-67	8	UCLA	FA/95	16/16
58	Russell, Twan	6-1/219	4-25-74	R	Miami (Fla.)	D5c/97	—
51	Smith, Derek	6-2/239	1-18-75	R	Arizona State	D3/97	—
	DEFENSIVE BACKS						
27	Barnes, Tomur (CB)	5-10/185	9-8-70	4	North Texas	FA/96	*10/0
37	Campbell, Jesse (S)	6-1/211	4-11-69	7	North Carolina State	FA/97	*16/16
6	Dishman, Cris (CB)	6-0/195	8-13-65	10	Purdue	FA/97	*16/16
31	Evans, Greg (S)	6-1/208	6-28-71	2	Texas Christian	FA/94	0/0
25	Evans, Leomont (S)	6-1/202	7-12-74	2	Clemson	D5/96	12/0
28	Green, Darrell (CB)	5-8/184	2-15-60	15	Texas A&I	D1/83	16/16
21	Pounds, Darryl (CB)	5-10/189	7-21-72	3	Nicholls State	D3/95	12/1
24	Richard, Stanley (S)	6-2/198	10-21-67	7	Texas	FA/95	16/15
22	Thibodeaux, Keith	5-11/189	5-16-74	R	Northwestern (La.) State	D5b/97	—
29	Turner, Scott (CB)	5-10/180	2-26-72	3	Illinois	D7/95	16/0
25	Walker, Brian (S)	6-2/193	5-31-72	2	Washington State	FA/96	16/4
22	Williams, Jamel	5-11/205	12-22-73	R	Nebraska	D5a/97	—

No.	SPECIALISTS	Ht./Wt.	Born	NFL Exp.	College	How acq.	'96 Games GP/GS
16	Blanton, Scott (K)	6-2/221	7-1-73	3	Oklahoma	FA/95	16/0
1	Turk, Matt (P)	6-5/237	6-16-68	3	Wisconsin-Whitewater	FA/95	16/0

*Barnes played 5 games with Oilers, 2 games with Vikings and 3 games with Redskins in '96; Campbell played 16 games with Giants; Dishman played 16 games with Oilers; Olive played 1 game with Colts.

Abbreviations: D1—draft pick, first round; SupD2—supplemental draft pick second round; W-Den—waivers acquisition from Denver; T-Sea—trade acquisition from Seattle; PlanB—Plan B free-agent acquisition; FA—free-agent acquisition (other than Plan B).

MISCELLANEOUS TEAM DATA

Stadium (capacity, surface):
Jack Kent Cooke
Stadium (78,600, grass)
Business address:
P.O. Box 17247
Dulles International Airport
Washington, D.C. 20041
Business phone:
703-478-8900
Ticket information:
TBA
Team colors:
Burgundy and gold
Flagship radio station:
WJFK, 106.7 FM
Training site:
Frostburg State University
Frostburg, Md.
301-687-7975

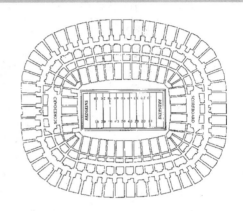

TSN REPORT CARD

Coaching staff — C +
Norv Turner has assembled a well-balanced offense. The special teams have excelled under assistant Pete Rodriguez. However, the defense was so bad despite seven millionaire starters that coordinator Ron Lynn and two of his aides were fired. It's up to new coordinator Mike Nolan, who did a great job with less talent the past four years with the New York Giants, to turn the defense around.

Offensive backfield — B
Terry Allen's hard-nosed running is the key to Washington's attack. Gus Frerotte's not flashy, but few quarterbacks are as efficient or as durable. If the Redskins acquire Jeff Hostetler from Oakland as expected they'll have a top backup. Marc Logan's not the ideal blocking back, but he's a threat on screen passes Third-down back Brian Mitchell's a weapon running or catching the ball.

Receivers — B -
No receiver had ever done what Henry Ellard did at 34 and 35, so why expect a dropoff at age 36? Michael Westbrook's still more potential than production, largely because of injuries. Leslie Shepherd's a decent third receiver. Jamie Asher's on the verge of being Washington's top receiving tight end since Jerry Smith's heyday in the late 1960s. James Jenkins and Scott Galbraith are solid blocking types.

Offensive line — B
They're not quite up to the standards of the Hogs, who made blocking famous in the 1980s, but Washington's line is big (325 pounds on average), young (right tackle Ed Simmons is the only projected starter to have hit 30) and good. Although Allen mostly runs behind Simmons and right guard Bob Dahl left guard Tre Johnson is the lineman the Redskins see as Pro Bowl-bound.

Defensive line — D
This has been Washington's sore point since Hall of Fame coach Joe Gibbs retired after the 1992 season Adding former Pro Bowl tackle Sean Gilbert didn't make a big difference last season nor did the emergence of end Rich Owens into a pass-rushing force in his second year. Maybe University of Miami end Kenard Lang, Washington's top draft pick, is the answer for this beleaguered unit.

Linebackers — C
Ken Harvey has been to three straight Pro Bowls. Marvcus Patton has led the Redskins in tackles the past two years. So Washington blamed middle man Rod Stephens for the inconsistent linebacker play and cut him. Stephens' replacement, Patrise Alexander, is as raw as sushi, but he'll start unless rookie outside backer Greg Jones progresses quickly and moves Patton inside.

Secondary — B -
Few teams have had two cornerbacks as talented and experienced as Darrell Green, coming off his sixth Pro Bowl, and 10-year man Cris Dishman, signed as a free agent from Houston. New strong safety Jesse Campbell knows the defense after four years with Nolan in New York. If free safety Stanley Richard can live up to his $2 million salary, the secondary could be second to none.

Special teams — A -
Although there was a bit of a dropoff last year, this is still Washington's strong suit. Return man Mitchell led the NFL in all-purpose yards for a third straight year. Punter Matt Turk went to the Pro Bowl after leading the NFL in net average. Kicker Scott Blanton was perfect inside the 40 and on extra points. The cover teams have plenty of speed, led by Darryl Pounds and Scott Turner.

SCHEDULE

PRESEASON
(All times are Eastern)

WEEK 1

SATURDAY, JULY 26

Minnesota vs. Seattle at Canton, O.*	2:30
Miami at Green Bay	6:30
Buffalo at Denver	9:00

*Hall of Fame Game.

SUNDAY, JULY 27

Chicago vs. Pittsburgh at Dublin, Ireland	1:00

WEEK 2

THURSDAY, JULY 31

New England at Green Bay	8:00

FRIDAY, AUGUST 1

Atlanta at Detroit	7:30
Cincinnati at Indianapolis	7:30

SATURDAY, AUGUST 2

Chicago at Buffalo	7:00
Washington vs. Tampa Bay at Orlando, Fla.	7:30
New Orleans vs. Tennessee at Memphis, Tenn.	8:00
Philadelphia at N.Y. Jets	8:00
N.Y. Giants at Baltimore	8:00
Pittsburgh at Kansas City	8:00
St. Louis at Minnesota	8:00
Arizona at Seattle	10:00
San Francisco at San Diego	10:00

SUNDAY, AUGUST 3

Carolina at Jacksonville	3:00
Oakland at Dallas	8:00

MONDAY, AUGUST 4

Denver vs. Miami at Guadalajara, Mexico	8:00

WEEK 3

FRIDAY, AUGUST 8

Cincinnati at Detroit	7:30
Baltimore at N.Y. Jets	8:00
Dallas at New England	8:00
Arizona at St. Louis	8:00
Green Bay at Oakland	TBA

SATURDAY, AUGUST 9

Washington vs. Tennessee at Nashville, Tenn.	7:00
Tampa Bay at Atlanta	7:30
Minnesota at Buffalo	7:30
Denver at Carolina	8:00
Jacksonville at N.Y. Giants	8:00
Kansas City at New Orleans	8:00
Seattle at San Francisco	9:00
Indianapolis at San Diego	10:00

SUNDAY, AUGUST 10

Chicago at Miami	8:00

MONDAY, AUGUST 11

Philadelphia at Pittsburgh	8:00

WEEK 4

THURSDAY, AUGUST 14

Carolina at Kansas City	8:00

FRIDAY, AUGUST 15

St. Louis at Dallas	8:00

SATURDAY, AUGUST 16

Buffalo vs. Green Bay at Toronto	4:00
New Orleans at Oakland	4:00
San Diego vs. Tennessee at Nashville, Tenn.	7:00
Minnesota at Cincinnati	7:30
Washington at Atlanta	7:30
Miami at Tampa Bay	7:30
N.Y. Jets at N.Y. Giants	8:00
Baltimore at Philadelphia	8:00
Arizona at Chicago	8:00
Indianapolis at Seattle	10:00

SUNDAY, AUGUST 17

Denver at New England	1:00
Detroit at Pittsburgh	8:00

MONDAY, AUGUST 18

Jacksonville at San Francisco	8:00

WEEK 5

THURSDAY, AUGUST 21

Detroit at Indianapolis	7:30
New England at Philadelphia	8:00
Washington at Miami	8:00
Kansas City at St. Louis	8:00

FRIDAY, AUGUST 22

Atlanta at Jacksonville	7:30
Buffalo at Baltimore	7:30
N.Y. Jets vs. Tampa Bay at Orlando, Fla.	7:30
Seattle at Cincinnati	7:30
N.Y. Giants vs. Green Bay at Madison, Wis.	8:00
San Diego at Minnesota	8:00
Pittsburgh at Carolina	8:00
New Orleans at Chicago	8:30

SATURDAY, AUGUST 23

Tennessee at Dallas	8:00
San Francisco at Denver	8:00
Oakland at Arizona	10:00

REGULAR SEASON
(All times local)

WEEK 1

SUNDAY, AUGUST 31

Arizona at Cincinnati	1:00
Atlanta at Detroit	1:00
Dallas at Pittsburgh	1:00
Indianapolis at Miami	1:00
Minnesota at Buffalo	1:00
New Orleans at St. Louis	12:00
Oakland at Tennessee	12:00
Philadelphia at N.Y. Giants	1:00
San Diego at New England	1:00
Jacksonville at Baltimore	4:00
Kansas City at Denver	2:00
N.Y. Jets at Seattle	1:00
San Francisco at Tampa Bay	4:00
Washington at Carolina	8:00

MONDAY, SEPTEMBER 1

Chicago at Green Bay	8:00

WEEK 2

SUNDAY, SEPTEMBER 7

Buffalo at N.Y. Jets	1:00
Carolina at Atlanta	1:00
Cincinnati at Baltimore	1:00
Tennessee at Miami	1:00
Minnesota at Chicago	12:00
New England at Indianapolis	12:00
San Diego at New Orleans	12:00
San Francisco at St. Louis	12:00
Tampa Bay at Detroit	1:00
Washington at Pittsburgh	1:00
Denver at Seattle	1:00
Green Bay at Philadelphia	4:00
N.Y. Giants at Jacksonville	4:00
Dallas at Arizona	5:00

MONDAY, SEPTEMBER 8

Kansas City at Oakland	6:00

WEEK 3

SUNDAY, SEPTEMBER 14

Arizona at Washington	1:00
Baltimore at N.Y. Giants	1:00
Buffalo at Kansas City	12:00
Detroit at Chicago	12:00
Miami at Green Bay	12:00
Oakland at Atlanta	1:00
Tampa Bay at Minnesota	12:00
Carolina at San Diego	1:00
New Orleans at San Francisco	1:00
St. Louis at Denver	2:00
Seattle at Indianapolis	3:00
N.Y. Jets at New England	8:00

MONDAY, SEPTEMBER 15

Philadelphia at Dallas	8:00

Open date: Cincinnati, Tennessee, Jacksonville, Pittsburgh

WEEK 4

SUNDAY, SEPTEMBER 21

Baltimore at Tennessee	12:00
Chicago at New England	1:00
Detroit at New Orleans	12:00
Kansas City at Carolina	1:00
Minnesota at Green Bay	12:00
Oakland at N.Y. Jets	1:00
Atlanta at San Francisco	1:00
Cincinnati at Denver	2:00
Indianapolis at Buffalo	4:00
N.Y. Giants at St. Louis	3:00
San Diego at Seattle	1:00
Miami at Tampa Bay	8:00

MONDAY, SEPTEMBER 22

Pittsburgh at Jacksonville	9:00

Open date: Arizona, Dallas, Philadelphia, Washington

WEEK 5

SUNDAY, SEPTEMBER 28

Arizona at Tampa Bay	1:00
Denver at Atlanta	1:00
Green Bay at Detroit	1:00
Tennessee at Pittsburgh	1:00
Jacksonville at Washington	1:00
New Orleans at N.Y. Giants	1:00
Baltimore at San Diego	1:00
Chicago at Dallas	3:00
N.Y. Jets at Cincinnati	4:00
St. Louis at Oakland	1:00
Seattle at Kansas City	3:00
Philadelphia at Minnesota	7:00

MONDAY, SEPTEMBER 29

San Francisco at Carolina	9:00■

Open date: Buffalo, Indianapolis, Miami, New England

WEEK 6

SUNDAY, OCTOBER 5

Cincinnati at Jacksonville	1:0■
Dallas at N.Y. Giants	1:0■
Detroit at Buffalo	1:0■
Kansas City at Miami	1:0C
Pittsburgh at Baltimore	1:0■
Tampa Bay at Green Bay	12:0■
Washington at Philadelphia	1:0■
Tennessee at Seattle	1:0■
Minnesota at Arizona	1:0C
N.Y. Jets at Indianapolis	3:0■
San Diego at Oakland	1:0■
New Orleans at Chicago	7:0■

MONDAY, OCTOBER 6

New England at Denver	7:0■

Open date: Atlanta, Carolina, St. Louis, San Francisco

WEEK 7

SUNDAY, OCTOBER 12

Atlanta at New Orleans	12:0■
Buffalo at New England	1:0C
Cincinnati at Tennessee	12:0■
Detroit at Tampa Bay	1:0■
Green Bay at Chicago	12:0■
Miami at N.Y. Jets	1:0■
N.Y. Giants at Arizona	1:0■
Philadelphia at Jacksonville	1:0■
Carolina at Minnesota	3:0■
St. Louis at San Francisco	1:0■
Indianapolis at Pittsburgh	8:0■

MONDAY, OCTOBER 13

Dallas at Washington	9:0■

Open date: Baltimore, Denver, Kansas City, Oakland, San Diego, Seattle

WEEK 8

THURSDAY, OCTOBER 16

San Diego at Kansas City	7:0■

SUNDAY, OCTOBER 19

Arizona at Philadelphia	1:0■
Carolina at New Orleans	12:0■
Jacksonville at Dallas	12:0■
New England at N.Y. Jets	1:0■
San Francisco at Atlanta	1:0■
Seattle at St. Louis	12:0■
Denver at Oakland	1:0■
Miami at Baltimore	4:0■
N.Y. Giants at Detroit	4:0■
Pittsburgh at Cincinnati	4:0■
Washington at Tennessee	12:0■

MONDAY, OCTOBER 20

Buffalo at Indianapolis	8:0■

Open date: Chicago, Green Bay, Minnesota, Tampa Bay

WEEK 9

SUNDAY, OCTOBER 26

Baltimore at Washington	1:0
Cincinnati at N.Y. Giants	1:0
Dallas at Philadelphia	1:0
Denver at Buffalo	1:0
Tennessee at Arizona	2:0
Indianapolis at San Diego	1:0
Kansas City at St. Louis	12:0
Minnesota at Tampa Bay	1:0

Oakland at Seattle 1:00
San Francisco at New Orleans 12:00
Chicago at Miami 4:00
Jacksonville at Pittsburgh................................. 4:00
Atlanta at Carolina 8:00

MONDAY, OCTOBER 27

Green Bay at New England 9:00
    Open date: Detroit, N.Y. Jets

WEEK 10

SUNDAY, NOVEMBER 2

Baltimore at N.Y. Jets 1:00
Dallas at San Francisco 1:00
Miami at Buffalo 1:00
New England at Minnesota 12:00
Oakland at Carolina.. 1:00
St. Louis at Atlanta 1:00
San Diego at Cincinnati 1:00
Tampa Bay at Indianapolis................................ 1:00
Washington at Chicago 12:00
Jacksonville at Tennessee................................ 3:00
Philadelphia at Arizona 2:00
Seattle at Denver 2:00
Detroit at Green Bay 7:00

MONDAY, NOVEMBER 3

Pittsburgh at Kansas City 8:00
    Open date: New Orleans, N.Y. Giants

WEEK 11

SUNDAY, NOVEMBER 9

Arizona at Dallas... 12:00
Chicago at Minnesota 12:00
Cincinnati at Indianapolis.................................. 1:00
Detroit at Washington....................................... 1:00
Kansas City at Jacksonville............................... 1:00
N.Y. Jets at Miami.. 1:00
St. Louis at Green Bay 12:00
Tampa Bay at Atlanta 1:00
Carolina at Denver 2:00
New England at Buffalo 4:00
New Orleans at Oakland.................................... 1:00
N.Y. Giants at Tennessee.................................. 3:00
Seattle at San Diego 1:00
Baltimore at Pittsburgh..................................... 8:00

MONDAY, NOVEMBER 10

San Francisco at Philadelphia........................... 9:00

WEEK 12

SUNDAY, NOVEMBER 16

Arizona at N.Y. Giants 1:00
Atlanta at St. Louis 12:00
Cincinnati at Pittsburgh 1:00
Denver at Kansas City..................................... 12:00
Green Bay at Indianapolis 1:00
Tennessee at Jacksonville................................. 1:00
Minnesota at Detroit... 1:00
New England at Tampa Bay 1:00
Philadelphia at Baltimore.................................. 1:00
Seattle at New Orleans.................................... 12:00
Washington at Dallas....................................... 12:00
Carolina at San Francisco 1:00
N.Y. Jets at Chicago.. 3:00
Oakland at San Diego 5:00

MONDAY, NOVEMBER 17

Buffalo at Miami 9:00

WEEK 13

SUNDAY, NOVEMBER 23

Arizona at Baltimore 1:00
Buffalo at Tennessee....................................... 12:00

Dallas at Green Bay 12:00
Indianapolis at Detroit 1:00
Miami at New England 1:00
Minnesota at N.Y. Jets...................................... 1:00
New Orleans at Atlanta 1:00
Pittsburgh at Philadelphia................................. 1:00
Tampa Bay at Chicago 12:00
Carolina at St. Louis 3:00
Jacksonville at Cincinnati.................................. 4:00
Kansas City at Seattle 1:00
San Diego at San Francisco 1:00
N.Y. Giants at Washington 8:00

MONDAY, NOVEMBER 24

Oakland at Denver 7:00

WEEK 14

THURSDAY, NOVEMBER 27

Chicago at Detroit... 12:30
Tennessee at Dallas 3:00

SUNDAY, NOVEMBER 30

Baltimore at Jacksonville 1:00
Cincinnati at Philadelphia.................................. 1:00
Indianapolis at New England 1:00
New Orleans at Carolina 1:00
N.Y. Jets at Buffalo 1:00
St. Louis at Washington 1:00
San Francisco at Kansas City.......................... 12:00
Atlanta at Seattle 1:00
Miami at Oakland... 1:00
Pittsburgh at Arizona 2:00
Tampa Bay at N.Y. Giants................................. 4:00
Denver at San Diego 5:00

MONDAY, DECEMBER 1

Green Bay at Minnesota.................................... 8:00

WEEK 15

THURSDAY, DECEMBER 4

Tennessee at Cincinnati 8:00

SUNDAY, DECEMBER 7

Buffalo at Chicago 12:00
Denver at Pittsburgh... 1:00
Green Bay at Tampa Bay................................... 1:00
New England at Jacksonville 1:00
N.Y. Giants at Philadelphia................................ 1:00
Oakland at Kansas City 12:00
St. Louis at New Orleans 12:00
Seattle at Baltimore 1:00
Atlanta at San Diego 1:00
Indianapolis at N.Y. Jets................................... 4:00
Minnesota at San Francisco.............................. 1:00
Washington at Arizona...................................... 2:00
Detroit at Miami... 8:00

MONDAY, DECEMBER 8

Carolina at Dallas.. 8:00

WEEK 16

SATURDAY, DECEMBER 13

Washington at N.Y. Giants 12:30
Pittsburgh at New England 4:00

SUNDAY, DECEMBER 14

Dallas at Cincinnati 1:00
Detroit at Minnesota 12:00
Tennessee at Baltimore 1:00
Jacksonville at Buffalo 1:00
Miami at Indianapolis 1:00
Philadelphia at Atlanta 1:00
Tampa Bay at N.Y. Jets 1:00
Arizona at New Orleans 3:00
Green Bay at Carolina 4:00
Kansas City at San Diego.................................. 1:00

Seattle at Oakland	1:00
Chicago at St. Louis	7:00

MONDAY, DECEMBER 15

Denver at San Francisco	6:00

WEEK 17

SATURDAY, DECEMBER 20

Buffalo at Green Bay	11:30
St. Louis at Carolina	4:00

SUNDAY, DECEMBER 21

Baltimore at Cincinnati	1:00
Chicago at Tampa Bay	1:00

Indianapolis at Minnesota	12:00
New Orleans at Kansas City	12:00
N.Y. Giants at Dallas	12:00
Philadelphia at Washington	1:00
Pittsburgh at Tennessee	12:00
Atlanta at Arizona	2:00
Jacksonville at Oakland	1:00
N.Y. Jets at Detroit	4:00
San Diego at Denver	2:00
San Francisco at Seattle	5:00

MONDAY, DECEMBER 22

New England at Miami	9:00

NATIONALLY TELEVISED GAMES

(All times local)

REGULAR SEASON

Sun. Aug. 31— Kansas City at Denver (2:00, NBC)
Washington at Carolina (8:00, TNT)
Mon. Sept. 1— Chicago at Green Bay (8:00, ABC)
Sun. Sept. 7— Green Bay at Philadelphia (4:00, FOX)
Dallas at Arizona (5:00, TNT)
Mon. Sept. 8— Kansas City at Oakland (6:00, ABC)
Sun. Sept. 14— St. Louis at Denver (2:00, FOX)
N.Y. Jets at New England (8:00, TNT)
Mon. Sept. 15— Philadelphia at Dallas (8:00, ABC)
Sun. Sept. 21— Cincinnati at Denver (2:00, NBC)
Miami at Tampa Bay (8:00, TNT)
Mon. Sept. 22— Pittsburgh at Jacksonville (9:00, ABC)
Sun. Sept. 28— Chicago at Dallas (3:00, FOX)
Philadelphia at Minnesota (7:00, TNT)
Mon. Sept. 29— San Francisco at Carolina (9:00, ABC)
Sun. Oct. 5— San Diego at Oakland (1:00, NBC)
New Orleans at Chicago (7:00, TNT)
Mon. Oct. 6— New England at Denver (7:00, ABC)
Sun. Oct. 12— Carolina at Minnesota (3:00, FOX)
Indianapolis at Pittsburgh (8:00, TNT)
Mon. Oct. 13— Dallas at Washington (9:00, ABC)
Thur. Oct. 16— San Diego at Kansas City (7:00, TNT)
Sun. Oct. 19— Denver at Oakland (1:00, NBC)
Mon. Oct. 20— Buffalo at Indianapolis (8:00, ABC)
Sun. Oct. 26— Oakland at Seattle (1:00, NBC)
Atlanta at Carolina (8:00, TNT)
Mon. Oct. 27— Green Bay at New England (9:00, ABC)
Sun. Nov. 2— Dallas at San Francisco (1:00, FOX)
Detroit at Green Bay (7:00, ESPN)
Mon. Nov. 3— Pittsburgh at Kansas City (8:00, ABC)
Sun. Nov. 9— New England at Buffalo (4:00, NBC)
Baltimore at Pittsburgh (8:00, ESPN)
Mon. Nov. 10— San Francisco at Philadelphia (9:00, ABC)

Sun. Nov. 16— Carolina at San Francisco (1:00, FOX)
Oakland at San Diego (5:00, ESPN)
Mon. Nov. 17— Buffalo at Miami (9:00, ABC)
Sun. Nov. 23— San Diego at San Francisco (1:00, NBC)
N.Y. Giants at Washington (8:00, ESPN)
Mon. Nov. 24— Oakland at Denver (7:00, ABC)
Thur. Nov. 27— Chicago at Detroit (12:30, FOX)
Tennessee at Dallas (3:00, NBC)
Sun. Nov. 30— Miami at Oakland (1:00, NBC)
Denver at San Diego (5:00, ESPN)
Mon. Dec. 1— Green Bay at Minnesota (8:00, ABC)
Thur. Dec. 4— Tennessee at Cincinnati (8:00, ESPN)
Sun. Dec. 7— Minnesota at San Francisco (1:00, FOX)
Detroit at Miami (8:00, ESPN)
Mon. Dec. 8— Carolina at Dallas (8:00, ABC)
Sat. Dec. 13— Washington at N.Y. Giants (12:30, FOX)
Pittsburgh at New England (4:00, NBC)
Sun. Dec. 14— Green Bay at Carolina (4:00, FOX)
Chicago at St. Louis (7:00, ESPN)
Mon. Dec. 15— Denver at San Francisco (6:00, ABC)
Sat. Dec. 20— Buffalo at Green Bay (11:30, NBC)
St. Louis at Carolina (4:00, FOX)
Sun. Dec. 21— San Diego at Denver (2:00, NBC)
San Francisco at Seattle (5:00, ESPN)
Mon. Dec. 22— New England at Miami (9:00, ABC)

POSTSEASON

Sat. Dec. 27— AFC, NFC wild-card playoffs (ABC)
Sun. Dec. 28— AFC, NFC wild-card playoffs (NBC, FOX)
Sat. Jan. 3— AFC, NFC divisional playoffs (NBC, FOX)
Sun. Jan. 4— AFC, NFC divisional playoffs (NBC, FOX)
Sun. Jan. 11— AFC, NFC championship games (NBC, FOX)
Sun. Jan. 25— Super Bowl XXXII at San Diego/Jack Murphy
Stadium (NBC)
Sun. Feb. 1— Pro Bowl at Honolulu (ABC)

INTERCONFERENCE GAMES

(All times local)

Sun.	Aug.	31—Arizona at Cincinnati	1:00				Jacksonville at Washington	1:00
		Dallas at Pittsburgh	1:00				St. Louis at Oakland	1:00
		Minnesota at Buffalo	1:00	Sun.	Oct.	6—Detroit at Buffalo	1:00
Sun.	Sept.	2—San Diego at New Orleans	12:00	Sun.	Oct.	7—Philadelphia at Jacksonville	1:00
		Washington at Pittsburgh	1:00	Sun.	Oct.	8—Jacksonville at Dallas	12:00
		N.Y. Giants at Jacksonville	4:00				Seattle at St. Louis	12:00
Sun.	Sept.	3—Baltimore at N.Y. Giants	1:00				Washington at Tennessee	12:00
		Miami at Green Bay	12:00	Sun.	Oct.	9—Baltimore at Washington	1:00
		Oakland at Atlanta	1:00				Cincinnati at N.Y. Giants	1:00
		Carolina at San Diego	1:00				Tennessee at Arizona	2:00
		St. Louis at Denver	2:00				Kansas City at St. Louis	12:00
Sun.	Sept.	4—Chicago at New England	1:00				Chicago at Miami	4:00
		Kansas City at Carolina	1:00	Mon.	Oct.	9—Green Bay at New England	9:00
		Miami at Tampa Bay	8:00	Sun.	Nov.	10—New England at Minnesota	12:00
Sun.	Sept.	5—Denver at Atlanta	1:00				Oakland at Carolina	1:00

– 98 –

		Tampa Bay at Indianapolis..............	1:00
Sun.	Nov. 11—	Carolina at Denver	2:00
		New Orleans at Oakland.................	1:00
		N.Y. Giants at Tennessee	3:00
Sun.	Nov. 12—	Green Bay at Indianapolis..............	1:00
		New England at Tampa Bay	1:00
		Philadelphia at Baltimore...............	1:00
		Seattle at New Orleans...................	12:00
		N.Y. Jets at Chicago.......................	3:00
Sun.	Nov. 13—	Arizona at Baltimore	1:00
		Indianapolis at Detroit	1:00
		Minnesota at N.Y. Jets...................	1:00
		Pittsburgh at Philadelphia..............	1:00
		San Diego at San Francisco............	1:00
Thur.	Nov. 14—	Tennessee at Dallas	3:00

Sun.	Nov. 14—	Cincinnati at Philadelphia	1:00
		San Francisco at Kansas City.........	12:00
		Atlanta at Seattle...........................	1:00
		Pittsburgh at Arizona......................	2:00
Sun.	Dec. 15—	Buffalo at Chicago	12:00
		Atlanta at San Diego	1:00
		Detroit at Miami..............................	8:00
Sun.	Dec. 16—	Dallas at Cincinnati	1:00
		Tampa Bay at N.Y. Jets	1:00
Mon.	Dec. 16—	Denver at San Francisco.................	6:00
Sat.	Dec. 17—	Buffalo at Green Bay......................	11:30
Sun.	Dec. 17—	Indianapolis at Minnesota..............	12:00
		New Orleans at Kansas City...........	12:00
		N.Y. Jets at Detroit.........................	4:00
		San Francisco at Seattle	5:00

1997 SEASON *Schedule*

COLLEGE DRAFT

ROUND-BY-ROUND SELECTIONS

FIRST ROUND

	Team	Player selected	Pos.	College	Draft pick origination
1.	St. Louis	Orlando Pace	T	Ohio State	From N.Y. Jets
2.	Oakland	Darrell Russell	DT	Southern California	From New Orleans
3.	Seattle	Shawn Springs	CB	Ohio State	From Atlanta
4.	Baltimore	Peter Boulware	DE	Florida State	
5.	Detroit	Bryant Westbrook	DB	Texas	
6.	Seattle	Walter Jones	T	Florida State	From St. Louis through NYJ and T.B.
7.	N.Y. Giants	Ike Hilliard	WR	Florida	
8.	N.Y. Jets	James Farrior	LB	Virginia	From Tampa Bay
9.	Arizona	Tom Knight	DB	Iowa	
10.	New Orleans	Chris Naeole	G	Colorado	From Oakland
11.	Atlanta	Michael Booker	DB	Nebraska	From Chicago through Seattle
12.	Tampa Bay	Warrick Dunn	RB	Florida State	From Seattle
13.	Kansas City	Tony Gonzalez	TE	California	From Houston
14.	Cincinnati	Reinard Wilson	LB	Florida State	
15.	Miami	Yatil Green	WR	Miami, Fla.	
16.	Tampa Bay	Reidel Anthony	WR	Florida	From San Diego
17.	Washington	Kenard Lang	DE	Miami, Fla.	
18.	Houston	Kenny Holmes	DE	Miami, Fla.	From Kansas City
19.	Indianapolis	Tarik Glenn	T	California	
20.	Minnesota	Dwayne Rudd	LB	Alabama	
21.	Jacksonville	Renaldo Wynn	DT	Notre Dame	
22.	Dallas	David LaFleur	TE	Louisiana State	From Philadelphia
23.	Buffalo	Antowain Smith	RB	Houston	
24.	Pittsburgh	Chad Scott	DB	Maryland	
25.	Philadelphia	Jon Harris	DE	Virginia	From Dallas
26.	San Francisco	Jim Druckenmiller	QB	Virginia Tech	
27.	Carolina	Rae Carruth	WR	Colorado	
28.	Denver	Trevor Pryce	DT	Clemson	
29.	New England	Chris Canty	DB	Kansas State	
30.	Green Bay	Ross Verba	T	Iowa	

SECOND ROUND

	Team	Player selected	Pos.	College	Draft pick origination
31.	N.Y. Jets	Rick Terry	DT	North Carolina	
32.	Atlanta	Nathan Davis	DE	Indiana	
33.	New Orleans	Rob Kelly	DB	Ohio State	
34.	Baltimore	Jamie Sharper	LB	Virginia	
35.	Detroit	Juan Roque	G	Arizona	
36.	N.Y. Giants	Tiki Barber	RB	Virginia	
37.	Tampa Bay	Jerry Wunsch	T	Wisconsin	
38.	Chicago	John Allred	TE	Southern California	From St. Louis
39.	New Orleans	Jared Tomich	DE	Nebraska	From Oakland
40.	St. Louis	Dexter McCleon	DB	Clemson	From Chicago
41.	Atlanta	Byron Hanspard	RB	Texas Tech	From Seattle
42.	Arizona	Jake Plummer	QB	Arizona State	
43.	Cincinnati	Corey Dillon	RB	Washington	
44.	Miami	Sam Madison	DB	Louisville	
45.	San Diego	Freddie Jones	TE	North Carolina	
46.	Houston	Joey Kent	WR	Tennessee	
47.	Kansas City	Kevin Lockett	WR	Kansas State	
48.	Indianapolis	Adam Meadows	T	Georgia	
49.	Minnesota	Torrian Gray	DB	Virginia Tech	
50.	Jacksonville	Mike Logan	DB	West Virginia	
51.	Washington	Greg Jones	LB	Colorado	
52.	Buffalo	Marcellus Wiley	DE	Columbia	
53.	Pittsburgh	Will Blackwell	WR	San Diego State	
54.	Detroit	Kevin Abrams	DB	Syracuse	From Dallas
55.	San Francisco	Marc Edwards	FB	Notre Dame	From Philadelphia
56.	Carolina	Mike Minter	DB	Nebraska	
57.	Philadelphia	James Darling	LB	Washington State	From San Francisco
58.	Baltimore	Kim Herring	DB	Penn State	From Denver
59.	New England	Brandon Mitchell	DT	Texas A&M	
60.	Green Bay	Darren Sharper	DB	William & Mary	

THIRD ROUND

Team	Player selected	Pos.	College	Draft pick origination
61. New England	Sedrick Shaw	RB	Iowa	From N.Y. Jets
62. New Orleans	Troy Davis	RB	Iowa State	
63. Tampa Bay	Frank Middleton	G	Arizona	From Atlanta through Seattle
64. Baltimore	Jay Graham	RB	Tennessee	
65. Dallas	Dexter Coakley	LB	Appalachian State	From Detroit
66. Tampa Bay	Ronde Barber	DB	Virginia	
67. Denver	Dan Neil	C	Texas	From St. Louis through N.Y. Jets
68. N.Y. Giants	Ryan Phillips	LB	Idaho	
69. Chicago	Bob Sapp	G	Washington	
70. Atlanta	O.J. Santiago	TE	Kent	From Seattle
71. Philadelphia	Duce Staley	RB	South Carolina	From Arizona
72. Oakland	Adam Treu	G	Nebraska	
73. Miami	Jason Taylor	DE	Akron	
74. San Diego	Michael Hamilton	LB	North Carolina A&T	
75. Houston	Denard Walker	DB	Louisiana State	
76. Cincinnati	Rod Payne	C	Michigan	
77. San Francisco	Greg Clark	TE	Stanford	From Indianapolis
78. Minnesota	Stalin Colinet	DE	Boston College	
79. Jacksonville	James Hamilton	LB	North Carolina	
80. Washington	Derek Smith	LB	Arizona State	
81. Houston	Scott Sanderson	T	Washington State	From Kansas City
82. Pittsburgh	Paul Wiggins	T	Oregon	
83. Dallas	Steve Scifres	T	Wyoming	
84. Arizona	Ty Howard	DB	Ohio State	From Philadelphia
85. Oakland	Tim Kohn	T	Iowa State	From Buffalo
86. Indianapolis	Bert Berry	LB	Notre Dame	From San Francisco
87. Carolina	Kinnon Tatum	LB	Notre Dame	
88. N.Y. Jets	Dedric Ward	WR	Northern Iowa	From Denver
89. New England	Chris Carter	DB	Texas	
90. Green Bay	Brett Conway	K	Penn State	
91. Pittsburgh*	Mike Vrabel	DE	Ohio State	
92. Miami*	Derrick Rodgers	LB	Arizona State	
93. Miami*	Ronnie Ward	LB	Kansas	
94. Dallas*	Kenny Wheaton	DB	Oregon	
95. N.Y. Giants*	Brad Maynard	P	Ball State	
96. Miami*	Brent Smith	T	Mississippi State	

FOURTH ROUND

Team	Player selected	Pos.	College	Draft pick origination
97. New England	Damon Denson	G	Michigan	From N.Y. Jets
98. Houston	Derrick Mason	WR	Michigan State	From Atlanta
99. New Orleans	Danny Wuerffel	QB	Florida	
100. Atlanta	Henri Crockett	LB	Florida State	From Baltimore through Seattle
101. Dallas	Antonio Anderson	DT	Syracuse	From Detroit
102. N.Y. Jets	Terry Day	DE	Mississippi State	From St. Louis
103. N.Y. Giants	Pete Monty	LB	Wisconsin	
104. N.Y. Jets	Leon Johnson	RB	North Carolina	From Tampa Bay
105. Chicago	Darnell Autry	RB	Northwestern	From Seattle
106. Arizona	Chris Dishman	G	Nebraska	
107. Houston	Pratt Lyons	DE	Troy State	From Oakland through New Orleans
108. Chicago	Marcus Robinson	WR	South Carolina	
109. San Diego	Raleigh Roundtree	T	South Carolina State	
110. Kansas City	Pat Barnes	QB	California	From Houston
111. Cincinnati	Tremain Mack	DB	Miami, Fla.	
112. St. Louis	Ryan Tucker	C	Texas Christian	From Miami
113. Minnesota	Antonio Banks	DB	Virginia Tech	
114. Jacksonville	Seth Payne	DT	Cornell	
115. Washington	Albert Connell	WR	Texas A&M	
116. New Orleans	Keith Poole	WR	Arizona State	From Kansas City through Houston
117. Indianapolis	Delmonico Montgomery	DB	Houston	
118. Baltimore	Tyrus McCloud	LB	Louisville	From Dallas
119. Philadelphia	Damien Robinson	DB	Iowa	
120. Buffalo	Jamie Nails	T	Florida A&M	
121. Miami	Jerome Daniels	T	Northeastern	From Pittsburgh through St. Louis
122. Carolina	Tarek Saleh	LB	Wisconsin	
123. Oakland	Chad Levitt	RB	Cornell	From San Francisco through Miami
124. Denver	Corey Gilliard	DB	Ball State	
125. New England	Ed Ellis	T	Buffalo	

Team	Player selected	Pos.	College	Draft pick origination
126. Green Bay	Jermaine Smith	DT	Georgia	
127. Dallas*	Macey Brooks	WR	James Madison	
128. Tampa Bay*	Alshermond Singleton	LB	Temple	
129. Dallas*	Nicky Sualua	RB	Ohio State	
130. Detroit*	Matt Russell	LB	Colorado	

FIFTH ROUND

Team	Player selected	Pos.	College	Draft pick origination
131. N.Y. Jets	Lamont Burns	G	East Carolina	
132. Washington	Jamel Williams	DB	Nebraska	From Houston
133. Atlanta	Marcus Wimberly	DB	Miami, Fla.	
134. Baltimore	Jeff Mitchell	C	Florida	
135. Detroit	Pete Chryplewicz	TE	Notre Dame	
136. N.Y. Giants	Sam Garnes	DB	Cincinnati	
137. Tampa Bay	Patrick Hape	TE	Alabama	
138. San Diego	Kenny Bynum	RB	South Carolina State	From St. Louis
139. Arizona	Chad Carpenter	WR	Washington State	
140. Washington	Keith Thibodeaux	DB	Northwestern (La.) State	From Oakland through Atlanta
141. Chicago	Van Hiles	DB	Kentucky	
142. Seattle	Eric Stokes	DB	Nebraska	
143. Houston	George McCullough	DB	Baylor	
144. Cincinnati	Andre Purvis	DT	North Carolina	
145. N.Y. Jets	Raymond Austin	DB	Tennessee	From Miami
146. San Diego	Paul Bradford	DB	Portland State	From San Diego through Pittsburgh
147. Jacksonville	Damon Jones	TE	Southern Illinois	
148. Washington	Twan Russell	LB	Miami, Fla.	
149. Miami	Barron Tanner	DT	Oklahoma	From Kansas City
150. Indianapolis	Nate Jacquet	WR	San Diego State	
151. Minnesota	Tony Williams	DT	Memphis	
152. Philadelphia	Ndukwe Kalu	DE	Rice	
153. Buffalo	Sean Woodson	DB	Jackson State	
154. Pittsburgh	George Jones	RB	San Diego State	
155. Philadelphia	Luther Broughton	TE	Furman	From Dallas
156. Indianapolis	Carl Powell	DE	Louisville	From San Francisco
157. Miami	Nicholas Lopez	DE	Texas Southern	From Carolina through Oakland
158. St. Louis	Taje Allen	DB	Texas	From Denver
159. New England	Vernon Crawford	LB	Florida State	
160. Green Bay	Anthony Hicks	LB	Arkansas	
161. Detroit*	Duane Ashman	DE	Virginia	
162. Washington*	Brad Badger	G	Stanford	
163. Kansas City*	June Henley	RB	Kansas	

SIXTH ROUND

Team	Player selected	Pos.	College	Draft pick origination
164. N.Y. Jets	Tim Scharf	LB	Northwestern	
165. New Orleans	Nicky Savoie	TE	Louisiana State	From Atlanta through Houston
166. Miami	John Fiala	LB	Washington	From New Orleans through Oakland
167. Baltimore	Steve Lee	RB	Indiana	
168. Detroit	Tony Ramirez	T	Northern Colorado	
169. Tampa Bay	Al Harris	DB	Texas A&M-Kingsville	
170. Miami	Brian Manning	WR	Stanford	From St. Louis
171. N.Y. Giants	Mike Cherry	QB	Murray State	
172. Oakland	Calvin Branch	RB	Colorado State	
173. Miami	Mike Crawford	LB	Nevada	From Chicago through St. Louis
174. Seattle	Itula Mili	TE	Brigham Young	
175. Arizona	Rod Brown	RB	North Carolina State	
176. Cincinnati	Canute Curtis	LB	West Virginia	
177. Miami	Ed Perry	TE	James Madison	
178. San Diego	Daniel Palmer	C	Air Force	
179. St. Louis	Muadianvita Kazadi	LB	Tulsa	From Houston
180. Atlanta	Calvin Collins	C	Texas A&M	From Washington
181. Houston	Dennis Stallings	LB	Illinois	From Kansas City
182. Indianapolis	Scott Von Der Ahe	LB	Arizona State	
183. Minnesota	Robert Tate	WR	Cincinnati	
184. Jacksonville	Daimon Shelton	RB	Cal State Sacramento	
185. Buffalo	Marcus Spriggs	T	Houston	
186. Pittsburgh	Daryl Porter	DB	Boston College	
187. Dallas	Lee Vaughn	DB	Wyoming	
188. Arizona	Tony McCombs	LB	Eastern Kentucky	From Philadelphia

Team	Player selected	Pos.	College	Draft pick origination
189. Carolina	Matt Finkes	DE	Ohio State	
190. Philadelphia	Antwuan Wyatt	WR	Bethune-Cookman	From San Francisco
191. N.Y. Jets	Chuck Clements	QB	Houston	From Denver
192. New England	Tony Gaiter	WR	Miami, Fla.	
193. Oakland	Grady Jackson	DE	Knoxville	From Green Bay
194. Baltimore*	Cornell Brown	LB	Virginia Tech	
195. Kansas City*	Isaac Byrd	WR	Kansas	
196. Chicago*	Shawn Swayda	DE	Arizona State	
197. Tampa Bay*	Nigea Carter	WR	Michigan State	
198. Philadelphia*	Edward Jasper	DT	Texas A&M	
199. Pittsburgh*	Rod Manuel	DE	Oklahoma	
200. Chicago*	Richard Hogans	LB	Memphis	
201. Chicago*	Ricky Parker	DB	San Diego State	

SEVENTH ROUND

Team	Player selected	Pos.	College	Draft pick origination
202. N.Y. Jets	Steve Rosga	DB	Colorado	
203. Miami	Hudhaifa Ismaeli	DB	Northwestern	From New Orleans through Oakland
204. Atlanta	Tony Graziani	QB	Oregon	
205. Baltimore	Chris Ward	DE	Kentucky	
206. Detroit	Terry Battle	RB	Arizona State	
207. Philadelphia	Koy Detmer	QB	Colorado	From St. Louis through N.Y. Jets
208. N.Y. Giants	Matt Keneley	DT	Southern California	
209. Tampa Bay	Anthony DeGrate	DT	Stephen F. Austin	
210. Chicago	Mike Miano	DT	Southwest Missouri State	
211. Seattle	Carlos Jones	DB	Miami, Fla.	
212. Arizona	Mark Smith	DE	Auburn	
213. Green Bay	Chris Miller	WR	Southern California	From Oakland
214. Kansas City	Nathan Parks	T	Stanford	From Miami
215. St. Louis	Cedric White	DE	North Carolina A&T	From San Diego
216. Houston	Armon Williams	DB	Arizona	
217. Cincinnati	William Carr	DT	Michigan	
218. San Diego	Toran James	LB	North Carolina A&T	From Kansas City through Pittsburgh
219. Indianapolis	Clarence Thompson	DB	Knoxville	
220. Minnesota	Artie Ulmer	LB	Valdosta State	
221. Jacksonville	Jon Hesse	LB	Nebraska	
222. Atlanta	Chris Bayne	DB	Fresno State	From Washington
223. Pittsburgh	Michael Adams	WR	Texas	
224. Dallas	Omar Stoutmire	DB	Fresno State	
225. Philadelphia	Byron Capers	DB	Florida State	
226. Buffalo	Pat Fitzgerald	TE	Texas	
227. Philadelphia	Deauntae Brown	DB	Central State (Ohio)	From San Francisco
228. Carolina	Kris Mangum	TE	Mississippi	
229. N.Y. Jets	Jason Ferguson	DT	Georgia	From Denver
230. New England	Scott Rehberg	T	Central Michigan	
231. Green Bay	Jerald Sowell	RB	Tulane	
232. Detroit*	Marcus Harris	WR	Wyoming	
233. Chicago*	Marvin Thomas	DE	Memphis	
234. Baltimore*	Wally Richardson	QB	Penn State	
235. Minnesota*	Matthew Hatchette	WR	Langston (Okla.)	
236. Baltimore*	Ralph Staten	DB	Alabama	
237. San Diego*	Tony Corbin	QB	Cal State Sacramento	
238. Baltimore*	Leland Taylor	DT	Louisville	
239. Detroit*	Richard Jordan	LB	Missouri Southern	
240. Green Bay*	Ronnie McAda	QB	Army	

*Pick awarded to team as compensation for loss of a free agent.

PLAYOFF PLAN

TIEBREAKING PROCEDURES

DIVISION TIES

TWO CLUBS

1. Head-to-head (best won-lost-tied percentage in games between the clubs).
2. Best won-lost-tied percentage in games played within the division.
3. Best won-lost-tied percentage in games played within the conference.
4. Best won-lost-tied percentage in common games, if applicable.
5. Best net points in division games.
6. Best net points in all games.
7. Strength of schedule.
8. Best net touchdowns in all games.
9. Coin toss.

THREE OR MORE CLUBS

(Note: If two clubs remain tied after other clubs are eliminated during any step, tie-breaker reverts to step 1 of two-club format.)
1. Head-to-head (best won-lost-tied percentage in games among the clubs).
2. Best won-lost-tied percentage in games played within the division.
3. Best won-lost-tied percentage in games played within the conference.
4. Best won-lost-tied percentage in common games.
5. Best net points in division games.
6. Best net points in all games.
7. Strength of schedule.
8. Best net touchdowns in all games.
9. Coin toss.

WILD-CARD TIES

If necessary to break ties to determine the three wild-card clubs from each conference, the following steps will be taken:
1. If all the tied clubs are from the same division, apply division tie-breaker.
2. If the tied clubs are from different divisions, apply the steps listed below.
3. When the first wild-card team has been identified, the procedure is repeated to name the second wild card (i.e., eliminate all but the highest-ranked club in each division prior to proceeding to step 2), and repeated a third time, if necessary, to identify the third wild card. In situations where three or more teams from the same division are involved in the procedure, the original seeding of the teams remains the same for subsequent applications of the tie-breaker if the top-ranked team in that division qualifies for a wild-card berth.

TWO CLUBS

1. Head-to-head, if applicable.
2. Best won-lost-tied percentage in games played within the conference.
3. Best won-lost-tied percentage in common games, minimum of four.
4. Best average net points in conference games.
5. Best net points in all games.
6. Strength of schedule.
7. Best net touchdowns in all games.
8. Coin toss.

THREE OR MORE CLUBS

(Note: If two clubs remain tied after other clubs are eliminated, tie-breaker reverts to step 1 of two-club format.)
1. Apply division tie-breaker to eliminate all but highest-ranked club in each division prior to proceeding to step 1. The original seeding within a division upon application of the division tie-breaker remains the same for all subsequent applications of the procedure that are necessary to identify the three wild-card participants.
2. Head-to-head sweep (applicable only if one club has defeated each of the others or one club has lost to each of the others).
3. Best won-lost-tied percentage in games played within the conference.
4. Best won-lost-tied percentage in common games, minimum of four.
5. Best average net points in conference games.
6. Best net points in all games.
7. Strength of schedule.
8. Best net touchdowns in all games.
9. Coin toss.

1996 REVIEW

Year in review
Final standings
Weeks 1 through 17
Wild-card games
Divisional playoffs
Conference championships
Super Bowl XXXI
Pro Bowl
Player participation
Attendance
Trades

YEAR IN REVIEW

THE TOP STORIES OF THE PAST YEAR

By VITO STELLINO

If the Green Bay Packers didn't exist, the NFL might have had to invent them in 1996.

The Packers were the feel-good story of the year at a time when the NFL was coping with turmoil and strife on and off the field during its 77th season.

Although the Packers play in the league's smallest city—Green Bay's population of slightly under 100,000 could fit comfortably into the Rose Bowl—the Packers are one team that will never skip town. The community-owned team, founded by the Indian Packing Company in 1919, has 1,195 stockholders who own 4,634 shares of stock. The shares, purchased for $25, never pay dividends, but they're heirlooms in Green Bay.

No team has a heritage to match the Packers, who have won an even dozen titles. Under Curly Lambeau, for whom their stadium is named, the Packers won three consecutive championships from 1929-31 before the league even had a championship game. Under Vince Lombardi, for whom the Super Bowl trophy is named, they won three consecutive NFL championships from 1965-67, including the first two Super Bowls.

That's why when the Packers beat the New England Patriots, 35-21, in Super Bowl XXXI in New Orleans on January, 26, 1997, their fans were awash in nostalgia. Even the fans who were too young to remember Lambeau and Lombardi and the "Ice Bowl" were caught up in the emotion of the moment.

"I think it's time the Lombardi Trophy goes home to Lambeau Field, where it belongs," team president Bob Harlan said.

Coach Mike Holmgren told his players, "This trophy, men, is named after Vince Lombardi. As important as it is to every player in this league, it's even more important to us. This is where it belongs."

There was a larger message in the Green Bay victory. It was that a well-managed, small-market team without a deep-pockets owner still could compete—and win—against the big-market teams in the free-agency era.

The man who ultimately made it all possible, former NFL commissioner Pete Rozelle, died at age 70 in Rancho Sante Fe, Calif., of brain cancer on December 6, less than two months before the Packers won the Super Bowl.

Rozelle convinced the owners to share all the TV revenue equally, which made it possible for all teams to compete on an equal level and for Green Bay to survive. Unfortunately, the league has had trouble coping in recent years with the success he helped create as teams continue to search for greener pastures with more luxury boxes and premium seats.

The league didn't even have a team the past two years in Los Angeles, the nation's second-largest market, or last year in Cleveland, a market whose NFL roots date to 1937. It had a lame-duck team in Houston that is heading to Tennessee.

In the past 15 years, five franchises—the Raiders, Colts, Cardinals, Rams and Browns—have relocated, with the Raiders going to Los Angeles in 1982 and returning to Oakland in 1995. The Colts left Baltimore for Indianapolis in 1984, the Cardinals left St. Louis for Phoenix in 1988 and the Rams left Anaheim for St. Louis in 1995. The Browns moved to Baltimore in 1996 and became the Ravens, leaving the Browns nickname and heritage behind for a new team that will play in Cleveland in 1999.

All that instability may be one of the reasons why attendance and TV ratings dropped slightly in 1996. But pro football has surpassed all its rivals to become the nation's most popular sport—the Super Bowl has become a virtual mid-winter holiday—and Green Bay's success showed the NFL can still remember its roots.

THE NFC IS STILL KING

For the first time since the Chicago Bears won Super Bowl XX after the 1985 season, the San Francisco 49ers, Dallas Cowboys, New York Giants and Washington Redskins were shut out of the Super Bowl. Those teams had combined to win 10 consecutive Super Bowls—three each by the 49ers and Cowboys and two each by the Giants and Redskins.

But the Packers' return to the top did keep alive the NFC's amazing string of Super Bowl victories. The conference has won every game since the Raiders beat Washington in Super Bowl XVIII after the 1983 season. The NFC has won 15 of the past 16, with three teams—the 49ers (five) and the Cowboys and Redskins (three each)—combining to win 11 of those 15 titles.

Nobody has yet come up with a clear explanation of why the NFC has managed to keep winning the Super Bowl even though all 30 teams draft from the same common pool, play each other in the regular season and allow executives, coaches and players to switch back and forth from one conference to another.

The Packers' rebuilding program even had its roots in the AFC because general manager Ron Wolf was a long-time Raiders aide and, later, worked for the Jets before he was hired to run the Packers at the end of the 1991 season. He hired coach Mike Holmgren, traded for quarterback Brett Favre in 1992 and signed defensive lineman Reggie White to a $17 million deal in 1993, proving the Packers could lure free agents to the league's smallest market.

The Packers put together an old-fashioned, five-year rebuilding program to get to the top, but the acquisition of Favre was the key. He was the league's MVP each of the past two seasons. He passed for 3,899 yards and 39 touchdowns in 1996. And the Packers are 57-30 with him as the starter.

The Packers, who had lost in Dallas in the playoffs each of the three previous years, found out during the '96 season that they still couldn't climb that hurdle. With their receiver corps depleted by injuries, they lost, 21-6, in Week 12 for their seventh consecutive loss in Dallas. But they won their last five regular-season games and beat San Francisco, 35-14, and Carolina, 30-13, in the playoffs to gain the Super Bowl berth.

In the Super Bowl, Favre burned New England with touchdown passes of 54 and 81 yards and ran for a third touchdown, but return man Desmond Howard won MVP honors by setting up two scores with punt returns and scored himself on a 99-yard kickoff return in the third quarter. That broke the game open after the Patriots had narrowed the deficit to 27-21.

THE OTHER CONFERENCE

The AFC continued to play the role of the Washington Generals to the NFC's Harlem Globetrotters, losing the Super Bowl for the 13th consecutive time. And for the second year in a row, the AFC team with the best record got knocked out at home in the first round of the playoffs.

In 1995, it was Kansas City, which posted a 13-3 regular-season record, then lost its first playoff game to Indianapolis, 10-7.

Last year, it was Denver, which also went 13-3 during the regular season, then lost its first playoff game to Jacksonville, 30-27. Mark Brunell passed for 245 yards and two touchdowns, and Natrone Means rushed for 140 yards as the Jaguars shredded the Denver defense.

The Jaguars then went to New England for the AFC championship game, where they lost to the Patriots, 20-6. The Patriots forced two turnovers in the last five minutes to wrap it up.

That put the Patriots in the Super Bowl for the first time since 1985. Even though they had a coach, Bill Parcells, who had previously led the New York Giants to two of the NFC's Super Bowl championships, the Patriots became No. 13 in the NFC's string of Super Bowl victims.

DETHRONED

The Dallas Cowboys failed in their attempt to become the first team to win four Super Bowls in a five-year span when they were eliminated in the second round of the playoffs at Carolina, 26-17.

But the real failure for the Cowboys was not on the field but off it, where the team was embarrassed by a series of sex, drug and alcohol problems that scarred its image.

It started early in the offseason with reports that the players had rented a so-called "White House" near their training facility where they had parties away from their wives.

Then came the indictment of wide receiver Michael Irvin on drug possession charges after Dallas police found him in a hotel room with two topless dancers and a former teammate. Irvin eventually pleaded no contest to felony cocaine charges in July, ending a trial that exposed several sordid scandals, including a murder-for-hire plot that targeted Irvin and was funded by a Dallas policeman.

Irvin was sentenced to four years' probation, 800 hours of community service, fined $10,000 and warned that he could face 20 years in jail for the next offense. Irvin then was suspended for the first five games by the

NFL for violating its substance-abuse policy.

Defensive tackle Leon Lett, who was suspended for four games in 1995 for violating the drug policy, was suspended for a year on December 3. Drug suspensions are nothing new for the Cowboys; of the league's previous 13 suspensions, seven involved Cowboys or ex-Cowboys.

There was another firestorm in late December, during the week before the Carolina playoff game, when a 23-year-old woman charged that offensive tackle Erik Williams raped her while Irvin held a gun to her head. The woman later recanted her charges and was charged with perjury. All charges were dropped against the players, and Williams filed a federal court suit against the city of Dallas and the police for violating his civil rights.

With all this turmoil going on, it was remarkable that the Cowboys still went 10-6, won the NFC Eastern Division and a first-round playoff game against Minnesota before losing in Carolina, where Irvin was injured early in the game after making his first reception.

The turbulent year led to much soul-searching about the future direction of the Cowboys. Owner Jerry Jones addressed the players at their final team meeting and warned them to clean up their act.

As quarterback Troy Aikman said, "With all the problems this team faced, I don't think anyone's real proud of the image. I don't think those in control are real proud."

In April 1997, Jones hired former Cowboys player Calvin Hill and his wife, Janet—better known to the younger generation as the parents of NBA star Grant Hill—to direct a department designed to improve player behavior. Robert Newhouse, another former Cowboy, was named the day-to-day director of the program.

Jones, who may have been concerned that the team's tarnished image would hurt his ability to negotiate lucrative marketing deals, warned that players who do not accept the program will become ex-Cowboys. "The fans of the Cowboys deserve this type of intense commitment to good behavior." he said.

UPS AND DOWNS

Seven of the 12 teams that made the playoffs in 1995 made it back last season. The three newcomers in the AFC were New England, Denver and Jacksonville; they replaced Miami, San Diego and Kansas City. The two newcomers in the NFC were Carolina and Minnesota; they replaced Detroit and Atlanta.

The biggest improvements were made by New England, which went from 6-10 in 1995 to an 11-5 mark and the AFC Eastern Division title; Jacksonville, from 4-12 to 9-7 and a wild-card playoff berth; Denver, from 8-8 to 13-3 and the AFC West title; and Carolina, from 7-9 to 12-4 and first place in the NFC West.

Three of the division champions—Pittsburgh (AFC Central), Dallas (NFC East) and Green Bay (NFC Central)—repeated. New England, Denver and Carolina replaced Buffalo, Kansas City and San Francisco, respectively, atop their divisions.

The biggest plunge was made by Atlanta, which went from a 9-7 wild-card mark in '95 to 3-13, which tied New Orleans for the second-worst record in the league.

EXPANSION TWINS

One of the most remarkable stories of the year was the rise of the Carolina Panthers and the Jacksonville Jaguars, the two 1995 expansion teams, who reached the conference title games in just their second seasons. Carolina won its division title with a 12-4 record. Jacksonville started out 4-7, then rallied to win its last five games and earn a wild-card spot.

The records were tributes to the organizations put together by the two owners, Jerry Richardson of Carolina and Wayne Weaver of Jacksonville.

But there were complaints around the league that the two clubs got deals that were too generous. Each was allotted 28 total draft picks in 1995 and 1996, compared to 14 for the established teams, and were allowed to spend a full salary cap once they counted the salaries of the players in the veteran allocation pool.

"They're not expansion teams, they're free-agency teams" grumbled Green Bay G.M. Ron Wolf, who was with Tampa Bay when the Buccaneers, who did not have similar advantages, started out 0-26.

The league didn't want the expansion teams to struggle the way the Buccaneers and Seattle Seahawks did when they were founded in 1976, but Carolina and Jacksonville weren't expected to become instant contenders.

Although San Diego general manager Bobby Beathard noted the teams had to be given credit for taking advantage of the hands they were dealt, he said, "In my mind, the league was too generous to give all of that for fear maybe it would be an embarrassment to have struggling expansion teams."

Michael Huyghue, the Jaguars' senior vice president of football operations, responded by saying, "What you've seen is two good organizations who have outhustled their competitors. All the teams could have thrown in all their cards and started over if they wanted to."

COACHING DERBY

If you like job security, an NFL coaching job is not an ideal one.

Eleven of the 30 coaches who began the 1996 season failed to keep their jobs. The exodus started with the departures of Jim Mora of the New Orleans Saints and David Shula of the Cincinnati Bengals on October 21, after Week 8. Mora resigned and Shula was fired.

By the time the smoke cleared, nine more coaches—George Seifert of San Francisco, Bill Parcells of New England, Bobby Ross of San Diego, June Jones of Atlanta, Dan Reeves of the Giants, Rich Brooks of St. Louis, Mike White of Oakland, Rich Kotite of the Jets and Wayne Fontes of Detroit—had departed.

Three of the coaches quickly got new jobs. Parcells moved to the Jets after club owner Leon Hess agreed to give the Patriots compensation for Parcells. Ross took the Lions' job and Reeves went to Atlanta.

Bruce Coslet, who led the Bengals to a 7-2 mark after replacing Shula on an interim basis, was named coach on a permanent basis. Coslet, fired by the Jets after the 1993 season, was one of five former coaches to return. Dick Vermeil, who had been away 14 years since quitting in Philadelphia after the 1982 season, got the St.

Louis job. Mike Ditka, who was fired in Chicago after the 1992 season, was named the New Orleans coach. Joe Bugel, who was fired by Arizona after the 1993 season, was promoted from assistant head coach/offense to coach in Oakland. And Pete Carroll, who lasted just one year (1994) with the Jets, took the New England job.

Three more coaches, Kevin Gilbride in San Diego, Steve Mariucci in San Francisco and Jim Fassel with the Giants, were named NFL coaches for the first time. This doesn't count Bill Belichick, who lasted six days as the Jets' coach before the team made a settlement with the Patriots to get Parcells.

"I asked (Jets team president) Steve Gutman if he was going to throw a retirement party for Belichick," joked Baltimore Ravens owner Art Modell, who fired Belichick in Cleveland after the 1995 season.

By the time the musical chairs game was over, the average tenure for a coach was 2.4 years in the AFC and 1.7 in the NFC. Marv Levy, who has coached the Bills for 11 years, is the leader in seniority.

The days when Tom Landry could coach 29 years in Dallas, Don Shula 26 years in Miami and Chuck Noll 23 years in Pittsburgh apparently are gone.

Rams president John Shaw, who fired Brooks after just two years on the job, said, "Teams are less patient. You only get four years with a player before he becomes a free agent. A lot of teams now view it as a two- or three-year program, especially when you look at this year's conference championship games."

He was referring to Carolina—which is in the Rams' division—and Jacksonville reaching the conference championship games in only their second seasons. When owners see teams reach success that quickly, they're less patient in waiting for five-year plans to materialize.

Sam Wyche, who has been fired both in Cincinnati and Tampa Bay and is now a TV analyst, said owners should get the blame.

"Any owner who hires a coach and fires him after one, two or three years—that's a failure of the owner," he said. "The owner picked a guy he shouldn't have picked. If an owner will not be patient enough, to me it's a failure of the guy doing the hiring."

FRONT-OFFICE BATTLES

Not all of the coaching changes were garden-variety firings because of losing records. Some were more complicated.

In San Diego, Bobby Ross clashed with G.M. Bobby Beathard; in New York, Dan Reeves couldn't work harmoniously with Giants G.M. George Young. Ross and Reeves wanted more control, and they got it in their new jobs.

In New England, Bill Parcells couldn't co-exist with owner Bob Kraft. When Parcells protested the decision of personnel chief Bobby Grier to select wide receiver Terry Glenn in the first round of the 1996 draft—Parcells felt the team needed defensive help—Kraft backed Grier, and the rift couldn't be healed.

The irony is that Parcells had planned to retire after the 1996 season in the wake of a disappointing 6-10 record in 1995. He even asked Kraft to delete a provision in his contract that obligated Parcells to pay $1.3 million if he didn't fulfill the final year. Kraft agreed, with the stipulation that Parcells couldn't coach any other team in 1997.

Parcells then was energized when the Patriots made the Super Bowl—with the help of Glenn's 90 receptions and six touchdowns—and wanted to return to New York to take the Jets' job.

After commissioner Paul Tagliabue ruled that Parcells' contract tied him to the Patriots in 1997 if he wanted to coach, Kraft refused to release him unless he got compensation. Parcells quit and was ready to sit out for a year if the Jets and Patriots couldn't agree on compensation.

In a deal brokered by Tagliabue, the Patriots, who wanted the first pick in the 1997 draft, instead got third- and fourth-round picks in '97, a second-round choice in '98 and and a first-round pick in '99, plus $300,000 to be donated to a Patriots' charity.

Then there was the San Francisco situation. George Seifert didn't want to go into the 1997 season, the final year of his contract, as a lame duck, so he quit when he didn't get an extension. The 49ers, who seem to think they should win the Super Bowl every year, didn't appreciate Seifert's 108-35 record in eight years, including two Super Bowl victories, and pushed him out the door with a golden parachute.

MINORITY HIRING

Frustrated by the fact that none of the 11 coaches hired was a minority, a group of nine black assistants met with commissioner Paul Tagliabue in New York in March to discuss the league's minority hiring problem.

Even though about 67 percent of the league's players are black, there are only three black coaches: Ray Rhodes in Philadelphia, Dennis Green in Minnesota and Tony Dungy in Tampa.

Art Shell, the former Raiders coach who didn't get an interview for any of the openings even though eight of the 11 coaches hired had previous NFL coaching experience, said of the meeting, "We do feel we had a good start."

Tagliabue, noting he doesn't do the hiring, said, "I told them my role was to make sure our clubs looked at a wide pool of candidates, a diverse pool of candidates."

One of the coaches bypassed was Sherm Lewis, offensive coordinator of the Packers, even though assistant coaches on Super Bowl teams often advance to coaching jobs. Lewis, who didn't attend the meeting in New York, took a low-key approach, at least publicly.

"If we just keep winning Super Bowls, somebody will eventually say, 'Hey, this guy deserves a shot,'" Lewis said.

But Dungy said of the snub of Lewis: "If Sherman Lewis were white, do you think he would have gotten a job?"

FAN SUPPORT

The fans sent the NFL a warning in 1996: It can no longer take them for granted.

Both attendance and TV ratings dipped slightly last year. Average attendance dropped from 62,682 to 60,885 per game, and the TV ratings slipped on all three networks. Fox dipped from a 12.5 rating to 11.3, NBC from 11.1 to 10.9 and ABC's Monday Night

Football dropped from 17.0 to 16.2.

Even the Super Bowl, which got a 46 rating and a 68 share in 1996, dropped to a 43.3 rating and a 65 share for the Green Bay-New England matchup. The audience dipped from 138.5 million to 128.9 million.

Although the networks complained about the way Nielsen compiled the ratings, the real problem could be that the league's instability and off-the-field problems turned off some fans.

But the drop in TV ratings won't hurt the league's leverage when the new TV contracts are negotiated after this season. The league got $4.4 billion for four years in the last TV contract and expects at least a 30 percent hike this time. That CBS will enter the bidding again virtually guarantees that the contracts will go up. Although there's virtually no chance CBS can wrest the NFC package back from Fox, it is likely to bid on one of the other packages.

THE HARD CAP

The NFL's salary cap, which has seemed squishy soft at times in recent years, got a bit harder. That's because the cap went up only slightly, from $40.8 million in 1996 to $41.454 million this year. The cap had jumped from $34.6 million in 1994 to $37.1 million in 1995 and to $40.8 million in '96.

The result was that teams didn't have much extra money to spend and they tended to be leery of free agency after the Jets, who went on a spending spree in 1996 that included a $25 million deal for quarterback Neil O'Donnell, had the league's worst record (1-15).

The conventional wisdom now is that teams are better off spending their money to keep their own players and foster a sense of team unity.

That helps explain why by April 30, 1997, 88 unrestricted free agents and 32 restricted free agents had re-signed with their old teams, while 73 players (69 unrestricted free agents, two transition players and two restricted free agents) had changed teams. Last year, 88 players changed teams by the end of April and a total of 105 changed teams by the time free agency ended on July 15.

Of course, some players cashed in on big deals to change teams. The Seahawks were quick to plunge into the market, signing Pittsburgh linebacker Chad Brown to a six-year, $24 million deal and then signing another Steeler, cornerback Willie Williams, to a four-year, $8.7 million deal.

Quarterback Elvis Grbac left San Francisco for a $20.4 million deal with the Kansas City Chiefs. Offensive lineman Kevin Gogan was lured across the Bay from Oakland to San Francisco for a six-year, $12 million deal. Linebacker Micheal Barrow got a $19 million deal to move from Houston to Carolina, and Chicago gave cornerback Tom Carter, a transition player, a five-year, $13.8 million deal that Washington declined to match.

But some of the best deals went to players who stayed home. Detroit quarterback Scott Mitchell signed a $21 million deal even before the free-agency market opened, and linebacker Derrick Thomas got a

$27 million pact in Kansas City. Two of the league's best running backs, Terry Allen of Washington and Jerome Bettis of Pittsburgh, stayed home for $14.8 million and $14.4 million contracts, respectively.

The league has had free agency since 1993, but the owners and players still are learning to live with it. A year ago, the two sides agreed to extend the current collective bargaining agreement through 2000, with options to extend it two more years.

By December 1, 1997, they must decide whether to extend it through 2001. The owners, who want restrictions placed on signing bonuses (which now account for 45 percent of all salaries), have threatened not to extend it. Meanwhile, the NFL Players Association has decided to stop rebating dues to put together a $50 million war chest in case it has to fight another labor war.

In another dispute, the two sides have agreed on a salary cap bank for 1998 that will reduce the increase in the cap after the new TV contract is negotiated. The owners say the reduction in the increase should be $3 million; the players say it should be much less. A special master will have to make the final determination.

STADIUM GAMES

Although voters have approved new stadiums in Cleveland, Cincinnati, Nashville, Detroit and Tampa, the battle to get stadiums constructed always is a difficult one.

In Tampa, even after construction was started, a judge ruled the stadium's financing plan was unconstitutional. The Florida Supreme Court will have to make the final ruling.

Voters in Seattle and San Francisco were to vote in June whether to approve new stadiums in those cities. If the Seattle vote is approved, Microsoft co-founder Paul Allen will exercise his option to buy the Seahawks from Ken Behring.

The owners passed a cross-ownership bill at their March meeting that will allow Allen to own the Seahawks even though he already owns the NBA's Portland Trail Blazers. The measure also allows Wayne Huizenga, who also owns baseball's Marlins and the NHL's Panthers, to keep the Dolphins.

Carolina opened Ericsson Stadium last year, Washington will open its new stadium this fall in suburban Landover, Md., and Baltimore's new stadium will be completed for the 1998 season.

New stadiums are scheduled to be completed in Nashville and Cleveland, which will get an expansion team in 1999 if an existing team doesn't move there first. Nashville will be the new home of the Houston Oilers, but until the new stadium is built, the Oilers will play in Memphis.

MILESTONES

Chiefs running back Marcus Allen is writing his page in the record book. He surpassed Jim Brown (106) and Walter Payton (110) to become the career rushing touchdowns leader with 112. Allen has 134 touchdowns overall and trails only San Francisco's Jerry Rice, who has 165.

Allen also topped Roger Craig (566) to become the career receptions leader for running backs with 576 and topped Mosi Tatupu (199) to become the leader in games played at running back with 205.

In other milestones, Miami's Dan Marino became the first quarterback to pass for 50,000 yards, Rice became the first receiver to top the 1,000-receptions mark and Detroit's Barry Sanders became the first player to rush for 1,000 yards in each of his first eight seasons.

THE LEGAL FILE

The NFL settled two major lawsuits last year.

It reached an agreement with former Patriots owner Billy Sullivan for $11.5 million rather than risk a third trial. Sullivan had won a $114 million judgment after the first trial that was overturned in appellate court; the second one ended in a hung jury. Sullivan sued because he contended the league forced him to sell by not allowing him to conduct a public stock sale.

The league also dropped its suits against Dallas owner Jerry Jones over his marketing deals. It means Jones is free to make his own deals.

But the league's legal woes are far from over. Victor Kiam, another former Patriots owner, is suing because he said he was forced to sell when the league didn't allow him to move his team.

Raiders owner Al Davis once again is suing the league because he says it scuttled his negotiations to remain in Los Angeles. The city of St. Louis is suing to overturn its $29 million relocation fee because Davis wasn't forced to pay one when he moved the Raiders back to Oakland.

Fran Murray, who was once a minority owner of the Patriots and negotiated a deal for the lease at the new stadium in St. Louis when he was trying to obtain an expansion team in that city, is suing the league because he contends the league squeezed him out of both markets. A jury was to hear the case in Philadelphia in the summer of 1997.

INSTANT REPLAY

The return of instant replay fell three votes shy of passing at the March meeting when the owners voted, 20-10, in favor of the measure.

Under the proposed challenge system, a coach would have had to ask for a replay and would have lost a timeout even if the call was overturned. That feature upset Jets coach Bill Parcells, who provided a critical "no" vote. Raiders owner Al Davis also didn't like the challenge feature. Once it was obvious instant replay was going to lose, Dallas owner Jerry Jones provided the 10th "no" vote. Jones opposed replay, but would have voted "yes" if 22 other teams had favored it.

Seven teams have remained opposed to replay under any circumstances, so proponents need to find a system the other 23 teams will support. The debate is likely to heat up every time there is a controversial call, so this issue won't go away.

FINES

The league continued to send a message to the players that conduct it deems detrimental to the game will bring stiff fines.

Chicago linebacker Bryan Cox was fined a record $87,500 for making an obscene gesture to an official in a game against Green Bay. Oakland guard Steve Wisniewski was fined $50,000 for his actions in a game against the Lions—$30,000 for launching himself into a pile and $20,000 for bumping an official. Earlier in the season, he was fined $10,000 and $5,000 for unnecessary roughness, bringing his tab to $65,000,

Minnesota cornerback Corey Fuller was fined $30,000 for poking Green Bay center Frank Winters in the eye, plus $7,500 for a late hit that provoked Winters.

Atlanta linebacker Chuck Smith was fined $7,500 for going at Dallas quarterback Troy Aikman's knees and $25,000 (although he was told $10,000 would be rebated if he had no further incidents) for doing the same thing to Carolina quarterback Kerry Collins.

The league also handed out multiple fines for brawls. A combined 35 Pittsburgh and Houston players were penalized a total of $145,000, although $92,000 was to be rebated if there were no further incidents; 17 Seahawks and Chiefs were fined $73,000; and 14 Packers and Cowboys were fined $64,000.

But the NFL could be nit-picking at times. It fined Dallas cornerback Deion Sanders $5,000 for putting Leon Lett's number on his wristband after Lett was suspended.

The league also decided to start fining players this season if they take their helmets off on the field to celebrate.

DRUG PROBLEMS

If suspensions are a barometer, Dallas is the team with the most serious drug problem. Five Cowboys and ex-Cowboys were suspended in the past year for violating the league's substance-abuse policy. No other team had more than one player suspended.

Cory Fleming, released by Dallas after the 1995 season, reportedly was suspended for four games, although the penalty wasn't carried out because no team signed him. Clayton Holmes, suspended for a year late in the 1995 season and then released by the Cowboys, sat out the 1996 season and was signed by the Dolphins during the offseason.

Michael Irvin was suspended for the first five games of the '96 season and Shante Carver for the first six. Leon Lett, who was suspended for four games in 1995, was suspended for a year on December 3 and will miss the first 13 games of the '97 season.

Larry Webster of the Ravens and Roosevelt Potts of the Colts also sat out the 1996 season under suspensions.

Bam Morris, who was suspended for four games after pleading guilty to a marijuana possession charge, wound up missing five games before he was allowed to take the field for the Ravens after he was released by Pittsburgh.

New Orleans' Darren Mickell, Carolina's Curtis Whitley and St. Louis' Jesse James each served four-game suspensions.

Green Bay quarterback Brett Favre spent several weeks during the 1996 offseason in a Kansas clinic, where he was treated for an addiction to painkillers. But he was not suspended and came back to win MVP honors again. Favre appealed when the league banned him from using alcohol and that prohibition was lifted after the season ended.

GOING NORTH

The NFL entered into a five-year agreement with the Canadian Football League in which the NFL will give the CFL $3 million and assistance in marketing the struggling league.

As part of the agreement, the CFL champion will meet the World League champion and players from the CFL will be eligible to join NFL teams at the end of the CFL season.

Commissioner Paul Tagliabue made this agreement without consulting the owners, and it did not get a warm reception in Buffalo, which is trying to attract fans from Toronto.

HALL OF FAME

Don Shula, the winningest coach in NFL history, headed this year's four-man delegation into the Hall of Fame. Elected with Shula were Wellington Mara, the co-owner of the New York Giants and one of the pioneers of the game; Pittsburgh and Kansas City center Mike Webster; and cornerback Mike Haynes, who played with the Patriots and Raiders.

The four were to be inducted into the Hall in Canton, Ohio, during ceremonies on July 26.

RETIREMENTS

Two of the top quarterbacks of the past decade, Jim Kelly and Bernie Kosar, were among the notable players to announce their retirements at the end of the 1996 season. Kelly is likely to go into TV. Kosar is heading a group trying to bring an expansion team to Cleveland.

Among the other players who retired were Buffalo center Kent Hull, Green Bay tight end Keith Jackson and defensive end Sean Jones, and linebacker Kyle Clifton, who spent 13 years with the Jets.

Offensive tackle Jim Lachey of the Redskins, fullback Steve Smith of the Seahawks and kicker Fuad Reveiz of the Vikings retired before the start of the '96 season.

DEATH OF AN ICON

Pete Rozelle, who did more than any one person to turn the NFL into the success story it is today, died at age 70 in December 1996.

During his tenure as commissioner from 1960-89, Rozelle presided over the growth of the league from 12 to 28 teams. He helped bring about the 1970 merger with the AFL and invented the Super Bowl and Monday Night Football, which are now permanent fixtures on the American sports landscape.

Two owners, Jack Kent Cooke of the Redskins and Robert Irsay of the Colts, also died. Their sons, John Kent Cooke and Jim Irsay, will keep the franchises in their respective families.

FINAL STANDINGS

AMERICAN FOOTBALL CONFERENCE

EASTERN DIVISION

	W	L	T	Pct.	Pts.	Opp.	Home	Away	Vs. AFC	Vs. NFC	Vs.AFC East
*New England	11	5	0	.687	418	313	6-2	5-3	9-3	2-2	6-2
†Buffalo	10	6	0	.625	319	266	7-1	3-5	6-6	4-0	4-4
†Indianapolis	9	7	0	.563	317	334	6-2	3-5	6-6	3-1	4-4
Miami	8	8	0	.500	339	325	4-4	4-4	7-5	1-3	6-2
N.Y. Jets	1	15	0	.063	279	454	0-8	1-7	0-12	1-3	0-8

CENTRAL DIVISION

	W	L	T	Pct.	Pts.	Opp.	Home	Away	Vs. AFC	Vs. NFC	Vs.AFC Central
*Pittsburgh	10	6	0	.625	344	257	7-1	3-5	8-4	2-2	4-4
†Jacksonville	9	7	0	.563	325	335	7-1	2-6	7-5	2-2	5-3
Cincinnati	8	8	0	.500	372	369	6-2	2-6	6-6	2-2	5-3
Houston	8	8	0	.500	345	319	2-6	6-2	6-6	2-2	5-3
Baltimore	4	12	0	.250	371	441	4-4	0-8	2-10	2-2	1-7

WESTERN DIVISION

	W	L	T	Pct.	Pts.	Opp.	Home	Away	Vs. AFC	Vs. NFC	Vs.AFC West
*Denver	13	3	0	.813	391	275	8-0	5-3	10-2	3-1	6-2
Kansas City	9	7	0	.563	297	300	5-3	4-4	5-7	4-0	4-4
San Diego	8	8	0	.500	310	376	5-3	3-5	7-5	1-3	5-3
Oakland	7	9	0	.438	340	293	4-4	3-5	6-6	1-3	3-5
Seattle	7	9	0	.438	317	376	4-4	3-5	5-7	2-2	2-6

*Division champion. †Wild-card team.

NATIONAL FOOTBALL CONFERENCE

EASTERN DIVISION

	W	L	T	Pct.	Pts.	Opp.	Home	Away	Vs. AFC	Vs. NFC	Vs.NFC East
*Dallas	10	6	0	.625	286	250	6-2	4-4	2-2	8-4	5-3
†Philadelphia	10	6	0	.625	363	341	5-3	5-3	2-2	8-4	5-3
Washington	9	7	0	.563	364	312	5-3	4-4	3-1	6-6	4-4
Arizona	7	9	0	.438	300	397	5-3	2-6	0-4	7-5	4-4
N.Y. Giants	6	10	0	.375	242	297	3-5	3-5	2-2	4-8	2-6

CENTRAL DIVISION

	W	L	T	Pct.	Pts.	Opp.	Home	Away	Vs. AFC	Vs. NFC	Vs.NFC Central
*Green Bay	13	3	0	.813	456	210	8-0	5-3	3-1	10-2	7-1
†Minnesota	9	7	0	.563	298	315	5-3	4-4	1-3	8-4	5-3
Chicago	7	9	0	.438	283	305	6-2	1-7	2-2	5-7	3-5
Tampa Bay	6	10	0	.375	221	293	5-3	1-7	2-2	4-8	2-6
Detroit	5	11	0	.313	302	368	4-4	1-7	1-3	4-8	3-5

WESTERN DIVISION

	W	L	T	Pct.	Pts.	Opp.	Home	Away	Vs. AFC	Vs. NFC	Vs.NFC West
*Carolina	12	4	0	.750	367	218	8-0	4-4	3-1	9-3	7-1
†San Francisco	12	4	0	.750	398	257	6-2	6-2	4-0	8-4	6-2
St. Louis	6	10	0	.375	303	409	4-4	2-6	2-2	4-8	4-4
Atlanta	3	13	0	.188	309	465	2-6	1-7	0-4	3-9	3-5
New Orleans	3	13	0	.188	229	339	2-6	1-7	1-3	2-10	0-8

*Division champion. †Wild-card team.

AFC PLAYOFFS

AFC wild card: Jacksonville 30, Buffalo 27
Pittsburgh 42, Indianapolis 14
AFC semifinals: Jacksonville 30, Denver 27
New England 28, Pittsburgh 3
AFC championship: New England 20, Jacksonville 16

NFC PLAYOFFS

NFC wild card: Dallas 40, Minnesota 15
San Francisco 14, Philadelphia 0
NFC semifinals: Green Bay 35, San Francisco 14
Carolina 26, Dallas 17
NFC championship: Green Bay 30, Carolina 13

SUPER BOWL
Green Bay 35, New England 21

WEEK 1

RESULTS

BALTIMORE 19, Oakland 14
Buffalo 23, N.Y. GIANTS 20 (OT)
CAROLINA 29, Atlanta 6
DENVER 31, N.Y. Jets 6
Green Bay 34, TAMPA BAY 3
INDIANAPOLIS 20, Arizona 13
JACKSONVILLE 24, Pittsburgh 9
Kansas City 20, HOUSTON 19
MIAMI 24, New England 10
MINNESOTA 17, Detroit 13
Philadelphia 17, WASHINGTON 14
ST. LOUIS 26, Cincinnati 16
SAN DIEGO 29, Seattle 7
SAN FRANCISCO 27, New Orleans 11
CHICAGO 22, Dallas 6

Note: All caps denotes home team.

STANDINGS

AFC EAST	W	L	T	Pct.
Buffalo	1	0	0	1.000
Indianapolis	1	0	0	1.000
Miami	1	0	0	1.000
New England	0	1	0	.000
N.Y. Jets	0	1	0	.000

AFC CENTRAL	W	L	T	Pct.
Baltimore	1	0	0	1.000
Jacksonville	1	0	0	1.000
Cincinnati	0	1	0	.000
Houston	0	1	0	.000
Pittsburgh	0	1	0	.000

AFC WEST	W	L	T	Pct.
Denver	1	0	0	1.000
Kansas City	1	0	0	1.000
San Diego	1	0	0	1.000
Oakland	0	1	0	.000
Seattle	0	1	0	.000

NFC EAST	W	L	T	Pct.
Philadelphia	1	0	0	1.000
Arizona	0	1	0	.000
Dallas	0	1	0	.000
N.Y. Giants	0	1	0	.000
Washington	0	1	0	.000

NFC CENTRAL	W	L	T	Pct.
Chicago	1	0	0	1.000
Green Bay	1	0	0	1.000
Minnesota	1	0	0	1.000
Detroit	0	1	0	.000
Tampa Bay	0	1	0	.000

NFC WEST	W	L	T	Pct.
Carolina	1	0	0	1.000
St. Louis	1	0	0	1.000
San Francisco	1	0	0	1.000
Atlanta	0	1	0	.000
New Orleans	0	1	0	.000

HIGHLIGHTS

Hero of the week: Green Bay quarterback Brett Favre picked up where he left off the year before, going 20-of-27 for 247 yards and four touchdowns in the Packers' 34-3 rout of Tampa Bay. Favre, the 1995 NFL MVP, showed no ill-effects after spending six weeks in a rehabilitation center during the summer to combat an addiction to pain-killing drugs.

Goat of the week: Despite throwing for 260 yards, Detroit quarterback Scott Mitchell also threw four interceptions, and they proved critical in the Lions' 17-13 loss at Minnesota. The first interception was returned for a touchdown by cornerback Dwayne Washington (after a lateral from linebacker Ed Brady), and the fourth—at the Vikings' 15 with 20 seconds left—ended the Lions' last scoring opportunity.

Sub of the week: In the first game of his NFL career, Miami running back Karim Abdul-Jabbar rushed for 115 yards on 26 carries in leading the Dolphins to a 24-10 win over New England. Abdul-Jabbar, a third-round pick from UCLA, got the start after veteran running back Irving Spikes was sidelined by a sore hamstring.

Comeback of the week: Buffalo rallied from a 17-0 deficit to defeat the Giants, 23-20, in overtime. Jim Kelly completed a 20-yard pass to Quinn Early on third-and-18 to set up a 39-yard, game-tying field goal by Steve Christie with 7:14 left in regulation. Kelly then drove the Bills into position for another Christie field goal (from 34 yards out) after Chris Spielman recovered a fumble by Dave Brown.

Blowout of the week: The Broncos sacked quarterbacks Neil O'Donnell and Frank Reich a combined nine times (one shy of a team record) in a 31-6 rout of the Jets. The Broncos converted three second-quarter turnovers into 17 points in building a 31-0 halftime lead. Denver outgained New York, 244-33, in the first half.

Nail-biter of the week: Colts cornerback Eugene Daniel broke up two passes intended for Rob Moore in the end zone in the final minute to preserve Indy's 20-13 victory over Arizona. After scoring on a two-yard run with 61 seconds left to pull his team to cut the lead to seven points, Arizona quarterback Boomer Esiason completed four consecutive passes (after a successful onsides kick) to put the Cardinals at the Colts' 22 with 15 seconds left. But Daniel's heroics kept the Cards from scoring.

Hit of the week: By Baltimore rookie linebacker Ray Lewis, who stuffed Oakland running back Harvey Williams for no gain on a third-and-1 play in the fourth period. The Raiders led 14-13 at the time, but the hit seemed to inspire the Ravens, who scored the game's go-ahead touchdown on their next possession.

Oddity of the week: Tommy Vardell, whose nickname at Stanford was "Touchdown Tommy," scored a touchdown on his first carry as a San Francisco 49er in their 27-11 win over New Orleans. Vardell needed more than 100 carries to score the first touchdown of first NFL career, for the then-Cleveland Browns, in 1993.

Top rusher: Barry Sanders ran for 163 yards on 24 carries in Detroit's 17-13 loss at Minnesota.

Top passer: Kelly was 24-of-41 for 313 yards in Buffalo's 23-20 overtime win against the Giants.

Top receiver: Herman Moore caught 12 passes for 157 yards and one touchdown in the Lions' loss to Minnesota.

Notes: The largest crowd in Baltimore football history (64,124) turned out to see the city's newest NFL team, the Ravens, defeat Oakland, 19-14. The Ravens, who moved from Cleveland after the 1995 season in a highly controversial move, outscored the Raiders 12-0 in the second half to win the first game played at Memorial Stadium since the then-Baltimore Colts defeated the Oilers, 20-10, on December 18, 1983. . . . In the first game played at Ericsson Stadium in downtown Charlotte, the Carolina Panthers whipped Atlanta, 29-6. The Panthers sacked Falcons quarterback Jeff George seven times and scored the most points in their two-year history. . . . The NFL's other second-year team, the Jacksonville Jaguars, opened their season with a 24-9 win over visiting Pittsburgh. The Jaguars set club records for fewest points allowed, sacks (four) and yards allowed (187). They also held an opponent without a touchdown for the first time in franchise history. . . . In their first regular-season game since they announced plans to move to Nashville, Tenn., in 1998, the Houston Oilers drew only 27,725 fans to the Astrodome for their game against Kansas City. It was the Oilers' smallest home crowd since 1982. The Chiefs won their seventh consecutive season-opener, 20-19. . . . Tampa Bay's 34-3 loss to Green Bay was its worst ever in a season-opening game. Favre's four touchdown passes increased his touchdown-to-interception ratio in eight career starts against the Buccaneers to 20-3. . . . The Rams scored six times (two touchdowns, four field goals) in their 26-16 win over Cincinnati, but their offense didn't move the ball more than 33 yards on any scoring drive. . . . San Diego beat Seattle for the ninth time in 10 games and Philadelphia beat Washington for the eighth consecutive time. The Eagles' eight wins have come by a total of 30 points. . . . Although Miami beat New England, Dolphins quarterback Dan Marino did not throw a touchdown pass for only the 24th time in 187 regular-season games. Miami's record in such games is 9-15. . . . Dallas' 22-6 loss at Chicago was only its ninth in 37 season-opening games. The Cowboys, playing without suspended Pro Bowl receiver Michael Irvin, were held without a touchdown for the first time in 69 games—a 38-6 loss to Detroit in the 1991 season playoffs.

Quote of the week: Buffalo's white-haired Marv Levy, at 71 the league's oldest coach, talking to reporters after the Bills' comeback win over the Giants: "Fellas, I'm really 34 years old. I just look like this."

GAME SUMMARIES

BILLS 23, GIANTS 20

Sunday, September 1

Buffalo	0	7	10	3	3—23
N.Y. Giants	3	14	3	0	0—20

First Quarter
NYG—FG, Daluiso 22, 6:33.
Second Quarter
NYG—Toomer 87 punt return (Daluiso kick), 4:46.
NYG—Way 37 pass from Brown (Daluiso kick), 7:33.
Buf.—T. Thomas 1 run (Christie kick), 11:46.
Third Quarter
NYG—FG, Daluiso 34, 5:11.
Buf.—FG, Christie 28, 8:30.
Buf.—Reed 60 pass from Kelly (Christie kick), 10:15.
Fourth Quarter
Buf.—FG, Christie 39, 7:46.
Overtime
Buf.—FG, Christie 34, 10:08.
Attendance—74,218.

TEAM STATISTICS

	Buffalo	N.Y. Giants
First downs	25	12
Rushes-yards	43-153	31-93
Passing	257	138
Punt returns	3-(-5)	4-113
Kickoff returns	1-15	4-70
Interception returns	0-0	1-19
Comp.-att.-int.	24-41-1	11-27-0
Sacked-yards lost	7-56	5-31

	Buffalo	N.Y. Giants
Punts	9-43	10-40
Fumbles-lost	5-1	1-1
Penalties-yards	5-34	5-30
Time of possession	40:30	29:38

INDIVIDUAL STATISTICS
RUSHING—Buffalo, T. Thomas 32-97, Holmes 7-31, Tasker 2-1, Reed 1-13, Moulds 1-11. New York, Hampton 18-50, Wheatley 5-9, Brown 4-26, Way 2-4, Calloway 1-2, Elias 1-2.
PASSING—Buffalo, Kelly 24-41-1-313. New York, Brown 11-27-0-169.
RECEIVING—Buffalo, Cline 6-41, Johnson 6-37, Reed 5-138, Early 3-67, T. Thomas 2-19, Tasker 1-9, Moulds 1-2. New York, Way 4-78, Lewis 3-45, Cross 1-19, Dawsey 1-13, Elias 1-7, Pierce 1-7.
MISSED FIELD GOAL ATTEMPTS—None.
INTERCEPTIONS—New York, Sparks 1-19.
KICKOFF RETURNS—Buffalo, Moulds 1-15. New York, Toomer 3-56, Wheatley 1-14.
PUNT RETURNS—Buffalo, Copeland 2-(minus 5), Burris 1-0. New York, Toomer 4-113.
SACKS—Buffalo, B. Smith 2, Washington 1, Paup 1, Jeffcoat 1. New York, Miller 2, Armstead 1, Harris 1, K. Hamilton 1, Sehorn 1, Strahan 1/2, Bratzke 1/2.

BRONCOS 31, JETS 6

Sunday, September 1

N.Y. Jets	0	0	0	6	6
Denver	7	24	0	0	31

First Quarter
Den.—Sharpe 13 pass from Elway (Elam kick), 7:03.
Second Quarter
Den.—McCaffrey 39 pass from Elway (Elam kick), :51.
Den.—Davis 1 run (Elam kick), 6:34.
Den.—Miller 26 run (Elam kick), 10:14.
Den.—FG, Elam 28, 12:54.
Fourth Quarter
NYJ—Slaughter 13 pass from Reich (pass failed), 12:53.
Attendance—70,595.

TEAM STATISTICS

	N.Y. Jets	Denver
First downs	12	21
Rushes-yards	25-102	37-200
Passing	72	167
Punt returns	3-11	6-70
Kickoff returns	3-54	1-12
Interception returns	2-2	1-(-6)
Comp.-att.-int.	11-25-1	16-34-2
Sacked-yards lost	9-61	2-16
Punts	9-45	7-45
Fumbles-lost	4-3	2-1
Penalties-yards	3-15	7-39
Time of possession	25:34	34:26

INDIVIDUAL STATISTICS
RUSHING—New York, Murrell 17-94, Anderson 3-9, O'Donnell 3-7, Cobb 1-6, Reich 1-(minus 14). Denver, Davis 19-72, Craver 7-59, Hebron 7-39, Miller 2-32, Musgrave 2-(minus 2).
PASSING—New York, O'Donnell 7-13-1-50, Reich 4-12-0-83. Denver, Elway 16-33-2-183, Musgrave 0-1-0-0.
RECEIVING—New York, Chrebet 4-20, Slaughter 3-30, Graham 2-26, Johnson 1-50, Van Dyke 1-7. Denver, McCaffrey 4-61, Sharpe 4-55, Sherrard 3-29, Davis 3-23, Miller 1-8, Craver 1-7.
MISSED FIELD GOAL ATTEMPTS—None.
INTERCEPTIONS—New York, Houston 1-3, Spindler 1-(minus 1). Denver, Washington 1-(minus 6).
KICKOFF RETURNS—New York, Carpenter 3-54. Denver, Hebron 1-12.
PUNT RETURNS—New York, Chrebet 3-11. Denver, Kinchen 6-70.
SACKS—New York, Douglas 2. Denver, Perry 2, Romanowski 1, Crockett 1, D. Williams 1, A. Williams 1, Geathers 1, Hasselbach 1, Tanuvasa 1.

RAMS 26, BENGALS 16

Sunday, September 1

Cincinnati	3	6	7	0	16
St. Louis	7	0	3	16	26

First Quarter
Cin.—FG, Pelfrey 27, 4:09.
St.L.—Phillips 1 run (Lohmiller kick), 8:35.

Second Quarter
Cin.—FG, Pelfrey 35, 4:22.
Cin.—FG, Pelfrey 47, 11:42.

Third Quarter
Cin.—Scott 6 pass from Blake (Pelfrey kick), 5:44.
St.L.—FG, Lohmiller 42, 10:15.

Fourth Quarter
St.L.—FG, Lohmiller 20, :06.
St.L.—FG, Lohmiller 29, 5:42.
St.L.—Phillips 1 run (Lohmiller kick), 7:27.
St.L.—FG, Lohmiller 20, 9:34.
Attendance—62,659.

TEAM STATISTICS

	Cincinnati	St.Louis
First downs	14	18
Rushes-yards	22-37	35-70
Passing	205	139
Punt returns	2-74	1-40
Kickoff returns	5-107	4-94
Interception returns	1-0	2-55
Comp.-att.-int.	23-40-2	13-35-1
Sacked-yards lost	3-21	2-15
Punts	3-26	3-45
Fumbles-lost	3-3	3-2
Penalties-yards	15-96	11-61
Time of possession	29:51	30:09

INDIVIDUAL STATISTICS
RUSHING—Cincinnati, Carter 14-14, Hearst 3-6, Bieniemy 2-12, Blake 2-4, Scott 1-1. St. Louis, Phillips 21-46, Green 5-15, Walsh 5-13, Robinson 3- (minus 4), D. Harris 1-0.

PASSING—Cincinnati, Blake 23-40-2-226. St. Louis, Walsh 13-35-1-154.

RECEIVING—Cincinnati, Pickens 6-91, Scott 6-76, Carter 5-22, McGee 2-19, Bieniemy 2-10, Battaglia 1-4, Cothran 1-4. St. Louis, Kennison 4-70, Bruce 4-40, Green 4-38, Robinson 1-6.

MISSED FIELD GOAL ATTEMPTS—St. Louis, Lohmiller 44.

INTERCEPTIONS—Cincinnati, Ambrose 1-0. St. Louis, Lyle 1-58, Jenkins 1-(minus 3).

KICKOFF RETURNS—Cincinnati, Dunn 4-81, Sawyer 1-26. St. Louis, Thomas 2-44, Phillips 1-35, Laing 1-15.

PUNT RETURNS—Cincinnati, Sawyer 2-74. St. Louis, Kennison 1-40.

SACKS—Cincinnati, Francis 1, Wilkinson 1. St. Louis, Carter 1, O'Neal 1, J. Jones 1.

CHARGERS 29, SEAHAWKS 7

Sunday, September 1

Seattle	0	7	0	0— 7
San Diego	7	6	3	13—29

First Quarter
S.D.—Martin 2 pass from Humphries (Carney kick), 12:45.

Second Quarter
Sea.—Mirer 6 run (Peterson kick), 2:59.
S.D.—FG, Carney 35, 13:34.
S.D.—FG, Carney 53, 15:00.

Third Quarter
S.D.—FG, Carney 22, 12:26.

Fourth Quarter
S.D.—FG, Carney 50, 1:26.
S.D.—Russell 6 run (Carney kick), 3:21.
S.D.—FG, Carney 31, 4:32.
Attendance—58,780.

TEAM STATISTICS

	Seattle	San Diego
First downs	16	27
Rushes-yards	19-106	38-185
Passing	251	202
Punt returns	1-9	3-62
Kickoff returns	5-65	2-35
Interception returns	0-0	2-21
Comp.-att.-int.	24-41-2	22-39-0
Sacked-yards lost	1-0	0-0
Punts	4-48	3-44
Fumbles-lost	3-2	0-0
Penalties-yards	8-63	5-34
Time of possession	25:30	34:30

INDIVIDUAL STATISTICS
RUSHING—Seattle, Warren 13-50, Mirer 4-49, Smith 1-4, Galloway 1-3. San Diego, Russell 13-46, Hayden 11-59, Fletcher 7-49, Bradley 5-23, Humphries 2-8.

PASSING—Seattle, Mirer 24-41-2-251. San Diego, Humphries 21-38-0-195, Salisbury 1-1-0-7.

RECEIVING—Seattle, Blades 5-49, Galloway 4-89, Crumpler 4-45, Proehl 3-29, Fauria 3-19, Pritchard 1-10, Strong 1-7. San Diego, Martin 7-66, A. Coleman 3-38, Pupunu 3-19, Russell 2-24, Jones 2-23, Mitchell 2-18, Fletcher 1-7, May 1-7, Reeves 1-0.

MISSED FIELD GOAL ATTEMPTS—None.

INTERCEPTIONS—San Diego, Shaw 1-22, Young 1-(minus 1).

KICKOFF RETURNS—Seattle, Broussard 5-65. San Diego, A. Coleman 2-35.

PUNT RETURNS—Seattle, Galloway 1-9. San Diego, Da. Gordon 3-62.

SACKS—San Diego, Seau 1.

49ERS 27, SAINTS 11

Sunday, September 1

New Orleans	0	0	3	8—11
San Francisco	14	10	0	3—27

First Quarter
S.F.—Vardell 1 run (Wilkins kick), 6:41.
S.F.—Rice 2 run (Wilkins kick), 12:49.

Second Quarter
S.F.—FG, Wilkins 29, 5:54.
S.F.—Loville 4 run (Wilkins kick), 11:02.

Third Quarter
N.O.—FG, Brien 35, 6:27.

Fourth Quarter
S.F.—FG, Wilkins 29, 2:38.
N.O.—Jeffires 3 pass from Everett (Wilmsmeyer run), 6:21.
Attendance—63,970.

TEAM STATISTICS

	New Orleans	San Francisco
First downs	14	23
Rushes-yards	18-56	38-157
Passing	175	181
Punt returns	3-16	3-37
Kickoff returns	4-115	3-68
Interception returns	0-0	1-14
Comp.-att.-int.	16-41-1	18-31-0
Sacked-yards lost	0-0	3-18
Punts	8-39	7-46
Fumbles-lost	1-1	0-0
Penalties-yards	6-64	10-79
Time of possession	23:03	36:57

INDIVIDUAL STATISTICS
RUSHING—New Orleans, Bates 14-30, Brown 2-6, Small 1-22, Everett 1-(minus 2). San Francisco, Loville 16-61, Vardell 8-33, S. Young 6-52, Grbac 3-(minus 3), Lynn 2-8, Kirby 2-4, Rice 1-2.

PASSING—New Orleans, Everett 16-41-1-175. San Francisco, S. Young 18-29-0-199, Grbac 0-2-0-0.

RECEIVING—New Orleans, Small 4-52, Jeffires 4-34, Haynes 3-24, Lusk 2-28, Green 1-16, I. Smith 1-15, Brown 1-6. San Francisco, Rice 5-88, Stokes 4-52, Vardell 4-26, Loville 3-15, Singleton 1-11, Jones 1-7.

MISSED FIELD GOAL ATTEMPTS—None.

INTERCEPTIONS—San Francisco, McDonald 1-14.

KICKOFF RETURNS—New Orleans, Hughes 4-115. San Francisco, D. Carter 3-68.

PUNT RETURNS—New Orleans, Hughes 3-16. San Francisco, Singleton 2-32, D. Carter 1-5.

SACKS—New Orleans, Turnbull 2, Martin 1.

DOLPHINS 24, PATRIOTS 10

Sunday, September 1

New England	0	3	7	0—10
Miami	10	7	7	0—24

First Quarter
Mia.—S. Hill 10 fumble return (Nedney kick), 3:54.
Mia.—FG, Nedney 34, 9:03.

Second Quarter
N.E.—FG, Vinatieri 25, 2:50.
Mia.—Abdul-Jabbar 3 run (Nedney kick), 14:25.

Third Quarter
Mia.—Miller fumble recovery in end zone (Nedney kick), 5:27.
N.E.—Coates 29 pass from Bledsoe (Vinatieri kick), 7:13.
Attendance—71,542.

TEAM STATISTICS

	New England	Miami
First downs	16	19
Rushes-yards	14-29	39-146
Passing	201	176
Punt returns	3-21	1-8
Kickoff returns	5-151	3-29
Interception returns	1-43	2-60
Comp.-att.-int.	19-38-2	16-22-1
Sacked-yards lost	4-21	0-0
Punts	2-47	5-42
Fumbles-lost	3-2	4-0
Penalties-yards	4-31	9-55
Time of possession	24:01	35:59

INDIVIDUAL STATISTICS

RUSHING—New England, Martin 11-23, Jefferson 1-6, Meggett 1-1, Bledsoe 1-(minus 1). Miami, Abdul-Jabbar 26-115, Parmalee 8-32, Marino 3-(minus 3), McPhail 2-2.

PASSING—New England, Bledsoe 19-38-2-222. Miami, Marino 16-22-1-176.

RECEIVING—New England, Coates 6-69, Jefferson 5-48, Graham 2-32, W. Moore 2-26, Meggett 2-17, Burke 1-19, Gash 1-11. Miami, Pritchett 6-77, McDuffie 3-43, Byars 2-18, Miller 2-15, Abdul-Jabbar 2-2, McPhail 1-21.

MISSED FIELD GOAL ATTEMPTS—None.

INTERCEPTIONS—New England, Ray 1-43. Miami, Oliver 1-60, Buckley 1-0.

KICKOFF RETURNS—New England, Meggett 4-131, T. Brown 1-20. Miami, McPhail 3-29.

PUNT RETURNS—New England, Meggett 3-21. Miami, McDuffie 1-8.

SACKS—Miami, Z. Thomas 1, Gardener 1, Bailey 1, Stubbs 1.

PACKERS 34, BUCCANEERS 3

Sunday, September 1

Green Bay	10	14	10	0—34
Tampa Bay	0	3	0	0— 3

First Quarter
G.B.—FG, Jacke 23, 8:17.
G.B.—Jackson 1 pass from Favre (Jacke kick), 10:53.

Second Quarter
T.B.—FG, Husted 48, :55.
G.B.—Jackson 4 pass from Favre (Jacke kick), 13:20.
G.B.—Jackson 51 pass from Favre (Jacke kick), 14:21.

Third Quarter
G.B.—FG, Jacke 40, 5:08.
G.B.—Levens 1 pass from Favre (Jacke kick), 9:25.
Attendance—54,102.

TEAM STATISTICS

	Green Bay	Tampa Bay
First downs	24	15
Rushes-yards	35-139	23-59
Passing	267	117
Punt returns	3-42	0-0
Kickoff returns	2-52	5-106
Interception returns	4-68	0-0
Comp.-att.-int.	21-28-0	13-30-4
Sacked-yards lost	1-4	1-6
Punts	2-45	3-46
Fumbles-lost	3-2	3-2
Penalties-yards	6-40	3-20
Time of possession	38:56	21:04

INDIVIDUAL STATISTICS

RUSHING—Green Bay, Bennett 13-62, Levens 12-48, Jervey 5-13, Henderson 3-13, R. Brooks 1-2, Favre 1-1. Tampa Bay, Ellison 8-10, R. Brooks 6-20, Alstott 5-15, Thompson 4-14.

PASSING—Green Bay, Favre 20-27-0-247, McMahon 1-1-0-24. Tampa Bay, Dilfer 13-30-4-123.

RECEIVING—Green Bay, Freeman 6-82, Jackson 5-76, R. Brooks 3-25, Chmura 2-24, Levens 2-20, Thomason 1-24, Henderson 1-12, Bennett 1-8. Tampa Bay, Alstott 4-42, Harper 3-35, Harris 2-19, Hawkins 2-16, Thompson 1-6, Moore 1-5.

MISSED FIELD GOAL ATTEMPTS—Green Bay, Jacke 46.

INTERCEPTIONS—Green Bay, Butler 2-59, Prior 1-7, Hollinquest 1-2.

KICKOFF RETURNS—Green Bay, Beebe 2-52. Tampa Bay, Silvan 5-106.

PUNT RETURNS—Green Bay, Howard 3-42.

SACKS—Green Bay, Holland 1. Tampa Bay, Sapp 1.

VIKINGS 17, LIONS 13

Sunday, September 1

Detroit	0	10	0	3—13
Minnesota	7	0	0	10—17

First Quarter
Min.—D. Washington 27 interception return (Sisson kick), 11:41.

Second Quarter
Det.—H. Moore 17 pass from Mitchell (Hanson kick), 5:26.
Det.—FG, Hanson 24, 12:45.

Fourth Quarter
Min.—FG, Sisson 25, 9:19.
Det.—FG, Hanson 39, 12:41.
Min.—Carter 31 pass from B. Johnson (Sisson kick), 13:54.
Attendance—52,972.

TEAM STATISTICS

	Detroit	Minnesota
First downs	27	16
Rushes-yards	29-191	27-128
Passing	244	183
Punt returns	4-38	1-7
Kickoff returns	3-82	2-55
Interception returns	0-0	4-57
Comp.-att.-int.	21-42-4	21-37-0
Sacked-yards lost	3-8	4-31
Punts	4-42	8-42
Fumbles-lost	2-1	1-0
Penalties-yards	6-40	9-60
Time of possession	29:04	30:56

INDIVIDUAL STATISTICS

RUSHING—Detroit, Sanders 24-163, Morton 3-25, Mitchell 1-3, Lynch 1-0. Minnesota, R. Smith 22-113, B. Johnson 3-14, Lee 1-1, Evans 1-0.

PASSING—Detroit, Mitchell 20-41-4-260, Royals 1-1-0-(minus 8). Minnesota, B. Johnson 16-23-0-157, Moon 5-14-0-57.

RECEIVING—Detroit, H. Moore 12-157, Perriman 5-41, Sloan 2-10, Sanders 1-28, Morton 1-16. Minnesota, Carter 8-88, Reed 4-53, Lee 4-27, Ismail 2-21, R. Smith 2-19, DeLong 1-6.

MISSED FIELD GOAL ATTEMPTS—Minnesota, Sisson 43.

INTERCEPTIONS—Minnesota, Brady 2-12, Edwards 1-18, Jackson 1-0. KICKOFF RETURNS—Detroit, Milburn 3-82. Minnesota, Ismail 1-32, Lee 1-23.

PUNT RETURNS—Detroit, Milburn 4-38. Minnesota, Palmer 1-7.

SACKS—Detroit, Thomas 2, Elliss 1, Scroggins 1. Minnesota, Edwards 1, Griffith 1, Randle 1.

JAGUARS 24, STEELERS 9

Sunday, September 1

Pittsburgh	3	3	3	0— 9
Jacksonville	7	7	0	10—24

First Quarter
Jac.—W. Jackson 38 pass from Brunell (Hollis kick), 6:34.
Pit.—FG, N. Johnson 48, 14:08.

Second Quarter
Pit.—FG, N. Johnson 29, 11:48.
Jac.—McCardell 15 pass from Brunell (Hollis kick), 14:44.

Third Quarter
Pit.—FG, N. Johnson 23, 13:41.

Fourth Quarter
Jac.—FG, Hollis 52, 6:35.
Jac.—Stewart 1 run (Hollis kick), 10:11.
Attendance—70,210.

TEAM STATISTICS

	Pittsburgh	Jacksonville
First downs	13	23
Rushes-yards	25-101	36-119
Passing	86	194
Punt returns	3-15	2-20
Kickoff returns	5-151	4-100
Interception returns	2-34	1-6
Comp.-att.-int.	12-23-1	20-31-2
Sacked-yards lost	4-21	4-18
Punts	6-40	5-41
Fumbles-lost	2-1	1-0
Penalties-yards	7-41	4-35
Time of possession	24:54	35:06

INDIVIDUAL STATISTICS

RUSHING—Pittsburgh, Bettis 14-57, Pegram 7-44, Stewart 3-4, Ji. Miller 1-(minus 4). Jacksonville, Stewart 25-77, Brunell 10-41, Maston 1-1.

PASSING—Pittsburgh, Ji. Miller 9-17-0-83, Tomczak 3-4-1-24, Stewart 0-2-0-0. Jacksonville, Brunell 20-31-2-212.

RECEIVING—Pittsburgh, Hastings 3-34, Bruener 2-23, C. Johnson 2-16, Bettis 2-14, Stewart 1-8, Lester 1-8, Arnold 1-4. Jacksonville, McCardell 5-53, Rison 4-42, Mitchell 3-27, Smith 3-25, Stewart 3-21, W. Jackson 1-38, Brown 1-6.

MISSED FIELD GOAL ATTEMPTS—None.

INTERCEPTIONS—Pittsburgh, Woodson 1-28, Kirkland 1-6. Jacksonville, Hardy 1-6.

KICKOFF RETURNS—Pittsburgh, Pegram 2-55, Arnold 2-54, Hastings 1-42. Jacksonville, W. Jackson 3-65, Jordan 1-35.

PUNT RETURNS—Pittsburgh, Hastings 3-15. Jacksonville, Hudson 2-20.

SACKS—Pittsburgh, Kirkland 1, Henry 1, Lloyd 1, Ravotti 1. Jacksonville, Lageman 2, Hardy 1, Simmons 1.

PANTHERS 29, FALCONS 6

Sunday, September 1

Atlanta	3	3	0	0— 6
Carolina	7	13	3	6—29

First Quarter

Car.—Carrier 12 pass from Collins (Kasay kick), 5:04.
Atl.—FG, Andersen 46, 12:39.

Second Quarter

Car.—FG, Kasay 32, 1:39.
Atl.—FG, Andersen 33, 5:00.
Car.—FG, Kasay 36, 11:33.
Car.—Walls 1 pass from Collins (Kasay kick), 14:34.

Third Quarter

Car.—FG, Kasay 53, 8:54.

Fourth Quarter

Car.—FG, Kasay 38, 1:09.
Car.—FG, Kasay 42, 13:04.
Attendance—69,522.

TEAM STATISTICS

	Atlanta	Carolina
First downs	12	23
Rushes-yards	19-119	37-129
Passing	162	186
Punt returns	1-5	3-63
Kickoff returns	5-105	2-68
Interception returns	0-0	0-0
Comp.-att.-int.	16-35-0	17-31-0
Sacked-yards lost	7-53	4-12
Punts	5-45	3-35
Fumbles-lost	1-1	2-1
Penalties-yards	9-79	7-55
Time of possession	26:50	33:10.

INDIVIDUAL STATISTICS

RUSHING—Atlanta, Anderson 14-108, Heyward 4-7, J. George 1-4. Carolina, Biakabutuka 26-69, Oliver 6-37, Griffith 3-3, Collins 1-14, Stone 1-6.

PASSING—Atlanta, J. George 16-35-0-215. Carolina, Collins 17-31-0-198.

RECEIVING—Atlanta, Metcalf 6-56, Mathis 4-123, Emanuel 2-16, Birden 2-14, Heyward 1-6, Anderson 1-0. Carolina, Carrier 6-78, Green 4-57, Walls 4-31, Griffith 2-21, Stone 1-11.

MISSED FIELD GOAL ATTEMPTS—Atlanta, Andersen 33.

INTERCEPTIONS—None.

KICKOFF RETURNS—Atlanta, Anderson 3-68, Metcalf 2-37. Carolina, Bates 1-35, Oliver 1-33.

PUNT RETURNS—Atlanta, Metcalf 1-5. Carolina, Oliver 3-63.

SACKS—Atlanta, Smith 2, Hall 1, Owens 1. Carolina, Lathon 3, Greene 2, Cook 1, Bickett 1.

CHIEFS 20, OILERS 19

Sunday, September 1

Kansas City	7	10	0	3—20
Houston	10	6	0	3—19

First Quarter

Hou.—FG, Del Greco 34, 4:39.
Hou.—Davis 34 pass from Chandler (Del Greco kick), 8:58.
K.C.—Vanover 11 pass from Bono (Stoyanovich kick), 10:27.

Second Quarter

K.C.—FG, Stoyanovich 35, 2:24.
Hou.—FG, Del Greco 44, 7:28.

Hou.—FG, Del Greco 33, 13:38.
K.C.—Dawson 23 pass from Bono (Stoyanovich kick), 14:34.

Fourth Quarter

K.C.—FG, Stoyanovich 43, 3:33.
Hou.—FG, Del Greco 22, 11:23.
Attendance—27,725.

TEAM STATISTICS

	Kansas City	Houston
First downs	17	16
Rushes-yards	24-79	26-72
Passing	169	191
Punt returns	2-7	3-33
Kickoff returns	6-128	4-76
Interception returns	1-17	0-0
Comp.-att.-int.	21-37-0	16-29-1
Sacked-yards lost	1-23	3-25
Punts	5-28	4-37
Fumbles-lost	2-2	0-0
Penalties-yards	7-50	9-118
Time of possession	25:41	34:19.

INDIVIDUAL STATISTICS

RUSHING—Kansas City, Allen 6-18, Hill 6-9, Anders 5-21, Bono 4-13, Bennett 2-12, Vanover 1-6. Houston, George 21-50, Chandler 3-13, Thomas 1-8, Harmon 1-1.

PASSING—Kansas City, Bono 21-37-0-192. Houston, Chandler 16-29-1-216.

RECEIVING—Kansas City, Vanover 7-76, Cash 4-29, Dawson 3-54, McNair 2-19, Anders 2-2, Hill 1-15, Penn 1-5, Bennett 1-(minus 8). Houston, Russell 4-52, Wycheck 4-36, Harmon 3-23, Sanders 2-58, Davis 1-34, Floyd 1-7, Thomas 1-6.

MISSED FIELD GOAL ATTEMPTS—Houston, Del Greco 55.

INTERCEPTIONS—Kansas City, D. Carter 1-17.

KICKOFF RETURNS—Kansas City, Woods 5-108, Hughes 1-20. Houston, Gray 4-76.

PUNT RETURNS—Kansas City, Vanover 2-7. Houston, Gray 3-33.

SACKS—Kansas City, Thomas 2, N. Smith 1. Houston, Bowden 1.

RAVENS 19, RAIDERS 14

Sunday, September 1

Oakland	0	14	0	0—14
Baltimore	7	0	6	6—19

First Quarter

Bal.—Testaverde 9 run (Stover kick), 14:21.

Second Quarter

Oak.—T. Brown 7 pass from Hobert (Ford kick), 3:59.
Oak.—T. Brown 10 pass from Hobert (Ford kick), 8:10.

Third Quarter

Bal.—FG, Stover 25, 7:05.
Bal.—FG, Stover 37, 13:43.

Fourth Quarter

Bal.—Byner 1 run (pass failed), 7:10.
Attendance—64,124.

TEAM STATISTICS

	Oakland	Baltimore
First downs	13	22
Rushes-yards	21-60	30-95
Passing	178	219
Punt returns	2-14	4-13
Kickoff returns	4-66	3-32
Interception returns	0-0	2-28
Comp.-att.-int.	17-26-2	19-33-0
Sacked-yards lost	3-14	3-35
Punts	7-44	6-38
Fumbles-lost	1-0	1-1
Penalties-yards	12-60	2-15
Time of possession	25:22	34:38.

INDIVIDUAL STATISTICS

RUSHING—Oakland, Williams 13-39, Kaufman 6-13, Fenner 1-17, T. Brown 1-(minus 9). Baltimore, Byner 14-43, Testaverde 8-42, Gardner 5-16, Hoard 2-7, Alexander 1-(minus 13).

PASSING—Oakland, Hobert 17-26-2-192. Baltimore, Testaverde 19-33-0-254.

RECEIVING—Oakland, Jett 4-65, Fenner 4-36, T. Brown 4-31, Hobbs 2-20, Dudley 1-30, Shedd 1-8, Williams 1-2. Baltimore, Kinchen 4-57, Byner 4-32, Gardner 4-16, Jackson 3-60, Alexander 2-57, Hunter 1-25, C. Williams 1-7.

MISSED FIELD GOAL ATTEMPTS—None.
INTERCEPTIONS—Baltimore, Langham 1-28, R. Lewis 1-0.
KICKOFF RETURNS—Oakland, Kaufman 4-66. Baltimore, Hunter 2-13, J. Lewis 1-19.
PUNT RETURNS—Oakland, T. Brown 2-14. Baltimore, J. Lewis 4-13.
SACKS—Oakland, Lewis 1, McGlockton 1, Smith 1. Baltimore, Burnett 1, Caldwell 1, J. Williams 1.

COLTS 20, CARDINALS 13

Sunday, September 1

Arizona	3	3	0	7—13
Indianapolis	0	10	0	10—20

First Quarter
Ariz.—FG, G. Davis 24, 8:43.

Second Quarter
Ariz.—FG, G. Davis 29, 3:16.
Ind.—Crockett 2 pass from Harbaugh (Blanchard kick), 7:24.
Ind.—FG, Blanchard 23, 14:57.

Fourth Quarter
Ind.—FG, Blanchard 40, 4:26.
Ind.—Harrison 35 pass from Harbaugh (Blanchard kick), 13:06.
Ariz.—Esiason 2 run (G. Davis kick), 13:59.
Attendance—48,133.

TEAM STATISTICS

	Arizona	Indianapolis
First downs	20	19
Rushes-yards	24-84	21-74
Passing	226	238
Punt returns	1-9	1-0
Kickoff returns	4-67	3-37
Interception returns	1-10	0-0
Comp.-att.-int.	25-38-0	21-33-1
Sacked-yards lost	2-11	1-11
Punts	4-42	3-39
Fumbles-lost	0-0	1-1
Penalties-yards	7-49	3-59
Time of possession	33:11	26:49.

INDIVIDUAL STATISTICS

RUSHING—Arizona, McElroy 17-63, Esiason 3-15, Centers 2-6, C. Smith 1-3, Johnson 1-(minus 3). Indianapolis, Faulk 12-46, Warren 5-5, Crockett 3-19, Harbaugh 1-4.
PASSING—Arizona, Esiason 25-38-0-237. Indianapolis, Harbaugh 16-25-1-196, Justin 5-8-0-53.
RECEIVING—Arizona, Centers 11-108, Sanders 7-72, Edwards 2-15, R. Moore 2-11, Carter 1-20, Dowdell 1-11, Terry 1-0. Indianapolis, Harrison 6-85, Faulk 4-62, Dawkins 4-40, Dilger 3-26, Bailey 1-19, Warren 1-9, Stablein 1-6, Crockett 1-2.
MISSED FIELD GOAL ATTEMPTS—Arizona, G. Davis 46.
INTERCEPTIONS—Arizona, Joyner 1-10.
KICKOFF RETURNS—Arizona, McElroy 4-67. Indianapolis, Bailey 1-19, Warren 1-18, Stablein 1-0.
PUNT RETURNS—Arizona, Dowdell 1-9. Indianapolis, Harrison 1-0.
SACKS—Arizona, B. Smith 1. Indianapolis, Belser 1, McCoy 1.

EAGLES 17, REDSKINS 14

Sunday, September 1

Philadelphia	7	10	0	0—17
Washington	7	0	7	0—14

First Quarter
Phi.—Fryar 18 pass from Peete (Anderson kick), 6:52.
Was.—Allen 2 run (Blanton kick), 9:47.

Second Quarter
Phi.—Jones 9 pass from Peete (Anderson kick), 11:57.
Phi.—FG, Anderson 26, 14:45.

Third Quarter
Was.—Allen 49 run (Blanton kick), 1:01.
Attendance—53,415.

TEAM STATISTICS

	Philadelphia	Washington
First downs	23	11
Rushes-yards	37-144	24-127

	Philadelphia	Washington
Passing	258	93
Punt returns	3-10	2-19
Kickoff returns	3-63	4-123
Interception returns	0-0	1-0
Comp.-att.-int.	20-34-1	12-25-0
Sacked-yards lost	2-11	3-26
Punts	5-40	7-49
Fumbles-lost	2-2	1-0
Penalties-yards	6-50	5-42
Time of possession	35:57	24:03.

INDIVIDUAL STATISTICS

RUSHING—Philadelphia, Watters 18-86, Garner 13-48, Peete 6-10. Washington, Allen 20-111, Mitchell 3-11, Shepherd 1-5.
PASSING—Philadelphia, Peete 20-34-1-269. Washington, Frerotte 12-25-0-119.
RECEIVING—Philadelphia, Jones 6-82, Fryar 5-74, Turner 2-14, West 2-10, Dunn 1-54, J. Johnson 1-19, Seay 1-11, Watters 1-3, Garner 1-2. Washington, Asher 3-23, Ellard 2-38, Shepherd 2-29, Mitchell 2-8, B. Brooks 1-11, Galbraith 1-7, Bowie 1-3.
MISSED FIELD GOAL ATTEMPTS—Washington, Blanton 53.
INTERCEPTIONS—Washington, D. Green 1-0.
KICKOFF RETURNS—Philadelphia, Seay 2-36, Witherspoon 1-27. Washington, Mitchell 3-110, Asher 1-13.
PUNT RETURNS—Philadelphia, Solomon 3-10. Washington, Mitchell 2-19.
SACKS—Philadelphia, Mamula 2, Fuller 1. Washington, Woods 1, Bandison 1.

BEARS 22, COWBOYS 6

Monday, September 2

Dallas	3	0	0	3— 6
Chicago	0	10	0	12—22

First Quarter
Dal.—FG, Boniol 28, 10:05.

Second Quarter
Chi.—R. Harris 33 pass from Conway (Huerta kick), 11:29.
Chi.—FG, Huerta 31, 14:49.

Fourth Quarter
Chi.—FG, Huerta 42, 3:04.
Chi.—FG, Huerta 34, 5:12.
Chi.—Cox fumble recovery in end zone (pass failed), 6:13.
Dal.—FG, Boniol 28, 11:27.
Attendance—63,076.

TEAM STATISTICS

	Dallas	Chicago
First downs	18	14
Rushes-yards	25-83	32-91
Passing	173	213
Punt returns	3-24	2-9
Kickoff returns	5-131	2-34
Interception returns	1-(-1)	1-29
Comp.-att.-int.	21-37-1	14-29-1
Sacked-yards lost	2-19	0-0
Punts	4-37	3-53
Fumbles-lost	4-3	1-1
Penalties-yards	9-64	6-57
Time of possession	30:36	29:24.

INDIVIDUAL STATISTICS

RUSHING—Dallas, E. Smith 18-70, Aikman 3-9, Johnston 2-6, K. Williams 2-(minus 2). Chicago, Green 17-62, R. Harris 10-21, Kramer 4-0, Timpson 1-8.
PASSING—Dallas, Aikman 21-37-1-192. Chicago, Kramer 12-27-1-133, Sauerbrun 1-1-0-47, Conway 1-1-0-33.
RECEIVING—Dallas, Sanders 9-87, K. Williams 3-32, Johnston 3-27, Walker 2-24, E. Smith 2-5, Martin 1-12, Ware 1-5. Chicago, Conway 4-33, R. Harris 3-103, Timpson 3-56, Green 2-8, Engram 1-7, Jennings 1-6.
MISSED FIELD GOAL ATTEMPTS—Dallas, Boniol 43. Chicago, Huerta 35.
INTERCEPTIONS—Dallas, K. Smith 1-(minus 1). Chicago, M. Carter 1-29.
KICKOFF RETURNS—Dallas, K. Williams 5-131. Chicago, Ja. Jackson 2-34.
PUNT RETURNS—Dallas, K. Williams 2-17, Martin 1-7. Chicago, Engram 2-9.
SACKS—Chicago, Flanigan 1, Miniefield 1.

WEEK 2

RESULTS

BUFFALO 17, New England 10
Carolina 22, NEW ORLEANS 20
DALLAS 27, N.Y. Giants 0
Denver 30, SEATTLE 20
DETROIT 21, Tampa Bay 6
Houston 34, JACKSONVILLE 27
Indianapolis 21, N.Y. JETS 7
KANSAS CITY 19, Oakland 3
Miami 38, ARIZONA 10
Minnesota 23, ATLANTA 17
PITTSBURGH 31, Baltimore 17
SAN DIEGO 27, Cincinnati 14
SAN FRANCISCO 34, St. Louis 0
WASHINGTON 10, Chicago 3
GREEN BAY 39, Philadelphia 13

STANDINGS

AFC EAST	W	L	T	Pct.
Buffalo	2	0	0	1.000
Indianapolis	2	0	0	1.000
Miami	2	0	0	1.000
New England	0	2	0	.000
N.Y. Jets	0	2	0	.000

AFC CENTRAL	W	L	T	Pct.
Baltimore	1	1	0	.500
Jacksonville	1	1	0	.500
Houston	1	1	0	.500
Pittsburgh	1	1	0	.500
Cincinnati	0	2	0	.000

AFC WEST	W	L	T	Pct.
Denver	2	0	0	1.000
Kansas City	2	0	0	1.000
San Diego	2	0	0	1.000
Oakland	0	2	0	.000
Seattle	0	2	0	.000

NFC EAST	W	L	T	Pct.
Dallas	1	1	0	.500
Philadelphia	1	1	0	.500
Washington	1	1	0	.500
Arizona	0	2	0	.000
N.Y. Giants	0	2	0	.000

NFC CENTRAL	W	L	T	Pct.
Green Bay	2	0	0	1.000
Minnesota	2	0	0	1.000
Chicago	1	1	0	.500
Detroit	1	1	0	.500
Tampa Bay	0	2	0	.000

NFC WEST	W	L	T	Pct.
Carolina	2	0	0	1.000
San Francisco	2	0	0	1.000
St. Louis	1	1	0	.500
Atlanta	0	2	0	.000
New Orleans	0	2	0	.000

HIGHLIGHTS

Hero of the week: Denver linebacker Bill Romanowski, a free-agent signee from Philadelphia, had eight tackles, two fumble recoveries and an interception in his second game as a Bronco, a 30-20 win at Seattle.

Goat of the week: Much-maligned Tampa Bay quarterback Trent Dilfer did little to quiet his critics in Week 2, going 14-of-34 for 176 yards, no touchdowns and two interceptions in the Bucs' 21-6 loss at Detroit. Dilfer had thrown one touchdown pass in his last 379 attempts.

Sub of the week: In the first start of his five-year NFL career, Minnesota quarterback Brad Johnson was superb, going 15-of-26 for 275 yards and two touchdowns in the Vikings' 23-17 win at Atlanta. Johnson, subbing for the injured Warren Moon, completed five of seven passes on a 13-play, 82-yard drive in the final minutes to set up an insurance field goal with 17 seconds left.

Comeback of the week: Trailing 20-19 midway through the fourth quarter, the Carolina Panthers drove 67 yards in 11 plays to defeat New Orleans, 22-20, on John Kasay's fifth field goal of the game, a 23-yarder with 2:09 left.

Blowout of the week: San Francisco held St. Louis to six first downs and 105 total yards in beating the Rams, 34-0. It was the 49ers' 12th consecutive win over the Rams and their first shutout in seven years. It was the fewest yards the 49ers allowed in a game since 1977. Three Rams quarterbacks combined to complete 11 of 27 passes for a net of 69 yards.

Nail-biter of the week: Buffalo beat New England, 17-10, as four Bills defenders—led by end Phil Hansen—gang-tackled running back David Meggett at the 2 as time expired. The Bills had taken the lead when Jim Kelly and Quinn Early hooked up for a 63-yard touchdown pass on a third-and-23 play with 5:21 left.

Hit of the week: By Colts strong safety David Tate, who stopped Kyle Brady short of the goal line after the Jets' tight end caught a pass inside the 5 and seemed certain to score. Instead, Brady fumbled and the Colts recovered.

Oddity of the week: For the second consecutive season, Chiefs cornerback James Hasty helped to defeat the Raiders at Arrowhead Stadium by scoring a touchdown. On September 17, 1995, he returned an interception 64 yards for an overtime touchdown to clinch a 23-17 victory. In Week 2, he returned a fumble 80 yards for a score in a 19-3 Kansas City win.

Top rusher: Rookie Eddie George carried 17 times for 143 yards and one touchdown in leading the Oilers to a 34-27 win over Jacksonville.

Top passer: Neil O'Donnell was 26-of-46 for 319 yards and one touchdown in the Jets' 21-7 loss to Indianapolis.

Top receiver: Ken Dilger caught seven passes for 156 yards and one touchdown in the Colts' win over the Jets.

Notes: Dilger's 156 yards broke John Mackey's 33-year-old record for most receiving yards in a game by a Colts tight end. . . . Kasay's five field-goal game was his second in two weeks. . . . San Francisco quarterback Steve Young had not thrown a touchdown pass in 18 quarters. . . . In the Cowboys' 27-0 win over the Giants, Troy Aikman threw three touchdown passes in a regular-season game for the first time since 1992. The Dallas quarterback also attained two career milestones: the 20,000-yard mark in passing yardage and 100 touchdown passes. . . . Eight of the Giants' 11 possessions against the Cowboys lasted three plays or less. . . . Heavy rain and lightning caused a 32-minute delay in the Colts-Jets game at Giants Stadium, believed to be the first delay ever in an NFL regular-season game. . . . The Cardinals have never beaten the Dolphins (0-7) in their history or won a home opener since moving to Arizona in 1988. . . . Vinny Testaverde is 0-7 with 11 interceptions in his career against the Steelers. . . . George had a 76-yard run against Jacksonville, the longest run from scrimmage by an Oilers player since Larry Moriarty went 80 yards against the Raiders in 1983. . . . The Raiders have lost eight consecutive regular-season games for the first time since Al Davis took over in 1963. . . . Washington did not allow a touchdown for the first time since 1993 in beating Chicago, 10-3. . . . Denver quarterback John

Elway broke Tom Jackson's team record by playing in his 192nd game. . . . A Lambeau Field record crowd of 60,666 saw the Packers defeat the Eagles, 39-13, in the first Monday night game at Lambeau since 1986.

Quote of the week: Dilger, on breaking Mackey's record: "I don't know much about John Mackey, but he's in the Hall of Fame, so he can't be too bad."

GAME SUMMARIES

DOLPHINS 38, CARDINALS 10

Sunday, September 8

Miami	7	17	7	7—38
Arizona	0	0	10	0—10

First Quarter
Mia.—Abdul-Jabbar 3 run (Nedney kick), 9:54.
Second Quarter
Mia.—Abdul-Jabbar 3 run (Nedney kick), 1:22.
Mia.—L. Thomas 20 pass from Marino (Nedney kick), 3:23.
Mia.—FG, Nedney 36, 14:55.
Third Quarter
Ariz.—C. Smith 1 pass from K. Graham (G. Davis kick), 3:55.
Ariz.—FG, G. Davis 26, 7:25.
Mia.—Spikes 1 run (Nedney kick), 12:02.
Fourth Quarter
Mia.—McDuffie 5 pass from Marino (Nedney kick), 2:08.
Attendance—55,444.

TEAM STATISTICS

	Miami	Arizona
First downs	25	13
Rushes-yards	32-128	19-27
Passing	203	176
Punt returns	2-27	2-14
Kickoff returns	3-67	5-113
Interception returns	3-70	0-0
Comp.-att.-int.	18-27-0	21-37-3
Sacked-yards lost	3-19	2-14
Punts	4-46	6-36
Fumbles-lost	2-1	4-1
Penalties-yards	4-30	8-59
Time of possession	33:14	26:46

INDIVIDUAL STATISTICS
RUSHING—Miami, Abdul-Jabbar 16-41, Spikes 11-79, Parmalee 5-8. Arizona, Centers 6-23, McElroy 6-(minus 5), C. Smith 4-2, Johnson 3-7.
PASSING—Miami, Marino 14-23-0-178, Kosar 4-4-0-44. Arizona, K. Graham 13-19-2-133, Esiason 8-18-1-57.
RECEIVING—Miami, L. Thomas 3-40, McDuffie 3-30, Jordan 2-51, Miller 2-38, Spikes 2-17, Byars 2-17, Pritchett 1-13, McPhail 1-12, Parmalee 1-2, Carolan 1-2. Arizona, Sanders 8-81, R. Moore 4-56, Centers 4-25, Carter 2-13, Dowdell 1-9, Edwards 1-5, C. Smith 1-1.
MISSED FIELD GOAL ATTEMPTS—Miami, Nedney 40, 30.
INTERCEPTIONS—Miami, Buckley 2-65, Oliver 1-5.
KICKOFF RETURNS—Miami, Jordan 2-43, McPhail 1-24. Arizona, McElroy 3-71, Terry 1-28, C. Smith 1-14.
PUNT RETURNS—Miami, Miller 1-15, McDuffie 1-12. Arizona, Dowdell 2-14.
SACKS—Miami, Burton 1, A. Jones 1. Arizona, Miller 1, Rice 1, Swann 1.

REDSKINS 10, BEARS 3

Sunday, September 8

Chicago	3	0	0	0— 3
Washington	0	3	7	0—10

First Quarter
Chi.—FG, Huerta 37, 13:37.
Second Quarter
Was.—FG, Blanton 50, 14:36.
Third Quarter
Was.—Allen 28 run (Blanton kick), 10:11.
Attendance—52,711.

TEAM STATISTICS

	Chicago	Washington
First downs	19	13
Rushes-yards	33-148	24-75

	Chicago	Washington
Passing	151	168
Punt returns	3-29	0-0
Kickoff returns	3-54	1-29
Interception returns	0-0	1-4
Comp.-att.-int.	20-37-1	18-29-0
Sacked-yards lost	4-32	1-9
Punts	7-47	8-43
Fumbles-lost	3-1	1-1
Penalties-yards	6-43	2-8
Time of possession	32:49	27:11

INDIVIDUAL STATISTICS
RUSHING—Chicago, Green 20-106, R. Harris 12-43, Kramer 1-(minus 1). Washington, Allen 21-83, Mitchell 2-(minus 7), Frerotte 1-(minus 1).
PASSING—Chicago, Kramer 20-37-1-183. Washington, Frerotte 18-29-0-177.
RECEIVING—Chicago, Timpson 7-91, Conway 6-69, R. Harris 3-15, Green 2-8, Engram 1-9, T. Carter 1-(minus 9). Washington, Ellard 4-70, Westbrook 4-38, Mitchell 3-27, Allen 3-12, Logan 2-17, Asher 1-7, Shepherd 1-6.
MISSED FIELD GOAL ATTEMPTS—Chicago, Huerta 39. Washington, Blanton 44.
INTERCEPTIONS—Washington, Morrison 1-4.
KICKOFF RETURNS—Chicago, Ja. Jackson 2-30, Engram 1-24. Washington, Mitchell 1-29.
PUNT RETURNS—Chicago, Engram 3-29.
SACKS—Chicago, Cox 1. Washington, Gilbert 1, Owens 1, Harvey 1, Stephens 1.

49ERS 34, RAMS 0

Sunday, September 8

St. Louis	0	0	0	0— 0
San Francisco	0	14	3	17—34

Second Quarter
S.F.—Safety, Banks tackled by B. Young in end zone, 3:16.
S.F.—Loville 2 run (Wilkins kick), 9:10.
S.F.—FG, Wilkins 38, 14:15.
S.F.—Safety, Landeta kicked ball out of end zone, 14:51.
Third Quarter
S.F.—FG, Wilkins 22, 11:13.
Fourth Quarter
S.F.—FG, Wilkins 21, 4:47.
S.F.—Vardell 1 run (Wilkins kick), 8:18.
S.F.—D. Carter 1 run (Wilkins kick), 11:45.
Attendance—63,624.

TEAM STATISTICS

	St. Louis	San Francisco
First downs	6	23
Rushes-yards	16-36	42-129
Passing	69	222
Punt returns	0-0	4-31
Kickoff returns	4-67	3-49
Interception returns	0-0	1-25
Comp.-att.-int.	11-27-1	21-30-0
Sacked-yards lost	7-45	1-2
Punts	6-39	3-42
Fumbles-lost	5-4	1-0
Penalties-yards	11-82	5-45
Time of possession	21:23	38:37

INDIVIDUAL STATISTICS
RUSHING—St. Louis, Phillips 9-15, Green 3-10, Robinson 2-6, D. Harris 1-3, Banks 1-2. San Francisco, Vardell 17-44, Loville 12-49, S. Young 4-14, D. Carter 3-(minus 5), Brohm 3-(minus 5), Lynn 1-8, Rice 1-3, Grbac 1-1.
PASSING—St. Louis, Banks 6-17-0-69, Walsh 2-6-1-13, Martin 3-4-0-32. San Francisco, S. Young 15-18-0-138, Grbac 6-12-0-86.
RECEIVING—St. Louis, Bruce 4-52, Laing 2-25, Green 2-15, Ross 1-13, Drayton 1-6, D. Harris 1-3. San Francisco, Rice 7-99, Vardell 6-31, Stoke 3-62, Jones 3-26, Loville 2-6.
MISSED FIELD GOAL ATTEMPTS—San Francisco, Wilkins 45.
INTERCEPTIONS—San Francisco, Pope 1-25.
KICKOFF RETURNS—St. Louis, Kennison 2-36, Thomas 2-31. San Francisco, D. Carter 1-27, Deese 1-12, Singleton 1-10.
PUNT RETURNS—San Francisco, D. Carter 4-31.
SACKS—St. Louis, Farr 1. San Francisco, B. Young 2, Doleman 1, Barke 1, D. Brown 1, Drakeford 1, Woodall 1.

CHIEFS 19, RAIDERS 3

Sunday, September 8

Oakland	0	0	0	3—	3
Kansas City	0	7	7	5—	19

Second Quarter
K.C.—To. Richardson 1 pass from Bono (Stoyanovich kick), 13:51.

Third Quarter
K.C.—Hasty 80 fumble return (Stoyanovich kick), 6:21.

Fourth Quarter
K.C.—FG, Stoyanovich 23, 1:21.
Oak.—FG, Ford 38, 7:59.
K.C.—Safety, Saleaumua tackled Robbins in end zone, 11:48.
Attendance—79,281.

TEAM STATISTICS

	Oakland	Kansas City
First downs	22	16
Rushes-yards	26-136	31-125
Passing	160	121
Punt returns	2-8	1-(-11)
Kickoff returns	4-81	1-13
Interception returns	0-0	1-2
Comp.-att.-int.	19-40-1	11-19-0
Sacked-yards lost	2-21	3-14
Punts	3-43	6-46
Fumbles-lost	3-1	3-0
Penalties-yards	7-58	11-82
Time of possession	31:05	28:55

INDIVIDUAL STATISTICS
RUSHING—Oakland, Williams 12-38, Kaufman 8-69, Aska 4-11, Gossett 9-18. Kansas City, Allen 12-34, Hill 7-50, Bennett 5-26, Anders 5-12, To. Richardson 1-2, McNair 1-1.
PASSING—Oakland, Hobert 19-40-1-181. Kansas City, Bono 11-19-0-135.
RECEIVING—Oakland, T. Brown 8-96, Hobbs 5-50, Dudley 3-16, Fenner 2-11, A. Glover 1-8, Williams 1-0. Kansas City, Hughes 3-45, Anders 2-28, Penn 2-23, Allen 1-29, Walker 1-6, Bennett 1-3, To. Richardson 1-1.
MISSED FIELD GOAL ATTEMPTS—Oakland, Ford 43. Kansas City, Stoyanovich 47.
INTERCEPTIONS—Kansas City, Simien 1-2.
KICKOFF RETURNS—Oakland, Kaufman 3-67, Shedd 1-14. Kansas City, Woods 1-13.
PUNT RETURNS—Oakland, T. Brown 2-8. Kansas City, Vanover 1-(minus 11).
SACKS—Oakland, Maryland 1, Bruce 1, McGlockton 1. Kansas City, Thomas 2.

CHARGERS 27, BENGALS 14

Sunday, September 8

Cincinnati	0	7	0	7—	14
San Diego	7	7	3	10—	27

First Quarter
S.D.—Russell 1 run (Carney kick), 12:49.

Second Quarter
S.D.—Martin 21 pass from Humphries (Carney kick), 4:08.
Cin.—Pickens 27 pass from Blake (Pelfrey kick), 13:07.

Third Quarter
S.D.—FG, Carney 47, 4:21.

Fourth Quarter
S.D.—FG, Carney 23, 1:47.
S.D.—Russell 1 run (Carney kick), 3:09.
Cin.—McGee 12 pass from Wilhelm (Pelfrey kick), 12:59.
Attendance—55,880.

TEAM STATISTICS

	Cincinnati	San Diego
First downs	14	25
Rushes-yards	22-63	34-114
Passing	187	269
Punt returns	2-0	4-96
Kickoff returns	6-116	0-0
Interception returns	2-4	1-21
Comp.-att.-int.	17-36-1	27-42-2
Sacked-yards lost	0-0	1-6
Punts	7-52	4-47
Fumbles-lost	2-1	0-0
Penalties-yards	5-30	8-79
Time of possession	27:19	32:41

INDIVIDUAL STATISTICS
RUSHING—Cincinnati, Hearst 7-16, Carter 7-13, Blake 3-8, Wilhelm 2-22, Scott 1-8, Pickens 1-2, Bieniemy 1-(minus 6). San Diego, Russell 16-62, Hayden 13-46, Humphries 2-4, Fletcher 2-3, Salisbury 1-(minus 1).
PASSING—Cincinnati, Blake 14-33-1-163, Wilhelm 3-3-0-24. San Diego, Humphries 27-41-2-275, Salisbury 0-1-0-0.
RECEIVING—Cincinnati, Pickens 4-63, Hearst 3-17, McGee 2-34, Battaglia 2-24, Carter 2-20, Cothran 2-12, Bieniemy 1-9, Dunn 1-8. San Diego, Martin 9-96, Fletcher 6-51, A. Coleman 5-70, Pupunu 3-22, Jones 2-23, Hayden 1-10, Reeves 1-3.
MISSED FIELD GOAL ATTEMPTS—None.
INTERCEPTIONS—Cincinnati, Ambrose 2-4. San Diego, Gouveia 1-21.
KICKOFF RETURNS—Cincinnati, Dunn 4-66, Sawyer 2-50.
PUNT RETURNS—Cincinnati, Sawyer 1-0, Myers 1-0. San Diego, Da. Gordon 4-96.
SACKS—Cincinnati, Wilkinson 1.

OILERS 34, JAGUARS 27

Sunday, September 8

Houston	10	14	7	3—	34
Jacksonville	10	3	7	7—	27

First Quarter
Jac.—FG, Hollis 38, 2:13.
Hou.—FG, Del Greco 32, 5:36.
Jac.—Stewart 5 run (Hollis kick), 11:35.
Hou.—George 1 run (Del Greco kick), 14:12.

Second Quarter
Hou.—Floyd 63 pass from Chandler (Del Greco kick), 1:50.
Jac.—FG, Hollis 37, 9:09.
Hou.—Wycheck 7 pass from Chandler (Del Greco kick), 14:13.

Third Quarter
Hou.—Davis 11 pass from Chandler (Del Greco kick), 7:52.
Jac.—Smith 5 pass from Brunell (Hollis kick), 12:13.

Fourth Quarter
Hou.—FG, Del Greco 29, 7:33.
Jac.—McCardell 3 pass from Brunell (Hollis kick), 12:27.
Attendance—66,468.

TEAM STATISTICS

	Houston	Jacksonville
First downs	21	26
Rushes-yards	31-181	21-72
Passing	220	298
Punt returns	1-0	2-47
Kickoff returns	4-133	6-160
Interception returns	2-17	0-0
Comp.-att.-int.	14-22-0	27-38-2
Sacked-yards lost	1-6	2-4
Punts	2-44	1-48
Fumbles-lost	2-1	2-1
Penalties-yards	7-60	6-55
Time of possession	28:45	31:15

INDIVIDUAL STATISTICS
RUSHING—Houston, George 17-143, Thomas 9-27, Chandler 4-6, Harmon 1-5. Jacksonville, Stewart 17-58, Brunell 2-7, Maston 2-7.
PASSING—Houston, Chandler 14-22-0-226. Jacksonville, Brunell 27-38-2-302.
RECEIVING—Houston, Floyd 3-90, Davis 3-32, Russell 2-34, Harmon 2-22, Wycheck 2-19, Sanders 1-20, George 1-9. Jacksonville, McCardell 8-100, Rison 6-81, Mitchell 5-44, Stewart 3-37, Smith 2-10, Maston 1-17, Brown 1-10, Griffith 1-3.
MISSED FIELD GOAL ATTEMPTS—Jacksonville, Hollis 31.
INTERCEPTIONS—Houston, Robertson 2-17.
KICKOFF RETURNS—Houston, Gray 4-133. Jacksonville, Jordan 4-109, W. Jackson 2-51.
PUNT RETURNS—Houston, Gray 1-0. Jacksonville, Hudson 2-47.
SACKS—Houston, Young 1½, Walker ½. Jacksonville, Hardy 1.

COLTS 21, JETS 7

Sunday, September 8

Indianapolis	7	7	0	7—	21
N.Y. Jets	0	7	0	0—	7

First Quarter
Ind.—Faulk 1 run (Blanchard kick), 11:59.

Second Quarter
Ind.—Dilger 22 pass from Harbaugh (Blanchard kick), 13:11.
NYJ—Johnson 11 pass from O'Donnell (Lowery kick), 14:29.

Fourth Quarter
Ind.—Harbaugh 12 run (Blanchard kick), 3:38.
  Attendance—63,534.

TEAM STATISTICS

	Indianapolis	N.Y. Jets
First downs	17	21
Rushes-yards	29-71	24-69
Passing	220	290
Punt returns	5-102	2-8
Kickoff returns	1-20	3-69
Interception returns	1-32	0-0
Comp.-att.-int.	15-20-0	26-46-1
Sacked-yards lost	3-22	3-29
Punts	5-50	7-48
Fumbles-lost	1-1	1-1
Penalties-yards	4-33	15-100
Time of possession	29:22	30:38

INDIVIDUAL STATISTICS

RUSHING—Indianapolis, Faulk 10-25, Crockett 6-15, Warren 6-6, Harbaugh 4-19, Workman 3-6. New York, Murrell 13-41, Anderson 5-14, Cobb 5-12, O'Donnell 1-2.

PASSING—Indianapolis, Harbaugh 15-20-0-242. New York, O'Donnell 26-46-1-319.

RECEIVING—Indianapolis, Dilger 7-156, Harrison 2-35, Crockett 2-18, Faulk 2-11, Bailey 1-15, Warren 1-7. New York, Chrebet 7-93, Johnson 5-53, Anderson 5-41, Slaughter 3-80, Graham 2-5, F. Baxter 1-23, Murrell 1-13, Brady 1-8, Cobb 1-3.

MISSED FIELD GOAL ATTEMPTS—None.

INTERCEPTIONS—Indianapolis, Buchanan 1-32.

KICKOFF RETURNS—Indianapolis, Bailey 1-20. New York, Moore 2-46, Van Dyke 1-23.

PUNT RETURNS—Indianapolis, Harrison 5-102. New York, Chrebet 2-8.

SACKS—Indianapolis, Siragusa 1, Buchanan ½, Bennett ½, Dent ½, McCoy ½. New York, Brock 1, Green 1, Chalenski 1.

BRONCOS 30, SEAHAWKS 20

Sunday, September 8

Denver	3	10	7	10—30
Seattle	3	3	7	7—20

First Quarter
Den.—FG, Elam 18, 7:52.
Sea.—FG, Peterson 27, 14:30.

Second Quarter
Sea.—FG, Peterson 40, 6:44.
Den.—Craver 39 pass from Elway (Elam kick), 9:31.
Den.—FG, Elam 28, 14:50.

Third Quarter
Sea.—Galloway 88 punt return (Peterson kick), 7:50.
Den.—Miller 7 pass from Elway (Elam kick), 13:54.

Fourth Quarter
Den.—FG, Elam 33, 4:28.
Sea.—Fauria 23 pass from Friesz (Peterson kick), 10:46.
Den.—Elway 1 run (Elam kick), 13:00.
  Attendance—43,671.

TEAM STATISTICS

	Denver	Seattle
First downs	22	10
Rushes-yards	40-180	19-39
Passing	194	172
Punt returns	3-40	2-88
Kickoff returns	4-84	7-156
Interception returns	1-1	0-0
Comp.-att.-int.	18-28-0	18-30-1
Sacked-yards lost	5-15	3-18
Punts	5-35	4-53
Fumbles-lost	2-1	4-2
Penalties-yards	3-19	8-50
Time of possession	36:44	23:16

INDIVIDUAL STATISTICS

RUSHING—Denver, Davis 28-111, Craver 9-47, Elway 3-22. Seattle, Warren 14-35, Friesz 2-3, Mirer 2-2, Strong 1-(minus 1).

PASSING—Denver, Elway 18-28-0-209. Seattle, Friesz 11-19-0-137, Mirer 7-11-1-53.

RECEIVING—Denver, Miller 4-49, Craver 4-45, Sharpe 3-40, Davis 3-37, McCaffrey 3-26, Sherrard 1-12. Seattle, Blades 4-57, Fauria 4-53, Galloway 3-42, Pritchard 3-26, Warren 3-11, Strong 1-1.

MISSED FIELD GOAL ATTEMPTS—None.
INTERCEPTIONS—Denver, Romanowski 1-1.
KICKOFF RETURNS—Denver, Hebron 4-84. Seattle, Broussard 5-137, Brown 2-19.
PUNT RETURNS—Denver, Kinchen 3-40. Seattle, Galloway 2-88.
SACKS—Denver, Crockett 1, Perry 1, Hasselbach 1. Seattle, Sinclair 4, C. Harris 1.

COWBOYS 27, GIANTS 0

Sunday, September 8

N.Y. Giants	0	0	0	0— 0
Dallas	14	7	3	3—27

First Quarter
Dal.—Sanders 8 pass from Aikman (Boniol kick), 7:00.
Dal.—K. Williams 19 pass from Aikman (Boniol kick), 13:37.

Second Quarter
Dal.—E. Smith 5 pass from Aikman (Boniol kick), 14:58.

Third Quarter
Dal.—FG, Boniol 23, 12:16.

Fourth Quarter
Dal.—FG, Boniol 29, 4:40.
  Attendance—63,069.

TEAM STATISTICS

	N.Y. Giants	Dallas
First downs	7	21
Rushes-yards	24-55	40-140
Passing	38	228
Punt returns	0-0	4-31
Kickoff returns	6-98	0-0
Interception returns	0-0	1-22
Comp.-att.-int.	10-19-1	19-27-0
Sacked-yards lost	3-17	0-0
Punts	8-48	5-36
Fumbles-lost	2-1	2-0
Penalties-yards	5-53	5-40
Time of possession	25:17	34:43

INDIVIDUAL STATISTICS

RUSHING—New York, Hampton 15-44, Wheatley 6-0, Brown 1-5, Way 1-4, Elias 1-2. Dallas, E. Smith 25-94, S. Williams 6-26, Walker 3-9, Wilson 2-(minus 3), Johnston 1-7, K. Williams 1-4, Sanders 1-3, Aikman 1-0.

PASSING—New York, Brown 10-19-1-55. Dallas, Aikman 19-27-0-228.

RECEIVING—New York, Elias 3-12, Calloway 2-15, Pierce 2-15, Hampton 2-1, Toomer 1-12. Dallas, K. Williams 6-86, Bjornson 4-41, Sanders 3-38, E. Smith 3-12, Johnston 2-13, Martin 1-38.

MISSED FIELD GOAL ATTEMPTS—None.
INTERCEPTIONS—Dallas, K. Smith 1-22.
KICKOFF RETURNS—New York, Wheatley 3-57, Toomer 2-36, Douglas 1-5.
PUNT RETURNS—Dallas, Martin 4-31.
SACKS—Dallas, D. Smith 1, Tolbert 1, Haley 1.

LIONS 21, BUCCANEERS 6

Sunday, September 8

Tampa Bay	3	3	0	0— 6
Detroit	0	14	7	0—21

First Quarter
T.B.—FG, Husted 30, 7:56.

Second Quarter
T.B.—FG, Husted 41, 1:40.
Det.—Sanders 54 run (Hanson kick), 10:22.
Det.—Raymond 24 interception return (Hanson kick), 11:32.

Third Quarter
Det.—H. Moore 23 pass from Mitchell (Hanson kick), 7:29.
  Attendance—54,229.

TEAM STATISTICS

	Tampa Bay	Detroit
First downs	13	12
Rushes-yards	29-74	26-120
Passing	200	114
Punt returns	6-50	3-15
Kickoff returns	3-59	3-74
Interception returns	0-0	2-24
Comp.-att.-int.	19-41-2	14-27-0
Sacked-yards lost	2-10	3-17
Punts	6-41	10-42

	Tampa Bay	Detroit
Fumbles-lost	3-2	1-1
Penalties-yards	4-20	8-49
Time of possession	33:54	26:06

INDIVIDUAL STATISTICS

RUSHING—Tampa Bay, Ellison 8-12, Thompson 8-8, Alstott 6-19, R. Brooks 4-17, Dilfer 2-18, Weldon 1-0. Detroit, Sanders 20-125, Mitchell 4-1, Morton 2-(minus 6).

PASSING—Tampa Bay, Dilfer 14-34-2-176, Weldon 3-4-0-25, Milanovich 2-3-0-9. Detroit, Mitchell 14-27-0-131.

RECEIVING—Tampa Bay, Hawkins 8-111, Harris 4-31, Alstott 2-23, Thompson 2-9, Ellison 1-20, Harper 1-11, Williams 1-5. Detroit, H. Moore 8-84, Sanders 3-13, Sloan 2-22, Perriman 1-12.

MISSED FIELD GOAL ATTEMPTS—Detroit, Hanson 53.

INTERCEPTIONS—Detroit, Raymond 1-24, Jeffries 1-0.

KICKOFF RETURNS—Tampa Bay, Silvan 3-59. Detroit, Milburn 3-74.

PUNT RETURNS—Tampa Bay, Silvan 6-50. Detroit, Milburn 3-15.

SACKS—Tampa Bay, Curry 1, Mayhew 1, Culpepper 1. Detroit, Elliss 1, Scroggins 1.

VIKINGS 23, FALCONS 17

Sunday, September 8

Minnesota	3	7	0	13—23
Atlanta	3	0	14	0—17

First Quarter
Min.—FG, Sisson 26, 6:05.
Atl.—FG, Andersen 20, 14:52.

Second Quarter
Min.—Carter 7 pass from B. Johnson (Sisson kick), 13:46.

Third Quarter
Atl.—Mathis 3 pass from J. George (Andersen kick), 5:46.
Atl.—Mathis 10 pass from J. George (Andersen kick), 13:21.

Fourth Quarter
Min.—FG, Sisson 30, :40.
Min.—Frisch 3 pass from B. Johnson (Sisson kick), 4:33.
Min.—FG, Sisson 21, 14:43.
Attendance—42,688.

TEAM STATISTICS

	Minnesota	Atlanta
First downs	18	21
Rushes-yards	33-99	19-79
Passing	266	245
Punt returns	1-6	4-57
Kickoff returns	2-36	3-80
Interception returns	1-0	1-0
Comp.-att.-int.	15-26-1	24-41-1
Sacked-yards lost	1-9	3-21
Punts	4-45	4-44
Fumbles-lost	3-1	3-1
Penalties-yards	10-77	9-75
Time of possession	29:11	30:49

INDIVIDUAL STATISTICS

RUSHING—Minnesota, R. Smith 30-90, Lee 3-9. Atlanta, Anderson 16-83, J. George 3-6.

PASSING—Minnesota, B. Johnson 15-26-1-275. Atlanta, J. George 24-41-1-266.

RECEIVING—Minnesota, Reed 4-148, Carter 4-75, Lee 2-19, Jordan 2-7, Evans 1-10, R. Smith 1-3, Frisch 1-3. Atlanta, Emanuel 9-116, Metcalf 5-52, Anderson 4-37, Birden 3-21, Mathis 2-13, Scott 1-27.

MISSED FIELD GOAL ATTEMPTS—Atlanta, Andersen 45.

INTERCEPTIONS—Minnesota, Thomas 1-0. Atlanta, Walker 1-0.

KICKOFF RETURNS—Minnesota, Ismail 2-36. Atlanta, Metcalf 2-65, Preston 1-15.

PUNT RETURNS—Minnesota, Palmer 1-6. Atlanta, Metcalf 4-57.

SACKS—Minnesota, F. Smith 1½, Randle 1, Tuaolo ½. Atlanta, Bennett 1.

BILLS 17, PATRIOTS 10

Sunday, September 8

New England	3	0	7	0—10
Buffalo	3	7	0	7—17

First Quarter
N.E.—FG, Vinatieri 42, 7:08.
Buf.—FG, Christie 33, 14:12.

Second Quarter
Buf.—T. Thomas 4 run (Christie kick), 1:56.

Third Quarter
N.E.—Glenn 37 pass from Bledsoe (Vinatieri kick), 11:07.

Fourth Quarter
Buf.—Early 63 pass from Kelly (Christie kick), 9:39.
Attendance—78,104.

TEAM STATISTICS

	New England	Buffalo
First downs	23	15
Rushes-yards	35-114	35-77
Passing	179	154
Punt returns	4-49	2-26
Kickoff returns	3-38	2-47
Interception returns	3-24	0-0
Comp.-att.-int.	21-47-0	14-27-3
Sacked-yards lost	4-31	2-19
Punts	4-46	7-42
Fumbles-lost	4-2	0-0
Penalties-yards	4-57	10-109
Time of possession	31:53	28:07

INDIVIDUAL STATISTICS

RUSHING—New England, Martin 28-90, Meggett 4-17, Gash 3-7. Buffalo, Holmes 15-49, T. Thomas 15-22, Moulds 4-7, Kelly 1-(minus 1).

PASSING—New England, Bledsoe 21-46-0-210, Tupa 0-1-0-0. Buffalo, Kelly 14-27-3-173.

RECEIVING—New England, Glenn 6-76, Meggett 4-35, Martin 4-20, Coates 3-31, Gash 2-26, Graham 1-11, W. Moore 1-11. Buffalo, Early 6-119, Johnson 3-21, Holmes 2-7, Copeland 1-14, T. Thomas 1-6, Moulds 1-6.

MISSED FIELD GOAL ATTEMPTS—New England, Vinatieri 45, 25, 47. Buffalo, Christie 37.

INTERCEPTIONS—New England, Clay 1-15, Reynolds 1-7, Slade 1-2.

KICKOFF RETURNS—New England, Meggett 2-21, T. Brown 1-17. Buffalo, Moulds 2-47.

PUNT RETURNS—New England, Meggett 4-49. Buffalo, Copeland 2-26.

SACKS—New England, Slade 1, McGinest 1. Buffalo, B. Smith 3, Hansen 1.

STEELERS 31, RAVENS 17

Sunday, September 8

Baltimore	7	10	0	0—17
Pittsburgh	14	14	3	0—31

First Quarter
Pit.—Woodson 43 interception return (N. Johnson kick), :54.
Bal.—Testaverde 6 run (Stover kick), 6:33.
Pit.—Bettis 1 run (N. Johnson kick), 11:09.

Second Quarter
Bal.—Alexander 17 pass from Testaverde (Stover kick), 2:03.
Pit.—C. Johnson 5 pass from Tomczak (N. Johnson kick), 6:51.
Pit.—Hastings 20 pass from Tomczak (N. Johnson kick), 11:47.
Bal.—FG, Stover 29, 14:41.

Third Quarter
Pit.—FG, N. Johnson 35, 7:38.
Attendance—57,241.

TEAM STATISTICS

	Baltimore	Pittsburgh
First downs	17	26
Rushes-yards	25-97	42-206
Passing	154	191
Punt returns	0-0	1-10
Kickoff returns	6-151	3-63
Interception returns	1-16	1-43
Comp.-att.-int.	13-24-1	18-25-1
Sacked-yards lost	2-5	1-7
Punts	4-49	2-38
Fumbles-lost	3-2	2-1
Penalties-yards	1-10	3-20
Time of possession	24:49	35:11

INDIVIDUAL STATISTICS

RUSHING—Baltimore, Hoard 13-54, Byner 8-30, Gardner 2-7, Testaverde 1-6, Hunter 1-0. Pittsburgh, Bettis 21-116, Pegram 11-60, Stewart 4-26, Tomczak 3-(minus 2), Lester 2-3, Hastings 1-3.

PASSING—Baltimore, Testaverde 13-24-1-159. Pittsburgh, Tomczak 18-25-1-198.

RECEIVING—Baltimore, Alexander 6-67, Jackson 3-46, Kinchen 2-30, Byner 1-12, Hoard 1-4. Pittsburgh, Hastings 7-76, C. Johnson 4-66, Stewart 2-22, Pegram 2-17, Bruener 2-11, Bettis 1-6.

MISSED FIELD GOAL ATTEMPTS—None.

INTERCEPTIONS—Baltimore, Adams 1-16. Pittsburgh, Woodson 1-43.

KICKOFF RETURNS—Baltimore, Hunter 4-95, J. Lewis 2-56. Pittsburgh, C. Johnson 1-23, Arnold 1-20, Wittman 1-20.

PUNT RETURNS—Pittsburgh, Hastings 1-10.

SACKS—Baltimore, Burnett 1. Pittsburgh, Ravotti 1, Henry ½, Emmons ½.

PANTHERS 22, SAINTS 20

Sunday, September 8

Carolina	7	6	3	6—22
New Orleans	7	7	3	3—20

First Quarter
N.O.—Small 9 pass from Everett (Brien kick), 6:38.
Car.—Oliver 84 punt return (Kasay kick), 14:32.

Second Quarter
N.O.—Jeffires 27 pass from Everett (Brien kick), 2:12.
Car.—FG, Kasay 51, 8:10.
Car.—FG, Kasay 22, 10:02.

Third Quarter
Car.—FG, Kasay 29, 4:29.
N.O.—FG, Brien 48, 13:36.

Fourth Quarter
Car.—FG, Kasay 51, :05.
N.O.—FG, Brien 43, 7:20.
Car.—FG, Kasay 23, 12:51.
Attendance—43,288.

TEAM STATISTICS

	Carolina	New Orleans
First downs	15	14
Rushes-yards	34-83	20-94
Passing	142	244
Punt returns	3-103	0-0
Kickoff returns	5-125	6-141
Interception returns	0-0	1-0
Comp.-att.-int.	13-21-1	22-32-0
Sacked-yards lost	3-29	2-11
Punts	4-37	5-43
Fumbles-lost	1-0	2-2
Penalties-yards	8-60	10-85
Time of possession	31:49	28:11

INDIVIDUAL STATISTICS
RUSHING—Carolina, Biakabutuka 21-74, Oliver 7-18, Collins 3-1, Beuerlein 3-(minus 10). New Orleans, Bates 15-69, Brown 3-13, Small 1-9, Whittle 1-3.

PASSING—Carolina, Collins 13-21-1-171. New Orleans, Everett 22-32-0-255.

RECEIVING—Carolina, Muhammad 6-96, Carrier 3-32, Walls 2-34, Green 1-7, Johnson 1-2. New Orleans, I. Smith 5-24, Jeffires 4-70, Brown 3-28, Lusk 3-24, Haynes 2-82, Small 2-21, Bates 2-9, Whittle 1-(minus 3).

MISSED FIELD GOAL ATTEMPTS—None.

INTERCEPTIONS—New Orleans, Newman 1-0.

KICKOFF RETURNS—Carolina, Bates 4-111, Oliver 1-14. New Orleans, Hughes 6-141.

PUNT RETURNS—Carolina, Oliver 3-103.

SACKS—Carolina, Lathon 2. New Orleans, Martin 2, B. Smith 1.

PACKERS 39, EAGLES 13

Monday, September 9

Philadelphia	0	7	0	6—13
Green Bay	10	20	7	2—39

First Quarter
G.B.—FG, Jacke 29, 2:25.
G.B.—R. Brooks 25 pass from Favre (Jacke kick), 13:20.

Second Quarter
G.B.—FG, Jacke 44, :04.
G.B.—Levens 1 run (Jacke kick), 5:40.
G.B.—FG, Jacke 38, 9:42.
Phi.—Watters 1 run (Anderson kick), 13:04.
G.B.—R. Brooks 20 pass from Favre (Jacke kick), 14:34.

Third Quarter
G.B.—Bennett 25 pass from Favre (Jacke kick), 8:46.

Fourth Quarter
G.B.—Safety, Peete sacked in end zone by S. Dotson and White, 3:54.
Phi.—Garner 1 run (pass failed), 14:30.
Attendance—60,666.

TEAM STATISTICS

	Philadelphia	Green Bay
First downs	14	23
Rushes-yards	17-59	38-171
Passing	200	261
Punt returns	2-14	5-25
Kickoff returns	5-99	3-47
Interception returns	0-0	3-11
Comp.-att.-int.	16-36-3	17-32-0
Sacked-yards lost	3-12	1-0
Punts	5-48	3-55
Fumbles-lost	1-1	2-0
Penalties-yards	8-49	5-23
Time of possession	23:33	36:27

INDIVIDUAL STATISTICS
RUSHING—Philadelphia, Watters 10-38, Garner 3-10, Detmer 2-7, Peete 2-4. Green Bay, Bennett 17-93, Levens 9-25, Henderson 6-40, Jervey 3-12 Favre 2-3, McMahon 1-(minus 2).

PASSING—Philadelphia, Peete 10-25-3-142, Detmer 6-11-0-70. Green Bay, Favre 17-31-0-261, Hentrich 0-1-0-0.

RECEIVING—Philadelphia, Jones 4-63, Garner 3-21, Ingram 2-33, Turner 2-14, Seay 2-12, Fryar 1-50, Dunn 1-18, Watters 1-1. Green Bay, R. Brooks 5-130, Bennett 5-49, Chmura 2-31, Jackson 2-27, Henderson 2-3, Freeman 1-21.

MISSED FIELD GOAL ATTEMPTS—None.

INTERCEPTIONS—Green Bay, Koonce 1-6, Dowden 1-5, Evans 1-0.

KICKOFF RETURNS—Philadelphia, Garner 5-99. Green Bay, Beebe 2-31 Freeman 1-16.

PUNT RETURNS—Philadelphia, Seay 2-14. Green Bay, Howard 5-25.

SACKS—Philadelphia, Taylor 1. Green Bay, S. Dotson 1½, McKenzie ½ White ½, Wilkins ½.

WEEK 3

RESULTS

CINCINNATI 30, New Orleans 15
DENVER 27, Tampa Bay 23
GREEN BAY 42, San Diego 10
HOUSTON 29, Baltimore 13
Indianapolis 25, DALLAS 24
Kansas City 35, SEATTLE 17
MIAMI 36, N.Y. Jets 27
Minnesota 20, CHICAGO 14
NEW ENGLAND 31, Arizona 0
OAKLAND 17, Jacksonville 3
PHILADELPHIA 24, Detroit 17
Washington 31, N.Y. GIANTS 10
PITTSBURGH 24, Buffalo 6
   Open date: Atlanta, Carolina, St. Louis, San Francisco

STANDINGS

AFC EAST

	W	L	T	Pct.
Indianapolis	3	0	0	1.000
Miami	3	0	0	1.000
Buffalo	2	1	0	.667
New England	1	2	0	.333
N.Y. Jets	0	3	0	.000

AFC CENTRAL

	W	L	T	Pct.
Houston	2	1	0	.667
Pittsburgh	2	1	0	.667
Baltimore	1	2	0	.333
Jacksonville	1	2	0	.333
Cincinnati	1	2	0	.333

AFC WEST

	W	L	T	Pct.
Denver	3	0	0	1.000
Kansas City	3	0	0	1.000
San Diego	2	1	0	.667
Oakland	1	2	0	.333
Seattle	0	3	0	.000

NFC EAST

	W	L	T	Pct.
Philadelphia	2	1	0	.500
Washington	2	1	0	.500
Dallas	1	2	0	.333
Arizona	0	3	0	.000
N.Y. Giants	0	3	0	.000

NFC CENTRAL

	W	L	T	Pct.
Green Bay	3	0	0	1.000
Minnesota	3	0	0	1.000
Chicago	1	2	0	.333
Detroit	1	2	0	.333
Tampa Bay	0	3	0	.000

NFC WEST

	W	L	T	Pct.
Carolina	2	0	0	1.000
San Francisco	2	0	0	1.000
St. Louis	1	1	0	.500
Atlanta	0	2	0	.000
New Orleans	0	3	0	.000

HIGHLIGHTS

Hero of the week: Philadelphia quarterback Rodney Peete was 25-of-30 for 284 yards and one touchdown in leading the Eagles to a 24-17 victory over Detroit. He also ran for a touchdown and did not throw an interception.

Goat of the week: New Orleans quarterback Jim Everett threw three interceptions in the second half and fumbled a snap in the Saints' 30-15 loss to previously winless Cincinnati.

Sub of the week: Linebacker Sammie Burroughs, subbing for the injured Steven Grant, had a team-high eight tackles in the Colts' 25-24 win at Dallas. Burroughs, a free-agent rookie from Portland State, also jarred the ball loose and forced a fumble by Cowboys star Emmitt Smith.

Comeback of the week: In the 38th fourth-quarter comeback of his career, Denver's John Elway drove the Broncos 80 yards in 14 plays in the final minutes for the winning touchdown and a 27-23 win over Tampa Bay. Although Elway directed the drive, running back Terrell Davis was its star, carrying eight times for 39 yards and scoring the go-ahead touchdown on a 3-yard run with 3:32 left. Twelve of the Broncos' 14 plays were runs, and the drive took more than eight minutes to complete.

Blowout of the week: New England limited Arizona to 26 first-half yards and one first down in whipping the Cardinals, 31-0. Pats running back Curtis Martin had two touchdowns before the Cardinals—who were outgained by more than 200 yards in the game—got their initial first down. It was the Patriots' first shutout in three years.

Nail-biter of the week: The Colts' 25-24 victory at Texas Stadium was a stunner. Playing without seven injured starters, they erased a 21-3 second-quarter deficit to take their first lead of the game when Jim Harbaugh capped a nine-play, 78-yard drive by throwing an eight-yard touchdown pass to Ken Dilger with :42 left in the third quarter. After Chris Boniol regained the lead for Dallas with a 52-yard field goal early in the fourth quarter, Cary Blanchard answered for Indianapolis by kicking a 43-yard field goal with 51

seconds left. A 57-yard field goal attempt by Boniol bounced off the crossbar as time expired.

Hit of the week: With the Raiders leading, 10-3, Oakland linebacker Rob Fredrickson blitzed Jacksonville quarterback Mark Brunell as he attempted to rally his team late in the game. Brunell, hit as he threw, fumbled the ball, and Jerry Ball lumbered 66 yards for an insurance touchdown with 2:15 left. The win snapped the Raiders' longest losing streak (eight games) in 33 years.

Oddity of the week: In Ray Rhodes' first 19 games as an NFL coach, the Eagles lost five games by a double-digit margin. In each case, they rebounded to win the following week.

Top rusher: Ricky Watters rushed 27 times for 153 yards and one touchdown in the Eagles' 24-17 win over Detroit.

Top passer: Neil O'Donnell was 25-of-44 passes for 325 yards and three touchdowns in the Jets' 36-27 loss at Miami.

Top receiver: Chris T. Jones caught a career-high nine passes in the Eagles' win over the Lions.

Notes: Green Bay was 3-0 for the first time since 1982 and had outscored its three opponents 115-26. The Packers did not trail in any game. . . . Elway joined Dan Marino and Fran Tarkenton as the only players in NFL history to have more than 45,000 yards in total offense. . . . Kansas City's Marcus Allen, at 36 the league's oldest starting running back, became the eighth NFL player to rush for more than 11,000 career yards. . . . The Bengals had two rushing touchdowns in the same game for the first time in two years. . . . Patriots quarterback Drew Bledsoe, 24, became the youngest player to throw for 11,000 yards. . . . Ten Washington players threw, carried or caught a ball for a first down in the Redskins' 31-10 win over the Giants. . . . Aaron Glenn's 100-yard interception return against Miami was the longest in Jets history. . . . San Diego's 42-10 loss at Green Bay was the Chargers' most lopsided since 1988. . . . Chicago's Erik Kramer, the only quarterback to take every snap in 1995, had to leave for one play in the second quarter of the Bears' 20-14 loss to

Minnesota after taking a hard hit. It ended a string of 1,190 consecutive snaps. . . . Before Week 3, the Colts hadn't beat the Cowboys since January 17, 1971, a 16-13 win in Super Bowl V.

Quote of the week: Dallas coach Barry Switzer, on the stunning one-point loss to Indianapolis: "Sometimes you bite the bear and sometimes the bear bites you. Today, the bear bit us."

GAME SUMMARIES

OILERS 29, RAVENS 13

Sunday, September 15

Baltimore	0	7	0	6	13
Houston	14	3	9	3	29

First Quarter
Hou.—Wycheck 3 pass from Chandler (Del Greco kick), 4:06.
Hou.—Davis 18 pass from Chandler (Del Greco kick), 14:29.
Second Quarter
Bal.—Jackson 7 pass from Testaverde (Stover kick), 5:21.
Hou.—FG, Del Greco 41, 12:04.
Third Quarter
Hou.—Safety, Montgomery stepped out of end zone, 4:01.
Hou.—Harmon 2 run (Del Greco kick), 13:06.
Fourth Quarter
Hou.—FG, Del Greco 44, 10:07.
Bal.—Arvie 1 pass from Testaverde (pass failed), 12:53.
Attendance—20,082.

TEAM STATISTICS

	Baltimore	Houston
First downs	19	19
Rushes-yards	22-73	32-140
Passing	208	172
Punt returns	0-0	0-0
Kickoff returns	6-130	3-66
Interception returns	0-0	3-41
Comp.-att.-int.	25-40-3	17-28-0
Sacked-yards lost	1-9	1-8
Punts	2-56	4-36
Fumbles-lost	1-0	0-0
Penalties-yards	4-35	6-48
Time of possession	26:12	33:48

INDIVIDUAL STATISTICS
RUSHING—Baltimore, Byner 19-68, Gardner 2-5, Montgomery 1-0. Houston, George 17-74, Thomas 10-32, Chandler 2-19, McNair 1-13, Harmon 1-2, Wycheck 1-0.
PASSING—Baltimore, Testaverde 25-40-3-217. Houston, Chandler 16-27-0-162, McNair 1-1-0-18.
RECEIVING—Baltimore, Jackson 6-86, Kinchen 6-54, Alexander 6-38, Byner 4-25, C. Williams 2-13, Arvie 1-1. Houston, Wycheck 6-64, Russell 3-35, Davis 2-32, Floyd 2-14, Sanders 1-29, Thomas 1-5, R. Lewis 1-4, George 1-(minus 3).
MISSED FIELD GOAL ATTEMPTS—None.
INTERCEPTIONS—Houston, D. Lewis 2-14, Robertson 1-27.
KICKOFF RETURNS—Baltimore, Hunter 3-70, J. Lewis 3-60. Houston, Gray 3-66.
PUNT RETURNS—None.
SACKS—Baltimore, Caldwell 1. Houston, Jackson 1.

BRONCOS 27, BUCCANEERS 23

Sunday, September 15

Tampa Bay	3	10	7	3	23
Denver	7	3	10	7	27

First Quarter
Den.—Braxton 69 interception return (Elam kick), 11:28.
T.B.—FG, Husted 24, 13:38.
Second Quarter
Den.—FG, Elam 45, 5:07.
T.B.—R. Brooks 8 run (Husted kick), 10:00.
T.B.—FG, Husted 35, 14:57.

Third Quarter
Den.—FG, Elam 20, 6:26.
Den.—Miller 17 pass from Elway (Elam kick), 11:42.
T.B.—Harper 40 pass from Dilfer (Husted kick), 13:03.
Fourth Quarter
T.B.—FG, Husted 28, 3:17.
Den.—Davis 3 run (Elam kick), 11:28.
Attendance—71,535.

TEAM STATISTICS

	Tampa Bay	Denver
First downs	15	20
Rushes-yards	22-121	39-194
Passing	186	180
Punt returns	2-2	4-6
Kickoff returns	5-150	3-76
Interception returns	2-7	1-69
Comp.-att.-int.	12-30-1	25-34-2
Sacked-yards lost	2-14	0-0
Punts	5-41	3-49
Fumbles-lost	3-1	3-1
Penalties-yards	8-52	8-98
Time of possession	24:06	35:54

INDIVIDUAL STATISTICS
RUSHING—Tampa Bay, R. Brooks 15-114, Dilfer 2-14, Alstott 2-3, Thompson 2-3, Hawkins 1-(minus 13). Denver, Davis 22-137, Craver 11-53, Elway 4-3, Hebron 2-1.
PASSING—Tampa Bay, Dilfer 12-30-1-200. Denver, Elway 25-34-2-180.
RECEIVING—Tampa Bay, Harris 5-96, Harper 2-77, Alstott 2-20, Hawkins 1-6, Ellison 1-3, R. Brooks 1-(minus 2). Denver, Miller 7-60, Craver 5-26, Sharpe 4-30, Davis 4-23, McCaffrey 2-21, Hebron 2-14, Carswell 1-6.
MISSED FIELD GOAL ATTEMPTS—None.
INTERCEPTIONS—Tampa Bay, D. Brooks 1-6, D. Abraham 1-1. Denver, Braxton 1-69.
KICKOFF RETURNS—Tampa Bay, Silvan 5-150. Denver, Hebron 2-58, Jeffers 1-18.
PUNT RETURNS—Tampa Bay, Silvan 2-2. Denver, Kinchen 4-6.
SACKS—Denver, A. Williams 2.

EAGLES 24, LIONS 17

Sunday, September 15

Detroit	0	3	7	7	17
Philadelphia	7	3	7	7	24

First Quarter
Phi.—Watters 11 run (Anderson kick), 4:41.
Second Quarter
Det.—FG, Hanson 50, 7:31.
Phi.—FG, Anderson 39, 12:16.
Third Quarter
Phi.—Jones 17 pass from Peete (Anderson kick), 8:30.
Det.—Sanders 8 run (Hanson kick), 12:25.
Fourth Quarter
Phi.—Peete 1 run (Anderson kick), 7:28.
Det.—Sanders 1 run (Hanson kick), 9:10.
Attendance—66,007.

TEAM STATISTICS

	Detroit	Philadelphia
First downs	17	25
Rushes-yards	19-60	39-175
Passing	173	271
Punt returns	2-16	2-17
Kickoff returns	4-115	4-94
Interception returns	0-0	1-0
Comp.-att.-int.	14-26-1	25-30-0
Sacked-yards lost	1-4	2-13
Punts	4-46	2-44
Fumbles-lost	0-0	0-0
Penalties-yards	6-50	11-73
Time of possession	20:38	39:22

INDIVIDUAL STATISTICS
RUSHING—Detroit, Sanders 16-49, Mitchell 3-11. Philadelphia, Watters 27-153, Peete 8-8, Turner 4-14.
PASSING—Detroit, Mitchell 14-26-1-177. Philadelphia, Peete 25-30-0-284.

RECEIVING—Detroit, H. Moore 6-88, Morton 5-39, Perriman 2-40, San-ers 1-10. Philadelphia, Jones 9-121, Fryar 6-63, Watters 6-57, Turner 4-43.
MISSED FIELD GOAL ATTEMPTS—Philadelphia, Anderson 38.
INTERCEPTIONS—Philadelphia, Taylor 1-0.
KICKOFF RETURNS—Detroit, Milburn 4-115. Philadelphia, Witherspoon -94.
PUNT RETURNS—Detroit, Milburn 2-16. Philadelphia, Solomon 2-17.
SACKS—Detroit, Porcher 1, London 1. Philadelphia, Hall 1.

RAIDERS 17, JAGUARS 3

Sunday, September 15

acksonville	0	0	3	0— 3
akland	0	10	0	7—17

Second Quarter
ak.—T. Brown 19 pass from Hostetler (Ford kick), 9:14.
ak.—FG, Ford 32, 14:02.
Third Quarter
c.—FG, Hollis 33, 10:20.
Fourth Quarter
ak.—Ball 66 interception return (Ford kick), 12:45.
Attendance—46,291.

TEAM STATISTICS

	Jacsonville	Oakland
st downs	14	18
ushes-yards	21-69	30-134
assing	201	197
unt returns	1-16	4-21
ckoff returns	2-35	1-19
terception returns	2-19	2-66
mp.-att.-int.	18-37-2	18-27-2
cked-yards lost	3-16	1-3
unts	7-37	5-42
mbles-lost	1-0	3-1
nalties-yards	8-58	10-90
me of possession	31:41	28:19

INDIVIDUAL STATISTICS
RUSHING—Jacksonville, Stewart 8-51, Means 8-12, Maston 3-2, Brunell 4. Oakland, Williams 16-54, Kaufman 7-54, Fenner 4-15, Aska 2-11, ostetler 1-0.
PASSING—Jacksonville, Brunell 18-37-2-217. Oakland, Hostetler 18-27-200.
RECEIVING—Jacksonville, McCardell 4-72, Smith 4-55, Mitchell 4-41, son 3-25, Stewart 2-12, W. Jackson 1-12. Oakland, T. Brown 5-60, Jett 4-, Hobbs 3-43, Fenner 2-25, Dudley 2-15, Kaufman 1-5, Williams 1-2.
MISSED FIELD GOAL ATTEMPTS—None.
INTERCEPTIONS—Jacksonville, V. Clark 1-15, Hudson 1-4. Oakland, Ball 66, Lewis 1-0.
KICKOFF RETURNS—Jacksonville, Smith 1-20, Bullard 1-15. Oakland, ufman 1-19.
PUNT RETURNS—Jacksonville, Hudson 1-16. Oakland, T. Brown 4-21.
SACKS—Jacksonville, Jurkovic 1. Oakland, Ball 1, Bruce 1, Harrison 1.

PATRIOTS 31, CARDINALS 0

Sunday, September 15

zona	0	0	0	0— 0
w England	7	13	8	3—31

First Quarter
E.—Martin 13 pass from Bledsoe (Vinatieri kick), 12:35.
Second Quarter
E.—Martin 1 run (Vinatieri kick), 5:31.
E.—Coates 2 pass from Bledsoe (kick failed), 14:40.
Third Quarter
E.—Martin 7 pass from Bledsoe (Martin pass from Bledsoe), 5:52.
Fourth Quarter
E.—FG, Vinatieri 31, 14:24.
Attendance—59,118.

TEAM STATISTICS

	Arizona	New England
st downs	9	26
shes-yards	16-46	43-163
ssing	124	221
nt returns	2-27	5-87

	Arizona	New England
Kickoff returns	5-84	1-19
Interception returns	0-0	3-7
Comp.-att.-int.	13-31-3	22-37-0
Sacked-yards lost	1-9	2-5
Punts	7-43	5-44
Fumbles-lost	1-1	0-0
Penalties-yards	5-45	6-45
Time of possession	20:39	39:21

INDIVIDUAL STATISTICS
RUSHING—Arizona, McElroy 8-11, Centers 6-31, K. Graham 1-2, C. Smith 1-2. New England, Martin 27-92, Meggett 7-26, Grier 5-28, Glenn 1-14, Bledsoe 1-2, Gash 1-1, Zolak 1-0.
PASSING—Arizona, K. Graham 9-19-1-111, Esiason 4-12-2-22. New England, Bledsoe 21-35-0-221, Meggett 0-1-0-0, Zolak 1-1-0-5.
RECEIVING—Arizona, Centers 5-56, Carter 3-30, Edwards 2-33, Sanders 2-10, R. Moore 1-4. New England, Coates 6-61, Glenn 5-66, Martin 5-33, Gash 3-32, Jefferson 1-19, Graham 1-10, Jells 1-5.
MISSED FIELD GOAL ATTEMPTS—New England, Vinatieri 47.
INTERCEPTIONS—New England, Collins 1-7, Clay 1-0, Reynolds 1-0.
KICKOFF RETURNS—Arizona, McElroy 3-59, Terry 2-25. New England, Meggett 1-19.
PUNT RETURNS—Arizona, Dowdell 2-27. New England, Meggett 5-87.
SACKS—Arizona, Joyner 1, Rice 1. New England, Slade 1.

REDSKINS 31, GIANTS 10

Sunday, September 15

Washington	3	14	0	14—31
N.Y. Giants	0	7	3	0—10

First Quarter
Was.—FG, Blanton 36, 11:12.
Second Quarter
Was.—Logan 3 run (Blanton kick), 3:32.
Was.—Galbraith 30 pass from Frerotte (Blanton kick), 11:19.
NYG—Pierce 7 pass from Brown (Daluiso kick), 14:04.
Third Quarter
NYG—FG, Daluiso 19, 11:10.
Fourth Quarter
Was.—Allen 7 run (Blanton kick), :04.
Was.—Davis 39 run (Blanton kick), 13:33.
Attendance—71,693.

TEAM STATISTICS

	Washington	N.Y. Giants
First downs	26	19
Rushes-yards	43-239	20-104
Passing	188	182
Punt returns	3-34	2-5
Kickoff returns	2-39	6-151
Interception returns	4-27	1-15
Comp.-att.-int.	15-23-1	17-31-4
Sacked-yards lost	3-9	4-19
Punts	4-44	4-45
Fumbles-lost	0-0	0-0
Penalties-yards	12-125	6-50
Time of possession	34:34	25:26

INDIVIDUAL STATISTICS
RUSHING—Washington, Allen 27-146, Davis 6-57, Logan 5-13, Mitchell 3-25, Westbrook 1-0, Frerotte 1-(minus 2). New York, Hampton 9-58, Wheatley 6-26, Brown 2-12, Elias 2-6, Way 1-2.
PASSING—Washington, Frerotte 15-23-1-197. New York, Brown 17-31-4-201.
RECEIVING—Washington, Mitchell 3-19, Allen 3-17, Asher 2-49, Logan 2-35, Westbrook 2-24, Galbraith 1-30, Ellard 1-16, Jenkins 1-7. New York, Calloway 5-72, Lewis 4-57, Pierce 2-22, Way 2-19, Dawsey 2-17, Cross 1-11, Hampton 1-3.
MISSED FIELD GOAL ATTEMPTS—New York, Daluiso 43.
INTERCEPTIONS—Washington, Carter 2-0, M. Patton 1-23, Turner 1-4. New York, Sehorn 1-15.
KICKOFF RETURNS—Washington, Mitchell 2-39. New York, Wheatley 4-106, Lewis 2-45.
PUNT RETURNS—Washington, Mitchell 3-34. New York, Toomer 2-5.
SACKS—Washington, Owens 2, Gilbert 1, Nottage 1. New York, K. Hamilton 1½, Strahan 1, Holsey ½.

CHIEFS 35, SEAHAWKS 17

Sunday, September 15

Kansas City	14	7	7	7—35
Seattle	0	10	0	7—17

First Quarter
K.C.—Penn 9 pass from Bono (Stoyanovich kick), 4:53.
K.C.—D. Carter 46 pass from Bono (Stoyanovich kick), 10:09.

Second Quarter
Sea.—FG, Peterson 47, 5:55.
Sea.—Smith 4 run (Peterson kick), 13:09.
K.C.—Penn 1 pass from Bono (Stoyanovich kick), 14:36.

Third Quarter
K.C.—Allen 2 run (Stoyanovich kick), 5:16.

Fourth Quarter
Sea.—Mirer 1 run (Peterson kick), 1:32.
K.C.—Allen 1 run (Stoyanovich kick), 11:41.
Attendance—39,790.

TEAM STATISTICS

	Kansas City	Seattle
First downs	24	17
Rushes-yards	30-157	32-97
Passing	166	141
Punt returns	5-65	2-(-2)
Kickoff returns	4-74	6-151
Interception returns	1-22	0-0
Comp.-att.-int.	18-27-0	15-31-1
Sacked-yards lost	3-19	7-18
Punts	6-47	6-48
Fumbles-lost	3-2	0-0
Penalties-yards	6-38	6-86
Time of possession	28:03	31:57

INDIVIDUAL STATISTICS

RUSHING—Kansas City, Allen 12-52, Hill 11-57, Anders 3-11, Bennett 2-40, Bono 2-(minus 3). Seattle, Warren 14-6, Smith 8-73, Mirer 6-14, Strong 2-1, Galloway 1-4, Broussard 1-(minus 1).

PASSING—Kansas City, Bono 18-27-0-185. Seattle, Mirer 15-31-1-159.

RECEIVING—Kansas City, Hughes 5-28, D. Carter 3-61, Johnson 3-30, Anders 2-29, Penn 2-10, Dawson 1-12, Allen 1-10, McNair 1-5. Seattle, Galloway 4-57, Warren 3-26, Blades 2-26, Strong 2-20, Fauria 1-19, Smith 1-6, Broussard 1-3, Crumpler 1-2.

MISSED FIELD GOAL ATTEMPTS—Seattle, Peterson 40.

INTERCEPTIONS—Kansas City, Collins 1-22.

KICKOFF RETURNS—Kansas City, Woods 4-74. Seattle, Broussard 4-135, Brown 1-8, Fauria 1-8.

PUNT RETURNS—Kansas City, Penn 5-65. Seattle, Galloway 1-0, R. Harris 1-(minus 2).

SACKS—Kansas City, Phillips 2, Davis 1, N. Smith 1, Booker 1, Browning 1, Thomas 1. Seattle, Sinclair 3.

DOLPHINS 36, JETS 27

Sunday, September 15

N.Y. Jets	0	14	0	13—27
Miami	0	14	12	10—36

Second Quarter
NYJ—Glenn 100 interception return (Lowery kick), 1:41.
NYJ—Slaughter 30 pass from O'Donnell (Lowery kick), 8:08.
Mia.—Pritchett 74 pass from Marino (Nedney kick), 8:32.
Mia.—Abdul-Jabbar 4 run (Nedney kick), 13:13.

Third Quarter
Mia.—Wainright 2 pass from Marino (kick failed), 9:26.
Mia.—Carolan 12 pass from Marino (pass failed), 12:28.

Fourth Quarter
Mia.—Abdul-Jabbar 7 run (Nedney kick), 5:38.
NYJ—Graham 78 pass from O'Donnell (run failed), 7:13.
NYJ—Johnson 29 pass from O'Donnell (Lowery kick), 10:08.
Mia.—FG, Nedney 29, 13:15.
Attendance—68,137.

TEAM STATISTICS

	N.Y. Jets	Miami
First downs	20	20
Rushes-yards	18-72	40-195
Passing	304	251
Punt returns	1-7	2-25
Kickoff returns	5-98	4-111
Interception returns	1-100	3-45
Comp.-att.-int.	25-44-3	13-23-1
Sacked-yards lost	2-21	1-6
Punts	4-45	3-46
Fumbles-lost	0-0	2-1
Penalties-yards	9-95	6-45
Time of possession	26:37	33:23

INDIVIDUAL STATISTICS

RUSHING—New York, Murrell 11-35, Anderson 3-13, Cobb 3-7, O'Donnell 1-17. Miami, Abdul-Jabbar 23-124, Spikes 15-64, Parmalee 2-7.

PASSING—New York, O'Donnell 25-44-3-325. Miami, Marino 13-23-1-257.

RECEIVING—New York, Chrebet 6-60, Johnson 6-59, Graham 5-136, Slaughter 3-56, Anderson 2-(minus 1), F. Baxter 1-11, Murrell 1-2, Cobb 1-2. Miami, McDuffie 7-86, Pritchett 1-74, McPhail 1-52, Spikes 1-17, Miller 1-14, Carolan 1-12, Wainright 1-2.

MISSED FIELD GOAL ATTEMPTS—New York, Lowery 49. Miami, Nedney 37.

INTERCEPTIONS—New York, Glenn 1-100. Miami, Oliver 1-45, Buckley 1-0, S. Hill 1-0.

KICKOFF RETURNS—New York, Carpenter 3-53, Van Dyke 2-45. Miami, Spikes 2-58, McPhail 2-53.

PUNT RETURNS—New York, Chrebet 1-7. Miami, McDuffie 2-25.

SACKS—New York, Spindler 1. Miami, S. Hill 1, Stubbs 1.

COLTS 25, COWBOYS 24

Sunday, September 15

Indianapolis	3	6	13	3—25
Dallas	7	14	0	3—24

First Quarter
Ind.—FG, Blanchard 23, 10:05.
Dal.—Johnston 5 pass from Aikman (Boniol kick), 14:51.

Second Quarter
Dal.—Sanders 22 fumble return (Boniol kick), :53.
Dal.—E. Smith 2 run (Boniol kick), 8:37.
Ind.—FG, Blanchard 25, 12:29.
Ind.—FG, Blanchard 52, 14:53.

Third Quarter
Ind.—Pollard 48 pass from Harbaugh (Blanchard kick), 5:12.
Ind.—Dilger 8 pass from Harbaugh (pass failed), 12:18.

Fourth Quarter
Dal.—FG, Boniol 52, 1:34.
Ind.—FG, Blanchard 43, 14:09.
Attendance—63,021.

TEAM STATISTICS

	Indianapolis	Dallas
First downs	18	18
Rushes-yards	28-103	30-111
Passing	218	184
Punt returns	0-0	2-12
Kickoff returns	5-172	3-71
Interception returns	0-0	1-15
Comp.-att.-int.	19-28-1	17-27-0
Sacked-yards lost	5-26	0-0
Punts	2-51	3-38
Fumbles-lost	3-1	1-1
Penalties-yards	6-50	2-30
Time of possession	31:18	28:42

INDIVIDUAL STATISTICS

RUSHING—Indianapolis, Crockett 10-36, Warren 8-14, Harbaugh 4-11, Groce 3-28, Workman 3-14. Dallas, E. Smith 26-101, Aikman 3-8, Johnston 1-2.

PASSING—Indianapolis, Harbaugh 19-28-1-244. Dallas, Aikman 17-27-0-184.

RECEIVING—Indianapolis, Crockett 4-60, Dawkins 4-57, Warren 4-23, Harrison 3-16, Dilger 2-34, Pollard 1-48, Workman 1-6. Dallas, Bjornson 5-54, Johnston 4-24, K. Williams 2-36, Martin 2-29, Sanders 2-27, E. Smith 2-14.

MISSED FIELD GOAL ATTEMPTS—Dallas, Boniol 40, 57.

INTERCEPTIONS—Dallas, Harper 1-15.

KICKOFF RETURNS—Indianapolis, Bailey 5-172. Dallas, K. Williams 3-71.

PUNT RETURNS—Dallas, Martin 2-12.

SACKS—Dallas, Tolbert 3, Lett 2.

BENGALS 30, SAINTS 15

Sunday, September 15

New Orleans	3	3	6	3—15
Cincinnati	3	14	3	10—30

First Quarter
Cin.—FG, Pelfrey 33, 6:35.
N.O.—FG, Brien 51, 12:18.

Second Quarter
Cin.—Scott 24 pass from Blake (Pelfrey kick), 4:12.
N.O.—FG, Brien 37, 11:16.
Cin.—Carter 31 run (Pelfrey kick), 13:17.

Third Quarter
N.O.—Zellars 3 run (pass failed), 1:33.
Cin.—FG, Pelfrey 21, 12:05.

Fourth Quarter
Cin.—FG, Pelfrey 35, :21.
N.O.—FG, Brien 25, 5:40.
Cin.—Bieniemy 5 run (Pelfrey kick), 11:00.
Attendance—45,412.

TEAM STATISTICS

	New Orleans	Cincinnati
First downs	15	24
Rushes-yards	15-27	37-101
Passing	287	218
Punt returns	1-8	1-12
Kickoff returns	7-205	3-72
Interception returns	0-0	3-48
Comp.-att.-int.	21-39-3	22-39-0
Sacked-yards lost	1-9	2-7
Punts	1-44	3-53
Fumbles-lost	1-1	0-0
Penalties-yards	6-47	4-31
Time of possession	23:28	36:32

INDIVIDUAL STATISTICS

RUSHING—New Orleans, Zellars 7-23, Bates 4-5, Brown 2-(minus 4), Small 1-3, Everett 1-0. Cincinnati, Carter 19-63, Bieniemy 7-33, Hearst 5-(minus 1), Blake 4-3, Cothran 2-3.

PASSING—New Orleans, Everett 21-39-3-296. Cincinnati, Blake 22-39-0-225.

RECEIVING—New Orleans, Haynes 5-156, Jeffires 4-34, Small 3-16, I. Smith 2-42, DeRamus 2-25, Brown 2-2, Neal 1-19, Lusk 1-4, Bates 1-(minus 2). Cincinnati, Pickens 8-89, Scott 7-83, Bieniemy 3-17, Carter 2-15, McGee 1-12, Battaglia 1-9.

MISSED FIELD GOAL ATTEMPTS—Cincinnati, Pelfrey 37.

INTERCEPTIONS—Cincinnati, Walker 1-35, Tovar 1-13, Rod W. Jones 1-0.

KICKOFF RETURNS—New Orleans, Hughes 7-205. Cincinnati, Dunn 3-72.

PUNT RETURNS—New Orleans, Hughes 1-8. Cincinnati, Myers 1-12.

SACKS—New Orleans, Martin 1, A. Robbins 1. Cincinnati, Wilkinson 1.

PACKERS 42, CHARGERS 10

Sunday, September 15

San Diego	3	0	0	7—10
Green Bay	7	14	7	14—42

First Quarter
G.B.—Bennett 10 run (Jacke kick), 5:09.
S.D.—FG, Carney 43, 13:55.

Second Quarter
G.B.—Freeman 19 pass from Favre (Jacke kick), 2:08.
G.B.—Henderson 8 pass from Favre (Jacke kick), 13:47.

Third Quarter
G.B.—Jackson 7 pass from Favre (Jacke kick), 13:08.

Fourth Quarter
S.D.—Martin 9 pass from Humphries (Carney kick), 6:44.
G.B.—Butler 90 interception return (Jacke kick), 8:29.
G.B.—Howard 65 punt return (Jacke kick), 10:01.
Attendance—60,584.

TEAM STATISTICS

	San Diego	Green Bay
First downs	11	23
Rushes-yards	13-33	36-132
Passing	108	217
Punt returns	0-0	7-118
Kickoff returns	5-114	1-24
Interception returns	2-9	2-90
Comp.-att.-int.	18-35-2	22-34-2
Sacked-yards lost	5-36	1-14
Punts	7-52	3-38
Fumbles-lost	2-1	2-1
Penalties-yards	8-55	10-90
Time of possession	21:22	38:38

INDIVIDUAL STATISTICS

RUSHING—San Diego, Russell 9-27, Fletcher 3-3, Hayden 1-3. Green Bay, Bennett 13-65, Levens 9-39, Jervey 4-14, Henderson 4-8, Favre 3-7, R. Brooks 2-(minus 1), McMahon 1-0.

PASSING—San Diego, Humphries 16-31-2-130, Salisbury 2-4-0-14. Green Bay, Favre 22-34-2-231.

RECEIVING—San Diego, A. Coleman 5-31, Fletcher 4-20, Martin 3-38, Jones 3-28, Pupunu 2-25, May 1-2. Green Bay, R. Brooks 8-108, Chmura 4-35, Henderson 4-26, Jackson 2-10, Beebe 1-28, Freeman 1-19, Bennett 1-4, Levens 1-1.

MISSED FIELD GOAL ATTEMPTS—San Diego, Carney 46. Green Bay, Jacke 48.

INTERCEPTIONS—San Diego, Clark 1-9, Harper 1-0. Green Bay, Butler 2-90.

KICKOFF RETURNS—San Diego, A. Coleman 3-58, Still 2-56. Green Bay, Beebe 1-24.

PUNT RETURNS—Green Bay, Howard 7-118.

SACKS—San Diego, M. Coleman 1. Green Bay, White 2, S. Jones 2, Wilkins ½, Clavelle ½.

VIKINGS 20, BEARS 14

Sunday, September 15

Minnesota	0	14	0	6—20
Chicago	7	7	0	0—14

First Quarter
Chi.—Engram 5 pass from Kramer (Huerta kick), 13:53.

Second Quarter
Min.—R. Smith 14 run (Sisson kick), 4:52.
Chi.—Woolford 28 interception return (Huerta kick), 6:48.
Min.—Reed 29 pass from Moon (Sisson kick), 13:06.

Fourth Quarter
Min.—FG, Sisson 33, 7:35.
Min.—FG, Sisson 34, 14:54.
Attendance—61,301.

TEAM STATISTICS

	Minnesota	Chicago
First downs	21	17
Rushes-yards	34-138	22-108
Passing	239	191
Punt returns	3-38	2-27
Kickoff returns	1-11	3-61
Interception returns	3-7	1-28
Comp.-att.-int.	22-44-1	18-40-3
Sacked-yards lost	0-0	1-8
Punts	9-35	7-51
Fumbles-lost	0-0	3-0
Penalties-yards	11-77	5-31
Time of possession	35:03	24:57

INDIVIDUAL STATISTICS

RUSHING—Minnesota, R. Smith 18-81, Lee 8-46, Graham 6-5, Moon 2-6. Chicago, Green 13-55, R. Harris 7-41, Conway 1-12, Krieg 1-0.

PASSING—Minnesota, Moon 22-44-1-239. Chicago, Kramer 18-40-3-199.

RECEIVING—Minnesota, Carter 5-74, Ismail 5-54, Lee 5-31, Reed 4-60, Evans 2-15, Jordan 1-5. Chicago, Timpson 5-54, Conway 4-69, Green 4-36, Wetnight 2-11, Engram 2-11, R. Harris 1-16.

MISSED FIELD GOAL ATTEMPTS—Chicago, Huerta 44.

INTERCEPTIONS—Minnesota, Brady 1-8, Fuller 1-0, Griffith 1-(minus 1). Chicago, Woolford 1-28.

KICKOFF RETURNS—Minnesota, Brown 1-11. Chicago, Ja. Jackson 3-61.

PUNT RETURNS—Minnesota, Lee 3-38. Chicago, Engram 2-27.

SACKS—Minnesota, Randle 1.

STEELERS 24, BILLS 6

Monday, September 16

Buffalo	3	0	3	0— 6
Pittsburgh	7	17	0	0—24

First Quarter
Buf.—FG, Christie 31, 7:29.
Pit.—Bettis 1 run (N. Johnson kick), 11:05.
Second Quarter
Pit.—FG, N. Johnson 30, 6:25.
Pit.—Bettis 43 run (N. Johnson kick), 13:12.
Pit.—Lake 47 interception return (N. Johnson kick), 15:00.
Third Quarter
Buf.—FG, Christie 45, 4:51.
Attendance—59,002.

TEAM STATISTICS

	Buffalo	Pittsburgh
First downs	11	22
Rushes-yards	23-86	49-222
Passing	99	160
Punt returns	0-0	0-0
Kickoff returns	3-69	3-74
Interception returns	0-0	4-68

	Buffalo	Pittsburgh
Comp.-att.-int.	15-31-4	14-21-0
Sacked-yards lost	2-17	0-0
Punts	4-42	3-26
Fumbles-lost	0-0	2-1
Penalties-yards	7-56	3-15
Time of possession	21:02	38:58

INDIVIDUAL STATISTICS

RUSHING—Buffalo, T. Thomas 16-68, Holmes 5-15, Tindale 1-3, Moulds 1-0. Pittsburgh, Bettis 20-133, Pegram 17-84, Witman 4-14, Stewart 4-(minus 5), Tomczak 3-(minus 4), Lester 1-0.

PASSING—Buffalo, Kelly 15-31-4-116. Pittsburgh, Tomczak 12-19-0-150, Stewart 2-2-0-10.

RECEIVING—Buffalo, Reed 5-31, Early 3-41, Johnson 2-13, Moulds 1-11, T. Thomas 1-6, Holmes 1-6, Copeland 1-5, Cline 1-3. Pittsburgh, Hastings 4-27, Stewart 3-65, Bettis 3-32, C. Johnson 2-17, Pegram 1-12, Hayes 1-7.

MISSED FIELD GOAL ATTEMPTS—Pittsburgh, N. Johnson 37, 24.

INTERCEPTIONS—Pittsburgh, Kirkland 2-2, Lake 1-47, Olsavsky 1-5.

KICKOFF RETURNS—Buffalo, Moulds 3-69. Pittsburgh, C. Johnson 2-5C Arnold 1-24.

PUNT RETURNS—None.

SACKS—Pittsburgh, Brown 1, Emmons 1.

WEEK 4

RESULTS

Arizona 28, NEW ORLEANS 14
BUFFALO 10, Dallas 7
CAROLINA 23, San Francisco 7
DETROIT 35, Chicago 16
KANSAS CITY 17, Denver 14
MINNESOTA 30, Green Bay 21
NEW ENGLAND 28, Jacksonville 25 (OT)
N.Y. Giants 13, N.Y. JETS 6
Philadelphia 33, ATLANTA 18
San Diego 40, OAKLAND 34
Seattle 17, TAMPA BAY 13
Washington 17, ST. LOUIS 10
INDIANAPOLIS 10, Miami 6
    Open date: Baltimore, Cincinnati, Houston,
Pittsburgh

STANDINGS

AFC EAST	W	L	T	Pct.
Indianapolis	4	0	0	1.000
Buffalo	3	1	0	.750
Miami	3	1	0	.750
New England	2	2	0	.500
N.Y. Jets	0	4	0	.000

AFC CENTRAL	W	L	T	Pct.
Houston	2	1	0	.667
Pittsburgh	2	1	0	.667
Baltimore	1	2	0	.333
Cincinnati	1	2	0	.333
Jacksonville	1	3	0	.250

AFC WEST	W	L	T	Pct.
Kansas City	4	0	0	1.000
Denver	3	1	0	.750
San Diego	3	1	0	.750
Oakland	1	3	0	.250
Seattle	1	3	0	.250

NFC EAST	W	L	T	Pct.
Philadelphia	3	1	0	.750
Washington	3	1	0	.750
Arizona	1	3	0	.250
Dallas	1	3	0	.250
N.Y. Giants	1	3	0	.250

NFC CENTRAL	W	L	T	Pct.
Minnesota	4	0	0	1.000
Green Bay	3	1	0	.750
Detroit	2	2	0	.500
Chicago	1	3	0	.250
Tampa Bay	0	4	0	.000

NFC WEST	W	L	T	Pct.
Carolina	3	0	0	1.000
San Francisco	2	1	0	.667
St. Louis	1	2	0	.333
Atlanta	0	3	0	.000
New Orleans	0	4	0	.000

HIGHLIGHTS

Hero of the week: LeShon Johnson rushed for a team-record 214 yards and two touchdowns on 21 carries to lead Arizona to its first win of the season, 28-14 over New Orleans. Johnson had 25 yards in the first half and 189 in the second half, including touchdown runs of 56 and 70 yards.

Goat of the week: Rams quarterback Steve Walsh, already in a fight with rookie Tony Banks for his starting job, did nothing to aid his cause in Week 4. In a 17-10 loss to Washington, Walsh threw three interceptions, completed half his passes and was practically booed off the field by St. Louis fans.

Sub of the week: Subbing for the injured Kerry Collins, veteran NFL backup Steve Beuerlein was superb, going 22-of-31 for 290 yards in leading Carolina to a 23-7 win over San Francisco. Beuerlein was 17-of-20 in the first half alone as the Panthers scored on their first three possessions en route to building a 17-0 lead.

Comeback of the week: Trailing 21-17 with five minutes left, Minnesota scored 13 unanswered points in less than four minutes to defeat Green Bay, 30-21. Robert Smith's 37-yard touchdown run with 4:13 left put the Vikings ahead for good, and Scott Sisson kicked two field goals in the final 2:31 to increase the lead.

Blowout of the week: Although the margin of victory was only six points, San Diego's 40-34 win over Oakland was not that close. The Chargers scored three consecutive touchdowns in the first period and led, 40-21, before the Raiders scored two touchdowns in the final 1:29 to narrow the score. In perhaps his best performance in five seasons with the Chargers, quarterback Stan Humphries threw four touchdown passes without an interception.

Nail-biter of the week: New England beat Jacksonville, 28-25, on Adam Vinatieri's fifth field goal of the game, a 40-yarder at 2:36 of overtime. Vinatieri, a rookie free agent from South Dakota State, entered the game on shaky ground, having made only three of his first seven field goal attempts. The Jaguars, who forced overtime on Mike Hollis' 27-yard field goal with 6:34 left, nearly won the game outright on the last play of regulation when Mark Brunell hit Willie Jackson on a desperation 58-yard pass at the goal line as time expired.

Hit of the week: By Vikings defensive tackle John Randle, who sacked and forced a fumble by Green Bay quarterback Brett Favre in the final minutes to preserve Minnesota's nine-point win over the Packers. Derrick Alexander recovered for the Vikings.

Oddity of the week: Before Week 4, Johnson had just 4 yards rushing in the Cardinals' first three games of the season and 101 in his three-year (19 games) NFL career.

Top rusher: Johnson's 214 yards broke the Cardinals' single-game record of 203 yards set by John David Crow in 1960.

Top passer: Jacksonville's Brunell was 23-of-39 for 432 yards and three touchdowns in the Jaguars' overtime loss at New England.

Top receiver: Johnnie Morton caught seven passes for a career-high 174 yards and two touchdowns in Detroit's 35-16 win over Chicago.

Notes: Johnson's record-breaking performance—the NFL's only 200-yard rushing performance of 1996—was witnessed by 34,316 people, the Saints' smallest home crowd since 1980. Both teams entered the game with losing records. . . . Only 30,212 people showed up at Tampa Stadium for the Seattle-Tampa Bay game, the Buccaneers' smallest crowd since the end of the 1991 season. . . . Emmitt Smith rushed for 25 yards on 15 carries in the Cowboys' 10-7 loss at Buffalo, his lowest output ever in a game he started and finished. . . . Dallas' 1-3 start was its worst since 1990. No team has gone on to win the Super Bowl after a 1-3 start. . . . Chicago was 1-3 for the first time since 1983. . . . Kansas City was 4-0 for the first time ever. The Chiefs beat Denver, 17-14, despite Terrell Davis' 141 yards rushing and Shannon Sharpe's 131 yards receiving. . . . New England's 28-25 victory over Jacksonville was coach Bill Parcells' 100th regular-season victory. At 100-78-1, he became the 22nd NFL coach to reach that plateau. . . . Minnesota was 4-0 for the first time since 1975 despite trailing after three quarters in each of its first four games.

Quote of the week: Giants defensive end Mike Strahan, on his team's first victory of the season, 13-6 over the crosstown (and winless) Jets: "I think we're just happy to win a game. We would not have cared whether it was against Parsippany High School."

1996 REVIEW Week 4

GAME SUMMARIES

EAGLES 33, FALCONS 18

Sunday, September 22

Philadelphia	3	10	10	10—33
Atlanta	0	10	0	8—18

First Quarter
Phi.—FG, Anderson 28, 14:21.

Second Quarter
Phi.—Watters 2 run (Anderson kick), 4:45.
Phi.—FG, Anderson 33, 10:46.
Atl.—Emanuel 23 pass from J. George (Andersen kick), 11:58.
Atl.—FG, Andersen 43, 14:56.

Third Quarter
Phi.—Watters 56 run (Anderson kick), 3:11.
Phi.—FG, Anderson 39, 9:11.

Fourth Quarter
Phi.—FG, Anderson 25, 3:00.
Atl.—Mathis 12 pass from Hebert (Mathis pass from Hebert), 10:49.
Phi.—Witherspoon 97 kickoff return (Anderson kick), 11:05.
Attendance—40,107.

TEAM STATISTICS

	Philadelphia	Atlanta
First downs	14	18
Rushes-yards	32-123	12-40
Passing	195	351
Punt returns	4-84	2-23
Kickoff returns	4-149	7-188
Interception returns	5-113	0-0
Comp.-att.-int.	16-29-0	33-49-5
Sacked-yards lost	2-4	2-15
Punts	6-38	6-42
Fumbles-lost	3-1	2-1
Penalties-yards	5-39	11-95
Time of possession	29:44	30:16

INDIVIDUAL STATISTICS
RUSHING—Philadelphia, Watters 26-121, Peete 4-0, Garner 2-2. Atlanta, Anderson 7-36, Heyward 3-4, J. George 1-0, Hebert 1-0.
PASSING—Philadelphia, Peete 16-29-0-199. Atlanta, Hebert 17-26-3-149, J. George 16-23-2-217.
RECEIVING—Philadelphia, Fryar 4-35, Turner 3-34, Watters 3-27, Jones 3-23, Dunn 1-58, Seay 1-14, J. Johnson 1-8. Atlanta, Emanuel 9-93, Brown 7-91, Mathis 7-58, Metcalf 5-97, Anderson 5-27.
MISSED FIELD GOAL ATTEMPTS—None.
INTERCEPTIONS—Philadelphia, W. Thomas 2-40, Vincent 1-31, Dawkins 1-30, Zordich 1-12.
KICKOFF RETURNS—Philadelphia, Witherspoon 3-144, Seay 1-5. Atlanta, Metcalf 6-176, Styles 1-12.
PUNT RETURNS—Philadelphia, Seay 4-84. Atlanta, Metcalf 2-23.
SACKS—Philadelphia, W. Fuller 2. Atlanta, Hall 2.

SEAHAWKS 17, BUCCANEERS 13

Sunday, September 22

Seattle	0	3	0	14—17
Tampa Bay	3	7	0	3—13

First Quarter
T.B.—FG, Husted 33, 9:06.

Second Quarter
Sea.—FG, Peterson 33, :47.
T.B.—R. Brooks 2 run (Husted kick), 13:48.

Fourth Quarter
T.B.—FG, Husted 28, 5:40.
Sea.—Blades 5 pass from Mirer (Peterson kick), 12:00.
Sea.—Smith 14 run (Peterson kick), 14:29.
Attendance—30,212.

TEAM STATISTICS

	Seattle	Tampa Bay
First downs	22	14
Rushes-yards	26-124	33-111
Passing	198	106
Punt returns	4-6	4-36
Kickoff returns	4-70	4-54
Interception returns	1-0	1-17
Comp.-att.-int.	20-37-1	15-26-1
Sacked-yards lost	3-11	2-12
Punts	5-47	4-44
Fumbles-lost	1-0	1-0
Penalties-yards	13-95	9-53
Time of possession	28:24	31:36

INDIVIDUAL STATISTICS
RUSHING—Seattle, Warren 12-38, Smith 7-32, Mirer 5-32, Galloway 2-22. Tampa Bay, R. Brooks 26-65, Dilfer 4-5, Lynch 1-40, Barnhardt 1-2, Alstott 1-(minus 1).
PASSING—Seattle, Mirer 20-37-1-209. Tampa Bay, Dilfer 15-26-1-118.
RECEIVING—Seattle, Blades 9-92, Galloway 3-33, Warren 2-18, R. Harris 1-21, Strong 1-20, Fauria 1-18, Broussard 1-6, Proehl 1-3, Smith 1-(minus 2). Tampa Bay, Alstott 4-25, Moore 4-21, Harper 3-48, Hawkins 2-11, Williams 1-7, R. Brooks 1-6.
MISSED FIELD GOAL ATTEMPTS—None.
INTERCEPTIONS—Seattle, D. Williams 1-0. Tampa Bay, Nickerson 1-17.
KICKOFF RETURNS—Seattle, Broussard 4-70. Tampa Bay, Silvan 4-54.
PUNT RETURNS—Seattle, Galloway 4-6. Tampa Bay, Silvan 4-36.
SACKS—Seattle, Moss 1, Kennedy 1. Tampa Bay, Sapp 2, Marts 1.

CHARGERS 40, RAIDERS 34

Sunday, September 22

San Diego	21	6	0	13—40
Oakland	0	14	7	13—34

First Quarter
S.D.—Fletcher 6 pass from Humphries (Carney kick), 10:57.
S.D.—Martin 7 pass from Humphries (Carney kick), 11:55.
S.D.—Martin 41 pass from Humphries (Carney kick), 14:02.

Second Quarter
Oak.—Fenner 4 pass from Hostetler (Ford kick), :49.
S.D.—FG, Carney 28, 5:39.
Oak.—Dudley 6 pass from Hostetler (Ford kick), 7:49.
S.D.—FG, Carney 39, 13:56.

Third Quarter
Oak.—T. Brown 6 pass from Hostetler (Ford kick), 9:19.

Fourth Quarter
S.D.—Martin 19 pass from Humphries (run failed), 6:56.
S.D.—Clark 83 interception return (Carney kick), 11:20.
Oak.—T. Brown 11 pass from Hobert (pass failed), 13:31.
Oak.—Shedd 28 pass from Hobert (Ford kick), 14:48.
Attendance—49,249.

TEAM STATISTICS

	San Diego	Oakland
First downs	20	28
Rushes-yards	30-103	22-182
Passing	218	371
Punt returns	4-68	4-44
Kickoff returns	2-48	4-98
Interception returns	2-92	0-0
Comp.-att.-int.	18-25-0	34-57-2
Sacked-yards lost	1-8	4-29
Punts	5-48	4-45
Fumbles-lost	2-0	1-1
Penalties-yards	4-40	9-77
Time of possession	26:53	33:07

INDIVIDUAL STATISTICS
RUSHING—San Diego, Russell 19-63, Hayden 5-20, Humphries 3-6, Fletcher 2-15, Salisbury 1-(minus 1). Oakland, Williams 9-8, Kaufman 7-116, Fenner 3-7, Aska 1-24, Hobert 1-14, Hostetler 1-13.
PASSING—San Diego, Humphries 18-25-0-226. Oakland, Hostetler 26-44-2-293, Hobert 8-12-0-107, Williams 0-1-0-0.
RECEIVING—San Diego, Martin 10-138, Jones 2-47, A. Coleman 2-25, Fletcher 2-12, Mitchell 1-4, Pupunu 1-0. Oakland, T. Brown 11-120, Jett 5-91, Hobbs 5-59, Aska 4-55, Williams 3-18, Dudley 2-14, Fenner 2-11, Shedd 1-28, Kaufman 1-4.
MISSED FIELD GOAL ATTEMPTS—San Diego, Carney 47. Oakland, Ford 54, 25.
INTERCEPTIONS—San Diego, Clark 1-83, Gouveia 1-9.
KICKOFF RETURNS—San Diego, A. Coleman 2-48. Oakland, Kaufman 3-81, Aska 1-17.
PUNT RETURNS—San Diego, Da. Gordon 4-68. Oakland, T. Brown 4-44.
SACKS—San Diego, Gouveia 1, Seau 1, R. Davis 1, Mims 1. Oakland, Ball 1.

PATRIOTS 28, JAGUARS 25

Sunday, September 22

Jacksonville	0	7	15	3	0—25
New England	9	13	3	0	3—28

First Quarter
N.E.—Coates 5 pass from Bledsoe (kick blocked), 8:22.
N.E.—FG, Vinatieri 23, 13:43.

Second Quarter
N.E.—FG, Vinatieri 30, 5:10.
N.E.—Martin 4 run (Vinatieri kick), 9:31.
N.E.—FG, Vinatieri 29, 13:54.
Jac.—Smith 51 pass from Brunell (Hollis kick), 15:00.

Third Quarter
Jac.—Rison 41 pass from Brunell (Hollis kick), 3:27.
N.E.—FG, Vinatieri 41, 13:25.
Jac.—Rison 61 pass from Brunell (Brunell run), 13:51.

Fourth Quarter
Jac.—FG, Hollis 27, 6:34.

Overtime
N.E.—FG, Vinatieri 40, 2:36.
Attendance—59,446.

TEAM STATISTICS

	Jacksonville	New England
First downs	12	26
Rushes-yards	11-29	31-123
Passing	413	230
Punt returns	1-16	3-70
Kickoff returns	7-168	5-100
Interception returns	1-8	1-14
Comp.-att.-int.	23-39-1	27-44-1
Sacked-yards lost	2-19	4-25
Punts	5-41	2-38
Fumbles-lost	2-1	1-1
Penalties-yards	17-148	6-30
Time of possession	24:58	37:38

INDIVIDUAL STATISTICS
RUSHING—Jacksonville, Stewart 9-5, Brunell 2-24. New England, Martin 24-95, Meggett 4-12, Bledsoe 3-16.
PASSING—Jacksonville, Brunell 23-39-1-432. New England, Bledsoe 27-44-1-255.
RECEIVING—Jacksonville, Smith 6-95, Rison 4-115, W. Jackson 4-101, Mitchell 4-53, McCardell 2-27, Stewart 1-20, Brown 1-12, Griffith 1-9. New England, Glenn 6-89, Jefferson 6-57, Gash 5-35, Meggett 4-33, Coates 4-27, Martin 2-14.
MISSED FIELD GOAL ATTEMPTS—Jacksonville, Hollis 42. New England, Vinatieri 44.
INTERCEPTIONS—Jacksonville, Thomas 1-8. New England, Hitchcock 1-14.
KICKOFF RETURNS—Jacksonville, Bullard 4-91, Jordan 2-42, Smith 1-9. New England, T. Brown 4-80, Meggett 1-20.
PUNT RETURNS—Jacksonville, Hudson 1-16. New England, Meggett 3-70.
SACKS—Jacksonville, Simmons 2, Hardy 1, Pritchett 1. New England, Slade 1, Wyman 1.

VIKINGS 30, PACKERS 21

Sunday, September 22

Green Bay	7	0	14	0	—21
Minnesota	7	7	3	13	—30

First Quarter
G.B.—R. Brooks 13 pass from Favre (Jacke kick), 4:14.
Min.—Reed 26 pass from Moon (Sisson kick), 9:00.

Second Quarter
Min.—Ismail 20 pass from Moon (Sisson kick), 9:59.

Third Quarter
Min.—FG, Sisson 34, 5:22.
G.B.—Beebe 80 pass from Favre (Jacke kick), 5:42.
G.B.—Koonce 75 interception return (Jacke kick), 11:02.

Fourth Quarter
Min.—R. Smith 37 run (Sisson kick), 10:47.
Min.—FG, Sisson 44, 12:29.
Min.—FG, Sisson 33, 14:32.
Attendance—64,168.

TEAM STATISTICS

	Green Bay	Minnesota
First downs	8	18
Rushes-yards	15-60	33-88
Passing	157	263
Punt returns	5-71	3-32
Kickoff returns	4-92	4-71
Interception returns	2-104	1-41
Comp.-att.-int.	14-27-1	24-41-2
Sacked-yards lost	7-41	2-17
Punts	8-48	6-46
Fumbles-lost	5-3	2-2
Penalties-yards	8-79	7-45
Time of possession	22:01	37:59

INDIVIDUAL STATISTICS
RUSHING—Green Bay, Bennett 11-33, Favre 2-25, Henderson 2-2. Minnesota, R. Smith 26-88, Lee 4-1, Moon 2-1, B. Johnson 1-(minus 2).
PASSING—Green Bay, Favre 14-27-1-198. Minnesota, Moon 24-40-2-280, B. Johnson 0-1-0-0.
RECEIVING—Green Bay, Beebe 3-96, Freeman 3-34, Bennett 3-10, Henderson 1-21, R. Brooks 1-13, Chmura 1-11, Howard 1-11, Levens 1-2. Minnesota, Reed 7-129, Carter 5-65, Lee 4-27, Jordan 3-21, Ismail 2-23, R. Smith 2-9, Evans 1-6.
MISSED FIELD GOAL ATTEMPTS—None.
INTERCEPTIONS—Green Bay, Koonce 1-75, Robinson 1-29. Minnesota, Griffith 1-41.
KICKOFF RETURNS—Green Bay, Beebe 4-92. Minnesota, Ismail 3-58, Lee 1-13.
PUNT RETURNS—Green Bay, Howard 5-71. Minnesota, Palmer 3-32.
SACKS—Green Bay, Butler 1, S. Dotson 1. Minnesota, Randle 2, Harrison 2, Alexander 1, F. Smith 1, Tuaolo 1.

LIONS 35, BEARS 16

Sunday, September 22

Chicago	0	16	0	0	—16
Detroit	0	21	7	7	—35

Second Quarter
Det.—Morton 15 pass from Mitchell (Hanson kick), :14.
Det.—Perriman 2 pass from Mitchell (Hanson kick), 1:38.
Chi.—FG, Jaeger 46, 6:51.
Chi.—Conway 58 pass from Kramer (Jaeger kick), 10:07.
Det.—Morton 62 pass from Mitchell (Hanson kick), 13:19.
Chi.—Flanigan 1 pass from Kramer (pass failed), 14:44.

Third Quarter
Det.—Mitchell 1 run (Hanson kick), 7:50.

Fourth Quarter
Det.—Perriman 24 pass from Mitchell (Hanson kick), 8:14.
Attendance—70,022.

TEAM STATISTICS

	Chicago	Detroit
First downs	19	19
Rushes-yards	24-70	29-85
Passing	248	309
Punt returns	5-52	2-18
Kickoff returns	5-128	4-70
Interception returns	1-0	1-15
Comp.-att.-int.	23-46-1	24-34-1
Sacked-yards lost	2-13	4-27
Punts	6-49	7-50
Fumbles-lost	3-1	1-0
Penalties-yards	6-31	8-76
Time of possession	28:52	31:08

INDIVIDUAL STATISTICS
RUSHING—Chicago, Salaam 10-27, Hicks 9-26, Kramer 3-5, Green 1-9, T. Carter 1-3. Detroit, Sanders 19-66, Mitchell 6-8, Rivers 3-5, Morton 1-6.
PASSING—Chicago, Kramer 23-46-1-261. Detroit, Mitchell 24-34-1-336.
RECEIVING—Chicago, Conway 8-126, Wetnight 4-40, Engram 3-39, Ja. Jackson 2-20, Salaam 2-13, T. Carter 2-12, Green 1-10, Flanigan 1-1. Detroit, Morton 7-174, H. Moore 7-74, Perriman 6-65, Sloan 3-19, Sanders 1-4.
MISSED FIELD GOAL ATTEMPTS—None.
INTERCEPTIONS—Chicago, W. Harris 1-0. Detroit, McNeil 1-15.
KICKOFF RETURNS—Chicago, Ja. Jackson 5-128. Detroit, Milburn 3-69, Metzelaars 1-1.
PUNT RETURNS—Chicago, Engram 5-52. Detroit, Milburn 2-18.
SACKS—Chicago, Cox 1, Miniefield 1, Simpson 1, A. Fontenot 1. Detroit, Bonham 1, Thomas 1.

BILLS 10, COWBOYS 7

Sunday, September 22

Dallas	0	0	0	7	—7
Buffalo	7	0	3	0	—10

First Quarter
Buf.—T. Thomas 2 run (Christie kick), 13:15.

Third Quarter
Buf.—FG, Christie 32, 7:13.

1996 REVIEW Week 4

Fourth Quarter

Dal.—E. Smith 2 run (Boniol kick), 9:07.
Attendance—78,098.

TEAM STATISTICS

	Dallas	Buffalo
First downs	12	14
Rushes-yards	18-32	43-135
Passing	160	89
Punt returns	2-10	3-36
Kickoff returns	2-59	2-47
Interception returns	1-12	3-35
Comp.-att.-int.	16-34-3	13-22-1
Sacked-yards lost	1-4	2-7
Punts	6-46	6-44
Fumbles-lost	1-1	1-1
Penalties-yards	8-39	4-37
Time of possession	22:32	37:28

INDIVIDUAL STATISTICS

RUSHING—Dallas, E. Smith 15-25, Aikman 1-5, Walker 1-3, Johnston 1-(minus 1). Buffalo, T. Thomas 22-51, Holmes 8-48, Collins 5-20, Tindale 4-14, Van Pelt 3-(minus 5), Early 1-7.

PASSING—Dallas, Aikman 16-33-3-164, S. Williams 0-1-0-0. Buffalo, Collins 11-17-1-87, Van Pelt 2-5-0-9.

RECEIVING—Dallas, Bjornson 6-48, Johnston 4-25, Martin 3-38, Walker 1-24, Sanders 1-20, E. Smith 1-9. Buffalo, Reed 5-36, Johnson 4-50, Cline 2-11, Louchiey 1-0, Tindale 1-(minus 1).

MISSED FIELD GOAL ATTEMPTS—Dallas, Boniol 36.

INTERCEPTIONS—Dallas, Woodson 1-12. Buffalo, Martin 2-35, T. Smith 1-0.

KICKOFF RETURNS—Dallas, K. Williams 2-59. Buffalo, Moulds 2-47.

PUNT RETURNS—Dallas, Martin 2-10. Buffalo, Copeland 3-36.

SACKS—Dallas, Strickland 1, McCormack 1. Buffalo, Paup 1.

PANTHERS 23, 49ERS 7

Sunday, September 22

San Francisco	0	0	7	0—	7
Carolina	10	7	3	3—23	

First Quarter

Car.—Walls 19 pass from Beuerlein (Kasay kick), 5:18.
Car.—FG, Kasay 28, 10:25.

Second Quarter

Car.—Walls 7 pass from Beuerlein (Kasay kick), 2:11.

Third Quarter

S.F.—Loville 44 pass from S. Young (Wilkins kick), 6:41.
Car.—FG, Kasay 35, 8:41.

Fourth Quarter

Car.—FG, Kasay 19, 14:22.
Attendance—72,224.

TEAM STATISTICS

	San Francisco	Carolina
First downs	15	21
Rushes-yards	13-48	29-117
Passing	252	272
Punt returns	2-6	5-48
Kickoff returns	5-102	1-41
Interception returns	1-0	1-35
Comp.-att.-int.	24-40-1	22-31-1
Sacked-yards lost	4-15	3-18
Punts	7-47	4-42
Fumbles-lost	0-0	1-0
Penalties-yards	7-42	3-20
Time of possession	26:34	33:26

INDIVIDUAL STATISTICS

RUSHING—San Francisco, Loville 7-20, Vardell 3-14, D. Carter 2-7, S. Young 1-7. Carolina, Biakabutuka 20-69, Johnson 6-44, Oliver 1-6, Beuerlein 1-(minus 1), Muhammad 1-(minus 1).

PASSING—San Francisco, S. Young 24-40-1-267. Carolina, Beuerlein 22-31-1-290.

RECEIVING—San Francisco, Rice 10-127, Loville 6-85, Stokes 4-47, Owens 2-6, Vardell 2-2. Carolina, Walls 6-81, Carrier 6-52, Green 3-64, Oliver 3-45, Muhammad 3-36, Ismail 1-12.

MISSED FIELD GOAL ATTEMPTS—None.

INTERCEPTIONS—San Francisco, Pope 1-0. Carolina, Maxie 1-35.

KICKOFF RETURNS—San Francisco, D. Carter 4-81, Uwaezuoke 1-21. Carolina, Bates 1-41.

PUNT RETURNS—San Francisco, D. Carter 2-6. Carolina, Oliver 5-48.

SACKS—San Francisco, McDonald 1, Doleman 1, D. Brown 1. Carolina, Fox 1 1/2, Mills 1, Lathon 1, Bailey 1/2.

REDSKINS 17, RAMS 10

Sunday, September 22

Washington	7	3	7	0—17
St. Louis	0	0	3	7—10

First Quarter

Was.—Galbraith 2 pass from Frerotte (Blanton kick), 8:06.

Second Quarter

Was.—FG, Blanton 38, 4:57.

Third Quarter

St.L.—FG, Lohmiller 19, 5:26.
Was.—Allen 9 run (Blanton kick), 11:29.

Fourth Quarter

St.L.—Ross 3 run (Lohmiller kick), 7:43.
Attendance—62,303.

TEAM STATISTICS

	Washington	St. Louis
First downs	16	17
Rushes-yards	32-106	28-112
Passing	151	173
Punt returns	3-25	4-15
Kickoff returns	2-47	4-77
Interception returns	3-5	2-43
Comp.-att.-int.	12-23-2	18-36-3
Sacked-yards lost	0-0	1-4
Punts	6-47	6-51
Fumbles-lost	2-0	0-0
Penalties-yards	5-30	13-82
Time of possession	29:50	30:10

INDIVIDUAL STATISTICS

RUSHING—Washington, Allen 23-78, Frerotte 5-(minus 1), Mitchell 3-27, Logan 1-2. St. Louis, Phillips 14-48, Green 6-38, Robinson 5-22, Moore 1-4, Ross 1-3, Walsh 1-(minus 3).

PASSING—Washington, Frerotte 12-23-2-151. St. Louis, Walsh 18-36-3-177.

RECEIVING—Washington, Logan 3-50, Allen 3-26, Mitchell 2-19, Galbraith 2-16, Asher 1-20, Shepherd 1-20. St. Louis, Bruce 11-136, Green 3-26, Kennison 1-12, Drayton 1-5, D. Harris 1-4, Phillips 1-(minus 6).

MISSED FIELD GOAL ATTEMPTS—St. Louis, Lohmiller 38.

INTERCEPTIONS—Washington, M. Patton 1-3, Harvey 1-2, Carter 1-0. St. Louis, Dorn 1-40, Lyght 1-3.

KICKOFF RETURNS—Washington, Mitchell 2-47. St. Louis, Kennison 3-64, Phillips 1-13.

PUNT RETURNS—Washington, Mitchell 3-25. St. Louis, Kennison 4-15.

SACKS—Washington, Owens 1.

CARDINALS 28, SAINTS 14

Sunday, September 22

Arizona	3	3	8	14—28
New Orleans	0	7	0	7—14

First Quarter

Ariz.—FG, G. Davis 25, 6:47.

Second Quarter

Ariz.—FG, G. Davis 27, 7:35.
N.O.—B. Jones 11 blocked punt return (Brien kick), 12:45.

Third Quarter

Ariz.—R. Moore 20 pass from K. Graham (R. Moore pass from K. Graham) 11:30.

Fourth Quarter

Ariz.—L. Johnson 56 run (G. Davis kick), :14.
Ariz.—L. Johnson 70 run (G. Davis kick), 2:07.
N.O.—Jeffires 23 pass from Everett (Brien kick), 4:33.
Attendance—34,316.

TEAM STATISTICS

	Arizona	New Orleans
First downs	20	15
Rushes-yards	44-267	27-76
Passing	165	142
Punt returns	3-44	5-20
Kickoff returns	3-62	6-117
Interception returns	1-0	0-0
Comp.-att.-int.	11-25-0	18-33-1
Sacked-yards lost	1-0	3-22
Punts	7-37	7-42
Fumbles-lost	2-1	2-2
Penalties-yards	7-57	8-41
Time of possession	32:24	27:36

RUSHING—Arizona, L. Johnson 21-214, Centers 9-42, K. Graham 6-2, McElroy 4-5, C. Smith 3-3, Sanders 1-1. New Orleans, Zellars 12-57, Bates 6-18, Everett 6-(minus 1), Whittle 2-(minus 3), Hayes 1-5.

PASSING—Arizona, K. Graham 11-25-0-165. New Orleans, Everett 18-33-1-164.

RECEIVING—Arizona, R. Moore 4-91, Sanders 2-35, Dowdell 2-28, Centers 2-3, L. Johnson 1-8. New Orleans, Whittle 4-47, Haynes 3-30, Jeffires 2-31, Small 2-13, I. Smith 2-13, DeRamus 1-21, Green 1-7, Lusk 1-2, Zellars 1-1, Neal 1-(minus 1).

MISSED FIELD GOAL ATTEMPTS—None.

INTERCEPTIONS—Arizona, Bradford 1-0.

KICKOFF RETURNS—Arizona, McElroy 3-62. New Orleans, Hughes 6-117.

PUNT RETURNS—Arizona, Dowdell 3-44. New Orleans, Hughes 5-20.

SACKS—Arizona, Swann 2, Rice 1. New Orleans, Johnson 1.

CHIEFS 17, BRONCOS 14

Sunday, September 22

Denver	7	7	0	0—14
Kansas City	3	7	0	7—17

First Quarter
Den.—Davis 6 run (Elam kick), 7:34.
K.C.—FG, Stoyanovich 37, 14:03.

Second Quarter
K.C.—Hughes 8 pass from Bono (Stoyanovich kick), 3:50.
Den.—Davis 65 run (Elam kick), 8:26.

Fourth Quarter
K.C.—Allen 2 run (Stoyanovich kick), 10:51.
Attendance—79,439.

TEAM STATISTICS

	Denver	Kansas City
First downs	17	20
Rushes-yards	27-161	29-75
Passing	138	231
Punt returns	4-74	3-26
Kickoff returns	4-111	3-59
Interception returns	1-0	2-23
Comp.-att.-int.	14-30-2	20-35-1
Sacked-yards lost	2-18	2-11
Punts	4-45	6-40
Fumbles-lost	0-0	0-0
Penalties-yards	7-35	5-24
Time of possession	27:39	32:21

INDIVIDUAL STATISTICS

RUSHING—Denver, Davis 19-141, Craver 5-(minus 1), Elway 3-21. Kansas City, Allen 17-55, Hill 6-15, Bono 4-5, To. Richardson 1-4, Anders 1-(minus 4).

PASSING—Denver, Elway 14-30-2-156. Kansas City, Bono 20-35-1-242.

RECEIVING—Denver, Sharpe 9-131, Miller 3-17, Craver 2-8. Kansas City, Penn 5-55, Anders 3-68, Hughes 3-25, Johnson 3-25, McNair 2-15, Dawson 1-17, D. Carter 1-13, Bailey 1-12, Allen 1-6.

MISSED FIELD GOAL ATTEMPTS—Denver, Elam 52, 34.

INTERCEPTIONS—Denver, Romanowski 1-0. Kansas City, Collins 1-23, D. Carter 1-0.

KICKOFF RETURNS—Denver, Hebron 4-111. Kansas City, Woods 3-59.

PUNT RETURNS—Denver, Kinchen 4-74. Kansas City, D. Carter 2-18, Penn 1-8.

SACKS—Denver, Crockett 1, Perry 1. Kansas City, Thomas 1, N. Smith 1.

GIANTS 13, JETS 6

Sunday, September 22

N.Y. Giants	0	7	0	6—13
N.Y. Jets	3	0	3	0— 6

First Quarter
NYJ—FG, Lowery 46, 8:51.

Second Quarter
NYG—Calloway 17 pass from Brown (Daluiso kick), 10:22.

Third Quarter
NYJ—FG, Lowery 39, 7:34.

Fourth Quarter
NYG—FG, Daluiso 20, 1:56.
NYG—FG, Daluiso 20, 10:25.
Attendance—58,339.

TEAM STATISTICS

	N.Y. Giants	N.Y. Jets
First downs	12	13
Rushes-yards	38-91	21-78
Passing	110	130
Punt returns	3-37	1-(-1)
Kickoff returns	3-88	3-57
Interception returns	1-23	0-0
Comp.-att.-int.	9-13-0	22-38-1
Sacked-yards lost	1-1	4-19
Punts	5-44	7-46
Fumbles-lost	2-2	2-1
Penalties-yards	2-15	7-71
Time of possession	29:13	30:47

INDIVIDUAL STATISTICS

RUSHING—Giants, Hampton 27-81, Brown 7-3, Wheatley 3-7, Way 1-0. Jets, Murrell 11-41, Cobb 8-34, Anderson 2-3.

PASSING—Giants, Brown 9-13-0-111. Jets, O'Donnell 22-38-1-149.

RECEIVING—Giants, Calloway 3-53, Hampton 3-12, Cross 2-25, Dawsey 1-21. Jets, Graham 5-49, Chrebet 4-31, Anderson 4-17, Murrell 4-9, Slaughter 2-19, Johnson 1-14, Cobb 1-6, F. Baxter 1-4.

MISSED FIELD GOAL ATTEMPTS—None.

INTERCEPTIONS—Giants, Armstead 1-23.

KICKOFF RETURNS—Giants, Wheatley 2-63, Toomer 1-25. Jets, Van Dyke 3-57.

PUNT RETURNS—Giants, Toomer 3-37. Jets, Chrebet 1-(minus 1).

SACKS—Giants, Strahan 2, Harris 1, Team 1. Jets, M. Jones 1.

COLTS 10, DOLPHINS 6

Monday, September 23

Miami	3	3	0	0— 6
Indianapolis	0	7	0	3—10

First Quarter
Mia.—FG, Nedney 24, 7:55.

Second Quarter
Ind.—Dilger 1 pass from Harbaugh (Blanchard kick), 6:09.
Mia.—FG, Nedney 29, 13:23.

Fourth Quarter
Ind.—FG, Blanchard 18, :46.
Attendance—60,891.

TEAM STATISTICS

	Miami	Indianapolis
First downs	12	20
Rushes-yards	15-28	32-171
Passing	162	106
Punt returns	1-5	3-22
Kickoff returns	3-105	1-22
Interception returns	0-0	0-0
Comp.-att.-int.	20-30-0	19-26-0
Sacked-yards lost	5-27	3-14
Punts	5-49	4-47
Fumbles-lost	1-0	3-1
Penalties-yards	6-46	4-25
Time of possession	29:30	30:30

INDIVIDUAL STATISTICS

RUSHING—Miami, Abdul-Jabbar 9-18, Spikes 5-4, Kosar 1-6. Indianapolis, Warren 14-69, Crockett 9-81, Harbaugh 4-(minus 1), Groce 3-2, Harrison 1-15, Workman 1-5.

PASSING—Miami, Kosar 15-22-0-122, Marino 5-8-0-67. Indianapolis, Harbaugh 19-25-0-120, Justin 0-1-0-0.

RECEIVING—Miami, McDuffie 4-62, Pritchett 4-20, Abdul-Jabbar 3-27, L. Thomas 2-21, Spikes 2-10, Jordan 1-15, Carolan 1-13, McPhail 1-13, Byars 1-5, Miller 1-3. Indianapolis, Dawkins 4-40, Harrison 4-11, Warren 3-18, Dilger 3-11, Stablein 2-21, Crockett 2-12, Workman 1-7.

MISSED FIELD GOAL ATTEMPTS—Miami, Nedney 53.

INTERCEPTIONS—None.

KICKOFF RETURNS—Miami, McPhail 2-70, Spikes 1-35. Indianapolis, Bailey 1-22.

PUNT RETURNS—Miami, McDuffie 1-5. Indianapolis, Harrison 3-22.

SACKS—Miami, Armstrong 1½, Stubbs 1, Emtman ½. Indianapolis, McCoy 2, Alexander 1, Whittington 1, Dent 1.

1996 REVIEW *Week 4*

WEEK 5

ARIZONA 31, St. Louis 28 (OT)
BALTIMORE 17, New Orleans 10
CHICAGO 19, Oakland 17
Denver 14, CINCINNATI 10
Detroit 27, TAMPA BAY 0
Green Bay 31, SEATTLE 10
JACKSONVILLE 24, Carolina 14
N.Y. GIANTS 15, Minnesota 10
PITTSBURGH 30, Houston 16
SAN DIEGO 22, Kansas City 19
SAN FRANCISCO 39, Atlanta 17
WASHINGTON 31, N.Y. Jets 16
Dallas 23, PHILADELPHIA 19
  Open date: Buffalo, Indianapolis, Miami, New England

STANDINGS

AFC EAST	W	L	T	Pct.
Indianapolis	4	0	0	1.000
Buffalo	3	1	0	.750
Miami	3	1	0	.750
New England	2	2	0	.500
N.Y. Jets	0	5	0	.000

AFC CENTRAL	W	L	T	Pct.
Pittsburgh	3	1	0	.750
Baltimore	2	2	0	.500
Houston	2	2	0	.500
Jacksonville	2	3	0	.400
Cincinnati	1	3	0	.250

AFC WEST	W	L	T	Pct.
Denver	4	1	0	.800
Kansas City	4	1	0	.800
San Diego	4	1	0	.800
Oakland	1	4	0	.200
Seattle	1	4	0	.200

NFC EAST	W	L	T	Pct.
Washington	4	1	0	.800
Philadelphia	3	2	0	.600
Arizona	2	3	0	.400
Dallas	2	3	0	.400
N.Y. Giants	2	3	0	.400

NFC CENTRAL	W	L	T	Pct.
Green Bay	4	1	0	.800
Minnesota	4	1	0	.800
Detroit	3	2	0	.600
Chicago	2	3	0	.400
Tampa Bay	0	5	0	.000

NFC WEST	W	L	T	Pct.
Carolina	3	1	0	.750
San Francisco	3	1	0	.750
St. Louis	1	3	0	.250
Atlanta	0	4	0	.000
New Orleans	0	5	0	.000

HIGHLIGHTS

Hero of the week: San Diego linebacker Junior Seau played like a man possessed in the Chargers' 22-19 victory over Kansas City, the Chiefs' first loss of the season. The seven-year veteran had 12 tackles, a fourth-quarter sack and two interceptions, including one with 5:50 left that resulted in John Carney's game-winning, 33-yard field goal with 3:17 left.

Goat of the week: Seattle quarterback Rick Mirer would just as soon forget his performance against Green Bay. Under pressure most of the game, he was 10-of-30 for 156 yards, no touchdowns and four interceptions in the Seahawks' 31-10 loss. Mirer, who also lost a fumble, finished the day with a quarterback rating of 11.9.

Sub of the week: Subbing for the injured Erik Kramer, veteran quarterback Dave Krieg directed a turnover-free offense on five scoring drives in the Bears' 19-17 win over Oakland.

Comeback of the week: In a battle of bad teams, the Cardinals edged the Rams, 31-28, on Greg Davis' 24-yard field goal at 1:54 of overtime. Kent Graham threw two touchdown passes in the final seven minutes to rally Arizona from a 28-14 deficit, the third 14-point deficit the Cardinals overcame in the game. LeShon Johnson set up Davis' winning field goal by running 66 yards to the St. Louis 8 on the second play of overtime.

Blowout of the week: Detroit whipped Tampa Bay, 27-0, by forcing four turnovers and continually harrassing Bucs quarterback Trent Dilfer, who had an interception returned for a touchdown for the third time in four weeks (this time, Bennie Blades—98 yards—did the deed). The Lions held the Bucs to 74 yards in the second half.

Nail-biter of the week: San Diego's 22-19 win over Kansas City was not sealed until the Chargers' Chris Mims blocked a 47-yard field-goal attempt by Pete Stoyanovich with 28 seconds left.

Hit of the week: By Giants cornerback Jason Sehorn, who hit and forced a fumble by Minnesota quarterback Warren Moon early in the third quarter with the Vikings leading, 7-6. Chad Bratzke recovered near mid-field, and the Giants drove 49 yards in 11 plays for the go-ahead touchdown.

Oddity of the week: The Giants improved their all-time record in games before a bye week (since 1990) to 7-1. Their regular-season record in the same span was 37-64.

Top rusher: Earnest Byner carried 24 times for 149 yards in Baltimore's 17-10 win over New Orleans.

Top passer: Kent Graham was 27-of-58 for 366 yards and four touchdowns in Arizona's 31-28 win over St. Louis.

Top receiver: Rob Moore caught nine passes from Graham for 143 yards and one touchdown.

Notes: The Rams had played a league-high 95 consecutive games without overtime before Week 5. . . . Denver running back Terrell Davis tied a team record with his fourth consecutive 100-yard game. . . . In the first regular-season meeting between the NFL's two 1995 expansion teams, Jacksonville beat Carolina, 24-14. Rookie end Tony Brackens had six tackles, two sacks, one pass deflection, two forced fumbles and two fumble recoveries for the Jaguars. . . . Kansas City had won 12 consecutive AFC Western Division games before losing at San Diego. . . . Jerome Bettis became the first Pittsburgh running back since Barry Foster in 1992 to rush for 100 yards in three consecutive games. The Steelers improved their record to 25-2 in games in which when a running back rushes for 100 yards in the Bill Cowher regime. . . . Despite scoring on four consecutive possessions, the Jets lost their ninth game in a row, 31-16 to Washington. . . . The Saints were off to a 0-5 start for the second consecutive year. . . . Jeff Wilkins kicked a team record-tying six field goals in San Francisco's 39-17 win over Atlanta. Ray Wersching kicked six field goals for the 49ers in a win over New Orleans in 1983.

Quote of the week: Steelers defensive end Brentson Buckner gave Oilers running back Eddie George, the 1995 Heisman Trophy winner from Ohio State, a less-than-warm NFL welcome while helping to hold George to 47 yards on 11 attempts: "You're not running against Iowa any more!"

GAME SUMMARIES

REDSKINS 31, JETS 16

Sunday, September 29

N.Y. Jets	0	13	3	0—16
Washington	0	10	7	14—31

Second Quarter
Was.—FG, Blanton 28, :46.
NYJ—Murrell 9 run (Lowery kick), 3:58.
NYJ—FG, Lowery 26, 9:10.
Was.—Shepherd 12 run (Blanton kick), 12:46.
NYJ—FG, Lowery 35, 14:52.

Third Quarter
Was.—Allen 8 run (Blanton kick), 2:36.
NYJ—FG, Lowery 33, 12:39.

Fourth Quarter
Was.—Shepherd 52 pass from Frerotte (Blanton kick), :07.
Was.—Allen 28 run (Blanton kick), 13:06.
Attendance—52,068.

TEAM STATISTICS

	N.Y. Jets	Washington
First downs	27	18
Rushes-yards	37-140	25-142
Passing	287	254
Punt returns	1-4	1-9
Kickoff returns	5-90	5-103
Interception returns	0-0	1-0
Comp.-att.-int.	27-40-1	15-22-0
Sacked-yards lost	1-5	1-3
Punts	1-52	2-44
Fumbles-lost	1-0	0-0
Penalties-yards	4-30	2-9
Time of possession	37:18	22:42

INDIVIDUAL STATISTICS
RUSHING—New York, Murrell 31-118, Anderson 5-19, Cobb 1-3. Washington, Allen 20-101, Logan 3-12, Shepherd 2-29.
PASSING—New York, O'Donnell 27-40-1-292. Washington, Frerotte 15-22-0-257.
RECEIVING—New York, Johnson 8-74, Graham 7-95, Slaughter 6-51, Chrebet 4-63, Anderson 1-12, Murrell 1-(minus 3). Washington, Ellard 4-88, Shepherd 3-76, Asher 3-30, B. Brooks 2-54, Allen 1-8, Galbraith 1-8.
MISSED FIELD GOAL ATTEMPTS—New York, Lowery 49.
INTERCEPTIONS—Washington, Carter 1-0.
KICKOFF RETURNS—New York, Moore 4-58, Bailey 1-32. Washington, Mitchell 4-92, W. Bell 1-11.
PUNT RETURNS—New York, Chrebet 1-4. Washington, Mitchell 1-9.
SACKS—New York. Washington, Harvey 1.

CARDINALS 31, RAMS 28

Sunday, September 29

St. Louis	7	14	7	0	0—28
Arizona	0	14	0	14	3—31

First Quarter
St.L.—Kennison 66 punt return (Lohmiller kick), 11:26.

Second Quarter
St.L.—Bruce 46 pass from Banks (Lohmiller kick), :07.
Ariz.—R. Moore 24 pass from K. Graham (G. Davis kick), 6:03.
St.L.—Kennison 34 pass from Banks (Lohmiller kick), 9:03.
Ariz.—L. Johnson 2 run from K. Graham (G. Davis kick), 13:41.

Third Quarter
St.L.—Bruce 49 pass from Banks (Lohmiller kick), 8:46.

Fourth Quarter
Ariz.—Centers 5 pass from K. Graham (G. Davis kick), 8:41.
Ariz.—Sanders 5 pass from K. Graham (G. Davis kick), 14:49.

Overtime
Ariz.—FG, G. Davis 24, 1:54.
Attendance—33,116.

TEAM STATISTICS

	St. Louis	Arizona
First downs	10	27
Rushes-yards	22-60	27-150
Passing	166	348
Punt returns	4-128	3-24
Kickoff returns	3-56	3-64
Interception returns	0-0	1-3
Comp.-att.-int.	10-18-1	37-58-0
Sacked-yards lost	2-20	4-18
Punts	5-51	6-43
Fumbles-lost	3-2	2-1
Penalties-yards	8-60	11-85
Time of possession	20:06	41:48

INDIVIDUAL STATISTICS
RUSHING—St. Louis, Green 10-39, Banks 6-20, Phillips 5-1, Moore 1-0. Arizona, Centers 13-33, L. Johnson 12-97, K. Graham 2-20.
PASSING—St. Louis, Banks 10-18-1-186. Arizona, K. Graham 37-58-0-366.
RECEIVING—St. Louis, Bruce 4-117, Ross 2-18, Phillips 2-9, Kennison 1-34, Green 1-8. Arizona, Centers 13-83, R. Moore 9-143, L. Johnson 6-55, Sanders 4-47, Edwards 3-18, Dowdell 2-20.
MISSED FIELD GOAL ATTEMPTS—Arizona, G. Davis 48.
INTERCEPTIONS—Arizona, Alexander 1-3.
KICKOFF RETURNS—St. Louis, Kennison 3-56. Arizona, McElroy 2-35, Terry 1-29.
PUNT RETURNS—St. Louis, Kennison 4-128. Arizona, Dowdell 3-24.
SACKS—St. Louis, Carter 2, J. Jones 1½, O'Neal ½. Arizona, Swann 1, Rice 1.

JAGUARS 24, PANTHERS 14

Sunday, September 29

Carolina	0	0	6	8—14
Jacksonville	14	3	0	7—24

First Quarter
Jac.—Stewart 1 run (Hollis kick), 5:40.
Jac.—Smith 8 pass from Brunell (Hollis kick), 13:01.

Second Quarter
Jac.—FG, Hollis 53, 15:00.

Third Quarter
Car.—Carrier 24 pass from Beuerlein (kick failed), 4:22.

Fourth Quarter
Jac.—Stewart 4 run (Hollis kick), 3:13.
Car.—Carrier 3 pass from Collins (Collins run), 10:53.
Attendance—71,537.

TEAM STATISTICS

	Carolina	Jacksonville
First downs	21	22
Rushes-yards	21-57	38-179
Passing	215	199
Punt returns	6-56	2-26
Kickoff returns	4-93	2-28
Interception returns	1-0	0-0
Comp.-att.-int.	17-36-0	15-27-1
Sacked-yards lost	5-46	3-15
Punts	7-43	6-52
Fumbles-lost	4-2	2-1
Penalties-yards	7-41	13-118
Time of possession	25:01	34:59

INDIVIDUAL STATISTICS
RUSHING—Carolina, Johnson 12-31, Biakabutuka 4-17, Beuerlein 2-4, Oliver 2-4, Griffith 1-1. Jacksonville, Stewart 21-96, Means 11-27, Brunell 6-56.
PASSING—Carolina, Beuerlein 15-30-0-219, Collins 2-6-0-42. Jacksonville, Brunell 15-27-1-214.
RECEIVING—Carolina, Carrier 8-124, Muhammad 5-96, Oliver 2-25, Walls 1-10, Green 1-6. Jacksonville, Smith 4-64, McCardell 3-67, Griffith 3-41, W. Jackson 1-14, Brown 1-10, Mitchell 1-8, Rison 1-6, Maston 1-4.
MISSED FIELD GOAL ATTEMPTS—Carolina, Kasay 45.
INTERCEPTIONS—Carolina, Terrell 1-0.
KICKOFF RETURNS—Carolina, Bates 4-93. Jacksonville, Jordan 2-28.
PUNT RETURNS—Carolina, Oliver 6-56. Jacksonville, Hudson 2-26.
SACKS—Carolina, Kragen 1, Mills 1, Greene 1. Jacksonville, Brackens 2, Smeenge 2, Robinson 1.

BRONCOS 14, BENGALS 10

Sunday, September 29

Denver	7	0	7	0—14
Cincinnati	3	7	0	0—10

First Quarter
Cin.—FG, Pelfrey 44, 5:20.
Den.—Sharpe 11 pass from Elway (Elam kick), 13:56.

Second Quarter
Cin.—Blake 2 run (Pelfrey kick), 2:28.

Third Quarter

Den.—Miller 23 pass from Elway (Elam kick), 12:42.

Attendance—51,798.

TEAM STATISTICS

	Denver	Cincinnati
First downs	22	17
Rushes-yards	27-114	24-106
Passing	288	147
Punt returns	2-18	2-9
Kickoff returns	1-27	3-71
Interception returns	1-0	1-0
Comp.-att.-int.	23-38-1	15-29-1
Sacked-yards lost	5-47	4-19
Punts	5-43	6-53
Fumbles-lost	2-2	1-0
Penalties-yards	6-52	6-40
Time of possession	31:15	28:45

INDIVIDUAL STATISTICS

RUSHING—Denver, Davis 24-112, Elway 2-(minus 1), Rivers 1-3. Cincinnati, Hearst 10-71, Blake 6-21, Carter 5-13, Bieniemy 2-(minus 1), Cothran 1-2.

PASSING—Denver, Elway 23-37-1-335, Craver 0-1-0-0. Cincinnati, Blake 15-29-1-166.

RECEIVING—Denver, Sharpe 6-60, Miller 5-131, McCaffrey 5-80, Sherrard 2-21, Carswell 2-5, Kinchen 1-27, Craver 1-12, Rivers 1-(minus 1). Cincinnati, McGee 4-48, Pickens 3-39, Bieniemy 3-24, Dunn 2-36, Carter 2-14, Scott 1-5.

MISSED FIELD GOAL ATTEMPTS—None.

INTERCEPTIONS—Denver, Braxton 1-0. Cincinnati, Walker 1-0.

KICKOFF RETURNS—Denver, Hebron 1-27. Cincinnati, Hill 2-49, Dunn 1-22.

PUNT RETURNS—Denver, Kinchen 2-18. Cincinnati, Sawyer 1-9, Myers 1-0.

SACKS—Denver, Geathers 2, Mobley 1, A. Williams 1. Cincinnati, Francis 1, Copeland 1, T. Johnson 1, Sawyer 1, Wilkinson 1.

CHARGERS 22, CHIEFS 19

Sunday, September 29

Kansas City	0	9	7	3—19
San Diego	6	0	10	6—22

First Quarter

S.D.—FG, Carney 33, 7:16.

S.D.—FG, Carney 38, 14:14.

Second Quarter

K.C.—FG, Stoyanovich 44, 2:43.

K.C.—FG, Stoyanovich 26, 12:12.

K.C.—FG, Stoyanovich 25, 14:37.

Third Quarter

S.D.—FG, Carney 44, 4:47.

S.D.—Da. Gordon 81 punt return (Carney kick), 7:46.

K.C.—Johnson 3 pass from Bono (Stoyanovich kick), 8:53.

Fourth Quarter

S.D.—FG, Carney 39, 2:54.

K.C.—FG, Stoyanovich 32, 5:10.

S.D.—FG, Carney 33, 11:43.

Attendance—59,384.

TEAM STATISTICS

	Kansas City	San Diego
First downs	19	18
Rushes-yards	19-58	29-75
Passing	257	238
Punt returns	2-19	3-84
Kickoff returns	5-176	6-151
Interception returns	0-0	2-18
Comp.-att.-int.	25-54-2	19-41-0
Sacked-yards lost	3-23	0-0
Punts	5-53	5-39
Fumbles-lost	1-0	3-2
Penalties-yards	5-36	7-54
Time of possession	30:48	29:12

INDIVIDUAL STATISTICS

RUSHING—Kansas City, Allen 9-35, Hill 6-(minus 1), Anders 3-17, Bono 1-7. San Diego, Russell 14-50, Hayden 8-24, Humphries 4-(minus 2), Fletcher 2-10, A. Coleman 1-(minus 7).

PASSING—Kansas City, Bono 25-54-2-280. San Diego, Humphries 19-41-0-238.

RECEIVING—Kansas City, Allen 6-88, LaChapelle 3-56, Penn 3-46, Johnson 3-29, McNair 2-15, Vanover 2-11, Anders 2-4, Bennett 1-10, D. Carter 1-8, Cash 1-8, Hughes 1-5. San Diego, Pupunu 5-83, Martin 4-48, A. Coleman 3-41, Jones 3-25, Fletcher 2-19, Russell 1-16, Roche 1-6.

MISSED FIELD GOAL ATTEMPTS—Kansas City, Stoyanovich 47.

INTERCEPTIONS—San Diego, Seau 2-18.

KICKOFF RETURNS—Kansas City, Woods 4-159, Manusky 1-17. San Diego, A. Coleman 4-126, Pupunu 1-15, Russell 1-10.

PUNT RETURNS—Kansas City, Penn 1-13, Vanover 1-6. San Diego, Da. Gordon 3-84.

SACKS—San Diego, Seau 1, R. Davis 1, Mims 1.

STEELERS 30, OILERS 16

Sunday, September 29

Houston	0	0	14	2—16
Pittsburgh	17	3	0	10—30

First Quarter

Pit.—Stewart 16 pass from Tomczak (N. Johnson kick), 1:50.

Pit.—FG, N. Johnson 33, 4:49.

Pit.—C. Johnson 62 pass from Tomczak (N. Johnson kick), 7:36.

Second Quarter

Pit.—FG, N. Johnson 36, 14:37.

Third Quarter

Hou.—Davis 4 pass from Chandler (Del Greco kick), 6:09.

Hou.—D. Lewis 36 interception return (Del Greco kick), 8:30.

Fourth Quarter

Pit.—FG, N. Johnson 36, 2:37.

Pit.—Perry 13 interception return (N. Johnson kick), 9:43.

Hou.—Safety, S. Edge forced out of end zone by S. Jackson, 13:12.

Attendance—58,608.

TEAM STATISTICS

	Houston	Pittsburgh
First downs	16	15
Rushes-yards	20-80	35-112
Passing	189	197
Punt returns	2-6	3-36
Kickoff returns	8-148	3-59
Interception returns	1-36	2-40
Comp.-att.-int.	24-42-2	15-28-1
Sacked-yards lost	2-18	1-5
Punts	6-48	6-34
Fumbles-lost	5-3	2-1
Penalties-yards	4-23	3-20
Time of possession	29:42	30:18

INDIVIDUAL STATISTICS

RUSHING—Houston, George 11-47, Thomas 4-7, Harmon 3-8, Chandler 2-18. Pittsburgh, Bettis 29-115, Stewart 3-15, Tomczak 2-(minus 2), Edge 1-(minus 16).

PASSING—Houston, Chandler 24-42-2-207. Pittsburgh, Tomczak 15-28-1-202.

RECEIVING—Houston, Harmon 6-53, Davis 5-44, Sanders 4-49, Russell 4-23, Thomas 2-19, Wycheck 2-15, George 1-4. Pittsburgh, Stewart 4-40, C. Johnson 3-87, Bruener 3-29, Arnold 1-21, Lester 1-19, McAfee 1-8, Hastings 1-4, Bettis 1-(minus 6).

MISSED FIELD GOAL ATTEMPTS—Houston, Del Greco 47.

INTERCEPTIONS—Houston, D. Lewis 1-36. Pittsburgh, Perry 2-40.

KICKOFF RETURNS—Houston, Gray 6-129, Roan 1-13, McKeehan 1-6. Pittsburgh, C. Johnson 2-29, Arnold 1-30.

PUNT RETURNS—Houston, Gray 2-6. Pittsburgh, Hastings 3-36.

SACKS—Houston, Walker 1. Pittsburgh, Lake 1, Williams 1.

RAVENS 17, SAINTS 10

Sunday, September 29

New Orleans	3	0	0	7—10
Baltimore	7	3	0	7—17

First Quarter

Bal.—Alexander 64 pass from Testaverde (Stover kick), 5:25.

N.O.—FG, Brien 23, 13:53.

Second Quarter

Bal.—FG, Stover 38, 12:40.

Fourth Quarter

N.O.—Haynes 31 pass from Everett (Brien kick), :12.

Bal.—Jackson 6 pass from Testaverde (Stover kick), 4:33.

Attendance—61,063.

TEAM STATISTICS

	New Orleans	Baltimore
First downs	18	16
Rushes-yards	29-96	33-165
Passing	202	178
Punt returns	0-0	3-31

	New Orleans	Baltimore
Kickoff returns	4-87	3-56
Interception returns	0-0	0-0
Comp.-att.-int.	23-30-0	11-20-0
Sacked-yards lost	1-5	1-8
Punts	4-47	3-45
Fumbles-lost	0-0	1-0
Penalties-yards	6-55	4-41
Time of possession	32:40	27:20

INDIVIDUAL STATISTICS

RUSHING—New Orleans, Bates 23-82, Brown 3-9, Everett 3-5. Baltimore, Byner 24-149, Gardner 6-19, Testaverde 3-(minus 3).

PASSING—New Orleans, Everett 23-30-0-207. Baltimore, Testaverde 11-20-0-186.

RECEIVING—New Orleans, Haynes 6-94, Lusk 3-16, Neal 3-14, Bates 3-9, Small 2-30, I. Smith 2-5, Brown 1-14, Green 1-13, DeRamus 1-6, Jeffires 1-6. Baltimore, Jackson 5-61, Alexander 2-83, F. Turner 2-9, Kinchen 1-29, C. Williams 1-4.

MISSED FIELD GOAL ATTEMPTS—New Orleans, Brien 38. Baltimore, Stover 48, 49.

INTERCEPTIONS—None.

KICKOFF RETURNS—New Orleans, Hughes 4-87. Baltimore, J. Lewis 2-35, Ethridge 1-21.

PUNT RETURNS—Baltimore, J. Lewis 3-31.

SACKS—New Orleans, Martin 1. Baltimore, Burnett 1.

49ERS 39, FALCONS 17

Sunday, September 29

Atlanta	3	0	7	7—17
San Francisco	6	21	9	3—39

First Quarter

Atl.—FG, Andersen 20, 7:00.
S.F.—FG, Wilkins 21, 11:34.
S.F.—FG, Wilkins 43, 13:54.

Second Quarter

S.F.—Pope 55 interception return (Wilkins kick), :15.
S.F.—Rice 24 pass from Kirby (Wilkins kick), 7:10.
S.F.—Popson 16 pass from Grbac (Wilkins kick), 14:01.

Third Quarter

S.F.—FG, Wilkins 46, 2:53.
S.F.—FG, Wilkins 29, 6:07.
Atl.—Brown 22 pass from Hebert (Andersen kick), 9:10.
S.F.—FG, Wilkins 29, 13:50.

Fourth Quarter

S.F.—FG, Wilkins 38, 9:41.
Atl.—Preston 17 pass from Hebert (Andersen kick), 13:05.
Attendance—62,995.

TEAM STATISTICS

	Atlanta	San Francisco
First downs	18	16
Rushes-yards	24-126	22-150
Passing	191	246
Punt returns	0-0	2-19
Kickoff returns	10-188	3-67
Interception returns	0-0	3-58
Comp.-att.-int.	17-32-3	23-37-0
Sacked-yards lost	2-15	0-0
Punts	4-38	2-34
Fumbles-lost	2-1	0-0
Penalties-yards	5-59	9-68
Time of possession	28:57	31:03

INDIVIDUAL STATISTICS

RUSHING—Atlanta, Anderson 14-67, Heyward 9-55, Metcalf 1-4. San Francisco, Loville 8-18, Kirby 4-14, Grbac 4-13, Vardell 3-6, Lynn 1-67, D. Carter 1-18, Rice 1-14.

PASSING—Atlanta, Hebert 17-32-3-206. San Francisco, Grbac 22-36-0-222, Kirby 1-1-0-24.

RECEIVING—Atlanta, Preston 6-65, Brown 4-59, Metcalf 3-44, Mathis 3-29, Anderson 1-9. San Francisco, Stokes 7-88, Rice 7-72, Vardell 5-35, Popson 2-20, Owens 1-26, Se. Manuel 1-5.

MISSED FIELD GOAL ATTEMPTS—None.

INTERCEPTIONS—San Francisco, Pope 1-55, Israel 1-3, McDonald 1-0.

KICKOFF RETURNS—Atlanta, Metcalf 9-176, Anderson 1-12. San Francisco, D. Carter 2-50, Owens 1-17.

PUNT RETURNS—San Francisco, D. Carter 2-19.

SACKS—San Francisco, Stubblefield 1, Barker 1.

GIANTS 15, VIKINGS 10

Sunday, September 29

Minnesota	0	7	0	3—10
N.Y. Giants	3	3	6	3—15

First Quarter

NYG—FG, Daluiso 25, 8:32.

Second Quarter

Min.—Palmer 69 punt return (Sisson kick), :39.
NYG—FG, Daluiso 27, 3:04.

Third Quarter

NYG—Pierce 1 run (pass failed), 12:07.

Fourth Quarter

Min.—FG, Sisson 28, 1:33.
NYG—FG, Daluiso 18, 7:21.
Attendance—70,970.

TEAM STATISTICS

	Minnesota	N.Y. Giants
First downs	10	21
Rushes-yards	20-87	40-144
Passing	140	146
Punt returns	1-69	3-38
Kickoff returns	4-84	3-91
Interception returns	0-0	1-0
Comp.-att.-int.	13-25-1	18-29-0
Sacked-yards lost	2-3	5-21
Punts	7-39	6-38
Fumbles-lost	2-1	2-0
Penalties-yards	7-79	4-20
Time of possession	22:17	37:43

INDIVIDUAL STATISTICS

RUSHING—Minnesota, R. Smith 17-86, Lee 2-1, Moon 1-0. New York, Hampton 24-82, Brown 6-18, Wheatley 3-24, Way 3-11, Elias 3-8, Pierce 1-1.

PASSING—Minnesota, Moon 13-25-1-143. New York, Brown 18-29-0-167.

RECEIVING—Minnesota, Carter 6-55, Reed 3-60, Lee 2-15, Jordan 1-7, Palmer 1-6. New York, Lewis 5-44, Pierce 3-45, Way 3-16, Calloway 2-38, Dawsey 2-13, Elias 2-11, Wheatley 1-0.

MISSED FIELD GOAL ATTEMPTS—None.

INTERCEPTIONS—New York, Sparks 1-0.

KICKOFF RETURNS—Minnesota, Ismail 4-84. New York, Lewis 1-47, Wheatley 1-22, Toomer 1-22.

PUNT RETURNS—Minnesota, Palmer 1-69. New York, Toomer 3-38.

SACKS—Minnesota, F. Smith 2, Edwards 1, Randle 1, Alexander 1. New York, Sehorn 2.

PACKERS 31, SEAHAWKS 10

Sunday, September 29

Green Bay	10	7	7	7—31
Seattle	0	7	3	0—10

First Quarter

G.B.—Freeman 13 pass from Favre (Jacke kick), 10:24.
G.B.—FG, Jacke 36, 14:26.

Second Quarter

G.B.—Levens 4 pass from Favre (Jacke kick), 11:06.
Sea.—Warren 37 run (Peterson kick), 13:04.

Third Quarter

G.B.—Jackson 10 pass from Favre (Jacke kick), 6:36.
Sea.—FG, Peterson 44, 9:25.

Fourth Quarter

G.B.—Freeman 4 pass from Favre (Jacke kick), 5:10.
Attendance—59,973.

TEAM STATISTICS

	Green Bay	Seattle
First downs	23	19
Rushes-yards	35-142	26-159
Passing	202	170
Punt returns	4-68	3-29
Kickoff returns	3-45	6-141
Interception returns	4-150	0-0
Comp.-att.-int.	20-34-0	11-34-4
Sacked-yards lost	2-7	1-1
Punts	7-43	6-47
Fumbles-lost	1-0	1-1
Penalties-yards	5-37	6-38
Time of possession	35:34	24:26

INDIVIDUAL STATISTICS

RUSHING—Green Bay, Bennett 22-94, Levens 6-28, Favre 5-15,

Henderson 2-5. Seattle, Warren 18-103, Galloway 2-22, Mirer 2-17, Smith 2-5, Broussard 1-10, Friesz 1-2.

PASSING—Green Bay, Favre 20-34-0-209. Seattle, Mirer 10-30-4-156, Friesz 1-4-0-15.

RECEIVING—Green Bay, Freeman 7-108, Chmura 3-36, Levens 3-18, Beebe 2-15, Bennett 2-9, Jackson 1-10, Henderson 1-8, Howard 1-5. Seattle, Warren 3-44, Fauria 3-36, Pritchard 2-54, Blades 2-22, Galloway 1-15.

MISSED FIELD GOAL ATTEMPTS—Green Bay, Jacke 38.

INTERCEPTIONS—Green Bay, Evans 1-63, White 1-46, Robinson 1-39, Newsome 1-2.

KICKOFF RETURNS—Green Bay, Beebe 2-36, Levens 1-9. Seattle, Broussard 6-141.

PUNT RETURNS—Green Bay, Howard 4-68. Seattle, Galloway 2-12, R. Harris 1-17.

SACKS—Green Bay, Simmons 1. Seattle, Sinclair 1, Kennedy 1.

BEARS 19, RAIDERS 17

Sunday, September 29

Oakland	0	10	7	0—17
Chicago	0	3	7	9—19

Second Quarter
Chi.—FG, Jaeger 44, 6:25.
Oak.—Fenner 1 run (Ford kick), 13:03.
Oak.—FG, Ford 28, 14:42.

Third Quarter
Oak.—T. Brown 5 pass from Hostetler (Ford kick), 6:21.
Chi.—Salaam 11 pass from Krieg (Jaeger kick), 9:46.

Fourth Quarter
Chi.—FG, Jaeger 24, :42.
Chi.—FG, Jaeger 40, 7:28.
Chi.—FG, Jaeger 30, 14:49.
Attendance—57,062.

TEAM STATISTICS

	Oakland	Chicago
First downs	17	15
Rushes-yards	25-117	33-107
Passing	166	188
Punt returns	5-62	4-43
Kickoff returns	6-142	3-74
Interception returns	0-0	4-20
Comp.-att.-int.	19-35-4	16-30-0
Sacked-yards lost	1-6	1-2
Punts	6-41	7-40
Fumbles-lost	0-0	1-0
Penalties-yards	10-87	9-51
Time of possession	29:17	30:43

INDIVIDUAL STATISTICS

RUSHING—Oakland, Aska 13-86, Kaufman 6-13, Fenner 4-14, Hostetler 2-4. Chicago, Salaam 24-76, Hicks 7-31, Conway 1-1, Krieg 1-(minus 1).

PASSING—Oakland, Hostetler 19-35-4-172. Chicago, Krieg 16-30-0-190.

RECEIVING—Oakland, T. Brown 6-51, Jett 5-56, Fenner 5-38, Hobbs 3-27. Chicago, T. Carter 5-32, Conway 4-49, Timpson 2-59, Wetnight 2-28, Neely 1-12, Salaam 1-11, Hicks 1-(minus 1).

MISSED FIELD GOAL ATTEMPTS—None.

INTERCEPTIONS—Chicago, Woolford 2-4, Burton 1-11, Minter 1-5.

KICKOFF RETURNS—Oakland, Kidd 5-123, Shedd 1-19. Chicago, Ja. Jackson 2-59, Faulkerson 1-15.

PUNT RETURNS—Oakland, T. Brown 3-14, Hobbs 2-48. Chicago, Engram 4-43.

SACKS—Oakland, Maryland 1. Chicago, Cain 1.

LIONS 27, BUCCANEERS 0

Sunday, September 29

Detroit	7	10	0	10—27
Tampa Bay	0	0	0	0— 0

First Quarter
Det.—Blades 98 interception return (Hanson kick), 13:42.

Second Quarter
Det.—FG, Hanson 20, :21.
Det.—Morton 31 pass from Mitchell (Hanson kick), 7:58.

Fourth Quarter
Det.—FG, Hanson 29, 6:54.
Det.—H. Moore 3 pass from Mitchell (Hanson kick), 11:18.
Attendance—34,961.

TEAM STATISTICS

	Detroit	Tampa Bay
First downs	20	13
Rushes-yards	27-129	26-70
Passing	221	156
Punt returns	1-13	1-14
Kickoff returns	1-24	5-114
Interception returns	3-104	0-0
Comp.-att.-int.	22-33-0	16-31-3
Sacked-yards lost	3-17	2-14
Punts	3-45	5-46
Fumbles-lost	1-0	1-1
Penalties-yards	5-45	4-25
Time of possession	29:09	30:51

INDIVIDUAL STATISTICS

RUSHING—Detroit, Sanders 15-73, Rivers 9-57, Mitchell 1-4, Majkowski 1-(minus 1), Morton 1-(minus 4). Tampa Bay, R. Brooks 14-37, Alstott 8-31, Dilfer 3-2, Thompson 1-0.

PASSING—Detroit, Mitchell 21-32-0-230, Majkowski 1-1-0-8. Tampa Bay, Dilfer 14-26-2-119, Weldon 2-5-1-51.

RECEIVING—Detroit, H. Moore 9-104, Perriman 5-42, Morton 3-58, Sanders 2-17, Metzelaars 2-9, Matthews 1-8. Tampa Bay, Harper 4-41, Alstott 4-30, Moore 3-17, Thompson 2-21, Ellison 1-42, Hawkins 1-12, Harris 1-7.

MISSED FIELD GOAL ATTEMPTS—Detroit, Hanson 39.

INTERCEPTIONS—Detroit, Blades 1-98, Malone 1-5, McNeil 1-1.

KICKOFF RETURNS—Detroit, Milburn 1-24. Tampa Bay, Silvan 5-114.

PUNT RETURNS—Detroit, Milburn 1-13. Tampa Bay, Silvan 1-14.

SACKS—Detroit, Porcher 1, Bonham 1. Tampa Bay, Sapp 1, Upshaw 1, Marts 1.

COWBOYS 23, EAGLES 19

Monday, September 30

Dallas	7	13	3	0—23
Philadelphia	10	0	7	2—19

First Quarter
Phi.—FG, Anderson 46, 5:13.
Phi.—Watters 2 run (Anderson kick), 11:12.
Dal.—Bjornson 5 pass from Aikman (Boniol kick), 14:43.

Second Quarter
Dal.—E. Smith 5 run (Boniol kick), 8:28.
Dal.—FG, Boniol 46, 11:32.
Dal.—FG, Boniol 30, 14:47.

Third Quarter
Phi.—Hall 32 interception return (Anderson kick), 1:24.
Dal.—FG, Boniol 21, 9:00.

Fourth Quarter
Phi.—Safety, Jett ran out of end zone, 14:52.
Attendance—67,201.

TEAM STATISTICS

	Dallas	Philadelphia
First downs	15	14
Rushes-yards	34-108	27-85
Passing	141	174
Punt returns	3-26	2-16
Kickoff returns	2-74	6-135
Interception returns	2-31	1-32
Comp.-att.-int.	13-23-1	16-30-2
Sacked-yards lost	1-8	6-42
Punts	4-40	3-46
Fumbles-lost	1-1	5-3
Penalties-yards	8-53	4-25
Time of possession	31:33	28:27

INDIVIDUAL STATISTICS

RUSHING—Dallas, E. Smith 22-92, S. Williams 7-27, Aikman 3-11, Johnston 1-1, Jett 1-(minus 23). Philadelphia, Watters 21-68, Turner 4-12, Peete 1-9, Fryar 1-(minus 4).

PASSING—Dallas, Aikman 13-23-1-149. Philadelphia, Peete 9-16-1-98, Detmer 7-14-1-118.

RECEIVING—Dallas, Sanders 3-55, Bjornson 3-33, E. Smith 3-30, Johnston 2-2, Martin 1-16, Walker 1-13. Philadelphia, Turner 4-79, Watters 4-26, Fryar 2-15, Jones 2-13, Seay 1-35, Dunn 1-34, West 1-10, McIntyre 1-4.

MISSED FIELD GOAL ATTEMPTS—Philadelphia, Anderson 29.

INTERCEPTIONS—Dallas, Teague 1-29, Sanders 1-2. Philadelphia, Hall 1-32.

KICKOFF RETURNS—Dallas, Walker 2-74. Philadelphia, Witherspoon 6-135.

PUNT RETURNS—Dallas, Martin 3-26. Philadelphia, Seay 2-16.

SACKS—Dallas, Tolbert 2, Woodson 1, Lett 1, Hennings 1, McCormack 1. Philadelphia, W. Fuller 1.

WEEK 6

BUFFALO 16, Indianapolis 13 (OT)
DENVER 28, San Diego 17
DETROIT 28, Atlanta 24
Green Bay 37, CHICAGO 6
Houston 30, CINCINNATI 27 (OT)
MINNESOTA 14, Carolina 12
New England 46, BALTIMORE 38
NEW ORLEANS 17, Jacksonville 13
Oakland 34, N.Y. JETS 13
San Francisco 28, ST. LOUIS 11
Seattle 22, MIAMI 15
Pittsburgh 17, KANSAS CITY 7
    Open date: Arizona, Dallas, N.Y. Giants,
Philadelphia, Tampa Bay, Washington

STANDINGS

AFC EAST	W	L	T	Pct.
Buffalo	4	1	0	.800
Indianapolis	4	1	0	.800
Miami	3	2	0	.600
New England	3	2	0	.600
N.Y. Jets	0	6	0	.000

AFC CENTRAL	W	L	T	Pct.
Pittsburgh	4	1	0	.800
Houston	3	2	0	.600
Baltimore	2	3	0	.400
Jacksonville	2	4	0	.333
Cincinnati	1	4	0	.200

AFC WEST	W	L	T	Pct.
Denver	5	1	0	.833
Kansas City	4	2	0	.667
San Diego	4	2	0	.667
Oakland	2	4	0	.333
Seattle	2	4	0	.333

NFC EAST	W	L	T	Pct.
Washington	4	1	0	.800
Philadelphia	3	2	0	.600
Arizona	2	3	0	.400
Dallas	2	3	0	.400
N.Y. Giants	2	3	0	.400

NFC CENTRAL	W	L	T	Pct.
Green Bay	5	1	0	.833
Minnesota	5	1	0	.833
Detroit	4	2	0	.667
Chicago	2	4	0	.333
Tampa Bay	0	5	0	.000

NFC WEST	W	L	T	Pct.
San Francisco	4	1	0	.800
Carolina	3	2	0	.600
St. Louis	1	4	0	.200
New Orleans	1	5	0	.167
Atlanta	0	5	0	.000

HIGHLIGHTS

Hero of the week: Green Bay wide receiver Antonio Freeman pierced Chicago for a pair of spectacular touchdown catches, one of which came on a Hail Mary to end the first half, in the Packers' 37-6 victory. Freeman, who finished with seven catches for 146 yards, went up in a tight group that included three players from each team to somehow make the 50-yard touchdown reception before halftime. In the second half, Freeman went right over Kevin Miniefield's back to claim a 35-yard touchdown reception.

Goat of the week: Carolina quarterback Kerry Collins, making his first start in three weeks because of a knee sprain, couldn't shake the rust in a 14-12 loss to Minnesota. He threw no touchdown passes and four interceptions, including one by Dewayne Washington at the Panthers' 36 with 3:08 left that sealed the Vikings' victory.

Sub of the week: Making his first start in place of the benched Rick Mirer, John Friesz led Seattle to a 22-15 upset victory in rainy Miami. Friesz was 18-of-32 for 299 yards and three long touchdown passes, including an 80-yarder to Brian Blades with 2:03 left that erased the Dolphins' 15-14 lead. Friesz also threw touchdown passes of 65 and 51 yards to Joey Galloway.

Comeback of the week: With the Broncos trailing 17-0 late in the first half, John Elway threw four touchdown passes and rallied Denver to a 28-17 victory over San Diego. Elway spurred the comeback by leading the Broncos on a five-play, 80-yard drive late in the first half that culminated with a 20-yard touchdown pass to Shannon Sharpe. Elway, who said he had been inspired by Junior Seau's pregame comment that the Broncos were a team of mostly "average players," threw two more touchdown passes to Sharpe and one to Ed McCaffrey in the second half.

Blowout of the week: Green Bay crushed Chicago, 37-6, in its most decisive victory ever at Soldier Field and one of the most lopsided outcomes in the history of the rivalry. The Packers were carried by Brett Favre's four touchdown passes and a ball-hawking defense that intercepted three passes, giving it 18 for the season.

Nail-biter of the week: Buffalo blew a 10-0 lead, then rallied to defeat Indianapolis, 16-13, in overtime on Steve Christie's 39-yard field goal. In addition to Christie's heroics and a ferocious defense that beat up Jim Harbaugh all day, the Bills received a boost from quarterback Todd Collins, who started in place of hamstring-troubled Jim Kelly. Collins moved the team 58 yards in 11 plays late in regulation to set up a 37-yard field goal by Christie with 15 seconds left in regulation. The victory gave the Bills a 5-0 record in overtime at Rich Stadium.

Hit of the week: With Denver ahead, 21-17, early in the fourth quarter, safety Steve Atwater separated San Diego receiver Charlie Jones from the ball on a fourth-down play from the Broncos' 38. Denver then went 62 yards in 12 plays for an insurance touchdown.

Oddity of the week: After Green Bay scored on Antonio Freeman's Hail Mary catch to end the first half, Chicago linebacker Bryan Cox raised his middle finger to on-field officials and threw his helmet. He then stood in the end zone, helmet in hands, during Chris Jacke's extra-point attempt. Jacke missed.

Top rusher: Rookie Eddie George rushed 26 times for 152 yards and a 45-yard touchdown in Houston's 30-27 overtime victory at Cincinnati.

Top passer: Elway was 32-of-41 for 323 yards and four touchdowns, with one interception, in Denver's 28-17 victory over San Diego.

Top receiver: Sharpe caught a career-high 13 passes (tying a club record) for 153 yards and three touchdowns in the Broncos' victory over the Chargers.

Notes: Buffalo's Thurman Thomas rushed for 68 yards and went over the 10,000-yard mark in his career. . . . San Diego's Darren Bennett boomed three 66-yard punts and added 59- and 56-yarders. All five of those punts were fielded in the air without bouncing. He finished with a 56.7 average on six punts. . . . The 49ers' 28-11 victory in St. Louis gave them a 13-game winning streak against the Rams, dating to 1990. The average score of those victories: 33-12. . . . Baltimore was penal-

ized 13 times for 146 yards in its 46-38 loss to New England. . . . San Francisco tight end Ted Popson, who entered the game with two receptions for 20 yards, caught five passes for 44 yards and two touchdowns against St. Louis. . . . The Rams started the NFL's first all-rookie backfield since 1976 with Tony Banks at quarterback, Lawrence Phillips at tailback and Derrick Harris at fullback. . . . At 19-50, Cincinnati's Dave Shula reached 50 losses faster than any coach in NFL history. . . . Houston's Mel Gray had 263 return yards on five kickoff and three punt returns at Cincinnati. . . . With his 107th career rushing touchdown, Kansas City's Marcus Allen moved past Jim Brown and into second place behind Walter Payton. Allen also moved past Tony Dorsett and into second place on the career combined yardage list. . . . Pittsburgh's Jerome Bettis recorded his fourth straight 100-yard rushing game.
Quote of the week: Jets kicker Nick Lowery, on his injury-riddled team: "I feel like I should be like Scotty on the Starship Enterprise and make sure I have enough 'dilithium' crystals to put a shield around me, so at least I don't get injured, too."

GAME SUMMARIES

SEAHAWKS 22, DOLPHINS 15
Sunday, October 6

Seattle	7	7	0	8—22
Miami	3	6	6	0—15

First Quarter
Mia.—FG, Nedney 20, 7:30.
Sea.—Galloway 65 pass from Friesz (Peterson kick), 15:00.
Second Quarter
Sea.—Galloway 51 pass from Friesz (Peterson kick), 2:55.
Mia.—R. Hill 33 pass from Erickson (run failed), 14:09.
Third Quarter
Mia.—Spikes 2 run (run failed), 14:05.
Fourth Quarter
Sea.—Blades 80 pass from Friesz (Smith run), 12:57.
Attendance—59,539.

TEAM STATISTICS
	Seattle	Miami
First downs	12	17
Rushes-yards	27-59	32-85
Passing	301	214
Punt returns	2-27	3-13
Kickoff returns	2-38	4-99
Interception returns	1-38	1-11
Comp.-att.-int.	18-32-1	16-28-1
Sacked-yards lost	0-0	4-29
Punts	6-39	7-48
Fumbles-lost	3-2	7-2
Penalties-yards	4-26	3-30
Time of possession	27:31	32:29

INDIVIDUAL STATISTICS
RUSHING—Seattle, Warren 12-18, Smith 7-35, Friesz 4-(minus 3), Strong 2-8, Broussard 1-4, Galloway 1-(minus 3). Miami, Spikes 19-48, Abdul-Jabbar 6-19, Erickson 4-5, McPhail 1-10, Pritchett 1-3, Ruddy 1-0.
PASSING—Seattle, Friesz 18-32-1-299. Miami, Erickson 16-28-1-243.
RECEIVING—Seattle, Galloway 5-137, Blades 4-95, Warren 3-18, Strong 2-18, Pritchard 2-14, Proehl 1-10, Smith 1-7. Miami, McPhail 6-86, McDuffie 3-34, R. Hill 2-51, Miller 2-38, Carolan 1-21, Spikes 1-8, Pritchett 1-5.
MISSED FIELD GOAL ATTEMPTS—None.
INTERCEPTIONS—Seattle, Blackmon 1-38. Miami, Hollier 1-11.
KICKOFF RETURNS—Seattle, Broussard 2-38. Miami, Spikes 3-100, McPhail 1-(minus 1).
PUNT RETURNS—Seattle, Galloway 2-27. Miami, McDuffie 3-13.
SACKS—Seattle, Kennedy 2, McCrary 1, Daniels 1.

SAINTS 17, JAGUARS 13
Sunday, October 6

Jacksonville	0	7	3	3—13
New Orleans	10	0	0	7—17

First Quarter
N.O.—Bates 1 run (Brien kick), 9:25.
N.O.—FG, Brien 27, 12:34.
Second Quarter
Jac.—Stewart 21 pass from Brunell (Hollis kick), 10:18.
Third Quarter
Jac.—FG, Hollis 36, 12:07.
Fourth Quarter
Jac.—FG, Hollis 19, 9:45.
N.O.—Small 6 pass from Everett (Brien kick), 13:15.
Attendance—34,231.

TEAM STATISTICS
	Jacksonville	New Orleans
First downs	22	11
Rushes-yards	34-141	19-36
Passing	243	161
Punt returns	4-70	1-8
Kickoff returns	2-37	4-118
Interception returns	1-0	0-0
Comp.-att.-int.	28-35-0	15-28-1
Sacked-yards lost	1-9	0-0
Punts	3-41	6-37
Fumbles-lost	3-2	0-0
Penalties-yards	10-99	10-68
Time of possession	37:19	22:41

INDIVIDUAL STATISTICS
RUSHING—Jacksonville, Stewart 24-79, Means 6-50, Brunell 4-12. New Orleans, Bates 16-39, Whittle 3-(minus 3).
PASSING—Jacksonville, Brunell 28-35-0-252. New Orleans, Everett 15-28-1-161.
RECEIVING—Jacksonville, McCardell 8-86, Smith 7-63, Mitchell 4-41, Stewart 4-31, W. Jackson 2-16, Rison 2-12, Brown 1-3. New Orleans, Small 4-59, Whittle 4-37, Lusk 3-32, Haynes 1-10, DeRamus 1-9, Jeffires 1-8, Green 1-6.
MISSED FIELD GOAL ATTEMPTS—Jacksonville, Hollis 48.
INTERCEPTIONS—Jacksonville, Davis 1-0.
KICKOFF RETURNS—Jacksonville, Jordan 2-37. New Orleans, Hughes 3-100, McCleskey 1-18.
PUNT RETURNS—Jacksonville, Hudson 4-70. New Orleans, Hughes 1-8.
SACKS—New Orleans, Turnbull 1.

OILERS 30, BENGALS 27
Sunday, October 6

Houston	3	7	7	10	3—30
Cincinnati	0	13	7	7	0—27

First Quarter
Hou.—FG, Del Greco 40, 11:06.
Second Quarter
Cin.—FG, Pelfrey 42, 1:34.
Hou.—Wycheck 9 pass from Chandler (Del Greco kick), 7:17.
Cin.—Spencer 59 fumble return (Pelfrey kick), 9:44.
Cin.—FG, Pelfrey 31, 14:35.
Third Quarter
Cin.—Cothran 2 run (Pelfrey kick), 5:11.
Hou.—George 45 run (Del Greco kick), 8:01.
Fourth Quarter
Hou.—FG, Del Greco 32, 1:33.
Cin.—Scott 1 pass from Blake (Pelfrey kick), 8:14.
Hou.—Russell 7 pass from Chandler (Del Greco kick), 9:45.
Overtime
Hou.—FG, Del Greco 49, 7:07.
Attendance—44,680.

TEAM STATISTICS
	Houston	Cincinnati
First downs	18	22
Rushes-yards	29-160	36-163
Passing	175	152
Punt returns	4-86	2-11
Kickoff returns	5-177	6-112
Interception returns	0-0	1-19

	Houston	Cincinnati
Comp.-att.-int.	18-32-1	18-37-0
Sacked-yards lost	2-18	4-18
Punts	4-44	7-46
Fumbles-lost	1-1	0-0
Penalties-yards	6-64	5-50
Time of possession	32:00	35:07

INDIVIDUAL STATISTICS

RUSHING—Houston, George 26-152, Harmon 3-8. Cincinnati, Hearst 15-90, Blake 7-35, Bieniemy 7-10, Cothran 5-25, Carter 2-3.

PASSING—Houston, Chandler 18-32-1-193. Cincinnati, Blake 18-37-0-170.

RECEIVING—Houston, Wycheck 7-59, George 3-22, Davis 2-40, Harmon 2-25, Sanders 2-25, Russell 2-22. Cincinnati, Pickens 6-48, Scott 5-56, McGee 4-49, Bieniemy 2-9, Sadowski 1-8.

MISSED FIELD GOAL ATTEMPTS—Cincinnati, Pelfrey 40.

INTERCEPTIONS—Cincinnati, Spencer 1-19.

KICKOFF RETURNS—Houston, Gray 5-177. Cincinnati, Dunn 3-62, Sawyer 2-39, Hill 1-11.

PUNT RETURNS—Houston, Gray 3-86, Floyd 1-0. Cincinnati, Sawyer 2-11.

SACKS—Houston, Cook 1, Roberson 1, Young 1, Walker 1. Cincinnati, McDonald 1, Wilkinson 1.

49ERS 28, RAMS 11

Sunday, October 6

San Francisco	7	14	0	7—28
St. Louis	0	0	3	8—11

First Quarter
S.F.—Popson 1 pass from Grbac (Wilkins kick), 11:01.

Second Quarter
S.F.—Kirby 1 run (Wilkins kick), 8:06.
S.F.—Popson 9 pass from Grbac (Wilkins kick), 9:12.

Third Quarter
St.L.—FG, Lohmiller 28, 9:45.

Fourth Quarter
S.F.—Rice 31 pass from Grbac (Wilkins kick), 1:33.
St.L.—Green 3 pass from Banks (Banks run), 13:20.
Attendance—61,260.

TEAM STATISTICS

	San Francisco	St. Louis
First downs	23	15
Rushes-yards	37-154	20-65
Passing	235	137
Punt returns	3-60	0-0
Kickoff returns	1-18	4-60
Interception returns	2-(-1)	2-14
Comp.-att.-int.	22-36-2	18-33-2
Sacked-yards lost	0-0	5-37
Punts	3-27	4-48
Fumbles-lost	0-0	4-2
Penalties-yards	9-64	8-53
Time of possession	34:02	25:58

INDIVIDUAL STATISTICS

RUSHING—San Francisco, Kirby 13-73, Vardell 8-30, Lynn 7-39, D. Carter 5-0, Brohm 4-12. St. Louis, Phillips 10-26, Green 5-28, Banks 4-9, D. Harris 1-2.

PASSING—San Francisco, Grbac 20-32-2-222, Brohm 2-4-0-13. St. Louis, Banks 18-33-2-174.

RECEIVING—San Francisco, Rice 7-108, Kirby 5-57, Popson 5-44, Lynn 2-14, Vardell 2-5, Se. Manuel 1-7. St. Louis, Green 5-10, Bruce 4-56, Kennison 4-54, Conwell 2-22, Ross 1-20, Laing 1-7, Phillips 1-5.

MISSED FIELD GOAL ATTEMPTS—San Francisco, Wilkins 46.

INTERCEPTIONS—San Francisco, Hanks 2-(minus 1). St. Louis, Lyght 1-14, Lyle 1-0.

KICKOFF RETURNS—San Francisco, Owens 1-18. St. Louis, Kennison 2-34, Phillips 2-26.

PUNT RETURNS—San Francisco, D. Carter 3-60.

SACKS—San Francisco, B. Young 3, Woodall 1, Doleman 1.

BILLS 16, COLTS 13

Sunday, October 6

Indianapolis	0	0	3	10	0—13
Buffalo	0	7	3	3	3—16

Second Quarter
Buf.—Reed 30 pass from Collins (Christie kick), 5:18.

Third Quarter
Buf.—FG, Christie 42, 5:01.
Ind.—FG, Blanchard 44, 7:44.

Fourth Quarter
Ind.—Faulk 1 run (Blanchard kick), :03.
Ind.—FG, Blanchard 41, 6:35.
Buf.—FG, Christie 37, 14:45.

Overtime
Buf.—FG, Christie 39, 9:22.
Attendance—79,401.

TEAM STATISTICS

	Indianapolis	Buffalo
First downs	16	20
Rushes-yards	30-86	34-113
Passing	163	299
Punt returns	4-26	6-56
Kickoff returns	4-75	4-95
Interception returns	0-0	0-0
Comp.-att.-int.	17-42-0	23-44-0
Sacked-yards lost	6-40	3-10
Punts	12-46	11-40
Fumbles-lost	0-0	1-1
Penalties-yards	3-20	13-95
Time of possession	34:32	34:50

INDIVIDUAL STATISTICS

RUSHING—Indianapolis, Faulk 20-55, Groce 4-10, Crockett 3-13, Harbaugh 3-8. Buffalo, T. Thomas 18-69, Holmes 10-31, Collins 3-12, Tindale 2-0, Moulds 1-1.

PASSING—Indianapolis, Harbaugh 17-42-0-203. Buffalo, Collins 23-44-0-309.

RECEIVING—Indianapolis, Harrison 5-88, Faulk 4-8, Dilger 3-53, Bailey 2-34, Crockett 2-4, Dawkins 1-16. Buffalo, T. Thomas 8-111, Moulds 5-56, Early 4-64, Reed 4-58, Johnson 2-20.

MISSED FIELD GOAL ATTEMPTS—Indianapolis, Blanchard 46.

INTERCEPTIONS—None.

KICKOFF RETURNS—Indianapolis, Bailey 2-39, Warren 2-36. Buffalo, Moulds 4-95.

PUNT RETURNS—Indianapolis, Harrison 3-9, Stablein 1-17. Buffalo, Copeland 4-34, Burris 2-22.

SACKS—Indianapolis, Bennett 1, Dent 1, Team 1. Buffalo, Paup 2, Northern 2, B. Smith 1, Washington 1/2, Hansen 1/2.

BRONCOS 28, CHARGERS 17

Sunday, October 6

San Diego	3	14	0	0—17
Denver	0	7	14	7—28

First Quarter
S.D.—FG, Carney 27, 8:20.

Second Quarter
S.D.—Fletcher 5 pass from Humphries (Carney kick), 8:06.
S.D.—Martin 6 pass from Humphries (Carney kick), 12:09.
Den.—Sharpe 20 pass from Elway (Elam kick), 13:41.

Third Quarter
Den.—Sharpe 20 pass from Elway (Elam kick), 6:25.
Den.—Sharpe 3 pass from Elway (Elam kick), 11:57.

Fourth Quarter
Den.—McCaffrey 9 pass from Elway (Elam kick), 6:38.
Attendance—75,058.

TEAM STATISTICS

	San Diego	Denver
First downs	14	23
Rushes-yards	16-35	26-94
Passing	210	312
Punt returns	2-2	5-73
Kickoff returns	4-78	2-65
Interception returns	1-29	0-0
Comp.-att.-int.	24-36-0	32-41-1
Sacked-yards lost	3-27	1-11
Punts	6-57	5-41
Fumbles-lost	3-0	1-0
Penalties-yards	7-61	8-84
Time of possession	24:31	35:29

INDIVIDUAL STATISTICS

RUSHING—San Diego, Russell 11-24, Hayden 3-8, Humphries 1-2, Fletcher 1-1. Denver, Davis 17-50, Elway 8-37, Hebron 1-7.

PASSING—San Diego, Humphries 23-35-0-237, Salisbury 1-1-0-0. Denver, Elway 32-41-1-323.

RECEIVING—San Diego, Fletcher 10-60, Pupunu 5-81, Martin 4-36, Roche 3-21, A. Coleman 2-39. Denver, Sharpe 13-153, Davis 6-42, McCaffrey 5-58, Sherrard 4-45, Chamberlain 2-18, Miller 1-4, Carswell 1-3.

MISSED FIELD GOAL ATTEMPTS—None.

INTERCEPTIONS—San Diego, Harrison 1-29.

KICKOFF RETURNS—San Diego, A. Coleman 4-78. Denver, Hebron 2-65.

PUNT RETURNS—San Diego, Da. Gordon 2-2. Denver, Kinchen 5-73.

SACKS—San Diego, Lee 1. Denver, A. Williams 1, Geathers 1, Tanuvasa 1.

RAIDERS 34, JETS 13

Sunday, October 6

Oakland	0	13	0	21—34
N.Y. Jets	0	3	3	7—13

Second Quarter
Oak.—FG, Ford 26, 1:35.
NYJ—FG, Lowery 43, 3:37.
Oak.—Dudley 23 pass from Hostetler (Ford kick), 8:17.
Oak.—FG, Ford 35, 14:39.

Third Quarter
NYJ—FG, Lowery 24, 4:49.

Fourth Quarter
Oak.—Hobbs 3 pass from Hostetler (Ford kick), :35.
Oak.—Dudley 2 pass from Hostetler (Ford kick), 7:45.
NYJ—Van Dyke 3 pass from Reich (Lowery kick), 11:12.
Oak.—Aska 30 run (Ford kick), 11:40.
Attendance—63,611.

TEAM STATISTICS

	Oakland	N.Y. Jets
First downs	26	20
Rushes-yards	43-222	24-111
Passing	182	171
Punt returns	2-14	1-5
Kickoff returns	3-55	5-85
Interception returns	2-72	1-0
Comp.-att.-int.	17-28-1	18-38-2
Sacked-yards lost	3-6	2-18
Punts	4-37	4-46
Fumbles-lost	0-0	0-0
Penalties-yards	8-89	5-35
Time of possession	35:26	24:34

INDIVIDUAL STATISTICS

RUSHING—Oakland, Aska 21-136, Fenner 12-46, Kaufman 6-34, Hall 3-7, Hobert 1-(minus 1). New York, Murrell 20-102, Anderson 1-5, O'Donnell 1-4, Moore 1-1, Reich 1-(minus 1).

PASSING—Oakland, Hostetler 17-28-1-188. New York, Reich 15-31-2-177, O'Donnell 3-7-0-12.

RECEIVING—Oakland, T. Brown 5-55, Dudley 4-60, Hobbs 2-10, Fenner 2-9, Jett 1-33, A. Glover 1-17, Aska 1-3, Kaufman 1-1. New York, Graham 4-35, Van Dyke 4-31, Bailey 3-42, Chrebet 3-28, Murrell 2-30, Anderson 2-23.

MISSED FIELD GOAL ATTEMPTS—New York, Lowery 45.

INTERCEPTIONS—Oakland, McDaniel 1-43, Lynch 1-29. New York, Glenn 1-0.

KICKOFF RETURNS—Oakland, Kidd 2-50, Shedd 1-5. New York, Bailey 4-72, Moore 1-13.

PUNT RETURNS—Oakland, Hobbs 1-10, T. Brown 1-4. New York, Chrebet 1-5.

SACKS—Oakland, McGlockton 1, Ball 1. New York, R. Hamilton 1½, Washington 1, Houston ½.

PATRIOTS 46, RAVENS 38

Sunday, October 6

New England	3	17	15	11—46
Baltimore	0	14	0	24—38

First Quarter
N.E.—FG, Vinatieri 22, 4:26.

Second Quarter
Bal.—Byner 4 run (Stover kick), 1:25.
N.E.—Jefferson 7 pass from Bledsoe (Vinatieri kick), 4:06.
Bal.—Jackson 5 pass from Testaverde (Stover kick), 9:36.
N.E.—Coates 1 pass from Bledsoe (Vinatieri kick), 11:28.
N.E.—FG, Vinatieri 35, 15:00.

Third Quarter
N.E.—Bartrum 1 pass from Bledsoe (Gash pass from Bledsoe), 3:12.
N.E.—Jefferson 35 pass from Bledsoe (Vinatieri kick), 5:52.

Fourth Quarter
N.E.—FG, Vinatieri 50, :05.
Bal.—Alexander 16 pass from Testaverde (Jackson pass from Testaverde), 2:37.
N.E.—Bruschi 4 blocked punt return (Coates pass from Bledsoe), 7:07.
Bal.—Byner 5 run (Jackson pass from Testaverde), 11:12.
Bal.—Jackson 27 pass from Testaverde (Gardner run), 13:02.
Attendance—63,569.

TEAM STATISTICS

	New England	Baltimore
First downs	26	28
Rushes-yards	23-54	28-133
Passing	310	330
Punt returns	4-48	3-16
Kickoff returns	4-105	7-167
Interception returns	1-0	0-0
Comp.-att.-int.	25-39-0	29-45-1
Sacked-yards lost	0-0	3-23
Punts	4-39	6-36
Fumbles-lost	1-0	1-0
Penalties-yards	8-44	13-146
Time of possession	27:39	32:21

INDIVIDUAL STATISTICS

RUSHING—New England, Martin 19-49, Gash 1-3, Meggett 1-2, Bledsoe 1-1, Glenn 1-(minus 1). Baltimore, Byner 21-86, Gardner 6-50, J. Lewis 1-(minus 3).

PASSING—New England, Bledsoe 25-39-0-310. Baltimore, Testaverde 29-45-1-353.

RECEIVING—New England, Coates 7-83, Glenn 6-88, Jefferson 4-88, Gash 4-26, Martin 2-17, Meggett 1-7, Bartrum 1-1. Baltimore, Jackson 8-128, C. Williams 7-54, Alexander 6-123, Kinchen 5-37, Gardner 2-12, Byner 1-(minus 1).

MISSED FIELD GOAL ATTEMPTS—None.

INTERCEPTIONS—New England, Clay 1-0.

KICKOFF RETURNS—New England, T. Brown 4-105. Baltimore, J. Lewis 6-138, Ethridge 1-29.

PUNT RETURNS—New England, Meggett 4-48. Baltimore, J. Lewis 3-16.

SACKS—New England, Bruschi 2, Ray 1.

VIKINGS 14, PANTHERS 12

Sunday, October 6

Carolina	0	0	9	3—12
Minnesota	0	7	7	0—14

Second Quarter
Min.—Carter 6 pass from Moon (Sisson kick), 2:57.

Third Quarter
Min.—Carter 3 pass from Moon (Sisson kick), 5:15.
Car.—Johnson 4 run (Kasay kick), 12:48.
Car.—Safety, punt blocked out of end zone by M. Bates, 13:57.

Fourth Quarter
Car.—FG, Kasay 22, 8:32.
Attendance—60,894.

TEAM STATISTICS

	Carolina	Minnesota
First downs	15	16
Rushes-yards	28-101	30-101
Passing	155	192
Punt returns	0-0	1-19
Kickoff returns	3-60	2-28
Interception returns	1-8	4-13
Comp.-att.-int.	15-30-4	19-34-1
Sacked-yards lost	1-0	4-17
Punts	4-39	5-32
Fumbles-lost	2-2	2-1
Penalties-yards	5-41	9-72
Time of possession	26:04	33:56

INDIVIDUAL STATISTICS

RUSHING—Carolina, Johnson 23-102, Oliver 3-(minus 1), Collins 1-0, Hoard 1-0. Minnesota, R. Smith 27-102, Moon 3-(minus 1).

PASSING—Carolina, Collins 15-30-4-155. Minnesota, Moon 19-34-1-209.

RECEIVING—Carolina, Walls 6-71, Muhammad 4-34, Carrier 2-28, Griffith 2-16, Oliver 1-6. Minnesota, Carter 7-90, Reed 5-58, Lee 2-12, R. Smith 2-8, Evans 1-16, Ismail 1-16, DeLong 1-9.

MISSED FIELD GOAL ATTEMPTS—Minnesota, Sisson 32.

INTERCEPTIONS—Carolina, Cota 1-8. Minnesota, D. Washington 2-0, Griffith 1-9, Jackson 1-4.

– 144 –

KICKOFF RETURNS—Carolina, Bates 2-44, Oliver 1-16. Minnesota, Lee 1-, Ismail 1-12.
PUNT RETURNS—Minnesota, Palmer 1-19.
SACKS—Carolina, Greene 2, Kragen 1, Lathon ¹/₂, Williams ¹/₂. innesota, F. Smith 1.

LIONS 28, FALCONS 24

Sunday, October 6

| lanta | 0 | 7 | 14 | 3—24 |
| troit | 7 | 21 | 0 | 0—28 |

First Quarter
t.—Mitchell 2 run (Hanson kick), 7:56.
Second Quarter
t.—Perriman 9 pass from Mitchell (Hanson kick), 1:17.
t.—H. Moore 25 pass from Mitchell (Hanson kick), 9:14.
t.—H. Moore 50 pass from Mitchell (Hanson kick), 13:03.
.—Anderson 9 run (Andersen kick), 14:53.
Third Quarter
.—Anderson 5 run (Andersen kick), 9:49.
.—Anderson 14 run (Andersen kick), 15:00.
Fourth Quarter
.—FG, Andersen 47, 9:03.
Attendance—58,666.

TEAM STATISTICS

	Atlanta	Detroit
st downs	19	23
shes-yards	22-116	32-95
ssing	165	262
nt returns	4-62	4-51
koff returns	3-87	4-64
erception returns	0-0	1-0
mp.-att.-int.	18-36-1	20-37-0
cked-yards lost	3-15	2-14
nts	7-46	6-41
mbles-lost	1-0	1-1
nalties-yards	7-75	7-51
ne of possession	27:57	32:03

INDIVIDUAL STATISTICS
RUSHING—Atlanta, Anderson 16-103, Heyward 4-9, Hebert 1-3, Metcalf . Detroit, Sanders 26-86, Mitchell 6-9.
PASSING—Atlanta, Hebert 18-36-1-180. Detroit, Mitchell 20-37-0-276.
RECEIVING—Atlanta, Preston 6-74, Mathis 5-54, Brown 4-28, Scott 2-21, ons 1-3. Detroit, Perriman 7-84, Morton 4-49, H. Moore 3-107, tzelaars 3-23, Sanders 3-13.
MISSED FIELD GOAL ATTEMPTS—None.
INTERCEPTIONS—Detroit, McNeil 1-0.
KICKOFF RETURNS—Atlanta, Metcalf 3-87. Detroit, Milburn 2-42, K. shington 1-14, Rivers 1-8.
PUNT RETURNS—Atlanta, Metcalf 4-62. Detroit, Milburn 4-51.
SACKS—Atlanta, Owens 2. Detroit, Porcher 1¹/₂, Thomas 1¹/₂.

PACKERS 37, BEARS 6

Sunday, October 6

| en Bay | 0 | 20 | 14 | 3—37 |
| icago | 0 | 3 | 3 | 0— 6 |

Second Quarter
.—R. Brooks 18 pass from Favre (Jacke kick), 5:33.
.—FG, Jaeger 40, 12:48.
.—Jackson 2 pass from Favre (Jacke kick), 14:25.
.—Freeman 50 pass from Favre (kick failed), 15:00.
Third Quarter
.—FG, Jaeger 41, 3:43.
.—Beebe 90 kickoff return (Jacke kick), 4:00.
.—Freeman 35 pass from Favre (Jacke kick), 10:53.
Fourth Quarter
.—FG, Jacke 32, 6:28.
Attendance—65,480.

TEAM STATISTICS

	Green Bay	Chicago
st downs	21	15
shes-yards	29-100	27-53

	Green Bay	Chicago
Passing	248	190
Punt returns	2-20	1-0
Kickoff returns	2-113	6-153
Interception returns	3-10	1-(-1)
Comp.-att.-int.	19-28-1	19-32-3
Sacked-yards lost	1-3	1-5
Punts	2-37	3-53
Fumbles-lost	0-0	1-0
Penalties-yards	4-25	7-68
Time of possession	28:49	31:11

INDIVIDUAL STATISTICS
RUSHING—Green Bay, Bennett 12-32, Jervey 6-25, Levens 5-23, Favre 3-15, Henderson 2-4, R. Brooks 1-1. Chicago, Salaam 20-43, Hicks 4-7, Krieg 3-3.
PASSING—Green Bay, Favre 18-27-1-246, McMahon 1-1-0-5. Chicago, Krieg 15-27-3-142, Stenstrom 3-4-0-37, Sauerbrun 1-1-0-16.
RECEIVING—Green Bay, Freeman 7-146, R. Brooks 6-68, Bennett 2-15, Jackson 2-11, Beebe 1-6, Thomason 1-5. Chicago, Conway 9-101, Timpson 4-54, T. Carter 3-8, Engram 2-30, Salaam 1-2.
MISSED FIELD GOAL ATTEMPTS—None.
INTERCEPTIONS—Green Bay, Evans 1-7, Koonce 1-3, Simmons 1-0. Chicago, M. Carter 1-(minus 1).
KICKOFF RETURNS—Green Bay, Beebe 1-90, Henderson 1-23. Chicago, Engram 4-125, Faulkerson 2-28.
PUNT RETURNS—Green Bay, Howard 2-20. Chicago, Engram 1-0.
SACKS—Green Bay, Wilkins 1. Chicago, Smith 1.

STEELERS 17, CHIEFS 7

Monday, October 7

| Pittsburgh | 0 | 6 | 8 | 3—17 |
| Kansas City | 0 | 7 | 0 | 0— 7 |

Second Quarter
K.C.—Allen 6 run (Stoyanovich kick), 7:22.
Pit.—FG, N. Johnson 21, 10:12.
Pit.—FG, N. Johnson 32, 14:29.
Third Quarter
Pit.—Bettis 5 run (Bruener pass from Tomczak), 12:19.
Fourth Quarter
Pit.—FG, N. Johnson 43, 13:50.
Attendance—79,189.

TEAM STATISTICS

	Pittsburgh	Kansas City
First downs	21	17
Rushes-yards	31-106	31-130
Passing	330	170
Punt returns	3-36	0-0
Kickoff returns	2-37	5-96
Interception returns	2-1	1-0
Comp.-att.-int.	20-32-1	18-29-2
Sacked-yards lost	1-8	0-0
Punts	2-43	5-48
Fumbles-lost	2-2	1-1
Penalties-yards	7-33	8-45
Time of possession	30:25	29:35

INDIVIDUAL STATISTICS
RUSHING—Pittsburgh, Bettis 27-103, Stewart 2-(minus 3), Witman 1-7, Tomczak 1-(minus 1). Kansas City, Allen 18-69, Bennett 4-29, Anders 4-21, Hill 4-9, McNair 1-2.
PASSING—Pittsburgh, Tomczak 20-32-1-338. Kansas City, Bono 18-29-2-170.
RECEIVING—Pittsburgh, C. Johnson 6-125, Bettis 5-40, Thigpen 3-56, Hastings 2-50, McAfee 2-10, Stewart 1-31, Arnold 1-26. Kansas City, Penn 7-80, Allen 4-29, Hughes 2-21, Anders 2-16, Vanover 1-24, Cash 1-0, Johnson 1-0.
MISSED FIELD GOAL ATTEMPTS—Pittsburgh, N. Johnson 28. Kansas City, Stoyanovich 43.
INTERCEPTIONS—Pittsburgh, Williams 1-1, Fuller 1-0. Kansas City, D. Carter 1-0.
KICKOFF RETURNS—Pittsburgh, Arnold 1-28, C. Johnson 1-9. Kansas City, Woods 4-73, Vanover 1-23.
PUNT RETURNS—Pittsburgh, Hastings 3-36.
SACKS—Kansas City, Booker ¹/₂, Saleaumua ¹/₂.

1996 REVIEW *Week 6*

RESULTS

CAROLINA 45, St. Louis 13
DALLAS 17, Arizona 3
Houston 23, ATLANTA 13
INDIANAPOLIS 26, Baltimore 21
JACKSONVILLE 21, N.Y. Jets 17
Miami 21, BUFFALO 7
NEW ORLEANS 27, Chicago 24
OAKLAND 37, Detroit 21
Philadelphia 19, N.Y. GIANTS 10
PITTSBURGH 20, Cincinnati 10
TAMPA BAY 24, Minnesota 13
Washington 27, NEW ENGLAND 22
GREEN BAY 23, San Francisco 20 (OT)
  Open date: Denver, Kansas City, San Diego, Seattle

STANDINGS

AFC EAST	W	L	T	Pct.
Indianapolis	5	1	0	.833
Buffalo	4	2	0	.667
Miami	4	2	0	.667
New England	3	3	0	.500
N.Y. Jets	0	7	0	.000

AFC CENTRAL	W	L	T	Pct.
Pittsburgh	5	1	0	.833
Houston	4	2	0	.667
Jacksonville	3	4	0	.429
Baltimore	2	4	0	.333
Cincinnati	1	5	0	.167

AFC WEST	W	L	T	Pct.
Denver	5	1	0	.833
Kansas City	4	2	0	.667
San Diego	4	2	0	.667
Oakland	3	4	0	.429
Seattle	2	4	0	.333

NFC EAST	W	L	T	Pct.
Washington	5	1	0	.833
Philadelphia	4	2	0	.667
Dallas	3	3	0	.500
Arizona	2	4	0	.333
N.Y. Giants	2	4	0	.333

NFC CENTRAL	W	L	T	Pct.
Green Bay	6	1	0	.857
Minnesota	5	2	0	.714
Detroit	4	3	0	.571
Chicago	2	5	0	.286
Tampa Bay	1	5	0	.167

NFC WEST	W	L	T	Pct.
Carolina	4	2	0	.667
San Francisco	4	2	0	.667
New Orleans	2	5	0	.286
St. Louis	1	5	0	.167
Atlanta	0	6	0	.000

HIGHLIGHTS

Hero of the week: Linebacker Chad Brown contributed 4½ sacks, four tackles, seven assists, a forced fumble and an interception in Pittsburgh's 20-10 victory over Cincinnati. It was only the fifth start at outside linebacker for Brown, who was moved from the inside after Greg Lloyd's season-ending knee injury in the opener.

Goat of the week: Jim Kelly's nightmarish season continued with a dismal ending in a 21-7 loss to Miami at Rich Stadium. With Buffalo trailing, 14-7, late in the fourth quarter, Kelly hit Andre Reed for a 49-yard reception to Miami's 2. But Kelly was flagged for intentional grounding on the next play, and on fourth-and-10, his pass for Reed was intercepted by Terrell Buckley, who raced 91 yards for a touchdown with 47 seconds left. Kelly suffered three pickoffs in the game, giving him 11 interceptions and two touchdown passes for the season.

Sub of the week: After Robert Brooks went down with a season-ending knee injury, veteran receiver Don Beebe came off the bench to catch 11 passes for a career-high 220 yards in Green Bay's 23-20 overtime victory over San Francisco. Beebe's disputed 59-yard touchdown reception—replays indicated that Beebe had been touched after making a diving reception at the 49ers' 30 and should not have been able to get up and run to the end zone—in the third quarter started the Packers' comeback from a 17-6 halftime deficit.

Comeback of the week: Beebe wasn't the only player to rally Green Bay from a 17-6 halftime deficit. Brett Favre, who threw a team-record 61 passes and completed 28 for 395 yards, led the team to a game-tying 31-yard field goal by Jacke with eight seconds left. Then, in overtime, Jacke connected on a 53-yard field goal that would have been good from 60. It was Jacke's fifth field goal of the game, matching a career high.

Blowout of the week: Carolina dominated every facet of a 45-13 victory over St. Louis. The Panthers' running game, behind Anthony Johnson's club-record 126 yards, pummeled the Rams; quarterback Kerry Collins threw three touchdown passes, including two to tight end Wesley Walls; the defense held the Rams to 219 net yards; linebacker Kevin Greene returned a fumble 66 yards for a touchdown; and Michael Bates returned a

kickoff 93 yards for a touchdown. The 45 points easily surpassed the franchise's previous best of 29.

Nail-biter of the week: The 49ers had a chance to a but put the Packers away late in regulation whe Marquez Pope intercepted a pass and returned it to th Packers' 13. But rather than go for a touchdown, th 49ers played it conservatively, settling for a 28-yard fie goal by Jeff Wilkins and a 20-17 lead with 1:50 left. The when Niners nickel back Steve Israel committed tw penalties on the ensuing drive, the Packers were set u for Chris Jacke's heroics.

Hit of the week: Indianapolis' Tony Bennett h Baltimore quarterback Vinny Testaverde just as h released the ball, helping cause an interception that Je Herrod returned 68 yards for a touchdown. The pla the longest return for a touchdown by a linebacker i Colts history, gave the team a 26-14 lead early in th fourth quarter and enough cushion to hold off th Ravens, 26-21.

Oddity of the week: When Houston quarterbac Chris Chandler tried to run for a first down late in th first half in Houston's 23-13 victory over Atlanta, h stumbled out of bounds and into Falcons coach Jun Jones. Georgia Dome fans cheered sarcastically a Jones tumbled to the turf on his head and shoulde Jones wasn't hurt, but Chandler limped off with strained groin muscle and didn't return.

Top rusher: New Orleans' Ray Zellars, who had bee suspended the previous week for arguing with coac Jim Mora, rushed for 174 yards in 20 carries and touchdown in the Saints' 27-24 victory over Chicago.

Top passer: Oakland's Jeff Hostetler was 27-of-38 fo 295 yards and four touchdowns, with no interception in the Raiders' 37-21 victory over Detroit. Hostetler als rushed four times for 44 yards, tying Joe Aska for th team lead in the game.

Top receiver: Veteran Henry Ellard, who had caugh only 11 passes in Washington's first five games, collec ed eight receptions for 152 yards and a touchdown i Washington's 27-22 victory over New England. Mos important, Ellard caught three passes for 65 yards o Washington's final time-draining drive that ended in field goal with 56 seconds left.

Notes: The Jets' Nick Lowery 20-yard field goal against Jacksonville was the 374th of his career, moving him past Jan Stenerud and into first place on the all-time list. . . Dallas wide receiver Michael Irvin, back after serving a five-game suspension for drugs, caught five passes for 51 yards in a 17-3 victory over Arizona. . . . With 133½ career sacks, Bruce Smith passed Lawrence Taylor and into second place on the all-time list.

Quote of the week: Running back Thurman Thomas, on Buffalo's 21-7 loss to Miami: "I felt like they were an average football team. The way they played, they made us look like we're an average football team."

GAME SUMMARIES

COLTS 26, RAVENS 21

Sunday, October 13

Baltimore	0	7	7	7—21
Indianapolis	3	10	7	6—26

First Quarter
Ind.—FG, Blanchard 27, 6:57.

Second Quarter
Ind.—Stablein 30 pass from Harbaugh (Blanchard kick), 1:16.
Bal.—Alexander 23 pass from Testaverde (Stover kick), 6:58.
Ind.—FG, Blanchard 30, 11:39.

Third Quarter
Bal.—Alexander 5 pass from Testaverde (Stover kick), 6:45.
Ind.—Faulk 1 run (Blanchard kick), 13:44.

Fourth Quarter
Ind.—Herrod 68 interception return (pass failed), :53.
Bal.—C. Williams 3 pass from Testaverde (Stover kick), 10:51.
Attendance—56,978.

TEAM STATISTICS

	Baltimore	Indianapolis
First downs	20	15
Rushes-yards	23-112	38-123
Passing	213	132
Punt returns	3-25	2-20
Kickoff returns	6-134	4-102
Interception returns	0-0	1-68
Comp.-att.-int.	17-30-1	9-15-0
Sacked-yards lost	2-22	4-23
Punts	5-44	5-44
Fumbles-lost	0-0	0-0
Penalties-yards	6-35	6-48
Time of possession	25:58	34:02

INDIVIDUAL STATISTICS
RUSHING—Baltimore, Byner 19-79, Testaverde 2-27, Gardner 2-6. Indianapolis, Faulk 19-44, Groce 11-55, Harbaugh 6-21, Workman 2-3.
PASSING—Baltimore, Testaverde 17-30-1-235. Indianapolis, Harbaugh 9-15-0-155.
RECEIVING—Baltimore, Alexander 5-96, Jackson 3-46, Byner 3-37, Bishop 2-22, C. Williams 2-7, J. Lewis 1-19, Kinchen 1-8. Indianapolis, Bailey 2-53, Dawkins 2-21, Stablein 1-30, Faulk 1-21, Harrison 1-20, Groce 1-7, Dilger 1-3.
MISSED FIELD GOAL ATTEMPTS—None. Indianapolis, Herrod 1-68.
KICKOFF RETURNS—Baltimore, J. Lewis 5-108, Baldwin 1-26. Indianapolis, Bailey 4-102.
PUNT RETURNS—Baltimore, J. Lewis 3-25. Indianapolis, Harrison 2-20.
SACKS—Baltimore, Goad 2, R. Lewis 1, J. Jones 1. Indianapolis, Siragusa 1, Dent 1.

RAIDERS 37, LIONS 21

Sunday, October 13

Detroit	0	0	21	0—21
Oakland	7	13	14	3—37

First Quarter
Oak.—Jett 4 pass from Hostetler (Ford kick), 8:24.

Second Quarter
Oak.—FG, Ford 29, 1:58.
Oak.—FG, Ford 23, 11:08.
Oak.—Kaufman 10 pass from Hostetler (Ford kick), 14:33.

Third Quarter
Oak.—Jett 58 pass from Hostetler (Ford kick), 1:38.
Oak.—Dudley 62 pass from Hostetler (Ford kick), 5:19.
Det.—H. Moore 11 pass from Mitchell (Hanson kick), 7:09.
Det.—H. Moore 6 pass from Mitchell (Hanson kick), 10:36.
Det.—Morton 19 pass from Mitchell (Hanson kick), 15:00.

Fourth Quarter
Oak.—FG, Ford 32, 13:14.
Attendance—50,037.

TEAM STATISTICS

	Detroit	Oakland
First downs	23	20
Rushes-yards	13-63	29-124
Passing	333	295
Punt returns	3-17	5-17
Kickoff returns	5-119	4-93
Interception returns	0-0	2-27
Comp.-att.-int.	31-50-2	27-38-0
Sacked-yards lost	2-10	0-0
Punts	5-40	5-38
Fumbles-lost	1-0	3-0
Penalties-yards	6-45	8-64
Time of possession	23:45	36:15

INDIVIDUAL STATISTICS
RUSHING—Detroit, Sanders 9-36, Mitchell 3-11, Rivers 1-16. Oakland, Aska 16-44, Kaufman 7-21, Hostetler 4-44, T. Brown 2-15.
PASSING—Detroit, Mitchell 31-50-2-343. Oakland, Hostetler 27-38-0-295.
RECEIVING—Detroit, H. Moore 10-109, Morton 8-109, Perriman 7-75, Metzelaars 3-15, Sanders 2-16, Rivers 1-19. Oakland, Jett 7-112, T. Brown 4-41, Hobbs 4-33, Davison 4-21, Kaufman 3-14, Aska 3-5, Dudley 2-69.
MISSED FIELD GOAL ATTEMPTS—None.
INTERCEPTIONS—Oakland, Trapp 1-23, L. Brown 1-4.
KICKOFF RETURNS—Detroit, Milburn 5-119. Oakland, Kidd 3-77, Shedd 1-16.
PUNT RETURNS—Detroit, Milburn 3-17. Oakland, Hobbs 5-17.
SACKS—Oakland, Bruce 1, Johnstone 1.

JAGUARS 21, JETS 17

Sunday, October 13

N.Y. Jets	7	7	0	3—17
Jacksonville	3	11	7	0—21

First Quarter
Jac.—FG, Hollis 35, 1:35.
NYJ—Murrell 14 pass from Reich (Lowery kick), 8:17.

Second Quarter
NYJ—Chrebet 12 pass from Reich (Lowery kick), :08.
Jac.—FG, Hollis 40, 7:33.
Jac.—Smith 15 pass from Brunell (McCardell pass from Brunell), 13:09.

Third Quarter
Jac.—W. Jackson 41 pass from Brunell (Hollis kick), 8:41.

Fourth Quarter
NYJ—FG, Lowery 20, 4:01.
Attendance—65,699.

TEAM STATISTICS

	N.Y. Jets	Jacksonville
First downs	24	10
Rushes-yards	30-91	23-72
Passing	276	217
Punt returns	5-43	2-7
Kickoff returns	5-111	4-134
Interception returns	0-0	2-12
Comp.-att.-int.	23-44-2	14-23-0
Sacked-yards lost	0-0	5-31
Punts	4-49	7-39
Fumbles-lost	1-0	2-0
Penalties-yards	3-25	15-123
Time of possession	33:03	26:57

INDIVIDUAL STATISTICS
RUSHING—New York, Murrell 21-49, Anderson 7-38, Reich 1-8, Bailey 1-(minus 4). Jacksonville, Stewart 12-55, Means 6-14, Brunell 2-3.
PASSING—New York, Reich 23-43-2-276, Foley 0-1-0-0. Jacksonville, Brunell 14-23-0-248.
RECEIVING—New York, Chrebet 12-162, Van Dyke 4-28, Anderson 3-24, Bailey 2-23, Brady 1-25, Murrell 1-14. Jacksonville, Smith 5-135, McCardell 4-38, Stewart 2-9, W. Jackson 1-41, Mitchell 1-17, Means 1-8.
MISSED FIELD GOAL ATTEMPTS—New York, Lowery 36.
INTERCEPTIONS—Jacksonville, Hardy 1-13, Thomas 1-(minus 1).
KICKOFF RETURNS—New York, Bailey 5-111. Jacksonville, Jordan 3-119, W. Jackson 1-15.

PUNT RETURNS—New York, Chrebet 5-43. Jacksonville, Hudson 1-6, Thomas 1-1.

SACKS—New York, B. Hamilton 2, Brock 1, Washington 1, Cascadden 1.

BUCCANEERS 24, VIKINGS 13

Sunday, October 13

Minnesota	7	0	3	3—13
Tampa Bay	0	0	7	17—24

First Quarter
Min.—R. Smith 26 run (Sisson kick), 14:31.
Third Quarter
T.B.—R. Thomas 31 pass from Dilfer (Husted kick), 8:31.
Min.—FG, Sisson 33, 11:35.
Fourth Quarter
T.B.—Alstott 12 pass from Dilfer (Husted kick), 1:06.
T.B.—R. Thomas 11 pass from Dilfer (Husted kick), 5:41.
Min.—FG, Sisson 32, 11:22.
T.B.—FG, Husted 35, 14:17.
Attendance—32,175.

TEAM STATISTICS

	Minnesota	Tampa Bay
First downs	17	20
Rushes-yards	21-139	31-76
Passing	255	208
Punt returns	3-5	1-11
Kickoff returns	3-57	2-42
Interception returns	0-0	1-24
Comp.-att.-int.	22-34-1	22-35-0
Sacked-yards lost	3-22	1-10
Punts	3-48	6-45
Fumbles-lost	3-2	0-0
Penalties-yards	8-92	3-30
Time of possession	28:29	31:31

INDIVIDUAL STATISTICS

RUSHING—Minnesota, R. Smith 18-133, Lee 1-7, Evans 1-0, Moon 1-(minus 1). Tampa Bay, R. Brooks 20-45, Alstott 8-16, Ellison 2-7, Dilfer 1-8.

PASSING—Minnesota, Moon 22-34-1-277. Tampa Bay, Dilfer 22-35-0-218.

RECEIVING—Minnesota, Reed 5-89, Lee 5-32, Ismail 2-48, Walsh 2-15, Palmer 1-4, DeLong 1-3. Tampa Bay, R. Thomas 5-73, Harris 5-38, Hawkins 5-33, Alstott 3-33, Harper 2-22, Ellison 2-19.

MISSED FIELD GOAL ATTEMPTS—Minnesota, Sisson 44. Tampa Bay, Husted 31.

INTERCEPTIONS—Tampa Bay, M. Johnson 1-24.

KICKOFF RETURNS—Minnesota, Palmer 1-20, Ismail 1-20, Lee 1-17. Tampa Bay, Silvan 2-42.

PUNT RETURNS—Minnesota, Palmer 3-5. Tampa Bay, Silvan 1-11.

SACKS—Minnesota, Edwards 1. Tampa Bay, Sapp 1½, Ahanotu 1, Upshaw ½.

STEELERS 20, BENGALS 10

Sunday, October 13

Cincinnati	0	0	3	7—10
Pittsburgh	3	0	7	10—20

First Quarter
Pit.—FG, N. Johnson 33, 6:05.
Third Quarter
Cin.—FG, Pelfrey 19, 7:57.
Pit.—Stewart 32 pass from Tomczak (N. Johnson kick), 9:57.
Fourth Quarter
Pit.—FG, N. Johnson 22, 3:25.
Pit.—Woodson 42 fumble return (N. Johnson kick), 11:31.
Cin.—Pickens 3 pass from Blake (Pelfrey kick), 13:40.
Attendance—58,875.

TEAM STATISTICS

	Cincinnati	Pittsburgh
First downs	20	17
Rushes-yards	23-94	32-124
Passing	163	182
Punt returns	2-5	4-32
Kickoff returns	4-75	3-55
Interception returns	2-0	1-4
Comp.-att.-int.	23-30-1	14-28-2
Sacked-yards lost	10-66	0-0
Punts	6-48	4-43
Fumbles-lost	2-1	1-0
Penalties-yards	7-58	4-27
Time of possession	32:41	27:19

INDIVIDUAL STATISTICS

RUSHING—Cincinnati, Hearst 14-51, Blake 4-14, Bieniemy 3-16, Carter 2-13. Pittsburgh, Bettis 28-109, Pegram 2-13, Tomczak 2-2.

PASSING—Cincinnati, Blake 23-30-1-229. Pittsburgh, Tomczak 14-28-2-182.

RECEIVING—Cincinnati, Pickens 9-81, Scott 6-59, McGee 3-37, Bieniemy 2-29, Cothran 2-17, Dunn 1-6. Pittsburgh, Hastings 7-85, Pegram 3-19, C. Johnson 2-47, Stewart 2-31.

MISSED FIELD GOAL ATTEMPTS—None.

INTERCEPTIONS—Cincinnati, Ambrose 1-0, Sawyer 1-0. Pittsburgh, Brown 1-4.

KICKOFF RETURNS—Cincinnati, Sawyer 3-61, Dunn 1-14. Pittsburgh, Arnold 2-47, Perry 1-8.

PUNT RETURNS—Cincinnati, Sawyer 2-5. Pittsburgh, Hastings 3-29, Jones 1-3.

SACKS—Pittsburgh, Brown 4½, Kirkland 2, Gildon 1, Emmons 1, Gibson 1, B. Johnson ½.

COWBOYS 17, CARDINALS 3

Sunday, October 13

Arizona	0	0	0	3— 3
Dallas	0	3	7	7—17

Second Quarter
Dal.—FG, Boniol 23, 14:55.
Third Quarter
Dal.—E. Smith 1 run (Boniol kick), 13:31.
Fourth Quarter
Ariz.—FG, G. Davis 49, 9:11.
Dal.—E. Smith 13 run (Boniol kick), 12:57.
Attendance—64,096.

TEAM STATISTICS

	Arizona	Dallas
First downs	13	22
Rushes-yards	22-58	29-125
Passing	120	199
Punt returns	3-18	3-42
Kickoff returns	4-66	2-54
Interception returns	1-0	1-0
Comp.-att.-int.	16-31-1	23-37-1
Sacked-yards lost	3-21	0-0
Punts	7-43	5-40
Fumbles-lost	0-0	0-0
Penalties-yards	2-20	3-28
Time of possession	27:05	32:55

INDIVIDUAL STATISTICS

RUSHING—Arizona, L. Johnson 14-21, Centers 5-24, K. Graham 3-13. Dallas, E. Smith 21-112, S. Williams 3-9, Johnston 3-6, Aikman 2-(minus 2).

PASSING—Arizona, K. Graham 16-31-1-141. Dallas, Aikman 23-37-1-199.

RECEIVING—Arizona, Centers 8-40, R. Moore 3-45, Carter 3-39, Sanders 2-17. Dallas, Irvin 5-51, Bjornson 5-49, Sanders 4-42, E. Smith 4-10, Johnston 3-17, Martin 1-25, Walker 1-5.

MISSED FIELD GOAL ATTEMPTS—None.

INTERCEPTIONS—Arizona, Williams 1-0. Dallas, K. Smith 1-0.

KICKOFF RETURNS—Arizona, McElroy 4-66. Dallas, Walker 1-28, Marion 1-26.

PUNT RETURNS—Arizona, Dowdell 3-18. Dallas, Martin 3-42.

SACKS—Dallas, Tolbert 2, Thomas 1.

EAGLES 19, GIANTS 10

Sunday, October 13

Philadelphia	0	3	3	13—19
N.Y. Giants	3	7	0	0—10

First Quarter
NYG—FG, Daluiso 39, 8:52.
Second Quarter
Phi.—FG, Anderson 39, 3:19.
NYG—Toomer 65 punt return (Daluiso kick), 8:18.
Third Quarter
Phi.—FG, Anderson 46, 11:33.
Fourth Quarter
Phi.—FG, Anderson 45, :59.
Phi.—FG, Anderson 29, 12:48.
Phi.—W. Thomas 23 fumble return (Anderson kick), 13:09.
Attendance—72,729.

TEAM STATISTICS

	Philadelphia	N.Y. Giants
First downs	17	9
Rushes-yards	35-140	23-87
Passing	164	63

	Philadelphia	N.Y. Giants
Punt returns	3-31	5-96
Kickoff returns	2-42	5-79
Interception returns	1-0	0-0
Comp.-att.-int.	18-33-0	11-25-1
Sacked-yards lost	1-6	8-42
Punts	7-44	9-44
Fumbles-lost	1-0	2-1
Penalties-yards	5-39	6-40
Time of possession	33:22	26:38

INDIVIDUAL STATISTICS

RUSHING—Philadelphia, Watters 27-110, Detmer 4-14, Garner 2-16, Turner 2-0. New York, Hampton 17-60, Brown 3-16, Wheatley 3-11.

PASSING—Philadelphia, Detmer 18-33-0-170. New York, Brown 11-25-1-105.

RECEIVING—Philadelphia, Fryar 6-73, Jones 4-54, Seay 2-23, Watters 2-8, Turner 2-5, Dunn 1-7. New York, Calloway 3-44, Lewis 3-32, Wheatley 3-23, Way 2-6.

MISSED FIELD GOAL ATTEMPTS—None.

INTERCEPTIONS—Philadelphia, Taylor 1-0.

KICKOFF RETURNS—Philadelphia, Witherspoon 2-42. New York, Wheatley 2-45, Toomer 1-12, Saxton 1-12, Way 1-10.

PUNT RETURNS—Philadelphia, Seay 3-31. New York, Toomer 5-96.

SACKS—Philadelphia, Mamula 2$\frac{1}{2}$, W. Fuller 2, W. Thomas 1$\frac{1}{2}$, Hall 1$\frac{1}{2}$, Griffin $\frac{1}{2}$. New York, Strahan $\frac{1}{2}$, Bratzke $\frac{1}{2}$.

REDSKINS 27, PATRIOTS 22

Sunday, October 13

Washington	3	7	14	3—27
New England	6	10	0	6—22

First Quarter
N.E.—FG, Vinatieri 24, 7:14.
Was.—FG, Blanton 21, 12:25.
N.E.—FG, Vinatieri 35, 14:42.

Second Quarter
Was.—Shepherd 32 run (Blanton kick), 1:56.
N.E.—Martin 3 run (Vinatieri kick), 4:19.
N.E.—FG, Vinatieri 29, 10:52.

Third Quarter
Was.—Asher 13 pass from Frerotte (Blanton kick), 4:32.
Was.—Ellard 13 pass from Frerotte (Blanton kick), 8:42.

Fourth Quarter
N.E.—Martin 2 run (run failed), 9:27.
Was.—FG, Blanton 24, 14:04.
Attendance—59,638.

TEAM STATISTICS
	Washington	New England
First downs	22	23
Rushes-yards	32-108	23-177
Passing	276	205
Punt returns	1-11	4-23
Kickoff returns	5-106	5-100
Interception returns	1-16	0-0
Comp.-att.-int.	18-34-0	23-48-1
Sacked-yards lost	1-4	2-17
Punts	5-44	2-47
Fumbles-lost	1-0	2-0
Penalties-yards	10-99	4-24
Time of possession	29:25	30:35

INDIVIDUAL STATISTICS

RUSHING—Washington, Allen 26-71, Mitchell 3-7, Shepherd 2-31, Frerotte 1-(minus 1). New England, Martin 17-164, Meggett 2-5, Bledsoe 2-, Glenn 1-5, Gash 1-2.

PASSING—Washington, Frerotte 18-33-0-280, Mitchell 0-1-0-0. New England, Bledsoe 23-48-1-222.

RECEIVING—Washington, Ellard 8-152, Logan 4-63, Asher 3-37, Shepherd 2-18, Allen 1-10. New England, Glenn 7-84, Coates 5-34, Jefferson 4-69, Meggett 3-21, Gash 2-11, T. Brown 1-9, Martin 1-(minus 6).

MISSED FIELD GOAL ATTEMPTS—Washington, Blanton 48. New England, Vinatieri 43.

INTERCEPTIONS—Washington, D. Green 1-16.

KICKOFF RETURNS—Washington, Mitchell 4-86, W. Bell 1-20. New England, Meggett 3-59, T. Brown 2-41.

PUNT RETURNS—Washington, Mitchell 1-11. New England, Meggett 4-23.

SACKS—Washington, Harvey 1, Owens 1. New England, McGinest 1.

SAINTS 27, BEARS 24

Sunday, October 13

Chicago	3	14	7	0—24
New Orleans	0	7	10	10—27

First Quarter
Chi.—FG, Jaeger 28, 11:59.

Second Quarter
Chi.—Conway 18 pass from Krieg (Jaeger kick), 3:33.
N.O.—DeRamus 28 pass from Everett (Brien kick), 7:47.
Chi.—Spears 1 pass from Krieg (Jaeger kick), 14:37.

Third Quarter
N.O.—FG, Brien 34, 4:06.
N.O.—Haynes 5 pass from Everett (Brien kick), 7:56.
Chi.—Conway 53 pass from Krieg (Jaeger kick), 9:33.

Fourth Quarter
N.O.—Zellars 3 run (Brien kick), 4:48.
N.O.—FG, Brien 54, 13:16.
Attendance—43,512.

TEAM STATISTICS
	Chicago	New Orleans
First downs	18	23
Rushes-yards	28-105	34-205
Passing	222	218
Punt returns	1-1	3-28
Kickoff returns	4-99	4-117
Interception returns	1-0	0-0
Comp.-att.-int.	19-28-0	22-31-1
Sacked-yards lost	2-25	1-5
Punts	5-44	1-43
Fumbles-lost	2-1	5-3
Penalties-yards	7-43	6-35
Time of possession	28:29	31:31

INDIVIDUAL STATISTICS

RUSHING—Chicago, Salaam 14-40, Hicks 7-28, T. Carter 6-37, Conway 1-0. New Orleans, Zellars 20-174, Neal 4-16, Everett 4-2, Bates 4-1, Whittle 2-12.

PASSING—Chicago, Krieg 19-28-0-247. New Orleans, Everett 22-31-1-223.

RECEIVING—Chicago, Conway 7-111, Timpson 5-52, Wetnight 2-48, T. Carter 2-12, Engram 1-22, Salaam 1-1, Spears 1-1. New Orleans, Small 6-59, I. Smith 4-48, Haynes 4-39, Lusk 2-19, Jeffires 2-18, Whittle 2-4, DeRamus 1-28, Zellars 1-8.

MISSED FIELD GOAL ATTEMPTS—Chicago, Jaeger 32.

INTERCEPTIONS—Chicago, Marshall 1-0.

KICKOFF RETURNS—Chicago, Engram 4-99. New Orleans, Hughes 4-117.

PUNT RETURNS—Chicago, Engram 1-1. New Orleans, Hughes 3-28.

SACKS—Chicago, Spellman 1. New Orleans, Harvey 1, Stokes 1.

DOLPHINS 21, BILLS 7

Sunday, October 13

Miami	0	7	7	7—21
Buffalo	0	0	7	0— 7

Second Quarter
Mia.—Abdul-Jabbar 3 run (Nedney kick), 5:00.

Third Quarter
Mia.—Spikes 1 run (Nedney kick), 10:46.
Buf.—T. Thomas 19 run (Christie kick), 14:12.

Fourth Quarter
Mia.—Buckley 91 interception return (Nedney kick), 14:13.
Attendance—79,642.

TEAM STATISTICS
	Miami	Buffalo
First downs	15	17
Rushes-yards	32-63	25-105
Passing	176	191
Punt returns	1-0	3-28
Kickoff returns	2-39	4-94
Interception returns	3-102	0-0
Comp.-att.-int.	14-29-0	21-32-3
Sacked-yards lost	3-16	7-56
Punts	8-48	7-47
Fumbles-lost	1-0	1-1
Penalties-yards	4-20	8-48
Time of possession	30:51	29:09

INDIVIDUAL STATISTICS

RUSHING—Miami, Abdul-Jabbar 25-37, Spikes 3-6, Pritchett 1-16, Kidd 1-3, Erickson 1-1, McDuffie 1-0. Buffalo, T. Thomas 16-85, Holmes 8-17, Early 1-3.

PASSING—Miami, Erickson 14-29-0-192. Buffalo, Kelly 21-32-3-247.

RECEIVING—Miami, R. Hill 4-94, Abdul-Jabbar 3-30, Drayton 3-27, McDuffie 2-26, McPhail 2-15. Buffalo, Reed 10-134, Early 3-52, Holmes 2-23, Moulds 2-1, Johnson 2-14, Copeland 1-4, T. Thomas 1-3.

MISSED FIELD GOAL ATTEMPTS—Miami, Nedney 33.

INTERCEPTIONS—Miami, Buckley 1-91, Z. Thomas 1-11, Jackson 1-0.

KICKOFF RETURNS—Miami, McPhail 2-39. Buffalo, Moulds 4-94.

PUNT RETURNS—Miami, McDuffie 1-0. Buffalo, Copeland 3-28.

SACKS—Miami, Armstrong 2½, Bowens 2, Z. Thomas 1, Stubbs 1, Hand ½. Buffalo, B. Smith 1, Paup 1, Jeffcoat 1.

PANTHERS 45, RAMS 13

Sunday, October 13

St. Louis	0	13	0	0—13
Carolina	14	14	10	7—45

First Quarter
Car.—Walls 9 pass from Collins (Kasay kick), 6:07.
Car.—Greene 66 fumble return (Kasay kick), 13:42.

Second Quarter
Car.—Muhammad 54 pass from Collins (Kasay kick), 8:56.
St.L.—Parker 22 interception return (Lohmiller kick), 12:35.
Car.—Bates 93 kickoff return (Kasay kick), 13:01.
St.L.—Kennison 12 pass from Banks (kick failed), 14:03.

Third Quarter
Car.—FG, Kasay 22, 10:08.
Car.—Walls 19 pass from Collins (Kasay kick), 14:51.

Fourth Quarter
Car.—Philyaw 2 run (Kasay kick), 11:04.
Attendance—70,535.

TEAM STATISTICS

	St. Louis	Carolina
First downs	15	21
Rushes-yards	20-78	42-184
Passing	141	177
Punt returns	0-0	6-80
Kickoff returns	7-144	3-135
Interception returns	1-22	2-52
Comp.-att.-int.	19-36-2	11-18-1
Sacked-yards lost	5-52	2-19
Punts	7-44	1-46
Fumbles-lost	3-1	0-0
Penalties-yards	3-35	3-15
Time of possession	26:17	33:43

INDIVIDUAL STATISTICS

RUSHING—St. Louis, Phillips 13-54, Robinson 2-12, Banks 2-8, Green 2-2, Martin 1-2. Carolina, Johnson 22-126, Philyaw 9-22, Oliver 5-6, Hoard 4-11, Ismail 1-17, Collins 1-2.

PASSING—St. Louis, Banks 15-29-1-163, Martin 4-7-1-30. Carolina, Collins 11-18-1-196.

RECEIVING—St. Louis, Kennison 8-93, Green 4-6, Bruce 3-34, Conwell 2-24, Ross 1-28, D. Harris 1-8. Carolina, Walls 5-68, Griffith 2-31, Johnson 2-14, Muhammad 1-54, Oliver 1-29.

MISSED FIELD GOAL ATTEMPTS—Carolina, Kasay 50, 51.

INTERCEPTIONS—St. Louis, Parker 1-22. Carolina, Lofton 1-42, Mills 1-10.

KICKOFF RETURNS—St. Louis, Thomas 4-79, Kennison 3-65. Carolina, Bates 1-93, Oliver 1-23, Hoard 1-19.

PUNT RETURNS—Carolina, Oliver 6-80.

SACKS—St. Louis, O'Neal 1, Farr 1. Carolina, Greene 2, Lathon 1, King 1, Thomas 1.

OILERS 23, FALCONS 13

Sunday, October 13

Houston	7	3	7	6—23
Atlanta	0	0	0	13—13

First Quarter
Hou.—Sanders 62 pass from Chandler (Del Greco kick), 14:04.

Second Quarter
Hou.—FG, Del Greco 27, 5:14.

Third Quarter
Hou.—McNair 10 run (Del Greco kick), 8:33.

Fourth Quarter
Hou.—FG, Del Greco 35, :07.
Atl.—Mathis 3 pass from Hebert (Andersen kick), 4:33.
Hou.—FG, Del Greco 33, 7:43.
Atl.—Mathis 1 pass from Hebert (pass failed), 13:04.
Attendance—35,401.

TEAM STATISTICS

	Houston	Atlanta
First downs	16	20
Rushes-yards	27-121	16-55
Passing	199	268
Punt returns	1-0	0-0
Kickoff returns	1-18	6-120
Interception returns	2-55	0-0
Comp.-att.-int.	14-23-0	31-46-2
Sacked-yards lost	2-5	1-11
Punts	3-45	6-31
Fumbles-lost	2-1	1-0
Penalties-yards	6-44	7-50
Time of possession	30:07	29:53

INDIVIDUAL STATISTICS

RUSHING—Houston, George 23-109, McNair 2-9, Chandler 2-3. Atlanta, Anderson 13-45, Heyward 2-8, Hebert 1-2.

PASSING—Houston, Chandler 9-13-0-146, McNair 5-10-0-58. Atlanta, Hebert 31-46-2-279.

RECEIVING—Houston, Sanders 4-100, Wycheck 4-42, Davis 3-25, Russell 2-23, George 1-14. Atlanta, Preston 9-69, Mathis 6-36, Brown 4-65, Scott 4-32, Anderson 3-53, Heyward 3-14, Metcalf 2-10.

MISSED FIELD GOAL ATTEMPTS—Houston, Del Greco 51.

INTERCEPTIONS—Houston, D. Lewis 1-53, Robinson 1-2.

KICKOFF RETURNS—Houston, Harmon 1-18. Atlanta, Metcalf 6-120.

PUNT RETURNS—Houston, Gray 1-0.

SACKS—Houston, Barrow 1. Atlanta, Bennett 1, Smith 1.

PACKERS 23, 49ERS 20

Monday, October 14

San Francisco	0	17	0	3	0—20
Green Bay	6	0	8	6	3—23

First Quarter
G.B.—FG, Jacke 30, 9:37.
G.B.—FG, Jacke 25, 12:02.

Second Quarter
S.F.—FG, Wilkins 48, 7:45.
S.F.—Rice 7 pass from Grbac (Wilkins kick), 12:40.
S.F.—Rice 13 pass from Grbac (Wilkins kick), 14:37.

Third Quarter
G.B.—Beebe 59 pass from Favre (Bennett pass from Favre), 7:46.

Fourth Quarter
G.B.—FG, Jacke 35, 11:25.
S.F.—FG, Wilkins 28, 13:10.
G.B.—FG, Jacke 31, 14:52.

Overtime
G.B.—FG, Jacke 53, 3:41.
Attendance—60,716.

TEAM STATISTICS

	San Francisco	Green Bay
First downs	14	24
Rushes-yards	28-74	26-68
Passing	179	378
Punt returns	1-12	6-28
Kickoff returns	7-149	5-94
Interception returns	2-27	2-0
Comp.-att.-int.	21-39-2	28-61-2
Sacked-yards lost	1-3	2-17
Punts	9-42	6-40
Fumbles-lost	0-0	1-0
Penalties-yards	9-65	2-24
Time of possession	28:57	34:44

INDIVIDUAL STATISTICS

RUSHING—San Francisco, Kirby 10-27, Vardell 8-31, Grbac 4-1, Lynn 3-11, Loville 3-4. Green Bay, Levens 10-16, Bennett 7-18, Favre 6-24, Henderson 3-10.

PASSING—San Francisco, Grbac 21-39-2-182. Green Bay, Favre 28-61-2-395.

RECEIVING—San Francisco, Rice 7-84, Vardell 6-44, Kirby 4-15, Popson 3-39, Loville 1-0. Green Bay, Beebe 11-220, Freeman 6-71, Howard 4-30, Jackson 2-53, Henderson 2-12, Mayes 1-5, Bennett 1-3, Levens 1-1.

MISSED FIELD GOAL ATTEMPTS—None.

INTERCEPTIONS—San Francisco, Stubblefield 1-15, Pope 1-12. Green Bay, Butler 1-0, Robinson 1-0.

KICKOFF RETURNS—San Francisco, D. Carter 6-141, Deese 1-8. Green Bay, Levens 4-75, Beebe 1-19.

PUNT RETURNS—San Francisco, D. Carter 1-12. Green Bay, Howard 6-28.

SACKS—San Francisco, Woodall 1, Barker 1. Green Bay, White 1.

WEEK 8

RESULTS

KANSAS CITY 34, Seattle 16
ARIZONA 13, Tampa Bay 9
Buffalo 25, N.Y. JETS 22
CAROLINA 19, New Orleans 7
DALLAS 32, Atlanta 28
DENVER 45, Baltimore 34
HOUSTON 23, Pittsburgh 13
New England 27, INDIANAPOLIS 9
PHILADELPHIA 35, Miami 28
ST. LOUIS 17, Jacksonville 14
SAN FRANCISCO 28, Cincinnati 21
WASHINGTON 31, N.Y. Giants 21
Oakland 23, SAN DIEGO 14
 Open date: Chicago, Detroit, Green Bay,
Minnesota

STANDINGS

AFC EAST

	W	L	T	Pct.
Buffalo	5	2	0	.714
Indianapolis	5	2	0	.714
Miami	4	3	0	.571
New England	4	3	0	.571
N.Y. Jets	0	8	0	.000

NFC EAST

	W	L	T	Pct.
Washington	6	1	0	.857
Philadelphia	5	2	0	.714
Dallas	4	3	0	.571
Arizona	3	4	0	.429
N.Y. Giants	2	5	0	.286

AFC CENTRAL

	W	L	T	Pct.
Houston	5	2	0	.714
Pittsburgh	5	2	0	.714
Jacksonville	3	5	0	.375
Baltimore	2	5	0	.286
Cincinnati	1	6	0	.143

NFC CENTRAL

	W	L	T	Pct.
Green Bay	6	1	0	.857
Minnesota	5	2	0	.714
Detroit	4	3	0	.571
Chicago	2	5	0	.286
Tampa Bay	1	6	0	.143

AFC WEST

	W	L	T	Pct.
Denver	6	1	0	.857
Kansas City	5	2	0	.714
San Diego	4	3	0	.571
Oakland	4	4	0	.500
Seattle	2	5	0	.286

NFC WEST

	W	L	T	Pct.
Carolina	5	2	0	.714
San Francisco	5	2	0	.714
St. Louis	2	5	0	.286
New Orleans	2	6	0	.250
Atlanta	0	7	0	.000

HIGHLIGHTS

Hero of the week: Philadelphia wide receiver Irving Fryar—spurned by new Miami coach Jimmy Johnson, who chose not to re-sign the veteran—burned his old team by catching four touchdown passes in the Eagles' 35-28 victory. Johnson didn't want to discuss Fryar's performance, saying only, "He just got behind us." Fryar tied an Eagles record with his four touchdown receptions.

Goat of the week: Jacksonville's Mark Brunell, who threw only eight interceptions in the first seven games, suffered five pickoffs in the Jaguars' 17-14 loss to St. Louis. Brunell threw for 421 yards and moved the Jaguars almost at will through much of the game, but all five of his interceptions occurred deep in Rams territory.

Sub of the week: Tight end Ted Popson, starting for the injured Brent Jones, caught eight passes for 116 yards and two touchdowns in San Francisco's 28-21 victory over Cincinnati. After the 49ers fell behind, 21-0, Popson helped jump-start the comeback by catching touchdown passes of 17 and 39 yards.

Comeback of the week: A hobbled Steve Young was the catalyst for the 49ers' rally from a 21-0 deficit against Cincinnati. Young, whose groin injury rendered him so ineffective early in the game that he was replaced by Elvis Grbac, was forced to return after Grbac was injured just before halftime. Young threw two touchdown passes in the second half, including a game-tying 5-yard pass to Terrell Owens with 2:08 left, then jumped into the end zone on a 15-yard run for the winning points with 1:08 left.

Blowout of the week: In a convincing 34-16 victory, Kansas City rung up Seattle for the 11th time in 12 games. The Chiefs battered the Seahawks for 27 first downs and 340 total yards while holding onto the ball for 35 minutes, 13 seconds.

Nail-biter of the week: Dallas was almost shot down by the run-and-shoot, but the Cowboys were rescued by a 60-yard touchdown catch by Kelvin Martin with 1:42 remaining to secure a 32-28 victory over winless Atlanta.

Hit of the week: With less than five minutes remaining and Houston leading, 16-13, Oilers defensive lineman Gary Walker stripped the ball from Pittsburgh quarterback Mike Tomczak and the Oilers recovered at the Steelers' 5. That set up a clinching 2-yard touchdown run by Eddie George in the Oilers' 23-13 victory.

Oddity of the week: How about these numbers? Jacksonville outgained St. Louis 538 yards to 204, had 36 first downs to the Rams' eight and controlled the ball 41 minutes, 34 seconds. As shockingly dominant as the second-year expansion team was, the Jaguars' ability to squander it all in a 17-14 loss was even more stunning.

Top rusher: Terrell Davis rushed 28 times for a club-record 194 yards and two touchdowns (71, 4) in Denver's 45-34 victory over Baltimore.

Top passer: Vinny Testaverde was 27-of-45 for 338 yards and four touchdowns, with one interception, in the Ravens' loss to Denver.

Top receiver: Jacksonville's Keenan McCardell beat St. Louis on slants all day, catching 16 passes for 232 yards, in the Jaguars' loss.

Notes: With his 92-yard interception return for a touchdown, St. Louis cornerback Anthony Parker tied Deion Sanders for the most touchdown returns (seven) by interception or fumble recovery. . . . With his 100th career victory, San Francisco's George Seifert replaced Vince Lombardi as the coach to reach that milestone the fastest. Lombardi needed 136 games; Seifert took 132. . . . Jerry Rice became the first receiver in history with 11 50 catch-seasons. . . . Steve Christie made a career- and team-record six field goals in the Bills' 25-22 victory over the Jets. . . . With 97 yards against the Jets, Thurman Thomas supplanted O.J. Simpson as the franchise's career rushing leader. Simpson had 10,183 yards from 1969 to 1977. . . . When John Elway drove the Broncos to a go-ahead touchdown against the Ravens, it marked his 39th fourth-quarter saving drive and his 32nd game-winning drive. . . . The Broncos had a club-record 548 yards, eclipsing the 543 set in 1976 against the Jets.

Quote of the week: New Orleans coach Jim Mora, after a 19-7 loss to Carolina (his last game before resigning): "I'm totally embarrassed and totally ashamed. Our coaches did a horrible job. Our players did a horrible job. The second half was an abomination. Terrible, terrible, terrible."

CHIEFS 34, SEAHAWKS 16

Thursday, October 17

Seattle	0	3	7	6—16
Kansas City	10	10	7	7—34

First Quarter
K.C.—FG, Stoyanovich 45, 4:32.
K.C.—Anders 15 run (Stoyanovich kick), 11:19.
Second Quarter
K.C.—Allen 1 run (Stoyanovich kick), 11:13.
Sea.—FG, Peterson 24, 14:34.
K.C.—FG, Stoyanovich 43, 15:00.
Third Quarter
Sea.—Warren 50 run (Peterson kick), 3:54.
K.C.—Allen 1 run (Stoyanovich kick), 14:39.
Fourth Quarter
K.C.—LaChapelle 4 pass from Bono (Stoyanovich kick), 8:20.
Sea.—Galloway 16 pass from Friesz (run failed), 13:59.
Attendance—76,057.

TEAM STATISTICS

	Seattle	Kansas City
First downs	18	27
Rushes-yards	20-110	39-146
Passing	213	194
Punt returns	1-12	3-28
Kickoff returns	6-112	3-86
Interception returns	0-0	1-30
Comp.-att.-int.	20-34-1	17-26-0
Sacked-yards lost	3-25	0-0
Punts	5-35	3-37
Fumbles-lost	0-0	1-1
Penalties-yards	13-118	9-70
Time of possession	24:47	35:13

INDIVIDUAL STATISTICS

RUSHING—Seattle, Warren 14-81, Smith 4-24, Galloway 1-4, Friesz 1-1. Kansas City, Allen 14-39, Bennett 10-32, Hill 7-27, Anders 4-38, Bono 4-10.

PASSING—Seattle, Friesz 20-34-1-238. Kansas City, Bono 17-26-0-194.

RECEIVING—Seattle, Warren 6-59, Galloway 3-65, Crumpler 3-47, Blades 3-25, Pritchard 2-28, Fauria 2-20, Broussard 1-(minus 6). Kansas City, Penn 5-69, Anders 4-21, Johnson 2-27, LaChapelle 2-22, McNair 1-29, Vanover 1-14, Bennett 1-7, Cash 1-5.

MISSED FIELD GOAL ATTEMPTS—None.

INTERCEPTIONS—Kansas City, Davis 1-30.

KICKOFF RETURNS—Seattle, Broussard 3-57, McKnight 2-31, Brown 1-24. Kansas City, Vanover 2-47, Woods 1-39.

PUNT RETURNS—Seattle, R. Harris 1-12. Kansas City, Penn 2-16, Vanover 1-12.

SACKS—Kansas City, Davis 1, Thomas 1, N. Smith 1.

PANTHERS 19, SAINTS 7

Sunday, October 20

New Orleans	0	7	0	0— 7
Carolina	3	3	10	3—19

First Quarter
Car.—FG, Kasay 23, 9:50.
Second Quarter
N.O.—Zellars 1 run (Brien kick), 8:22.
Car.—FG, Kasay 40, 14:10.
Third Quarter
Car.—FG, Kasay 26, 7:32.
Car.—Carrier 13 pass from Collins (Kasay kick), 12:30.
Fourth Quarter
Car.—FG, Kasay 39, 12:21.
Attendance—70,888.

TEAM STATISTICS

	New Orleans	Carolina
First downs	10	21
Rushes-yards	20-71	42-159
Passing	103	155
Punt returns	3-7	2-12
Kickoff returns	6-134	2-53
Interception returns	0-0	1-0
Comp.-att.-int.	14-29-1	14-30-0
Sacked-yards lost	1-14	3-21
Punts	5-45	3-44
Fumbles-lost	1-1	1-0
Penalties-yards	8-52	5-30
Time of possession	21:38	38:22

INDIVIDUAL STATISTICS

RUSHING—New Orleans, Zellars 17-61, Whittle 2-8, Bates 1-2. Carolina, Johnson 29-123, Collins 8-3, Oliver 5-33.

PASSING—New Orleans, Everett 14-29-1-117. Carolina, Collins 14-30-0-176.

RECEIVING—New Orleans, Whittle 3-8, Small 2-18, Jeffires 2-14, Lusk 2-8, DeRamus 1-16, Neal 1-16, Bates 1-15, Zellars 1-12, Haynes 1-10. Carolina, Johnson 5-41, Carrier 3-51, Muhammad 3-46, Griffith 2-16, Walls 1-22.

MISSED FIELD GOAL ATTEMPTS—Carolina, Kasay 52.

INTERCEPTIONS—Carolina, Pieri 1-0.

KICKOFF RETURNS—New Orleans, Hughes 6-134. Carolina, Bates 1-27, Oliver 1-26.

PUNT RETURNS—New Orleans, Hughes 3-7. Carolina, Oliver 2-12.

SACKS—New Orleans, Johnson 1½, M. Fields 1, Martin ½. Carolina, Thomas 1.

PATRIOTS 27, COLTS 9

Sunday, October 20

New England	0	10	14	3—27
Indianapolis	3	3	0	3— 9

First Quarter
Ind.—FG, Blanchard 21, 12:11.
Second Quarter
Ind.—FG, Blanchard 35, 8:48.
N.E.—Glenn 8 pass from Bledsoe (Vinatieri kick), 12:49.
N.E.—FG, Vinatieri 44, 14:10.
Third Quarter
N.E.—Martin 1 run (Vinatieri kick), 3:11.
N.E.—Martin 6 run (Vinatieri kick), 13:03.
Fourth Quarter
Ind.—FG, Blanchard 38, 1:51.
N.E.—FG, Vinatieri 36, 6:59.
Attendance—58,725.

TEAM STATISTICS

	New England	Indianapolis
First downs	15	27
Rushes-yards	31-80	18-49
Passing	142	319
Punt returns	2-46	4-24
Kickoff returns	4-108	3-75
Interception returns	0-0	0-0
Comp.-att.-int.	14-24-0	36-55-0
Sacked-yards lost	0-0	4-23
Punts	6-46	2-50
Fumbles-lost	3-2	5-4
Penalties-yards	9-75	6-49
Time of possession	25:56	34:04

INDIVIDUAL STATISTICS

RUSHING—New England, Martin 25-75, Bledsoe 5-2, Gash 1-3. Indianapolis, Warren 10-18, Groce 6-18, Harbaugh 1-10, Workman 1-3.

PASSING—New England, Bledsoe 14-24-0-142. Indianapolis, Harbaugh 26-43-0-223, Justin 10-12-0-119.

RECEIVING—New England, Jefferson 5-79, Glenn 3-29, Meggett 2-16, Gash 2-12, Coates 1-7, Martin 1-(minus 1). Indianapolis, Dawkins 8-84, Warren 7-50, Stablein 5-47, Bailey 4-48, Harrison 4-42, Groce 4-28, Dilger 3-25, Workman 1-18.

MISSED FIELD GOAL ATTEMPTS—None.

INTERCEPTIONS—None.

KICKOFF RETURNS—New England, Meggett 2-55, T. Brown 2-53. Indianapolis, Bailey 3-75.

PUNT RETURNS—New England, Meggett 2-46. Indianapolis, Harrison 4-24.

SACKS—New England, McGinest 2, Jones 1, Sagapolutele 1.

BILLS 25, JETS 22

Sunday, October 20

Buffalo	3	3	16—25
N.Y. Jets	7	0	8	7—22

First Quarter
NYJ—Johnson 16 pass from Reich (Lowery kick), 9:39.
Buf.—FG, Christie 48, 13:20.
Second Quarter
Buf.—FG, Christie 32, 9:47.

Third Quarter

Buf.—FG, Christie 47, 4:52.
NYJ—Johnson 9 pass from Reich (Brady pass from Reich), 12:25.

Fourth Quarter

Buf.—FG, Christie 23, 4:50.
Buf.—Holmes 1 run (Christie kick), 7:02.
Buf.—FG, Christie 33, 11:58.
NYJ—Chrebet 21 pass from Reich (Lowery kick), 13:17.
Buf.—FG, Christie 47, 14:50.
Attendance—49,775.

TEAM STATISTICS

	Buffalo	N.Y. Jets
First downs	23	19
Rushes-yards	43-138	22-64
Passing	195	253
Punt returns	3-46	2-14
Kickoff returns	4-84	8-116
Interception returns	2-28	0-0
Comp.-att.-int.	19-36-0	21-36-2
Sacked-yards lost	3-26	0-0
Punts	3-34	3-42
Fumbles-lost	1-1	3-3
Penalties-yards	5-40	3-20
Time of possession	36:24	23:36

INDIVIDUAL STATISTICS

RUSHING—Buffalo, T. Thomas 24-97, Holmes 10-7, Kelly 3-27, Tindale 4-9, Reed 2-(minus 7), Moulds 1-5. New York, Murrell 13-49, Anderson 6-6, Reich 3-(minus 1).
PASSING—Buffalo, Kelly 19-36-0-221. New York, Reich 21-36-2-253.
RECEIVING—Buffalo, Johnson 6-90, Early 3-34, Reed 3-26, Moulds 2-31, T. Thomas 2-17, Cline 2-11, Coons 1-12. New York, Johnson 8-94, Chrebet 7-73, Anderson 3-55, F. Baxter 1-12, Brady 1-12, Davis 1-6, Murrell 1-1.
MISSED FIELD GOAL ATTEMPTS—Buffalo, Christie 36. New York, Lowery 43.
INTERCEPTIONS—Buffalo, Burris 1-28, Stevens 1-0.
KICKOFF RETURNS—Buffalo, Moulds 4-84. New York, Bailey 6-115, Moore 1-1, R. Hamilton 1-0.
PUNT RETURNS—Buffalo, Burris 3-46. New York, Chrebet 2-14.
SACKS—New York, Gunn 2, Green 1.

COWBOYS 32, FALCONS 28

Sunday, October 20

Atlanta	3	15	7	3—28
Dallas	7	10	8	7—32

First Quarter

Dal.—E. Smith 9 pass from Aikman (Boniol kick), 1:28.
Atl.—FG, Andersen 23, 9:20.

Second Quarter

Dal.—E. Smith 1 run (Boniol kick), :04.
Atl.—FG, Andersen 54, 4:06.
Dal.—FG, Boniol 49, 5:06.
Atl.—Hebert 1 run (run failed), 11:31.
Atl.—FG, Andersen 32, 13:18.
Atl.—FG, Andersen 28, 14:24.

Third Quarter

Atl.—Emanuel 4 pass from Hebert (Andersen kick), 10:17.
Dal.—E. Smith 3 run (Irvin pass from Aikman), 13:26.

Fourth Quarter

Atl.—FG, Andersen 37, 7:51.
Dal.—Martin 60 pass from Aikman (Boniol kick), 13:18.
Attendance—64,091.

TEAM STATISTICS

	Atlanta	Dallas
First downs	22	17
Rushes-yards	31-113	16-56
Passing	256	250
Punt returns	3-9	0-0
Kickoff returns	5-85	7-235
Interception returns	0-0	0-0
Comp.-att.-int.	25-40-0	17-24-0
Sacked-yards lost	3-16	2-15
Punts	3-44	3-42
Fumbles-lost	1-0	2-2
Penalties-yards	10-60	6-70
Time of possession	41:22	18:38

INDIVIDUAL STATISTICS

RUSHING—Atlanta, Anderson 26-97, Heyward 3-14, Hebert 2-2. Dallas, Smith 15-50, Johnston 1-6.

PASSING—Atlanta, Hebert 25-40-0-271. Dallas, Aikman 17-24-0-265.
RECEIVING—Atlanta, Emanuel 8-71, Anderson 7-45, Mathis 5-101, Heyward 2-28, Metcalf 2-21, Birden 1-6. Dallas, Irvin 7-119, Bjornson 4-24, Martin 3-96, E. Smith 2-7, Sanders 1-19.
MISSED FIELD GOAL ATTEMPTS—None.
INTERCEPTIONS—None.
KICKOFF RETURNS—Atlanta, Metcalf 5-85. Dallas, Walker 6-198, Marion 1-37.
PUNT RETURNS—Atlanta, Mathis 2-9, Heyward 1-0.
SACKS—Atlanta, McKyer 1, Bennett 1. Dallas, Thomas 2, Carver 1.

EAGLES 35, DOLPHINS 28

Sunday, October 20

Miami	3	8	0	17—28
Philadelphia	14	7	7	7—35

First Quarter

Phi.—Fryar 38 pass from Detmer (Anderson kick), 1:41.
Phi.—Fryar 2 pass from Detmer (Anderson kick), 9:04.
Mia.—FG, Nedney 37, 14:19.

Second Quarter

Mia.—R. Hill 6 pass from Erickson (Drayton pass from Erickson), 13:05.
Phi.—Fryar 12 pass from Detmer (Anderson kick), 14:55.

Third Quarter

Phi.—Fryar 36 pass from Detmer (Anderson kick), 7:38.

Fourth Quarter

Mia.—McDuffie 24 pass from Erickson (Nedney kick), 2:53.
Mia.—FG, Nedney 39, 8:04.
Phi.—Watters 49 run (Anderson kick), 12:32.
Mia.—McDuffie 17 pass from Kosar (Nedney kick), 13:56.
Attendance—66,240.

TEAM STATISTICS

	Miami	Philadelphia
First downs	18	21
Rushes-yards	24-93	30-196
Passing	254	223
Punt returns	1-12	4-34
Kickoff returns	6-133	3-53
Interception returns	1-0	1-11
Comp.-att.-int.	23-37-1	18-24-1
Sacked-yards lost	4-27	1-3
Punts	4-44	4-50
Fumbles-lost	0-0	0-0
Penalties-yards	9-69	8-80
Time of possession	32:31	27:29

INDIVIDUAL STATISTICS

RUSHING—Miami, Abdul-Jabbar 22-80, Erickson 2-13. Philadelphia, Watters 25-173, Garner 4-22, Turner 1-1.
PASSING—Miami, Erickson 18-31-1-239, Kosar 5-6-0-42. Philadelphia, Detmer 18-24-1-226.
RECEIVING—Miami, McDuffie 7-121, McPhail 6-71, R. Hill 3-44, Drayton 3-19, Barnett 2-27, Abdul-Jabbar 1-3, Pritchett 1-(minus 4). Philadelphia, Fryar 8-116, Jones 3-35, Watters 3-23, Seay 2-22, Dunn 1-25, West 1-5.
MISSED FIELD GOAL ATTEMPTS—None.
INTERCEPTIONS—Miami, Wooden 1-0. Philadelphia, Dawkins 1-11.
KICKOFF RETURNS—Miami, Spikes 3-71, McPhail 2-52, Wainright 1-10. Philadelphia, Witherspoon 2-35, Garner 1-18.
PUNT RETURNS—Miami, McDuffie 1-12. Philadelphia, Seay 4-34.
SACKS—Miami, Stubbs 1. Philadelphia, Hall 1, Jefferson 1, Mamula 1, Harmon 1.

REDSKINS 31, GIANTS 21

Sunday, October 20

N.Y. Giants	0	0	14	7—21
Washington	7	21	0	3—31

First Quarter

Was.—Allen 2 run (Blanton kick), 4:06.

Second Quarter

Was.—Allen 1 run (Blanton kick), :46.
Was.—Allen 2 run (Blanton kick), 11:03.
Was.—D. Green 68 interception return (Blanton kick), 12:00.

Third Quarter

NYG—Lewis 31 pass from Brown (Daluiso kick), 5:20.
NYG—Calloway 13 pass from Brown (Daluiso kick), 9:21.

Fourth Quarter

NYG—Wheatley 1 run (Daluiso kick), 8:25.
Was.—FG, Blanton 45, 12:27.
Attendance—52,684.

TEAM STATISTICS

	N.Y. Giants	Washington
First downs	24	20
Rushes-yards	28-107	34-123
Passing	287	207
Punt returns	1-9	1-3
Kickoff returns	6-108	3-63
Interception returns	1-33	2-68
Comp.-att.-int.	26-43-2	14-24-1
Sacked-yards lost	2-11	0-0
Punts	5-42	5-43
Fumbles-lost	1-0	1-0
Penalties-yards	8-70	4-20
Time of possession	33:18	26:42

INDIVIDUAL STATISTICS

RUSHING—New York, Hampton 16-50, Wheatley 11-54, Brown 1-3. Washington, Allen 28-89, Frerotte 4-(minus 2), Shepherd 1-31, Mitchell 1-5.

PASSING—New York, Brown 26-43-2-298. Washington, Frerotte 14-24-1-207.

RECEIVING—New York, Lewis 9-125, Calloway 9-108, Cross 3-36, Way 2-25, Wheatley 2-(minus 2), Hampton 1-6. Washington, Ellard 5-119, Mitchell 3-26, Asher 2-19, Logan 2-19, Shepherd 1-24, Allen 1-0.

MISSED FIELD GOAL ATTEMPTS—New York, Daluiso 41.

INTERCEPTIONS—New York, Ellsworth 1-33. Washington, D. Green 1-68, Richard 1-0.

KICKOFF RETURNS—New York, Wheatley 3-68, Toomer 3-40. Washington, W. Bell 3-63.

PUNT RETURNS—New York, Toomer 1-9. Washington, Mitchell 1-3.

SACKS—Washington, Nottage 2.

CARDINALS 13, BUCCANEERS 9

Sunday, October 20

Tampa Bay	0	0	3	6— 9
Arizona	3	7	3	0—13

First Quarter
Ariz.—FG, G. Davis 22, 8:40.

Second Quarter
Ariz.—Centers 5 pass from K. Graham (G. Davis kick), 4:36.

Third Quarter
T.B.—FG, Husted 41, 6:32.
Ariz.—FG, G. Davis 37, 12:53.

Fourth Quarter
T.B.—Alstott 1 run (kick blocked), 7:26.
Attendance—27,738.

TEAM STATISTICS

	Tampa Bay	Arizona
First downs	19	21
Rushes-yards	26-95	33-104
Passing	218	133
Punt returns	0-0	1-12
Kickoff returns	4-101	2-17
Interception returns	0-0	0-0
Comp.-att.-int.	22-35-0	17-26-0
Sacked-yards lost	1-11	2-13
Punts	1-51	2-42
Fumbles-lost	1-0	1-0
Penalties-yards	14-114	2-15
Time of possession	29:49	30:11

INDIVIDUAL STATISTICS

RUSHING—Tampa Bay, R. Brooks 14-43, Alstott 9-27, Ellison 2-20, Dilfer 1-5. Arizona, L. Johnson 14-26, Centers 9-23, K. Graham 6-40, McElroy 3-12, C. Smith 1-3.

PASSING—Tampa Bay, Dilfer 22-35-0-229. Arizona, K. Graham 17-26-0-146.

RECEIVING—Tampa Bay, Hawkins 6-74, R. Thomas 4-67, Williams 4-38, Alstott 4-30, Ellison 2-8, R. Brooks 1-9, Moore 1-3. Arizona, Sanders 4-40, Centers 4-16, R. Moore 2-26, L. Johnson 2-24, Edwards 2-19, Dowdell 2-13, Carter 1-8.

MISSED FIELD GOAL ATTEMPTS—Tampa Bay, Husted 49, 52.

INTERCEPTIONS—None.

KICKOFF RETURNS—Tampa Bay, Silvan 4-101. Arizona, McElroy 2-17.

PUNT RETURNS—Arizona, Dowdell 1-12.

SACKS—Tampa Bay, Lynch 1, Marts 1. Arizona, Joyner 1.

49ERS 28, BENGALS 21

Sunday, October 20

Cincinnati	14	7	0	0—21
San Francisco	0	7	7	14—28

First Quarter
Cin.—McGee 5 pass from Blake (Pelfrey kick), 6:02.
Cin.—Hearst 15 pass from Blake (Pelfrey kick), 9:52.

Second Quarter
Cin.—Scott 50 pass from Blake (Pelfrey kick), 6:18.
S.F.—Popson 17 pass from Grbac (Wilkins kick), 9:00.

Third Quarter
S.F.—Popson 39 pass from S. Young (Wilkins kick), 3:27.

Fourth Quarter
S.F.—Owens 45 pass from S. Young (Wilkins kick), 12:52.
S.F.—S. Young 15 run (Wilkins kick), 13:52.
Attendance—63,218.

TEAM STATISTICS

	Cincinnati	San Francisco
First downs	18	20
Rushes-yards	36-149	23-80
Passing	196	338
Punt returns	3-7	1-8
Kickoff returns	4-56	3-52
Interception returns	4-0	1-0
Comp.-att.-int.	15-34-1	27-42-4
Sacked-yards lost	1-4	4-23
Punts	10-42	4-51
Fumbles-lost	1-0	1-1
Penalties-yards	9-70	3-15
Time of possession	32:30	27:30

INDIVIDUAL STATISTICS

RUSHING—Cincinnati, Hearst 21-88, Bieniemy 6-34, Carter 4-14, Cothran 3-6, Blake 2-7. San Francisco, S. Young 10-45, Kirby 4-13, Loville 4-(minus 3), Floyd 2-7, D. Carter 1-18, Grbac 1-2, Lynn 1-(minus 2).

PASSING—Cincinnati, Blake 15-34-1-200. San Francisco, S. Young 19-30-3-274, Grbac 8-12-1-87.

RECEIVING—Cincinnati, McGee 3-26, Carter 3-25, Scott 2-66, Hearst 2-25, Pickens 2-25, Dunn 1-14, Battaglia 1-12, Bieniemy 1-7. San Francisco, Popson 8-116, Rice 7-82, Kirby 5-31, Owens 4-94, Floyd 2-26, Uwaezuoke 1-12.

MISSED FIELD GOAL ATTEMPTS—None.

INTERCEPTIONS—Cincinnati, Ambrose 1-0, Orlando 1-0, Spencer 1-0, Tovar 1-0. San Francisco, Dodge 1-0.

KICKOFF RETURNS—Cincinnati, Dunn 2-30, Sawyer 2-26. San Francisco, Loville 1-25, D. Carter 1-15, Owens 1-12.

PUNT RETURNS—Cincinnati, Sawyer 3-7. San Francisco, D. Carter 1-8.

SACKS—Cincinnati, McDonald 2, Tovar 1, Copeland 1. San Francisco, Barker 1.

BRONCOS 45, RAVENS 34

Sunday, October 20

Baltimore	0	13	21	0—34
Denver	14	14	3	14—45

First Quarter
Den.—McCaffrey 4 pass from Elway (Elam kick), 7:07.
Den.—Davis 71 run (Elam kick), 9:34.

Second Quarter
Bal.—FG, Stover 45, 2:28.
Den.—Davis 4 run (Elam kick), 6:33.
Bal.—Byner 4 pass from Testaverde (Stover kick), 11:23.
Bal.—FG, Stover 33, 13:09.
Den.—McCaffrey 8 pass from Elway (Elam kick), 14:46.

Third Quarter
Bal.—F. Turner 11 pass from Testaverde (Stover kick), 2:15.
Bal.—Jackson 25 pass from Testaverde (pass failed), 6:03.
Den.—FG, Elam 34, 9:58.
Bal.—Jackson 25 pass from Testaverde (Testaverde run), 14:32.

Fourth Quarter
Den.—McCaffrey 6 pass from Elway (Elam kick), 4:03.
Den.—Elway 9 run (Elam kick), 13:44.
Attendance—70,453.

TEAM STATISTICS

	Baltimore	Denver
First downs	23	26
Rushes-yards	18-75	34-222
Passing	317	326
Punt returns	2-23	2-19
Kickoff returns	7-147	7-154
Interception returns	1-26	1-12
Comp.-att.-int.	27-45-1	25-39-1
Sacked-yards lost	3-21	0-0
Punts	3-48	2-46
Fumbles-lost	2-0	2-0

	Baltimore	Denver
Penalties-yards	4-25	4-35
Time of possession	27:09	32:51

INDIVIDUAL STATISTICS

RUSHING—Baltimore, Byner 13-42, Morris 4-15, Testaverde 1-18. Denver, Davis 28-194, Craver 3-10, Elway 2-11, Miller 1-7.

PASSING—Baltimore, Testaverde 27-45-1-338. Denver, Elway 25-39-1-326.

RECEIVING—Baltimore, Jackson 7-92, F. Turner 7-57, Alexander 6-126, Byner 4-33, Green 3-30. Denver, Sharpe 9-161, McCaffrey 7-76, Davis 3-19, Craver 3-16, R. Smith 1-35, Miller 1-18, Carswell 1-1.

MISSED FIELD GOAL ATTEMPTS—None.

INTERCEPTIONS—Baltimore, Langham 1-26. Denver, Braxton 1-12.

KICKOFF RETURNS—Baltimore, J. Lewis 4-91, Ethridge 1-28, Baldwin 1-19, Byner 1-9. Denver, Hebron 6-125, R. Smith 1-29.

PUNT RETURNS—Baltimore, J. Lewis 2-23. Denver, Kinchen 2-19.

SACKS—Denver, A. Williams 2, Romanowski 1/2, Geathers 1/2.

RAMS 17, JAGUARS 14

Sunday, October 20

Jacksonville	0	7	7	0—14
St. Louis	10	0	7	0—17

First Quarter
St.L.—Parker 92 interception return (Lohmiller kick), 5:40.
St.L.—FG, Lohmiller 25, 7:52.

Second Quarter
Jac.—Stewart 1 run (Hollis kick), 7:47.

Third Quarter
Jac.—Stewart 8 run (Hollis kick), 3:34.
St.L.—Kennison 29 pass from Banks (Lohmiller kick), 8:16.
Attendance—60,066.

TEAM STATISTICS

	Jacksonville	St. Louis
First downs	36	8
Rushes-yards	33-118	20-83
Passing	420	121
Punt returns	2-21	0-0
Kickoff returns	4-78	3-66
Interception returns	1-20	5-177
Comp.-att.-int.	37-52-5	9-17-1
Sacked-yards lost	2-1	2-8
Punts	0-0	5-49
Fumbles-lost	2-1	2-0
Penalties-yards	3-16	7-55
Time of possession	41:34	18:26

INDIVIDUAL STATISTICS

RUSHING—Jacksonville, Stewart 29-112, Brunell 2-2, Maston 1-7, Means 1-(minus 3). St. Louis, Phillips 12-37, Banks 7-46, Moore 1-0.

PASSING—Jacksonville, Brunell 37-52-5-421. St. Louis, Banks 9-17-1-129.

RECEIVING—Jacksonville, McCardell 16-232, Smith 7-65, Stewart 4-18, W. Jackson 3-52, Mitchell 3-25, Rison 3-25, Maston 1-4. St. Louis, Kennison 2-71, Bruce 2-30, Ross 2-13, Phillips 1-6, Green 1-5, Conwell 1-4.

MISSED FIELD GOAL ATTEMPTS—None.

INTERCEPTIONS—Jacksonville, Hall 1-20. St. Louis, Parker 2-106, Lyle 2-68, McBurrows 1-3.

KICKOFF RETURNS—Jacksonville, Bullard 2-51, Jordan 2-27. St. Louis, Kennison 2-46, Thomas 1-20.

PUNT RETURNS—Jacksonville, Hudson 2-21.

SACKS—Jacksonville, Smeenge 1, Lageman 1. St. Louis, Phifer 1, Goss 1.

OILERS 23, STEELERS 13

Sunday, October 20

Pittsburgh	7	3	0	3—13
Houston	3	6	0	14—23

First Quarter
Hou.—FG, Del Greco 22, 6:14.
Pit.—C. Johnson 70 pass from Tomczak (N. Johnson kick), 7:15.

Second Quarter
Pit.—FG, N. Johnson 26, 3:50.
Hou.—FG, Del Greco 32, 13:28.
Hou.—FG, Del Greco 48, 15:00.

Fourth Quarter
Pit.—FG, N. Johnson 29, 3:21.
Hou.—Davis 34 pass from Chandler (Del Greco kick), 9:59.
Hou.—George 2 run (Del Greco kick), 11:55.
Attendance—50,337.

TEAM STATISTICS

	Pittsburgh	Houston
First downs	12	23
Rushes-yards	23-83	30-91
Passing	192	237
Punt returns	4-5	4-25
Kickoff returns	5-91	4-69
Interception returns	1-4	0-0
Comp.-att.-int.	13-30-0	23-38-1
Sacked-yards lost	2-7	4-21
Punts	5-43	5-45
Fumbles-lost	5-2	1-1
Penalties-yards	3-25	4-63
Time of possession	25:43	34:17

INDIVIDUAL STATISTICS

RUSHING—Pittsburgh, Bettis 18-65, Tomczak 2-1, Hastings 1-14, Stewart 1-6, Arnold 1-(minus 3). Houston, George 25-65, Chandler 4-21, Harmon 1-5.

PASSING—Pittsburgh, Tomczak 13-29-0-199, Stewart 0-1-0-0. Houston, Chandler 23-38-1-258.

RECEIVING—Pittsburgh, C. Johnson 5-155, Hastings 2-12, McAfee 2-3, Bettis 2-2, Arnold 1-14, Bruener 1-13. Houston, Sanders 7-85, Davis 6-88, Wycheck 3-29, George 3-22, Russell 2-24, Harmon 2-10.

MISSED FIELD GOAL ATTEMPTS—Pittsburgh, N. Johnson 38.

INTERCEPTIONS—Pittsburgh, Kirkland 1-4.

KICKOFF RETURNS—Pittsburgh, Arnold 5-91. Houston, Gray 3-49, Harmon 1-20.

PUNT RETURNS—Pittsburgh, Hastings 4-5. Houston, Gray 3-20, Floyd 1-5.

SACKS—Pittsburgh, Brown 1, M. Bell 1, Woodson 1, Gibson 1. Houston, Barrow 1, Walker 1.

RAIDERS 23, CHARGERS 14

Monday, October 21

Oakland	7	3	10	3—23
San Diego	7	0	0	7—14

First Quarter
Oak.—Kaufman 12 run (Ford kick), 3:01.
S.D.—Martin 11 pass from Salisbury (Carney kick), 14:57.

Second Quarter
Oak.—FG, Ford 36, 3:33.

Third Quarter
Oak.—Fenner 17 pass from Hostetler (Ford kick), 6:58.
Oak.—FG, Ford 32, 11:48.

Fourth Quarter
S.D.—Martin 12 pass from Salisbury (Carney kick), 1:55.
Oak.—FG, Ford 34, 12:49.
Attendance—62,350.

TEAM STATISTICS

	Oakland	San Diego
First downs	22	16
Rushes-yards	34-131	20-29
Passing	179	253
Punt returns	1-9	2-7
Kickoff returns	3-78	3-71
Interception returns	1-19	1-20
Comp.-att.-int.	20-33-1	23-40-1
Sacked-yards lost	2-12	1-11
Punts	4-30	5-47
Fumbles-lost	2-0	2-2
Penalties-yards	11-97	9-84
Time of possession	35:30	24:30

INDIVIDUAL STATISTICS

RUSHING—Oakland, Kaufman 13-56, Williams 10-30, Hostetler 7-25, Fenner 3-7, T. Brown 1-13. San Diego, Russell 13-19, Hayden 4-(minus 1), Fletcher 1-6, Humphries 1-5, Salisbury 1-0.

PASSING—Oakland, Hostetler 20-33-1-191. San Diego, Salisbury 22-35-1-252, Humphries 1-5-0-12.

RECEIVING—Oakland, T. Brown 5-68, Williams 4-40, Fenner 4-35, Hobbs 4-31, Kaufman 3-17. San Diego, Martin 5-81, Jones 5-52, Fletcher 5-20, Mitchell 2-27, May 2-20, A. Coleman 2-17, Still 1-37, Russell 1-10.

MISSED FIELD GOAL ATTEMPTS—San Diego, Carney 44.

INTERCEPTIONS—Oakland, McDaniel 1-19. San Diego, Shaw 1-20.

KICKOFF RETURNS—Oakland, Kidd 2-49, Kaufman 1-29. San Diego, A. Coleman 3-71.

PUNT RETURNS—Oakland, Hobbs 1-9. San Diego, Da. Gordon 2-7.

SACKS—Oakland, M. Jones 1. San Diego, M. Coleman 1, R. Davis 1.

WEEK 9

BALTIMORE 37, St. Louis 31 (OT)
CINCINNATI 28, Jacksonville 21
Dallas 29, MIAMI 10
DENVER 34, Kansas City 7
GREEN BAY 13, Tampa Bay 7
NEW ENGLAND 28, Buffalo 25
N.Y. Giants 35, DETROIT 7
N.Y. Jets 31, ARIZONA 21
PHILADELPHIA 20, Carolina 9
Pittsburgh 20, ATLANTA 17
San Francisco 10, HOUSTON 9
SEATTLE 32, San Diego 13
WASHINGTON 31, Indianapolis 16
Chicago 15, MINNESOTA 13
   Open date: New Orleans, Oakland

STANDINGS

AFC EAST	W	L	T	Pct.
Buffalo	5	3	0	.625
Indianapolis	5	3	0	.625
New England	5	3	0	.625
Miami	4	4	0	.500
N.Y. Jets	1	8	0	.111

AFC CENTRAL	W	L	T	Pct.
Pittsburgh	6	2	0	.750
Houston	5	3	0	.625
Baltimore	3	5	0	.375
Jacksonville	3	6	0	.333
Cincinnati	2	6	0	.250

AFC WEST	W	L	T	Pct.
Denver	7	1	0	.875
Kansas City	5	3	0	.625
Oakland	4	4	0	.500
San Diego	4	4	0	.500
Seattle	3	5	0	.375

NFC EAST	W	L	T	Pct.
Washington	7	1	0	.875
Philadelphia	6	2	0	.750
Dallas	5	3	0	.625
Arizona	3	5	0	.375
N.Y. Giants	3	5	0	.375

NFC CENTRAL	W	L	T	Pct.
Green Bay	7	1	0	.875
Minnesota	5	3	0	.625
Detroit	4	4	0	.500
Chicago	3	5	0	.375
Tampa Bay	1	7	0	.125

NFC WEST	W	L	T	Pct.
San Francisco	6	2	0	.750
Carolina	5	3	0	.625
New Orleans	2	6	0	.250
St. Louis	2	6	0	.250
Atlanta	0	8	0	.000

HIGHLIGHTS

Hero of the week: San Francisco defensive end Chris Doleman intercepted a Steve McNair pass in the final minute and produced two sacks in a 10-9 victory over the Oilers. Doleman led a defensive charge that allowed the 49ers to win without quarterback Steve Young, who suffered a concussion on the third play of the game, and No. 2 quarterback Elvis Grbac, who was inactive with a shoulder injury. Doleman's interception occurred at the Oilers' 15 after Junior Bryant batted McNair's pass. The 49ers then ran out the clock. Earlier in the quarter, Doleman pushed through and sacked McNair for a 10-yard loss on third-and-2 at the 49ers' 30.

Goat of the week: San Diego quarterback Sean Salisbury, starting in place of injured Stan Humphries, suffered four interceptions in a 32-13 loss at Seattle. One of the interceptions was returned 79 yards for a touchdown by safety Darryl Williams, putting the Seahawks up 20-6 at halftime. It was the first start for Salisbury since 1994, when he was with the Vikings.

Sub of the week: Third-string quarterback Jeff Brohm, forced into action after Steve Young was injured early in the game, threw a 20-yard touchdown pass to rookie wide receiver Terrell Owens with 4:27 left to lift San Francisco to a 10-9 victory over Houston. Brohm was 19-of-30 for 176 yards, one touchdown and no interceptions. Backup quarterback Elvis Grbac was inactive with a shoulder injury.

Comeback of the week: Trailing 18-15 in the fourth quarter, New England rallied with a 10-yard touchdown run by Curtis Martin with 1:25 left, then scored again on a 46-yard interception return by Willie McGinest in a 28-25 victory over Buffalo. The Bills scored with 24 seconds left on a 48-yard touchdown reception by Andre Reed to finish the flurry of points in the final two minutes.

Blowout of the week: The Giants scored 23 points in a 4:54 span of the second quarter to hammer Detroit, 35-7, ending the Lions' 10-game home winning streak. Chris Calloway opened the second-period blitz by catching a 24-yard touchdown pass from Tyrone Wheatley on a halfback option. After a field goal, the

Giants scored on a 32-yard interception return by Maurice Douglass and a 23-yard touchdown reception by Thomas Lewis. Five Giants intercepted passes.

Nail-biter of the week: For the second consecutive week, winless Atlanta came up a little short against one of the league's best teams. After falling to Dallas in the final two minutes the previous week, the Falcons lost to Pittsburgh, 20-17. The Steelers broke 17-17 tie on Norm Johnson's 20-yard field goal as time expired. That capped a 13-play, 66-yard, 5:55 drive in which Jerome Bettis carried seven times for 32 yards.

Hit of the week: Middle linebacker Bryan Cox forced a fumble from Brad Johnson and recovered it with 1:47 left, preserving Chicago's 15-13 Monday night victory over Minnesota. After Vikings defensive tackle Jason Fisk intercepted a pass near midfield, the Vikings were in position to drive for a game-winning field goal. But Cox sacked and stripped Johnson and recovered the fumble.

Oddity of the week: In a baseball-like move, Detroit coach Wayne Fontes pulled quarterback Scott Mitchell during a second-quarter series against the Giants. Mitchell had thrown three interceptions when he came back on the field with five minutes left in the second quarter. But after Mitchell threw an incomplete pass, Fontes sent in Don Majkowski to replace him. When Mitchell returned to the sideline, he was visibly frustrated and threw his helmet.

Top rusher: Adrian Murrell rushed 31 times for 199 yards and a touchdown to lead the Jets to their first victory of the season, a 31-21 win over Arizona.

Top passer: Dallas' Troy Aikman was 33-of-41 for 363 yards and three touchdowns (with no interceptions) in a 29-10 victory over his former coach, Jimmy Johnson, and the Dolphins.

Top receiver: Wide receiver Michael Irvin caught 12 passes for 186 yards and a 2-yard touchdown in the Cowboys' victory at Miami.

Notes: Denver's John Elway ran for 62 yards in a 34-7 victory over Kansas City, giving him 3,001 yards rushing in his career. He and Fran Tarkenton are the only wo quarterbacks to accumulate 3,000 yards rushing and 40,000 yards passing. . . . The Broncos' 27-point victory margin over the Chiefs was Denver's biggest ever against Kansas City. . . . For the first time, the Bills lost a game in which Thurman Thomas gained 100 yards rushing and Andre Reed had 100 yards receiving. With 119 yards, Thomas moved past Ottis Anderson into 10th place on the career rushing list. . . . When the Bills completed a 48-yard desperation touchdown pass to Reed in the final minute of a loss to New England, it marked the third time this season that the Patriots had allowed successful Hail Marys. . . . Washington running back Terry Allen scored three touchdowns in his second consecutive game. The last back to accomplish that was the Giants' Joe Morris in 1985. . . . In Green Bay's 13-7 victory over Tampa Bay, Brett Favre was held without a touchdown pass for the first time in 17 games. . . . Al Del Greco's 56-yard field goal for the Oilers was a franchise and personal record, breaking the 55-yard record set by George Blanda in 1961. . . . The Bears scored their first rushing touchdown of the season. . . . The Falcons opened the season with nine losses for the first time since their first season (1966). The nine consecutive losses also tied the club record matched in 1984. . . . Irving Fryar became the 15th player in history to record 600 receptions.

Quote of the week: Kansas City safety Brian Washington, after the Chiefs' 34-7 loss to Denver: "It's not something we can't come back from, but it's definitely devastating. After the Pittsburgh game (a 17-7 loss three weeks before), we said we had to go back to basics. Hell, I don't know what to go back to now."

GAME SUMMARIES

STEELERS 20, FALCONS 17

Sunday, October 27

ttsburgh	3	0	14	3—20
lanta	7	3	0	7—17

First Quarter
t.—FG, N. Johnson 27, 5:05.
l.—Tobeck 1 pass from Hebert (Andersen kick), 10:46.

Second Quarter
l.—FG, Andersen 41, 14:11.

Third Quarter
t.—Hastings 12 pass from Tomczak (N. Johnson kick), 6:05.
.—Bettis 1 run (N. Johnson kick), 12:57.

Fourth Quarter
.—Emanuel 4 pass from Hebert (Andersen kick), 9:05.
.—FG, N. Johnson 20, 15:00.
Attendance—58,760.

TEAM STATISTICS

	Pittsburgh	Atlanta
st downs	20	19
shes-yards	28-133	16-67
ssing	178	234
nt returns	0-0	3-11
:koff returns	3-76	4-80
erception returns	1-23	0-0
mp.-att.-int.	23-29-0	24-36-1
cked-yards lost	4-49	0-0
nts	4-50	4-50
mbles-lost	0-0	0-0
nalties-yards	5-50	6-59
ne of possession	30:51	29:09

INDIVIDUAL STATISTICS

RUSHING—Pittsburgh, Bettis 26-126, Witman 1-5, Pegram 1-2. Atlanta, Anderson 12-55, Heyward 3-10, Hebert 1-2.
PASSING—Pittsburgh, Tomczak 22-27-0-214, Stewart 1-2-0-13. Atlanta, Hebert 24-36-1-234.
RECEIVING—Pittsburgh, C. Johnson 8-110, Hastings 6-59, Lester 2-25, Bruener 2-22, Pegram 2-5, Bettis 2-2, Stewart 1-4. Atlanta, Mathis 8-76, Anderson 5-53, Emanuel 4-54, Metcalf 3-21, Birden 2-25, Heyward 1-4, Tobeck 1-1.
MISSED FIELD GOAL ATTEMPTS—None.
INTERCEPTIONS—Pittsburgh, Perry 1-23.
KICKOFF RETURNS—Pittsburgh, Arnold 3-76. Atlanta, Metcalf 4-80.
PUNT RETURNS—Atlanta, Metcalf 3-11.
SACKS—Atlanta, Smith 1½, Matthews 1½, Bennett 1.

49ERS 10, OILERS 9

Sunday, October 27

San Francisco	3	0	0	7—10
Houston	0	6	3	0—9

First Quarter
S.F.—FG, Wilkins 27, 8:33.

Second Quarter
Hou.—FG, Del Greco 38, 9:31.
Hou.—FG, Del Greco 56, 14:33.

Third Quarter
Hou.—FG, Del Greco 39, 10:22.

Fourth Quarter
S.F.—Owens 20 pass from Brohm (Wilkins kick), 10:33.
Attendance—53,664.

TEAM STATISTICS

	San Francisco	Houston
First downs	12	12
Rushes-yards	28-63	27-107
Passing	175	77
Punt returns	4-21	2-14
Kickoff returns	4-78	2-24
Interception returns	1-0	0-0
Comp.-att.-int.	20-32-0	12-27-1
Sacked-yards lost	2-10	3-25
Punts	6-41	5-44
Fumbles-lost	1-0	2-1
Penalties-yards	10-60	6-40
Time of possession	30:19	29:41

INDIVIDUAL STATISTICS

RUSHING—San Francisco, Kirby 12-23, Brohm 9-35, Floyd 3-(minus 4), Loville 2-6, Rice 1-3, Lynn 1-0. Houston, George 22-77, McNair 1-10, Harmon 1-7, Thomas 1-6, Chandler 1-4, Wycheck 1-3.
PASSING—San Francisco, Brohm 19-30-0-176, Kirby 0-1-0-0, S. Young 1-1-0-9. Houston, Chandler 7-18-0-57, McNair 5-9-1-45.
RECEIVING—San Francisco, Kirby 5-61, Rice 5-36, Owens 4-42, Floyd 4-31, Popson 1-9, Se. Manuel 1-6. Houston, Russell 3-45, Wycheck 3-9, Harmon 2-31, Davis 2-9, Sanders 1-10, George 1-(minus 2).
MISSED FIELD GOAL ATTEMPTS—None.
INTERCEPTIONS—San Francisco, Doleman 1-0.
KICKOFF RETURNS—San Francisco, D. Carter 2-40, Loville 2-38. Houston, Archie 2-24.
PUNT RETURNS—San Francisco, D. Carter 4-21. Houston, Floyd 2-14.
SACKS—San Francisco, Doleman 2, B. Young 1. Houston, Cook 1, Walker 1.

REDSKINS 31, COLTS 16

Sunday, October 27

Indianapolis	0	13	3	0—16
Washington	10	7	7	7—31

First Quarter
Was.—FG, Blanton 20, 6:17.
Was.—Allen 4 run (Blanton kick), 11:59.

Second Quarter
Ind.—FG, Blanchard 21, 5:18.
Was.—Shepherd 7 pass from Frerotte (Blanton kick), 10:03.
Ind.—Faulk 1 run (Blanchard kick), 13:03.
Ind.—FG, Blanchard 49, 15:00.

Third Quarter
Was.—Allen 1 run (Blanton kick), 12:19.
Ind.—FG, Blanchard 51, 14:57.

Fourth Quarter
Was.—Allen 32 run (Blanton kick), 4:37.
Attendance—54,254.

TEAM STATISTICS

	Indianapolis	Washington
First downs	18	25
Rushes-yards	24-100	37-215
Passing	198	173
Punt returns	0-0	2-79
Kickoff returns	5-102	4-101
Interception returns	1-20	0-0
Comp.-att.-int.	17-33-0	18-25-1
Sacked-yards lost	1-0	1-5
Punts	3-51	2-39
Fumbles-lost	2-1	0-0
Penalties-yards	6-45	6-53
Time of possession	27:59	32:01

INDIVIDUAL STATISTICS

RUSHING—Indianapolis, Faulk 13-53, Harbaugh 5-28, Warren 5-23, Harrison 1-(minus 4). Washington, Allen 22-124, Logan 5-43, Davis 4-25, Mitchell 3-22, Frerotte 3-1.

PASSING—Indianapolis, Harbaugh 17-33-0-198. Washington, Frerotte 18-25-1-178.

RECEIVING—Indianapolis, Dawkins 5-61, Faulk 4-39, Dilger 3-58, Harrison 2-18, Stock 1-13, Warren 1-8, Groce 1-1. Washington, Shepherd 4-34, Ellard 3-55, Logan 3-30, Mitchell 3-26, Westbrook 2-21, Asher 1-8, Allen 1-7, Galbraith 1-(minus 3).

MISSED FIELD GOAL ATTEMPTS—Indianapolis, Blanchard 42.

INTERCEPTIONS—Indianapolis, Morrison 1-20.

KICKOFF RETURNS—Indianapolis, Stock 5-102. Washington, Mitchell 4-101.

PUNT RETURNS—Washington, Mitchell 2-79.

SACKS—Indianapolis, Grant 1. Washington, Harvey 1.

RAVENS 37, RAMS 31

Sunday, October 27

St. Louis	7	6	7	11	0—31
Baltimore	0	6	11	14	6—37

First Quarter
St.L.—Bruce 8 pass from Banks (Lohmiller kick), 12:19.

Second Quarter
St.L.—FG, Lohmiller 50, 2:44.
St.L.—FG, Lohmiller 38, 10:06.
Bal.—F. Turner 27 pass from Testaverde (kick failed), 13:41.

Third Quarter
St.L.—Lyght 25 interception return (Lohmiller kick), 4:28.
Bal.—FG, Stover 50, 5:47.
Bal.—Morris 3 run (Alexander pass from Testaverde), 9:41.

Fourth Quarter
St.L.—FG, Lohmiller 36, :05.
Bal.—Alexander 13 pass from Testaverde (Stover kick), 1:43.
Bal.—Morris 10 run (Stover kick), 8:24.
St.L.—Green 1 run (Green run), 11:53.

Overtime
Bal.—Jackson 22 pass from Testaverde, 14:50.
Attendance—60,256.

TEAM STATISTICS

	St. Louis	Baltimore
First downs	26	25
Rushes-yards	46-165	17-74
Passing	321	404
Punt returns	2-43	2-20
Kickoff returns	6-108	6-117
Interception returns	2-47	2-11
Comp.-att.-int.	26-40-2	31-51-2
Sacked-yards lost	6-32	3-25
Punts	5-43	6-48
Fumbles-lost	4-2	2-2
Penalties-yards	14-104	8-51
Time of possession	45:43	29:07

INDIVIDUAL STATISTICS

RUSHING—St. Louis, Phillips 31-83, Banks 8-50, Green 6-32, Martin 1-0. Baltimore, Byner 11-18, Morris 6-56.

PASSING—St. Louis, Banks 26-40-2-353. Baltimore, Testaverde 31-51-2-429.

RECEIVING—St. Louis, Bruce 11-229, Kennison 4-49, Green 4-31, Thomas 2-15, Ross 2-14, Clay 2-8, Conwell 1-7. Baltimore, Jackson 7-113, F. Turner 6-108, Byner 6-96, Alexander 4-64, Kinchen 4-35, Green 3-10, Morris 1-3.

MISSED FIELD GOAL ATTEMPTS—Baltimore, Stover 43, 32.

INTERCEPTIONS—St. Louis, Lyght 1-25, Lyle 1-22. Baltimore, Moore 1-10, E. Turner 1-1.

KICKOFF RETURNS—St. Louis, Thomas 5-81, Kennison 1-27. Baltimore, J. Lewis 4-79, Baldwin 1-19, Kinchen 1-19.

PUNT RETURNS—St. Louis, Kennison 2-43. Baltimore, J. Lewis 2-20.

SACKS—St. Louis, Carter 2, O'Neal 1. Baltimore, Caldwell 2, Croel 1¹/₂, Pleasant 1¹/₂, J. Williams 1.

BENGALS 28, JAGUARS 21

Sunday, October 27

Jacksonville	0	7	7	7—21	
Cincinnati	0	7	0	21—28	

Second Quarter
Jac.—Brunell 14 run (Hollis kick), 2:21.
Cin.—Pickens 11 pass from Blake (Pelfrey kick), 7:06.

Third Quarter
Jac.—Means 11 pass from Brunell (Hollis kick), 12:19.

Fourth Quarter
Cin.—Pickens 10 pass from Blake (Pelfrey kick), :06.
Cin.—Carter 1 run (Pelfrey kick), 8:50.
Cin.—Carter 4 run (Pelfrey kick), 11:28.
Jac.—Smith 11 pass from Brunell (Hollis kick), 13:25.
Attendance—45,890.

TEAM STATISTICS

	Jacksonville	Cincinnati
First downs	19	18
Rushes-yards	28-149	31-60
Passing	189	207
Punt returns	5-41	2-8
Kickoff returns	4-75	3-57
Interception returns	0-0	2-0
Comp.-att.-int.	18-31-2	20-31-0
Sacked-yards lost	4-26	5-42
Punts	7-44	6-48
Fumbles-lost	2-0	0-0
Penalties-yards	8-48	5-33
Time of possession	28:24	31:36

INDIVIDUAL STATISTICS

RUSHING—Jacksonville, Stewart 14-80, Brunell 7-45, Means 7-24. Cincinnati, Carter 8-27, Hearst 8-18, Bieniemy 5-8, Blake 4-14, Wilhelm 3-(minus 2), Cothran 2-0, Scott 1-(minus 5).

PASSING—Jacksonville, Brunell 18-31-2-215. Cincinnati, Blake 19-30-0-244, Wilhelm 1-1-0-5.

RECEIVING—Jacksonville, McCardell 5-52, Rison 3-74, Smith 3-47, Stewart 2-5, Brown 1-12, Means 1-11, Mitchell 1-7, Hallock 1-5, W. Jackson 1-2. Cincinnati, Pickens 6-51, Bieniemy 6-47, Dunn 3-66, Scott 2-51, McGee 1-18, Carter 1-8, Battaglia 1-8.

MISSED FIELD GOAL ATTEMPTS—None.

INTERCEPTIONS—Cincinnati, Orlando 1-0, Francis 1-0.

KICKOFF RETURNS—Jacksonville, R. Bell 2-39, Jordan 1-24, W. Jackson 1-12. Cincinnati, Sawyer 2-39, Dunn 1-18.

PUNT RETURNS—Jacksonville, Hudson 4-39, McCardell 1-2. Cincinnati, Myers 2-8.

SACKS—Jacksonville, Simmons 3, Brackens 1, Smeenge 1. Cincinnati, Johnson 1, Copeland 1, Wilkinson 1, Stallings 1.

PACKERS 13, BUCCANEERS 7

Sunday, October 27

Tampa Bay	0	0	0	7—7	
Green Bay	3	10	0	0—13	

First Quarter
G.B.—FG, Jacke 40, 9:19.

Second Quarter
G.B.—Levens 1 run (Jacke kick), :52.
G.B.—FG, Jacke 48, 14:01.

Fourth Quarter
T.B.—Moore 11 pass from Dilfer (Husted kick), 9:32.
Attendance—60,627.

TEAM STATISTICS

	Tampa Bay	Green Bay
First downs	14	24
Rushes-yards	26-57	37-124
Passing	139	165
Punt returns	1-26	2-2
Kickoff returns	4-113	2-3

	Tampa Bay	Green Bay
Interception returns	1-1	2-0
Comp.-att.-int.	15-29-2	19-31-1
Sacked-yards lost	3-25	2-9
Punts	5-30	2-43
Fumbles-lost	2-0	4-1
Penalties-yards	6-45	4-20
Time of possession	29:30	30:30

INDIVIDUAL STATISTICS

RUSHING—Tampa Bay, Rhett 12-29, R. Brooks 7-14, Alstott 4-8, Dilfer 2-3, Ellison 1-3. Green Bay, Bennett 20-93, Levens 7-21, Favre 7-2, Henderson 3-13.

PASSING—Tampa Bay, Dilfer 15-29-2-164. Green Bay, Favre 19-31-1-178.

RECEIVING—Tampa Bay, Alstott 4-34, Williams 3-38, Moore 2-28, R. Thomas 2-28, Hawkins 2-25, Harper 1-7, Ellison 1-4. Green Bay, Howard 5-0, Chmura 3-59, Beebe 3-23, Mayes 2-20, Levens 2-10, Bennett 2-7, Henderson 1-16, Jackson 1-13.

MISSED FIELD GOAL ATTEMPTS—Tampa Bay, Husted 27. Green Bay, Jacke 46.

INTERCEPTIONS—Tampa Bay, Lynch 1-1. Green Bay, Robinson 1-0, Evans 1-0.

KICKOFF RETURNS—Tampa Bay, Williams 4-113. Green Bay, Howard 2-38.

PUNT RETURNS—Tampa Bay, Williams 1-26. Green Bay, Howard 2-24.

SACKS—Tampa Bay, Marts 1, Ahanotu 1. Green Bay, Butler 1 1/2, White 1, Williams 1/2.

SEAHAWKS 32, CHARGERS 13

Sunday, October 27

San Diego	3	3	0	7—13
Seattle	3	17	3	9—32

First Quarter
Sea.—FG, Peterson 33, 3:45.
S.D.—FG, Carney 41, 8:00.

Second Quarter
S.D.—FG, Carney 43, 1:30.
Sea.—FG, Peterson 44, 4:00.
Sea.—Smith 10 run (Peterson kick), 8:18.
Sea.—D. Williams 79 interception return (Peterson kick), 12:21.

Third Quarter
Sea.—FG, Peterson 47, 10:43.

Fourth Quarter
Sea.—FG, Peterson 27, 1:15.
S.D.—Jones 27 pass from Salisbury (Carney kick), 2:24.
Sea.—Warren 37 run (run failed), 10:12.
Attendance—38,143.

TEAM STATISTICS

	San Diego	Seattle
First downs	15	18
Rushes-yards	21-69	34-208
Passing	253	196
Punt returns	4-38	5-40
Kickoff returns	8-206	3-74
Interception returns	0-0	4-78
Comp.-att.-int.	21-43-4	16-33-0
Sacked-yards lost	4-38	2-10
Punts	6-50	7-36
Fumbles-lost	3-1	2-1
Penalties-yards	7-51	7-52
Time of possession	27:31	32:29

INDIVIDUAL STATISTICS

RUSHING—San Diego, Russell 10-33, Fletcher 8-36, Hayden 3-0. Seattle, Warren 19-146, Smith 11-54, Friesz 2-(minus 2), Broussard 1-6, Galloway 1-4.

PASSING—San Diego, Salisbury 21-43-4-291. Seattle, Friesz 16-33-0-206.

RECEIVING—San Diego, Jones 7-79, Fletcher 4-51, Martin 3-43, Still 2-, A. Coleman 2-22, Russell 1-20, May 1-6, Pupunu 1-6. Seattle, Blades 4-, Warren 4-40, Proehl 4-29, Strong 2-12, Pritchard 1-41, Galloway 1-18.

MISSED FIELD GOAL ATTEMPTS—None.

INTERCEPTIONS—Seattle, D. Williams 2-75, Bellamy 1-2, Blackmon 1-1.

KICKOFF RETURNS—San Diego, A. Coleman 8-206, Broussard 3-74.

PUNT RETURNS—San Diego, Da. Gordon 4-38. Seattle, R. Harris 5-40.

SACKS—San Diego, Bush 1, Johnson 1. Seattle, Kennedy 1, McCrary 1, Sims 1, Sinclair 1.

BRONCOS 34, CHIEFS 7

Sunday, October 27

Kansas City	7	0	0	0— 7
Denver	17	7	7	3—34

First Quarter
Den.—Sharpe 46 pass from Elway (Elam kick), 5:24.
Den.—FG, Elam 40, 9:03.
K.C.—Vanover 97 kickoff return (Stoyanovich kick), 9:22.
Den.—Sharpe 10 pass from Elway (Elam kick), 12:11.

Second Quarter
Den.—Sherrard 25 pass from Elway (Elam kick), 14:14.

Third Quarter
Den.—Craver 1 run (Elam kick), 12:51.

Fourth Quarter
Den.—FG, Elam 29, 5:02.
Attendance—75,652.

TEAM STATISTICS

	Kansas City	Denver
First downs	10	26
Rushes-yards	12-24	43-213
Passing	208	286
Punt returns	0-0	7-99
Kickoff returns	7-200	2-48
Interception returns	2-3	2-0
Comp.-att.-int.	21-49-2	16-32-2
Sacked-yards lost	1-5	0-0
Punts	8-48	3-40
Fumbles-lost	0-0	2-1
Penalties-yards	12-88	7-60
Time of possession	25:59	34:01

INDIVIDUAL STATISTICS

RUSHING—Kansas City, Allen 7-22, Anders 3-(minus 2), Bennett 1-2, McNair 1-2. Denver, Davis 21-77, Elway 8-62, Hebron 7-73, Musgrave 4-(minus 3), Craver 3-4.

PASSING—Kansas City, Bono 21-49-2-213. Denver, Elway 16-31-1-286, Musgrave 0-1-1-0.

RECEIVING—Kansas City, Cash 4-26, Penn 3-52, Vanover 3-40, Allen 3-29, Johnson 2-27, LaChapelle 2-15, Hughes 1-12, Horn 1-9, McNair 1-2, Bennett 1-1. Denver, Sharpe 6-99, Miller 3-88, R. Smith 2-22, Craver 2-20, Sherrard 1-25, Davis 1-22, McCaffrey 1-10.

MISSED FIELD GOAL ATTEMPTS—Kansas City, Stoyanovich 54. Denver, Elam 47.

INTERCEPTIONS—Kansas City, Washington 1-3, Collins 1-0. Denver, Braxton 1-0, Crockett 1-0.

KICKOFF RETURNS—Kansas City, Vanover 5-163, Woods 1-21, McNair 1-16. Denver, Hebron 2-48.

PUNT RETURNS—Denver, R. Smith 7-99.

SACKS—Denver, A. Williams 1.

COWBOYS 29, DOLPHINS 10

Sunday, October 27

Dallas	3	6	13	7—29
Miami	0	10	0	0—10

First Quarter
Dal.—FG, Boniol 33, 7:14.

Second Quarter
Dal.—FG, Boniol 29, :04.
Mia.—Pritchett 16 pass from Marino (Nedney kick), 4:28.
Mia.—FG, Nedney 26, 13:11.
Dal.—FG, Boniol 24, 15:00.

Third Quarter
Dal.—Bjornson 4 pass from Aikman (Boniol kick), 5:34.
Dal.—Irvin 2 pass from Aikman (kick failed), 10:20.

Fourth Quarter
Dal.—E. Smith 10 pass from Aikman (Boniol kick), 2:11.
Attendance—75,283.

TEAM STATISTICS

	Dallas	Miami
First downs	27	10
Rushes-yards	36-123	13-48
Passing	359	173
Punt returns	5-54	1-5
Kickoff returns	2-40	6-161
Interception returns	1-0	0-0
Comp.-att.-int.	33-41-0	12-27-1
Sacked-yards lost	1-4	0-0
Punts	4-45	5-54
Fumbles-lost	1-0	2-2
Penalties-yards	9-65	3-22
Time of possession	41:58	18:02

INDIVIDUAL STATISTICS

RUSHING—Dallas, E. Smith 22-74, S. Williams 8-48, Aikman 4-4, Johnston 1-1, Sanders 1-(minus 4). Miami, Abdul-Jabbar 7-29, Spikes 3-6, McPhail 2-14, Erickson 1-(minus 1).

PASSING—Dallas, Aikman 33-41-0-363. Miami, Marino 12-27-1-173.

RECEIVING—Dallas, Irvin 12-186, E. Smith 7-44, Sanders 5-60, Bjornson 4-19, Johnston 2-28, Martin 2-23, Walker 1-3. Miami, McDuffie 3-32, R. Hill 2-46, Pritchett 2-24, Parmalee 2-23, McPhail 2-12, Jordan 1-36.

MISSED FIELD GOAL ATTEMPTS—None.

INTERCEPTIONS—Dallas, K. Smith 1-0.

KICKOFF RETURNS—Dallas, Walker 2-40. Miami, Spikes 4-92, McPhail 2-69.

PUNT RETURNS—Dallas, Martin 5-54. Miami, McDuffie 1-5.

SACKS—Miami, Stubbs 1.

JETS 31, CARDINALS 21

Sunday, October 27

N.Y. Jets	3	14	0	14—31
Arizona	0	0	14	7—21

First Quarter
NYJ—FG, Lowery 37, 12:13.

Second Quarter
NYJ—Johnson 34 pass from Reich (Lowery kick), :07.
NYJ—Anderson 1 run (Lowery kick), 14:44.

Third Quarter
Ariz.—Centers 1 pass from K. Graham (G. Davis kick), 7:25.
Ariz.—Centers 2 pass from K. Graham (G. Davis kick), 9:13.

Fourth Quarter
NYJ—Murrell 1 run (Lowery kick), 2:09.
Ariz.—R. Moore 6 pass from K. Graham (G. Davis kick), 3:13.
NYJ—Cobb 2 run (Lowery kick), 10:05.
Attendance—28,088.

TEAM STATISTICS

	N.Y. Jets	Arizona
First downs	27	19
Rushes-yards	38-208	21-107
Passing	246	246
Punt returns	1-2	2-6
Kickoff returns	4-59	4-156
Interception returns	1-0	2-23
Comp.-att.-int.	22-31-2	17-32-1
Sacked-yards lost	1-8	1-9
Punts	2-44	4-41
Fumbles-lost	1-1	0-0
Penalties-yards	8-76	8-108
Time of possession	37:10	22:50

INDIVIDUAL STATISTICS

RUSHING—New York, Murrell 31-199, Reich 3-3, Cobb 2-5, Anderson 2-1. Arizona, L. Johnson 12-85, Centers 6-8, McElroy 2-6, K. Graham 1-8.

PASSING—New York, Reich 22-31-2-254. Arizona, K. Graham 17-32-1-255.

RECEIVING—New York, Johnson 7-94, Chrebet 5-46, Anderson 3-35, Graham 3-34, F. Baxter 1-18, Brady 1-18, Van Dyke 1-5, Murrell 1-4. Arizona, R. Moore 7-143, Centers 6-58, Edwards 2-24, Sanders 1-19, Dowdell 1-11.

MISSED FIELD GOAL ATTEMPTS—Arizona, G. Davis 28, 33.

INTERCEPTIONS—New York, Young 1-0. Arizona, Williams 2-23.

KICKOFF RETURNS—New York, Bailey 4-59. Arizona, McElroy 4-156.

PUNT RETURNS—New York, Chrebet 1-2. Arizona, Dowdell 2-6.

SACKS—New York, Lewis 1/2, Washington 1/2. Arizona, Joyner 1.

EAGLES 20, PANTHERS 9

Sunday, October 27

Carolina	0	3	6	0— 9
Philadelphia	7	7	3	3—20

First Quarter
Phi.—Watters 3 run (Anderson kick), 9:39.

Second Quarter
Phi.—Dunn 9 pass from Detmer (Anderson kick), 13:58.
Car.—FG, Kasay 47, 15:00.

Third Quarter
Phi.—FG, Anderson 46, 5:31.
Car.—FG, Kasay 39, 8:06.
Car.—FG, Kasay 29, 11:24.

Fourth Quarter
Phi.—FG, Anderson 21, 5:31.
Attendance—65,982.

TEAM STATISTICS

	Carolina	Philadelphia
First downs	10	16
Rushes-yards	26-61	27-30
Passing	239	329
Punt returns	3-30	3-11
Kickoff returns	5-149	1-20
Interception returns	1-10	0-0
Comp.-att.-int.	16-34-0	23-38-1
Sacked-yards lost	1-9	2-13
Punts	7-39	9-43
Fumbles-lost	3-2	1-0
Penalties-yards	6-39	7-73
Time of possession	26:39	33:21

INDIVIDUAL STATISTICS

RUSHING—Carolina, Johnson 18-45, Collins 4-16, Oliver 3-2, Griffith 1-(minus 2). Philadelphia, Watters 21-33, Detmer 4-1, Garner 1-(minus 2) Turner 1-(minus 2).

PASSING—Carolina, Collins 16-34-0-248. Philadelphia, Detmer 23-38-1-342

RECEIVING—Carolina, Carrier 5-82, Muhammad 3-45, Johnson 2-64, Griffith 2-28, Walls 2-18, Oliver 2-11. Philadelphia, Fryar 7-143, Jones 5-72, Dunn 3-26, Turner 3-14, Watters 2-9, West 1-29, J. Johnson 1-26, Solomon 1-23.

MISSED FIELD GOAL ATTEMPTS—Carolina, Kasay 51.

INTERCEPTIONS—Carolina, Davis 1-10.

KICKOFF RETURNS—Carolina, Bates 4-138, Baker 1-11. Philadelphia Witherspoon 1-20.

PUNT RETURNS—Carolina, Oliver 3-30. Philadelphia, Seay 3-13.

SACKS—Carolina, Lathon 1, Bickett 1. Philadelphia, H. Thomas 1.

PATRIOTS 28, BILLS 25

Sunday, October 27

Buffalo	0	0	10	15—25
New England	7	6	2	13—28

First Quarter
N.E.—Martin 4 pass from Bledsoe (Vinatieri kick), 13:43.

Second Quarter
N.E.—FG, Vinatieri 40, 5:01.
N.E.—FG, Vinatieri 32, 15:00.

Third Quarter
Buf.—FG, Christie 33, 6:40.
Buf.—Holmes 6 pass from Kelly (Christie kick), 11:09.
N.E.—Safety, Kelly called for intentional grounding in the end zone as h was being sacked, 13:08.

Fourth Quarter
Buf.—T. Thomas 1 run (Holmes run), 6:10.
N.E.—Martin 10 run (kick failed), 13:35.
N.E.—McGinest 46 interception return (Vinatieri kick), 14:19.
Buf.—Reed 48 pass from Kelly (Christie kick), 14:36.
Attendance—58,858.

TEAM STATISTICS

	Buffalo	New England
First downs	18	23
Rushes-yards	32-141	28-59
Passing	196	358
Punt returns	2-5	4-14
Kickoff returns	5-108	6-81
Interception returns	0-0	1-46
Comp.-att.-int.	15-32-1	32-45-0
Sacked-yards lost	1-8	2-15
Punts	7-44	4-50
Fumbles-lost	0-0	1-1
Penalties-yards	9-67	9-63
Time of possession	26:53	33:07

INDIVIDUAL STATISTICS

RUSHING—Buffalo, T. Thomas 26-119, Holmes 3-6, Kelly 1-12, Tindale 1-4, Tasker 1-0. New England, Martin 21-54, Meggett 4-6, Bledsoe 3-(minus 1).

PASSING—Buffalo, Kelly 15-32-1-204. New England, Bledsoe 32-45-0-373.

RECEIVING—Buffalo, Johnson 6-47, Reed 4-121, Early 3-32, Holmes 1-6, Cline 1-(minus 2). New England, Byars 7-52, Martin 5-21, Jefferson 4-95, Glenn 4-65, Coates 4-40, Gash 4-31, T. Brown 3-43, Meggett 1-26.

MISSED FIELD GOAL ATTEMPTS—New England, Vinatieri 54.

INTERCEPTIONS—New England, McGinest 1-46.

KICKOFF RETURNS—Buffalo, Moulds 5-108. New England, T. Brown 3-56, Meggett 1-16, Gisler 1-9, Byars 1-0.

PUNT RETURNS—Buffalo, Burris 2-5. New England, Meggett 4-14.

SACKS—Buffalo, Hansen 1, Northern 1. New England, McGinest 1.

GIANTS 35, LIONS 7

Sunday, October 27

N.Y. Giants	2	23	0	10—35
Detroit	7	0	0	0— 7

First Quarter
Det.—Mitchell 1 run (Hanson kick), 3:18.
NYG—Safety, punt blocked out of end zone by T. Wooten for a safety, 9:07.

Second Quarter
NYG—Calloway 24 pass from Wheatley (run failed), 4:43.
NYG—FG, Daluiso 38, 7:01.
NYG—Douglass 32 interception return (Daluiso kick), 8:11.
NYG—Lewis 23 pass from Brown (Daluiso kick), 9:37.

Fourth Quarter
NYG—FG, Daluiso 32, 6:24.
NYG—Agnew 34 interception return (Daluiso kick), 12:57.
Attendance—63,501.

TEAM STATISTICS

	N.Y. Giants	Detroit
First downs	18	14
Rushes-yards	39-100	20-67
Passing	235	185
Punt returns	2-9	3-30
Kickoff returns	3-62	5-158
Interception returns	5-125	1-(-2)
Comp.-att.-int.	16-28-1	20-47-5
Sacked-yards lost	2-10	2-12
Punts	6-43	5-40
Fumbles-lost	3-1	2-1
Penalties-yards	7-67	9-65
Time of possession	35:39	24:21

INDIVIDUAL STATISTICS

RUSHING—New York, Hampton 27-76, Wheatley 5-18, Brown 3-2, Kanell 3-(minus 3), Way 1-7. Detroit, Sanders 16-47, Majkowski 3-19, Mitchell 1-1.

PASSING—New York, Brown 15-27-1-221, Wheatley 1-1-0-24. Detroit, Majkowski 11-28-2-126, Mitchell 9-19-3-71.

RECEIVING—New York, Lewis 5-76, Calloway 4-92, Way 3-22, Pierce 2-31, Hampton 2-24. Detroit, Perriman 8-88, H. Moore 4-49, Metzelaars 3-31, Sanders 3-20, Morton 2-9.

MISSED FIELD GOAL ATTEMPTS—New York, Daluiso 43.

INTERCEPTIONS—New York, Wooten 1-35, Agnew 1-34, Douglass 1-32, Beamon 1-20, Widmer 1-4. Detroit, McNeil 1-(minus 2).

KICKOFF RETURNS—New York, Wheatley 2-47, Lewis 1-15. Detroit, Milburn 4-143, Lynch 1-15.

PUNT RETURNS—New York, Lewis 2-9. Detroit, Milburn 3-30.

SACKS—New York, Armstead 1, Widmer 1. Detroit, London 1, Porcher 1.

BEARS 15, VIKINGS 13

Monday, October 28

Chicago	2	13	0	0—15
Minnesota	3	0	10	0—13

First Quarter
Min.—FG, Sisson 41, 9:07.
Chi.—Safety, punt blocked out of end zone by K. Miniefield for a safety, 13:38.

Second Quarter
Chi.—FG, Jaeger 41, 11:19.
Chi.—Salaam 1 run (Jaeger kick), 14:22.
Chi.—FG, Jaeger 44, 14:55.

Third Quarter
Min.—Ismail 54 pass from Moon (Sisson kick), 3:31.
Min.—FG, Sisson 43, 13:05.
Attendance—58,143.

TEAM STATISTICS

	Chicago	Minnesota
First downs	18	16
Rushes-yards	29-96	14-11
Passing	180	268
Punt returns	0-0	2-11
Kickoff returns	5-129	4-63
Interception returns	1-0	2-0
Comp.-att.-int.	23-35-2	25-41-1
Sacked-yards lost	1-7	5-29
Punts	3-40	4-31
Fumbles-lost	0-0	4-1
Penalties-yards	6-63	12-75
Time of possession	32:39	27:21

INDIVIDUAL STATISTICS

RUSHING—Chicago, R. Harris 15-61, Salaam 11-36, Krieg 2-(minus 1), T. Carter 1-0. Minnesota, Graham 4-8, R. Smith 4-(minus 1), Lee 4-(minus 2), Evans 2-6.

PASSING—Chicago, Krieg 23-35-2-187. Minnesota, Moon 15-26-1-218, B. Johnson 10-15-0-79.

RECEIVING—Chicago, Timpson 7-78, Conway 5-68, Wetnight 5-19, Jennings 3-19, T. Carter 2-1, Engram 1-2. Minnesota, Reed 11-153, Lee 5-36, Carter 5-34, Ismail 3-70, Evans 1-4.

MISSED FIELD GOAL ATTEMPTS—Chicago, Jaeger 44, 46. Minnesota, Sisson 48.

INTERCEPTIONS—Chicago, Carrier 1-0. Minnesota, Thomas 1-0, Fisk 1-0.

KICKOFF RETURNS—Chicago, Engram 5-129. Minnesota, Ismail 3-51, Brown 1-12.

PUNT RETURNS—Minnesota, Palmer 2-11.

SACKS—Chicago, Cox 1, Flanigan 1, A. Fontenot 1, Spellman 1, Thierry 1. Minnesota, Griffith 1.

RESULTS

ATLANTA 20, Carolina 17
BUFFALO 38, Washington 13
CHICAGO 13, Tampa Bay 10
Cincinnati 24, BALTIMORE 21
GREEN BAY 28, Detroit 18
Kansas City 21, MINNESOTA 6
NEW ENGLAND 42, Miami 23
N.Y. GIANTS 16, Arizona 8
Philadelphia 31, DALLAS 21
PITTSBURGH 42, St. Louis 6
San Diego 26, INDIANAPOLIS 19
San Francisco 24, NEW ORLEANS 17
SEATTLE 23, Houston 16
Denver 22, OAKLAND 21

Open date: Jacksonville, N.Y. Jets

STANDINGS

AFC EAST	W	L	T	Pct.
Buffalo	6	3	0	.667
New England	6	3	0	.667
Indianapolis	5	4	0	.556
Miami	4	5	0	.444
N.Y. Jets	1	8	0	.111

AFC CENTRAL	W	L	T	Pct.
Pittsburgh	7	2	0	.778
Houston	5	4	0	.556
Baltimore	3	6	0	.333
Cincinnati	3	6	0	.333
Jacksonville	3	6	0	.333

AFC WEST	W	L	T	Pct.
Denver	8	1	0	.889
Kansas City	6	3	0	.667
San Diego	5	4	0	.556
Oakland	4	5	0	.444
Seattle	4	5	0	.444

NFC EAST	W	L	T	Pct.
Philadelphia	7	2	0	.778
Washington	7	2	0	.778
Dallas	5	4	0	.556
N.Y. Giants	4	5	0	.444
Arizona	3	6	0	.333

NFC CENTRAL	W	L	T	Pct.
Green Bay	8	1	0	.889
Minnesota	5	4	0	.556
Chicago	4	5	0	.444
Detroit	4	5	0	.444
Tampa Bay	1	8	0	.111

NFC WEST	W	L	T	Pct.
San Francisco	7	2	0	.778
Carolina	5	4	0	.556
New Orleans	2	7	0	.222
St. Louis	2	7	0	.222
Atlanta	1	8	0	.111

HIGHLIGHTS

Hero of the week: San Francisco wide receiver Jerry Rice caught a 36-yard touchdown pass, set up another score with the 1,000th reception of his career and recovered an onside kick late in the game, helping seal the 49ers' 24-17 victory over New Orleans. Rice became the first player in NFL history to catch 1,000 passes.

Goat of the week: Indianapolis quarterback Jim Harbaugh, who had only five passes intercepted in 1995, was picked off four times as the Colts fell to San Diego, 26-19. Harbaugh, who was intercepted on four of the Colts' first five possessions, also was sacked six times and fumbled once. He was only 18-of-44.

Sub of the week: Quarterback Danny Kanell, who never had taken a snap in an NFL game other than to kneel down, came on in relief for an injured Dave Brown and helped the New York Giants beat NFC East division rival Arizona, 16-8. Kanell, who came into the game in the first quarter when Brown went to the sideline with a bruised back and back spasms, was 14-of-27 for 128 yards and did not turn the ball over despite being blitzed frequently. His 24-yard scoring pass to Thomas Lewis in the third quarter put the Giants comfortably ahead, 13-0.

Comeback of the week: Visiting Cincinnati rallied from an 18-point halftime deficit and beat Baltimore, 24-21 in dramatic fashion when Doug Pelfrey kicked a 34-yard field goal as time expired. The Bengals trailed, 21-3, at halftime, had drives of 88, 77, 45 and 56 yards in the second half. Quarterback Jeff Blake (22-of-39 for 255 yards and one touchdown) led Cincinnati from its 28 to the Ravens' 16 in six plays, setting up Pelfrey's game-winning kick.

Blowout of the week: Jerome Bettis was a one-man steamroller as Pittsburgh flattened St. Louis, 42-6. Bettis gained a huge measure of revenge on his former team as he rushed 19 times for 129 yards and two touchdowns. The Steelers outrushed the Rams, 248 yards to 64, and rookie Lawrence Phillips, drafted to replace Bettis in the St. Louis lineup, rushed for only 6 yards.

Nail-biter of the week: Just when Dallas appeared to be moving in for the game-winning touchdown or, at the least, getting in position for a tying field goal, middle linebacker James Willis saved the day for Philadelphia. With time running out in regulation, Willis intercepted Troy Aikman's pass four yards deep in the end zone, ran it out to the 10 and lateralled to Troy Vincent, who went the final 90 yards for a touchdown that gave the Eagles a 31-21 triumph over their NFC East rivals. The victory vaulted Philadelphia into a first-place tie with Washington.

Hit of the week: With Tampa Bay leading Chicago, 10-6, in the third quarter, Buccaneers running back Errict Rhett was hit by linebacker Joe Cain and fumbled at Chicago's 47. Players from both teams stood around momentarily until Bears linebacker Vinson Smith, realizing the whistle hadn't blown, picked up the ball and returned it 34 yards to Tampa Bay's 19. That led to Raymont Harris' game-winning, 1-yard touchdown run as the Bears won 13-10.

Oddity of the week: Quarterbacks Dave Brown of the Giants and Kent Graham of the Cardinals were supposed to do battle in a showdown of former teammates, but both left the game with injuries in the first quarter. Brown suffered a bruised back and back spasms and Graham suffered a knee injury. They ended up in the Giants' training room, where they watched the rest of the game on television.

Top rusher: Barry Sanders gained 152 yards on 20 carries, including an 18-yard run during which he eluded four tacklers, in Detroit's 28-18 loss to Green Bay.

Top passer: Drew Bledsoe was 30-of-41 for 419 yards and three touchdowns in directing New England to a 42-23 win over Miami.

Top receiver: Tight end Ben Coates caught five passes for 135 yards and two touchdowns in the Patriots' victory.

Notes: The screen pass was a particularly effective weapon for New England. Coates scored an 84-yard touchdown, running the last 80 yards, and running back Curtis Martin turned another screen pass into a 41-yard gain. . . . The milestones continued to pile up for Kansas

City running back Marcus Allen. In the Chiefs' 21-6 win over Minnesota, Allen rushed for his 110th career touchdown, tying Walter Payton's NFL record; caught his 566th pass, matching Roger Craig's record for a running back; and played in his 199th game, equaling Mosi Tatupu's mark for backs. . . . Pittsburgh's five rushing touchdowns matched the team record in one game. . . . Green Bay improved to 8-1 for the first time since 1963. . . . Packers quarterback Brett Favre threw four touchdown passes, giving him 25 for the season. . . . Atlanta became the last team to win this season when it upset Carolina, 20-19. The Falcons thus avoided tying the worst start in franchise history—0-9 by the 1966 expansion team. . . . Washington's winning streak was stopped at seven games as the Redskins were routed in Buffalo, 38-13. . . . Quarterback John Elway ran for a career-high 70 yards in Denver's victory over Oakland. . . . The Raiders lost a Monday night game at home for the first time. They had been 8-0 in Oakland and 4-0 in Los Angeles. . . . Buffalo's Jim Kelly became the 11th quarterback in NFL history to surpass 34,000 passing yards. . . . Philadelphia kicker Gary Anderson became the fourth player to score 1,500 points. . . . Minnesota scored 14 or fewer points for the fourth consecutive game.

Quote of the week: Marcus Allen, after the Chiefs rushed for a season-high 202 yards in the victory over Minnesota: "The big picture is to wear a team down. That's what the running game is all about. Passing does not destroy a team's will. You destroy a team's will by running the ball."

GAME SUMMARIES

EAGLES 31, COWBOYS 21

Sunday, November 3

Philadelphia	7	7	7	10—31
Dallas	7	3	3	8—21

First Quarter
Dal.—E. Smith 1 run (Boniol kick), 1:06.
Phi.—Watters 5 run (Anderson kick), 7:25.

Second Quarter
Dal.—FG, Boniol 19, 3:48.
Phi.—Detmer 6 run (Anderson kick), 14:01.

Third Quarter
Dal.—FG, Boniol 37, 6:48.
Phi.—Fryar 14 pass from Detmer (Anderson kick), 13:03.

Fourth Quarter
Dal.—E. Smith 7 run (Bjornson pass from Aikman), 4:46.
Phi.—FG, Anderson 30, 11:41.
Phi.—Vincent 90 interception return (Anderson kick), 14:45.
Attendance—64,952.

TEAM STATISTICS

	Philadelphia	Dallas
First downs	22	22
Rushes-yards	30-130	31-117
Passing	217	179
Punt returns	1-8	3-19
Kickoff returns	5-76	6-164
Interception returns	2-108	0-0
Comp.-att.-int.	19-33-0	21-33-2
Sacked-yards lost	0-0	0-0
Punts	3-49	2-52
Fumbles-lost	0-0	2-0
Penalties-yards	12-71	3-34
Time of possession	30:02	29:58

INDIVIDUAL STATISTICS

RUSHING—Philadelphia, Watters 24-116, Detmer 5-12, Garner 1-2. Dallas, E. Smith 24-113, Aikman 3-4, S. Williams 3-(minus 3), Johnston 1-3.

PASSING—Philadelphia, Detmer 19-33-0-217. Dallas, Aikman 21-33-2-179.

RECEIVING—Philadelphia, Fryar 9-120, Jones 3-23, Seay 2-36, West 1-18, J. Johnson 1-9, Garner 1-4, Turner 1-4, Watters 1-3. Dallas, Irvin 7-89, Martin 4-42, E. Smith 4-4, Bjornson 3-14, Sanders 2-24, Johnston 1-6.

MISSED FIELD GOAL ATTEMPTS—None.

INTERCEPTIONS—Philadelphia, Willis 1-14, J. Fuller 1-4.

KICKOFF RETURNS—Philadelphia, Witherspoon 4-66, Seay 1-10. Dallas, Walker 6-159.

PUNT RETURNS—Philadelphia, Seay 1-8. Dallas, Martin 3-19.

SACKS—None.

GIANTS 16, CARDINALS 8

Sunday, November 3

Arizona	0	0	0	8— 8
N.Y. Giants	3	0	3	10—16

First Quarter
NYG—FG, Daluiso 31, 5:53.

Third Quarter
NYG—FG, Daluiso 32, 13:00.

Fourth Quarter
NYG—Lewis 24 pass from Kanell (Daluiso kick), 6:26.
NYG—FG, Daluiso 45, 9:30.
Ariz.—Sanders 7 pass from Esiason (Esiason run), 14:20.
Attendance—68,262.

TEAM STATISTICS

	Arizona	N.Y. Giants
First downs	14	17
Rushes-yards	18-29	39-135
Passing	216	144
Punt returns	5-75	3-9
Kickoff returns	3-50	1-21
Interception returns	0-0	2-14
Comp.-att.-int.	22-43-2	16-30-0
Sacked-yards lost	2-9	2-17
Punts	8-47	8-42
Fumbles-lost	1-0	1-0
Penalties-yards	4-34	5-31
Time of possession	24:58	35:02

INDIVIDUAL STATISTICS

RUSHING—Arizona, L. Johnson 10-29, Centers 5-8, C. Smith 2-0, Edwards 1-(minus 8). New York, Hampton 24-94, Wheatley 11-27, Kanell 2-(minus 4), Brown 1-12, Way 1-6.

PASSING—Arizona, Esiason 20-40-2-196, K. Graham 2-3-0-29. New York, Kanell 14-27-0-128, Brown 2-3-0-33.

RECEIVING—Arizona, Centers 8-56, Sanders 5-61, Dowdell 3-41, R. Moore 2-36, Carter 2-16, Edwards 1-9, L. Johnson 1-6. New York, Lewis 7-77, Hampton 3-25, Pierce 1-24, Way 1-15, Calloway 1-10, Douglas 1-8, Cross 1-5, Wheatley 1-(minus 3).

MISSED FIELD GOAL ATTEMPTS—Arizona, G. Davis 28.

INTERCEPTIONS—New York, Campbell 2-14.

KICKOFF RETURNS—Arizona, McElroy 2-36, Dowdell 1-14. New York, Wheatley 1-21.

PUNT RETURNS—Arizona, Dowdell 5-75. New York, Lewis 3-9.

SACKS—Arizona, Rice 1, Miller ¹/₂, Wilson ¹/₂. New York, Armstead 1, Bratzke 1.

PACKERS 28, LIONS 18

Sunday, November 3

Detroit	3	7	0	8—18
Green Bay	7	7	14	0—28

First Quarter
Det.—FG, Hanson 48, 6:11.
G.B.—Levens 1 pass from Favre (Jacke kick), 15:00.

Second Quarter
Det.—Sanders 18 run (Hanson kick), 3:37.
G.B.—Mickens 1 pass from Favre (Jacke kick), 7:14.

Third Quarter
G.B.—Mickens 6 pass from Favre (Jacke kick), 10:27.
G.B.—Beebe 65 pass from Favre (Jacke kick), 13:52.

Fourth Quarter
Det.—Perriman 8 pass from Majkowski (H. Moore pass from Majkowski), 10:33.
Attendance—60,695.

TEAM STATISTICS

	Detroit	Green Bay
First downs	18	23
Rushes-yards	26-166	24-101
Passing	127	254
Punt returns	0-0	3-43
Kickoff returns	5-110	1-27
Interception returns	1-0	0-0
Comp.-att.-int.	15-32-0	24-35-1
Sacked-yards lost	5-26	4-27
Punts	5-37	5-31
Fumbles-lost	1-0	0-0
Penalties-yards	10-91	8-55
Time of possession	26:42	33:18

INDIVIDUAL STATISTICS

RUSHING—Detroit, Sanders 20-152, Majkowski 5-12, Rivers 1-2. Green Bay, Bennett 17-68, Levens 4-25, Henderson 2-7, Favre 1-1.

PASSING—Detroit, Majkowski 15-32-0-153. Green Bay, Favre 24-35-1-281.

RECEIVING—Detroit, Perriman 7-87, H. Moore 4-50, Morton 3-17, Sanders 1-(minus 1). Green Bay, Mickens 7-52, Beebe 4-106, Jackson 3-35, Bennett 3-27, Chmura 2-28, Henderson 2-13, Levens 2-11, Howard 1-9.

MISSED FIELD GOAL ATTEMPTS—None.

INTERCEPTIONS—Detroit, McNeil 1-0.

KICKOFF RETURNS—Detroit, Milburn 5-110. Green Bay, Howard 1-27.

PUNT RETURNS—Green Bay, Howard 3-43.

SACKS—Detroit, Elliss 2, Porcher 1, London 1. Green Bay, S. Dotson 2, Butler 1, Evans 1, White 1/2, S. Jones 1/2.

FALCONS 20, PANTHERS 17

Sunday, November 3

Carolina	3	7	0	7—17
Atlanta	10	3	0	7—20

First Quarter
Atl.—FG, Andersen 25, 5:49.
Atl.—Anderson 32 run (Andersen kick), 6:12.
Car.—FG, Kasay 40, 8:20.

Second Quarter
Car.—Johnson 6 run (Kasay kick), 2:11.
Atl.—FG, Andersen 45, 15:00.

Fourth Quarter
Atl.—Birden 15 pass from Hebert (Andersen kick), 1:19.
Car.—Carrier 12 pass from Beuerlein (Kasay kick), 12:38.
Attendance—42,726.

TEAM STATISTICS

	Carolina	Atlanta
First downs	17	16
Rushes-yards	21-104	27-124
Passing	243	189
Punt returns	5-37	3-28
Kickoff returns	3-91	3-64
Interception returns	1-0	0-0
Comp.-att.-int.	21-36-0	19-32-1
Sacked-yards lost	6-48	4-23
Punts	7-46	9-42
Fumbles-lost	3-3	3-1
Penalties-yards	4-21	7-56
Time of possession	27:01	32:59

INDIVIDUAL STATISTICS

RUSHING—Carolina, Johnson 13-61, Oliver 5-32, Griffith 2-(minus 1), Beuerlein 1-12. Atlanta, Anderson 22-109, Heyward 4-13, Hebert 1-2.

PASSING—Carolina, Collins 14-21-0-222, Beuerlein 7-15-0-69. Atlanta, Hebert 19-32-1-212.

RECEIVING—Carolina, Green 9-96, Ismail 5-108, Carrier 4-54, Walls 2-27, Griffith 1-6. Atlanta, Mathis 5-52, Anderson 3-71, Emanuel 3-39, Birden 3-23, Metcalf 3-15, Heyward 1-7, Lyons 1-5.

MISSED FIELD GOAL ATTEMPTS—None.

INTERCEPTIONS—Carolina, Davis 1-0.

KICKOFF RETURNS—Carolina, Bates 3-91. Atlanta, Metcalf 3-64.

PUNT RETURNS—Carolina, Oliver 5-37. Atlanta, Metcalf 3-28.

SACKS—Carolina, Lathon 1, K. Greene 1, Cook 1, Miller 1/2, Williams 1/2. Atlanta, Matthews 3, R. George 2, Archambeau 1.

BENGALS 24, RAVENS 21

Sunday, November 3

Cincinnati	0	3	7	14—24
Baltimore	7	14	0	0—21

First Quarter
Bal.—Alexander 17 pass from Testaverde (Stover kick), 10:57.

Second Quarter
Cin.—FG, Pelfrey 41, 6:40.
Bal.—Morris 1 run (Stover kick), 10:50.
Bal.—Jackson 26 pass from Testaverde (Stover kick), 14:27.

Third Quarter
Cin.—Carter 1 run (Pelfrey kick), 7:05.

Fourth Quarter
Cin.—Blake 4 run (Pickens pass from Blake), :43.
Cin.—FG, Pelfrey 49, 13:11.
Cin.—FG, Pelfrey 34, 15:00.
Attendance—60,743.

TEAM STATISTICS

	Cincinnati	Baltimore
First downs	33	23
Rushes-yards	39-168	24-92
Passing	265	279
Punt returns	2-8	2-27
Kickoff returns	3-46	5-93
Interception returns	4-28	1-0
Comp.-att.-int.	23-40-1	20-43-4
Sacked-yards lost	1-2	0-0
Punts	4-35	3-45
Fumbles-lost	3-1	0-0
Penalties-yards	5-35	7-38
Time of possession	39:13	20:47

INDIVIDUAL STATISTICS

RUSHING—Cincinnati, Hearst 23-80, Blake 7-49, Bieniemy 5-30, Carter 3-3, Cothran 1-6. Baltimore, Byner 12-44, Morris 11-48, Cothran 1-6.

PASSING—Cincinnati, Blake 22-39-1-255, Pickens 1-1-0-12. Baltimore, Testaverde 20-43-4-279.

RECEIVING—Cincinnati, Scott 6-70, Pickens 6-65, Bieniemy 4-37, McGee 3-34, Dunn 2-43, Battaglia 1-13, Cothran 1-5. Baltimore, F. Turner 6-104, Alexander 4-56, Jackson 3-52, Green 2-31, Morris 2-18, Byner 2-9, Ethridge 1-9.

MISSED FIELD GOAL ATTEMPTS—None.

INTERCEPTIONS—Cincinnati, Ambrose 1-28, Wilkinson 1-7, Sawyer 1-0, Spencer 1-(minus 7). Baltimore, E. Turner 1-0.

KICKOFF RETURNS—Cincinnati, Dunn 2-35, Cothran 1-11. Baltimore, J. Lewis 2-38, Baldwin 2-36, Byner 1-19.

PUNT RETURNS—Cincinnati, Myers 2-8. Baltimore, J. Lewis 2-27.

SACKS—Baltimore, J. Williams 1.

STEELERS 42, RAMS 6

Sunday, November 3

St. Louis	0	3	3	0— 6
Pittsburgh	14	7	14	7—42

First Quarter
Pit.—Bettis 3 run (N. Johnson kick), 6:29.
Pit.—Bettis 50 run (N. Johnson kick), 11:09.

Second Quarter
St.L.—FG, Lohmiller 25, :25.
Pit.—Stewart 7 run (N. Johnson kick), 7:21.

Third Quarter
St.L.—FG, Lohmiller 27, 9:06.
Pit.—Pegram 91 kickoff return (N. Johnson kick), 9:26.
Pit.—Stewart 2 run (N. Johnson kick), 13:06.

Fourth Quarter
Pit.—Pegram 17 run (N. Johnson kick), 3:28.
Attendance—58,148.

TEAM STATISTICS

	St. Louis	Pittsburgh
First downs	18	20
Rushes-yards	27-64	41-248
Passing	137	100
Punt returns	2-5	2-9
Kickoff returns	6-136	2-110
Interception returns	0-0	0-0
Comp.-att.-int.	16-35-2	10-15-0
Sacked-yards lost	6-47	0-0
Punts	6-37	5-38
Fumbles-lost	1-1	2-1
Penalties-yards	4-35	7-49
Time of possession	29:28	30:32

INDIVIDUAL STATISTICS

RUSHING—St. Louis, Green 11-26, Robinson 6-25, Phillips 5-6, Moore 3-9, Banks 2-(minus 2). Pittsburgh, Bettis 19-129, Pegram 9-53, Witman 7-33, Stewart 3-12, Hastings 1-17, Lester 1-4, Ji. Miller 1-0.

PASSING—St. Louis, Banks 16-35-2-184. Pittsburgh, Ji. Miller 4-8-0-40, Tomczak 6-7-0-60.

RECEIVING—St. Louis, Bruce 7-108, Kennison 6-67, Moore 2-8, Green 1-1. Pittsburgh, Hastings 4-37, C. Johnson 2-29, Pegram 2-19, Lester 1-8, Hayes 1-7.

MISSED FIELD GOAL ATTEMPTS—None.

INTERCEPTIONS—Pittsburgh, Woodson 1-0, Figures 1-0.

KICKOFF RETURNS—St. Louis, Thomas 4-90, Kennison 2-46. Pittsburgh, Pegram 2-110.

PUNT RETURNS—St. Louis, Kennison 2-5. Pittsburgh, Hastings 2-9.

SACKS—Pittsburgh, Kirkland 1, Buckner 1, Brown 1, Oldham 1, M. Bell 1, Olsavsky 1/2, Gibson 1/2.

CHARGERS 26, COLTS 19

Sunday, November 3

San Diego	7	9	3	7—26
Indianapolis	0	6	6	7—19

First Quarter
S.D.—Jones 41 pass from Salisbury (Carney kick), 4:19.

Second Quarter
S.D.—FG, Carney 28, :05.
S.D.—FG, Carney 30, 4:17.
Ind.—FG, Blanchard 47, 9:52.
Ind.—FG, Blanchard 39, 13:57.
S.D.—FG, Carney 47, 14:48.

Third Quarter
S.D.—FG, Carney 22, 5:33.
Ind.—FG, Blanchard 33, 9:23.
Ind.—FG, Blanchard 20, 12:14.

Fourth Quarter
S.D.—Martin 22 pass from Salisbury (Carney kick), 2:17.
Ind.—Harrison 9 pass from Harbaugh (Blanchard kick), 11:40.
Attendance—58,484.

TEAM STATISTICS

	San Diego	Indianapolis
First downs	14	22
Rushes-yards	25-75	28-91
Passing	237	173
Punt returns	1-13	5-141
Kickoff returns	5-135	7-152
Interception returns	4-46	0-0
Comp.-att.-int.	19-31-0	18-44-4
Sacked-yards lost	0-0	6-30
Punts	7-48	1-60
Fumbles-lost	2-0	3-1
Penalties-yards	15-133	5-35
Time of possession	25:03	34:57

INDIVIDUAL STATISTICS

RUSHING—San Diego, Russell 17-53, Hayden 4-8, Fletcher 3-13, Salisbury 1-1. Indianapolis, Faulk 14-37, Harbaugh 6-42, Warren 5-9, Groce 3-3.

PASSING—San Diego, Salisbury 19-31-0-237. Indianapolis, Harbaugh 18-44-4-203.

RECEIVING—San Diego, Martin 6-128, Jones 3-60, Fletcher 3-13, Russell 2-8, May 1-13, A. Coleman 1-7, Pupunu 1-7, Roche 1-4, Mitchell 1-(minus 3). Indianapolis, Dawkins 5-63, Faulk 4-37, Harrison 3-35, Groce 3-31, Dilger 1-11, Pollard 1-11, Stablein 1-9.

MISSED FIELD GOAL ATTEMPTS—None.

INTERCEPTIONS—San Diego, Shaw 1-36, Gouveia 1-11, Ross 1-0, Lee 1-(minus 1).

KICKOFF RETURNS—San Diego, A. Coleman 5-135. Indianapolis, Stock 7-152.

PUNT RETURNS—San Diego, Da. Gordon 1-13. Indianapolis, Buchanan 5-141.

SACKS—San Diego, Seau 2, Johnson 1, Parrella 1, M. Coleman 1, Mims 1.

BEARS 13, BUCCANEERS 10

Sunday, November 3

Tampa Bay	0	10	0	0—10
Chicago	3	3	7	0—13

First Quarter
Chi.—FG, Jaeger 27, 11:03.

Second Quarter
T.B.—Moore 17 pass from Dilfer (Husted kick), 4:55.
Chi.—FG, Jaeger 23, 9:16.
T.B.—FG, Husted 45, 13:49.

Third Quarter
Chi.—R. Harris 1 run (Jaeger kick), 6:50.
Attendance—58,727.

TEAM STATISTICS

	Tampa Bay	Chicago
First downs	14	18
Rushes-yards	23-67	38-185
Passing	178	84
Punt returns	4-14	4-16
Kickoff returns	3-56	3-47
Interception returns	1-4	1-0
Comp.-att.-int.	15-32-1	11-25-1
Sacked-yards lost	1-6	0-0
Punts	6-40	7-42
Fumbles-lost	3-1	1-0
Penalties-yards	8-75	4-30
Time of possession	27:33	32:27

INDIVIDUAL STATISTICS

RUSHING—Tampa Bay, Rhett 20-67, Dilfer 2-2, Alstott 1-(minus 2). Chicago, R. Harris 19-118, Salaam 16-54, Timpson 1-13, T. Carter 1-0, Krieg 1-0.

PASSING—Tampa Bay, Dilfer 15-32-1-184. Chicago, Krieg 11-25-1-84.

RECEIVING—Tampa Bay, R. Thomas 6-76, Moore 5-62, Alstott 2-9, Williams 1-25, Hawkins 1-12. Chicago, T. Carter 4-6, Jennings 2-31, Engram 2-28, Timpson 2-8, Conway 1-11.

MISSED FIELD GOAL ATTEMPTS—Chicago, Jaeger 47.

INTERCEPTIONS—Tampa Bay, D. Abraham 1-4. Chicago, Carrier 1-0.

KICKOFF RETURNS—Tampa Bay, Williams 3-56. Chicago, Ja. Jackson 1-21, Faulkerson 1-20, Engram 1-6.

PUNT RETURNS—Tampa Bay, Williams 3-15, Hawkins 1-(minus 1). Chicago, Engram 4-16.

SACKS—Chicago, Spellman 1.

CHIEFS 21, VIKINGS 6

Sunday, November 3

Kansas City	0	7	0	14—21
Minnesota	0	0	0	6— 6

Second Quarter
K.C.—Allen 1 run (Stoyanovich kick), 14:34.

Fourth Quarter
K.C.—Hill 17 run (Stoyanovich kick), 11:28.
K.C.—Hill 10 run (Stoyanovich kick), 11:53.
Min.—Carter 1 pass from B. Johnson (pass failed), 13:32.
Attendance—59,552.

TEAM STATISTICS

	Kansas City	Minnesota
First downs	23	13
Rushes-yards	43-202	14-48
Passing	157	210
Punt returns	2-27	3-17
Kickoff returns	2-29	4-50
Interception returns	2-34	1-2
Comp.-att.-int.	19-33-1	22-42-2
Sacked-yards lost	1-8	1-8
Punts	7-43	8-37
Fumbles-lost	0-0	0-0
Penalties-yards	12-85	5-26
Time of possession	36:33	23:27

INDIVIDUAL STATISTICS

RUSHING—Kansas City, Allen 18-89, Hill 15-100, Anders 3-4, Bono 3-(minus 2), To. Richardson 2-4, Bennett 1-4, D. Carter 1-3. Minnesota, Lee 5-22, Graham 4-5, B. Johnson 3-12, Palmer 1-8, Evans 1-1.

PASSING—Kansas City, Bono 19-32-1-165, Allen 0-1-0-0. Minnesota, B. Johnson 22-42-2-218.

RECEIVING—Kansas City, Anders 7-48, LaChapelle 4-41, Walker 2-13, Johnson 1-26, Hill 1-11, Penn 1-11, Vanover 1-7, Bennett 1-6, Allen 1-2. Minnesota, Carter 9-89, Lee 3-20, Reed 2-55, Jordan 2-9, Palmer 2-7, Ismail 1-32, DeLong 1-5, Evans 1-3, Graham 1-(minus 2).

MISSED FIELD GOAL ATTEMPTS—Kansas City, Stoyanovich 31, 22. Minnesota, Sisson 35.

INTERCEPTIONS—Kansas City, Washington 1-34, Collins 1-0. Minnesota, Fuller 1-2.

KICKOFF RETURNS—Kansas City, Vanover 1-24, McNair 1-5. Minnesota, Palmer 4-50.

PUNT RETURNS—Kansas City, Vanover 2-27. Minnesota, Palmer 3-17.

SACKS—Kansas City, Bayless 1. Minnesota, Harrison 1.

BILLS 38, REDSKINS 13

Sunday, November 3

Washington	7	0	0	6—13
Buffalo	0	17	14	7—38

First Quarter

Was.—Allen 1 run (Blanton kick), 7:09.

Second Quarter

Buf.—T. Thomas 10 run (Christie kick), 3:24.

Buf.—FG, Christie 33, 7:29.

Buf.—Holmes 3 run (Christie kick), 12:24.

Third Quarter

Buf.—Holmes 5 run (Christie kick), 6:20.

Buf.—Kelly 4 run (Christie kick), 13:52.

Fourth Quarter

Was.—Allen 1 run (pass failed), 2:25.

Buf.—Holmes 13 run (Christie kick), 6:38.

Attendance—78,002.

TEAM STATISTICS

	Washington	Buffalo
First downs	16	31
Rushes-yards	24-75	56-266
Passing	159	210
Punt returns	1-(-10)	1-28
Kickoff returns	7-149	3-57
Interception returns	0-0	0-0
Comp.-att.-int.	13-28-0	20-24-0
Sacked-yards lost	1-12	1-2
Punts	7-42	4-38
Fumbles-lost	3-2	1-0
Penalties-yards	9-56	4-68
Time of possession	23:49	36:11

INDIVIDUAL STATISTICS

RUSHING—Washington, Allen 15-49, Davis 5-22, Mitchell 2-3, Logan 1-1, Frerotte 1-0. Buffalo, T. Thomas 23-107, Holmes 22-122, Kelly 5-20, Collins 3-(minus 4), Tindale 1-15, Tasker 1-11, Reed 1-(minus 5).

PASSING—Washington, Frerotte 13-28-0-171. Buffalo, Kelly 19-23-0-206, Collins 1-1-0-6.

RECEIVING—Washington, Allen 3-14, Ellard 2-31, Shepherd 2-30, Asher 2-17, Westbrook 1-27, Logan 1-21, Galbraith 1-21, Mitchell 1-10. Buffalo, Reed 5-94, Early 3-31, Tasker 3-16, T. Thomas 3-1, Moulds 2-24, Johnson 2-21, Holmes 1-19, Cline 1-6.

MISSED FIELD GOAL ATTEMPTS—Buffalo, Christie 50.

INTERCEPTIONS—None.

KICKOFF RETURNS—Washington, Mitchell 7-149. Buffalo, Moulds 3-57.

PUNT RETURNS—Washington, Mitchell 1-(minus 10). Buffalo, Burris 1-28.

SACKS—Washington, Nottage 1. Buffalo, Paup 1.

SEAHAWKS 23, OILERS 16

Sunday, November 3

Houston	3	0	3	10—16
Seattle	3	3	3	14—23

First Quarter

Hou.—FG, Del Greco 35, 6:17.

Sea.—FG, Peterson 25, 12:07.

Second Quarter

Sea.—FG, Peterson 35, 8:59.

Third Quarter

Hou.—FG, Del Greco 36, 9:57.

Sea.—FG, Peterson 44, 12:29.

Fourth Quarter

Hou.—FG, Del Greco 45, :05.

Hou.—Sanders 65 pass from McNair (Del Greco kick), 6:48.

Sea.—Galloway 14 pass from Friesz (Peterson kick), 11:30.

Sea.—Blackmon 61 blocked FG return (Peterson kick), 14:56.

Attendance—36,320.

TEAM STATISTICS

	Houston	Seattle
First downs	13	19
Rushes-yards	33-128	21-32
Passing	225	310
Punt returns	2-20	1-0
Kickoff returns	5-95	5-123
Interception returns	1-0	1-13
Comp.-att.-int.	12-18-1	24-38-1
Sacked-yards lost	0-0	3-13
Punts	4-40	3-50
Fumbles-lost	0-0	2-0
Penalties-yards	6-40	3-20
Time of possession	28:59	31:01

INDIVIDUAL STATISTICS

RUSHING—Houston, George 25-91, McNair 5-22, Harmon 2-17, Thomas 1-(minus 2). Seattle, Warren 16-34, Smith 4-(minus 2), Friesz 1-0.

PASSING—Houston, McNair 12-18-1-225. Seattle, Friesz 24-38-1-323.

RECEIVING—Houston, Davis 3-61, Thomas 3-57, Russell 2-38, Harmon 2-3, Sanders 1-65, R. Lewis 1-1. Seattle, Galloway 8-94, Blades 4-69, Pritchard 3-61, Crumpler 3-22, Warren 3-10, Proehl 1-30, Smith 1-22, Fauria 1-15.

MISSED FIELD GOAL ATTEMPTS—Houston, Del Greco 37. Seattle, Peterson 47, 23.

INTERCEPTIONS—Houston, D. Lewis 1-0. Seattle, Wooden 1-13.

KICKOFF RETURNS—Houston, Gray 3-72, Thomas 2-23. Seattle, Broussard 4-111, Barber 1-12.

PUNT RETURNS—Houston, Gray 1-15, Floyd 1-5. Seattle, R. Harris 1-0.

SACKS—Houston, Barrow 1, Bowden 1, Walker 1.

PATRIOTS 42, DOLPHINS 23

Sunday, November 3

Miami	7	7	3	6—23
New England	7	7	7	21—42

First Quarter

N.E.—Martin 1 run (Vinatieri kick), 7:20.

Mia.—Abdul-Jabbar 4 run (Nedney kick), 13:33.

Second Quarter

Mia.—Abdul-Jabbar 3 run (Nedney kick), 7:09.

N.E.—Martin 1 run (Vinatieri kick), 14:56.

Third Quarter

Mia.—FG, Nedney 39, 3:33.

N.E.—Coates 23 pass from Bledsoe (Vinatieri kick), 6:43.

Fourth Quarter

N.E.—Coates 84 pass from Bledsoe (Vinatieri kick), 7:30.

N.E.—Gash 5 pass from Bledsoe (Vinatieri kick), 9:13.

N.E.—Martin 2 run (Vinatieri kick), 12:24.

Mia.—McDuffie 29 pass from Erickson (pass failed), 14:05.

Attendance—58,942.

TEAM STATISTICS

	Miami	New England
First downs	22	28
Rushes-yards	33-115	21-59
Passing	315	409
Punt returns	2-30	5-31
Kickoff returns	7-120	3-77
Interception returns	2-23	1-0
Comp.-att.-int.	24-42-1	30-41-2
Sacked-yards lost	2-16	1-10
Punts	6-44	5-49
Fumbles-lost	2-2	2-2
Penalties-yards	14-105	6-62
Time of possession	35:08	24:52

INDIVIDUAL STATISTICS

RUSHING—Miami, Abdul-Jabbar 29-104, Spikes 2-(minus 3), Parmalee 1-12, McPhail 1-2. New England, Martin 18-53, Meggett 3-6.

PASSING—Miami, Marino 17-34-1-225, Erickson 7-8-0-106. New England, Bledsoe 30-41-2-419.

RECEIVING—Miami, McDuffie 5-84, Parmalee 4-48, Pritchett 4-35, L. Thomas 3-71, Jordan 3-50, Abdul-Jabbar 3-16, Spikes 1-19, Drayton 1-8. New England, Glenn 10-112, Coates 5-135, Meggett 3-34, T. Brown 3-30, Martin 2-56, Byars 2-22, Jefferson 2-13, Gash 2-6, Graham 1-11.

MISSED FIELD GOAL ATTEMPTS—Miami, Nedney 45.

INTERCEPTIONS—Miami, Wooden 1-15, Buckley 1-8. New England, Hitchcock 1-0.

KICKOFF RETURNS—Miami, Spikes 3-65, Jordan 2-38, Z. Thomas 1-17, R. Hill 1-0. New England, Meggett 3-77.

PUNT RETURNS—Miami, McDuffie 2-30. New England, Meggett 5-31.

SACKS—Miami, Stubbs 1. New England, McGinest 2.

49ERS 24, SAINTS 17

Sunday, November 3

San Francisco	3	11	3	7—24
New Orleans	0	7	0	10—17

First Quarter

S.F.—FG, Wilkins 34, 8:32.

Second Quarter

S.F.—FG, Wilkins 35, 1:46.
N.O.—Zellars 1 run (Brien kick), 4:40.
S.F.—Rice 36 pass from S. Young (S. Young run), 8:14.

Third Quarter

S.F.—FG, Wilkins 27, 13:49.

Fourth Quarter

N.O.—Haynes 50 pass from Everett (Brien kick), 1:12.
S.F.—S. Young 2 run (Wilkins kick), 3:29.
N.O.—FG, Brien 37, 12:44.
Attendance—53,297.

TEAM STATISTICS

	San Francisco	New Orleans
First downs	17	18
Rushes-yards	32-191	28-64
Passing	115	229
Punt returns	4-32	4-18
Kickoff returns	3-106	6-146
Interception returns	2-26	0-0
Comp.-att.-int.	12-23-0	20-40-2
Sacked-yards lost	6-34	4-31
Punts	6-43	6-43
Fumbles-lost	0-0	4-1
Penalties-yards	9-70	6-48
Time of possession	29:28	30:32

INDIVIDUAL STATISTICS

RUSHING—San Francisco, Kirby 18-90, Floyd 6-43, S. Young 5-9, Rice 1-38, Lynn 1-6, Loville 1-5. New Orleans, Zellars 20-49, Brown 3-6, Neal 3-4, Whittle 2-5.

PASSING—San Francisco, S. Young 12-23-0-149. New Orleans, Everett 20-40-2-260.

RECEIVING—San Francisco, Rice 3-45, Popson 2-32, Owens 2-26, Kirby 2-18, Floyd 1-13, Uwaezuoke 1-9, Jones 1-6. New Orleans, Haynes 5-121, Small 4-45, Lusk 3-30, DeRamus 2-18, Whittle 2-15, Neal 1-12, Green 1-9, Zellars 1-6, Brown 1-4.

MISSED FIELD GOAL ATTEMPTS—None.

INTERCEPTIONS—San Francisco, Dodge 1-26, Hanks 1-0.

KICKOFF RETURNS—San Francisco, D. Carter 3-106. New Orleans, Hughes 6-146.

PUNT RETURNS—San Francisco, D. Carter 4-32. New Orleans, Hughes 4-18.

SACKS—San Francisco, Barker 3, B. Young 1. New Orleans, Broughton 2, Martin 1, Johnson 1, B. Smith 1, Turnbull 1.

BRONCOS 22, RAIDERS 21

Monday, November 4

Denver	7	6	0	9—22
Oakland	7	0	0	14—21

First Quarter

Oak.—Hostetler 5 run (Ford kick), 3:00.
Den.—Sharpe 10 pass from Elway (Elam kick), 12:45.

Second Quarter

Den.—FG, Elam 36, 10:57.
Den.—FG, Elam 43, 14:29.

Fourth Quarter

Den.—FG, Elam 28, 4:52.
Oak.—Fenner 15 pass from Hostetler (Ford kick), 7:40.
Oak.—T. Brown 42 pass from Hostetler (Ford kick), 9:59.
Den.—R. Smith 49 pass from Elway (pass failed), 10:46.
Attendance—61,179.

TEAM STATISTICS

	Denver	Oakland
First downs	18	17
Rushes-yards	31-152	16-105
Passing	160	216
Punt returns	2-0	1-10
Kickoff returns	3-60	6-104
Interception returns	0-0	1-11
Comp.-att.-int.	16-33-1	22-34-0
Sacked-yards lost	2-22	4-34
Punts	4-44	6-39
Fumbles-lost	0-0	0-0
Penalties-yards	5-50	11-82
Time of possession	32:17	27:43

INDIVIDUAL STATISTICS

RUSHING—Denver, Davis 19-85, Elway 9-70, Craver 2-(minus 4), R. Smith 1-1. Oakland, Kaufman 6-38, Williams 6-25, Fenner 2-24, Hostetler 2-18.

PASSING—Denver, Elway 16-33-1-182. Oakland, Hostetler 22-34-0-250.

RECEIVING—Denver, Sharpe 5-57, R. Smith 4-72, Miller 3-23, Craver 2-5, Davis 1-17, Sherrard 1-8. Oakland, T. Brown 8-126, Williams 5-32, Kaufman 3-36, Hobbs 3-19, Fenner 1-15, Dudley 1-13, Jett 1-9.

MISSED FIELD GOAL ATTEMPTS—Oakland, Ford 30.

INTERCEPTIONS—Oakland, Lynch 1-11.

KICKOFF RETURNS—Denver, Hebron 3-60. Oakland, Kidd 6-104.

PUNT RETURNS—Denver, R. Smith 2-0. Oakland, T. Brown 1-10.

SACKS—Denver, Romanowski 1, Crockett 1, Tanuvasa 1, Lodish 1/2, D. Williams 1/2. Oakland, Swilling 2.

1996 REVIEW Week 10

WEEK 11

RESULTS

Arizona 37, WASHINGTON 34 (OT)
Buffalo 24, PHILADELPHIA 17
CAROLINA 27, N.Y. Giants 17
CINCINNATI 34, Pittsburgh 24
Dallas 20, SAN FRANCISCO 17 (OT)
DENVER 17, Chicago 12
Houston 31, NEW ORLEANS 14
JACKSONVILLE 30, Baltimore 27
KANSAS CITY 27, Green Bay 20
MIAMI 37, Indianapolis 13
New England 31, N.Y. JETS 27
ST. LOUIS 59, Atlanta 16
SEATTLE 42, Minnesota 23
TAMPA BAY 20, Oakland 17 (OT)
SAN DIEGO 27, Detroit 21

STANDINGS

AFC EAST

	W	L	T	Pct.
Buffalo	7	3	0	.700
New England	7	3	0	.700
Indianapolis	5	5	0	.500
Miami	5	5	0	.500
N.Y. Jets	1	9	0	.100

AFC CENTRAL

	W	L	T	Pct.
Pittsburgh	7	3	0	.700
Houston	6	4	0	.600
Cincinnati	4	6	0	.400
Jacksonville	4	6	0	.400
Baltimore	3	7	0	.300

AFC WEST

	W	L	T	Pct.
Denver	9	1	0	.900
Kansas City	7	3	0	.700
San Diego	6	4	0	.600
Seattle	5	5	0	.500
Oakland	4	6	0	.400

NFC EAST

	W	L	T	Pct.
Philadelphia	7	3	0	.700
Washington	7	3	0	.700
Dallas	6	4	0	.600
Arizona	4	6	0	.400
N.Y. Giants	4	6	0	.400

NFC CENTRAL

	W	L	T	Pct.
Green Bay	8	2	0	.800
Minnesota	5	5	0	.500
Chicago	4	6	0	.400
Detroit	4	6	0	.400
Tampa Bay	2	8	0	.200

NFC WEST

	W	L	T	Pct.
San Francisco	7	3	0	.700
Carolina	6	4	0	.600
St. Louis	3	7	0	.300
New Orleans	2	8	0	.200
Atlanta	1	9	0	.100

HIGHLIGHTS

Hero of the week: Mark Brunell led Jacksonville to two touchdowns in the final 3:50 as the Jaguars rallied from a 17-point deficit and beat Baltimore, 30-27. Brunell was 24-of-37 for 354 yards, led the Jaguars with 58 yards rushing and scored the game-winning touchdown on a 1-yard run with 41 seconds left.

Goat of the week: Pittsburgh's Norm Johnson was supposed to squib his kickoff with five seconds left in the first half after the Steelers had taken a 17-10 lead over Cincinnati. Instead, he kicked it deep and David Dunn returned it 90 yards for a touchdown that propelled the Bengals to a 34-24 triumph. It was the third consecutive victory for Cincinnati since Bruce Coslet replaced David Shula as coach.

Sub of the week: San Diego wide receiver Andre Coleman, who had lost his starting job to Charlie Jones one week earlier, came into the game after Jones suffered bruised ribs and caught a 46-yard touchdown pass on a desperation throw by Stan Humphries on the final play of the first half. The score gave the Chargers a 17-14 lead en route to a 27-21 win over Detroit.

Comeback of the week: New England climbed out of a hole at Giants Stadium, where it spotted the Jets a 21-0 lead only to roar back for a 31-27 victory. The Patriots rang up 342 offensive yards in the final three quarters. The victory was their fourth in a row over an AFC East rival.

Blowout of the week: One week after getting pounded, 42-6, by Pittsburgh, St. Louis turned around and mauled Atlanta, 59-16. The Rams took a 28-0 lead just three minutes into the second quarter. It was the most points by a Rams team since December 1976 and the most points by any NFL team since Cincinnati beat Houston, 61-7, in December 1989.

Nail-biter of the week: Chicago had first-and-goal at Denver's 1 but failed to score despite getting four cracks in the final 40 seconds, and the Broncos held on for a 17-12 decision. Bears running back Raymont Harris was dropped for losses of 1 and 2 yards on the first two plays; defensive lineman Jim Flanigan, lined up at tight end, dropped a pass in the end zone on third down; and quarterback Dave Krieg couldn't connect with Curtis Conway on a fourth-down pass in the end zone.

Hit of the week: Carolina defensive lineman Greg Kragen punched the ball from the arms of Giants running back Rodney Hampton and recovered the fumble at New York's 14. Four plays later, John Kasay's 28-yard field goal snapped a 17-17 tie and the Panthers went on to win, 27-17.

Oddity of the week: Tampa Bay is only 29-72 in regulation games in the '90s but 5-0 in overtime games after Michael Husted's 23-yard field goal with 3:04 left in OT lifted the Buccaneers to a 20-17 verdict over the Raiders.

Top rusher: Adrian Murrell rushed 31 times for 128 yards and two touchdowns for the Jets, but it wasn't enough to prevent a 31-27 loss to Indianapolis.

Top passer: Boomer Esiason, making his first start since being benched in Week 4, was 35-of-59 for 522 yards and three touchowns, directing the Cardinals to a 37-34 overtime victory in Washington. Esiason, 35, passed for 351 yards in the fourth quarter and overtime combined.

Top receiver: Minnesota's Cris Carter had seven receptions for 142 yards. Unfortunately, his defensive teammates couldn't hold up their end, surrendering 452 yards to Seattle in a 42-23 loss.

Notes: Not even the Washington team that lost, 73-0, to Chicago in the 1940 NFL championship game gave up as many offensive yards as the Redskins surrendered to Arizona (615). . . . Esiason's passing performance was the third-most prolific in NFL history, surpassed only by Norm Van Brocklin's 554 yards for the Rams against the New York Yanks in 1951 and Warren Moon's 527 yards for Houston against Kansas City in 1990. . . . The Vikings were held to 15 rushing yards in 12 carries and suffered their fourth consecutive loss, the first time that has happened in Dennis Green's five seasons as coach. . . . Carl Pickens' 12 receptions in Cincinnati's victory over Pittsburgh tied a team single-game record. . . . Dan Marino reached two more passing milestones—4,000 completions and 50,000 yards—in Miami's 37-13 win over Indianapolis. . . . Chicago's Dave Krieg was sacked only once, but it was enough to tie Fran Tarkenton's

NFL record for most times sacked (483).

Quote of the week: Patriots tight end Keith Byars, after New England's come-from-behind victory over the Jets: "We weren't going to panic. If you panic now, in November, you won't get a chance to panic in January, when they hand out the awards."

GAME SUMMARIES

PATRIOTS 31, JETS 27

Sunday, November 10

New England	0	7 10	14—31
N.Y. Jets	7	14 3	3—27

First Quarter
NYJ—Graham 26 pass from Reich (Lowery kick), 6:17.
Second Quarter
NYJ—Murrell 1 run (Lowery kick), 2:01.
NYJ—Murrell 1 run (Lowery kick), 9:02.
N.E.—Glenn 26 pass from Bledsoe (Vinatieri kick), 13:05.
Third Quarter
N.E.—Martin 1 run (Vinatieri kick), 3:56.
N.E.—FG, Vinatieri 30, 8:34.
NYJ—FG, Lowery 26, 14:38.
Fourth Quarter
N.E.—Coates 17 pass from Bledsoe (Vinatieri kick), 3:35.
NYJ—FG, Lowery 32, 6:43.
N.E.—Byars 2 pass from Bledsoe (Vinatieri kick), 10:57.
Attendance—61,715.

TEAM STATISTICS

	New England	N.Y. Jets
First Downs	21	28
Rushes-Yards	17-68	36-142
Passing	275	280
Punt Returns	1-14	0-0
Kickoff Returns	4-106	6-106
Interception Returns	1-35	2-9
Comp-Att-Int	24-34-2	22-44-1
Sacked-Yards Lost	2-22	1-1
Punts	1-47	2-35
Fumbles-Lost	1-1	1-0
Penalties-Yards	7-48	4-35
Time of Possession	24:15	35:45

INDIVIDUAL STATISTICS
RUSHING—New England, Martin 15-43, Glenn 1-26, Bledsoe 1-(minus 1). New York, Murrell 31-128, Anderson 3-5, Reich 2-9.
PASSING—New England, Bledsoe 24-34-2-297. New York, Reich 22-44-1-281.
RECEIVING—New England, Glenn 6-83, Martin 5-81, Coates 4-27, Byars 4-22, Jefferson 3-42, Meggett 1-26, T. Brown 1-16. New York, Graham 6-95, Anderson 6-85, Johnson 4-44, Chrebet 3-33, Van Dyke 1-10, Murrell 1-7, Brady 1-7.
MISSED FIELD GOAL ATTEMPTS—New York, Lowery 48.
INTERCEPTIONS—New England, Clay 1-35. New York, Green 1-9, Glenn 1-0.
KICKOFF RETURNS—New England, Meggett 3-78, T. Brown 1-28. New York, Bailey 4-81, Van Dyke 2-25.
PUNT RETURNS—New England, Meggett 1-14.
SACKS—New England, McGinest 1. New York, Cascadden 1, Douglas 1.

CHIEFS 27, PACKERS 20

Sunday, November 10

Green Bay	3	3 7	7—20
Kansas City	3	17 7	0—27

First Quarter
K.C.—FG, Stoyanovich 26, 2:01.
G.B.—FG, Jacke 24, 8:08.
Second Quarter
K.C.—FG, Stoyanovich 22, :56.
K.C.—Hill 8 run (Stoyanovich kick), 4:42.
K.C.—Hill 34 pass from Bono (Stoyanovich kick), 7:15.
G.B.—FG, Jacke 49, 15:00.

Third Quarter
K.C.—Hill 24 run (Stoyanovich kick), :22.
G.B.—Beebe 25 pass from Favre (Jacke kick), 11:10.
Fourth Quarter
G.B.—Mayes 6 pass from Favre (Jacke kick), 13:58.
Attendance—79,281.

TEAM STATISTICS

	Green Bay	Kansas City
First Downs	24	19
Rushes-Yards	20-75	40-182
Passing	285	201
Punt Returns	3-19	2-29
Kickoff Returns	5-100	3-62
Interception Returns	0-0	1-2
Comp-Att-Int	27-49-1	9-22-0
Sacked-Yards Lost	4-25	1-3
Punts	6-42	7-36
Fumbles-Lost	2-1	1-0
Penalties-Yards	7-82	9-81
Time of Possession	29:09	30:51

INDIVIDUAL STATISTICS
RUSHING—Green Bay, Bennett 12-37, Levens 5-25, Favre 2-10, Henderson 1-3. Kansas City, Hill 14-94, Allen 10-48, Bennett 8-22, Bono 4-(minus 2), Anders 3-17, McNair 1-3.
PASSING—Green Bay, Favre 27-49-1-314. Kansas City, Bono 9-22-0-204.
RECEIVING—Green Bay, Levens 5-83, Henderson 5-62, Bennett 4-10, Beebe 3-52, Jackson 3-33, Mickens 3-31, Mayes 2-18, Chmura 1-11, Howard 1-10. Kansas City, LaChapelle 2-89, Anders 2-41, Hill 1-34, Horn 1-21, Penn 1-12, McNair 1-5, Johnson 1-2.
MISSED FIELD GOAL ATTEMPTS—None.
INTERCEPTIONS—Kansas City, Washington 1-2.
KICKOFF RETURNS—Green Bay, Howard 5-100. Kansas City, Vanover 2-42, Anders 1-20.
PUNT RETURNS—Green Bay, Howard 3-19. Kansas City, Vanover 2-29.
SACKS—Green Bay, S. Dotson 1. Kansas City, Thomas 2, Hasty 1, N. Smith 1.

BILLS 24, EAGLES 17

Sunday, November 10

Buffalo	7	10 7	0—24
Philadelphia	10	0 0	7—17

First Quarter
Phi.—Turner 23 pass from Detmer (Anderson kick), 4:38.
Buf.—Northern 18 blocked punt return (Christie kick), 6:29.
Phi.—FG, Anderson 23, 13:40.
Second Quarter
Buf.—T. Thomas 5 run (Christie kick), 12:37.
Buf.—FG, Christie 38, 14:24.
Third Quarter
Buf.—Early 5 pass from Kelly (Christie kick), 13:44.
Fourth Quarter
Phi.—Fryar 10 pass from Detmer (Anderson kick), 4:33.
Attendance—66,613.

TEAM STATISTICS

	Buffalo	Philadelphia
First Downs	18	25
Rushes-Yards	37-140	29-111
Passing	112	274
Punt Returns	1-12	2-10
Kickoff Returns	4-99	5-109
Interception Returns	1-6	1-0
Comp-Att-Int	11-22-1	26-44-1
Sacked-Yards Lost	0-0	5-41
Punts	3-46	4-24
Fumbles-Lost	1-1	1-0
Penalties-Yards	6-40	5-40
Time of Possession	23:46	36:14

INDIVIDUAL STATISTICS
RUSHING—Buffalo, T. Thomas 22-90, Holmes 10-30, Reed 2-16, Kelly 2-(minus 2), Tasker 1-6. Philadelphia, Watters 19-51, Garner 10-60.
PASSING—Buffalo, Kelly 11-22-1-112. Philadelphia, Detmer 26-44-1-315.
RECEIVING—Buffalo, Tasker 4-46, Early 4-38, Reed 2-22, Cline 1-6. Philadelphia, Fryar 8-92, Watters 5-47, Turner 5-43, Jones 4-60, Dunn 1-6, Seay 1-19, J. Johnson 1-17, Garner 1-13.
MISSED FIELD GOAL ATTEMPTS—None.
INTERCEPTIONS—Buffalo, Kerner 1-6. Philadelphia, Dawkins 1-0.

KICKOFF RETURNS—Buffalo, Moulds 4-99. Philadelphia, Witherspoon 5-109.
PUNT RETURNS—Buffalo, Burris 1-12. Philadelphia, Seay 2-10.
SACKS—Buffalo, B. Smith 2, Kerner 1, Rogers 1, Jeffcoat 1.

DOLPHINS 37, COLTS 13

Sunday, November 10

Indianapolis	3	3	0	7—13
Miami	7	14	16	0—37

First Quarter
Ind.—FG, Blanchard 48, 7:20.
Mia.—McDuffie 12 pass from Marino (Nedney kick), 14:24.
Second Quarter
Mia.—Abdul-Jabbar 1 run (Nedney kick), 6:54.
Mia.—Barnett 15 pass from Marino (Nedney kick), 11:02.
Ind.—FG, Blanchard 22, 14:33.
Third Quarter
Mia.—Safety, intentional grounding by Harbaugh in the end zone, 1:38.
Mia.—Barnett 12 pass from Marino (Nedney kick), 6:44.
Mia.—Abdul-Jabbar 3 run (Nedney kick), 10:52.
Fourth Quarter
Ind.—Dawkins 16 pass from Justin (Blanchard kick), 9:59.
Attendance—66,623.

TEAM STATISTICS

	Indianapolis	Miami
First Downs	15	19
Rushes-Yards	15-33	35-111
Passing	260	196
Punt Returns	5-40	2-22
Kickoff Returns	2-52	3-67
Interception Returns	0-0	2-50
Comp-Att-Int	23-41-2	17-25-0
Sacked-Yards Lost	0-0	1-8
Punts	4-46	5-49
Fumbles-Lost	1-0	1-0
Penalties-Yards	8-48	5-35
Time of Possession	26:53	33:07

INDIVIDUAL STATISTICS

RUSHING—Indianapolis, Faulk 10-13, Warren 4-9, Harbaugh 1-11. Miami, Abdul-Jabbar 19-67, Spikes 7-31, Parmalee 5-17, Erickson 2-(minus 2), R. Wilson 1-0, Marino 1-(minus 2).
PASSING—Indianapolis, Harbaugh 13-24-2-126, Justin 10-17-0-134. Miami, Marino 17-23-0-204, Erickson 0-2-0-0.
RECEIVING—Indianapolis, Dawkins 5-96, Dilger 5-36, Harrison 4-38, Faulk 3-10, Warren 2-28, Groce 2-20, Stablein 1-17, Bailey 1-15. Miami, McDuffie 6-106, Barnett 4-42, Pritchett 2-26, Drayton 2-17, Abdul-Jabbar 2-11, R. Wilson 1-2.
MISSED FIELD GOAL ATTEMPTS—Miami, Nedney 44.
INTERCEPTIONS—Miami, J. Brown 1-29, Jackson 1-21.
KICKOFF RETURNS—Indianapolis, Bailey 2-52. Miami, Buckley 1-48, Spikes 1-15, R. Hill 1-4.
PUNT RETURNS—Indianapolis, Buchanan 5-40. Miami, McDuffie 2-22.
SACKS—Indianapolis, McCoy 1.

BUCCANEERS 20, RAIDERS 17

Sunday, November 10

Oakland	0	10	7	0	0—17
Tampa Bay	7	3	0	7	3—20

First Quarter
T.B.—Rhett 5 pass from Dilfer (Husted kick), 9:32.
Second Quarter
Oak.—Jett 18 pass from Williams (Ford kick), 1:20.
T.B.—FG, Husted 44, 14:21.
Oak.—FG, Ford 45, 15:00.
Third Quarter
Oak.—Hobbs 8 pass from Hostetler (Ford kick), 14:36.
Fourth Quarter
T.B.—Alstott 2 pass from Dilfer (Husted kick), 7:35.
Overtime
T.B.—FG, Husted 23, 11:56.
Attendance—45,392.

TEAM STATISTICS

	Oakland	Tampa Bay
First Downs	17	27
Rushes-Yards	22-89	49-162
Passing	182	177
Punt Returns	2-13	4-24
Kickoff Returns	4-74	4-79
Interception Returns	1-14	1-7
Comp-Att-Int	16-23-1	20-28-1
Sacked-Yards Lost	4-17	2-15
Punts	5-42	3-47
Fumbles-Lost	1-0	1-1
Penalties-Yards	12-75	6-91
Time of Possession	23:47	48:09

INDIVIDUAL STATISTICS

RUSHING—Oakland, Fenner 7-31, Kaufman 6-32, Hostetler 6-10, Williams 3-16. Tampa Bay, Rhett 33-95, Alstott 10-54, Dilfer 4-13, Ellison 1-3, Williams 1-(minus 3).
PASSING—Oakland, Hostetler 15-22-1-181, Williams 1-1-0-18. Tampa Bay, Dilfer 20-28-1-192.
RECEIVING—Oakland, T. Brown 5-89, Jett 3-47, Hobbs 3-27, Williams 2-20, Kaufman 2-13, Fenner 1-3. Tampa Bay, Alstott 8-67, Williams 5-63, Moore 3-29, Marshall 2-27, Rhett 2-6.
MISSED FIELD GOAL ATTEMPTS—Oakland, Ford 28. Tampa Bay, Husted 53.
INTERCEPTIONS—Oakland, McDaniel 1-14. Tampa Bay, Nickerson 1-7.
KICKOFF RETURNS—Oakland, Kidd 3-62, Kaufman 1-12. Tampa Bay, Marshall 4-79.
PUNT RETURNS—Oakland, T. Brown 2-13. Tampa Bay, Marshall 4-24.
SACKS—Oakland, McGlockton 1, Smith 1. Tampa Bay, Marts 2, Ahanotu 1, M. Jones 1.

BENGALS 34, STEELERS 24

Sunday, November 10

Pittsburgh	0	17	7	0—24
Cincinnati	3	14	7	10—34

First Quarter
Cin.—FG, Pelfrey 32, 10:28.
Second Quarter
Pit.—FG, N. Johnson 46, :06.
Pit.—Bettis 6 run (N. Johnson kick), 7:23.
Cin.—Carter 1 run (Pelfrey kick), 13:45.
Pit.—Stewart 1 run (N. Johnson kick), 14:55.
Cin.—Dunn 90 kickoff return (Pelfrey kick), 15:00.
Third Quarter
Pit.—Bettis 1 run (N. Johnson kick), 8:42.
Cin.—Bieniemy 33 run (Pelfrey kick), 10:32.
Fourth Quarter
Cin.—Carter 12 pass from Blake (Pelfrey kick), 8:21.
Cin.—FG, Pelfrey 34, 12:28.
Attendance—57,265.

TEAM STATISTICS

	Pittsburgh	Cincinnati
First Downs	18	24
Rushes-Yards	28-137	32-112
Passing	180	260
Punt Returns	1-13	3-20
Kickoff Returns	6-115	4-151
Interception Returns	3-48	3-25
Comp-Att-Int	13-28-3	24-39-3
Sacked-Yards Lost	1-0	2-15
Punts	3-43	3-43
Fumbles-Lost	1-1	1-0
Penalties-Yards	10-99	7-50
Time of Possession	24:11	35:49

INDIVIDUAL STATISTICS

RUSHING—Pittsburgh, Bettis 21-111, Stewart 3-0, Pegram 2-15, Witman 1-8, Tomczak 1-3. Cincinnati, Hearst 19-61, Blake 5-3, Bieniemy 4-42, Carter 4-6.
PASSING—Pittsburgh, Tomczak 13-28-3-180. Cincinnati, Blake 24-39-3-275.
RECEIVING—Pittsburgh, Hastings 6-56, Thigpen 3-63, C. Johnson 2-21, Stewart 1-36, Lester 1-4. Cincinnati, Pickens 12-103, Dunn 5-79, Scott 3-32, Hearst 2-38, Carter 1-12, Cothran 1-11.
MISSED FIELD GOAL ATTEMPTS—Pittsburgh, N. Johnson 42.
INTERCEPTIONS—Pittsburgh, Woodson 2-32, Brown 1-16. Cincinnati, Rog. Jones 1-30, Ambrose 1-0, Spencer 1-(minus 5).
KICKOFF RETURNS—Pittsburgh, Pegram 5-99, Mills 1-16. Cincinnati, Hill 3-52, Dunn 1-99.
PUNT RETURNS—Pittsburgh, Hastings 1-13. Cincinnati, Sawyer 2-9, Myers 1-11.
SACKS—Pittsburgh, Gildon 1, Team 1. Cincinnati, McDonald 1.

RAMS 59, FALCONS 16

Sunday, November 10

Atlanta	0	7	9	0—16
St. Louis	14	17	7	21—59

First Quarter
St.L.—Kennison 78 punt return (Lohmiller kick), 2:54.
St.L.—Bruce 22 pass from Banks (Lohmiller kick), 8:52.

Second Quarter
St.L.—Phillips 1 run (Lohmiller kick), 3:18.
St.L.—T. Wright 19 interception return (Lohmiller kick), 3:36.
Atl.—Birden 18 pass from Hebert (Andersen kick), 9:28.
St.L.—FG, Lohmiller 42, 15:00.

Third Quarter
Atl.—Anderson 2 pass from Hebert (conversion failed), 3:48.
St.L.—Kennison 1 pass from Banks (Lohmiller kick), 8:51.
Atl.—FG, Andersen 47, 12:47.

Fourth Quarter
St.L.—Green 1 run (Lohmiller kick), 4:10.
St.L.—Green 35 run (Lohmiller kick), 9:46.
St.L.—Robinson 13 run (Lohmiller kick), 11:27.
Attendance—58,776.

TEAM STATISTICS

	Atlanta	St.Louis
First Downs	15	29
Rushes-Yards	16-44	38-279
Passing	248	185
Punt Returns	1-10	5-111
Kickoff Returns	9-144	2-34
Interception Returns	0-0	2-22
Comp-Att-Int	22-38-2	15-24-0
Sacked-Yards Lost	4-24	1-3
Punts	6-41	2-49
Fumbles-Lost	1-1	1-1
Penalties-Yards	6-53	5-34
Time of Possession	28:35	31:25

INDIVIDUAL STATISTICS

RUSHING—Atlanta, Anderson 13-23, Heyward 3-21. St. Louis, Phillips 14-106, Green 13-106, Robinson 8-56, Banks 2-12, Martin 1-(minus 1).
PASSING—Atlanta, Hebert 19-33-1-241, Nagle 3-5-1-31. St. Louis, Banks 15-24-0-188.
RECEIVING—Atlanta, Birden 8-75, Mathis 5-42, Emanuel 4-109, Metcalf 2-21, Anderson 2-11, Heyward 1-14. St. Louis, Bruce 5-91, Kennison 4-53, Green 2-18, Ross 2-11, Thomas 1-11, Laing 1-1.
MISSED FIELD GOAL ATTEMPTS—None.
INTERCEPTIONS—St. Louis, T. Wright 1-19, Lincoln 1-3.
KICKOFF RETURNS—Atlanta, Metcalf 9-144. St. Louis, Thomas 1-19, Kennison 1-15.
PUNT RETURNS—Atlanta, Mathis 1-10. St. Louis, Kennison 5-111.
SACKS—Atlanta, Owens 1. St. Louis, O'Neal 1, Carter 1, J. Harris 1, J. Jones 1.

COWBOYS 20, 49ERS 17

Sunday, November 10

Dallas	0	7	0	10	3—20
San Francisco	10	0	0	7	0—17

First Quarter
S.F.—FG, Wilkins 28, 7:35.
S.F.—Uwaezuoke 29 pass from S. Young (Wilkins kick), 11:42.

Second Quarter
Dal.—Aikman 3 run (Boniol kick), 14:28.

Fourth Quarter
Dal.—FG, Boniol 26, :04.
S.F.—Kirby 27 run (Wilkins kick), 3:22.
Dal.—Bjornson 6 pass from Aikman (Boniol kick), 12:15.

Overtime
Dal.—FG, Boniol 29, 6:17.
Attendance—68,919.

TEAM STATISTICS

	Dallas	San Francisco
First Downs	20	16
Rushes-Yards	31-94	26-111
Passing	222	156
Punt Returns	4-54	4-64
Kickoff Returns	5-87	3-59
Interception Returns	2-2	1-6
Comp-Att-Int	24-39-1	17-30-2
Sacked-Yards Lost	2-8	3-15
Punts	7-47	5-48
Fumbles-Lost	0-0	1-1
Penalties-Yards	10-80	8-45
Time of Possession	39:20	26:57

INDIVIDUAL STATISTICS

RUSHING—Dallas, E. Smith 26-81, Aikman 3-8, S. Williams 1-4, Johnston 1-1. San Francisco, Kirby 12-55, Floyd 10-55, S. Young 2-4, Rice 1-(minus 1), D. Carter 1-(minus 2).
PASSING—Dallas, Aikman 24-39-1-230. San Francisco, Grbac 10-17-2-88, S. Young 7-13-0-83.
RECEIVING—Dallas, Bjornson 8-45, Irvin 6-88, Johnston 5-33, Sanders 2-34, Martin 2-19, E. Smith 1-11. San Francisco, Rice 5-49, Floyd 4-36, Kirby 3-18, Uwaezuoke 2-39, Popson 2-24, Owens 1-5.
MISSED FIELD GOAL ATTEMPTS—None.
INTERCEPTIONS—Dallas, K. Smith 1-2, Strickland 1-0. San Francisco, Pope 1-6.
KICKOFF RETURNS—Dallas, Walker 5-87. San Francisco, D. Carter 2-33, Loville 1-26.
PUNT RETURNS—Dallas, Martin 3-50, Sanders 1-4. San Francisco, D. Carter 4-64.
SACKS—Dallas, Woodson 1, Hennings 1, Thomas 1. San Francisco, B. Young 1, Doleman 1.

JAGUARS 30, RAVENS 27

Sunday, November 10

Baltimore	7	10	3	7—27
Jacksonville	0	3	10	17—30

First Quarter
Bal.—Jackson 5 pass from Testaverde (Stover kick), 8:45.

Second Quarter
Jac.—FG, Hollis 23, 8:27.
Bal.—Morris 52 pass from Testaverde (Stover kick), 9:21.
Bal.—FG, Stover 21, 14:55.

Third Quarter
Jac.—Stewart 10 run (Hollis kick), 2:07.
Bal.—FG, Stover 21, 7:59.
Jac.—FG, Hollis 33, 10:55.

Fourth Quarter
Jac.—FG, Hollis 24, 3:49.
Bal.—Alexander 21 pass from Testaverde (Stover kick), 8:37.
Jac.—Stewart 8 pass from Brunell (pass failed), 11:10.
Jac.—Brunell 1 run (McCardell pass from Brunell), 14:19.
Attendance—64,628.

TEAM STATISTICS

	Baltimore	Jacksonville
First Downs	24	22
Rushes-Yards	36-152	20-86
Passing	235	332
Punt Returns	4-45	1-21
Kickoff Returns	7-155	6-97
Interception Returns	1-0	0-0
Comp-Att-Int	17-27-0	24-37-1
Sacked-Yards Lost	4-18	6-22
Punts	5-36	4-49
Fumbles-Lost	3-3	1-1
Penalties-Yards	6-78	8-65
Time of Possession	33:33	26:27

INDIVIDUAL STATISTICS

RUSHING—Baltimore, Morris 26-109, Byner 7-29, Testaverde 3-14. Jacksonville, Stewart 9-23, Brunell 7-58, Means 3-3, W. Jackson 1-2.
PASSING—Baltimore, Testaverde 17-27-0-253. Jacksonville, Brunell 24-37-1-354.
RECEIVING—Baltimore, Alexander 4-65, Kinchen 4-36, Morris 3-73, Green 3-50, Jackson 2-13, J. Lewis 1-16. Jacksonville, Mitchell 6-80, Rison 6-62, Smith 3-74, McCardell 3-41, Stewart 3-19, W. Jackson 2-62, Brown 1-16.
MISSED FIELD GOAL ATTEMPTS—None.
INTERCEPTIONS—Baltimore, E. Turner 1-0.
KICKOFF RETURNS—Baltimore, J. Lewis 4-85, Baldwin 3-70. Jacksonville, Jordan 5-69, R. Bell 1-28.
PUNT RETURNS—Baltimore, J. Lewis 4-45. Jacksonville, Hudson 1-21.
SACKS—Baltimore, Thompson 3, R. Lewis 1, Goad 1, Brady 1/2, Caldwell 1/2. Jacksonville, Hardy 1, Brackens 1, Smeenge 1, Simmons 1.

BRONCOS 17, BEARS 12

Sunday, November 10

Chicago	3	0	6	3—12
Denver	7	7	0	3—17

First Quarter
Chi.—FG, Jaeger 35, 5:26.
Den.—Sharpe 15 pass from Elway (Elam kick), 11:17.
Second Quarter
Den.—Davis 1 run (Elam kick), 9:23.
Third Quarter
Chi.—Conway 11 pass from Krieg (pass failed), 8:51.
Fourth Quarter
Den.—FG, Elam 24, 1:49.
Chi.—FG, Jaeger 48, 5:37.
Attendance—75,555.

TEAM STATISTICS

	Chicago	Denver
First Downs	24	17
Rushes-Yards	39-174	26-92
Passing	172	192
Punt Returns	2-26	1-25
Kickoff Returns	4-71	1-21
Interception Returns	0-0	2-27
Comp-Att-Int	17-35-2	19-32-0
Sacked-Yards Lost	1-9	1-6
Punts	3-49	5-42
Fumbles-Lost	1-1	0-0
Penalties-Yards	7-48	8-71
Time of Possession	32:51	27:09

INDIVIDUAL STATISTICS
RUSHING—Chicago, R. Harris 23-112, Salaam 11-53, Krieg 3-4, Conway 1-5, T. Carter 1-0. Denver, Davis 21-76, Craver 4-13, Elway 1-3.
PASSING—Chicago, Krieg 17-35-2-181. Denver, Elway 19-32-0-198.
RECEIVING—Chicago, Conway 5-59, T. Carter 4-19, Timpson 3-42, R. Harris 3-31, Engram 1-21, Salaam 1-9. Denver, Miller 8-65, Sharpe 5-92, Davis 2-10, Craver 2-9, R. Smith 1-14, Carswell 1-8.
MISSED FIELD GOAL ATTEMPTS—None.
INTERCEPTIONS—Denver, Hilliard 1-27, Braxton 1-0.
KICKOFF RETURNS—Chicago, Engram 3-54, Ja. Jackson 1-17. Denver, Hebron 1-21.
PUNT RETURNS—Chicago, Engram 2-26. Denver, R. Smith 1-25.
SACKS—Chicago, Flanigan 1. Denver, A. Williams 1.

PANTHERS 27, GIANTS 17

Sunday, November 10

N.Y. Giants	14	0	3	0—17
Carolina	7	3	10	7—27

First Quarter
Car.—Ismail 35 run (Kasay kick), 3:35.
NYG—Calloway 13 pass from Brown (Daluiso kick), 7:44.
NYG—Lewis 23 pass from Brown (Daluiso kick), 12:55.
Second Quarter
Car.—FG, Kasay 42, 7:32.
Third Quarter
NYG—FG, Daluiso 22, 5:03.
Car.—Johnson 1 run (Kasay kick), 9:34.
Car.—FG, Kasay 28, 12:11.
Fourth Quarter
Car.—Griffith 17 pass from Collins (Kasay kick), 3:24.
Attendance—70,298.

TEAM STATISTICS

	N.Y. Giants	Carolina
First Downs	14	23
Rushes-Yards	20-74	40-142
Passing	215	208
Punt Returns	3-12	3-17
Kickoff Returns	5-115	4-126
Interception Returns	1-0	3-28
Comp-Att-Int	15-31-3	20-34-1
Sacked-Yards Lost	1-8	0-0
Punts	5-43	5-37
Fumbles-Lost	1-1	0-0
Penalties-Yards	10-94	5-40
Time of Possession	24:35	35:25

INDIVIDUAL STATISTICS
RUSHING—New York, Hampton 19-73, Brown 1-1. Carolina, Johnson 23-67, Oliver 8-23, Collins 5-1, Philyaw 3-16, Ismail 1-35.
PASSING—New York, Brown 15-31-3-223. Carolina, Collins 19-33-1-202, Beuerlein 1-1-0-6.
RECEIVING—New York, Calloway 7-95, Lewis 4-76, Cross 2-13, Dawsey 1-28, Elias 1-11. Carolina, Walls 6-73, Griffith 4-36, Green 4-35, Johnson 3-24, Ismail 1-30, Carrier 1-9, Oliver 1-1.
MISSED FIELD GOAL ATTEMPTS—Carolina, Kasay 49.
INTERCEPTIONS—New York, Armstead 1-0. Carolina, Terrell 2-6, Cook 1-22.
KICKOFF RETURNS—New York, C. Hamilton 5-115. Carolina, Bates 3-93, Oliver 1-33.
PUNT RETURNS—New York, Lewis 3-12. Carolina, Oliver 3-17.
SACKS—Carolina, Mills 1.

OILERS 31, SAINTS 14

Sunday, November 10

Houston	14	7	7	3—31
New Orleans	3	3	0	8—14

First Quarter
Hou.—Sanders 42 pass from Chandler (Del Greco kick), 3:07.
Hou.—Harmon 11 pass from Chandler (Del Greco kick), 6:43.
N.O.—FG, Brien 29, 12:54.
Second Quarter
Hou.—Norgard 1 pass from Chandler (Del Greco kick), 13:49.
N.O.—FG, Brien 49, 14:59.
Third Quarter
Hou.—George 1 run (Del Greco kick), 7:47.
Fourth Quarter
N.O.—Haynes 34 pass from Everett (Haynes run), 1:32.
Hou.—FG, Del Greco 25, 13:22.
Attendance—34,121.

TEAM STATISTICS

	Houston	New Orleans
First Downs	20	14
Rushes-Yards	37-148	21-73
Passing	161	159
Punt Returns	2-50	2-21
Kickoff Returns	4-57	6-141
Interception Returns	0-0	1-10
Comp-Att-Int	13-21-1	16-33-0
Sacked-Yards Lost	1-12	1-10
Punts	5-48	7-43
Fumbles-Lost	1-0	3-2
Penalties-Yards	4-33	8-69
Time of Possession	35:25	24:35

INDIVIDUAL STATISTICS
RUSHING—Houston, George 25-91, Harmon 5-47, Chandler 4-9, Thomas 3-1. New Orleans, Zellars 17-60, Neal 3-14, Hunter 1-(minus 1).
PASSING—Houston, Chandler 13-21-1-173. New Orleans, Everett 16-33-0-169.
RECEIVING—Houston, Harmon 7-108, Davis 2-3, Sanders 1-42, Wycheck 1-16, George 1-3, Norgard 1-1. New Orleans, Hunter 5-39, Haynes 2-48, DeRamus 2-24, Lusk 2-13, Small 2-11, T. Johnson 1-15, Neal 1-12, Zellars 1-7.
MISSED FIELD GOAL ATTEMPTS—None.
INTERCEPTIONS—New Orleans, G. Jackson 1-10.
KICKOFF RETURNS—Houston, Thomas 3-57, Wycheck 1-0. New Orleans, Hughes 4-111, Hayes 2-30.
PUNT RETURNS—Houston, Floyd 2-50. New Orleans, Hughes 2-21.
SACKS—Houston, Barrow 1. New Orleans, Martin 1.

SEAHAWKS 42, VIKINGS 23

Sunday, November 10

Minnesota	0	7	0	16—23
Seattle	10	18	7	7—42

First Quarter
Sea.—FG, Peterson 54, 4:24.
Sea.—Smith 1 run (Peterson kick), 10:13.
Second Quarter
Sea.—FG, Peterson 38, 5:26.
Min.—Reed 38 pass from Moon (Sisson kick), 11:12.
Sea.—Galloway 7 pass from Friesz (Smith run), 14:05.
Sea.—Broussard 26 run (Peterson kick), 14:49.
Third Quarter
Sea.—Warren 1 run (Peterson kick), 5:22.

Fourth Quarter
Sea.—Proehl 22 pass from Friesz (Peterson kick), 2:15.
Min.—B. Johnson 1 run (Jordan pass from B. Johnson), 12:20.
Min.—Reed 14 pass from B. Johnson (Walsh pass from B. Johnson), 13:26.
Attendance—50,794.

TEAM STATISTICS

	Minnesota	Seattle
First Downs	16	26
Rushes-Yards	12-15	37-199
Passing	300	253
Punt Returns	2-4	5-95
Kickoff Returns	8-180	2-31
Interception Returns	0-0	2-1
Comp-Att-Int	22-42-2	23-34-0
Sacked-Yards Lost	1-10	2-15
Punts	8-44	6-40
Fumbles-Lost	2-2	1-1
Penalties-Yards	9-81	13-98
Time of Possession	22:23	37:37

INDIVIDUAL STATISTICS

RUSHING—Minnesota, Graham 6-9, Lee 3-2, B. Johnson 2-3, Palmer 1-1. Seattle, Smith 15-90, Warren 14-61, Broussard 4-49, Mirer 2-(minus 2), O. Gray 1-2, Galloway 1-(minus 1).

PASSING—Minnesota, Moon 14-30-2-187, B. Johnson 8-12-0-123. Seattle, Friesz 22-33-0-263, Mirer 1-1-0-5.

RECEIVING—Minnesota, Carter 7-142, Lee 4-26, Reed 3-78, Jordan 3-18, Evans 3-15, Palmer 1-20, Graham 1-11. Seattle, Galloway 8-91, Proehl 6-95, Fauria 3-34, Warren 3-11, Pritchard 2-32, R. Harris 1-5.

MISSED FIELD GOAL ATTEMPTS—Seattle, Peterson 50.

INTERCEPTIONS—Seattle, Moss 1-1, Bellamy 1-0.

KICKOFF RETURNS—Minnesota, Palmer 4-114, Ismail 3-50, Lee 1-16. Seattle, Broussard 1-17, R. Harris 1-14.

PUNT RETURNS—Minnesota, Palmer 2-4. Seattle, R. Harris 5-95.

SACKS—Minnesota, F. Smith 1, Randle 1. Seattle, McCrary 1.

CARDINALS 37, REDSKINS 34

Sunday, November 10

| Arizona | 3 | 10 | 0 | 21 | 3—37 |
| Washington | 3 | 10 | 14 | 7 | 0—34 |

First Quarter
Ariz.—FG, Butler 26, 7:19.
Was.—FG, Blanton 53, 14:04.

Second Quarter
Was.—Logan 36 run (Blanton kick), 4:57.
Ariz.—FG, Butler 39, 10:12.
Ariz.—Dowdell 64 pass from Esiason (Butler kick), 13:48.
Was.—FG, Blanton 24, 15:00.

Third Quarter
Was.—Westbrook 17 pass from Frerotte (Blanton kick), 4:57.
Was.—Allen 1 run (Blanton kick), 12:13.

Fourth Quarter
Ariz.—Centers 1 run (Butler kick), 1:25.
Was.—Allen 1 run (Blanton kick), 4:23.
Ariz.—McWilliams 13 pass from Esiason (Butler kick), 7:23.
Ariz.—Edwards 12 pass from Esiason (Butler kick), 14:40.

Overtime
Ariz.—FG, Butler 32, 14:27.
Attendance—51,929.

TEAM STATISTICS

	Arizona	Washington
First Downs	32	25
Rushes-Yards	33-108	39-204
Passing	507	212
Punt Returns	3-24	2-11
Kickoff Returns	7-129	7-138
Interception Returns	1-20	4-16
Comp-Att-Int	35-59-4	18-36-1
Sacked-Yards Lost	2-15	0-0
Punts	3-45	6-48

	Arizona	Washington
Fumbles-Lost	4-1	2-1
Penalties-Yards	9-100	8-49
Time of Possession	42:23	32:04

INDIVIDUAL STATISTICS

RUSHING—Arizona, L. Johnson 20-65, Centers 9-39, Esiason 3-1, McElroy 1-3. Washington, Allen 31-124, Mitchell 5-25, Logan 1-36, Frerotte 1-17, Westbrook 1-2.

PASSING—Arizona, Esiason 35-59-4-522. Washington, Frerotte 18-36-1-212.

RECEIVING—Arizona, Sanders 6-79, Centers 6-55, Edwards 5-70, McWilliams 5-54, Carter 4-48, Dowdell 3-92, R. Moore 3-91, L. Johnson 3-33. Washington, Westbrook 6-91, Mitchell 4-49, Allen 3-15, Asher 2-20, Logan 2-18, Ellard 1-19.

MISSED FIELD GOAL ATTEMPTS—Arizona, Butler 32. Washington, Blanton 48.

INTERCEPTIONS—Arizona, Lassiter 1-20. Washington, Pounds 2-11, Richard 1-5, Boutte 1-0.

KICKOFF RETURNS—Arizona, McElroy 7-103. Washington, Mitchell 7-138.

PUNT RETURNS—Arizona, Dowdell 3-24. Washington, Mitchell 2-11.

SACKS—Washington, Owens 1, Palmer 1.

CHARGERS 27, LIONS 21

Monday, November 11

| Detroit | 7 | 7 | 0 | 7—21 |
| San Diego | 7 | 10 | 7 | 3—27 |

First Quarter
S.D.—Martin 32 pass from Humphries (Carney kick), 10:00.
Det.—Sanders 2 run (Hanson kick), 13:13.

Second Quarter
Det.—Sanders 11 run (Hanson kick), 1:20.
S.D.—FG, Carney 29, 8:33.
S.D.—A. Coleman 46 pass from Humphries (Carney kick), 15:00.

Third Quarter
S.D.—Pupunu 9 pass from Humphries (Carney kick), 6:16.

Fourth Quarter
S.D.—FG, Carney 20, 2:36.
Det.—Perriman 1 pass from Majkowski (Hanson kick), 13:08.
Attendance—60,425.

TEAM STATISTICS

	Detroit	San Diego
First Downs	19	27
Rushes-Yards	19-82	40-127
Passing	140	279
Punt Returns	2-26	2-33
Kickoff Returns	5-148	3-65
Interception Returns	0-0	0-0
Comp-Att-Int	15-27-0	24-32-0
Sacked-Yards Lost	4-19	3-32
Punts	4-48	4-37
Fumbles-Lost	3-1	2-0
Penalties-Yards	7-61	11-129
Time of Possession	19:21	40:39

INDIVIDUAL STATISTICS

RUSHING—Detroit, Sanders 16-51, Morton 1-18, Perriman 1-13, Majkowski 1-0. San Diego, Russell 20-80, Fletcher 11-22, Bradley 7-25, Humphries 2-0.

PASSING—Detroit, Majkowski 10-18-0-110, Mitchell 5-9-0-49. San Diego, Humphries 24-32-0-311.

RECEIVING—Detroit, Perriman 7-70, H. Moore 3-39, Morton 3-32, Metzelaars 1-11, Sanders 1-7. San Diego, Martin 8-113, A. Coleman 3-63, Fletcher 3-35, Pupunu 3-28, Russell 2-33, Jones 2-21, May 1-12, Still 1-7, Mitchell 1-(minus 1).

MISSED FIELD GOAL ATTEMPTS—Detroit, Hanson 53. San Diego, Carney 49.

INTERCEPTIONS—None.

KICKOFF RETURNS—Detroit, Milburn 5-148. San Diego, A. Coleman 3-65.

PUNT RETURNS—Detroit, Milburn 2-26. San Diego, Da. Gordon 2-33.

SACKS—Detroit, Porcher 1, Thomas 1, Waldroup 1. San Diego, Da. Gordon 2, Mims 1, M. Coleman 1.

WEEK 12

ARIZONA 31, N.Y. Giants 23
ATLANTA 17, New Orleans 15
BUFFALO 31, Cincinnati 17
Carolina 20, ST. LOUIS 10
Denver 34, NEW ENGLAND 8
DETROIT 17, Seattle 16
INDIANAPOLIS 34, N.Y. Jets 29
KANSAS CITY 14, Chicago 10
Miami 23, HOUSTON 20
Minnesota 16, OAKLAND 13 (OT)
PITTSBURGH 28, Jacksonville 3
SAN FRANCISCO 38, Baltimore 20
Tampa Bay 25, SAN DIEGO 17
Washington 26, PHILADELPHIA 21
DALLAS 21, Green Bay 6

STANDINGS

AFC EAST	W	L	T	Pct.
Buffalo	8	3	0	.727
New England	7	4	0	.636
Indianapolis	6	5	0	.545
Miami	6	5	0	.545
N.Y. Jets	1	10	0	.091

AFC CENTRAL	W	L	T	Pct.
Pittsburgh	8	3	0	.727
Houston	6	5	0	.545
Cincinnati	4	7	0	.363
Jacksonville	4	7	0	.363
Baltimore	3	8	0	.273

AFC WEST	W	L	T	Pct.
Denver	10	1	0	.909
Kansas City	8	3	0	.727
San Diego	6	5	0	.545
Seattle	5	6	0	.454
Oakland	4	7	0	.363

NFC EAST	W	L	T	Pct.
Washington	8	3	0	.727
Dallas	7	4	0	.636
Philadelphia	7	4	0	.636
Arizona	5	6	0	.454
N.Y. Giants	4	7	0	.363

NFC CENTRAL	W	L	T	Pct.
Green Bay	8	3	0	.727
Minnesota	6	5	0	.545
Detroit	5	6	0	.454
Chicago	4	7	0	.363
Tampa Bay	3	8	0	.273

NFC WEST	W	L	T	Pct.
San Francisco	8	3	0	.727
Carolina	7	4	0	.636
St. Louis	3	8	0	.273
New Orleans	2	9	0	.181
Atlanta	2	9	0	.181

HIGHLIGHTS

Hero of the week: Making his third start of the season in place of Steve Young, San Francisco quarterback Elvis Grbac was 26-of-31 for 268 yards and one touchdown and ran for another in helping the 49ers beat the Ravens, 38-20. His 84 percent completion rate was the fourth best in team history. Grbac's performance came one week after his costly interception in a 20-17 loss to Dallas led San Francisco mayor Willie Brown to call Grbac "an embarrassment to mankind."

Goat of the week: Houston's John Henry Mills, a Pro Bowl special teams alternate the last two seasons, made two costly mistakes in the Oilers' 23-20 loss to Miami. First, Mills missed blocking Kirby Dar Dar, who blocked Reggie Roby's punt, setting up a Dolphins touchdown. Later, Mills failed to see Larry Izzo carrying the ball when Miami faked a punt on fourth-and-9. Izzo gained 26 yards on the play.

Sub of the week: In another attempt to replace injured Robert Smith, Minnesota started peripatetic Leroy Hoard at running back against Oakland. Hoard, playing for his third team this season, sparked a Vikings offense that came into the game ranked 28th in the league in rushing. Hoard carried 20 times for 108 yards and the Vikings rushed for 182 yards overall as they defeated the Raiders, 16-13, in overtime.

Comeback of the week: Tampa Bay spotted San Diego a 14-0 lead, then held the Chargers to only a field goal in the final 49 minutes and 12 seconds as the Buccaneers rallied for a 25-17 victory. Trent Dilfer was 30-of-40 for 327 yards—his completions, yards and percentage (75.0) were career bests—as Tampa Bay won back-to-back games for the first time under coach Tony Dungy.

Blowout of the week: Denver took a 24-0 halftime lead en route to a 34-8 trouncing of New England. The victory improved the Broncos' record to an NFL-best 10-1. Quarterback John Elway, who has never lost to the Patriots in nine games, was 14-of-23 for 175 yards before giving way to backup Bill Musgrave in the fourth quarter. The Patriots rushed a franchise-low nine times for 17 yards.

Nail-biter of the week: Washington, last in defense in the NFL, forced Philadelphia quarterback Ty Detmer to throw four consecutive incompletions from the Redskins' 20 in the final 24 seconds and held on for a 26-21 win. The victory moved Washington into first place in the NFC East.

Hit of the week: A safety blitz by Carnell Lake turned out to be a pivotal play in Pittsburgh's 28-3 victory over Jacksonville. Trailing 14-3, Jacksonville started the second half by driving to the Steelers' 7 as Mark Brunell completed five consecutive passes. But the Jaguars failed to pick up Lake, who forced a Brunell fumble and returned it 85 yards for a touchdown. It was the fifth touchdown of the season by the Steelers' defense.

Oddity of the week: Seattle cornerback Selwyn Jones lost both shoes chasing down Detroit running back Barry Sanders during the third quarter of the Lions' 17-16 victory. Eventually, "Shoeless Selwyn" helped push Sanders out of bounds at the 6 after a 40-yard gain.

Top rusher: Terrell Davis carried 32 times for 154 yards and two touchdowns in Denver's victory over New England. Davis also caught four passes for 56 yards. His 210 total yards were eight less than the Patriots' team total.

Top passer: Frank Reich was 20-of-42 for a career-best 352 yards and three touchdowns for the Jets. But he also was intercepted four times as Indianapolis won 34-29.

Top receiver: Jeff Graham of the Jets caught nine passes for 189 yards and three touchdowns.

Notes: Jacksonville's road record fell to 0-6 with the loss to Pittsburgh. During the game, the Jaguars faced long shot situations of third-and-32, third-and-34 and third-and-39. . . . Making his first start since the Super Bowl, Steelers wide receiver Yancy Thigpen caught four passes for 79 yards and one touchdown. He missed the first half of the season with injuries. . . . The Raiders lost by a field goal in overtime for the second week in a row. Six of their seven losses have been by a combined 19 points. . . . Miami scored a touchdown following a blocked punt for the fifth time this season. . . .

New Orleans' Ray Zellars rushed four times for minus-10 yards and also lost a fumble. . . . Atlanta's Morten Andersen—who equaled his NFL record by kicking three field goals of 50 or more yards in a game against New Orleans, his old team, last season—missed three attempts of 50 or more yards in the Falcons' 17-15 victory over the Saints. . . . San Francisco's win over Baltimore gave coach George Seifert 103 victories—one more than former 49ers coach Bill Walsh.—Washington's victory snapped a string of eight consecutive losses to Philadelphia. . . . Houston guard Bruce Matthews played in his club-record 211th game. . . . Cincinnati was penalized on four of the first five snaps in a 31-17 loss to Buffalo. . . . Arizona scored a touchdown in the first quarter for the first time in 19 games. . . . Chris Boniol tied an NFL record by kicking seven field goals in Dallas' 21-6 victory over Green Bay. It was the Cowboys' eighth consecutive victory over the Packers. . . . Tampa Bay won on the West Coast for only the second time in 21 games.

Quote of the week: Denver tight end Shannon Sharpe, after the Broncos' victory over New England in Foxboro: "We are the bullies. Even in someone else's backyard, we come in and beat them up."

GAME SUMMARIES

FALCONS 17, SAINTS 15

Sunday, November 17

New Orleans	0	3 3	9—15
Atlanta	10	7 0	0—17

First Quarter
Atl.—Metcalf 8 pass from Hebert (Andersen kick), 7:39.
Atl.—FG, Andersen 38, 14:57.

Second Quarter
N.O.—FG, Brien 42, 11:42.
Atl.—Mathis 5 pass from Hebert (Andersen kick), 14:44.

Third Quarter
N.O.—FG, Brien 37, 6:09.

Fourth Quarter
N.O.—Neal 19 pass from Everett (run failed), 3:35.
N.O.—FG, Brien 30, 12:22.
Attendance—43,119.

TEAM STATISTICS
	New Orleans	Atlanta
First Downs	15	18
Rushes-Yards	16-34	22-74
Passing	233	219
Punt Returns	1-0	0-0
Kickoff Returns	4-94	5-116
Interception Returns	1-0	2-3
Comp-Att-Int	23-33-2	26-39-1
Sacked-Yards Lost	2-11	1-10
Punts	2-45	3-40
Fumbles-Lost	1-1	0-0
Penalties-Yards	5-29	7-60
Time of Possession	26:36	33:24

INDIVIDUAL STATISTICS
RUSHING—New Orleans, Zellars 10-(minus 4), Everett 1-(minus 1), Bates 4-38, Neal 1-1, Hebert 1-(minus 1). Atlanta, Anderson 13-35, Heyward 7-37, Metcalf 1-3.

PASSING—New Orleans, Everett 23-33-2-244. Atlanta, Hebert 26-39-1-229.

RECEIVING—New Orleans, Haynes 6-79, Neal 6-40, Small 4-51, T. Johnson 4-48, Hunter 2-9, Hayes 1-17. Atlanta, Emanuel 8-76, Metcalf 5-60, Anderson 4-21, Mathis 4-21, Heyward 3-24, Tobeck 1-14, Birden 1-13.

MISSED FIELD GOAL ATTEMPTS—Atlanta, Andersen 55, 52, 52.

INTERCEPTIONS—New Orleans, Molden 1-0. Atlanta, Bennett 1-3, Edwards 1-0.

KICKOFF RETURNS—New Orleans, Hughes 3-74, Hunter 1-20. Atlanta, Preston 5-116.

PUNT RETURNS—New Orleans, Hughes 1-0.

SACKS—New Orleans, Mickell 1. Atlanta, McGill 1, Riddick 1.

BRONCOS 34, PATRIOTS 8

Sunday, November 17

Denver	14	10 7	3—34
New England	0	0 8	0— 8

First Quarter
Den.—Davis 15 pass from Elway (Elam kick), 4:43.
Den.—Davis 10 run (Elam kick), 7:13.

Second Quarter
Den.—Davis 2 run (Elam kick), 4:02.
Den.—FG, Elam 28, 14:52.

Third Quarter
N.E.—Martin 7 run (Byars pass from Bledsoe), 6:04.
Den.—Elway 1 run (Elam kick), 11:17.

Fourth Quarter
Den.—FG, Elam 47, 4:39.
Attendance—59,452.

TEAM STATISTICS
	Denver	New England
First Downs	26	11
Rushes-Yards	45-198	9-17
Passing	224	201
Punt Returns	3-45	0-0
Kickoff Returns	2-42	7-152
Interception Returns	1-11	1-14
Comp-Att-Int	16-27-1	22-42-1
Sacked-Yards Lost	1-6	2-11
Punts	3-45	5-45
Fumbles-Lost	2-0	1-0
Penalties-Yards	5-52	6-34
Time of Possession	39:00	21:00

INDIVIDUAL STATISTICS
RUSHING—Denver, Davis 32-154, Hebron 11-43, Elway 1-1, Craver 1-0. New England, Martin 7-13, Bledsoe 1-3, Meggett 1-1.

PASSING—Denver, Elway 14-23-1-175, Musgrave 2-4-0-55. New England, Bledsoe 22-41-1-212, Tupa 0-1-0-0.

RECEIVING—Denver, Miller 4-78, Davis 4-56, Sharpe 3-37, Craver 2-24, McCaffrey 2-24, Carswell 1-11. New England, Martin 7-23, Coates 5-48, Jefferson 2-56, Glenn 2-22, T. Brown 2-14, Meggett 2-13, Byars 1-27, Gash 1-9.

MISSED FIELD GOAL ATTEMPTS—Denver, Elam 52. New England, Vinatieri 40.

INTERCEPTIONS—Denver, Atwater 1-11. New England, Milloy 1-14.

KICKOFF RETURNS—Denver, Hebron 1-27, Chamberlain 1-15. New England, T. Brown 4-83, Meggett 3-69.

PUNT RETURNS—Denver, R. Smith 3-45.

SACKS—Denver, A. Williams 1, Tanuvasa 1. New England, Slade 1.

CHIEFS 14, BEARS 10

Sunday, November 17

Chicago	7	3 0	0—10
Kansas City	7	7 0	0—14

First Quarter
Chi.—R. Harris 14 run (Jaeger kick), 3:28.
K.C.—Penn 20 pass from Bono (Stoyanovich kick), 6:04.

Second Quarter
K.C.—Anders 10 run (Stoyanovich kick), 10:30.
Chi.—FG, Jaeger 49, 14:45.
Attendance—76,762.

TEAM STATISTICS
	Chicago	Kansas City
First Downs	14	20
Rushes-Yards	19-35	40-149
Passing	221	151
Punt Returns	1-9	5-46
Kickoff Returns	3-46	2-35
Interception Returns	1-0	1-0
Comp-Att-Int	21-36-1	15-25-1
Sacked-Yards Lost	2-11	4-33

	Chicago	Kansas City
Punts	7-50	6-40
Fumbles-Lost	2-1	1-1
Penalties-Yards	7-56	8-50
Time of Possession	26:28	33:32

INDIVIDUAL STATISTICS

RUSHING—Chicago, R. Harris 17-35, Green 2-0. Kansas City, Allen 16-64, Hill 15-52, Anders 3-17, McNair 2-10, Bennett 2-(minus 1), Horn 1-8, Bono 1-(minus 1).

PASSING—Chicago, Krieg 21-36-1-232. Kansas City, Bono 14-24-1-154, Hughes 1-1-0-30.

RECEIVING—Chicago, Engram 5-57, Neely 5-55, Conway 4-58, T. Carter 4-45, Timpson 1-11, Green 1-8, R. Harris 1-(minus 2). Kansas City, Penn 5-71, LaChapelle 3-46, Anders 2-8, Walker 1-24, To. Richardson 1-17, Hughes 1-8, D. Carter 1-7, Cash 1-3.

MISSED FIELD GOAL ATTEMPTS—None.

INTERCEPTIONS—Chicago, W. Harris 1-0. Kansas City, Collins 1-0.

KICKOFF RETURNS—Chicago, Engram 3-46. Kansas City, Woods 2-35.

PUNT RETURNS—Chicago, Engram 1-9. Kansas City, Penn 5-46.

SACKS—Chicago, A. Fontenot 1, Spellman 1, Thierry 1, Flanigan 1. Kansas City, Thomas 2.

REDSKINS 26, EAGLES 21

Sunday, November 17

Washington	3	10	10	3—26
Philadelphia	0	7	7	7—21

First Quarter

Was.—FG, Blanton 37, 14:56.

Second Quarter

Was.—Asher 12 pass from Frerotte (Blanton kick), 8:01.
Phi.—Watters 1 run (Anderson kick), 12:55.
Was.—FG, Blanton 22, 15:00.

Third Quarter

Was.—Asher 7 pass from Frerotte (Blanton kick), 4:24.
Phi.—Jones 13 pass from Detmer (Anderson kick), 9:46.
Was.—FG, Blanton 30, 11:58.

Fourth Quarter

Phi.—Watters 1 run (Anderson kick), 7:15.
Was.—FG, Blanton 33, 13:40.
Attendance—66,834.

TEAM STATISTICS

	Washington	Philadelphia
First Downs	19	27
Rushes-Yards	30-98	30-129
Passing	202	235
Punt Returns	1-23	2-0
Kickoff Returns	3-67	5-119
Interception Returns	1-42	1-0
Comp-Att-Int	18-33-1	21-33-1
Sacked-Yards Lost	3-10	3-16
Punts	3-50	4-45
Fumbles-Lost	1-0	1-1
Penalties-Yards	7-47	7-52
Time of Possession	28:08	31:52

INDIVIDUAL STATISTICS

RUSHING—Washington, Allen 25-84, Mitchell 3-13, Frerotte 2-1. Philadelphia, Watters 26-87, Garner 3-41, Detmer 1-1.

PASSING—Washington, Frerotte 18-33-1-212. Philadelphia, Detmer 21-33-1-251.

RECEIVING—Washington, Asher 5-48, Westbrook 4-39, Ellard 3-69, Mitchell 2-16, B. Brooks 1-18, Galbraith 1-10, Allen 1-6, Logan 1-6. Philadelphia, Jones 7-103, Watters 6-78, Fryar 5-40, Dunn 1-21, Garner 1-6, Turner 1-3.

MISSED FIELD GOAL ATTEMPTS—None.

INTERCEPTIONS—Washington, Richard 1-42. Philadelphia, Vincent 1-0.

KICKOFF RETURNS—Washington, Mitchell 3-67. Philadelphia, Witherspoon 5-119.

PUNT RETURNS—Washington, Mitchell 1-23. Philadelphia, Seay 2-0.

SACKS—Washington, Harvey 2, Owens 1. Philadelphia, Dawkins 1, W. Thomas 1, Team 1.

LIONS 17, SEAHAWKS 16

Sunday, November 17

Seattle	7	3	3	3—16
Detroit	0	7	7	3—17

First Quarter

Sea.—Smith 1 run (Peterson kick), 8:20.

Second Quarter

Sea.—FG, Peterson 24, 5:04.
Det.—Sanders 11 run (Hanson kick), 12:14.

Third Quarter

Sea.—FG, Peterson 25, 2:22.
Det.—H. Moore 6 pass from Majkowski (Hanson kick), 13:08.

Fourth Quarter

Sea.—FG, Peterson 21, 5:55.
Det.—FG, Hanson 43, 10:28.
Attendance—51,194.

TEAM STATISTICS

	Seattle	Detroit
First Downs	24	17
Rushes-Yards	41-184	21-144
Passing	194	141
Punt Returns	2-12	1-20
Kickoff Returns	2-48	5-145
Interception Returns	1-25	1-14
Comp-Att-Int	13-25-1	18-23-1
Sacked-Yards Lost	1-6	2-16
Punts	3-42	4-42
Fumbles-Lost	3-0	1-0
Penalties-Yards	6-46	7-66
Time of Possession	35:07	24:53

INDIVIDUAL STATISTICS

RUSHING—Seattle, Smith 33-148, Broussard 6-31, Galloway 1-5, Friesz 1-0. Detroit, Sanders 16-134, Majkowski 4-8, Lynch 1-2.

PASSING—Seattle, Friesz 8-18-1-148, Mirer 5-7-0-52. Detroit, Majkowski 18-23-1-157.

RECEIVING—Seattle, Crumpler 3-41, Galloway 3-22, Broussard 2-15, McKnight 1-73, Pritchard 1-24, Smith 1-19, O. Gray 1-5, R. Williams 1-1. Detroit, H. Moore 6-55, Perriman 4-51, Morton 4-35, Sanders 3-12, Metzelaars 1-4.

MISSED FIELD GOAL ATTEMPTS—Seattle, Peterson 42.

INTERCEPTIONS—Seattle, C. Harris 1-25. Detroit, Stewart 1-14.

KICKOFF RETURNS—Seattle, Broussard 2-48. Detroit, Milburn 5-145.

PUNT RETURNS—Seattle, R. Harris 2-12. Detroit, Milburn 1-20.

SACKS—Seattle, Kennedy 1, McCrary 1. Detroit, Elliss 1.

STEELERS 28, JAGUARS 3

Sunday, November 17

Jacksonville	0	3	0	0— 3
Pittsburgh	0	14	14	0—28

Second Quarter

Pit.—Thigpen 12 pass from Tomczak (N. Johnson kick), 1:39.
Pit.—Bettis 3 run (N. Johnson kick), 2:44.
Jac.—FG, Hollis 40, 15:00.

Third Quarter

Pit.—Lake 85 fumble return (N. Johnson kick), 6:42.
Pit.—Thigpen 27 pass from Tomczak (N. Johnson kick), 14:04.
Attendance—58,879.

TEAM STATISTICS

	Jacksonville	Pittsburgh
First Downs	20	15
Rushes-Yards	18-78	32-108
Passing	161	90
Punt Returns	2-0	6-59
Kickoff Returns	5-94	1-21
Interception Returns	1-0	2-17
Comp-Att-Int	28-47-2	7-25-1
Sacked-Yards Lost	6-54	2-19
Punts	8-43	6-40
Fumbles-Lost	5-2	1-0
Penalties-Yards	12-84	6-58
Time of Possession	33:21	26:39

INDIVIDUAL STATISTICS

RUSHING—Jacksonville, Stewart 14-62, Means 4-16. Pittsburgh, Bettis 21-53, Pegram 6-43, Tomczak 3-(minus 4), Mills 1-15, Stewart 1-1.

PASSING—Jacksonville, Brunell 28-47-2-215. Pittsburgh, Tomczak 7-24-1-109, Stewart 0-1-0-0.

RECEIVING—Jacksonville, W. Jackson 8-69, Smith 6-60, Stewart 5-4, McCardell 4-37, Mitchell 2-20, Rison 2-16, Brown 1-9. Pittsburgh, Thigpen 4-79, Mills 1-22, Bruener 1-7, Bettis 1-1.

MISSED FIELD GOAL ATTEMPTS—Pittsburgh, N. Johnson 51.
INTERCEPTIONS—Jacksonville, T. Davis 1-0. Pittsburgh, Figures 1-13, Woodson 1-4.
KICKOFF RETURNS—Jacksonville, Jordan 3-47, R. Bell 2-47. Pittsburgh, Mills 1-21.
PUNT RETURNS—Jacksonville, Hudson 2-0. Pittsburgh, Hastings 6-59.
SACKS—Jacksonville, Brackens 1, T. Davis ½, Hudson ½. Pittsburgh, Brown 3, Gildon 2, Lake 1.

CARDINALS 31, GIANTS 23

Sunday, November 17

N.Y. Giants	0	6	7	10—23
Arizona	14	7	7	3—31

First Quarter
Ariz.—R. Moore 18 pass from Esiason (Butler kick), 5:33.
Ariz.—C. Smith 1 run (Butler kick), 9:04.
Second Quarter
NYG—FG, Daluiso 25, :33.
Ariz.—Sanders 2 pass from Esiason (Butler kick), 4:24.
NYG—FG, Daluiso 22, 13:04.
Third Quarter
NYG—Wheatley 4 pass from Brown (Daluiso kick), 8:27.
Ariz.—L. Johnson 1 run (Butler kick), 14:22.
Fourth Quarter
NYG—Wheatley 9 pass from Brown (Daluiso kick), 5:04.
Ariz.—FG, Butler 18, 10:34.
NYG—FG, Daluiso 27, 13:35.
Attendance—34,924.

TEAM STATISTICS

	N.Y. Giants	Arizona
First Downs	24	21
Rushes-Yards	28-86	34-100
Passing	240	250
Punt Returns	3-(-12)	4-29
Kickoff Returns	6-98	4-77
Interception Returns	1-0	2-1
Comp-Att-Int	22-41-2	18-26-1
Sacked-Yards Lost	4-22	2-10
Punts	4-43	4-46
Fumbles-Lost	3-2	2-2
Penalties-Yards	4-19	9-54
Time of Possession	30:55	29:05

INDIVIDUAL STATISTICS
RUSHING—New York, Wheatley 13-50, Hampton 7-3, Brown 6-27, Elias 6-6. Arizona, L. Johnson 17-49, Centers 10-43, Esiason 5-6, C. Smith 2-2.
PASSING—New York, Brown 22-41-2-262. Arizona, Esiason 18-26-1-260.
RECEIVING—New York, Calloway 6-95, Wheatley 5-33, Lewis 3-35, Dawsey 2-22, Way 2-20, Saxton 2-14, Alexander 1-33, Elias 1-10. Arizona, Sanders 5-49, L. Johnson 2-50, Centers 2-42, R. Moore 2-37, Carter 2-28, Dowdell 2-25, Edwards 2-22, McElroy 1-7.
MISSED FIELD GOAL ATTEMPTS—None.
INTERCEPTIONS—New York, Ellsworth 1-0. Arizona, Williams 1-1, Alexander 1-0.
KICKOFF RETURNS—New York, C. Hamilton 4-82, Wheatley 2-16. Arizona, McElroy 4-77.
PUNT RETURNS—New York, Lewis 2-6, Sehorn 1-(minus 18). Arizona, Dowdell 4-29.
SACKS—New York, Widmer 1, Rudolph 1. Arizona, Rice 2, Swann 1, Joyner ½, Bankston ½.

49ERS 38, RAVENS 20

Sunday, November 17

Baltimore	7	6	7	0—20
San Francisco	10	7	7	14—38

First Quarter
Bal.—Jackson 65 pass from Testaverde (Stover kick), 1:11.
S.F.—Kirby 8 run (Wilkins kick), 4:06.
S.F.—FG, Wilkins 27, 7:07.
Second Quarter
S.F.—Rice 34 pass from Grbac (Wilkins kick), :05.
Bal.—FG, Stover 43, 12:16.
Bal.—FG, Stover 25, 15:00.
Third Quarter
Bal.—J. Jones 2 pass from Zeier (Stover kick), 1:45.
S.F.—Floyd 1 run (Wilkins kick), 10:39.

Fourth Quarter
S.F.—Doleman recovered fumble in end zone (Wilkins kick), 2:52.
S.F.—Grbac 1 run (Wilkins kick), 14:44.
Attendance—51,596.

TEAM STATISTICS

	Baltimore	San Francisco
First Downs	16	22
Rushes-Yards	28-109	31-110
Passing	159	262
Punt Returns	2-18	3-25
Kickoff Returns	7-112	4-63
Interception Returns	2-0	1-8
Comp-Att-Int	14-30-1	26-31-2
Sacked-Yards Lost	5-35	2-6
Punts	7-39	4-44
Fumbles-Lost	3-2	2-2
Penalties-Yards	8-66	4-45
Time of Possession	26:11	33:49

INDIVIDUAL STATISTICS
RUSHING—Baltimore, Morris 20-62, Byner 5-27, Zeier 2-8, Alexander 1-12. San Francisco, Kirby 17-56, Floyd 8-43, Grbac 3-8, Loville 3-3.
PASSING—Baltimore, Zeier 10-21-1-97, Testaverde 4-9-0-97. San Francisco, Grbac 26-31-2-268.
RECEIVING—Baltimore, F. Turner 4-37, Jackson 3-91, Alexander 3-32, Green 2-26, Kinchen 1-6, J. Jones 1-2. San Francisco, Jones 6-74, Rice 6-58, Kirby 5-31, Owens 4-68, Floyd 4-32, Uwaezuoke 1-5.
MISSED FIELD GOAL ATTEMPTS—None.
INTERCEPTIONS—Baltimore, E. Turner 1-0, Langham 1-0. San Francisco, Hanks 1-8.
KICKOFF RETURNS—Baltimore, Ethridge 4-67, J. Lewis 2-32, Alexander 1-13. San Francisco, Loville 2-37, D. Carter 2-26.
PUNT RETURNS—Baltimore, Alexander 1-15, Ethridge 1-3. San Francisco, D. Carter 3-25.
SACKS—Baltimore, Croel 1, Lyle 1. San Francisco, Doleman 3, Mitchell 1, Barker 1.

COLTS 34, JETS 29

Sunday, November 17

N.Y. Jets	3	12	6	8—29
Indianapolis	3	7	16	8—34

First Quarter
NYJ—FG, Lowery 23, 5:53.
Ind.—FG, Blanchard 25, 11:25.
Second Quarter
Ind.—Warren 1 run (Blanchard kick), :06.
NYJ—Graham 52 pass from Reich (kick failed), 10:13.
NYJ—Graham 17 pass from Reich (pass failed), 14:34.
Third Quarter
Ind.—Harrison 4 pass from Harbaugh (pass failed), 3:49.
Ind.—Daniel 35 interception return (Blanchard kick), 4:52.
NYJ—Murrell 1 run (pass failed), 9:29.
Ind.—FG, Blanchard 49, 12:57.
Fourth Quarter
NYJ—Graham 32 pass from Reich (Johnson pass from Reich), :48.
Ind.—Safety, Dent tackled Reich in end zone, 4:04.
Ind.—FG, Blanchard 37, 6:50.
Ind.—FG, Blanchard 50, 13:36.
Attendance—48,322.

TEAM STATISTICS

	N.Y. Jets	Indianapolis
First Downs	21	14
Rushes-Yards	27-87	31-152
Passing	332	151
Punt Returns	1-0	2-20
Kickoff Returns	6-149	6-133
Interception Returns	0-0	4-50
Comp-Att-Int	20-42-4	15-30-0
Sacked-Yards Lost	3-20	2-12
Punts	2-47	4-47
Fumbles-Lost	2-1	3-3
Penalties-Yards	9-72	7-61
Time of Possession	28:50	31:10

INDIVIDUAL STATISTICS
RUSHING—New York, Murrell 20-66, Cobb 4-16, Anderson 3-5. Indianapolis, Faulk 18-46, Groce 6-23, Warren 4-64, Harbaugh 3-19.

PASSING—New York, Reich 20-42-4-352. Indianapolis, Harbaugh 13-26-0-130, Justin 2-4-0-33.

RECEIVING—New York, Graham 9-189, Johnson 5-91, Chrebet 3-32, Anderson 2-28, Cobb 1-12. Indianapolis, Dawkins 4-70, Harrison 3-39, Faulk 3-22, Dilger 3-15, Warren 1-11, Pollard 1-6.

MISSED FIELD GOAL ATTEMPTS—None.

INTERCEPTIONS—Indianapolis, Daniel 2-35, Belser 1-15, Buchanan 1-0.

KICKOFF RETURNS—New York, Cobb 6-149. Indianapolis, Bailey 4-97, Buchanan 1-20, Hetherington 1-16.

PUNT RETURNS—New York, Chrebet 1-0. Indianapolis, Buchanan 2-20.

SACKS—New York, Douglas 2. Indianapolis, Martin 1, Bennett 1, Dent 1.

BILLS 31, BENGALS 17

Sunday, November 17

Cincinnati	0	7	0	10	17
Buffalo	7	17	7	0	31

First Quarter
Buf.—T. Thomas 1 run (Christie kick); 3:34.

Second Quarter
Buf.—Kelly 1 run (Christie kick); 3:05.
Cin.—Ambrose 31 interception return (Pelfrey kick); 8:26.
Buf.—White 12 fumble return (Christie kick); 11:09.
Buf.—FG, Christie 22, 14:51.

Third Quarter
Buf.—Tasker 22 pass from Kelly (Christie kick); 3:49.

Fourth Quarter
Cin.—Carter 1 run (Pelfrey kick); 7:15.
Cin.—FG, Pelfrey 30, 8:40.
Attendance—75,549.

TEAM STATISTICS

	Cincinnati	Buffalo
First Downs	13	23
Rushes-Yards	28-115	51-134
Passing	109	174
Punt Returns	5-1	5-69
Kickoff Returns	6-100	4-80
Interception Returns	2-65	3-19
Comp-Att-Int	11-31-3	14-25-2
Sacked-Yards Lost	7-47	3-21
Punts	8-45	8-45
Fumbles-Lost	3-1	0-0
Penalties-Yards	6-33	5-26
Time of Possession	26:21	33:39

INDIVIDUAL STATISTICS

RUSHING—Cincinnati, Hearst 11-55, Carter 6-12, Bieniemy 4-34, Blake 4-8, Wilhelm 1-4, Cothran 1-2, Pickens 1-0. Buffalo, Holmes 28-46, T. Thomas 19-78, Kelly 4-10.

PASSING—Cincinnati, Blake 8-22-1-95, Wilhelm 3-9-2-61. Buffalo, Kelly 13-22-1-199, Collins 1-3-1-(minus 4).

RECEIVING—Cincinnati, Pickens 5-62, Scott 3-62, Bieniemy 1-13, Hearst 1-12, McGee 1-7. Buffalo, Reed 6-115, Johnson 3-22, Tasker 2-42, Early 1-18, Brantley 1-12, Holmes 1-(minus 4).

MISSED FIELD GOAL ATTEMPTS—None.

INTERCEPTIONS—Cincinnati, Spencer 1-34, Ambrose 1-31. Buffalo, Schulz 2-19, Stevens 1-0.

KICKOFF RETURNS—Cincinnati, Hill 3-61, Dunn 2-32, Sadowski 1-7. Buffalo, Moulds 4-80.

PUNT RETURNS—Cincinnati, Sawyer 2-2, Dunn 2-(minus 3), Pickens 1-2. Buffalo, Burris 3-51, Tasker 2-18.

SACKS—Cincinnati, Tovar 1, Stallings 1, Smith 1. Buffalo, B. Smith 1½, Rogers 1½, Irvin 1, Jeffcoat 1, Northern 1, Hansen 1.

BUCCANEERS 25, CHARGERS 17

Sunday, November 17

Tampa Bay	3	10	0	12	25
San Diego	14	0	3	0	17

First Quarter
S.D.—Jones 63 pass from Humphries (Carney kick); 1:25.
S.D.—Russell 14 run (Carney kick); 10:48.
T.B.—FG, Husted 33, 14:16.

Second Quarter
T.B.—Alstott 4 run (Husted kick); 7:45.
T.B.—FG, Husted 29, 15:00.

Third Quarter
S.D.—FG, Carney 42, 7:43.

Fourth Quarter
T.B.—FG, Husted 27, 6:28.
T.B.—Rhett 1 run (pass failed), 8:58.
T.B.—FG, Husted 19, 13:49.
Attendance—57,526.

TEAM STATISTICS

	Tampa Bay	San Diego
First Downs	23	1?
Rushes-Yards	34-99	19-9?
Passing	324	18?
Punt Returns	3-38	1-?
Kickoff Returns	4-115	5-10?
Interception Returns	3-47	1-?
Comp-Att-Int	30-40-1	15-33-?
Sacked-Yards Lost	1-3	2-2?
Punts	2-54	6-3?
Fumbles-Lost	2-2	2-?
Penalties-Yards	6-45	4-2?
Time of Possession	39:02	20:5?

INDIVIDUAL STATISTICS

RUSHING—Tampa Bay, Rhett 20-24, Alstott 9-39, Ellison 2-11, Dilfer ?-0, Barnhardt 1-25. San Diego, Russell 14-76, Fletcher 4-13, Humphries 1-?

PASSING—Tampa Bay, Dilfer 30-40-1-327. San Diego, Humphries 15-3?-3-203.

RECEIVING—Tampa Bay, Hawkins 7-94, Alstott 6-53, R. Thomas 5-5? Moore 3-38, Williams 3-29, Harris 2-5, Harper 1-27, Ellison 1-1? San Diego, Fletcher 6-46, May 2-44, Roche 2-14, Ellison 2-9, Jones 1-6? Martin 1-18, A. Coleman 1-9.

MISSED FIELD GOAL ATTEMPTS—Tampa Bay, Husted 33.

INTERCEPTIONS—Tampa Bay, Lynch 1-25, D. Abraham 1-21, Dimry 1-? San Diego, Harrison 1-0.

KICKOFF RETURNS—Tampa Bay, Marshall 4-115. San Diego, A. Colema? 5-107.

PUNT RETURNS—Tampa Bay, Marshall 3-38. San Diego, Da. Gordon 1-3?

SACKS—Tampa Bay, Marts 1, Upshaw 1. San Diego, Mims 1.

DOLPHINS 23, OILERS 20

Sunday, November 17

Miami	0	10	3	10	2?
Houston	14	0	3	3	2?

First Quarter
Hou.—Russell 18 pass from Chandler (Del Greco kick); 5:29.
Hou.—Wycheck 15 pass from Chandler (Del Greco kick); 10:46.

Second Quarter
Mia.—Spikes 10 pass from Marino (Nedney kick); 9:31.
Mia.—FG, Nedney 34, 15:00.

Third Quarter
Mia.—FG, Nedney 44, 8:25.
Hou.—FG, Del Greco 30, 14:06.

Fourth Quarter
Mia.—Z. Thomas 26 interception return (Nedney kick); 4:18.
Hou.—FG, Del Greco 33, 11:40.
Mia.—FG, Nedney 29, 15:00.
Attendance—47,358.

TEAM STATISTICS

	Miami	Houston
First Downs	17	1?
Rushes-Yards	26-94	23-97
Passing	209	16?
Punt Returns	2-17	2-?
Kickoff Returns	5-107	4-85
Interception Returns	1-26	0-?
Comp-Att-Int	21-28-0	15-27-1?
Sacked-Yards Lost	3-28	2-?
Punts	3-45	5-38
Fumbles-Lost	3-2	1-?
Penalties-Yards	6-40	4-47
Time of Possession	31:31	28:29

INDIVIDUAL STATISTICS

RUSHING—Miami, Abdul-Jabbar 18-59, Spikes 5-12, Marino 2-(minu? 3), Izzo 1-26. Houston, George 15-60, Chandler 3-14, Harmon 3-11, Dav? 1-15, Thomas 1-(minus 3).

PASSING—Miami, Marino 21-28-0-237. Houston, Chandler 15-27-1-16?

RECEIVING—Miami, McDuffie 8-86, Barnett 5-53, Parmalee 3-2? Drayton 2-63, Spikes 1-10, R. Hill 1-5, Abdul-Jabbar 1-0. Houston, Wyche? 5-54, George 3-34, Davis 2-22, Sanders 2-21, Harmon 2-18, Russell 1-18?

MISSED FIELD GOAL ATTEMPTS—Miami, Nedney 39.

INTERCEPTIONS—Miami, Z. Thomas 1-26.

KICKOFF RETURNS—Miami, Dar Dar 4-72, Spikes 1-35. Houston, Gray 4-85.

PUNT RETURNS—Miami, McDuffie 2-17. Houston, Gray 2-4.

SACKS—Miami, Stubbs 1, Armstrong 1/2, Emtman 1/2. Houston, Wortham 1, Roberson 1, Bowden 1.

PANTHERS 20, RAMS 10

Sunday, November 17

| Carolina | 0 | 3 | 14 | 3—20 |
| St. Louis | 0 | 10 | 0 | 0—10 |

Second Quarter
St.L.—FG, Lohmiller 41, 2:41.
Car.—FG, Kasay 38, 7:54.
St.L.—Phillips 11 pass from Banks (Lohmiller kick), 13:07.

Third Quarter
Car.—Walls 9 pass from Beuerlein (Kasay kick), 4:50.
Car.—Johnson 7 run (Kasay kick), 13:29.

Fourth Quarter
Car.—FG, Kasay 34, 12:17.
Attendance—60,652.

TEAM STATISTICS

	Carolina	St.Louis
First Downs	22	15
Rushes-Yards	33-147	28-122
Passing	108	121
Punt Returns	4-30	1-12
Kickoff Returns	2-20	4-79
Interception Returns	1-6	1-1
Comp-Att-Int	13-28-1	14-33-1
Sacked-Yards Lost	4-22	6-39
Punts	5-41	5-44
Fumbles-Lost	2-1	1-0
Penalties-Yards	11-91	8-96
Time of Possession	31:09	28:51

INDIVIDUAL STATISTICS

RUSHING—Carolina, Johnson 27-123, Ismail 3-24, Beuerlein 3-0. St. Louis, Phillips 14-56, Green 9-32, Banks 3-17, Lyle 1-17, Landeta 1-0.

PASSING—Carolina, Beuerlein 13-28-1-130. St. Louis, Banks 14-33-1-160.

RECEIVING—Carolina, Green 3-28, Walls 3-27, Carrier 2-32, Griffith 2-16, Oliver 1-11, Ismail 1-9, Johnson 1-7. St. Louis, Bruce 4-59, Conwell 4-54, Green 2-14, Kennison 1-12, Phillips 1-11, Thomas 1-8, D. Harris 1-2.

MISSED FIELD GOAL ATTEMPTS—St. Louis, Lohmiller 45.

INTERCEPTIONS—Carolina, Cook 1-6. St. Louis, Lyght 1-1.

KICKOFF RETURNS—Carolina, Ismail 1-16, S. Greene 1-4. St. Louis, Thomas 3-62, Kennison 1-17.

PUNT RETURNS—Carolina, Poole 3-26, Oliver 1-4. St. Louis, Kennison 1-12.

SACKS—Carolina, K. Greene 2 1/2, Thomas 2, Miller 1, Mills 1/2. St. Louis, O'Neal 1 1/2, J. Jones 1, Osborne 1, Carter 1/2.

VIKINGS 16, RAIDERS 13

Sunday, November 17

| Minnesota | 10 | 0 | 0 | 3 | 3—16 |
| Oakland | 0 | 7 | 3 | 3 | 0—13 |

First Quarter
Min.—FG, Sisson 22, 12:15.
Min.—Reed 82 pass from B. Johnson (Sisson kick), 15:00.

Second Quarter
Oak.—McDaniel 56 interception return (Ford kick), 5:30.

Third Quarter
Oak.—FG, Ford 26, 10:15.

Fourth Quarter
Min.—FG, Sisson 25, :40.
Oak.—FG, Ford 41, 7:11.

Overtime
Min.—FG, Sisson 31, 11:53.
Attendance—41,183.

TEAM STATISTICS

	Minnesota	Oakland
First Downs	20	13
Rushes-Yards	44-182	32-125
Passing	263	112
Punt Returns	2-10	1-8
Kickoff Returns	4-75	3-82
Interception Returns	1-23	2-91
Comp-Att-Int	20-33-2	14-27-1
Sacked-Yards Lost	1-12	4-27
Punts	4-40	7-37
Fumbles-Lost	1-0	0-0
Penalties-Yards	4-53	5-40
Time of Possession	39:16	32:37

INDIVIDUAL STATISTICS

RUSHING—Minnesota, Hoard 20-108, Graham 13-42, B. Johnson 7-18, Lee 4-14. Oakland, Kaufman 20-63, Williams 6-36, Hostetler 5-23, Fenner 1-3.

PASSING—Minnesota, B. Johnson 20-33-2-275. Oakland, Hostetler 14-27-1-139.

RECEIVING—Minnesota, Carter 6-56, Reed 4-134, Ismail 2-44, Jordan 2-17, Lee 2-12, Evans 2-4, Graham 1-5, DeLong 1-3. Oakland, Jett 4-38, T. Brown 3-48, Dudley 3-33, Williams 2-18, Kaufman 2-2.

MISSED FIELD GOAL ATTEMPTS—Minnesota, Sisson 38.

INTERCEPTIONS—Minnesota, Thomas 1-23. Oakland, McDaniel 1-56, Lynch 1-35.

KICKOFF RETURNS—Minnesota, Ismail 3-58, Morrow 1-17. Oakland, Kaufman 2-58, Kidd 1-24.

PUNT RETURNS—Minnesota, Lee 2-10. Oakland, T. Brown 1-8.

SACKS—Minnesota, Randle 2, Brady 1, Fisk 1. Oakland, Swilling 1.

COWBOYS 21, PACKERS 6

Monday, November 18

| Green Bay | 0 | 0 | 0 | 6— 6 |
| Dallas | 6 | 9 | 0 | 6—21 |

First Quarter
Dal.—FG, Boniol 45, 3:38.
Dal.—FG, Boniol 37, 10:13.

Second Quarter
Dal.—FG, Boniol 42, :59.
Dal.—FG, Boniol 45, 8:30.
Dal.—FG, Boniol 35, 14:53.

Fourth Quarter
Dal.—FG, Boniol 39, 6:24.
G.B.—Mayes 3 pass from Favre (pass failed), 13:07.
Dal.—FG, Boniol 28, 14:40.
Attendance—65,032.

TEAM STATISTICS

	Green Bay	Dallas
First Downs	15	15
Rushes-Yards	21-90	28-112
Passing	164	205
Punt Returns	3-14	6-50
Kickoff Returns	8-155	0-0
Interception Returns	0-0	0-0
Comp-Att-Int	21-37-0	24-35-0
Sacked-Yards Lost	4-30	1-1
Punts	7-45	4-45
Fumbles-Lost	1-0	2-0
Penalties-Yards	6-28	5-25
Time of Possession	27:01	32:59

INDIVIDUAL STATISTICS

RUSHING—Green Bay, Levens 9-26, Bennett 8-48, Favre 3-14, Henderson 1-2. Dallas, E. Smith 20-76, S. Williams 4-29, Johnston 3-9, Aikman 1-(minus 2).

PASSING—Green Bay, Favre 21-37-0-194. Dallas, Aikman 24-35-0-206.

RECEIVING—Green Bay, Jackson 7-98, Mickens 5-38, Levens 3-21, Bennett 2-5, Thomason 1-16, Beebe 1-10, Henderson 1-3, Mayes 1-3. Dallas, E. Smith 6-16, Irvin 5-66, Johnston 4-18, K. Williams 3-47, Bjornson 3-40, Sanders 2-14, Martin 1-5.

MISSED FIELD GOAL ATTEMPTS—Green Bay, Jacke 32.

INTERCEPTIONS—None.

KICKOFF RETURNS—Green Bay, Howard 6-120, Thomason 1-20, Henderson 1-15.

PUNT RETURNS—Green Bay, Howard 3-14. Dallas, Martin 6-50.

SACKS—Green Bay, S. Dotson 1. Dallas, Hennings 1, Tolbert 1, Carver 1, Thomas 1.

WEEK 13

RESULTS

ARIZONA 36, Philadelphia 30
BUFFALO 35, N.Y. Jets 10
Carolina 31, HOUSTON 6
CHICAGO 31, Detroit 14
CINCINNATI 41, Atlanta 31
Denver 21, MINNESOTA 17
Green Bay 24, ST. LOUIS 9
Jacksonville 28, BALTIMORE 25 (OT)
NEW ENGLAND 27, Indianapolis 13
N.Y. GIANTS 20, Dallas 6
Oakland 27, SEATTLE 21
San Diego 28, KANSAS CITY 14
San Francisco 19, WASHINGTON 16 (OT)
TAMPA BAY 13, New Orleans 7
Pittsburgh 24, MIAMI 17

STANDINGS

AFC EAST	W	L	T	Pct.
Buffalo	9	3	0	.750
New England	8	4	0	.667
Indianapolis	6	6	0	.500
Miami	6	6	0	.500
N.Y. Jets	1	11	0	.083

AFC CENTRAL	W	L	T	Pct.
Pittsburgh	9	3	0	.750
Houston	6	6	0	.500
Cincinnati	5	7	0	.417
Jacksonville	5	7	0	.417
Baltimore	3	9	0	.250

AFC WEST	W	L	T	Pct.
Denver	11	1	0	.917
Kansas City	8	4	0	.667
San Diego	7	5	0	.583
Seattle	5	7	0	.417
Oakland	5	7	0	.417

NFC EAST	W	L	T	Pct.
Washington	8	4	0	.667
Dallas	7	5	0	.583
Philadelphia	7	5	0	.583
Arizona	6	6	0	.500
N.Y. Giants	5	7	0	.417

NFC CENTRAL	W	L	T	Pct.
Green Bay	9	3	0	.750
Minnesota	6	6	0	.500
Chicago	5	7	0	.417
Detroit	5	7	0	.417
Tampa Bay	4	8	0	.333

NFC WEST	W	L	T	Pct.
San Francisco	9	3	0	.750
Carolina	8	4	0	.667
St. Louis	3	9	0	.250
Atlanta	2	10	0	.167
New Orleans	2	10	0	.167

HIGHLIGHTS

Hero of the week: Buffalo's Steve Tasker, a special teams player nonpareil in his previous 11 years who is playing his first full season as a wide receiver, caught six passes for 160 yards and two touchdowns in helping the Bills to a 35-10 rout of the Jets. Tasker, whose sliding catch in the end zone just before halftime gave Buffalo a 21-3 lead, eventually had to leave the game when he suffered a sprained knee on a reverse.

Goat of the week: Following a safety that gave St. Louis a 9-0 lead late in the first half, Rams return man Herman O'Berry watched the ensuing free kick hit the turf and allowed Green Bay's Mike Prior to recover at St. Louis' 37. That eventually led to a 37-yard Chris Jacke field goal on the final play of the half that started the Packers on the way to a 24-9 victory.

Sub of the week: Carolina's Steve Beuerlein, playing in place of the injured Kerry Collins, threw touchdown passes of 30 and 12 yards to Willie Green and a 40-yarder to Wesley Walls as the Panthers routed Houston, 31-6. Beuerlein was 11-of-18 for 165 yards as the Panthers won their third game in a row and stayed in position for a playoff berth.

Comeback of the week: Jacksonville rallied from a 15-point deficit with 13 minutes left in regulation and defeated Baltimore, 28-25, on Mike Hollis' 34-yard field goal with 5:57 left in overtime. Mark Brunell threw fourth-quarter touchdown passes to Pete Mitchell and Willie Jackson—the last one coming with 1:24 left in regulation—then ran for the two-point conversion that tied the game. It was the Jaguars' first road victory since October 1995.

Blowout of the week: San Diego played a near-perfect game as it decisively carved up Kansas City, 28-14. The Chargers allowed no sacks, had no turnovers and committed only two penalties during a game in which they rolled up a 28-0 lead midway through the third quarter. Leonard Russell rushed for two touchdowns and Tony Martin had a pair of touchdowns among his five receptions for 148 yards.

Nail-biter of the week: Arizona survived a wild finish against Philadelphia—the teams combined for 37 points in the fourth quarter—and won, 36-30, when Boomer Esiason threw a 24-yard touchdown pass to Marcus McDowell with 14 seconds left. With the Cardinals out of timeouts, Esiason completed five passes in the game's final minute. Larry Centers' 2-yard scoring reception gave the Cardinals a 29-20 lead with 2:45 left. The Eagles recaptured the lead, 30-29, on Derrick Witherspoon's 95-yard kickoff return and Gary Anderson's 32-yard field goal before Esiason's last-minute heroics.

Hit of the week: New York Giants linebacker Corey Widmer slammed into Dallas wide receiver Michael Irving after a short reception, forcing a fumble that Tito Wooten scooped up and returned 54 yards for a touchdown just before halftime. That gave the Giants a 13-3 lead, and they went on to beat the listless Cowboys, 20-6.

Oddity of the week: Assistants from both the Jaguars and Ravens, making their way from the locker rooms to the press box after halftime, got stuck in an elevator and didn't get to their seats until midway through the third quarter.

Top rusher: One week after rushing just seven times in a 34-8 loss to Denver, New England's Curtis Martin had a season-high 35 carries and gained 141 yards in sparking the Patriots to a 27-13 win over Indianapolis. Martin carried on each of the Patriots' first six plays from scrimmage and on 18 of their first 22 snaps.

Top passer: Esiason was 24-of-43 for 367 yards in the Cardinals' wild win over Philadelphia. He was 13-of-16 for 180 yards in the fourth quarter.

Top receiver: Cincinnati's Carl Pickens caught 11 passes for 176 yards, including touchdown receptions of 61, 7 and 14 yards, as the Bengals outlasted Atlanta, 41-31.

Notes: Detroit's Barry Sanders, who rushed 21 times for 107 yards in a 31-14 loss to Chicago, became the first NFL back to gain 1,000 yards in eight consecutive seasons. He also moved past O.J. Simpson and into eighth place on the career rushing list. . . . Dave Krieg's three touchdown passes for Chicago gave him 255 for his career, tying him with Sonny Jurgensen for fifth place on the career list. . . . Indianapolis kicker Cary Blanchard set a team record by converting his 13th consecutive field-goal attempt. . . . Jacksonville's victory over Baltimore gave it a 4-0 record over the Ravens (nee: Browns) in two seasons. The Jaguars are just 5-9 against the rest of the NFL. . . . For the second game in a row, kicker Chris Boniol accounted for all of Dallas's points. He has hit on his last 21 field-goal attempts. . . . After gaining just 18 yards on 11 carries, Cowboys running back Emmitt Smith was benched for the first time in his NFL career. . . . With 19 carries for 103 yards, Adrian Murrell became the first Jets running back since Freeman McNeil in 1985 to rush for 1,000 yards in a season. . . . Brett Favre's two touchdown passes in Green Bay's victory over St. Louis gave him 30 in a season for the third time in his career. Miami's Dan Marino is the only other NFL quarterback to have accomplished that feat. . . . San Francisco quarterback Steve Young was 33-of-41, including 20 in a row, during the 49ers' 19-16 overtime triumph in Washington. . . . The Jets have been alone or tied for last place in the AFC East for 32 consecutive weeks.

Quote: Tampa Bay defensive end Chidi Ahanotu, after a 13-7 victory over New Orleans, the seventh consecutive game the Buccaneers had held their opponent to 7 points or less and the sixth game in a row in which the opponent gained fewer than 300 yards: "In past years, there would be wide eyes in the huddle—wide eyes and nervous. You'd wonder what was going to happen. Now, no eyes get wide. They close and get slanted because we're going for the kill. Nothing fazes this defense."

GAME SUMMARIES

BRONCOS 21, VIKINGS 17
Sunday, November 24

Denver	7	7	0	7—21
Minnesota	0	10	7	0—17

First Quarter
Den.—Davis 1 run (Elam kick), 8:28.
Second Quarter
Min.—FG, Sisson 27, :39.
Min.—Walsh 7 pass from B. Johnson (Sisson kick), 5:38.
Den.—Davis 1 pass from Elway (Elam kick), 14:07.
Third Quarter
Min.—Carter 11 pass from B. Johnson (Sisson kick), 14:37.
Fourth Quarter
Den.—McCaffrey 5 pass from Elway (Elam kick), 14:41.
Attendance—59,142.

TEAM STATISTICS

	Denver	Minnesota
First Downs	22	20
Rushes-Yards	23-79	28-50
Passing	309	246
Punt Returns	0-0	0-0
Kickoff Returns	4-91	4-71
Interception Returns	2-29	1-34
Comp-Att-Int	27-36-1	24-35-2
Sacked-Yards Lost	3-25	2-20
Punts	4-40	5-33
Fumbles-Lost	3-2	0-0

	Denver	Minnesota
Penalties-Yards	5-50	2-18
Time of Possession	27:49	32:11

INDIVIDUAL STATISTICS
RUSHING—Denver, Davis 19-68, Elway 2-8, Craver 2-3. Minnesota, Hoard 13-10, Graham 6-19, Evans 4-11, B. Johnson 3-5, Lee 2-5.
PASSING—Denver, Elway 27-36-1-334. Minnesota, B. Johnson 24-35-2-266.
RECEIVING—Denver, McCaffrey 6-83, Davis 6-37, Miller 5-81, Craver 5-32, Sharpe 4-90, Carswell 1-11. Minnesota, Carter 8-74, Lee 4-55, Reed 3-62, Graham 2-23, DeLong 2-3, Frisch 1-21, Ismail 1-9, Evans 1-8, Walsh 1-7, Hoard 1-4.
MISSED FIELD GOAL ATTEMPTS—Denver, Elam 42.
INTERCEPTIONS—Denver, Braxton 1-21, Mobley 1-8. Minnesota, Thomas 1-34.
KICKOFF RETURNS—Denver, Hebron 4-91. Minnesota, Ismail 3-54, Morrow 1-17.
PUNT RETURNS—None.
SACKS—Denver, A. Williams 2. Minnesota, F. Smith 2, Harrison 1.

BENGALS 41, FALCONS 31
Sunday, November 24

Atlanta	0	10	7	14—31
Cincinnati	17	3	7	14—41

First Quarter
Cin.—FG, Pelfrey 36, 2:28.
Cin.—Scott 20 pass from Blake (Pelfrey kick), 9:45.
Cin.—Pickens 61 pass from Blake (Pelfrey kick), 11:43.
Second Quarter
Atl.—FG, Andersen 33, 5:05.
Atl.—Emanuel 15 pass from Hebert (Andersen kick), 11:25.
Cin.—FG, Pelfrey 20, 14:40.
Third Quarter
Atl.—Anderson 4 run (Andersen kick), 1:38.
Cin.—Pickens 7 pass from Blake (Pelfrey kick), 11:22.
Fourth Quarter
Atl.—Metcalf 26 pass from Hebert (Andersen kick), :07.
Cin.—Milne 1 run (Pelfrey kick), 4:00.
Cin.—Pickens 14 pass from Blake (Pelfrey kick), 5:27.
Atl.—Metcalf 27 pass from Hebert (Andersen kick), 8:46.
Attendance—44,868.

TEAM STATISTICS

	Atlanta	Cincinnati
First Downs	21	24
Rushes-Yards	20-112	35-121
Passing	305	342
Punt Returns	2-9	1-20
Kickoff Returns	7-176	5-95
Interception Returns	0-0	3-29
Comp-Att-Int	24-42-3	21-36-0
Sacked-Yards Lost	1-3	1-7
Punts	3-41	5-40
Fumbles-Lost	1-1	1-0
Penalties-Yards	8-55	4-43
Time of Possession	31:03	28:57

INDIVIDUAL STATISTICS
RUSHING—Atlanta, Anderson 16-86, Heyward 4-26. Cincinnati, Hearst 23-67, Blake 5-13, Bieniemy 4-37, Milne 3-4.
PASSING—Atlanta, Hebert 23-40-2-304, Nagle 1-2-1-4. Cincinnati, Blake 21-36-0-349.
RECEIVING—Atlanta, Metcalf 9-122, Mathis 7-70, Emanuel 5-50, Birden 2-55, Brown 1-11. Cincinnati, Pickens 11-176, Scott 4-79, Bieniemy 2-52, Dunn 2-30, Battaglia 1-9, Sadowski 1-3.
MISSED FIELD GOAL ATTEMPTS—Atlanta, Andersen 54.
INTERCEPTIONS—Cincinnati, Tovar 2-29, Langford 1-0.
KICKOFF RETURNS—Atlanta, Preston 7-176. Cincinnati, Hundon 4-85, Dunn 1-10.
PUNT RETURNS—Atlanta, Metcalf 2-9. Cincinnati, Dunn 1-20.
SACKS—Atlanta, Owens 1. Cincinnati, Langford 1.

BUCCANEERS 13, SAINTS 7
Sunday, November 24

New Orleans	0	0	7	0— 7
Tampa Bay	3	3	7	0—13

First Quarter
T.B.—FG, Husted 43, 6:54.

Second Quarter

T.B.—FG, Husted 38, 12:29.

Third Quarter

T.B.—Alstott 17 pass from Dilfer (Husted kick), 4:44.
N.O.—T. Johnson 1 pass from Everett (Brien kick), 12:30.
Attendance—40,203.

TEAM STATISTICS

	New Orleans	Tampa Bay
First Downs	14	15
Rushes-Yards	20-58	31-130
Passing	184	251
Punt Returns	2-20	3-19
Kickoff Returns	4-79	2-31
Interception Returns	0-0	3-1
Comp-Att-Int	20-31-3	20-34-0
Sacked-Yards Lost	1-12	1-2
Punts	6-50	5-43
Fumbles-Lost	2-1	3-2
Penalties-Yards	4-24	3-30
Time of Possession	27:16	32:44

INDIVIDUAL STATISTICS

RUSHING—New Orleans, Zellars 12-41, Neal 3-8, Bates 2-5, Everett 2-2, Hayes 1-2. Tampa Bay, Rhett 21-87, Alstott 5-8, Dilfer 2-21, Ellison 2-13, R. Brooks 1-1.

PASSING—New Orleans, Everett 20-31-3-196. Tampa Bay, Dilfer 20-34-0-253.

RECEIVING—New Orleans, Small 6-85, Lusk 4-30, Zellars 4-11, Neal 3-29, Hayes 1-24, Haynes 1-16, T. Johnson 1-1. Tampa Bay, Alstott 7-91, Harris 4-63, R. Thomas 3-46, Hawkins 3-24, Williams 2-13, Moore 1-16.

MISSED FIELD GOAL ATTEMPTS—None.

INTERCEPTIONS—Tampa Bay, D. Abraham 1-1, M. Johnson 1-0, Lynch 1-0.

KICKOFF RETURNS—New Orleans, Hughes 4-79. Tampa Bay, Marshall 1-17, Alstott 1-14.

PUNT RETURNS—New Orleans, Hughes 2-20. Tampa Bay, Marshall 3-19.

SACKS—New Orleans, Mickell 1. Tampa Bay, Ahanotu 1.

PANTHERS 31, OILERS 6

Sunday, November 24

Carolina	0	10	7	14—31
Houston	0	3	0	3— 6

Second Quarter

Car.—Green 30 pass from Beuerlein (Kasay kick), 6:04.
Hou.—FG, Del Greco 24, 13:50.
Car.—FG, Kasay 49, 14:54.

Third Quarter

Car.—Green 12 pass from Beuerlein (Kasay kick), 9:14.

Fourth Quarter

Hou.—FG, Del Greco 45, :45.
Car.—Mills 41 fumble return (Kasay kick), 7:42.
Car.—Walls 40 pass from Beuerlein (Kasay kick), 9:53.
Attendance—20,107.

TEAM STATISTICS

	Carolina	Houston
First Downs	12	17
Rushes-Yards	30-94	25-85
Passing	160	186
Punt Returns	3-38	1-3
Kickoff Returns	3-70	6-115
Interception Returns	2-11	0-0
Comp-Att-Int	11-18-0	23-39-2
Sacked-Yards Lost	1-5	4-21
Punts	6-45	6-52
Fumbles-Lost	2-1	3-2
Penalties-Yards	7-40	8-72
Time of Possession	24:36	35:24

INDIVIDUAL STATISTICS

RUSHING—Carolina, Johnson 27-86, Beuerlein 2-12, Ismail 1-(minus 4). Houston, George 19-62, Thomas 3-15, McNair 2-5, Chandler 1-3.

PASSING—Carolina, Beuerlein 11-18-0-165. Houston, Chandler 13-22-1-116, McNair 10-17-1-91.

RECEIVING—Carolina, Walls 3-60, Carrier 3-47, Green 2-42, Griffith 2-11, Johnson 1-5. Houston, Sanders 4-44, Wycheck 4-44, Floyd 3-29, Thomas 3-17, R. Lewis 2-27, Davis 2-13, Harmon 2-13, Wilson 1-14, Russell 1-6, George 1-0.

MISSED FIELD GOAL ATTEMPTS—None.

INTERCEPTIONS—Carolina, Davis 1-11, Cota 1-0.

KICKOFF RETURNS—Carolina, Ismail 3-70. Houston, Gray 5-110, Wycheck 1-5.

PUNT RETURNS—Carolina, Oliver 3-38. Houston, Gray 1-3.

SACKS—Carolina, K. Greene 1½, Bailey 1, King 1, Miller ½. Houston, Ford 1.

CARDINALS 36, EAGLES 30

Sunday, November 24

Philadelphia	7	3	3	17—30
Arizona	3	10	3	20—36

First Quarter

Phi.—Watters 1 run (Anderson kick), 3:54.
Ariz.—FG, Butler 21, 8:27.

Second Quarter

Phi.—FG, Anderson 44, 1:26.
Ariz.—McElroy 4 run (Butler kick), 3:52.
Ariz.—FG, Butler 36, 14:30.

Third Quarter

Phi.—FG, Anderson 25, 8:05.
Ariz.—FG, Butler 27, 13:26.

Fourth Quarter

Ariz.—Carter 6 pass from Esiason (kick failed), 4:02.
Phi.—Watters 4 run (Anderson kick), 6:37.
Ariz.—Centers 2 pass from Esiason (Butler kick), 12:15.
Phi.—Witherspoon 95 kickoff return (Anderson kick), 12:34.
Phi.—FG, Anderson 32, 14:08.
Ariz.—Dowdell 24 pass from Esiason (Butler kick), 14:46.
Attendance—36,175.

TEAM STATISTICS

	Philadelphia	Arizona
First Downs	23	27
Rushes-Yards	26-67	29-107
Passing	292	340
Punt Returns	2-12	2-9
Kickoff Returns	8-253	7-181
Interception Returns	0-0	1-(-2)
Comp-Att-Int	21-38-1	24-43-0
Sacked-Yards Lost	4-30	3-27
Punts	4-36	3-40
Fumbles-Lost	1-1	3-2
Penalties-Yards	11-105	3-25
Time of Possession	29:03	30:57

INDIVIDUAL STATISTICS

RUSHING—Philadelphia, Watters 25-64, Turner 1-3. Arizona, Centers 13-45, McElroy 7-16, L. Johnson 6-14, Esiason 3-32.

PASSING—Philadelphia, Detmer 21-38-1-322. Arizona, Esiason 24-43-0-367.

RECEIVING—Philadelphia, Fryar 7-131, Turner 4-40, Solomon 3-54, Watters 3-36, Seay 2-28, Dunn 1-32, West 1-1. Arizona, R. Moore 9-156, Sanders 6-90, Carter 3-46, Centers 3-29, Dowdell 2-42, Edwards 1-4.

MISSED FIELD GOAL ATTEMPTS—Arizona, Butler 31.

INTERCEPTIONS—Arizona, Williams 1-(minus 2).

KICKOFF RETURNS—Philadelphia, Witherspoon 8-253. Arizona, McElroy 4-124, Dowdell 2-60, Edwards 1-(minus 3).

PUNT RETURNS—Philadelphia, Seay 2-12. Arizona, Dowdell 2-9.

SACKS—Philadelphia, W. Thomas 2, Mamula ½, W. Fuller ½. Arizona, Williams 1, Joyner 1, Ottis 1, Bankston ½, Rice ½.

RAIDERS 27, SEAHAWKS 21

Sunday, November 24

Oakland	0	14	3	10—27
Seattle	3	7	3	8—21

First Quarter

Sea.—FG, Peterson 21, 7:49.

Second Quarter

Oak.—Jett 17 pass from Hostetler (Ford kick), 3:09.
Sea.—R. Williams 2 pass from Mirer (Peterson kick), 5:47.
Oak.—Cunningham 3 pass from Hostetler (Ford kick), 10:59.

Third Quarter

Oak.—FG, Ford 47, 4:37.
Sea.—FG, Peterson 32, 10:05.

Fourth Quarter

Oak.—Fenner 1 run (Ford kick), 1:27.
Sea.—Warren 2 run (Warren run), 3:50.
Oak.—FG, Ford 26, 13:04.
Attendance—47,506.

TEAM STATISTICS

	Oakland	Seattle
First Downs	19	17
Rushes-Yards	43-200	28-130
Passing	149	166
Punt Returns	0-0	1-5
Kickoff Returns	5-120	6-104
Interception Returns	0-0	0-0
Comp-Att-Int	13-23-0	16-25-0
Sacked-Yards Lost	4-29	3-15
Punts	3-38	3-38
Fumbles-Lost	3-1	1-1
Penalties-Yards	9-102	4-30
Time of Possession	34:12	25:48

INDIVIDUAL STATISTICS

RUSHING—Oakland, Kaufman 15-104, Williams 11-33, Fenner 9-24, Hostetler 7-29, Gossett 1-10. Seattle, Warren 18-88, Mirer 6-33, Smith 2-2, Broussard 1-7, Galloway 1-0.

PASSING—Oakland, Hostetler 13-23-0-178. Seattle, Mirer 16-25-0-181.

RECEIVING—Oakland, T. Brown 6-77, Jett 2-33, A. Glover 2-24, Hobbs 1-9, Dudley 1-12, Cunningham 1-3. Seattle, Blades 4-32, Galloway 3-99, Warren 3-10, Pritchard 2-19, Broussard 1-8, Crumpler 1-6, Proehl 1-5, R. Williams 1-2.

MISSED FIELD GOAL ATTEMPTS—None.

INTERCEPTIONS—None.

KICKOFF RETURNS—Oakland, Kaufman 4-102, Kidd 1-18. Seattle, Broussard 4-68, R. Harris 2-36.

PUNT RETURNS—Seattle, R. Harris 1-5.

SACKS—Oakland, McGlockton 1, Bruce 1, Swilling 1. Seattle, Adams 2, McCrary 1, Wells 1.

BILLS 35, JETS 10
Sunday, November 24

N.Y. Jets	3	0	0	7—10
Buffalo	7	14	7	7—35

First Quarter
NYJ—FG, Lowery 25, 6:54.
Buf.—Reed 3 pass from Kelly (Christie kick), 10:43.

Second Quarter
Buf.—Reed 22 pass from Kelly (Christie kick), 1:41.
Buf.—Tasker 19 pass from Kelly (Christie kick), 14:45.

Third Quarter
Buf.—Tasker 18 pass from Collins (Christie kick), 7:14.

Fourth Quarter
NYJ—Graham 8 pass from Reich (Lowery kick), 3:55.
Buf.—Moulds 97 kickoff return (Christie kick), 4:12.
Attendance—60,854.

TEAM STATISTICS

	N.Y. Jets	Buffalo
First Downs	22	17
Rushes-Yards	24-112	35-84
Passing	229	264
Punt Returns	1-(-16)	2-9
Kickoff Returns	6-104	3-158
Interception Returns	1-18	3-5
Comp-Att-Int	25-50-3	16-24-1
Sacked-Yards Lost	5-38	1-3
Punts	6-42	7-41
Fumbles-Lost	2-2	2-1
Penalties-Yards	8-45	7-49
Time of Possession	33:49	26:11

INDIVIDUAL STATISTICS

RUSHING—New York, Murrell 19-103, Anderson 4-10, Reich 1-(minus 1). Buffalo, Holmes 22-58, Bratton 4-8, Collins 4-(minus 4), T. Thomas 3-8, Tasker 1-8, Moulds 1-6.

PASSING—New York, Reich 25-50-3-267. Buffalo, Kelly 10-14-1-176, Collins 6-10-0-91.

RECEIVING—New York, Chrebet 10-75, Graham 7-124, Anderson 4-14, Brady 2-21, F. Baxter 1-23, Johnson 1-10. Buffalo, Tasker 6-160, Reed 4-61, Early 2-24, Holmes 2-14, Moulds 1-8, Johnson 1-0.

MISSED FIELD GOAL ATTEMPTS—None.

INTERCEPTIONS—New York, Green 1-18. Buffalo, Schulz 2-5, Jackson 1-0.

KICKOFF RETURNS—New York, Cobb 4-79, Brady 1-16, Van Dyke 1-9. Buffalo, Copeland 2-61, Moulds 1-97.

PUNT RETURNS—New York, Chrebet 1-(minus 16). Buffalo, Burris 2-9.

SACKS—New York, Douglas 1. Buffalo, Hansen 1½, B. Smith 1, Rogers 1, Northern 1, White ½.

49ERS 19, REDSKINS 16
Sunday, November 24

San Francisco	3	3	0	10	3—19
Washington	0	6	3	7	0—16

First Quarter
S.F.—FG, Wilkins 20, 7:28.

Second Quarter
Was.—FG, Blanton 19, 9:44.
Was.—FG, Blanton 22, 14:21.
S.F.—FG, Wilkins 48, 14:56.

Third Quarter
Was.—FG, Blanton 31, 13:39.

Fourth Quarter
S.F.—FG, Wilkins 44, 3:19.
Was.—Asher 20 pass from Frerotte (Blanton kick), 7:32.
S.F.—Floyd 1 run (Wilkins kick), 13:03.

Overtime
S.F.—FG, Wilkins 38, 3:24.
Attendance—54,235.

TEAM STATISTICS

	San Francisco	Washington
First Downs	27	15
Rushes-Yards	28-117	25-64
Passing	275	282
Punt Returns	1-11	0-0
Kickoff Returns	5-118	5-73
Interception Returns	0-0	0-0
Comp-Att-Int	33-41-0	18-26-0
Sacked-Yards Lost	4-20	2-12
Punts	3-39	5-42
Fumbles-Lost	6-1	2-0
Penalties-Yards	3-35	2-20
Time of Possession	36:58	26:26

INDIVIDUAL STATISTICS

RUSHING—San Francisco, Kirby 13-69, Floyd 7-18, S. Young 4-25, Rice 3-12, D. Carter 1-(minus 7). Washington, Allen 21-67, Mitchell 2-7, Logan 1-4, Shepherd 1-(minus 14).

PASSING—San Francisco, S. Young 33-41-0-295. Washington, Frerotte 18-26-0-294.

RECEIVING—San Francisco, Kirby 11-74, Rice 8-87, Jones 5-70, Floyd 5-15, Owens 3-39, Popson 1-10. Washington, Westbrook 7-126, Shepherd 3-61, Ellard 3-52, Asher 3-43, Allen 2-12.

MISSED FIELD GOAL ATTEMPTS—San Francisco, Wilkins 46.

INTERCEPTIONS—None.

KICKOFF RETURNS—San Francisco, D. Carter 5-118. Washington, Mitchell 3-40, W. Bell 2-33.

PUNT RETURNS—San Francisco, D. Carter 1-11.

SACKS—San Francisco, Drakeford 1, Barker 1. Washington, Owens 2, B. Walker 1, Nottage 1.

CHARGERS 28, CHIEFS 14
Sunday, November 24

San Diego	7	14	7	0—28
Kansas City	0	0	0	14—14

First Quarter
S.D.—Martin 20 pass from Humphries (Carney kick), 8:36.

Second Quarter
S.D.—Russell 4 run (Carney kick), 3:53.
S.D.—Martin 10 pass from Humphries (Carney kick), 11:23.

Third Quarter
S.D.—Russell 1 run (Carney kick), 7:26.

Fourth Quarter
K.C.—Penn 17 pass from Gannon (Stoyanovich kick), 6:06.
K.C.—McNair 10 pass from Gannon (Stoyanovich kick), 12:06.
Attendance—69,472.

TEAM STATISTICS

	San Diego	Kansas City
First Downs	20	26
Rushes-Yards	39-128	16-102
Passing	252	332
Punt Returns	2-17	1-(-2)
Kickoff Returns	3-25	5-106
Interception Returns	2-6	0-0
Comp-Att-Int	13-26-0	32-54-2
Sacked-Yards Lost	0-0	0-0

	San Diego	Kansas City
Punts	4-43	4-40
Fumbles-Lost	1-0	0-0
Penalties-Yards	2-25	5-54
Time of Possession	31:03	28:57

INDIVIDUAL STATISTICS

RUSHING—San Diego, Russell 32-88, Fletcher 6-39, Humphries 1-1. Kansas City, Hill 6-45, Allen 6-30, Anders 2-1, Gannon 1-19, McNair 1-7.

PASSING—San Diego, Humphries 13-26-0-252. Kansas City, Gannon 22-31-0-226, Bono 10-23-2-106.

RECEIVING—San Diego, Martin 5-148, May 4-40, Fletcher 2-39, Roche 1-18, Mitchell 1-7. Kansas City, Allen 7-60, Penn 6-90, McNair 6-64, Anders 6-50, Vanover 3-35, LaChapelle 1-19, Johnson 1-12, Walker 1-5, Bennett 1-(minus 3).

MISSED FIELD GOAL ATTEMPTS—San Diego, Carney 28.

INTERCEPTIONS—San Diego, Harrison 2-6.

KICKOFF RETURNS—San Diego, A. Coleman 1-15, Harrison 1-10, Roche 1-0. Kansas City, Vanover 4-84, Hughes 1-22.

PUNT RETURNS—San Diego, Da. Gordon 2-17. Kansas City, Vanover 1-(minus 2).

SACKS—None.

GIANTS 20, COWBOYS 6
Sunday, November 24

Dallas	3	0	0	3—	6
N.Y. Giants	0	13	0	7—	20

First Quarter
Dal.—FG, Boniol 31, 10:30.

Second Quarter
NYG—FG, Daluiso 45, 4:32.
NYG—FG, Daluiso 46, 10:03.
NYG—Wooten 54 fumble return (Daluiso kick), 13:07.

Fourth Quarter
Dal.—FG, Boniol 37, 3:17.
NYG—Kozlowski 4 pass from Brown (Daluiso kick), 8:59.
Attendance—77,081.

TEAM STATISTICS

	Dallas	N.Y. Giants
First Downs	15	14
Rushes-Yards	16-33	38-111
Passing	272	104
Punt Returns	2-23	1-10
Kickoff Returns	3-62	3-69
Interception Returns	1-24	2-53
Comp-Att-Int	28-39-2	12-18-1
Sacked-Yards Lost	1-8	1-6
Punts	4-39	6-38
Fumbles-Lost	3-3	1-0
Penalties-Yards	6-35	7-60
Time of Possession	27:08	32:52

INDIVIDUAL STATISTICS

RUSHING—Dallas, E. Smith 11-18, Johnston 2-5, S. Williams 1-8, Sanders 1-3, Aikman 1-(minus 1). New York, Wheatley 21-69, Hampton 14-38, Brown 3-4.

PASSING—Dallas, Aikman 28-39-2-280. New York, Brown 12-18-1-110.

RECEIVING—Dallas, Johnston 7-57, Irvin 6-77, K. Williams 5-34, E. Smith 4-24, S. Williams 3-27, Sanders 2-55, Martin 1-6. New York, Calloway 4-48, Cross 3-25, Dawsey 1-10, Alexander 1-9, Way 1-9, Downs 1-5, Kozlowski 1-4.

MISSED FIELD GOAL ATTEMPTS—None.

INTERCEPTIONS—Dallas, K. Smith 1-24. New York, Ellsworth 1-29, Sehorn 1-24.

KICKOFF RETURNS—Dallas, Walker 2-41, C. Williams 1-21. New York, C. Hamilton 3-65.

PUNT RETURNS—Dallas, Martin 2-23. New York, Marshall 1-10.

SACKS—Dallas, Tolbert 1. New York, Harris 1.

BEARS 31, LIONS 14
Sunday, November 24

Detroit	14	0	0	0—	14
Chicago	14	10	7	0—	31

First Quarter
Chi.—Conway 19 pass from Krieg (Jaeger kick), 1:40.
Det.—Mitchell 1 run (Hanson kick), 10:11.
Chi.—Faulkerson 1 pass from Krieg (Jaeger kick), 11:25.
Det.—Sanders 22 run (Hanson kick), 14:14.

Second Quarter
Chi.—Engram 5 pass from Krieg (Jaeger kick), 6:16.
Chi.—FG, Jaeger 42, 14:29.

Third Quarter
Chi.—R. Harris 3 run (Jaeger kick), 8:46.
Attendance—55,864.

	Detroit	Chicago
First Downs	27	22
Rushes-Yards	25-114	37-139
Passing	208	219
Punt Returns	1-(-1)	1-11
Kickoff Returns	5-103	3-153
Interception Returns	0-0	3-11
Comp-Att-Int	18-35-3	18-28-0
Sacked-Yards Lost	3-22	0-0
Punts	2-42	3-20
Fumbles-Lost	2-0	2-2
Penalties-Yards	5-30	9-94
Time of Possession	25:41	34:19

INDIVIDUAL STATISTICS

RUSHING—Detroit, Sanders 21-107, Mitchell 2-2, Rivers 1-9, Morton 1-(minus 4). Chicago, R. Harris 27-122, Salaam 6-9, Green 1-3, Sauerbrun 3, Krieg 1-2, Timpson 1-0.

PASSING—Detroit, Mitchell 18-35-3-230. Chicago, Krieg 18-28-0-219.

RECEIVING—Detroit, Perriman 8-85, H. Moore 5-61, Metzelaars 3-4, Morton 1-25, Sanders 1-5, Roberts 0-5. Chicago, Timpson 5-76, Conway 58, R. Harris 3-38, T. Carter 2-16, Neely 1-13, Ja. Jackson 1-12, Engram 5, Faulkerson 1-1.

MISSED FIELD GOAL ATTEMPTS—None.

INTERCEPTIONS—Chicago, Woolford 2-5, M. Carter 1-6.

KICKOFF RETURNS—Detroit, Milburn 5-103. Chicago, Engram 3-78.

PUNT RETURNS—Detroit, Milburn 1-(minus 1). Chicago, Engram 1-11.

SACKS—Chicago, A. Fontenot 1½, Minter 1, Mangum ½.

JAGUARS 28, RAVENS 25
Sunday, November 24

Jacksonville	0	10	0	15	3—28
Baltimore	7	9	9	0	0—25

First Quarter
Bal.—Caldwell 45 interception return (Stover kick), 2:30.

Second Quarter
Bal.—FG, Stover 21, :42.
Jac.—Stewart 1 run (Hollis kick), 2:00.
Bal.—FG, Stover 29, 9:44.
Jac.—FG, Hollis 29, 13:57.
Bal.—FG, Stover 41, 14:54.

Third Quarter
Bal.—Morris 1 run (run failed), 4:21.
Bal.—FG, Stover 33, 13:25.

Fourth Quarter
Jac.—Mitchell 11 pass from Brunell (Hollis kick), 2:56.
Jac.—W. Jackson 7 pass from Brunell (Brunell run), 13:36.

Overtime
Jac.—FG, Hollis 34, 9:06.
Attendance—57,384.

TEAM STATISTICS

	Jacksonville	Baltimore
First Downs	23	21
Rushes-Yards	25-86	30-100
Passing	281	35
Punt Returns	0-0	2-24
Kickoff Returns	7-143	5-111
Interception Returns	0-0	2-45
Comp-Att-Int	28-46-2	31-50-0
Sacked-Yards Lost	4-25	1-1
Punts	4-51	3-4
Fumbles-Lost	0-0	2-
Penalties-Yards	13-80	8-100
Time of Possession	35:25	33:4

INDIVIDUAL STATISTICS

RUSHING—Jacksonville, Means 10-39, Brunell 8-29, Stewart 7-1, Baltimore, Morris 22-60, Testaverde 4-34, Byner 3-4, F. Turner 1-6.

PASSING—Jacksonville, Brunell 28-46-2-306. Baltimore, Testaverde 31-50-0-366.

RECEIVING—Jacksonville, McCardell 9-107, Smith 8-131, W. Jackson 31, Mitchell 2-17, Means 2-9, Maston 1-8, Brown 1-3. Baltimore, Jackson 150, Kinchen 9-71, Alexander 4-68, F. Turner 4-40, Byner 3-20, Morris 2-1

MISSED FIELD GOAL ATTEMPTS—Jacksonville, Hollis 41. Baltimore, over 49.

INTERCEPTIONS—Baltimore, Caldwell 1-45, E. Turner 1-0.

KICKOFF RETURNS—Jacksonville, B. Brooks 4-103, Griffith 2-24, Jordan 16. Baltimore, J. Lewis 4-93, Ethridge 1-26.

PUNT RETURNS—Baltimore, J. Lewis 2-20.

SACKS—Jacksonville, Simmons 1. Baltimore, Croel 1, R. Lewis 1, J. nes 1, Pleasant 1.

PATRIOTS 27, COLTS 13
Sunday, November 24

dianapolis	0	3	3	7—13
w England	10	7	3	7—27

First Quarter
E.—FG, Vinatieri 26, 6:15.
E.—Jefferson 13 pass from Bledsoe (Vinatieri kick), 14:10.

Second Quarter
E.—Glenn 5 pass from Bledsoe (Vinatieri kick), 10:23.
J.—FG, Blanchard 42, 14:58.

Third Quarter
J.—FG, Blanchard 50, 4:34.
E.—FG, Vinatieri 22, 10:21.

Fourth Quarter
E.—Martin 12 run (Vinatieri kick), 3:18.
J.—Harrison 5 pass from Justin (Blanchard kick), 12:03.
Attendance—58,226.

TEAM STATISTICS
	Indianapolis	New England
st Downs	15	25
shes-Yards	13-44	44-195
ssing	247	234
nt Returns	3-32	4-59
koff Returns	6-134	4-83
erception Returns	0-0	1-0
mp-Att-Int	22-40-1	21-30-0
cked-Yards Lost	0-0	2-8
nts	5-45	4-39
mbles-Lost	1-1	2-0
nalties-Yards	5-40	3-30
ne of Possession	21:53	38:07

INDIVIDUAL STATISTICS
RUSHING—Indianapolis, Faulk 10-25, Harbaugh 3-19. New England, artin 35-141, Grier 3-35, Meggett 3-13, Byars 2-2, Bledsoe 1-4.

PASSING—Indianapolis, Justin 11-22-0-128, Harbaugh 11-18-1-119. w England, Bledsoe 21-30-0-242.

RECEIVING—Indianapolis, Harrison 6-93, Stablein 5-38, Dawkins 4-52, ulk 3-18, Dilger 2-26, Warren 2-20. New England, Glenn 7-82, Gash 4-56, artin 3-28, T. Brown 3-26, Jefferson 2-20, Meggett 1-18, Coates 1-12.

MISSED FIELD GOAL ATTEMPTS—None.

INTERCEPTIONS—New England, Sabb 1-0.

KICKOFF RETURNS—Indianapolis, Bailey 6-134. New England, T. Brown 56, Meggett 1-27, C. Brown 1-0.

PUNT RETURNS—Indianapolis, Stablein 3-32. New England, Meggett 4-

SACKS—Indianapolis, Bennett 1½, Dent ½.

PACKERS 24, RAMS 9
Sunday, November 24

een Bay	0	3	14	7—24
Louis	0	9	0	0— 9

Second Quarter
L.—Bruce 6 pass from Banks (Lohmiller kick), 12:31.
L.—Safety, Favre called for intentional grounding in end zone, 12:52.
B.—FG, Jacke 37, 15:00.

Third Quarter
B.—Evans 32 interception return (Jacke kick), :55.
B.—Jackson 6 pass from Favre (Jacke kick), 11:01.

Fourth Quarter
B.—Levens 5 pass from Favre (Jacke kick), :52.
Attendance—61,499.

	Green Bay	St.Louis
st Downs	15	15
shes-Yards	27-58	23-65

	Green Bay	St.Louis
Passing	185	165
Punt Returns	3-53	5-16
Kickoff Returns	2-34	2-28
Interception Returns	1-32	2-0
Comp-Att-Int	25-38-2	17-37-1
Sacked-Yards Lost	1-7	3-5
Punts	6-44	7-49
Fumbles-Lost	0-0	3-2
Penalties-Yards	6-47	7-36
Time of Possession	32:40	27:20

INDIVIDUAL STATISTICS
RUSHING—Green Bay, Bennett 15-31, Levens 4-23, Henderson 4-4, Favre 4-0. St. Louis, Green 12-43, Phillips 9-23, Banks 1-0, Thomas 1- (minus 1).

PASSING—Green Bay, Favre 25-38-2-192. St. Louis, Banks 17-37-1-170.

RECEIVING—Green Bay, Rison 5-44, Beebe 4-46, Bennett 4-28, Levens 4-18, Mickens 3-36, Jackson 3-17, Henderson 2-3. St. Louis, Bruce 6-53, Conwell 5-53, Green 3-32, Laing 2-19, A. Wright 1-13.

MISSED FIELD GOAL ATTEMPTS—None.

INTERCEPTIONS—Green Bay, Evans 1-32. St. Louis, R. Jones 1-0, Lyle 1-0.

KICKOFF RETURNS—Green Bay, Howard 1-17, Jervey 1-17. St. Louis, Crawford 2-28.

PUNT RETURNS—Green Bay, Howard 3-53. St. Louis, O'Berry 5-16.

SACKS—Green Bay, Butler 2, Wilkins 1. St. Louis, Carter 1.

STEELERS 24, DOLPHINS 17
Monday, November 25

Pittsburgh	3	7	7	7—24
Miami	7	7	3	0—17

First Quarter
Mia.—McDuffie 2 pass from Marino (Nedney kick), 9:45.
Pit.—FG, N. Johnson 47, 13:45.

Second Quarter
Mia.—Jackson 61 interception return (Nedney kick), 7:12.
Pit.—Lester 5 run (N. Johnson kick), 11:30.

Third Quarter
Pit.—Stewart 1 run (N. Johnson kick), 7:00.
Mia.—FG, Nedney 41, 12:26.

Fourth Quarter
Pit.—Mills 20 pass from Tomczak (N. Johnson kick), 12:50.
Attendance—73,489.

TEAM STATISTICS
	Pittsburgh	Miami
First Downs	23	15
Rushes-Yards	36-142	20-75
Passing	242	237
Punt Returns	2-7	1-16
Kickoff Returns	3-39	5-95
Interception Returns	0-0	1-61
Comp-Att-Int	16-29-1	22-37-0
Sacked-Yards Lost	1-10	2-17
Punts	3-50	4-47
Fumbles-Lost	2-2	1-1
Penalties-Yards	1-26	9-54
Time of Possession	32:07	27:53

INDIVIDUAL STATISTICS
RUSHING—Pittsburgh, Bettis 27-119, Stewart 4-5, Pegram 2-5, Mills 1-9, Lester 1-5, Tomczak 1-(minus 1). Miami, Abdul-Jabbar 16-57, Pritchett 2-8, Parmalee 1-10, Spikes 1-0.

PASSING—Pittsburgh, Tomczak 16-29-1-252. Miami, Marino 22-37-0-254.

RECEIVING—Pittsburgh, C. Johnson 5-60, Hastings 4-57, Bettis 2-28, Bruener 1-36, Thigpen 1-34, Mills 1-20, Witman 1-11, Lester 1-6. Miami, Barnett 8-98, McDuffie 5-33, Drayton 3-47, R. Hill 2-51, Parmalee 2-17, Miller 1-8, Pritchett 1-0.

MISSED FIELD GOAL ATTEMPTS—Pittsburgh, N. Johnson 47. Miami, Nedney 56, 48.

INTERCEPTIONS—Miami, Jackson 1-61.

KICKOFF RETURNS—Pittsburgh, Pegram 2-24, Mills 1-15. Miami, Spikes 3-66, Dar Dar 1-17, R. Wilson 1-12.

PUNT RETURNS—Pittsburgh, Hastings 2-7. Miami, McDuffie 1-16.

SACKS—Pittsburgh, Brown 1, Raybon 1. Miami, Emtman 1.

WEEK 14

RESULTS

DALLAS 21, Washington 10
Kansas City 28, DETROIT 24
BALTIMORE 31, Pittsburgh 17
CAROLINA 24, Tampa Bay 0
DENVER 34, Seattle 7
GREEN BAY 28, Chicago 17
Houston 35, N.Y. JETS 10
INDIANAPOLIS 13, Buffalo 10 (OT)
JACKSONVILLE 30, Cincinnati 27
MINNESOTA 41, Arizona 17
New England 45, SAN DIEGO 7
OAKLAND 17, Miami 7
PHILADELPHIA 24, N.Y. Giants 0
St. Louis 26, NEW ORLEANS 10
San Francisco 34, ATLANTA 10

STANDINGS

AFC EAST

	W	L	T	Pct.
Buffalo	9	4	0	.692
New England	9	4	0	.692
Indianapolis	7	6	0	.538
Miami	6	7	0	.462
N.Y. Jets	1	12	0	.077

AFC CENTRAL

	W	L	T	Pct.
Pittsburgh	9	4	0	.692
Houston	7	6	0	.538
Jacksonville	6	7	0	.462
Cincinnati	5	8	0	.385
Baltimore	4	9	0	.308

AFC WEST

	W	L	T	Pct
Denver	12	1	0	.923
Kansas City	9	4	0	.692
San Diego	7	6	0	.538
Oakland	6	7	0	.462
Seattle	5	8	0	.385

NFC EAST

	W	L	T	Pct.
Dallas	8	5	0	.615
Philadelphia	8	5	0	.615
Washington	8	5	0	.615
Arizona	6	7	0	.462
N.Y. Giants	5	8	0	.385

NFC CENTRAL

	W	L	T	Pct.
Green Bay	10	3	0	.769
Minnesota	7	6	0	.538
Chicago	5	8	0	.385
Detroit	5	8	0	.385
Tampa Bay	4	9	0	.308

NFC WEST

	W	L	T	Pct.
San Francisco	10	3	0	.769
Carolina	9	4	0	.692
St. Louis	4	9	0	.308
Atlanta	2	11	0	.154
New Orleans	2	11	0	.154

HIGHLIGHTS

Hero of the week: Green Bay's Desmond Howard broke open a 7-7 game against Chicago with a 75-yard punt return for a touchdown in the third quarter. Howard—aided by excellent blocks—scampered untouched, holding the football up in his right hand at Chicago's 40 after punter Todd Sauerbrun slipped. The Packers added two fourth-quarter touchdowns for a 28-17 victory.

Goat of the week: Miami quarterback Dan Marino turned in a terrible performance against the Raiders, fumbling once and throwing three interceptions. Marino managed a fourth-quarter touchdown pass to Randal Hill, but it wasn't enough as Oakland prevailed, 17-7.

Sub of the week: Kansas City quarterback Rich Gannon, in his first start of the season, led the Chiefs to a 28-24 Thanksgiving Day win over the Lions. Gannon, who started for the benched Steve Bono, was 15-of-18, threw two touchdown passes and rushed seven times for 45 yards.

Comeback of the week: Against Buffalo, Colts kicker Cary Blanchard connected on a 25-yard field goal to tie the game, 10-10, on the second play of the fourth quarter. Neither team scored again in regulation. On the initial drive of overtime, the Bills stalled and punted. The Colts started at their 16, and quarterback Paul Justin—who started for the injured Jim Harbaugh—completed four passes for 59 yards, including a 28-yard pass to receiver Aaron Bailey, to move the Colts to Buffalo's 33. Four plays later, Blanchard booted a 49-yarder for a 13-10 victory.

Blowout of the week: The Patriots crushed San Diego, 45-7, at Jack Murphy Stadium. Quarterback Drew Bledsoe connected on three first-half touchdown passes to three different receivers (Terry Glenn, Keith Byars and Sam Gash) as New England rolled to a 31-7 halftime lead. Two plays into the second half, cornerback Otis Smith picked off a Stan Humphries' pass, setting up Bledsoe's fourth touchdown pass—an 11-yarder to former Chargers receiver Shawn Jefferson—for a 38-7 lead.

Nail-biter of the week: Jacksonville jumped out to a 10-0 lead over the Bengals before Cincinnati quarter-

back Jeff Blake connected with receiver Carl Picken for two touchdowns, helping the Bengals to a 17-1 lead at halftime. Both teams hit field goals in the thir quarter. On a third-and-10 play late in the quarte Jaguars quarterback Mark Brunell rolled out an tossed a 48-yard touchdown pass to receiver Keena McCardell and added a two-point conversion to receiv er Willie Jackson for a 27-20 lead. Jaguars kicker Mik Hollis made a 20-yard field goal with about two minute left in the fourth quarter, extending the lead to 30-2C Blake hit Pickens with a 25-yard touchdown strike wit 15 seconds left, but it wasn't enough as the Jaguar held on, 30-27.

Hit of the week: By Patriots defensive end Mik Jones, who knocked San Diego quarterback Sta Humphries out of the game with a concussion. Ne England led 38-7 in the third quarter when Jone knocked Humphries out of the game. Jones was calle for a roughing-the-passer penalty on the play.

Oddity of the week: In the first quarter agains Pittsburgh, Ravens quarterback Vinny Testaverd threw a 1-yard touchdown pass to rookie offensive lin man Jonathan Ogden. It was the third time this seaso Baltimore scored on the tackle-eligible play.

Top rusher: Emmitt Smith rushed 29 times for 15 yards and three touchdowns in Dallas' 21-10 victor over Washington on Thanksgiving.

Top passer: Jacksonville's Brunell was 21-of-34 fc 356 yards and one touchdown in the Jaguars' victor over Cincinnati.

Top receiver: Derrick Alexander caught seven passe for 198 yards and a touchdown in Baltimore's 31-17 vic tory over the Steelers.

Notes: Kansas City's Marcus Allen scored two touc downs to become the NFL's career leader in rushin touchdowns with 112, passing Walter Payton's mark o 110. . . . At the 70,852-seat Superdome, the Sain played the Rams before 26,310 fans—the smalle home crowd in the team's history. . . . John Elwa became the ninth quarterback in NFL history to pas

or 250 touchdowns and surpassed 3,000 passing yards
a season for the 11th time in his career, tying
Marino. . . . Running back Terry Kirby gained 105
ards to become the first 49er to rush for more than
00 yards in a game since Ricky Watters in 1994. . . .
an Diego's Tony Martin caught his 14th touchdown
ass of the season, tying Lance Alworth's club record
et in 1965. . . . Emmitt Smith became the 12th player
a history to rush for 10,000 yards. . . . Minnesota run-
ing back Leroy Hoard scored his first touchdown
nce a January 1, 1995, playoff game. . . . Against the
agles, the Giants were 1-of-10 on third-down conver-
ions. . . . Jets quarterback Neil O'Donnell, who was set
return after missing six games with a shoulder
jury, suffered a pulled calf muscle when he slipped
n the wet turf during warmups and did not play
gainst Houston. . . . Jacksonville's Hollis set a team
ngle-game record with five field goals against the
engals. . . . Buffalo quarterback Todd Collins con-
ected with Quinn Early for a 95-yard touchdown pass
gainst Indianapolis. . . . The Chargers' 45-7 loss to the
atriots was the club's worst defeat since November
7, 1988, when the 49ers beat them, 48-10. . . . With its
in over Seattle, Denver clinched home-field advan-
ge throughout the AFC playoffs.

uote of the week: Jets defensive end Hugh Douglas,
ter the team's 35-10 loss to the Oilers, on O'Donnell's
eak pregame injury and the team's misfortunes: "It
nd of makes you want to cry, man, because nothing
er goes your way. What did I do to deserve this?
hat's going on? That's how you feel. When he went
wn, I thought, 'That's crazy.' It's so rough. We need
put this on Unsolved Mysteries or something."

GAME SUMMARIES

CHIEFS 28, LIONS 24
Thursday, November 28

nsas City	7	7	0	14—28
troit	0	14	7	3—24

First Quarter
.—Allen 1 run (Stoyanovich kick), 11:11.
Second Quarter
t.—Morton 16 pass from Mitchell (Hanson kick), :06.
t.—Wells fumble recovery in end zone (Hanson kick), 2:40.
.—Penn 17 pass from Gannon (Stoyanovich kick), 6:56.
Third Quarter
.—Sanders 13 run (Hanson kick), 14:39.
Fourth Quarter
.—Walker 9 pass from Gannon (Stoyanovich kick), 4:06.
t.—FG, Hanson 21, 6:19.
.—Allen 1 run (Stoyanovich kick), 14:14.
Attendance—75,079.

TEAM STATISTICS

	Kansas City	Detroit
st Downs	26	21
shes-Yards	45-243	24-81
ssing	95	237
t Returns	0-0	2-14
koff Returns	5-98	5-123
rception Returns	3-31	0-0
np-Att-Int	15-18-0	18-30-3
ked-Yards Lost	2-25	2-10
ts	3-40	1-45
bles-Lost	2-1	1-0

	Kansas City	Detroit
Penalties-Yards	6-47	6-44
Time of Possession	32:50	27:10

INDIVIDUAL STATISTICS
RUSHING—Kansas City, Hill 17-103, Allen 15-73, Gannon 7-45, Anders 2-16, McNair 2-7, Vanover 2-(minus 1). Detroit, Sanders 20-77, Mitchell 3-10, Rivers 1-(minus 6).
PASSING—Kansas City, Gannon 15-18-0-120. Detroit, Mitchell 18-29-2-247, Sanders 0-1-1-0.
RECEIVING—Kansas City, Anders 5-44, Walker 3-20, LaChapelle 2-20, McNair 2-3, Penn 1-17, Johnson 1-11, Bennett 1-5. Detroit, Perriman 8-131, H. Moore 7-84, Morton 2-27, Metzelaars 1-5.
MISSED FIELD GOAL ATTEMPTS—None.
INTERCEPTIONS—Kansas City, Edwards 1-22, Stargell 1-9, Collins 1-0.
KICKOFF RETURNS—Kansas City, Vanover 4-83, Manusky 1-15. Detroit, Milburn 5-123.
PUNT RETURNS—Detroit, Milburn 2-14.
SACKS—Kansas City, Traylor 1, Washington 1/2, N. Smith 1/2. Detroit, Porcher 1, Waldroup 1.

COWBOYS 21, REDSKINS 10
Thursday, November 28

Washington	0	3	7	0—10
Dallas	0	7	7	7—21

Second Quarter
Dal.—E. Smith 4 run (Boniol kick), 12:57.
Was.—FG, Blanton 21, 14:37.
Third Quarter
Was.—Shepherd 26 pass from Frerotte (Blanton kick), 4:35.
Dal.—E. Smith 4 run (Boniol kick), 8:58.
Fourth Quarter
Dal.—E. Smith 3 run (Boniol kick), 7:11.
Attendance—64,955.

TEAM STATISTICS

	Washington	Dallas
First Downs	13	19
Rushes-Yards	16-46	48-201
Passing	163	46
Punt Returns	2-4	4-28
Kickoff Returns	4-91	3-37
Interception Returns	1-0	2-22
Comp-Att-Int	17-33-2	9-19-1
Sacked-Yards Lost	2-12	2-17
Punts	6-51	7-43
Fumbles-Lost	2-1	0-0
Penalties-Yards	4-30	7-68
Time of Possession	23:25	36:35

INDIVIDUAL STATISTICS
RUSHING—Washington, Allen 12-34, Mitchell 2-12, Frerotte 1-0, Logan 1-0. Dallas, E. Smith 29-155, S. Williams 13-46, Aikman 4-(minus 1), Johnston 2-1.
PASSING—Washington, Frerotte 17-33-2-175. Dallas, Aikman 9-19-1-63.
RECEIVING—Washington, Asher 4-55, Shepherd 4-46, B. Brooks 3-41, Mitchell 3-17, Logan 2-0, Ellard 1-16. Dallas, K. Williams 2-22, Johnston 2-11, E. Smith 2-9, Martin 1-10, Bjornson 1-6, Irvin 1-5.
MISSED FIELD GOAL ATTEMPTS—Washington, Blanton 40.
INTERCEPTIONS—Washington, Stephens 1-0. Dallas, Teague 1-22, Sanders 1-0.
KICKOFF RETURNS—Washington, Mitchell 4-91. Dallas, K. Williams 2-37, Walker 1-0.
PUNT RETURNS—Washington, Mitchell 2-4. Dallas, Martin 4-28.
SACKS—Washington, Harvey 2. Dallas, Tolbert 1, Carver 1.

VIKINGS 41, CARDINALS 17
Sunday, December 1

Arizona	0	3	0	14—17
Minnesota	3	10	14	14—41

First Quarter
Min.—FG, Sisson 38, 12:19.
Second Quarter
Min.—FG, Sisson 26, 6:45.
Min.—Lee 19 pass from B. Johnson (Sisson kick), 10:01.
Ariz.—FG, Butler 38, 14:53.
Third Quarter
Min.—Reed 40 pass from B. Johnson (Sisson kick), 6:51.
Min.—Ismail 13 pass from B. Johnson (Sisson kick), 11:55.

Fourth Quarter
Min.—Carter 4 pass from B. Johnson (Sisson kick), :03.
Ariz.—Centers 9 pass from Esiason (Butler kick), 3:32.
Min.—Hoard 1 run (Sisson kick), 7:25.
Ariz.—Centers 1 run (Butler kick), 10:55.
Attendance—45,767.

TEAM STATISTICS

	Arizona	Minnesota
First Downs	18	29
Rushes-Yards	12-35	45-149
Passing	245	263
Punt Returns	1-10	2-16
Kickoff Returns	7-163	2-14
Interception Returns	0-0	2-19
Comp-Att-Int	26-40-2	21-29-0
Sacked-Yards Lost	3-25	1-6
Punts	3-51	1-49
Fumbles-Lost	1-1	2-0
Penalties-Yards	10-77	3-10
Time of Possession	22:14	37:46

INDIVIDUAL STATISTICS
RUSHING—Arizona, L. Johnson 7-18, Centers 4-21, McKinnon 1-(minus 4). Minnesota, Hoard 22-94, Graham 9-21, Lee 4-15, Evans 4-11, B. Johnson 4-7, R. McDaniel 2-1.

PASSING—Arizona, Esiason 26-40-2-270. Minnesota, B. Johnson 19-26-0-238, Walker 2-2-0-31, Walsh 0-1-0-0.

RECEIVING—Arizona, Centers 10-85, Anderson 3-47, R. Moore 3-28, Edwards 3-27, Sanders 3-26, Carter 2-52, McWilliams 1-5, C. Smith 1-0. Minnesota, Carter 5-40, Reed 4-79, Lee 4-42, Hoard 2-44, Ismail 2-25, Evans 2-10, Goodwin 1-24, Jordan 1-5.

MISSED FIELD GOAL ATTEMPTS—Minnesota, Sisson 45.

INTERCEPTIONS—Minnesota, Griffith 1-18, Fuller 1-1.

KICKOFF RETURNS—Arizona, McElroy 7-163. Minnesota, Ismail 1-11, DeLong 1-3.

PUNT RETURNS—Arizona, Edwards 1-10. Minnesota, Lee 2-16.

SACKS—Arizona, Rice 1. Minnesota, Harrison 1, Randle 1, Tuaolo 1.

COLTS 13, BILLS 10
Sunday, December 1

Buffalo	0	10	0	0	0—10
Indianapolis	7	0	0	3	3—13

First Quarter
Ind.—Faulk 1 run (Blanchard kick), 10:42.

Second Quarter
Buf.—Early 95 pass from Collins (Christie kick), 6:56.
Buf.—FG, Christie 24, 10:30.

Fourth Quarter
Ind.—FG, Blanchard 25, :06.

Overtime
Ind.—FG, Blanchard 49, 10:46.
Attendance—53,804.

TEAM STATISTICS

	Buffalo	Indianapolis
First Downs	11	18
Rushes-Yards	38-124	32-85
Passing	183	203
Punt Returns	4-20	5-13
Kickoff Returns	4-88	3-62
Interception Returns	0-0	2-21
Comp-Att-Int	9-17-2	22-40-0
Sacked-Yards Lost	3-21	3-25
Punts	9-38	8-46
Fumbles-Lost	2-1	0-0
Penalties-Yards	9-65	5-33
Time of Possession	25:07	45:39

INDIVIDUAL STATISTICS
RUSHING—Buffalo, Holmes 30-96, Collins 4-13, Moulds 3-14, Reed 1-1. Indianapolis, Faulk 23-46, Groce 4-21, Warren 4-17, Justin 1-1.

PASSING—Buffalo, Collins 9-17-2-204. Indianapolis, Justin 22-40-0-228.

RECEIVING—Buffalo, Holmes 4-29, Early 3-113, Moulds 1-47, Cline 1-15. Indianapolis, Faulk 10-78, Dawkins 4-64, Harrison 3-22, Bailey 2-34, Pollard 2-19, Stock 1-11.

MISSED FIELD GOAL ATTEMPTS—Indianapolis, Blanchard 33, 41.

INTERCEPTIONS—Indianapolis, Watts 1-21, Daniel 1-0.

KICKOFF RETURNS—Buffalo, Moulds 2-52, Copeland 2-36. Indianapolis, Bailey 3-62.

PUNT RETURNS—Buffalo, Burris 4-20. Indianapolis, Stock 5-13.

SACKS—Buffalo, Washington 2, B. Smith 1. Indianapolis, Bennett 1, Whittington 1, Dent 1.

PANTHERS 24, BUCCANEERS 0
Sunday, December 1

Tampa Bay	0	0	0	0— 0
Carolina	3	7	7	7—24

First Quarter
Car.—FG, Kasay 23, 13:01.

Second Quarter
Car.—King 12 fumble return (Kasay kick), :06.

Third Quarter
Car.—Griffith 1 run (Kasay kick), 6:58.

Fourth Quarter
Car.—Johnson 25 run (Kasay kick), 11:50.
Attendance—57,623.

TEAM STATISTICS

	Tampa Bay	Carolina
First Downs	17	13
Rushes-Yards	23-78	30-132
Passing	206	83
Punt Returns	3-14	2-18
Kickoff Returns	3-53	1-14
Interception Returns	0-0	2-40
Comp-Att-Int	23-41-2	14-24-0
Sacked-Yards Lost	4-30	0-0
Punts	5-41	7-35
Fumbles-Lost	2-2	1-0
Penalties-Yards	6-55	4-48
Time of Possession	31:03	28:57

INDIVIDUAL STATISTICS
RUSHING—Tampa Bay, Rhett 18-68, Ellison 3-9, Alstott 2-1. Carolina, Johnson 26-111, Oliver 1-14, Griffith 1-1, Collins 1-(minus 1).

PASSING—Tampa Bay, Dilfer 23-41-2-236. Carolina, Collins 14-24-0-83.

RECEIVING—Tampa Bay, R. Thomas 6-66, Alstott 5-52, Harris 4-52, Ellison 4-32, Hawkins 2-15, Williams 1-12, Moore 1-7. Carolina, Walls 4-32, Carrier 3-31, Johnson 3-2, Green 2-20, Griffith 1-2, Oliver 1-(minus 4).

MISSED FIELD GOAL ATTEMPTS—None.

INTERCEPTIONS—Carolina, Davis 1-39, King 1-1.

KICKOFF RETURNS—Tampa Bay, Marshall 3-53. Carolina, Ismail 1-14.

PUNT RETURNS—Tampa Bay, Marshall 3-14. Carolina, Oliver 2-18.

SACKS—Carolina, Lathon 1, K. Greene 1, Cook 1, King 1/2, Rod. Smith 1.

RAVENS 31, STEELERS 17
Sunday, December 1

Pittsburgh	7	3	7	0—17
Baltimore	7	17	0	7—31

First Quarter
Bal.—Ogden 1 pass from Testaverde (Stover kick), 4:00.
Pit.—Hastings 30 pass from Tomczak (N. Johnson kick), 6:04.

Second Quarter
Pit.—FG, N. Johnson 22, 3:01.
Bal.—Alexander 24 pass from Testaverde (Stover kick), 11:35.
Bal.—Byner 7 run (Stover kick), 13:36.
Bal.—FG, Stover 40, 15:00.

Third Quarter
Pit.—Hastings 5 pass from Tomczak (N. Johnson kick), 3:29.

Fourth Quarter
Bal.—Green 3 pass from Testaverde (Stover kick), 2:38.
Attendance—51,822.

TEAM STATISTICS

	Pittsburgh	Baltimore
First Downs	18	17
Rushes-Yards	30-119	35-127
Passing	214	257
Punt Returns	1-9	3-7
Kickoff Returns	4-118	3-63
Interception Returns	1-24	1-1
Comp-Att-Int	18-36-1	17-24-1
Sacked-Yards Lost	1-7	1-4
Punts	6-40	5-41
Fumbles-Lost	1-0	1-1
Penalties-Yards	3-15	5-29
Time of Possession	30:58	29:02

RUSHING—Pittsburgh, Bettis 24-105, Pegram 3-4, Lester 1-5, Tomczak 1-3, Stewart 1-2. Baltimore, Morris 28-100, Byner 2-11, Gardner 2-7, Testaverde 2-(minus 2), F. Turner 1-6.

PASSING—Pittsburgh, Tomczak 18-36-1-221. Baltimore, Testaverde 17-4-1-259.

RECEIVING—Pittsburgh, C. Johnson 8-117, Hastings 6-74, Mills 2-19, Holliday 1-7, Pegram 1-4. Baltimore, Alexander 7-198, Morris 3-22, Kinchen 2-22, F. Turner 2-13, Green 2-3, Ogden 1-1.

MISSED FIELD GOAL ATTEMPTS—None.

INTERCEPTIONS—Pittsburgh, Perry 1-24. Baltimore, Croel 1-16.

KICKOFF RETURNS—Pittsburgh, Pegram 2-72, Mills 2-46. Baltimore, Baldwin 2-54, Byner 1-15.

PUNT RETURNS—Pittsburgh, Hastings 1-9. Baltimore, J. Lewis 3-71.

SACKS—Pittsburgh, Jones 1. Baltimore, Pleasant 1.

PACKERS 28, BEARS 17
Sunday, December 1

Chicago	0	7	3	7—17
Green Bay	0	7	7	14—28

Second Quarter
Chi.—Engram 15 pass from Krieg (Jaeger kick), 13:30.
G.B.—Jackson 19 pass from Favre (Jacke kick), 14:06.

Third Quarter
G.B.—Howard 75 punt return (Jacke kick), 9:30.
Chi.—FG, Jaeger 34, 12:46.

Fourth Quarter
G.B.—Levens 10 run (Jacke kick), 2:20.
G.B.—Favre 1 run (Jacke kick), 9:21.
Chi.—Engram 5 pass from Krieg (Jaeger kick), 13:05.
Attendance—59,682.

TEAM STATISTICS

	Chicago	Green Bay
First Downs	21	20
Rushes-Yards	25-84	26-126
Passing	208	216
Punt Returns	1-8	1-75
Kickoff Returns	3-72	3-73
Interception Returns	0-0	1-2
Comp-Att-Int	29-45-1	19-27-0
Sacked-Yards Lost	1-10	2-15
Punts	5-40	4-40
Fumbles-Lost	1-0	3-0
Penalties-Yards	3-30	2-10
Time of Possession	32:22	27:38

INDIVIDUAL STATISTICS

RUSHING—Chicago, R. Harris 24-79, Conway 1-5. Green Bay, Bennett 16-51, Levens 5-69, Favre 4-4, Henderson 1-2.

PASSING—Chicago, Krieg 29-45-1-218. Green Bay, Favre 19-27-0-231.

RECEIVING—Chicago, Conway 7-65, R. Harris 5-28, Engram 4-46, Simpson 4-38, T. Carter 4-21, Green 3-8, Neely 2-12. Green Bay, Freeman 8-156, Jackson 3-34, Beebe 2-18, Rison 2-14, Levens 1-8, Henderson 1-1.

MISSED FIELD GOAL ATTEMPTS—Green Bay, Jacke 46.

INTERCEPTIONS—Green Bay, E. Robinson 1-2.

KICKOFF RETURNS—Chicago, Ja. Jackson 3-72. Green Bay, Howard 3-73.

PUNT RETURNS—Chicago, Engram 1-8. Green Bay, Howard 1-75.

SACKS—Chicago, Minter 1, Spellman 1. Green Bay, S. Jones ½, White ½.

OILERS 35, JETS 10
Sunday, December 1

Houston	14	7	0	14—35
N.Y. Jets	0	10	0	0—10

First Quarter
Hou.—Wycheck 23 pass from McNair (Del Greco kick), 10:47.
Hou.—Sanders 83 pass from McNair (Del Greco kick), 14:26.

Second Quarter
NYJ—FG, Lowery 30, 6:27.
Hou.—George 35 run (Del Greco kick), 11:12.
NYJ—Johnson 18 pass from Reich (Lowery kick), 13:50.

Fourth Quarter
Hou.—George 1 run (Del Greco kick), 4:31.
Hou.—Thomas 24 run (Del Greco kick), 10:59.
Attendance—21,731.

TEAM STATISTICS

	Houston	N.Y. Jets
First Downs	18	15
Rushes-Yards	48-243	21-79
Passing	142	185

	Houston	N.Y. Jets
Punt Returns	1-6	3-26
Kickoff Returns	3-66	6-122
Interception Returns	1-7	0-0
Comp-Att-Int	6-17-0	19-39-1
Sacked-Yards Lost	0-0	2-5
Punts	6-45	7-39
Fumbles-Lost	1-1	3-2
Penalties-Yards	4-20	5-35
Time of Possession	34:35	25:25

INDIVIDUAL STATISTICS

RUSHING—Houston, George 28-141, Thomas 9-54, McNair 8-38, Harmon 3-10. New York, Murrell 14-63, Reich 5-13, Anderson 2-3.

PASSING—Houston, McNair 6-17-0-142. New York, Reich 13-27-0-154, Foley 6-12-1-36.

RECEIVING—Houston, Sanders 3-102, Wycheck 1-23, Russell 1-13, Harmon 1-4. New York, Slaughter 5-44, Chrebet 5-41, Johnson 3-48, Anderson 3-21, Van Dyke 2-13, F. Baxter 1-23.

MISSED FIELD GOAL ATTEMPTS—None.

INTERCEPTIONS—Houston, Dishman 1-7.

KICKOFF RETURNS—Houston, Gray 3-66. New York, Cobb 3-62, Van Dyke 2-50, Brady 1-10.

PUNT RETURNS—Houston, Gray 1-6. New York, Chrebet 3-26.

SACKS—Houston, Barrow 1, Cook 1.

BRONCOS 34, SEAHAWKS 7
Sunday, December 1

Seattle	7	0	0	0— 7
Denver	14	13	7	0—34

First Quarter
Den.—Sharpe 1 pass from Elway (Elam kick), 3:24.
Sea.—Pritchard 8 pass from Mirer (Peterson kick), 9:35.
Den.—Elway 2 run (Elam kick), 13:09.

Second Quarter
Den.—FG, Elam 44, 5:44.
Den.—FG, Elam 18, 13:13.
Den.—McCaffrey 4 pass from Elway (Elam kick), 14:30.

Third Quarter
Den.—Davis 5 run (Elam kick), 8:07.
Attendance—74,982.

TEAM STATISTICS

	Seattle	Denver
First Downs	13	31
Rushes-Yards	19-105	45-205
Passing	172	236
Punt Returns	0-0	4-58
Kickoff Returns	5-106	2-100
Interception Returns	0-0	2-12
Comp-Att-Int	13-28-2	23-34-0
Sacked-Yards Lost	1-5	1-4
Punts	5-55	2-38
Fumbles-Lost	1-1	0-0
Penalties-Yards	6-44	7-52
Time of Possession	18:36	41:24

INDIVIDUAL STATISTICS

RUSHING—Seattle, Smith 8-42, Warren 7-32, Mirer 4-31. Denver, Davis 26-106, Hebron 8-60, Craver 5-32, Musgrave 3-(minus 3), Elway 2-7, Rivers 1-3.

PASSING—Seattle, Mirer 13-28-2-177. Denver, Elway 17-27-0-189, Musgrave 6-7-0-51.

RECEIVING—Seattle, Galloway 5-108, Crumpler 4-31, Blades 2-23, Pritchard 1-8, R. Williams 1-7. Denver, McCaffrey 5-43, Sharpe 4-21, Craver 3-66, Miller 3-20, Chamberlain 2-28, Sherrard 2-23, Davis 2-15, R. Smith 1-13, Hebron 1-11.

MISSED FIELD GOAL ATTEMPTS—None.

INTERCEPTIONS—Denver, Braxton 1-12, James 1-0.

KICKOFF RETURNS—Seattle, R. Harris 4-85, C. Harris 1-21. Denver, Hebron 2-100.

PUNT RETURNS—Denver, R. Smith 4-58.

SACKS—Seattle, McCrary ½, Kennedy ½. Denver, Lodish ½, Robinson ½.

RAMS 26, SAINTS 10
Sunday, December 1

St. Louis	3	10	10	3—26
New Orleans	3	7	0	0—10

First Quarter
St.L.—FG, Lohmiller 35, 4:44.
N.O.—FG, Brien 30, 12:31.

Second Quarter

St.L.—FG, Lohmiller 32, :38.
N.O.—Small 17 run (Brien kick), 2:28.
St.L.—Bruce 10 pass from Banks (Lohmiller kick), 12:09.

Third Quarter

St.L.—FG, Lohmiller 49, 9:20.
St.L.—Green 1 run (Lohmiller kick), 15:00.

Fourth Quarter

St.L.—FG, Lohmiller 27, 10:53.
    Attendance—26,310

TEAM STATISTICS

	St.Louis	New Orleans
First Downs	15	14
Rushes-Yards	35-92	24-86
Passing	220	142
Punt Returns	3-13	0-0
Kickoff Returns	3-107	7-166
Interception Returns	0-0	1-8
Comp-Att-Int	11-23-1	15-31-0
Sacked-Yards Lost	1-11	3-27
Punts	2-23	5-38
Fumbles-Lost	4-1	3-1
Penalties-Yards	10-85	6-55
Time of Possession	32:35	27:25

INDIVIDUAL STATISTICS

RUSHING—St. Louis, Green 20-65, Banks 9-10, Robinson 6-17. New Orleans, Bates 8-29, Zellars 6-11, Hunter 4-23, Nussmeier 3-6, Small 1-17, Everett 1-0, Neal 1-0.

PASSING—St. Louis, Banks 11-23-1-231. New Orleans, Everett 8-16-0-68, Nussmeier 7-15-0-101.

RECEIVING—St. Louis, Bruce 4-112, Kennison 2-39, Green 2-31, Clay 1-34, A. Wright 1-11, Ross 1-4. New Orleans, Neal 5-22, Hunter 4-37, Small 3-38, Hayes 2-60, Guess 1-12.

MISSED FIELD GOAL ATTEMPTS—New Orleans, Brien 48.

INTERCEPTIONS—New Orleans, G. Jackson 1-8.

KICKOFF RETURNS—St. Louis, Thomas 3-107. New Orleans, Hughes 6-150, Lusk 1-16.

PUNT RETURNS—St. Louis, Kennison 2-19, P. Davis 1-(minus 6).

SACKS—St. Louis, Carter 1, J. Jones 1, J. Harris 1. New Orleans, J. Johnson 1/2, Turnbull 1/2.

JAGUARS 30, BENGALS 27

Sunday, December 1

Cincinnati	7	10	3	7—27
Jacksonville	13	3	11	3—30

First Quarter

Jac.—Washington 65 blocked FG return (Hollis kick), 3:32.
Jac.—FG, Hollis 25, 8:36.
Cin.—Pickens 23 pass from Blake (Pelfrey kick), 11:34.
Jac.—FG, Hollis 46, 12:55.

Second Quarter

Cin.—FG, Pelfrey 22, 3:25.
Cin.—Pickens 8 pass from Blake (Pelfrey kick), 7:33.
Jac.—FG, Hollis 40, 14:55.

Third Quarter

Jac.—FG, Hollis 39, 4:51.
Cin.—FG, Pelfrey 34, 10:18.
Jac.—McCardell 48 pass from Brunell (W. Jackson pass from Brunell), 13:27.

Fourth Quarter

Jac.—FG, Hollis 20, 12:56.
Cin.—Pickens 25 pass from Blake (Pelfrey kick), 14:45.
    Attendance—57,408.

TEAM STATISTICS

	Cincinnati	Jacksonville
First Downs	27	19
Rushes-Yards	31-172	23-66
Passing	313	356
Punt Returns	2-19	2-9
Kickoff Returns	8-160	5-121
Interception Returns	0-0	2-1
Comp-Att-Int	23-39-2	21-34-0
Sacked-Yards Lost	0-0	1-0
Punts	3-34	3-52
Fumbles-Lost	0-0	1-0
Penalties-Yards	4-25	5-44
Time of Possession	32:38	27:22

INDIVIDUAL STATISTICS

RUSHING—Cincinnati, Hearst 18-78, Blake 6-50, Carter 4-36, Bieniemy 3-8. Jacksonville, Means 21-56, Brunell 2-10.

PASSING—Cincinnati, Blake 23-39-2-313. Jacksonville, Brunell 21-34-0-356.

RECEIVING—Cincinnati, Pickens 7-109, McGee 4-52, Bieniemy 4-13, Scott 2-60, Dunn 2-27, Hearst 2-20, Carter 1-17, Milne 1-15. Jacksonville, Smith 7-162, McCardell 4-79, Mitchell 4-55, W. Jackson 2-24, Brown 2-16, Maston 1-13, Means 1-7.

MISSED FIELD GOAL ATTEMPTS—Cincinnati, Pelfrey 42.

INTERCEPTIONS—Jacksonville, Washington 1-1, Beasley 1-0.

KICKOFF RETURNS—Cincinnati, Dunn 6-142, Hundon 1-18, Sadowski 1-0. Jacksonville, B. Brooks 5-121.

PUNT RETURNS—Cincinnati, Dunn 2-19. Jacksonville, Hudson 2-9.

SACKS—Cincinnati, Tovar 1.

RAIDERS 17, DOLPHINS 7

Sunday, December 1

Miami	0	0	0	7— 7
Oakland	0	14	0	3—17

Second Quarter

Oak.—Fenner 6 run (Ford kick), 7:28.
Oak.—T. Brown 22 pass from Hostetler (Ford kick), 14:18.

Fourth Quarter

Oak.—FG, Ford 38, 10:10.
Mia.—R. Hill 4 pass from Marino (Nedney kick), 12:26.
    Attendance—60,591.

TEAM STATISTICS

	Miami	Oakland
First Downs	21	20
Rushes-Yards	20-34	34-156
Passing	281	158
Punt Returns	3-30	4-21
Kickoff Returns	3-56	0-0
Interception Returns	0-0	3-31
Comp-Att-Int	22-39-3	21-29-0
Sacked-Yards Lost	1-9	4-14
Punts	6-45	7-42
Fumbles-Lost	1-1	1-1
Penalties-Yards	11-75	11-64
Time of Possession	24:21	35:39

INDIVIDUAL STATISTICS

RUSHING—Miami, Abdul-Jabbar 18-39, Marino 1-0, Parmalee 1-(minus 5). Oakland, Fenner 12-45, Kaufman 11-42, Williams 9-49, T. Brown 1-12, Hostetler 1-8.

PASSING—Miami, Marino 22-39-3-290. Oakland, Hostetler 20-28-0-165, Hobbs 1-1-0-7.

RECEIVING—Miami, Barnett 6-95, McDuffie 5-44, Parmalee 4-50, L. Thomas 2-34, R. Hill 2-17, Drayton 1-33, Pritchett 1-10, Abdul-Jabbar 1-7. Oakland, Dudley 6-54, T. Brown 5-53, Jett 2-19, A. Glover 2-16, Kaufman 2-13, Fenner 2-4, Hobbs 1-9, Williams 1-4.

MISSED FIELD GOAL ATTEMPTS—Miami, Nedney 42. Oakland, Ford 48.

INTERCEPTIONS—Oakland, McDaniel 1-18, Morton 1-13, Lewis 1-0.

KICKOFF RETURNS—Miami, Spikes 3-56.

PUNT RETURNS—Miami, McDuffie 2-17, Buckley 1-13. Oakland, T. Brown 4-21.

SACKS—Miami, Burton 2, Hollier 1, Jackson 1. Oakland, Harrison 1.

EAGLES 24, GIANTS 0

Sunday, December 1

N.Y. Giants	0	0	0	0— 0
Philadelphia	10	14	0	0—24

First Quarter

Phi.—FG, Anderson 44, 6:53.
Phi.—Dunn 14 pass from Detmer (Anderson kick), 12:14.

Second Quarter

Phi.—Fryar 19 pass from Detmer (Anderson kick), 2:09.
Phi.—Jones 2 pass from Detmer (Anderson kick), 14:32.
    Attendance—51,468.

TEAM STATISTICS

	N.Y. Giants	Philadelphia
First Downs	9	24
Rushes-Yards	21-84	43-139
Passing	47	271
Punt Returns	1-0	5-29
Kickoff Returns	4-63	0-0
Interception Returns	1-0	2-23
Comp-Att-Int	7-24-2	25-33-1

	N.Y. Giants	Philadelphia
cked-Yards Lost	5-31	2-13
nts	7-41	2-45
mbles-Lost	3-2	3-2
nalties-Yards	2-20	5-29
ne of Possession	20:08	39:52

INDIVIDUAL STATISTICS

RUSHING—New York, Wheatley 9-39, Hampton 8-20, Brown 3-12, Kanell 3. Philadelphia, Watters 29-104, Garner 6-36, Detmer 5-(minus 1), ner 3-0.

PASSING—New York, Kanell 4-13-0-47, Brown 3-11-2-31. Philadelphia, mer 25-33-1-284.

RECEIVING—New York, Calloway 2-26, Way 2-10, Dawsey 1-17, Cross 1-Alexander 1-11. Philadelphia, Watters 6-77, Fryar 6-59, Jones 5-36, nn 3-33, Seay 2-36, West 1-18, J. Johnson 1-17, Garner 1-8.

MISSED FIELD GOAL ATTEMPTS—Philadelphia, Anderson 44.

INTERCEPTIONS—New York, Sehorn 1-0. Philadelphia, Vincent 1-23, mer 1-0.

KICKOFF RETURNS—New York, C. Hamilton 3-54, Saxton 1-9.

PUNT RETURNS—New York, Marshall 1-0. Philadelphia, Seay 5-29.

SACKS—New York, Bratzke 1, Harris 1. Philadelphia, W. Fuller 2, Farmer K. Johnson 1, Jefferson 1.

PATRIOTS 45, CHARGERS 7
Sunday, December 1

w England		14	17	14	0—45
a Diego		7	0	0	0— 7

First Quarter
.—Glenn 8 pass from Bledsoe (Vinatieri kick), 3:47.
.—Byars 19 pass from Bledsoe (Vinatieri kick), 9:32.
.—Martin 46 pass from Humphries (Carney kick), 12:02.

Second Quarter
.—Gash 7 pass from Bledsoe (Vinatieri kick), 1:40.
.—McGinest fumble recovery in end zone (Vinatieri kick), 12:28.
.—FG, Vinatieri 47, 14:07.

Third Quarter
.—Jefferson 11 pass from Bledsoe (Vinatieri kick), 2:14.
.—C. Brown 42 fumble return (Vinatieri kick), 13:37.
Attendance—59,209.

TEAM STATISTICS
	New England	San Diego
t Downs	15	15
hes-Yards	36-84	15-32
sing	229	204
t Returns	3-18	4-29
Koff Returns	2-38	7-165
rception Returns	4-16	0-0
mp-Att-Int	19-29-0	22-51-4
ked-Yards Lost	2-3	6-58
its	7-46	7-45
nbles-Lost	1-0	2-2
nalties-Yards	8-65	6-48
e of Possession	36:06	23:54

INDIVIDUAL STATISTICS

RUSHING—New England, Martin 19-63, Grier 12-23, Zolak 3-(minus 3), ggett 1-2, Bledsoe 1-(minus 1). San Diego, Russell 10-35, Fletcher 4-nus 4), Bradley 1-1.

PASSING—New England, Bledsoe 19-29-0-232. San Diego, Humphries 35-3-204, Salisbury 6-16-1-58.

RECEIVING—New England, Coates 6-71, Glenn 5-63, Jefferson 4-52, Byars 3, Martin 1-14, Gash 1-7, Meggett 1-6. San Diego, Martin 5-84, Jones 5-Fletcher 4-49, May 3-16, Still 2-34, Russell 2-27, A. Coleman 1-8.

MISSED FIELD GOAL ATTEMPTS—None.

INTERCEPTIONS—New England, O. Smith 1-9, Henderson 1-7, Milloy 1-0, Johnson 1-0.

KICKOFF RETURNS—New England, T. Brown 2-38. San Diego, A. Coleman 5-108, Still 2-57.

PUNT RETURNS—New England, Meggett 3-18. San Diego, Da. Gordon 3-28, Still 1-1.

SACKS—New England, Bruschi 1, Sagapolutele 1, Eaton 1, Slade 1, Wheeler 1, McGinest ½, McGruder ½. San Diego, Mims 1, Parrella 1.

49ERS 34, FALCONS 10
Monday, December 2

San Francisco		6	19	7	2—34
Atlanta		3	0	0	7—10

First Quarter
S.F.—FG, Wilkins 39, 4:49.
Atl.—FG, Andersen 32, 8:11.
S.F.—FG, Wilkins 26, 13:48.

Second Quarter
S.F.—S. Young 26 run (Wilkins kick), 1:32.
S.F.—FG, Wilkins 43, 6:59.
S.F.—S. Young 5 run (pass failed), 14:19.
S.F.—FG, Wilkins 23, 15:00.

Third Quarter
S.F.—Kirby 10 pass from S. Young (Wilkins kick), 5:30.

Fourth Quarter
S.F.—Safety, Young sacked Nagle in end zone, 10:07.
Atl.—Mathis 7 pass from Nagle (Andersen kick), 12:37.
Attendance—46,318.

TEAM STATISTICS
	San Francisco	Atlanta
First Downs	25	9
Rushes-Yards	38-202	15-61
Passing	264	117
Punt Returns	2-3	0-0
Kickoff Returns	2-41	6-103
Interception Returns	2-1	1-21
Comp-Att-Int	26-38-1	12-30-2
Sacked-Yards Lost	4-15	4-20
Punts	3-34	5-44
Fumbles-Lost	1-1	2-2
Penalties-Yards	9-70	3-40
Time of Possession	40:19	19:41

INDIVIDUAL STATISTICS

RUSHING—San Francisco, Kirby 12-105, Vardell 8-29, S. Young 6-43, Lynn 5-13, Floyd 4-14, Grbac 2-(minus 2), D. Carter 1-0. Atlanta, Anderson 13-55, Hebert 2-6.

PASSING—San Francisco, S. Young 23-30-0-254, Grbac 3-7-1-25, Rice 0-1-0-0. Atlanta, Hebert 10-25-2-113, Nagle 2-5-0-24.

RECEIVING—San Francisco, Rice 8-78, Owens 5-55, Floyd 4-36, Jones 3-56, Vardell 2-23, Kirby 2-10, Cooper 1-11, Uwaezuoke 1-10. Atlanta, Emanuel 3-35, Anderson 3-33, Mathis 3-27, Metcalf 2-35, Birden 1-7.

MISSED FIELD GOAL ATTEMPTS—None.

INTERCEPTIONS—San Francisco, Dodge 1-1, Pope 1-0. Atlanta, Smith 1-21.

KICKOFF RETURNS—San Francisco, D. Carter 2-41. Atlanta, Preston 6-103.

PUNT RETURNS—San Francisco, D. Carter 2-3.

SACKS—San Francisco, B. Young 2, Barker 1, Doleman 1. Atlanta, Smith 1, Owens 1, Zgonina 1, Brandon 1.

WEEK 15

RESULTS

INDIANAPOLIS 37, Philadelphia 10
Atlanta 31, NEW ORLEANS 15
Carolina 30, SAN FRANCISCO 24
CHICAGO 35, St. Louis 9
CINCINNATI 21, Baltimore 14
Dallas 10, ARIZONA 6
GREEN BAY 41, Denver 6
Jacksonville 23, HOUSTON 17
Minnesota 24, DETROIT 22
NEW ENGLAND 34, N.Y. Jets 10
N.Y. Giants 17, MIAMI 7
PITTSBURGH 16, San Diego 3
SEATTLE 26, Buffalo 18
TAMPA BAY 24, Washington 10
OAKLAND 26, Kansas City 7

STANDINGS

AFC EAST	W	L	T	Pct.
New England	10	4	0	.714
Buffalo	9	5	0	.643
Indianapolis	8	6	0	.571
Miami	6	8	0	.429
N.Y. Jets	1	13	0	.071

AFC CENTRAL	W	L	T	Pct.
Pittsburgh	10	4	0	.714
Houston	7	7	0	.500
Jacksonville	7	7	0	.500
Cincinnati	6	8	0	.429
Baltimore	4	10	0	.286

AFC WEST	W	L	T	Pct.
Denver	12	2	0	.85
Kansas City	9	5	0	.64
Oakland	7	7	0	.50
San Diego	7	7	0	.50
Seattle	6	8	0	.42

NFC EAST	W	L	T	Pct.
Dallas	9	5	0	.643
Philadelphia	8	6	0	.571
Washington	8	6	0	.571
Arizona	6	8	0	.429
N.Y. Giants	6	8	0	.429

NFC CENTRAL	W	L	T	Pct.
Green Bay	11	3	0	.786
Minnesota	8	6	0	.571
Chicago	6	8	0	.429
Detroit	5	9	0	.357
Tampa Bay	5	9	0	.357

NFC WEST	W	L	T	Pct.
Carolina	10	4	0	.71
San Francisco	10	4	0	.71
St. Louis	4	10	0	.28
Atlanta	3	11	0	.21
New Orleans	2	12	0	.14

HIGHLIGHTS

Heroes of the week: Quarterback Kerry Collins and cornerback Eric Davis led the Panthers to a big win over the 49ers, 30-24. Collins played one of his best games as a pro, going 22-of-37 for 327 yards and three touchdowns—with no interceptions. Davis, a former 49er, made a one-handed interception of a Steve Young pass to stop a potential game-winning drive with 4:35 left.

Goat of the week: Chargers quarterback Sean Salisbury, subbing for the injured Stan Humphries, struggled mightily against Pittsburgh, going 10-of-29 for 125 yards and an interception in a 16-3 loss. He also fumbled to stop a Chargers drive and was sacked on consecutive plays to end San Diego's last drive of the game.

Sub of the week: Quarterback Kerwin Bell, who had never thrown an NFL pass, stepped in for the injured Paul Justin in the third quarter and led the Colts on a scoring drive against Philadelphia. Starting at his 10, Bell moved the team down the field—culminating the drive in a 20-yard touchdown pass to receiver Marvin Harrison for a 30-3 lead. For the game, Bell was 5-of-5 for 75 yards.

Comeback of the week: The Cowboys' defense, which lost defensive end Leon Lett on December 3 to a one-year suspension for violating the NFL's drug policy, was further depleted by Deion Sanders' absence for most of the first half because of back spasms, as the Cardinals took a 6-0 lead into halftime. Late in the third quarter, quarterback Troy Aikman hit Michael Irvin with a sideline pass, which the receiver broke for a 50-yard touchdown to put Dallas up, 7-6. In the fourth quarter, safety Darren Woodson picked off a Boomer Esiason pass and returned it to Arizona's 23. Chris Boniol made a 31-yard field goal to put Dallas ahead, 10-6, for the final margin.

Blowout of the week: In a game billed as a Super Bowl preview, Green Bay crushed the Broncos, 41-6. Denver, which clinched AFC home-field advantage a week earlier, rested John Elway and his sore hamstring and backup Bill Musgrave got his first NFL start. Green Bay led 6-3 with 51 seconds left in the first half, when Brett Favre moved the Packers down the field

and connected with receiver Antonio Freeman on a 1 yard touchdown pass for a 13-3 halftime lead. Early the third quarter, Jason Elam kicked a 39-yard fie goal to keep the Broncos close, but the Packers reel off 28 consecutive points—including three Favi touchdown passes—to close out the game.

Nail-biter of the week: Detroit's Jason Hanson made 31-yard field goal midway through the fourth quarter cut the Vikings' lead to 17-16. With five minutes le Vikings quarterback Brad Johnson threw a 30-ya touchdown pass to receiver Cris Carter for a 24-16 lea The Lions countered with a four-play, 71-yard driv capped by Barry Sanders' 2-yard touchdown ru Detroit tried a two-point conversion, but Scott Mitchel pass to receiver Johnnie Morton was batted away safety Robert Griffith to seal the Vikings' victory.

Hit of the week: By Bengals safety Sam Shade, wl stopped Ravens fullback Carwell Gardner short of tl goal-line with 23 seconds left in the Bengals' 21-14 v tory. Ravens quarterback Vinny Testaverde faked handoff to running back Bam Morris, looked for lir man Jonathan Ogden on a tackle-eligible play, the completed a pass to Gardner, who was dropped Shade to end the game.

Oddity of the week: Saints quarterback Doug Nus meier, who made his first NFL start in place of tl injured Jim Everett, hooked up with rookie Ter Guess on a 57-yard touchdown pass for a pair firsts—Nussmeier's first NFL touchdown pass a Guess' first NFL touchdown reception.

Top rusher: Detroit's Sanders rushed 20 times for 1 yards and one touchdown in the Lions' loss to Minneso

Top passer: Steve Young was 27-of-41 for 393 yards w three touchdowns in the 49ers' 30-24 loss to Carolina.

Top receiver: Irvin caught eight passes for 198 yards a one touchdown in Dallas' 10-6 victory over the Cardina

Notes: Colts kicker Cary Blanchard, who made thr field goals against the Eagles, has scored 123 poi this season, a club single-season record for points. . For the eighth time in nine games, Tampa Bay held opponent to 17 points or less. . . . Denver's 41-6 loss to the Packers was its worst regular-season loss since 1988, when the Saints beat them, 42-0. . . . For just the third time in Dan Marino's career, the Dolphins scored fewer than 10 points in consecutive games. . . . 24-year old Drew Bledsoe became the youngest player in NFL history to surpass 14,000 career passing yards. . . . The Rams had 13 penalties for 102 yards and two ejections against the Bears. . . . Against the Oilers, Jacksonville quarterback Mark Brunell failed to pass for 200 yards for the first time in 15 games; he finished with 172 yards. . . . Seattle running back Chris Warren, with his 116-yard performance against Buffalo, became the Seahawks' career leader in 100-yard rushing games with 24. . . . Barry Sanders moved into seventh place on the NFL's career rushing list, pushing his career total to 11,472. . . . The Cowboys recorded their 13th consecutive victory over the Cardinals. . . . San Diego's 13 possessions against the Steelers ended with eight punts, two fumbles, an interception, a loss of downs and a 25-yard field goal by John Carney. . . . With its win against the 49ers, Carolina became the first second-year expansion team to make the playoffs. . . . Despite their Monday night loss to Oakland, the Chiefs are 13-2 against the Raiders in the '90s.

Quote of the week: Washington linebacker Marvcus Patton, on the Redskins' loss to the Buccaneers: "We played like crap. Everybody, myself included. With the talent we have and the start we got off to, we should do much better than this. It basically comes down to what we did to ourselves. We played like babies. We didn't tackle. We didn't chase down people. We let it slip away."

GAME SUMMARIES

COLTS 37, EAGLES 10
Thursday, December 5

Philadelphia	3	0	0	7—10
Indianapolis	7	16	7	7—37

First Quarter
Ind.—Faulk 13 run (Blanchard kick), 5:17.
Phi.—FG, Anderson 31, 12:45.
Second Quarter
Ind.—FG, Blanchard 30, 5:55.
Ind.—Belser 44 interception return (Blanchard kick), 8:12.
Ind.—FG, Blanchard 42, 13:00.
Ind.—FG, Blanchard 51, 14:57.
Third Quarter
Ind.—Harrison 20 pass from Bell (Blanchard kick), 8:49.
Fourth Quarter
Ind.—Faulk 7 run (Blanchard kick), :46.
Phi.—Fryar 8 pass from Rypien (Anderson kick), 14:55.
Attendance—52,689.

TEAM STATISTICS
	Philadelphia	Indianapolis
First Downs	18	19
Rushes-Yards	15-76	34-151
Passing	254	210
Punt Returns	3-40	1-0
Kickoff Returns	5-85	2-25
Interception Returns	0-0	3-64
Comp-Att-Int	27-47-3	19-28-0
Sacked-Yards Lost	1-4	1-9
Punts	6-46	4-43
Fumbles-Lost	0-0	1-0
Penalties-Yards	6-84	4-25
Time of Possession	25:54	34:06

INDIVIDUAL STATISTICS
RUSHING—Philadelphia, Watters 7-33, Garner 6-32, Detmer 2-11. Indianapolis, Faulk 16-101, Workman 13-38, Groce 2-3, Justin 1-6, Harrison 1-4, Bell 1-(minus 1).
PASSING—Philadelphia, Detmer 17-34-3-182, Rypien 10-13-0-76. Indianapolis, Justin 14-23-0-144, Bell 5-5-0-75.
RECEIVING—Philadelphia, Fryar 6-44, Jones 5-70, Turner 5-56, Solomon 3-39, Watters 3-22, Garner 3-18, Seay 2-9. Indianapolis, Faulk 7-40, Harrison 6-106, Dawkins 3-45, Bailey 1-13, Stablein 1-10, Workman 1-5.
MISSED FIELD GOAL ATTEMPTS—None.
INTERCEPTIONS—Indianapolis, Belser 2-45, Alberts 1-19.
KICKOFF RETURNS—Philadelphia, Witherspoon 5-85. Indianapolis, Bailey 2-25.
PUNT RETURNS—Philadelphia, Seay 3-40. Indianapolis, Stablein 1-0.
SACKS—Philadelphia, W. Fuller 1. Indianapolis, Bennett 1.

FALCONS 31, SAINTS 15
Sunday, December 8

Atlanta	7	7	7	10—31
New Orleans	3	0	6	6—15

First Quarter
N.O.—FG, Brien 34, 8:36.
Atl.—Lyons 3 pass from Hebert (Andersen kick), 13:00.
Second Quarter
Atl.—Metcalf 4 pass from Hebert (Andersen kick), 14:31.
Third Quarter
Atl.—Heyward 1 run (Andersen kick), 3:08.
N.O.—Guess 57 pass from Nussmeier (pass failed), 12:35.
Fourth Quarter
Atl.—Emanuel 3 pass from Hebert (Andersen kick), 4:53.
Atl.—FG, Andersen 33, 8:57.
N.O.—Bates 4 run (pass failed), 12:55.
Attendance—32,923.

TEAM STATISTICS
	Atlanta	New Orleans
First Downs	19	14
Rushes-Yards	25-122	21-83
Passing	182	168
Punt Returns	3-43	1-7
Kickoff Returns	3-59	5-114
Interception Returns	1-2	2-17
Comp-Att-Int	20-29-2	21-36-1
Sacked-Yards Lost	2-16	1-3
Punts	4-43	7-39
Fumbles-Lost	3-1	2-1
Penalties-Yards	9-70	12-76
Time of Possession	30:31	29:29

INDIVIDUAL STATISTICS
RUSHING—Atlanta, Anderson 13-71, Heyward 9-47, Hebert 3-4. New Orleans, Bates 14-70, Whittle 4-8, Hunter 2-6, Guess 1-(minus 1).
PASSING—Atlanta, Hebert 20-29-2-198. New Orleans, Nussmeier 21-35-1-171, Hunter 0-1-0-0.
RECEIVING—Atlanta, Emanuel 5-22, Anderson 4-39, Mathis 3-42, Birden 3-30, Heyward 2-49, Metcalf 2-13, Lyons 1-3. New Orleans, Neal 6-19, Whittle 4-23, DeRamus 3-49, Bates 3-6, Guess 1-57, T. Johnson 1-12, Small 1-12, Hunter 1-9, Lusk 1-4.
MISSED FIELD GOAL ATTEMPTS—New Orleans, Brien 41.
INTERCEPTIONS—Atlanta, Bush 1-2. New Orleans, Tubbs 1-11, G. Jackson 1-6.
KICKOFF RETURNS—Atlanta, Preston 2-41, Heyward 1-18. New Orleans, Hughes 4-106, B. Smith 1-8.
PUNT RETURNS—Atlanta, Metcalf 3-43. New Orleans, Guess 1-7.
SACKS—Atlanta, Hall 1. New Orleans, Mickell 1, Martin 1.

GIANTS 17, DOLPHINS 7
Sunday, December 8

N.Y. Giants	7	7	3	0—17
Miami	7	0	0	0— 7

First Quarter
NYG—Hampton 4 run (Daluiso kick), 6:08.
Mia.—R. Wilson 3 pass from Marino (Nedney kick), 14:24.
Second Quarter
NYG—Cross 1 pass from Brown (Daluiso kick), 13:45.
Third Quarter
NYG—FG, Daluiso 37, 13:22.
Attendance—63,889.

TEAM STATISTICS

	N.Y. Giants	Miami
First Downs	21	15
Rushes-Yards	41-131	20-103
Passing	149	191
Punt Returns	3-34	1-1
Kickoff Returns	1-21	1-22
Interception Returns	2-33	0-0
Comp-Att-Int	21-28-0	16-30-2
Sacked-Yards Lost	4-20	3-18
Punts	4-46	4-42
Fumbles-Lost	2-1	1-0
Penalties-Yards	3-16	7-47
Time of Possession	36:28	23:32

INDIVIDUAL STATISTICS

RUSHING—New York, Hampton 20-60, Wheatley 13-59, Way 4-9, Brown 4-3. Miami, Abdul-Jabbar 17-96, Marino 1-7, Pritchett 1-1, Parmalee 1-(minus 1).

PASSING—New York, Brown 21-28-0-169. Miami, Marino 16-30-2-209.

RECEIVING—New York, Way 6-56, Cross 5-23, Dawsey 3-40, Lewis 2-17, Calloway 2-13, Hampton 2-6, Saxton 1-14. Miami, Barnett 4-139, McDuffie 3-22, Abdul-Jabbar 2-14, Parmalee 2-14, Pritchett 2-6, R. Hill 1-8, Drayton 1-3, R. Wilson 1-3.

MISSED FIELD GOAL ATTEMPTS—None.

INTERCEPTIONS—New York, C. Hamilton 1-29, Widmer 1-4.

KICKOFF RETURNS—New York, Wheatley 1-21. Miami, Spikes 1-22.

PUNT RETURNS—New York, Marshall 3-34. Miami, Buckley 1-1.

SACKS—New York, K. Hamilton 1, Bratzke 1, Strahan 1. Miami, Armstrong 2½, Bowens 1, Jackson ½.

PACKERS 41, BRONCOS 6
Sunday, December 8

Denver	3	0	3	0— 6
Green Bay	3	10	7	21—41

First Quarter
G.B.—FG, Jacke 33, 7:03.
Den.—FG, Elam 40, 12:11.

Second Quarter
G.B.—FG, Jacke 22, 13:06.
G.B.—Freeman 14 pass from Favre (Jacke kick), 14:43.

Third Quarter
Den.—FG, Elam 39, 3:04.
G.B.—Freeman 51 pass from Favre (Jacke kick), 6:12.

Fourth Quarter
G.B.—Jackson 1 pass from Favre (Jacke kick), :44.
G.B.—Freeman 25 pass from Favre (Jacke kick), 7:39.
G.B.—Beebe fumble recovery in end zone (Jacke kick), 9:33.
Attendance—60,712.

TEAM STATISTICS

	Denver	Green Bay
First Downs	9	22
Rushes-Yards	24-93	29-103
Passing	83	276
Punt Returns	1-6	2-24
Kickoff Returns	8-153	3-45
Interception Returns	2-14	0-0
Comp-Att-Int	13-24-0	20-38-2
Sacked-Yards Lost	3-23	1-4
Punts	5-35	2-39
Fumbles-Lost	4-3	2-0
Penalties-Yards	10-65	7-45
Time of Possession	27:25	32:35

INDIVIDUAL STATISTICS

RUSHING—Denver, Davis 14-54, Hebron 7-30, Musgrave 1-6, Lewis 1-4, Craver 1-(minus 1). Green Bay, Levens 14-86, Bennett 9-5, Jervey 3-7, Favre 2-2, Henderson 1-3.

PASSING—Denver, Musgrave 12-21-0-101, Lewis 1-3-0-5. Green Bay, Favre 20-38-2-280.

RECEIVING—Denver, Sharpe 4-34, McCaffrey 3-41, Miller 2-18, Sherrard 1-7, R. Smith 1-6, Hebron 1-5, Craver 1-(minus 5). Green Bay, Freeman 9-175, Chmura 4-70, Jackson 3-20, Levens 2-7, Rison 1-7, Henderson 1-1.

MISSED FIELD GOAL ATTEMPTS—None.

INTERCEPTIONS—Denver, Braxton 1-14, Atwater 1-0.

KICKOFF RETURNS—Denver, Hebron 6-119, Chamberlain 2-34. Green Bay, Howard 3-45.

PUNT RETURNS—Denver, R. Smith 1-6. Green Bay, Howard 2-24.

SACKS—Denver, A. Williams ½, Mobley ½. Green Bay, Evans 2, Butler 1.

BUCCANEERS 24, REDSKINS 10
Sunday, December 8

Washington	0	3	0	7—10
Tampa Bay	10	3	11	0—24

First Quarter
T.B.—Harris 22 pass from Dilfer (Husted kick), 6:02.
T.B.—FG, Husted 42, 10:35.

Second Quarter
Was.—FG, Blanton 29, :05.
T.B.—FG, Husted 35, 15:00.

Third Quarter
T.B.—FG, Husted 19, 3:38.
T.B.—Alstott 13 run (Harris pass from Dilfer), 11:48.

Fourth Quarter
Was.—Ellard 3 pass from Frerotte (Blanton kick), 12:11.
Attendance—44,733.

TEAM STATISTICS

	Washington	Tampa Bay
First Downs	17	18
Rushes-Yards	16-41	45-209
Passing	206	92
Punt Returns	0-0	3-24
Kickoff Returns	5-69	2-84
Interception Returns	0-0	1-5
Comp-Att-Int	20-39-1	8-15-0
Sacked-Yards Lost	2-13	3-20
Punts	3-46	2-43
Fumbles-Lost	1-1	1-0
Penalties-Yards	4-30	5-42
Time of Possession	24:35	35:25

INDIVIDUAL STATISTICS

RUSHING—Washington, Allen 14-36, Mitchell 2-5. Tampa Bay, Rhett 28-97, Alstott 8-67, Dilfer 4-27, R. Brooks 3-10, Ellison 2-8.

PASSING—Washington, Frerotte 20-39-1-219. Tampa Bay, Dilfer 8-15-0-112.

RECEIVING—Washington, Ellard 5-93, B. Brooks 5-54, Asher 5-31, Mitchell 3-29, Allen 2-12. Tampa Bay, Alstott 3-24, Ellison 2-30, Hawkins 1-33, Harris 1-22, Moore 1-3.

MISSED FIELD GOAL ATTEMPTS—Washington, Blanton 45. Tampa Bay, Husted 35.

INTERCEPTIONS—Tampa Bay, Mayhew 1-5.

KICKOFF RETURNS—Washington, Mitchell 4-66, W. Bell 1-3. Tampa Bay, Williams 2-84.

PUNT RETURNS—Tampa Bay, Williams 3-24.

SACKS—Washington, Owens 2, Harvey 1. Tampa Bay, Nickerson 1, Curry 1.

BENGALS 21, RAVENS 14
Sunday, December 8

Baltimore	0	7	0	7—14
Cincinnati	0	10	0	11—21

Second Quarter
Bal.—Kinchen 23 pass from Testaverde (Stover kick), 1:27.
Cin.—Pickens 14 pass from Blake (Pelfrey kick), 6:53.
Cin.—FG, Pelfrey 23, 14:39.

Fourth Quarter
Cin.—FG, Pelfrey 26, 1:57.
Bal.—J. Lewis 6 pass from Testaverde (Stover kick), 5:20.
Cin.—McGee 1 pass from Blake (Hearst run), 11:51.
Attendance—43,022.

TEAM STATISTICS

	Baltimore	Cincinnati
First Downs	21	25
Rushes-Yards	25-123	31-93
Passing	199	267
Punt Returns	2-29	2-18
Kickoff Returns	5-72	2-28
Interception Returns	0-0	1-10
Comp-Att-Int	21-39-1	26-42-0
Sacked-Yards Lost	1-6	2-5
Punts	4-44	4-45
Fumbles-Lost	1-0	0-0
Penalties-Yards	4-37	1-5
Time of Possession	24:13	35:47

INDIVIDUAL STATISTICS

RUSHING—Baltimore, Morris 21-117, Testaverde 2-7, Alexander 1-1, Gardner 1-(minus 2). Cincinnati, Hearst 20-50, Blake 7-34, Milne 2-5, Carter 2-4.

PASSING—Baltimore, Testaverde 21-39-1-205. Cincinnati, Blake 26-42-0-272.

RECEIVING—Baltimore, Jackson 7-81, Morris 5-22, J. Lewis 4-50, Kinchen 2-32, Alexander 2-20, Gardner 1-0. Cincinnati, Scott 8-103, Pickens 7-75, Dunn 3-46, Milne 2-14, Carter 2-13, Hearst 1-11, Bieniemy 1-5, Sadowski 1-4, McGee 1-1.

MISSED FIELD GOAL ATTEMPTS—Baltimore, Stover 45. Cincinnati, Pelfrey 49.

INTERCEPTIONS—Cincinnati, Myers 1-10.

KICKOFF RETURNS—Baltimore, J. Lewis 2-49, Baldwin 1-18, Morris 1-3, Isaia 1-2. Cincinnati, Dunn 1-20, Battaglia 1-8.

PUNT RETURNS—Baltimore, J. Lewis 2-29. Cincinnati, Dunn 2-18.

SACKS—Baltimore, R. Lewis 1, Pleasant 1. Cincinnati, Orlando 1.

BEARS 35, RAMS 9
Sunday, December 8

St. Louis	0	3	0	6— 9
Chicago	7	0	14	14—35

First Quarter
Chi.—Conway 27 pass from Krieg (Jaeger kick), 9:49.

Second Quarter
St.L.—FG, Lohmiller 25, 13:03.

Third Quarter
Chi.—Salaam 3 run (Jaeger kick), 7:00.
Chi.—Krieg 1 run (Jaeger kick), 11:22.

Fourth Quarter
Chi.—Lowery fumble recovery in end zone (Jaeger kick), 1:36.
Chi.—Salaam 4 run (Jaeger kick), 10:34.
St.L.—Kennison 19 pass from Martin (run failed), 13:10.
Attendance—45,075.

TEAM STATISTICS

	St.Louis	Chicago
First Downs	17	22
Rushes-Yards	19-94	37-162
Passing	229	222
Punt Returns	5-34	2-15
Kickoff Returns	4-49	1-14
Interception Returns	1-0	1-0
Comp-Att-Int	24-42-1	17-25-1
Sacked-Yards Lost	2-12	1-4
Punts	5-36	5-43
Fumbles-Lost	1-1	2-0
Penalties-Yards	13-102	4-21
Time of Possession	26:52	33:08

INDIVIDUAL STATISTICS
RUSHING—St. Louis, Green 11-65, Phillips 5-8, Banks 2-1, Lyle 1-20. Chicago, Salaam 19-115, R. Harris 10-26, Green 5-14, Krieg 2-3, Conway 1-4.

PASSING—St. Louis, Banks 20-38-1-194, Martin 4-4-0-47. Chicago, Krieg 17-25-1-226.

RECEIVING—St. Louis, Kennison 8-102, Bruce 6-87, Laing 4-17, Thomas 2-12, Ross 1-19, Clay 1-9, Phillips 1-(minus 5). Chicago, Timpson 6-111, T. Carter 4-49, Conway 3-43, R. Harris 2-9, Engram 1-9, Krieg 1-5.

MISSED FIELD GOAL ATTEMPTS—St. Louis, Lohmiller 45.

INTERCEPTIONS—St. Louis, M. Walker 1-0. Chicago, Marshall 1-0.

KICKOFF RETURNS—St. Louis, Thomas 2-35, Kennison 1-11, Crawford 1-3. Chicago, Ja. Jackson 1-14.

PUNT RETURNS—St. Louis, Kennison 5-34. Chicago, Engram 2-15.

SACKS—St. Louis, Carter 1. Chicago, Flanigan 1, Spellman 1.

SEAHAWKS 26, BILLS 18
Sunday, December 8

Buffalo	0	8	0	10—18
Seattle	10	6	3	7—26

First Quarter
Sea.—Galloway 27 pass from Mirer (Peterson kick), 3:03.
Sea.—FG, Peterson 41, 11:15.

Second Quarter
Sea.—FG, Peterson 38, 1:01.
Sea.—FG, Peterson 22, 6:48.
Buf.—Moulds 37 pass from Kelly (Early pass from Kelly), 13:55.

Third Quarter
Sea.—FG, Peterson 30, 6:27.

Fourth Quarter
Buf.—FG, Christie 22, 3:24.
Sea.—Smith 12 run (Peterson kick), 6:19.
Buf.—Brantley 22 pass from Collins (Christie kick), 11:19.
Attendance—41,373.

TEAM STATISTICS

	Buffalo	Seattle
First Downs	21	11
Rushes-Yards	24-70	35-170
Passing	312	132
Punt Returns	4-67	3-15
Kickoff Returns	7-140	3-67
Interception Returns	0-0	3-89
Comp-Att-Int	28-48-3	9-23-0
Sacked-Yards Lost	9-58	2-15
Punts	7-39	9-46
Fumbles-Lost	2-2	0-0
Penalties-Yards	4-25	2-10
Time of Possession	30:45	29:15

INDIVIDUAL STATISTICS
RUSHING—Buffalo, T. Thomas 17-65, Holmes 4-4, Kelly 2-1, Collins 1-0. Seattle, Warren 21-116, Smith 10-27, Mirer 2-15, Pritchard 1-7, Galloway 1-5.

PASSING—Buffalo, Kelly 24-41-2-324, Collins 4-7-1-46. Seattle, Mirer 9-23-0-147.

RECEIVING—Buffalo, Early 6-79, Moulds 5-89, Copeland 4-62, Brantley 4-35, Johnson 3-59, Cline 3-22, T. Thomas 2-17, Reed 1-7. Seattle, Proehl 4-91, Warren 3-18, Galloway 1-27, R. Williams 1-11.

MISSED FIELD GOAL ATTEMPTS—Seattle, Peterson 27.

INTERCEPTIONS—Seattle, D. Williams 2-73, Bellamy 1-16.

KICKOFF RETURNS—Buffalo, Moulds 6-116, Copeland 1-24. Seattle, R. Harris 3-67.

PUNT RETURNS—Buffalo, Burris 4-67. Seattle, R. Harris 2-15, Galloway 1-0.

SACKS—Buffalo, Rogers 1, Irvin 1. Seattle, Sinclair 3, Kennedy 2, Edwards 2, McCrary 1, Blackmon 1.

PATRIOTS 34, JETS 10
Sunday, December 8

N.Y. Jets	0	3	7	0—10
New England	7	13	7	7—34

First Quarter
N.E.—Coates 2 pass from Bledsoe (Vinatieri kick), 9:17.

Second Quarter
N.E.—FG, Vinatieri 19, 1:53.
NYJ—FG, Lowery 27, 9:16.
N.E.—Martin 19 run (Vinatieri kick), 11:56.
N.E.—FG, Vinatieri 41, 14:58.

Third Quarter
NYJ—Johnson 4 pass from Foley (Lowery kick), 9:32.
N.E.—Law 38 interception return (Vinatieri kick), 12:36.

Fourth Quarter
N.E.—Grier 1 run (Vinatieri kick), 10:41.
Attendance—54,621.

TEAM STATISTICS

	N.Y. Jets	New England
First Downs	16	27
Rushes-Yards	14-42	33-119
Passing	202	248
Punt Returns	1-7	4-19
Kickoff Returns	7-132	3-70
Interception Returns	1-0	2-38
Comp-Att-Int	22-45-2	24-43-1
Sacked-Yards Lost	4-25	1-3
Punts	5-42	4-36
Fumbles-Lost	0-0	2-0
Penalties-Yards	10-64	9-55
Time of Possession	24:38	35:22

INDIVIDUAL STATISTICS
RUSHING—New York, Murrell 12-30, Foley 1-11, Hansen 1-1. New England, Martin 21-94, Grier 7-19, Bledsoe 2-3, Gash 2-2, Meggett 1-1.

PASSING—New York, Foley 22-45-2-227. New England, Bledsoe 24-42-1-251, Grier 0-1-0-0.

RECEIVING—New York, Johnson 7-91, Chrebet 4-52, Slaughter 3-40, Brady 3-19, Van Dyke 2-17, Anderson 2-14, Murrell 1-(minus 6). New England, Glenn 7-66, Jefferson 5-91, Byars 4-37, Martin 3-13, Coates 2-18, Gash 2-14, Meggett 1-12.

MISSED FIELD GOAL ATTEMPTS—None.

INTERCEPTIONS—New York, Houston 1-0. New England, Law 1-38, Henderson 1-0.

KICKOFF RETURNS—New York, Cobb 5-102, Van Dyke 2-30. New England, Meggett 2-55, T. Brown 1-15.

PUNT RETURNS—New York, Chrebet 1-7. New England, Meggett 4-19.

SACKS—New York, B. Hamilton 1. New England, Sagapolutele 1, Bruschi 1, Milloy 1, Slade 1.

PANTHERS 30, 49ERS 24

Sunday, December 8

Carolina	10	17	3	0—30
San Francisco	0	17	0	7—24

First Quarter
Car.—Walls 5 pass from Collins (Kasay kick), 3:21.
Car.—FG, Kasay 18, 12:21.

Second Quarter
S.F.—Jones 1 pass from S. Young (Wilkins kick), 5:21.
Car.—Walls 5 pass from Collins (Kasay kick), 7:05.
S.F.—Owens 46 pass from S. Young (Wilkins kick), 10:46.
Car.—Green 20 pass from Collins (Kasay kick), 12:10.
Car.—FG, Kasay 26, 14:32.
S.F.—FG, Wilkins 31, 15:00.

Third Quarter
Car.—FG, Kasay 33, 7:46.

Fourth Quarter
S.F.—Rice 5 pass from S. Young (Wilkins kick), 8:38.
Attendance—66,291.

	Carolina	San Francisco
First Downs	22	23
Rushes-Yards	33-58	13-75
Passing	324	375
Punt Returns	2-13	2-6
Kickoff Returns	4-105	7-130
Interception Returns	2-35	0-0
Comp-Att-Int	22-37-0	27-41-2
Sacked-Yards Lost	1-3	5-18
Punts	3-46	4-46
Fumbles-Lost	0-0	2-2
Penalties-Yards	7-35	14-121
Time of Possession	32:30	27:30

INDIVIDUAL STATISTICS
RUSHING—Carolina, Johnson 25-52, Collins 5-3, Griffith 2-2, Ismail 1-1. San Francisco, Kirby 6-10, S. Young 5-63, Floyd 2-2.
PASSING—Carolina, Collins 22-37-0-327. San Francisco, S. Young 27-41-2-393.
RECEIVING—Carolina, Green 7-157, Walls 5-35, Carrier 4-83, Ismail 2-40, Oliver 2-9, Griffith 1-3, Johnson 1-0. San Francisco, Rice 10-129, Jones 6-68, Owens 5-110, Kirby 5-80, Popson 1-6.
MISSED FIELD GOAL ATTEMPTS—Carolina, Kasay 45, 31.
INTERCEPTIONS—Carolina, Cota 1-35, Davis 1-0.
KICKOFF RETURNS—Carolina, Bates 3-99, S. Greene 1-6. San Francisco, D. Carter 7-130.
PUNT RETURNS—Carolina, Oliver 2-13. San Francisco, D. Carter 2-6.
SACKS—Carolina, Lathon 2, Mills 1, Cook 1, K. Greene 1. San Francisco, Barker 1.

STEELERS 16, CHARGERS 3

Sunday, December 8

San Diego	0	0	3	0— 3
Pittsburgh	6	7	0	3—16

First Quarter
Pit.—FG, N. Johnson 49, 4:51.
Pit.—FG, N. Johnson 39, 11:31.

Second Quarter
Pit.—Hastings 11 pass from Tomczak (N. Johnson kick), 13:57.

Third Quarter
S.D.—FG, Carney 25, 11:04.

Fourth Quarter
Pit.—FG, N. Johnson 21, :48.
Attendance—56,368.

TEAM STATISTICS

	San Diego	Pittsburgh
First Downs	8	21
Rushes-Yards	23-65	37-167
Passing	83	160
Punt Returns	2-53	5-4
Kickoff Returns	2-39	1-24
Interception Returns	3-62	1-28
Comp-Att-Int	10-29-1	16-33-3
Sacked-Yards Lost	5-42	0-0
Punts	8-41	5-47
Fumbles-Lost	4-3	3-1
Penalties-Yards	7-74	6-43
Time of Possession	24:06	35:54

INDIVIDUAL STATISTICS
RUSHING—San Diego, Russell 16-35, Fletcher 3-17, Salisbury 2-15, Hayden 2-(minus 2). Pittsburgh, Pegram 17-83, Bettis 16-71, Stewart 2-14, Lester 1-1, Tomczak 1-(minus 2).
PASSING—San Diego, Salisbury 10-29-1-125. Pittsburgh, Tomczak 15-31-3-153, Stewart 1-2-0-7.
RECEIVING—San Diego, Fletcher 3-24, Jones 2-19, Martin 2-10, A. Coleman 1-50, Roche 1-19, Mitchell 1-3. Pittsburgh, Hastings 6-63, C. Johnson 4-67, Pegram 2-16, Bettis 2-6, Botkin 1-4, Witman 1-4.
MISSED FIELD GOAL ATTEMPTS—None.
INTERCEPTIONS—San Diego, Da. Gordon 2-55, Ross 1-7. Pittsburgh, Perry 1-28.
KICKOFF RETURNS—San Diego, A. Coleman 2-39. Pittsburgh, Pegram 1-24.
PUNT RETURNS—San Diego, Da. Gordon 2-53. Pittsburgh, Hastings 5-4.
SACKS—Pittsburgh, Brown 2, Gildon 2, Oldham 1.

JAGUARS 23, OILERS 17

Sunday, December 8

Jacksonville	7	3	7	6—23
Houston	0	7	0	10—17

First Quarter
Jac.—Means 1 run (Hollis kick), 6:04.

Second Quarter
Hou.—Harmon 23 pass from McNair (Del Greco kick), 3:27.
Jac.—FG, Hollis 34, 13:11.

Third Quarter
Jac.—Means 5 run (Hollis kick), 14:00.

Fourth Quarter
Hou.—George 6 run (Del Greco kick), 1:49.
Jac.—FG, Hollis 38, 8:47.
Jac.—FG, Hollis 31, 13:04.
Hou.—FG, Del Greco 27, 14:49.
Attendance—20,196.

TEAM STATISTICS

	Jacksonville	Houston
First Downs	18	21
Rushes-Yards	35-114	21-74
Passing	165	289
Punt Returns	1-20	1-7
Kickoff Returns	3-70	5-124
Interception Returns	1-21	0-0
Comp-Att-Int	15-25-0	24-37-1
Sacked-Yards Lost	3-7	4-19
Punts	3-47	3-44
Fumbles-Lost	1-1	4-3
Penalties-Yards	2-10	5-45
Time of Possession	30:44	29:16

INDIVIDUAL STATISTICS
RUSHING—Jacksonville, Means 25-67, Brunell 10-47. Houston, George 16-45, McNair 3-20, Harmon 2-9.
PASSING—Jacksonville, Brunell 15-25-0-172. Houston, McNair 24-37-1-308.
RECEIVING—Jacksonville, Smith 5-61, McCardell 3-68, Mitchell 3-23, Brown 2-7, W. Jackson 1-11, Means 1-2. Houston, Sanders 7-127, Harmon 6-75, Wycheck 3-24, R. Lewis 2-19, George 2-18, Davis 2-16, Russell 1-19, Wilson 1-10.
MISSED FIELD GOAL ATTEMPTS—Jacksonville, Hollis 51. Houston, De Greco 44.
INTERCEPTIONS—Jacksonville, Hudson 1-21.
KICKOFF RETURNS—Jacksonville, B. Brooks 3-70. Houston, Gray 3-93, Harmon 2-31.
PUNT RETURNS—Jacksonville, Hudson 1-20. Houston, Gray 1-7.
SACKS—Jacksonville, Hardy 1½, Brackens 1, Pritchett 1, Davey ½. Houston, Cook 2, Wortham 1.

COWBOYS 10, CARDINALS 6

Sunday, December 8

Dallas	0	0	7	3—10
Arizona	3	3	0	0— 6

First Quarter
Ariz.—FG, Butler 33, 7:54.

Second Quarter
Ariz.—FG, Butler 28, 14:58.

Third Quarter
Dal.—Irvin 50 pass from Aikman (Boniol kick), 9:53.

Fourth Quarter
Dal.—FG, Boniol 31, 6:19.
Attendance—70,763.

TEAM STATISTICS

	Dallas	Arizona
First Downs	15	20
Rushes-Yards	35-80	26-134
Passing	254	213
Punt Returns	1-6	2-11
Kickoff Returns	3-53	3-61
Interception Returns	2-8	0-0
Comp-Att-Int	15-24-0	18-36-2
Sacked-Yards Lost	1-1	2-11
Punts	6-44	5-51
Fumbles-Lost	2-2	4-2
Penalties-Yards	5-55	7-50
Time of Possession	30:22	29:38

INDIVIDUAL STATISTICS

RUSHING—Dallas, E. Smith 27-70, S. Williams 3-8, Aikman 3-1, Johnston 2-1. Arizona, McElroy 14-90, Centers 8-34, L. Johnson 3-10, Siason 1-0.

PASSING—Dallas, Aikman 15-24-0-255. Arizona, Esiason 18-36-2-224.

RECEIVING—Dallas, Irvin 8-198, K. Williams 3-29, Martin 1-12, Bjornson 2-11, Armstrong 1-6, E. Smith 1-(minus 1). Arizona, Sanders 5-75, R. Moore 4-94, Centers 3-8, Carter 2-22, Anderson 1-17, Edwards 1-12, C. Smith 1-2, McElroy 1-(minus 6).

MISSED FIELD GOAL ATTEMPTS—None.

INTERCEPTIONS—Dallas, Woodson 1-7, Teague 1-0.

KICKOFF RETURNS—Dallas, K. Williams 2-53, Walker 1-0. Arizona, McElroy 2-50, L. Johnson 1-11.

PUNT RETURNS—Dallas, Martin 1-6. Arizona, Edwards 2-11.

SACKS—Dallas, Hennings 1, Tolbert 1. Arizona, Rice 1.

VIKINGS 24, LIONS 22
Sunday, December 8

Minnesota	3	14	0	7—24
Detroit	0	10	3	9—22

First Quarter
Min.—FG, Sisson 31, 7:44.

Second Quarter
Min.—Lee 3 pass from B. Johnson (Sisson kick), 2:48.
Det.—Morton 15 pass from Mitchell (Hanson kick), 6:00.
Min.—Reed 13 pass from B. Johnson (Sisson kick), 12:33.
Det.—FG, Hanson 30, 14:44.

Third Quarter
Det.—FG, Hanson 48, 13:44.

Fourth Quarter
Det.—FG, Hanson 31, 6:29.
Min.—Carter 30 pass from B. Johnson (Sisson kick), 10:04.
Det.—Sanders 2 run (pass failed), 12:26.
Attendance—46,043.

TEAM STATISTICS

	Minnesota	Detroit
First Downs	21	23
Rushes-Yards	31-116	23-145
Passing	173	235
Punt Returns	1-11	1-2
Kickoff Returns	5-95	4-130
Interception Returns	0-0	0-0
Comp-Att-Int	19-29-0	21-31-0
Sacked-Yards Lost	2-22	3-15
Punts	3-43	2-39
Fumbles-Lost	0-0	0-0

	Minnesota	Detroit
Penalties-Yards	2-20	7-56
Time of Possession	31:39	28:21

INDIVIDUAL STATISTICS

RUSHING—Minnesota, Hoard 17-66, B. Johnson 7-18, Graham 4-19, Lee 3-13. Detroit, Sanders 20-134, Mitchell 2-10, Rivers 1-1.

PASSING—Minnesota, B. Johnson 19-29-0-195. Detroit, Mitchell 21-31-0-250.

RECEIVING—Minnesota, Carter 7-83, Lee 3-33, Reed 3-32, Evans 2-11, Palmer 2-9, Hoard 1-18, Ismail 1-9. Detroit, H. Moore 9-126, Perriman 7-42, Morton 4-68, Price 1-14.

MISSED FIELD GOAL ATTEMPTS—Detroit, Hanson 48.

INTERCEPTIONS—None.

KICKOFF RETURNS—Minnesota, Palmer 2-60, Ismail 1-20, Brown 1-12, Carter 1-3. Detroit, Milburn 4-130.

PUNT RETURNS—Minnesota, Palmer 1-11. Detroit, Milburn 1-2.

SACKS—Minnesota, F. Smith 2, Barnett 1. Detroit, Elliss 1, Porcher 1.

RAIDERS 26, CHIEFS 7
Monday, December 9

Kansas City	0	0	0	7— 7
Oakland	10	0	16	0—26

First Quarter
Oak.—A. Glover 1 pass from Hostetler (Ford kick), 8:01.
Oak.—FG, Ford 43, 11:13.

Third Quarter
Oak.—Safety, Gannon tackled in end zone, :27.
Oak.—Fenner 23 pass from Hostetler (Ford kick), 10:29.
Oak.—T. Brown 34 pass from Hostetler (Ford kick), 14:08.

Fourth Quarter
K.C.—LaChapelle 12 pass from Gannon (Stoyanovich kick), :37.
Attendance—57,082.

TEAM STATISTICS

	Kansas City	Oakland
First Downs	13	15
Rushes-Yards	23-98	37-170
Passing	71	145
Punt Returns	3-29	2-49
Kickoff Returns	5-118	3-58
Interception Returns	0-0	1-21
Comp-Att-Int	12-33-1	13-27-0
Sacked-Yards Lost	3-17	1-5
Punts	7-40	5-42
Fumbles-Lost	0-0	1-0
Penalties-Yards	11-96	6-39
Time of Possession	25:45	34:15

INDIVIDUAL STATISTICS

RUSHING—Kansas City, Allen 14-64, Hill 6-22, Gannon 3-12. Oakland, Williams 18-35, Kaufman 8-109, Aska 4-14, Fenner 4-3, Hostetler 1-5, T. Brown 1-4, Araguz 1-0.

PASSING—Kansas City, Gannon 12-33-1-88. Oakland, Hostetler 13-27-0-150.

RECEIVING—Kansas City, Anders 5-25, McNair 3-24, LaChapelle 2-31, Allen 1-4, Cash 1-4. Oakland, Dudley 4-27, T. Brown 3-67, A. Glover 2-11, Fenner 1-23, Kaufman 1-10, Jett 1-8, Williams 1-4.

MISSED FIELD GOAL ATTEMPTS—Kansas City, Stoyanovich 37. Oakland, Ford 48.

INTERCEPTIONS—Oakland, Carrington 1-21.

KICKOFF RETURNS—Kansas City, Vanover 4-101, Anders 1-17. Oakland, Kaufman 2-34, T. Brown 1-24.

PUNT RETURNS—Kansas City, Vanover 3-29. Oakland, T. Brown 2-49.

SACKS—Kansas City, N. Smith 1. Oakland, McGlockton 2, Lewis 1.

WEEK 16

RESULTS

CHICAGO 27, San Diego 14
Philadelphia 21, N.Y. JETS 20
ARIZONA 27, Washington 26
CAROLINA 27, Baltimore 16
Cincinnati 21, HOUSTON 13
DALLAS 12, New England 6
DENVER 24, Oakland 19
Green Bay 31, DETROIT 3
Indianapolis 24, KANSAS CITY 19
JACKSONVILLE 20, Seattle 13
MINNESOTA 21, Tampa Bay 10
New Orleans 17, N.Y. GIANTS 3
St. Louis 34, ATLANTA 27
San Francisco 25, PITTSBURGH 15
MIAMI 16, Buffalo 14

STANDINGS

AFC EAST

	W	L	T	Pct.
New England	10	5	0	.667
Buffalo	9	6	0	.600
Indianapolis	9	6	0	.600
Miami	7	8	0	.467
N.Y. Jets	1	14	0	.067

AFC CENTRAL

	W	L	T	Pct.
Pittsburgh	10	5	0	.667
Jacksonville	8	7	0	.533
Cincinnati	7	8	0	.467
Houston	7	8	0	.467
Baltimore	4	11	0	.267

AFC WEST

	W	L	T	Pct.
Denver	13	2	0	.867
Kansas City	9	6	0	.600
Oakland	7	8	0	.467
San Diego	7	8	0	.467
Seattle	6	9	0	.400

NFC EAST

	W	L	T	Pct.
Dallas	10	5	0	.667
Philadelphia	9	6	0	.600
Washington	8	7	0	.533
Arizona	7	8	0	.467
N.Y. Giants	6	9	0	.400

NFC CENTRAL

	W	L	T	Pct.
Green Bay	12	3	0	.800
Minnesota	9	6	0	.600
Chicago	7	8	0	.467
Detroit	5	10	0	.333
Tampa Bay	5	10	0	.333

NFC WEST

	W	L	T	Pct.
Carolina	11	4	0	.733
San Francisco	11	4	0	.733
St. Louis	5	10	0	.333
Atlanta	3	12	0	.200
New Orleans	3	12	0	.200

HIGHLIGHTS

Hero of the week: Steve Young, who had suffered a number of injuries during the season—including a career-threatening concussion—turned in a vintage performance in the 49ers' 25-15 victory over the Steelers. Young threw three first-half touchdown passes, including a 20-yarder to Terrell Owens to push the 49ers' lead to 22-0 right before halftime. For the game, Young was 24-of-36 for 253 yards.

Goat of the week: Atlanta quarterback Bobby Hebert threw a last-second interception in the end zone in the Falcons' 34-27 loss to the Rams. The Falcons had the ball at the Rams' 7 with one second left, when Hebert dropped back and tossed a desperation pass into the end zone that was picked off by safety Keith Lyle. The interception was Hebert's sixth of the day, overshadowing his career-best 363 passing yards.

Sub of the week: Pittsburgh's Erric Pegram rushed 20 times for 103 yards in a losing effort against San Francisco. Pegram stepped in for Jerome Bettis, who was limited to six carries because of a sprained ankle. Pegram's performance was the first 100-yard game allowed by the 49ers in 21 games.

Comeback of the week: The Jets, fueled by derogatory remarks by Eagles quarterback Ty Detmer earlier in the week, held a 20-7 lead after three quarters. Detmer, aided by four interceptions by the defense, helped save the day by throwing two fourth-quarter touchdown passes to pull the Eagles even at 20-20. Kicker Gary Anderson tacked on the extra point to complete the comeback, 21-20.

Blowout of the week: The Packers, powered by the punt returns of Desmond Howard and the passing of Brett Favre, cruised by division rival Detroit, 31-3. Green Bay opened quietly, with a 20-yard field goal by Chris Jacke, before Howard busted a 92-yard punt return for a touchdown in the second quarter—striking a Heisman pose once he reached the end zone. Howard finished with 167 yards on punt returns to complement Favre's two touchdowns—a 1-yard run and a 27-yard strike to receiver Antonio Freeman.

Nail-biter of the week: Washington's Scott Blanton connected on his fourth field goal for a 26-24 lead mid way through the fourth quarter. On the ensuing drive quarterback Kent Graham moved the Cardinals down field, picking up first downs on 16- and 12-yard completions and a facemask penalty. Leeland McElroy ran a 21-yard sweep to Washington's 14 to set up kicker Kevin Butler, who hit a 28-yarder for the 27-26 victory. The loss eliminated the Redskins from playoff contention.

Hit of the week: In the fourth quarter against Seattle Jaguars quarterback Mark Brunell passed to receiver Jimmy Smith in the end zone. But cornerback Fred Thomas had Smith covered and appeared to have intercepted the pass, when teammate Darryl Williams ran into him, jarring the ball loose to Smith, who held on for a 39-yard touchdown reception. Kicker Mike Hollis added the extra point to give the Jaguars a 14-13 lead.

Oddity of the week: Against Denver, the Raiders nearly achieved a dubious record. Oakland committed 20 penalties, two short of the NFL record of 22 shared by the Brooklyn Dodgers and Chicago Bears, who set the mark in games played in 1944. Oakland's 20 penalties were the most since October 27, 1976, when Tampa Bay was called for 20 against Seattle.

Top rusher: The Saints' Mario Bates rushed 32 times for 129 yards and one touchdown in a 17-3 win over the Giants.

Top passer: Atlanta's Hebert was 28-of-49 for 363 yards and two touchdown passes in the Falcons' loss to St. Louis.

Top receiver: Rookie Eddie Kennison caught five passes for 226 yards and three touchdowns in the Rams' victory.

Notes: Colts receiver Marvin Harrison tied a team record with three touchdown receptions against the Chiefs. . . . Houston's Al Del Greco made his 30th and 31st field goals of the season, breaking his club single season record of 29. . . . Isaac Bruce's two receptions against Atlanta pushed his career total to 217 receptions setting an NFL record for most receptions in the first three years of a career, breaking Andre Rison's mark of 215. . . . Tampa Bay's defense surrendered more than 300 yards for the first time in eight games. . . . John Elway recorded his 126th career victory, passing Fran Tarkenton for the most in NFL history. . . . Buffalo's Steve Christie missed a field goal inside the 30 for just the fourth time in 60 career attempts. . . . The Cowboys' offense failed to score a touchdown for the third time in five games. . . . Desmond Howard's 167 yards on punt returns pushed his season total to 791 yards, shattering the single-season NFL record of 692 by Miami's Fulton Walker in 1985. . . . Saints coach Rick Venturi won his second game in 18 tries as an NFL coach.

Quote of the week: Detroit safety Bennie Blades, on seeing Packers fans in the Silverdome: "Every time I looked up, I saw those cheeseheads and that awful green color. No matter where you go, you're fighting like you're in a doghouse. But, hey, they support their team."

GAME SUMMARIES

EAGLES 21, JETS 20
Saturday, December 14

Philadelphia	0	0	7	14—21
N.Y. Jets	7	3	10	0—20

First Quarter
NYJ—Johnson 46 pass from Foley (Lowery kick), 12:54.
Second Quarter
NYJ—FG, Lowery 27, 10:38.
Third Quarter
Phi.—Fryar 40 pass from Detmer (Anderson kick), 7:17.
NYJ—Glenn 13 interception return (Lowery kick), 10:55.
NYJ—FG, Lowery 29, 14:57.
Fourth Quarter
Phi.—Jones 3 pass from Detmer (Anderson kick), 7:56.
Phi.—Fryar 14 pass from Detmer (Anderson kick), 9:31.
Attendance—29,178.

TEAM STATISTICS
	Philadelphia	N.Y. Jets
First Downs	15	14
Rushes-Yards	33-151	23-53
Passing	172	173
Punt Returns	1-9	2-15
Kickoff Returns	4-80	4-73
Interception Returns	4-20	2-36
Comp-Att-Int	17-34-2	16-26-4
Sacked-Yards Lost	4-26	2-13
Punts	7-37	5-52
Fumbles-Lost	4-2	1-1
Penalties-Yards	10-87	8-41
Time of Possession	32:09	27:51

INDIVIDUAL STATISTICS
RUSHING—Philadelphia, Watters 17-75, Garner 8-58, Detmer 7-12, Turner 1-6. New York, Murrell 18-46, Foley 5-7.
PASSING—Philadelphia, Detmer 17-34-2-198. New York, Foley 16-26-4-186.
RECEIVING—Philadelphia, Fryar 4-92, Jones 4-39, Watters 3-13, Turner 3-11, Garner 2-12, J. Johnson 1-31. New York, Johnson 4-77, Chrebet 4-59, Brady 3-15, Slaughter 2-30, Anderson 2-3, Murrell 1-2.
MISSED FIELD GOAL ATTEMPTS—Philadelphia, Anderson 48. New York, Lowery 48.
INTERCEPTIONS—Philadelphia, Zordich 2-14, W. Thomas 1-7, Taylor 1- (minus 1). New York, Coleman 1-23, Glenn 1-13.
KICKOFF RETURNS—Philadelphia, Witherspoon 4-80. New York, Cobb 2-18, Murrell 1-32, Van Dyke 1-23.
PUNT RETURNS—Philadelphia, Seay 1-9. New York, Chrebet 2-15.
SACKS—Philadelphia, W. Thomas 1, Mamula 1. New York, Douglas 3, Cascadden 1.

BEARS 27, CHARGERS 14
Saturday, December 14

San Diego	7	7	0	0—14
Chicago	14	0	3	10—27

First Quarter
S.D.—A. Coleman 20 pass from Humphries (Carney kick), 2:22.
Chi.—Engram 7 pass from Krieg (Jaeger kick), 6:33.
Chi.—Conway 7 pass from Krieg (Jaeger kick), 13:23.
Second Quarter
S.D.—Russell 1 run (Carney kick), 2:33.
Third Quarter
Chi.—FG, Jaeger 45, 8:55.
Fourth Quarter
Chi.—Wetnight 8 pass from Krieg (Jaeger kick), :07.
Chi.—FG, Jaeger 40, 13:56.
Attendance—49,763.

TEAM STATISTICS
	San Diego	Chicago
First Downs	17	19
Rushes-Yards	23-66	28-91
Passing	217	203
Punt Returns	3-33	2-36
Kickoff Returns	5-56	2-95
Interception Returns	0-0	1-0
Comp-Att-Int	23-38-1	24-38-0
Sacked-Yards Lost	0-0	2-14
Punts	4-42	4-43
Fumbles-Lost	0-0	0-0
Penalties-Yards	3-24	7-71
Time of Possession	27:31	32:29

INDIVIDUAL STATISTICS
RUSHING—San Diego, Fletcher 17-37, Russell 5-22, A. Coleman 1-7. Chicago, R. Harris 21-64, Salaam 5-7, Conway 1-19, Krieg 1-1.
PASSING—San Diego, Humphries 23-38-1-217. Chicago, Krieg 24-38-0-217.
RECEIVING—San Diego, Martin 9-74, A. Coleman 4-61, Fletcher 4-13, Russell 2-42, May 1-13, Ellison 1-6, Roche 1-6, Mitchell 1-2. Chicago, Engram 5-61, Timpson 5-51, R. Harris 5-36, T. Carter 3-15, Cash 2-27, Wetnight 2-14, Conway 2-13.
MISSED FIELD GOAL ATTEMPTS—San Diego, Carney 48, 26.
INTERCEPTIONS—Chicago, Woolford 1-0.
KICKOFF RETURNS—San Diego, A. Coleman 4-56, Edwards 1-0. Chicago, Ja. Jackson 2-95.
PUNT RETURNS—San Diego, Da. Gordon 3-33. Chicago, Engram 2-36.
SACKS—San Diego, Seau 2.

COWBOYS 12, PATRIOTS 6
Sunday, December 15

New England	6	0	0	0— 6
Dallas	3	3	6	0—12

First Quarter
N.E.—FG, Vinatieri 21, 5:46.
N.E.—FG, Vinatieri 30, 9:04.
Dal.—FG, Boniol 23, 13:40.
Second Quarter
Dal.—FG, Boniol 36, 12:54.
Third Quarter
Dal.—FG, Boniol 35, 7:34.
Dal.—FG, Boniol 29, 10:02.
Attendance—64,578.

TEAM STATISTICS
	New England	Dallas
First Downs	16	16
Rushes-Yards	21-101	35-107
Passing	178	144
Punt Returns	3-27	2-15
Kickoff Returns	5-78	3-106
Interception Returns	2-7	3-37
Comp-Att-Int	20-40-3	16-28-2
Sacked-Yards Lost	0-0	3-25
Punts	3-38	4-46
Fumbles-Lost	1-1	0-0
Penalties-Yards	4-29	8-67
Time of Possession	24:57	35:03

INDIVIDUAL STATISTICS
RUSHING—New England, Martin 20-91, Meggett 1-10. Dallas, E. Smith 27-85, S. Williams 4-15, Aikman 3-(minus 2), K. Williams 1-9.

PASSING—New England, Bledsoe 20-40-3-178. Dallas, Aikman 16-28-2-169.

RECEIVING—New England, Glenn 8-83, Byars 5-46, Martin 3-19, Jefferson 2-21, T. Brown 1-9, Meggett 1-0. Dallas, Irvin 6-76, E. Smith 5-55, Johnston 3-15, K. Williams 1-19, Bjornson 1-4.

MISSED FIELD GOAL ATTEMPTS—None.

INTERCEPTIONS—New England, Law 2-7. Dallas, Woodson 2-22, Harper 1-15.

KICKOFF RETURNS—New England, Meggett 5-78. Dallas, Walker 2-89, K. Williams 1-17.

PUNT RETURNS—New England, Meggett 3-27. Dallas, Martin 2-15.

SACKS—New England, McGinest 1, Slade 1, Collons 1/2, Sabb 1/2.

49ERS 25, STEELERS 15
Sunday, December 15

San Francisco	16	6	0	3—25
Pittsburgh	0	0	8	7—15

First Quarter
S.F.—Rice 4 pass from S. Young (Wilkins kick), 3:31.
S.F.—Safety, Tomczak sacked by B. Young, 4:55.
S.F.—Floyd 4 pass from S. Young (Wilkins kick), 5:53.

Second Quarter
S.F.—Owens 20 pass from S. Young (pass failed), 13:25.

Third Quarter
Pit.—Bettis 1 run (C. Johnson pass from Tomczak), 11:34.

Fourth Quarter
S.F.—FG, Wilkins 22, 7:04.
Pit.—Stewart 42 pass from Tomczak (N. Johnson kick), 8:56.
Attendance—59,823.

TEAM STATISTICS

	San Francisco	Pittsburgh
First Downs	21	23
Rushes-Yards	24-56	28-120
Passing	232	248
Punt Returns	1-3	2-9
Kickoff Returns	3-67	5-63
Interception Returns	2-12	0-0
Comp-Att-Int	24-36-0	23-43-2
Sacked-Yards Lost	3-21	1-5
Punts	6-44	4-42
Fumbles-Lost	0-0	1-1
Penalties-Yards	5-40	7-85
Time of Possession	31:30	28:30

INDIVIDUAL STATISTICS

RUSHING—San Francisco, Kirby 11-20, S. Young 6-22, Floyd 5-8, Rice 2-6. Pittsburgh, Pegram 20-103, Bettis 6-9, Tomczak 1-6, Lester 1-2.

PASSING—San Francisco, S. Young 24-36-0-253. Pittsburgh, Tomczak 23-43-2-253.

RECEIVING—San Francisco, Rice 8-63, Jones 6-93, Kirby 5-44, Owens 3-45, Floyd 2-8. Pittsburgh, Hastings 8-63, C. Johnson 4-57, Pegram 4-20, Mills 3-31, Stewart 2-56, Botkin 2-26.

MISSED FIELD GOAL ATTEMPTS—San Francisco, Wilkins 39.

INTERCEPTIONS—San Francisco, Drakeford 1-11, Doleman 1-1.

KICKOFF RETURNS—San Francisco, Loville 2-45, Kirby 1-22. Pittsburgh, Pegram 3-35, Mills 2-28.

PUNT RETURNS—San Francisco, Kirby 1-3. Pittsburgh, Hastings 2-9.

SACKS—San Francisco, B. Young 1. Pittsburgh, Buckner 1 1/2, Gildon 1, B. Johnson 1/2.

VIKINGS 21, BUCCANEERS 10
Sunday, December 15

Tampa Bay	7	0	3	0—10
Minnesota	0	7	7	7—21

First Quarter
T.B.—Rhett 5 run (Husted kick), 12:13.

Second Quarter
Min.—Hoard 5 run (Sisson kick), 7:39.

Third Quarter
T.B.—FG, Husted 36, 8:18.
Min.—Hoard 22 run (Sisson kick), 13:01.

Fourth Quarter
Min.—Carter 36 pass from B. Johnson (Sisson kick), 13:06.
Attendance—49,302.

TEAM STATISTICS

	Tampa Bay	Minnesota
First Downs	8	21
Rushes-Yards	20-92	31-148

	Tampa Bay	Minnesota
Passing	77	191
Punt Returns	4-109	6-55
Kickoff Returns	3-81	3-67
Interception Returns	2-0	2-10
Comp-Att-Int	13-32-2	25-35-2
Sacked-Yards Lost	3-27	4-30
Punts	10-43	7-46
Fumbles-Lost	1-0	3-2
Penalties-Yards	6-45	4-25
Time of Possession	25:26	34:34

INDIVIDUAL STATISTICS

RUSHING—Tampa Bay, Rhett 10-28, Alstott 7-50, Ellison 2-9, Dilfer 1-5. Minnesota, Hoard 20-101, Lee 5-22, Graham 4-8, B. Johnson 2-17.

PASSING—Tampa Bay, Dilfer 13-32-2-104. Minnesota, B. Johnson 25-35-2-221.

RECEIVING—Tampa Bay, Alstott 5-10, Ellison 3-31, R. Thomas 2-17, Hawkins 1-23, Williams 1-16, Harris 1-7. Minnesota, Carter 8-89, Reed 5-56, Lee 3-15, Hoard 2-17, Graham 2-11, Evans 2-5, Walsh 1-17, Jordan 1-6, DeLong 1-5.

MISSED FIELD GOAL ATTEMPTS—None.

INTERCEPTIONS—Tampa Bay, D. Abraham 1-0, Dimry 1-0. Minnesota, Talley 1-10, Thomas 1-0.

KICKOFF RETURNS—Tampa Bay, Williams 3-81. Minnesota, Palmer 2-48, Ismail 1-19.

PUNT RETURNS—Tampa Bay, Williams 4-109. Minnesota, Palmer 4-35, Lee 2-20.

SACKS—Tampa Bay, Sapp 2, Ahanotu 1, Culpepper 1/2, Upshaw 1/2. Minnesota, Brady 1, Edwards 1, Randle 1.

SAINTS 17, GIANTS 3
Sunday, December 15

New Orleans	0	7	0	10—17
N.Y. Giants	0	0	3	0—3

Second Quarter
N.O.—Neal 1 run (Brien kick), 4:37.

Third Quarter
NYG—FG, Daluiso 30, 6:50.

Fourth Quarter
N.O.—FG, Brien 51, 6:01.
N.O.—Bates 22 run (Brien kick), 11:13.
Attendance—52,530.

TEAM STATISTICS

	New Orleans	N.Y. Giants
First Downs	11	10
Rushes-Yards	41-155	23-90
Passing	106	48
Punt Returns	3-3	5-57
Kickoff Returns	2-35	4-53
Interception Returns	3-23	1-(-1)
Comp-Att-Int	12-22-1	13-38-3
Sacked-Yards Lost	0-0	7-46
Punts	10-36	9-38
Fumbles-Lost	2-2	3-1
Penalties-Yards	6-45	4-25
Time of Possession	31:45	28:15

INDIVIDUAL STATISTICS

RUSHING—New Orleans, Bates 32-129, Neal 4-6, Whittle 3-24, Everett 1-(minus 1), Guess 1-(minus 3). New York, Hampton 9-38, Downs 7-42, Wheatley 3-(minus 1), Brown 2-11, Kanell 1-0, Way 1-0.

PASSING—New Orleans, Everett 12-22-1-106. New York, Kanell 5-20-1-52, Brown 8-18-2-42.

RECEIVING—New Orleans, Hunter 3-35, Neal 2-9, Whittle 2-7, Bates 2-4, Green 1-23, Small 1-16, Haynes 1-12. New York, Lewis 3-26, Dawsey 2-29, Downs 2-15, Cross 2-5, Calloway 1-9, Hampton 1-5, Saxton 1-3, Way 1-2.

MISSED FIELD GOAL ATTEMPTS—New Orleans, Brien 53.

INTERCEPTIONS—New Orleans, Newman 1-21, Molden 1-2, McMillian 1-0. New York, Sehorn 1-(minus 1).

KICKOFF RETURNS—New Orleans, Hughes 1-29, B. Smith 1-6. New York, C. Hamilton 2-25, Wheatley 1-19, Way 1-9.

PUNT RETURNS—New Orleans, Hughes 3-3. New York, Marshall 5-57.

SACKS—New Orleans, Martin 3, J. Johnson 1, M. Fields 1, Harvey 1, Turnbull 1.

PACKERS 31, LIONS 3
Sunday, December 15

Green Bay	3	7	6	15—31
Detroit	0	0	3	0—3

First Quarter
G.B.—FG, Jacke 20, 14:07.

Second Quarter
G.B.—Howard 92 punt return (Jacke kick), 3:11.

Third Quarter
G.B.—Favre 1 run (kick failed), 4:42.
Det.—FG, Hanson 39, 10:10.

Fourth Quarter
G.B.—Levens 1 run (Bennett pass from Favre), :05.
G.B.—Freeman 27 pass from Favre (Jacke kick), 12:28.
Attendance—73,214.

TEAM STATISTICS

	Green Bay	Detroit
First Downs	20	18
Rushes-Yards	26-111	23-79
Passing	225	186
Punt Returns	5-167	2-15
Kickoff Returns	1-29	6-140
Interception Returns	1-37	1-14
Comp-Att-Int	16-25-1	23-40-1
Sacked-Yards Lost	3-15	4-21
Punts	2-44	5-44
Fumbles-Lost	1-0	1-0
Penalties-Yards	11-75	7-60
Time of Possession	27:01	32:59

INDIVIDUAL STATISTICS

RUSHING—Green Bay, Bennett 12-60, Levens 11-39, Favre 2-3, Henderson 1-9. Detroit, Sanders 21-78, Mitchell 1-2, Rivers 1-(minus 1).

PASSING—Green Bay, Favre 16-25-1-240. Detroit, Mitchell 23-40-1-207.

RECEIVING—Green Bay, Beebe 4-79, Freeman 3-60, Rison 2-24, Chmura 2-22, Levens 2-18, Jackson 1-35, Bennett 1-1, Henderson 1-1. Detroit, Perriman 8-77, Morton 6-40, H. Moore 5-50, Matthews 2-33, Rivers 1-9, Sanders 1-(minus 2).

MISSED FIELD GOAL ATTEMPTS—None.

INTERCEPTIONS—Green Bay, E. Robinson 1-37. Detroit, Blades 1-14.

KICKOFF RETURNS—Green Bay, Beebe 1-29. Detroit, Milburn 6-140.

PUNT RETURNS—Green Bay, Howard 5-167. Detroit, Milburn 2-15.

SACKS—Green Bay, White 2, S. Jones 1, Gi. Brown 1. Detroit, Thomas 1, Porcher 1, Waldroup 1/2, Elliss 1/2.

BRONCOS 24, RAIDERS 19
Sunday, December 15

Oakland	3	0	9	7—19
Denver	7	17	0	0—24

First Quarter
Den.—Davis 3 run (Elam kick), 7:00.
Oak.—FG, Ford 38, 11:55.

Second Quarter
Den.—Craver 1 run (Elam kick), :55.
Den.—R. Smith 20 pass from Elway (Elam kick), 4:22.
Den.—FG, Elam 28, 10:43.

Third Quarter
Oak.—FG, Ford 35, 5:18.
Oak.—Johnstone 1 fumble return (run failed), 10:37.

Fourth Quarter
Oak.—Hobbs 7 pass from Hostetler (Ford kick), 11:22.
Attendance—75,466.

TEAM STATISTICS

	Oakland	Denver
First Downs	18	23
Rushes-Yards	13-105	37-99
Passing	150	186
Punt Returns	1-19	2-11
Kickoff Returns	5-95	2-46
Interception Returns	1-1	3-34
Comp-Att-Int	19-39-3	19-31-1
Sacked-Yards Lost	1-8	2-20
Punts	4-44	3-43
Fumbles-Lost	2-1	2-2
Penalties-Yards	20-157	10-101
Time of Possession	23:54	36:06

INDIVIDUAL STATISTICS

RUSHING—Oakland, Kaufman 9-44, Williams 3-61, Fenner 1-0. Denver, Davis 27-80, Craver 6-17, Elway 4-2.

PASSING—Oakland, Hostetler 18-36-2-146, Hobert 1-3-1-12. Denver, Elway 19-31-1-206.

RECEIVING—Oakland, T. Brown 7-57, Hobbs 6-52, Kaufman 3-28, Dudley 3-21. Denver, Chamberlain 5-61, Carswell 4-16, Miller 3-48, McCaffrey 3-20, R. Smith 2-44, Sherrard 1-15, Sharpe 1-2.

MISSED FIELD GOAL ATTEMPTS—Denver, Elam 40.

INTERCEPTIONS—Oakland, Kidd 1-1. Denver, Crockett 1-34, Braxton 1-0, Atwater 1-0.

KICKOFF RETURNS—Oakland, Kidd 3-54, Kaufman 2-41. Denver, Hebron 2-46.

PUNT RETURNS—Oakland, T. Brown 1-19. Denver, R. Smith 2-11.

SACKS—Oakland, Holmberg 1, Swilling 1. Denver, Romanowski 1/2, Geathers 1/2.

COLTS 24, CHIEFS 19
Sunday, December 15

Indianapolis	14	0	0	10—24
Kansas City	0	10	0	9—19

First Quarter
Ind.—Harrison 3 pass from Harbaugh (Blanchard kick), 8:01.
Ind.—Harrison 37 pass from Harbaugh (Blanchard kick), 13:46.

Second Quarter
K.C.—Anders 18 pass from Gannon (Stoyanovich kick), 2:03.
K.C.—FG, Stoyanovich 30, 10:53.

Fourth Quarter
Ind.—FG, Blanchard 22, 2:08.
K.C.—FG, Stoyanovich 30, 4:34.
Ind.—Harrison 5 pass from Harbaugh (Blanchard kick), 11:12.
K.C.—Anders 5 pass from Bono (run failed), 13:43.
Attendance—71,136.

TEAM STATISTICS

	Indianapolis	Kansas City
First Downs	19	20
Rushes-Yards	27-89	27-120
Passing	222	237
Punt Returns	1-7	2-14
Kickoff Returns	4-65	5-175
Interception Returns	0-0	0-0
Comp-Att-Int	16-28-0	23-41-0
Sacked-Yards Lost	2-5	2-14
Punts	3-45	3-33
Fumbles-Lost	0-0	1-1
Penalties-Yards	0-0	5-30
Time of Possession	29:46	30:14

INDIVIDUAL STATISTICS

RUSHING—Indianapolis, Faulk 20-71, Groce 3-12, Harbaugh 3-5, Workman 1-1. Kansas City, Allen 12-51, Hill 8-46, Anders 4-17, Bono 2-1, Gannon 1-5.

PASSING—Indianapolis, Harbaugh 16-28-0-227. Kansas City, Bono 18-33-0-194, Gannon 5-8-0-57.

RECEIVING—Indianapolis, Harrison 6-103, Faulk 4-18, Groce 2-19, Dawkins 1-42, Bailey 1-29, Stablein 1-14, Pollard 1-2. Kansas City, Anders 9-96, LaChapelle 6-83, Penn 4-44, Vanover 2-16, Allen 1-7, Cash 1-5.

MISSED FIELD GOAL ATTEMPTS—None.

INTERCEPTIONS—None.

KICKOFF RETURNS—Indianapolis, Bailey 3-47, Groce 1-18. Kansas City, Vanover 5-175.

PUNT RETURNS—Indianapolis, Stablein 1-7. Kansas City, Vanover 2-14.

SACKS—Indianapolis, Whittington 1, McCoy 1. Kansas City, Collins 1, Browning 1.

PANTHERS 27, RAVENS 16
Sunday, December 15

Baltimore	7	6	0	3—16
Carolina	3	7	10	7—27

First Quarter
Car.—FG, Kasay 29, 2:48.
Bal.—Jackson 23 pass from Testaverde (Stover kick), 8:10.

Second Quarter
Car.—Johnson 2 run (Kasay kick), 1:18.
Bal.—FG, Stover 37, 9:59.
Bal.—FG, Stover 46, 14:31.

Third Quarter
Car.—Carrier 6 pass from Collins (Kasay kick), 7:54.
Car.—FG, Kasay 44, 11:59.

Fourth Quarter
Bal.—FG, Stover 25, 2:33.
Car.—S. Greene 1 pass from Collins (Kasay kick), 11:22.
Attendance—70,075.

TEAM STATISTICS

	Baltimore	Carolina
First Downs	17	21
Rushes-Yards	25-99	28-82
Passing	220	268
Punt Returns	4-17	3-30
Kickoff Returns	5-96	5-89
Interception Returns	2-5	2-55
Comp-Att-Int	20-37-2	26-39-2
Sacked-Yards Lost	4-20	0-0
Punts	4-45	5-38
Fumbles-Lost	1-1	1-0
Penalties-Yards	5-40	5-30
Time of Possession	25:45	34:15

INDIVIDUAL STATISTICS

RUSHING—Baltimore, Morris 22-89, Testaverde 3-10. Carolina, Johnson 26-81, Collins 2-1.

PASSING—Baltimore, Testaverde 20-37-2-240. Carolina, Collins 26-39-2-268.

RECEIVING—Baltimore, Kinchen 6-87, Jackson 5-65, Morris 5-44, F. Turner 3-38, Alexander 1-6. Carolina, Walls 6-81, Carrier 6-80, Green 5-45, Griffith 3-25, Johnson 2-10, S. Greene 2-7, Oliver 1-11, Ismail 1-9.

MISSED FIELD GOAL ATTEMPTS—None.

INTERCEPTIONS—Baltimore, Langham 2-5. Carolina, Poole 1-35, Cota 1-20.

KICKOFF RETURNS—Baltimore, Baldwin 5-96. Carolina, Bates 4-74, Oliver 1-15.

PUNT RETURNS—Baltimore, J. Lewis 4-17. Carolina, Oliver 3-30.

SACKS—Carolina, Lathon 1, Miller 1, K. Greene 1, Bailey 1/2, Thomas 1/2.

RAMS 34, FALCONS 27
Sunday, December 15

St. Louis	7	17	3	7—34
Atlanta	3	7	10	7—27

First Quarter
Atl.—FG, Andersen 34, 4:44.
St.L.—Kennison 72 pass from Banks (Lohmiller kick), 5:56.

Second Quarter
St.L.—Kennison 77 pass from Banks (Lohmiller kick), 2:17.
St.L.—FG, Lohmiller 25, 4:48.
St.L.—Phillips 6 run (Lohmiller kick), 12:14.
Atl.—Emanuel 5 pass from Hebert (Andersen kick), 13:26.

Third Quarter
Atl.—Heyward 1 run (Andersen kick), :22.
St.L.—FG, Lohmiller 25, 4:41.
Atl.—FG, Andersen 31, 9:50.

Fourth Quarter
St.L.—Kennison 41 pass from Banks (Lohmiller kick), 7:51.
Atl.—Metcalf 2 pass from Hebert (Andersen kick), 11:44.
Attendance—26,519.

TEAM STATISTICS

	St.Louis	Atlanta
First Downs	17	24
Rushes-Yards	44-174	15-63
Passing	306	360
Punt Returns	0-0	2-40
Kickoff Returns	3-77	5-107
Interception Returns	6-6	1-15
Comp-Att-Int	12-17-1	28-49-6
Sacked-Yards Lost	2-13	3-3
Punts	4-48	2-41
Fumbles-Lost	5-3	2-1
Penalties-Yards	11-86	5-55
Time of Possession	32:58	27:02

INDIVIDUAL STATISTICS

RUSHING—St. Louis, Phillips 22-112, Banks 10-27, Green 8-13, Moore 3-18, Bruce 1-4. Atlanta, Anderson 13-37, Hebert 1-25, Heyward 1-1.

PASSING—St. Louis, Banks 11-16-1-304, Bruce 1-1-0-15. Atlanta, Hebert 28-49-6-363.

RECEIVING—St. Louis, Kennison 5-226, Bruce 2-37, Laing 2-35, Ross 2-20, Green 1-1. Atlanta, Emanuel 9-173, Anderson 7-74, Birden 4-50, Metcalf 4-28, Mathis 2-27, Brown 2-11.

MISSED FIELD GOAL ATTEMPTS—None.

INTERCEPTIONS—St. Louis, Lyle 3-1, Farr 1-5, Lyght 1-0, Parker 1-0. Atlanta, Edwards 1-15.

KICKOFF RETURNS—St. Louis, Thomas 2-58, Crawford 1-19. Atlanta, Preston 5-107.

PUNT RETURNS—Atlanta, Metcalf 2-40.

SACKS—St. Louis, Farr 2, O'Neal 1. Atlanta, Hall 1, Matthews 1.

CARDINALS 27, REDSKINS 26
Sunday, December 15

Washington	3	13	7	3—26
Arizona	7	7	3	10—27

First Quarter
Ariz.—Centers 6 pass from K. Graham (Butler kick), 6:48.
Was.—FG, Blanton 20, 12:11.

Second Quarter
Ariz.—Miller 26 fumble return (Butler kick), 4:21.
Was.—Turner fumble recovery in end zone (Blanton kick), 6:17.
Was.—FG, Blanton 22, 12:19.
Was.—FG, Blanton 23, 14:53.

Third Quarter
Was.—Allen 14 run (Blanton kick), 7:26.
Ariz.—FG, Butler 22, 12:34.

Fourth Quarter
Ariz.—Sanders 21 pass from K. Graham (Butler kick), 2:22.
Was.—FG, Blanton 35, 7:46.
Ariz.—FG, Butler 28, 15:00.
Attendance—34,260.

TEAM STATISTICS

	Washington	Arizona
First Downs	19	20
Rushes-Yards	24-80	27-78
Passing	249	221
Punt Returns	2-32	3-25
Kickoff Returns	5-141	7-155
Interception Returns	1-24	0-0
Comp-Att-Int	22-40-0	20-46-1
Sacked-Yards Lost	2-9	1-11
Punts	5-46	6-40
Fumbles-Lost	2-1	1-1
Penalties-Yards	7-52	4-28
Time of Possession	27:42	32:18

INDIVIDUAL STATISTICS

RUSHING—Washington, Allen 17-69, Frerotte 2-13, Logan 2-0, Mitchell 2-(minus 2), Turk 1-0. Arizona, McElroy 18-59, Centers 6-17, K. Graham 3-2.

PASSING—Washington, Frerotte 22-40-0-258. Arizona, K. Graham 20-46-1-232.

RECEIVING—Washington, Westbrook 4-59, Asher 4-53, Allen 4-30, Ellard 3-41, B. Brooks 3-27, Mitchell 2-35, Logan 1-10, W. Bell 1-3. Arizona, Centers 8-59, Sanders 6-82, R. Moore 2-34, Dowdell 1-26, McElroy 1-12, Edwards 1-12, Carter 1-7.

MISSED FIELD GOAL ATTEMPTS—None.

INTERCEPTIONS—Washington, Carter 1-24.

KICKOFF RETURNS—Washington, Mitchell 5-141. Arizona, L. Johnson 5-113, McElroy 1-26, McDonald 1-16.

PUNT RETURNS—Washington, Mitchell 2-32. Arizona, Edwards 2-25, Dowdell 1-0.

SACKS—Washington, M. Patton 1. Arizona, Rice 2.

BENGALS 21, OILERS 13
Sunday, December 15

Cincinnati	0	0	14	7—21
Houston	3	3	0	7—13

First Quarter
Hou.—FG, Del Greco 46, 8:27.

Second Quarter
Hou.—FG, Del Greco 42, 9:07.

Third Quarter
Cin.—Hundon 14 pass from Blake (Pelfrey kick), 10:26.
Cin.—Francis 42 interception return (Pelfrey kick), 12:53.

Fourth Quarter
Cin.—Carter 9 run (Pelfrey kick), 11:13.
Hou.—Wycheck 16 pass from McNair (Del Greco kick), 14:23.
Attendance—15,131.

TEAM STATISTICS

	Cincinnati	Houston
First Downs	12	22
Rushes-Yards	21-79	31-106
Passing	126	235
Punt Returns	0-0	2-17
Kickoff Returns	3-79	4-101
Interception Returns	3-61	0-0

	Cincinnati	Houston
Comp-Att-Int	13-23-0	22-39-3
Sacked-Yards Lost	4-32	3-15
Punts	5-36	2-46
Fumbles-Lost	0-0	1-1
Penalties-Yards	3-49	6-40
Time of Possession	24:53	35:07

INDIVIDUAL STATISTICS

RUSHING—Cincinnati, Hearst 11-24, Carter 4-25, Blake 3-19, Milne 2-8, Bieniemy 1-3. Houston, George 24-76, Thomas 2-13, Chandler 2-3, Harmon -3, McNair 1-11.

PASSING—Cincinnati, Blake 13-23-0-158. Houston, Chandler 16-29-3-78, McNair 6-10-0-72.

RECEIVING—Cincinnati, Dunn 7-95, Pickens 2-10, McGee 1-16, Carter 1-5, Hundon 1-14, Hearst 1-8. Houston, Sanders 6-89, Wycheck 5-57, George 3-32, Russell 3-30, Harmon 2-31, Thomas 1-7, Floyd 1-5, R. Lewis -(minus 1).

MISSED FIELD GOAL ATTEMPTS—Cincinnati, Pelfrey 47. Houston, Del Greco 34.

INTERCEPTIONS—Cincinnati, Francis 2-61, Myers 1-0.

KICKOFF RETURNS—Cincinnati, Dunn 3-79. Houston, Gray 4-101.

PUNT RETURNS—Houston, Gray 2-17.

SACKS—Cincinnati, Francis 1, von Oelhoffen 1, Sawyer 1/2, Morabito 1/2. Houston, Cook 21/2, Young 11/2.

JAGUARS 20, SEAHAWKS 13
Sunday, December 15

Seattle	0	10	3	0—13
Jacksonville	7	0	0	13—20

First Quarter
Jac.—Smith 12 pass from Brunell (Hollis kick), 12:55.

Second Quarter
Sea.—FG, Peterson 27, 4:31.
Sea.—Proehl 10 pass from Mirer (Peterson kick), 14:24.

Third Quarter
Sea.—FG, Peterson 24, 13:06.

Fourth Quarter
Jac.—Smith 39 pass from Brunell (Hollis kick), :07.
Jac.—FG, Hollis 19, 5:05.
Jac.—FG, Hollis 39, 12:12.
Attendance—66,134.

TEAM STATISTICS

	Seattle	Jacksonville
First Downs	19	18
Rushes-Yards	29-159	31-133
Passing	147	218
Punt Returns	1-11	4-25
Kickoff Returns	5-124	3-68
Interception Returns	0-0	1-27
Comp-Att-Int	16-31-1	19-26-0
Sacked-Yards Lost	2-9	3-13
Punts	4-42	3-37
Fumbles-Lost	1-0	2-0
Penalties-Yards	5-33	2-21
Time of Possession	29:25	30:35

INDIVIDUAL STATISTICS

RUSHING—Seattle, Smith 16-59, Warren 11-47, Galloway 1-51, O. Gray -2. Jacksonville, Means 23-92, Brunell 7-34, Stewart 1-7.

PASSING—Seattle, Mirer 16-31-1-156. Jacksonville, Brunell 19-26-0-231.

RECEIVING—Seattle, Crumpler 6-58, Galloway 3-51, Proehl 2-17, Smith 2-10, Pritchard 1-11, Warren 1-5, R. Williams 1-4. Jacksonville, Smith 8-124, Mitchell 5-71, McCardell 3-23, Means 1-8, Brown 1-4, Stewart 1-1.

MISSED FIELD GOAL ATTEMPTS—Jacksonville, Hollis 36.

INTERCEPTIONS—Jacksonville, Brackens 1-27.

KICKOFF RETURNS—Seattle, C. Harris 3-86, R. Harris 2-38. Jacksonville, B. Brooks 3-68.

PUNT RETURNS—Seattle, Galloway 1-11. Jacksonville, Hudson 4-25.

SACKS—Seattle, McCrary 3. Jacksonville, Brackens 1, Lageman 1.

DOLPHINS 16, BILLS 14
Monday, December 16

Buffalo	0	7	0	7—14
Miami	3	3	3	7—16

First Quarter
Mia.—FG, Nedney 29, 14:29.

Second Quarter
Mia.—FG, Nedney 41, 12:55.
Buf.—Reed 67 pass from Kelly (Christie kick), 13:17.

Third Quarter
Mia.—FG, Nedney 18, 9:08.

Fourth Quarter
Mia.—McDuffie 5 pass from Marino (Nedney kick), 3:49.
Buf.—Moulds 16 pass from Kelly (Christie kick), 10:51.
Attendance—67,016.

TEAM STATISTICS

	Buffalo	Miami
First Downs	15	22
Rushes-Yards	17-51	40-145
Passing	223	249
Punt Returns	1-10	0-0
Kickoff Returns	4-94	0-0
Interception Returns	0-0	1-27
Comp-Att-Int	17-29-1	26-37-0
Sacked-Yards Lost	3-17	2-14
Punts	4-40	3-46
Fumbles-Lost	2-1	0-0
Penalties-Yards	3-30	8-92
Time of Possession	18:05	41:55

INDIVIDUAL STATISTICS

RUSHING—Buffalo, T. Thomas 11-34, Holmes 3-10, Tindale 2-4, Tasker 1-3. Miami, Abdul-Jabbar 27-76, Spikes 10-58, McDuffie 1-7, Pritchett 1-4, Parmalee 1-0.

PASSING—Buffalo, Kelly 17-29-1-240. Miami, Marino 26-37-0-263.

RECEIVING—Buffalo, Reed 6-127, T. Thomas 5-47, Johnson 2-15, Early 1-23, Moulds 1-16, Tasker 1-12, Holmes 1-0. Miami, Barnett 5-68, Drayton 5-47, McDuffie 5-43, Pritchett 4-47, Abdul-Jabbar 4-23, Parmalee 2-10, R. Hill 1-25.

MISSED FIELD GOAL ATTEMPTS—Buffalo, Christie 20.

INTERCEPTIONS—Miami, Z. Thomas 1-27.

KICKOFF RETURNS—Buffalo, Moulds 3-79, Copeland 1-15.

PUNT RETURNS—Buffalo, Burris 1-10.

SACKS—Buffalo, Hansen 2. Miami, Armstrong 2, Stubbs 1.

RESULTS

New England 23, N.Y. GIANTS 22
ST. LOUIS 14, New Orleans 13
BUFFALO 20, Kansas City 9
CAROLINA 18, Pittsburgh 14
CINCINNATI 31, Indianapolis 24
Denver 10, SAN DIEGO 16
GREEN BAY 38, Minnesota 10
Houston 24, BALTIMORE 21
JACKSONVILLE 19, Atlanta 17
Miami 31, N.Y. JETS 28
PHILADELPHIA 29, Arizona 19
Seattle 28, OAKLAND 21
TAMPA BAY 34, Chicago 19
WASHINGTON 37, Dallas 10
SAN FRANCISCO 24, Detroit 14

STANDINGS

AFC EAST

	W	L	T	Pct.
New England	11	5	0	.688
Buffalo	10	6	0	.625
Indianapolis	9	7	0	.563
Miami	8	8	0	.500
N.Y. Jets	1	15	0	.063

AFC CENTRAL

	W	L	T	Pct.
Pittsburgh	10	6	0	.625
Jacksonville	9	7	0	.563
Cincinnati	8	8	0	.500
Houston	8	8	0	.500
Baltimore	4	12	0	.250

AFC WEST

	W	L	T	Pct.
Denver	14	2	0	.875
Kansas City	9	7	0	.563
Oakland	7	9	0	.438
San Diego	7	9	0	.438
Seattle	7	9	0	.438

NFC EAST

	W	L	T	Pct.
Dallas	10	6	0	.625
Philadelphia	10	6	0	.625
Washington	8	8	0	.500
Arizona	7	9	0	.438
N.Y. Giants	6	10	0	.375

NFC CENTRAL

	W	L	T	Pct.
Green Bay	13	3	0	.813
Minnesota	9	7	0	.563
Chicago	7	9	0	.438
Detroit	5	11	0	.314
Tampa Bay	6	10	0	.375

NFC WEST

	W	L	T	Pct.
Carolina	12	4	0	.750
San Francisco	12	4	0	.750
St. Louis	6	10	0	.375
Atlanta	3	13	0	.188
New Orleans	3	13	0	.188

HIGHLIGHTS

Hero of the week: Carolina safety Chad Cota picked off a pass in the end zone to secure the Panthers' 18-14 victory over the Steelers. The Steelers faced third-and-goal from the Panthers' 8 when Kordell Stewart dropped back to pass. Cota recognized the Steelers' pass as a play they used earlier in the game, moved inside and made a diving interception with 29 seconds left. Cota's play clinched the NFC West title for Carolina and a first-round bye in the playoffs.

Goat of the week: Kicker Morten Andersen missed a chip shot that would have given the Falcons a 20-19 victory over the Jaguars, who qualified for the playoffs because of Andersen's miss. Andersen, one of the best kickers in NFL history, had not missed a field goal from 30 yards or less since 1989, a streak of 59 in a row. But with four seconds left, Andersen slipped on his follow-through and the ball sailed wide of the left upright, preserving Jacksonville's 19-17 victory.

Sub of the week: Quarterback Steve McNair, starting in place of Chris Chandler, turned in an excellent performance in the Oilers' 24-21 victory over the Ravens. McNair threw a 19-yard touchdown and ran for a 24-yard touchdown to stake the Oilers to a 24-7 lead after three quarters. In his sixth career start, the second-year quarterback completed passes to seven different receivers and was 19-of-24 for 238 yards with no interceptions.

Comeback of the week: The Giants led the Patriots, 22-3, early in the fourth quarter, but quarterback Drew Bledsoe found receiver Terry Glenn for a 26-yard touchdown pass to cut the lead to 22-10. The Giants went four and out and punted to New England's Dave Meggett. who returned the punt 60 yards for a touchdown to cut the lead to 22-17. With 1:23 left, New England faced fourth-and-7, but Bledsoe hit tight end Ben Coates with a 13-yard touchdown pass for the victory.

Blowout of the week: After being eliminated from the playoff picture a week earlier, the Redskins piled up 483 yards and 32 first downs against the Cowboys, who rested starters such as Troy Aikman and Emmitt Smith for the playoffs. Behind Gus Frerotte's passing and Terry Allen's running, Washington rolled to a 37-3

lead, before Herschel Walker scored on a 39-yard touchdown run in the fourth quarter, Dallas' lone offensive highlight.

Nail-biter of the week: In the fourth quarter against the Bengals, the Colts' Aaron Bailey returned a kickoff 95 yards for a touchdown, tying the game at 24. With 5:27 left, Cincinnati's Jeff Blake passed to Tony McGee for a 9-yard touchdown and a 31-24 lead. The Colts then drove to the Bengals' 19 and faced a fourth down, but couldn't convert. The Colts got another shot, but Jim Harbaugh's desperation pass from midfield was intercepted as time ran out.

Hit of the week: On the second play of the game, Eagles defensive end Mike Mamula got around Arizona tackle Lomas Brown and slapped the football out of quarterback Kent Graham's hand. Mamula picked up the loose ball and ran it back for a 4-yard touchdown—his first in the NFL.

Oddity of the week: Stewart saw significant action as Pittsburgh's quarterback for the first time this season. Once again, Stewart proved why he is the league's most versatile player, as he broke out of the pocket for an 80-yard touchdown run and a 14-9 halftime lead.

Top rusher: Detroit's Barry Sanders rushed 28 times for 175 yards, including a 54-yard touchdown run, in the Lions' loss to the 49ers.

Top passer: Washington's Frerotte threw for a career-high 346 yards on 22-of-31 passing in the Redskins' victory.

Top receiver: Henry Ellard caught seven of Frerotte's passes for 155 yards.

Notes: The Bengals finished 8-8, which included a 7-2 mark after Bruce Coslet replaced Dave Shula as coach, their best record since 1990. . . . Denver's Terrell Davis set club single-season records for most touchdowns (15) and most rushing touchdowns (13). . . . The Redskins, in their final game at RFK Stadium, recorded their 229th consecutive sellout. . . . The Packers won 13 games for just the second time in their history; they were 13-1 in 1962. . . . For the third consecutive game Eagles quarterback Ty Detmer threw an interception that was returned for a touchdown. . . . For the first time in 16 seasons, the Saints failed to win a game against an NFC West opponent. . . . Rookie Karim Abdul-Jabbar became the first Dolphin to rush for 1,000 yards in a season since Delvin Williams had 1,258 in 1978. . . . The Chiefs failed to make the playoffs for the first time since 1989. . . . Buffalo's Thurman Thomas joined Detroit's Barry Sanders as the only running backs to record eight consecutive 1,000-yard seasons. . . . Curtis Conway became the first Bears receiver to have back-to-back 1,000-yard seasons. . . . For the first time since 1988, Tampa Bay avoided a last-place finish in the NFC Central. . . . The Raiders' 156 penalties tied the NFL single-season record they set two seasons ago. . . . Seattle's Gino Torretta, the 1992 Heisman Trophy winner, played in his first NFL game and threw his first NFL touchdown pass—a 32-yarder to Joey Galloway. . . . Before its 6-2 road record this season, Houston had never had more than five road victories in a season in its 36-year history. . . . Baltimore's Vinny Testaverde became the eighth quarterback in NFL history to throw for 4,000 yards and at least 30 touchdown passes in a season—and the first quarterback to do it with a sub .500 team (4-12). . . . Detroit's Sanders finished the season with 1,553 yards to win his third rushing title and became the first player in league history to rush for 1,500 yards or more in three consecutive seasons. . . . San Francisco's Steve Young won his fifth passing title in six seasons with a 97.2 quarterback rating.

Quote of the week: Atlanta quarterback Bobby Hebert, on Andersen's missed field goal and the team's loss to Jacksonville: "If I was a betting man, I would have bet my life that we win that game. But, shoot, I would be dead right now."

GAME SUMMARIES

PATRIOTS 23, GIANTS 22
Saturday, December 21

New England	0	0	3	20—23
N.Y. Giants	2	20	0	0—22

First Quarter
NYG—Safety, Bledsoe called for intentional grounding in end zone, 14:50.
Second Quarter
NYG—Way 1 run (Daluiso kick), 2:32.
NYG—FG, Daluiso 30, 8:33.
NYG—FG, Daluiso 27, 12:00.
NYG—Sehorn 23 interception return (Daluiso kick), 12:15.
Third Quarter
N.E.—FG, Vinatieri 40, 10:48.
Fourth Quarter
N.E.—Glenn 26 pass from Bledsoe (Vinatieri kick), 2:40.
N.E.—Meggett 60 punt return (Vinatieri kick), 3:51.
N.E.—Coates 13 pass from Bledsoe (pass failed), 13:37.
Attendance—65,387.

TEAM STATISTICS

	New England	N.Y. Giants
First Downs	17	17
Rushes-Yards	18-26	32-97
Passing	282	199
Punt Returns	3-62	3-43
Kickoff Returns	5-118	6-94
Interception Returns	1-11	2-27
Comp-Att-Int	31-47-2	14-34-1
Sacked-Yards Lost	2-19	2-16

	New England	N.Y. Giants
Punts	6-36	6-40
Fumbles-Lost	0-0	0-0
Penalties-Yards	4-24	8-56
Time of Possession	29:25	30:35

INDIVIDUAL STATISTICS
RUSHING—New England, Martin 8-9, Meggett 7-20, Bledsoe 2-(minus 1), Glenn 1-(minus 2). New York, Downs 22-52, Way 7-36, Brown 3-9.
PASSING—New England, Bledsoe 31-47-2-301. New York, Brown 14-34-1-215.
RECEIVING—New England, Glenn 8-124, T. Brown 7-75, Meggett 6-28, Byars 3-24, Coates 3-19, Martin 2-1, Jefferson 1-22, Grier 1-8. New York, Lewis 5-84, Way 3-50, Dawsey 2-23, Calloway 2-21, Alexander 1-35, Cross 1-2.
MISSED FIELD GOAL ATTEMPTS—None.
INTERCEPTIONS—New England, O. Smith 1-11. New York, Sehorn 1-23, Sparks 1-4.
KICKOFF RETURNS—New England, Meggett 3-76, T. Brown 2-42. New York, C. Hamilton 2-41, Alexander 2-27, Kozlowski 1-16, Saxton 1-10.
PUNT RETURNS—New England, Meggett 3-62. New York, Marshall 3-43.
SACKS—New England, O. Smith 1, Jones 1. New York, Bratzke 1, Harris 1/2, Agnew 1/2.

RAMS 14, SAINTS 13
Saturday, December 21

New Orleans	10	0	0	3—13
St. Louis	0	0	7	7—14

First Quarter
N.O.—Bates 1 run (Brien kick), 1:06.
N.O.—FG, Brien 43, 11:59.
Third Quarter
St.L.—Bruce 22 pass from Martin (Huerta kick), 10:31.
Fourth Quarter
N.O.—FG, Brien 35, :41.
St.L.—Kennison 15 pass from Martin (Huerta kick), 9:30.
Attendance—57,681.

TEAM STATISTICS

	New Orleans	St.Louis
First Downs	12	14
Rushes-Yards	33-93	25-51
Passing	148	136
Punt Returns	2-3	3-16
Kickoff Returns	3-80	3-54
Interception Returns	3-56	0-0
Comp-Att-Int	17-26-0	16-29-3
Sacked-Yards Lost	1-8	6-35
Punts	7-35	6-50
Fumbles-Lost	2-1	0-0
Penalties-Yards	7-60	1-10
Time of Possession	32:25	27:35

INDIVIDUAL STATISTICS
RUSHING—New Orleans, Bates 21-67, Hunter 7-16, Neal 2-9, DeRamus 1-2, Everett 1-1, Whittle 1-(minus 2). St. Louis, Phillips 9-11, Green 6-9, Martin 4-13, Banks 3-15, Moore 2-1, Lyle 1-2.
PASSING—New Orleans, Everett 17-26-0-156. St. Louis, Martin 12-19-1-132, Banks 4-9-1-39, Bruce 0-1-1-0.
RECEIVING—New Orleans, Haynes 4-65, Small 4-32, Whittle 4-24, Hunter 2-9, Green 1-17, DeRamus 1-6, Bates 1-3. St. Louis, Bruce 7-97, Kennison 4-42, Green 2-10, Laing 1-9, Phillips 1-8, Moore 1-5.
MISSED FIELD GOAL ATTEMPTS—None.
INTERCEPTIONS—New Orleans, Allen 1-33, Newman 1-19, McMillian 1-4.
KICKOFF RETURNS—New Orleans, Hughes 3-80. St. Louis, Kennison 2-37, Thomas 1-17.
PUNT RETURNS—New Orleans, Hughes 2-3. St. Louis, Kennison 3-16.
SACKS—New Orleans, J. Johnson 2, Molden 2, Tubbs 1, A. Robbins 1. St. Louis, Farr 1.

OILERS 24, RAVENS 21
Sunday, December 22

Houston	10	7	7	0—24
Baltimore	7	0	0	14—21

First Quarter
Hou.—George 1 run (Del Greco kick), 4:39.
Bal.—Jackson 86 pass from Testaverde (Stover kick), 8:50.
Hou.—FG, Del Greco 37, 13:48.
Second Quarter
Hou.—Davis 19 pass from McNair (Del Greco kick), 13:08.
Third Quarter
Hou.—McNair 24 run (Del Greco kick), 13:41.

Fourth Quarter
Bal.—Jackson 8 pass from Testaverde (Stover kick), 1:24.
Bal.—Jackson 4 pass from Testaverde (Stover kick), 14:47.
Attendance—52,704.

TEAM STATISTICS

	Houston	Baltimore
First Downs	18	20
Rushes-Yards	36-117	17-120
Passing	234	257
Punt Returns	1-8	2-2
Kickoff Returns	4-67	5-85
Interception Returns	2-6	0-0
Comp-Att-Int	19-24-0	23-32-2
Sacked-Yards Lost	1-4	4-50
Punts	4-39	3-48
Fumbles-Lost	2-0	0-0
Penalties-Yards	6-55	10-64
Time of Possession	36:31	23:29

INDIVIDUAL STATISTICS

RUSHING—Houston, George 21-85, McNair 9-41, Thomas 5-(minus 7), Harmon 1-(minus 2). Baltimore, Morris 12-81, Testaverde 4-35, Byner 1-4.
PASSING—Houston, McNair 19-24-0-238. Baltimore, Testaverde 23-32-2-307.
RECEIVING—Houston, Davis 4-45, Harmon 3-72, Russell 3-39, Wycheck 3-20, George 2-29, Thomas 2-17, Sanders 2-16. Baltimore, Kinchen 7-70, Jackson 5-117, F. Turner 4-55, Morris 4-43, Byner 2-7, Ethridge 1-15.
MISSED FIELD GOAL ATTEMPTS—None.
INTERCEPTIONS—Houston, Bishop 1-6, Robertson 1-0.
KICKOFF RETURNS—Houston, Gray 3-67, McKeehan 1-0. Baltimore, Baldwin 4-67, Byner 1-18.
PUNT RETURNS—Houston, Gray 1-8. Baltimore, J. Lewis 2-2.
SACKS—Houston, Barrow 1, Jackson 1, Mix 1, Roberson 1. Baltimore, Fortune 1.

PACKERS 38, VIKINGS 10
Sunday, December 22

Minnesota	7	3	0	0—10
Green Bay	7	3	14	14—38

First Quarter
G.B.—Bennett 5 run (Jacke kick), 7:10.
Min.—Carter 43 pass from B. Johnson (Sisson kick), 12:40.
Second Quarter
G.B.—FG, Jacke 45, 9:53.
Min.—FG, Sisson 34, 15:00.
Third Quarter
G.B.—Levens 13 pass from Favre (Jacke kick), 3:00.
G.B.—Rison 22 pass from Favre (Jacke kick), 8:55.
Fourth Quarter
G.B.—Jackson 23 pass from Favre (Jacke kick), :05.
G.B.—Levens 11 run (Jacke kick), 9:03.
Attendance—59,306.

TEAM STATISTICS

	Minnesota	Green Bay
First Downs	12	29
Rushes-Yards	17-49	41-233
Passing	203	207
Punt Returns	1-0	4-84
Kickoff Returns	6-118	2-70
Interception Returns	0-0	1-20
Comp-Att-Int	17-34-1	16-25-0
Sacked-Yards Lost	2-8	2-5
Punts	8-42	3-41
Fumbles-Lost	1-1	3-2
Penalties-Yards	5-25	2-10
Time of Possession	22:50	37:10

INDIVIDUAL STATISTICS

RUSHING—Minnesota, Hoard 13-41, Lee 2-5, Graham 1-2, B. Johnson 1-1. Green Bay, Bennett 18-109, Levens 11-73, Jervey 5-35, Henderson 3-5, Favre 2-10, McMahon 2-1.
PASSING—Minnesota, B. Johnson 17-34-1-211. Green Bay, Favre 15-23-0-202, McMahon 1-2-0-10.
RECEIVING—Minnesota, Reed 5-74, Hoard 4-46, Carter 3-46, Evans 2-22, Lee 2-20, Frisch 1-3. Green Bay, Chmura 4-43, Freeman 3-61, Rison 3-46, Jackson 2-33, Henderson 2-21, Levens 2-8.
MISSED FIELD GOAL ATTEMPTS—None.
INTERCEPTIONS—Green Bay, Newsome 1-20.
KICKOFF RETURNS—Minnesota, Morrow 4-83, Ismail 1-22, Gerak 1-13. Green Bay, Howard 1-40, Beebe 1-30.

PUNT RETURNS—Minnesota, Lee 1-0. Green Bay, Howard 4-84.
SACKS—Minnesota, Alexander 2. Green Bay, S. Jones 1, White 1.

BUCCANEERS 34, BEARS 19
Sunday, December 22

Chicago	7	0	0	12—19
Tampa Bay	7	24	0	3—34

First Quarter
Chi.—R. Harris 1 run (Jaeger kick), 7:40.
T.B.—Moore 2 pass from Dilfer (Husted kick), 13:41.
Second Quarter
T.B.—Rhett 3 run (Husted kick), 1:35.
T.B.—K. Williams 88 punt return (Husted kick), 6:15.
T.B.—Hawkins 15 pass from Dilfer (Husted kick), 10:28.
T.B.—FG, Husted 50, 14:38.
Fourth Quarter
T.B.—FG, Husted 22, 1:20.
Chi.—Engram 6 pass from Matthews (pass failed), 12:46.
Chi.—Matthews 2 run (pass failed), 14:42.
Attendance—51,572.

TEAM STATISTICS

	Chicago	Tampa Bay
First Downs	25	15
Rushes-Yards	19-67	31-89
Passing	272	92
Punt Returns	0-0	2-100
Kickoff Returns	6-107	2-49
Interception Returns	0-0	1-26
Comp-Att-Int	30-43-1	11-14-0
Sacked-Yards Lost	4-25	1-12
Punts	3-43	3-43
Fumbles-Lost	2-1	1-0
Penalties-Yards	12-75	4-40
Time of Possession	32:31	27:29

INDIVIDUAL STATISTICS

RUSHING—Chicago, R. Harris 9-26, Salaam 7-35, T. Carter 1-3, Matthews 1-2, Krieg 1-1. Tampa Bay, Rhett 14-44, Alstott 11-42, R. Brooks 2-2, Ellison 2-1, Dilfer 1-1, Weldon 1-(minus 1).
PASSING—Chicago, Krieg 17-26-1-139, Matthews 13-17-0-158. Tampa Bay, Dilfer 11-14-0-104.
RECEIVING—Chicago, Conway 9-120, R. Harris 6-22, Wetnight 4-61, Timpson 4-35, Engram 2-23, Cash 2-15, Salaam 1-8, Ja. Jackson 1-7, T. Carter 1-6. Tampa Bay, Hawkins 4-55, Harper 2-21, Alstott 2-14, Moore 2-8, Harris 1-6.
MISSED FIELD GOAL ATTEMPTS—None.
INTERCEPTIONS—Tampa Bay, Mincy 1-26.
KICKOFF RETURNS—Chicago, Ja. Jackson 5-88, Engram 1-19. Tampa Bay, K. Williams 2-49.
PUNT RETURNS—Tampa Bay, K. Williams 2-100.
SACKS—Chicago, Spellman 1. Tampa Bay, Nickerson 2, Upshaw 1, Sapp 1.

EAGLES 29, CARDINALS 19
Sunday, December 22

Arizona	0	3	3	13—19
Philadelphia	13	10	3	3—29

First Quarter
Phi.—Mamula 4 fumble return (Anderson kick), :41.
Phi.—FG, Anderson 23, 6:42.
Phi.—FG, Anderson 22, 13:45.
Second Quarter
Phi.—FG, Anderson 43, 1:14.
Ariz.—FG, Butler 41, 8:29.
Phi.—Watters 1 run (Anderson kick), 14:12.
Third Quarter
Ariz.—FG, Butler 41, 4:08.
Phi.—FG, Anderson 26, 9:45.
Fourth Quarter
Phi.—FG, Anderson 39, 1:45.
Ariz.—McElroy 2 pass from Esiason (kick failed), 4:59.
Ariz.—Williams 65 interception return (Butler kick), 8:54.
Attendance—63,658.

TEAM STATISTICS

	Arizona	Philadelphia
First Downs	15	22
Rushes-Yards	16-71	40-127
Passing	158	216
Punt Returns	2-5	1-5

	Arizona	Philadelphia
Kickoff Returns	8-132	4-62
Interception Returns	1-65	1-28
Comp-Att-Int	16-41-1	20-32-1
Sacked-Yards Lost	4-26	0-0
Punts	3-39	3-44
Fumbles-Lost	3-1	1-1
Penalties-Yards	10-67	7-67
Time of Possession	21:20	38:40

INDIVIDUAL STATISTICS

RUSHING—Arizona, McElroy 9-45, Centers 5-28, L. Johnson 1-3, Sanders 1-(minus 5). Philadelphia, Watters 31-99, Garner 7-21, Turner 1-5, Detmer 1-2.

PASSING—Arizona, Esiason 12-26-0-138, K. Graham 4-15-1-46. Philadelphia, Detmer 20-32-1-216.

RECEIVING—Arizona, Centers 6-43, Edwards 3-41, Sanders 3-30, McElroy 2-28, McWilliams 1-21, R. Moore 1-21. Philadelphia, Jones 5-65, Turner 4-49, Fryar 4-48, Watters 2-14, C. Williams 2-8, Seay 1-15, Solomon 1-9, Garner 1-8.

MISSED FIELD GOAL ATTEMPTS—Arizona, Butler 38.

INTERCEPTIONS—Arizona, Williams 1-65. Philadelphia, Zordich 1-28.

KICKOFF RETURNS—Arizona, L. Johnson 4-74, McElroy 3-36, Dowdell 1-22. Philadelphia, Witherspoon 3-62, Brooks 1-0.

PUNT RETURNS—Arizona, Dowdell 2-5. Philadelphia, Seay 1-5.

SACKS—Philadelphia, W. Fuller 3, Mamula 1.

BENGALS 31, COLTS 24

Sunday, December 22

Indianapolis	7	3	7	7—24
Cincinnati	7	3	7	14—31

First Quarter

Cin.—Dunn 10 pass from Blake (Pelfrey kick), 2:44.
Ind.—Belser 21 interception return (Blanchard kick), 7:57.

Second Quarter

Cin.—FG, Pelfrey 25, 6:26.
Ind.—FG, Blanchard 32, 13:28.

Third Quarter

Cin.—Carter 1 run (Pelfrey kick), 9:19.
Ind.—Dilger 1 pass from Harbaugh (Blanchard kick), 14:17.

Fourth Quarter

Cin.—Pickens 2 pass from Blake (Pelfrey kick), 4:06.
Ind.—Bailey 95 kickoff return (Blanchard kick), 4:22.
Cin.—McGee 9 pass from Blake (Pelfrey kick), 9:33.
Attendance—49,389.

TEAM STATISTICS

	Indianapolis	Cincinnati
First Downs	16	26
Rushes-Yards	19-35	31-157
Passing	231	284
Punt Returns	0-0	2-5
Kickoff Returns	6-199	5-134
Interception Returns	1-21	2-12
Comp-Att-Int	23-34-2	22-37-1
Sacked-Yards Lost	3-13	0-0
Punts	3-32	2-53
Fumbles-Lost	0-0	2-2
Penalties-Yards	5-36	4-30
Time of Possession	29:14	30:46

INDIVIDUAL STATISTICS

RUSHING—Indianapolis, Faulk 13-25, Harbaugh 3-1, Warren 2-(minus 2), Groce 1-11. Cincinnati, Hearst 17-93, Carter 7-18, Blake 4-31, Bieniemy 2-10, Milne 1-5.

PASSING—Indianapolis, Harbaugh 23-34-2-244. Cincinnati, Blake 22-37-1-284.

RECEIVING—Indianapolis, Faulk 7-64, Harrison 6-85, Dilger 6-43, Bailey 3-42, Doering 1-10. Cincinnati, McGee 8-93, Pickens 6-93, Dunn 3-59, Scott 3-31, Carter 2-8.

MISSED FIELD GOAL ATTEMPTS—None.

INTERCEPTIONS—Indianapolis, Belser 1-21. Cincinnati, Dixon 1-10, Rod W. Jones 1-2.

KICKOFF RETURNS—Indianapolis, Bailey 6-199. Cincinnati, Hundon 5-134.

PUNT RETURNS—Cincinnati, Myers 1-12, Hundon 1-(minus 7).

SACKS—Cincinnati, T. Johnson 1, Langford 1, Copeland ¹/₂, Wilkinson ¹/₂.

JAGUARS 19, FALCONS 17

Sunday, December 22

Atlanta	0	3	7	7—17
Jacksonville	7	6	3	3—19

First Quarter

Jac.—Brunell 11 run (Hollis kick), 7:06.

Second Quarter

Atl.—FG, Andersen 46, 2:35.
Jac.—FG, Hollis 23, 8:48.
Jac.—FG, Hollis 26, 14:18.

Third Quarter

Jac.—FG, Hollis 22, 6:49.
Atl.—Metcalf 4 pass from Hebert (Andersen kick), 12:26.

Fourth Quarter

Jac.—FG, Hollis 42, 2:00.
Atl.—Heyward 2 run (Andersen kick), 9:21.
Attendance—71,449.

TEAM STATISTICS

	Atlanta	Jacksonville
First Downs	21	21
Rushes-Yards	31-146	32-143
Passing	163	214
Punt Returns	3-18	2-12
Kickoff Returns	6-123	3-55
Interception Returns	0-0	0-0
Comp-Att-Int	17-26-0	18-29-0
Sacked-Yards Lost	1-9	3-8
Punts	4-44	3-45
Fumbles-Lost	0-0	0-0
Penalties-Yards	2-10	1-3
Time of Possession	29:17	30:43

INDIVIDUAL STATISTICS

RUSHING—Atlanta, Heyward 16-69, Anderson 11-55, Hebert 2-14, Huntley 2-8. Jacksonville, Means 27-110, Brunell 4-28, Maston 1-5.

PASSING—Atlanta, Hebert 17-25-0-172, Nagle 0-1-0-0. Jacksonville, Brunell 18-29-0-222.

RECEIVING—Atlanta, Emanuel 6-67, Brown 6-60, Heyward 2-22, Huntley 1-14, Lyons 1-5, Metcalf 1-4. Jacksonville, Smith 5-75, McCardell 4-47, Mitchell 4-46, Brown 3-33, W. Jackson 1-13, Maston 1-8.

MISSED FIELD GOAL ATTEMPTS—Atlanta, Andersen 30.

INTERCEPTIONS—None.

KICKOFF RETURNS—Atlanta, Preston 6-123. Jacksonville, B. Brooks 2-50, R. Bell 1-5.

PUNT RETURNS—Atlanta, Metcalf 3-18. Jacksonville, Hudson 2-12.

SACKS—Atlanta, Archambeau 1, Hall 1, Matthews 1. Jacksonville, Beasley 1.

BILLS 20, CHIEFS 9

Sunday, December 22

Kansas City	3	3	3	0— 9
Buffalo	0	3	3	14—20

First Quarter

K.C.—FG, Stoyanovich 19, 9:42.

Second Quarter

K.C.—FG, Stoyanovich 24, 4:14.
Buf.—FG, Christie 41, 12:06.

Third Quarter

K.C.—FG, Stoyanovich 26, 3:38.
Buf.—FG, Christie 42, 12:44.

Fourth Quarter

Buf.—Cline 4 pass from Kelly (Christie kick), 2:37.
Buf.—Early 4 pass from Kelly (Christie kick), 10:47.
Attendance—68,671.

TEAM STATISTICS

	Kansas City	Buffalo
First Downs	15	15
Rushes-Yards	39-119	26-78
Passing	130	257
Punt Returns	2-5	3-16
Kickoff Returns	5-112	4-66
Interception Returns	1-7	2-20
Comp-Att-Int	14-28-2	20-29-1
Sacked-Yards Lost	1-8	2-22
Punts	7-40	5-39
Fumbles-Lost	2-1	6-2
Penalties-Yards	4-34	7-42
Time of Possession	35:01	24:59

INDIVIDUAL STATISTICS

RUSHING—Kansas City, Allen 20-87, Anders 9-15, Hill 7-17, Vanover 1-1, Bennett 1-0, Bono 1-(minus 1). Buffalo, T. Thomas 17-43, Holmes 4-1, Tasker 2-2, Early 1-29, Reed 1-4, Kelly 1-(minus 1).

PASSING—Kansas City, Bono 14-28-2-138. Buffalo, Kelly 20-29-1-279.

RECEIVING—Kansas City, Anders 7-49, Penn 3-43, Vanover 1-18, Hughes 1-17, Allen 1-6, Walker 1-5. Buffalo, Reed 6-76, Tasker 4-87, Johnson 4-48, Early 3-35, T. Thomas 1-27, Cline 1-4, Holmes 1-2.

MISSED FIELD GOAL ATTEMPTS—Buffalo, Christie 48.

INTERCEPTIONS—Kansas City, Davis 1-7. Buffalo, Spielman 1-14, Perry 1-6.

KICKOFF RETURNS—Kansas City, Vanover 5-112. Buffalo, Moulds 4-66.

PUNT RETURNS—Kansas City, Vanover 2-5. Buffalo, Burris 3-16.

SACKS—Kansas City, Thomas 2. Buffalo, B. Smith 1.

REDSKINS 37, COWBOYS 10
Sunday, December 22

Dallas	0	3	0	7—10
Washington	3	13	7	14—37

First Quarter
Was.—FG, Blanton 45, 8:37.
Second Quarter
Was.—FG, Blanton 29, :32.
Dal.—FG, Boniol 34, 2:46.
Was.—Allen 1 run (Blanton kick), 10:04.
Was.—FG, Blanton 18, 15:00.
Third Quarter
Was.—Allen 2 run (Blanton kick), 3:13.
Fourth Quarter
Was.—Allen 6 run (Blanton kick), 1:48.
Was.—Davis 4 run (Blanton kick), 7:28.
Dal.—Walker 39 run (Boniol kick), 8:19.
Attendance—56,454.

TEAM STATISTICS

	Dallas	Washington
First Downs	14	32
Rushes-Yards	23-119	39-157
Passing	116	326
Punt Returns	0-0	2-18
Kickoff Returns	7-166	3-62
Interception Returns	1-(-4)	1-12
Comp-Att-Int	11-21-1	22-31-1
Sacked-Yards Lost	1-7	3-20
Punts	6-41	3-36
Fumbles-Lost	1-1	1-0
Penalties-Yards	10-80	8-70
Time of Possession	24:25	35:35

INDIVIDUAL STATISTICS
RUSHING—Dallas, S. Williams 15-40, Walker 6-71, Wilson 2-8. Washington, Allen 26-87, Davis 8-35, Mitchell 4-33, Frerotte 1-2.

PASSING—Dallas, Wilson 8-18-1-79, Garrett 3-3-0-44. Washington, Frerotte 22-31-1-346.

RECEIVING—Dallas, K. Williams 2-18, S. Williams 2-14, St. Williams 1-32, Walker 1-20, Mitchell 1-17, Martin 1-9, Irvin 1-7, Armstrong 1-4, Johnston 1-2. Washington, Ellard 7-155, Westbrook 4-80, Allen 3-32, W. Bell 2-20, B. Brooks 2-19, Bowie 2-14, Asher 1-21, Mitchell 1-5.

MISSED FIELD GOAL ATTEMPTS—None.

INTERCEPTIONS—Dallas, Teague 1-(minus 4). Washington, Turner 1-12.

KICKOFF RETURNS—Dallas, K. Williams 6-103, Walker 1-63. Washington, Mitchell 3-62.

PUNT RETURNS—Washington, Mitchell 2-18.

SACKS—Dallas, McCormack 1, Childress 1, Woodson 1. Washington, M. Patton 1.

DOLPHINS 31, JETS 28
Sunday, December 22

Miami	0	7	17	7—31
N.Y. Jets	14	0	7	7—28

First Quarter
NYJ—Douglas 62 fumble return (Lowery kick), 4:15.
NYJ—Murrell 1 run (Lowery kick), 10:48.
Second Quarter
Mia.—McDuffie 1 pass from Marino (Nedney kick), 14:54.
Third Quarter
Mia.—Barnett 33 pass from Marino (Nedney kick), 2:04.
NYJ—Brady 11 pass from Foley (Lowery kick), 5:43.
Mia.—Abdul-Jabbar 17 run (Nedney kick), 9:45.
Mia.—FG, Nedney 37, 12:46.
Fourth Quarter
Mia.—R. Hill 50 pass from Marino (Nedney kick), 3:43.
NYJ—Chrebet 9 pass from Reich (Lowery kick), 10:15.
Attendance—49,933.

TEAM STATISTICS

	Miami	N.Y. Jets
First Downs	26	21
Rushes-Yards	40-157	22-83
Passing	259	195
Punt Returns	3-36	3-8
Kickoff Returns	5-109	4-79
Interception Returns	0-0	0-0
Comp-Att-Int	20-43-0	20-41-0
Sacked-Yards Lost	1-3	2-23
Punts	6-44	6-44
Fumbles-Lost	3-1	3-2
Penalties-Yards	7-87	8-50
Time of Possession	34:42	25:18

INDIVIDUAL STATISTICS
RUSHING—Miami, Abdul-Jabbar 30-152, Spikes 6-12, Marino 2-(minus 2), Pritchett 2-(minus 5). New York, Murrell 19-69, Anderson 1-9, Foley 1-4, Reich 1-1.

PASSING—Miami, Marino 20-42-0-262, Erickson 0-1-0-0. New York, Foley 10-26-0-110, Reich 10-15-0-108.

RECEIVING—Miami, McDuffie 5-66, Drayton 5-56, R. Hill 3-68, Pritchett 3-21, Barnett 2-40, Abdul-Jabbar 1-6, Parmalee 1-5. New York, Slaughter 5-84, Chrebet 4-41, Johnson 3-45, Brady 2-19, Anderson 2-14, Murrell 2-8, Van Dyke 2-7.

MISSED FIELD GOAL ATTEMPTS—None.

INTERCEPTIONS—None.

KICKOFF RETURNS—Miami, Spikes 3-66, Dar Dar 2-43. New York, Cobb 2-46, Van Dyke 1-27, Glenn 1-6.

PUNT RETURNS—Miami, McDuffie 2-26, Buckley 1-10. New York, Chrebet 3-8.

SACKS—Miami, Armstrong 2. New York, B. Hamilton 1.

PANTHERS 18, STEELERS 14
Sunday, December 22

Pittsburgh	0	14	0	0—14
Carolina	7	2	6	3—18

First Quarter
Car.—Walls 9 pass from Collins (Kasay kick), 4:51.
Second Quarter
Car.—Safety, Tomczak penalized for intentional grounding in end zone, :46.
Pit.—Hastings 6 pass from Tomczak (N. Johnson kick), 5:28.
Pit.—Stewart 80 run (N. Johnson kick), 7:53.
Third Quarter
Car.—FG, Kasay 35, 3:05.
Car.—FG, Kasay 30, 10:26.
Fourth Quarter
Car.—FG, Kasay 29, 1:24.
Attendance—72,217.

TEAM STATISTICS

	Pittsburgh	Carolina
First Downs	12	15
Rushes-Yards	26-185	28-79
Passing	80	148
Punt Returns	3-7	5-49
Kickoff Returns	4-75	3-71
Interception Returns	0-0	2-0
Comp-Att-Int	14-31-2	21-39-0
Sacked-Yards Lost	4-22	2-18
Punts	8-40	7-38
Fumbles-Lost	0-0	2-2
Penalties-Yards	9-60	7-32
Time of Possession	29:23	30:37

INDIVIDUAL STATISTICS
RUSHING—Pittsburgh, Stewart 7-102, McAfee 7-17, T. Richardson 5-17, Bettis 3-10, Witman 3-2, Hastings 1-37. Carolina, Johnson 23-68, Griffith 2-3, Oliver 1-9, Green 1-1, Collins 1-(minus 2).

PASSING—Pittsburgh, Stewart 8-21-2-77, Tomczak 6-10-0-25. Carolina, Collins 21-39-0-166.

RECEIVING—Pittsburgh, Hastings 7-54, C. Johnson 3-34, Arnold 2-11, Botkin 1-6, Bettis 1-(minus 3). Carolina, Green 5-57, Walls 5-43, Johnson 5-23, Griffith 3-12, Carrier 2-25, Ismail 1-6.

MISSED FIELD GOAL ATTEMPTS—None.

INTERCEPTIONS—Carolina, Cota 1-0, Cook 1-0.

KICKOFF RETURNS—Pittsburgh, Arnold 3-55, Mills 1-20. Carolina, Bates 2-59, Bickett 1-12.

PUNT RETURNS—Pittsburgh, Arnold 2-6, Hastings 1-1. Carolina, Oliver 5-49.

SACKS—Pittsburgh, Holmes 1, Perry 1. Carolina, Mills 1, Kragen 1, Cota 1, King 1.

SEAHAWKS 28, RAIDERS 21
Sunday, December 22

Seattle	0	13	15	0—28
Oakland	8	6	7	0—21

First Quarter
Oak.—FG, Ford 47, 5:25.
Oak.—Safety, Dan Land tackled J. Bellamy in end zone, 6:52.
Oak.—FG, Ford 23, 9:18.

Second Quarter
Oak.—FG, Ford 28, 1:55.
Sea.—FG, Peterson 45, 4:03.
Oak.—FG, Ford 24, 13:48.
Sea.—Smith 27 run (Peterson kick), 14:05.
Sea.—FG, Peterson 52, 15:00.

Third Quarter
Sea.—Galloway 32 pass from Torretta (Smith run), 1:08.
Sea.—Smith 3 run (Peterson kick), 7:03.
Oak.—Fenner 1 run (Ford kick), 15:00.
Attendance—33,455.

TEAM STATISTICS
	Seattle	Oakland
First Downs	8	21
Rushes-Yards	29-116	30-116
Passing	13	240
Punt Returns	1-5	6-94
Kickoff Returns	4-114	5-111
Interception Returns	1-12	1-0
Comp-Att-Int	5-18-1	22-47-1
Sacked-Yards Lost	4-28	6-22
Punts	10-39	4-37
Fumbles-Lost	1-1	9-6
Penalties-Yards	8-59	7-85
Time of Possession	23:49	36:11

INDIVIDUAL STATISTICS
RUSHING—Seattle, Smith 25-87, Torretta 2-12, Galloway 1-11, Pritchard 1-6. Oakland, Kaufman 15-66, Klingler 5-34, Williams 5-7, Fenner 4-9, Aska 1-0.
PASSING—Seattle, Torretta 5-16-1-41, Gelbaugh 0-2-0-0. Oakland, Klingler 10-24-0-87, Hobert 12-23-1-175.
RECEIVING—Seattle, Galloway 2-39, Smith 2-(minus 4), Crumpler 1-6. Oakland, Fenner 6-42, T. Brown 5-65, Jett 4-40, Dudley 2-22, Hobbs 2-14, Shedd 1-51, A. Glover 1-25, Williams 1-3.
MISSED FIELD GOAL ATTEMPTS—None.
INTERCEPTIONS—Seattle, Blackmon 1-9. Oakland, Morton 1-0.
KICKOFF RETURNS—Seattle, C. Harris 3-59, Crumpler 1-55. Oakland, Kidd 2-58, Kaufman 2-39, Hobbs 1-14.
PUNT RETURNS—Seattle, Galloway 1-5. Oakland, T. Brown 5-47, Hobbs 1-0.
SACKS—Seattle, McCrary 3, Adams 1, Sinclair 1, Daniels 1. Oakland, Morton 1, McGlockton 1, Lewis 1, Swilling 1.

CHARGERS 16, BRONCOS 10
Sunday, December 22

Denver	10	0	0	0—10
San Diego	7	3	6	0—16

First Quarter
Den.—FG, Elam 51, 1:11.
Den.—Davis 1 run (Elam kick), 6:40.
S.D.—Jones 9 pass from Humphries (Carney kick), 13:14.

Second Quarter
S.D.—FG, Carney 50, 6:29.

Third Quarter
S.D.—FG, Carney 21, 5:36.
S.D.—FG, Carney 22, 14:27.
Attendance—46,801.

TEAM STATISTICS
	Denver	San Diego
First Downs	13	14
Rushes-Yards	21-66	27-81
Passing	148	163
Punt Returns	3-39	1-21
Kickoff Returns	4-105	2-33
Interception Returns	3-38	2-21
Comp-Att-Int	25-43-2	17-36-3
Sacked-Yards Lost	3-20	1-7
Punts	5-41	6-46
Fumbles-Lost	2-2	1-0
Penalties-Yards	9-86	7-51
Time of Possession	33:06	26:54

INDIVIDUAL STATISTICS
RUSHING—Denver, Davis 9-21, Hebron 6-9, Lewis 3-35, Musgrave 2-(minus 2), Elway 1-3. San Diego, Bradley 19-60, Humphries 4-(minus 1), Fletcher 3-21, Hayden 1-1.
PASSING—Denver, Musgrave 11-18-1-69, Lewis 8-14-1-53, Elway 6-11-0-46. San Diego, Humphries 17-36-3-170.
RECEIVING—Denver, Craver 6-32, R. Smith 4-31, Miller 3-27, Carswell 3-24, Chamberlain 3-22, Hebron 3-13, McCaffrey 2-10, Davis 1-9. San Diego, Martin 4-50, Jones 4-40, Roche 3-23, Fletcher 2-17, May 2-15, Bradley 1-20, A. Coleman 1-5.
MISSED FIELD GOAL ATTEMPTS—Denver, Elam 45.
INTERCEPTIONS—Denver, Washington 1-23, James 1-15, Romanowski 1-0. San Diego, Harrison 1-21, Clark 1-0.
KICKOFF RETURNS—Denver, Hebron 4-105. San Diego, A. Coleman 2-33.
PUNT RETURNS—Denver, R. Smith 3-39. San Diego, Jones 1-21.
SACKS—Denver, Tanuvasa 1. San Diego, Harrison 1, Johnson 1, Edwards 1.

49ERS 24, LIONS 14
Monday, December 23

Detroit	7	0	7	0—14
San Francisco	7	7	7	3—24

First Quarter
S.F.—Popson 1 pass from S. Young (Wilkins kick), 7:02.
Det.—Sanders 54 run (Hanson kick), 9:08.

Second Quarter
S.F.—Loville 1 pass from S. Young (Wilkins kick), 9:08.

Third Quarter
S.F.—Grbac 6 run (Wilkins kick), 4:58.
Det.—H. Moore 5 pass from Mitchell (Hanson kick), 13:07.

Fourth Quarter
S.F.—FG, Wilkins 49, 8:32.
Attendance—61,921.

TEAM STATISTICS
	Detroit	San Francisco
First Downs	18	18
Rushes-Yards	33-189	31-129
Passing	88	152
Punt Returns	3-10	2-14
Kickoff Returns	5-70	3-91
Interception Returns	0-0	0-0
Comp-Att-Int	15-27-0	17-23-0
Sacked-Yards Lost	3-22	0-0
Punts	4-42	3-46
Fumbles-Lost	1-0	1-0
Penalties-Yards	5-34	6-61
Time of Possession	29:56	30:04

INDIVIDUAL STATISTICS
RUSHING—Detroit, Sanders 28-175, Mitchell 4-11, Rivers 1-3. San Francisco, Loville 14-66, Grbac 5-1, D. Carter 4-17, S. Young 3-26, Vardell 3-5, Lynn 2-14.
PASSING—Detroit, Mitchell 15-27-0-110. San Francisco, S. Young 11-14-0-96, Grbac 6-9-0-56.
RECEIVING—Detroit, H. Moore 8-59, Perriman 4-31, Morton 2-16, Sanders 1-4. San Francisco, Rice 5-49, Loville 4-32, Jones 2-28, Caldwell 2-9, Uwaezuoke 1-16, Vardell 1-13, Owens 1-4, Popson 1-1.
MISSED FIELD GOAL ATTEMPTS—Detroit, Hanson 41.
INTERCEPTIONS—None.
KICKOFF RETURNS—Detroit, Milburn 5-70. San Francisco, Loville 2-58, D. Carter 1-33.
PUNT RETURNS—Detroit, Milburn 3-10. San Francisco, D. Carter 2-14.
SACKS—San Francisco, Doleman $1^{1}/_{2}$, Barker 1, B. Young $^{1}/_{2}$.

WILD-CARD GAMES

PITTSBURGH 42, INDIANAPOLIS 14

Why the Steelers won: After trailing, 14-13, at halftime, the team held the Colts to just 22 yards in the second half, including just 2 yards on the ground. While the defense was at work, the offense was using its high-powered ground game to wear down the Colts. The Steelers gained 182 of their 228 rushing yards in the second half, led by Jerome Bettis (55), Kordell Stewart (48) and Jon Witman (48). Bettis tallied two 1-yard touchdown runs, Stewart had a 3-yarder and Witman rambled 31 yards for a score, all in the second half.

Why the Colts lost: They couldn't move the ball in the second half. The Steelers led 13-0 before the Colts scored twice in the second quarter to take a 14-13 lead before the half. Running back Marshall Faulk finished with 25 yards on nine carries and Jim Harbaugh was 12-of-32 for 134 yards.

The turning points:

1. With the Colts trailing, 13-0, in the second period, Indianapolis cornerback Eugene Daniel intercepted a Mike Tomczak pass and returned it 59 yards for a touchdown. Tomczak then threw an interception to cornerback Ray McElroy, setting up a 9-yard touchdown pass from Harbaugh to Aaron Bailey. The two touchdowns enabled the Colts to take a 14-13 halftime lead, although they were outplayed in the first two periods.

2. The Colts might have had the lead at the half, but they never stood a chance when the whistle was blown to start the second half. The Steelers opened the half with a 16-play, 91-yard touchdown drive that lasted 9:30. Bettis scored from the 1 to cap the drive, and Stewart's two-point conversion pass to John Farquhar gave Pittsburgh a 21-14 lead. Harbaugh was intercepted by Levon Kirkland two plays later, then fumbled the ball away on the Colts' next possession.

Notable: The Steelers set team playoff records for most points scored (42), fewest first downs allowed (eight) and fewest rushing first downs allowed (none). . . . Bettis, in the first playoff game of his career, ran nine times for 44 yards on the Steelers' game-winning march, including an 18-yard jaunt up the middle. . . . Pittsburgh had the second-ranked defense in the NFL during the regular season, allowing 273 yards per game. . . . With the loss, the Colts fell to 0-4 at Three Rivers Stadium since 1992. . . . After rushing for 69 yards and zero touchdowns in the regular season, Pittsburgh's Witman had 48 yards and one score against the Colts.

Quotable: Steelers linebacker Chad Brown about his outlook: "The next logical step is to win the Super Bowl. I don't want us to get ahead of ourselves, because we have New England next. But I like our chances." . . . Coach Bill Cowher on th quarterback situation between Kordell Stewart an Mike Tomczak: "They're both going to play in th upcoming weeks. How much, I can't answer." . . Cowher on the team's effort: "This is one of the be ter games we've played in a while." . . . Harbaug after being sacked four times and having a chippe tooth and a cut in his mouth that needed 15-2 stitches: "It got to be a matter of survival out there and my mouth didn't. I've got some dental work t be done." . . . Colts coach Lindy Infante on the los "We battled for 30 minutes, had ourselves one poir ahead at halftime. In the second half, Pittsburgh dominated us on both sides of the football and ou played us. It's sad for our guys, we had such a ga lant season. It's unfortunate it had to end this way.

STEELERS 42, COLTS 14
Sunday, December 29

Indianapolis	0	14	0	0—14
Pittsburgh	10	3	8	21—42

First Quarter
Pit.—FG, N. Johnson 29, 6:41.
Pit.—Stewart 1 run (N. Johnson kick), 10:05.
Second Quarter
Pit.—FG, N. Johnson 50, :10.
Ind.—Daniel 59 interception return (Blanchard kick), 10:25.
Ind.—Bailey 9 pass from Harbaugh (Blanchard kick), 14:29.
Third Quarter
Pit.—Bettis 1 run (Farquhar pass from Stewart), 9:30.
Fourth Quarter
Pit.—Bettis 1 run (N. Johnson kick), :30.
Pit.—Witman 31 run (N. Johnson kick), 7:31.
Pit.—Stewart 3 run (N. Johnson kick), 11:50.
Attendance—58,078.

TEAM STATISTICS
	Indianapolis	Pittsburgl
First downs	8	24
Rushes-yards	15-41	51-231
Passing	105	176
Punt returns	1-4	5-77
Kickoff returns	7-127	3-67
Interception returns	2-59	1-0
Comp.-att.-int.	13-33-1	14-22-2
Sacked-yards lost	4-35	0-0
Punts	8-42	2-42
Fumbles-lost	1-1	2-1
Penalties-yards	6-30	1-19
Time of possession	22:24	37:36

INDIVIDUAL STATISTICS
RUSHING—Indianapolis, Faulk 9-25, Harbaugh 3-6, Groce 2-11, Warre 1-(minus 1). Pittsburgh, Bettis 25-102, Stewart 9-48, Witman 7-48, McAfe 5-21, Hastings 2-7, Mills 1-4, Lester 1-2, Tomczak 1-(minus 1).

PASSING—Indianapolis, Harbaugh 12-32-1-134, Justin 1-1-0-4 Pittsburgh, Tomczak 13-21-2-176, Stewart 1-1-0-0.

RECEIVING—Indianapolis, Harrison 3-71, Stablein 3-28, Faulk 3-1 Dawkins 2-18, Bailey 1-9, Dilger 1-4. Pittsburgh, C. Johnson 5-10 Hastings 3-30, Botkin 2-26, Lester 2-7, Bettis 1-4, McAfee 1-0.

MISSED FIELD GOAL ATTEMPTS—None.

INTERCEPTIONS—Indianapolis, Daniel 1-59, McElroy 1-0. Pittsburg Kirkland 1-0.

KICKOFF RETURNS—Indianapolis, Warren 4-68, Stock 2-38, Bailey 1-1 Pittsburgh, Arnold 2-38, Mills 1-29.

PUNT RETURNS—Indianapolis, Buchanan 1-4. Pittsburgh, Arnold 5-77

SACKS—Pittsburgh, Brown 3, Gildon 1.

1996 REVIEW *Wild-card games*

JACKSONVILLE 30, BUFFALO 27

Why the Jaguars won: In Week 17, the Jaguars defeated Atlanta, 19-17, when Morten Andersen missed a 30-yard field goal with four seconds left. Andersen had not missed a kick from 30 yards or less since the 1989 season. Jacksonville followed that little bit of luck into its wild-card matchup with the Bills. With the game tied at 7 and 3:07 left in the game, Mike Hollis kicked a 45-yard field goal for what turned out to be the winning points. On the kick, Hollis watched from the ground as the ball hit off the the right upright before going through. Jacksonville was able to use a 175-yard rushing performance from Natrone Means and 239 passing yards from Mark Brunell to control the ball for 33:06. Hollis' field goal marked the fourth and final lead change for the Jaguars.

Why the Bills lost: Buffalo couldn't hold a lead, and when push came to shove, Means shoved the Bills to the ground. The Bills' aging stars—Jim Kelly and Thurman Thomas—showed in the first half why Buffalo had played in four Super Bowls. But in the second half, the two were shut down. Kelly threw for 166 yards in the first half, including a 7-yard touchdown pass to Thomas, but was held to only 10 yards in the final two quarters. And Thomas was held to 19 yards after 31 in the first half.

The turning points:
1. With the Bills leading, 7-0, in the first quarter, Kelly attempted a shovel pass to Thomas. This was the second time the Bills had tried this play and Jaguars defensive end Clyde Simmons was prepared. He stepped in front of Thomas for the interception and returned it 20 yards for a touchdown.
2. The Bills took a 14-10 lead late in the first quarter after a 2-yard touchdown run by Thomas. On the ensuing possession, Brunell was intercepted by Thomas Smith. The Bills promptly drove to the Jaguars' 16, where they were faced with a fourth-and-1. A quarterback sneak by Kelly is stopped short of the first-down marker. Six plays later, following a 47-yard pass play from Brunell to tight end Pete Mitchell, Means ran 30 yards for a score to give the Jaguars a 17-14 advantage.
3. After a 38-yard interception return for a touchdown by the Bills' Jeff Burris, Brunell responded by leading Jacksonville on a 65-yard touchdown drive, taking 5:37 off the clock. The drive was capped off with a 2-yard touchdown pass from Brunell to Jimmy Smith to tie the game at 27.

Notable: Brunell threw two interceptions, snapping his streak of 129 consecutive passes without an interception. . . . The Jaguars became the first team to beat the Bills at Rich Stadium in the postseason. The Bills had won their nine previous playoff games at Rich Stadium. . . . Means' 175 rushing yards was a team record and marked the first time in team history a Jacksonville player rushed for 100 yards in consecutive games. . . . Thomas' two touchdowns kept him tied with Dallas' Emmitt Smith for the postseason career record with 20.

. . . In the regular season, Bills defensive end Bruce Smith was tied for the AFC lead in sacks with 13.5, but he was held to just two quarterback pressures in this game. Second-year tackle Tony Boselli was matched against Smith for most of the game.

Quotable: Bills center Kent Hull on the Jaguars: "They seem like the team we used to be. That was an opportunistic team, and they made the plays when they had to have them. That's the reason they won." . . . Jaguars wide receiver Keenan McCardell on the win: "Everybody said we're too young and we're supposed to lose, but we're hungry and we kept on scratching and clawing to go on." . . . Bills coach Marv Levy on the loss: "We lost a game that was a very bitter loss. This game hurts the most." . . . Jaguars coach Tom Coughlin on the Bills losing: "The end of an era? Well, it's the beginning of one maybe for us. If it's the end or the beginning, I'd rather choose to talk about the beginning."

JAGUARS 30, BILLS 27
Saturday, December 28

Jacksonville	10	7	3	10—30
Buffalo	14	3	3	7—27

First Quarter
Buf.—T. Thomas 7 pass from Kelly (Christie kick), 3:30.
Jac.—Simmons 20 interception return (Hollis kick), 8:34.
Buf.—T. Thomas 2 run (Christie kick), 12:34.
Jac.—FG, Hollis 27, 14:50.

Second Quarter
Jac.—Means 30 run (Hollis kick), 11:15.
Buf.—FG, Christie 33, 13:04.

Third Quarter
Buf.—FG, Christie 47, 4:40.
Jac.—FG, Hollis 24, 12:15.

Fourth Quarter
Buf.—Burris 38 interception return (Christie kick), :43.
Jac.—Smith 2 pass from Brunell (Hollis kick), 6:20.
Jac.—FG, Hollis 45, 11:53.
Attendance—70,213.

TEAM STATISTICS

	Jacksonville	Buffalo
First downs	18	19
Rushes-yards	35-184	29-92
Passing	225	216
Punt returns	2-11	5-32
Kickoff returns	5-99	7-172
Interception returns	1-20	2-38
Comp.-att.-int.	18-33-2	22-36-1
Sacked-yards lost	2-14	3-30
Punts	5-51	5-43
Fumbles-lost	0-0	4-2
Penalties-yards	6-42	6-39
Time of possession	33:06	26:54

INDIVIDUAL STATISTICS
RUSHING—Jacksonville, Means 31-175, Brunell 3-9, Stewart 1-0. Buffalo, T. Thomas 14-50, Holmes 9-10, Kelly 4-18, Tasker 1-9, Tindale 1-5.
PASSING—Jacksonville, Brunell 18-33-2-239. Buffalo, Kelly 21-32-1-239, Collins 1-4-0-7.
RECEIVING—Jacksonville, Smith 5-58, McCardell 4-76, Mitchell 3-64, Maston 2-21, W. Jackson 1-11, Brown 1-8, Stewart 1-5, Means 1-(minus 4). Buffalo, Early 9-122, Reed 3-32, Tasker 3-30, Johnson 3-27, T. Thomas 3-24, Holmes 1-11.
MISSED FIELD GOAL ATTEMPTS—Jacksonville, Hollis 58.
INTERCEPTIONS—Jacksonville, Simmons 1-20. Buffalo, Burris 1-38, T. Smith 1-0.
KICKOFF RETURNS—Jacksonville, B. Brooks 4-74, R. Bell 1-25. Buffalo, Moulds 5-142, Copeland 1-26, Coons 1-4.
PUNT RETURNS—Jacksonville, Hudson 2-11. Buffalo, Burris 5-32.
SACKS—Jacksonville, Simmons 2, Brackens 1. Buffalo, Covington 1, White 1.

DALLAS 40, MINNESOTA 15

Why the Cowboys won: Dallas played its most complete game of the season. The defense took control early, forcing four turnovers in the first half. The Cowboys were able to capitalize, scoring 20 points off the turnovers to take a 30-0 halftime lead. The offense had their best game of the season, controlling the line of scrimmage and rushing for 255 yards. As a result of the line's dominance, Emmitt Smith rushed for 116 yards and two touchdowns. The 40 points were a season-high for the Cowboys, exceeding the previous best of 32.

Why the Vikings lost: Minnesota's five turnovers allowed Dallas to score early and often. Not helping the matter was Brad Johnson starting his first postseason game. His inexperience was evident in the second quarter, as he threw two costly interceptions. To make matters worse, the team's defensive front lost the battle in the trenches They allowed 255 yards on the ground, more than double the season average (122.9). The Vikings controlled the ball for only 18 minutes, compared to the Cowboys' 42.

The turning points:

1. After forcing the Vikings to punt, the Cowboys scored on their opening drive when Troy Aikman followed a block from Larry Allen and scored from the 2. The early score was especially important for Dallas since it had scored only 32 points in the last three regular-season games.

2. With the Cowboys leading, 7-0, early, Minnesota running back Amp Lee caught a short pass from Brad Johnson and was on his way to the end zone to tie the game. Before he could get the ball over the goal line, Dallas safety George Teague reached in, forcing a fumble at the 2. The ball bounced out of the end zone, giving the Cowboys possession on the touchback. After the turnover, Dallas drove 70 yards and went up 10-0 on a 28-yard field goal by Chris Boniol.

3. On the Vikings' first possession following a 37-yard touchdown run by Emmitt Smith (made possible by another forced fumble from Teague), Teague intercepted an errant Johnson pass and returned it 29 yards for a touchdown. The touchdown made it 24-0 with just over eight minutes remaining in the first half.

Notable: Teague's interception return for a touchdown was the second in his career. The first was an NFL postseason record 101-yarder in 1994 while playing for the Green Bay Packers. . . . Smith's two rushing touchdowns allowed him to take sole possession of the postseason record for rushing touchdowns with 18. The scores were his 19th and 20th overall, keeping him in a first-place tie with Buffalo's Thurman Thomas. Smith rushed for 100 yards for the seventh time in the postseason, another record. . . . The Vikings' loss was their sixth in a row in the playoffs, including four in a row under coach Dennis Green.

Quotable: Cornerback Deion Sanders on the Cowboys' performance: "We sent a message out there to everybody. Dallas is still the team to beat." . . . Vikings linebacker Jeff Brady on the Dallas offensive line: "What their offensive line did to us was just an awesome display of power." . . . Lee on his early fumble: "You can't put a play like that out of your mind. It was a big turning point, and I accept responsibility for what happened." . . . Aikman on expectations placed on Dallas: "We realize it doesn't matter what we do in the regular season. We're judged on what takes place in the postseason." . . . Wide receiver Michael Irvine on the Cowboys' ability to "turn it on" when they needed to: "When you say you're going to turn it up, that's not physical. That's mental. I think the mind plays a big role in any sport, and we feel we can pretty much accomplish anything if we put our mind to it."

COWBOYS 40, VIKINGS 15
Saturday, December 28

Minnesota	0	0	7	8—15
Dallas	7	23	7	3—40

First Quarter
Dal.—Aikman 2 run (Boniol kick), 9:57.
Second Quarter
Dal.—FG, Boniol 28, 4:56.
Dal.—E. Smith 37 run (Boniol kick), 5:24.
Dal.—Teague 29 interception return (Boniol kick), 6:24.
Dal.—FG, Boniol 31, 9:41.
Dal.—FG, Boniol 22, 14:37.
Third Quarter
Min.—Carter 30 pass from B. Johnson (Sisson kick), 4:12.
Dal.—E. Smith 1 run (Boniol kick), 13:19.
Fourth Quarter
Dal.—FG, Boniol 25, 5:31.
Min.—B. Johnson 5 run (Carter pass from B. Johnson), 8:01.
Attendance—64,682.

TEAM STATISTICS

	Minnesota	Dallas
First downs	12	27
Rushes-yards	15-63	46-255
Passing	205	183
Punt returns	1-8	1-6
Kickoff returns	8-153	1-21
Interception returns	1-4	2-51
Comp.-att.-int.	15-27-2	21-31-1
Sacked-yards lost	2-3	1-9
Punts	2-40	1-43
Fumbles-lost	4-4	2-1
Penalties-yards	3-15	5-54
Time of possession	17:57	42:03

INDIVIDUAL STATISTICS

RUSHING—Minnesota, Lee 7-26, Hoard 3-21, B. Johnson 3-14, Graham 2-2. Dallas, E. Smith 17-116, S. Williams 17-67, Walker 8-62, Aikman 2-4, Johnston 1-5, K. Williams 1-1.

PASSING—Minnesota, B. Johnson 15-27-2-208. Dallas, Aikman 19-29-1-178, Garrett 2-2-0-14.

RECEIVING—Minnesota, Ismail 3-78, Carter 3-36, Evans 3-9, Lee 2-38, Jordan 1-10, Reed 1-10, Hoard 1-7, Graham 1-(minus 1). Dallas, Irvin 8-103, E. Smith 4-26, Bjornson 3-16, Martin 2-30, Johnston 2-7, Walker 1-8, S. Williams 1-2.

MISSED FIELD GOAL ATTEMPTS—None.

INTERCEPTIONS—Minnesota, Thomas 1-4. Dallas, Teague 1-29, Sanders 1-22.

KICKOFF RETURNS—Minnesota, Palmer 6-130, Gerak 1-12, Lee 1-11. Dallas, Walker 1-21.

PUNT RETURNS—Minnesota, Palmer 1-8. Dallas, Martin 1-6.

SACKS—Minnesota, Alexander 1. Dallas, Carver 1, Thomas 1.

SAN FRANCISCO 14, PHILADELPHIA 0

Why the 49ers won: Three words—Young, Rice, defense. Steve Young led the Niners to both of their touchdowns. The first came on a 9-yard run. The second was a 3-yard pass to Jerry Rice. The touchdown pass was the result of Rice's one-handed, 26-yard reception on the previous play. The 49ers were outgained by the Eagles, but the defense made the necessary big plays and stiffened in the second half. They made two key interceptions with the Eagles in the red zone and held Philadelphia to 8 rushing yards in the second half.

Why the Eagles lost: Starting his first postseason game, Ty Detmer threw two second-quarter interceptions with the Eagles inside the 49ers' 10. Even though the Eagles controlled the ball for 19 minutes in the first half, their inability to score set the tone for the game. After coming up empty in the red zone, the offense stalled in the second half, totaling only 102 yards. Former San Francisco running back Ricky Watters was held in check by his old teammates, rushing for 57 yards on 20 carries.

The turning points:

1. After being forced to punt on the opening drive, Steve Young guided the 49ers on a 74-yard touchdown drive on their second possession. Young completed six of seven passes and finished the drive with a 9-yard run up the middle. He suffered bruised ribs and had the wind knocked out of him on the touchdown run.

2. With the score 7-0 in the second quarter, the Eagles forced the 49ers to punt. A 22-yard return by Mark Seay allows Philadelphia to start with the ball on its 40. Using a balanced attack (five runs, four passes), the Eagles take 5:37 and drive to the 49ers' 7. On third-and-1, Philadelphia chose to use a surprise pass instead of the more conventional running play. The call resulted in an interception by Marquez Pope in the end zone.

3. The Eagles' defense held tough after Pope's interception and forced San Francisco to punt with 2:56 left. Ricky Watters touched the ball on five consecutive plays to start the drive, rushing for 29 yards and two first downs. With two minutes left and the ball on San Francisco's 40, the Eagles decided to try and pass their way into the end zone. Detmer completed three of his next four passes for 30 yards to lead the Eagles to the 5. But two plays later, Detmer's pass intended for Chris T. Jones was intercepted in the end zone by defensive end Roy Barker.

Notable: Eagles coach Ray Rhodes was an assistant in all five of the 49ers' Super Bowl championship teams. And six players on Philadelphia's roster were former 49ers. . . . The shutout was the first for the Eagles in postseason play. . . . The 14 combined points were a record low for a wild-card game. The game was played in rain and winds that reached 51 mph. Conditions were so bad that fans were advised to take public transporation to the game. . . . The game was the first time since 1985 the 49ers did not receive a first-round bye. . . . Young carried the ball 11 times and led the 49ers with 65 yards. . . . Watters led the Eagles with 57 yards rushing. The Eagles are 10-0 when Watters rushes for at least 100 yards and 30-0-1 in the last 31 games in which an Eagles running back has at least 100 yards rushing. . . . San Francisco had its first postseason shutout since a 23-0 victory against the Chicago Bears in the 1984 NFC championship game.

Quotable: 49ers safety Merton Hanks on the team's experience: "We've all been here before. We have guys with Super Bowl rings, and we understand what it takes to get back there." . . . San Francisco safety Tim McDonald on wanting to play the Green Bay Packers again: "We got that shot now. We got a chance to do something about it." . . . Watters on the Eagles' running game: "Up until halftime, we were running on them. We didn't do much of anything the second half." . . . Rhodes on Detmer's game: "That was not a good game for Ty and I think everyone knows that. The turnovers in the red area, you can't do that. You can't leave that area without any points." . . . Eagles guard Guy McIntyre on calling a pass instead of a run on third-and-1 on the 49ers' 7: "I kind of cringed a little when the call came in. I thought we could run it in."

49ERS 14, EAGLES 0

Sunday, December 29

Philadelphia	0	0	0	0— 0
San Francisco	0	7	7	0—14

Second Quarter
S.F.—S. Young 9 run (Wilkins kick), 3:50.
Third Quarter
S.F.—Rice 3 pass from S. Young (Wilkins kick), 10:13.
Attendance—56,460.

TEAM STATISTICS

	Philadelphia	San Francisco
First downs	16	17
Rushes-yards	26-71	34-118
Passing	212	161
Punt returns	3-17	2-10
Kickoff returns	2-48	1-11
Interception returns	0-0	3-6
Comp.-att.-int.	19-33-3	14-21-0
Sacked-yards lost	3-13	1-0
Punts	5-36	6-37
Fumbles-lost	1-0	0-0
Penalties-yards	3-20	4-38
Time of possession	30:15	29:45

INDIVIDUAL STATISTICS

RUSHING—Philadelphia, Watters 20-57, Garner 3-10, Turner 3-4. San Francisco, Kirby 16-43, S. Young 11-65, Floyd 5-13, Loville 2-(minus 3).

PASSING—Philadelphia, Detmer 14-21-2-148, Rypien 5-12-1-77. San Francisco, S. Young 14-21-0-161.

RECEIVING—Philadelphia, Fryar 5-62, Watters 5-45, J. Johnson 3-37, C. Williams 2-40, Jones 2-23, Turner 2-18. San Francisco, Rice 4-50, Floyd 4-41, Kirby 2-24, Jones 2-22, Cooper 1-17, Owens 1-7.

MISSED FIELD GOAL ATTEMPTS—Philadelphia, Anderson 40.

INTERCEPTIONS—San Francisco, Barker 1-5, McDonald 1-1, Pope 1-0.

KICKOFF RETURNS—Philadelphia, Witherspoon 1-26, Seay 1-22. San Francisco, Loville 1-11.

PUNT RETURNS—Philadelphia, Seay 2-17, C. Williams 1-0. San Francisco, Kirby 2-10.

SACKS—Philadelphia, W. Thomas 1. San Francisco, B. Young 2, Woodall 1.

DIVISIONAL PLAYOFFS

JACKSONVILLE 30, DENVER 27

Why the Jaguars won: Coming off an upset at Buffalo in the wild-card playoffs, Jacksonville and quarterback Mark Brunell simply wouldn't be denied at a site—Mile High Stadium—where visiting teams usually have nightmares. Not even a 12-0 first-quarter deficit and 75,000-plus screaming Denver zealots could shake the second-year expansion team. The Jaguars, spurred by Brunell's deft passing and running and Natrone Means' brute-force rushing, rebounded for two second-quarter field goals by Mike Hollis and an 8-yard touchdown run by Means to seize a lead they never relinquished.

Why the Broncos lost: After playing solid defense in the regular season after some sieve-like performances in preceding years, Denver reverted to form and could not stop the Jaguars at key junctures. The Jags wouldn't and couldn't be contained. Most telling was the Broncos' inability to corral Brunell on a fourth-quarter play—Jacksonville was nursing a 23-20 lead—in which the quarterback eluded four Denver defenders and scrambled 29 yards to the Broncos' 21. The play set up the Jaguars' final and clinching touchdown, which came on Brunell's 16-yard strike to Jimmy Smith on third-and-5.

The turning points:

1. When Jacksonville's Keenan McCardell slipped into the clear to take a 31-yard scoring pitch from Brunell in the third period. The play boosted the Jaguars into a 20-12 lead, and any thought that it was inevitable that Jacksonville would crack against this Denver team—the Broncos had started the season with 12 victories in 13 games—was now being reassessed.

2. When Hollis kicked a 22-yard field goal early in the fourth quarter, giving Jacksonville a 23-12 lead and making it five consecutive series in which the Jaguars had scored on Denver's supposedly sturdy defense. The 17-play, 88-yard drive, featuring Brunell's short passes and Means' bullish rushes, seemed to take the stuffing out of the Broncos, who could only trade scores with the Jags the rest of the way.

Notable: Denver, seemingly mapping its Super Bowl plans since midseason, never seemed to have its head in the game. Defensive lineman Michael Dean Perry's casual jaunt off the field preceding a Jaguars punt near the end of the third quarter told the story. The too-many-men-on-the-field penalty gave Jacksonville a first down when the Broncos should have taken possession, and the blunder led to Hollis' field goal that stretched the Jags' lead to 11 points. . . . Means rumbled for 140 yards on 21 carries, and Brunell threw for 245 yards in an 18-for-29 passing performance. . . . The defeat was only the Broncos' second playoff loss at home in franchise history. . . . Denver's Terrell Davis, who ran for an AFC-high 1,538 yards in the regular season, rushed for 56 yards in the first quarter but, hobbled by a knee strain thereafter, gained only 35 the rest of the game. Davis' ineffectiveness altered the Broncos' game plan, leaving quarterback John Elway—as has been the case so often in his storied career—to carry most of the offensive burden.

Quotable: "Without question, this is the toughest loss I've ever faced," Broncos coach Mike Shanahan said. . . "Time heals a lot of wounds," said an obviously hurting Elway, "but this is as disappointed as I've been. I thought we had a team that would make it happen." . . ."I don't know if I'll ever be able to completely get over this," moaned Broncos tight end Shannon Sharpe, who had an 18-yard touchdown reception. . . . "People thought we would just be happy to be (in the playoffs) after we beat Buffalo, and this proved we're not," Jaguars defensive end Clyde Simmons said. "We're for real, and we're taking everything very seriously. We believed all year that we could get in, and once you get in anything can happen."

JAGUARS 30, BRONCOS 27

Saturday, January 4

Jacksonville	0	13	7	10—30
Denver	12	0	0	15—27

First Quarter
Den.—Hebron 1 run (kick blocked), 8:38.
Den.—Sharpe 18 pass from Elway (pass failed), 14:27.

Second Quarter
Jac.—FG, Hollis 46, 3:45.
Jac.—Means 8 run (Hollis kick), 12:02.
Jac.—FG, Hollis 42, 14:50.

Third Quarter
Jac.—McCardell 31 pass from Brunell (Hollis kick), 6:09.

Fourth Quarter
Jac.—FG, Hollis 22, 4:09.
Den.—Davis 2 run (Davis run), 7:23.
Jac.—Smith 16 pass from Brunell (Hollis kick), 11:21.
Den.—McCaffrey 15 pass from Elway (Elam kick), 13:10.
Attendance—75,678.

TEAM STATISTICS

	Jacksonville	Denver
First downs	22	21
Rushes-yards	36-203	21-126
Passing	240	225
Punt returns	1-3	2-12
Kickoff returns	4-75	6-123
Interception returns	0-0	0-0
Comp.-att.-int.	18-29-0	25-38-0
Sacked-yards lost	2-5	1-1
Punts	3-40	5-43
Fumbles-lost	0-0	1-0
Penalties-yards	3-18	8-64
Time of possession	32:24	27:36

INDIVIDUAL STATISTICS

RUSHING—Jacksonville, Means 21-140, Stewart 8-19, Brunell 7-44. Denver, Davis 14-91, Elway 5-30, Hebron 2-5.

PASSING—Jacksonville, Brunell 18-29-0-245. Denver, Elway 25-38-0-226.

RECEIVING—Jacksonville, McCardell 5-59, Means 4-46, Smith 3-71, W. Jackson 3-35, Mitchell 2-9, Stewart 1-25. Denver, Davis 7-24, Miller 5-67, McCaffrey 5-54, Craver 3-17, Sharpe 2-31, Carswell 2-18, R. Smith 1-15.

MISSED FIELD GOAL ATTEMPTS—None.

INTERCEPTIONS—None.

KICKOFF RETURNS—Jacksonville, B. Brooks 4-75. Denver, Hebron 3-85, Chamberlain 1-15, Burns 1-14, Jeffers 1-9.

PUNT RETURNS—Jacksonville, Hudson 1-3. Denver, R. Smith 2-12.

SACKS—Jacksonville, Robinson 1. Denver, Aldridge 1, D. Williams 1.

NEW ENGLAND 28, PITTSBURGH 3

Why the Patriots won: They took it to the Steelers' highly touted zone-blitz defense from the get-go. New England, seemingly not fazed by Pittsburgh's press clippings, scored touchdowns on three of its first four possessions against a defense that had ranked second in the NFL.

Why the Steelers lost: Their offense was, basically, a zero. Pittsburgh's only points—coming on a Norm Johnson field goal—were set up by Chad Brown's third-quarter interception of a Drew Bledsoe pass.

The turning points:

1. When, on the first offensive play of the game, Bledsoe went right at standout Steelers cornerback Rod Woodson and completed a 53-yard pass to rookie Terry Glenn. On the next play, running back Curtis Martin scored from the 2.

2. When, after the Patriots had extended their lead 14-0 on a Bledsoe-to-Keith Byars pass play later in the first period, Martin set sail on a 78-yard touchdown run in the second quarter. Forced into a dire catch-up situation after New England had bolted to the 21-0 lead, the ground-oriented Steelers were in deep trouble.

Notable: Pittsburgh simply didn't have the wherewithal to mount a comeback—not with backup quarterback Kordell Stewart failing to complete any of his 10 pass attempts, starting quarterback Mike Tomczak hitting on only two completions of more than 15 yards and battering ram Jerome Bettis being slowed by a groin injury. Bettis, coming off a 102-yard performance in Pittsburgh's 42-14 drubbing of Indianapolis in the wild-card round, managed only 43 yards on 13 carries against the Pats. . . . Martin made a third touchdown run in the fourth quarter, a jaunt covering 23 yards, and finished with 166 yards rushing. . . . The Patriots needed a total of only seven plays to score their first three touchdowns. . . . Bledsoe completed his first seven passes for 123 yards. The rest of the afternoon, he threw for only 41 yards—but by then, the damage had been done. . . . Facing a fourth-and-4 on New England's 24 with time running out in the second quarter, the Steelers gambled on a Tomczak pass to Fred McAfee instead of settling for a field-goal attempt. Coach Bill Cowher's decision, coming with his team down by 21 points, went awry as the Pats' Tedy Bruschi threw McAfee for a 2-yard loss. . . . The game at Foxboro Stadium was played in a dense fog, an apt description for the way the Steelers played on both sides of the ball. The conditions were never really a factor in the game, though. . . . The victory meant the Patriots would play host to the AFC championship game. Heading into the weekend, it was assumed that Denver, scourge of the conference in the regular season, would be the home team for the title clash, but the Broncos' surprising loss to Jacksonville and the Pats' easy victory thrust New England into the host role.

Quotable: "That first play (the strike to Glenn) loosened us up," New England guard William Roberts said. "We showed them it was time to get it on." . . . "We hit a few plays early and got a little momentum," Patriots coach Bill Parcells said. "We felt that was important because they would have liked, I'm sure, to run Bettis and play the way they played last week." . . . Parcells said he and the Pats targeted Woodson, one of the best defenders in NFL history. "We wanted him to know we'd throw his way," Parcells said of the game-opening bomb. . . . "You could see their frustration growing," Pats safety Willie Clay said of the Steelers' woeful attempt to play catch-up ball. "(Quarterback) has been their problem all year." . . . "Everybody talked about Denver (as the probable AFC representative in Super Bowl XXXI)," New England offensive tackle Bruce Armstrong said. "And everybody talked about Pittsburgh. But then Denver loses. And now the Pittsburgh people are out, too. The Patriots are still here."

PATRIOTS 28, STEELERS 3

Sunday, January 5

Pittsburgh	0	0	3	0— 3
New England	14	7	0	7—28

First Quarter
N.E.—Martin 2 run (Vinatieri kick), 3:02.
N.E.—Byars 34 pass from Bledsoe (Vinatieri kick), 7:05.
Second Quarter
N.E.—Martin 78 run (Vinatieri kick), 5:05.
Third Quarter
Pit.—FG, N. Johnson 29, 11:10.
Fourth Quarter
N.E.—Martin 23 run (Vinatieri kick), 2:29.
Attendance—60,188.

TEAM STATISTICS

	Pittsburgh	New England
First downs	12	17
Rushes-yards	27-123	32-194
Passing	90	152
Punt returns	5-34	7-72
Kickoff returns	5-99	2-54
Interception returns	2-0	2-14
Comp.-att.-int.	16-39-2	15-26-2
Sacked-yards lost	3-20	2-15
Punts	9-42	7-44
Fumbles-lost	0-0	0-0
Penalties-yards	3-15	2-21
Time of possession	28:39	31:21

INDIVIDUAL STATISTICS

RUSHING—Pittsburgh, Bettis 13-43, McAfee 5-30, Stewart 4-19, Witman 3-11, Tomczak 2-20. New England, Martin 19-166, Grier 5-7, Zolak 3-(minus 4), Meggett 2-18, Byars 2-8, Bledsoe 1-(minus 1).

PASSING—Pittsburgh, Tomczak 16-29-2-110, Stewart 0-10-0-0. New England, Bledsoe 14-24-2-164, Zolak 1-2-0-3.

RECEIVING—Pittsburgh, Hastings 5-55, Botkin 2-20, Arnold 2-16, Mills 2-15, McAfee 2-7, Bettis 2-(minus 1), Witman 1-(minus 2). New England, Byars 4-53, Glenn 3-69, Coates 3-18, Jefferson 3-18, Martin 2-9.

MISSED FIELD GOAL ATTEMPTS—None.

INTERCEPTIONS—Pittsburgh, Brown 1-0, Williams 1-0. New England, Clay 1-14, Milloy 1-0.

KICKOFF RETURNS—Pittsburgh, Mills 5-99. New England, T. Brown 2-54.

PUNT RETURNS—Pittsburgh, Arnold 5-34. New England, Meggett 7-72.

SACKS—Pittsburgh, Brown 1, Roye 1. New England, Johnson 1, Slade 1, Eaton ½, Jones ½.

GREEN BAY 35, SAN FRANCISCO 14

Why the Packers won: Green Bay took advantage of rain-soaked, mud-filled Lambeau Field and pounced on the 49ers early, running up a 21-0 lead late in the second quarter. The Packers' running game dominated in every way, from the 139 yards rushing gained by Edgar Bennett and Dorsey Levens to the 117 punt return yards racked up by Desmond Howard, including a 71-yarder for a touchdown.

Why the 49ers lost: The Packers ran all over them. As late as December 10, San Francisco led the NFC in run defense (84.9 yards per game). But in the three games since that date, including this playoff loss, the run defense collapsed and gave up an average of 149.3 yards on the ground.

The turning points:

1. Two minutes and 15 seconds into the game, Desmond Howard fielded a punt and ran through a half-dozen tackles for a 71-yard touchdown. Two failed 49ers possessions later, Howard took another punt and returned it 46 yards, setting up the Packers' second touchdown.

2. After the 49ers took advantage of a pair of miscues on special teams and cut the lead to 21-14, the Packers answered with a 12-play, 72-yard touchdown drive—a drive in which they passed only twice—to put it out of reach.

Notable: The attendance at Lambeau Field of 60,787 included three no-shows. . . . 49ers quarterback Steve Young lasted only two series before the pain of cracked rib forced him to the sideline. . . . Packers quarterback Brett Favre passed for only 79 yards. . . . The 49ers' loss was the third to the Packers in less than a year. . . . It was the second year in a row the 49ers were knocked out of the playoffs by the Packers.

Quotable: 49ers coach George Seifert: "When you come to an opposing team's home stadium and you're down 14 points right away, against such a good football team, it's pretty tough odds to overcome." . . . Seifert on the Packers' drive that put the game away: "The drive following our second touchdown that Green Bay put together demonstrated what type of team they are. They were a damn good football team to take the ball and respond the way they did." . . . Young on the decision to take him out of the game: "It was apparent we were going to need to throw the ball downfield. That just wasn't in my game today. As much as I wish it was. Believe me, it's a very painful thing to watch the season end." . . . Seifert on the decision to play Young: "I'm a little upset with myself for maybe pushing Steve into that situation. He really didn't practice and he's taking shots and he's coming on the field and off the field. I had a sense he might not (stay in). But at the same time, he's such a great competitor." . . . Packers coach Mike Holmgren on the field conditions: "It was hard to throw. It was hard to make breaks. It was hard to han-dle the football. We changed our approach a little b We got some turnovers. It was going to be that kind game." . . . 49ers strong safety Tim McDonald on th loss: "I thought we had a good enough team to win. thought we'd come in here and beat these guys."

PACKERS 35, 49ERS 14

Saturday, January 4

San Francisco	0	7	7	0—	
Green Bay	14	7	7	7—	

First Quarter
G.B.—Howard 71 punt return (Jacke kick), 2:15.
G.B.—Rison 4 pass from Favre (Jacke kick), 8:44.
Second Quarter
G.B.—Bennett 2 run (Jacke kick), 11:42.
S.F.—Kirby 8 pass from Grbac (Wilkins kick), 14:36.
Third Quarter
S.F.—Grbac 4 run (Wilkins kick), :16.
G.B.—Freeman fumble recovery in end zone (Jacke kick), 8:10.
Fourth Quarter
G.B.—Bennett 11 run (Jacke kick), 9:29.
Attendance—60,787.

TEAM STATISTICS

	San Francisco	Green Ba
First downs	12	1
Rushes-yards	18-68	39-13
Passing	128	
Punt returns	3-23	3-1
Kickoff returns	4-75	2-4
Interception returns	0-0	3
Comp.-att.-int.	21-41-3	11-15
Sacked-yards lost	1-5	1
Punts	6-36	6-4
Fumbles-lost	3-2	5
Penalties-yards	6-42	1
Time of possession	26:02	33:

INDIVIDUAL STATISTICS

RUSHING—San Francisco, Kirby 6-14, Floyd 5-13, Grbac 4-32, Vardel 6, S. Young 1-3. Green Bay, Bennett 17-80, Levens 15-46, Favre 5 Henderson 2-4.

PASSING—San Francisco, Grbac 19-36-3-125, S. Young 2-5-0-8. Gr Bay, Favre 11-15-0-79.

RECEIVING—San Francisco, Kirby 6-35, Floyd 6-30, Rice 5-36, Jones 32. Green Bay, Freeman 2-26, Levens 2-16, Bennett 2-14, Rison 2- Henderson 1-4, Jackson 1-4, Beebe 1-2.

MISSED FIELD GOAL ATTEMPTS—None.

INTERCEPTIONS—Green Bay, E. Robinson 2-0, Newsome 1-5.

KICKOFF RETURNS—San Francisco, Loville 3-75, Pollack 1-0. Green E Beebe 1-25, Howard 1-19.

PUNT RETURNS—San Francisco, Kirby 3-23. Green Bay, Howard 2-1 Hayes 1-0.

SACKS—San Francisco, Stubblefield 1. Green Bay, Evans 1.

1996 REVIEW Divisional playoffs

CAROLINA 26, DALLAS 17

hy the Panthers won: Carolina stopped Emmitt
mith. The league's career leader in playoff touch-
wns was stopped six times on three drives inside the
anthers' 5. Combine that with the Cowboys' loss of
ichael Irvin to injury early, and the Panthers' defense
led the day. In addition, Carolina—led by Anthony
hnson's 104 yards—was able to run the football.

hy the Cowboys lost: Dallas' offense was lacklus-
r. It had trouble making third downs and couldn't get
touchdown when it needed one, particularly without
ar receiver Michael Irvin.

rning points:

1. On the Cowboys' second offensive play, wide
ceiver Michael Irvin broke his collarbone while mak-
g a 22-yard catch and was lost for the game. Without
vin, the passing game was severely hampered. Dallas
arterback Troy Aikman completed only 50 percent
his passes for 165 yards.

2. In the second quarter, on third-and-goal from the
allas 10, Carolina's Willie Green fights off Kevin
nith and makes a diving touchdown catch. That
eant that Dallas had allowed touchdowns on consec-
ive drives to fall behind, 14-3.

otable: The Panthers made the playoffs in only their
cond season in the NFL. . . . The Panthers were 9-0
Ericsson Stadium's inaugural season. . . . The
anthers allowed the Cowboys only six points—two
ld goals—in the second half. . . . The Cowboys' sea-
n ended the same way it began—without Michael
vin. Irvin was suspended for the first five games after
eading no contest to cocaine possession, then broke
s right collarbone on the second offensive play and
issed the rest of the game. . . . Troy Aikman, the
FL's most accurate passer, struggled. He was sacked
ice and intercepted three times.

uotable: Panthers coach Dom Capers: "This team
s a strong will. They rise to the occasion in the sec-
d half. They've been doing it all year long." . . .
anthers safety Pat Terrell: "Everyone in this locker
om believed that this is where we were going to be at
e end of the season. That's not arrogance. It's just
at we have a bunch of believers on this team." . . .
wboys coach Barry Switzer: "The same old story we
d all year long finally caught up with us. You've got
get the ball in the end zone. Simple as that." . . .
anthers linebacker Sam Mills on stopping Emmitt
nith: "That takes a lot of wind out of a team when you
something like that. That was critical for us. We had
em on their heels." . . . Panthers linebacker Carlton
iley on his team's reputation: "I think the whole
untry put us out of nearly every (big) game. We won
ght straight at home, and we were still underdogs. I
n't understand it. We proved to everyone there is a
od football team in Charlotte."

PANTHERS 26, COWBOYS 17
Sunday, January 5

Dallas	3	8	3	3—17
Carolina	7	10	3	6—26

First Quarter
Dal.—FG, Boniol 22, 6:33.
Car.—Walls 1 pass from Collins (Kasay kick), 9:32.

Second Quarter
Car.—Green 10 pass from Collins (Kasay kick), 2:11.
Dal.—Johnston 2 pass from Aikman (pass failed), 10:41.
Dal.—Safety, ball snapped out of end zone on punt attempt, 11:49.
Car.—FG, Kasay 24, 14:57.

Third Quarter
Dal.—FG, Boniol 21, 4:53.
Car.—FG, Kasay 40, 10:02.

Fourth Quarter
Car.—FG, Kasay 40, 3:19.
Dal.—FG, Boniol 21, 9:27.
Car.—FG, Kasay 32, 13:12.
Attendance—72,808.

TEAM STATISTICS

	Dallas	Carolina
First downs	21	18
Rushes-yards	24-96	37-127
Passing	148	100
Punt returns	0-0	2-17
Kickoff returns	6-101	5-155
Interception returns	1-0	3-122
Comp.-att.-int.	18-36-3	12-22-1
Sacked-yards lost	2-17	0-0
Punts	3-51	1-39
Fumbles-lost	1-0	2-1
Penalties-yards	6-61	5-38
Time of possession	30:37	29:23

INDIVIDUAL STATISTICS
RUSHING—Dallas, E. Smith 22-80, Sanders 1-16, Aikman 1-0. Carolina, Johnson 26-104, Collins 6-5, Oliver 3-11, Ismail 1-7, Stark 1-0.
PASSING—Dallas, Aikman 18-36-3-165. Carolina, Collins 12-22-1-100.
RECEIVING—Dallas, K. Williams 6-89, Johnston 4-18, Martin 3-31, E. Smith 3-(minus 2), Irvin 1-22, Bjornson 1-7. Carolina, Green 5-53, Walls 3-25, Johnson 1-9, Carrier 1-7, Oliver 1-5, Griffith 1-1.
MISSED FIELD GOAL ATTEMPTS—None.
INTERCEPTIONS—Dallas, Woodson 1-0. Carolina, Terrell 1-49, Cota 1-49, Mills 1-24.
KICKOFF RETURNS—Dallas, K. Williams 3-44, Walker 2-29, Sanders 1-28. Carolina, Bates 5-155.
PUNT RETURNS—Carolina, Oliver 2-17.
SACKS—Carolina, Lathon 1, Miller 1.

CONFERENCE CHAMPIONSHIPS

NEW ENGLAND 20, JACKSONVILLE 6

Why the Patriots won: Their defense came up with big plays to offset a sub-par effort by the offense. The defense forced three turnovers in the final four minutes and helped the offense convert Jaguars mistakes and turnovers into 10 points while scoring six points of its own. Quarterback Drew Bledsoe passed for only 178 yards while Curtis Martin rushed for only 59 yards. But Willie Clay intercepted a Mark Brunell pass in the end zone to thwart a possible game-tying drive late in the fourth quarter, and the Patriots' Otis Smith returned James Stewart's fumble 47 yards for a touchdown with 2:24 left to seal the victory.

Why the Jaguars lost: Their offense kept putting the defense under pressure to come up with a big play. And although the defense responded by forcing two turnovers and holding the Patriots to 234 net yards, it couldn't provide enough opportunities for the struggling offense. After gaining 184 and 203 yards rushing in previous playoff games against Buffalo and Denver, respectively, the Jaguars ran for just 101 yards against the Patriots.

The turning points:

1. After the Jaguars' opening drive of the game stalled, Rich Griffith snapped the ball high to punter Bryan Barker, who couldn't get the punt off and was tackled on the 4. Two plays later, Curtis Martin scored on a 1-yard run to give the Patriots a 7-0 lead.

2. With the Patriots leading 13-6 and less than four minutes to play, the Jaguars marched to the Patriots' 5. But Clay made a leaping interception of Brunell's pass intended for tight end Derek Brown in the end zone. Clay came off his double-team of outside receiver Jimmy Smith, sensing the Jaguars would run a crossing route underneath, to make the play.

3. With 2 1/2 minutes left and the Patriots clinging to the 13-6 lead, linebacker Chris Slade jarred the ball from Stewart. Smith recovered the fumble and went 47 yards for a touchdown, icing the team's second trip to the Super Bowl in 11 years.

Notable: With the win, Bill Parcells joined Don Shula as the only coaches to lead different teams to the Super Bowl. Shula did it with the Colts and Dolphins, while Parcells accomplished the feat with the Giants and Patriots. . . . For 11 minutes during the first half the lights went out at Foxboro Stadium, leaving the game in the dark but adding more fuel to Patriots owner Robert Kraft's fire to lobby for a new stadium. . . . The Patriots gave up nine points in their two playoff games; they held the Jaguars to 289 net yards and three trips inside the 20 without a touchdown. . . . A group of 10,000 fans showed up at Jacksonville Municipal Stadium to watch the game on the stadium's big-screen TVs.

Quotable: Parcells on the ability of the Patriots to limit Brunell's out-of-pocket exploits: "I thought our kids did a great job, especially on their bootleg play. They tried five or six of those today, and we were giving them a lot of trouble." . . . Slade on forcing Stewart to fumble late in the game: "I knew it was a draw play. I just stuck my head in there. Otis made a heads-up play to run it back." . . . Stewart on the fumble: "It's a heart-wrenching feeling for me. The game was so close. Everything was on the line. It's one of those things you're going to think about for a long time." . . . Jaguars coach Tom Coughlin on the team's missed opportunities and mistakes: "The very thing that brought us here left us today." . . . Parcells on the challenge he issued to the team before the season: "At the beginning of the season, we talked about trying to either be club fighters or trying to play like champions. Club fighters have a certain mentality where they go to the gym and work hard and they take a beating and go home. I just told the players that they can't call themselves club fighters anymore. They have shown bigger hearts than that."

PATRIOTS 20, JAGUARS 6

Sunday, January 12

Jacksonville	0	3	3	0— 6
New England	7	6	0	7—20

First Quarter
N.E.—Martin 1 run (Vinatieri kick), 2:26.

Second Quarter
Jac.—FG, Hollis 32, 4:27.
N.E.—FG, Vinatieri 29, 7:37.
N.E.—FG, Vinatieri 20, 15:00.

Third Quarter
Jac.—FG, Hollis 28, 12:23.

Fourth Quarter
N.E.—O. Smith 47 fumble return (Vinatieri kick), 12:36.
Attendance—60,190.

TEAM STATISTICS

	Jacksonville	New England
First downs	18	13
Rushes-yards	33-101	24-73
Passing	188	161
Punt returns	4-15	3-29
Kickoff returns	4-69	3-52
Interception returns	1-15	2-12
Comp.-att.-int.	20-38-2	20-33-1
Sacked-yards lost	1-2	2-17
Punts	5-36	6-40
Fumbles-lost	3-2	2-1
Penalties-yards	4-23	2-5
Time of possession	34:43	25:17

INDIVIDUAL STATISTICS

RUSHING—Jacksonville, Means 19-43, Stewart 7-40, Brunell 6-34, Barker (minus 16). New England, Martin 19-59, Meggett 3-9, Bledsoe 1-4, Byars 1-1.

PASSING—Jacksonville, Brunell 20-38-2-190. New England, Bledsoe 20-33-1-178.

RECEIVING—Jacksonville, Mitchell 7-63, McCardell 6-62, Smith 3-4, Stewart 2-8, Brown 1-10, Barlow 1-2. New England, Glenn 5-33, Jefferson 91, Byars 4-16, Martin 3-18, Meggett 3-15, Coates 1-5.

MISSED FIELD GOAL ATTEMPTS—New England, Vinatieri 46.

INTERCEPTIONS—Jacksonville, Beasley 1-15. New England, Bruschi 12, Clay 1-0.

KICKOFF RETURNS—Jacksonville, B. Brooks 4-69. New England, Megg 3-52.

PUNT RETURNS—Jacksonville, Hudson 4-15. New England, Meggett 3-2

SACKS—Jacksonville, Davey 1, Robinson 1/2, Simmons 1/2. New Englan Slade 1.

GREEN BAY 30, CAROLINA 13

Why the Packers won: After a slow start, during which the Panthers converted two Brett Favre turnovers into 10 points, the Packers stuck to a game plan of running out of four-receiver sets and passing out of the I-formation, which helped to neutralize the Panthers' zone-blitz. Edgar Bennett and Dorsey Levens combined for 187 of the 201 net rushing yards, the third-highest total in Packers playoff history, and Favre threw for 292 yards and was sacked only once. The Packers outgained the Panthers 479 yards to 251 and held the ball 16:06 longer than the Panthers.

Why the Panthers lost: Fullback Anthony Johnson and tight end Wesley Walls, two key players in the Panthers' offense, each had a sub-par game. Johnson gained 31 yards on 11 carries and Walls had three catches for 33 yards. The Panthers' 45 net rushing yards were a season-low. The failure to establish the running game put the pressure to move the offense on second-year quarterback Kerry Collins, who played hesitantly. With the Panthers choosing to go with short drops and quick passing plays, the Packers adjusted by dropping eight men into coverage to blanket the short-pass routes and limit Walls' effectiveness.

The turning points:

. When Levens bounced outside to gain 14 yards on his first carry, the Packers had found a way to attack the Panthers' zone-blitzing style. With linebackers Kevin Greene and Lamar Lathon clogging the middle, the Packers could run sweeps to the outside effectively. Levens gained 35 yards on a run that set up the Packers' first score, a 29-yard pass in the second quarter from Favre to Levens, who used spectacular body control to keep his feet inbounds. After the early success, the Packers kept going to Levens, who set career highs in rushing yards, 88, and receiving yards, 117.

. With the Packers leading 14-10 and 48 seconds left in the first half, Collins threw for receiver Willie Green on the left sideline. But the pass was too long and the Packers' Tyrone Williams made a leaping, one-handed interception at the Packers' 38. It was Williams' first career interception and led to Chris Jacke's 31-yard field goal with 10 seconds left in the half that gave the Packers a 17-10 lead.

. With the Packers leading 20-13 late in the third quarter, the Panthers' defense appeared to have finally gotten pressure on Favre with their blitz. But Favre threw a screen pass to Levens, who turned what looked like near-disaster into a 66-yard gain to the Panthers' 4. On the next play, Bennett scored to give the Packers a commanding 27-13 lead.

Quotable: Favre improved his record to 19-0 as a starter in games played when the temperature is below 35 degrees. The game-time temperature at Lambeau Field was 3 degrees, with a minus-17 degree wind chill. . . . The Packers have won an NFL-record 11 consecutive home playoff games, which includes a 9-0 record at Lambeau and a 2-0 record at Milwaukee's County Stadium. . . . The Packers converted 53 percent of their third-down plays into first downs against the Panthers, who were the stingiest team in the league on third down, giving up first downs 32 percent of the time. . . . In a 15-minute span from the second quarter to the fourth quarter, the Packers scored on five consecutive possessions. . . . The Packers wore down the Panthers' defense with drives of 73, 71, 73, 73 and 74 yards.

Quotable: Packers president Bob Harlan on ending the Cowboys and 49ers' dominance in the NFC: "This is the real America's team." . . . Levens on his increased role in the Packers' offense: "I thought I would contribute a little bit. I never dreamed I would have a game like this. This is definitely a career game." . . . Favre on the long screen pass to Levens: "That was a great call for the blitz. Kevin Greene came from the outside and I just dumped it over his head. There was no one out there really except our linemen to block people."

PACKERS 30, PANTHERS 13
Sunday, January 12

Carolina	7	3	3	0—13
Green Bay	0	17	10	3—30

First Quarter
Car.—Griffith 3 pass from Collins (Kasay kick), 9:50.
Second Quarter
G.B.—Levens 29 pass from Favre (Jacke kick), :06.
Car.—FG, Kasay 22, 6:20.
G.B.—Freeman 6 pass from Favre (Jacke kick), 14:12.
G.B.—FG, Jacke 31, 14:50.
Third Quarter
G.B.—FG, Jacke 32, 6:44.
Car.—FG, Kasay 23, 11:37.
G.B.—Bennett 4 run (Jacke kick), 13:02.
Fourth Quarter
G.B.—FG, Jacke 28, 4:58.
Attendance—60,216.

TEAM STATISTICS

	Carolina	Green Bay
First downs	12	22
Rushes-yards	14-45	45-201
Passing	206	278
Punt returns	1-4	1-3
Kickoff returns	7-86	4-104
Interception returns	1-10	2-35
Comp.-att.-int.	19-37-2	19-29-1
Sacked-yards lost	2-9	1-14
Punts	5-36	2-36
Fumbles-lost	2-1	2-1
Penalties-yards	4-25	5-45
Time of possession	21:57	38:03

INDIVIDUAL STATISTICS
RUSHING—Carolina, Johnson 11-31, Oliver 2-15, Collins 1-(minus 1). Green Bay, Bennett 25-99, Levens 10-88, Favre 5-14, McMahon 4-0, Henderson 1-0.

PASSING—Carolina, Collins 19-37-2-215. Green Bay, Favre 19-29-1-292.

RECEIVING—Carolina, Green 5-51, Carrier 4-65, Griffith 4-23, Walls 3-33, Ismail 1-24, Johnson 1-14, Oliver 1-5. Green Bay, Levens 5-117, Freeman 4-43, Rison 3-53, Jackson 3-30, Bennett 2-5, Beebe 1-29, Chmura 1-15.

MISSED FIELD GOAL ATTEMPTS—Green Bay, Jacke 46.

INTERCEPTIONS—Carolina, Mills 1-10. Green Bay, Newsome 1-35, T. Williams 1-0.

KICKOFF RETURNS—Carolina, Bates 4-59, S. Greene 1-14, Oliver 1-13, Baker 1-0. Green Bay, Howard 4-104.

PUNT RETURNS—Carolina, Oliver 1-4. Green Bay, Howard 1-3.

SACKS—Carolina. Green Bay, Simmons 1, McKenzie 1.

SUPER BOWL XXXI

GREEN BAY 35, NEW ENGLAND 21

Why the Packers won: They did it with the electrifying returns of Desmond Howard—seven punts for 90 yards and four kickoffs for 154. They did it with Reggie White and the NFL's best defense intercepting Drew Bledsoe four times, sacking him five times and batting down or deflecting 10 passes (the interceptions resulted in 10 Packers points). And they did it with Brett Favre's brilliant playmaking ability—14-of-27, 246 yards, two touchdowns and no interceptions and a 2-yard TD run.

Why the Patriots lost: For a team that had not allowed a touchdown in the postseason (the Patriots allowed one field goal against Pittsburgh and two against Jacksonville), New England allowed far too many big plays— starting with 34- and 32-yard punt returns and a 99-yard kickoff return by Howard, and 54- and 81-yard touchdown receptions by Andre Rison and Antonio Freeman, respectively. Offensively, despite having 1,000-yard rusher Curtis Martin, the Patriots abandoned the running game early in the proceedings— rushing just 13 times for 43 yards while passing 48 times against a defense that could ignore the run and concentrate on putting pressure on Bledsoe.

The turning points:

1. On their second offensive play from scrimmage, the Packers caught New England showing a blitz. A pass was designed to go to tight end Keith Jackson, but Favre recognized the blitz and audibled to a pass to Andre Rison, who turned around cornerback Otis Smith with a fake at the New England 40, caught the ball at the 20 and raced untouched for a 54-yard score just 3:32 into the game.

2. Just 56 seconds into the second quarter, the Packers took a 17-14 lead when Favre gambled that the speedy Freeman could beat Lawyer Milloy in one-on-one coverage. Freeman ran a stop-and-go route and sprinted into the clear for an 81-yard touchdown, the longest from scrimmage in Super Bowl history.

3. In recent playoff games, Favre never had the luxury of a running game to keep the defense honest. A drive at the end of the first half that gave Green Bay a 27-14 lead was highlighted by runs of 9, 6, 8 and 8 yards by Dorsey Levens. Favre took the ball in the end zone himself from the 2. It was the start of a 61-yard rushing day for Levens, who combined with Edgar Bennett (40 yards) for the bulk of the team's 115 yards rushing.

4. With the Patriots scoring what seemed to be a momentum-changing touchdown on Martin's 18-yard run, shrinking the Packers' lead to 27-21 with 3:27 left in the third quarter, Howard dropped back at the goal line to take the kick from Adam Vinatieri. He burst up the middle of the field, bounced off a tackle by Hason Graham at the 30 and dashed to daylight for the back-breaking touchdown.

5. White, put the exclamation point on the victory on the series immediately following Howard's return. Two of his Super Bowl-record three sacks came back-to-back to prevent the Patriots from regaining momentum.

Notable: The Packers, who won the first two Super Bowls, became the NFL champion for the first time in 2 years. . . . The loss marked Bill Parcells' last game a coach of the Patriots. . . . Howard became the first return man to be named Most Valuable Player in the Super Bow The 1991 Heisman Trophy winner returned three punt for touchdowns during the regular season, then got anoth er in a divisional playoff victory over San Francisco. But h had never brought a kick back all the way during his fiv year NFL career. He also became the first player to retur both a punt and kickoff for touchdowns in the playoffs.

Quotables: Parcells: "That kickoff was the difference. thought we might have had them rocking a bit. We wer down by six points and had momentum. But he made th big play." . . . Bledsoe: "Year in and year out, Super Bow are won on big plays. The Packers made more big play than we did—and they didn't turn the ball over." . . Freeman: "It's the Vince Lombardi Trophy and now it going back home."

PACKERS 35, PATRIOTS 21
Sunday, January 26

New England	14	0	7	0—2
Green Bay	10	17	8	0—3

First Quarter
G.B.—Rison 54 pass from Favre (Jacke kick), 3:32.
G.B.—FG, Jacke 37, 6:18.
N.E.—Byars 1 pass from Bledsoe (Vinatieri kick), 8:25.
N.E.—Coates 4 pass from Bledsoe (Vinatieri kick), 12:27.
Second Quarter
G.B.—Freeman 81 pass from Favre (Jacke kick), :56.
G.B.—FG, Jacke 31, 6:45.
G.B.—Favre 2 run (Jacke kick), 13:49.
Third Quarter
N.E.—Martin 18 run (Vinatieri kick), 11:33.
G.B.—Howard 99 kickoff return (Chmura pass from Favre), 11:50.
Attendance—72,301.

TEAM STATISTICS
	New England	Green Ba
First downs	16	1
Rushes-yards	13-43	36-11
Passing	214	20
Punt returns	4-30	6-9
Kickoff returns	6-135	4-15
Interception returns	0-0	4-2
Comp.-att.-int.	25-48-4	14-27-
Sacked-yards lost	5-39	5-3
Punts	8-45	7-4
Fumbles-lost	0-0	0-
Penalties-yards	2-22	3-4
Time of possession	25:45	34:1

INDIVIDUAL STATISTICS
RUSHING—New England, Martin 11-42, Bledsoe 1-1, Meggett 1-0. Gre Bay, Bennett 17-40, Levens 14-61, Favre 4-12, Henderson 1-2.
PASSING—New England, Bledsoe 25-48-4-253. Green Bay, Favre 14-27-0-24
RECEIVING—New England, Coates 6-67, Glenn 4-62, Byars 4-32, Jeffers 3-34, Martin 3-28, Meggett 3-8, Brisby 2-12. Green Bay, Freeman 3-105, Leve 3-23, Rison 2-77, Henderson 2-14, Chmura 2-13, Jackson 1-10, Bennett 1-4
MISSED FIELD GOAL ATTEMPTS—Green Bay, Jacke 47.
INTERCEPTIONS—Green Bay, B. Williams 1-16, Prior 1-8, Evans 1 Newsome 1-0.
KICKOFF RETURNS—New England, Meggett 5-117, Graham 1-18. Gre Bay, Howard 4-154.
PUNT RETURNS—New England, Meggett 4-30. Green Bay, Howard 6-90.
SACKS—New England, Bruschi 2, McGinest 1, Collons 1, O. Smith 1. Gre Bay, White 3, Butler 1, S. Dotson 1.

PRO BOWL

AFC 26, NFC 23

hy the AFC won: Mark Brunell got a chance to play ad Cary Blanchard got a second chance to kick. runell, who led Jacksonville on its march into the ayoffs, was rewarded with a Pro Bowl berth as an jury replacement for Denver's John Elway. Wise oice. Brunell was 12-of-22 for 236 yards, including an -yard touchdown that helped send the game into vertime and a 44-yard pass that set up the game-winng field goal. Brunell was named MVP. Blanchard, of dianapolis, missed his first attempt at win the game overtime, from 41 yards. After Brunell's final pass, lanchard kicked a 37-yard field goal for the winner.

hy the NFC lost: John Kasay couldn't get in sync th his snapper and holder. Kasay, Carolina's kicker, ffered the same problem Blanchard encountered— ck of familiarity and practice time with his specialams partners. As a result, both found their timing paired. Kasay missed field-goal attempts from 60, 40 d 39 yards. Washington's Gus Frerotte almost saved e day. He first threw a 52-yard touchdown pass to Cris rter with four minutes left in regulation, then direct l a late drive that put Kasay in position to win the me. Kasay lined up a 39-yard attempt—and missed.

e turning points:
1. With the AFC trailing 15-3, the Patriots' Curtis artin scored on a 3-yard run at 8:05 of the third period. e AFC had failed to generate much offense in the first lf, getting only a Blanchard field goal late in the sec d quarter. Patriots quarterback Drew Bledsoe and ltimore's Vinny Testaverde were a combined 9-for-22 135 yards before Brunell provided some spark.
. The Bengals' Ashley Ambrose started an exciting irth-quarter rally. Ambrose stepped in front of ceiver Irving Fryar to intercept Kerry Collins' pass d went into the end zone untouched. His 54-yard turn for a touchdown was a Pro Bowl record and lped put the AFC ahead, 16-15.
. Carter's touchdown and Frerotte's two-point con rsion pass to Carolina's Wesley Walls staked the 'C to a 23-16 lead with 4:07 left. That set up a furious ish, featuring Brunell's 80-yard touchdown pass to kland's Tim Brown and the late missed field-goal empt by Kasay. Carter, of the Vikings, executed a rfect stop-and-go move on cornerback Terry cDaniel, and Frerotte delivered the ball as Carter eaked down the sideline. That looked like it would e the winning score until Brown and Brunell went to rk. Brown raced past Aeneas Williams of the rdinals and went down the right sideline. Brunell's ss found Brown in stride for the 80-yard score with seconds left in regulation. Blanchard's extra point d the game.

table: Two-time NFL MVP Brett Favre hit lineman ndall McDaniel with a 5-yard touchdown pass on a kle-eligible play. . . . Lance Alstodt proved to be the best kicker of the day. In a halftime promotion, Alstodt, an investment banker by trade, kicked a 35-yard field goal to win $1 million. OK, so the ball was on a tee, and there were no defenders rushing him. But Alstodt, 26, a former high school soccer player, calmly banged the kick through the uprights.

Quotable: Blanchard, on kicking in the Pro Bowl: "Your rhythm really isn't there because of different guys in different places. I just pulled through it (his first overtime kick), but the second one was beautiful. The snap was perfect, the hold was perfect." . . . Kasay, on his kicking: "We tried the best we could, but it didn't work out. We didn't get a chance to work on it that much." . . . Kasay, on Alstodt's kick: "That was exciting. He handled the pressure well. He shouldn't give up his day job. But he made more in one day than I did this season."

AFC 26, NFC 23
Sunday, February 2

AFC	0	3	7	13	3—26
NFC	9	0	6	8	0—23

First Quarter
NFC—FG, Kasay 20, 4:41.
NFC—McDaniel 5 pass from Favre (kick failed), 11:16.
Second Quarter
AFC—FG, Blanchard 28, 14:33.
Third Quarter
NFC—Sanders 6 run (pass failed), 6:09.
AFC—C. Martin 3 run (Blanchard kick), 8:05.
Fourth Quarter
AFC—Ambrose 54 interception return (pass failed), :11.
NFC—C. Carter 53 pass from Frerotte (Frerotte to Walls), 10:53.
AFC—T. Brown 80 pass from Brunell (Blanchard kick), 14:16.
Overtime
AFC—FG, Blanchard 37, 8:15.
Attendance—50,031.

TEAM STATISTICS

	AFC	NFC
First downs	20	24
Rushes-yards	31-97	35-130
Passing	369	366
Punt returns	2-51	2-33
Kickoff returns	6-173	5-152
Interception returns	2-54	0-0
Comp.-att.-int.	21-44-0	23-44-2
Sacked-yards lost	1-2	0-0
Punts	6-42	6-49
Fumbles-lost	2-0	1-0
Penalties-yards	8-43	5-32
Time of possession	33:29	34:47

INDIVIDUAL STATISTICS
RUSHING—AFC, C. Martin 13-48, Davis 7-21, Bettis 4-9, Testaverde 2-7, Brunell 1-6, T. Brown 1-4, Anders 2-2, Bledsoe 1-0. NFC, Sanders 11-59, Centers 9-38, Allen 6-20, Watters 7-13, Frerotte 2-0.

PASSING—AFC, Brunell 12-22-0-236, Testaverde, 6-14-0-68, Bledsoe, 3-8-0-67. NFC, Favre 6-11-0-143, Collins 4-8-1-30, Frerotte 13-25-1-193.

RECEIVING—AFC, T. Brown 5-137, Sharpe 3-43, McCardell 3-40, Coates 2-46, Meggett 2-24, C. Martin 2-8, T. Martin 1-41, Bettis 1-18, Anders 1-17, Davis 1-7. NFC, Bruce 7-104, Carter 4-87, Moore 3-48, Sanders 1-40, McDaniel 1-5, Fryar 2-25, Walls 2-40, Centers 1-12, Allen 1-5, Watters 1-0.

MISSED FIELD GOAL ATTEMPTS—AFC, Blanchard 55, 41. NFC, Kasay 66, 40, 39.

INTERCEPTIONS—AFC, Ambrose 1-54, McDaniel 1-0.
KICKOFF RETURNS—AFC, Meggett 6-173. NFC, Bates 5-152.
PUNT RETURNS—AFC, Meggett 2-51. NFC, Bruce 1-13, Green 1-8.
SACKS—NFC, Swann 1.

AFC SQUAD

OFFENSE

WR—Carl Pickens, Cincinnati*
Tony Martin, San Diego*
Tim Brown, Oakland
Keenan McCardell, Jacksonville
TE— Shannon Sharpe, Denver*
Ben Coates, New England
T— Gary Zimmerman, Denver*
Bruce Armstrong, New England*
Richmond Webb, Miami
Tony Boselli, Jacksonville
G— Bruce Matthews, Houston*
Will Shields, Kansas City*
Ruben Brown, Buffalo
C— Dermontti Dawson, Pittsburgh*
Mark Stepnoski, Houston
QB— John Elway, Denver*
Drew Bledsoe, New England
Mark Brunell, Jacksonville
Vinny Testaverde, Baltimore
RB— Terrell Davis, Denver*
Jerome Bettis, Pittsburgh*
Curtis Martin, New England
FB— Kimble Anders, Kansas City
NOTE: T Zimmerman replaced due to injury by Tony Boselli,
Jacksonville; QB Elway replaced due to injury by Mark
Brunell, Jacksonville.

DEFENSE

DE— Bruce Smith, Buffalo*
Alfred Williams, Denver*
Michael Sinclair, Seattle
Willie McGinest, New England
DT— Cortez Kennedy, Seattle*
Chester McGlockton, Oakland*
Michael Dean Perry, Denver
OLB—Derrick Thomas, Kansas City*
Chad Brown, Pittsburgh*
Bryce Paup, Buffalo
Bill Romanowski, Denver†
ILB— Junior Seau, San Diego*
Levon Kirkland, Pittsburgh
CB— Dale Carter, Kansas City*
Ashley Ambrose, Cincinnati*
Rod Woodson, Pittsburgh
Terry McDaniel, Oakland
S— Carnell Lake, Pittsburgh*
Steve Atwater, Denver*
Blaine Bishop, Houston
Eric Turner, Baltimore
Tyrone Braxton, Denver
NOTE: DE Smith replaced due to injury by Willie McGinest, New
England; CB Carter replaced due to injury by Terry
McDaniel, Oakland; S Atwater replaced due to injury by
Eric Turner, Baltimore; S Bishop replaced due to injury
by Tyrone Braxton, Denver.

SPECIALISTS

P— Chris Gardocki, Indianapolis
K— Cary Blanchard, Indianapolis
KR—David Meggett, New England
ST— John Henry Mills, Houston

NFC SQUAD

OFFENSE

WR—Jerry Rice, San Francisco*
Herman Moore, Detroit*
Isaac Bruce, St. Louis
Cris Carter, Minnesota
Irving Fryar, Philadelphia
TE—Wesley Walls, Carolina*
Keith Jackson, Green Bay
T— Erik Williams, Dallas
William Roaf, New Orleans*
Lomas Brown, Arizona
G— Larry Allen, Dallas*
Randall McDaniel, Minnesota*
Nate Newton, Dallas
C— Kevin Glover, Detroit*
Ray Donaldson, Dallas
Frank Winters, Green Bay
QB—Brett Favre, Green Bay*
Troy Aikman, Dallas
Gus Frerotte, Washington
Steve Young, San Francisco
Kerry Collins, Carolina
RB—Barry Sanders, Detroit*
Terry Allen, Washington*
Ricky Watters, Philadelphia
FB— Larry Centers, Arizona
NOTE: WR Rice replaced due to injury by Irving Fryar,
Philadelphia; C Donaldson replaced due to injury by
Frank Winters, Green Bay; QB Aikman replaced due to
injury by Gus Frerotte; QB Young replaced due to injury
by Kerry Collins, Carolina.

DEFENSE

DE— Reggie White, Green Bay*
Tony Tolbert, Dallas*
William Fuller, Philadelphia
DT— John Randle, Minnesota*
Bryant Young, San Francisco*
Eric Swann, Arizona
OLB—Kevin Greene, Carolina*
Lamar Lathon, Carolina*
Ken Harvey, Washington
William Thomas, Philadelphia†
ILB— Sam Mills, Carolina*
Hardy Nickerson, Tampa Bay
CB— Deion Sanders, Dallas*
Aeneas Williams, Arizona*
Eric Davis, Carolina
Darrell Green, Washington
S— Leroy Butler, Green Bay*
Merton Hanks, San Francisco*
Darren Woodson, Dallas
NOTE: CB Sanders replaced due to injury by Darrell Green,
Washington.

SPECIALISTS

P— Matt Turk, Washington
K— John Kasay, Carolina
KR—Michael Bates, Carolina
ST—Jim Schwantz, Dallas
*Elected starter.
†Selected as need player.

– 222 –

PLAYER PARTICIPATION

Player, Team	GP	GS	Player, Team	GP	GS	Player, Team	GP	GS
ᴐdul-Jabbar, Karim, Miami	16	14	Bandison, Romeo, Washington	10	0	Blake, Jeff, Cincinnati	16	16
ᴐraham, Clifton, Chicago	2	0	Banks, Tony, St. Louis	14	13	Blanchard, Cary, Indianapolis	16	0
ᴐraham, Donnie, Tampa Bay	16	12	Bankston, Michael, Arizona	16	16	Blanton, Scott, Washington	16	0
ᴄkerman, Tom, New Orleans	2	0	Banta, Bradford, Indianapolis	13	0	Bledsoe, Drew, New England	16	16
ᴅams, Sam, Seattle	16	15	Barber, Michael, Seattle	13	7	Boatswain, Harry, N.Y. Jets	16	4
ᴅams, Scott, Tampa Bay	7	2	Barber, Bryan, Jacksonville	16	0	Bock, John, Miami	2	0
ᴅams, Vashone, Baltimore	16	2	Barker, Roy, San Francisco	16	16	Bolden, Juran, Atlanta	9	0
ᴣnew, Ray, N.Y. Giants	13	2	Barlow, Reggie, Jacksonville	7	0	Bonham, Shane, Detroit	15	2
ᴣuiar, Louie, Kansas City	16	0	Barndt, Tom, Kansas City	13	0	Boniol, Chris, Dallas	16	0
ᴅanotu, Chidi, Tampa Bay	13	13	Barnes, Tomur, Hou.-Min.-Was.	10	0	Bono, Steve, Kansas City	13	13
ᴋman, Troy, Dallas	15	15	Barnett, Fred, Miami	9	7	Booker, Vaughn, Kansas City	14	12
ᴏerts, Trev, Indianapolis	9	4	Barnett, Harlon, Minnesota	16	4	Booth, Issac, Baltimore	11	3
ᴏright, Ethan, Buffalo	16	0	Barnett, Troy, N.E.-Was.	4	0	Borgella, Jocelyn, Detroit	11	0
ᴅridge, Allen, Denver	16	16	Barnhardt, Tommy, Tampa Bay	16	0	Boselli, Tony, Jacksonville	16	16
ᴇ, Arnold, San Diego	7	0	Barrow, Micheal, Houston	16	16	Botkin, Kirk, Pittsburgh	16	0
ᴇxander, Brent, Arizona	16	15	Barton, Harris, San Francisco	13	13	Bouie, Kevin, San Diego	1	0
ᴇxander, David, N.Y. Jets	7	7	Bartrum, Mike, New England	16	0	Bouie, Tony, Tampa Bay	16	0
ᴇxander, Derrick, Minnesota	12	9	Bates, Bill, Dallas	14	0	Boutte, Marc, Washington	10	10
ᴇxander, Derrick A., Baltimore	15	14	Bates, Mario, New Orleans	14	10	Bowden, Joe, Houston	16	16
ᴇxander, Elijah, Indianapolis	14	3	Bates, Michael, Carolina	14	0	Bowens, Tim, Miami	16	16
ᴇxander, Kevin, N.Y. Giants	4	0	Bates, Patrick, Atlanta	15	9	Bowie, Larry, Washington	3	0
ᴇxander, Patrise, Washington	16	1	Battaglia, Marco, Cincinnati	16	0	Boyd, Sean, Atlanta	2	0
ᴇn, Eric, New Orleans	16	16	Baxter, Fred, N.Y. Jets	16	4	Boyd, Stephen, Detroit	8	5
ᴇn, Larry, Dallas	16	16	Bayless, Martin, Kansas City	16	1	Boyer, Brant, Jacksonville	12	0
ᴇn, Marcus, Kansas City	16	15	Beamon, Willie, N.Y. Giants	5	0	Boykin, Deral, Philadelphia	10	0
ᴇn, Terry, Washington	16	16	Beasley, Aaron, Jacksonville	9	7	Brackens, Tony, Jacksonville	16	1
ᴤtott, Mike, Tampa Bay	16	16	Beavers, Aubrey, N.Y. Jets	7	0	Bradford, Ronnie, Arizona	15	11
ᴋ, John, Kansas City	12	11	Beckles, Ian, Tampa Bay	13	13	Bradley, Freddie, San Diego	10	1
ᴧbrose, Ashley, Cincinnati	16	16	Beebe, Don, Green Bay	16	6	Bradley, Kyle, N.Y. Jets	16	16
ᴅers, Kimble, Kansas City	16	15	Beede, Frank, Seattle	14	2	Braham, Rich, Cincinnati	16	16
ᴅdersen, Morten, Atlanta	16	0	Beer, Tom, Detroit	16	1	Brandon, David, Atlanta	16	2
ᴅderson, Darren, Kansas City	11	3	Belin, Chuck, St. Louis	1	0	Brandon, Michael, San Francisco	4	0
ᴅderson, Eddie, Oakland	7	5	Bell, Kerwin, Indianapolis	1	0	Brantley, Chris, Buffalo	10	0
ᴅderson, Flipper, Washington	2	0	Bell, Myron, Pittsburgh	16	4	Bratton, Jason, Buffalo	2	0
ᴅderson, Gary, Philadelphia	16	0	Bell, Ricky, Jacksonville	12	0	Bratzke, Chad, N.Y. Giants	16	16
ᴅderson, Jamal, Atlanta	16	12	Bell, William, Washington	16	0	Braxton, Tyrone, Denver	16	16
ᴅderson, Richie, N.Y. Jets	16	13	Bellamy, Jay, Seattle	16	0	Brew, Dorian, Baltimore	7	0
ᴅderson, Stevie, Arizona	8	0	Belser, Jason, Indianapolis	16	16	Brice, Alundis, Dallas	14	1
ᴅderson, Willie, Cincinnati	16	10	Bender, Carey, Buffalo	1	0	Brien, Doug, New Orleans	16	0
ᴅguz, Leo, Oakland	3	0	Benefield, Daved, San Francisco	15	0	Brigance, O.J., Miami	12	0
ᴄhambeau, Lester, Atlanta	15	15	Bennett, Cornelius, Atlanta	13	13	Briggs, Greg, Chicago	14	0
ᴁmstead, Jessie, N.Y. Giants	16	16	Bennett, Darren, San Diego	16	0	Brilz, Darrick, Cincinnati	13	13
ᴁmstrong, Bruce, New England	16	16	Bennett, Donnell, Kansas City	16	0	Brisby, Vincent, New England	3	0
ᴁmstrong, Trace, Miami	16	9	Bennett, Edgar, Green Bay	16	15	Brock, Matt, N.Y. Jets	16	16
ᴁmstrong, Tyji, Dallas	16	7	Bennett, Tommy, Arizona	16	1	Brockermeyer, Blake, Carolina	12	12
ᴁnold Jahine, Pittsburgh	9	0	Bennett, Tony, Indianapolis	14	13	Brohm, Jeff, San Francisco	3	0
ᴁthur, Mike, Green Bay	5	0	Bercich, Pete, Minnesota	15	1	Brooks, Barrett, Philadelphia	16	15
ᴀvie, Herman, Baltimore	14	1	Berger, Mitch, Minnesota	16	0	Brooks, Bill, Washington	16	2
ᴀher, Jamie, Washington	16	12	Berti, Tony, San Diego	16	14	Brooks, Bucky, G.B.-Jac.	8	1
ᴀhmore, Darryl, St.L.-Was.	11	0	Bettis, Jerome, Pittsburgh	16	12	Brooks, Derrick, Tampa Bay	16	16
ᴋa, Joe, Oakland	15	2	Beuerlein, Steve, Carolina	8	4	Brooks, Ethan, Atlanta	2	0
ᴋins, Gene, Miami	5	5	Biakabutuka, Tim, Carolina	4	4	Brooks, Michael, Detroit	4	4
ᴋins, James, Seattle	16	16	Bickett, Duane, Carolina	16	0	Brooks, Reggie, Tampa Bay	11	4
ᴠater, Steve, Denver	16	16	Biekert, Greg, Oakland	16	15	Brooks, Robert, Green Bay	7	7
ᴤtin, Eric, Tampa Bay	2	0	Bieniemy, Eric, Cincinnati	16	0	Brooks, Steve, Detroit	1	0
ᴢenne, Troy, Indianapolis	12	5	Binn, David, San Diego	16	0	Brostek, Bern, St. Louis	16	16
ᴉley, Aaron, Indianapolis	14	2	Birden, J.J., Atlanta	12	12	Broughton, Willie, New Orleans	14	5
ᴉley, Carlton, Carolina	16	14	Bishop, Blaine, Houston	15	15	Broussard, Steve, Seattle	12	0
ᴉley, Henry, N.Y. Jets	8	0	Bishop, Greg, N.Y. Giants	16	16	Brown, Anthony, Cincinnati	7	0
ᴉley, Robert, Miami	14	0	Bishop, Harold, Baltimore	8	2	Brown, Chad, Pittsburgh	14	14
ᴉley, Victor, Kansas City	2	0	Bjornson, Eric, Dallas	14	10	Brown, Corwin, New England	14	0
ᴋer, Myron, Carolina	16	0	Blackman, Ken, Cincinnati	14	10	Brown, Dave, N.Y. Giants	16	16
ᴅwin, Randy, Baltimore	9	0	Blackmon, Robert, Seattle	16	16	Brown, Dennis, San Francisco	15	0
ᴵ, Jerry, Oakland	16	0	Blackshear, Jeff, Baltimore	16	12	Brown, Derek D., New Orleans	11	0
ᴵard, Howard, Seattle	16	16	Blades, Bennie, Detroit	15	15			
			Blades, Brian, Seattle	11	9			

1996 REVIEW *Player participation*

Player, Team	GP	GS
Brown, Derek V., Jacksonville ...	16	14
Brown, Gary, Green Bay	8	5
Brown, Gilbert, Green Bay	16	16
Brown, J.B., Miami..................	14	1
Brown, James, Miami	16	16
Brown, Jamie, Denver	12	2
Brown, Lance, Arizona	1	0
Brown, Larry, Oakland.............	8	1
Brown, Lomas, Arizona	16	16
Brown, Monty, New England	11	7
Brown, Orlando, Baltimore	16	16
Brown, Ray, San Francisco	16	16
Brown, Reggie, Seattle	7	0
Brown, Reggie D., Detroit	10	10
Brown, Richard, Minnesota	14	0
Brown, Ruben, Buffalo	14	14
Brown, Tim, Oakland	16	16
Brown, Troy, New England	16	0
Brown, Tyrone, Atlanta	9	4
Browning, John, Kansas City	13	2
Brownlow, Darrick, Washington..	16	0
Bruce, Aundray, Oakland	16	0
Bruce, Isaac, St. Louis	16	16
Bruener, Mark, Pittsburgh	12	12
Brumfield, Scott, Cincinnati	9	8
Brunell, Mark, Jacksonville.......	16	16
Bruschi, Tedy, New England	16	0
Bryant, Junior, San Francisco...	16	1
Buchanan, Ray, Indianapolis	13	13
Buckey, Jeff, Miami	15	1
Buckley, Curtis, San Francisco .	15	0
Buckley, Marcus, N.Y. Giants.....	15	2
Buckley, Terrell, Miami	16	16
Buckner, Brentson, Pittsburgh ..	15	14
Bullard, Kendricke, Jacksonville..	12	0
Burger, Todd, Chicago	11	8
Burke, John, New England	11	2
Burnett, Rob, Baltimore............	6	6
Burns, Keith, Denver	16	0
Burris, Jeff, Buffalo	15	15
Burrough, John, Atlanta	16	1
Burroughs, Sammie, Ind.	16	1
Burton, James, Chicago	16	3
Burton, Kendrick, Houston	4	2
Burton, Shane, Miami	16	8
Bush, Devin, Atlanta	16	15
Bush, Lewis, San Diego	16	16
Butcher, Paul, Oakland	16	0
Butler, Kevin, Arizona	7	0
Butler, LeRoy, Green Bay..........	16	16
Byars, Keith, Mia.-N.E.	14	10
Byner, Earnest, Baltimore	16	8
Cadrez, Glenn, Denver	16	0
Cain, Joe, Chicago	16	15
Caldwell, Mike I., Baltimore.......	9	9
Caldwell, Mike T., San Francisco..	1	0
Calloway, Chris, N.Y. Giants	16	15
Camarillo, Rich, Oakland	1	0
Campbell, Jesse, N.Y. Giants	16	16
Campbell, Matthew, Carolina......	9	8
Campos, Alan, Dallas	15	0
Carney, John, San Diego	16	0
Carolan, Brett, Miami	6	2
Carpenter, Ron, N.Y. Jets	2	0
Carrier, Mark A., Chicago	13	13
Carrier, Mark J., Carolina.........	16	15
Carrington, Darren, Oakland.....	14	9
Carswell, Dwayne, Denver	16	2
Carter, Cris, Minnesota	16	16
Carter, Dale, Kansas City	14	14
Carter, Dexter, San Francisco ...	16	0
Carter, Kevin, St. Louis.............	16	16
Carter, Ki-Jana, Cincinnati	16	4
Carter, Marty, Chicago	16	16
Carter, Pat, Arizona..................	16	16
Carter, Perry, Oakland..............	4	0
Carter, Tom, Washington...........	16	16
Carter, Tony, Chicago...............	16	11
Carver, Shante, Dallas	10	7
Cascadden, Chad, N.Y. Jets.......	16	8
Cash, Keith, Kansas City	9	5
Cash, Kerry, Chicago	4	2
Casillas, Tony, Dallas...............	16	3
Castle, Eric, San Diego	16	0
Catanho, Alcides, Washington...	15	0
Centers, Larry, Arizona	16	14
Chalenski, Mike, N.Y. Jets	15	7
Chamberlain, Byron, Denver......	11	0
Chandler, Chris, Houston	12	12
Cheever, Michael, Jacksonville..	11	2
Cherry, Je'Rod, New Orleans.....	13	0
Childress, Ray, Dallas..............	3	0
Chmura, Mark, Green Bay	13	13
Chrebet, Wayne, N.Y. Jets	16	9
Christie, Steve, Buffalo	16	0
Christopherson, Ryan, Jac.-Ariz. .	8	0
Christy, Jeff, Minnesota............	16	16
Clark, Jon, Chicago	1	0
Clark, Reggie, Jacksonville........	5	0
Clark, Sedric, Baltimore............	6	0
Clark, Vinnie, Jacksonville........	4	4
Clark, Willie, San Diego	16	4
Clavelle, Shannon, Green Bay ..	8	0
Clay, Hayward, St. Louis	11	4
Clay, Willie, New England	16	16
Clemons, Duane, Minnesota......	13	0
Clifton, Kyle, N.Y. Jets	16	0
Cline, Tony, Buffalo.................	16	7
Coates, Ben, New England	16	15
Cobb, Reggie, N.Y. Jets	15	0
Cocozzo, Joe, San Diego	16	11
Cole, Lee, Houston	3	0
Coleman, Andre, San Diego	16	10
Coleman, Ben, Jacksonville......	16	16
Coleman, Marco, San Diego	16	15
Coleman, Marcus, N.Y. Jets	13	4
Collins, Andre, Cincinnati	14	0
Collins, Kerry, Carolina............	13	12
Collins, Mark, Kansas City........	16	15
Collins, Todd, Buffalo	7	3
Collins, Todd F., New England ...	16	9
Collons, Ferric, New England	15	5
Colman, Doug, N.Y. Giants	13	0
Colston, Tim, Carolina..............	2	0
Compton, Mike, Detroit.............	15	15
Conley, Steven, Pittsburgh	2	0
Conner, Darion, Philadelphia	7	0
Conover, Scott, Detroit.............	10	7
Conway, Curtis, Chicago	16	16
Conwell, Ernie, St. Louis	10	8
Cook, Anthony, Houston	12	11
Cook, Toi, Carolina.................	15	1
Coons, Robert, Buffalo	16	0
Cooper, Adrian, San Francisco ..	6	0
Cooper, Richard, Philadelphia ...	16	16
Copeland, John, Cincinnati	13	13
Copeland, Russell, Buffalo	11	0
Coryatt, Quentin, Indianapolis ...	8	7
Cota, Chad, Carolina...............	16	2
Cothran, Jeff, Cincinnati	11	11
Covington, Damien, Buffalo.......	9	2
Cox, Bryan, Chicago................	9	9
Cox, Ron, Green Bay	16	
Craver, Aaron, Denver	15	1
Crawford, Keith, St. Louis	16	
Crisman, Joel, Tampa Bay	9	
Criswell, Jeff, Kansas City	15	
Crockett, Ray, Denver..............	15	1
Crockett, Zack, Indianapolis	5	
Croel, Mike, Baltimore..............	16	1
Cross, Howard, N.Y. Giants	16	
Crumpler, Carlester, Seattle......	16	
Culpepper, Brad, Tampa Bay	13	1
Cummings, Joe, San Diego	3	
Cunningham, Ed, Seattle	11	
Cunningham, Rick, Oakland	13	
Cunningham, T.J., Seattle..........	9	
Curry, Eric, Tampa Bay	12	
Dafney, Bernard, Pittsburgh	14	
D'Agostino, Lou, N.Y. Jets........	9	
Dahl, Bob, Washington.............	15	1
Dalman, Chris, San Francisco ...	16	
Daluiso, Brad, N.Y. Giants........	16	
Daniel, Eugene, Indianapolis	16	
Daniels, Dexter, Baltimore........	4	
Daniels, Phillip, Seattle	15	
Dar Dar, Kirby, Miami	11	
Darby, Matt, Arizona................	15	1
Davey, Don, Jacksonville..........	16	1
Davidson, Kenny, Cincinnati	3	
Davis, Andre, Jacksonville........	2	
Davis, Anthony, Kansas City	16	
Davis, Antone, Atlanta	16	1
Davis, Billy, Dallas	13	
Davis, Don, New Orleans	11	
Davis, Eric, Carolina...............	16	
Davis, Greg, Arizona	9	
Davis, Isaac, San Diego	14	
Davis, Paschall, St. Louis	10	
Davis, Reuben, San Diego	15	1
Davis, Rob, Chicago................	16	
Davis, Stephen, Washington	12	
Davis, Terrell, Denver..............	16	1
Davis, Travis, Jacksonville........	16	
Davis, Tyrone, N.Y. Jets...........	2	
Davis, Wendell, Dallas	13	
Davis, Willie, Houston	16	1
Davison, Jerone, Oakland	2	
Dawkins, Brian, Philadelphia	14	1
Dawkins, Sean, Indianapolis	15	1
Dawsey, Lawrence, N.Y. Giants..	16	
Dawson, Dermontti, Pittsburgh..	16	
Dawson, Lake, Kansas City	4	
Deese, Derrick, San Francisco...	16	1
Del Greco, Al, Houston.............	16	
Dellenbach, Jeff, N.E.-G.B.	5	
DeLong, Greg, Minnesota.........	16	
DeMarco, Brian, Jacksonville	10	
Dennis, Mark, Carolina	16	
Dent, Richard, Indianapolis	16	
DeRamus, Lee, New Orleans	15	
Detmer, Ty, Philadelphia	13	
Devlin, Mike, Arizona	11	1
Dexter, James, Arizona	6	
Diaz, Jorge, Tampa Bay	11	
Diaz-Infante, David, Denver	9	
Dilfer, Trent, Tampa Bay	16	
Dilger, Ken, Indianapolis	16	
Dill, Scott, Minnesota	9	
Dimry, Charles, Tampa Bay	16	
Dingle, Hunter, Jacksonville	2	
Dishman, Chris, Houston	16	
Dixon, Cal, Miami	11	

Player, Team	GP	GS
Dixon, David, Minnesota	13	6
Dixon, Ernest, New Orleans	16	0
Dixon, Gerald, Cincinnati	16	1
Dixon, Ronnie, Philadelphia	16	4
Dodge, Dedrick, San Francisco	16	3
Doering, Chris, Indianapolis	1	0
Dogins, Kevin, Tampa Bay	1	0
Doleman, Chris, San Francisco	16	16
Dombrowski, Jim, New Orleans	10	10
Donaldson, Ray, Dallas	16	16
Donnalley, Kevin, Houston	16	16
Dorn, Torin, St. Louis	9	0
Dorsett, Anthony, Houston	8	0
Dotson, Earl, Green Bay	15	15
Dotson, Santana, Green Bay	16	15
Douglas, Hugh, N.Y. Jets	10	10
Douglas, Omar, N.Y. Giants	4	0
Douglass, Maurice, N.Y. Giants	15	0
Dowdell, Marcus, Arizona	15	0
Dowden, Corey, G.B.-Bal.	12	0
Downs, Gary, N.Y. Giants	6	1
Drake, Jerry, Arizona	11	0
Drake, Troy, Philadelphia	11	0
Drakeford, Tyronne, S.F.	16	16
Drayton, Troy, St.L.-Mia.	13	13
Dronett, Shane, Atl.-Det.	12	0
DuBose, Demetrius, Tampa Bay	14	0
Dudley, Rickey, Oakland	16	15
Duffy, Roger, N.Y. Jets	16	16
Dumas, Troy, Kansas City	6	0
Dunn, David, Cincinnati	16	0
Dunn, Jason, Philadelphia	16	12
Dye, Ernest, Arizona	8	0
Early, Quinn, Buffalo	16	13
Eatman, Irv, Houston	16	16
Eaton, Chad, New England	4	0
Edge, Shayne, Pittsburgh	4	0
Edwards, Anthony, Arizona	16	1
Edwards, Antonio, Seattle	12	3
Edwards, Brad, Atlanta	16	7
Edwards, Dixon, Minnesota	14	13
Edwards, Donnie, Kansas City	15	1
Edwards, Vernon, San Diego	5	1
Elam, Jason, Denver	16	0
Elias, Keith, N.Y. Giants	9	0
Ellard, Henry, Washington	16	16
Elliott, Jumbo, N.Y. Jets	14	14
Elliott, Matt, Carolina	16	12
Ellis, Kwame, N.Y. Jets	8	0
Ellison, 'Omar, San Diego	10	1
Ellison, Jerry, Tampa Bay	16	2
Elliss, Luther, Detroit	14	14
Ellsworth, Percy, N.Y. Giants	14	4
El-Mashtoub, Hicham, Houston	1	0
Elway, John, Denver	15	15
Emanuel, Bert, Atlanta	14	13
Emmons, Carlos, Pittsburgh	15	0
Emtman, Steve, Miami	13	4
Engel, Greg, San Diego	12	9
England, Eric, Arizona	11	1
Ingram, Bobby, Chicago	16	2
Erickson, Craig, Miami	7	3
Esiason, Boomer, Arizona	10	8
Ethridge, Ray, Baltimore	14	1
Evans, Chuck, Minnesota	16	6
Evans, Doug, Green Bay	16	16
Evans, Josh, Houston	8	0
Evans, Leomont, Washington	12	0
Everett, Jim, New Orleans	15	15
Everitt, Steve, Baltimore	8	7
Farmer, Ray, Philadelphia	16	11
Farquhar, John, T.B.-Pit.	5	0
Farr, D'Marco, St. Louis	16	16
Faulk, Marshall, Indianapolis	13	13
Faulkerson, Mike, Chicago	16	0
Faulkner, Jeff, N.Y. Jets	4	0
Fauria, Christian, Seattle	10	9
Favre, Brett, Green Bay	16	16
Feagles, Jeff, Arizona	16	0
Fenner, Derrick, Oakland	16	11
Fields, Mark, New Orleans	16	15
Fields, Scott, Atlanta	6	0
Figaro, Cedric, St. Louis	15	0
Figures, Deon, Pittsburgh	16	3
Fina, John, Buffalo	15	15
Fisk, Jason, Minnesota	16	6
Flanigan, Jim, Chicago	14	14
Flannery, John, Dallas	1	0
Fletcher, Terrell, San Diego	16	0
Flowers, Lethon, Pittsburgh	16	0
Floyd, Malcolm, Houston	16	0
Floyd, William, San Francisco	9	8
Foley, Glenn, N.Y. Jets	5	3
Folston, James, Oakland	12	0
Fontenot, Al, Chicago	16	15
Fontenot, Jerry, Chicago	16	16
Footman, Dan, Baltimore	10	8
Forbes, Marlon, Chicago	15	0
Ford, Brad, Detroit	14	0
Ford, Cole, Oakland	16	0
Ford, Henry, Houston	15	14
Fortin, Roman, Atlanta	16	16
Fortune, Elliott, Baltimore	14	0
Fox, Mike, Carolina	11	11
Francis, James, Cincinnati	16	15
Frase, Paul, Jacksonville	14	0
Frazier, Derrick, Indianapolis	6	4
Frederick, Mike, Baltimore	16	11
Fredrickson, Rob, Oakland	10	10
Freeman, Antonio, Green Bay	12	12
Frerotte, Gus, Washington	16	16
Friesz, John, Seattle	8	6
Frisch, David, Minnesota	10	1
Fryar, Irving, Philadelphia	16	16
Fuller, Corey, Minnesota	16	14
Fuller, James, Philadelphia	13	2
Fuller, Randy, Pittsburgh	14	1
Fuller, William, Philadelphia	16	16
Gaines, William, Washington	16	6
Galbraith, Scott, Washington	16	6
Galbreath, Harry, N.Y. Jets	15	8
Galloway, Joey, Seattle	16	16
Galyon, Scott, N.Y. Giants	16	0
Gammon, Kendall, New Orleans	16	0
Gandy, Wayne, St. Louis	16	16
Gannon, Rich, Kansas City	4	3
Gant, Kenneth, Tampa Bay	16	0
Garcia, Frank, Carolina	14	8
Gardener, Daryl, Miami	16	12
Gardner, Carwell, Baltimore	13	3
Gardner, Moe, Atlanta	10	10
Gardocki, Chris, Indianapolis	16	0
Garner, Charlie, Philadelphia	15	1
Garnett, Dave, Minnesota	12	4
Garrett, Jason, Dallas	1	0
Garrido, Norberto, Carolina	12	8
Gash, Sam, New England	14	9
Gaskins, Percell, St. Louis	15	0
Gayle, Rashid, Jacksonville	2	0
Geathers, Jumpy, Denver	16	0
Gelbaugh, Stan, Seattle	1	1
George, Eddie, Houston	16	16
George, Jeff, Atlanta	3	3
George, Ron, Atlanta	16	15
Gerak, John, Minnesota	14	10
Gibson, Oliver, Pittsburgh	16	0
Gilbert, Sean, Washington	16	16
Gildon, Jason, Pittsburgh	14	13
Gisler, Mike, New England	14	0
Glenn, Aaron, N.Y. Jets	16	16
Glenn, Terry, New England	15	15
Glover, Andrew, Oakland	14	4
Glover, Kevin, Detroit	16	16
Glover, La'Roi, Oakland	2	0
Goad, Tim, Baltimore	16	5
Godfrey, Randall, Dallas	16	6
Goeas, Leo, St. Louis	16	13
Goff, Robert, Minnesota	5	0
Gogan, Kevin, Oakland	16	16
Goganious, Keith, Baltimore	13	8
Gooch, Jeff, Tampa Bay	15	0
Goodwin, Hunter, Minnesota	9	6
Gordon, Darrien, San Diego	16	6
Gordon, Dwayne, San Diego	13	0
Goss, Antonio, St. Louis	8	3
Gossett, Jeff, Oakland	12	0
Gouveia, Kurt, San Diego	16	16
Gragg, Scott, N.Y. Giants	16	16
Graham, Aaron, Arizona	16	7
Graham, Derrick, Seattle	16	16
Graham, Hason, New England	9	0
Graham, Jeff, N.Y. Jets	11	9
Graham, Kent, Arizona	10	8
Graham, Roger, Jacksonville	1	0
Graham, Scottie, Minnesota	11	0
Grant, Steve, Indianapolis	11	11
Grasmanis, Paul, Chicago	14	3
Gray, Carlton, Seattle	16	16
Gray, Chris, Miami	11	11
Gray, Derwin, Indianapolis	10	1
Gray, Mel, Houston	14	0
Gray, Oscar, Seattle	9	0
Grbac, Elvis, San Francisco	15	4
Green, Darrell, Washington	16	16
Green, Eric, Baltimore	6	3
Green, Harold, St. Louis	16	5
Green, Paul, New Orleans	14	5
Green, Robert, Chicago	10	3
Green, Victor, N.Y. Jets	16	16
Green, Willie, Carolina	15	10
Greene, Kevin, Carolina	16	16
Greene, Scott, Carolina	8	0
Greenwood, Carl, N.Y. Jets	14	2
Grier, Marrio, New England	16	0
Griffin, Don, Philadelphia	16	1
Griffith, Howard, Carolina	16	14
Griffith, Richard, Jacksonville	16	2
Griffith, Robert, Minnesota	14	14
Groce, Clif, Indianapolis	15	8
Gruber, Paul, Tampa Bay	13	13
Grunhard, Tim, Kansas City	16	16
Gruttadauria, Mike, St. Louis	9	3
Guess, Terry, New Orleans	3	2
Gunn, Mark, Phi.-NYJ	12	0
Habib, Brian, Denver	16	16
Hager, Britt, Denver	2	0
Halapin, Mike, Houston	9	0
Haley, Charles, Dallas	5	5
Hall, Courtney, San Diego	7	7
Hall, Dana, Jacksonville	16	10
Hall, Lemanski, Houston	3	0
Hall, Rhett, Philadelphia	16	16
Hall, Steve, Min.-Ind.	3	0

Player, Team	GP	GS
Hall, Tim, Oakland	2	0
Hall, Travis, Atlanta	14	13
Hallock, Ty, Jacksonville	7	0
Hamilton, Bobby, N.Y. Jets	15	11
Hamilton, Conrad, N.Y. Giants	15	1
Hamilton, Keith, N.Y. Giants	14	14
Hamilton, Rick, N.Y. Jets	15	4
Hampton, Rodney, N.Y. Giants	15	15
Hand, Norman, Miami	9	0
Hanks, Ben, Minnesota	12	0
Hanks, Merton, San Francisco	16	16
Hansen, Brian, N.Y. Jets	16	0
Hansen, Phil, Buffalo	16	16
Hanshaw, Tim, San Francisco	1	0
Hanson, Jason, Detroit	16	0
Harbaugh, Jim, Indianapolis	14	14
Hardin, Steve, Indianapolis	1	0
Hardy, Kevin, Jacksonville	16	15
Harlow, Pat, Oakland	10	9
Harmon, Andy, Philadelphia	2	2
Harmon, Ronnie, Houston	16	6
Harper, Alvin, Tampa Bay	12	7
Harper, Dwayne, San Diego	6	6
Harper, Roger, Dallas	14	0
Harris, Anthony, Miami	7	3
Harris, Bernardo, Green Bay	16	0
Harris, Corey, Seattle	16	16
Harris, Derrick, St. Louis	11	6
Harris, Jackie, Tampa Bay	13	12
Harris, James, St. Louis	16	0
Harris, Mark, San Francisco	1	0
Harris, Raymont, Chicago	12	10
Harris, Robert, N.Y. Giants	16	16
Harris, Ronnie, Seattle	15	0
Harris, Sean, Chicago	15	0
Harris, Walt, Chicago	15	13
Harrison, Chris, Detroit	2	0
Harrison, Martin, Minnesota	16	8
Harrison, Marvin, Indianapolis	16	15
Harrison, Nolan, Oakland	15	2
Harrison, Rodney, San Diego	16	16
Hartings, Jeff, Detroit	11	10
Hartley, Frank, Baltimore	8	0
Harvey, Ken, Washington	16	16
Harvey, Richard, New Orleans	14	7
Hasselbach, Harald, Denver	16	1
Hastings, Andre, Pittsburgh	16	10
Hasty, James, Kansas City	15	14
Hauck, Tim, Denver	16	0
Hawkins, Courtney, Tampa Bay	16	16
Hayden, Aaron, San Diego	11	0
Hayes, Brandon, Carolina	7	0
Hayes, Chris, Green Bay	2	0
Hayes, Jarius, Arizona	4	0
Hayes, Jonathan, Pittsburgh	16	6
Hayes, Melvin, N.Y. Jets	1	0
Hayes, Mercury, New Orleans	7	0
Haynes, Michael, New Orleans	16	10
Hearst, Garrison, Cincinnati	16	12
Hebert, Bobby, Atlanta	14	13
Hebron, Vaughn, Denver	16	0
Heck, Andy, Chicago	16	16
Hegamin, George, Dallas	16	1
Hellestrae, Dale, Dallas	16	0
Hempstead, Hessley, Detroit	13	0
Henderson, Jerome, N.E.	7	0
Henderson, William, Green Bay	16	11
Hendrix, David, San Diego	14	0
Hennings, Chad, Dallas	15	15
Henry, Kevin, Pittsburgh	12	10
Hentrich, Craig, Green Bay	16	0
Herrod, Jeff, Indianapolis	14	14
Hetherington, Chris, Indianapolis	6	0
Heyward, Craig, Atlanta	15	5
Hicks, Michael, Chicago	4	0
Hill, Eric, Arizona	16	16
Hill, Greg, Kansas City	15	1
Hill, Jeff, Cincinnati	10	0
Hill, Randal, Miami	14	5
Hill, Sean, Miami	12	5
Hilliard, Randy, Denver	13	3
Hills, Keno, New Orleans	1	0
Hinton, Marcus, Oakland	2	0
Hitchcock, Jimmy, New England	13	5
Hoage, Terry, Arizona	5	3
Hoard, Leroy, Bal.-Car.-Min.	11	7
Hobbs, Daryl, Oakland	16	1
Hobert, Billy Joe, Oakland	8	3
Holland, Darius, Green Bay	16	0
Holliday, Corey, Pittsburgh	11	0
Holliday, Marcus, St. Louis	1	0
Hollier, Dwight, Miami	16	15
Hollinquest, Lamont, Green Bay	16	0
Hollis, Mike, Jacksonville	16	0
Holmberg, Rob, Oakland	13	1
Holmes, Darick, Buffalo	16	1
Holmes, Earl, Pittsburgh	3	1
Holmes, Lester, Philadelphia	16	14
Holsey, Bernard, N.Y. Giants	16	0
Homco, Thomas, St. Louis	3	0
Hopkins, Brad, Houston	16	16
Horan, Mike, N.Y. Giants	16	0
Horn, Joe, Kansas City	9	0
Hoskins, Derrick, New Orleans	1	0
Hostetler, Jeff, Oakland	13	13
Houston, Bobby, N.Y. Jets	15	15
Howard, Dana, Chicago	3	0
Howard, Desmond, Green Bay	16	0
Howard, Erik, N.Y. Jets	1	1
Hoying, Bobby, Philadelphia	1	0
Hudson, Chris, Jacksonville	16	16
Hudson, John, N.Y. Jets	16	0
Huerta, Carlos, Chi.-St.L.	4	0
Hughes, Danan, Kansas City	15	2
Hughes, Tyrone, New Orleans	16	1
Hull, Kent, Buffalo	16	16
Humphries, Stan, San Diego	13	13
Hundon, James, Cincinnati	5	0
Hunter, Ernest, Bal.-N.O.	11	0
Huntington, Greg, Jacksonville	2	0
Huntley, Richard, Atlanta	1	0
Husted, Michael, Tampa Bay	16	0
Hutton, Tom, Philadelphia	16	0
Ifeanyi, Israel, San Francisco	3	0
Ingram, Mark, Philadelphia	5	0
Innocent, Dou, Seattle	4	0
Irvin, Ken, Buffalo	16	1
Irvin, Michael, Dallas	11	11
Irving, Terry, Arizona	16	0
Isaia, Sale, Baltimore	9	0
Ismail, Qadry, Minnesota	16	2
Ismail, Raghib, Carolina	13	5
Israel, Steve, San Francisco	14	2
Izzo, Larry, Miami	16	0
Jacke, Chris, Green Bay	16	0
Jackson, Alfred M., Minnesota	14	2
Jackson, Calvin, Miami	16	15
Jackson, Greg, New Orleans	16	15
Jackson, Jack, Chicago	12	0
Jackson, John, Chicago	5	0
Jackson, John, Pittsburgh	16	16
Jackson, Keith, Green Bay	16	5
Jackson, Michael, Baltimore	16	16
Jackson, Raymond, Buffalo	12	0
Jackson, Steve, Houston	16	1
Jackson, Tyoka, Tampa Bay	13	2
Jackson, Willie, Jacksonville	16	2
Jacobs, Tim, Miami	12	0
Jaeger, Jeff, Chicago	13	0
James, Jesse, St. Louis	1	0
James, Tory, Denver	16	2
Jamison, George, Kansas City	5	0
Jeffcoat, Jim, Buffalo	16	0
Jeffers, Patrick, Denver	4	0
Jefferson, Greg, Philadelphia	11	0
Jefferson, Shawn, New England	15	15
Jeffires, Haywood, New Orleans	9	1
Jeffries, Greg, Detroit	16	4
Jells, Dietrich, New England	7	1
Jenkins, Carlos, St. Louis	13	10
Jenkins, DeRon, Baltimore	15	2
Jenkins, James, Washington	16	5
Jenkins, Robert, Oakland	10	6
Jenkins, Trezelle, Kansas City	6	0
Jennings, Keith, Chicago	6	5
Jervey, Travis, Green Bay	16	0
Jeter, Tommy, Carolina	1	0
Jett, James, Oakland	16	16
Jett, John, Dallas	16	0
Johnson, Anthony, Carolina	16	11
Johnson, Bill, Pittsburgh	15	8
Johnson, Brad, Minnesota	12	8
Johnson, Charles, Pittsburgh	16	12
Johnson, Chris, Minnesota	5	0
Johnson, D.J., Atl.-Ariz.	9	0
Johnson, Darrius, Denver	13	0
Johnson, Ellis, Indianapolis	12	6
Johnson, Jimmie, Philadelphia	16	3
Johnson, Joe, New Orleans	13	13
Johnson, Kevin, Philadelphia	12	5
Johnson, Keyshawn, N.Y. Jets	14	11
Johnson, Lee, Cincinnati	16	0
Johnson, LeShon, Arizona	15	8
Johnson, Lonnie, Buffalo	16	15
Johnson, Melvin, Tampa Bay	16	16
Johnson, Norm, Pittsburgh	16	0
Johnson, Pepper, Detroit	15	12
Johnson, Raylee, San Diego	16	1
Johnson, Reggie, Kansas City	11	3
Johnson, Rob, Jacksonville	2	0
Johnson, Ted, New England	16	16
Johnson, Tim, Cincinnati	14	13
Johnson, Tony, New Orleans	9	7
Johnson, Tracy, Tampa Bay	10	0
Johnson, Tre', Washington	15	15
Johnston, Daryl, Dallas	16	15
Johnstone, Lance, Oakland	16	0
Jones, Aaron, Miami	8	0
Jones, Brent, San Francisco	11	10
Jones, Brian, New Orleans	16	1
Jones, Calvin, Green Bay	1	0
Jones, Cedric, N.Y. Giants	16	0
Jones, Charlie, San Diego	14	4
Jones, Chris T., Philadelphia	16	16
Jones, Clarence, New Orleans	16	16
Jones, Donta, Pittsburgh	15	2
Jones, Ernest, Denver	6	0
Jones, Gary, N.Y. Jets	15	15
Jones, Henry, Buffalo	5	5
Jones, James, Baltimore	16	11
Jones, Jeff, Detroit	7	0
Jones, Jimmie, St. Louis	14	14
Jones, LaCurtis, Tampa Bay	10	0

Player, Team	GP	GS
ones, Lenoy, Houston	11	0
ones, Marcus, Tampa Bay	16	3
ones, Marvin, N.Y. Jets	12	12
ones, Mike A., Oakland	15	15
ones, Mike D., New England	16	12
ones, Richard, Indianapolis	4	0
ones, Robert, St. Louis	16	13
ones, Rod E., Cincinnati	5	1
ones, Rod W., Cincinnati	6	1
ones, Roger, Cincinnati	14	1
ones, Rondell, Denver	16	0
ones, Sean, Green Bay	15	15
ones, Selwyn, Seattle	16	1
ones, Tony, Baltimore	15	15
ordan, Andrew, Minnesota	13	9
ordan, Charles, Miami	6	0
ordan, Kevin, Arizona	1	0
ordan, Randy, Jacksonville	15	0
oseph, Vance, Indianapolis	4	0
oyce, Matt, Arizona	2	0
oyner, Seth, Arizona	16	16
unkin, Trey, Oak.-Ariz.	16	0
urkovic, John, Jacksonville	16	14
ustin, Paul, Indianapolis	8	2
anell, Danny, N.Y. Giants	4	0
asay, John, Carolina	16	0
aufman, Napoleon, Oakland	16	9
eeney, Brad, N.Y. Jets	1	0
elly, Jim, Buffalo	13	13
elly, Joe, Philadelphia	16	2
elly, Todd, Cin.-Atl.	4	0
endall, Pete, Seattle	12	11
ennard, Derek, Dallas	1	0
ennedy, Cortez, Seattle	16	16
ennedy, Lincoln, Oakland	16	16
ennison, Eddie, St. Louis	15	14
erner, Marlon, Buffalo	15	0
eyes, Marcus, Chicago	2	0
idd, Carl, Oakland	16	0
idd, John, Miami	16	0
illens, Terry, Houston	14	0
inchen, Brian, Baltimore	16	16
inchen, Todd, Denver	7	0
ing, Ed, New Orleans	16	16
ing, Shawn, Carolina	16	0
irby, Terry, San Francisco	14	10
irk, Randy, San Francisco	16	0
irkland, Levon, Pittsburgh	16	16
irksey, Jon, St. Louis	11	1
ingler, David, Oakland	1	0
napp, Lindsay, Green Bay	9	0
oonce, George, Green Bay	16	16
opp, Jeff, Jacksonville	12	0
osar, Bernie, Miami	3	0
owalkowski, Scott, Detroit	16	1
ozlowski, Brian, N.Y. Giants	5	0
ragen, Greg, Carolina	16	16
ramer, Erik, Chicago	4	4
ratch, Bob, New England	8	4
rieg, Dave, Chicago	13	12
uberski, Bob, Green Bay	1	0
uehl, Ryan, Washington	2	0
yle, Jason, Seattle	16	0
aBounty, Matt, Seattle	3	0
aChapelle, Sean, Kansas City	12	8
acina, Corbin, Buffalo	12	2
ageman, Jeff, Jacksonville	12	9
aing, Aaron, St. Louis	12	8
ake, Carnell, Pittsburgh	13	13
and, Dan, Oakland	16	2
andeta, Sean, St. Louis	16	0
Lane, Max, New England	16	16
Langford, Jevon, Cincinnati	12	3
Langham, Antonio, Baltimore	15	14
Lassiter, Kwamie, Arizona	14	0
Lathon, Lamar, Carolina	16	16
Law, Ty, New England	13	12
Layman, Jason, Houston	16	0
Leasy, Wesley, Arizona	16	0
LeBel, Harper, Atlanta	16	0
Lee, Amp, Minnesota	16	3
Lee, Kevin, San Francisco	2	0
Lee, Shawn, San Diego	15	7
Leeuwenburg, Jay, Indianapolis	15	7
Legette, Tyrone, Tampa Bay	15	0
Lester, Tim, Pittsburgh	16	13
Lett, Leon, Dallas	13	13
Levens, Dorsey, Green Bay	16	1
Lewis, Albert, Oakland	16	13
Lewis, Darryll, Houston	16	16
Lewis, Jeff, Denver	2	0
Lewis, Jermaine, Baltimore	16	1
Lewis, Mo, N.Y. Jets	9	9
Lewis, Ray, Baltimore	14	13
Lewis, Roderick, Houston	16	7
Lewis, Thomas, N.Y. Giants	13	11
Lewis, Vernon, New England	7	0
Lincoln, Jeremy, St. Louis	13	1
Lloyd, Greg, Pittsburgh	1	1
Lodish, Mike, Denver	16	16
Lofton, Steve, Carolina	11	3
Logan, Ernie, Jacksonville	4	0
Logan, James, Seattle	6	0
Logan, Marc, Washington	14	9
Lohmiller, Chip, St. Louis	15	0
London, Antonio, Detroit	14	12
Louchiey, Corey, Buffalo	16	4
Love, Duval, Arizona	9	9
Loville, Derek, San Francisco	12	6
Lowdermilk, Kirk, Indianapolis	16	16
Lowery, Michael, Chicago	16	0
Lowery, Nick, N.Y. Jets	16	0
Lucas, Ray, New England	2	0
Lumpkin, Sean, New Orleans	7	1
Lusk, Henry, New Orleans	16	3
Lyght, Todd, St. Louis	16	16
Lyle, Keith, St. Louis	16	16
Lyle, Rick, Baltimore	11	3
Lynch, Eric, Detroit	16	0
Lynch, John, Tampa Bay	16	14
Lynch, Lorenzo, Oakland	16	16
Lynn, Anthony, San Francisco	16	1
Lyons, Lamar, Oakland	6	0
Lyons, Mitch, Atlanta	14	4
Maddox, Mark, Buffalo	14	14
Mahlum, Eric, Indianapolis	13	9
Majkowski, Don, Detroit	5	2
Malamala, Siupeli, N.Y. Jets	4	1
Malone, Van, Detroit	15	15
Mamula, Mike, Philadelphia	16	16
Mandarich, Tony, Indianapolis	15	6
Mangum, John, Chicago	16	2
Maniecki, Jason, Tampa Bay	5	0
Manuel, Sean, San Francisco	11	0
Manusky, Greg, Kansas City	16	1
Marino, Dan, Miami	13	13
Marion, Brock, Dallas	10	10
Marsh, Curtis, Jacksonville	1	0
Marshall, Anthony, Chicago	13	3
Marshall, Arthur, N.Y. Giants	5	1
Marshall, Marvin, Tampa Bay	5	0
Marshall, Whit, Philadelphia	1	0
Martin, Chris, Chicago	1	0
Martin, Curtis, New England	16	15
Martin, Emanuel, Buffalo	16	1
Martin, Jamie, St. Louis	6	0
Martin, Kelvin, Dallas	16	1
Martin, Steve, Indianapolis	14	5
Martin, Tony, San Diego	16	16
Martin, Wayne, New Orleans	16	16
Marts, Lonnie, Tampa Bay	16	13
Maryland, Russell, Oakland	16	16
Massey, Robert, Jacksonville	16	2
Maston, Le'Shai, Jacksonville	15	7
Mathews, Jason, Indianapolis	16	15
Mathis, Dedric, Indianapolis	16	6
Mathis, Terance, Atlanta	16	16
Matich, Trevor, Washington	16	0
Matthews, Aubrey, Detroit	16	0
Matthews, Bruce, Houston	16	16
Matthews, Clay, Atlanta	15	1
Matthews, Shane, Chicago	2	0
Maumalanga, Chris, Arizona	1	0
Mawae, Kevin, Seattle	16	16
Maxie, Brett, Carolina	13	13
May, Deems, San Diego	16	12
May, Sherriden, N.Y. Jets	8	0
Mayberry, Jermane, Philadelphia	3	1
Mayberry, Tony, Tampa Bay	16	16
Mayes, Derrick, Green Bay	7	0
Mayhew, Martin, Tampa Bay	16	16
McAfee, Fred, Pittsburgh	14	0
McBride, Oscar, Arizona	2	1
McBurrows, Gerald, St. Louis	16	7
McCaffrey, Ed, Denver	15	15
McCardell, Keenan, Jacksonville	15	15
McCleskey, J.J., N.O.-Ariz.	10	0
McCollum, Andy, New Orleans	16	16
McCormack, Hurvin, Dallas	16	4
McCorvey, Kez, Detroit	1	0
McCoy, Tony, Indianapolis	15	15
McCrary, Michael, Seattle	16	13
McDaniel, Emmanuel, Carolina	2	0
McDaniel, Randall, Minnesota	16	16
McDaniel, Terry, Oakland	16	15
McDaniels, Pellom, Kansas City	9	1
McDonald, Devon, Arizona	16	0
McDonald, Ricardo, Cincinnati	16	15
McDonald, Tim, San Francisco	16	16
McDuffie, O.J., Miami	16	16
McElroy, Leeland, Arizona	16	6
McElroy, Ray, Indianapolis	16	5
McElroy, Reggie, Denver	7	0
McGee, Tony, Cincinnati	16	16
McGill, Lenny, Atlanta	16	8
McGinest, Willie, New England	16	16
McGlockton, Chester, Oakland	16	16
McGruder, Mike, New England	14	0
McGuire, Gene, Green Bay	8	0
McIntyre, Guy, Philadelphia	15	2
McIver, Everett, Miami	7	5
McKeehan, James, Houston	14	0
McKenzie, Keith, Green Bay	10	0
McKenzie, Raleigh, Philadelphia	16	16
McKinnon, Ronald, Arizona	16	0
McKnight, James, Seattle	16	0
McKyer, Tim, Atlanta	8	7
McMahon, Jim, Green Bay	5	0
McManus, Tom, Jacksonville	16	11
McMillian, Henry, Seattle	3	0
McMillian, Mark, New Orleans	16	16
McNair, Steve, Houston	9	4
McNair, Todd, Kansas City	16	0

1996 REVIEW · Player participation

Player, Team	GP	GS
McNeil, Ryan, Detroit	16	16
McPhail, Jerris, Miami	9	1
McRae, Charles, Oakland	13	1
McWilliams, Johnny, Arizona	12	0
Means, Natrone, Jacksonville	14	4
Meggett, Dave, New England	16	1
Metcalf, Eric, Atlanta	16	11
Metzelaars, Pete, Detroit	15	11
Michels, John, Green Bay	15	9
Mickell, Darren, New Orleans	12	12
Mickens, Arnold, Indianapolis	3	0
Mickens, Ray, N.Y. Jets	15	10
Mickens, Terry, Green Bay	8	5
Milanovich, Scott, Tampa Bay	1	0
Milburn, Glyn, Detroit	16	0
Miller, Anthony, Denver	16	16
Miller, Corey, N.Y. Giants	14	13
Miller, Fred, St. Louis	14	0
Miller, Jamir, Arizona	16	16
Miller, Jim, Pittsburgh	2	1
Miller, Josh, Pittsburgh	12	0
Miller, Les, Carolina	15	5
Miller, Scott, Miami	12	1
Milloy, Lawyer, New England	16	10
Mills, Ernie, Pittsburgh	9	3
Mills, Jim, San Diego	1	0
Mills, John Henry, Houston	16	0
Mills, Sam, Carolina	16	16
Milne, Brian, Cincinnati	6	5
Milner, Billy, Mia.-St.L.	14	0
Milstead, Rod, San Francisco	11	0
Mims, Chris, San Diego	15	15
Mincy, Charles, Tampa Bay	2	0
Miniefield, Kevin, Chicago	13	3
Minter, Barry, Chicago	16	7
Mirer, Rick, Seattle	11	9
Mitchell, Brian, Washington	16	2
Mitchell, Johnny, Dallas	4	1
Mitchell, Kevin, San Francisco	12	3
Mitchell, Pete, Jacksonville	16	7
Mitchell, Scott, Detroit	14	14
Mitchell, Shannon, San Diego	16	11
Mix, Bryant, Houston	6	2
Mobley, John, Denver	16	16
Mohr, Chris, Buffalo	16	0
Molden, Alex, New Orleans	14	2
Montgomery, Glenn, Seattle	7	1
Montgomery, Greg, Baltimore	16	0
Montreuil, Mark, San Diego	13	0
Moon, Warren, Minnesota	8	8
Moore, Dave, Tampa Bay	16	8
Moore, Herman, Detroit	16	16
Moore, Jerald, St. Louis	11	4
Moore, Marty, New England	16	0
Moore, Rob, Arizona	16	16
Moore, Ronald, N.Y. Jets	16	0
Moore, Stevon, Baltimore	16	16
Moore, Will, New England	2	1
Morabito, Tim, Cincinnati	7	1
Moran, Sean, Buffalo	16	0
Morgan, Anthony, Green Bay	3	0
Morris, Bam, Baltimore	11	7
Morris, Mike, Minnesota	16	0
Morrison, Darryl, Washington	12	12
Morrison, Steve, Indianapolis	16	8
Morrow, Harold, Minnesota	8	0
Morton, Johnnie, Detroit	16	15
Morton, Mike, Oakland	16	6
Moss, Winston, Seattle	16	16
Moss, Zefross, Detroit	15	15
Moten, Eric, San Diego	15	15
Moulds, Eric, Buffalo	16	5
Muhammad, Muhsin, Carolina	9	5
Mullen, Roderick, Green Bay	14	0
Murrell, Adrian, N.Y. Jets	16	16
Musgrave, Bill, Denver	6	1
Myers, Greg, Cincinnati	14	0
Myles, Godfrey, Dallas	16	0
Myslinski, Tom, Pittsburgh	8	6
Nagle, Browning, Atlanta	5	0
Nalen, Tom, Denver	16	16
Nash, Joe, Seattle	8	0
Neal, Lorenzo, New Orleans	16	11
Neal, Randy, Cincinnati	1	0
Nedney, Joe, Miami	16	0
Neely, Bobby, Chicago	11	5
Neujahr, Quentin, Baltimore	5	0
Newman, Anthony, New Orleans	16	16
Newsome, Craig, Green Bay	16	16
Newton, Nate, Dallas	16	16
Nickerson, Hardy, Tampa Bay	16	16
Norgard, Erik, Houston	13	0
Northern, Gabe, Buffalo	16	2
Norton, Ken, San Francisco	16	16
Nottage, Dexter, Washington	16	4
Novak, Jeff, Jacksonville	5	0
Novitsky, Craig, New Orleans	16	6
Nunn, Freddie Joe, Indianapolis	5	0
Nussmeier, Doug, New Orleans	2	1
Oben, Roman, N.Y. Giants	2	0
O'Berry, Herman, St. Louis	9	0
Odom, Jason, Tampa Bay	12	7
Odomes, Nate, Atlanta	7	4
O'Donnell, Neil, N.Y. Jets	6	6
O'Dwyer, Matt, N.Y. Jets	16	16
Ogden, Jonathan, Baltimore	16	16
Oldham, Chris, Pittsburgh	16	0
Olive, Bobby, Indianapolis	1	0
Oliver, Louis, Miami	16	12
Oliver, Winslow, Carolina	16	0
Olsavsky, Jerry, Pittsburgh	15	13
O'Neal, Leslie, St. Louis	16	16
Orlando, Bo, Cincinnati	16	16
Osborne, Chuck, St. Louis	15	1
Ostroski, Jerry, Buffalo	16	16
Ottis, Brad, Arizona	11	1
Owens, Dan, Atlanta	16	9
Owens, Rich, Washington	16	16
Owens, Terrell, San Francisco	16	10
Pahukoa, Jeff, Atlanta	14	3
Palmer, David, Minnesota	11	1
Palmer, Emile, New England	1	0
Palmer, Sterling, Washington	6	5
Panos, Joe, Philadelphia	16	16
Parker, Anthony, St. Louis	14	14
Parker, Glenn, Buffalo	14	13
Parker, Vaughn, San Diego	16	16
Parmalee, Bernie, Miami	16	16
Parrella, John, San Diego	16	9
Parrish, James, N.Y. Jets	1	0
Patton, Joe, Washington	16	15
Patton, Marvcus, Washington	16	16
Paul, Tito, Arizona	16	3
Paup, Bryce, Buffalo	12	11
Pederson, Doug, Green Bay	1	0
Peete, Rodney, Philadelphia	5	5
Pegram, Erric, Pittsburgh	12	4
Pelfrey, Doug, Cincinnati	16	0
Penn, Chris, Kansas City	16	16
Perriman, Brett, Detroit	16	16
Perry, Darren, Pittsburgh	16	16
Perry, Marlo, Buffalo	13	0
Perry, Michael Dean, Denver	15	15
Perry, Todd, Chicago	16	16
Peterson, Todd, Seattle	16	0
Peterson, Tony, San Francisco	13	0
Phifer, Roman, St. Louis	15	15
Phillips, Anthony, Atlanta	7	5
Phillips, Joe, Kansas City	16	16
Phillips, Lawrence, St. Louis	15	11
Philyaw, Dino, Carolina	9	0
Pickens, Carl, Cincinnati	16	16
Pierce, Aaron, N.Y. Giants	10	3
Pieri, Damon, Carolina	16	1
Pierson, Pete, Tampa Bay	11	2
Pike, Mark, Buffalo	16	0
Pilgrim, Evan, Chicago	6	0
Pittman, Kavika, Dallas	15	0
Pleasant, Anthony, Baltimore	12	12
Plummer, Gary, San Francisco	13	11
Pollack, Frank, San Francisco	16	2
Pollard, Marcus, Indianapolis	16	4
Poole, Tyrone, Carolina	15	15
Pope, Marquez, San Francisco	16	16
Popson, Ted, San Francisco	15	6
Porcher, Robert, Detroit	16	16
Porter, Rufus, New Orleans	13	9
Pounds, Darryl, Washington	12	1
Pourdanesh, Shar, Washington	16	8
Powell, Craig, Baltimore	9	0
Preston, Roell, Atlanta	15	2
Price, Daryl, San Francisco	14	0
Price, Derek, Detroit	13	1
Price, Shawn, Buffalo	15	0
Prior, Anthony, Minnesota	3	0
Prior, Mike, Green Bay	16	0
Pritchard, Mike, Seattle	16	5
Pritchett, Kelvin, Jacksonville	13	4
Pritchett, Stanley, Miami	16	16
Proehl, Ricky, Seattle	16	7
Pupunu, Alfred, San Diego	9	8
Purnell, Lovett, New England	2	0
Pyne, Jim, Tampa Bay	12	11
Randle, John, Minnesota	16	16
Randolph, Thomas, N.Y. Giants	16	2
Rasby, Walter, Carolina	16	0
Ravotti, Eric, Pittsburgh	15	2
Ray, Terry, New England	16	7
Raybon, Israel, Pittsburgh	3	0
Raymer, Cory, Washington	6	5
Raymond, Corey, Detroit	13	13
Redmon, Anthony, Arizona	16	16
Reed, Andre, Buffalo	16	16
Reed, Jake, Minnesota	16	15
Reed, Michael, Carolina	2	0
Reeves, Carl, Chicago	5	0
Reeves, Walter, San Diego	9	2
Regular, Moses, N.Y. Giants	16	0
Reich, Frank, N.Y. Jets	10	7
Reynolds, Jerry, N.Y. Giants	8	0
Reynolds, Ricky, New England	11	9
Rhett, Errict, Tampa Bay	9	7
Rice, Jerry, San Francisco	16	16
Rice, Ron, Detroit	13	2
Rice, Simeon, Arizona	16	15
Richard, Stanley, Washington	16	15
Richards, David, Atl.-N.E.	11	6
Richardson, Terry, Pittsburgh	1	0
Richardson, Tony, Kansas City	13	0
Riddick, Louis, Atlanta	16	1
Riesenberg, Doug, Tampa Bay	10	10
Riley, Phillip, N.Y. Jets	1	0
Rison, Andre, Jac.-G.B.	15	13

Player, Team	GP	GS	Player, Team	GP	GS	Player, Team	GP	GS
ivers, Reggie, Denver	16	0	Scroggins, Tracy, Detroit	6	6	Smith, Vinson, Chicago	15	12
ivers, Ron, Detroit	15	0	Scurlock, Mike, St. Louis	16	0	Solomon, Ariel, Minnesota	16	0
oaf, Willie, New Orleans	13	13	Searcy, Leon, Jacksonville	16	16	Solomon, Freddie, Philadelphia	12	0
oan, Michael, Houston	15	1	Seau, Junior, San Diego	15	15	Sparks, Phillippi, N.Y. Giants	14	14
obbins, Austin, New Orleans	15	7	Seay, Mark, Philadelphia	16	0	Spears, Marcus, Chicago	9	0
obbins, Barret, Oakland	14	14	Sedoris, Chris, Washington	9	0	Spellman, Alonzo, Chicago	16	15
oberson, James, Houston	15	5	Sehorn, Jason, N.Y. Giants	16	15	Spencer, Jimmy, Cincinnati	15	14
oberts, Ray, Detroit	16	16	Seigler, Dexter, Seattle	12	0	Spielman, Chris, Buffalo	16	16
oberts, William, New England	16	16	Selby, Rob, Arizona	13	4	Spikes, Irving, Miami	15	1
obertson, Marcus, Houston	16	16	Semple, Tony, Detroit	15	1	Spindler, Marc, N.Y. Jets	15	5
obinson, Eddie, Jacksonville	16	15	Shade, Sam, Cincinnati	12	0	Stablein, Brian, Indianapolis	16	0
obinson, Eugene, Green Bay	16	16	Sharpe, Shannon, Denver	15	15	Stai, Brenden, Pittsburgh	9	9
obinson, Greg, St. Louis	11	0	Shaw, Terrance, San Diego	16	16	Stallings, Ramondo, Cincinnati	13	3
obinson, Jeff, Denver	16	0	Shedd, Kenny, Oakland	16	1	Stargell, Tony, Kansas City	8	4
obinson, Mike, Green Bay	6	0	Shelley, Elbert, Atlanta	12	0	Stark, Rohn, Carolina	16	0
obinson, Rafael, Houston	16	2	Shelling, Chris, Cincinnati	1	0	Staten, Robert, Tampa Bay	6	0
oby, Reggie, Houston	16	0	Shello, Kendall, Indianapolis	1	0	Staysniak, Joe, Arizona	9	0
oche, Brian, San Diego	13	0	Shepherd, Leslie, Washington	12	6	Steed, Joel, Pittsburgh	16	14
odenhauser, Mark, Carolina	16	0	Sherrard, Mike, Denver	15	0	Stenstrom, Steve, Chicago	1	0
oe, James, Baltimore	1	0	Shields, Will, Kansas City	16	16	Stephens, Darnell, Tampa Bay	1	0
ogers, Sam, Buffalo	14	14	Shiver, Clay, Dallas	14	0	Stephens, Rod, Seattle	16	15
ogers, Tracy, Kansas City	3	1	Shuler, Heath, Washington	1	0	Stepnoski, Mark, Houston	16	16
omanowski, Bill, Denver	16	16	Sienkiewicz, Troy, San Diego	7	0	Steussie, Todd, Minnesota	16	16
oss, Dominique, Dallas	2	0	Siglar, Ricky, Kansas City	16	16	Stevens, Matt, Buffalo	13	11
oss, Jermaine, St. Louis	15	0	Silvan, Nilo, Tampa Bay	7	0	Stewart, James, Jacksonville	13	11
oss, Kevin, San Diego	16	16	Silvestri, Don, N.Y. Jets	12	0	Stewart, Kordell, Pittsburgh	16	2
ouen, Tom, Denver	16	0	Simien, Tracy, Kansas City	16	13	Stewart, Michael, Miami	9	0
oyal, Andre, Carolina	16	0	Simmons, Clyde, Jacksonville	16	14	Stewart, Rayna, Houston	15	0
oyals, Mark, Detroit	16	0	Simmons, Ed, Washington	11	11	Stewart, Ryan, Detroit	14	2
oye, Orpheus, Pittsburgh	13	1	Simmons, Wayne, Green Bay	16	16	Still, Bryan, San Diego	16	0
ucci, Todd, New England	16	12	Simpson, Carl, Chicago	16	16	Stock, Mark, Indianapolis	14	0
uddy, Tim, Miami	16	16	Sims, Keith, Miami	15	15	Stocz, Eric, Detroit	1	0
udolph, Coleman, N.Y. Giants	16	1	Sinclair, Michael, Seattle	16	16	Stokes, Fred, New Orleans	9	0
uettgers, Ken, Green Bay	4	1	Singleton, Chris, Miami	14	13	Stokes, J.J., San Francisco	6	6
unyan, Jon, Houston	10	0	Singleton, Nate, San Francisco	2	0	Stoltenberg, Bryan, San Diego	9	0
usk, Reggie, Tampa Bay	1	0	Siragusa, Tony, Indianapolis	10	10	Stone, Dwight, Carolina	16	0
ussell, Derek, Houston	16	5	Sisson, Scott, Minnesota	16	0	Stone, Ron, N.Y. Giants	16	16
ussell, Leonard, San Diego	15	15	Skrepenak, Greg, Carolina	16	16	Stover, Matt, Baltimore	16	0
yans, Larry, Tampa Bay	3	0	Slade, Chris, New England	16	9	Stoyanovich, Pete, Kansas City	16	0
ypien, Mark, Philadelphia	1	0	Slaughter, Webster, N.Y. Jets	10	1	Strahan, Mike, N.Y. Giants	16	16
abb, Dwayne, New England	16	7	Sloan, David, Detroit	4	4	Strickland, Fred, Dallas	16	16
adowski, Troy, Cincinnati	16	0	Slutzker, Scott, Indianapolis	15	0	Stringer, Korey, Minnesota	16	15
agapolutele, Pio, New England	15	10	Small, Torrance, New Orleans	16	13	Strong, Mack, Seattle	14	8
alaam, Rashaan, Chicago	12	6	Smedley, Eric, Buffalo	6	0	Strong, William, New Orleans	9	0
aleaumua, Dan, Kansas City	15	14	Smeenge, Joel, Jacksonville	10	10	Stryzinski, Dan, Atlanta	16	0
alisbury, Sean, San Diego	16	3	Smith, Al, Houston	1	1	Strzelczyk, Justin, Pittsburgh	16	16
amson, Michael, Philadelphia	2	0	Smith, Anthony, Oakland	6	4	Stubblefield, Dana, S.F.	15	15
anders, Barry, Detroit	16	16	Smith, Artie, Cincinnati	16	12	Stubbs, Danny, Miami	16	15
anders, Chris, Houston	16	15	Smith, Ben, Arizona	2	0	Studstill, Darren, Jacksonville	7	0
anders, Deion, Dallas	16	15	Smith, Brady, New Orleans	16	4	Styles, Lorenzo, Atlanta	16	0
anders, Frank, Arizona	16	16	Smith, Bruce, Buffalo	16	16	Sullivan, Chris, New England	16	0
apolu, Jesse, San Francisco	16	16	Smith, Cedric, Arizona	15	2	Sutter, Eddie, Baltimore	16	4
app, Patrick, San Diego	16	0	Smith, Chuck, Atlanta	15	15	Sutton, Eric, Washington	4	0
app, Warren, Tampa Bay	15	14	Smith, Darrin, Dallas	16	16	Swann, Eric, Arizona	16	15
asa, Don, San Diego	4	1	Smith, Detron, Denver	13	0	Swayne, Harry, San Diego	16	3
atterfield, Brian, Green Bay	1	0	Smith, Emmitt, Dallas	15	15	Sweeney, Jim, Pittsburgh	16	16
auer, Craig, Atlanta	16	1	Smith, Fernando, Minnesota	16	16	Swilling, Pat, Oakland	16	16
auerbrun, Todd, Chicago	16	0	Smith, Frankie, San Francisco	14	0	Szott, David, Kansas City	16	16
awyer, Corey, Cincinnati	15	2	Smith, Herman, Tampa Bay	5	0	Talley, Darryl, Minnesota	12	12
axton, Brian, N.Y. Giants	16	2	Smith, Irv, New Orleans	7	7	Tamm, Ralph, Denver	9	0
chlereth, Mark, Denver	14	14	Smith, Jimmy, Jacksonville	16	9	Tanuvasa, Maa, Denver	16	1
chlesinger, Cory, Detroit	16	1	Smith, Kevin L., Green Bay	1	0	Tasker, Steve, Buffalo	8	5
chreiber, Adam, N.Y. Giants	15	2	Smith, Kevin R., Dallas	16	16	Tate, David, Indianapolis	10	10
chulz, Kurt, Buffalo	15	15	Smith, Lamar, Seattle	16	2	Tate, Willy, Tampa Bay	13	0
chwantz, Jim, Dallas	16	0	Smith, Lance, N.Y. Giants	16	10	Taylor, Aaron, Green Bay	16	16
chwartz, Bryan, Jacksonville	4	3	Smith, Neil, Kansas City	16	16	Taylor, Bobby, Philadelphia	16	16
cott, Darnay, Cincinnati	16	16	Smith, Otis, NYJ-N.E.	13	6	Taylor, Keith, Washington	3	0
cott, Freddie, Atlanta	10	0	Smith, Robert, Minnesota	8	7	Teague, George, Dallas	16	8
cott, Todd, Tampa Bay	2	2	Smith, Rod, Carolina	8	1	Terrell, Pat, Carolina	16	16
cott, Walter, New England	1	0	Smith, Rod, Denver	10	1	Terry, Ryan, Arizona	5	0
crafford, Kirk, San Francisco	7	1	Smith, Thomas, Buffalo	16	16	Testaverde, Vinny, Baltimore	16	16

Player, Team	GP	GS
Theirry, John, Chicago	16	2
Thigpen, Yancey, Pittsburgh	6	2
Thomas, Broderick, Dallas	16	9
Thomas, Dave, Jacksonville	9	5
Thomas, Derrick, Kansas City	16	13
Thomas, Fred, Seattle	15	0
Thomas, Henry, Detroit	15	15
Thomas, Hollis, Philadelphia	16	5
Thomas, J.T., St. Louis	16	1
Thomas, Johnny, Philadelphia	9	0
Thomas, Lamar, Miami	9	3
Thomas, Mark, Carolina	12	0
Thomas, Orlanda, Minnesota	16	16
Thomas, Robb, Tampa Bay	12	8
Thomas, Rodney, Houston	16	0
Thomas, Thurman, Buffalo	15	15
Thomas, William, Philadelphia	16	16
Thomas, Zach, Miami	16	16
Thomason, Jeff, Green Bay	16	1
Thompson, Bennie, Baltimore	16	0
Thompson, Broderick, Denver	16	16
Thompson, Leroy, Tampa Bay	5	0
Thompson, Tommy, S.F.	16	0
Timmerman, Adam, Green Bay	16	16
Timpson, Michael, Chicago	15	15
Tindale, Tim, Buffalo	14	3
Tobeck, Robbie, Atlanta	16	16
Tolbert, Tony, Dallas	16	16
Tomczak, Mike, Pittsburgh	16	15
Tongue, Reggie, Kansas City	16	0
Toomer, Amani, N.Y. Giants	7	1
Torretta, Gino, Seattle	1	0
Tovar, Steve, Cincinnati	13	13
Trapp, James, Oakland	12	4
Traylor, Keith, Kansas City	15	2
Truitt, Greg, Cincinnati	16	0
Truitt, Olanda, Oakland	10	0
Tuaolo, Esera, Minnesota	14	9
Tubbs, Winfred, New Orleans	16	13
Tuggle, Jessie, Atlanta	16	16
Tuinei, Mark, Dallas	15	15
Tumulty, Tom, Cincinnati	16	3
Tupa, Tom, New England	16	0
Turk, Dan, Oakland	16	2
Turk, Matt, Washington	16	0
Turnbull, Renaldo, New Orleans	12	7
Turner, Eric, Baltimore	14	14
Turner, Floyd, Baltimore	11	6
Turner, Kevin, Philadelphia	16	12
Turner, Scott, Washington	16	0
Tuten, Melvin, Cincinnati	16	7
Tuten, Rick, Seattle	16	0
Tylski, Rich, Jacksonville	16	7
Uhlenhake, Jeff, Washington	12	11
Ulufale, Mike, Dallas	3	0
Unutoa, Morris, Philadelphia	16	0
Unverzagt, Eric, Seattle	8	0
Upshaw, Regan, Tampa Bay	16	16
Uwaezuoke, Iheanyi, S.F.	14	0
Valerio, Joe, St. Louis	1	0
Van Dyke, Alex, N.Y. Jets	15	1
Van Pelt, Alex, Buffalo	1	0
Vanderbeek, Matt, Washington	1	0
Vanhorse, Sean, Minnesota	9	0
Vanover, Tamarick, Kansas City	13	6
Vardell, Tommy, San Francisco	11	7
Verstegen, Mike, New Orleans	8	4
Vickers, Kipp, Indianapolis	10	6
Villa, Danny, Kansas City	16	0
Villarrial, Chris, Chicago	14	8
Vinatieri, Adam, New England	16	0
Vincent, Troy, Philadelphia	16	16
Von Oelhoffen, Kimo, Cincinnati	11	1
Wainright, Frank, Miami	16	0
Waldroup, Kerwin, Detroit	16	10
Walker, Adam, Philadelphia	13	0
Walker, Bracey, Cincinnati	16	16
Walker, Brian, Washington	16	4
Walker, Darnell, Atlanta	15	9
Walker, Derrick, Kansas City	11	9
Walker, Gary, Houston	16	16
Walker, Hershel, Dallas	16	1
Walker, Jay, Minnesota	1	0
Walker, Marquis, St.L.-Was.	9	4
Walker, Robert, N.Y. Giants	1	0
Wallace, Steve, San Francisco	16	16
Walls, Wesley, Carolina	16	15
Walsh, Chris, Minnesota	15	0
Walsh, Steve, St. Louis	3	3
Walter, Joe, Cincinnati	15	0
Ware, Derek, Dallas	5	1
Warren, Chris, Seattle	14	14
Warren, Lamont, Indianapolis	13	3
Washington, Brian, Kansas City	16	16
Washington, Dewayne, Min.	16	16
Washington, Keith, Detroit	12	0
Washington, Lionel, Denver	14	12
Washington, Marvin, N.Y. Jets	14	14
Washington, Mickey, Jac.	16	16
Washington, Ted, Buffalo	16	16
Watters, Ricky, Philadelphia	16	16
Watts, Damon, Indianapolis	10	0
Way, Charles, N.Y. Giants	16	12
Webb, Richmond, Miami	16	16
Weldon, Casey, Tampa Bay	3	0
Wells, Dean, Seattle	16	15
Wells, Mike, Detroit	16	1
West, Derek, Indianapolis	1	0
West, Ed, Philadelphia	16	4
Westbrook, Michael, Was.	11	6
Wetnight, Ryan, Chicago	11	5
Wheatley, Tyrone, N.Y. Giants	14	0
Wheeler, Leonard, Cincinnati	13	0
Wheeler, Mark, New England	16	15
Whigham, Larry, New England	16	1
White, Alberto, St. Louis	3	0
White, David, Buffalo	16	5
White, Dwayne, St. Louis	16	16
White, Reggie, Green Bay	16	16
White, Steve, Tampa Bay	4	0
White, William, Kansas City	12	2
Whitfield, Bob, Atlanta	16	16
Whitley, Curtis, Carolina	11	8
Whittington, Bernard, Ind.	16	14
Whittle, Ricky, New Orleans	10	0
Widell, Dave, Jacksonville	15	14
Widell, Doug, Indianapolis	16	16
Widmer, Corey, N.Y. Giants	16	16
Wiegert, Zach, St. Louis	16	16
Wilburn, Barry, Philadelphia	7	2
Wilhelm, Erik, Cincinnati	3	0
Wilkerson, Bruce, Green Bay	14	2
Wilkins, Gabe, Green Bay	16	1
Wilkins, Jeff, San Francisco	16	0
Wilkinson, Dan, Cincinnati	16	16
Williams, Aeneas, Arizona	16	16
Williams, Alfred, Denver	16	16
Williams, Billy, St. Louis	1	0
Williams, Brent, N.Y. Jets	5	0
Williams, Brian, Green Bay	16	16
Williams, Brian S., N.Y. Giants	14	14
Williams, Calvin, Bal.-Phi.	8	2
Williams, Charlie, Dallas	7	0
Williams, Dan, Denver	15	15
Williams, Darryl, Seattle	16	16
Williams, David, N.Y. Jets	14	14
Williams, Erik, Dallas	16	16
Williams, Gene, Atlanta	10	
Williams, Gerald, Carolina	16	14
Williams, Grant, Seattle	8	
Williams, Harvey, Oakland	13	5
Williams, James E., S.F.	1	0
Williams, James O., Chicago	16	16
Williams, Jay, St. Louis	2	0
Williams, Jerrol, Baltimore	9	
Williams, Karl, Tampa Bay	16	
Williams, Kevin, Dallas	10	9
Williams, Mark, St. Louis	2	
Williams, Moe, Minnesota	9	
Williams, Ronnie, Seattle	14	3
Williams, Sherman, Dallas	16	1
Williams, Stepfret, Dallas	5	0
Williams, Tyrone, Green Bay	16	
Williams, Wally, Baltimore	15	13
Williams, Willie, Pittsburgh	15	14
Willig, Matt, Atlanta	12	
Willis, Donald, New Orleans	4	
Willis, James, Philadelphia	16	13
Wilmsmeyer, Klaus, N.O.	16	
Wilson, Bernard, Arizona	16	16
Wilson, Jerry, Miami	15	
Wilson, Robert, Miami	15	
Wilson, Sheddrick, Houston	11	0
Wilson, Wade, Dallas	3	1
Winans, Tydus, Cincinnati	2	
Winters, Frank, Green Bay	16	16
Wisniewski, Steve, Oakland	16	16
Witherspoon, Derrick, Phi.	16	0
Witman, Jon, Pittsburgh	16	4
Wohlabaugh, Dave, N.E.	16	16
Wolf, Joe, Arizona	16	16
Wolford, Will, Pittsburgh	16	16
Woodall, Lee, San Francisco	16	13
Woodard, Marc, Philadelphia	16	2
Wooden, Shawn, Miami	16	11
Wooden, Terry, Seattle	9	5
Woodley, Richard, Detroit	11	
Woods, Jerome, Kansas City	16	
Woods, Tony, Washington	13	2
Woodson, Darren, Dallas	16	16
Woodson, Rod, Pittsburgh	16	16
Woolford, Donnell, Chicago	15	15
Wooten, Tito, N.Y. Giants	13	14
Workman, Vince, Indianapolis	9	0
Wortham, Barron, Houston	15	14
Wright, Alexander, St. Louis	3	0
Wright, Sylvester, Philadelphia	16	0
Wright, Toby, St. Louis	12	12
Wycheck, Frank, Houston	16	16
Wyman, Devin, New England	9	2
Yeboah-Kodie, Phil, Indianapolis	2	
Young, Bryant, San Francisco	16	16
Young, Glen, San Diego	6	
Young, Lonnie, N.Y. Jets	15	
Young, Robert, Houston	15	13
Young, Rodney, N.Y. Giants	12	
Young, Steve, San Francisco	16	12
Zandofsky, Mike, Atlanta	14	14
Zatechka, Rob, N.Y. Giants	15	6
Zeier, Eric, Baltimore	1	0
Zeigler, Dusty, Buffalo	16	
Zellars, Ray, New Orleans	9	
Zgonina, Jeff, Atlanta	8	0
Zimmerman, Gary, Denver	14	14
Zolak, Scott, New England	3	0
Zomalt, Eric, Phi.-NYJ	13	
Zordich, Mike, Philadelphia	16	16

Player, Team	GP	GS	Player, Team	GP	GS	Player, Team	GP	GS
Ashmore, Darryl, St. Louis	6	0	Dronett, Shane, Atlanta	5	0	Kelly, Todd, Cincinnati	2	0
Ashmore, Darryl, Washington	5	0	Dronett, Shane, Detroit	7	0	Kelly, Todd, Atlanta	2	0
Barnes, Tomur, Houston	5	0	Farquhar, John, Tampa Bay	1	0	McCleskey, J.J., New Orleans	5	0
Barnes, Tomur, Minnesota	2	0	Farquhar, John, Pittsburgh	4	0	McCleskey, J.J., Arizona	5	0
Barnes, Tomur, Washington	3	0	Gunn, Mark, Philadelphia	3	0	Milner, Billy, Miami	4	0
Barnett, Troy, New England	1	0	Gunn, Mark, N.Y. Jets	9	0	Milner, Billy, St. Louis	10	0
Barnett, Troy, Washington	3	0	Hall, Steve, Minnesota	1	0	Richards, David, Atlanta	6	6
Brooks, Bucky, Green Bay	2	0	Hall, Steve, Indianapolis	2	0	Richards, David, New England	5	0
Brooks, Bucky, Jacksonville	6	1	Hoard, Leroy, Baltimore	2	1	Rison, Andre, Jacksonville	10	9
Byars, Keith, Miami	4	4	Hoard, Leroy, Carolina	3	0	Rison, Andre, Green Bay	5	4
Byars, Keith, New England	10	6	Hoard, Leroy, Minnesota	6	6	Smith, Otis, N.Y. Jets	2	0
Christopherson, Ryan, Jac.	2	0	Huerta, Carlos, Chicago	3	0	Smith, Otis, New England	11	6
Christopherson, Ryan, Arizona	6	0	Huerta, Carlos, St. Louis	1	0	Walker, Marquis, St. Louis	8	4
Dellenbach, Jeff, New England	2	0	Hunter, Ernest, Baltimore	5	0	Walker, Marquis, Washington	1	0
Dellenbach, Jeff, Green Bay	3	0	Hunter, Ernest, New Orleans	6	0	Williams, Calvin, Baltimore	7	2
Dowden, Corey, Green Bay	9	0	Johnson, D.J., Atlanta	2	0	Williams, Calvin, Philadelphia	1	0
Dowden, Corey, Baltimore	3	0	Johnson, D.J., Arizona	7	0	Zomalt, Eric, Philadelphia	3	2
Drayton, Troy, St. Louis	3	3	Junkin, Trey, Oakland	6	0	Zomalt, Eric, N.Y. Jets	10	1
Drayton, Troy, Miami	10	10	Junkin, Trey, Arizona	10	0			

1996 REVIEW *Player participation*

ATTENDANCE

REGULAR SEASON

Team	Home Attendance	Average	NFL Rank	Road Attendance	Average	NFL Rank
Arizona	320,508	40,064	28	435,279	54,410	22
Atlanta	335,638	41,955	26	463,290	57,911	11
Baltimore	471,665	58,958	14	434,075	54,259	24
Buffalo	598,321	74,790	2	470,659	58,832	10
Carolina	553,382	69,173	4	431,477	53,935	25
Chicago	456,348	57,044	18	487,959	60,995	7
Cincinnati	382,324	47,791	24	449,463	56,183	18
Dallas	513,794	64,224	9	556,875	69,609	1
Denver	589,296	73,662	3	462,194	57,774	13
Detroit	491,948	61,494	11	442,882	55,360	20
Green Bay	482,988	60,374	13	522,749	65,344	3
Houston	254,600	31,825	30	350,033	43,754	30
Indianapolis	438,026	54,753	20	505,584	63,198	5
Jacksonville	533,533	66,692	7	382,383	47,798	29
Kansas City	610,617	76,327	1	462,935	57,867	12
Miami	545,518	68,190	6	479,041	59,880	9
Minnesota	449,940	56,243	19	404,460	50,558	27
N.Y. Giants	552,870	69,109	5	458,172	57,272	15
N.Y. Jets	397,816	49,727	23	448,384	56,048	19
New England	468,301	58,538	15	522,829	65,354	2
New Orleans	301,998	37,750	29	434,866	54,358	23
Oakland	398,915	49,864	22	494,792	61,849	6
Philadelphia	514,003	64,250	8	409,911	51,239	26
Pittsburgh	466,944	58,368	16	513,289	64,161	4
San Diego	460,355	57,544	17	456,969	57,121	16
San Francisco	502,534	62,817	10	461,537	57,692	14
Seattle	357,570	44,696	25	450,353	56,294	17
St. Louis	484,896	60,612	12	383,583	47,948	28
Tampa Bay	333,350	41,669	27	437,307	54,663	21
Washington	427,750	53,469	21	482,418	60,302	8
NFL total	13,695,748	57,066		13,695,748	57,066	

Note: Attendance figures are unofficial and are based on box scores of games.

HISTORICAL
TOP REGULAR-SEASON HOME CROWDS

Team	Attendance	Date	Site	Opponent
Arizona	73,400	October 30, 1994	Sun Devil Stadium	Pittsburgh
Atlanta	71,253	November 21, 1993	Georgia Dome	Dallas
Buffalo	80,368	October 4, 1992	Rich Stadium	Miami
Carolina	76,136	December 10, 1995	Clemson Memorial Stadium	San Francisco
Chicago	66,900	September 5, 1993	Soldier Field	N.Y. Giants
Cincinnati	60,284	October 17, 1971	Riverfront Stadium	Cleveland
Cleveland	85,703	September 21, 1970	Cleveland Stadium	New York Jets
Dallas	80,259	November 24, 1966	Cotton Bowl	Cleveland
Denver	76,089	October 26,1986	Mile High Stadium	Seattle
Detroit	80,444	December 20, 1981	Pontiac Silverdome	Tampa Bay
Green Bay	60,716	October 14, 1996	Lambeau Field	San Francisco
Houston	63,713	September 6, 1992	Astrodome	Pittsburgh
Indianapolis	60,891	September 23, 1996	RCA Dome	Miami
Jacksonville	72,363	September 3, 1995	Jacksonville Municipal Stadium	Houston
Kansas City	82,094	November 5, 1972	Arrowhead Stadium	Oakland
Miami	78,914	November 19, 1972	Orange Bowl	New York Jets
Minnesota	64,168	September 22, 1996	Metrodome	Green Bay
New England	61,457	December 5, 1971	Schaefer Stadium*	Miami
New Orleans	83,437	November 12, 1967	Tulane Stadium	Dallas
		November 26, 1967	Tulane Stadium	Atlanta
New York Giants	77,454	September 4, 1995	Giants Stadium	Dallas
New York Jets	75,606	November 27, 1994	Giants Stadium	Miami
Oakland	74,121	September 23, 1973	Memorial Stadium; Berkeley, Cal.	Miami
Philadelphia	72,111	November 1, 1981	Veterans Stadium	Dallas
Pittsburgh	60,808	December 18, 1994	Three Rivers Stadium	Cleveland
St. Louis	65,598	November 12, 1995	Trans World Dome	Carolina

1996 REVIEW Attendance

Team	Attendance	Date	Site	Opponent
San Diego..........................	63,012	December 5, 1994	San Diego Jack Murphy Stadium	L.A. Raiders
San Francisco....................	69,014	November 13, 1994	Candlestick Park	Dallas
Seattle	65,902	December 13, 1992	Kingdome	Philadelphia
Tampa Bay.........................	72,077	October 8, 1989	Tampa Stadium	Chicago
Washington	56,454	September 4, 1994	Robert F. Kennedy Memorial Stadium	Seattle
	56,454	December 22, 1996	Robert F. Kennedy Memorial Stadium	Dallas

*Now known as Foxboro Stadium.

SECOND ROUND

NATIONAL FOOTBALL LEAGUE

Year	Regular season*		Average	Postseason†	
1934	492,684	(60)	8,211	35,059	(1)
1935	638,178	(53)	12,041	15,000	(1)
1936	816,007	(54)	15,111	29,545	(1)
1937	963,039	(55)	17,510	15,878	(1)
1938	937,197	(55)	17,040	48,120	(1)
1939	1,071,200	(55)	19,476	32,279	(1)
1940	1,063,025	(55)	19,328	36,034	(1)
1941	1,108,615	(55)	20,157	55,870	(2)
1942	887,920	(55)	16,144	36,006	(1)
1943	969,128	(50)	19,383	71,315	(2)
1944	1,019,649	(50)	20,393	46,016	(1)
1945	1,270,401	(50)	25,408	32,178	(1)
1946	1,732,135	(55)	31,493	58,346	(1)
1947	1,837,437	(60)	30,624	66,268	(2)
1948	1,525,243	(60)	25,421	36,309	(1)
1949	1,391,735	(60)	23,196	27,980	(1)
1950	1,977,753	(78)	25,356	136,647	(3)
1951	1,913,019	(72)	26,570	57,522	(1)
1952	2,052,126	(72)	28,502	97,507	(2)
1953	2,164,585	(72)	30,064	54,577	(1)
1954	2,190,571	(72)	30,425	43,827	(1)
1955	2,521,836	(72)	35,026	85,693	(1)
1956	2,551,263	(72)	35,434	56,836	(1)
1957	2,836,318	(72)	39,393	119,579	(2)
1958	3,006,124	(72)	41,752	123,659	(2)
1959	3,140,000	(72)	43,617	57,545	(1)
1960	3,128,296	(78)	40,106	67,325	(1)
1961	3,986,159	(98)	40,675	39,029	(1)
1962	4,003,421	(98)	40,851	64,892	(1)
1963	4,163,643	(98)	42,486	45,801	(1)
1964	4,563,049	(98)	46,562	79,544	(1)
1965	4,634,021	(98)	47,296	100,304	(2)
1966	5,337,044	(105)	50,829	135,098	(2)
1967	5,938,924	(112)	53,026	241,754	(4)
1968	5,882,313	(112)	52,521	291,279	(4)
1969	6,096,127	(112)	54,430	242,841	(4)
1970	9,533,333	(182)	52,381	410,371	(7)
1971	10,076,035	(182)	55,363	430,244	(7)
1972	10,445,827	(182)	57,395	435,466	(7)
1973	10,730,933	(182)	58,961	458,515	(7)
1974	10,236,322	(182)	56,224	412,180	(7)
1975	10,213,193	(182)	56,116	443,811	(7)
1976	11,070,543	(196)	56,482	428,733	(7)
1977	11,018,632	(196)	56,218	483,588	(7)
1978	12,771,800	(224)	57,017	578,107	(9)
1979	13,182,039	(224)	58,848	582,266	(9)
1980	13,392,230	(224)	59,787	577,186	(9)
1981	13,606,990	(224)	60,745	587,361	(9)
1982§	7,367,438	(126)	58,472	985,952	(15)
1983	13,277,222	(224)	59,273	625,068	(9)
1984	13,398,112	(224)	59,813	614,809	(9)
1985	13,345,047	(224)	59,567	660,667	(9)
1986	13,588,551	(224)	60,663	683,901	(9)
1987∞	10,032,493	(168)	59,717	606,864	(9)
1988	13,539,848	(224)	60,446	608,204	(9)
1989	13,625,662	(224)	60,829	635,326	(9)
1990	14,266,240	(224)	63,689	797,198	(11)
1991	13,187,478	(224)	58,873	758,186	(11)
1992	13,159,387	(224)	58,747	756,005	(11)
1993	13,328,760	(224)	59,503	755,625	(11)
1994	13,479,680	(224)	60,177	719,143	(11)
1995	14,196,205	(240)	59,151	733,729	(11)
1996	13,695,748	(240)	57,066	711,601	(11)

*Number of tickets sold, including no-shows; number of regular-season games in parentheses.

†Includes conference, league championship and Super Bowl games, but not Pro Bowl; number of postseason games in parentheses.

‡A 57-day players strike reduced 224-game schedule to 126 games.

§A 24-day players strike reduced 224-game schedule to 168 non-strike games.

AMERICAN FOOTBALL LEAGUE

Year	Regular season*	Average	AFL Champ. Game
1960	926,156 (56)	16,538	32,183
1961	1,002,657 (56)	17,904	29,556
1962	1,147,302 (56)	20,487	37,981
1963	1,241,741 (56)	22,174	30,127
1964	1,447,875 (56)	25,855	40,242
1965	1,782,384 (56)	31,828	30,361
1966	2,160,369 (63)	34,291	42,080
1967	2,295,697 (63)	36,439	53,330
1968	2,635,004 (70)	37,643	62,627
1969	2,843,373 (70)	40,620	53,564

*Number of regular-season games in parentheses.

TRADES

(Covering June 1996 through May 1997)

JUNE 6
Atlanta traded RB Robert Baldwin to Green Bay for CB Lenny McGill.

JUNE 27
Seattle traded S Eugene Robinson to Green Bay for DE Matt LaBounty.

JULY 16
Green Bay traded S George Teague to Atlanta for a conditional draft choice.

JULY 17
St. Louis traded DE Robert Young to Houston for a 1997 conditional pick. St. Louis selected LB Muadianvita Kazadi (Tulsa) in the sixth round of the 1997 draft.

AUGUST 6
Green Bay traded DE Wendall Gaines to St. Louis for a conditional draft choice.

AUGUST 7
Acquired CB Carlos Yancy from New England for past considerations.

AUGUST 20
Miami traded RB Terry Kirby to San Francisco for an undisclosed draft choice. Miami later traded the pick to Oakland.

Miami traded K Pete Stoyanovich to Kansas City for an undisclosed draft choice. Kansas City selected DT Barron Tanner (Oklahoma) in the fifth round of the 1997 draft.

AUGUST 24
New Orleans traded an undisclosed draft choice to Oakland for DT Austin Robbins. Oakland later traded the pick to Miami.

Oakland traded WR-KR Rocket Ismail to Carolina for an undisclosed draft choice. Oakland later traded the pick to Miami.

AUGUST 26
St. Louis traded WR Todd Kinchen to Denver for an undisclosed draft choice. St. Louis selected DB Taje Allen (Texas) in the fifth round of the 1997 draft.

FEBRUARY 10
The NFL announced Bill Parcells can coach the New York Jets immediately. New England received New York's third- and fourth-round picks in the 1997 draft, a second-round pick in the 1998 draft, a first-round pick in the 1999 draft and a $300,000 contribution to the Patriots' charitable foundation as compensation. New England selected RB Sedrick Shaw (Iowa) in the third round and G Damon Denson (Michigan) in the fourth round of the 1997 draft.

FEBRUARY 14
Denver traded a 1997 second-round draft choice to Baltimore for T Tony Jones. Baltimore selected DB Kim Herring (Penn State).

FEBRUARY 17
Oakland traded QB Billy Joe Hobert to Buffalo for an undisclosed draft choice. Oakland selected T Tim Kohn (Iowa State) in the third round of the 1997 draft.

FEBRUARY 18
Chicago traded a 1997 first-round draft choice to Seattle for QB Rick Mirer. Seattle later traded the pick to Atlanta.

FEBRUARY 24
Houston traded QB Chris Chandler to Atlanta for two undisclosed 1997 draft choices. Houston later traded a 1997 sixth round pick

to New Orleans and selected WR Derrick Mason (Michigan State) in the fourth round.

MARCH 28
Seattle traded 1997 first-, second-, third- and fourth-round draft choices to Atlanta for 1997 first- and third-round draft choices. Seattle selected CB Shawn Springs (Ohio State) in the first round and traded the third-round pick to Tampa Bay. Atlanta selected DB Michael Booker (Nebraska) in the first round, RB Byron Hanspard (Texas Tech) in the second round, TE O.J. Santiago (Kent) in the third round and LB Henri Crockett (Florida State) in the fourth round.

MARCH 31
Oakland traded WR Daryl Hobbs and their first-, second- and fourth-round 1997 draft choices to New Orleans for their first- and sixth-round 1997 draft choices. Oakland selected DT Darrell Russell (Southern California) in the first round and traded the sixth-round pick to Miami. New Orleans selected G Chris Naeole (Colorado) in the first round, DE Jared Tomich (Nebraska) in the second round and traded their fourth-round pick to Houston.

APRIL 4
Pittsburgh traded DL Brentson Buckner to Kansas City for a 1997 seventh-round draft choice. Pittsburgh traded the seventh-round pick to San Diego.

APRIL 17
N.Y. Jets traded their 1997 first-round pick to St. Louis for their 1997 first-, third-, fourth- and seventh-round picks. St. Louis selected T Orlando Pace (Ohio State) with their pick. New York selected DE Terry Day (Mississippi State) in the fourth round, and traded their first-round pick to Seattle, their third-round pick to Denver and their seventh-round pick to Philadelphia.

APRIL 18
N.Y. Jets traded a 1997 seventh-round draft choice to Philadelphia for DT Ronnie Dixon. Philadelphia selected QB Koy Detmer (Colorado).

APRIL 19
N.Y. Jets traded a 1997 first-round draft choice to Tampa Bay for 1997 first- and fourth-round draft choices. Tampa Bay traded its pick to Seattle. New York selected LB James Farrior (Virginia) in the first round and RB Leon Johnson (North Carolina) in the fourth round.

Tampa Bay traded a 1997 first-round draft choice to Seattle for 1997 first- and third-round draft choices. Seattle selected T Walter Jones (Florida State). Tampa Bay selected RB Warrick Dunn (Florida State) in the first round and G Frank Middleton (Arizona) in the third round.

Houston traded 1997 first- and fourth-round draft choices to Kansas City for 1997 first-, third-, fourth- and sixth-round draft choices. Kansas City chose TE Tony Gonzalez (California) in the first round and QB Pat Barnes (California) in the fourth round. Houston chose DE Kenny Holmes (Miami, Fla.) in the first round, T Scott Sanderson (Washington State) in the third round, LB Dennis Stallings (Illinois) in the sixth round and traded the fourth-round pick to New Orleans.

Philadelphia traded a 1997 first-round draft choice to Dallas for 1997 first- and fifth-round draft choices and a 1998 third round draft choice. Dallas selected TE David LaFleur (Louisiana State). Philadelphia selected DE Jon Harris (Virginia) in the first round and TE Luther Broughton (Furman) in the fifth round.

St. Louis traded a 1997 second-round draft choice to Chicago for 1997 second- and sixth-round draft choices. Chicago selected TE

John Allred (Southern California). St. Louis selected DB Dexter McCleon (Clemson) in the second round and traded the sixth-round pick to Miami.

Dallas traded a 1997 second-round draft choice to Detroit for 1997 third- and fourth-round draft choices. Detroit selected DB Kevin Abrams (Syracuse). Dallas selected LB Dexter Coakley (Appalachian State) in the third round and DT Antonio Anderson (Syracuse) in the fourth round.

Philadelphia traded a 1997 second-round draft choice to San Francisco for 1997 second-, sixth- and seventh-round draft choices. San Francisco selected FB Marc Edwards (Notre Dame). Philadelphia selected LB James Darling (Washington State) in the second round, WR Antwuan Wyatt (Bethune-Cookman) in the sixth round and DB Deauntae Brown (Central State, O.) in the seventh round.

N.Y. Jets traded a 1997 third-round draft choice to Denver for 1997 third-, sixth- and seventh-round draft choices and a 1998 sixth-round draft choice. Denver selected C Dan Neil (Texas). New York selected WR Dedric Ward (Northern Iowa) in the third round, QB Chuck Clements (Houston) in the sixth round and DT Jason Ferguson (Georgia) in the seventh round.

Arizona traded a 1997 third-round draft choice to Philadelphia for 1997 third- and sixth-round draft choices. Philadelphia selected RB Duce Staley (South Carolina). Arizona selected DB Ty Howard (Ohio State) in the third round and LB Tony McCombs (Eastern Kentucky) in the sixth round.

Indianapolis traded a 1997 third-round draft choice to San Francisco for 1997 third- and fifth-round draft choices. San Francisco selected TE Greg Clark (Stanford). Indianapolis selected LB Bert Berry (Notre Dame) in the third round and DE Carl Powell (Louisville) in the fifth round.

APRIL 20

New Orleans traded a 1997 fourth-round draft choice to Houston for 1997 fourth- and sixth- round draft choices. Houston select-ed DE Pratt Lyons (Troy State). New Orleans selected WR Keith Poole (Arizona State) in the fourth round and TE Nicky Savoie (Louisiana State) in the sixth round.

Miami traded a 1997 fourth-round draft choice to St. Louis for 1997 fourth- and two sixth-round draft choices. St. Louis select-ed C Ryan Tucker (Texas Christian). Miami selected T Jerome Daniels (Northeastern) in the fourth round and WR Brian Manning (Stanford) and LB Mike Crawford (Nevada) in the sixth round.

Miami traded its 1997 fourth-round draft choice to Oakland for 1997 fifth-, sixth- and seventh-round draft choices. Oakland selected RB Chad Levitt (Cornell). Miami selected DE Nicholas Lopez (Texas Southern) in the fifth round, LB John Fiala (Washington) in the sixth round and DB Hudhaifa Ismaeli (Northwestern) in the seventh round.

St. Louis traded a 1997 fifth-round draft choice to San Diego for a 1997 seventh-round draft choice and a 1998 fourth-round draft choice. San Diego selected RB Kenny Bynum (South Carolina State). St. Louis selected DE Cedric White (North Carolina A&T).

Atlanta traded a 1997 fifth-round draft choice to Washington for 1997 sixth- and seventh-round draft choices. Washington select-ed DB Keith Thibodeaux (Northwestern State, La.). Atlanta select-ed C Calvin Collins (Texas A&M) in the sixth round and DB Chris Bayne (Fresno State) in the seventh round.

Pittsburgh traded 1997 fifth- and seventh-round draft choices to San Diego for a 1998 third-round draft choice. San Diego select-ed DB Paul Bradford (Portland State) in the fifth round and LB Toran James (North Carolina A&T) in the seventh round.

Green Bay traded a 1997 sixth-round draft choice to Oakland for a 1997 seventh-round draft choice. Oakland selected DE Grady Jackson (Knoxville). Green Bay selected WR Chris Miller (Southern California).

1996 STATISTICS

Rushing
Passing
Receiving
Scoring
Interceptions
Sacks
Fumbles
Field goals
Punting
Punt returns
Kickoff returns
Miscellaneous

RUSHING

TEAM

AFC

Team	Att.	Yds.	Avg.	Long	TD
Denver	525	2362	4.5	t71	20
Pittsburgh	525	2299	4.4	t80	18
Oakland	456	2174	4.8	77	7
Kansas City	488	2009	4.1	35	15
Seattle	442	1997	4.5	51	16
Houston	475	1950	4.1	76	12
Buffalo	563	1901	3.4	37	14
Cincinnati	478	1793	3.8	t33	14
Baltimore	416	1745	4.2	42	10
Jacksonville	431	1650	3.8	35	13
Miami	460	1622	3.5	49	14
N.Y. Jets	407	1583	3.9	78	8
New England	427	1468	3.4	57	15
Indianapolis	420	1448	3.4	53	9
San Diego	412	1312	3.2	21	7
AFC total	6925	27313	3.9	t80	192
AFC average	461.7	1820.9	3.9	....	12.8

t—touchdown.

NFC

Team	Att.	Yds.	Avg.	Long	TD
Washington	467	1910	4.1	t49	2?
Philadelphia	489	1882	3.8	t56	1?
San Francisco	454	1847	4.1	67	1?
Green Bay	465	1838	4.0	24	?
Detroit	389	1810	4.7	t54	1?
Carolina	502	1729	3.4	t35	?
Chicago	472	1720	3.6	32	?
Dallas	475	1641	3.5	42	1?
St. Louis	448	1607	3.6	38	1?
N.Y. Giants	485	1603	3.3	37	?
Tampa Bay	472	1589	3.4	56	?
Minnesota	435	1546	3.6	57	?
Arizona	401	1502	3.7	t70	?
Atlanta	329	1461	4.4	34	?
New Orleans	386	1308	3.4	63	1?
NFC total	6669	24993	3.7	t70	17?
NFC average	444.6	1666.2	3.7	....	11.?
NFL total	13594	52306	....	t80	36?
NFL average	453.1	1743.5	3.8	....	12.?

INDIVIDUAL

BESTS OF THE SEASON

Yards, season
NFC: 1553—Barry Sanders, Detroit.
AFC: 1538—Terrell Davis, Denver.

Yards, game
NFC: 214—LeShon Johnson, Arizona at New Orleans, Sept. 22 (21 attempts, 2 TDs).
AFC: 199—Adrian Murrell, N.Y. Jets at Arizona, Oct. 27 (31 attempts, 1 TD).

Longest gain
AFC: 80— Kordell Stewart, Pittsburgh at Carolina, Dec. 22 (TD).
NFC: 70— LeShon Johnson, Arizona at New Orleans, Sept. 22 (TD).

Attempts, season
NFC: 353—Ricky Watters, Philadelphia.
AFC: 345—Terrell Davis, Denver.

Attempts, game
AFC: 35—Curtis Martin, New England vs. Indianapolis, Nov. 24 (141 yards, 1 TD).
NFC: 33— Errict Rhett, Tampa Bay vs. Oakland, Nov. 10 (95 yards, 0 TDs).

Yards per attempt, season
AFC: 5.8—Napoleon Kaufman, Oakland.
NFC: 5.1—Barry Sanders, Detroit.

Touchdowns, season
NFC: 21—Terry Allen, Washington.
AFC: 14—Curtis Martin, New England.

Team leaders, yards
AFC:

Team	Yds.	Player
Baltimore	737	Bam Morris
Buffalo	1033	Thurman Thomas
Cincinnati	847	Garrison Hearst
Denver	1538	Terrell Davis
Houston	1368	Eddie George
Indianapolis	587	Marshall Faulk
Jacksonville	723	James Stewart
Kansas City	830	Marcus Allen
Miami	1116	Karim Abdul-Jabbar
New England	1152	Curtis Martin
N.Y. Jets	1249	Adrian Murrell
Oakland	874	Napoleon Kaufman
Pittsburgh	1431	Jerome Bettis
San Diego	713	Leonard Russell
Seattle	855	Chris Warren

NFC:

Team	Yds.	Player
Arizona	634	LeShon Johnson
Atlanta	1055	Jamal Anderson
Carolina	1120	Anthony Johnson
Chicago	748	Raymont Harris
Dallas	1204	Emmitt Smith
Detroit	1553	Barry Sanders
Green Bay	899	Edgar Bennett
Minnesota	692	Robert Smith
New Orleans	584	Mario Bates
N.Y. Giants	827	Rodney Hampton
Philadelphia	1411	Ricky Watters
St. Louis	632	Lawrence Phillips
San Francisco	559	Terry Kirby
Tampa Bay	539	Errict Rhett
Washington	1353	Terry Allen

NFL LEADERS

Player, Team	Att.	Yds.	Avg.	Long	TD
Sanders, Barry, Detroit	307	1553	5.1	t54	11
Davis, Terrell, Denver*	345	1538	4.5	t71	13
Bettis, Jerome, Pittsburgh*	320	1431	4.5	t50	11
Watters, Ricky, Philadelphia	353	1411	4.0	t56	13
George, Eddie, Houston*	335	1368	4.1	76	8
Allen, Terry, Washington	347	1353	3.9	t49	21
Murrell, Adrian, N.Y.Jets*	301	1249	4.1	78	6
Smith, Emmitt, Dallas	327	1204	3.7	42	12
Martin, Curtis, New England*	316	1152	3.6	57	14
Johnson, Anthony, Carolina	300	1120	3.7	29	6
Abdul-Jabbar, Karim, Miami*	307	1116	3.6	29	11
Anderson, Jamal, Atlanta	232	1055	4.5	t32	5
Thomas, Thurman, Buffalo*	281	1033	3.7	36	8
Bennett, Edgar, Green Bay*	222	899	4.0	23	2
Kaufman, Napoleon, Oakland*	150	874	5.8	77	1
Warren, Chris, Seattle*	203	855	4.2	51	5
Hearst, Garrison, Cincinnati*	225	847	3.8	24	0
Allen, Marcus, Kansas City*	206	830	4.0	35	9
Hampton, Rodney, N.Y. Giants	254	827	3.3	25	1
Harris, Raymont, Chicago	194	748	3.9	23	4

Player, Team	Att.	Yds.	Avg.	Long	TD
Morris, Bam, Baltimore*	172	737	4.3	19	4
Stewart, James, Jacksonville*	190	723	3.8	34	8
Russell, Leonard, San Diego*	219	713	3.3	21	7
Smith, Robert, Minnesota	162	692	4.3	57	3
Smith, Lamar, Seattle*	153	680	4.4	29	8
Hill, Greg, Kansas City*	135	645	4.8	28	4
Byner, Earnest, Baltimore*	159	634	4.0	42	4
Johnson, LeShon, Arizona	141	634	4.5	t70	3
Phillips, Lawrence, St. Louis	193	632	3.3	38	4
Faulk, Marshall, Indianapolis*	198	587	3.0	43	7

*AFC.
t—touchdown.
Leader based on yards gained.

AFC

Player, Team	Att.	Yds.	Avg.	Long	TD
Abdul-Jabbar, Karim, Miami	307	1116	3.6	29	11
Alexander, Derrick, Baltimore	3	0	0.0	12	0
Allen, Marcus, Kansas City	206	830	4.0	35	9
Anders, Kimble, Kansas City	54	201	3.7	t15	2
Anderson, Richie, N.Y. Jets	47	150	3.2	11	1
Araguz, Leo, Oakland	1	0	0.0	0	0
Arnold, Jahine, Pittsburgh	1	-3	-3.0	-3	0
Aska, Joe, Oakland	62	326	5.3	38	1
Bailey, Henry, N.Y. Jets	1	-4	-4.0	-4	0
Bell, Kerwin, Indianapolis	1	-1	-1.0	-1	0
Bennett, Donnell, Kansas City	36	166	4.6	34	0
Bettis, Jerome, Pittsburgh	320	1431	4.5	t50	11
Bieniemy, Eric, Cincinnati	56	269	4.8	t33	2
Blake, Jeff, Cincinnati	72	317	4.4	18	2
Bledsoe, Drew, New England	24	27	1.1	8	0
Bono, Steve, Kansas City	26	27	1.0	17	0
Bradley, Freddie, San Diego	32	109	3.4	17	0
Bratton, Jason, Buffalo	4	8	2.0	5	0
Broussard, Steve, Seattle	15	106	7.1	t26	1
Brown, Tim, Oakland	6	35	5.8	15	0
Brunell, Mark, Jacksonville	80	396	5.0	33	3
Byars, Keith, New England	2	2	1.0	3	0
Byner, Earnest, Baltimore	159	634	4.0	42	4
Carter, Dale, Kansas City	1	3	3.0	3	0
Carter, Ki-Jana, Cincinnati	91	264	2.9	t31	8
Chandler, Chris, Houston	28	113	4.0	16	0
Cobb, Reggie, N.Y. Jets	25	85	3.4	9	1
Coleman, Andre, San Diego	2	0	0.0	7	0
Collins, Todd, Buffalo	21	43	2.0	10	0
Cothran, Jeff, Cincinnati	15	44	2.9	9	1
Craver, Aaron, Denver	59	232	3.9	28	2
Crockett, Zack, Indianapolis	31	164	5.3	25	0
Davis, Terrell, Denver	345	1538	4.5	t71	13
Davis, Willie, Houston	1	15	15.0	15	0
Early, Quinn, Buffalo	3	39	13.0	29	0
Edge, Shayne, Pittsburgh	1	-16	-16.0	-16	0
Elway, John, Denver	50	249	5.0	22	4
Erickson, Craig, Miami	11	16	1.5	12	0
Faulk, Marshall, Indianapolis	198	587	3.0	43	7
Fenner, Derrick, Oakland	67	245	3.7	17	4
Fletcher, Terrell, San Diego	77	282	3.7	19	0
Foley, Glenn, N.Y. Jets	7	40	5.7	12	0
Friesz, John, Seattle	12	1	0.1	3	0
Galloway, Joey, Seattle	15	127	8.5	51	0
Gannon, Rich, Kansas City	12	81	6.8	19	0
Gardner, Carwell, Baltimore	26	108	4.2	19	0
Gash, Sam, New England	8	15	1.9	3	0
George, Eddie, Houston	335	1368	4.1	76	8
Glenn, Terry, New England	5	42	8.4	26	0
Gossett, Jeff, Oakland	3	28	9.3	18	0
Gray, Oscar, Seattle	2	4	2.0	2	0
Grier, Marrio, New England	27	105	3.9	26	1
Groce, Clif, Indianapolis	46	184	4.0	24	0
Hall, Tim, Oakland	3	7	2.3	4	0
Hansen, Brian, N.Y. Jets	1	1	1.0	1	0
Harbaugh, Jim, Indianapolis	48	192	4.0	21	1
Harmon, Ronnie, Houston	29	131	4.5	25	1
Harrison, Marvin, Indianapolis	3	15	5.0	15	0
Hastings, Andre, Pittsburgh	4	71	17.8	37	0
Hayden, Aaron, San Diego	55	166	3.0	13	0
Hearst, Garrison, Cincinnati	225	847	3.8	24	0
Hebron, Vaughn, Denver	49	262	5.3	47	0
Hill, Greg, Kansas City	135	645	4.8	28	4
Hobert, Billy Joe, Oakland	2	13	6.5	14	0
Holmes, Darick, Buffalo	189	571	3.0	37	4
Horn, Joe, Kansas City	1	8	8.0	8	0
Hostetler, Jeff, Oakland	37	179	4.8	17	1
Humphries, Stan, San Diego	21	28	1.3	7	0
Izzo, Larry, Miami	1	26	26.0	26	0
Jackson, Willie, Jacksonville	1	2	2.0	2	0
Jefferson, Shawn, New England	1	6	6.0	6	0
Justin, Paul, Indianapolis	2	7	3.5	6	0
Kaufman, Napoleon, Oakland	150	874	5.8	77	1
Kelly, Jim, Buffalo	19	66	3.5	22	2
Kidd, John, Miami	1	3	3.0	3	0
Klingler, David, Oakland	4	36	9.0	14	0
Kosar, Bernie, Miami	1	6	6.0	6	0
Lester, Tim, Pittsburgh	8	20	2.5	t5	1
Lewis, Jeff, Denver	4	39	9.8	18	0
Lewis, Jermaine, Baltimore	1	-3	-3.0	-3	0
Marino, Dan, Miami	11	-3	-.3	7	0
Martin, Curtis, New England	316	1152	3.6	57	14
Maston, Le'Shai, Jacksonville	8	22	2.8	7	0
McAfee, Fred, Pittsburgh	7	17	2.4	5	0
McDuffie, O.J., Miami	2	7	3.5	7	0
McNair, Steve, Houston	31	169	5.5	t24	2
McNair, Todd, Kansas City	9	32	3.6	9	0
McPhail, Jerris, Miami	6	28	4.7	10	0
Means, Natrone, Jacksonville	152	507	3.3	35	2
Meggett, David, New England	40	122	3.1	12	0
Miller, Anthony, Denver	3	39	13.0	t26	1
Miller, Jim, Pittsburgh	2	-4	-2.0	0	0
Mills, Ernie, Pittsburgh	2	24	12.0	15	0
Milne, Brian, Cincinnati	8	22	2.8	5	1
Mirer, Rick, Seattle	33	191	5.8	33	2
Montgomery, Greg, Baltimore	1	0	0.0	0	0
Moore, Ronald, N.Y. Jets	1	1	1.0	1	0
Morris, Bam, Baltimore	172	737	4.3	19	4
Moulds, Eric, Buffalo	12	44	3.7	11	0
Murrell, Adrian, N.Y. Jets	301	1249	4.1	78	6
Musgrave, Bill, Denver	12	-4	-.3	6	0
O'Donnell, Neil, N.Y. Jets	6	30	5.0	17	0
Parmalee, Bernie, Miami	25	80	3.2	17	0
Pegram, Erric, Pittsburgh	97	509	5.2	27	1
Pickens, Carl, Cincinnati	2	2	1.0	2	0
Pritchard, Mike, Seattle	2	13	6.5	7	0
Pritchett, Stanley, Miami	7	27	3.9	16	0
Reed, Andre, Buffalo	8	22	2.8	13	0
Reich, Frank, N.Y. Jets	18	31	1.7	10	0
Richardson, Terry, Pittsburgh	5	17	3.4	8	0
Richardson, Tony, Kansas City	4	10	2.5	4	0
Rivers, Reggie, Denver	2	6	3.0	3	0
Russell, Leonard, San Diego	219	713	3.3	21	7
Salisbury, Sean, San Diego	6	14	2.3	11	0
Scott, Darnay, Cincinnati	3	4	1.3	8	0
Smith, Lamar, Seattle	153	680	4.4	29	8
Smith, Rod, Denver	1	1	1.0	1	0
Spikes, Irving, Miami	87	316	3.6	49	3
Stewart, James, Jacksonville	190	723	3.8	34	8
Stewart, Kordell, Pittsburgh	39	171	4.4	t80	5
Strong, Mack, Seattle	5	8	1.6	4	0
Tasker, Steve, Buffalo	9	31	3.4	11	0
Testaverde, Vinny, Baltimore	34	188	5.5	22	2
Thomas, Rodney, Houston	49	151	3.1	t24	1
Thomas, Thurman, Buffalo	281	1033	3.7	36	8
Tindale, Tim, Buffalo	14	49	3.5	15	0
Tomczak, Mike, Pittsburgh	22	-7	-.3	6	0

1996 STATISTICS Rushing

Player, Team	Att.	Yds.	Avg.	Long	TD
Torretta, Gino, Seattle	2	12	6.0	13	0
Turner, Floyd, Baltimore	2	12	6.0	6	0
Van Pelt, Alex, Buffalo	3	-5	-1.7	-1	0
Vanover, Tamarick, Kansas City	4	6	1.5	6	0
Warren, Chris, Seattle	203	855	4.2	51	5
Warren, Lamont, Indianapolis	67	230	3.4	53	1
Wilhelm, Erik, Cincinnati	6	24	4.0	18	0
Williams, Harvey, Oakland	121	431	3.6	44	0
Wilson, Robert, Miami	1	0	0.0	0	0
Witman, Jon, Pittsburgh	17	69	4.1	15	0
Workman, Vince, Indianapolis	24	70	2.9	11	0
Wycheck, Frank, Houston	2	3	1.5	3	0
Zeier, Eric, Baltimore	2	8	4.0	5	0
Zolak, Scott, New England	4	-3	-.8	0	0

t—touchdown.

NFC

Player, Team	Att.	Yds.	Avg.	Long	TD
Aikman, Troy, Dallas	35	42	1.2	10	1
Allen, Terry, Washington	347	1353	3.9	t49	21
Alstott, Mike, Tampa Bay	96	377	3.9	39	3
Anderson, Jamal, Atlanta	232	1055	4.5	t32	5
Banks, Tony, St. Louis	61	212	3.5	22	0
Barnhardt, Tommy, Tampa Bay	2	27	13.5	25	0
Bates, Mario, New Orleans	164	584	3.6	33	4
Bennett, Edgar, Green Bay	222	899	4.0	23	2
Beuerlein, Steve, Carolina	12	17	1.4	13	0
Biakabutuka, Tim, Carolina	71	229	3.2	17	0
Brohm, Jeff, San Francisco	16	43	2.7	22	0
Brooks, Reggie, Tampa Bay	112	368	3.3	56	2
Brooks, Robert, Green Bay	4	2	0.5	6	0
Brown, Dave, N.Y. Giants	50	170	3.4	18	0
Brown, Derek, New Orleans	13	30	2.3	12	0
Bruce, Isaac, St. Louis	1	4	4.0	4	0
Calloway, Chris, N.Y. Giants	1	2	2.0	2	0
Carter, Dexter, San Francisco	19	66	3.5	18	1
Carter, Tony, Chicago	11	43	3.9	23	0
Centers, Larry, Arizona	116	425	3.7	24	2
Collins, Kerry, Carolina	32	38	1.2	14	0
Conway, Curtis, Chicago	8	50	6.3	19	0
Davis, Stephen, Washington	23	139	6.0	t39	2
DeRamus, Lee, New Orleans	1	2	2.0	2	0
Detmer, Ty, Philadelphia	31	59	1.9	9	1
Dilfer, Trent, Tampa Bay	32	124	3.9	19	0
Downs, Gary, N.Y. Giants	29	94	3.2	27	0
Edwards, Anthony, Arizona	1	-8	-8.0	-8	0
Elias, Keith, N.Y. Giants	9	24	2.7	8	0
Ellison, Jerry, Tampa Bay	35	106	3.0	13	0
Esiason, Boomer, Arizona	15	52	3.5	13	1
Evans, Charles, Minnesota	13	29	2.2	9	0
Everett, Jim, New Orleans	22	3	0.1	3	0
Favre, Brett, Green Bay	49	136	2.8	23	2
Feagles, Jeff, Arizona	1	0	0.0	0	0
Floyd, William, San Francisco	47	186	4.0	12	2
Frerotte, Gus, Washington	28	16	0.6	17	0
Fryar, Irving, Philadelphia	1	-4	-4.0	-4	0
Garner, Charlie, Philadelphia	66	346	5.2	46	1
George, Jeff, Atlanta	5	10	2.0	5	0
Graham, Kent, Arizona	21	87	4.1	19	0
Graham, Scottie, Minnesota	57	138	2.4	12	0
Grbac, Elvis, San Francisco	23	21	0.9	12	2
Green, Harold, St. Louis	127	523	4.1	t35	4
Green, Robert, Chicago	60	249	4.2	19	0
Green, Willie, Carolina	1	1	1.0	1	0
Griffith, Howard, Carolina	12	7	0.6	3	1
Guess, Terry, New Orleans	2	-4	-2.0	-1	0
Hampton, Rodney, N.Y. Giants	254	827	3.3	25	1
Harris, Derrick, St. Louis	3	5	1.7	3	0
Harris, Raymont, Chicago	194	748	3.9	23	4
Hawkins, Courtney, Tampa Bay	1	-13	-13.0	-13	0
Hayes, Mercury, New Orleans	2	7	3.5	5	0
Hebert, Bobby, Atlanta	15	59	3.9	25	1
Henderson, William, Green Bay	39	130	3.3	14	0
Heyward, Craig, Atlanta	72	321	4.5	34	3
Hicks, Michael, Chicago	27	92	3.4	23	0
Hoard, Leroy, Bal.-Car.-Min.*	125	492	3.9	25	3
Hunter, Earnest, Bal.-N.O.*	15	44	2.9	9	0
Huntley, Richard, Atlanta	2	8	4.0	5	0
Ismail, Raghib, Carolina	8	80	10.0	t35	1
Jervey, Travis, Green Bay	26	106	4.1	12	0
Jett, John, Dallas	1	-23	-23.0	-23	0
Johnson, Anthony, Carolina	300	1120	3.7	29	6
Johnson, Brad, Minnesota	34	90	2.6	13	1
Johnson, LeShon, Arizona	141	634	4.5	t70	3
Johnston, Daryl, Dallas	22	48	2.2	7	0
Kanell, Danny, N.Y. Giants	7	6	0.9	13	0
Kirby, Terry, San Francisco	134	559	4.2	31	3
Kramer, Erik, Chicago	8	4	0.5	3	0
Krieg, Dave, Chicago	16	12	0.8	2	1
Landeta, Sean, St. Louis	2	0	0.0	0	0
Lee, Amp, Minnesota	51	161	3.2	12	0
Levens, Dorsey, Green Bay	121	566	4.7	24	5
Logan, Marc, Washington	20	111	5.6	t36	2
Loville, Derek, San Francisco	70	229	3.3	16	2
Lyle, Keith, St. Louis	3	39	13.0	20	0
Lynch, Eric, Detroit	2	2	1.0	2	0
Lynch, John, Tampa Bay	1	40	40.0	40	0
Lynn, Anthony, San Francisco	24	164	6.8	67	0
Majkowski, Don, Detroit	14	38	2.7	12	0
Martin, Jamie, St. Louis	7	14	2.0	11	0
Matthews, Shane, Chicago	1	2	2.0	t2	1
McDaniel, Randall, Minnesota	2	1	0.5	1	0
McElroy, Leeland, Arizona	89	305	3.4	32	1
McKinnon, Ronald, Arizona	1	-4	-4.0	-4	0
McMahon, Jim, Green Bay	4	-1	-.3	2	0
Metcalf, Eric, Atlanta	3	8	2.7	4	0
Mitchell, Brian, Washington	39	193	4.9	32	0
Mitchell, Scott, Detroit	37	83	2.2	9	4
Moon, Warren, Minnesota	9	6	0.7	5	0
Moore, Jerald, St. Louis	11	32	2.9	14	0
Morton, Johnnie, Detroit	9	35	3.9	18	0
Muhammad, Muhsin, Carolina	1	-1	-1.0	-1	0
Neal, Lorenzo, New Orleans	21	58	2.8	11	1
Nussmeier, Doug, New Orleans	3	6	2.0	6	0
Oliver, Winslow, Carolina	47	183	3.9	16	0
Palmer, David, Minnesota	2	9	4.5	8	0
Peete, Rodney, Philadelphia	20	31	1.6	11	1
Perriman, Brett, Detroit	1	13	13.0	13	0
Phillips, Lawrence, St. Louis	193	632	3.3	38	4
Philyaw, Dino, Carolina	12	38	3.2	8	1
Pierce, Aaron, N.Y. Giants	1	1	1.0	t1	1
Rhett, Errict, Tampa Bay	176	539	3.1	35	3
Rice, Jerry, San Francisco	11	77	7.0	38	1
Rivers, Ron, Detroit	19	86	4.5	26	0
Robinson, Greg, St. Louis	32	134	4.2	24	1
Ross, Jermaine, St. Louis	1	3	3.0	t3	1
Salaam, Rashaan, Chicago	143	496	3.5	32	3
Sanders, Barry, Detroit	307	1553	5.1	t54	11
Sanders, Deion, Dallas	3	2	0.7	3	0
Sanders, Frank, Arizona	2	-4	-2.0	1	0
Sauerbrun, Todd, Chicago	1	3	3.0	3	0
Shepherd, Leslie, Washington	6	96	16.0	t32	2
Shuler, Heath, Washington	1	0	0.0	0	0
Small, Torrance, New Orleans	4	51	12.8	22	1
Smith, Cedric, Arizona	14	15	1.1	3	1
Smith, Emmitt, Dallas	327	1204	3.7	42	12
Smith, Robert, Minnesota	162	692	4.3	57	3
Stone, Dwight, Carolina	1	6	6.0	6	0
Thomas, J.T., St. Louis	1	-1	-1.0	-1	0
Thompson, Leroy, Tampa Bay	14	25	1.8	10	0
Timpson, Michael, Chicago	3	21	7.0	13	0
Turk, Matt, Washington	1	0	0.0	0	0
Turner, Kevin, Philadelphia	18	39	2.2	7	0

1996 STATISTICS *Rushing*

layer, Team	Att.	Yds.	Avg.	Long	TD
ardell, Tommy, San Francisco	58	192	3.3	17	2
Jalker, Herschel, Dallas	10	83	8.3	t39	1
Jalsh, Steve, St. Louis	6	10	1.7	13	0
Jatters, Ricky, Philadelphia	353	1411	4.0	t56	13
Jay, Charles, N.Y. Giants	22	79	3.6	18	1
Jeldon, Casey, Tampa Bay	2	-1	-.5	0	0
Jestbrook, Michael, Washington ...	2	2	1.0	2	0
Jheatley, Tyrone, N.Y. Giants	112	400	3.6	37	1
Jhittle, Ricky, New Orleans	20	52	2.6	15	0
Jilliams, Karl, Tampa Bay	1	-3	-3.0	-3	0
Jilliams, Kevin, Dallas	4	11	2.8	9	0
Jilliams, Sherman, Dallas	69	269	3.9	27	0
Jilson, Wade, Dallas	4	5	1.3	8	0

Player, Team	Att.	Yds.	Avg.	Long	TD
Young, Steve, San Francisco	52	310	6.0	33	4
Zellars, Ray, New Orleans..............	120	475	4.0	63	4

*Includes both NFC and AFC statistics.
t—touchdown.

PLAYERS WITH TWO CLUBS

Player, Team	Att.	Yds.	Avg.	Long	TD
Hoard, Leroy, Baltimore................	15	61	4.1	10	0
Hoard, Leroy, Carolina..................	5	11	2.2	5	0
Hoard, Leroy, Minnesota	105	420	4.0	25	3
Hunter, Earnest, Baltimore............	1	0	0.0	0	0
Hunter, Earnest, New Orleans	14	44	3.1	9	0

PASSING

TEAM

AFC

Team	Att.	Comp.	Pct. Comp.	Gross Yds.	Sack	Yds. Lost	Net Yds.	Yds./ Att.	Yds./ Comp.	TD	Pct. TD	Long	Had Int.	P
Jacksonville	557	353	63.4	4367	50	257	4110	7.84	12.37	19	3.41	62	20	3
Baltimore	570	335	58.8	4274	38	296	3978	7.50	12.76	34	5.96	t86	20	3
New England........	628	374	59.6	4091	30	190	3901	6.51	10.94	27	4.30	t84	15	2
N.Y. Jets..............	629	339	53.9	3911	41	286	3625	6.22	11.54	22	3.50	t78	30	4
Miami....................	504	300	59.5	3783	36	240	3543	7.51	12.61	22	4.37	t74	11	2
Cincinnati	563	316	56.1	3726	47	294	3432	6.62	11.79	25	4.44	t61	16	2
Denver	536	327	61.0	3662	31	233	3429	6.83	11.20	26	4.85	51	17	3
San Diego	577	314	54.4	3654	33	296	3358	6.33	11.64	23	3.99	t63	21	3
Buffalo	483	279	57.8	3558	48	340	3218	7.37	12.75	18	3.73	t95	24	5
Indianapolis	537	311	57.9	3544	43	248	3296	6.60	11.40	16	2.98	51	11	2
Oakland	533	311	58.3	3327	45	249	3078	6.24	10.70	28	5.25	t62	19	3
Houston	463	272	58.7	3296	34	198	3098	7.12	12.12	22	4.75	t83	15	3
Seattle..................	494	261	52.8	3216	38	189	3027	6.51	12.32	14	2.83	t80	17	3
Kansas City..........	530	290	54.7	3093	27	203	2890	5.84	10.67	18	3.40	69	14	2
Pittsburgh	456	246	53.9	2990	21	149	2841	6.56	12.15	15	3.29	t70	19	4
AFC total............	8060	4628	....	54492	562	3668	50824	....	....	329	....	t95	269	3
AFC average.......	537.3	308.5	57.4	3632.8	37.5	244.5	3388.3	6.76	11.77	21.9	4.1	....	17.9	3

t—touchdown.

NFC

Team	Att.	Comp.	Pct. Comp.	Gross Yds.	Sack	Yds. Lost	Net Yds.	Yds./ Att.	Yds./ Comp.	TD	Pct. TD	Long	Had Int.	P
Philadelphia	548	328	59.9	3979	39	234	3745	7.26	12.13	19	3.47	62	18	3
Green Bay	548	328	59.9	3938	40	241	3697	7.19	12.01	39	7.12	t80	13	2
Arizona.................	613	336	54.8	3917	36	229	3688	6.39	11.66	23	3.75	69	21	3
Atlanta..................	600	356	59.3	3909	42	254	3655	6.52	10.98	26	4.33	67	30	5
Minnesota	561	331	59.0	3899	34	241	3658	6.95	11.78	24	4.28	t82	19	3
San Francisco	550	358	65.1	3859	42	200	3659	7.02	10.78	24	4.36	52	16	2
Detroit...................	541	309	57.1	3463	46	260	3203	6.40	11.21	20	3.70	t62	21	3
Washington...........	471	270	57.3	3453	22	134	3319	7.33	12.79	12	2.55	t52	11	2
Chicago................	551	318	57.7	3350	23	165	3185	6.08	10.53	19	3.45	t58	18	3
Carolina................	487	273	56.1	3333	36	250	3083	6.84	12.21	22	4.52	55	11	2
Dallas...................	487	307	63.0	3249	19	127	3122	6.67	10.58	12	2.46	61	14	2
St. Louis	481	249	51.8	3144	57	379	2765	6.54	12.63	18	3.74	t77	23	4
New Orleans.........	515	295	57.3	3069	22	171	2898	5.96	10.40	13	2.52	t57	17	3
Tampa Bay	494	274	55.5	2944	30	217	2727	5.96	10.74	12	2.43	45	20	4
N.Y. Giants...........	459	238	51.9	2663	56	324	2339	5.80	11.19	14	3.05	t37	21	4
NFC total	7906	4570	....	52169	544	3426	48743	....	....	297	....	t82	273	3
NFC average.......	527.1	304.7	57.8	3477.9	36.3	228.4	3249.5	6.60	11.42	19.8	3.8	....	18.2	3
NFL total.............	15966	9198	....	106661	1106	7094	99567	....	....	626	....	t95	542	
NFL average.......	532.2	306.6	57.6	3555.4	36.9	236.5	3318.9	6.68	11.60	20.9	3.9	....	18.1	3

INDIVIDUAL

BESTS OF THE SEASON

Highest rating, season
NFC: 97.2—Steve Young, San Francisco.
AFC: 89.2—John Elway, Denver.

Completion percentage, season
NFC: 67.7—Steve Young, San Francisco.
AFC: 63.4—Mark Brunell, Jacksonville.

Attempts, season
AFC: 623—Drew Bledsoe, New England.
NFC: 543—Brett Favre, Green Bay.

Completions, season
AFC: 373—Drew Bledsoe, New England.
NFC: 325—Brett Favre, Green Bay.

Yards, season
AFC: 4367—Mark Brunell, Jacksonville.
NFC: 3899—Brett Favre, Green Bay.

Yards, game
NFC: 522—Boomer Esiason, Arizona at Washington, Nov. 10 (35-59, 3 TDs).
AFC: 432—Mark Brunell, Jacksonville at New England, Sept. 2 (23-39, 3 TDs).

Longest gain
AFC: 95—Todd Collins (to Quinn Early), Buffalo at Indianapolis, Dec. 1 (TD).
NFC: 82—Brad Johnson (to Jake Reed), Minnesota at Oakland, Nov. 17 (TD).

Yards per attempt, season
AFC: 7.84—Mark Brunell, Jacksonville.
NFC: 7.63—Steve Young, San Francisco.

Touchdown passes, season
NFC: 39—Brett Favre, Green Bay.
AFC: 33—Vinny Testaverde, Baltimore.

Touchdown passes, game
NFC: 4—Stan Humphries, San Diego at Oakland, Sept. 22 (18-25, 226 yards); John Elway, Denver vs. San Diego, Oct

6 (32-41, 323 yards); Drew Bledsoe, New England at Baltimore, Oct. 6 (25-39, 310 yards); Jeff Hostetler, Oakland vs. Detroit, Oct. 13 (27-38, 295 yards); Vinny Testaverde, Baltimore at Denver, October 20 (27-45, 338 yards); Jeff Blake, Cincinnati vs. Atlanta, Nov. 24 (21-36, 349 yards); Drew Bledsoe, New England at San Diego, Dec. 1 (19-29, 232 yards).

TC: 4—Brett Favre, Green Bay at Tampa Bay, Sept. 1 (20-27, 247 yards); Scott Mitchell, Detroit vs. Chicago, Sept. 22 (24-34, 336 yards); Kent Graham, Arizona vs. St. Louis, Sept. 29 (37-58, 366 yards); Brett Favre, Green Bay at

Seattle, Sept. 29 (20-34, 209 yards); Brett Favre, Green Bay at Chicago, Oct. 6 (18-27, 246 yards); Ty Detmer, Philadelphia vs. Miami, Oct. 20 (18-24, 226 yards); Brett Favre, Green Bay vs. Detroit, Nov. 3 (24-35, 281 yards); Brad Johnson, Minnesota vs. Arizona, Dec. 1 (19-26, 238 yards); Brett Favre, Green Bay vs. Denver, Dec. 8 (20-38, 280 yards).

Lowest interception percentage, season
NFC: 1.9—Steve Young, San Francisco.
AFC: 2.4—Drew Bledsoe, New England.

NFL LEADERS

Player, Team	Att.	Comp.	Pct. Comp.	Yds.	Avg. Gain	TD	Pct. TD	Long	Int.	Pct. Int.	Sack	Yds. Lost	Rat. Pts.
Young, Steve, San Francisco	316	214	67.7	2410	7.63	14	4.4	52	6	1.9	34	160	97.2
Favre, Brett, Green Bay	543	325	59.9	3899	7.18	39	7.2	t80	13	2.4	40	241	95.8
Johnson, Brad, Minnesota	311	195	62.7	2258	7.26	17	5.5	t82	10	3.2	15	119	89.4
Elway, John, Denver*	466	287	61.6	3328	7.14	26	5.6	51	14	3.0	26	194	89.2
Testaverde, Vinny, Baltimore*	549	325	59.2	4177	7.61	33	6.0	t86	19	3.5	34	270	88.7
Marino, Dan, Miami*	373	221	59.2	2795	7.49	17	4.6	t74	9	2.4	18	131	87.8
Brunell, Mark, Jacksonville*	557	353	63.4	4367	7.84	19	3.4	62	20	3.6	50	257	84.0
Bledsoe, Drew, New England*	623	373	59.9	4086	6.56	27	4.3	t84	15	2.4	30	190	83.7
Hostetler, Jeff, Oakland*	402	242	60.2	2548	6.34	23	5.7	t62	14	3.5	32	181	83.2
Detmer, Ty, Philadelphia	401	238	59.4	2911	7.26	15	3.7	42	13	3.2	27	171	80.8
Blake, Jeff, Cincinnati*	549	308	56.1	3624	6.60	24	4.4	t61	14	2.6	44	278	80.3
Aikman, Troy, Dallas	465	296	63.7	3126	6.72	12	2.6	61	13	2.8	18	120	80.1
Chandler, Chris, Houston*	320	184	57.5	2099	6.56	16	5.0	t63	11	3.4	25	153	79.7
Collins, Kerry, Carolina	364	204	56.0	2454	6.74	14	3.8	55	9	2.5	18	114	79.4
Frerotte, Gus, Washington	470	270	57.4	3453	7.35	12	2.6	t52	11	2.3	22	134	79.3
Humphries, Stan, San Diego*	416	232	55.8	2670	6.42	18	4.3	t63	13	3.1	20	187	76.7
Krieg, Dave, Chicago	377	226	59.9	2278	6.04	14	3.7	t53	12	3.2	14	104	76.3
Harbaugh, Jim, Indianapolis*	405	232	57.3	2630	6.49	13	3.2	51	11	2.7	36	190	76.3
Graham, Kent, Arizona	274	146	53.3	1624	5.93	12	4.4	69	7	2.6	19	120	75.1
Mitchell, Scott, Detroit	437	253	57.9	2917	6.68	17	3.9	t62	17	3.9	36	199	74.9
Kelly, Jim, Buffalo*	379	222	58.6	2810	7.41	14	3.7	t67	19	5.0	37	287	73.2
Hebert, Bobby, Atlanta	488	294	60.2	3152	6.46	22	4.5	57	25	5.1	27	150	72.9
Tomczak, Mike, Pittsburgh*	401	222	55.4	2767	6.90	15	3.7	t70	17	4.2	16	105	71.8
Banks, Tony, St. Louis	368	192	52.2	2544	6.91	15	4.1	t77	15	4.1	48	306	71.0
Esiason, Boomer, Arizona	339	190	56.0	2293	6.76	11	3.2	t64	14	4.1	17	109	70.6
Everett, Jim, New Orleans	464	267	57.5	2797	6.03	12	2.6	51	16	3.4	19	154	69.4
Reich, Frank, N.Y. Jets*	331	175	52.9	2205	6.66	15	4.5	t52	16	4.8	14	94	68.9
Moon, Warren, Minnesota	247	134	54.3	1610	6.52	7	2.8	t54	9	3.6	19	122	68.7
Bono, Steve, Kansas City*	438	235	53.7	2572	5.87	12	2.7	69	13	3.0	22	161	68.0
Dilfer, Trent, Tampa Bay	482	267	55.4	2859	5.93	12	2.5	45	19	3.9	28	207	64.8

*AFC.
t—touchdown.
Leader based on rating points, minimum 224 attempts.

AFC

Player, Team	Att.	Comp.	Pct. Comp.	Yds.	Avg. Gain	TD	Pct. TD	Long	Int.	Pct. Int.	Sack	Yds. Lost	Rat. Pts.
Abdul-Jabbar, Karim, Miami	0	0	....	0	....	0	....	....	0	....	1	3	....
Allen, Marcus, Kansas City	1	0	0.0	0	0.00	0	0.0	0	0	0.0	0	0	39.6
Bell, Kerwin, Indianapolis	5	5	100.0	75	15.00	1	20.0	30	0	0.0	0	0	158.3
Blake, Jeff, Cincinnati	549	308	56.1	3624	6.60	24	4.4	t61	14	2.6	44	278	80.3
Bledsoe, Drew, New England	623	373	59.9	4086	6.56	27	4.3	t84	15	2.4	30	190	83.7
Bono, Steve, Kansas City	438	235	53.7	2572	5.87	12	2.7	69	13	3.0	22	161	68.0
Brunell, Mark, Jacksonville	557	353	63.4	4367	7.84	19	3.4	62	20	3.6	50	257	84.0
Chandler, Chris, Houston	320	184	57.5	2099	6.56	16	5.0	t63	11	3.4	25	153	79.7
Collins, Todd, Buffalo	99	55	55.6	739	7.46	4	4.0	t95	5	5.1	11	53	71.9
Craver, Aaron, Denver	1	0	0.0	0	0.00	0	0.0	0	0	0.0	0	0	39.6
Elway, John, Denver	466	287	61.6	3328	7.14	26	5.6	51	14	3.0	26	194	89.2
Erickson, Craig, Miami	99	55	55.6	780	7.88	4	4.0	61	2	2.0	11	72	86.3
Foley, Glenn, N.Y. Jets	110	54	49.1	559	5.08	3	2.7	t46	7	6.4	9	65	46.7
Friesz, John, Seattle	211	120	56.9	1629	7.72	8	3.8	t80	4	1.9	12	77	86.4
Gannon, Rich, Kansas City	90	54	60.0	491	5.46	6	6.7	25	1	1.1	5	42	92.4
Gelbaugh, Stan, Seattle	2	0	0.0	0	0.00	0	0.0	0	0	0.0	1	11	39.6
Grier, Marrio, New England	1	0	0.0	0	0.00	0	0.0	0	0	0.0	0	0	39.6
Harbaugh, Jim, Indianapolis	405	232	57.3	2630	6.49	13	3.2	51	11	2.7	36	190	76.3
Hobbs, Daryl, Oakland	1	1	100.0	7	7.00	0	0.0	7	0	0.0	0	0	95.8

1996 STATISTICS Passing

Player, Team	Att.	Comp.	Pct. Comp.	Yds.	Avg. Gain	TD	Pct. TD	Long	Int.	Pct. Int.	Sack	Yds. Lost	Ra Pts
Hobert, Billy Joe, Oakland	104	57	54.8	667	6.41	4	3.8	51	5	4.8	9	52	67
Hostetler, Jeff, Oakland	402	242	60.2	2548	6.34	23	5.7	t62	14	3.5	32	181	83
Hughes, Danan, Kansas City	1	1	100.0	30	30.00	0	0.0	30	0	0.0	0	0	118
Humphries, Stan, San Diego	416	232	55.8	2670	6.42	18	4.3	t63	13	3.1	20	187	76
Justin, Paul, Indianapolis	127	74	58.3	839	6.61	2	1.6	38	0	0.0	7	58	83
Kelly, Jim, Buffalo	379	222	58.6	2810	7.41	14	3.7	t67	19	5.0	37	287	73
Klingler, David, Oakland	24	10	41.7	87	3.63	0	0.0	20	0	0.0	4	16	51
Kosar, Bernie, Miami	32	24	75.0	208	6.50	1	3.1	20	0	0.0	6	34	102
Lewis, Jeff, Denver	17	9	52.9	58	3.41	0	0.0	11	1	5.9	1	7	35
Marino, Dan, Miami	373	221	59.2	2795	7.49	17	4.6	t74	9	2.4	18	131	87
McNair, Steve, Houston	143	88	61.5	1197	8.37	6	4.2	t83	4	2.8	9	45	90
Meggett, David, New England	1	0	0.0	0	0.00	0	0.0	0	0	0.0	0	0	39
Miller, Jim, Pittsburgh	25	13	52.0	123	4.92	0	0.0	17	0	0.0	2	7	65
Mirer, Rick, Seattle	265	136	51.3	1546	5.83	5	1.9	60	12	4.5	22	84	56
Musgrave, Bill, Denver	52	31	59.6	276	5.31	0	0.0	46	2	3.8	4	32	57
O'Donnell, Neil, N.Y. Jets	188	110	58.5	1147	6.10	4	2.1	t78	7	3.7	18	127	67
Pickens, Carl, Cincinnati	1	1	100.0	12	12.00	0	0.0	12	0	0.0	0	0	116
Reich, Frank, N.Y. Jets	331	175	52.9	2205	6.66	15	4.5	t52	16	4.8	14	94	68
Salisbury, Sean, San Diego	161	82	50.9	984	6.11	5	3.1	56	8	5.0	13	109	59
Stewart, Kordell, Pittsburgh	30	11	36.7	100	3.33	0	0.0	15	2	6.7	3	37	18
Testaverde, Vinny, Baltimore	549	325	59.2	4177	7.61	33	6.0	t86	19	3.5	34	270	88
Tomczak, Mike, Pittsburgh	401	222	55.4	2767	6.90	15	3.7	t70	17	4.2	16	105	71
Torretta, Gino, Seattle	16	5	31.3	41	2.56	1	6.3	t32	1	6.3	3	17	35
Tupa, Tom, New England	2	0	0.0	0	0.00	0	0.0	0	0	0.0	0	0	39
Van Pelt, Alex, Buffalo	5	2	40.0	9	1.80	0	0.0	5	0	0.0	0	0	47
Wilhelm, Erik, Cincinnati	13	7	53.8	90	6.92	1	7.7	38	2	15.4	3	16	61
Williams, Harvey, Oakland	2	1	50.0	18	9.00	1	50.0	t18	0	0.0	0	0	120
Zeier, Eric, Baltimore	21	10	47.6	97	4.62	1	4.8	15	1	4.8	4	26	57
Zolak, Scott, New England	1	1	100.0	5	5.00	0	0.0	5	0	0.0	0	0	87

t—touchdown.

NFC

Player, Team	Att.	Comp.	Pct. Comp.	Yds.	Avg. Gain	TD	Pct. TD	Long	Int.	Pct. Int.	Sack	Yds. Lost	Ra Pts
Aikman, Troy, Dallas	465	296	63.7	3126	6.72	12	2.6	61	13	2.8	18	120	80
Banks, Tony, St. Louis	368	192	52.2	2544	6.91	15	4.1	t77	15	4.1	48	306	71
Beuerlein, Steve, Carolina	123	69	56.1	879	7.15	8	6.5	t40	2	1.6	18	136	93
Brohm, Jeff, San Francisco	34	21	61.8	189	5.56	1	2.9	49	0	0.0	2	10	86
Brown, Dave, N.Y. Giants	398	214	53.8	2412	6.06	12	3.0	t37	20	5.0	49	276	61
Bruce, Isaac, St. Louis	2	1	50.0	15	7.50	0	0.0	15	1	50.0	0	0	35
Collins, Kerry, Carolina	364	204	56.0	2454	6.74	14	3.8	55	9	2.5	18	114	79
Conway, Curtis, Chicago	1	1	100.0	33	33.00	1	100.0	t33	0	0.0	0	0	158
Detmer, Ty, Philadelphia	401	238	59.4	2911	7.26	15	3.7	42	13	3.2	27	171	80
Dilfer, Trent, Tampa Bay	482	267	55.4	2859	5.93	12	2.5	45	19	3.9	28	207	64
Esiason, Boomer, Arizona	339	190	56.0	2293	6.76	11	3.2	t64	14	4.1	17	109	70
Everett, Jim, New Orleans	464	267	57.5	2797	6.03	12	2.6	51	16	3.4	19	154	69
Favre, Brett, Green Bay	543	325	59.9	3899	7.18	39	7.2	t80	13	2.4	40	241	95
Frerotte, Gus, Washington	470	270	57.4	3453	7.35	12	2.6	t52	11	2.3	22	134	79
Garrett, Jason, Dallas	3	3	100.0	44	14.67	0	0.0	32	0	0.0	0	0	118
George, Jeff, Atlanta	99	56	56.6	698	7.05	3	3.0	67	3	3.0	11	84	76
Graham, Kent, Arizona	274	146	53.3	1624	5.93	12	4.4	69	7	2.6	19	120	75
Grbac, Elvis, San Francisco	197	122	61.9	1236	6.27	8	4.1	40	10	5.1	6	30	72
Hebert, Bobby, Atlanta	488	294	60.2	3152	6.46	22	4.5	57	25	5.1	27	150	72
Hentrich, Craig, Green Bay	1	0	0.0	0	0.00	0	0.0	0	0	0.0	0	0	39
Hoying, Bobby, Philadelphia	0	0	....	0	....	0	....	....	0	....	1	10	..
Hunter, Earnest, New Orleans	1	0	0.0	0	0.00	0	0.0	0	0	0.0	0	0	39
Johnson, Brad, Minnesota	311	195	62.7	2258	7.26	17	5.5	t82	10	3.2	15	119	89
Kanell, Danny, N.Y. Giants	60	23	38.3	227	3.78	1	1.7	25	1	1.7	7	48	48
Kirby, Terry, San Francisco	2	1	50.0	24	12.00	1	50.0	t24	0	0.0	0	0	133
Kramer, Erik, Chicago	150	73	48.7	781	5.21	3	2.0	t58	6	4.0	7	53	54
Krieg, Dave, Chicago	377	226	59.9	2278	6.04	14	3.7	t53	12	3.2	14	104	76
Majkowski, Don, Detroit	102	55	53.9	554	5.43	3	2.9	27	3	2.9	10	61	67
Martin, Jamie, St. Louis	34	23	67.6	241	7.09	3	8.8	t22	2	5.9	4	34	92
Matthews, Shane, Chicago	17	13	76.5	158	9.29	1	5.9	26	0	0.0	1	3	124
McMahon, Jim, Green Bay	4	3	75.0	39	9.75	0	0.0	24	0	0.0	0	0	105
Milanovich, Scott, Tampa Bay	3	2	66.7	9	3.00	0	0.0	8	0	0.0	0	0	70
Mitchell, Brian, Washington	1	0	0.0	0	0.00	0	0.0	0	0	0.0	0	0	39
Mitchell, Scott, Detroit	437	253	57.9	2917	6.68	17	3.9	t62	17	3.9	36	199	74
Moon, Warren, Minnesota	247	134	54.3	1610	6.52	7	2.8	t54	9	3.6	19	122	68
Nagle, Browning, Atlanta	13	6	46.2	59	4.54	1	7.7	17	2	15.4	4	20	45

Player, Team	Att.	Comp.	Pct. Comp.	Yds.	Avg. Gain	TD	Pct. TD	Long	Int.	Pct. Int.	Sack	Yds. Lost	Rat. Pts.
Nussmeier, Doug, New Orleans	50	28	56.0	272	5.44	1	2.0	t57	1	2.0	3	17	69.8
Peete, Rodney, Philadelphia	134	80	59.7	992	7.40	3	2.2	62	5	3.7	11	53	74.6
Phillips, Lawrence, St. Louis	0	0	....	0	....	0	....	....	0	....	1	12	....
Rice, Jerry, San Francisco	1	0	0.0	0	0.00	0	0.0	0	0	0.0	0	0	39.6
Royals, Mark, Detroit	1	1	100.0	-8	-8.00	0	0.0	-8	0	0.0	0	0	79.2
Rypien, Mark, Philadelphia	13	10	76.9	76	5.85	1	7.7	16	0	0.0	0	0	116.2
Sanders, Barry, Detroit	1	0	0.0	0	0.00	0	0.0	0	1	100.0	0	0	0.0
Sauerbrun, Todd, Chicago	2	2	100.0	63	31.50	0	0.0	47	0	0.0	0	0	118.8
Stenstrom, Steve, Chicago	4	3	75.0	37	9.25	0	0.0	28	0	0.0	1	5	103.1
Walker, Jay, Minnesota	2	2	100.0	31	15.50	0	0.0	19	0	0.0	0	0	118.8
Walsh, Chris, Minnesota	1	0	0.0	0	0.00	0	0.0	0	0	0.0	0	0	39.6
Walsh, Steve, St. Louis	77	33	42.9	344	4.47	0	0.0	32	5	6.5	4	27	29.4
Weldon, Casey, Tampa Bay	9	5	55.6	76	8.44	0	0.0	42	1	11.1	2	10	44.0
Wheatley, Tyrone, N.Y. Giants	1	1	100.0	24	24.00	1	100.0	t24	0	0.0	0	0	158.3
Williams, Sherman, Dallas	1	0	0.0	0	0.00	0	0.0	0	0	0.0	0	0	39.6
Wilson, Wade, Dallas	18	8	44.4	79	4.39	0	0.0	20	1	5.6	1	7	34.3
Young, Steve, San Francisco	316	214	67.7	2410	7.63	14	4.4	52	6	1.9	34	160	97.2

t—touchdown.

RECEIVING

INDIVIDUAL

BESTS OF THE SEASON

Receptions, season
NFC: 108—Jerry Rice, San Francisco.
AFC: 100—Carl Pickens, Cincinnati.

Receptions, game
AFC: 16—Keenan McCardell, Jacksonville at St. Louis, Oct. 20 (232 yards, 0 TDs).
NFC: 13—Larry Centers, Arizona vs. St. Louis, Sept. 29 (83 yards, 1 TD).

Yards, season
NFC: 1338—Isaac Bruce, St. Louis.
AFC: 1244—Jimmy Smith, Jacksonville.

Yards, game
AFC: 232—Keenan McCardell, Jacksonville at St. Louis, Oct. 20 (16 receptions, 0 TDs).
NFC: 229—Isaac Bruce, St. Louis at Baltimore, Oct. 27 (11 receptions, 1 TD).

Longest gain
AFC: 95—Quinn Early, (from Todd Collins), Buffalo at Indianapolis, Dec. 1 (TD).
NFC: 82—Jake Reed, (from Brad Johnson), Minnesota at Oakland, Nov. 17 (TD).

Yards per reception, season
NFC: 19.5—Henry Ellard, Washington.
AFC: 18.4—Chris Sanders, Houston.

Touchdowns, season
AFC: 14—Tony Martin, San Diego; Michael Jackson, Baltimore.
NFC: 11—Irving Fryar, Philadelphia.

Team leaders, receptions
AFC:

Baltimore	76	Michael Jackson
Buffalo	66	Andre Reed
Cincinnati	100	Carl Pickens
Denver	80	Shannon Sharpe
Houston	53	Frank Wycheck
Indianapolis	64	Marvin Harrison
Jacksonville	85	Keenan McCardell
Kansas City	60	Kimble Anders
Miami	74	O.J. McDuffie
New England	90	Terry Glenn
N.Y. Jets	84	Wayne Chrebet
Oakland	90	Tim Brown
Pittsburgh	72	Andre Hastings
San Diego	85	Tony Martin
Seattle	57	Joey Galloway

NFC:

Arizona	99	Larry Centers
Atlanta	75	Bert Emanuel
Carolina	61	Wesley Walls
Chicago	81	Curtis Conway
Dallas	64	Michael Irvin
Detroit	106	Herman Moore
Green Bay	56	Antonio Freeman
Minnesota	96	Cris Carter
New Orleans	50	Torrance Small
N.Y. Giants	53	Chris Calloway
		Thomas Lewis
Philadelphia	88	Irving Fryar
San Francisco	108	Jerry Rice
St. Louis	84	Isaac Bruce
Tampa Bay	65	Mike Alstott
Washington	52	Henry Ellard

NFL LEADERS

Player, Team	No.	Yds.	Avg.	Long	TD
Rice, Jerry, San Francisco	108	1254	11.6	39	8
Moore, Herman, Detroit	106	1296	12.2	t50	9

Player, Team	No.	Yds.	Avg.	Long	T
Pickens, Carl, Cincinnati*	100	1180	11.8	t61	1
Centers, Larry, Arizona	99	766	7.7	39	
Carter, Cris, Minnesota	96	1163	12.1	t43	1
Perriman, Brett, Detroit	94	1021	10.9	44	
Glenn, Terry, New England*	90	1132	12.6	t37	
Brown, Tim, Oakland*	90	1104	12.3	t42	
Fryar, Irving, Philadelphia	88	1195	13.6	42	1
Martin, Tony, San Diego*	85	1171	13.8	55	1
McCardell, Keenan, Jacksonville*	85	1129	13.3	52	
Bruce, Isaac, St. Louis	84	1338	15.9	70	
Chrebet, Wayne, N.Y. Jets*	84	909	10.8	44	
Smith, Jimmy, Jacksonville*	83	1244	15.0	62	
Conway, Curtis, Chicago	81	1049	13.0	t58	
Sharpe, Shannon, Denver*	80	1062	13.3	51	1
Jackson, Michael, Baltimore*	76	1201	15.8	t86	1
Emanuel, Bert, Atlanta	75	921	12.3	53	
McDuffie, O.J., Miami*	74	918	12.4	36	
Reed, Jake, Minnesota	72	1320	18.3	t82	
Hastings, Andre, Pittsburgh*	72	739	10.3	38	
Jones, Chris T., Philadelphia	70	859	12.3	38	
Sanders, Frank, Arizona	69	813	11.8	34	
Mathis, Terance, Atlanta	69	771	11.2	55	
Reed, Andre, Buffalo*	66	1036	15.7	t67	
Alstott, Mike, Tampa Bay	65	557	8.6	29	
Irvin, Michael, Dallas	64	962	15.0	61	
Harrison, Marvin, Indianapolis*	64	836	13.1	41	
Johnson, Keyshawn, N.Y. Jets*	63	844	13.4	50	
Alexander, Derrick, Baltimore*	62	1099	17.7	t64	

*AFC.
t—touchdown.
Leader based on most passes caught.

AFC

Player, Team	No.	Yds.	Avg.	Long	T
Abdul-Jabbar, Karim, Miami	23	139	6.0	23	
Alexander, Derrick, Baltimore	62	1099	17.7	t64	
Allen, Marcus, Kansas City	27	270	10.0	59	
Anders, Kimble, Kansas City	60	529	8.8	45	
Anderson, Richie, N.Y. Jets	44	385	8.8	48	
Arnold, Jahine, Pittsburgh	6	76	12.7	26	
Arvie, Herman, Baltimore	1	1	1.0	t1	
Aska, Joe, Oakland	8	63	7.9	22	
Bailey, Aaron, Indianapolis	18	302	16.8	40	
Bailey, Henry, N.Y. Jets	5	65	13.0	28	
Bailey, Victor, Kansas City	1	12	12.0	12	
Barnett, Fred, Miami	36	562	15.6	66	
Bartrum, Mike, New England	1	1	1.0	t1	
Battaglia, Marco, Cincinnati	8	79	9.9	17	
Baxter, Fred, N.Y. Jets	7	114	16.3	23	
Bennett, Donnell, Kansas City	8	21	2.6	10	
Bettis, Jerome, Pittsburgh	22	122	5.5	16	
Bieniemy, Eric, Cincinnati	32	272	8.5	42	
Bishop, Harold, Baltimore	2	22	11.0	13	
Blades, Brian, Seattle	43	556	12.9	t80	
Botkin, Kirk, Pittsburgh	4	36	9.0	17	
Bradley, Freddie, San Diego	1	20	20.0	20	
Brady, Kyle, N.Y. Jets	15	144	9.6	22	
Brantley, Chris, Buffalo	5	47	9.4	t22	
Broussard, Steve, Seattle	6	26	4.3	9	
Brown, Derek, Jacksonville	17	141	8.3	16	
Brown, Tim, Oakland	90	1104	12.3	t42	
Brown, Troy, New England	21	222	10.6	38	
Bruener, Mark, Pittsburgh	12	141	11.8	36	
Burke, John, New England	1	19	19.0	19	
Byars, Keith, Mia.-N.E.	32	289	9.0	27	

layer, Team	No.	Yds.	Avg.	Long	TD
yner, Earnest, Baltimore	30	270	9.0	40	1
arolan, Brett, Miami	4	48	12.0	21	1
arswell, Dwayne, Denver	15	85	5.7	11	0
arter, Dale, Kansas City	6	89	14.8	t46	1
arter, Ki-Jana, Cincinnati	22	169	7.7	20	1
ash, Keith, Kansas City	14	80	5.7	20	0
hamberlain, Byron, Denver	12	129	10.8	17	0
hrebet, Wayne, N.Y. Jets	84	909	10.8	44	3
ine, Tony, Buffalo	19	117	6.2	15	1
bates, Ben, New England	62	682	11.0	t84	9
obb, Reggie, N.Y. Jets	4	23	5.8	12	0
oleman, Andre, San Diego	36	486	13.5	50	2
oons, Rob, Buffalo	1	12	12.0	12	0
opeland, Russell, Buffalo	7	85	12.1	31	0
othran, Jeff, Cincinnati	7	49	7.0	14	0
raver, Aaron, Denver	39	297	7.6	t39	1
rockett, Zack, Indianapolis	11	96	8.7	32	1
rumpler, Carlester, Seattle	26	258	9.9	26	0
unningham, Rick, Oakland	1	3	3.0	t3	1
avis, Terrell, Denver	36	310	8.6	23	2
avis, Tyrone, N.Y. Jets	1	6	6.0	6	0
avis, Willie, Houston	39	464	11.9	49	6
avison, Jerone, Oakland	4	21	5.3	8	0
awkins, Sean, Indianapolis	54	751	13.9	42	1
awson, Lake, Kansas City	5	83	16.6	25	1
ilger, Ken, Indianapolis	42	503	12.0	51	4
oering, Chris, Indianapolis	1	10	10.0	10	0
rayton, Troy, Stl.-Mia.*	28	331	11.8	51	0
udley, Rickey, Oakland	34	386	11.4	t62	4
unn, David, Cincinnati	32	509	15.9	40	1
arly, Quinn, Buffalo	50	798	16.0	t95	4
lison, 'OMar, San Diego	3	15	5.0	6	0
thridge, Ray, Baltimore	2	24	12.0	15	0
aulk, Marshall, Indianapolis	56	428	7.6	30	0
auria, Christian, Seattle	18	214	11.9	t23	1
enner, Derrick, Oakland	31	252	8.1	t23	4
etcher, Terrell, San Diego	61	476	7.8	41	2
oyd, Malcolm, Houston	10	145	14.5	t63	1
alloway, Joey, Seattle	57	987	17.3	t65	7
ardner, Carwell, Baltimore	7	28	4.0	7	0
ash, Sam, New England	33	276	8.4	28	2
eorge, Eddie, Houston	23	182	7.9	17	0
lenn, Terry, New England	90	1132	12.6	t37	6
lover, Andrew, Oakland	9	101	11.2	25	1
raham, Hason, New England	5	64	12.8	23	0
raham, Jeff, N.Y. Jets	50	788	15.8	t78	6
ray, Oscar, Seattle	1	5	5.0	5	0
reen, Eric, Baltimore	15	150	10.0	23	1
rier, Marrio, New England	1	8	8.0	8	0
riffith, Rich, Jacksonville	5	53	10.6	18	0
roce, Clif, Indianapolis	13	106	8.2	24	0
allock, Ty, Jacksonville	1	5	5.0	5	0
armon, Ronnie, Houston	42	488	11.6	43	2
arris, Ronnie, Seattle	2	26	13.0	21	0
arrison, Marvin, Indianapolis	64	836	13.1	41	8
astings, Andre, Pittsburgh	72	739	10.3	38	6
ayden, Aaron, San Diego	1	10	10.0	10	0
ayes, Jonathan, Pittsburgh	2	14	7.0	7	0
earst, Garrison, Cincinnati	12	131	10.9	40	1
ebron, Vaughn, Denver	7	43	6.1	11	0
ill, Greg, Kansas City	3	60	20.0	t34	1
ill, Randal, Miami	21	409	19.5	61	4
obbs, Daryl, Oakland	44	423	9.6	29	3
olliday, Corey, Pittsburgh	1	7	7.0	7	0
olmes, Darick, Buffalo	16	102	6.4	20	1
orn, Joe, Kansas City	2	30	15.0	21	0
ughes, Danan, Kansas City	17	167	9.8	26	1
undon, James, Cincinnati	1	14	14.0	t14	1
ackson, Michael, Baltimore	76	1201	15.8	t86	14
ackson, Willie, Jacksonville	33	486	14.7	58	3
efferson, Shawn, New England	50	771	15.4	42	4
ells, Dietrich, New England	1	5	5.0	5	0

Player, Team	No.	Yds.	Avg.	Long	TD
Jett, James, Oakland	43	601	14.0	t58	4
Johnson, Charles, Pittsburgh	60	1008	16.8	t70	3
Johnson, Keyshawn, N.Y. Jets	63	844	13.4	50	8
Johnson, Lonnie, Buffalo	46	457	9.9	33	0
Johnson, Reggie, Kansas City	18	189	10.5	26	1
Jones, Charlie, San Diego	41	524	12.8	t63	4
Jones, James, Baltimore	1	2	2.0	t2	1
Jordan, Charles, Miami	7	152	21.7	43	0
Kaufman, Napoleon, Oakland	22	143	6.5	19	1
Kinchen, Brian, Baltimore	55	581	10.6	29	1
Kinchen, Todd, Denver	1	27	27.0	27	0
LaChapelle, Sean, Kansas City	27	422	15.6	69	2
Lester, Tim, Pittsburgh	7	70	10.0	19	0
Lewis, Jermaine, Baltimore	5	78	15.6	24	1
Lewis, Roderick, Houston	7	50	7.1	18	0
Louchiey, Corey, Buffalo	1	0	0.0	0	0
Martin, Curtis, New England	46	333	7.2	41	3
Martin, Tony, San Diego	85	1171	13.8	55	14
Maston, Le'Shai, Jacksonville	6	54	9.0	17	0
May, Deems, San Diego	19	188	9.9	39	0
McAfee, Fred, Pittsburgh	5	21	4.2	9	0
McCaffrey, Ed, Denver	48	553	11.5	t39	7
McCardell, Keenan, Jacksonville	85	1129	13.3	52	3
McDuffie, O.J., Miami	74	918	12.4	36	8
McGee, Tony, Cincinnati	38	446	11.7	22	4
McKnight, James, Seattle	1	73	73.0	73	0
McNair, Todd, Kansas City	21	181	8.6	29	1
McPhail, Jerris, Miami	20	282	14.1	52	0
Means, Natrone, Jacksonville	7	45	6.4	t11	1
Meggett, David, New England	33	292	8.8	26	0
Miller, Anthony, Denver	56	735	13.1	46	3
Miller, Scott, Miami	9	116	12.9	22	0
Mills, Ernie, Pittsburgh	7	92	13.1	22	1
Milne, Brian, Cincinnati	3	29	9.7	15	0
Mitchell, Pete, Jacksonville	52	575	11.1	30	1
Mitchell, Shannon, San Diego	10	57	5.7	25	0
Moore, Will, New England	3	37	12.3	16	0
Morris, Bam, Baltimore	25	242	9.7	t52	1
Moulds, Eric, Buffalo	20	279	14.0	47	2
Murrell, Adrian, N.Y. Jets	17	81	4.8	30	1
Norgard, Erik, Houston	1	1	1.0	t1	1
Ogden, Jonathan, Baltimore	1	1	1.0	t1	1
Parmalee, Bernie, Miami	21	189	9.0	17	0
Pegram, Erric, Pittsburgh	17	112	6.6	14	0
Penn, Chris, Kansas City	49	628	12.8	22	5
Pickens, Carl, Cincinnati	100	1180	11.8	t61	12
Pollard, Marcus, Indianapolis	6	86	14.3	t48	1
Pritchard, Mike, Seattle	21	328	15.6	44	1
Pritchett, Stanley, Miami	33	354	10.7	t74	2
Proehl, Ricky, Seattle	23	309	13.4	56	2
Pupunu, Alfred, San Diego	24	271	11.3	41	1
Reed, Andre, Buffalo	66	1036	15.7	t67	6
Reeves, Walter, San Diego	1	3	3.0	3	0
Richardson, Tony, Kansas City	2	18	9.0	17	1
Rivers, Reggie, Denver	1	-1	-1.0	-1	0
Roche, Brian, San Diego	13	111	8.5	19	0
Russell, Derek, Houston	34	421	12.4	29	2
Russell, Leonard, San Diego	13	180	13.8	35	0
Sadowski, Troy, Cincinnati	3	15	5.0	8	0
Sanders, Chris, Houston	48	882	18.4	t83	4
Scott, Darnay, Cincinnati	58	833	14.4	t50	5
Sharpe, Shannon, Denver	80	1062	13.3	51	10
Shedd, Kenny, Oakland	3	87	29.0	51	1
Sherrard, Mike, Denver	16	185	11.6	t25	1
Slaughter, Webster, N.Y. Jets	32	434	13.6	53	2
Smith, Jimmy, Jacksonville	83	1244	15.0	62	7
Smith, Lamar, Seattle	9	58	6.4	22	0
Smith, Rod, Denver	16	237	14.8	t49	2
Spikes, Irving, Miami	8	81	10.1	19	1
Stablein, Brian, Indianapolis	18	192	10.7	t30	1
Stewart, James, Jacksonville	30	177	5.9	t21	2
Stewart, Kordell, Pittsburgh	17	293	17.2	48	3

1996 STATISTICS Receiving

Player, Team	No.	Yds.	Avg.	Long	TD
Still, Bryan, San Diego	6	142	23.7	56	0
Stock, Mark, Indianapolis	2	24	12.0	13	0
Strong, Mack, Seattle	9	78	8.7	20	0
Tasker, Steve, Buffalo	21	372	17.7	62	3
Thigpen, Yancey, Pittsburgh	12	244	20.3	39	2
Thomas, Lamar, Miami	10	166	16.6	34	1
Thomas, Rodney, Houston	13	128	9.8	33	0
Thomas, Thurman, Buffalo	26	254	9.8	69	0
Tindale, Tim, Buffalo	1	-1	-1.0	-1	0
Turner, Floyd, Baltimore	38	461	12.1	t27	2
Van Dyke, Alex, N.Y. Jets	17	118	6.9	12	1
Vanover, Tamarick, Kansas City	21	241	11.5	24	1
Wainright, Frank, Miami	1	2	2.0	t2	1
Walker, Derrick, Kansas City	9	73	8.1	24	1
Warren, Chris, Seattle	40	273	6.8	33	0
Warren, Lamont, Indianapolis	22	174	7.9	17	0
Williams, Harvey, Oakland	22	143	6.5	20	0
Williams, Ronnie, Seattle	5	25	5.0	11	1
Wilson, Robert, Miami	2	5	2.5	t3	1
Wilson, Sheddrick, Houston	2	24	12.0	14	0
Witman, Jon, Pittsburgh	2	15	7.5	11	0
Workman, Vince, Indianapolis	4	36	9.0	18	0
Wycheck, Frank, Houston	53	511	9.6	29	6

*Includes both NFC and AFC statistics.
t—touchdown.

NFC

Player, Team	No.	Yds.	Avg.	Long	TD
Alexander, Kevin, N.Y. Giants	4	88	22.0	35	0
Allen, Terry, Washington	32	194	6.1	28	0
Alstott, Mike, Tampa Bay	65	557	8.6	29	3
Anderson, Jamal, Atlanta	49	473	9.7	34	1
Anderson, Stevie, Arizona	4	64	16.0	19	0
Armstrong, Tyji, Dallas	2	10	5.0	6	0
Asher, Jamie, Washington	42	481	11.5	34	4
Bates, Mario, New Orleans	13	44	3.4	15	0
Beebe, Don, Green Bay	39	699	17.9	t80	4
Bell, William, Washington	3	23	7.7	12	0
Bennett, Edgar, Green Bay	31	176	5.7	t25	1
Birden, J.J., Atlanta	30	319	10.6	57	2
Bjornson, Eric, Dallas	48	388	8.1	25	3
Bowie, Larry, Washington	3	17	5.7	8	0
Brooks, Bill, Washington	17	224	13.2	31	0
Brooks, Reggie, Tampa Bay	3	13	4.3	9	0
Brooks, Robert, Green Bay	23	344	15.0	38	4
Brown, Derek, New Orleans	8	54	6.8	18	0
Brown, Tyrone, Atlanta	28	325	11.6	38	1
Bruce, Isaac, St. Louis	84	1338	15.9	70	7
Caldwell, Mike, San Francisco	2	9	4.5	8	0
Calloway, Chris, N.Y. Giants	53	739	13.9	36	4
Carrier, Mark, Carolina	58	808	13.9	39	6
Carter, Cris, Minnesota	96	1163	12.1	t43	10
Carter, Pat, Arizona	26	329	12.7	36	1
Carter, Tony, Chicago	41	233	5.7	29	0
Cash, Kerry, Chicago	4	42	10.5	14	0
Centers, Larry, Arizona	99	766	7.7	39	7
Chmura, Mark, Green Bay	28	370	13.2	29	0
Clay, Hayward, St. Louis	4	51	12.8	34	0
Conway, Curtis, Chicago	81	1049	13.0	t58	7
Conwell, Ernie, St. Louis	15	164	10.9	26	0
Cooper, Adrian, San Francisco	1	11	11.0	11	0
Cross, Howard, N.Y. Giants	22	178	8.1	19	1
Dawsey, Lawrence, N.Y. Giants	18	233	12.9	28	0
DeLong, Greg, Minnesota	8	34	4.3	9	0
DeRamus, Lee, New Orleans	15	182	12.1	t28	1
Douglas, Omar, N.Y. Giants	1	8	8.0	8	0
Dowdell, Marcus, Arizona	20	318	15.9	t64	2
Downs, Gary, N.Y. Giants	3	20	6.7	13	0
Dunn, Jason, Philadelphia	15	332	22.1	58	2
Edwards, Anthony, Arizona	29	311	10.7	31	0
Elias, Keith, N.Y. Giants	8	51	6.4	11	0

Player, Team	No.	Yds.	Avg.	Long	T*
Ellard, Henry, Washington	52	1014	19.5	51	
Ellison, Jerry, Tampa Bay	18	208	11.6	42	
Emanuel, Bert, Atlanta	75	921	12.3	53	
Engram, Bobby, Chicago	33	389	11.8	24	
Evans, Charles, Minnesota	22	135	6.1	16	
Faulkerson, Mike, Chicago	1	1	1.0	t1	
Flanigan, Jim, Chicago	1	1	1.0	t1	
Floyd, William, San Francisco	26	197	7.6	24	
Freeman, Antonio, Green Bay	56	933	16.7	t51	
Frisch, David, Minnesota	3	27	9.0	21	
Fryar, Irving, Philadelphia	88	1195	13.6	42	1
Galbraith, Scott, Washington	8	89	11.1	t30	
Garner, Charlie, Philadelphia	14	92	6.6	13	
Goodwin, Hunter, Minnesota	1	24	24.0	24	
Graham, Scottie, Minnesota	7	48	6.9	18	
Green, Harold, St. Louis	37	246	6.6	19	
Green, Paul, New Orleans	7	91	13.0	23	
Green, Robert, Chicago	13	78	6.0	18	
Green, Willie, Carolina	46	614	13.3	50	
Greene, Scott, Carolina	2	7	3.5	6	
Griffith, Howard, Carolina	27	223	8.3	21	
Guess, Terry, New Orleans	2	69	34.5	t57	
Hampton, Rodney, N.Y. Giants	15	82	5.5	16	
Harper, Alvin, Tampa Bay	19	289	15.2	t40	
Harris, Derrick, St. Louis	4	17	4.3	8	
Harris, Jackie, Tampa Bay	30	349	11.6	36	
Harris, Raymont, Chicago	32	296	9.3	47	
Hawkins, Courtney, Tampa Bay	46	544	11.8	45	
Hayes, Mercury, New Orleans	4	101	25.3	50	
Haynes, Michael, New Orleans	44	786	17.9	51	
Henderson, William, Green Bay	27	203	7.5	27	
Heyward, Craig, Atlanta	16	168	10.5	25	
Hicks, Michael, Chicago	1	-1	-1.0	-1	
Hoard, Leroy, Bal.-Min.*	11	133	12.1	37	
Howard, Desmond, Green Bay	13	95	7.3	12	
Hunter, Earnest, Bal.-N.O.*	18	163	9.1	25	
Huntley, Richard, Atlanta	1	14	14.0	14	
Ingram, Mark, Philadelphia	2	33	16.5	20	
Irvin, Michael, Dallas	64	962	15.0	61	
Ismail, Qadry, Minnesota	22	351	16.0	t54	
Ismail, Raghib, Carolina	12	214	17.8	51	
Jackson, Jack, Chicago	4	39	9.8	14	
Jackson, Keith, Green Bay	40	505	12.6	t51	1
Jeffires, Haywood, New Orleans	20	215	10.8	t27	
Jenkins, James, Washington	1	7	7.0	7	
Jennings, Keith, Chicago	6	56	9.3	20	
Johnson, Anthony, Carolina	26	192	7.4	55	
Johnson, Jimmie, Philadelphia	7	127	18.1	31	
Johnson, LeShon, Arizona	15	176	11.7	35	
Johnson, Tony, New Orleans	7	76	10.9	17	
Johnston, Daryl, Dallas	43	278	6.5	23	
Jones, Brent, San Francisco	33	428	13.0	39	
Jones, Chris T., Philadelphia	70	859	12.3	38	
Jordan, Andrew, Minnesota	19	128	6.7	15	
Kennison, Eddie, St. Louis	54	924	17.1	t77	
Kirby, Terry, San Francisco	52	439	8.4	52	
Kozlowski, Brian, N.Y. Giants	1	4	4.0	t4	
Krieg, Dave, Chicago	1	5	5.0	5	
Laing, Aaron, St. Louis	13	116	8.9	22	
Lee, Amp, Minnesota	54	422	7.8	21	
Levens, Dorsey, Green Bay	31	226	7.3	19	
Lewis, Thomas, N.Y. Giants	53	694	13.1	34	
Logan, Marc, Washington	23	269	11.7	26	
Loville, Derek, San Francisco	16	138	8.6	t44	
Lusk, Henry, New Orleans	27	210	7.8	24	
Lynn, Anthony, San Francisco	2	14	7.0	8	
Lyons, Mitch, Atlanta	4	16	4.0	5	
Manuel, Sean, San Francisco	3	18	6.0	7	
Marshall, Marvin, Tampa Bay	2	27	13.5	20	
Martin, Kelvin, Dallas	25	380	15.2	t60	
Mathis, Terance, Atlanta	69	771	11.2	55	
Matthews, Aubrey, Detroit	3	41	13.7	21	

ayer, Team	No.	Yds.	Avg.	Long	TD
ayes, Derrick, Green Bay	6	46	7.7	12	2
cElroy, Leeland, Arizona	5	41	8.2	t22	1
cIntyre, Guy, Philadelphia	1	4	4.0	4	0
cWilliams, Johnny, Arizona	7	80	11.4	21	1
etcalf, Eric, Atlanta	54	599	11.1	67	6
etzelaars, Pete, Detroit	17	146	8.6	20	0
ckens, Terry, Green Bay	18	161	8.9	19	2
tchell, Brian, Washington	32	286	8.9	20	0
tchell, Johnny, Dallas	1	17	17.0	17	0
oore, Dave, Tampa Bay	27	237	8.8	23	3
oore, Herman, Detroit	106	1296	12.2	t50	9
oore, Jerald, St. Louis	3	13	4.3	7	0
oore, Rob, Arizona	58	1016	17.5	69	4
orton, Johnnie, Detroit	55	714	13.0	t62	6
uhammad, Muhsin, Carolina	25	407	16.3	t54	1
al, Lorenzo, New Orleans	31	194	6.3	23	1
ely, Bobby, Chicago	9	92	10.2	21	0
iver, Winslow, Carolina	15	144	9.6	29	0
vens, Terrell, San Francisco	35	520	14.9	t46	4
lmer, David, Minnesota	6	40	6.7	20	0
rriman, Brett, Detroit	94	1021	10.9	44	5
illips, Lawrence, St. Louis	8	28	3.5	t11	1
erce, Aaron, N.Y. Giants	11	144	13.1	30	1
pson, Ted, San Francisco	26	301	11.6	t39	6
eston, Roell, Atlanta	21	208	9.9	t17	1
ce, Derek, Detroit	1	14	14.0	14	0
ed, Jake, Minnesota	72	1320	18.3	t82	7
ett, Errict, Tampa Bay	4	11	2.8	t5	1
ce, Jerry, San Francisco	108	1254	11.6	39	8
son, Andre, Jac.-G.B.*	47	593	12.6	t61	3
vers, Ron, Detroit	2	28	14.0	19	0
berts, Ray, Detroit	0	5	...	5	0
binson, Greg, St. Louis	1	6	6.0	6	0
ss, Jermaine, St. Louis	15	160	10.7	28	0
laam, Rashaan, Chicago	7	44	6.3	t11	1
nders, Barry, Detroit	24	147	6.1	28	0
nders, Deion, Dallas	36	475	13.2	41	1
nders, Frank, Arizona	69	813	11.8	34	4
xton, Brian, N.Y. Giants	4	31	7.8	14	0
ott, Freddie, Atlanta	7	80	11.4	27	0
ay, Mark, Philadelphia	19	260	13.7	35	0
epherd, Leslie, Washington	23	344	15.0	t52	3
ngleton, Nate, San Francisco	1	11	11.0	11	0
oan, David, Detroit	7	51	7.3	18	0
all, Torrance, New Orleans	50	558	11.2	41	2
nith, Cedric, Arizona	3	3	1.0	2	1
nith, Emmitt, Dallas	47	249	5.3	21	3
nith, Irv, New Orleans	15	144	9.6	37	0
nith, Robert, Minnesota	7	39	5.6	16	0
lomon, Freddie, Philadelphia	8	125	15.6	23	0

Player, Team	No.	Yds.	Avg.	Long	TD
Spears, Marcus, Chicago	1	1	1.0	t1	1
Stokes, J.J., San Francisco	18	249	13.8	40	0
Stone, Dwight, Carolina	1	11	11.0	11	0
Terry, Ryan, Arizona	1	0	0.0	0	0
Thomas, J.T., St. Louis	7	46	6.6	11	0
Thomas, Robb, Tampa Bay	33	427	12.9	t31	2
Thomason, Jeff, Green Bay	3	45	15.0	24	0
Thompson, Leroy, Tampa Bay	5	36	7.2	12	0
Timpson, Michael, Chicago	62	802	12.9	49	0
Tobeck, Robbie, Atlanta	2	15	7.5	14	1
Toomer, Amani, N.Y. Giants	1	12	12.0	12	0
Turner, Kevin, Philadelphia	43	409	9.5	41	1
Uwaezuoke, Iheanyi, S.F.	7	91	13.0	t29	1
Vardell, Tommy, San Francisco	28	179	6.4	22	0
Walker, Herschel, Dallas	7	89	12.7	24	0
Walls, Wesley, Carolina	61	713	11.7	t40	10
Walsh, Chris, Minnesota	4	39	9.8	17	1
Ware, Derek, Dallas	1	5	5.0	5	0
Watters, Ricky, Philadelphia	51	444	8.7	36	0
Way, Charles, N.Y. Giants	32	328	10.3	t37	1
West, Ed, Philadelphia	8	91	11.4	29	0
Westbrook, Michael, Washington	34	505	14.9	45	1
Wetnight, Ryan, Chicago	21	223	10.6	38	1
Wheatley, Tyrone, N.Y. Giants	12	51	4.3	13	2
Whittle, Ricky, New Orleans	26	162	6.2	28	0
Williams, Calvin, Bal.-Phi.*	15	93	6.2	19	1
Williams, Karl, Tampa Bay	22	246	11.2	25	0
Williams, Kevin, Dallas	27	323	12.0	31	1
Williams, Sherman, Dallas	5	41	8.2	13	0
Williams, Stepfret, Dallas	1	32	32.0	32	0
Wright, Alexander, St. Louis	2	24	12.0	13	0
Zellars, Ray, New Orleans	9	45	5.0	12	0

*Includes both NFC and AFC statistics.
t—touchdown.

PLAYERS WITH TWO CLUBS

Player, Team	No.	Yds.	Avg.	Long	TD
Byars, Keith, Miami	5	40	8.0	16	0
Byars, Keith, New England	27	249	9.2	27	2
Drayton, Troy, St. Louis	2	11	5.5	6	0
Drayton, Troy, Miami	26	320	12.3	51	0
Hoard, Leroy, Baltimore	1	4	4.0	4	0
Hoard, Leroy, Minnesota	10	129	12.9	37	0
Hunter, Earnest, Baltimore	1	25	25.0	25	0
Hunter, Earnest, New Orleans	17	138	8.1	22	0
Rison, Andre, Jacksonville	34	458	13.5	t61	2
Rison, Andre, Green Bay	13	135	10.4	t22	1
Williams, Calvin, Baltimore	13	85	6.5	19	1
Williams, Calvin, Philadelphia	2	8	4.0	4	0

SCORING

AFC

Team	Total TD	TD Rush	TD Pass	TD Misc.	XP	2Pt.	XPA	FG	FGA	Safeties	Total Pts
New England	48	15	27	6	39	4	42	27	35	1	41
Denver	47	20	26	1	46	0	46	21	28	0	39
Cincinnati	43	14	25	4	41	2	41	23	28	0	37
Baltimore	45	10	34	1	34	5	35	19	25	0	37
Houston	35	12	22	1	35	0	35	32	38	2	34
Pittsburgh	39	18	15	6	37	2	37	23	30	0	34
Oakland	38	7	28	3	36	0	36	24	31	2	34
Miami	41	14	22	5	35	1	36	18	29	1	33
Jacksonville	33	13	19	1	27	5	27	30	36	0	32
Buffalo	35	14	18	3	33	2	33	24	29	0	31
Indianapolis	30	9	16	5	27	0	27	36	40	1	31
Seattle	33	16	14	3	27	4	27	28	34	0	31
San Diego	32	7	23	2	31	0	31	29	36	0	31
Kansas City	35	15	18	2	34	0	34	17	24	1	29
N.Y. Jets	33	8	22	3	26	2	27	17	24	0	27
AFC total	567	192	329	46	508	27	514	368	467	8	508
AFC average	37.8	12.8	21.9	3.1	33.9	1.8	34.3	24.5	31.1	0.5	338

NFC

Team	Total TD	TD Rush	TD Pass	TD Misc.	XP	2Pt.	XPA	FG	FGA	Safeties	Total Pts
Green Bay	56	9	39	8	51	2	53	21	27	1	45
San Francisco	43	17	24	2	40	1	40	30	34	4	39
Carolina	36	9	22	5	34	1	35	37	45	2	36
Washington	41	27	12	2	40	0	40	26	32	0	36
Philadelphia	41	16	19	6	40	0	40	25	29	1	36
Atlanta	35	9	26	0	31	1	31	22	29	0	30
St. Louis	34	10	18	6	30	2	31	21	25	1	30
Detroit	38	15	20	3	36	1	36	12	17	0	30
Arizona	33	8	23	2	29	2	31	23	31	0	30
Minnesota	33	7	24	2	30	2	30	22	29	0	29
Dallas	27	14	12	1	24	2	25	32	36	0	28
Chicago	31	9	19	3	26	0	26	23	30	1	28
N.Y. Giants	24	4	14	6	22	0	22	24	27	2	24
New Orleans	24	10	13	1	18	2	18	21	25	0	22
Tampa Bay	21	8	12	1	18	1	19	25	32	0	22
NFC total	517	172	297	48	469	17	477	364	448	12	472
NFC average	34.5	11.5	19.8	3.2	31.3	1.1	31.8	24.3	29.9	0.8	314.
NFL total	1084	364	626	94	977	44	991	732	915	20	980
NFL average	36.1	12.1	20.9	3.1	32.6	1.5	33.0	24.4	30.5	0.7	326

INDIVIDUAL

BESTS OF THE SEASON

Points, season
NFC: 145—John Kasay, Carolina.
AFC: 135—Cary Blanchard, Indianapolis.

Touchdowns, season
NFC: 21—Terry Allen, Washington.
AFC: 17—Curtis Martin, New England.

Extra points, season
NFC: 51—Chris Jacke, Green Bay.
AFC: 46—Jason Elam, Denver.

Field goals, season
NFC: 37—John Kasay, Carolina.
AFC: 36—Cary Blanchard, Indianapolis.

Field goal attempts, season
NFC: 45—John Kasay, Carolina.
AFC: 40—Cary Blanchard, Indianapolis.

Longest field goal
AFC: 56—Al Del Greco, Houston vs. San Francisco, Oct. 27.
NFC: 54—Doug Brien, New Orleans vs. Chicago, Oct. 13; Morten Andersen, Atlanta at Dallas, Oct. 20.

Most points, game
NFC: 24—Irving Fryar, Philadelphia vs. Miami, Oct. 20.
AFC: 20—Curtis Martin, New England vs. Arizona, Sept. 15.

Team leaders, points
AFC:

Baltimore	91	Matt Stover
Buffalo	105	Steve Christie
Cincinnati	110	Doug Pelfrey
Denver	109	Jason Elam
Houston	131	Al Del Greco
Indianapolis	135	Cary Blanchard
Jacksonville	117	Mike Hollis
Kansas City	85	Pete Stoyanovich
Miami	89	Joe Nedney

ew England	120	Adam Vinatieri
Y. Jets	77	Nick Lowery
akland	108	Cole Ford
ttsburgh	106	Norm Johnson
an Diego	118	John Carney
attle	111	Todd Peterson
FC:		
izona	59	Kevin Butler
anta	97	Morten Andersen
arolina	145	John Kasay
icago	80	Jeff Jaeger
allas	120	Chris Boniol
etroit	72	Jason Hanson
een Bay	114	Chris Jacke
innesota	96	Scott Sisson
ew Orleans	81	Doug Brien
Y. Giants	94	Brad Daluiso
iladelphia	115	Gary Anderson
n Francisco	130	Jeff Wilkins
Louis	91	Chip Lohmiller
mpa Bay	93	Michael Husted
ashington	126	Terry Allen

NFL LEADERS

KICKERS

ayer, Team	XPM	XPA	FGM	FGA	Tot. Pts.
say, John, Carolina	34	35	37	45	145
anchard, Cary, Indianapolis*	27	27	36	40	135
l Greco, Al, Houston*	35	35	32	38	131
ilkins, Jeff, San Francisco	40	40	30	34	130
oniol, Chris, Dallas	24	25	32	36	120
natieri, Adam, New England*	39	42	27	35	120
rney, John, San Diego*	31	31	29	36	118
anton, Scott, Washington	40	40	26	32	118
ollis, Mike, Jacksonville*	27	27	30	36	117
derson, Gary, Philadelphia	40	40	25	29	115
cke, Chris, Green Bay	51	53	21	27	114
terson, Todd, Seattle*	27	27	28	34	111
lfrey, Doug, Cincinnati*	41	41	23	28	110
am, Jason, Denver*	46	46	21	28	109
rd, Cole, Oakland*	36	36	24	31	108
hnson, Norm, Pittsburgh*	37	37	23	30	106
ristie, Steve, Buffalo*	33	33	24	29	105
dersen, Morten, Atlanta	31	31	22	29	97
sson, Scott, Minnesota	30	30	22	29	96
luiso, Brad, N.Y. Giants	22	22	24	27	94

*AFC.

NON-KICKERS

ayer, Team	TD	RTD	PTD	MTD	2Pt.	Tot. Pts.
en, Terry, Washington	21	21	0	0	0	126
rtin, Curtis, New England*	17	14	3	0	1	104
ith, Emmitt, Dallas	15	12	3	0	0	90
vis, Terrell, Denver*	15	13	2	0	0	90
ckson, Michael, Baltimore*	14	0	14	0	2	88
rtin, Tony, San Diego*	14	0	14	0	0	84
tters, Ricky, Philadelphia	13	13	0	0	0	78
kens, Carl, Cincinnati*	12	0	12	0	1	74
ar, Irving, Philadelphia	11	0	11	0	0	66
nders, Barry, Detroit	11	11	0	0	0	66
ttis, Jerome, Pittsburgh*	11	11	0	0	0	66
nnison, Eddie, St. Louis	11	0	9	2	0	66
dul-Jabbar, Karim, Miami*	11	11	0	0	0	66
ckson, Keith, Green Bay	10	0	10	0	0	60
rter, Cris, Minnesota	10	0	10	0	0	60
lls, Wesley, Carolina	10	0	10	0	0	60
arpe, Shannon, Denver*	10	0	10	0	0	60
vens, Dorsey, Green Bay	10	5	5	0	0	60
wart, James, Jacksonville*	10	8	2	0	0	60
ore, Herman, Detroit	9	0	9	0	1	56

*AFC.

Player, Team	TD	RTD	PTD	MTD	2Pt.	Tot. Pts.
Coates, Ben, New England*	9	0	9	0	1	56
Alexander, Derrick, Baltimore*	9	0	9	0	1	56
Rice, Jerry, San Francisco	9	1	8	0	0	54
Allen, Marcus, Kansas City*	9	9	0	0	0	54
Brown, Tim, Oakland*	9	0	9	0	0	54
Centers, Larry, Arizona	9	2	7	0	0	54
Smith, Lamar, Seattle*	8	8	0	0	3	54
Carter, Ki-Jana, Cincinnati*	9	8	1	0	0	54
Freeman, Antonio, Green Bay	9	0	9	0	0	54
Johnson, Keyshawn, N.Y. Jets*	8	0	8	0	1	50

*AFC.

AFC

KICKERS

Player, Team	XPM	XPA	FGM	FGA	Tot. Pts.
Blanchard, Cary, Indianapolis	27	27	36	40	135
Carney, John, San Diego	31	31	29	36	118
Christie, Steve, Buffalo	33	33	24	29	105
Del Greco, Al, Houston	35	35	32	38	131
Elam, Jason, Denver	46	46	21	28	109
Ford, Cole, Oakland	36	36	24	31	108
Hollis, Mike, Jacksonville	27	27	30	36	117
Johnson, Norm, Pittsburgh	37	37	23	30	106
Lowery, Nick, N.Y. Jets	26	27	17	24	77
Nedney, Joe, Miami	35	36	18	29	89
Pelfrey, Doug, Cincinnati	41	41	23	28	110
Peterson, Todd, Seattle	27	27	28	34	111
Stover, Matt, Baltimore	34	35	19	25	91
Stoyanovich, Pete, Kansas City	34	34	17	24	85
Vinatieri, Adam, New England	39	42	27	35	120

NON-KICKERS

Player, Team	TD	RTD	PTD	MTD	2Pt.	Tot. Pts.
Abdul-Jabbar, Karim, Miami	11	11	0	0	0	66
Alexander, Derrick, Baltimore	9	0	9	0	1	56
Allen, Marcus, Kansas City	9	9	0	0	0	54
Ambrose, Ashley, Cincinnati	1	0	0	1	0	6
Anders, Kimble, Kansas City	4	2	2	0	0	24
Anderson, Richie, N.Y. Jets	1	1	0	0	0	6
Arvie, Herman, Baltimore	1	0	1	0	0	6
Aska, Joe, Oakland	1	1	0	0	0	6
Bailey, Aaron, Indianapolis	1	0	0	1	0	6
Ball, Jerry, Oakland	1	0	0	1	0	6
Barnett, Fred, Miami	3	0	3	0	0	18
Bartrum, Mike, New England	1	0	1	0	0	6
Belser, Jason, Indianapolis	2	0	0	2	0	12
Bettis, Jerome, Pittsburgh	11	11	0	0	0	66
Bieniemy, Eric, Cincinnati	2	2	0	0	0	12
Blackmon, Robert, Seattle	1	0	0	1	0	6
Blades, Brian, Seattle	2	0	2	0	0	12
Blake, Jeff, Cincinnati	2	2	0	0	0	12
Brady, Kyle, N.Y. Jets	1	0	1	0	1	8
Brantley, Chris, Buffalo	1	0	1	0	0	6
Braxton, Tyrone, Denver	1	0	0	1	0	6
Broussard, Steve, Seattle	1	1	0	0	0	6
Brown, Corwin, New England	1	0	0	1	0	6
Brown, Tim, Oakland	9	0	9	0	0	54
Bruener, Mark, Pittsburgh	0	0	0	0	1	2
Brunell, Mark, Jacksonville	3	3	0	0	2	22
Bruschi, Tedy, New England	1	0	0	1	0	6
Buckley, Terrell, Miami	1	0	0	1	0	6
Byars, Keith, New England	2	0	2	0	1	14
Byner, Earnest, Baltimore	5	4	1	0	0	30
Caldwell, Mike, Baltimore	1	0	0	1	0	6
Carolan, Brett, Miami	1	0	1	0	0	6
Carter, Dale, Kansas City	1	0	1	0	0	6
Carter, Ki-Jana, Cincinnati	9	8	1	0	0	54
Chrebet, Wayne, N.Y. Jets	3	0	3	0	0	18

Player, Team	Tot. TD	RTD	PTD	MTD	2Pt.	Tot. Pts.
Clark, Willie, San Diego	1	0	0	1	0	6
Cline, Tony, Buffalo	1	0	1	0	0	6
Coates, Ben, New England	9	0	9	0	1	56
Cobb, Reggie, N.Y. Jets	1	1	0	0	0	6
Coleman, Andre, San Diego	2	0	2	0	0	12
Cothran, Jeff, Cincinnati	1	1	0	0	0	6
Craver, Aaron, Denver	3	2	1	0	0	18
Crockett, Zack, Indianapolis	1	0	1	0	0	6
Cunningham, Rick, Oakland	1	0	1	0	0	6
Daniel, Eugene, Indianapolis	1	0	0	1	0	6
Davis, Terrell, Denver	15	13	2	0	0	90
Davis, Willie, Houston	6	0	6	0	0	36
Dawkins, Sean, Indianapolis	1	0	1	0	0	6
Dawson, Lake, Kansas City	1	0	1	0	0	6
Dent, Richard, Indianapolis	0	0	0	0	0	*2
Dilger, Ken, Indianapolis	4	0	4	0	0	24
Douglas, Hugh, N.Y. Jets	1	0	0	1	0	6
Drayton, Troy, Miami	0	0	0	0	1	2
Dudley, Rickey, Oakland	4	0	4	0	0	24
Dunn, David, Cincinnati	2	0	1	1	0	12
Early, Quinn, Buffalo	4	0	4	0	1	26
Elway, John, Denver	4	4	0	0	0	24
Faulk, Marshall, Indianapolis	7	7	0	0	0	42
Fauria, Christian, Seattle	1	0	1	0	0	6
Fenner, Derrick, Oakland	8	4	4	0	0	48
Fletcher, Terrell, San Diego	2	0	2	0	0	12
Floyd, Malcolm, Houston	1	0	1	0	0	6
Francis, James, Cincinnati	1	0	0	1	0	6
Galloway, Joey, Seattle	8	0	7	1	0	48
Gardner, Carwell, Baltimore	0	0	0	0	1	2
Gash, Sam, New England	2	0	2	0	1	14
George, Eddie, Houston	8	8	0	0	0	48
Glenn, Aaron, N.Y. Jets	2	0	0	2	0	12
Glenn, Terry, New England	6	0	6	0	0	36
Glover, Andrew, Oakland	1	0	1	0	0	6
Gordon, Darrien, San Diego	1	0	0	1	0	6
Graham, Jeff, N.Y. Jets	6	0	6	0	0	36
Green, Eric, Baltimore	1	0	1	0	0	6
Grier, Marrio, New England	1	1	0	0	0	6
Harbaugh, Jim, Indianapolis	1	1	0	0	0	6
Harmon, Ronnie, Houston	3	1	2	0	0	18
Harrison, Marvin, Indianapolis	8	0	8	0	0	48
Hastings, Andre, Pittsburgh	6	0	6	0	0	36
Hasty, James, Kansas City	1	0	0	1	0	6
Hearst, Garrison, Cincinnati	1	0	1	0	1	8
Herrod, Jeff, Indianapolis	1	0	0	1	0	6
Hill, Greg, Kansas City	5	4	1	0	0	30
Hill, Randal, Miami	4	0	4	0	0	24
Hill, Sean, Miami	1	0	0	1	0	6
Hobbs, Daryl, Oakland	3	0	3	0	0	18
Holmes, Darick, Buffalo	5	4	1	0	1	32
Hostetler, Jeff, Oakland	1	1	0	0	0	6
Hughes, Danan, Kansas City	1	0	1	0	0	6
Hundon, James, Cincinnati	1	0	1	0	0	6
Jackson, Calvin, Miami	1	0	0	1	0	6
Jackson, Michael, Baltimore	14	0	14	0	2	88
Jackson, Steve, Houston	0	0	0	0	0	*2
Jackson, Willie, Jacksonville	3	0	3	0	0	18
Jefferson, Shawn, N.E.	4	0	4	0	0	24
Jett, James, Oakland	4	0	4	0	0	24
Johnson, Charles, Pittsburgh	3	0	3	0	1	20
Johnson, Keyshawn, N.Y. Jets	8	0	8	0	1	50
Johnson, Reggie, Kansas City	1	0	1	0	0	6
Johnstone, Lance, Oakland	1	0	0	1	0	6
Jones, Charlie, San Diego	4	0	4	0	0	24
Jones, James, Baltimore	1	0	1	0	0	6
Kaufman, Napoleon, Oakland	2	1	1	0	0	12
Kelly, Jim, Buffalo	2	2	0	0	0	12
Kinchen, Brian, Baltimore	1	0	1	0	0	6
LaChapelle, Sean, Kansas City	2	0	2	0	0	12
Lake, Carnell, Pittsburgh	2	0	0	2	0	12

Player, Team	Tot. TD	RTD	PTD	MTD	2Pt.	Tot Pts
Law, Ty, New England	1	0	0	1	0	6
Lester, Tim, Pittsburgh	1	1	0	0	0	6
Lewis, Darryll, Houston	1	0	0	1	0	6
Lewis, Jermaine, Baltimore	1	0	1	0	0	6
Martin, Curtis, New England	17	14	3	0	1	104
Martin, Tony, San Diego	14	0	14	0	0	84
McCaffrey, Ed, Denver	7	0	7	0	0	42
McCardell, Keenan, Jac.	3	0	3	0	2	22
McDaniel, Terry, Oakland	1	0	0	1	0	6
McDuffie, O.J., Miami	8	0	8	0	0	48
McGee, Tony, Cincinnati	4	0	4	0	0	24
McGinest, Willie, New England	2	0	0	2	0	12
McNair, Steve, Houston	2	2	0	0	0	12
McNair, Todd, Kansas City	1	0	1	0	0	6
Means, Natrone, Jacksonville	3	2	1	0	0	18
Meggett, David, New England	1	0	0	1	0	6
Miller, Anthony, Denver	4	1	3	0	0	24
Miller, Scott, Miami	1	0	0	1	0	6
Mills, Ernie, Pittsburgh	1	0	1	0	0	6
Milne, Brian, Cincinnati	1	1	0	0	0	6
Mirer, Rick, Seattle	2	2	0	0	0	12
Mitchell, Pete, Jacksonville	1	0	1	0	0	6
Morris, Bam, Baltimore	5	4	1	0	0	30
Moulds, Eric, Buffalo	3	0	2	1	0	18
Murrell, Adrian, N.Y. Jets	7	6	1	0	0	42
Norgard, Erik, Houston	1	0	1	0	0	6
Northern, Gabe, Buffalo	1	0	0	1	0	6
Ogden, Jonathan, Baltimore	1	0	1	0	0	6
Pegram, Erric, Pittsburgh	2	1	0	1	0	12
Penn, Chris, Kansas City	5	0	5	0	0	30
Perry, Darren, Pittsburgh	1	0	0	1	0	6
Pickens, Carl, Cincinnati	12	0	12	0	1	74
Pollard, Marcus, Indianapolis	1	0	1	0	0	6
Pritchard, Mike, Seattle	1	0	1	0	0	6
Pritchett, Stanley, Miami	2	0	2	0	0	12
Proehl, Ricky, Seattle	2	0	2	0	0	12
Pupunu, Alfred, San Diego	1	0	1	0	0	6
Reed, Andre, Buffalo	6	0	6	0	0	36
Richardson, Tony, Kansas City	1	0	1	0	0	6
Russell, Derek, Houston	2	0	2	0	0	12
Russell, Leonard, San Diego	7	7	0	0	0	42
Sanders, Chris, Houston	4	0	4	0	0	24
Scott, Darnay, Cincinnati	5	0	5	0	0	30
Sharpe, Shannon, Denver	10	0	10	0	0	60
Shedd, Kenny, Oakland	1	0	1	0	0	*
Sherrard, Mike, Denver	1	0	1	0	0	6
Slaughter, Webster, N.Y. Jets	2	0	2	0	0	12
Smith, Jimmy, Jacksonville	7	0	7	0	0	42
Smith, Lamar, Seattle	8	8	0	0	3	54
Smith, Rod, Denver	2	0	2	0	0	12
Spencer, Jimmy, Cincinnati	1	0	0	1	0	6
Spikes, Irving, Miami	4	3	1	0	0	24
Stablein, Brian, Indianapolis	1	0	1	0	0	6
Stewart, James, Jacksonville	10	8	2	0	0	60
Stewart, Kordell, Pittsburgh	8	5	3	0	0	48
Tasker, Steve, Buffalo	3	0	3	0	0	18
Testaverde, Vinny, Baltimore	2	2	0	0	1	14
Thigpen, Yancey, Pittsburgh	2	0	2	0	0	12
Thomas, Derrick, Kansas City	0	0	0	0	0	*2
Thomas, Lamar, Miami	1	0	1	0	0	6
Thomas, Rodney, Houston	1	1	0	0	0	6
Thomas, Thurman, Buffalo	8	8	0	0	0	48
Thomas, Zach, Miami	1	0	0	1	0	6
Turner, Floyd, Baltimore	2	0	2	0	0	12
Van Dyke, Alex, N.Y. Jets	1	0	1	0	0	6
Vanover, Tamarick, Kansas City	2	0	1	1	0	12
Wainright, Frank, Miami	1	0	1	0	0	6
Walker, Derrick, Kansas City	1	0	1	0	0	6
Warren, Chris, Seattle	5	5	0	0	1	32
Warren, Lamont, Indianapolis	1	1	0	0	0	6
Washington, Mickey, Jac.	1	0	0	1	0	6

ayer, Team	Tot. TD	RTD	PTD	MTD	2Pt.	Tot. Pts.
ite, David, Buffalo	1	0	0	1	0	6
lliams, Calvin, Baltimore	1	0	1	0	0	6
lliams, Darryl, Seattle	1	0	0	1	0	6
lliams, Ronnie, Seattle	1	0	1	0	0	6
lson, Robert, Miami	1	0	1	0	0	6
oodson, Rod, Pittsburgh	2	0	0	2	0	12
ycheck, Frank, Houston	6	0	6	0	0	36

*Includes safety.
NOTE: One team safety apiece credited to Houston, Oakland, ami and New England.

NFC

KICKERS

ayer, Team	XPM	XPA	FGM	FGA	Tot. Pts.
dersen, Morten, Atlanta	31	31	22	29	97
derson, Gary, Philadelphia	40	40	25	29	115
nton, Scott, Washington	40	40	26	32	118
niol, Chris, Dallas	24	25	32	36	120
en, Doug, New Orleans	18	18	21	25	81
tler, Kevin, Arizona	17	19	14	17	59
uiso, Brad, N.Y. Giants	22	22	24	27	94
vis, Greg, Arizona	12	12	9	14	39
nson, Jason, Detroit	36	36	12	17	72
erta, Carlos, Chi.-St.L.*	5	5	4	7	17
sted, Michael, Tampa Bay	18	19	25	32	93
ke, Chris, Green Bay	51	53	21	27	114
ger, Jeff, Chicago	23	23	19	23	80
say, John, Carolina	34	35	37	45	145
miller, Chip, St. Louis	28	29	21	25	91
son, Scott, Minnesota	30	30	22	29	96
kins, Jeff, San Francisco	40	40	30	34	130

NON-KICKERS

ayer, Team	Tot. TD	RTD	PTD	MTD	2Pt.	Tot. Pts.
ew, Ray, N.Y. Giants	1	0	0	1	0	6
man, Troy, Dallas	1	1	0	0	0	6
en, Terry, Washington	21	21	0	0	0	126
tott, Mike, Tampa Bay	6	3	3	0	0	36
derson, Jamal, Atlanta	6	5	1	0	0	36
ner, Jamie, Washington	4	0	4	0	0	24
ks, Tony, St. Louis	0	0	0	0	1	2
es, Mario, New Orleans	4	4	0	0	0	24
es, Michael, Carolina	1	0	0	1	0	6
be, Don, Green Bay	6	0	4	2	0	36
nett, Edgar, Green Bay	3	2	1	0	2	22
den, J.J., Atlanta	2	0	2	0	0	12
rnson, Eric, Dallas	3	0	3	0	1	20
des, Bennie, Detroit	1	0	0	1	0	6
oks, Reggie, Tampa Bay	2	2	0	0	0	12
oks, Robert, Green Bay	4	0	4	0	0	24
wn, Tyrone, Atlanta	1	0	1	0	0	6
ce, Isaac, St. Louis	7	0	7	0	0	42
ler, LeRoy, Green Bay	1	0	0	1	0	6
oway, Chris, N.Y. Giants	4	0	4	0	0	24
rier, Mark, Carolina	6	0	6	0	0	36
ter, Cris, Minnesota	10	0	10	0	0	60
ter, Dexter, San Francisco	1	1	0	0	0	6
ter, Pat, Arizona	1	0	1	0	0	6
ters, Larry, Arizona	9	2	7	0	0	54
lins, Kerry, Carolina	0	0	0	0	1	2
way, Curtis, Chicago	7	0	7	0	0	42
x, Bryan, Chicago	1	0	0	1	0	6
ss, Howard, N.Y. Giants	1	0	1	0	0	6
is, Stephen, Washington	2	2	0	0	0	12
amus, Lee, New Orleans	1	0	1	0	0	6
mer, Ty, Philadelphia	1	1	0	0	0	6
eman, Chris, San Francisco	1	0	0	1	0	6
glass, Maurice, N.Y. Giants	1	0	0	1	0	6

Player, Team	Tot. TD	RTD	PTD	MTD	2Pt.	Tot. Pts.
Dowdell, Marcus, Arizona	2	0	2	0	0	12
Dunn, Jason, Philadelphia	2	0	2	0	0	12
Edwards, Anthony, Arizona	1	0	1	0	0	6
Ellard, Henry, Washington	2	0	2	0	0	12
Emanuel, Bert, Atlanta	6	0	6	0	0	36
Engram, Bobby, Chicago	6	0	6	0	0	36
Esiason, Boomer, Arizona	1	1	0	0	1	8
Evans, Doug, Green Bay	1	0	0	1	0	6
Faulkerson, Mike, Chicago	1	0	1	0	0	6
Favre, Brett, Green Bay	2	2	0	0	0	12
Flanigan, Jim, Chicago	1	0	1	0	0	6
Floyd, William, San Francisco	3	2	1	0	0	18
Freeman, Antonio, Green Bay	9	0	9	0	0	54
Frisch, David, Minnesota	1	0	1	0	0	6
Fryar, Irving, Philadelphia	11	0	11	0	0	66
Galbraith, Scott, Washington	2	0	2	0	0	12
Garner, Charlie, Philadelphia	1	1	0	0	0	6
Grbac, Elvis, San Francisco	2	2	0	0	0	12
Green, Darrell, Washington	1	0	0	1	0	6
Green, Harold, St. Louis	5	4	1	0	1	32
Green, Willie, Carolina	3	0	3	0	0	18
Greene, Kevin, Carolina	1	0	0	1	0	6
Greene, Scott, Carolina	1	0	1	0	0	6
Griffith, Howard, Carolina	2	1	1	0	0	12
Guess, Terry, New Orleans	1	0	1	0	0	6
Hall, Rhett, Philadelphia	1	0	0	1	0	6
Hampton, Rodney, N.Y. Giants	1	1	0	0	0	6
Harper, Alvin, Tampa Bay	1	0	1	0	0	6
Harris, Jackie, Tampa Bay	1	0	1	0	1	8
Harris, Raymont, Chicago	5	4	1	0	0	30
Hawkins, Courtney, Tampa Bay	1	0	1	0	0	6
Haynes, Michael, New Orleans	4	0	4	0	1	26
Hebert, Bobby, Atlanta	1	1	0	0	0	6
Henderson, William, Green Bay	1	0	1	0	0	6
Heyward, Craig, Atlanta	3	3	0	0	0	18
Hoard, Leroy, Minnesota	3	3	0	0	0	18
Howard, Desmond, Green Bay	3	0	0	3	0	18
Irvin, Michael, Dallas	2	0	2	0	1	14
Ismail, Qadry, Minnesota	3	0	3	0	0	18
Ismail, Raghib, Carolina	1	1	0	0	0	6
Jackson, Keith, Green Bay	10	0	10	0	0	60
Jeffires, Haywood, N.O.	3	0	3	0	0	18
Johnson, Anthony, Carolina	6	6	0	0	0	36
Johnson, Brad, Minnesota	1	1	0	0	0	6
Johnson, LeShon, Arizona	4	3	1	0	0	24
Johnson, Tony, New Orleans	1	0	1	0	0	6
Johnston, Daryl, Dallas	1	0	1	0	0	6
Jones, Brent, San Francisco	1	0	1	0	0	6
Jones, Brian, New Orleans	1	0	0	1	0	6
Jones, Chris T., Philadelphia	5	0	5	0	0	30
Jordan, Andrew, Minnesota	0	0	0	0	1	2
Kennison, Eddie, St. Louis	11	0	9	2	0	66
King, Shawn, Carolina	1	0	0	1	0	6
Kirby, Terry, San Francisco	4	3	1	0	0	24
Koonce, George, Green Bay	1	0	0	1	0	6
Kozlowski, Brian, N.Y. Giants	1	0	1	0	0	6
Krieg, Dave, Chicago	1	1	0	0	0	6
Lee, Amp, Minnesota	2	0	2	0	0	12
Levens, Dorsey, Green Bay	10	5	5	0	0	60
Lewis, Thomas, N.Y. Giants	4	0	4	0	0	24
Logan, Marc, Washington	2	2	0	0	0	12
Loville, Derek, San Francisco	4	2	2	0	0	24
Lowery, Michael, Chicago	1	0	0	1	0	6
Lyght, Todd, St. Louis	1	0	0	1	0	6
Lyons, Mitch, Atlanta	1	0	1	0	0	6
Mamula, Mike, Philadelphia	1	0	0	1	0	6
Martin, Kelvin, Dallas	1	0	1	0	0	6
Mathis, Terance, Atlanta	7	0	7	0	1	44
Matthews, Shane, Chicago	1	1	0	0	0	6
Mayes, Derrick, Green Bay	2	0	2	0	0	12
McElroy, Leeland, Arizona	2	1	1	0	0	12

Player, Team	Tot. TD	RTD	PTD	MTD	2Pt.	Tot. Pts.
McWilliams, Johnny, Arizona..	1	0	1	0	0	6
Metcalf, Eric, Atlanta..............	6	0	6	0	0	36
Mickens, Terry, Green Bay	2	0	2	0	0	12
Miller, Jamir, Arizona	1	0	0	1	0	6
Mills, Sam, Carolina..............	1	0	0	1	0	6
Mitchell, Scott, Detroit...........	4	4	0	0	0	24
Moore, Dave, Tampa Bay	3	0	3	0	0	18
Moore, Herman, Detroit..........	9	0	9	0	1	56
Moore, Rob, Arizona.............	4	0	4	0	1	26
Morton, Johnnie, Detroit	6	0	6	0	0	36
Muhammad, Muhsin, Carolina..	1	0	1	0	0	6
Neal, Lorenzo, New Orleans....	2	1	1	0	0	12
Oliver, Winslow, Carolina........	1	0	0	1	0	6
Owens, Terrell, San Francisco.	4	0	4	0	0	24
Palmer, David, Minnesota.......	1	0	0	1	0	6
Parker, Anthony, St. Louis	2	0	0	2	0	12
Peete, Rodney, Philadelphia....	1	1	0	0	0	6
Perriman, Brett, Detroit	5	0	5	0	0	30
Phillips, Lawrence, St. Louis ..	5	4	1	0	0	30
Philyaw, Dino, Carolina..........	1	1	0	0	0	6
Pierce, Aaron, N.Y. Giants.......	2	1	1	0	0	12
Pope, Marquez, San Francisco..	1	0	0	1	0	6
Popson, Ted, San Francisco ...	6	0	6	0	0	36
Preston, Roell, Atlanta..........	1	0	1	0	0	6
Raymond, Corey, Detroit	1	0	0	1	0	6
Reed, Jake, Minnesota...........	7	0	7	0	0	42
Rhett, Errict, Tampa Bay	4	3	1	0	0	24
Rice, Jerry, San Francisco	9	1	8	0	0	54
Rison, Andre, Jac.-G.B.^	3	0	3	0	0	18
Robinson, Greg, St. Louis	1	1	0	0	0	6
Ross, Jermaine, St. Louis.......	1	1	0	0	0	6
Salaam, Rashaan, Chicago	4	3	1	0	0	24
Sanders, Barry, Detroit	11	11	0	0	0	66
Sanders, Deion, Dallas...........	2	0	1	1	0	12
Sanders, Frank, Arizona.........	4	0	4	0	0	24
Sehorn, Jason, N.Y. Giants	1	0	0	1	0	6
Shepherd, Leslie, Washington..	5	2	3	0	0	30
Small, Torrance, New Orleans..	3	1	2	0	0	18

Player, Team	Tot. TD	RTD	PTD	MTD	2Pt.	Tot. Pts.
Smith, Cedric, Arizona............	2	1	1	0	0	1
Smith, Emmitt, Dallas.............	15	12	3	0	0	9
Smith, Robert, Minnesota.......	3	3	0	0	0	1
Spears, Marcus, Chicago........	1	0	1	0	0	
Thomas, Robb, Tampa Bay	2	0	2	0	0	1
Thomas, William, Philadelphia .	1	0	0	1	0	
Tobeck, Robbie, Atlanta	1	0	1	0	0	
Toomer, Amani, N.Y. Giants	2	0	0	2	0	1
Turner, Kevin, Philadelphia......	1	0	1	0	0	
Turner, Scott, Washington	1	0	0	1	0	
Uwaezuoke, Iheanyi, S.F.	1	0	1	0	0	
Vardell, Tommy, San Francisco..	2	2	0	0	0	1
Vincent, Troy, Philadelphia.......	1	0	0	1	0	
Walker, Herschel, Dallas	1	1	0	0	0	
Walls, Wesley, Carolina...........	10	0	10	0	0	6
Walsh, Chris, Minnesota..........	1	0	1	0	1	
Washington, Dewayne, Min......	1	0	0	1	0	
Watters, Ricky, Philadelphia ...	13	13	0	0	0	7
Way, Charles, N.Y. Giants	2	1	1	0	0	1
Wells, Mike, Detroit	1	0	0	1	0	
Westbrook, Michael, Was........	1	0	1	0	0	
Wetnight, Ryan, Chicago	1	0	1	0	0	
Wheatley, Tyrone, N.Y. Giants..	3	1	2	0	0	1
Williams, Aeneas, Arizona.......	1	0	0	1	0	
Williams, Karl, Tampa Bay	1	0	0	1	0	
Williams, Kevin, Dallas	1	0	1	0	0	
Wilmsmeyer, Klaus, N.O.	0	0	0	0	1	
Witherspoon, Derrick, Phi.......	2	0	0	2	0	1
Woolford, Donnell, Chicago....	1	0	0	1	0	
Wooten, Tito, N.Y. Giants........	1	0	0	1	0	*
Wright, Toby, St. Louis	1	0	0	1	0	*
Young, Bryant, San Francisco..	0	0	0	0	0	*
Young, Steve, San Francisco ..	4	4	0	0	1	2
Zellars, Ray, New Orleans.......	4	4	0	0	0	2

*Includes safety.

NOTE: Two team safeties apiece credited to Carolina and St. Louis, and one apiece to Chicago, Green Bay, N.Y. Giants, Philadelphia and St. Louis.

INTERCEPTIONS

TEAM

AFC

am	No.	Yds.	Avg.	Long	TD
ιcinnati	34	308	9.1	t42	2
ttsburgh	23	334	14.5	t47	3
w England	23	255	11.1	t46	2
nver	23	241	10.5	t69	1
n Diego	22	336	15.3	t83	1
ami	20	475	23.8	t91	3
kland	17	353	20.8	t66	2
nsas City	17	171	10.1	34	0
ltimore	15	147	9.8	t45	1
attle	14	256	18.3	t79	1
ffalo	14	113	8.1	31	0
dianapolis	13	276	21.2	t68	4
cksonville	13	114	8.8	27	0
uston	12	162	13.5	53	1
Y.Jets	11	165	15.0	t100	2
AFC total	271	3706	13.7	t100	23
AFC average	18.1	247.1	13.7	....	1.5

t—touchdown.

NFC

Team	No.	Yds.	Avg.	Long	TD
Green Bay	26	524	20.2	t90	3
St. Louis	26	390	15.0	t92	4
N.Y.Giants	22	341	15.5	35	3
Carolina	22	277	12.6	42	0
Minnesota	22	206	9.4	41	1
Washington	21	214	10.2	t68	1
San Francisco	20	176	8.8	t55	1
Philadelphia	19	303	15.9	t104	1
Dallas	19	168	8.8	24	0
Tampa Bay	17	139	8.2	26	0
Chicago	17	107	6.3	29	1
New Orleans	12	114	9.5	33	0
Detroit	11	169	15.4	t98	2
Arizona	11	122	11.1	t65	1
Atlanta	6	41	6.8	21	0
NFC total	271	3291	12.1	t104	18
NFC average	18.1	219.4	12.1	....	1.2
NFL total	542	6997	....	t104	41
NFL average	18.1	233.2	12.9	....	1.4

INDIVIDUAL

BESTS OF THE SEASON

erceptions, season
C: 9—Tyrone Braxton, Denver.
C: 9—Keith Lyle, St. Louis.

erceptions, game
C: 3—Keith Lyle, St. Louis at Atlanta, Dec. 15.
C: 2—Held by many players.

rds, season
C: 164—Terrell Buckley, Miami.
C: 152—Keith Lyle, St. Louis.

ngest
C: 100—Aaron Glenn, N.Y. Jets at Miami, Sept. 15 (TD).
C: 98—Bennie Blades, Detroit at Tampa Bay, Sept. 29 (TD).

uchdowns, season
C: 2—Jason Belser, Indianapolis; Aaron Glenn, N.Y. Jets.
C: 2—Anthony Parker, St. Louis.

am leaders, interceptions
C:

timore	5	Antonio Langham
		Eric Turner
ffalo	4	Kurt Schulz
icinnati	8	Ashley Ambrose
nver	9	Tyrone Braxton
uston	5	Darryll Lewis
dianapolis	4	Jason Belser
cksonville	2	Chris Hudson
		Kevin Hardy
		Dave Thomas
		Travis Davis
nsas City	6	Mark Collins
ami	6	Terrell Buckley
Y. Jets	4	Aaron Glenn
w England	4	Willie Clay
kland	5	Terry McDaniel
tsburgh	6	Rod Woodson
n Diego	5	Rodney Harrison
attle	5	Darryl Williams

C:

zona	6	Aeneas Williams
nta	2	Brad Edwards
Carolina	5	Chad Cota
		Eric Davis
Chicago	6	Donnell Woolford
Dallas	5	Kevin Smith
		Darren Woodson
Detroit	5	Ryan McNeil
Green Bay	6	Eugene Robinson
Minnesota	5	Orlando Thomas
N.Y. Giants	5	Jason Sehorn
New Orleans	3	Anthony Newman
		Greg Jackson
Philadelphia	4	Michael Zordich
San Francisco	6	Marquez Pope
St. Louis	9	Keith Lyle
Tampa Bay	5	Donnie Abraham
Washington	5	Tom Carter

NFL LEADERS

Player, Team	No.	Yds.	Avg.	Long	TD
Lyle, Keith, St. Louis	9	152	16.9	68	0
Braxton, Tyrone, Denver*	9	128	14.2	t69	1
Ambrose, Ashley, Cincinnati*	8	63	7.9	t31	1
Buckley, Terrell, Miami*	6	164	27.3	t91	1
Woodson, Rod, Pittsburgh*	6	121	20.2	t43	1
Robinson, Eugene, Green Bay	6	107	17.8	39	0
Pope, Marquez, San Francisco	6	98	16.3	t55	1
Williams, Aeneas, Arizona	6	89	14.8	t65	1
Collins, Mark, Kansas City*	6	45	7.5	23	0
Woolford, Donnell, Chicago	6	37	6.2	t28	1

*AFC.
t—touchdown.
Leader based on most interceptions.

AFC

Player, Team	No.	Yds.	Avg.	Long	TD
Adams, Vashone, Baltimore	1	16	16.0	16	0
Alberts, Trev, Indianapolis	1	19	19.0	19	0
Ambrose, Ashley, Cincinnati	8	63	7.9	t31	1
Atwater, Steve, Denver	3	11	3.7	11	0
Ball, Jerry, Oakland	1	66	66.0	t66	1
Beasley, Aaron, Jacksonville	1	0	0.0	0	0

Player, Team	No.	Yds.	Avg.	Long	TD
Bellamy, Jay, Seattle	3	18	6.0	16	0
Belser, Jason, Indianapolis	4	81	20.3	t44	2
Bishop, Blaine, Houston	1	6	6.0	6	0
Blackmon, Robert, Seattle	3	48	16.0	38	0
Brackens, Tony, Jacksonville	1	27	27.0	27	0
Braxton, Tyrone, Denver	9	128	14.2	t69	1
Brown, Chad, Pittsburgh	2	20	10.0	16	0
Brown, J.B., Miami	1	29	29.0	29	0
Brown, Larry, Oakland	1	4	4.0	4	0
Buchanan, Ray, Indianapolis	2	32	16.0	32	0
Buckley, Terrell, Miami	6	164	27.3	t91	1
Burris, Jeff, Buffalo	1	28	28.0	28	0
Caldwell, Mike, Baltimore	1	45	45.0	t45	1
Carrington, Darren, Oakland	1	21	21.0	21	0
Carter, Dale, Kansas City	3	17	5.7	17	0
Clark, Vinnie, Jacksonville	1	15	15.0	15	0
Clark, Willie, San Diego	2	83	41.5	t83	1
Clay, Willie, New England	4	50	12.5	35	0
Coleman, Marcus, N.Y. Jets	1	23	23.0	23	0
Collins, Mark, Kansas City	6	45	7.5	23	0
Collins, Todd, New England	1	7	7.0	7	0
Crockett, Ray, Denver	2	34	17.0	34	0
Croel, Mike, Baltimore	1	16	16.0	16	0
Daniel, Eugene, Indianapolis	3	35	11.7	t35	1
Davis, Anthony, Kansas City	2	37	18.5	30	0
Davis, Travis, Jacksonville	2	0	0.0	0	0
Dishman, Cris, Houston	1	7	7.0	7	0
Dixon, Gerald, Cincinnati	1	10	10.0	10	0
Edwards, Donnie, Kansas City	1	22	22.0	22	0
Figures, Deon, Pittsburgh	2	13	6.5	13	0
Francis, James, Cincinnati	3	61	20.3	t42	1
Fuller, Randy, Pittsburgh	1	0	0.0	0	0
Glenn, Aaron, N.Y. Jets	4	113	28.3	t100	2
Gordon, Darrien, San Diego	2	55	27.5	55	0
Gouveia, Kurt, San Diego	3	41	13.7	21	0
Gray, Carlton, Seattle	0	3	....	3	0
Green, Victor, N.Y. Jets	2	27	13.5	18	0
Hall, Dana, Jacksonville	1	20	20.0	20	0
Hardy, Kevin, Jacksonville	2	19	9.5	13	0
Harper, Dwayne, San Diego	1	0	0.0	0	0
Harris, Corey, Seattle	1	25	25.0	25	0
Harrison, Rodney, San Diego	5	56	11.2	29	0
Henderson, Jerome, New England	2	7	3.5	7	0
Herrod, Jeff, Indianapolis	1	68	68.0	t68	1
Hill, Sean, Miami	1	0	0.0	0	0
Hilliard, Randy, Denver	1	27	27.0	27	0
Hitchcock, Jimmy, New England	2	14	7.0	14	0
Hollier, Dwight, Miami	1	11	11.0	11	0
Houston, Bobby, N.Y. Jets	2	3	1.5	3	0
Hudson, Chris, Jacksonville	2	25	12.5	21	0
Jackson, Calvin, Miami	3	82	27.3	t61	1
Jackson, Ray, Buffalo	1	0	0.0	0	0
James, Tory, Denver	2	15	7.5	15	0
Johnson, Ted, New England	1	0	0.0	0	0
Jones, Rod, Cincinnati	2	2	1.0	2	0
Jones, Roger, Cincinnati	1	30	30.0	30	0
Kerner, Marlon, Buffalo	1	6	6.0	6	0
Kidd, Carl, Oakland	1	1	1.0	1	0
Kirkland, Levon, Pittsburgh	4	12	3.0	6	0
Lake, Carnell, Pittsburgh	1	47	47.0	t47	1
Langford, Jevon, Cincinnati	1	0	0.0	0	0
Langham, Antonio, Baltimore	5	59	11.8	28	0
Law, Ty, New England	3	45	15.0	t38	1
Lee, Shawn, San Diego	1	-1	-1.0	0	0
Lewis, Albert, Oakland	2	0	0.0	0	0
Lewis, Darryll, Houston	5	103	20.6	53	1
Lewis, Ray, Baltimore	1	0	0.0	0	0
Lynch, Lorenzo, Oakland	3	75	25.0	35	0
Martin, Emanuel, Buffalo	2	35	17.5	31	0
McDaniel, Terry, Oakland	5	150	30.0	t56	1
McGinest, Willie, New England	1	46	46.0	t46	1
Milloy, Lawyer, New England	2	14	7.0	14	0

Player, Team	No.	Yds.	Avg.	Long	TD
Mobley, John, Denver	1	8	8.0	8	
Moore, Stevon, Baltimore	1	10	10.0	10	
Morrison, Steve, Indianapolis	1	20	20.0	20	
Morton, Mike, Oakland	2	13	6.5	13	
Moss, Winston, Seattle	1	1	1.0	1	
Myers, Greg, Cincinnati	2	10	5.0	10	
Oliver, Louis, Miami	3	110	36.7	60	
Olsavsky, Jerry, Pittsburgh	1	5	5.0	5	
Orlando, Bo, Cincinnati	2	0	0.0	0	
Perry, Darren, Pittsburgh	5	115	23.0	28	
Perry, Marlo, Buffalo	1	6	6.0	6	
Ray, Terry, New England	1	43	43.0	43	
Reynolds, Ricky, New England	2	7	3.5	7	
Robertson, Marcus, Houston	4	44	11.0	27	
Robinson, Rafael, Houston	1	2	2.0	2	
Romanowski, Bill, Denver	3	1	0.3	1	
Ross, Kevin, San Diego	2	7	3.5	7	
Sabb, Dwayne, New England	1	0	0.0	0	
Sawyer, Corey, Cincinnati	2	0	0.0	0	
Schulz, Kurt, Buffalo	4	24	6.0	19	
Seau, Junior, San Diego	2	18	9.0	10	
Shaw, Terrance, San Diego	3	78	26.0	36	
Simien, Tracy, Kansas City	1	2	2.0	2	
Slade, Chris, New England	1	2	2.0	2	
Smith, Otis, New England	2	20	10.0	11	
Smith, Thomas, Buffalo	1	0	0.0	0	
Spencer, Jimmy, Cincinnati	5	48	9.6	34	
Spielman, Chris, Buffalo	1	14	14.0	14	
Spindler, Marc, N.Y. Jets	1	-1	-1.0	0	
Stargell, Tony, Kansas City	1	9	9.0	9	
Stevens, Matt, Buffalo	2	0	0.0	0	
Thomas, Dave, Jacksonville	2	7	3.5	8	
Thomas, Zach, Miami	3	64	21.3	27	
Tovar, Steve, Cincinnati	4	42	10.5	24	
Trapp, James, Oakland	1	23	23.0	23	
Turner, Eric, Baltimore	5	1	0.2	1	
Walker, Bracey, Cincinnati	2	35	17.5	35	
Washington, Brian, Kansas City	3	39	13.0	34	
Washington, Lionel, Denver	2	17	8.5	23	
Washington, Mickey, Jacksonville	1	1	1.0	1	
Watts, Damon, Indianapolis	1	21	21.0	21	
Wilkinson, Dan, Cincinnati	1	7	7.0	7	
Williams, Darryl, Seattle	5	148	29.6	t79	
Williams, Willie, Pittsburgh	1	1	1.0	1	
Wooden, Shawn, Miami	2	15	7.5	15	
Wooden, Terry, Seattle	1	13	13.0	13	
Woodson, Rod, Pittsburgh	6	121	20.2	t43	
Young, Glen, San Diego	1	-1	-1.0	0	
Young, Lonnie, N.Y. Jets	1	0	0.0	0	

t—touchdown.

NFC

Player, Team	No.	Yds.	Avg.	Long	TD
Abraham, Donnie, Tampa Bay	5	27	5.4	21	
Agnew, Ray, N.Y. Giants	1	34	34.0	t34	
Alexander, Brent, Arizona	2	3	1.5	3	
Allen, Eric, New Orleans	1	33	33.0	33	
Armstead, Jesse, N.Y. Giants	2	23	11.5	23	
Beamon, Willie, N.Y. Giants	1	20	20.0	20	
Bennett, Cornelius, Atlanta	1	3	3.0	3	
Blades, Bennie, Detroit	2	112	56.0	t98	
Boutte, Marc, Washington	1	0	0.0	0	
Bradford, Ronnie, Arizona	1	0	0.0	0	
Brady, Jeff, Minnesota	3	20	6.7	8	
Brooks, Derrick, Tampa Bay	1	6	6.0	6	
Burton, James, Chicago	1	11	11.0	11	
Bush, Devin, Atlanta	1	2	2.0	2	
Butler, LeRoy, Green Bay	5	149	29.8	t90	
Campbell, Jesse, N.Y. Giants	2	14	7.0	14	
Carrier, Mark, Chicago	2	0	0.0	0	
Carter, Marty, Chicago	3	34	11.3	29	

Player, Team	No.	Yds.	Avg.	Long	TD
Carter, Tom, Washington	5	24	4.8	24	0
Cook, Toi, Carolina	3	28	9.3	22	0
Cota, Chad, Carolina	5	63	12.6	35	0
Davis, Eric, Carolina	5	57	11.4	36	0
Dawkins, Brian, Philadelphia	3	41	13.7	30	0
Dimry, Charles, Tampa Bay	2	1	0.5	1	0
Dodge, Dedrick, San Francisco	3	27	9.0	26	0
Doleman, Chris, San Francisco	2	1	0.5	1	0
Dorn, Torin, St. Louis	1	40	40.0	40	0
Douglass, Maurice, N.Y. Giants	1	32	32.0	t32	1
Dowden, Corey, Green Bay	1	5	5.0	5	0
Drakeford, Tyronne, San Francisco	1	11	11.0	11	0
Edwards, Brad, Atlanta	2	15	7.5	15	0
Edwards, Dixon, Minnesota	1	18	18.0	18	0
Ellsworth, Percy, N.Y. Giants	3	62	20.7	33	0
Evans, Doug, Green Bay	5	102	20.4	63	1
Farmer, Ray, Philadelphia	1	0	0.0	0	0
Farr, D'Marco, St. Louis	1	5	5.0	5	0
Fisk, Jason, Minnesota	1	0	0.0	0	0
Fuller, Corey, Minnesota	3	3	1.0	2	0
Fuller, James, Philadelphia	1	4	4.0	4	0
Green, Darrell, Washington	3	84	28.0	t68	1
Griffith, Robert, Minnesota	4	67	16.8	41	0
Hamilton, Conrad, N.Y. Giants	1	29	29.0	29	0
Hanks, Merton, San Francisco	4	7	1.8	8	0
Harper, Roger, Dallas	2	30	15.0	15	0
Harris, Walt, Chicago	2	0	0.0	0	0
Harvey, Ken, Washington	1	2	2.0	2	0
Hollinquest, Lamont, Green Bay	1	2	2.0	2	0
Israel, Steve, San Francisco	1	3	3.0	3	0
Jackson, Alfred, Minnesota	2	4	2.0	4	0
Jackson, Greg, New Orleans	3	24	8.0	10	0
Jeffries, Greg, Detroit	1	0	0.0	0	0
Jenkins, Carlos, St. Louis	1	-3	-3.0	0	0
Johnson, Melvin, Tampa Bay	2	24	12.0	24	0
Jones, Robert, St. Louis	1	0	0.0	0	0
Joyner, Seth, Arizona	1	10	10.0	10	0
King, Shawn, Carolina	1	1	1.0	1	0
Loonce, George, Green Bay	3	84	28.0	t75	1
Lassiter, Kwamie, Arizona	1	20	20.0	20	0
Lincoln, Jeremy, St. Louis	1	3	3.0	3	0
Lofton, Steve, Carolina	1	42	42.0	42	0
Lyght, Todd, St. Louis	5	43	8.6	t25	1
Lyle, Keith, St. Louis	9	152	16.9	68	0
Lynch, John, Tampa Bay	3	26	8.7	25	0
Malone, Van, Detroit	1	5	5.0	5	0
Marshall, Anthony, Chicago	2	20	10.0	20	0
Maxie, Brett, Carolina	1	35	35.0	35	0
Mayhew, Martin, Tampa Bay	1	5	5.0	5	0
McBurrows, Gerald, St. Louis	1	3	3.0	3	0
McDonald, Tim, San Francisco	2	14	7.0	14	0
McMillian, Mark, New Orleans	2	4	2.0	4	0
McNeil, Ryan, Detroit	5	14	2.8	15	0
Mills, Sam, Carolina	1	10	10.0	10	0
Mincy, Charles, Tampa Bay	1	26	26.0	26	0
Minter, Barry, Chicago	1	5	5.0	5	0
Molden, Alex, New Orleans	2	2	1.0	2	0
Morrison, Darryl, Washington	1	4	4.0	4	0
Newman, Anthony, New Orleans	3	40	13.3	21	0
Newsome, Craig, Green Bay	2	22	11.0	20	0
Nickerson, Hardy, Tampa Bay	2	24	12.0	17	0
Parker, Anthony, St. Louis	4	128	32.0	t92	2
Patton, Marvcus, Washington	2	26	13.0	23	0
Pieri, Damon, Carolina	1	0	0.0	0	0
Poole, Tyrone, Carolina	1	35	35.0	35	0
Pope, Marquez, San Francisco	6	98	16.3	t55	1
Pounds, Darryl, Washington	2	11	5.5	11	0
Prior, Mike, Green Bay	1	7	7.0	7	0
Raymond, Corey, Detroit	1	24	24.0	t24	1
Richard, Stanley, Washington	3	47	15.7	42	0
Robinson, Eugene, Green Bay	6	107	17.8	39	0
Sanders, Deion, Dallas	2	3	1.5	2	0
Sehorn, Jason, N.Y. Giants	5	61	12.2	24	1
Simmons, Wayne, Green Bay	1	0	0.0	0	0
Smith, Chuck, Atlanta	1	21	21.0	21	0
Smith, Kevin, Dallas	5	45	9.0	24	0
Sparks, Phillippi, N.Y. Giants	3	23	7.7	19	0
Stephens, Rod, Green Bay	1	0	0.0	0	0
Stewart, Ryan, Detroit	1	14	14.0	14	0
Strickland, Fred, Dallas	1	0	0.0	0	0
Stubblefield, Dana, San Francisco	1	15	15.0	15	0
Talley, Darryl, Minnesota	1	10	10.0	10	0
Taylor, Bobby, Philadelphia	3	-1	-.3	0	0
Teague, George, Dallas	4	47	11.8	22	0
Terrell, Pat, Carolina	3	6	2.0	6	0
Thomas, Orlando, Minnesota	5	57	11.4	34	0
Thomas, William, Philadelphia	3	47	15.7	37	0
Tubbs, Winfred, New Orleans	1	11	11.0	11	0
Turner, Scott, Washington	2	16	8.0	12	0
Vincent, Troy, Philadelphia	3	144	48.0	t90	1
Walker, Darnell, Atlanta	1	0	0.0	0	0
Walker, Marquis, St. Louis	1	0	0.0	0	0
Washington, Dewayne, Minnesota	2	27	13.5	t27	1
White, Reggie, Green Bay	1	46	46.0	46	0
Widmer, Corey, N.Y. Giants	2	8	4.0	4	0
Williams, Aeneas, Arizona	6	89	14.8	t65	1
Willis, James, Philadelphia	1	14	14.0	14	0
Woodson, Darren, Dallas	5	43	8.6	21	0
Woolford, Donnell, Chicago	6	37	6.2	t28	1
Wooten, Tito, N.Y. Giants	1	35	35.0	35	0
Wright, Toby, St. Louis	1	19	19.0	t19	1
Zordich, Michael, Philadelphia	4	54	13.5	28	0

t—touchdown.

SACKS

AFC

Team	Sacks	Yards
Pittsburgh	51	369
Buffalo	48	341
Seattle	48	285
Denver	40	274
Jacksonville	37	237
Miami	37	233
Houston	35	242
Oakland	34	252
New England	33	252
San Diego	33	201
Cincinnati	32	202
Kansas City	31	193
Baltimore	30	146
Indianapolis	29	182
N.Y.Jets	28	178
AFC total	**546**	**3587**
AFC average	**36.4**	**239.1**

NFC

Team	Sacks	Yards
Carolina	60	371
San Francisco	45	297
Minnesota	43	263
New Orleans	41	283
Philadelphia	40	264
Dallas	37	219
Green Bay	37	202
Atlanta	36	208
Tampa Bay	35	207
Washington	34	207
Detroit	32	233
St. Louis	32	181
Chicago	30	209
N.Y.Giants	30	178
Arizona	28	185
NFC total	**560**	**3507**
NFC average	**37.3**	**233.8**
NFL total	**1106**	**7094**
NFL average	**36.9**	**236.5**

INDIVIDUAL

BESTS OF THE SEASON

Sacks, season
NFC: 14.5—Kevin Greene, Carolina.
AFC: 13.5—Bruce Smith, Buffalo; Michael McCrary, Seattle.
Sacks, game
AFC: 4.5—Chad Brown, Pittsburgh vs. Cincinnati, Oct. 13.
NFC: 3.5—John Randle, Minnesota vs. Green Bay, Sept. 22.

NFL LEADERS

Player, Team	No.
Greene, Kevin, Carolina	14.5
Smith, Bruce, Buffalo*	13.5
Lathon, Lamar, Carolina	13.5
McCrary, Michael, Seattle*	13.5
Thomas, Derrick, Kansas City*	13.0
Williams, Alfred, Denver*	13.0
Brown, Chad, Pittsburgh*	13.0
Fuller, William, Philadelphia	13.0
Sinclair, Michael, Seattle*	13.0
Barker, Roy, San Francisco	12.5
Rice, Simeon, Arizona	12.5
Armstrong, Trace, Miami*	12.0
Tolbert, Tony, Dallas	12.0
Young, Bryant, San Francisco	11.5
Randle, John, Minnesota	11.5
Martin, Wayne, New Orleans	11.0
Doleman, Chris, San Francisco	11.0
Owens, Rich, Washington	11.0
Porcher, Robert, Detroit	10.0
Carter, Kevin, St. Louis	9.5
McGinest, Willie, New England*	9.5
Smith, Fernando, Minnesota	9.5
*AFC.	

AFC

Player, Team	No.
Adams, Sam, Seattle	5.5
Alexander, Elijah, Indianapolis	1.0
Armstrong, Trace, Miami	12.0
Bailey, Robert, Miami	1.0
Ball, Jerry, Oakland	3.0

Player, Team	No.
Barrow, Micheal, Houston	6.0
Bayless, Martin, Kansas City	1.0
Beasley, Aaron, Jacksonville	1.0
Bell, Myron, Pittsburgh	2.0
Belser, Jason, Indianapolis	1.0
Bennett, Tony, Indianapolis	6.0
Blackmon, Robert, Seattle	1.0
Booker, Vaughn, Kansas City	1.0
Bowden, Joe, Houston	3.0
Bowens, Tim, Miami	3.0
Brackens, Tony, Jacksonville	7.0
Brady, Donny, Baltimore	0.5
Brock, Matt, N.Y. Jets	2.0
Brown, Chad, Pittsburgh	13.0
Browning, John, Kansas City	2.0
Bruce, Aundray, Oakland	4.0
Bruschi, Tedy, New England	4.0
Buchanan, Ray, Indianapolis	0.5
Buckner, Brentson, Pittsburgh	3.0
Burnett, Rob, Baltimore	3.0
Burton, Shane, Miami	3.0
Bush, Lewis, San Diego	1.0
Caldwell, Mike, Baltimore	4.5
Cascadden, Chad, N.Y. Jets	3.0
Chalenski, Mike, N.Y. Jets	0.5
Coleman, Marco, San Diego	4.0
Collins, Mark, Kansas City	1.0
Collons, Ferric, New England	0.5
Cook, Anthony, Houston	7.5
Copeland, John, Cincinnati	3.0
Crockett, Ray, Denver	4.0
Croel, Mike, Baltimore	3.0
Daniels, Phillip, Seattle	2.0
Davey, Don, Jacksonville	0.5
Davis, Anthony, Kansas City	2.5
Davis, Reuben, San Diego	3.0
Davis, Travis, Jacksonville	0.5
Dent, Richard, Indianapolis	6.5
Douglas, Hugh, N.Y. Jets	8.0
Eaton, Chad, New England	1.0
Edwards, Antonio, Seattle	2.0
Edwards, Vernon, San Diego	1.1

Player, Team	No.
mmons, Carlos, Pittsburgh	2.5
mtman, Steve, Miami	2.0
ootman, Dan, Baltimore	0.5
ord, Henry, Houston	1.0
ortune, Elliott, Baltimore	1.0
rancis, James, Cincinnati	3.0
ardener, Daryl, Miami	1.0
eathers, Jumpy, Denver	5.0
ibson, Oliver, Pittsburgh	2.5
ildon, Jason, Pittsburgh	7.0
oad, Tim, Baltimore	3.0
ordon, Darrien, San Diego	2.0
ouveia, Kurt, San Diego	1.0
rant, Stephen, Indianapolis	1.0
reen, Victor, N.Y. Jets	2.0
unn, Mark, N.Y. Jets	2.0
amilton, Bobby, N.Y. Jets	4.5
amilton, Rick, N.Y. Jets	1.5
and, Norman, Miami	0.5
ansen, Phil, Buffalo	8.0
ardy, Kevin, Jacksonville	5.5
arris, Corey, Seattle	1.0
arrison, Nolan, Oakland	2.0
arrison, Rodney, San Diego	1.0
asselbach, Harald, Denver	2.0
asty, James, Kansas City	1.0
enry, Kevin, Pittsburgh	1.5
ill, Sean, Miami	1.0
ollier, Dwight, Miami	1.0
olmberg, Rob, Oakland	1.0
olmes, Earl, Pittsburgh	1.0
udson, Chris, Jacksonville	0.5
vin, Ken, Buffalo	2.0
ackson, Calvin, Miami	1.5
ackson, Steve, Houston	2.0
effcoat, Jim, Buffalo	5.0
ohnson, Bill, Pittsburgh	1.0
ohnson, Raylee, San Diego	3.0
ohnson, Tim, Cincinnati	2.5
ohnstone, Lance, Oakland	1.0
ones, Donta, Pittsburgh	1.0
ones, James, Baltimore	1.0
ones, Marvin, N.Y. Jets	1.0
ones, Mike, Oakland	1.0
ones, Mike, New England	2.0
urkovic, John, Jacksonville	1.0
ennedy, Cortez, Seattle	8.0
erner, Marlon, Buffalo	1.0
irkland, Levon, Pittsburgh	4.0
ageman, Jeff, Jacksonville	4.5
ake, Carnell, Pittsburgh	2.0
angford, Jevon, Cincinnati	2.0
ee, Shawn, San Diego	1.0
ewis, Albert, Oakland	3.0
ewis, Mo, N.Y. Jets	0.5
ewis, Ray, Baltimore	2.5
oyd, Greg, Pittsburgh	1.0
odish, Mike, Denver	1.5
yle, Rick, Baltimore	1.0
artin, Steve, Indianapolis	1.0
aryland, Russell, Oakland	2.0
cCoy, Tony, Indianapolis	5.0
cCrary, Michael, Seattle	13.5
cDonald, Ricardo, Cincinnati	5.0
cGinest, Willie, New England	9.5
cGlockton, Chester, Oakland	8.0
cGruder, Michael, New England	0.5
illoy, Lawyer, New England	1.0
ims, Chris, San Diego	6.0
ix, Bryant, Houston	1.0
obley, John, Denver	1.5
orabito, Tim, Cincinnati	0.5
orton, Mike, Oakland	1.0

Player, Team	No.
Moss, Winston, Seattle	1.0
Northern, Gabe, Buffalo	5.0
Oldham, Chris, Pittsburgh	2.0
Olsavsky, Jerry, Pittsburgh	0.5
Orlando, Bo, Cincinnati	1.0
Parrella, John, San Diego	2.0
Paup, Bryce, Buffalo	6.0
Perry, Darren, Pittsburgh	1.0
Perry, Michael Dean, Denver	3.5
Phillips, Joe, Kansas City	2.0
Pleasant, Anthony, Baltimore	4.0
Pritchett, Kelvin, Jacksonville	2.0
Ravotti, Eric, Pittsburgh	2.0
Ray, Terry, New England	1.0
Raybon, Israel, Pittsburgh	1.0
Roberson, James, Houston	3.0
Robinson, Eddie, Jacksonville	1.0
Robinson, Jeff, Denver	0.5
Rogers, Sam, Buffalo	3.5
Romanowski, Bill, Denver	3.0
Sabb, Dwayne, New England	0.5
Sagapolutele, Pio, New England	3.0
Sawyer, Corey, Cincinnati	1.5
Seau, Junior, San Diego	7.0
Simmons, Clyde, Jacksonville	7.5
Sinclair, Michael, Seattle	13.0
Siragusa, Tony, Indianapolis	2.0
Slade, Chris, New England	7.0
Smeenge, Joel, Jacksonville	5.0
Smith, Anthony, Oakland	2.0
Smith, Artie, Cincinnati	1.0
Smith, Bruce, Buffalo	13.5
Smith, Neil, Kansas City	6.0
Smith, Otis, New England	1.0
Spindler, Marc, N.Y. Jets	0.5
Stallings, Ramondo, Cincinnati	2.0
Stubbs, Daniel, Miami	9.0
Swilling, Pat, Oakland	6.0
Tanuvasa, Maa, Denver	5.0
Tate, David, Indianapolis	1.0
Thomas, Derrick, Kansas City	13.0
Thomas, Zach, Miami	2.0
Thompson, Bennie, Baltimore	3.0
Tovar, Steve, Cincinnati	3.0
Traylor, Keith, Kansas City	1.0
von Oelhoffen, Kimo, Cincinnati	1.0
Walker, Gary, Houston	5.5
Washington, Brian, Kansas City	0.5
Washington, Marvin, N.Y. Jets	2.5
Washington, Ted, Buffalo	3.5
Wells, Dean, Seattle	1.0
Wheeler, Mark, New England	1.0
White, David, Buffalo	0.5
Whittington, Bernard, Indianapolis	3.0
Wilkinson, Dan, Cincinnati	6.5
Williams, Alfred, Denver	13.0
Williams, Dan, Denver	1.0
Williams, Jerrol, Baltimore	3.0
Williams, Willie, Pittsburgh	1.0
Woodson, Rod, Pittsburgh	1.0
Wortham, Barron, Houston	2.0
Wyman, Devin, New England	1.0
Young, Robert, Houston	4.0

NFC

Player, Team	No.
Agnew, Ray, N.Y. Giants	0.5
Ahanotu, Chidi, Tampa Bay	5.5
Alexander, Derrick, Minnesota	3.5
Archambeau, Lester, Atlanta	2.0
Armstead, Jesse, N.Y. Giants	3.0
Bailey, Carlton, Carolina	2.5

Player, Team	No.	Player, Team	No.
Bankston, Michael, Arizona	0.5	McCormack, Hurvin, Dallas	2.5
Barker, Roy, San Francisco	12.5	McDonald, Tim, San Francisco	1.0
Barnett, Harlon, Minnesota	1.0	McKenzie, Keith, Green Bay	1.0
Bennett, Cornelius, Atlanta	3.0	McKyer, Tim, Atlanta	1.0
Bickett, Duane, Carolina	2.0	Mickell, Darren, New Orleans	3.0
Bonham, Shane, Detroit	2.0	Miller, Corey, N.Y. Giants	2.0
Brady, Jeff, Minnesota	1.5	Miller, Jamir, Arizona	1.0
Brandon, David, Atlanta	1.0	Miller, Les, Carolina	3.0
Bratzke, Chad, N.Y. Giants	5.0	Mills, Sam, Carolina	5.5
Broughton, Willie, New Orleans	2.0	Miniefield, Kevin, Chicago	1.5
Brown, Dennis, San Francisco	2.0	Minter, Barry, Chicago	1.5
Brown, Gilbert, Green Bay	1.0	Mitchell, Kevin, San Francisco	1.0
Bryant, Junior, San Francisco	0.5	Molden, Alex, New Orleans	2.0
Butler, LeRoy, Green Bay	6.5	Nickerson, Hardy, Tampa Bay	3.0
Cain, Joe, Chicago	1.0	Nottage, Dexter, Washington	5.0
Carter, Kevin, St. Louis	9.5	O'Neal, Leslie, St. Louis	7.0
Carver, Shante, Dallas	3.0	Osborne, Chuck, St. Louis	1.0
Childress, Ray, Dallas	1.0	Ottis, Brad, Arizona	1.0
Clavelle, Shannon, Green Bay	0.5	Owens, Dan, Atlanta	5.5
Cook, Toi, Carolina	4.0	Owens, Rich, Washington	11.0
Cota, Chad, Carolina	1.0	Palmer, Sterling, Washington	1.0
Cox, Bryan, Chicago	3.0	Patton, Marvcus, Washington	2.0
Culpepper, Brad, Tampa Bay	1.5	Phifer, Roman, St. Louis	1.5
Curry, Eric, Tampa Bay	2.0	Porcher, Robert, Detroit	10.0
Dawkins, Brian, Philadelphia	1.0	Randle, John, Minnesota	11.5
Doleman, Chris, San Francisco	11.0	Rice, Simeon, Arizona	12.5
Dotson, Santana, Green Bay	5.5	Riddick, Louis, Atlanta	1.0
Drakeford, Tyronne, San Francisco	2.0	Robbins, Austin, New Orleans	1.0
Edwards, Dixon, Minnesota	3.5	Rudolph, Coleman, N.Y. Giants	1.0
Elliss, Luther, Detroit	6.5	Sapp, Warren, Tampa Bay	9.0
Evans, Doug, Green Bay	3.0	Scroggins, Tracy, Detroit	2.0
Farmer, Ray, Philadelphia	1.0	Sehorn, Jason, N.Y. Giants	3.0
Farr, D'Marco, St. Louis	4.5	Simmons, Wayne, Green Bay	2.5
Fields, Mark, New Orleans	2.0	Simpson, Carl, Chicago	1.5
Fisk, Jason, Minnesota	1.0	Smith, Ben, Arizona	1.0
Flanigan, Jim, Chicago	5.0	Smith, Brady, New Orleans	2.0
Fontenot, Al, Chicago	4.5	Smith, Chuck, Atlanta	6.0
Fox, Mike, Carolina	2.0	Smith, Darrin, Dallas	1.0
Fuller, William, Philadelphia	13.0	Smith, Fernando, Minnesota	9.5
George, Ron, Atlanta	2.0	Smith, Rod, Carolina	1.0
Gilbert, Sean, Washington	3.0	Smith, Vinson, Chicago	1.0
Goss, Antonio, St. Louis	1.0	Spellman, Alonzo, Chicago	8.0
Greene, Kevin, Carolina	14.5	Stephens, Rod, Washington	1.0
Griffin, Don, Philadelphia	0.5	Stokes, Fred, New Orleans	1.0
Griffith, Robert, Minnesota	2.0	Strahan, Michael, N.Y. Giants	5.0
Haley, Charles, Dallas	1.0	Strickland, Fred, Dallas	1.0
Hall, Rhett, Philadelphia	4.5	Stubblefield, Dana, San Francisco	1.0
Hall, Travis, Atlanta	6.0	Swann, Eric, Arizona	5.0
Hamilton, Keith, N.Y. Giants	3.0	Taylor, Bobby, Philadelphia	1.0
Harmon, Andy, Philadelphia	1.0	Thierry, John, Chicago	2.0
Harris, James, St. Louis	2.0	Thomas, Broderick, Dallas	4.5
Harris, Robert, N.Y. Giants	4.5	Thomas, Henry, Detroit	6.0
Harrison, Martin, Minnesota	7.0	Thomas, Hollis, Philadelphia	1.0
Harvey, Ken, Washington	9.0	Thomas, Mark, Carolina	4.0
Harvey, Richard, New Orleans	2.0	Thomas, William, Philadelphia	5.5
Hennings, Chad, Dallas	4.5	Tolbert, Tony, Dallas	12.0
Jefferson, Greg, Philadelphia	2.5	Tuaolo, Esera, Minnesota	2.5
Johnson, Joe, New Orleans	7.5	Tubbs, Winfred, New Orleans	1.0
Johnson, Kevin, Philadelphia	1.0	Tuggle, Jessie, Atlanta	1.0
Jones, Jimmie, St. Louis	5.5	Turnbull, Renaldo, New Orleans	6.5
Jones, Marcus, Tampa Bay	1.0	Upshaw, Regan, Tampa Bay	4.0
Jones, Sean, Green Bay	5.0	Waldroup, Kerwin, Detroit	2.5
Joyner, Seth, Arizona	5.0	Walker, Bryan, Washington	1.0
King, Shawn, Carolina	3.0	White, Reggie, Green Bay	8.5
Kragen, Greg, Carolina	3.0	Widmer, Corey, N.Y. Giants	2.0
Lathon, Lamar, Carolina	13.5	Wilkins, Gabe, Green Bay	3.0
Lett, Leon, Dallas	3.5	Williams, Aeneas, Arizona	1.0
London, Antonio, Detroit	3.0	Williams, Brian, Green Bay	0.5
Lynch, John, Tampa Bay	1.0	Williams, Gerald, Carolina	1.0
Mamula, Mike, Philadelphia	8.0	Wilson, Bernard, Arizona	1.0
Mangum, John, Chicago	1.0	Woodall, Lee, San Francisco	2.5
Martin, Wayne, New Orleans	11.0	Woods, Tony, Washington	1.0
Marts, Lonnie, Tampa Bay	7.0	Woodson, Darren, Dallas	3.0
Matthews, Clay, Atlanta	6.5	Young, Bryant, San Francisco	11.5
Mayhew, Martin, Tampa Bay	1.0	Zgonina, Jeff, Atlanta	1.0

FUMBLES

TEAM

AFC

eam	Fum.	Own Fum. Rec.	Own Fum. *O.B.	Own Fum. Lost	TD	Opp Fum. Rec.	TD	†Yards	Total Rec.
incinnati	19	7	3	9	0	10	1	46	17
ansas City	17	6	1	10	0	10	1	87	16
acksonville	29	17	2	10	0	14	0	-1	31
an Diego	30	15	4	11	0	14	0	-10	29
uffalo	25	11	2	12	0	14	1	12	25
ew England	25	11	2	12	0	11	2	93	22
eattle	24	10	2	12	0	18	0	97	28
akland	30	16	2	12	0	9	1	5	25
dianapolis	24	11	0	13	0	10	0	4	21
iami	31	15	3	13	2	16	0	12	31
altimore	23	8	2	13	0	7	0	18	15
ittsburgh	27	12	1	14	0	17	2	160	29
enver	27	10	2	15	0	9	0	27	19
ouston	26	10	1	15	0	14	0	14	24
.Y. Jets	25	7	2	16	0	15	1	-14	22
AFC total	382	166	29	187	2	188	9	550	354
AFC average	25.5	11.1	1.9	12.5	0.1	12.5	0.6	36.7	23.6

*Fumbled out of bounds.
†Includes all fumble yardage (aborted plays and recoveries of own and opponents' fumbles).

NFC

am	Fum.	Own Fum. Rec.	Own Fum. *O.B.	Own Fum. Lost	TD	Opp Fum. Rec.	TD	†Yards	Total Rec.
etroit	21	15	1	5	0	8	1	-9	23
ashington	21	13	1	7	0	9	1	-2	22
an Francisco	16	6	2	8	0	14	1	89	20
hicago	25	15	1	9	0	11	2	34	26
tlanta	23	11	1	11	0	17	0	-10	28
reen Bay	33	19	3	11	1	12	0	18	31
innesota	26	12	2	12	0	13	0	7	25
.Y. Giants	27	12	2	13	0	13	1	57	25
hiladelphia	24	8	2	14	0	12	3	101	20
rizona	29	11	4	14	0	14	1	27	25
mpa Bay	28	11	3	14	0	12	0	-2	23
arolina	25	10	1	14	0	16	3	151	26
allas	24	6	3	15	0	13	1	72	19
ew Orleans	30	8	2	20	0	10	1	38	18
. Louis	42	19	2	21	0	13	0	-38	32
NFC total	394	176	30	188	1	187	15	533	363
NFC average	26.3	11.7	2.0	12.5	0.1	12.5	1.0	35.5	24.2
NFL total	776	342	59	375	3	375	24	1083	717
NFL average	25.9	11.4	2.0	12.5	0.1	12.5	0.8	36.1	23.9

INDIVIDUAL

BESTS OF THE SEASON

mbles, season
C: 21—Tony Banks, St. Louis.
C: 14—Mark Brunell, Jacksonville.

mbles, game
C: 4—Craig Erickson, Miami vs. Seattle, Oct. 6.
C: 4—Steve Beuerlein, Carolina at Jacksonville, Sept. 29; Tony Banks, St. Louis at Atlanta, Dec. 15.

wn fumbles recovered, season
C: 5—Jeff Hostetler, Oakland; Mark Brunell, Jacksonville.
C: 5—Scott Mitchell, Detroit; Brett Favre, Green Bay.

wn fumbles recovered, game
C: 3—Craig Erickson, Miami vs. Seattle, Oct. 6; Lonnie Johnson, Buffalo vs. Kansas City, Dec. 22.
C: 2—Jeff George, Atlanta vs. Minnesota, Sept. 8; Brett Favre, Green Bay vs. Tampa Bay, Oct. 27; Scott Mitchell, Detroit at Chicago, Nov. 24; LeShon Johnson, Arizona vs. Dallas, Dec. 8.

Opponents' fumbles recovered, season
AFC: 4—Louis Oliver, Miami.
NFC: 3—Held by 14 players.

Opponents' fumbles recovered, game
AFC: 2—Bill Romanowski, Denver at Seattle, Sept. 8; Tony Brackens, Jacksonville vs. Carolina, Sept. 29; Junior Seau, San Diego vs. Denver, Dec. 22; Terry Wooden, Seattle at Oakland, Dec. 22.
NFC: 2—Held by 5 players.

Yards returning fumbles, season
AFC: 85—Carnell Lake, Pittsburgh.
NFC: 66—Kevin Greene, Carolina.

1996 STATISTICS Fumbles

Longest fumble return
AFC: 85—Carnell Lake, Pittsburgh vs. Jacksonville, Nov. 17 (TD).
NFC: 66—Kevin Greene, Carolina vs. St. Louis, Oct. 13 (TD).

AFC

Player, Team	Fum.	Own Rec.	Opp. Rec.	Yds.	Tot. Rec.	TD
Abdul-Jabbar, Karim, Miami ...	4	0	0	0	0	0
Adams, Sam, Seattle	0	0	1	2	1	0
Allen, Marcus, Kansas City	2	0	0	0	0	0
Anderson, Darren, Kansas City..	0	0	1	0	1	0
Anderson, Richie, N.Y. Jets.....	0	0	1	0	1	0
Araguz, Leo, Oakland	0	1	0	0	1	0
Armstrong, Trace, Miami	0	0	2	0	2	0
Arnold, Jahine, Pittsburgh	1	0	0	0	0	0
Arvie, Herman, Baltimore........	0	1	0	0	1	0
Aska, Joe, Oakland	1	0	0	0	0	0
Atkins, James, Seattle.............	0	2	0	0	2	0
Atwater, Steve, Denver............	1	0	0	0	0	0
Bailey, Aaron, Indianapolis......	3	1	0	0	1	0
Baldwin, Randy, Baltimore......	1	0	0	0	0	0
Ball, Jerry, Oakland	0	0	1	0	1	0
Ballard, Howard, Seattle	0	1	0	0	1	0
Barber, Michael, Seattle	0	0	1	0	1	0
Barnett, Fred, Miami	1	0	0	0	0	0
Barrow, Micheal, Houston	0	0	1	0	1	0
Battaglia, Marco, Cincinnati	0	0	1	0	1	0
Baxter, Fred, N.Y. Jets............	1	0	0	0	0	0
Bell, Myron, Pittsburgh...........	0	0	2	0	2	0
Bell, Ricky, Jacksonville.........	1	0	0	0	0	0
Belser, Jason, Indianapolis	0	0	1	0	1	0
Bettis, Jerome, Pittsburgh.......	7	2	0	0	2	0
Biekert, Greg, Oakland	0	0	1	0	1	0
Bieniemy, Eric, Cincinnati	1	0	0	0	0	0
Blackmon, Robert, Seattle	0	0	1	5	1	0
Blades, Brian, Seattle.............	1	0	0	0	0	0
Blake, Jeff, Cincinnati	7	1	0	-5	1	0
Bledsoe, Drew, New England..	9	1	0	-2	1	0
Boatswain, Harry, N.Y. Jets.....	0	1	0	0	1	0
Bono, Steve, Kansas City	5	0	0	0	0	0
Booker, Vaughn, Kansas City ..	0	0	1	0	1	0
Boselli, Tony, Jacksonville	0	1	0	0	1	0
Bowens, Tim, Miami	0	0	1	0	1	0
Brackens, Tony, Jacksonville ..	0	0	3	0	3	0
Brady, Donny, Baltimore	0	0	1	0	1	0
Brady, Kyle, N.Y. Jets.............	1	0	0	0	0	0
Braxton, Tyrone, Denver	0	0	1	20	1	0
Brock, Matt, N.Y. Jets.............	0	0	1	5	1	0
Broussard, Steve, Seattle........	2	0	0	0	0	0
Brown, Chad, Pittsburgh	1	0	2	0	2	0
Brown, Corwin, New England..	0	0	1	42	1	1
Brown, Tim, Oakland	3	1	0	0	1	0
Bruce, Aundray, Oakland	0	0	1	3	1	0
Brunell, Mark, Jacksonville.....	14	5	0	-14	5	0
Buckley, Terrell, Miami...........	1	1	1	0	2	0
Buckner, Brentson, Pittsburgh..	1	0	1	13	1	0
Bullard, Kendricke, Jacksonville.	1	0	0	0	0	0
Burris, Jeff, Buffalo.................	1	0	1	0	1	0
Burton, Kendrick, Houston	0	0	1	9	1	0
Burton, Shane, Miami.............	0	0	1	0	1	0
Bush, Lewis, San Diego..........	0	0	2	0	2	0
Butcher, Paul, Oakland...........	0	1	0	0	1	0
Byner, Earnest, Baltimore	1	0	0	0	0	0
Cadrez, Glenn, Denver	0	1	0	0	1	0
Carter, Dale, Kansas City........	1	1	1	7	2	0
Carter, Ki-Jana, Cincinnati	2	2	0	-8	2	0
Cascadden, Chad, N.Y. Jets	0	0	1	0	1	0
Cash, Keith, Kansas City.........	1	0	0	0	0	0
Chalenski, Mike, N.Y. Jets.......	0	0	1	0	1	0
Chamberlain, Byron, Denver...	1	0	0	0	0	0
Chandler, Chris, Houston........	8	3	0	-4	3	0

Player, Team	Fum.	Own Rec.	Opp. Rec.	Yds.	Tot. Rec.	TD
Chrebet, Wayne, N.Y. Jets.......	5	2	0	0	2	■
Clark, Willie, San Diego	0	0	1	9	1	■
Clay, Willie, New England	0	0	1	17	1	■
Coates, Ben, New England......	1	0	0	0	0	■
Coleman, Andre, San Diego....	4	3	0	0	3	■
Collins, Mark, Kansas City	0	0	1	0	1	■
Collins, Todd, Buffalo.............	3	0	0	0	0	■
Copeland, Russell, Buffalo......	2	1	0	0	1	■
Coryatt, Quentin, Indianapolis..	0	0	2	7	2	■
Craver, Aaron, Denver............	1	0	0	0	0	■
Crockett, Zack, Indianapolis....	2	0	0	0	0	■
Crumpler, Carlester, Seattle	1	0	0	0	0	■
Cunningham, T.J., Seattle	0	0	1	0	1	■
Daniel, Eugene, Indianapolis...	0	0	1	0	1	■
Daniels, Phillip, Seattle	0	0	1	0	1	■
Davey, Don, Jacksonville	0	0	1	0	1	■
Davidson, Kenny, Cincinnati ...	0	0	1	0	1	■
Davis, Reuben, San Diego	0	0	1	0	1	■
Davis, Terrell, Denver..............	5	2	0	0	2	■
Davis, Travis, Jacksonville	0	1	1	0	2	■
Davis, Willie, Houston.............	1	0	0	0	0	■
Dawkins, Sean, Indianapolis ...	1	0	0	0	0	■
Dilger, Ken, Indianapolis	1	0	0	0	0	■
Dishman, Cris, Houston..........	0	0	2	0	2	■
Douglas, Hugh, N.Y. Jets	0	0	3	64	3	■
Drayton, Troy, Miami	0	1	0	0	1	■
Dudley, Rickey, Oakland	1	0	0	0	0	■
Duffy, Roger, N.Y. Jets...........	0	1	0	0	1	■
Dunn, David, Cincinnati	1	0	0	0	0	■
Eatman, Irv, Houston..............	0	1	0	0	1	■
Elway, John, Denver...............	6	2	0	-4	2	■
Emmons, Carlos, Pittsburgh...	0	1	0	0	1	■
Emtman, Steve, Miami............	0	0	1	0	1	■
Erickson, Craig, Miami............	4	3	0	-3	3	■
Ethridge, Ray, Baltimore	0	1	0	0	1	■
Faulk, Marshall, Indianapolis ..	2	0	0	0	0	■
Figures, Deon, Pittsburgh.......	0	1	0	0	1	■
Fina, John, Buffalo..................	0	1	1	-1	2	■
Fletcher, Terrell, San Diego	1	0	1	0	1	■
Floyd, Malcolm, Houston........	1	0	0	0	0	■
Foley, Glenn, N.Y. Jets	1	0	0	-4	0	■
Francis, James, Cincinnati	0	0	3	0	3	■
Friesz, John, Seattle................	7	2	0	-6	2	■
Galloway, Joey, Seattle	2	0	0	0	0	■
Gannon, Rich, Kansas City	1	0	0	0	0	■
Gardener, Daryl, Miami...........	0	0	1	0	1	■
George, Eddie, Houston..........	3	1	0	0	1	■
Glenn, Terry, New England......	1	0	0	0	0	■
Gogan, Kevin, Oakland............	0	1	0	0	1	■
Gordon, Darrien, San Diego....	3	0	0	0	0	■
Gossett, Jeff, Oakland..............	1	1	0	-19	1	■
Grant, Stephen, Indianapolis ..	0	0	1	0	1	■
Gray, Carlton, Seattle..............	0	0	1	62	1	■
Gray, Mel, Houston	4	0	0	0	0	■
Green, Victor, N.Y. Jets	0	0	3	0	3	■
Grier, Marrio, New England	0	0	1	4	1	■
Griffith, Rich, Jacksonville	0	1	0	0	1	■
Groce, Clif, Indianapolis..........	2	1	0	0	1	■
Grunhard, Tim, Kansas City	0	1	0	0	1	■
Hall, Dana, Jacksonville..........	0	1	1	0	2	■
Hamilton, Bobby, N.Y. Jets.....	0	0	1	7	1	■
Hamilton, Rick, N.Y. Jets	0	0	1	0	1	■
Hand, Norman, Miami	0	0	1	8	1	■
Hansen, Phil, Buffalo	0	0	2	0	2	■
Harbaugh, Jim, Indianapolis....	8	4	0	-3	4	■
Hardy, Kevin, Jacksonville	0	0	1	13	1	■
Harris, Anthony, Miami...........	0	0	1	0	1	■
Harris, Corey, Seattle..............	0	0	3	28	3	■
Harrison, Marvin, Indianapolis..	1	0	0	0	0	■
Harrison, Rodney, San Diego..	1	1	1	4	2	■

Player, Team	Fum.	Own Rec.	Opp. Rec.	Yds.	Tot. Rec.	TD
Hastings, Andre, Pittsburgh....	3	1	0	0	1	0
Hasty, James, Kansas City	0	0	1	80	1	1
Hayden, Aaron, San Diego	1	1	0	0	1	0
Hearst, Garrison, Cincinnati	1	1	0	0	1	0
Hebron, Vaughn, Denver	3	1	0	0	1	0
Henry, Kevin, Pittsburgh	0	0	1	4	1	0
Hill, Greg, Kansas City	1	0	0	0	0	0
Hill, Jeff, Cincinnati	1	0	1	0	1	0
Hill, Randal, Miami	1	0	0	0	0	0
Hill, Sean, Miami	0	1	0	10	1	1
Hilliard, Randy, Denver	0	1	0	0	1	0
Hobbs, Daryl, Oakland	4	2	0	0	2	0
Hobert, Billy Joe, Oakland	6	0	0	0	0	0
Holmes, Darick, Buffalo	2	1	0	0	1	0
Hopkins, Brad, Houston	0	1	0	0	1	0
Hostetler, Jeff, Oakland	4	5	0	-3	5	0
Houston, Bobby, N.Y. Jets	0	0	1	0	1	0
Hudson, Chris, Jacksonville....	3	1	1	0	2	0
Hull, Kent, Buffalo	0	1	0	1	1	0
Humphries, Stan, San Diego...	7	4	0	-6	4	0
Hundon, James, Cincinnati	1	0	0	0	0	0
Irvin, Ken, Buffalo	0	0	1	0	1	0
Isaia, Sale, Baltimore	1	1	0	0	1	0
Jackson, Calvin, Miami	1	0	0	0	0	0
Jackson, John, Pittsburgh	0	1	0	0	1	0
Jackson, Michael, Baltimore	0	0	1	0	1	0
Jackson, Steve, Houston	0	0	1	0	1	0
James, Tory, Denver	0	0	1	15	1	0
Jefferson, Shawn, N.E.	2	0	0	0	0	0
Jenkins, DeRon, Baltimore	0	0	1	0	1	0
Johnson, Bill, Pittsburgh	0	0	1	0	1	0
Johnson, Charles, Pittsburgh..	1	0	0	0	0	0
Johnson, Lonnie, Buffalo	1	3	1	0	4	0
Johnson, Ted, New England ...	0	0	1	0	1	0
Johnstone, Lance, Oakland	0	0	1	1	1	1
Jones, Gary, N.Y. Jets	0	0	1	0	1	0
Jones, Lenoy, Houston	0	0	1	0	1	0
Jones, Mike, New England	0	0	1	31	1	0
Jordan, Randy, Jacksonville	1	1	0	0	1	0
Jurkovic, John, Jacksonville ...	0	0	2	0	2	0
Justin, Paul, Indianapolis	1	1	0	0	1	0
Kaufman, Napoleon, Oakland..	3	0	0	0	0	0
Kelly, Jim, Buffalo	9	0	0	0	0	0
Kennedy, Lincoln, Oakland	0	1	0	0	1	0
Kidd, Carl, Oakland	2	1	0	0	1	0
Kinchen, Brian, Baltimore	1	0	0	-20	0	0
Kinchen, Todd, Denver	5	1	0	0	1	0
Klingler, David, Oakland	1	1	0	0	1	0
Lake, Carnell, Pittsburgh	0	0	2	85	2	1
Land, Dan, Oakland	0	0	2	0	2	0
Lane, Max, New England	0	3	0	0	3	0
Langford, Jevon, Cincinnati	0	0	1	0	1	0
Lester, Tim, Pittsburgh	1	0	0	0	0	0
Lewis, Jermaine, Baltimore	4	1	0	0	1	0
Mahlum, Eric, Indianapolis	0	1	0	0	1	0
Manusky, Greg, Kansas City ...	1	1	2	0	3	0
Marino, Dan, Miami	4	1	0	-3	1	0
Martin, Curtis, New England ...	4	1	0	0	1	0
Martin, Steve, Indianapolis	0	0	1	0	1	0
Mathews, Jason, Indianapolis..	0	1	0	0	1	0
Mawae, Kevin, Seattle	0	2	0	0	2	0
May, Deems, San Diego	0	0	1	0	1	0
McCardell, Keenan, Jac.	1	3	0	0	3	0
McCoy, Tony, Indianapolis	0	0	1	0	1	0
McCrary, Michael, Seattle	0	0	1	0	1	0
McDuffie, O.J., Miami	6	3	0	0	3	0
McGinest, Willie, New England..	0	0	2	0	2	1
McKnight, James, Seattle	0	0	1	0	1	0
McNair, Steve, Houston	7	4	0	0	4	0
McPhail, Jerris, Miami	2	1	0	0	1	0
Means, Natrone, Jacksonville..	3	1	0	0	1	0
Meggett, David, New England..	7	3	0	0	4	0
Miller, Jim, Pittsburgh	1	0	0	-4	0	0
Miller, Scott, Miami	0	1	0	0	1	1
Milloy, Lawyer, New England ..	0	0	1	0	1	0
Mills, Ernie, Pittsburgh	0	0	1	5	1	0
Mills, John Henry, Houston	0	0	2	0	2	0
Mims, Chris, San Diego	0	0	2	0	2	0
Mirer, Rick, Seattle	4	0	0	0	0	0
Mitchell, Pete, Jacksonville	1	0	0	0	0	0
Mitchell, Shannon, San Diego..	1	0	0	0	0	0
Montgomery, Greg, Baltimore..	1	1	0	0	1	0
Moore, Stevon, Baltimore	0	0	1	0	1	0
Morrison, Steve, Indianapolis..	0	0	2	0	2	0
Moten, Eric, San Diego	0	1	0	0	1	0
Moulds, Eric, Buffalo	1	0	0	0	0	0
Murrell, Adrian, N.Y. Jets	6	2	0	-16	2	0
Musgrave, Bill, Denver	3	0	0	-4	0	0
Myers, Greg, Cincinnati	1	0	0	0	0	0
Neujahr, Quentin, Baltimore	0	1	0	0	1	0
O'Donnell, Neil, N.Y. Jets	2	0	0	0	0	0
Oliver, Louis, Miami	1	1	4	7	5	0
Olsavsky, Jerry, Pittsburgh	0	0	1	6	1	0
Orlando, Bo, Cincinnati	0	1	0	0	1	0
Ostroski, Jerry, Buffalo	0	1	0	0	1	0
Parker, Glenn, Buffalo	0	2	0	0	2	0
Parker, Vaughn, San Diego	0	1	0	0	1	0
Parmalee, Bernie, Miami	1	0	0	0	0	0
Pegram, Erric, Pittsburgh	1	1	0	0	1	0
Penn, Chris, Kansas City	3	0	0	0	0	0
Perry, Darren, Pittsburgh	1	1	1	0	2	0
Perry, Michael Dean, Denver ..	0	0	1	0	1	0
Pleasant, Anthony, Baltimore..	0	0	1	36	1	0
Pollard, Marcus, Indianapolis..	0	1	0	0	1	0
Pritchett, Kelvin, Jacksonville..	0	0	2	0	2	0
Pritchett, Stanley, Miami	3	1	0	0	1	0
Pupunu, Alfred, San Diego	1	2	0	0	2	0
Ravotti, Eric, Pittsburgh	0	0	1	9	1	0
Reed, Andre, Buffalo	1	0	0	0	0	0
Reich, Frank, N.Y. Jets	9	1	0	-70	1	0
Richardson, Tony, Kansas City..	0	1	0	0	1	0
Rivers, Reggie, Denver	0	1	0	0	1	0
Robbins, Barret, Oakland	0	1	0	0	1	0
Roberson, James, Houston	0	0	1	4	1	0
Robertson, Marcus, Houston..	0	0	1	5	1	0
Robinson, Eddie, Jacksonville..	0	0	1	0	1	0
Robinson, Jeff, Denver	0	1	0	0	1	0
Robinson, Rafael, Houston	0	0	1	0	1	0
Rogers, Sam, Buffalo	0	0	2	0	2	0
Romanowski, Bill, Denver	0	0	3	0	3	0
Ross, Kevin, San Diego	0	0	1	0	1	0
Roye, Orpheus, Pittsburgh	0	1	0	0	1	0
Ruddy, Tim, Miami	1	0	0	-14	0	0
Russell, Leonard, San Diego...	6	2	0	-7	2	0
Salisbury, Sean, San Diego	3	0	0	-10	0	0
Sawyer, Corey, Cincinnati	2	1	0	0	1	0
Searcy, Leon, Jacksonville	0	1	0	0	1	0
Seau, Junior, San Diego	0	0	3	0	3	0
Sharpe, Shannon, Denver	1	0	0	0	0	0
Simien, Tracy, Kansas City	0	0	1	0	1	0
Simmons, Clyde, Jacksonville..	0	0	1	0	1	0
Siragusa, Tony, Indianapolis ...	0	0	1	0	1	0
Slade, Chris, New England	1	0	0	0	0	0
Smith, Anthony, Oakland	0	0	1	3	1	0
Smith, Artie, Cincinnati	0	0	1	0	1	0
Smith, Bruce, Buffalo	0	0	1	0	1	0
Smith, Jimmy, Jacksonville	1	0	0	0	0	0
Smith, Lamar, Seattle	4	1	0	0	1	0
Smith, Rod, Denver	1	0	0	0	0	0
Spencer, Jimmy, Cincinnati.....	0	0	1	59	1	1
Spielman, Chris, Buffalo	0	0	2	0	2	0
Spikes, Irving, Miami	1	0	0	0	0	0

1996 STATISTICS Fumbles

Player, Team	Fum.	Own Rec.	Opp. Rec.	Yds.	Tot. Rec.	TD
Spindler, Marc, N.Y. Jets	0	0	1	0	1	0
Steed, Joel, Pittsburgh	0	0	1	0	1	0
Stevens, Matt, Buffalo	0	0	1	0	1	0
Stewart, James, Jacksonville	2	1	0	0	1	0
Stewart, Kordell, Pittsburgh	1	0	0	0	0	0
Still, Bryan, San Diego	2	0	0	0	0	0
Strong, Mack, Seattle	0	0	1	0	1	0
Sullivan, Chris, New England	0	1	0	0	1	0
Sutter, Eddie, Baltimore	0	0	1	0	1	0
Swilling, Pat, Oakland	0	0	1	49	1	0
Tanuvasa, Maa, Denver	0	0	1	0	1	0
Tasker, Steve, Buffalo	3	0	0	0	0	0
Testaverde, Vinny, Baltimore	9	0	0	-11	0	0
Thomas, Dave, Jacksonville	1	0	0	0	0	0
Thomas, Derrick, Kansas City	0	0	1	0	1	0
Thomas, Thurman, Buffalo	1	1	0	0	1	0
Thomas, Zach, Miami	0	0	2	7	2	0
Tindale, Tim, Buffalo	1	0	0	0	0	0
Tomczak, Mike, Pittsburgh	7	2	0	0	2	0
Tovar, Steve, Cincinnati	1	0	0	0	0	0
Turk, Dan, Oakland	1	0	1	-29	1	0
Vanover, Tamarick, Kansas City	1	0	0	0	0	0
Walker, Derrick, Kansas City	0	1	0	0	1	0
Walker, Gary, Houston	0	0	1	0	1	0
Walter, Joe, Cincinnati	0	1	0	0	1	0
Warren, Chris, Seattle	3	2	0	4	2	0
Warren, Lamont, Indianapolis	3	1	0	0	1	0
Washington, Brian, Kansas City	0	0	1	0	1	0
Wells, Dean, Seattle	0	0	2	0	2	0
Wheeler, Mark, New England	0	0	1	0	1	0
Whigham, Larry, New England	0	0	1	0	1	0
White, David, Buffalo	0	0	2	12	2	1
Wilkinson, Dan, Cincinnati	1	0	1	0	1	0
Williams, Alfred, Denver	0	0	1	0	1	0
Williams, Dan, Denver	0	0	1	0	1	0
Williams, Darryl, Seattle	0	0	1	2	1	0
Williams, Harvey, Oakland	3	0	0	0	0	0
Williams, Jerrol, Baltimore	1	1	1	13	2	0
Williams, Ronnie, Seattle	0	0	1	0	1	0
Williams, Willie, Pittsburgh	0	0	1	0	1	0
Wohlabaugh, Dave, N.E.	0	2	0	1	2	0
Wooden, Shawn, Miami	0	1	1	0	2	0
Wooden, Terry, Seattle	0	0	2	0	2	0
Woods, Jerome, Kansas City	1	1	0	0	1	0
Woodson, Rod, Pittsburgh	1	1	2	42	3	1
Wortham, Barron, Houston	0	0	2	0	2	0
Wycheck, Frank, Houston	2	0	0	0	0	0
Young, Glen, San Diego	0	0	1	0	1	0
Zeier, Eric, Baltimore	2	1	0	0	1	0

NFC

Player, Team	Fum.	Own Rec.	Opp. Rec.	Yds.	Tot. Rec.	TD
Abraham, Donnie, Tampa Bay	0	0	2	3	2	0
Ahanotu, Chidi, Tampa Bay	0	0	1	0	1	0
Aikman, Troy, Dallas	6	2	0	-8	2	0
Alexander, Derrick, Minnesota	0	0	1	3	1	0
Allen, Terry, Washington	4	0	0	0	0	0
Alstott, Mike, Tampa Bay	4	0	0	0	0	0
Anderson, Jamal, Atlanta	4	0	1	0	1	0
Armstead, Jesse, N.Y. Giants	1	0	2	0	2	0
Arthur, Mike, Green Bay	1	0	0	0	0	0
Asher, Jamie, Washington	0	2	0	0	2	0
Baker, Myron, Carolina	0	1	0	0	1	0
Banks, Tony, St. Louis	21	4	0	-17	4	0
Bankston, Michael, Arizona	0	0	1	0	1	0
Barnett, Harlon, Minnesota	0	0	1	0	1	0
Bates, Mario, New Orleans	4	0	0	0	0	0
Bates, Michael, Carolina	2	0	0	0	0	0
Bates, Patrick, Atlanta	0	0	1	0	1	0

Player, Team	Fum.	Own Rec.	Opp. Rec.	Yds.	Tot. Rec.	TD
Beebe, Don, Green Bay	1	1	0	0	1	1
Bennett, Cornelius, Atlanta	0	0	2	0	2	0
Bennett, Edgar, Green Bay	2	1	0	0	1	0
Bercich, Pete, Minnesota	0	0	1	0	1	0
Beuerlein, Steve, Carolina	9	2	0	-7	2	0
Birden, J.J., Atlanta	2	0	0	0	0	0
Bishop, Greg, N.Y. Giants	0	1	0	0	1	0
Bjornson, Eric, Dallas	1	0	0	0	0	0
Bradford, Ronnie, Arizona	0	0	1	0	1	0
Brady, Jeff, Minnesota	0	0	3	0	3	0
Bratzke, Chad, N.Y. Giants	0	0	2	0	2	0
Brohm, Jeff, San Francisco	1	1	0	0	1	0
Brooks, Barrett, Philadelphia	0	1	0	0	1	0
Brooks, Bill, Washington	0	1	0	0	1	0
Brooks, Reggie, Tampa Bay	1	0	0	0	0	0
Brown, Dave, N.Y. Giants	9	1	0	-3	1	0
Brown, Dennis, San Francisco	0	0	1	0	1	0
Bruce, Isaac, St. Louis	1	0	0	0	0	0
Bryant, Junior, San Francisco	0	1	0	0	1	0
Buckley, Curtis, San Francisco	0	1	1	0	2	0
Burger, Todd, Chicago	0	0	1	0	1	0
Bush, Devin, Atlanta	0	0	1	0	1	0
Butler, LeRoy, Green Bay	0	1	1	2	2	0
Calloway, Chris, N.Y. Giants	1	1	0	7	1	0
Campbell, Jesse, N.Y. Giants	0	0	1	0	1	0
Carrier, Mark, Chicago	0	0	1	0	1	0
Carter, Cris, Minnesota	1	0	1	0	1	0
Carter, Dexter, San Francisco	5	0	0	0	0	0
Carter, Kevin, St. Louis	0	1	1	0	2	0
Carter, Tony, Chicago	1	1	0	0	1	0
Centers, Larry, Arizona	1	1	0	0	1	0
Cherry, Je'Rod, New Orleans	0	0	1	0	1	0
Clay, Hayward, St. Louis	0	1	0	0	1	0
Clemons, Duane, Minnesota	0	0	1	8	1	0
Collins, Kerry, Carolina	6	1	0	0	1	0
Compton, Mike, Detroit	1	0	0	0	0	0
Conway, Curtis, Chicago	1	0	0	0	0	0
Conwell, Ernie, St. Louis	0	0	1	0	1	0
Cook, Toi, Carolina	0	0	1	3	1	0
Cooper, Adrian, San Francisco	1	0	0	0	0	0
Cota, Chad, Carolina	0	1	0	0	1	0
Cox, Bryan, Chicago	0	0	3	0	3	1
Cross, Howard, N.Y. Giants	1	0	0	0	0	0
Dahl, Bob, Washington	0	1	0	0	1	0
Darby, Matt, Arizona	0	0	1	0	1	0
Davis, Don, New Orleans	0	0	1	0	1	0
Dawkins, Brian, Philadelphia	0	0	2	23	2	0
Dawsey, Lawrence, N.Y. Giants	0	1	0	0	1	0
DeLong, Greg, Minnesota	0	1	0	0	1	0
Dennis, Mark, Carolina	0	1	0	0	1	0
Detmer, Ty, Philadelphia	7	1	0	0	1	0
Dilfer, Trent, Tampa Bay	10	4	0	-4	4	0
Dimry, Charles, Tampa Bay	0	0	1	0	1	0
Dixon, Ernest, New Orleans	0	0	1	22	1	0
Doleman, Chris, San Francisco	0	0	3	13	3	1
Donaldson, Ray, Dallas	2	0	0	-3	0	0
Dotson, Earl, Green Bay	0	1	0	0	1	0
Dotson, Santana, Green Bay	0	0	1	8	1	0
Douglass, Maurice, N.Y. Giants	0	0	1	1	1	0
Dowdell, Marcus, Arizona	6	0	0	0	0	0
Downs, Gary, N.Y. Giants	1	1	0	0	1	0
Drakeford, Tyronne, S.F.	0	0	1	8	1	0
Dunn, Jason, Philadelphia	0	1	0	0	1	0
Edwards, Anthony, Arizona	1	0	1	0	1	0
Elliott, Matt, Carolina	0	1	0	0	1	0
Ellison, Jerry, Tampa Bay	2	1	0	0	1	0
Ellsworth, Percy, N.Y. Giants	0	0	1	0	1	0
Engram, Bobby, Chicago	2	0	0	0	0	0
Esiason, Boomer, Arizona	5	1	0	-8	1	0
Evans, Doug, Green Bay	1	0	1	2	1	0

Player, Team	Fum.	Own Rec.	Opp. Rec.	Yds.	Tot. Rec.	TD
Everett, Jim, New Orleans	10	1	0	-9	1	0
Farmer, Ray, Philadelphia	1	0	3	10	3	0
Favre, Brett, Green Bay	11	5	0	-10	5	0
Feagles, Jeff, Arizona	1	0	0	-7	0	0
Fields, Mark, New Orleans	0	0	1	20	1	0
Figaro, Cedric, St. Louis	1	1	0	0	1	0
Fisk, Jason, Minnesota	0	0	1	0	1	0
Floyd, William, San Francisco	4	1	0	0	1	0
Forbes, Marlon, Chicago	0	1	0	0	1	0
Fortin, Roman, Atlanta	0	2	0	0	2	0
Freeman, Antonio, Green Bay	3	1	0	14	1	0
Frerotte, Gus, Washington	12	1	0	-12	1	0
Fuller, William, Philadelphia	0	0	1	0	1	0
Garcia, Frank, Carolina	0	2	0	0	2	0
Gardner, Moe, Atlanta	0	0	1	0	1	0
Garner, Charlie, Philadelphia	1	0	0	0	0	0
Garnett, Dave, Minnesota	0	0	1	0	1	0
Gaskins, Percell, St. Louis	0	0	1	0	1	0
George, Jeff, Atlanta	3	2	0	-24	2	0
George, Ron, Atlanta	0	0	3	14	3	0
Gerak, John, Minnesota	0	1	0	0	1	0
Glover, Kevin, Detroit	0	2	0	0	2	0
Goeas, Leo, St. Louis	0	1	0	0	1	0
Gooch, Jeff, Tampa Bay	0	1	0	0	1	0
Graham, Kent, Arizona	5	0	0	0	0	0
Green, Darrell, Washington	0	0	1	15	1	0
Green, Harold, St. Louis	2	1	0	0	1	0
Green, Robert, Chicago	3	3	0	0	3	0
Greene, Kevin, Carolina	0	0	3	66	3	1
Griffith, Howard, Carolina	1	0	1	0	1	0
Griffith, Robert, Minnesota	1	0	0	0	0	0
Hall, Rhett, Philadelphia	0	0	2	32	2	1
Hall, Travis, Atlanta	0	0	1	0	1	0
Hampton, Rodney, N.Y. Giants	3	1	0	0	1	0
Harper, Alvin, Tampa Bay	1	0	0	0	0	0
Harris, Derrick, St. Louis	0	1	0	0	1	0
Harris, Jackie, Tampa Bay	1	0	0	0	0	0
Harris, James, St. Louis	0	0	1	22	1	0
Harris, Raymont, Chicago	3	0	0	0	0	0
Harris, Walt, Chicago	0	0	2	8	2	0
Hartings, Jeff, Detroit	0	1	0	0	1	0
Harvey, Ken, Washington	1	0	2	0	2	0
Hawkins, Courtney, Tampa Bay	1	0	0	0	0	0
Hayes, Mercury, New Orleans	1	0	0	0	0	0
Haynes, Michael, New Orleans	1	0	0	0	0	0
Hebert, Bobby, Atlanta	10	2	0	0	2	0
Henderson, William, Green Bay	1	0	0	0	0	0
Hennings, Chad, Dallas	0	0	1	0	1	0
Hentrich, Craig, Green Bay	0	1	0	0	1	0
Hicks, Michael, Chicago	1	0	0	0	0	0
Hoage, Terry, Arizona	0	0	1	0	1	0
Hoard, Leroy, Minnesota	3	0	0	0	0	0
Howard, Desmond, Green Bay	2	1	0	0	1	0
Hoying, Bobby, Philadelphia	1	0	0	0	0	0
Hughes, Tyrone, New Orleans	2	0	0	0	0	0
Hunter, Earnest, Bal.-N.O.*	4	1	0	0	1	0
Hutton, Tom, Philadelphia	0	1	0	0	1	0
Irvin, Michael, Dallas	1	0	0	0	0	0
Irving, Terry, Arizona	0	0	1	5	1	0
Ismail, Qadry, Minnesota	2	1	0	0	1	0
Israel, Steve, San Francisco	0	0	1	0	1	0
Jackson, Greg, New Orleans	1	0	0	0	0	0
Jackson, Jack, Chicago	2	0	0	0	0	0
Jeffires, Haywood, N.O.	1	0	0	0	0	0
Jenkins, Carlos, St. Louis	0	0	2	0	2	0
Jenkins, James, Washington	0	1	0	0	1	0
Jervey, Travis, Green Bay	4	1	0	0	1	0
Johnson, Anthony, Carolina	2	0	0	0	0	0
Johnson, Brad, Minnesota	5	3	0	-8	3	0
Johnson, LeShon, Arizona	5	2	0	0	2	0

Player, Team	Fum.	Own Rec.	Opp. Rec.	Yds.	Tot. Rec.	TD
Johnson, Melvin, Tampa Bay	0	0	1	0	1	0
Johnson, Tre, Washington	0	1	0	0	1	0
Johnston, Daryl, Dallas	1	1	0	0	1	0
Jones, Brian, New Orleans	0	0	1	11	1	1
Jones, Chris T., Philadelphia	1	0	0	0	0	0
Jones, Jimmie, St. Louis	0	0	2	0	2	0
Jones, Sean, Green Bay	0	0	1	0	1	0
Joyner, Seth, Arizona	0	0	1	0	1	0
Kanell, Danny, N.Y. Giants	2	0	0	-1	0	0
Kennison, Eddie, St. Louis	5	0	0	0	0	0
King, Ed, New Orleans	0	1	0	0	1	0
King, Shawn, Carolina	0	0	1	12	1	1
Kirby, Terry, San Francisco	1	0	0	0	0	0
Koonce, George, Green Bay	0	0	1	0	1	0
Kowalkowski, Scott, Detroit	0	0	1	0	1	0
Kragen, Greg, Carolina	0	0	2	0	2	0
Kramer, Erik, Chicago	1	1	0	-1	1	0
Krieg, Dave, Chicago	6	3	0	-9	3	0
Laing, Aaron, St. Louis	0	1	0	0	1	0
Landeta, Sean, St. Louis	1	1	0	-11	1	0
Lathon, Lamar, Carolina	0	0	2	4	2	0
Le Bel, Harper, Atlanta	0	0	1	0	1	0
Lee, Amp, Minnesota	2	1	0	0	1	0
Lett, Leon, Dallas	0	0	2	0	2	0
Levens, Dorsey, Green Bay	2	1	0	0	1	0
Lincoln, Jeremy, St. Louis	0	1	0	0	1	0
Logan, Marc, Washington	1	0	0	0	0	0
Lowery, Michael, Chicago	0	0	1	0	1	1
Lusk, Henry, New Orleans	1	0	0	0	0	0
Lyght, Todd, St. Louis	1	0	0	0	0	0
Lyle, Keith, St. Louis	1	0	0	0	0	0
Lynch, Eric, Detroit	1	0	0	0	0	0
Lynch, John, Tampa Bay	0	1	0	0	1	0
Majkowski, Don, Detroit	5	1	0	-6	1	0
Mamula, Mike, Philadelphia	0	1	2	4	3	1
Marion, Brock, Dallas	1	0	1	45	1	0
Marshall, Marvin, Tampa Bay	1	0	0	0	0	0
Martin, Jamie, St. Louis	2	1	0	-2	1	0
Martin, Kelvin, Dallas	1	0	0	0	0	0
Martin, Wayne, New Orleans	0	0	1	0	1	0
Marts, Lonnie, Tampa Bay	0	1	1	0	2	0
Mathis, Terance, Atlanta	0	1	0	0	1	0
Mayberry, Tony, Tampa Bay	0	1	0	0	1	0
McCollum, Andy, New Orleans	0	1	0	0	1	0
McDonald, Tim, San Francisco	0	0	1	0	1	0
McElroy, Leeland, Arizona	3	1	0	0	1	0
McGill, Lenny, Atlanta	0	0	1	0	1	0
McKyer, Tim, Atlanta	0	1	1	0	2	0
McMahon, Jim, Green Bay	1	1	0	0	1	0
McMillian, Mark, New Orleans	0	1	0	-6	1	0
McNeil, Ryan, Detroit	0	0	2	0	2	0
Metcalf, Eric, Atlanta	3	0	0	0	0	0
Mickens, Terry, Green Bay	1	1	0	0	1	0
Miller, Jamir, Arizona	0	0	1	26	1	1
Miller, Les, Carolina	0	0	1	14	1	0
Mills, Sam, Carolina	0	0	2	41	2	1
Mitchell, Brian, Washington	1	2	0	0	2	0
Mitchell, Kevin, San Francisco	0	0	1	0	1	0
Mitchell, Scott, Detroit	9	5	0	-3	5	0
Moon, Warren, Minnesota	7	2	0	0	2	0
Morrison, Darryl, Washington	0	1	3	14	4	0
Morton, Johnnie, Detroit	1	0	0	0	0	0
Nagle, Browning, Atlanta	1	0	0	0	0	0
Neal, Lorenzo, New Orleans	1	2	0	0	2	0
Newman, Anthony, N.O.	0	0	2	0	2	0
Newsome, Craig, Green Bay	0	1	0	0	1	0
Nickerson, Hardy, Tampa Bay	0	0	2	0	2	0
Norton, Ken, San Francisco	0	0	1	21	1	0
Nussmeier, Doug, New Orleans	2	0	0	0	0	0
O'Berry, Herman, St. Louis	1	0	0	0	0	0

Player, Team	Fum.	Own Rec.	Opp. Rec.	Yds.	Tot. Rec.	TD
O'Neal, Leslie, St. Louis..........	0	0	3	0	3	0
Odom, Jason, Tampa Bay	0	1	0	0	1	0
Oliver, Winslow, Carolina	4	0	0	0	0	0
Owens, Dan, Atlanta	0	0	1	0	1	0
Owens, Terrell, San Francisco..	1	0	0	0	0	0
Palmer, David, Minnesota	3	1	0	0	1	0
Parker, Anthony, St. Louis	0	0	1	0	1	0
Patton, Joe, Washington.........	0	1	0	0	1	0
Paul, Tito, Arizona.................	0	1	0	0	1	0
Peete, Rodney, Philadelphia....	2	1	0	0	1	0
Perry, Todd, Chicago	0	1	0	0	1	0
Phillips, Lawrence, St. Louis ..	2	1	0	0	1	0
Pierce, Aaron, N.Y. Giants	0	1	0	0	1	0
Poole, Tyrone, Carolina..........	0	0	1	0	1	0
Pope, Marquez, San Francisco..	0	0	1	4	1	0
Popson, Ted, San Francisco ...	0	1	0	0	1	0
Porcher, Robert, Detroit..........	0	0	2	0	2	0
Pounds, Darryl, Washington...	0	0	1	0	1	0
Price, Daryl, San Francisco.....	0	0	1	0	1	0
Randolph, Thomas, N.Y. Giants .	0	0	1	17	1	0
Rasby, Walter, Carolina..........	0	1	0	0	1	0
Raymer, Cory, Washington	0	1	0	0	1	0
Redmon, Anthony, Arizona	0	1	0	0	1	0
Rhett, Errict, Tampa Bay	3	1	0	0	1	0
Rice, Simeon, Arizona	0	0	1	0	1	0
Richards, Dave, Atlanta	0	1	0	0	1	0
Rison, Andre, Green Bay.........	1	0	0	0	0	0
Roaf, William, New Orleans	0	1	0	0	1	0
Roberts, Ray, Detroit	0	2	0	0	2	0
Robinson, Greg, St. Louis	1	0	0	0	0	0
Ross, Jermaine, St. Louis.......	0	0	1	0	1	0
Royal, Andre, Carolina	0	1	0	0	1	0
Royals, Mark, Detroit.............	0	1	0	0	1	0
Salaam, Rashaan, Chicago	3	1	0	0	1	0
Sanders, Barry, Detroit	4	2	0	0	2	0
Sanders, Deion, Dallas...........	2	0	3	15	3	1
Sanders, Frank, Arizona	1	1	0	0	1	0
Sapp, Warren, Tampa Bay	0	0	1	0	1	0
Saxton, Brian, N.Y. Giants......	0	1	0	0	1	0
Scott, Todd, Tampa Bay	0	0	1	0	1	0
Scroggins, Tracy, Detroit	0	0	1	0	1	0
Seay, Mark, Philadelphia........	2	0	0	0	0	0
Sehorn, Jason, N.Y. Giants	1	1	0	0	1	0
Shelley, Elbert, Atlanta	0	0	1	0	1	0
Shepherd, Leslie, Washington..	0	1	0	0	1	0
Shuler, Heath, Washington	1	0	0	-14	0	0
Simpson, Carl, Chicago	0	0	2	2	2	0
Sloan, David, Detroit..............	0	1	0	0	1	0
Small, Torrance, New Orleans..	1	0	0	0	0	0
Smith, Chuck, Atlanta	0	0	1	0	1	0
Smith, Emmitt, Dallas............	5	1	0	0	1	0
Smith, Fernando, Minnesota...	0	0	2	4	2	0
Smith, Robert, Minnesota.......	2	1	0	0	1	0
Smith, Vinson, Chicago	0	0	2	34	2	0
Stephens, Rod, Washington ...	0	0	1	0	1	0
Steussie, Todd, Minnesota......	0	1	0	0	1	0
Strickland, Fred, Dallas..........	0	0	1	0	1	0
Stubblefield, Dana, S.F...........	0	0	1	0	1	0
Swann, Eric, Arizona..............	0	0	3	11	3	0
Taylor, Aaron, Green Bay	0	1	0	0	1	0

Player, Team	Fum.	Own Rec.	Opp. Rec.	Yds.	Tot. Rec.	TD
Taylor, Bobby, Philadelphia.....	1	1	1	9	2	0
Terry, Ryan, Arizona...............	1	1	0	0	1	0
Thomas, Broderick, Dallas......	0	0	3	23	3	0
Thomas, Henry, Detroit...........	0	0	1	0	1	0
Thomas, J.T., St. Louis	1	0	0	0	0	0
Thomas, Mark, Carolina..........	0	0	1	18	1	0
Thomas, Orlando, Minnesota..	0	0	1	0	1	0
Thomas, William, Philadelphia..	0	0	1	23	1	1
Timpson, Michael, Chicago.....	2	1	0	0	1	0
Tolbert, Tony, Dallas..............	0	0	2	0	2	0
Toomer, Amani, N.Y. Giants	1	2	0	0	2	0
Tubbs, Winfred, New Orleans ..	0	0	1	0	1	0
Turk, Matt, Washington	1	0	0	-5	0	0
Turnbull, Renaldo, N.O...........	0	0	1	0	1	0
Turner, Kevin, Philadelphia......	1	0	0	0	0	0
Turner, Scott, Washington	0	0	1	0	1	1
Unutoa, Morris, Philadelphia ..	1	0	0	0	0	0
Upshaw, Regan, Tampa Bay ...	0	0	1	0	1	0
Valerio, Joe, St. Louis............	1	0	0	-30	0	0
Walker, Darnell, Atlanta..........	0	1	0	0	1	0
Walker, Herschel, Dallas	0	1	0	0	1	0
Walsh, Steve, St. Louis..........	1	1	0	0	1	0
Watters, Ricky, Philadelphia ...	5	0	0	0	0	0
Way, Charles, N.Y. Giants	0	0	3	0	3	0
Weldon, Casey, Tampa Bay	1	0	0	-1	0	0
Wells, Mike, Detroit	0	0	1	0	1	1
Wheatley, Tyrone, N.Y. Giants..	6	1	0	-18	1	0
White, Dwayne, St. Louis........	0	1	0	0	1	0
White, Reggie, Green Bay	2	0	3	2	3	0
Whitfield, Bob, Atlanta	0	1	0	0	1	0
Whittle, Ricky, New Orleans....	1	0	0	0	0	0
Widmer, Corey, N.Y. Giants.....	1	0	1	0	1	0
Wiegert, Zach, St. Louis	0	2	0	0	2	0
Williams, Aeneas, Arizona.......	0	0	1	0	1	0
Williams, Brian, Green Bay	0	0	3	0	3	0
Williams, Charlie, Dallas	1	0	0	0	0	0
Williams, James, Chicago.......	0	2	0	0	2	0
Williams, Karl, Tampa Bay	2	1	0	0	1	0
Williams, Sherman, Dallas......	2	0	0	0	0	0
Williams, Tyrone, Green Bay...	0	0	1	0	1	0
Wilson, Bernard, Arizona	0	0	1	0	1	0
Winters, Frank, Green Bay	0	1	0	0	1	0
Witherspoon, Derrick, Phi.......	1	0	0	0	0	0
Wolf, Joe, Arizona..................	0	2	0	0	2	0
Woodard, Marc, Philadelphia..	0	1	0	0	1	0
Woodson, Darren, Dallas........	1	1	0	0	1	0
Wooten, Tito, N.Y. Giants........	0	0	1	54	1	1
Young, Bryant, San Francisco.	0	0	1	43	1	0
Young, Steve, San Francisco ..	3	1	0	0	1	0
Zellars, Ray, New Orleans	2	0	0	0	0	0
Zgonina, Jeff, Atlanta..............	0	0	1	0	1	0

*Includes both NFC and AFC statistics.

PLAYERS WITH TWOO CLUBS

Player, Team	Fum.	Own Rec.	Opp. Rec.	Yds.	Tot. Rec.	TD
Hunter, Earnest, Baltimore......	2	0	0	0	0	0
Hunter, Earnest, New Orleans ..	2	1	0	0	1	0

FIELD GOALS

TEAM

AFC

Team	Made	Att.	Pct.	Long
Indianapolis	36	40	.900	52
Houston	32	38	.842	56
Jacksonville	30	36	.833	53
Buffalo	24	29	.828	48
Seattle	28	34	.824	54
Cincinnati	23	28	.821	49
San Diego	29	36	.806	53
Oakland	24	31	.774	47
New England	27	35	.771	50
Pittsburgh	23	30	.767	49
Baltimore	19	25	.760	50
Denver	21	28	.750	51
N.Y.Jets	17	24	.708	46
Kansas City	17	24	.708	45
Miami	18	29	.621	44
AFC total	368	467	....	56
AFC average	24.5	31.1	.788	....

NFC

Team	Made	Att.	Pct.	Long
Dallas	32	36	.889	52
N.Y.Giants	24	27	.889	46
San Francisco	30	34	.882	49
Philadelphia	25	29	.862	46
New Orleans	21	25	.840	54
St. Louis	21	25	.840	50
Carolina	37	45	.822	53
Washington	26	32	.813	53
Tampa Bay	25	32	.781	50
Green Bay	21	27	.778	53
Chicago	23	30	.767	49
Atlanta	22	29	.759	54
Minnesota	22	29	.759	44
Arizona	23	31	.742	49
Detroit	12	17	.706	51
NFC total	364	448	....	54
NFC average	24.3	29.9	.813	....
NFL total	732	915	....	56
NFL average	24.4	30.5	.800	....

INDIVIDUAL

BESTS OF THE SEASON

Field goal percentage, season
AFC: .900—Cary Blanchard, Indianapolis.
NFC: .889—Chris Boniol, Dallas; Brad Daluiso, N.Y. Giants.
Field goals, season
NFC: 37—John Kasay, Carolina.
AFC: 36—Cary Blanchard, Indianapolis.
Field goal attempts, season
NFC: 45—John Kasay, Carolina.
AFC: 40—Cary Blanchard, Indianapolis.
Longest field goal
AFC: 56—Al Del Greco, Houston vs. San Francisco, Oct. 27.
NFC: 54—Doug Brien, New Orleans vs. Chicago, Oct. 13;
    Morten Andersen, Atlanta at Dallas, Oct. 20.
Average yards made, season
NFC: 37.9—Jeff Jaeger, Chicago.
AFC: 36.1—Al Del Greco, Houston.

NFL LEADERS

Team	Made	Att.	Pct.	Long
Blanchard, Cary, Indianapolis*	36	40	.900	52
Daluiso, Brad, N.Y. Giants	24	27	.889	46
Boniol, Chris, Dallas	32	36	.889	52
Wilkins, Jeff, San Francisco	30	34	.882	49
Anderson, Gary, Philadelphia	25	29	.862	46
Del Greco, Al, Houston*	32	38	.842	56
Lohmiller, Chip, St. Louis	21	25	.840	50
Brien, Doug, New Orleans	21	25	.840	54
Hollis, Mike, Jacksonville*	30	36	.833	53
Christie, Steve, Buffalo*	24	29	.828	48

*AFC.
Leader based on percentage, minimum 16 attempts.

AFC

Player, Team	1-19	20-29	30-39	40-49	Over	Totals	Avg. Yds. Att.	Avg. Yds. Made	Avg. Yds. Miss	Long
Blanchard, Cary	1-1	11-11	8-9	11-14	5-5	36-40	36.4	35.9	40.5	52
Indianapolis	1.000	1.000	.889	.786	1.000	.900				
Carney, John	0-0	11-13	8-8	7-12	3-3	29-36	35.9	34.7	41.1	53
San Diego	....	.846	1.000	.583	1.000	.806				
Christie, Steve	0-0	5-6	12-14	7-8	0-1	24-29	35.7	35.2	38.2	48
Buffalo	....	.833	.857	.875	.000	.828				
Del Greco, Al	0-0	7-7	14-16	10-12	1-3	32-38	37.4	36.1	44.7	56
Houston	....	1.000	.875	.833	.333	.842				
Elam, Jason	2-2	8-8	4-5	6-10	1-3	21-28	36.2	33.4	44.6	51
Denver	1.000	1.000	.800	.600	.333	.750				
Ford, Cole	0-0	9-11	10-11	5-8	0-1	24-31	34.9	33.6	39.4	47
Oakland	....	.818	.909	.625	.000	.774				
Hollis, Mike	2-2	9-9	12-14	5-8	2-3	30-36	34.6	33.2	41.5	53
Jacksonville	1.000	1.000	.857	.625	.667	.833				
Johnson, Norm	0-0	10-12	8-10	5-7	0-1	23-30	33.8	32.5	38.1	49
Pittsburgh	....	.833	.800	.714	.000	.767				
Lowery, Nick	0-0	9-9	6-7	2-8	0-0	17-24	35.0	30.7	45.4	46
N.Y. Jets	....	1.000	.857	.250	....	.708				

Player, Team	1-19	20-29	30-39	40-49	Over	Totals	Avg. Yds. Att.	Avg. Yds. Made	Avg. Yds. Miss	Long
Nedney, Joe	1-1	7-7	7-11	3-8	0-2	18-29	36.3	32.6	42.5	44
Miami	1.000	1.000	.636	.375	.000	.621				
Pelfrey, Doug	1-1	7-7	10-11	5-9	0-0	23-28	34.1	32.2	43.0	49
Cincinnati	1.000	1.000	.909	.556	....	.821				
Peterson, Todd	0-0	11-13	7-7	8-11	2-3	28-34	35.1	34.4	38.2	54
Seattle	....	.846	1.000	.727	.667	.824				
Stover, Matt	0-0	8-8	5-6	5-10	1-1	19-25	36.2	33.6	44.3	50
Baltimore	....	1.000	.833	.500	1.000	.760				
Stoyanovich, Pete	1-1	7-8	5-7	4-7	0-1	17-24	33.8	31.2	40.1	45
Kansas City	1.000	.875	.714	.571	.000	.708				
Vinatieri, Adam	1-1	9-10	8-8	8-14	1-2	27-35	35.1	32.7	43.1	50
New England	1.000	.900	1.000	.571	.500	.771				

NFC

Player, Team	1-19	20-29	30-39	40-49	Over	Totals	Avg. Yds. Att.	Avg. Yds. Made	Avg. Yds. Miss	Long
Andersen, Morten	0-0	5-5	9-11	7-8	1-5	22-29	38.2	35.8	45.9	54
Atlanta	....	1.000	.818	.875	.200	.759				
Anderson, Gary	0-0	10-11	8-9	7-9	0-0	25-29	34.6	33.8	39.8	46
Philadelphia	....	.909	.889	.778	....	.862				
Blanton, Scott	2-2	13-13	7-7	2-7	2-3	26-32	32.9	29.8	46.3	53
Washington	1.000	1.000	1.000	.286	.667	.813				
Boniol, Chris	1-1	13-13	12-13	5-7	1-2	32-36	34.1	32.9	44.0	52
Dallas	1.000	1.000	.923	.714	.500	.889				
Brien, Doug	0-0	4-4	9-10	5-7	3-4	21-25	39.0	37.8	45.0	54
New Orleans	....	1.000	.900	.714	.750	.840				
Butler, Kevin	1-1	6-6	5-8	2-2	0-0	14-17	31.2	30.7	33.7	41
Arizona	1.000	1.000	.625	1.000	....	.824				
Daluiso, Brad	2-2	10-10	9-9	3-6	0-0	24-27	31.1	29.7	42.3	46
N.Y. Giants	1.000	1.000	1.000	.500	....	.889				
Davis, Greg	0-0	7-9	1-2	1-3	0-0	9-14	31.9	29.2	36.6	49
Arizona	....	.778	.500	.333	....	.643				
Hanson, Jason	0-0	4-4	4-5	3-5	1-3	12-17	38.6	35.3	46.8	51
Detroit	....	1.000	.800	.600	.333	.706				
Huerta, Carlos	0-0	0-0	3-5	1-2	0-0	4-7	37.4	36.0	39.3	42
Chicago	....	....	.600	.500	....	.571				
Husted, Michael	2-2	7-8	8-11	7-8	1-3	25-32	35.3	33.9	40.0	50
Tampa Bay	1.000	.875	.727	.875	.333	.781				
Jacke, Chris	0-0	6-6	9-11	5-9	1-1	21-27	36.3	34.5	42.7	53
Green Bay	....	1.000	.818	.556	1.000	.778				
Jaeger, Jeff	0-0	4-4	3-4	12-15	0-0	19-23	38.7	37.9	42.3	49
Chicago	....	1.000	.750	.800	....	.826				
Kasay, John	2-2	14-14	11-12	7-10	3-7	37-45	36.0	33.6	46.8	53
Carolina	1.000	1.000	.917	.700	.429	.822				
Lohmiller, Chip	1-1	11-11	4-5	4-7	1-1	21-25	33.3	31.4	43.0	50
St. Louis	1.000	1.000	.800	.571	1.000	.840				
Sisson, Scott	0-0	8-8	11-14	3-7	0-0	22-29	33.7	31.4	40.7	44
Minnesota	....	1.000	.786	.429	....	.759				
Wilkins, Jeff	0-0	16-16	7-8	7-10	0-0	30-34	34.1	32.7	44.0	49
San Francisco	....	1.000	.875	.700	....	.882				

PUNTING

TEAM

AFC

Team	Total Punts	Yards	Long	Avg.	TB	Blocked	Opp. Ret.	Ret. Yards	Inside 20	Net Avg.
Miami	78	3611	63	46.3	11	0	48	368	26	38.8
Indianapolis	68	3105	61	45.7	2	0	38	413	23	39.0
San Diego	87	3967	66	45.6	6	0	51	612	23	37.2
N.Y. Jets	74	3293	69	44.5	8	0	40	429	13	36.5
Cincinnati	82	3634	67	44.3	17	1	38	502	16	34.0
Houston	68	2973	68	43.7	7	1	31	251	25	38.0
Jacksonville	69	3016	62	43.7	8	0	44	400	16	35.6
Seattle	86	3746	66	43.6	7	1	52	640	20	34.5
New England	64	2766	62	43.2	7	0	34	334	15	35.8
Baltimore	69	2980	67	43.2	5	1	27	273	23	37.8
Denver	65	2714	57	41.8	5	0	23	261	16	36.2
Kansas City	88	3667	68	41.7	10	0	42	492	25	33.8
Buffalo	101	4194	80	41.5	13	0	40	246	27	36.5
Pittsburgh	72	2931	61	40.7	11	0	32	284	25	33.7
Oakland	79	3169	64	40.1	8	0	38	272	24	34.6
AFC total	1150	49766	80	....	125	4	578	5777	317	....
AFC average	76.7	3317.7	....	43.3	8.3	0.3	38.5	385.1	21.1	36.1

Leader based on average.

NFC

Team	Total Punts	Yards	Long	Avg.	TB	Blocked	Opp. Ret.	Ret. Yards	Inside 20	Net Avg.
Washington	77	3470	63	45.1	12	0	35	235	25	38.9
Chicago	78	3491	72	44.8	12	0	42	527	15	34.9
St. Louis	78	3491	70	44.8	9	0	41	495	23	36.1
Arizona	77	3328	68	43.2	6	1	37	403	23	36.4
San Francisco	75	3217	65	42.9	6	2	36	235	20	38.2
Detroit	71	3044	60	42.9	8	1	42	519	12	33.3
Dallas	74	3150	60	42.6	9	0	32	249	22	36.8
Tampa Bay	71	3015	62	42.5	4	1	38	248	24	37.8
Green Bay	68	2886	65	42.4	9	0	29	237	28	36.3
N.Y. Giants	102	4289	63	42.0	10	0	45	432	32	35.9
Atlanta	75	3152	58	42.0	4	0	32	413	22	35.5
Philadelphia	74	3107	60	42.0	9	1	36	330	17	35.1
New Orleans	87	3551	63	40.8	9	0	43	546	16	32.5
Carolina	78	3158	60	40.5	10	0	32	173	21	35.7
Minnesota	90	3616	63	40.2	6	2	37	577	26	32.4
NFC total	1175	49965	72	....	123	8	557	5619	326	....
NFC average	78.3	3331.0	....	42.5	8.2	0.5	37.1	374.6	21.7	35.6
NFL total	2325	99731	80	....	248	12	1135	11396	643	....
NFL average	77.5	3324.4	....	42.9	8.3	0.4	37.8	379.9	21.4	35.9

INDIVIDUAL

BESTS OF THE SEASON

Average yards per punt, season
AFC: 46.3—John Kidd, Miami.
NFC: 45.1—Matt Turk, Washington.
Net average yards per punt, season
NFC: 39.2—Matt Turk, Washington.
AFC: 39.0—Chris Gardocki, Indianapolis.
Longest
AFC: 80—Chris Mohr, Miami vs. Buffalo, Oct. 13.
NFC: 72—Todd Sauerbrun, Chicago at Washington, Sept. 8.

Punts, season
NFC: 102—Mike Horan, N.Y. Giants.
AFC: 101—Chris Mohr, Buffalo.
Punts, game
AFC: 12—Chris Gardocki, Indianapolis at Buffalo, Oct. 6 (OT).
NFC: 10—Mike Horan, N.Y. Giants vs. Buffalo, Sept. 1 (OT);
Mark Royals, Detroit vs. Tampa Bay, Sept. 8; Tommy
Barnhardt, Tampa Bay at Minnesota, Dec. 15; Klaus
Wilmsmeyer, New Orleans at N.Y. Giants, Dec. 15.

NFL LEADERS

Player, Team	Net Punts	Yards	Long	Avg.	Total Punts	TB	Blk.	Opp. Ret.	Ret. Yds.	In 20	Net Avg.
Kidd, John, Miami	78	3611	63	46.3	78	11	0	48	368	26	38.8
Gardocki, Chris, Indianapolis	68	3105	61	45.7	68	2	0	38	413	23	39.0

Player, Team	Net Punts	Yards	Long	Avg.	Total Punts	TB	Blk.	Opp. Ret.	Ret. Yds.	In 20	Net Avg.
Bennett, Darren, San Diego	87	3967	66	45.6	87	6	0	51	612	23	37.2
Johnson, Lee, Cincinnati	80	3630	67	45.4	81	17	1	38	502	16	34.4
Turk, Matt, Washington	75	3386	63	45.1	75	11	0	34	224	25	39.2
Landeta, Sean, St. Louis	78	3491	70	44.8	78	9	0	41	495	23	36.1
Sauerbrun, Todd, Chicago	78	3491	72	44.8	78	12	0	42	527	15	34.9
Hanson, Jason, Detroit	1	24	24	24.0	1	0	0	0	0	1	24.0
Roby, Reggie, Houston	67	2973	68	44.4	68	7	1	31	251	25	38.0
Tuten, Rick, Seattle	85	3746	66	44.1	86	7	1	52	640	20	34.5

*AFC.
Leader based on average, minimum 40 punts.

AFC

Player, Team	Net Punts	Yards	Long	Avg.	Total Punts	TB	Blk.	Opp. Ret.	Ret. Yds.	In 20	Net Avg.
Aguiar, Louis, Kansas City	88	3667	68	41.7	88	10	0	42	492	25	33.8
Araguz, Leo, Oakland	13	534	52	41.1	13	2	0	6	45	4	34.5
Barker, Bryan, Jacksonville	69	3016	62	43.7	69	8	0	44	400	16	35.6
Bennett, Darren, San Diego	87	3967	66	45.6	87	6	0	51	612	23	37.2
Edge, Shayne, Pittsburgh	17	675	48	39.7	17	3	0	8	36	7	34.1
Gardocki, Chris, Indianapolis	68	3105	61	45.7	68	2	0	38	413	23	39.0
Gossett, Jeff, Oakland	57	2264	64	39.7	57	5	0	28	192	19	34.6
Hansen, Brian, N.Y.Jets	74	3293	69	44.5	74	8	0	40	429	13	36.5
Hobert, Billy Joe, Oakland	9	371	53	41.2	9	1	0	4	35	1	35.1
Johnson, Lee, Cincinnati	80	3630	67	45.4	81	17	1	38	502	16	34.4
Kidd, John, Miami	78	3611	63	46.3	78	11	0	48	368	26	38.8
Miller, Josh, Pittsburgh	55	2256	61	41.0	55	8	0	24	248	18	33.6
Mohr, Chris, Buffalo	101	4194	80	41.5	101	13	0	40	246	27	36.5
Montgomery, Greg, Baltimore	68	2980	67	43.8	69	5	1	27	273	23	37.8
Pelfrey, Doug, Cincinnati	1	4	4	4.0	1	0	0	0	0	0	4.0
Roby, Reggie, Houston	67	2973	68	44.4	68	7	1	31	251	25	38.0
Rouen, Tom, Denver	65	2714	57	41.8	65	5	0	23	261	16	36.2
Tupa, Tom, New England	63	2739	62	43.5	63	7	0	34	334	14	36.0
Tuten, Rick, Seattle	85	3746	66	44.1	86	7	1	52	640	20	34.5
Vinatieri, Adam, New England	1	27	27	27.0	1	0	0	0	0	1	27.0

NFC

Player, Team	Net Punts	Yards	Long	Avg.	Total Punts	TB	Blk.	Opp. Ret.	Ret. Yds.	In 20	Net Avg.
Barnhardt, Tommy, Tampa Bay	70	3015	62	43.1	71	4	1	38	248	24	37.8
Berger, Mitch, Minnesota	88	3616	63	41.1	90	6	2	37	577	26	32.4
Blanton, Scott, Washington	2	84	45	42.0	2	1	0	1	11	0	26.5
Feagles, Jeff, Arizona	76	3328	68	43.8	77	6	1	37	403	23	36.4
Hanson, Jason, Detroit	1	24	24	24.0	1	0	0	0	0	1	24.0
Hentrich, Craig, Green Bay	68	2886	65	42.4	68	9	0	29	237	28	36.3
Horan, Mike, N.Y.Giants	102	4289	63	42.0	102	10	0	45	432	32	35.9
Hutton, Tom, Philadelphia	73	3107	60	42.6	74	9	1	36	330	17	35.1
Jett, John, Dallas	74	3150	60	42.6	74	9	0	32	249	22	36.8
Kasay, John, Carolina	1	30	30	30.0	1	1	0	0	0	0	10.0
Landeta, Sean, St. Louis	78	3491	70	44.8	78	9	0	41	495	23	36.1
Royals, Mark, Detroit	69	3020	60	43.8	70	8	1	42	519	11	33.4
Sauerbrun, Todd, Chicago	78	3491	72	44.8	78	12	0	42	527	15	34.9
Stark, Rohn, Carolina	77	3128	60	40.6	77	9	0	32	173	21	36.0
Stryzinski, Dan, Atlanta	75	3152	58	42.0	75	4	0	32	413	22	35.5
Thompson, Tommy, San Francisco	73	3217	65	44.1	75	6	2	36	235	20	38.2
Turk, Matt, Washington	75	3386	63	45.1	75	11	0	34	224	25	39.2
Wilmsmeyer, Klaus, New Orleans	87	3551	63	40.8	87	9	0	43	546	16	32.5

PUNT RETURNS

TEAM

AFC

Team	No.	FC	Yds.	Avg.	Long	TD
San Diego	38	14	559	14.7	t81	1
Denver	49	19	583	11.9	40	0
New England	52	9	588	11.3	t60	1
Indianapolis	41	15	447	10.9	82	0
Seattle	34	15	352	10.4	t88	1
Jacksonville	34	13	351	10.3	60	0
Buffalo	43	15	423	9.8	45	0
Miami	26	25	251	9.7	19	0
Houston	29	18	279	9.6	40	0
Oakland	42	24	403	9.6	50	0
Baltimore	38	14	357	9.4	46	0
Kansas City	33	16	282	8.5	24	0
Cincinnati	33	8	217	6.6	62	0
Pittsburgh	40	12	251	6.3	33	0
N.Y. Jets	28	16	139	5.0	15	0
AFC total	560	233	5482	9.8	t88	3
AFC average	37.3	15.5	365.5	9.8	....	0.2

t—touchdown.

NFC

Team	No.	FC	Yds.	Avg.	Long	TD
Green Bay	58	17	875	15.1	t92	3
St. Louis	35	16	439	12.5	t78	2
Tampa Bay	41	9	481	11.7	t88	1
N.Y. Giants	42	23	478	11.4	t87	2
Carolina	55	17	624	11.3	t84	1
Washington	23	16	258	11.2	71	0
Atlanta	31	10	315	10.2	39	0
Minnesota	32	31	300	9.4	t69	1
Chicago	31	19	282	9.1	34	0
San Francisco	39	21	352	9.0	52	0
Dallas	44	11	394	9.0	22	0
Arizona	39	9	343	8.8	35	0
Detroit	34	19	284	8.4	33	0
Philadelphia	40	17	330	8.3	56	0
New Orleans	31	20	159	5.1	16	0
NFC total	575	255	5914	10.3	t92	10
NFC average	38.3	17.0	394.3	10.3	....	0.7
NFL total	1135	488	11396	....	t92	13
NFL average	37.8	16.3	379.9	10.0	....	0.4

INDIVIDUAL

BESTS OF THE SEASON

Yards per attempt, season
NFC: 15.1—Desmond Howard, Green Bay.
AFC: 14.9—Darrien Gordon, San Diego.

Yards, season
NFC: 875—Desmond Howard, Green Bay.
AFC: 588—David Meggett, New England.

Yards, game
NFC: 167—Desmond Howard, Green Bay at Detroit, Dec. 15 (5 returns, 1 TD).
AFC: 141—Ray Buchanan, Indianapolis vs. San Diego, Nov. 3 (5 returns).

Longest
NFC: 92—Desmond Howard, Green Bay at Detroit, Dec. 15 (TD).
AFC: 88—Joey Galloway, Seattle vs. Denver, Sept. 8 (TD).

Returns, season
NFC: 58—Desmond Howard, Green Bay.
AFC: 52—David Meggett, New England.

Returns, game
AFC: 7—Rod Smith, Denver vs. Kansas City, Oct. 27 (99 yards).
NFC: 7—Desmond Howard, Green Bay vs. San Diego, Sept. 15 (118 yards, 1 TD).

Fair catches, season
AFC: 24—O.J. McDuffie, Miami.
NFC: 20—David Palmer, Minnesota; Tyrone Hughes, New Orleans.

Touchdowns, season
NFC: 3—Desmond Howard, Green Bay.
AFC: 1—Joey Galloway, Seattle; Darrien Gordon, San Diego; David Meggett, New England.

NFL LEADERS

Player, Team	No.	FC	Yds.	Avg.	Long	TD
Howard, Desmond, Green Bay	58	16	875	15.1	t92	3
Gordon, Darrien, San Diego*	36	13	537	14.9	t81	1
Kennison, Eddie, St. Louis	29	16	423	14.6	t78	2
Smith, Rod, Denver*	23	15	283	12.3	36	0
Kinchen, Todd, Denver*	26	4	300	11.5	40	0
Oliver, Winslow, Carolina	52	17	598	11.5	t84	1
Meggett, David, New England*	52	9	588	11.3	t60	1
Mitchell, Brian, Washington	23	16	258	11.2	71	0

Player, Team	No.	FC	Yds.	Avg.	Long	TD
Metcalf, Eric, Atlanta	27	9	296	11.0	39	0
Hudson, Chris, Jacksonville*	32	12	348	10.9	60	0
Burris, Jeff, Buffalo*	27	7	286	10.6	45	0
Palmer, David, Minnesota	22	20	216	9.8	t69	1
McDuffie, O.J., Miami*	22	24	212	9.6	19	0
Lewis, Jermaine, Baltimore*	36	13	339	9.4	46	0
Gray, Mel, Houston*	22	15	205	9.3	40	0

*AFC.

t—touchdown.

Leader based on average return, minimum 20.

AFC

Player, Team	No.	FC	Yds.	Avg.	Long	TD
Alexander, Derrick, Baltimore	1	0	15	15.0	15	0
Arnold, Jahine, Pittsburgh	2	0	6	3.0	5	0
Brown, Tim, Oakland	32	21	272	8.5	36	0
Buchanan, Ray, Indianapolis	12	3	201	16.8	82	0
Buckley, Terrell, Miami	3	1	24	8.0	13	0
Burris, Jeff, Buffalo	27	7	286	10.6	45	0
Carter, Dale, Kansas City	2	0	18	9.0	15	0
Chrebet, Wayne, N.Y. Jets	28	16	139	5.0	15	0
Copeland, Russell, Buffalo	14	7	119	8.5	19	0
Dunn, David, Cincinnati	7	1	54	7.7	20	0
Ethridge, Ray, Baltimore	1	0	3	3.0	3	0
Floyd, Malcolm, Houston	7	3	74	10.6	32	0
Galloway, Joey, Seattle	15	5	158	10.5	t88	1
Gordon, Darrien, San Diego	36	13	537	14.9	t81	1
Gray, Mel, Houston	22	15	205	9.3	40	0
Harris, Ronnie, Seattle	19	10	194	10.2	35	0
Harrison, Marvin, Indianapolis	18	9	177	9.8	31	0
Hastings, Andre, Pittsburgh	37	12	242	6.5	33	0
Hobbs, Daryl, Oakland	10	3	84	8.4	33	0
Hudson, Chris, Jacksonville	32	12	348	10.9	60	0
Hundon, James, Cincinnati	1	0	-7	-7.0	-7	0
Hunter, Earnest, Baltimore	0	1	0	....	....	0
Jones, Charlie, San Diego	1	1	21	21.0	21	0
Jones, Donta, Pittsburgh	1	0	3	3.0	3	0
Kidd, Carl, Oakland	0	0	47	....	47	0
Kinchen, Todd, Denver	26	4	300	11.5	40	0
Lewis, Jermaine, Baltimore	36	13	339	9.4	46	0

Player, Team	No.	FC	Yds.	Avg.	Long	TD
McCardell, Keenan, Jacksonville .	1	1	2	2.0	2	0
McDuffie, O.J., Miami	22	24	212	9.6	19	0
Meggett, David, New England ..	52	9	588	11.3	t60	1
Miller, Scott, Miami	1	0	15	15.0	15	0
Myers, Greg, Cincinnati	9	2	51	5.7	12	0
Penn, Chris, Kansas City	14	4	148	10.6	20	0
Pickens, Carl, Cincinnati	1	0	2	2.0	2	0
Sawyer, Corey, Cincinnati	15	5	117	7.8	62	0
Smith, Rod, Denver	23	15	283	12.3	36	0
Stablein, Brian, Indianapolis	6	2	56	9.3	30	0
Still, Bryan, San Diego	1	0	1	1.0	1	0
Stock, Mark, Indianapolis	5	1	13	2.6	9	0
Tasker, Steve, Buffalo	2	1	18	9.0	12	0
Thomas, Dave, Jacksonville	1	0	1	1.0	1	0
Vanover, Tamarick, Kansas City..	17	12	116	6.8	24	0

t—touchdown.

NFC

Player, Team	No.	FC	Yds.	Avg.	Long	TD
Carter, Dexter, San Francisco ...	36	17	317	8.8	52	0
Dowdell, Marcus, Arizona	34	8	297	8.7	35	0
Edwards, Anthony, Arizona	5	1	46	9.2	20	0
Engram, Bobby, Chicago	31	19	282	9.1	34	0
Figaro, Cedric, St. Louis	1	0	0	0.0	0	0
Guess, Terry, New Orleans	1	0	7	7.0	7	0
Hawkins, Courtney, Tampa Bay	1	1	-1	-1.0	-1	0
Heyward, Craig, Atlanta	1	0	0	0.0	0	0
Howard, Desmond, Green Bay ..	58	16	875	15.1	t92	3

Player, Team	No.	FC	Yds.	Avg.	Long	TD
Hughes, Tyrone, New Orleans..	30	20	152	5.1	16	0
Kennison, Eddie, St. Louis	29	16	423	14.6	t78	2
Kirby, Terry, San Francisco	1	4	3	3.0	3	0
Lee, Amp, Minnesota	10	11	84	8.4	18	0
Lewis, Thomas, N.Y. Giants	10	4	36	3.6	8	0
Marshall, Arthur, N.Y. Giants....	13	9	144	11.1	36	0
Marshall, Marvin, Tampa Bay...	13	1	95	7.3	29	0
Martin, Kelvin, Dallas	41	10	373	9.1	22	0
Mathis, Terance, Atlanta	3	1	19	6.3	10	0
Metcalf, Eric, Atlanta	27	9	296	11.0	39	0
Milburn, Glyn, Detroit	34	19	284	8.4	33	0
Mitchell, Brian, Washington	23	16	258	11.2	71	0
O'Berry, Herman, St. Louis	5	0	16	3.2	8	0
Oliver, Winslow, Carolina	52	17	598	11.5	t84	1
Palmer, David, Minnesota	22	20	216	9.8	t69	1
Poole, Tyrone, Carolina	3	0	26	8.7	12	0
Prior, Mike, Green Bay	0	1	0	....	....	0
Sanders, Deion, Dallas	1	1	4	4.0	4	0
Seay, Mark, Philadelphia	35	14	305	8.7	56	0
Sehorn, Jason, N.Y. Giants	1	0	0	0.0	0	0
Silvan, Nilo, Tampa Bay	14	5	113	8.1	17	0
Singleton, Nate, San Francisco.	2	0	32	16.0	21	0
Solomon, Freddie, Philadelphia ..	5	3	27	5.4	9	0
Toomer, Amani, N.Y. Giants	18	10	298	16.6	t87	2
Vincent, Troy, Philadelphia	0	0	-2	....	-2	0
Williams, Karl, Tampa Bay	13	2	274	21.1	t88	1
Williams, Kevin, Dallas	2	0	17	8.5	9	0

t—touchdown.

KICKOFF RETURNS

TEAM

AFC

Team	No.	Yds.	Avg.	Long	TD
Denver	50	1195	23.9	59	0
Kansas City	66	1567	23.7	t97	1
Buffalo	58	1341	23.1	t97	1
Indianapolis	61	1403	23.0	t95	1
New England	64	1424	22.3	54	0
Pittsburgh	53	1171	22.1	t91	1
Miami	60	1320	22.0	59	0
Jacksonville	67	1463	21.8	73	0
Seattle	71	1542	21.7	86	0
San Diego	63	1358	21.6	57	0
Houston	66	1421	21.5	88	0
Oakland	61	1276	20.9	48	0
Cincinnati	70	1459	20.8	t90	1
Baltimore	86	1734	20.2	44	0
N.Y.Jets	79	1504	19.0	37	0
AFC total	975	21178	21.7	t97	5
AFC average	65.0	1411.9	21.7	....	0.3

t—touchdown.

NFC

Team	No.	Yds.	Avg.	Long	TD
Carolina	50	1310	26.2	t93	1
Dallas	53	1339	25.3	89	0
New Orleans	78	1899	24.3	58	0
Detroit	69	1675	24.3	65	0
Chicago	56	1337	23.9	88	0
Tampa Bay	55	1287	23.4	63	0
Philadelphia	64	1439	22.5	t97	2
Green Bay	47	1038	22.1	t90	1
Washington	65	1401	21.6	50	0
San Francisco	59	1258	21.3	71	0
Arizona	75	1582	21.1	92	0
Atlanta	87	1825	21.0	55	0
St. Louis	62	1233	19.9	44	0
N.Y.Giants	66	1287	19.5	47	0
Minnesota	58	1075	18.5	60	0
NFC total	944	20985	22.2	t97	4
NFC average	62.9	1399.0	22.2	....	0.3
NFL total	1919	42163	....	t97	9
NFL average	64.0	1405.4	22.0	....	0.3

INDIVIDUAL

BESTS OF THE SEASON

Yards per attempt, season
AFC: 30.2—Michael Bates, Carolina.
NFC: 25.9—Tamarick Vanover, Kansas City.

Yards, season
NFC: 1791—Tyrone Hughes, New Orleans.
AFC: 1224—Mel Gray, Houston.

Yards, game
NFC: 253—Derrick Witherspoon, Philadelphia at Arizona, Nov. 24 (8 returns, 1 TD).
AFC: 206—Andre Coleman, San Diego at Seattle, Oct. 27 (8 returns).

Longest
NFC: 97—Tamarick Vanover, Kansas City at Denver, Oct. 27 (TD); Eric Moulds, Buffalo vs. N.Y. Jets, Nov. 24 (TD).
NFC: 97—Derrick Witherspoon, Philadelphia at Atlanta, Sept. 22 (TD).

Returns, season
NFC: 70—Tyrone Hughes, New Orleans.
AFC: 55—Andre Coleman, San Diego.

Returns, game
NFC: 9—Eric Metcalf, Atlanta at San Francisco, Sept. 29 (176 yards); Eric Metcalf, Atlanta at St. Louis, Nov. 10 (144 yards).
AFC: 8—Andre Coleman, San Diego at Seattle, Oct. 27 (206 yards).

Touchdowns, season
NFC: 2—Derrick Witherspoon, Philadelphia.
AFC: 1—Held by five players.

NFL LEADERS

Player, Team	No.	Yds.	Avg.	Long	TD
Bates, Michael, Carolina	33	998	30.2	t93	1
Walker, Herschel, Dallas	27	779	28.9	89	0
Vanover, Tamarick, Kansas City*	33	854	25.9	t97	1
Hughes, Tyrone, New Orleans	70	1791	25.6	58	0
Milburn, Glyn, Detroit	64	1627	25.4	65	0
Gray, Mel, Houston*	50	1224	24.5	88	0

Player, Team	No.	Yds.	Avg.	Long	TD
Hebron, Vaughn, Denver*	45	1099	24.4	59	0
Spikes, Irving, Miami*	28	681	24.3	59	0
Bailey, Aaron, Indianapolis*	43	1041	24.2	t95	1
Witherspoon, Derrick, Philadelphia	53	1271	24.0	t97	2
Woods, Jerome, Kansas City*	25	581	23.2	66	0
Engram, Bobby, Chicago	25	580	23.2	45	0
Moulds, Eric, Buffalo*	52	1205	23.2	t97	1
Meggett, David, New England*	34	781	23.0	54	0
Jackson, Jack, Chicago	27	619	22.9	60	0

*AFC.
t—touchdown.
Leader based on average return, minimum 20.

AFC

Player, Team	No.	Yds.	Avg.	Long	TD
Alexander, Derrick, Baltimore	1	13	13.0	13	0
Anders, Kimble, Kansas City	f2	37	18.5	20	0
Archie, Mike, Houston	2	24	12.0	13	0
Arnold, Jahine, Pittsburgh	19	425	22.4	30	0
Aska, Joe, Oakland	1	17	17.0	17	0
Bailey, Aaron, Indianapolis	43	1041	24.2	t95	1
Bailey, Henry, N.Y. Jets	24	470	19.6	34	0
Baldwin, Randy, Baltimore	20	405	20.3	34	0
Barber, Michael, Seattle	1	12	12.0	12	0
Battaglia, Marco, Cincinnati	1	8	8.0	8	0
Bell, Ricky, Jacksonville	6	119	19.8	28	0
Brady, Kyle, N.Y. Jets	f2	26	13.0	16	0
Brooks, Bucky, Jacksonville	17	412	24.2	36	0
Broussard, Steve, Seattle	43	979	22.8	86	0
Brown, Reggie, Seattle	4	51	12.8	24	0
Brown, Tim, Oakland	1	24	24.0	24	0
Brown, Troy, New England	29	634	21.9	51	0
Buchanan, Ray, Indianapolis	1	20	20.0	20	0
Buckley, Terrell, Miami	1	48	48.0	48	0
Bullard, Kendricke, Jacksonville	7	157	22.4	36	0
Byner, Earnest, Baltimore	4	61	15.3	19	0
Carpenter, Ron, N.Y. Jets	6	107	17.8	21	0
Chamberlain, Byron, Denver	3	49	16.3	21	0
Cobb, Reggie, N.Y. Jets	23	488	21.2	34	0
Coleman, Andre, San Diego	55	1210	22.0	57	0

Player, Team	No.	Yds.	Avg.	Long	TD
Copeland, Russell, Buffalo.............	6	136	22.7	47	0
Cothran, Jeff, Cincinnati	1	11	11.0	11	0
Dar Dar, Kirby, Miami	7	132	18.9	25	0
Dunn, David, Cincinnati	35	782	22.3	t90	1
Edwards, Vernon, San Diego	1	0	0.0	0	0
Ethridge, Ray, Baltimore	8	171	21.4	29	0
Fauria, Christian, Seattle...............	1	8	8.0	8	0
Frederick, Mike, Baltimore.............	0	-1	....	-1	0
Gisler, Mike, New England	1	9	9.0	9	0
Glenn, Aaron, N.Y. Jets	1	6	6.0	6	0
Gossett, Jeff, Oakland	1	0	0.0	0	0
Gray, Mel, Houston.......................	50	1224	24.5	88	0
Griffith, Rich, Jacksonville	2	24	12.0	16	0
Groce, Clif, Indianapolis	1	18	18.0	18	0
Harmon, Ronnie, Houston.............	4	69	17.3	20	0
Harris, Corey, Seattle...................	7	166	23.7	41	0
Harris, Ronnie, Seattle..................	12	240	20.0	29	0
Harrison, Rodney, San Diego	1	10	10.0	10	0
Hastings, Andre, Pittsburgh	1	42	42.0	42	0
Hebron, Vaughn, Denver	45	1099	24.4	59	0
Hetherington, Chris, Indianapolis ..	1	16	16.0	16	0
Hill, Jeff, Cincinnati	9	173	19.2	29	0
Hill, Randal, Miami	2	4	2.0	4	0
Hobbs, Daryl, Oakland..................	1	14	14.0	14	0
Hughes, Danan, Kansas City	2	42	21.0	22	0
Hundon, James, Cincinnati...........	10	237	23.7	31	0
Isaia, Sale, Baltimore...................	1	2	2.0	2	0
Jackson, Willie, Jacksonville	7	149	21.3	27	0
Jeffers, Patrick, Denver	1	18	18.0	18	0
Johnson, Charles, Pittsburgh	6	111	18.5	31	0
Jordan, Charles, Miami	4	81	20.3	22	0
Jordan, Randy, Jacksonville	26	553	21.3	73	0
Kaufman, Napoleon, Oakland	25	548	21.9	39	0
Kidd, Carl, Oakland	29	622	21.4	48	0
Kinchen, Brian, Baltimore.............	1	19	19.0	19	0
Lewis, Jermaine, Baltimore	41	883	21.5	44	0
Manusky, Greg, Kansas City........	2	32	16.0	17	0
McKeehan, James, Houston..........	2	6	3.0	6	0
McKnight, James, Seattle.............	3	86	28.7	55	0
McNair, Todd, Kansas City............	2	21	10.5	16	0
McPhail, Jerris, Miami...................	15	335	22.3	40	0
Meggett, David, New England	34	781	23.0	54	0
Mills, Ernie, Pittsburgh................	8	146	18.3	27	0
Moore, Ronald, N.Y. Jets..............	8	118	14.8	28	0
Morris, Bam, Baltimore	1	3	3.0	3	0
Moulds, Eric, Buffalo....................	52	1205	23.2	t97	1
Pegram, Erric, Pittsburgh.............	17	419	24.6	t91	1
Perry, Darren, Pittsburgh..............	1	8	8.0	8	0
Pupunu, Alfred, San Diego	1	15	15.0	15	0
Roan, Michael, Houston................	1	13	13.0	13	0
Russell, Leonard, San Diego	1	10	10.0	10	0
Sadowski, Troy, Cincinnati............	2	7	3.5	7	0
Sawyer, Corey, Cincinnati	12	241	20.1	33	0
Shedd, Kenny, Oakland.................	3	51	17.0	19	0
Smith, Jimmy, Jacksonville	2	49	24.5	29	0
Smith, Rod, Denver	1	29	29.0	29	0
Spikes, Irving, Miami	28	681	24.3	59	0
Still, Bryan, San Diego.................	4	113	28.3	37	0
Stock, Mark, Indianapolis..............	12	254	21.2	28	0
Thomas, Rodney, Houston............	5	80	16.0	35	0
Thomas, Zach, Miami	1	17	17.0	17	0
Van Dyke, Alex, N.Y. Jets..............	15	289	19.3	37	0
Vanover, Tamarick, Kansas City.....	33	854	25.9	t97	1
Wainright, Frank, Miami	1	10	10.0	10	0
Warren, Lamont, Indianapolis	3	54	18.0	18	0
Wilson, Robert, Miami...................	1	12	12.0	12	0
Witman, Jon, Pittsburgh	1	20	20.0	20	0
Woods, Jerome, Kansas City.........	25	581	23.2	66	0
Wycheck, Frank, Houston..............	2	5	2.5	5	0

t—touchdown.
f—includes at least one fair catch.

NFC

Player, Team	No.	Yds.	Avg.	Long	T
Alexander, Kevin, N.Y. Giants.........	2	27	13.5	14	
Alstott, Mike, Tampa Bay..............	1	14	14.0	14	
Anderson, Jamal, Atlanta..............	4	80	20.0	27	
Asher, Jamie, Washington	1	13	13.0	13	
Baker, Myron, Carolina	1	11	11.0	11	
Bates, Michael, Carolina	33	998	30.2	t93	
Beebe, Don, Green Bay.................	15	403	26.9	t90	
Bell, William, Washington..............	8	130	16.3	27	
Bickett, Duane, Carolina	1	12	12.0	12	
Brooks, Barrett, Philadelphia.........	1	0	0.0	0	
Brown, Derek, New Orleans	1	10	10.0	10	
Brown, Richard, Minnesota	3	35	11.7	12	
Carter, Cris, Minnesota.................	1	3	3.0	3	
Carter, Dexter, San Francisco........	41	909	22.2	71	
Crawford, Keith, St. Louis	4	47	11.8	19	
Deese, Derrick, San Francisco.......	2	20	10.0	12	
DeLong, Greg, Minnesota..............	1	3	3.0	3	
Douglas, Omar, N.Y. Giants	1	11	11.0	11	
Dowdell, Marcus, Arizona..............	5	122	24.4	31	
Engram, Bobby, Chicago	25	580	23.2	45	
Faulkerson, Mike, Chicago............	4	63	15.8	20	
Freeman, Antonio, Green Bay........	1	16	16.0	16	
Garner, Charlie, Philadelphia.........	6	117	19.5	28	
Gerak, John, Minnesota.................	1	13	13.0	13	
Greene, Scott, Carolina.................	2	10	5.0	6	
Hamilton, Conrad, N.Y. Giants	19	382	20.1	29	
Hayes, Mercury, New Orleans	2	30	15.0	17	
Henderson, William, Green Bay.....	2	38	19.0	23	
Heyward, Craig, Atlanta................	1	18	18.0	18	
Hoard, Leroy, Carolina..................	1	19	19.0	19	
Howard, Desmond, Green Bay	22	460	20.9	40	
Hughes, Tyrone, New Orleans	70	1791	25.6	58	
Hunter, Earnest, Bal.-N.O.*	10	198	19.8	29	
Ismail, Qadry, Minnesota..............	28	527	18.8	32	
Ismail, Raghib, Carolina	5	100	20.0	30	
Jackson, Jack, Chicago.................	27	619	22.9	60	
Jervey, Travis, Green Bay	1	17	17.0	17	
Johnson, LeShon, Arizona.............	10	198	19.8	27	
Kennison, Eddie, St. Louis	23	454	19.7	44	
Kirby, Terry, San Francisco...........	1	22	22.0	22	
Kozlowski, Brian, N.Y. Giants........	1	16	16.0	16	
Laing, Aaron, St. Louis..................	1	15	15.0	15	
Lee, Amp, Minnesota....................	5	85	17.0	23	
Levens, Dorsey, Green Bay...........	5	84	16.8	29	
Lewis, Thomas, N.Y. Giants	4	107	26.8	47	
Loville, Derek, San Francisco	10	229	22.9	35	
Lusk, Henry, New Orleans	1	16	16.0	16	
Lynch, Eric, Detroit.......................	1	15	15.0	15	
Marion, Brock, Dallas	3	68	22.7	37	
Marshall, Anthony, Chicago...........	0	75	....	75	
Marshall, Marvin, Tampa Bay	12	264	22.0	37	
Matthews, Aubrey, Detroit	1	10	10.0	10	
McCleskey, J.J., New Orleans.......	1	18	18.0	18	
McDonald, Devon, Arizona	1	16	16.0	16	
McElroy, Leeland, Arizona	54	1148	21.3	92	
Metcalf, Eric, Atlanta	49	1034	21.1	55	
Metzelaars, Pete, Detroit	1	1	1.0	1	
Milburn, Glyn, Detroit....................	64	1627	25.4	65	
Mitchell, Brian, Washington	56	1258	22.5	50	
Morrow, Harold, Minnesota...........	6	117	19.5	26	
Oliver, Winslow, Carolina..............	7	160	22.9	33	
Owens, Terrell, San Francisco	3	47	15.7	18	
Palmer, David, Minnesota.............	13	292	22.5	60	
Phillips, Lawrence, St. Louis	4	74	18.5	35	
Preston, Roell, Atlanta..................	32	681	21.3	50	
Rivers, Ron, Detroit.......................	1	8	8.0	8	
Saxton, Brian, N.Y. Giants	3	31	10.3	17	
Seay, Mark, Philadelphia	4	51	12.8	22	
Silvan, Nilo, Tampa Bay................	28	626	22.4	54	

Player, Team	No.	Yds.	Avg.	Long	TD
Singleton, Nate, San Francisco......	1	10	10.0	10	0
Smith, Brady, New Orleans...........	2	14	7.0	8	0
Smith, Cedric, Arizona................	1	14	14.0	14	0
Styles, Lorenzo, Atlanta.....................	1	12	12.0	12	0
Terry, Ryan, Arizona	4	84	21.0	30	0
Thomas, J.T., St. Louis.................	30	643	21.4	43	0
Thomason, Jeff, Green Bay	1	20	20.0	20	0
Toomer, Amani, N.Y. Giants..........	11	191	17.4	25	0
Uwaezuoke, Iheanyi, San Francisco..	1	21	21.0	21	0
Walker, Herschel, Dallas................	27	779	28.9	89	0
Washington, Keith, Detroit	1	14	14.0	14	0
Way, Charles, N.Y. Giants	2	19	9.5	10	0
Wheatley, Tyrone, N.Y. Giants........	23	503	21.9	43	0

Player, Team	No.	Yds.	Avg.	Long	TD
Williams, Charlie, Dallas................	2	21	10.5	21	0
Williams, Karl, Tampa Bay	14	383	27.4	63	0
Williams, Kevin, Dallas	21	471	22.4	39	0
Witherspoon, Derrick, Philadelphia..	53	1271	24.0	t97	2

*Includes both NFC and AFC statistics.
t—touchdown.
f—includes at least one fair catch.

PLAYERS WITH TWO CLUBS

Player, Team	No.	Yds.	Avg.	Long	TD
Hunter, Earnest, Baltimore............	9	178	19.8	29	0
Hunter, Earnest, New Orleans........	1	20	20.0	20	0

1996 STATISTICS *Kickoff returns*

MISCELLANEOUS

CLUB RANKINGS BY YARDS

Team	Offense Total	Rush	Pass	Defense Total	Rush	Pass
Arizona	13	25	6	21	21	21
Atlanta	17	27	9	29	26	27
Baltimore	3	14	2	30	23	30
Buffalo	16	8	17	9	14	8
Carolina	23	15	22	10	8	12
Chicago	21	16	19	12	11	14
Cincinnati	10	13	12	25	12	29
Dallas	24	18	20	3	9	2
Denver	*1	*1	13	4	*1	10
Detroit	20	12	18	20	25	18
Green Bay	5	11	5	*1	4	*1
Houston	18	6	21	6	2	13
Indianapolis	25	28	16	22	18	23
Jacksonville	2	17	*1	15	19	16
Kansas City	22	4	26	18	13	22
Miami	14	19	11	17	7	24
Minnesota	12	24	8	16	24	9
New England	7	26	3	19	6	28
New Orleans	29	30	25	13	27	3
N.Y. Giants	30	21	30	14	16	15
N.Y. Jets	11	23	10	27	29	19
Oakland	8	3	23	8	15	7
Philadelphia	4	9	4	5	10	6
Pittsburgh	15	2	27	2	3	5
San Diego	26	29	14	23	17	25
San Francisco	6	10	7	7	5	11
Seattle	19	5	24	24	28	17
St. Louis	27	20	28	26	20	26
Tampa Bay	28	22	29	11	22	4
Washington	9	7	15	28	30	20

*NFL leader.
†Tied for position.

Team	Takeaways Int	Fum.	Tot.	Giveaways Int	Fum.	Tot.	Net Diff.
Minnesota	22	13	35	19	13	32	3
Chicago	17	11	28	18	9	27	1
N.Y. Giants	22	13	35	21	13	34	1
Philadelphia	19	12	31	18	14	32	-1
St. Louis	26	13	39	23	21	44	-5
Tampa Bay	17	12	29	20	14	34	-5
Detroit	11	8	19	21	5	26	-7
Arizona	11	14	25	21	14	35	-10
New Orleans	12	10	22	17	20	37	-15
Atlanta	6	17	23	30	11	41	-18

CLUB LEADERS

	Offense	Defense
First downs	N.E. 339	G.B. 24
Rushing	Pit. 138	Den. 6
Passing	Ari. 214	Dal. 14
Penalty	Car. 39	Ind.
Rushes	Buf. 563	Den. 34
Net yards gained	Den. 2362	Den. 133
Average gain	Oak. 4.8	Buf. 3.
Passes attempted	NYJ 629	NYJ 45
Completed	N.E. 374	NYJ 25
Percent completed	S.F. 65.1	S.F. 51.
Total yards gained	Jac. 4367	G.B. 294
Times sacked	Dal. 19	Car. 6
Yards lost	Dal. 127	Car. 37
Net yards gained	Jac. 4110	G.B. 274
Net yards per pass play	Jac. 6.77	G.B. 4.
Yds. gained per completion	Was. 12.79	T.B. 10.0
Combined net yards gained	Den. 5791	G.B. 415
Percent total yards rushing	Pit. 44.7	N.E. 28.
Percent total yards passing	N.E. 72.7	N.O. 57.
Ball-control plays	Buf. 1094	Den. 95
Average yards per play	Bal. 5.6	G.B. 4.
Avg. time of possession	Den. 33:17	Car. 32.
Third-down efficiency	Den. 48.9	Car. 32.
Interceptions	—	Cin. 3
Yards returned	—	G.B. 52
Returned for TD	—	Ind., St.L.
Punts	NYG 102	—
Yards punted	NYG 4289	—
Average yards per punt	Sea. 46.3	—
Punt returns	G.B. 58	Den. 2
Yards returned	G.B. 875	Car. 17
Average yds. per return	G.B. 15.1	Car. 5.
Returned for TD	G.B. 3	—
Kickoff returns	Atl. 87	NYG 4
Yards returned	N.O. 1899	NYG 94
Average yards per return	Car. 26.2	S.F. 18.
Returned for TD	Phi. 2	—
Total points scored	G.B. 456	G.B. 21
Total TDs	G.B. 56	G.B. 1
TDs rushing	Was. 27	S.F.
TDs passing	G.B. 39	Dal. 1
TDs on ret. and recov.	G.B. 8	3 tied with
Extra points	G.B. 51	G.B. 1
2-pt. conversions	Bal., Jac. 5	—
Safeties	S.F. 4	—
Field goals made	Car. 37	Mia. 1
Field goals attempted	Car. 45	Mia. 1
Percent successful	Ind. 90.0	Buf. 63.

TAKEAWAYS/GIVEAWAYS

AFC

	Takeaways Int	Fum.	Tot.	Giveaways Int	Fum.	Tot.	Net Diff.
Cincinnati	34	10	44	16	9	25	19
Miami	20	16	36	11	13	24	12
New England	23	11	34	15	12	27	7
Pittsburgh	23	17	40	19	14	33	7
San Diego	22	14	36	21	11	32	4
Kansas City	17	10	27	14	10	24	3
Seattle	14	18	32	17	12	29	3
Denver	23	9	32	17	15	32	0
Indianapolis	13	10	23	11	13	24	-1
Jacksonville	13	14	27	20	10	30	-3
Houston	12	14	26	15	15	30	-4
Oakland	17	9	26	19	12	31	-5
Buffalo	14	14	28	24	13	37	-9
Baltimore	15	7	22	20	13	33	-11
N.Y. Jets	11	15	26	30	16	46	-20

NFC

	Takeaways Int	Fum.	Tot.	Giveaways Int	Fum.	Tot.	Net Diff.
Green Bay	26	13	39	13	11	24	15
Carolina	22	16	38	11	14	25	13
Washington	21	9	30	11	7	18	12
San Francisco	20	14	34	16	8	24	10
Dallas	19	14	33	14	15	29	4

TEAM-BY-TEAM SUMMARIES
AFC
OFFENSE

	Bal.	Buf.	Cin.	Den.	Hou.	Ind.	Jac.	K.C.	Mia.	N.E.	NYJ	Oak.	Pit.	S.D.	Sea.
st downs	338	294	332	336	287	288	325	312	294	339	319	306	296	272	268
Rushing	108	128	114	134	110	89	90	111	92	103	94	98	138	80	94
Passing	208	149	190	180	157	172	208	168	173	206	191	172	146	168	147
Penalty	22	17	28	22	20	27	27	33	29	30	34	36	12	24	27
shes	416	563	478	525	475	420	431	488	460	427	407	456	525	412	442
Net yards gained	1745	1901	1793	2362	1950	1448	1650	2009	1622	1468	1583	2174	2299	1312	1997
Average gain	4.2	3.4	3.8	4.5	4.1	3.4	3.8	4.1	3.5	3.4	3.9	4.8	4.4	3.2	4.5
Average yards per game	109.1	118.8	112.1	147.6	121.9	90.5	103.1	125.6	101.4	91.8	98.9	135.9	143.7	82.0	124.8
sses attempted	570	483	563	536	463	537	557	530	504	628	629	533	456	577	494
Completed	335	279	316	327	272	311	353	290	300	374	339	311	246	314	261
Percent completed	58.8	57.8	56.1	61.0	58.7	57.9	63.4	54.7	59.5	59.6	53.9	58.3	53.9	54.4	52.8
Total yards gained	4274	3558	3726	3662	3296	3544	4367	3093	3783	4091	3911	3327	2990	3654	3216
Times sacked	38	48	47	31	34	43	50	27	36	30	41	45	21	33	38
Yards lost	296	340	294	233	198	248	257	203	240	190	286	249	149	296	189
Net yards gained	3978	3218	3432	3429	3098	3296	4110	2890	3543	3901	3625	3078	2841	3358	3027
Average yards per game	248.6	201.1	214.5	214.3	193.6	206.0	256.9	180.6	221.4	243.8	226.6	192.4	177.6	209.9	189.2
Net yards per pass play	6.54	6.06	5.63	6.05	6.23	5.68	6.77	5.19	6.56	5.93	5.41	5.33	5.96	5.50	5.69
Yards gained per completion	12.76	12.75	11.79	11.20	12.12	11.40	12.37	10.67	12.61	10.94	11.54	10.70	12.15	11.64	12.32
mbined net yards gained	5723	5119	5225	5791	5048	4744	5760	4899	5165	5369	5208	5252	5140	4670	5024
Percent total yards rushing	30.5	37.1	34.3	40.8	38.6	30.5	28.6	41.0	31.4	27.3	30.4	41.4	44.7	28.1	39.7
Percent total yards passing	69.5	62.9	65.7	59.2	61.4	69.5	71.4	59.0	68.6	72.7	69.6	58.6	55.3	71.9	60.3
Average yards per game	357.7	319.9	326.6	361.9	315.5	296.5	360.0	306.2	322.8	335.6	325.5	328.3	321.3	291.9	314.0
ll-control plays	1024	1094	1088	1092	972	1000	1038	1045	1000	1085	1077	1034	1002	1022	974
Average yards per play	5.6	4.7	4.8	5.3	5.2	4.7	5.5	4.7	5.2	4.9	4.8	5.1	5.1	4.6	5.2
Average time of possession	27:05	28:40	31:33	33:17	32:02	30:44	31:18	30:39	31:08	30:11	29:26	30:39	30:08	27:35	28:01
rd-down efficiency	43.8	34.9	43.2	48.9	38.3	37.7	41.8	34.8	40.3	36.8	40.9	40.6	40.4	33.9	30.2
d intercepted	20	24	16	17	15	11	20	14	11	15	30	19	19	21	17
Yards opponents returned	349	498	172	171	222	133	370	68	256	191	384	257	234	320	305
Returned by oppponents for TD	3	4	1	0	3	0	3	0	1	1	2	1	2	2	0
nts	69	101	82	65	68	68	69	88	78	64	74	79	72	87	86
Yards punted	2980	4194	3634	2714	2973	3105	3016	3667	3611	2766	3293	3169	2931	3967	3746
Average yards per punt	43.2	41.5	44.3	41.8	43.7	45.7	43.7	41.7	46.3	43.2	44.5	40.1	40.7	45.6	43.6
nt returns	38	43	33	49	29	41	34	33	26	52	28	42	40	38	34
Yards returned	357	423	217	583	279	447	351	282	251	588	139	403	251	559	352
Average yards per return	9.4	9.8	6.6	11.9	9.6	10.9	10.3	8.5	9.7	11.3	5.0	9.6	6.3	14.7	10.4
Returned for TD	0	0	0	0	0	0	0	0	0	1	0	0	0	1	1
koff returns	86	58	70	50	66	61	67	66	60	64	79	61	53	63	71
Yards returned	1734	1341	1459	1195	1421	1403	1463	1567	1320	1424	1504	1276	1171	1358	1542
Average yards per return	20.2	23.1	20.8	23.9	21.5	23.0	21.8	23.7	22.0	22.3	19.0	20.9	22.1	21.6	21.7
Returned for TD	0	1	1	0	0	1	0	1	0	0	0	0	1	0	0
mbles	23	25	19	27	26	24	29	17	31	25	25	30	27	30	24
Lost	13	13	9	15	15	13	10	10	13	12	16	12	14	11	12
Out of bounds	2	2	3	2	1	0	2	1	3	2	2	2	1	4	2
Recovered for TD	0	0	0	0	0	0	0	0	2	0	0	0	0	0	0
nalties	94	106	90	109	91	76	127	122	111	97	110	156	83	110	112
Yards penalized	818	831	678	949	812	615	1006	901	852	716	819	1266	665	969	879
al Points Scored	371	319	372	391	345	317	325	297	339	418	279	340	344	310	317
Total TDs	45	35	43	47	35	30	33	35	41	48	33	38	39	32	33
TDs rushing	10	14	14	20	12	9	13	15	14	15	8	7	18	7	16
TDs passing	34	18	25	26	22	16	19	18	22	27	22	28	15	23	14
TDs on returns and recoveries	1	3	4	1	1	5	1	2	5	6	3	3	6	2	3
Extra point kicks	34	33	41	46	35	27	27	34	35	39	26	36	37	31	27
Extra point kick att.	35	33	41	46	35	27	27	34	36	42	27	36	37	31	27
2-Pt. conversions	5	2	2	0	0	0	5	0	1	4	2	0	2	0	4
2-Pt. conversion att.	9	2	2	1	0	3	6	1	5	6	6	2	1	6	6
Safeties	0	0	0	0	2	1	0	1	1	1	0	2	0	0	0
Field goals made	19	24	23	21	32	36	30	17	18	27	17	24	23	29	28
Field goals attempted	25	29	28	28	38	40	36	24	29	35	24	31	30	36	34
Percent successful	76.0	82.8	82.1	75.0	84.2	90.0	83.3	70.8	62.1	77.1	70.8	77.4	76.7	80.6	82.4
Extra points	39	35	43	46	35	27	32	34	36	43	28	36	39	31	31
Field goals blocked	0	0	1	0	1	1	0	2	0	1	0	1	3	1	0

1996 STATISTICS Miscellaneous

DEFENSE

	Bal.	Buf.	Cin.	Den.	Hou.	Ind.	Jac.	K.C.	Mia.	N.E.	NYJ	Oak.	Pit.	S.D.	S
First downs	351	283	317	261	271	305	315	296	306	305	304	292	286	321	3
Rushing	115	94	109	67	78	108	110	84	91	102	119	97	80	92	1
Passing	213	168	196	165	169	189	180	184	191	178	157	162	174	199	1
Penalty	23	21	12	29	24	8	25	28	24	25	28	33	32	30	
Rushes	508	495	444	345	397	459	447	441	411	434	539	463	411	431	5
Net yards gained	1920	1669	1643	1331	1385	1760	1781	1666	1536	1502	2200	1676	1415	1755	2(
Average gain	3.8	3.4	3.7	3.9	3.5	3.8	4.0	3.8	3.7	3.5	4.1	3.6	3.4	4.1	
Average yards per game	120.0	104.3	102.7	83.2	86.6	110.0	111.3	104.1	96.0	93.9	137.5	104.8	88.4	109.7	13
Passes attempted	537	562	571	566	524	534	508	536	539	596	456	513	547	636	5
Completed	350	292	319	302	312	318	290	289	337	322	257	284	322	369	3
Percent completed	65.2	52.0	55.9	53.4	59.5	59.6	57.1	53.9	62.5	54.0	56.4	55.4	58.9	58.0	5
Total yards gained	4115	3409	4028	3413	3467	3825	3541	3731	3888	4055	3542	3273	3316	3867	36
Times sacked	30	48	32	40	35	29	37	31	37	33	28	34	51	33	
Yards lost	146	341	202	274	242	182	237	193	233	252	178	252	369	201	2
Net yards gained	3969	3068	3826	3139	3225	3643	3304	3538	3655	3803	3364	3021	2947	3666	33
Average yards per game	248.1	191.8	239.1	196.2	201.6	227.7	206.5	221.1	228.4	237.7	210.3	188.8	184.2	229.1	20
Net yards per pass play	7.00	5.03	6.34	5.18	5.77	6.47	6.06	6.24	6.35	6.05	6.95	5.52	4.93	5.48	5
Yards gained per completion	11.76	11.67	12.63	11.30	11.11	12.03	12.21	12.91	11.54	12.59	13.78	11.52	10.30	10.48	11
Combined net yards gained	5889	4737	5469	4470	4610	5403	5085	5204	5191	5305	5564	4697	4362	5421	5
Percent total yards rushing	32.6	35.2	30.0	29.8	30.0	32.6	35.0	32.0	29.6	28.3	39.5	35.7	32.4	32.4	3
Percent total yards passing	67.4	64.8	70.0	70.2	70.0	67.4	65.0	68.0	70.4	71.7	60.5	64.3	67.6	67.6	6
Average yards per game	368.1	296.1	341.8	279.4	288.1	337.7	317.8	325.3	324.4	331.6	347.8	293.6	272.6	338.8	33
Ball-control plays	1075	1105	1047	951	956	1022	992	1008	987	1063	1023	1010	1009	1100	1
Average yards per play	5.5	4.3	5.2	4.7	4.8	5.3	5.1	5.2	5.3	5.0	5.4	4.7	4.3	4.9	
Average time of possession	32:55	31:20	28:27	26:43	27:58	29:16	28:42	29:21	28:52	29:49	30:34	29:21	29:52	32:25	31
Third-down efficiency	48.2	35.5	43.9	35.9	35.2	39.8	44.1	42.2	33.7	36.0	40.0	34.1	36.2	42.0	3
Intercepted by	15	14	34	23	12	13	13	17	20	23	11	17	23	22	
Yards returned by	147	113	308	241	162	276	114	171	475	255	165	353	334	336	2
Returned for TD	1	0	2	1	1	4	0	0	3	2	2	2	3	1	
Punts	68	102	61	83	75	81	71	71	75	82	75	85	86	71	
Yards punted	2881	4406	2706	3825	3073	3525	2979	2969	3283	3483	3158	3562	3771	3145	32
Average yards per punt	42.4	43.2	44.4	46.1	41.0	43.5	42.0	41.8	43.8	42.5	42.1	41.9	43.8	44.3	4
Punt returns	27	40	38	23	31	38	44	42	48	34	40	38	32	51	
Yards returned	273	246	502	261	251	413	400	492	368	334	429	272	284	612	6
Average yards per return	10.1	6.2	13.2	11.3	8.1	10.9	9.1	11.7	7.7	9.8	10.7	7.2	8.9	12.0	1
Returned for TD	0	1	0	1	0	0	0	1	0	0	0	0	0	1	
Kickoff returns	70	65	69	76	78	67	71	64	48	81	58	55	69	59	
Yards returned	1402	1255	1642	1602	1675	1666	1674	1300	1058	1683	1485	1129	1509	1497	1
Average yards per return	20.0	19.3	23.8	21.1	21.5	24.9	23.6	20.3	22.0	20.8	25.6	20.5	21.9	25.4	2
Returned for TD	0	0	1	1	0	0	0	0	0	0	1	0	1	0	
Fumbles	23	23	16	26	29	20	26	23	29	23	26	18	28	29	
Recovered by	7	14	10	9	14	10	14	10	16	11	15	9	17	14	
Out of bounds	3	3	0	6	1	2	1	0	2	1	1	1	4	0	
Recovered for TD	1	0	2	1	2	1	1	1	1	0	0	1	0	2	
Penalties	104	86	102	119	88	121	97	103	98	139	107	113	97	115	
Yards penalized	744	607	768	834	672	970	800	876	786	1189	902	965	746	991	8
Total points scored	441	266	369	275	319	334	335	300	325	313	454	293	257	376	3
Total TDs	50	28	42	31	35	38	37	32	41	34	55	31	27	43	
TDs rushing	18	12	15	5	5	12	9	11	10	14	19	7	7	10	
TDs passing	27	11	22	22	24	25	24	19	29	17	33	22	17	28	
TDs on returns and recoveries	5	5	5	4	6	1	4	2	2	3	3	2	3	5	
Extra point kicks	41	25	40	25	32	33	33	29	38	28	51	26	26	40	
Extra point kick att.	41	26	40	25	32	34	35	29	39	28	52	26	26	40	
2-Pt. conversions	7	1	1	2	1	1	1	1	1	5	1	2	0	0	
2-Pt. conversion att.	9	2	2	6	3	4	2	3	2	6	3	5	1	3	
Safeties	1	1	0	0	1	0	1	0	1	0	1	1	1	3	0
Field goals made	28	23	25	20	25	23	26	25	13	23	23	25	21	26	
Field goals attempted	31	36	30	23	33	28	34	36	17	29	28	34	26	33	
Percent successful	90.3	63.9	83.3	87.0	75.8	82.1	76.5	69.4	76.5	79.3	82.1	73.5	80.8	78.8	9
Extra points	48	26	41	27	33	34	34	30	39	33	52	28	26	40	
Field goals blocked	0	5	0	0	0	0	1	3	0	0	0	0	0	1	

OFFENSE

	Ari.	Atl.	Car.	Chi.	Dal.	Det.	G.B.	Min.	N.O.	NYG	Phi.	S.F.	Stl.	T.B.	Was.
st downs	308	292	292	300	286	317	338	284	232	248	319	315	255	260	307
Rushing	70	67	93	104	105	105	118	75	77	82	107	108	93	90	106
Passing	214	202	160	176	163	180	197	186	135	145	196	188	141	152	174
Penalty	24	23	39	20	18	32	23	23	20	21	16	19	21	18	27
shes	401	329	502	472	475	389	465	435	386	485	489	454	448	472	467
Net yards gained	1502	1461	1729	1720	1641	1810	1838	1546	1308	1603	1882	1847	1607	1589	1910
Average gain	3.7	4.4	3.4	3.6	3.5	4.7	4.0	3.6	3.4	3.3	3.8	4.1	3.6	3.4	4.1
Average yards per game	93.9	91.3	108.1	107.5	102.6	113.1	114.9	96.6	81.8	100.2	117.6	115.4	100.4	99.3	119.4
ses attempted	613	600	487	551	487	541	548	561	515	459	548	550	481	494	471
Completed	336	356	273	318	307	309	328	331	295	238	328	358	249	274	270
Percent completed	54.8	59.3	56.1	57.7	63.0	57.1	59.9	59.0	57.3	51.9	59.9	65.1	51.8	55.5	57.3
Total yards gained	3917	3909	3333	3350	3249	3463	3938	3899	3069	2663	3979	3859	3144	2944	3453
Times sacked	36	42	36	23	19	46	40	34	22	56	39	42	57	30	22
Yards lost	229	254	250	165	127	260	241	241	171	324	234	200	379	217	134
Net yards gained	3688	3655	3083	3185	3122	3203	3697	3658	2898	2339	3745	3659	2765	2727	3319
Average yards per game	230.5	228.4	192.7	199.1	195.1	200.2	231.1	228.6	181.1	146.2	234.1	228.7	172.8	170.4	207.4
Net yards per pass play	5.68	5.69	5.89	5.55	6.17	5.46	6.29	6.15	5.40	4.54	6.38	6.18	5.14	5.20	6.73
Yards gained per completion	11.66	10.98	12.21	10.53	10.58	11.21	12.01	11.78	10.40	11.19	12.13	10.78	12.63	10.74	12.79
nbined net yards gained	5190	5116	4812	4905	4763	5013	5535	5204	4206	3942	5627	5506	4372	4316	5229
Percent total yards rushing	28.9	28.6	35.9	35.1	34.5	36.1	33.2	29.7	31.1	40.7	33.4	33.5	36.8	36.8	36.5
Percent total yards passing	71.1	71.4	64.1	64.9	65.5	63.9	66.8	70.3	68.9	59.3	66.6	66.5	63.2	63.2	63.5
Average yards per game	324.4	319.8	300.8	306.6	297.7	313.3	345.9	325.3	262.9	246.4	351.7	344.1	273.3	269.8	326.8
-control plays	1050	971	1025	1046	981	976	1053	1030	923	1000	1076	1046	986	996	960
Average yards per play	4.9	5.3	4.7	4.7	4.9	5.1	5.3	5.1	4.6	3.9	5.2	5.3	4.4	4.3	5.4
Average time of possession	28:45	29:52	30:48	30:51	30:53	27:06	31:44	30:14	27:33	29:48	32:12	31:28	27:58	30:58	27:29
rd-down efficiency	41.7	39.5	37.2	33.8	41.8	38.4	44.3	42.1	31.4	27.7	37.9	35.2	37.5	39.6	37.9
intercepted	21	30	11	18	14	21	13	19	17	21	18	16	23	20	11
Yards opponents returned	186	324	41	94	250	313	98	339	93	225	265	107	252	326	154
Returned by opponents for TD	0	2	1	0	1	3	0	3	0	1	3	0	1	3	0
ts	77	75	78	78	74	71	68	90	87	102	74	75	78	71	77
Yards punted	3328	3152	3158	3491	3150	3044	2886	3616	3551	4289	3107	3217	3491	3015	3470
Average yards per punt	43.2	42.0	40.5	44.8	42.6	42.9	42.4	40.2	40.8	42.0	42.0	42.9	44.8	42.5	45.1
t returns	39	31	55	31	44	34	58	32	31	42	40	39	35	41	23
Yards returned	343	315	624	282	394	284	875	300	159	478	330	352	439	481	258
Average yards per return	8.8	10.2	11.3	9.1	9.0	8.4	15.1	9.4	5.1	11.4	8.3	9.0	12.5	11.7	11.2
Returned for TD	0	0	1	0	0	0	3	1	0	2	0	0	2	1	0
koff returns	75	87	50	56	53	69	47	58	78	66	64	59	62	55	65
Yards returned	1582	1825	1310	1337	1339	1675	1038	1075	1899	1287	1439	1258	1233	1287	1401
Average yards per return	21.1	21.0	26.2	23.9	25.3	24.3	22.1	18.5	24.3	19.5	22.5	21.3	19.9	23.4	21.6
Returned for TD	0	0	1	0	0	0	1	0	0	0	2	0	0	0	0
nbles	29	23	25	25	24	21	33	26	30	27	24	16	42	28	21
ost	14	11	14	9	15	5	11	13	20	13	14	8	21	14	7
ut of bounds	4	1	1	1	3	1	3	2	2	2	2	2	2	3	1
ecovered for TD	0	0	0	0	0	0	1	0	0	0	0	0	0	0	0
alties	106	111	94	103	103	108	92	106	114	85	117	119	133	95	95
Yards penalized	873	961	638	808	832	863	714	835	853	666	963	925	1015	787	740
al points scored	300	309	367	283	286	302	456	298	229	242	363	398	303	221	364
Total TDs	33	35	36	31	27	38	56	33	24	24	41	43	34	21	41
TDs rushing	8	9	9	9	14	15	9	7	10	4	16	17	10	8	27
TDs passing	23	26	22	19	12	20	39	24	13	14	19	24	18	12	12
TDs on returns and recoveries	2	0	5	3	1	3	8	2	1	6	6	2	6	1	2
xtra point kicks	29	31	34	26	24	36	51	30	18	22	40	40	30	18	40
xtra point kick att.	31	31	35	26	25	36	53	30	18	22	40	40	31	19	40
-Pt. conversions	2	1	1	0	2	1	2	2	2	0	0	1	2	1	0
-Pt. conversion att.	2	4	1	5	2	2	3	3	6	2	1	3	3	2	1
afeties	0	0	2	1	0	0	1	0	0	2	1	4	1	0	0
ield goals made	23	22	37	23	32	12	21	22	21	24	25	30	21	25	26
ield goals attempted	31	29	45	30	36	17	27	29	25	27	29	34	25	32	32
ercent successful	74.2	75.9	82.2	76.7	88.9	70.6	77.8	75.9	84.0	88.9	86.2	88.2	84.0	78.1	81.3
xtra points	31	32	35	26	26	37	53	32	20	22	40	41	32	19	40
ield goals blocked	2	0	0	0	1	1	0	1	0	0	1	0	0	0	1

1996 STATISTICS Miscellaneous

DEFENSE

	Ari.	Atl.	Car.	Chi.	Dal.	Det.	G.B.	Min.	N.O.	N.Y.G.	Phi.	S.F.	Stl.	T.B.	W
First downs	337	309	251	295	260	324	247	309	287	285	264	269	329	296	
Rushing	120	102	69	87	89	126	74	117	104	98	87	76	114	114	
Passing	192	182	167	183	144	172	151	169	152	174	150	164	191	156	
Penalty	25	25	15	25	27	26	23	23	31	13	27	29	24	26	
Rushes	514	473	374	427	437	510	400	445	521	487	421	418	478	438	
Net yards gained	1862	2041	1562	1617	1576	2007	1416	1966	2076	1748	1583	1497	1854	1889	2
Average gain	3.6	4.3	4.2	3.8	3.6	3.9	3.5	4.4	4.0	3.6	3.8	3.6	3.9	4.3	
Average yards per game	116.4	127.6	97.6	101.1	98.5	125.4	88.5	122.9	129.8	109.3	98.9	93.6	115.9	118.1	14
Passes attempted	520	485	556	524	484	502	544	537	465	533	500	558	558	503	
Completed	311	302	307	314	271	311	283	314	267	317	271	287	341	311	
Percent completed	59.8	62.3	55.2	59.9	56.0	62.0	52.0	58.5	57.4	59.5	54.2	51.4	61.1	61.8	5
Total yards gained	3684	3953	3585	3476	3025	3577	2942	3384	3117	3477	3243	3461	3856	3132	3
Times sacked	28	36	60	30	37	32	37	43	41	30	40	45	32	35	
Yards lost	185	208	371	209	219	233	202	263	283	178	264	297	181	207	
Net yards gained	3499	3745	3214	3267	2806	3344	2740	3121	2834	3299	2979	3164	3675	2925	3
Average yards per game	218.7	234.1	200.9	204.2	175.4	209.0	171.3	195.1	177.1	206.2	186.2	197.8	229.7	182.8	21
Net yards per pass play	6.39	7.19	5.22	5.90	5.39	6.26	4.72	5.38	5.60	5.86	5.52	5.25	6.23	5.44	5
Yards gained per completion ..	11.85	13.09	11.68	11.07	11.16	11.50	10.40	10.78	11.67	10.97	11.97	12.06	11.31	10.07	1
Combined net yards gained	5361	5786	4776	4884	4382	5351	4156	5087	4910	5047	4562	4661	5529	4814	5
Percent total yards rushing	34.7	35.3	32.7	33.1	36.0	37.5	34.1	38.6	42.3	34.6	34.7	32.1	33.5	39.2	3
Percent total yards passing	65.3	64.7	67.3	66.9	64.0	62.5	65.9	61.4	57.7	65.4	65.3	67.9	66.5	60.8	6
Average yards per game	335.1	361.6	298.5	305.3	273.9	334.4	259.8	317.9	306.9	315.4	285.1	291.3	345.6	300.9	35
Ball-control plays	1062	994	990	981	958	1044	981	1025	1027	1050	961	1021	1068	976	1
Average yards per play	5.0	5.8	4.8	5.0	4.6	5.1	4.2	5.0	4.8	4.8	4.7	4.6	5.2	4.9	
Average time of possession	31:15	30:08	29:12	29:09	29:07	32:54	28:16	29:46	32:27	30:12	27:48	28:32	32:02	29:02	3
Third-down efficiency	41.3	42.2	32.4	38.3	34.4	43.2	32.7	33.2	36.6	34.2	39.1	33.6	42.0	40.7	
Intercepted by	11	6	22	17	19	11	26	22	12	22	19	20	26	17	
Yards returned by	122	41	277	107	168	169	524	206	114	341	303	176	390	139	
Returned for TD	1	0	0	1	0	2	3	1	0	3	1	1	4	0	
Punts	69	64	95	76	75	71	90	84	74	92	74	88	69	74	
Yards punted	3022	2697	4159	3047	3459	2927	3876	3596	3184	3801	3287	3695	2801	3210	2
Average yards per punt	43.8	42.1	43.8	40.1	46.1	41.2	43.1	42.8	43.0	41.3	44.4	42.0	40.6	43.4	
Punt returns	37	32	32	42	32	42	29	37	43	45	36	36	41	38	
Yards returned	403	413	173	527	249	519	237	577	546	432	330	235	495	248	
Average yards per return	10.9	12.9	5.4	12.5	7.8	12.4	8.2	15.6	12.7	9.6	9.2	6.5	12.1	6.5	
Returned for TD	1	1	0	2	0	1	0	0	1	2	1	0	0	0	
Kickoff returns	61	53	71	52	70	52	76	53	52	42	73	77	58	51	
Yards returned	1290	1314	1429	1115	1431	1298	1649	1314	1155	948	1715	1414	1290	972	1
Average yards per return	21.1	24.8	20.1	21.4	20.4	25.0	21.7	24.8	22.2	22.6	23.5	18.4	22.2	19.1	
Returned for TD	1	1	0	1	0	0	0	0	0	0	0	0	2	0	
Fumbles	24	27	25	29	26	26	25	27	25	27	26	29	26	31	
Recovered	14	17	16	11	14	8	13	13	10	13	12	14	13	12	
Out of bounds	2	0	3	3	1	1	1	1	0	6	4	4	0	1	
Recovered for TD	3	0	0	0	3	0	0	0	0	1	0	0	2	1	
Penalties	104	106	133	113	94	114	107	105	102	100	99	97	111	101	
Yards penalized	841	816	1155	849	717	938	797	840	823	781	710	819	832	810	
Total points scored	397	461	218	305	250	368	210	315	339	297	341	257	409	293	
Total TDs	44	48	24	37	24	44	19	36	34	33	35	25	50	34	
TDs rushing	18	18	6	13	10	12	7	15	11	14	12	4	22	13	
TDs passing	21	26	17	21	10	28	12	18	22	15	18	21	23	17	
TDs on returns and recoveries	5	4	1	3	4	4	0	3	1	4	5	0	5	4	
Extra point kicks	41	43	23	35	20	40	17	33	32	31	30	21	46	32	
Extra point kick att.	43	43	24	36	20	41	17	33	32	31	32	21	47	32	
2-Pt. conversions	1	1	0	0	0	1	1	1	2	1	3	4	1	0	
2-Pt. conversion att.	1	5	0	1	4	3	2	3	2	2	3	4	2	2	
Safeties	0	1	0	0	1	1	1	2	0	0	1	0	2	0	
Field goals made	30	42	17	16	28	20	25	20	33	22	31	26	19	19	
Field goals attempted	37	44	20	23	32	25	27	30	42	26	36	29	27	27	
Percent successful	81.1	95.5	85.0	69.6	87.5	80.0	92.6	66.7	78.6	84.6	86.1	89.7	70.4	70.4	
Extra points	42	44	23	35	20	41	18	34	34	32	33	25	47	32	
Field goals blocked	0	0	0	1	2	0	0	1	0	1	1	0	0	1	

AFC, NFC, AND NFL SUMMARIES

	AFC Offense Total	AFC Offense Average	AFC Defense Total	AFC Defense Average	NFC Offense Total	NFC Offense Average	NFC Defense Total	NFC Defense Average	NFL Total	NFL Average
t downs	4606	307.1	4538	302.5	4353	290.2	4421	294.7	8959	298.6
ushing	1583	105.5	1460	97.3	1400	93.3	1523	101.5	2983	99.4
assing	2635	175.7	2706	180.4	2609	173.9	2538	169.2	5244	174.8
enalty	388	25.9	372	24.8	344	22.9	360	24.0	732	24.4
hes	6925	461.7	6731	448.7	6669	444.6	6863	457.5	13594	453.1
et yards gained	27313	1820.9	25337	1689.1	24993	1666.2	26969	1797.9	52306	1743.5
verage gain	....	3.9	....	3.8	....	3.7	....	3.9	....	3.8
verage yards per game	....	113.8	....	105.6	....	104.1	....	112.4	....	109.0
ses attempted	8060	537.3	8137	542.5	7906	527.1	7829	521.9	15966	532.2
ompleted	4628	308.5	4666	311.1	4570	304.7	4532	302.1	9198	306.6
ercent completed	....	57.4	....	57.3	....	57.8	....	57.9	....	57.6
otal yards gained	54492	3632.8	55094	3672.9	52169	3477.9	51567	3437.8	106661	3555.4
mes sacked	562	37.5	546	36.4	544	36.3	560	37.3	1106	36.9
Yards lost	3668	244.5	3587	239.1	3426	228.4	3507	233.8	7094	236.5
et yards gained	50824	3388.3	51507	3433.8	48743	3249.5	48060	3204.0	99567	3318.9
verage yards per game	....	211.8	....	214.6	....	203.1	....	200.3	....	207.4
et yards per pass play	....	5.89	....	5.93	....	5.77	....	5.73	....	5.83
ards gained per completion	....	11.77	....	11.81	....	11.42	....	11.38	....	11.60
bined net yards gained	78137	5209.1	76844	5122.9	73736	4915.7	75029	5001.9	151873	5062.4
ercent total yards rushing	....	35.0	....	33.0	....	33.9	....	35.9	....	34.4
ercent total yards passing	....	65.0	....	67.0	....	66.1	....	64.1	....	65.6
verage yards per game	....	325.6	....	320.2	....	307.2	....	312.6	....	316.4
control plays	15547	1036.5	15414	1027.6	15119	1007.9	15252	1016.8	30666	1022.2
verage yards per play	....	5.0	....	5.0	....	4.9	....	4.9	....	5.0
hird-down efficiency	....	39.1	....	39.0	....	37.7	....	37.8	....	38.4
rceptions	269	17.9	271	18.1	273	18.2	271	18.1	542	18.1
ards returned	3930	262.0	3706	247.1	3067	204.5	3291	219.4	6997	233.2
eturned for TD	23	1.5	23	1.5	18	1.2	18	1.2	41	1.4
ts	1150	76.7	1162	77.5	1175	78.3	1163	77.5	2325	77.5
ards punted	49766	3317.7	49980	3332.0	49965	3331.0	49751	3316.7	99731	3324.4
verage yards per punt	....	43.3	....	43.0	....	42.5	....	42.8	....	42.9
t returns	560	37.3	578	38.5	575	38.3	557	37.1	1135	37.8
ards returned	5482	365.5	5777	385.1	5914	394.3	5619	374.6	11396	379.9
verage yards per return	....	9.8	....	10.0	....	10.3	....	10.1	....	10.0
eturned for TD	3	0.2	4	0.3	10	0.7	9	0.6	13	0.4
off returns	975	65.0	1002	66.8	944	62.9	917	61.1	1919	64.0
ards returned	21178	1411.9	22219	1481.3	20985	1399.0	19944	1329.6	42163	1405.4
verage yards per return	....	21.7	....	22.2	....	22.2	....	21.7	....	22.0
eturned for TD	5	0.3	4	0.3	4	0.3	5	0.3	9	0.3
bles	382	25.5	376	25.1	394	26.3	400	26.7	776	25.9
ıst	188	12.5	188	12.5	189	12.6	189	12.6	377	12.6
ıt of bounds	29	1.9	30	2.0	30	2.0	29	1.9	59	2.0
wn recovered for TD	2	0.1	3	0.2	1	0.1	0	0.0	3	0.1
pponents recovered by	188	12.5	187	12.5	187	12.5	188	12.5	375	12.5
pponents recovered for TD	9	0.6	13	0.9	15	1.0	11	0.7	24	0.8
alties	1594	106.3	1587	105.8	1581	105.4	1588	105.9	3175	105.8
ards penalized	12776	851.7	12654	843.6	12473	831.5	12595	839.7	25249	841.6
l points scored	5084	338.9	5033	335.5	4721	314.7	4772	318.1	9805	326.8
tal TDs	567	37.8	564	37.6	517	34.5	520	34.7	1084	36.1
s rushing	192	12.8	169	11.3	172	11.5	195	13.0	364	12.1
s passing	329	21.9	345	23.0	297	19.8	281	18.7	626	20.9
s on returns and recoveries	46	3.1	50	3.3	48	3.2	44	2.9	94	3.1
tra point kicks	508	33.9	502	33.5	469	31.3	475	31.7	977	32.6
tra point kick att	514	34.3	508	33.9	477	31.8	483	32.2	991	33.0
Pt. conversions	27	1.8	27	1.8	17	1.1	17	1.1	44	1.5
Pt. conversion att	52	3.5	56	3.7	40	2.7	36	2.4	92	3.1
afeties	8	0.5	11	0.7	12	0.8	9	0.6	20	0.7
eld goals made	368	24.5	357	23.8	364	24.3	375	25.0	732	24.4
eld goals attempted	467	31.1	452	30.1	448	29.9	463	30.9	915	30.5
ercent successful	....	78.8	....	79.0	....	81.3	....	81.0	....	80.0
tra points	535	33.9	529	33.5	486	31.3	492	31.7	1021	32.6
eld goals blocked	11	0.7	11	0.7	7	0.5	7	0.5	18	0.6

Player, Team	Opponent	Date	Att.	Yds.
LeShon Johnson, Arizona	at New Orleans	September 22	21	214
Adrian Murrell, N.Y. Jets	at Arizona	October 27	31	199
Terrell Davis, Denver	vs. Baltimore	October 20	28	194
Barry Sanders, Detroit	at San Francisco	December 23	28	175
Ray Zellars, New Orleans	vs. Chicago	October 13	20	174
Ricky Watters, Philadelphia	vs. Miami	October 20	25	173
Curtis Martin, New England	vs. Washington	October 13	17	164
Barry Sanders, Detroit	at Minnesota	September 1	24	163
Emmitt Smith, Dallas	vs. Washington	November 28	29	155
Terrell Davis, Denver	at New England	November 17	32	154
Ricky Watters, Philadelphia	vs. Detroit	September 15	27	153
Eddie George, Houston	at Cincinnati	October 6*	26	152
Barry Sanders, Detroit	at Green Bay	November 3	20	152
Karim Abdul-Jabbar, Miami	at N.Y. Jets	December 22	30	152
Earnest Byner, Baltimore	vs. New Orleans	September 29	24	149
Lamar Smith, Seattle	at Detroit	November 17	33	148
Terry Allen, Washington	at N.Y. Giants	September 15	27	146
Chris Warren, Seattle	vs. San Diego	October 27	19	146
Eddie George, Houston	at Jacksonville	September 8	17	143
Terrell Davis, Denver	at Kansas City	September 22	19	141
Curtis Martin, New England	vs. Indianapolis	November 24	35	141
Eddie George, Houston	at N.Y. Jets	December 1	28	141
Terrell Davis, Denver	vs. Tampa Bay	September 15	22	137
Joe Aska, Oakland	at N.Y. Jets	October 6	21	136
Barry Sanders, Detroit	vs. Seattle	November 17	16	134
Barry Sanders, Detroit	vs. Minnesota	December 8	20	134
Jerome Bettis, Pittsburgh	s. Buffalo	September 16	20	133
Robert Smith, Minnesota	at Tampa Bay	October 13	18	133
Jerome Bettis, Pittsburgh	vs. St. Louis	November 3	19	129
Mario Bates, New Orleans	at N.Y. Giants	December 15	32	129
Adrian Murrell, N.Y. Jets	vs. New England	November 10	31	128
Anthony Johnson, Carolina	vs. St. Louis	October 13	22	126
Jerome Bettis, Pittsburgh	at Atlanta	October 27	26	126
Barry Sanders, Detroit	vs. Tampa Bay	September 8	20	125
Karim Abdul-Jabbar, Miami	vs. N.Y. Jets	September 15	23	124
Terry Allen, Washington	vs. Indianapolis	October 27	22	124
Terry Allen, Washington	vs. Arizona	November 10*	31	124
Anthony Johnson, Carolina	vs. New Orleans	October 20	29	123
Anthony Johnson, Carolina	at St. Louis	November 17	27	123
Darick Holmes, Buffalo	vs. Washington	November 3	22	122
Raymont Harris, Chicago	vs. Detroit	November 24	27	122
Ricky Watters, Philadelphia	at Atlanta	September 22	26	121
Thurman Thomas, Buffalo	at New England	October 27	26	119
Jerome Bettis, Pittsburgh	at Miami	November 25	27	119
Adrian Murrell, N.Y. Jets	at Washington	September 29	31	118
Raymont Harris, Chicago	vs. Tampa Bay	November 3	19	118
Bam Morris, Baltimore	at Cincinnati	December 8	21	117
Jerome Bettis, Pittsburgh	vs. Baltimore	September 8	21	116
Napoleon Kaufman, Oakland	vs. San Diego	September 22	7	116
Ricky Watters, Philadelphia	at Dallas	November 3	24	116
Chris Warren, Seattle	vs. Buffalo	December 8	21	116
Karim Abdul-Jabbar, Miami	vs. New England	September 1	26	115
Jerome Bettis, Pittsburgh	vs. Houston	September 29	29	115
Rashaan Salaam, Chicago	vs. St. Louis	December 8	19	115
Reggie Brooks, Tampa Bay	at Denver	September 15	15	114
Robert Smith, Minnesota	vs. Detroit	September 1	22	113
Emmitt Smith, Dallas	vs. Philadelphia	November 3	24	113
Terrell Davis, Denver	at Cincinnati	September 29	24	112
Emmitt Smith, Dallas	vs. Arizona	October 13	21	112
James Stewart, Jacksonville	at St. Louis	October 20	29	112
Raymont Harris, Chicago	at Denver	November 10	23	112
Lawrence Phillips, St. Louis	at Atlanta	December 15	22	112
Terry Allen, Washington	vs. Philadelphia	September 1	20	111
Terrell Davis, Denver	at Seattle	September 8	28	111
Jerome Bettis, Pittsburgh	at Cincinnati	November 10	21	111
Anthony Johnson, Carolina	vs. Tampa Bay	December 1	26	111
Ricky Watters, Philadelphia	at N.Y. Giants	October 13	27	110
Natrone Means, Jacksonville	vs. Atlanta	December 22	27	110
Eddie George, Houston	at Atlanta	October 13	23	109
Jerome Bettis, Pittsburgh	vs. Cincinnati	October 13	28	109
Jamal Anderson, Atlanta	vs. Carolina	November 3	22	109
Bam Morris, Baltimore	at Jacksonville	November 10	26	109

ayer, Team	Opponent	Date	Att.	Yds.	TD
poleon Kaufman, Oakland	vs. Kansas City	December 9	8	109	0
gar Bennett, Green Bay	vs. Minnesota	December 22	18	109	1
nal Anderson, Atlanta	at Carolina	September 1	14	108	0
roy Hoard, Minnesota	at Oakland	November 17*	20	108	0
urman Thomas, Buffalo	vs. Washington	November 3	23	107	1
rry Sanders, Detroit	at Chicago	November 24	21	107	1
bert Green, Chicago	at Washington	September 8	20	106	0
wrence Phillips, St. Louis	vs. Atlanta	November 10	14	106	1
rold Green, St. Louis	vs. Atlanta	November 10	13	106	2
rrell Davis, Denver	vs. Seattle	December 1	26	106	1
rome Bettis, Pittsburgh	at Baltimore	December 1	24	105	0
rry Kirby, San Francisco	at Atlanta	December 2	12	105	0
rim Abdul-Jabbar, Miami	at New England	November 3	29	104	2
poleon Kaufman, Oakland	at Seattle	November 24	15	104	0
cky Watters, Philadelphia	vs. N.Y. Giants	December 1	29	104	0
ris Warren, Seattle	vs. Green Bay	September 29	18	103	1
nal Anderson, Atlanta	at Detroit	October 6	16	103	3
rome Bettis, Pittsburgh	at Kansas City	October 7	27	103	1
rian Murrell, N.Y. Jets	at Buffalo	November 24	19	103	0
eg Hill, Kansas City	at Detroit	November 28	17	103	0
ric Pegram, Pittsburgh	vs. San Francisco	December 15	20	103	0
thony Johnson, Carolina	at Minnesota	October 6	23	102	1
rian Murrell, N.Y. Jets	vs. Oakland	October 6	20	102	0
bert Smith, Minnesota	vs. Carolina	October 6	27	102	0
rdell Stewart, Pittsburgh	at Carolina	December 22	7	102	1
mitt Smith, Dallas	vs. Indianapolis	September 15	26	101	1
rry Allen, Washington	vs. N.Y. Jets	September 29	20	101	2
rshall Faulk, Indianapolis	vs. Philadelphia	December 5	16	101	2
roy Hoard, Minnesota	vs. Tampa Bay	December 15	20	101	2
eg Hill, Kansas City	at Minnesota	November 3	15	100	2
m Morris, Baltimore	vs. Pittsburgh	December 1	28	100	0

*Overtime game.

PASSING

ayer, Team	Opponent	Date	Att.	Comp.	Yds.	TD	Int.
omer Esiason, Arizona	at Washington	November 10*	59	35	522	3	4
rk Brunell, Jacksonville	at New England	September 22	39	23	432	3	1
ny Testaverde, Baltimore	vs. St. Louis	October 27*	51	31	429	3	2
rk Brunell, Jacksonville	at St. Louis	October 20	52	37	421	0	5
ew Bledsoe, New England	vs. Miami	November 3	41	30	419	3	2
tt Favre, Green Bay	vs. San Francisco	October 14*	61	28	395	1	2
ve Young, San Francisco	vs. Carolina	December 8	41	27	393	3	2
ew Bledsoe, New England	vs. Buffalo	October 27	45	32	373	1	0
omer Esiason, Arizona	vs. Philadelphia	November 24	43	24	367	3	0
nt Graham, Arizona	vs. St. Louis	September 29*	58	37	366	4	0
ny Testaverde, Baltimore	vs. Jacksonville	November 24*	50	31	366	0	0
y Aikman, Dallas	at Miami	October 27	41	33	363	3	0
oby Hebert, Atlanta	vs. St. Louis	December 15	49	28	363	2	6
rk Brunell, Jacksonville	vs. Cincinnati	December 1	34	21	356	1	0
rk Brunell, Jacksonville	vs. Baltimore	November 10	37	24	354	1	1
ny Testaverde, Baltimore	vs. New England	October 6	45	29	353	3	1
y Banks, St. Louis	at Baltimore	October 27*	40	26	353	1	2
nk Reich, N.Y. Jets	at Indianapolis	November 17	42	20	352	3	4
f Blake, Cincinnati	vs. Atlanta	November 24	36	21	349	4	0
s Frerotte, Washington	vs. Dallas	December 22	31	22	346	0	1
ott Mitchell, Detroit	at Oakland	October 13	50	31	343	3	2
Detmer, Philadelphia	vs. Carolina	October 27	38	23	342	1	1
ke Tomczak, Pittsburgh	at Kansas City	October 7	32	20	338	0	1
ny Testaverde, Baltimore	at Denver	October 20	45	27	338	4	1
ott Mitchell, Detroit	vs. Chicago	September 22	34	24	336	4	0
n Elway, Denver	at Cincinnati	September 29	37	23	335	2	1
n Elway, Denver	at Minnesota	November 24	36	27	334	2	1
nt Dilfer, Tampa Bay	at San Diego	November 17	40	30	327	0	1
ry Collins, Carolina	at San Francisco	December 8	37	22	327	3	0
n Elway, Denver	vs. Baltimore	October 20	39	25	326	3	1
l O'Donnell, N.Y. Jets	at Miami	September 15	44	25	325	3	3
Kelly, Buffalo	at Seattle	December 8	41	24	324	1	2
n Elway, Denver	vs. San Diego	October 6	41	32	323	4	1
n Friesz, Seattle	vs. Houston	November 3	38	24	323	1	1
Detmer, Philadelphia	at Arizona	November 24	38	21	322	0	1
l O'Donnell, N.Y. Jets	vs. Indianapolis	September 8	46	26	319	1	1
Detmer, Philadelphia	vs. Buffalo	November 10	44	26	315	2	1
tt Favre, Green Bay	at Kansas City	November 10	49	27	314	2	1
Kelly, Buffalo	at N.Y. Giants	September 1*	41	24	313	1	1
f Blake, Cincinnati	at Jacksonville	December 1	39	23	313	3	2
n Humphries, San Diego	vs. Detroit	November 10	32	24	311	3	0

Player, Team	Opponent	Date	Att.	Comp.	Yds.	TD	In
Drew Bledsoe, New England	at Baltimore	October 6	39	25	310	4	
Todd Collins, Buffalo	vs. Indianapolis	October 6*	44	23	309	1	
Steve McNair, Houston	vs. Jacksonville	December 8	37	24	308	1	
Vinny Testaverde, Baltimore	vs. Houston	December 22	32	23	307	3	
Mark Brunell, Jacksonville	at Baltimore	November 24*	46	28	306	2	
Bobby Hebert, Atlanta	at Cincinnati	November 24	40	23	304	3	
Tony Banks, St. Louis	at Atlanta	December 15	16	11	304	3	
Mark Brunell, Jacksonville	vs. Houston	September 8	38	27	302	2	
Drew Bledsoe, New England	at N.Y. Giants	December 21	47	31	301	2	

*Overtime game.

RECEIVING

Player, Team	Opponent	Date	Rec.	Yds.	T
Keenan McCardell, Jacksonville	at St. Louis	October 20	16	232	
Isaac Bruce, St. Louis	at Baltimore	October 27*	11	229	
Eddie Kennison, St. Louis	at Atlanta	December 15	5	226	
Don Beebe, Green Bay	vs. San Francisco	October 14*	11	220	
Derrick Alexander, Baltimore	vs. Pittsburgh	December 1	7	198	
Michael Irvin, Dallas	at Arizona	December 8	8	198	
Jeff Graham, N.Y. Jets	at Indianapolis	November 17	9	189	
Michael Irvin, Dallas	at Miami	October 27	12	186	
Carl Pickens, Cincinnati	vs. Atlanta	November 24	11	176	
Antonio Freeman, Green Bay	vs. Denver	December 8	9	175	
Johnnie Morton, Detroit	vs. Chicago	September 22	7	174	
Bert Emanuel, Atlanta	vs. St. Louis	December 15	9	173	
Wayne Chrebet, N.Y. Jets	at Jacksonville	October 13	12	162	
Jimmy Smith, Jacksonville	vs. Cincinnati	December 1	7	162	
Shannon Sharpe, Denver	vs. Baltimore	October 20	9	161	
Steve Tasker, Buffalo	vs. N.Y. Jets	November 24	6	160	
Herman Moore, Detroit	at Minnesota	September 1	12	157	
Willie Green, Carolina	at San Francisco	December 8	7	157	
Ken Dilger, Indianapolis	at N.Y. Jets	September 8	7	156	
Michael Haynes, New Orleans	at Cincinnati	September 15	5	156	
Rob Moore, Arizona	vs. Philadelphia	November 24	9	156	
Antonio Freeman, Green Bay	vs. Chicago	December 1	10	156	
Charles Johnson, Pittsburgh	at Houston	October 20	5	155	
Henry Ellard, Washington	vs. Dallas	December 22	7	155	
Shannon Sharpe, Denver	vs. San Diego	October 6	13	153	
Jake Reed, Minnesota	at Chicago	October 28	11	153	
Henry Ellard, Washington	at New England	October 13	8	152	
Michael Jackson, Baltimore	vs. Jacksonville	November 24*	9	150	
Jake Reed, Minnesota	at Atlanta	September 8	4	148	
Tony Martin, San Diego	at Kansas City	November 24	5	148	
Antonio Freeman, Green Bay	at Chicago	October 6	7	146	
Rob Moore, Arizona	vs. St. Louis	September 29*	9	143	
Rob Moore, Arizona	vs. N.Y. Jets	October 27	7	143	
Irving Fryar, Philadelphia	vs. Carolina	October 27	7	143	
Cris Carter, Minnesota	at Seattle	November 10	7	142	
Fred Barnett, Miami	vs. N.Y. Giants	December 8	4	139	
Andre Reed, Buffalo	at N.Y. Giants	September 1	5	138	
Tony Martin, San Diego	at Oakland	September 22	10	138	
Joey Galloway, Seattle	at Miami	October 6	5	137	
Isaac Bruce, St. Louis	vs. Washington	September 22	11	136	
Jeff Graham, N.Y. Jets	at Miami	September 15	5	136	
Jimmy Smith, Jacksonville	vs. N.Y. Jets	October 13	5	135	
Ben Coates, New England	vs. Miami	November 3	5	135	
Andre Reed, Buffalo	vs. Miami	October 13	10	134	
Jake Reed, Minnesota	at Oakland	November 17*	4	134	
Shannon Sharpe, Denver	at Kansas City	September 22	9	131	
Anthony Miller, Denver	at Cincinnati	September 29	5	131	
Irving Fryar, Philadelphia	at Arizona	November 24	7	131	
Jimmy Smith, Jacksonville	at Baltimore	November 24*	8	131	
Brett Perriman, Detroit	vs. Kansas City	November 28	8	131	
Robert Brooks, Green Bay	vs. Philadelphia	September 9	5	130	
Jake Reed, Minnesota	vs. Green Bay	September 22	7	129	
Jerry Rice, San Francisco	vs. Carolina	December 8	10	129	
Michael Jackson, Baltimore	vs. New England	October 6	8	128	
Tony Martin, San Diego	at Indianapolis	November 3	6	128	
Jerry Rice, San Francisco	at Carolina	September 22	10	127	
Chris Sanders, Houston	vs. Jacksonville	December 8	7	127	
Andre Reed, Buffalo	at Miami	December 16	6	127	
Curtis Conway, Chicago	at Detroit	September 22	8	126	
Derrick Alexander, Baltimore	at Denver	October 20	6	126	
Tim Brown, Oakland	vs. Denver	November 4	8	126	
Michael Westbrook, Washington	vs. San Francisco	November 24*	7	126	
Herman Moore, Detroit	vs. Minnesota	December 8	9	126	

ayer, Team	Opponent	Date	Rec.	Yds.	TD
arles Johnson, Pittsburgh	at Kansas City	October 7	6	125	0
omas Lewis, N.Y. Giants	at Washington	October 20	9	125	1
ark Carrier, Carolina	at Jacksonville	September 29	8	124	2
ff Graham, N.Y. Jets	at Buffalo	November 24	7	124	1
mmy Smith, Jacksonville	vs. Seattle	December 15	8	124	2
rry Glenn, New England	at N.Y. Giants	December 21	8	124	1
rance Mathis, Atlanta	at Carolina	September 1	4	123	0
rrick Alexander, Baltimore	vs. New England	October 6	6	123	1
ic Metcalf, Atlanta	at Cincinnati	November 24	9	122	2
ris T. Jones, Philadelphia	vs. Detroit	September 15	9	121	1
J. McDuffie, Miami	at Philadelphia	October 20	7	121	2
dre Reed, Buffalo	at New England	October 27	4	121	1
chael Haynes, New Orleans	vs. San Francisco	November 3	5	121	1
m Brown, Oakland	vs. San Diego	September 22	11	120	2
ing Fryar, Philadelphia	at Dallas	November 3	9	120	1
rtis Conway, Chicago	at Tampa Bay	December 22	9	120	0
inn Early, Buffalo	vs. New England	September 8	6	119	1
chael Irvin, Dallas	vs. Atlanta	October 20	7	119	0
nry Ellard, Washington	vs. N.Y. Giants	October 20	5	119	0
ac Bruce, St. Louis	at Arizona	September 29*	4	117	2
arles Johnson, Pittsburgh	at Baltimore	December 1	8	117	0
chael Jackson, Baltimore	vs. Houston	December 22	5	117	3
rt Emanuel, Atlanta	vs. Minnesota	September 8	9	116	0
ing Fryar, Philadelphia	vs. Miami	October 20	8	116	4
d Popson, San Francisco	vs. Cincinnati	October 20	8	116	2
dre Rison, Jacksonville	at New England	September 22	4	115	2
chael Jackson, Baltimore	vs. St. Louis	October 27*	7	113	1
ny Martin, San Diego	vs. Detroit	November 11	8	113	1
inn Early, Buffalo	at Indianapolis	December 1*	3	113	1
mes Jett, Oakland	vs. Detroit	October 13	7	112	2
rry Glenn, New England	vs. Miami	November 3	10	112	0
ac Bruce, St. Louis	at New Orleans	December 1	4	112	1
urtney Hawkins, Tampa Bay	at Detroit	September 8	8	111	0
urman Thomas, Buffalo	vs. Indianapolis	October 6*	8	111	0
rtis Conway, Chicago	at New Orleans	October 13	7	111	2
chael Timpson, Chicago	vs. St. Louis	December 8	6	111	0
arles Johnson, Pittsburgh	at Atlanta	October 27	8	110	0
rell Owens, San Francisco	vs. Carolina	December 8	5	110	1
rman Moore, Detroit	at Oakland	October 13	10	109	2
nnie Morton, Detroit	at Oakland	October 13	8	109	1
rt Emanuel, Atlanta	at St. Louis	November 10	4	109	0
l Pickens, Cincinnati	at Jacksonville	December 1	7	109	3
ry Centers, Arizona	at Indianapolis	September 1	11	108	0
tonio Freeman, Green Bay	at Seattle	September 29	7	108	2
ry Rice, San Francisco	at St. Louis	October 6	7	108	1
ris Calloway, N.Y. Giants	at Washington	October 20	9	108	1
bert Brooks, Green Bay	vs. San Diego	September 15	8	108	0
yd Turner, Baltimore	vs. St. Louis	October 27*	6	108	1
cket Ismail, Carolina	at Atlanta	November 3	5	108	0
ac Bruce, St. Louis	at Pittsburgh	November 3	7	108	0
nnie Harmon, Houston	at New Orleans	November 10	7	108	1
y Galloway, Seattle	at Denver	December 1	5	108	0
rman Moore, Detroit	vs. Atlanta	October 6	3	107	2
nan McCardell, Jacksonville	at Baltimore	November 24*	9	107	0
n Beebe, Green Bay	vs. Detroit	November 3	4	106	1
. McDuffie, Miami	vs. Indianapolis	November 10	6	106	1
vin Harrison, Indianapolis	vs. Philadelphia	December 5	6	106	1
dre Reed, Buffalo	vs. Cincinnati	November 17	6	105	0
rman Moore, Detroit	at Tampa Bay	September 29	9	104	1
yd Turner, Baltimore	vs. Cincinnati	November 3	6	104	0
mont Harris, Chicago	vs. Dallas	September 2	3	103	1
is T. Jones, Philadelphia	vs. Washington	November 17	7	103	1
nay Scott, Cincinnati	vs. Baltimore	December 8	8	103	0
vin Harrison, Indianapolis	at Kansas City	December 15	6	103	3
l Pickens, Cincinnati	vs. Pittsburgh	November 10	12	103	0
is Sanders, Houston	at N.Y. Jets	December 1	3	102	1
ie Kennison, St. Louis	at Chicago	December 8	8	102	1
ie Jackson, Jacksonville	at New England	September 22	4	101	1
rtis Conway, Chicago	vs. Green Bay	October 6	9	101	0
ince Mathis, Atlanta	at Dallas	October 20	5	101	0
nan McCardell, Jacksonville	vs. Houston	September 8	8	100	1
s Sanders, Houston	at Atlanta	October 13	4	100	1

Overtime game.

1996 STATISTICS Miscellaneous

OFFENSE

TOTAL SCORES

Team	Series	TD Rush	TD Pass	Total TDs	TD Efficiency Pct.	FGM	Total Scores	Scoring Efficiency Pct.
New England	63	15	20	35	55.56	20	55	87.3
Green Bay	61	10	26	36	59.02	16	52	85.2
Washington	52	20	9	29	55.77	22	51	98.0
Carolina	58	7	17	24	41.38	27	51	87.9
Cincinnati	55	12	19	31	56.36	19	50	90.9
San Francisco	63	15	13	28	44.44	22	50	79.3
Denver	56	17	17	34	60.71	14	48	85.7
Baltimore	55	10	23	33	60.00	15	48	87.2
Dallas	55	13	10	23	41.82	24	47	85.4
Philadelphia	57	14	15	29	50.88	17	46	80.7
Arizona	53	6	18	24	45.28	21	45	84.9
Jacksonville	58	13	11	24	41.38	21	45	77.5
Atlanta	53	8	22	30	56.60	14	44	83.0
Houston	47	8	13	21	44.68	22	43	91.4
Miami	50	14	17	31	62.00	12	43	86.0
Oakland	52	6	21	27	51.92	16	43	82.6
Kansas City	49	14	15	29	59.18	13	42	85.7
Buffalo	47	14	9	23	48.94	18	41	87.2
Pittsburgh	52	15	8	23	44.23	18	41	78.8
San Diego	48	7	15	22	45.83	17	39	81.2
Minnesota	46	4	14	18	39.13	20	38	82.6
N.Y. Jets	46	8	15	23	50.00	15	38	82.6
Indianapolis	46	9	10	19	41.30	18	37	80.4
Seattle	45	11	8	19	42.22	18	37	82.2
St. Louis	39	9	9	18	46.15	17	35	89.7
Tampa Bay	45	8	9	17	37.78	17	34	75.5
Chicago	44	9	15	24	54.55	9	33	75.0
Detroit	42	12	14	26	61.90	7	33	78.5
N.Y. Giants	35	4	8	12	34.29	19	31	88.5
New Orleans	33	10	6	16	48.48	13	29	87.8
Totals	1505	322	426	748	49.70	521	1269	84.3
Average	50.2	10.7	14.2	24.9	49.70	17.4	42.3	84.3

SCORING EFFICIENCY

Team	Series	TD Rush	TD Pass	Total TDs	TD Efficiency Pct.	FGM	Total Scores	Scoring Efficiency Pct.
Washington	52	20	9	29	55.77	22	51	98.0
Houston	47	8	13	21	44.68	22	43	91.4
Cincinnati	55	12	19	31	56.36	19	50	90.9
St. Louis	39	9	9	18	46.15	17	35	89.7
N.Y. Giants	35	4	8	12	34.29	19	31	88.5
Carolina	58	7	17	24	41.38	27	51	87.9
New Orleans	33	10	6	16	48.48	13	29	87.8
New England	63	15	20	35	55.56	20	55	87.3
Baltimore	55	10	23	33	60.00	15	48	87.2
Buffalo	47	14	9	23	48.94	18	41	87.2
Miami	50	14	17	31	62.00	12	43	86.0
Denver	56	17	17	34	60.71	14	48	85.7
Kansas City	49	14	15	29	59.18	13	42	85.7
Dallas	55	13	10	23	41.82	24	47	85.4
Green Bay	61	10	26	36	59.02	16	52	85.2
Arizona	53	6	18	24	45.28	21	45	84.9
Atlanta	53	8	22	30	56.60	14	44	83.0
Oakland	52	6	21	27	51.92	16	43	82.6
Minnesota	46	4	14	18	39.13	20	38	82.6
N.Y. Jets	46	8	15	23	50.00	15	38	82.6
Seattle	45	11	8	19	42.22	18	37	82.2
San Diego	48	7	15	22	45.83	17	39	81.2
Philadelphia	57	14	15	29	50.88	17	46	80.7
Indianapolis	46	9	10	19	41.30	18	37	80.4
San Francisco	63	15	13	28	44.44	22	50	79.3
Pittsburgh	52	15	8	23	44.23	18	41	78.8
Detroit	42	12	14	26	61.90	7	33	78.5
Jacksonville	58	13	11	24	41.38	21	45	77.5
Tampa Bay	45	8	9	17	37.78	17	34	75.5
Chicago	44	9	15	24	54.55	9	33	75.0
Totals	1505	322	426	748	49.70	521	1269	84.3
Average	50.2	10.7	14.2	24.9	49.70	17.4	42.3	84.3

TOTAL SCORES

m	Series	TD Rush	TD Pass	Total TDs	TD Efficiency Pct.	FGM	Total Scores	Scoring Efficiency Pct.
en Bay	32	4	9	13	40.63	10	23	71.88
olina	39	4	12	16	41.03	10	26	66.67
falo	46	11	6	17	36.96	17	34	73.91
cago	40	11	12	23	57.50	11	34	85.00
las	42	9	6	15	35.71	20	35	83.33
. Giants	43	12	12	24	55.81	11	35	81.40
sburgh	44	6	14	20	45.45	15	35	79.55
npa Bay	40	9	12	21	52.50	14	35	87.50
sas City	47	9	12	21	44.68	15	36	76.60
mi	43	9	17	26	60.47	10	36	83.72
ver	45	6	16	22	48.89	15	37	82.22
uston	45	5	17	22	48.89	17	39	86.67
v England	52	13	9	22	42.31	18	40	76.92
land	44	6	17	23	52.27	17	40	90.91
Francisco	46	3	14	17	36.96	24	41	89.13
adelphia	52	11	10	21	40.38	21	42	80.77
cinnati	55	14	12	26	47.27	17	43	78.18
roit	51	12	19	31	60.78	13	44	86.27
esota	49	14	15	29	59.18	15	44	89.80
shington	54	19	8	27	50.00	19	46	85.19
ksonville	51	9	16	25	49.02	21	46	90.20
anapolis	53	11	18	29	54.72	19	48	90.57
v Orleans	55	8	15	23	41.82	27	50	90.91
Diego	57	9	25	34	59.65	16	50	87.72
. Jets	61	14	20	34	55.74	17	51	83.61
ttle	55	15	17	32	58.18	19	51	92.73
ona	61	17	11	28	45.90	26	54	88.52
Louis	69	21	18	39	56.52	15	54	78.26
timore	67	16	22	38	56.72	20	58	86.57
nta	67	15	15	30	44.78	32	62	92.54
tals	1505	322	426	748	49.70	521	1269	84.32
erage	50.2	10.7	14.2	24.9	49.70	17.4	42.3	84.32

SCORING EFFICIENCY

m	Series	TD Rush	TD Pass	Total TDs	TD Efficiency Pct.	FGM	Total Scores	Scoring Efficiency Pct.
olina	39	4	12	16	41.03	10	26	66.67
en Bay	32	4	9	13	40.63	10	23	71.88
falo	46	11	6	17	36.96	17	34	73.91
sas City	47	9	12	21	44.68	15	36	76.60
v England	52	13	9	22	42.31	18	40	76.92
cinnati	55	14	12	26	47.27	17	43	78.18
Louis	69	21	18	39	56.52	15	54	78.26
sburgh	44	6	14	20	45.45	15	35	79.55
adelphia	52	11	10	21	40.38	21	42	80.77
Giants	43	12	12	24	55.81	11	35	81.40
ver	45	6	16	22	48.89	15	37	82.22
as	42	9	6	15	35.71	20	35	83.33
Jets	61	14	20	34	55.74	17	51	83.61
mi	43	9	17	26	60.47	10	36	83.72
cago	40	11	12	23	57.50	11	34	85.00
shington	54	19	8	27	50.00	19	46	85.19
roit	51	12	19	31	60.78	13	44	86.27
imore	67	16	22	38	56.72	20	58	86.57
ston	45	5	17	22	48.89	17	39	86.67
npa Bay	40	9	12	21	52.50	14	35	87.50
Diego	57	9	25	34	59.65	16	50	87.72
ona	61	17	11	28	45.90	26	54	88.52
Francisco	46	3	14	17	36.96	24	41	89.13
nesota	49	14	15	29	59.18	15	44	89.80
ksonville	51	9	16	25	49.02	21	46	90.20
anapolis	53	11	18	29	54.72	19	48	90.57
land	44	6	17	23	52.27	17	40	90.91
v Orleans	55	8	15	23	41.82	27	50	90.91
nta	67	15	15	30	44.78	32	62	92.54
ttle	55	15	17	32	58.18	19	51	92.73
tals	1505	322	426	748	49.70	521	1269	84.32
erage	50.2	10.7	14.2	24.9	49.70	17.4	42.3	84.32

1996 STATISTICS *Miscellaneous*

HISTORY

Championship games
Year-by-year standings
Super Bowls
Pro Bowls
Records
Statistical leaders
Coaching records
Hall of Fame
The Sporting News awards
Team by team

CHAMPIONSHIP GAMES

NFL (1933-1969); NFC (1970-1996)
RESULTS

Sea.	Date	Winner (Share)	Loser (Share)	Score	Site	Attendance
1933	Dec. 17	Chicago Bears ($210.34)	N.Y. Giants ($140.22)	23-21	Chicago	26,00
1934	Dec. 9	N.Y. Giants ($621)	Chicago Bears ($414.02)	30-13	N.Y. Giants	35,05
1935	Dec. 15	Detroit ($313.35)	N.Y. Giants ($200.20)	26-7	Detroit	15,00
1936	Dec. 13	Green Bay ($250)	Boston Redskins ($180)	21-6	N.Y. Giants	29,54
1937	Dec. 12	Washington ($225.90)	Chicago Bears ($127.78)	28-21	Chicago	15,87
1938	Dec. 11	N.Y. Giants ($504.45)	Green Bay ($368.81)	23-17	N.Y. Giants	48,12
1939	Dec. 10	Green Bay ($703.97)	N.Y. Giants ($455.57)	27-0	Milwaukee	32,27
1940	Dec. 8	Chicago Bears ($873)	Washington ($606)	73-0	Washington	36,03
1941	Dec. 21	Chicago Bears ($430)	N.Y. Giants ($288)	37-9	Chicago	13,34
1942	Dec. 13	Washington ($965)	Chicago Bears ($637)	14-6	Washington	36,00
1943	Dec. 26	Chicago Bears ($1,146)	Washington ($765)	41-21	Chicago	34,32
1944	Dec. 17	Green Bay ($1,449)	N.Y. Giants ($814)	14-7	N.Y. Giants	46,01
1945	Dec. 16	Cleveland Rams ($1,469)	Washington ($902)	15-14	Cleveland	32,17
1946	Dec. 15	Chicago Bears ($1,975)	N.Y. Giants ($1,295)	24-14	N.Y. Giants	58,34
1947	Dec. 28	Chi. Cardinals ($1,132)	Philadelphia ($754)	28-21	Chicago	30,75
1948	Dec. 19	Philadelphia ($1,540)	Chi. Cardinals ($874)	7-0	Philadelphia	36,30
1949	Dec. 18	Philadelphia ($1,094)	L.A. Rams ($739)	14-0	L.A. Rams	27,98
1950	Dec. 24	Cleveland Browns ($1,113)	L.A. Rams ($686)	30-28	Cleveland	29,75
1951	Dec. 23	L. A. Rams ($2,108)	Cleve. Browns ($1,483)	24-17	L.A. Rams	57,52
1952	Dec. 28	Detroit ($2,274)	Cleveland Browns ($1,712)	17-7	Cleveland	50,93
1953	Dec. 27	Detroit ($2,424)	Cleveland Browns ($1,654)	17-16	Detroit	54,57
1954	Dec. 26	Cleveland Browns ($2,478)	Detroit ($1,585)	56-10	Cleveland	43,83
1955	Dec. 26	Cleveland Browns ($3,508)	L.A. Rams ($2,316)	38-14	L.A. Rams	85,69
1956	Dec. 30	N.Y. Giants ($3,779)	Chicago Bears ($2,485)	47-7	N.Y. Giants	56,83
1957	Dec. 29	Detroit ($4,295)	Cleveland Browns ($2,750)	59-14	Detroit	55,26
1958	Dec. 28	Baltimore ($4,718)	N.Y. Giants ($3,111)	23-17*	N.Y. Giants	64,18
1959	Dec. 27	Baltimore ($4,674)	N.Y. Giants ($3,083)	31-16	Baltimore	57,54
1960	Dec. 26	Philadelphia ($5,116)	Green Bay ($3,105)	17-13	Philadelphia	67,32
1961	Dec. 31	Green Bay ($5,195)	N.Y. Giants ($3,339)	37-0	Green Bay	39,02
1962	Dec. 30	Green Bay ($5,888)	N.Y. Giants ($4,166)	16-7	N.Y. Giants	64,89
1963	Dec. 29	Chicago Bears ($5,899)	N.Y. Giants ($4,218)	14-10	Chicago	45,80
1964	Dec. 27	Cleveland Browns ($8,052)	Baltimore ($5,571)	27-0	Cleveland	79,54
1965	Jan. 2	Green Bay ($7,819)	Cleveland Browns ($5,288)	23-12	Green Bay	50,77
1966	Jan. 1	Green Bay ($9,813)	Dallas ($6,527)	34-27	Dallas	74,15
1967	Dec. 31	Green Bay ($7,950)	Dallas ($5,299)	21-17	Green Bay	50,86
1968	Dec. 29	Baltimore ($9,306)	Cleveland Browns ($5,963)	34-0	Cleveland	78,41
1969	Jan. 4	Minnesota ($7,930)	Cleveland Browns ($5,118)	27-7	Minnesota	46,50
1970	Jan. 3	Dallas ($8,500)	San Francisco ($5,500)	17-10	San Francisco	59,36
1971	Jan. 2	Dallas ($8,500)	San Francisco ($5,500)	14-3	Dallas	63,40
1972	Dec. 31	Washington ($8,500)	Dallas ($5,500)	26-3	Washington	53,12
1973	Dec. 30	Minnesota ($8,500)	Dallas ($5,500)	27-10	Dallas	64,42
1974	Dec. 29	Minnesota ($8,500)	L.A. Rams ($5,500)	14-10	Minnesota	48,44
1975	Jan. 4	Dallas ($8,500)	L.A. Rams ($5,500)	37-7	L.A. Rams	88,91
1976	Dec. 26	Minnesota ($8,500)	L.A. Rams ($5,500)	24-13	Minnesota	48,37
1977	Jan. 1	Dallas ($9,000)	Minnesota ($9,000)	23-6	Dallas	64,24
1978	Jan. 7	Dallas ($9,000)	L.A. Rams ($9,000)	28-0	L.A. Rams	71,04
1979	Jan. 6	L.A. Rams ($9,000)	Tampa Bay ($9,000)	9-0	Tampa Bay	72,03
1980	Jan. 11	Philadelphia ($9,000)	Dallas ($9,000)	20-7	Philadelphia	70,69
1981	Jan. 10	San Francisco ($9,000)	Dallas ($9,000)	28-27	San Francisco	60,53
1982	Jan. 22	Washington ($18,000)	Dallas ($18,000)	31-17	Washington	55,05
1983	Jan. 8	Washington ($18,000)	San Francisco ($18,000)	24-21	Washington	55,36
1984	Jan. 6	San Francisco ($18,000)	Chicago Bears ($18,000)	23-0	San Francisco	61,05
1985	Jan. 12	Chicago Bears ($18,000)	L.A. Rams ($18,000)	24-0	Chicago	63,52
1986	Jan. 11	N. Y. Giants ($18,000)	Washington ($18,000)	17-0	N.Y. Giants	76,63
1987	Jan. 17	Washington ($18,000)	Minnesota ($18,000)	17-10	Washington	55,21
1988	Jan. 8	San Francisco ($18,000)	Chicago Bears ($18,000)	28-3	Chicago	64,83
1989	Jan. 14	San Francisco ($18,000)	L.A. Rams ($18,000)	30-3	San Francisco	64,76
1990	Jan. 20	N. Y. Giants ($18,000)	San Francisco ($18,000)	15-13	San Francisco	65,75
1991	Jan. 12	Washington ($18,000)	Detroit ($18,000)	41-10	Washington	55,58
1992	Jan. 17	Dallas ($18,000)	San Francisco ($18,000)	30-20	San Francisco	64,92
1993	Jan. 23	Dallas ($18,000)	San Francisco ($18,000)	38-21	Dallas	64,90
1994	Jan. 15	San Francisco ($18,000)	Dallas ($18,000)	38-28	San Francisco	69,12
1995	Jan. 14	Dallas ($18,000)	Green Bay ($18,000)	38-27	Dallas	65,17
1996	Jan. 12	Green Bay ($18,000)	Carolina ($18,000)	30-13	Green Bay	60,21

*Sudden-death overtime.

COMPOSITE STANDINGS

	W	L	Pct.	PF	PA		W	L	Pct.	PF	PA
hiladelphia Eagles	4	1	.800	79	48	Phoenix Cardinals*	1	1	.500	28	28
reen Bay Packers..........	9	3	.750	280	167	San Francisco 49ers	5	6	.455	235	199
altimore Colts	3	1	.750	88	60	Cleveland Browns	4	7	.364	224	253
etroit Lions	4	2	.667	139	141	New York Giants	5	11	.313	240	322
innesota Vikings...........	4	2	.667	108	80	Los Angeles Rams‡........	3	9	.250	123	270
ashington Redskins†	7	5	.583	222	255	Carolina Panthers............	0	1	.000	13	30
hicago Bears.................	7	6	.538	286	245	Tampa Bay Buccaneers	0	1	.000	0	9
allas Cowboys...............	8	8	.500	361	319						

*Both games played when franchise was in Chicago; won 28-21, lost 7-0.
†One game played when franchise was in Boston; lost 21-6.
‡One game played when franchise was in Cleveland; won 15-14.

AFL (1960-1969); AFC (1970-1996)
RESULTS

ea.	Date	Winner (Share)	Loser (Share)	Score	Site	Attendance
960	Jan. 1	Houston ($1,025)	L.A. Chargers ($718)	24-16	Houston	32,183
961	Dec. 24	Houston ($1,792)	San Diego ($1,111)	10-3	San Diego	29,556
962	Dec. 23	Dallas Texans ($2,206)	Houston ($1,471)	20-17*	Houston	37,981
963	Jan. 5	San Diego ($2,498)	Boston Patriots ($1,596)	51-10	San Diego	30,127
964	Dec. 26	Buffalo ($2,668)	San Diego ($1,738)	20-7	Buffalo	40,242
965	Dec. 26	Buffalo ($5,189)	San Diego ($3,447)	23-0	San Diego	30,361
966	Jan. 1	Kansas City ($5,309)	Buffalo ($3,799)	31-7	Buffalo	42,080
967	Dec. 31	Oakland ($6,321)	Houston ($4,996)	40-7	Oakland	53,330
968	Dec. 29	N.Y. Jets ($7,007)	Oakland ($5,349)	27-23	New York	62,627
969	Jan. 4	Kansas City ($7,755)	Oakland ($6,252)	17-7	Oakland	53,564
970	Jan. 3	Baltimore ($8,500)	Oakland ($5,500)	27-17	Baltimore	54,799
971	Jan. 2	Miami ($8,500)	Baltimore ($5,500)	21-0	Miami	76,622
972	Dec. 31	Miami ($8,500)	Pittsburgh ($5,500)	21-17	Pittsburgh	50,845
973	Dec. 30	Miami ($8,500)	Oakland ($5,500)	27-10	Miami	79,325
974	Dec. 29	Pittsburgh ($8,500)	Oakland ($5,500)	24-13	Oakland	53,800
975	Jan. 4	Pittsburgh ($8,500)	Oakland ($5,500)	16-10	Pittsburgh	50,609
976	Dec. 28	Oakland ($8,500)	Pittsburgh ($5,500)	24-7	Oakland	53,821
977	Jan. 1	Denver ($9,000)	Oakland ($9,000)	20-17	Denver	75,044
978	Jan. 7	Pittsburgh ($9,000)	Houston ($9,000)	34-5	Pittsburgh	50,725
979	Jan. 6	Pittsburgh ($9,000)	Houston ($9,000)	27-13	Pittsburgh	50,475
980	Jan. 11	Oakland ($9,000)	San Diego ($9,000)	34-27	San Diego	52,428
981	Jan. 10	Cincinnati ($9,000)	San Diego ($9,000)	27-7	Cincinnati	46,302
982	Jan. 23	Miami ($18,000)	N.Y. Jets ($18,000)	14-0	Miami	67,396
983	Jan. 8	L.A. Raiders ($18,000)	Seattle ($18,000)	30-14	Los Angeles	88,734
984	Jan. 6	Miami ($18,000)	Pittsburgh ($18,000)	45-28	Miami	76,029
985	Jan. 12	New England ($18,000)	Miami ($18,000)	31-14	Miami	74,978
986	Jan. 11	Denver ($18,000)	Cleveland ($18,000)	23-20*	Cleveland	79,915
987	Jan. 17	Denver ($18,000)	Cleveland ($18,000)	38-33	Denver	75,993
988	Jan. 8	Cincinnati ($18,000)	Buffalo ($18,000)	21-10	Cincinnati	59,747
989	Jan. 14	Denver ($18,000)	Cleveland ($18,000)	37-21	Denver	76,046
990	Jan. 20	Buffalo ($18,000)	L.A. Raiders ($18,000)	51-3	Buffalo	80,234
991	Jan. 12	Buffalo ($18,000)	Denver ($18,000)	10-7	Buffalo	80,272
992	Jan. 17	Buffalo ($18,000)	Miami ($18,000)	29-10	Miami	72,703
993	Jan. 23	Buffalo ($18,000)	Kansas City ($18,000)	30-13	Buffalo	76,642
994	Jan. 15	San Diego ($18,000)	Pittsburgh ($18,000)	17-13	Pittsburgh	61,545
995	Jan. 14	Pittsburgh ($18,000)	Indianapolis ($18,000)	20-16	Pittsburgh	61,062
996	Jan. 12	New England ($18,000)	Jacksonville ($18,000)	20-6	New England	60,190

*Sudden-death overtime.

COMPOSITE STANDINGS

	W	L	Pct.	PF	PA		W	L	Pct.	PF	PA
incinnati Bengals...........	2	0	1.000	48	17	Houston Oilers	2	4	.333	76	140
enver Broncos	4	1	.800	125	101	Indianapolis Colts∞..........	1	2	.333	43	58
uffalo Bills	6	2	.750	180	92	Oakland Raiders§.............	4	8	.333	228	264
ansas City Chiefs†	3	1	.750	81	61	San Diego Chargers*	2	6	.250	128	161
iami Dolphins.................	5	2	.714	152	115	Seattle Seahawks	0	1	.000	14	30
ew England Patriots‡.....	2	1	.667	61	71	Jacksonville Jaguars........	0	1	.000	6	20
ittsburgh Steelers	5	4	.556	186	164	Cleveland Browns	0	3	.000	74	98
ew York Jets	1	1	.500	27	37						

*One game played when franchise was in Los Angeles; lost 24-16.
†One game played when franchise was in Dallas (Texans); won 20-17.
‡One game played when franchise was in Boston; lost 51-10.
§Two games played when franchise was in Los Angeles; record of 1-1.
∞Two games played when franchise was in Baltimore; record of 1-1.

POSTSEASON GAME COMPOSITE STANDINGS

	W	L	Pct.	PF	PA		W	L	Pct.	PF	PA
Green Bay Packers	20	8	.714	677	480	Philadelphia Eagles	9	11	.450	356	369
Jacksonville Jaguars	2	1	.667	66	74	Kansas City Chiefs*	8	10	.444	291	37
San Francisco 49ers	22	13	.629	888	667	New York Giants	14	18	.438	529	59
Dallas Cowboys	32	19	.627	1254	932	New England Patriots§	6	8	.429	287	322
Washington Redskins§	21	14	.600	738	625	Seattle Seahawks	3	4	.429	128	13
Pittsburgh Steelers	20	14	.588	773	677	Cincinnati Bengals	5	7	.417	246	25
Oakland Raiders◆	21	15	.583	855	659	Houston Oilers	9	13	.409	371	53
Miami Dolphins	17	14	.548	697	633	Minnesota Vikings	13	19	.406	568	68
Buffalo Bills	14	13	.519	648	612	St. Louis Rams†	13	20	.394	501	69
Chicago Bears	14	14	.500	579	552	San Diego Chargers▲	7	11	.389	332	42
Indianapolis Colts■	10	10	.500	360	389	Cleveland Browns	11	19	.367	596	70
Carolina Panthers	1	1	.500	39	47	Atlanta Falcons	2	5	.286	139	18
Detroit Lions	7	8	.467	342	357	Tampa Bay Buccaneers	1	3	.250	41	9
New York Jets	5	6	.455	216	200	Arizona Cardinals∞	1	4	.200	81	13
Denver Broncos	9	11	.450	407	532	New Orleans Saints	0	4	.000	56	12

*One game played when franchise was in Dallas (Texans); won 20-17.
†One game played when franchise was in Cleveland; won 15-14.
‡One game played when franchise was in Boston; lost 21-6.
§Two games played when franchise was in Boston; won 26-8, lost 51-10.
∞Two games played when franchise was in Chicago; won 28-21, lost 7-0. Three games played when franchise was in St. Louis; lost 35-23, lost 30-14, lost 41-16.
▲One game played when franchise was in Los Angeles; lost 24-16.
◆12 games played when franchise was in Los Angeles; record of 6-6.
■15 games played when franchise was in Baltimore; record of 8-7.

HISTORY Championship games

YEAR-BY-YEAR STANDINGS

1920

am	W	L	T	Pct.
ron Pros*	8	0	3	1.000
ecatur Staleys	10	1	2	.909
ffalo All-Americans	9	1	1	.900
icago Cardinals	6	2	2	.750
ck Island Independents	6	2	2	.750
yton Triangles	5	2	2	.714
ochester Jeffersons	6	3	2	.667
nton Bulldogs	7	4	2	.636
troit Heralds	2	3	3	.400
eveland Tigers	2	4	2	.333
icago Tigers	2	5	1	.286
mmond Pros	2	5	0	.286
lumbus Panhandles	2	6	2	.250
ncie Flyers	0	1	0	.000

*No official standings were maintained for the 1920 season, and the championship was awarded to the Akron Pros in a League meeting on April 30, 1921. ubs played schedules which included games against non-league opponents. cords of clubs against all opponents are listed above.

1921

am	W	L	T	Pct.
icago Staleys	9	1	1	.900
ffalo All-Americans	9	1	2	.900
ron Pros	8	3	1	.727
nton Bulldogs	5	2	3	.714
ck Island Independents	4	2	1	.667
ansville Crimson Giants	3	2	0	.600
een Bay Packers	3	2	1	.600
yton Triangles	4	4	1	.500
icago Cardinals	3	3	2	.500
ochester Jeffersons	2	3	0	.400
eveland Indians	3	5	0	.375
ashington Senators	1	2	0	.333
ncinnati Celts	1	3	0	.250
mmond Pros	1	3	1	.250
nneapolis Marines	1	3	1	.250
troit Heralds	1	5	1	.167
lumbus Panhandles	1	8	0	.111
nawanda Kardex	0	1	0	.000
ncie Flyers	0	2	0	.000
uisville Brecks	0	2	0	.000
w York Giants	0	2	0	.000

1922

am	W	L	T	Pct.
nton Bulldogs	10	0	2	1.000
icago Bears	9	3	0	.750
icago Cardinals	8	3	0	.727
edo Maroons	5	2	2	.714
ck Island Independents	4	2	1	.667
cine Legion	6	4	1	.600
yton Triangles	4	3	1	.571
een Bay Packers	4	3	3	.571
ffalo All-Americans	5	4	1	.556
ron Pros	3	5	2	.375
lwaukee Badgers	2	4	3	.333
rang Indians	2	6	0	.250
nneapolis Marines	1	3	0	.250
uisville Brecks	1	3	0	.250
ansville Crimson Giants	0	3	0	.000
ochester Jeffersons	0	4	1	.000
mmond Pros	0	5	1	.000
lumbus Panhandles	0	7	0	.000

1923

Team	W	L	T	Pct.
Canton Bulldogs	11	0	1	1.000
Chicago Bears	9	2	1	.818
Green Bay Packers	7	2	1	.778
Milwaukee Badgers	7	2	3	.778
Cleveland Indians	3	1	3	.750
Chicago Cardinals	8	4	0	.667
Duluth Kelleys	4	3	0	.571
Columbus Tigers	5	4	1	.556
Buffalo All-Americans	4	4	3	.500
Racine Legion	4	4	2	.500
Toledo Maroons	2	3	2	.400
Rock Island Independents	2	3	3	.400
Minneapolis Marines	2	5	2	.286
St. Louis All-Stars	1	4	2	.200
Hammond Pros	1	5	1	.167
Dayton Triangles	1	6	1	.143
Akron Indians	1	6	0	.143
Oorang Indians	1	10	0	.091
Rochester Jeffersons	0	2	0	.000
Louisville Brecks	0	3	0	.000

1924

Team	W	L	T	Pct.
Cleveland Bulldogs	7	1	1	.875
Chicago Bears	6	1	4	.857
Frankford Yellow Jackets	11	2	1	.846
Duluth Kelleys	5	1	0	.833
Rock Island Independents	6	2	2	.750
Green Bay Packers	7	4	0	.636
Racine Legion	4	3	3	.571
Chicago Cardinals	5	4	1	.556
Buffalo Bisons	6	5	0	.545
Columbus Tigers	4	4	0	.500
Hammond Pros	2	2	1	.500
Milwaukee Badgers	5	8	0	.385
Akron Indians	2	6	0	.250
Dayton Triangles	2	6	0	.250
Kansas City Blues	2	7	0	.222
Kenosha Maroons	0	5	1	.000
Minneapolis Marines	0	6	0	.000
Rochester Jeffersons	0	7	0	.000

1925

Team	W	L	T	Pct.
Chicago Cardinals	11	2	1	.846
Pottsville Maroons	10	2	0	.833
Detroit Panthers	8	2	2	.800
New York Giants	8	4	0	.667
Akron Indians	4	2	2	.667
Frankford Yellow Jackets	13	7	0	.650
Chicago Bears	9	5	3	.643
Rock Island Independents	5	3	3	.625
Green Bay Packers	8	5	0	.615
Providence Steam Roller	6	5	1	.545
Canton Bulldogs	4	4	0	.500
Cleveland Bulldogs	5	8	1	.385
Kansas City Cowboys	2	5	1	.286
Hammond Pros	1	4	0	.200
Buffalo Bisons	1	6	2	.143
Duluth Kelleys	0	3	0	.000
Rochester Jeffersons	0	6	1	.000
Milwaukee Badgers	0	6	0	.000
Dayton Triangles	0	7	1	.000
Columbus Tigers	0	9	0	.000

1926

Team	W	L	T	Pct.
Frankford Yellow Jackets	14	1	1	.933
Chicago Bears	12	1	3	.923
Pottsville Maroons	10	2	1	.833
Kansas City Cowboys	8	3	0	.727
Green Bay Packers	7	3	3	.700
Los Angeles Buccaneers	6	3	1	.667
New York Giants	8	4	1	.667
Duluth Eskimos	6	5	3	.545
Buffalo Rangers	4	4	2	.500
Chicago Cardinals	5	6	1	.455
Providence Steam Roller	5	7	1	.417
Detroit Panthers	4	6	2	.400
Hartford Blues	3	7	0	.300
Brooklyn Lions	3	8	0	.273
Milwaukee Badgers	2	7	0	.222
Akron Pros	1	4	3	.200
Dayton Triangles	1	4	1	.200
Racine Tornadoes	1	4	0	.200
Columbus Tigers	1	6	0	.143
Canton Bulldogs	1	9	3	.100
Hammond Pros	0	4	0	.000
Louisville Colonels	0	4	0	.000

1927

Team	W	L	T	Pct.
New York Giants	11	1	1	.917
Green Bay Packers	7	2	1	.778
Chicago Bears	9	3	2	.750
Cleveland Bulldogs	8	4	1	.667
Providence Steam Roller	8	5	1	.615
New York Yankees	7	8	1	.467
Frankford Yellow Jackets	6	9	3	.400
Pottsville Maroons	5	8	0	.385
Chicago Cardinals	3	7	1	.300
Dayton Triangles	1	6	1	.143
Duluth Eskimos	1	8	0	.111
Buffalo Bisons	0	5	0	.000

1928

Team	W	L	T	Pct.
Providence Steam Roller	8	1	2	.889
Frankford Yellow Jackets	11	3	2	.786
Detroit Wolverines	7	2	1	.778
Green Bay Packers	6	4	3	.600
Chicago Bears	7	5	1	.583
New York Giants	4	7	2	.364
New York Yankees	4	8	1	.333
Pottsville Maroons	2	8	0	.200
Chicago Cardinals	1	5	0	.167
Dayton Triangles	0	7	0	.000

1929

Team	W	L	T	Pe
Green Bay Packers	12	0	1	1.00
New York Giants	13	1	1	.92
Frankford Yellow Jackets	9	4	5	.69
Chicago Cardinals	6	6	1	.50
Boston Bulldogs	4	4	0	.50
Orange Tornadoes	3	4	4	.42
Staten Island Stapletons	3	4	3	.42
Providence Steam Roller	4	6	2	.40
Chicago Bears	4	9	2	.30
Buffalo Bisons	1	7	1	.12
Minneapolis Red Jackets	1	9	0	.10
Dayton Triangles	0	6	0	.00

1930

Team	W	L	T	Pe
Green Bay Packers	10	3	1	.76
New York Giants	13	4	0	.76
Chicago Bears	9	4	1	.69
Brooklyn Dodgers	7	4	1	.63
Providence Steam Roller	6	4	1	.60
Staten Island Stapletons	5	5	2	.50
Chicago Cardinals	5	6	2	.45
Portsmouth Spartans	5	6	3	.45
Frankford Yellow Jackets	4	13	1	.22
Minneapolis Red Jackets	1	7	1	.12
Newark Tornadoes	1	10	1	.09

1931

Team	W	L	T	Pe
Green Bay Packers	12	2	0	.85
Portsmouth Spartans	11	3	0	.78
Chicago Bears	8	5	0	.61
Chicago Cardinals	5	4	0	.55
New York Giants	7	6	1	.53
Providence Steam Roller	4	4	3	.50
Staten Island Stapletons	4	6	1	.40
Cleveland Indians	2	8	0	.20
Brooklyn Dodgers	2	12	0	.14
Frankford Yellow Jackets	1	6	1	.14

1932

Team	W	L	T	Pc
Chicago Bears	7	1	6	.87
Green Bay Packers	10	3	1	.76
Portsmouth Spartans	6	2	4	.75
Boston Braves	4	4	2	.50
New York Giants	4	6	2	.40
Brooklyn Dodgers	3	9	0	.25
Chicago Cardinals	2	6	2	.25
Staten Island Stapletons	2	7	3	.22

NOTE: Chicago Bears and Portsmouth finished regularly scheduled gam■ tied for first place. Bears won playoff game, which counted in standings, 9-0.

1933

EASTERN DIVISION

Team	W	L	T	Pct.	PF	PA
N.Y. Giants	11	3	0	.786	244	101
Brooklyn	5	4	1	.556	93	54
Boston	5	5	2	.500	103	97
Philadelphia	3	5	1	.375	77	158
Pittsburgh	3	6	2	.333	67	208

WESTERN DIVISION

Team	W	L	T	Pct.	PF	PA
Chicago Bears	10	2	1	.833	133	82
Portsmouth	6	5	0	.545	128	87
Green Bay	5	7	1	.417	170	107
Cincinnati	3	6	1	.333	38	110
Chi. Cardinals	1	9	1	.100	52	101

PLAYOFFS

NFL championship

Chicago Bears 23 vs. N.Y. Giants 21

1934

EASTERN DIVISION

Team	W	L	T	Pct.	PF	PA
N.Y. Giants	8	5	0	.615	147	107
Boston	6	6	0	.500	107	94
Brooklyn	4	7	0	.364	61	153
Philadelphia	4	7	0	.364	127	85
Pittsburgh	2	10	0	.167	51	206

WESTERN DIVISION

Team	W	L	T	Pct.	PF	PA
Chicago Bears	13	0	0	1.000	286	86
Detroit	10	3	0	.769	238	59
Green Bay	7	6	0	.538	156	112
Chi. Cardinals	5	6	0	.455	80	84
St. Louis	1	2	0	.333	27	61
Cincinnati	0	8	0	.000	10	243

PLAYOFFS

NFL championship
N.Y. Giants 30 vs. Chicago Bears 13

1935

EASTERN DIVISION

Team	W	L	T	Pct.	PF	PA
N.Y. Giants	9	3	0	.750	180	96
Brooklyn	5	6	1	.455	90	141
Pittsburgh	4	8	0	.333	100	209
Boston	2	8	1	.200	65	123
Philadelphia	2	9	0	.182	60	179

WESTERN DIVISION

Team	W	L	T	Pct.	PF	PA
Detroit	7	3	2	.700	191	111
Green Bay	8	4	0	.667	181	96
Chicago Bears	6	4	2	.600	192	106
Chi. Cardinals	6	4	2	.600	99	97

PLAYOFFS

NFL championship
Detroit 26 vs. N.Y. Giants 7

NOTE: One game between Boston and Philadelphia was cancelled.

1936

EASTERN DIVISION

Team	W	L	T	Pct.	PF	PA
Boston	7	5	0	.583	149	110
Pittsburgh	6	6	0	.500	98	187
N.Y. Giants	5	6	1	.455	115	163
Brooklyn	3	8	1	.273	92	161
Philadelphia	1	11	0	.083	51	206

WESTERN DIVISION

Team	W	L	T	Pct.	PF	PA
Green Bay	10	1	1	.909	248	118
Chicago Bears	9	3	0	.750	222	94
Detroit	8	4	0	.667	235	102
Chi. Cardinals	3	8	1	.273	74	143

PLAYOFFS

NFL championship
Green Bay 21, Boston 6, at New York.

1937

EASTERN DIVISION

Team	W	L	T	Pct.	PF	PA
Washington	8	3	0	.727	195	120
N.Y. Giants	6	3	2	.667	128	109
Pittsburgh	4	7	0	.364	122	145
Brooklyn	3	7	1	.300	82	174
Philadelphia	2	8	1	.200	86	177

WESTERN DIVISION

Team	W	L	T	Pct.	PF	PA
Chicago Bears	9	1	1	.900	201	100
Green Bay	7	4	0	.636	220	122
Detroit	7	4	0	.636	180	105
Chi. Cardinals	5	5	1	.500	135	165
Cleveland	1	10	0	.091	75	207

PLAYOFFS

NFL championship
Washington 28 at Chicago Bears 21

1938

EASTERN DIVISION

Team	W	L	T	Pct.	PF	PA
N.Y. Giants	8	2	1	.800	194	79
Washington	6	3	2	.667	148	154
Brooklyn	4	4	3	.500	131	161
Philadelphia	5	6	0	.455	154	164
Pittsburgh	2	9	0	.182	79	169

WESTERN DIVISION

Team	W	L	T	Pct.	PF	PA
Green Bay	8	3	0	.727	223	118
Detroit	7	4	0	.636	119	108
Chicago Bears	6	5	0	.545	194	148
Cleveland	4	7	0	.364	131	215
Chi. Cardinals	2	9	0	.182	111	168

PLAYOFFS

NFL championship
N.Y. Giants 23 vs. Green Bay 17

1939

EASTERN DIVISION

Team	W	L	T	Pct.	PF	PA
N.Y. Giants	9	1	1	.900	168	85
Washington	8	2	1	.800	242	94
Brooklyn	4	6	1	.400	108	219
Philadelphia	1	9	1	.100	105	200
Pittsburgh	1	9	1	.100	114	216

WESTERN DIVISION

Team	W	L	T	Pct.	PF	PA
Green Bay	9	2	0	.818	233	153
Chicago Bears	8	3	0	.727	298	157
Detroit	6	5	0	.545	145	150
Cleveland	5	5	1	.500	195	164
Chi. Cardinals	1	10	0	.091	84	254

PLAYOFFS

NFL championship
Green Bay 27 vs. N.Y. Giants 0

1940

EASTERN DIVISION

Team	W	L	T	Pct.	PF	PA
Washington	9	2	0	.818	245	142
Brooklyn	8	3	0	.727	186	120
N.Y. Giants	6	4	1	.600	131	133
Pittsburgh	2	7	2	.222	60	178
Philadelphia	1	10	0	.091	111	211

WESTERN DIVISION

Team	W	L	T	Pct.	PF	PA
Chicago Bears	8	3	0	.727	238	152
Green Bay	6	4	1	.600	238	155
Detroit	5	5	1	.500	138	153
Cleveland	4	6	1	.400	171	191
Chi. Cardinals	2	7	2	.222	139	222

PLAYOFFS

NFL championship
Chicago Bears 73 at Washington 0

1941

EASTERN DIVISION						WESTERN DIVISION						PLAYOFFS
Team	W	L	T	Pct.	PF	PA						**Western Division playoff**
N.Y. Giants	8	3	0	.727	238	114						Chicago Bears 33 vs. Green Bay 14
Brooklyn	7	4	0	.636	158	127						**NFL championship**
Washington	6	5	0	.545	176	174						Chicago Bears 37 vs. N.Y. Giants 9
Philadelphia	2	8	1	.200	119	218						
Pittsburgh	1	9	1	.100	103	276						

Team	W	L	T	Pct.	PF	PA
Chicago Bears	10	1	0	.909	396	147
Green Bay	10	1	0	.909	258	120
Detroit	4	6	1	.400	121	195
Chi. Cardinals	3	7	1	.300	127	197
Cleveland	2	9	0	.182	116	244

1942

EASTERN DIVISION						
Team	W	L	T	Pct.	PF	PA
Washington	10	1	0	.909	227	102
Pittsburgh	7	4	0	.636	167	119
N.Y. Giants	5	5	1	.500	155	139
Brooklyn	3	8	0	.273	100	168
Philadelphia	2	9	0	.182	134	239

WESTERN DIVISION						
Team	W	L	T	Pct.	PF	PA
Chicago Bears	11	0	0	1.000	376	84
Green Bay	8	2	1	.800	300	215
Cleveland	5	6	0	.455	150	207
Chi. Cardinals	3	8	0	.273	98	209
Detroit	0	11	0	.000	38	263

PLAYOFFS

NFL championship
Washington 14 vs. Chicago Bears 6

1943

EASTERN DIVISION						
Team	W	L	T	Pct.	PF	PA
Washington	6	3	1	.667	229	137
N.Y. Giants	6	3	1	.667	197	170
Phil.-Pitt.	5	4	1	.556	225	230
Brooklyn	2	8	0	.200	65	234

NOTE: Cleveland Rams did not play in 1943.

WESTERN DIVISION						
Team	W	L	T	Pct.	PF	PA
Chicago Bears	8	1	1	.889	303	157
Green Bay	7	2	1	.778	264	172
Detroit	3	6	1	.333	178	218
Chi. Cardinals	0	10	0	.000	95	238

PLAYOFFS

Eastern Division playoff
Washington 28 at N.Y. Giants 0

NFL championship
Chicago Bears 41 vs. Washington 21

1944

EASTERN DIVISION						
Team	W	L	T	Pct.	PF	PA
N.Y. Giants	8	1	1	.889	206	74
Philadelphia	7	1	2	.875	267	131
Washington	6	3	1	.667	169	180
Boston	2	8	0	.200	82	233
Brooklyn	0	10	0	.000	69	166

WESTERN DIVISION						
Team	W	L	T	Pct.	PF	PA
Green Bay	8	2	0	.800	238	141
Chicago Bears	6	3	1	.667	258	172
Detroit	6	3	1	.667	216	151
Cleveland	4	6	0	.400	188	224
Card-Pitt	0	10	0	.000	108	328

PLAYOFFS

NFL championship
Green Bay 14 at N.Y. Giants 7

1945

EASTERN DIVISION						
Team	W	L	T	Pct.	PF	PA
Washington	8	2	0	.800	209	121
Philadelphia	7	3	0	.700	272	133
N.Y. Giants	3	6	1	.333	179	198
Boston	3	6	1	.333	123	211
Pittsburgh	2	8	0	.200	79	220

WESTERN DIVISION						
Team	W	L	T	Pct.	PF	PA
Cleveland	9	1	0	.900	244	136
Detroit	7	3	0	.700	195	194
Green Bay	6	4	0	.600	258	173
Chicago Bears	3	7	0	.300	192	235
Chi. Cardinals	1	9	0	.100	98	228

PLAYOFFS

NFL championship
Cleveland 15 vs. Washington 14

1946

AAFC

EASTERN DIVISION						
Team	W	L	T	Pct.	PF	PA
New York	10	3	1	.769	270	192
Brooklyn	3	10	1	.231	226	339
Buffalo	3	10	1	.231	249	370
Miami	3	11	0	.154	167	378

WESTERN DIVISION						
Team	W	L	T	Pct.	PF	PA
Cleveland	12	2	0	.857	423	137
San Francisco	9	5	0	.643	307	189
Los Angeles	7	5	2	.583	305	290
Chicago	5	6	3	.455	263	315

PLAYOFFS

AAFC championship
Cleveland 14 vs. New York 9

NFL

EASTERN DIVISION						
Team	W	L	T	Pct.	PF	PA
N.Y. Giants	7	3	1	.700	236	162
Philadelphia	6	5	0	.545	231	220
Washington	5	5	1	.500	171	191
Pittsburgh	5	5	1	.500	136	117
Boston	2	8	1	.200	189	273

WESTERN DIVISION						
Team	W	L	T	Pct.	PF	PA
Chicago Bears	8	2	1	.800	289	193
Los Angeles	6	4	1	.600	277	257
Green Bay	6	5	0	.545	148	158
Chi. Cardinals	6	5	0	.545	260	198
Detroit	1	10	0	.091	142	310

PLAYOFFS

NFL championship
Chicago Bears 24 at N.Y. Giants 14

1947

AAFC

<table>
<tr><td colspan="6">EASTERN DIVISION</td><td colspan="6">WESTERN DIVISION</td><td>PLAYOFFS</td></tr>
<tr><td>Team</td><td>W</td><td>L</td><td>T</td><td>Pct.</td><td>PF</td><td>PA</td><td>Team</td><td>W</td><td>L</td><td>T</td><td>Pct.</td><td>PF</td><td>PA</td><td>AAFC championship</td></tr>
<tr><td>New York</td><td>11</td><td>2</td><td>1</td><td>.846</td><td>378</td><td>239</td><td>Cleveland</td><td>12</td><td>1</td><td>1</td><td>.923</td><td>410</td><td>185</td><td>Cleveland 14 at New York 3</td></tr>
<tr><td>Buffalo</td><td>8</td><td>4</td><td>2</td><td>.667</td><td>320</td><td>288</td><td>San Francisco</td><td>8</td><td>4</td><td>2</td><td>.667</td><td>327</td><td>264</td><td></td></tr>
<tr><td>Brooklyn</td><td>3</td><td>10</td><td>1</td><td>.231</td><td>181</td><td>340</td><td>Los Angeles</td><td>7</td><td>7</td><td>0</td><td>.500</td><td>328</td><td>256</td><td></td></tr>
<tr><td>Baltimore</td><td>2</td><td>11</td><td>1</td><td>.154</td><td>167</td><td>377</td><td>Chicago</td><td>1</td><td>13</td><td>0</td><td>.071</td><td>263</td><td>425</td><td></td></tr>
</table>

NFL

<table>
<tr><td colspan="6">EASTERN DIVISION</td><td colspan="6">WESTERN DIVISION</td><td>PLAYOFFS</td></tr>
<tr><td>Team</td><td>W</td><td>L</td><td>T</td><td>Pct.</td><td>PF</td><td>PA</td><td>Team</td><td>W</td><td>L</td><td>T</td><td>Pct.</td><td>PF</td><td>PA</td><td>Eastern Division playoff</td></tr>
<tr><td>Philadelphia</td><td>8</td><td>4</td><td>0</td><td>.667</td><td>308</td><td>242</td><td>Chi. Cardinals</td><td>9</td><td>3</td><td>0</td><td>.750</td><td>306</td><td>231</td><td>Philadelphia 21 at Pittsburgh 0</td></tr>
<tr><td>Pittsburgh</td><td>8</td><td>4</td><td>0</td><td>.667</td><td>240</td><td>259</td><td>Chicago Bears</td><td>8</td><td>4</td><td>0</td><td>.667</td><td>363</td><td>241</td><td>NFL championship</td></tr>
<tr><td>Boston</td><td>4</td><td>7</td><td>1</td><td>.364</td><td>168</td><td>256</td><td>Green Bay</td><td>6</td><td>5</td><td>1</td><td>.545</td><td>274</td><td>210</td><td>Chicago Cardinals 28 vs. Philadelphia 21</td></tr>
<tr><td>Washington</td><td>4</td><td>8</td><td>0</td><td>.333</td><td>295</td><td>367</td><td>Los Angeles</td><td>6</td><td>6</td><td>0</td><td>.500</td><td>259</td><td>214</td><td></td></tr>
<tr><td>N.Y. Giants</td><td>2</td><td>8</td><td>2</td><td>.200</td><td>190</td><td>309</td><td>Detroit</td><td>3</td><td>9</td><td>0</td><td>.250</td><td>231</td><td>305</td><td></td></tr>
</table>

1948

AAFC

<table>
<tr><td colspan="6">EASTERN DIVISION</td><td colspan="6">WESTERN DIVISION</td><td>PLAYOFFS</td></tr>
<tr><td>Team</td><td>W</td><td>L</td><td>T</td><td>Pct.</td><td>PF</td><td>PA</td><td>Team</td><td>W</td><td>L</td><td>T</td><td>Pct.</td><td>PF</td><td>PA</td><td>Eastern Division playoff</td></tr>
<tr><td>Buffalo</td><td>7</td><td>7</td><td>0</td><td>.500</td><td>360</td><td>358</td><td>Cleveland</td><td>14</td><td>0</td><td>0</td><td>1.000</td><td>389</td><td>190</td><td>Buffalo 28 vs. Baltimore 17</td></tr>
<tr><td>Baltimore</td><td>7</td><td>7</td><td>0</td><td>.500</td><td>333</td><td>327</td><td>San Francisco</td><td>12</td><td>2</td><td>0</td><td>.857</td><td>495</td><td>248</td><td>AAFC championship</td></tr>
<tr><td>New York</td><td>6</td><td>8</td><td>0</td><td>.429</td><td>265</td><td>301</td><td>Los Angeles</td><td>7</td><td>7</td><td>0</td><td>.500</td><td>258</td><td>305</td><td>Cleveland 49 vs. Buffalo 7</td></tr>
<tr><td>Brooklyn</td><td>2</td><td>12</td><td>0</td><td>.143</td><td>253</td><td>387</td><td>Chicago</td><td>1</td><td>13</td><td>0</td><td>.071</td><td>202</td><td>439</td><td></td></tr>
</table>

NFL

<table>
<tr><td colspan="6">EASTERN DIVISION</td><td colspan="6">WESTERN DIVISION</td><td>PLAYOFFS</td></tr>
<tr><td>Team</td><td>W</td><td>L</td><td>T</td><td>Pct.</td><td>PF</td><td>PA</td><td>Team</td><td>W</td><td>L</td><td>T</td><td>Pct.</td><td>PF</td><td>PA</td><td>NFL championship</td></tr>
<tr><td>Philadelphia</td><td>9</td><td>2</td><td>1</td><td>.818</td><td>376</td><td>156</td><td>Chi. Cardinals</td><td>11</td><td>1</td><td>0</td><td>.917</td><td>395</td><td>226</td><td>Philadelphia 7 vs. Chicago Cardinals 0</td></tr>
<tr><td>Washington</td><td>7</td><td>5</td><td>0</td><td>.583</td><td>291</td><td>287</td><td>Chicago Bears</td><td>10</td><td>2</td><td>0</td><td>.833</td><td>375</td><td>151</td><td></td></tr>
<tr><td>N.Y. Giants</td><td>4</td><td>8</td><td>0</td><td>.333</td><td>297</td><td>388</td><td>Los Angeles</td><td>6</td><td>5</td><td>1</td><td>.545</td><td>327</td><td>269</td><td></td></tr>
<tr><td>Pittsburgh</td><td>4</td><td>8</td><td>0</td><td>.333</td><td>200</td><td>243</td><td>Green Bay</td><td>3</td><td>9</td><td>0</td><td>.250</td><td>154</td><td>290</td><td></td></tr>
<tr><td>Boston</td><td>3</td><td>9</td><td>0</td><td>.250</td><td>174</td><td>372</td><td>Detroit</td><td>2</td><td>10</td><td>0</td><td>.167</td><td>200</td><td>407</td><td></td></tr>
</table>

1949

AAFC

<table>
<tr><td>Team</td><td>W</td><td>L</td><td>T</td><td>Pct.</td><td>PF</td><td>PA</td><td>PLAYOFFS</td></tr>
<tr><td>Cleveland</td><td>9</td><td>1</td><td>2</td><td>.900</td><td>339</td><td>171</td><td>AAFC Semifinals</td></tr>
<tr><td>San Francisco</td><td>9</td><td>3</td><td>0</td><td>.750</td><td>416</td><td>227</td><td>Cleveland 31 vs. Buffalo 21</td></tr>
<tr><td>Brooklyn-N.Y.</td><td>8</td><td>4</td><td>0</td><td>.667</td><td>196</td><td>206</td><td>San Francisco 17 vs. Brooklyn-N.Y. 7</td></tr>
<tr><td>Buffalo</td><td>5</td><td>5</td><td>2</td><td>.500</td><td>236</td><td>256</td><td>AAFC championship</td></tr>
<tr><td>Chicago</td><td>4</td><td>8</td><td>0</td><td>.333</td><td>179</td><td>268</td><td>Cleveland 21 vs. San Francisco 7</td></tr>
<tr><td>Los Angeles</td><td>4</td><td>8</td><td>0</td><td>.333</td><td>253</td><td>322</td><td></td></tr>
<tr><td>Baltimore</td><td>1</td><td>11</td><td>0</td><td>.083</td><td>172</td><td>341</td><td></td></tr>
</table>

NFL

<table>
<tr><td colspan="6">EASTERN DIVISION</td><td colspan="6">WESTERN DIVISION</td><td>PLAYOFFS</td></tr>
<tr><td>Team</td><td>W</td><td>L</td><td>T</td><td>Pct.</td><td>PF</td><td>PA</td><td>Team</td><td>W</td><td>L</td><td>T</td><td>Pct.</td><td>PF</td><td>PA</td><td>NFL championship</td></tr>
<tr><td>Philadelphia</td><td>11</td><td>1</td><td>0</td><td>.917</td><td>364</td><td>134</td><td>Los Angeles</td><td>8</td><td>2</td><td>2</td><td>.800</td><td>360</td><td>239</td><td>Philadelphia 14 at Los Angeles 0</td></tr>
<tr><td>Pittsburgh</td><td>6</td><td>5</td><td>1</td><td>.545</td><td>224</td><td>214</td><td>Chicago Bears</td><td>9</td><td>3</td><td>0</td><td>.750</td><td>332</td><td>218</td><td></td></tr>
<tr><td>N.Y. Giants</td><td>6</td><td>6</td><td>0</td><td>.500</td><td>287</td><td>298</td><td>Chi. Cardinals</td><td>6</td><td>5</td><td>1</td><td>.545</td><td>360</td><td>301</td><td></td></tr>
<tr><td>Washington</td><td>4</td><td>7</td><td>1</td><td>.364</td><td>268</td><td>339</td><td>Detroit</td><td>4</td><td>8</td><td>0</td><td>.333</td><td>237</td><td>259</td><td></td></tr>
<tr><td>N.Y. Bulldogs</td><td>1</td><td>10</td><td>1</td><td>.091</td><td>153</td><td>365</td><td>Green Bay</td><td>2</td><td>10</td><td>0</td><td>.167</td><td>114</td><td>329</td><td></td></tr>
</table>

1950

<table>
<tr><td colspan="6">AMERICAN CONFERENCE</td><td colspan="6">NATIONAL CONFERENCE</td><td>PLAYOFFS</td></tr>
<tr><td>Team</td><td>W</td><td>L</td><td>T</td><td>Pct.</td><td>PF</td><td>PA</td><td>Team</td><td>W</td><td>L</td><td>T</td><td>Pct.</td><td>PF</td><td>PA</td><td>American Conference playoff</td></tr>
<tr><td>Cleveland</td><td>10</td><td>2</td><td>0</td><td>.833</td><td>310</td><td>144</td><td>Los Angeles</td><td>9</td><td>3</td><td>0</td><td>.750</td><td>466</td><td>309</td><td>Cleveland 8 vs. N.Y. Giants 3</td></tr>
<tr><td>N.Y. Giants</td><td>10</td><td>2</td><td>0</td><td>.833</td><td>268</td><td>150</td><td>Chicago Bears</td><td>9</td><td>3</td><td>0</td><td>.750</td><td>279</td><td>207</td><td>National Conference playoff</td></tr>
<tr><td>Philadelphia</td><td>6</td><td>6</td><td>0</td><td>.500</td><td>254</td><td>141</td><td>N.Y. Yanks</td><td>7</td><td>5</td><td>0</td><td>.583</td><td>366</td><td>367</td><td>Los Angeles 24 vs. Chicago Bears 14</td></tr>
<tr><td>Pittsburgh</td><td>6</td><td>6</td><td>0</td><td>.500</td><td>180</td><td>195</td><td>Detroit</td><td>6</td><td>6</td><td>0</td><td>.500</td><td>321</td><td>285</td><td>NFL championship</td></tr>
<tr><td>Chi. Cardinals</td><td>5</td><td>7</td><td>0</td><td>.417</td><td>233</td><td>287</td><td>Green Bay</td><td>3</td><td>9</td><td>0</td><td>.250</td><td>244</td><td>406</td><td>Cleveland 30 vs. Los Angeles 28</td></tr>
<tr><td>Washington</td><td>3</td><td>9</td><td>0</td><td>.250</td><td>232</td><td>326</td><td>San Francisco</td><td>3</td><td>9</td><td>0</td><td>.250</td><td>213</td><td>300</td><td></td></tr>
<tr><td></td><td></td><td></td><td></td><td></td><td></td><td></td><td>Baltimore</td><td>1</td><td>11</td><td>0</td><td>.083</td><td>213</td><td>462</td><td></td></tr>
</table>

1951

AMERICAN CONFERENCE

Team	W	L	T	Pct.	PF	PA
Cleveland	11	1	0	.917	331	152
N.Y. Giants	9	2	1	.818	254	161
Washington	5	7	0	.417	183	296
Pittsburgh	4	7	1	.364	183	235
Philadelphia	4	8	0	.333	234	264
Chi. Cardinals	3	9	0	.250	210	287

NATIONAL CONFERENCE

Team	W	L	T	Pct.	PF	PA
Los Angeles	8	4	0	.667	392	261
Detroit	7	4	1	.636	336	259
San Francisco	7	4	1	.636	255	205
Chicago Bears	7	5	0	.583	286	282
Green Bay	3	9	0	.250	254	375
N.Y. Yanks	1	9	2	.100	241	382

PLAYOFFS

NFL championship
Los Angeles 24 vs. Cleveland 17

1952

AMERICAN CONFERENCE

Team	W	L	T	Pct.	PF	PA
Cleveland	8	4	0	.667	310	213
N.Y. Giants	7	5	0	.583	234	231
Philadelphia	7	5	0	.583	252	271
Pittsburgh	5	7	0	.417	300	273
Chi. Cardinals	4	8	0	.333	172	221
Washington	4	8	0	.333	240	287

NATIONAL CONFERENCE

Team	W	L	T	Pct.	PF	PA
Detroit	9	3	0	.750	344	192
Los Angeles	9	3	0	.750	349	234
San Francisco	7	5	0	.583	285	221
Green Bay	6	6	0	.500	295	312
Chicago Bears	5	7	0	.417	245	326
Dallas Texans	1	11	0	.083	182	427

PLAYOFFS

National Conference playoff
Detroit 31 vs. Los Angeles 21

NFL championship
Detroit 17 at Cleveland 7

1953

EASTERN CONFERENCE

Team	W	L	T	Pct.	PF	PA
Cleveland	11	1	0	.917	348	162
Philadelphia	7	4	1	.636	352	215
Washington	6	5	1	.545	208	215
Pittsburgh	6	6	0	.500	211	263
N.Y. Giants	3	9	0	.250	179	277
Chi. Cardinals	1	10	1	.091	190	337

WESTERN CONFERENCE

Team	W	L	T	Pct.	PF	PA
Detroit	10	2	0	.833	271	205
San Francisco	9	3	0	.750	372	237
Los Angeles	8	3	1	.727	366	236
Chicago Bears	3	8	1	.273	218	262
Baltimore	3	9	0	.250	182	350
Green Bay	2	9	1	.182	200	338

PLAYOFFS

NFL championship
Detroit 17 vs. Cleveland 16

1954

EASTERN CONFERENCE

Team	W	L	T	Pct.	PF	PA
Cleveland	9	3	0	.750	336	162
Philadelphia	7	4	1	.636	284	230
N.Y. Giants	7	5	0	.583	293	184
Pittsburgh	5	7	0	.417	219	263
Washington	3	9	0	.250	207	432
Chi. Cardinals	2	10	0	.167	183	347

WESTERN CONFERENCE

Team	W	L	T	Pct.	PF	PA
Detroit	9	2	1	.818	337	189
Chicago Bears	8	4	0	.667	301	279
San Francisco	7	4	1	.636	313	251
Los Angeles	6	5	1	.545	314	285
Green Bay	4	8	0	.333	234	251
Baltimore	3	9	0	.250	131	279

PLAYOFFS

NFL championship
Cleveland 56 vs. Detroit 10

1955

EASTERN CONFERENCE

Team	W	L	T	Pct.	PF	PA
Cleveland	9	2	1	.818	349	218
Washington	8	4	0	.667	246	222
N.Y. Giants	6	5	1	.545	267	223
Chi. Cardinals	4	7	1	.364	224	252
Philadelphia	4	7	1	.364	248	231
Pittsburgh	4	8	0	.333	195	285

WESTERN CONFERENCE

Team	W	L	T	Pct.	PF	PA
Los Angeles	8	3	1	.727	260	231
Chicago Bears	8	4	0	.667	294	251
Green Bay	6	6	0	.500	258	276
Baltimore	5	6	1	.455	214	239
San Francisco	4	8	0	.333	216	298
Detroit	3	9	0	.250	230	275

PLAYOFFS

NFL championship
Cleveland 38 at Los Angeles 14

1956

EASTERN CONFERENCE

Team	W	L	T	Pct.	PF	PA
N.Y. Giants	8	3	1	.727	264	197
Chi. Cardinals	7	5	0	.583	240	182
Washington	6	6	0	.500	183	225
Cleveland	5	7	0	.417	167	177
Pittsburgh	5	7	0	.417	217	250
Philadelphia	3	8	1	.273	143	215

WESTERN CONFERENCE

Team	W	L	T	Pct.	PF	PA
Chicago Bears	9	2	1	.818	363	246
Detroit	9	3	0	.750	300	188
San Francisco	5	6	1	.455	233	284
Baltimore	5	7	0	.417	270	322
Green Bay	4	8	0	.333	264	342
Los Angeles	4	8	0	.333	291	307

PLAYOFFS

NFL championship
N.Y. Giants 47 vs. Chicago Bears 7

1957

EASTERN CONFERENCE

Team	W	L	T	Pct.	PF	PA
Cleveland	9	2	1	.818	269	172
N.Y. Giants	7	5	0	.583	254	211
Pittsburgh	6	6	0	.500	161	178
Washington	5	6	1	.455	251	230
Philadelphia	4	8	0	.333	173	230
Chi. Cardinals	3	9	0	.250	200	299

WESTERN CONFERENCE

Team	W	L	T	Pct.	PF	PA
Detroit	8	4	0	.667	251	231
San Francisco	8	4	0	.667	260	264
Baltimore	7	5	0	.583	303	235
Los Angeles	6	6	0	.500	307	278
Chicago Bears	5	7	0	.417	203	211
Green Bay	3	9	0	.250	218	311

PLAYOFFS

Western Conference playoff
Detroit 31 at San Francisco 27

NFL championship
Detroit 59 vs. Cleveland 14

1958

EASTERN CONFERENCE

Team	W	L	T	Pct.	PF	PA
N.Y. Giants	9	3	0	.750	246	183
Cleveland	9	3	0	.750	302	217
Pittsburgh	7	4	1	.636	261	230
Washington	4	7	1	.364	214	268
Chi. Cardinals	2	9	1	.182	261	356
Philadelphia	2	9	1	.182	235	306

WESTERN CONFERENCE

Team	W	L	T	Pct.	PF	PA
Baltimore	9	3	0	.750	381	203
Chicago Bears	8	4	0	.667	298	230
Los Angeles	8	4	0	.667	344	278
San Francisco	6	6	0	.500	257	324
Detroit	4	7	1	.364	261	276
Green Bay	1	10	1	.091	193	382

PLAYOFFS

Eastern Conference playoff
N.Y. Giants 10 vs. Cleveland 0

NFL championship
Baltimore 23 at N.Y. Giants 17 (OT)

1959

EASTERN CONFERENCE

Team	W	L	T	Pct.	PF	PA
N.Y. Giants	10	2	0	.833	284	170
Cleveland	7	5	0	.583	270	214
Philadelphia	7	5	0	.583	268	278
Pittsburgh	6	5	1	.545	257	216
Washington	3	9	0	.250	185	350
Chi. Cardinals	2	10	0	.167	234	324

WESTERN CONFERENCE

Team	W	L	T	Pct.	PF	PA
Baltimore	9	3	0	.750	374	251
Chicago Bears	8	4	0	.667	252	196
Green Bay	7	5	0	.583	248	246
San Francisco	7	5	0	.583	255	237
Detroit	3	8	1	.273	203	275
Los Angeles	2	10	0	.167	242	315

PLAYOFFS

NFL championship
Baltimore 31 vs. N.Y. Giants 16

1960

AFL

EASTERN DIVISION

Team	W	L	T	Pct.	PF	PA
Houston	10	4	0	.714	379	285
N.Y. Titans	7	7	0	.500	382	399
Buffalo	5	8	1	.385	296	303
Boston Patriots	5	9	0	.357	286	349

WESTERN DIVISION

Team	W	L	T	Pct.	PF	PA
L.A. Chargers	10	4	0	.714	373	336
Dallas Texans	8	6	0	.571	362	253
Oakland	6	8	0	.429	319	388
Denver	4	9	1	.308	309	393

PLAYOFFS

AFL championship
Houston 24 vs. L.A. Chargers 16

NFL

EASTERN CONFERENCE

Team	W	L	T	Pct.	PF	PA
Philadelphia	10	2	0	.833	321	246
Cleveland	8	3	1	.727	362	217
N.Y. Giants	6	4	2	.600	271	261
St. Louis	6	5	1	.545	288	230
Pittsburgh	5	6	1	.455	240	275
Washington	1	9	2	.100	178	309

WESTERN CONFERENCE

Team	W	L	T	Pct.	PF	PA
Green Bay	8	4	0	.667	332	209
Detroit	7	5	0	.583	239	212
San Francisco	7	5	0	.583	208	205
Baltimore	6	6	0	.500	288	234
Chicago	5	6	1	.455	194	299
L.A. Rams	4	7	1	.364	265	297
Dallas Cowboys	0	11	1	.000	177	369

PLAYOFFS

NFL championship
Philadelphia 17 vs. Green Bay 13

1961

AFL

EASTERN DIVISION

Team	W	L	T	Pct.	PF	PA
Houston	10	3	1	.769	513	242
Boston Patriots	9	4	1	.692	413	313
N.Y. Titans	7	7	0	.500	301	390
Buffalo	6	8	0	.429	294	342

WESTERN DIVISION

Team	W	L	T	Pct.	PF	PA
San Diego	12	2	0	.857	396	219
Dallas Texans	6	8	0	.429	334	343
Denver	3	11	0	.214	251	432
Oakland	2	12	0	.143	237	458

PLAYOFFS

AFL championship
Houston 10 at San Diego 3

NFL

EASTERN CONFERENCE

Team	W	L	T	Pct.	PF	PA
N.Y. Giants	10	3	1	.769	368	220
Philadelphia	10	4	0	.714	361	297
Cleveland	8	5	1	.615	319	270
St. Louis	7	7	0	.500	279	267
Pittsburgh	6	8	0	.429	295	287
Dallas Cowboys	4	9	1	.308	236	380
Washington	1	12	1	.077	174	392

WESTERN CONFERENCE

Team	W	L	T	Pct.	PF	PA
Green Bay	11	3	0	.786	391	223
Detroit	8	5	1	.615	270	258
Baltimore	8	6	0	.571	302	307
Chicago	8	6	0	.571	326	302
San Francisco	7	6	1	.538	346	272
Los Angeles	4	10	0	.286	263	333
Minnesota	3	11	0	.214	285	407

PLAYOFFS

NFL championship
Green Bay 37 vs. N.Y. Giants 0

1962

AFL

EASTERN DIVISION

Team	W	L	T	Pct.	PF	PA
Houston	11	3	0	.786	387	270
Boston Patriots	9	4	1	.692	346	295
Buffalo	7	6	1	.538	309	272
N.Y. Titans	5	9	0	.357	278	423

WESTERN DIVISION

Team	W	L	T	Pct.	PF	PA
Dallas Texans	11	3	0	.786	389	233
Denver	7	7	0	.500	353	334
San Diego	4	10	0	.286	314	392
Oakland	1	13	0	.071	213	370

PLAYOFFS

AFL championship
Dallas Texans 20 at Houston 17 (OT)

NFL

EASTERN CONFERENCE

Team	W	L	T	Pct.	PF	PA
N.Y. Giants	12	2	0	.857	398	283
Pittsburgh	9	5	0	.643	312	363
Cleveland	7	6	1	.538	291	257
Washington	5	7	2	.417	305	376
Dallas Cowboys	5	8	1	.385	398	402
St. Louis	4	9	1	.308	287	361
Philadelphia	3	10	1	.231	282	356

WESTERN CONFERENCE

Team	W	L	T	Pct.	PF	PA
Green Bay	13	1	0	.929	415	148
Detroit	11	3	0	.786	315	177
Chicago	9	5	0	.643	321	287
Baltimore	7	7	0	.500	293	288
San Francisco	6	8	0	.429	282	331
Minnesota	2	11	1	.154	254	410
Los Angeles	1	12	1	.077	220	334

PLAYOFFS

NFL championship
Green Bay 16 at N.Y. Giants 7

1963

AFL

EASTERN DIVISION

Team	W	L	T	Pct.	PF	PA
Boston Patriots	7	6	1	.538	327	257
Buffalo	7	6	1	.538	304	291
Houston	6	8	0	.429	302	372
N.Y. Jets	5	8	1	.385	249	399

WESTERN DIVISION

Team	W	L	T	Pct.	PF	PA
San Diego	11	3	0	.786	399	256
Oakland	10	4	0	.714	363	288
Kansas City	5	7	2	.417	347	263
Denver	2	11	1	.154	301	473

PLAYOFFS

Eastern Division playoff
Boston 26 at Buffalo 8

AFL championship
San Diego 51 vs. Boston 10

NFL

EASTERN CONFERENCE

Team	W	L	T	Pct.	PF	PA
N.Y. Giants	11	3	0	.786	448	280
Cleveland	10	4	0	.714	343	262
St. Louis	9	5	0	.643	341	283
Pittsburgh	7	4	3	.636	321	295
Dallas	4	10	0	.286	305	378
Washington	3	11	0	.214	279	398
Philadelphia	2	10	2	.167	242	381

WESTERN CONFERENCE

Team	W	L	T	Pct.	PF	PA
Chicago	11	1	2	.917	301	144
Green Bay	11	2	1	.846	369	206
Baltimore	8	6	0	.571	316	285
Detroit	5	8	1	.385	326	265
Minnesota	5	8	1	.385	309	390
Los Angeles	5	9	0	.357	210	350
San Francisco	2	12	0	.143	198	391

PLAYOFFS

NFL championship
Chicago 14 vs. N.Y. Giants 10

1964

AFL

EASTERN DIVISION

Team	W	L	T	Pct.	PF	PA
Buffalo	12	2	0	.857	400	242
Boston Patriots	10	3	1	.769	365	297
N.Y. Jets	5	8	1	.385	278	315
Houston	4	10	0	.286	310	355

WESTERN DIVISION

Team	W	L	T	Pct.	PF	PA
San Diego	8	5	1	.615	341	300
Kansas City	7	7	0	.500	366	306
Oakland	5	7	2	.417	303	350
Denver	2	11	1	.154	240	438

PLAYOFFS

AFL championship
Buffalo 20 vs. San Diego 7

NFL

EASTERN CONFERENCE

Team	W	L	T	Pct.	PF	PA
Cleveland	10	3	1	.769	415	293
St. Louis	9	3	2	.750	357	331
Philadelphia	6	8	0	.429	312	313
Washington	6	8	0	.429	307	305
Dallas	5	8	1	.385	250	289
Pittsburgh	5	9	0	.357	253	315
N.Y. Giants	2	10	2	.167	241	399

WESTERN CONFERENCE

Team	W	L	T	Pct.	PF	PA
Baltimore	12	2	0	.857	428	225
Green Bay	8	5	1	.615	342	245
Minnesota	8	5	1	.615	355	296
Detroit	7	5	2	.583	280	260
Los Angeles	5	7	2	.417	283	339
Chicago	5	9	0	.357	260	379
San Francisco	4	10	0	.286	236	330

PLAYOFFS

NFL championship
Cleveland 27 vs. Baltimore 0

1965

AFL

EASTERN DIVISION

Team	W	L	T	Pct.	PF	PA
Buffalo	10	3	1	.769	313	226
N.Y. Jets	5	8	1	.385	285	303
Boston Patriots	4	8	2	.333	244	302
Houston	4	10	0	.286	298	429

WESTERN DIVISION

Team	W	L	T	Pct.	PF	PA
San Diego	9	2	3	.818	340	227
Oakland	8	5	1	.615	298	239
Kansas City	7	5	2	.583	322	285
Denver	4	10	0	.286	303	392

PLAYOFFS

AFL championship
Buffalo 23 at San Diego 0

NFL

EASTERN CONFERENCE

Team	W	L	T	Pct.	PF	PA
Cleveland	11	3	0	.786	363	325
Dallas	7	7	0	.500	325	280
N.Y. Giants	7	7	0	.500	270	338
Washington	6	8	0	.429	257	301
Philadelphia	5	9	0	.357	363	359
St. Louis	5	9	0	.357	296	309
Pittsburgh	2	12	0	.143	202	397

WESTERN CONFERENCE

Team	W	L	T	Pct.	PF	PA
Green Bay	10	3	1	.769	316	224
Baltimore	10	3	1	.769	389	284
Chicago	9	5	0	.643	409	275
San Francisco	7	6	1	.538	421	402
Minnesota	7	7	0	.500	383	403
Detroit	6	7	1	.462	257	295
Los Angeles	4	10	0	.286	269	328

PLAYOFFS

Western Conference playoff
Green Bay 13 vs. Baltimore 10 (OT)
NFL championship
Green Bay 23 vs. Cleveland 12

1966

AFL

EASTERN DIVISION

Team	W	L	T	Pct.	PF	PA
Buffalo	9	4	1	.692	358	255
Boston Patriots	8	4	2	.667	315	283
N.Y. Jets	6	6	2	.500	322	312
Houston	3	11	0	.214	335	396
Miami	3	11	0	.214	213	362

WESTERN DIVISION

Team	W	L	T	Pct.	PF	PA
Kansas City	11	2	1	.846	448	276
Oakland	8	5	1	.615	315	288
San Diego	7	6	1	.538	335	284
Denver	4	10	0	.286	196	381

PLAYOFFS

AFL championship
Kansas City 31 at Buffalo 7

NFL

EASTERN CONFERENCE

Team	W	L	T	Pct.	PF	PA
Dallas	10	3	1	.769	445	239
Cleveland	9	5	0	.643	403	259
Philadelphia	9	5	0	.643	326	340
St. Louis	8	5	1	.615	264	265
Washington	7	7	0	.500	351	355
Pittsburgh	5	8	1	.385	316	347
Atlanta	3	11	0	.214	204	437
N.Y. Giants	1	12	1	.077	263	501

WESTERN CONFERENCE

Team	W	L	T	Pct.	PF	PA
Green Bay	12	2	0	.857	335	163
Baltimore	9	5	0	.643	314	226
Los Angeles	8	6	0	.571	289	212
San Francisco	6	6	2	.500	320	325
Chicago	5	7	2	.417	234	272
Detroit	4	9	1	.308	206	317
Minnesota	4	9	1	.308	292	304

PLAYOFFS

NFL championship
Green Bay 34 at Dallas 27
Super Bowl I
Green Bay 35, Kansas City 10, at Los Angeles.

1967

AFL

EASTERN DIVISION

Team	W	L	T	Pct.	PF	PA
Houston	9	4	1	.692	258	199
N.Y. Jets	8	5	1	.615	371	329
Buffalo	4	10	0	.286	237	285
Miami	4	10	0	.286	219	407
Boston Patriots	3	10	1	.231	280	389

WESTERN DIVISION

Team	W	L	T	Pct.	PF	PA
Oakland	13	1	0	.929	468	233
Kansas City	9	5	0	.643	408	254
San Diego	8	5	1	.615	360	352
Denver	3	11	0	.214	256	409

PLAYOFFS

AFL championship
Oakland 40 vs. Houston 7

NFL

EASTERN CONFERENCE

CAPITOL DIVISION

Team	W	L	T	Pct.	PF	PA
Dallas	9	5	0	.643	342	268
Philadelphia	6	7	1	.462	351	409
Washington	5	6	3	.455	347	353
New Orleans	3	11	0	.214	233	379

CENTURY DIVISION

Team	W	L	T	Pct.	PF	PA
Cleveland	9	5	0	.643	334	297
N.Y. Giants	7	7	0	.500	369	379
St. Louis	6	7	1	.462	333	356
Pittsburgh	4	9	1	.308	281	320

WESTERN CONFERENCE

COASTAL DIVISION

Team	W	L	T	Pct.	PF	PA
Los Angeles	11	1	2	.917	398	196
Baltimore	11	1	2	.917	394	198
San Francisco	7	7	0	.500	273	337
Atlanta	1	12	1	.077	175	422

CENTRAL DIVISION

Team	W	L	T	Pct.	PF	PA
Green Bay	9	4	1	.692	332	209
Chicago	7	6	1	.538	239	218
Detroit	5	7	2	.417	260	259
Minnesota	3	8	3	.273	233	294

PLAYOFFS

Conference championships
Dallas 52 vs. Cleveland 14
Green Bay 28 vs. Los Angeles 7
NFL championship
Green Bay 21 vs. Dallas 17
Super Bowl II
Green Bay 33, Oakland 14, at Miami.

1968

AFL

EASTERN DIVISION

Team	W	L	T	Pct.	PF	PA
N.Y. Jets	11	3	0	.786	419	280
Houston	7	7	0	.500	303	248
Miami	5	8	1	.385	276	355
Boston Patriots	4	10	0	.286	229	406
Buffalo	1	12	1	.077	199	367

WESTERN DIVISION

Team	W	L	T	Pct.	PF	PA
Oakland	12	2	0	.857	453	233
Kansas City	12	2	0	.857	371	170
San Diego	9	5	0	.643	382	310
Denver	5	9	0	.357	255	404
Cincinnati	3	11	0	.214	215	329

PLAYOFFS

Western Division playoff
Oakland 41 vs. Kansas City 6
AFL championship
N.Y. Jets 27 vs. Oakland 23

NFL

EASTERN CONFERENCE

CAPITOL DIVISION

Team	W	L	T	Pct.	PF	PA
Dallas	12	2	0	.857	431	186
N.Y. Giants	7	7	0	.500	294	325
Washington	5	9	0	.357	249	358
Philadelphia	2	12	0	.143	202	351

CENTURY DIVISION

Team	W	L	T	Pct.	PF	PA
Cleveland	10	4	0	.714	394	273
St. Louis	9	4	1	.692	325	289
New Orleans	4	9	1	.308	246	327
Pittsburgh	2	11	1	.154	244	397

WESTERN CONFERENCE

COASTAL DIVISION

Team	W	L	T	Pct.	PF	PA
Baltimore	13	1	0	.929	402	144
Los Angeles	10	3	1	.769	312	200
San Francisco	7	6	1	.538	303	310
Atlanta	2	12	0	.143	170	389

CENTRAL DIVISION

Team	W	L	T	Pct.	PF	PA
Minnesota	8	6	0	.571	282	242
Chicago	7	7	0	.500	250	333
Green Bay	6	7	1	.462	281	227
Detroit	4	8	2	.333	207	241

PLAYOFFS

Conference championships
Cleveland 31 vs. Dallas 20
Baltimore 24 vs. Minnesota 14
NFL championship
Baltimore 34 at Cleveland 0
Super Bowl III
N.Y. Jets 16, Baltimore 7, at Miami.

1968

AFL

EASTERN DIVISION

Team	W	L	T	Pct.	PF	PA
N.Y. Jets	10	4	0	.714	353	269
Houston	6	6	2	.500	278	279
Boston Patriots	4	10	0	.286	266	316
Buffalo	4	10	0	.286	230	359
Miami	3	10	1	.231	233	332

WESTERN DIVISION

Team	W	L	T	Pct.	PF	PA
Oakland	12	1	1	.923	377	242
Kansas City	11	3	0	.786	359	177
San Diego	8	6	0	.571	288	276
Denver	5	8	1	.385	297	344
Cincinnati	4	9	1	.308	280	367

PLAYOFFS

Divisional games
Kansas City 13 at N.Y. Jets 6
Oakland 56 vs. Houston 7
AFL championship
Kansas City 17 at Oakland 7

NFL

EASTERN CONFERENCE

CAPITOL DIVISION

Team	W	L	T	Pct.	PF	PA
Dallas	11	2	1	.846	369	223
Washington	7	5	2	.583	307	319
New Orleans	5	9	0	.357	311	393
Philadelphia	4	9	1	.308	279	377

CENTURY DIVISION

Team	W	L	T	Pct.	PF	PA
Cleveland	10	3	1	.769	351	300
N.Y. Giants	6	8	0	.429	264	298
St. Louis	4	9	1	.308	314	389
Pittsburgh	1	13	0	.071	218	404

WESTERN CONFERENCE

COASTAL DIVISION

Team	W	L	T	Pct.	PF	PA
Los Angeles	11	3	0	.786	320	243
Baltimore	8	5	1	.615	279	268
Atlanta	6	8	0	.429	276	268
San Francisco	4	8	2	.333	277	319

CENTRAL DIVISION

Team	W	L	T	Pct.	PF	PA
Minnesota	12	2	0	.857	379	133
Detroit	9	4	1	.692	259	188
Green Bay	8	6	0	.571	269	221
Chicago	1	13	0	.071	210	339

PLAYOFFS

Conference championships
Cleveland 38 at Dallas 14
Minnesota 23 vs. Los Angeles 20
NFL championship
Minnesota 27 vs. Cleveland 7
Super Bowl IV
Kansas City 23, Minnesota 7, at New Orleans.

AMERICAN CONFERENCE
EASTERN DIVISION

Team	W	L	T	Pct.	PF	PA
Baltimore*	11	2	1	.846	321	234
Miami†	10	4	0	.714	297	228
N.Y. Jets	4	10	0	.286	255	286
Buffalo	3	10	1	.231	204	337
Boston Patriots	2	12	0	.143	149	361

CENTRAL DIVISION

Team	W	L	T	Pct.	PF	PA
Cincinnati*	8	6	0	.571	312	255
Cleveland	7	7	0	.500	286	265
Pittsburgh	5	9	0	.357	210	272
Houston	3	10	1	.231	217	352

WESTERN DIVISION

Team	W	L	T	Pct.	PF	PA
Oakland*	8	4	2	.667	300	293
Kansas City	7	5	2	.583	272	244
San Diego	5	6	3	.455	282	278
Denver	5	8	1	.385	253	264

*Division champion.
†Wild-card team.

NATIONAL CONFERENCE
EASTERN DIVISION

Team	W	L	T	Pct.	PF	PA
Dallas*	10	4	0	.714	299	221
N.Y. Giants	9	5	0	.643	301	270
St. Louis	8	5	1	.615	325	228
Washington	6	8	0	.429	297	314
Philadelphia	3	10	1	.231	241	332

CENTRAL DIVISION

Team	W	L	T	Pct.	PF	PA
Minnesota*	12	2	0	.857	335	143
Detroit†	10	4	0	.714	347	202
Chicago	6	8	0	.429	256	261
Green Bay	6	8	0	.429	196	293

WESTERN DIVISION

Team	W	L	T	Pct.	PF	PA
San Francisco*	10	3	1	.769	352	267
Los Angeles	9	4	1	.692	325	202
Atlanta	4	8	2	.333	206	261
New Orleans	2	11	1	.154	172	347

PLAYOFFS

AFC divisional games
Baltimore 17 vs. Cincinnati 0
Oakland 21 vs. Miami 14

AFC championship
Baltimore 27 vs. Oakland 17

NFC divisional games
Dallas 5 vs. Detroit 0
San Francisco 17 at Minnesota 14

NFC championship
Dallas 17 at San Francisco 10

Super Bowl V
Baltimore 16, Dallas 13, at Miami.

AMERICAN CONFERENCE
EASTERN DIVISION

Team	W	L	T	Pct.	PF	PA
Miami*	10	3	1	.769	315	174
Baltimore†	10	4	0	.714	313	140
New England	6	8	0	.429	238	325
N.Y. Jets	6	8	0	.429	212	299
Buffalo	1	13	0	.071	184	394

CENTRAL DIVISION

Team	W	L	T	Pct.	PF	PA
Cleveland*	9	5	0	.643	285	273
Pittsburgh	6	8	0	.429	246	292
Houston	4	9	1	.308	251	330
Cincinnati	4	10	0	.286	284	265

WESTERN DIVISION

Team	W	L	T	Pct.	PF	PA
Kansas City*	10	3	1	.769	302	208
Oakland	8	4	2	.667	344	278
San Diego	6	8	0	.429	311	341
Denver	4	9	1	.308	203	275

*Division champion.
†Wild-card team.

NATIONAL CONFERENCE
EASTERN DIVISION

Team	W	L	T	Pct.	PF	PA
Dallas*	11	3	0	.786	406	222
Washington†	9	4	1	.692	276	190
Philadelphia	6	7	1	.462	221	302
St. Louis	4	9	1	.308	231	279
N.Y. Giants	4	10	0	.286	228	362

CENTRAL DIVISION

Team	W	L	T	Pct.	PF	PA
Minnesota*	11	3	0	.786	245	139
Detroit	7	6	1	.538	341	286
Chicago	6	8	0	.429	185	276
Green Bay	4	8	2	.333	274	298

WESTERN DIVISION

Team	W	L	T	Pct.	PF	PA
San Francisco*	9	5	0	.643	300	216
Los Angeles	8	5	1	.615	313	260
Atlanta	7	6	1	.538	274	277
New Orleans	4	8	2	.333	266	347

PLAYOFFS

AFC divisional games
Miami 27 at Kansas City 24 (OT)
Baltimore 20 at Cleveland 3

AFC championship
Miami 21 vs. Baltimore 0

NFC divisional games
Dallas 20 at Minnesota 12
San Francisco 24 vs. Washington 20

NFC championship
Dallas 14 vs. San Francisco 3

Super Bowl VI
Dallas 24, Miami 3, at New Orleans.

BROADWAY JOE

Jets quarterback Joe Namath "guaranteed" a victory over the Baltimore Colts in Super Bowl III and delivered, leading New York to a 16-7 victory. Although Namath's statistics for the game were modest—17 completions in 28 attempts for 206 yards and no touchdowns—the victory wasn't. It was a landmark win for an American Football League team over the more established NFL, which had won the first two Super Bowl games with ease.

1972

AMERICAN CONFERENCE

EASTERN DIVISION

Team	W	L	T	Pct.	PF	PA
Miami*	14	0	0	1.000[ce7]	385	171
N.Y. Jets	7	7	0	.500	367	324
Baltimore	5	9	0	.357	235	252
Buffalo	4	9	1	.321	257	377
New England	3	11	0	.214	192	446

CENTRAL DIVISION

Team	W	L	T	Pct.	PF	PA
Pittsburgh*	11	3	0	.786	343	175
Cleveland†	10	4	0	.714	268	249
Cincinnati	8	6	0	.571	299	229
Houston	1	13	0	.071	164	380

WESTERN DIVISION

Team	W	L	T	Pct.	PF	PA
Oakland*	10	3	1	.750	365	248
Kansas City	8	6	0	.571	287	254
Denver	5	9	0	.357	325	350
San Diego	4	9	1	.321	264	344

*Division champion.
†Wild-card team.

NATIONAL CONFERENCE

EASTERN DIVISION

Team	W	L	T	Pct.	PF	PA
Washington*	11	3	0	.786	336	218
Dallas†	10	4	0	.714	319	240
N.Y. Giants	8	6	0	.571	331	247
St. Louis	4	9	1	.321	193	303
Philadelphia	2	11	1	.179	145	352

CENTRAL DIVISION

Team	W	L	T	Pct.	PF	PA
Green Bay*	10	4	0	.714	304	226
Detroit	8	5	1	.607	339	290
Minnesota	7	7	0	.500	301	252
Chicago	4	9	1	.321	225	275

WESTERN DIVISION

Team	W	L	T	Pct.	PF	PA
San Francisco*	8	5	1	.607	353	249
Atlanta	7	7	0	.500	269	274
Los Angeles	6	7	1	.464	291	286
New Orleans	2	11	1	.179	215	361

PLAYOFFS

AFC divisional games
Pittsburgh 13 vs. Oakland 7
Miami 20 vs. Cleveland 14

AFC championship
Miami 21 at Pittsburgh 17

NFC divisional games
Dallas 30 at San Francisco 28
Washington 16 vs. Green Bay 3

NFC championship
Washington 26 vs. Dallas 3

Super Bowl VII
Miami 14, Washington 7, at Los Angeles.

1973

AMERICAN CONFERENCE

EASTERN DIVISION

Team	W	L	T	Pct.	PF	PA
Miami*	12	2	0	.857	343	150
Buffalo	9	5	0	.643	259	230
New England	5	9	0	.357	258	300
Baltimore	4	10	0	.286	226	341
N.Y. Jets	4	10	0	.286	240	306

CENTRAL DIVISION

Team	W	L	T	Pct.	PF	PA
Cincinnati*	10	4	0	.714	286	231
Pittsburgh†	10	4	0	.714	347	210
Cleveland	7	5	2	.571	234	255
Houston	1	13	0	.071	199	447

WESTERN DIVISION

Team	W	L	T	Pct.	PF	PA
Oakland*	9	4	1	.679	292	175
Denver	7	5	2	.571	354	296
Kansas City	7	5	2	.571	231	192
San Diego	2	11	1	.179	188	386

*Division champion.
†Wild-card team.

NATIONAL CONFERENCE

EASTERN DIVISION

Team	W	L	T	Pct.	PF	PA
Dallas*	10	4	0	.714	382	203
Washington†	10	4	0	.714	325	198
Philadelphia	5	8	1	.393	310	393
St. Louis	4	9	1	.321	286	365
N.Y. Giants	2	11	1	.179	226	362

CENTRAL DIVISION

Team	W	L	T	Pct.	PF	PA
Minnesota*	12	2	0	.857	296	168
Detroit	6	7	1	.464	271	247
Green Bay	5	7	2	.429	202	259
Chicago	3	11	0	.214	195	334

WESTERN DIVISION

Team	W	L	T	Pct.	PF	PA
Los Angeles*	12	2	0	.857	388	178
Atlanta	9	5	0	.643	318	224
New Orleans	5	9	0	.357	163	312
San Francisco	5	9	0	.357	262	319

PLAYOFFS

AFC divisional games
Oakland 33 vs. Pittsburgh 14
Miami 34 vs. Cincinnati 16

AFC championship
Miami 27 vs. Oakland 10

NFC divisional games
Minnesota 27 vs. Washington 20
Dallas 27 vs. Los Angeles 16

NFC championship
Minnesota 27 at Dallas 10

Super Bowl VIII
Miami 24, Minnesota 7, at Houston.

1974

AMERICAN CONFERENCE

EASTERN DIVISION

Team	W	L	T	Pct.	PF	PA
Miami*	11	3	0	.786	327	216
Buffalo†	9	5	0	.643	264	244
New England	7	7	0	.500	348	289
N.Y. Jets	7	7	0	.500	279	300
Baltimore	2	12	0	.143	190	329

CENTRAL DIVISION

Team	W	L	T	Pct.	PF	PA
Pittsburgh*	10	3	1	.750	305	189
Cincinnati	7	7	0	.500	283	259
Houston	7	7	0	.500	236	282
Cleveland	4	10	0	.286	251	344

WESTERN DIVISION

Team	W	L	T	Pct.	PF	PA
Oakland*	12	2	0	.857	355	228
Denver	7	6	1	.536	302	294
Kansas City	5	9	0	.357	233	293
San Diego	5	9	0	.357	212	285

*Division champion.
†Wild-card team.

NATIONAL CONFERENCE

EASTERN DIVISION

Team	W	L	T	Pct.	PF	PA
St. Louis*	10	4	0	.714	285	218
Washington†	10	4	0	.714	320	196
Dallas	8	6	0	.571	297	235
Philadelphia	7	7	0	.500	242	217
N.Y. Giants	2	12	0	.143	195	299

CENTRAL DIVISION

Team	W	L	T	Pct.	PF	PA
Minnesota*	10	4	0	.714	310	195
Detroit	7	7	0	.500	256	270
Green Bay	6	8	0	.429	210	206
Chicago	4	10	0	.286	152	279

WESTERN DIVISION

Team	W	L	T	Pct.	PF	PA
Los Angeles*	10	4	0	.714	263	181
San Francisco	6	8	0	.429	226	236
New Orleans	5	9	0	.357	166	263
Atlanta	3	11	0	.214	111	271

PLAYOFFS

AFC divisional games
Oakland 28 vs. Miami 26
Pittsburgh 32 vs. Buffalo 14

AFC championship
Pittsburgh 24 at Oakland 13

NFC divisional games
Minnesota 30 vs. St. Louis 14
Los Angeles 19 vs. Washington 10

NFC championship
Minnesota 14 vs. Los Angeles 10

Super Bowl IX
Pittsburgh 16, Minnesota 6, at New Orleans.

1975

AMERICAN CONFERENCE

EASTERN DIVISION

am	W	L	T	Pct.	PF	PA
ltimore*	10	4	0	.714	395	269
ami	10	4	0	.714	357	222
ffalo	8	6	0	.571	420	355
w England	3	11	0	.214	258	358
Y. Jets	3	11	0	.214	258	433

CENTRAL DIVISION

am	W	L	T	Pct.	PF	PA
tsburgh*	12	2	0	.857	373	162
ncinnati†	11	3	0	.786	340	246
uston	10	4	0	.714	293	226
eveland	3	11	0	.214	218	372

WESTERN DIVISION

am	W	L	T	Pct.	PF	PA
kland*	11	3	0	.786	375	255
nver	6	8	0	.429	254	307
nsas City	5	9	0	.357	282	341
n Diego	2	12	0	.143	189	345

*Division champion.
†Wild-card team.

NATIONAL CONFERENCE

EASTERN DIVISION

Team	W	L	T	Pct.	PF	PA
St. Louis*	11	3	0	.786	356	276
Dallas†	10	4	0	.714	350	268
Washington	8	6	0	.571	325	276
N.Y. Giants	5	9	0	.357	216	306
Philadelphia	4	10	0	.286	225	302

CENTRAL DIVISION

Team	W	L	T	Pct.	PF	PA
Minnesota*	12	2	0	.857	377	180
Detroit	7	7	0	.500	245	262
Chicago	4	10	0	.286	191	379
Green Bay	4	10	0	.286	226	285

WESTERN DIVISION

Team	W	L	T	Pct.	PF	PA
Los Angeles*	12	2	0	.857	312	135
San Francisco	5	9	0	.357	255	286
Atlanta	4	10	0	.286	240	289
New Orleans	2	12	0	.143	165	360

PLAYOFFS

AFC divisional games
Pittsburgh 28 vs. Baltimore 10
Oakland 31 vs. Cincinnati 28

AFC championship
Pittsburgh 16 vs. Oakland 10

NFC divisional games
Los Angeles 35 vs. St. Louis 23
Dallas 17 at Minnesota 14

NFC championship
Dallas 37 at Los Angeles 7

Super Bowl X
Pittsburgh 21, Dallas 17, at Miami.

1976

AMERICAN CONFERENCE

EASTERN DIVISION

am	W	L	T	Pct.	PF	PA
ltimore*	11	3	0	.786	417	246
w England†	11	3	0	.786	376	236
ami	6	8	0	.429	263	264
Y. Jets	3	11	0	.214	169	383
ffalo	2	12	0	.143	245	363

CENTRAL DIVISION

am	W	L	T	Pct.	PF	PA
ttsburgh*	10	4	0	.714	342	138
ncinnati	10	4	0	.714	335	210
eveland	9	5	0	.643	267	287
ouston	5	9	0	.357	222	273

WESTERN DIVISION

am	W	L	T	Pct.	PF	PA
kland*	13	1	0	.929	350	237
nver	9	5	0	.643	315	206
n Diego	6	8	0	.429	248	285
nsas City	5	9	0	.357	290	376
mpa Bay	0	14	0	.000	125	412

*Division champion.
†Wild-card team.

NATIONAL CONFERENCE

EASTERN DIVISION

Team	W	L	T	Pct.	PF	PA
Dallas*	11	3	0	.786	296	194
Washington†	10	4	0	.714	350	217
St. Louis	10	4	0	.714	309	267
Philadelphia	4	10	0	.286	165	286
N.Y. Giants	3	11	0	.214	170	250

CENTRAL DIVISION

Team	W	L	T	Pct.	PF	PA
Minnesota*	11	2	1	.821	305	176
Chicago	7	7	0	.500	253	216
Detroit	6	8	0	.429	262	220
Green Bay	5	9	0	.357	218	299

WESTERN DIVISION

Team	W	L	T	Pct.	PF	PA
Los Angeles*	10	3	1	.750	351	190
San Francisco	8	6	0	.571	270	190
Atlanta	4	10	0	.286	172	312
New Orleans	4	10	0	.286	253	346
Seattle	2	12	0	.143	229	429

PLAYOFFS

AFC divisional games
Oakland 24 vs. New England 21
Pittsburgh 40 at Baltimore 14

AFC championship
Oakland 24 vs. Pittsburgh 7

NFC divisional games
Minnesota 35 vs. Washington 20
Los Angeles 14 at Dallas 12

NFC championship
Minnesota 24 vs. Los Angeles 13

Super Bowl XI
Oakland 32, Minnesota 14, at Pasadena, Calif.

A LONG WAIT ENDS

The Pittsburgh Steelers won their first NFL title with a 16-6 victory over Minnesota in Super Bowl IX. Franco Harris carried 34 times for a Super Bowl-record 158 yards to help Steelers founder Art Rooney visualize his dream of an NFL championship after 42 years of ownership. Before winning the AFC Central Division title in 1972 (their first championship of any kind, their second came in 1974), Rooney's Steelers had finished last 11 times, fourth 10 times and second six times since entering the NFL in 1933.

1977

AMERICAN CONFERENCE

EASTERN DIVISION

Team	W	L	T	Pct.	PF	PA
Baltimore*	10	4	0	.714	295	221
Miami	10	4	0	.714	313	197
New England	9	5	0	.643	278	217
N.Y. Jets	3	11	0	.214	191	300
Buffalo	3	11	0	.214	160	313

CENTRAL DIVISION

Team	W	L	T	Pct.	PF	PA
Pittsburgh*	9	5	0	.643	283	243
Houston	8	6	0	.571	299	230
Cincinnati	8	6	0	.571	238	235
Cleveland	6	8	0	.429	269	267

WESTERN DIVISION

Team	W	L	T	Pct.	PF	PA
Denver*	12	2	0	.857	274	148
Oakland†	11	3	0	.786	351	230
San Diego	7	7	0	.500	222	205
Seattle	5	9	0	.357	282	373
Kansas City	2	12	0	.143	225	349

*Division champion.
†Wild-card team.

NATIONAL CONFERENCE

EASTERN DIVISION

Team	W	L	T	Pct.	PF	PA
Dallas*	12	2	0	.857	345	212
Washington	9	5	0	.643	196	189
St. Louis	7	7	0	.500	272	287
Philadelphia	5	9	0	.357	220	207
N.Y. Giants	5	9	0	.357	181	265

CENTRAL DIVISION

Team	W	L	T	Pct.	PF	PA
Minnesota*	9	5	0	.643	231	227
Chicago†	9	5	0	.643	255	253
Detroit	6	8	0	.429	183	252
Green Bay	4	10	0	.286	134	219
Tampa Bay	2	12	0	.143	103	223

WESTERN DIVISION

Team	W	L	T	Pct.	PF	PA
Los Angeles*	10	4	0	.714	302	146
Atlanta	7	7	0	.500	179	129
San Francisco	5	9	0	.357	220	260
New Orleans	3	11	0	.214	232	336

PLAYOFFS

AFC divisional games
Denver 34 vs. Pittsburgh 21
Oakland 37 at Baltimore 31 (OT)

AFC championship
Denver 20 vs. Oakland 17

NFC divisional games
Dallas 37 vs. Chicago 7
Minnesota 14 at Los Angeles 7

NFC championship
Dallas 23 vs. Minnesota 6

Super Bowl XII
Dallas 27, Denver 10, at New Orleans.

1978

AMERICAN CONFERENCE

EASTERN DIVISION

Team	W	L	T	Pct.	PF	PA
New England*	11	5	0	.688	358	286
Miami†	11	5	0	.688	372	254
N.Y. Jets	8	8	0	.500	359	364
Buffalo	5	11	0	.313	302	354
Baltimore	5	11	0	.313	239	421

CENTRAL DIVISION

Team	W	L	T	Pct.	PF	PA
Pittsburgh*	14	2	0	.875	356	195
Houston†	10	6	0	.625	283	298
Cleveland	8	8	0	.500	334	356
Cincinnati	4	12	0	.250	252	284

WESTERN DIVISION

Team	W	L	T	Pct.	PF	PA
Denver*	10	6	0	.625	282	198
Oakland	9	7	0	.563	311	283
Seattle	9	7	0	.563	345	358
San Diego	9	7	0	.563	355	309
Kansas City	4	12	0	.250	243	327

*Division champion.
†Wild-card team.

NATIONAL CONFERENCE

EASTERN DIVISION

Team	W	L	T	Pct.	PF	PA
Dallas*	12	4	0	.750	384	208
Philadelphia†	9	7	0	.563	270	250
Washington	8	8	0	.500	273	283
St. Louis	6	10	0	.375	248	296
N.Y. Giants	6	10	0	.375	264	298

CENTRAL DIVISION

Team	W	L	T	Pct.	PF	PA
Minnesota*	8	7	1	.531	294	306
Green Bay	8	7	1	.531	249	269
Detroit	7	9	0	.438	290	300
Chicago	7	9	0	.438	253	274
Tampa Bay	5	11	0	.313	241	259

WESTERN DIVISION

Team	W	L	T	Pct.	PF	PA
Los Angeles*	12	4	0	.750	316	245
Atlanta†	9	7	0	.563	240	290
New Orleans	7	9	0	.438	281	298
San Francisco	2	14	0	.125	219	350

PLAYOFFS

AFC wild-card game
Houston 17 at Miami 9

AFC divisional games
Houston 31 at New England 14
Pittsburgh 33 vs. Denver 10

AFC championship
Pittsburgh 34 vs. Houston 5

NFC wild-card game
Atlanta 14 vs. Philadelphia 13

NFC divisional games
Dallas 27 vs. Atlanta 20
Los Angeles 34 vs. Minnesota 10

NFC championship
Dallas 28 at Los Angeles 0

Super Bowl XIII
Pittsburgh 35, Dallas 31, at Miami.

A SUPER SLUMP

The Minnesota Vikings' knack for losing Super Bowls continued in January 1977 as the Vikings lost in the NFL's big game for the fourth time in eight years, including three of the past four seasons. Minnesota's latest setback was a 32-14 loss to the Oakland Raiders, who jumped out to a 16-0 halftime lead and never looked back. The Raiders rolled up 429 total yards in offense and held Chuck Foreman, the Vikings' star running back, to 44 yards on 17 attempts.

1979

AMERICAN CONFERENCE

EASTERN DIVISION

am	W	L	T	Pct.	PF	PA
ami*	10	6	0	.625	341	257
w England	9	7	0	.563	411	326
V. Jets	8	8	0	.500	337	383
ffalo	7	9	0	.438	268	279
ltimore	5	11	0	.313	271	351

CENTRAL DIVISION

am	W	L	T	Pct.	PF	PA
tsburgh*	12	4	0	.750	416	262
uston†	11	5	0	.688	362	331
eveland	9	7	0	.563	359	352
cinnati	4	12	0	.250	337	421

WESTERN DIVISION

am	W	L	T	Pct.	PF	PA
n Diego*	12	4	0	.750	411	246
nver†	10	6	0	.625	289	262
attle	9	7	0	.563	378	372
kland	9	7	0	.563	365	337
nsas City	7	9	0	.438	238	262

*Division champion.
†Wild-card team.

NATIONAL CONFERENCE

EASTERN DIVISION

Team	W	L	T	Pct.	PF	PA
Dallas*	11	5	0	.688	371	313
Philadelphia†	11	5	0	.688	339	282
Washington	10	6	0	.625	348	295
N.Y. Giants	6	10	0	.375	237	323
St. Louis	5	11	0	.313	307	358

CENTRAL DIVISION

Team	W	L	T	Pct.	PF	PA
Tampa Bay*	10	6	0	.625	273	237
Chicago†	10	6	0	.625	306	249
Minnesota	7	9	0	.438	259	337
Green Bay	5	11	0	.313	246	316
Detroit	2	14	0	.125	219	365

WESTERN DIVISION

Team	W	L	T	Pct.	PF	PA
Los Angeles*	9	7	0	.563	323	309
New Orleans	8	8	0	.500	370	360
Atlanta	6	10	0	.375	300	388
San Francisco	2	14	0	.125	308	416

PLAYOFFS

AFC wild-card game
Houston 13 vs. Denver 7

AFC divisional games
Houston 17 at San Diego 14
Pittsburgh 34 vs. Miami 14

AFC championship
Pittsburgh 27 vs. Houston 13

NFC wild-card game
Philadelphia 27 vs. Chicago 17

NFC divisional games
Tampa Bay 24 vs. Philadelphia 17
Los Angeles 21 at Dallas 19

NFC championship
Los Angeles 9 at Tampa Bay 0

Super Bowl XIV
Pittsburgh 31, Los Angeles 19, at Pasadena, Calif.

1980

AMERICAN CONFERENCE

EASTERN DIVISION

am	W	L	T	Pct.	PF	PA
ffalo*	11	5	0	.688	320	260
w England	10	6	0	.625	441	325
ami	8	8	0	.500	266	305
timore	7	9	0	.438	355	387
V. Jets	4	12	0	.250	302	395

CENTRAL DIVISION

am	W	L	T	Pct.	PF	PA
veland*	11	5	0	.688	357	310
uston†	11	5	0	.688	295	251
tsburgh	9	7	0	.563	352	313
cinnati	6	10	0	.375	244	312

WESTERN DIVISION

am	W	L	T	Pct.	PF	PA
n Diego*	11	5	0	.688	418	327
kland†	11	5	0	.688	364	306
nsas City	8	8	0	.500	319	336
nver	8	8	0	.500	310	323
attle	4	12	0	.250	291	408

*Division champion.
†Wild-card team.

NATIONAL CONFERENCE

EASTERN DIVISION

Team	W	L	T	Pct.	PF	PA
Philadelphia*	12	4	0	.750	384	222
Dallas†	12	4	0	.750	454	311
Washington	6	10	0	.375	261	293
St. Louis	5	11	0	.313	299	350
N.Y. Giants	4	12	0	.250	249	425

CENTRAL DIVISION

Team	W	L	T	Pct.	PF	PA
Minnesota*	9	7	0	.563	317	308
Detroit	9	7	0	.563	334	272
Chicago	7	9	0	.438	304	264
Tampa Bay	5	10	1	.344	271	341
Green Bay	5	10	1	.344	231	371

WESTERN DIVISION

Team	W	L	T	Pct.	PF	PA
Atlanta*	12	4	0	.750	405	272
Los Angeles†	11	5	0	.688	424	289
San Francisco	6	10	0	.375	320	415
New Orleans	1	15	0	.063	291	487

PLAYOFFS

AFC wild-card game
Oakland 27 vs. Houston 7

AFC divisional games
San Diego 20 vs. Buffalo 14
Oakland 14 at Cleveland 12

AFC championship
Oakland 34 at San Diego 27

NFC wild-card game
Dallas 34 vs. Los Angeles 13

NFC divisional games
Philadelphia 31 vs. Minnesota 16
Dallas 30 at Atlanta 27

NFC championship
Philadelphia 20 vs. Dallas 7

Super Bowl XV
Oakland 27, Philadelphia 10, at New Orleans.

THE BEST EVER?

Such things are subjective, but the 1978 Pittsburgh Steelers could make a legitimate claim for being the best team in NFL history. With Terry Bradshaw at quarterback, Franco Harris at running back and Lynn Swann and John Stallworth at wide receiver, the '78 Steelers steamrolled the rest of the league. Of their 17 victories (including playoffs), 11 were by 10 points or more. The club's two defeats totaled 10 points. Pittsburgh's "Steel Curtain" defense of Joe Greene, Jack Ham, Jack Lambert and Mel Blount (all Hall of Famers) yielded a league-low 195 points during the regular season. When the Steelers edged Dallas, 35-31, in Super Bowl XIII, it marked their third league championship in five years.

1981

AMERICAN CONFERENCE

EASTERN DIVISION

Team	W	L	T	Pct.	PF	PA
Miami*	11	4	1	.719	345	275
N.Y. Jets†	10	5	1	.656	355	287
Buffalo†	10	6	0	.625	311	276
Baltimore	2	14	0	.125	259	533
New England	2	14	0	.125	322	370

CENTRAL DIVISION

Team	W	L	T	Pct.	PF	PA
Cincinnati*	12	4	0	.750	421	304
Pittsburgh	8	8	0	.500	356	297
Houston	7	9	0	.438	281	355
Cleveland	5	11	0	.313	276	375

WESTERN DIVISION

Team	W	L	T	Pct.	PF	PA
San Diego*	10	6	0	.625	478	390
Denver	10	6	0	.625	321	289
Kansas City	9	7	0	.563	343	290
Oakland	7	9	0	.438	273	343
Seattle	6	10	0	.375	322	388

*Division champion.
†Wild-card team.

NATIONAL CONFERENCE

EASTERN DIVISION

Team	W	L	T	Pct.	PF	PA
Dallas*	12	4	0	.750	367	277
Philadelphia†	10	6	0	.625	368	221
N.Y. Giants†	9	7	0	.563	295	257
Washington	8	8	0	.500	347	349
St. Louis	7	9	0	.438	315	408

CENTRAL DIVISION

Team	W	L	T	Pct.	PF	PA
Tampa Bay*	9	7	0	.563	315	268
Detroit	8	8	0	.500	397	322
Green Bay	8	8	0	.500	324	361
Minnesota	7	9	0	.438	325	369
Chicago	6	10	0	.375	253	324

WESTERN DIVISION

Team	W	L	T	Pct.	PF	PA
San Francisco*	13	3	0	.813	357	250
Atlanta	7	9	0	.438	426	355
Los Angeles	6	10	0	.375	303	351
New Orleans	4	12	0	.250	207	378

PLAYOFFS

AFC wild-card game
Buffalo 31 at New York Jets 27

AFC divisional games
San Diego 41 at Miami 38 (OT)
Cincinnati 28 vs. Buffalo 21

AFC championship
Cincinnati 27 vs. San Diego 7

NFC wild-card game
N.Y. Giants 27 at Philadelphia 21

NFC divisional games
Dallas 38 vs. Tampa Bay 0
San Francisco 38 vs. N.Y. Giants 24

NFC championship
San Francisco 28 vs. Dallas 27

Super Bowl XVI
San Francisco 26, Cincinnati 21, at Pontiac, Mich.

1982

AMERICAN CONFERENCE

Team	W	L	T	Pct.	PF	PA
L.A. Raiders	8	1	0	.889	260	200
Miami	7	2	0	.778	198	131
Cincinnati	7	2	0	.778	232	177
Pittsburgh	6	3	0	.667	204	146
San Diego	6	3	0	.667	288	221
N.Y. Jets	6	3	0	.667	245	166
New England	5	4	0	.556	143	157
Cleveland	4	5	0	.444	140	182
Buffalo	4	5	0	.444	150	154
Seattle	4	5	0	.444	127	147
Kansas City	3	6	0	.333	176	184
Denver	2	7	0	.222	148	226
Houston	1	8	0	.111	136	245
Baltimore	0	8	1	.056	113	236

NATIONAL CONFERENCE

Team	W	L	T	Pct.	PF	PA
Washington	8	1	0	.889	190	128
Dallas	6	3	0	.667	226	145
Green Bay	5	3	1	.611	226	169
Minnesota	5	4	0	.556	187	198
Atlanta	5	4	0	.556	183	199
St. Louis	5	4	0	.556	135	170
Tampa Bay	5	4	0	.556	158	178
Detroit	4	5	0	.444	181	176
New Orleans	4	5	0	.444	129	160
N.Y. Giants	4	5	0	.444	164	160
San Francisco	3	6	0	.333	209	206
Chicago	3	6	0	.333	141	174
Philadelphia	3	6	0	.333	191	195
L.A. Rams	2	7	0	.222	200	250

As a result of a 57-day players' strike, the 1982 NFL regular season schedule was reduced from 16 weeks to 9. At the conclusion of the regular season, a 16-team Super Bowl Tournament was held. Eight teams from each conference were seeded 1 through 8 based on their records during regular season play.

Miami finished ahead of Cincinnati based on a better conference record. Pittsburgh won common games tiebreaker with San Diego after New York Jets were eliminated from three-way tie based on conference record. Cleveland finished ahead of Buffalo and Seattle based on better conference record. Minnesota, Atlanta, St. Louis and Tampa Bay seeds were determined by best won-lost record in conference games. Detroit finished ahead of New Orleans and the New York Giants based on a better conference record.

PLAYOFFS

AFC first round
Miami 28 vs. New England 13
L.A. Raiders 27 vs. Cleveland 10
New York Jets 44 at Cincinnati 17
San Diego 31 at Pittsburgh 28

AFC second round
N.Y. Jets 17 at L.A. Raiders 14
Miami 34 vs. San Diego 13

AFC championship
Miami 14 vs. New York Jets 0

NFC first round
Washington 31 vs. Detroit 7
Green Bay 41 vs. St. Louis 16
Minnesota 30 vs. Atlanta 24
Dallas 30 vs. Tampa Bay 17

NFC second round
Washington 21 vs. Minnesota 7
Dallas 37 vs. Green Bay 26

NFC championship
Washington 31 vs. Dallas 17

Super Bowl XVII
Washington 27, Miami 17, at Pasadena, Calif.

PRO FOOTBALL STRIKES OUT

The NFL was hit by its first in-season work stoppage in history on September 20, 1982, when the players union, unhappy that an impasse had been reached on a new collective bargaining agreement with management, called a strike. When play resumed November 21, the two-month layoff seemed to have had a varying effect. Tampa Bay, for example, may have been helped. After an 0-2 start, the Buccaneers righted themselves to win five of their last six games and qualify for the playoffs. Defending league-champion San Francisco, however, was hurt. The 49ers began the year 0-2 and didn't regain their footing when the season resumed. The Dallas Cowboys, losers of the previous two NFC title games, weren't affected much at all. They went on to lose their third consecutive conference championship game.

1983

AMERICAN CONFERENCE

EASTERN DIVISION

am	W	L	T	Pct.	PF	PA
ami*	12	4	0	.750	389	250
w England	8	8	0	.500	274	289
ffalo	8	8	0	.500	283	351
timore	7	9	0	.438	264	354
Y. Jets	7	9	0	.438	313	331

CENTRAL DIVISION

am	W	L	T	Pct.	PF	PA
tsburgh*	10	6	0	.625	355	303
eveland	9	7	0	.563	356	342
ncinnati	7	9	0	.438	346	302
uston	2	14	0	.125	288	460

WESTERN DIVISION

am	W	L	T	Pct.	PF	PA
. Raiders*	12	4	0	.750	442	338
attle†	9	7	0	.563	403	397
nver†	9	7	0	.563	302	327
n Diego	6	10	0	.375	358	462
nsas City	6	10	0	.375	386	367

*Division champion.
†Wild-card team.

NATIONAL CONFERENCE

EASTERN DIVISION

Team	W	L	T	Pct.	PF	PA
Washington*	14	2	0	.875	541	332
Dallas†	12	4	0	.750	479	360
St. Louis	8	7	1	.531	374	428
Philadelphia	5	11	0	.313	233	322
N.Y. Giants	3	12	1	.219	267	347

CENTRAL DIVISION

Team	W	L	T	Pct.	PF	PA
Detroit*	9	7	0	.563	347	286
Green Bay	8	8	0	.500	429	439
Chicago	8	8	0	.500	311	301
Minnesota	8	8	0	.500	316	348
Tampa Bay	2	14	0	.125	241	380

WESTERN DIVISION

Team	W	L	T	Pct.	PF	PA
San Francisco*	10	6	0	.625	432	293
L.A. Rams†	9	7	0	.563	361	344
New Orleans	8	8	0	.500	319	337
Atlanta	7	9	0	.438	370	389

PLAYOFFS

AFC wild-card game
Seattle 31 vs. Denver 7

AFC divisional games
Seattle 27 at Miami 20
L.A. Raiders 38 vs. Pittsburgh 10

AFC championship game
L.A. Raiders 30 vs. Seattle 14

NFC wild-card game
Los Angeles Rams 24 at Dallas 17

NFC divisional games
San Francisco 24 vs. Detroit 23
Washington 51 vs. L.A. Rams 7

NFC championship
Washington 24 vs. San Francisco 21

Super Bowl XVIII
L.A. Raiders 38, Washington 9, at Tampa, Fla.

1984

AMERICAN CONFERENCE

EASTERN DIVISION

am	W	L	T	Pct.	PF	PA
ami*	14	2	0	.875	513	298
w England	9	7	0	.563	362	352
Y. Jets	7	9	0	.438	332	364
dianapolis	4	12	0	.250	239	414
ffalo	2	14	0	.125	250	454

CENTRAL DIVISION

am	W	L	T	Pct.	PF	PA
ttsburgh*	9	7	0	.563	387	310
ncinnati	8	8	0	.500	339	339
eveland	5	11	0	.313	250	297
uston	3	13	0	.188	240	437

WESTERN DIVISION

am	W	L	T	Pct.	PF	PA
nver*	13	3	0	.813	353	241
attle†	12	4	0	.750	418	282
A. Raiders†	11	5	0	.688	368	278
nsas City	8	8	0	.500	314	324
n Diego	7	9	0	.438	394	413

*Division champion.
†Wild-card team.

NATIONAL CONFERENCE

EASTERN DIVISION

Team	W	L	T	Pct.	PF	PA
Washington*	11	5	0	.688	426	310
N.Y. Giants†	9	7	0	.563	299	301
St. Louis	9	7	0	.563	423	345
Dallas	9	7	0	.563	308	308
Philadelphia	6	9	1	.406	278	320

CENTRAL DIVISION

Team	W	L	T	Pct.	PF	PA
Chicago*	10	6	0	.625	325	248
Green Bay	8	8	0	.500	390	309
Tampa Bay	6	10	0	.375	335	380
Detroit	4	11	1	.281	283	408
Minnesota	3	13	0	.188	276	484

WESTERN DIVISION

Team	W	L	T	Pct.	PF	PA
San Francisco*	15	1	0	.938	475	227
L.A. Rams†	10	6	0	.625	346	316
New Orleans	7	9	0	.438	298	361
Atlanta	4	12	0	.250	281	382

PLAYOFFS

AFC wild-card game
Seattle 13 vs. Los Angeles Raiders 7

AFC divisional games
Miami 31 vs. Seattle 10
Pittsburgh 24 at Denver 17

AFC championship
Miami 45 vs. Pittsburgh 28

NFC wild-card game
N.Y. Giants 16 at L.A. Rams 13

NFC divisional games
San Francisco 21 vs. N.Y. Giants 10
Chicago 23 at Washington 19

NFC championship
San Francisco 23 vs. Chicago 0

Super Bowl XIX
San Francisco 38, Miami 16, at Palo Alto, Calif.

BIG BAD BEARS

The Chicago Bears dominated pro football in 1985 like few teams in NFL history, winning all but one game during the regular season and outscoring three opponents, 91-10, in the playoffs (two by shutout). The Bears, in fact, were so confident of their eventual Super Bowl triumph that a number of them recorded a video, The Super Bowl Shuffle, weeks before the playoffs even began. As it turned out, the players were right. The Bears' 46-10 victory over New England was the most lopsided in Super Bowl history. Chicago's defense allowed the fewest points in the league, its offense scored the second-most, and a league-high nine Bears made the Pro Bowl.

1985

AMERICAN CONFERENCE

EASTERN DIVISION

Team	W	L	T	Pct.	PF	PA
Miami*	12	4	0	.750	428	320
N.Y. Jets†	11	5	0	.688	393	264
New England†	11	5	0	.688	362	290
Indianapolis	5	11	0	.313	320	386
Buffalo	2	14	0	.125	200	381

CENTRAL DIVISION

Team	W	L	T	Pct.	PF	PA
Cleveland*	8	8	0	.500	287	294
Cincinnati	7	9	0	.438	441	437
Pittsburgh	7	9	0	.438	379	355
Houston	5	11	0	.313	284	412

WESTERN DIVISION

Team	W	L	T	Pct.	PF	PA
L.A. Raiders*	12	4	0	.750	354	308
Denver	11	5	0	.688	380	329
Seattle	8	8	0	.500	349	303
San Diego	8	8	0	.500	467	435
Kansas City	6	10	0	.375	317	360

*Division champion.
†Wild-card team.

NATIONAL CONFERENCE

EASTERN DIVISION

Team	W	L	T	Pct.	PF	PA
Dallas*	10	6	0	.625	357	333
N.Y. Giants†	10	6	0	.625	399	283
Washington	10	6	0	.625	297	312
Philadelphia	7	9	0	.438	286	310
St. Louis	5	11	0	.313	278	414

CENTRAL DIVISION

Team	W	L	T	Pct.	PF	PA
Chicago*	15	1	0	.938	456	198
Green Bay	8	8	0	.500	337	355
Minnesota	7	9	0	.438	346	359
Detroit	7	9	0	.438	307	366
Tampa Bay	2	14	0	.125	294	448

WESTERN DIVISION

Team	W	L	T	Pct.	PF	PA
L.A. Rams*	11	5	0	.688	340	277
San Francisco†	10	6	0	.625	411	263
New Orleans	5	11	0	.313	294	401
Atlanta	4	12	0	.250	282	452

PLAYOFFS

AFC wild-card game
New England 26 at N.Y. Jets 14

AFC divisional games
Miami 24 vs. Cleveland 21
New England 27 at L.A. Raiders 20

AFC championship
New England 31 at Miami 14

NFC wild-card game
N.Y. Giants 17 vs. San Francisco 3

NFC divisional games
Los Angeles Rams 20 vs. Dallas 0
Chicago 21 vs. New York Giants 0

NFC championship
Chicago 24 vs. Los Angeles Rams 0

Super Bowl XX
Chicago 46, New England 10, at New Orleans.

1986

AMERICAN CONFERENCE

EASTERN DIVISION

Team	W	L	T	Pct.	PF	PA
New England*	11	5	0	.688	412	307
N.Y. Jets†	10	6	0	.625	364	386
Miami	8	8	0	.500	430	405
Buffalo	4	12	0	.250	287	348
Indianapolis	3	13	0	.188	229	400

CENTRAL DIVISION

Team	W	L	T	Pct.	PF	PA
Cleveland*	12	4	0	.750	391	310
Cincinnati	10	6	0	.625	409	394
Pittsburgh	6	10	0	.375	307	336
Houston	5	11	0	.313	274	329

WESTERN DIVISION

Team	W	L	T	Pct.	PF	PA
Denver*	11	5	0	.688	378	327
Kansas City†	10	6	0	.625	358	326
Seattle	10	6	0	.625	366	293
L.A. Raiders	8	8	0	.500	323	346
San Diego	4	12	0	.250	335	396

*Division champion.
†Wild-card team.

NATIONAL CONFERENCE

EASTERN DIVISION

Team	W	L	T	Pct.	PF	PA
N.Y. Giants*	14	2	0	.875	371	236
Washington†	12	4	0	.750	368	296
Dallas	7	9	0	.438	346	337
Philadelphia	5	10	1	.344	256	312
St. Louis	4	11	1	.281	218	351

CENTRAL DIVISION

Team	W	L	T	Pct.	PF	PA
Chicago*	14	2	0	.875	352	187
Minnesota	9	7	0	.563	398	273
Detroit	5	11	0	.313	277	326
Green Bay	4	12	0	.250	254	418
Tampa Bay	2	14	0	.125	239	473

WESTERN DIVISION

Team	W	L	T	Pct.	PF	PA
San Francisco*	10	5	1	.656	374	247
L.A. Rams†	10	6	0	.625	309	267
Atlanta	7	8	1	.469	280	280
New Orleans	7	9	0	.438	288	287

PLAYOFFS

AFC wild-card game
N.Y. Jets 35 vs. Kansas City 15

AFC divisional games
Cleveland 23 vs. N.Y. Jets 20 (OT)
Denver 22 vs. New England 17

AFC championship
Denver 23 at Cleveland 20 (OT)

NFC wild-card game
Washington 19 vs. L.A. Rams 7

NFC divisional games
Washington 27 at Chicago 13
N.Y. Giants 49 vs. San Francisco 3

NFC championship
N.Y. Giants 17 vs. Washington 0

Super Bowl XXI
New York Giants 39, Denver 20, at Pasadena, Ca.

COWBOYS' STREAK ENDS

In 1986, sports fans witnessed something they hadn't seen in a generation—a losing season by the Dallas Cowboys. Beginning with their 10-3-1 record in 1966, the Cowboys compiled a string of 20 consecutive winning seasons, the longest of any NFL team, and the third-longest such streak in pro sports history. Only the New York Yankees, who had a 39-year streak from 1926-64, and the Montreal Canadiens, who had a 32-year streak from 1952-83, put together longer streaks of consecutive winning seasons.

1987

AMERICAN CONFERENCE

EASTERN DIVISION

m	W	L	T	Pct.	PF	PA
anapolis*	9	6	0	.600	300	238
w England	8	7	0	.533	320	293
mi	8	7	0	.533	362	335
*alo	7	8	0	.467	270	305
Jets	6	9	0	.400	334	360

CENTRAL DIVISION

m	W	L	T	Pct.	PF	PA
veland*	10	5	0	.667	390	239
stont	9	6	0	.600	345	349
sburgh	8	7	0	.533	285	299
cinnati	4	11	0	.267	285	370

WESTERN DIVISION

m	W	L	T	Pct.	PF	PA
ver*	10	4	1	.700	379	288
ttlet	9	6	0	.600	371	314
Diego	8	7	0	.533	253	317
Raiders	5	10	0	.333	301	289
sas City	4	11	0	.267	273	388

*Division champion.
†Wild-card team.
NOTE: The 1987 NFL regular season was reduced from 224 games to 210 (16 to 15 for each team) to players' strike.

NATIONAL CONFERENCE

EASTERN DIVISION

Team	W	L	T	Pct.	PF	PA
Washington*	11	4	0	.733	379	285
Dallas	7	8	0	.467	340	348
St. Louis	7	8	0	.467	362	368
Philadelphia	7	8	0	.467	337	380
N.Y. Giants	6	9	0	.400	280	312

CENTRAL DIVISION

Team	W	L	T	Pct.	PF	PA
Chicago*	11	4	0	.733	356	282
Minnesotat	8	7	0	.533	336	335
Green Bay	5	9	1	.367	255	300
Tampa Bay	4	11	0	.267	286	360
Detroit	4	11	0	.267	269	384

WESTERN DIVISION

Team	W	L	T	Pct.	PF	PA
San Francisco*	13	2	0	.867	459	253
New Orleanst	12	3	0	.800	422	283
L.A. Rams	6	9	0	.400	317	361
Atlanta	3	12	0	.200	205	436

PLAYOFFS

AFC wild-card game
Houston 23 vs. Seattle 20 (OT)

AFC divisional games
Cleveland 38 vs. Indianapolis 21
Denver 34 vs. Houston 10

AFC championship
Denver 38 vs. Cleveland 33

NFC wild-card game
Minnesota 44 at New Orleans 10

NFC divisional games
Minnesota 36 at San Francisco 24
Washington 21 at Chicago 17

NFC championship
Washington 17 vs. Minnesota 10

Super Bowl XXII
Washington 42, Denver 10, at San Diego.

1988

AMERICAN CONFERENCE

EASTERN DIVISION

m	W	L	T	Pct.	PF	PA
alo	12	4	0	.750	329	237
anapolis	9	7	0	.563	354	315
w England	9	7	0	.563	250	284
Jets	8	7	1	.531	372	354
mi	6	10	0	.375	319	380

CENTRAL DIVISION

m	W	L	T	Pct.	PF	PA
cinnati*	12	4	0	.750	448	329
velandt	10	6	0	.625	304	288
stont	10	6	0	.625	424	365
sburgh	5	11	0	.313	336	421

WESTERN DIVISION

m	W	L	T	Pct.	PF	PA
ttle*	9	7	0	.563	339	329
ver	8	8	0	.500	327	352
Raiders	7	9	0	.438	325	369
Diego	6	10	0	.375	231	332
sas City	4	11	1	.281	254	320

*Division champion.
†Wild-card team.

NATIONAL CONFERENCE

EASTERN DIVISION

Team	W	L	T	Pct.	PF	PA
Philadelphia*	10	6	0	.625	379	319
N.Y. Giants	10	6	0	.625	359	304
Washington	7	9	0	.438	345	387
Phoenix	7	9	0	.438	344	398
Dallas	3	13	0	.188	265	381

CENTRAL DIVISION

Team	W	L	T	Pct.	PF	PA
Chicago*	12	4	0	.750	312	215
Minnesotat	11	5	0	.688	406	233
Tampa Bay	5	11	0	.313	261	350
Detroit	4	12	0	.250	220	313
Green Bay	4	12	0	.250	240	315

WESTERN DIVISION

Team	W	L	T	Pct.	PF	PA
San Francisco*	10	6	0	.625	369	294
L.A. Ramst	10	6	0	.625	407	293
New Orleans	10	6	0	.625	312	283
Atlanta	5	11	0	.313	244	315

PLAYOFFS

AFC wild-card game
Houston 24 at Cleveland 23

AFC divisional games
Cincinnati 21 vs. Seattle 13
Buffalo 17 vs. Houston 10

AFC championship
Cincinnati 21 vs. Buffalo 10

NFC wild-card game
Minnesota 28 vs. L.A. Rams 17

NFC divisional games
Chicago 20 vs. Philadelphia 12
San Francisco 34 vs. Minnesota 9

NFC championship
San Francisco 28 at Chicago 3

Super Bowl XXIII
San Francisco 20, Cincinnati 16, at Miami.

NINERS ARE FINER

In 1988 and '89, the San Francisco 49ers became the first team since the Pittsburgh Steelers a decade earlier to win back-to-back Super Bowl titles. San Francisco's latest two Super Bowl victories, however, were as dissimilar as night and day. The 49ers' 20-16 victory over Cincinnati in January 1989 was one of the most dramatic in Super Bowl history, undecided until Joe Montana hit John Taylor with a 10-yard scoring pass with 34 seconds left. A year later, San Francisco beat Denver, 55-10, as Montana threw five TD passes in one of the worst thrashings in Super Bowl history.

1989

AMERICAN CONFERENCE

EASTERN DIVISION

Team	W	L	T	Pct.	PF	PA
Buffalo*	9	7	0	.563	409	317
Indianapolis	8	8	0	.500	298	301
Miami	8	8	0	.500	331	379
New England	5	11	0	.313	297	391
N.Y. Jets	4	12	0	.250	253	411

CENTRAL DIVISION

Team	W	L	T	Pct.	PF	PA
Cleveland*	9	6	1	.594	334	254
Houston†	9	7	0	.563	365	412
Pittsburgh†	9	7	0	.563	265	326
Cincinnati	8	8	0	.500	404	285

WESTERN DIVISION

Team	W	L	T	Pct.	PF	PA
Denver*	11	5	0	.688	362	226
Kansas City	8	7	1	.531	318	286
L.A. Raiders	8	8	0	.500	315	297
Seattle	7	9	0	.438	241	327
San Diego	6	10	0	.375	266	290

*Division champion.
†Wild-card team.

NATIONAL CONFERENCE

EASTERN DIVISION

Team	W	L	T	Pct.	PF	PA
N.Y. Giants*	12	4	0	.750	348	252
Philadelphia†	11	5	0	.688	342	274
Washington	10	6	0	.625	386	308
Phoenix	5	11	0	.313	258	377
Dallas	1	15	0	.063	204	393

CENTRAL DIVISION

Team	W	L	T	Pct.	PF	PA
Minnesota*	10	6	0	.625	351	275
Green Bay	10	6	0	.625	362	356
Detroit	7	9	0	.438	312	364
Chicago	6	10	0	.375	358	377
Tampa Bay	5	11	0	.313	320	419

WESTERN DIVISION

Team	W	L	T	Pct.	PF	PA
San Francisco*	14	2	0	.875	442	253
L.A. Rams†	11	5	0	.688	426	344
New Orleans	9	7	0	.563	386	301
Atlanta	3	13	0	.188	279	437

PLAYOFFS

AFC wild-card game
Pittsburgh 26 at Houston 23 (OT)

AFC divisional games
Cleveland 34 vs. Buffalo 30
Denver 24 vs. Pittsburgh 23

AFC championship
Denver 37 vs. Cleveland 21

NFC wild-card game
L.A. Rams 21 at Philadelphia 7

NFC divisional games
L.A. Rams 19 at N.Y. Giants 13 (OT)
San Francisco 41 vs. Minnesota 13

NFC championship
San Francisco 30 vs. L.A. Rams 3

Super Bowl XXIV
San Francisco 55, Denver 10, at New Orleans.

1990

AMERICAN CONFERENCE

EASTERN DIVISION

Team	W	L	T	Pct.	PF	PA
Buffalo*	13	3	0	.813	428	263
Miami†	12	4	0	.750	336	242
Indianapolis	7	9	0	.438	281	353
N.Y. Jets	6	10	0	.375	295	345
New England	1	15	0	.063	181	446

CENTRAL DIVISION

Team	W	L	T	Pct.	PF	PA
Cincinnati*	9	7	0	.563	360	352
Houston†	9	7	0	.563	405	307
Pittsburgh	9	7	0	.563	292	240
Cleveland	3	13	0	.188	228	462

WESTERN DIVISION

Team	W	L	T	Pct.	PF	PA
L.A. Raiders*	12	4	0	.750	337	268
Kansas City†	11	5	0	.688	369	257
Seattle	9	7	0	.563	306	286
San Diego	6	10	0	.375	315	281
Denver	5	11	0	.313	331	374

*Division champion.
†Wild-card team.

NATIONAL CONFERENCE

EASTERN DIVISION

Team	W	L	T	Pct.	PF	PA
N.Y. Giants*	13	3	0	.813	335	211
Philadelphia†	10	6	0	.625	396	299
Washington†	10	6	0	.625	381	301
Dallas	7	9	0	.438	244	308
Phoenix	5	11	0	.313	268	396

CENTRAL DIVISION

Team	W	L	T	Pct.	PF	PA
Chicago*	11	5	0	.688	348	280
Tampa Bay	6	10	0	.375	264	367
Detroit	6	10	0	.375	373	413
Green Bay	6	10	0	.375	271	347
Minnesota	6	10	0	.375	351	326

WESTERN DIVISION

Team	W	L	T	Pct.	PF	PA
San Francisco*	14	2	0	.875	353	239
New Orleans†	8	8	0	.500	274	275
L.A. Rams	5	11	0	.313	345	412
Atlanta	5	11	0	.313	348	365

PLAYOFFS

AFC wild-card playoffs
Miami 17 vs. Kansas City 16
Cincinnati 41 vs. Houston 14

AFC divisional playoffs
Buffalo 44 vs. Miami 34
L.A. Raiders 20 vs. Cincinnati 10

AFC championship
Buffalo 51 vs. L.A. Raiders 3

NFC wild-card playoffs
Washington 20 at Philadelphia 6
Chicago 16 vs. New Orleans 6

NFC divisional playoffs
San Francisco 28 vs. Washington 10
N.Y. Giants 31 vs. Chicago 3

NFC championship
N.Y. Giants 15 at San Francisco 13

Super Bowl XXV
N.Y. Giants 20 vs. Buffalo 19, at Tampa, Fla.

BILLS BUFFALOED

Symmetry-wise, the 1990 NFL season was a strange one. In the AFC, all three division races were close, with the Buffalo Bills and Los Angeles Raiders winning their divisions by one game and the Central Division winding up in a three-way tie for first. In the NFC, the races looked more like runaways as the Giants, Bears and 49ers dominated. So what happened in the two conference title games? The Bills blew out the Raiders and the Giants edged the 49ers, setting the stage for one of the most memorable Super Bowls ever. The Giants nipped the Bills, 20-19, when Buffalo's Scott Norwood misfired on a 47-yard field goal attempt with eight second left.

1991

AMERICAN CONFERENCE

EASTERN DIVISION

	W	L	T	Pct.	PF	PA
alo*	13	3	0	.813	458	318
Jets†	8	8	0	.500	314	293
mi	8	8	0	.500	343	349
England	6	10	0	.375	211	305
anapolis	1	15	0	.063	143	381

CENTRAL DIVISION

	W	L	T	Pct.	PF	PA
ston*	11	5	0	.688	386	251
sburgh	7	9	0	.438	292	344
eland	6	10	0	.375	293	298
innati	3	13	0	.188	263	435

WESTERN DIVISION

	W	L	T	Pct.	PF	PA
ver*	12	4	0	.750	304	235
sas City†	10	6	0	.625	322	252
Raiders†	7	9	0	.563	298	297
ttle	7	9	0	.438	276	261
Diego	4	12	0	.250	274	342

*Division champion.
†Wild-card team.

NATIONAL CONFERENCE

EASTERN DIVISION

Team	W	L	T	Pct.	PF	PA
Washington*	14	2	0	.875	485	224
Dallas†	11	5	0	.688	342	310
Philadelphia	10	6	0	.625	285	244
N.Y. Giants	8	8	0	.500	281	297
Phoenix	4	12	0	.250	196	344

CENTRAL DIVISION

Team	W	L	T	Pct.	PF	PA
Detroit*	12	4	0	.750	339	295
Chicago†	11	5	0	.688	299	269
Minnesota	8	8	0	.500	301	306
Green Bay	4	12	0	.250	273	313
Tampa Bay	3	13	0	.188	199	365

WESTERN DIVISION

Team	W	L	T	Pct.	PF	PA
New Orleans*	11	5	0	.688	341	211
Atlanta†	10	6	0	.625	361	338
San Francisco	10	6	0	.625	393	239
L.A. Rams	3	13	0	.188	234	390

PLAYOFFS

AFC wild-card playoffs
Kansas City 10 vs. L.A. Raiders 6
Houston 17 vs. N.Y. Jets 10

AFC divisional playoffs
Denver 26 vs. Houston 24
Buffalo 37 vs. Kansas City 14

AFC championship
Buffalo 10 vs. Denver 7

NFC wild-card playoffs
Atlanta 27 at New Orleans 20
Dallas 17 at Chicago 13

NFC divisional playoffs
Washington 24 vs. Atlanta 7
Detroit 38 vs. Dallas 6

NFC championship
Washington 41 vs. Detroit 10

Super Bowl XXVI
Washington 37 vs. Buffalo 24, at Minneapolis.

1992

AMERICAN CONFERENCE

EASTERN DIVISION

	W	L	T	Pct.	PF	PA
mi*	11	5	0	.688	340	281
alo†	11	5	0	.688	381	283
anapolis	9	7	0	.563	216	302
Jets	4	12	0	.250	220	315
England	2	14	0	.125	205	363

CENTRAL DIVISION

	W	L	T	Pct.	PF	PA
sburgh*	11	5	0	.688	299	225
ston†	10	6	0	.625	352	258
eland	7	9	0	.438	272	275
innati	5	11	0	.313	274	364

WESTERN DIVISION

	W	L	T	Pct.	PF	PA
Diego*	11	5	0	.688	335	241
sas City†	10	6	0	.625	348	282
ver	8	8	0	.500	262	329
Raiders	7	9	0	.438	249	281
ttle	2	14	0	.125	140	312

*Division champion.
†Wild-card team.

NATIONAL CONFERENCE

EASTERN DIVISION

Team	W	L	T	Pct.	PF	PA
Dallas*	13	3	0	.813	409	243
Philadelphia†	11	5	0	.688	354	245
Washington†	9	7	0	.563	300	255
N.Y. Giants	6	10	0	.375	306	367
Phoenix	4	12	0	.250	243	332

CENTRAL DIVISION

Team	W	L	T	Pct.	PF	PA
Minnesota*	11	5	0	.688	374	249
Green Bay	9	7	0	.563	276	296
Tampa Bay	5	11	0	.313	267	365
Chicago	5	11	0	.313	295	361
Detroit	5	11	0	.313	273	332

WESTERN DIVISION

Team	W	L	T	Pct.	PF	PA
San Francisco*	14	2	0	.875	431	236
New Orleans†	12	4	0	.750	330	202
Atlanta	6	10	0	.375	327	414
L.A. Rams	6	10	0	.375	313	383

PLAYOFFS

AFC wild-card playoffs
San Diego 17 vs. Kansas City 0
Buffalo 41 vs. Houston 38 (OT)

AFC divisional playoffs
Buffalo 24 at Pittsburgh 3
Miami 31 vs. San Diego 0

AFC championship
Buffalo 29 at Miami 10

NFC wild-card playoffs
Washington 24 at Minnesota 7
Philadelphia 36 at New Orleans 20

NFC divisional playoffs
San Francisco 20 vs. Washington 13
Dallas 34 vs. Philadelphia 10

NFC championship
Dallas 30 at San Francisco 20

Super Bowl XXVII
Dallas 52 vs. Buffalo 17, at Pasadena, Calif.

COACHING CAROUSEL

The biggest coaching turnover in 14 years occurred in 1992 as nine coaches debuted with new teams. Two of them—Chuck Knox f the Rams and Ted Marchibroda of the Colts—were returning to clubs they had coached previously, while two others (Seattle's om Flores and Tampa Bay's Sam Wyche) had prior NFL head-coaching experience. Of the five first-time coaches, three led their eams to division championships: Pittsburgh's Bill Cowher, Minnesota's Dennis Green and San Diego's Bobby Ross.

1993

AMERICAN CONFERENCE

EASTERN DIVISION

Team	W	L	T	Pct.	PF	PA
Buffalo*	12	4	0	.750	329	242
Miami	9	7	0	.563	349	351
N.Y. Jets	8	8	0	.500	270	247
New England	5	11	0	.313	238	286
Indianapolis	4	12	0	.250	189	378

CENTRAL DIVISION

Team	W	L	T	Pct.	PF	PA
Houston*	12	4	0	.750	368	238
Pittsburgh†	9	7	0	.563	308	281
Cleveland	7	9	0	.438	304	307
Cincinnati	3	13	0	.188	187	319

WESTERN DIVISION

Team	W	L	T	Pct.	PF	PA
Kansas City*	11	5	0	.688	328	291
L.A. Raiders†	10	6	0	.625	306	326
Denver†	9	7	0	.563	373	284
San Diego	8	8	0	.500	322	290
Seattle	6	10	0	.375	280	314

*Division champion.
†Wild-card team.

NATIONAL CONFERENCE

EASTERN DIVISION

Team	W	L	T	Pct.	PF	PA
Dallas*	12	4	0	.750	376	229
N.Y. Giants†	11	5	0	.688	288	205
Philadelphia	8	8	0	.500	293	315
Phoenix	7	9	0	.438	326	269
Washington	4	12	0	.250	230	345

CENTRAL DIVISION

Team	W	L	T	Pct.	PF	PA
Detroit*	10	6	0	.625	298	292
Minnesota†	9	7	0	.563	277	290
Green Bay†	9	7	0	.563	340	282
Chicago	7	9	0	.438	234	230
Tampa Bay	5	11	0	.313	237	376

WESTERN DIVISION

Team	W	L	T	Pct.	PF	PA
San Francisco*	10	6	0	.625	473	295
New Orleans	8	8	0	.500	317	343
Atlanta	6	10	0	.375	316	385
L.A. Rams	5	11	0	.313	221	367

PLAYOFFS

AFC wild-card playoffs
Kansas City 27 vs. Pittsburgh 24 (OT)
L.A. Raiders 42 vs. Denver 24
AFC divisional playoffs
Buffalo 29 vs. L.A. Raiders 23
Kansas City 28 at Houston 20
AFC championship
Buffalo 30 vs. Kansas City 13
NFC wild-card playoffs
Green Bay 28 at Detroit 24
N.Y. Giants 17 vs. Minnesota 10
NFC divisional playoffs
San Francisco 44 vs. N.Y. Giants 3
Dallas 27 vs. Green Bay 17
NFC championship
Dallas 38 vs. San Francisco 21
Super Bowl XXVIII
Dallas 30 vs. Buffalo 13, at Atlanta.

1994

AMERICAN CONFERENCE

EASTERN DIVISION

Team	W	L	T	Pct.	PF	PA
Miami*	10	6	0	.625	389	327
New England†	10	6	0	.625	351	312
Indianapolis	8	8	0	.500	307	320
Buffalo	7	9	0	.438	340	356
N.Y. Jets	6	10	0	.375	264	320

CENTRAL DIVISION

Team	W	L	T	Pct.	PF	PA
Pittsburgh*	12	4	0	.750	316	234
Cleveland†	11	5	0	.688	340	204
Cincinnati	3	13	0	.188	276	406
Houston	2	14	0	.125	226	352

WESTERN DIVISION

Team	W	L	T	Pct.	PF	PA
San Diego*	11	5	0	.688	381	306
Kansas City†	9	7	0	.563	319	298
L.A. Raiders	9	7	0	.563	303	327
Denver	7	9	0	.438	347	396
Seattle	6	10	0	.375	287	323

*Division champion.
†Wild-card team.

NATIONAL CONFERENCE

EASTERN DIVISION

Team	W	L	T	Pct.	PF	PA
Dallas*	12	4	0	.750	414	248
N.Y. Giants	9	7	0	.563	279	305
Arizona	8	8	0	.500	235	267
Philadelphia	7	9	0	.438	308	308
Washington	3	13	0	.188	320	412

CENTRAL DIVISION

Team	W	L	T	Pct.	PF	PA
Minnesota*	10	6	0	.625	356	314
Detroit†	9	7	0	.563	357	342
Green Bay†	9	7	0	.563	382	287
Chicago†	9	7	0	.563	271	307
Tampa Bay	6	10	0	.375	251	351

WESTERN DIVISION

Team	W	L	T	Pct.	PF	PA
San Francisco*	13	3	0	.813	505	296
New Orleans	7	9	0	.438	348	407
Atlanta	7	9	0	.438	313	389
L.A. Rams	4	12	0	.250	286	365

PLAYOFFS

AFC wild-card playoffs
Miami 27 vs. Kansas City 17
Cleveland 20 vs. New England 13
AFC divisional playoffs
Pittsburgh 29 vs. Cleveland 9
San Diego 22 vs. Miami 21
AFC championship
San Diego 17 at Pittsburgh 13
NFC wild-card playoffs
Green Bay 16 vs. Detroit 12
Chicago 35 at Minnesota 18
NFC divisional playoffs
San Francisco 44 vs. Chicago 15
Dallas 35 vs. Green Bay 9
NFC championship
San Francisco 38 vs. Dallas 28
Super Bowl XXIX
San Francisco 49 vs. San Diego 26 at Miami.

EX-NINER DOESN'T STRIKE GOLD

After a stellar career with the San Francisco 49ers, quarterback Joe Montana moved east in 1993 in hopes of leading a second team, the Kansas City Chiefs, to a Super Bowl championship. But it never happened. In Montana's first season, the Chiefs won a division title and advanced to the AFC championship game before losing to Buffalo. In 1994 Kansas City finished second to San Diego in the AFC's Western Division and lost in the first round of the playoffs.

AMERICAN CONFERENCE

EASTERN DIVISION

	W	L	T	Pct.	Pts.	Opp.
ffalo	10	6	0	.625	350	335
dianapolis	9	7	0	.563	331	316
ami	9	7	0	.563	398	332
England	6	10	0	.375	294	377
Jets	3	13	0	.188	233	384

CENTRAL DIVISION

	W	L	T	Pct.	Pts.	Opp.
tsburgh	11	5	0	.689	407	327
cinnati	7	9	0	.438	349	374
ston	7	9	0	.438	348	324
eland	5	11	0	.313	289	356
ksonville	4	12	0	.250	275	404

WESTERN DIVISION

	W	L	T	Pct.	Pts.	Opp.
nsas City	13	3	0	.813	358	241
n Diego	9	7	0	.563	321	323
ttle	8	8	0	.500	363	366
ver	8	8	0	.500	388	345
land	8	8	0	.500	348	332

*Division champion.
Wild-card team.

NATIONAL CONFERENCE

EASTERN DIVISION

	W	L	T	Pct.	Pts.	Opp.
*Dallas	12	4	0	.750	435	291
†Philadelphia	10	6	0	.625	318	338
Washington	6	10	0	.375	326	359
N.Y. Giants	5	11	0	.313	290	340
Arizona	4	12	0	.250	275	422

CENTRAL DIVISION

	W	L	T	Pct.	Pts.	Opp.
*Green Bay	11	5	0	.689	404	314
†Detroit	10	6	0	.625	436	336
Chicago	9	7	0	.563	392	360
Minnesota	8	8	0	.500	412	385
Tampa Bay	7	9	0	.438	238	335

WESTERN DIVISION

	W	L	T	Pct.	Pts.	Opp.
*San Francisco	11	5	0	.688	457	258
†Atlanta	9	7	0	.563	362	349
St. Louis	7	9	0	.438	309	418
Carolina	7	9	0	.438	289	325
New Orleans	7	9	0	.438	319	348

PLAYOFFS

AFC wild-card playoffs
Buffalo 37 vs. Miami 22
Indianapolis 35 at San Diego 20
AFC divisional playoffs
Pittsburgh 40 vs. Buffalo 21
Indianapolis 10 at Kansas City 7
AFC championship
Pittsburgh 20 vs. Indianapolis 16
NFC wild-card playoffs
Philadelphia 58 vs. Detroit 37
Green Bay 37 vs. Atlanta 20
NFC divisional playoffs
Green Bay 27 at San Francisco 17
Dallas 30 vs. Philadelphia 11
NFC championship
Dallas 38 vs. Green Bay 27
Super Bowl XXX
Dallas 27 vs Pittsburgh 17, at Tempe, Ariz.

SUPER BOWLS

SUMMARIES

SUPER BOWL I
JANUARY 15, 1967, AT LOS ANGELES

Kansas City (AFL)	0	10	0	0 — 10
Green Bay (NFL)	7	7	14	7 — 35

Winning coach—Vince Lombardi.
Most Valuable Player—Bart Starr.
Attendance—61,946.

SUPER BOWL II
JANUARY 14, 1968, AT MIAMI

Green Bay (NFL)	3	13	10	7 — 33
Oakland (AFL)	0	7	0	7 — 14

Winning coach—Vince Lombardi.
Most Valuable Player—Bart Starr.
Attendance—75,546.

SUPER BOWL III
JANUARY 12, 1969, AT MIAMI

New York (AFL)	0	7	6	3 — 16
Baltimore (NFL)	0	0	0	7 — 7

Winning coach—Weeb Ewbank.
Most Valuable Player—Joe Namath.
Attendance—75,389.

SUPER BOWL IV
JANUARY 11, 1970, AT NEW ORLEANS

Minnesota (NFL)	0	0	7	0 — 7
Kansas City (AFL)	3	13	7	0 — 23

Winning coach—Hank Stram.
Most Valuable Player—Len Dawson.
Attendance—80,562.

SUPER BOWL V
JANUARY 17, 1971, AT MIAMI

Baltimore (AFC)	0	6	0	10 — 16
Dallas (NFC)	3	10	0	0 — 13

Winning coach—Don McCafferty.
Most Valuable Player—Chuck Howley.
Attendance—79,204.

SUPER BOWL VI
JANUARY 16, 1972, AT NEW ORLEANS

Dallas (NFC)	3	7	7	7 — 24
Miami (AFC)	0	3	0	0 — 3

Winning coach—Tom Landry.
Most Valuable Player—Roger Staubach.
Attendance—81,023.

SUPER BOWL VII
JANUARY 14, 1973, AT LOS ANGELES

Miami (AFC)	7	7	0	0 — 14
Washington (NFC)	0	0	0	7 — 7

Winning coach—Don Shula.
Most Valuable Player—Jake Scott.
Attendance—90,182.

SUPER BOWL VIII
JANUARY 13, 1974, AT HOUSTON

Minnesota (NFC)	0	0	0	7 — 7
Miami (AFC)	14	3	7	0 — 24

Winning coach—Don Shula.
Most Valuable Player—Larry Csonka.
Attendance—71,882.

SUPER BOWL IX
JANUARY 12, 1975, AT NEW ORLEANS

Pittsburgh (AFC)	0	2	7	7 — 16
Minnesota (NFC)	0	0	0	6 — 6

Winning coach—Chuck Noll.
Most Valuable Player—Franco Harris.
Attendance—80,997.

SUPER BOWL X
JANUARY 18, 1976, AT MIAMI

Dallas (NFC)	7	3	0	7 — 17
Pittsburgh (AFC)	7	0	0	14 — 21

Winning coach—Chuck Noll.
Most Valuable Player—Lynn Swann.
Attendance—80,187.

SUPER BOWL XI
JANUARY 9, 1977, AT PASADENA, CALIF.

Oakland (AFC)	0	16	3	13 — 32
Minnesota (NFC)	0	0	7	7 — 14

Winning coach—John Madden.
Most Valuable Player—Fred Biletnikoff.
Attendance—103,428.

SUPER BOWL XII
JANUARY 15, 1978, AT NEW ORLEANS

Dallas (NFC)	10	3	7	7 — 27
Denver (AFC)	0	0	10	0 — 10

Winning coach—Tom Landry.
Most Valuable Players—Harvey Martin and Randy White.
Attendance—75,804.

SUPER BOWL XIII
JANUARY 21, 1979, AT MIAMI

Pittsburgh (AFC)	7	14	0	14 — 35
Dallas (NFC)	7	7	3	14 — 31

Winning coach—Chuck Noll.
Most Valuable Player—Terry Bradshaw.
Attendance—78,656.

SUPER BOWL XIV
JANUARY 20, 1980, PASADENA, CALIF.

Los Angeles (NFC)	7	6	6	0 — 19
Pittsburgh (AFC)	3	7	7	14 — 31

Winning coach—Chuck Noll.
Most Valuable Player—Terry Bradshaw.
Attendance—103,985.

SUPER BOWL XV
JANUARY 25, 1981, AT NEW ORLEANS

Oakland (AFC)	14	0	10	3 — 27
Philadelphia (NFC)	0	3	0	7 — 10

Winning coach—Tom Flores.
Most Valuable Player—Jim Plunkett.
Attendance—75,500.

SUPER BOWL XVI
JANUARY 24, 1982, AT PONTIAC, MICH.

San Francisco (NFC)	7	13	0	6 — 26
Cincinnati (AFC)	0	0	7	14 — 21

Winning coach—Bill Walsh.
Most Valuable Player—Joe Montana.
Attendance—81,270.

SUPER BOWL XVII
JANUARY 30, 1983, AT PASADENA, CALIF.

ami (AFC)	7	10	0	0 — 17
ashington (NFC)	0	10	3	14 — 27

Winning coach—Joe Gibbs.
Most Valuable Player—John Riggins.
Attendance—103,667.

SUPER BOWL XVIII
JANUARY 22, 1984, AT TAMPA

ashington (NFC)	0	3	6	0 — 9
s Angeles (AFC)	7	14	14	3 — 38

Winning coach—Tom Flores.
Most Valuable Player—Marcus Allen.
Attendance—72,920.

SUPER BOWL XIX
JANUARY 20, 1985, AT PALO ALTO, CALIF.

ami (AFC)	10	6	0	0 — 16
n Francisco (NFC)...............	7	21	10	0 — 38

Winning coach—Bill Walsh.
Most Valuable Player—Joe Montana.
Attendance—84,059.

SUPER BOWL XX
JANUARY 26, 1986, AT NEW ORLEANS

icago (NFC)	13	10	21	2 — 46
w England (AFC)	3	0	0	7 — 10

Winning coach—Mike Ditka.
Most Valuable Player—Richard Dent.
Attendance—73,818.

SUPER BOWL XXI
JANUARY 25, 1987, AT PASADENA, CALIF.

nver (AFC)	10	0	0	10 — 20
Y. Giants (NFC)...................	7	2	17	13 — 39

Winning coach—Bill Parcells.
Most Valuable Player—Phil Simms.
Attendance—101,063.

SUPER BOWL XXII
JANUARY 31, 1988, AT SAN DIEGO

ashington (NFC)	0	35	0	7 — 42
nver (AFC)	10	0	0	0 — 10

Winning coach—Joe Gibbs.
Most Valuable Player—Doug Williams.
Attendance—73,302.

SUPER BOWL XXIII
JANUARY 22, 1989, AT MIAMI

icinnati (AFC)......................	0	3	10	3 — 16
n Francisco (NFC)...............	3	0	3	14 — 20

Winning coach—Bill Walsh.
Most Valuable Player—Jerry Rice.
Attendance—75,179.

SUPER BOWL XXIV
JANUARY 28, 1990, AT NEW ORLEANS

n Francisco (NFC)...............	13	14	14	14 — 55
nver (AFC)	3	0	7	0 — 10

Winning coach—George Seifert.
Most Valuable Player—Joe Montana.
Attendance—72,919.

SUPER BOWL XXV
JANUARY 27, 1991, AT TAMPA

Buffalo (AFC)........................	3	9	0	7 — 19
New York (NFC).....................	3	7	7	3 — 20

Winning coach—Bill Parcells.
Most Valuable Player—Ottis Anderson.
Attendance—73,813.

SUPER BOWL XXVI
JANUARY 26, 1992, AT MINNEAPOLIS

Washington (NFC)	0	17	14	6 — 37
Buffalo (AFC)	0	0	10	14 — 24

Winning coach—Joe Gibbs.
Most Valuable Player—Mark Rypien.
Attendance—63,130.

SUPER BOWL XXVII
JANUARY 31, 1993, AT PASADENA, CALIF.

Buffalo (AFC)........................	7	3	7	0 — 17
Dallas (NFC)	14	14	3	21 — 52

Winning coach—Jimmy Johnson.
Most Valuable Player—Troy Aikman.
Attendance—98,374.

SUPER BOWL XXVIII
JANUARY 30, 1994, AT ATLANTA, GA.

Dallas (NFC)	6	0	14	10 — 30
Buffalo (AFC)	3	10	0	0 — 13

Winning coach—Jimmy Johnson.
Most Valuable Player—Emmitt Smith.
Attendance—72,817.

SUPER BOWL XXIX
JANUARY 29, 1995, AT MIAMI, FLA.

San Diego (AFC)...................	7	3	8	8 — 26
San Francisco (NFC).............	14	14	14	7 — 49

Winning coach—George Seifert.
Most Valuable Player—Steve Young.
Attendance—74,107.

SUPER BOWL XXX
JANUARY 28, 1996, AT TEMPE, ARIZ.

Dallas (NFC)	10	3	7	7 — 27
Pittsburgh (AFC)....................	0	7	0	10 — 17

Winning coach—Barry Switzer.
Most Valuable Player—Larry Brown.
Attendance—76,347.

SUPER BOWL XXXI
JANUARY 26, 1997, AT NEW ORLEANS

New England (AFC)	14	0	7	0 — 21
Green Bay (NFC)...................	10	17	8	0 — 35

Winning coach—Mike Holmgren.
Most Valuable Player—Desmond Howard.
Attendance—72,301.

PRO BOWLS

RESULTS

Date	Site	Winning team, score	Losing team, score	A
1-15-39	Wrigley Field, Los Angeles	New York Giants, 13	Pro All-Stars, 10	†20,00
1-14-40	Gilmore Stadium, Los Angeles	Green Bay Packers, 16	NFL All-Stars, 7	†18,0
12-29-40	Gilmore Stadium, Los Angeles	Chicago Bears, 28	NFL All-Stars, 14	21,6
1-4-42	Polo Grounds, New York	Chicago Bears, 35	NFL All-Stars, 24	17,7
12-27-42	Shibe Park, Philadelphia	NFL All-Stars, 17	Washington Redskins, 14	18,6
1943-50	No game was played.			
1-14-51	Los Angeles Memorial Coliseum	American Conference, 28	National Conference, 27	53,6
1-12-52	Los Angeles Memorial Coliseum	National Conference, 30	American Conference, 13	19,4
1-10-53	Los Angeles Memorial Coliseum	National Conference, 27	American Conference, 7	34,2
1-17-54	Los Angeles Memorial Coliseum	East, 20	West, 9	44,2
1-16-55	Los Angeles Memorial Coliseum	West, 26	East, 19	43,9
1-15-56	Los Angeles Memorial Coliseum	East, 31	West, 30	37,8
1-13-57	Los Angeles Memorial Coliseum	West, 19	East, 10	44,1
1-12-58	Los Angeles Memorial Coliseum	West, 26	East, 7	66,6
1-11-59	Los Angeles Memorial Coliseum	East, 28	West, 21	72,2
1-17-60	Los Angeles Memorial Coliseum	West, 38	East, 21	56,8
1-15-61	Los Angeles Memorial Coliseum	West, 35	East, 31	62,9
1-7-62*	Balboa Stadium, San Diego	West, 47	East, 27	20,9
1-14-62	Los Angeles Memorial Coliseum	West, 31	East, 30	57,4
1-13-63*	Balboa Stadium, San Diego	West, 21	East, 14	27,6
1-13-63	Los Angeles Memorial Coliseum	East, 30	West, 20	61,3
1-12-64	Los Angeles Memorial Coliseum	West, 31	East, 17	67,2
1-19-64*	Balboa Stadium, San Diego	West, 27	East, 24	20,0
1-10-65	Los Angeles Memorial Coliseum	West, 34	East, 14	60,5
1-16-65*	Jeppesen Stadium, Houston	West, 38	East, 14	15,4
1-15-66*	Rice Stadium, Houston	AFL All-Stars, 30	Buffalo Bills, 19	35,5
1-15-66	Los Angeles Memorial Coliseum	East, 36	West, 7	60,1
1-21-67*	Oakland-Alameda County Coliseum	East, 30	West, 23	18,8
1-22-67	Los Angeles Memorial Coliseum	East, 20	West, 10	15,0
1-21-68*	Gator Bowl, Jacksonville, Fla.	East, 25	West, 24	40,1
1-21-68	Los Angeles Memorial Coliseum	West, 38	East, 20	53,2
1-19-69*	Gator Bowl, Jacksonville, Fla.	West, 38	East, 25	41,0
1-19-69	Los Angeles Memorial Coliseum	West, 10	East, 7	32,0
1-17-70*	Astrodome, Houston	West, 26	East, 3	30,1
1-18-70	Los Angeles Memorial Coliseum	West, 16	East, 13	57,7
1-24-71	Los Angeles Memorial Coliseum	NFC, 27	AFC, 6	48,2
1-23-72	Los Angeles Memorial Coliseum	AFC, 26	NFC, 13	53,6
1-21-73	Texas Stadium, Irving	AFC, 33	NFC, 28	37,0
1-20-74	Arrowhead Stadium, Kansas City	AFC, 15	NFC, 13	66,9
1-20-75	Orange Bowl, Miami	NFC, 17	AFC, 10	26,4
1-26-76	Louisiana Superdome, New Orleans	NFC, 23	AFC, 20	30,5
1-17-77	Kingdome, Seattle	AFC, 24	NFC, 14	64,7
1-23-78	Tampa Stadium	NFC, 14	AFC, 13	51,3
1-29-79	Los Angeles Memorial Coliseum	NFC, 13	AFC, 7	46,2
1-27-80	Aloha Stadium, Honolulu	NFC, 37	AFC, 27	49,8
2-1-81	Aloha Stadium, Honolulu	NFC, 21	AFC, 7	50,3
1-31-82	Aloha Stadium, Honolulu	AFC, 16	NFC, 13	50,4
2-6-83	Aloha Stadium, Honolulu	NFC, 20	AFC, 19	49,8
1-29-84	Aloha Stadium, Honolulu	NFC, 45	AFC, 3	50,4
1-27-85	Aloha Stadium, Honolulu	AFC, 22	NFC, 14	50,3
2-2-86	Aloha Stadium, Honolulu	NFC, 28	AFC, 24	50,1
2-1-87	Aloha Stadium, Honolulu	AFC, 10	NFC, 6	50,1
2-7-88	Aloha Stadium, Honolulu	AFC, 15	NFC, 6	50,1
1-29-89	Aloha Stadium, Honolulu	NFC, 34	AFC, 3	50,1
2-4-90	Aloha Stadium, Honolulu	NFC, 27	AFC, 21	50,4
2-3-91	Aloha Stadium, Honolulu	AFC, 23	NFC, 21	50,3
2-2-92	Aloha Stadium, Honolulu	NFC, 21	AFC, 15	50,2
2-7-93	Aloha Stadium, Honolulu	AFC, 23 (OT)	NFC, 20	50,0
2-6-94	Aloha Stadium, Honolulu	NFC, 17	AFC, 3	50,0
2-5-95	Aloha Stadium, Honolulu	AFC, 41	NFC, 13	49,1
2-4-96	Aloha Stadium, Honolulu	NFC, 20	AFC, 13	50,0
2-2-97	Aloha Stadium, Honolulu	AFC, 26 (OT)	NFC, 23	50,0

*AFL game.
†Estimated figure.

OUTSTANDING PLAYER AWARDS

r—Name, team

1— Otto Graham, Cleveland Browns
2— Dan Towler, Los Angeles Rams
3— Dan Doll, Detroit Lions
4— Chuck Bednarik, Philadelphia Eagles
5— Billy Wilson, San Francisco 49ers
6— Ollie Matson, Chicago Cardinals
7— Bert Rechichar, Baltimore Colts (back)
   Ernie Stautner, Pittsburgh Steelers (lineman)
8— Hugh McElhenny, San Francisco 49ers (back)
   Gene Brito, Washington Redskins (lineman)
9— Frank Gifford, New York Giants (back)
   Doug Atkins, Chicago Bears (lineman)
0— Johnny Unitas, Baltimore Colts (back)
   Gene Lipscomb, Baltimore Colts (lineman)
1— Johnny Unitas, Baltimore Colts (back)
   Sam Huff, New York Giants (lineman)
2— Cotton Davidson, Dallas Texans*
   Jim Brown, Cleveland Browns (back)
   Henry Jordan, Green Bay Packers (lineman)
3— Curtis McClinton, Dallas Texans* (offense)
   Earl Faison, San Diego Chargers* (defense)
   Jim Brown, Cleveland Browns (back)
   Gene Lipscomb, Pittsburgh Steelers (lineman)
4— Keith Lincoln, San Diego Chargers* (offense)
   Archie Matsos, Oakland Raiders* (defense)
   Johnny Unitas, Baltimore Colts (back)
   Gino Marchetti, Baltimore Colts (lineman)
5— Keith Lincoln, San Diego Chargers* (offense)
   Willie Brown, Denver Broncos* (defense)
   Fran Tarkenton, Minnesota Vikings (back)
   Terry Barr, Detroit Lions (lineman)
6— Joe Namath, New York Jets* (offense)
   Frank Buncom, San Diego Chargers* (defense)
   Jim Brown, Cleveland Browns (back)
   Dale Meinert, St. Louis Cardinals (lineman)
7— Babe Parilli, Boston Patriots* (offense)
   Verlon Biggs, New York Jets* (defense)
   Gale Sayers, Chicago Bears (back)
   Floyd Peters, Philadelphia Eagles (lineman)
8— Joe Namath, New York Jets* (offense)
   Don Maynard, New York Jets* (offense)
   Speedy Duncan, San Diego Chargers (defense)
   Gale Sayers, Chicago Bears (back)
   Dave Robinson, Green Bay Packers (lineman)

Year—Name, team

1969— Len Dawson, Kansas City Chiefs* (offense)
   George Webster, Houston* (defense)
   Roman Gabriel, Los Angeles Rams (back)
   Merlin Olsen, Los Angeles Rams (lineman)
1970— John Hadl, San Diego Chargers*
   Gale Sayers, Chicago Bears (back)
   George Andrie, Dallas Cowboys (lineman)
1971— Mel Renfro, Dallas Cowboys (back)
   Fred Carr, Green Bay Packers (lineman)
1972— Jan Stenerud, Kansas City Chiefs (offense)
   Willie Lanier, Kansas City Chiefs (defense)
1973— O.J. Simpson, Buffalo Bills
1974— Garo Yepremian, Miami Dolphins
1975— James Harris, Los Angeles Rams
1976— Billy Johnson, Houston Oilers
1977— Mel Blount, Pittsburgh Steelers
1978— Walter Payton, Chicago Bears
1979— Ahmad Rashad, Minnesota Vikings
1980— Chuck Muncie, New Orleans Saints
1981— Eddie Murray, Detroit Lions
1982— Kellen Winslow, San Diego Chargers
   Lee Roy Selmon, Tampa Bay Buccaneers
1983— Dan Fouts, San Diego Chargers
   John Jefferson, Green Bay Packers
1984— Joe Theismann, Washington Redskins
1985— Mark Gastineau, New York Jets
1986— Phil Simms, New York Giants
1987— Reggie White, Philadelphia Eagles
1988— Bruce Smith, Buffalo Bills
1989— Randall Cunningham, Philadelphia Eagles
1990— Jerry Gray, Los Angeles Rams
1991— Jim Kelly, Buffalo Bills
1992— Michael Irvin, Dallas Cowboys
1993— Steve Tasker, Buffalo Bills
1994— Andre Rison, Atlanta Falcons
1995— Marshall Faulk, Indianapolis Colts
1996— Jerry Rice, San Francisco 49ers
1997— Mark Brunell, Jacksonville Jaguars
   *AFL game.

HISTORY *Pro Bowls*

RECORDS

INDIVIDUAL SERVICE

PLAYERS

Most years played
26—George Blanda, Chicago Bears, Baltimore, Houston, Oakland, 1949 through 1975, except 1959.
Most years with one club
20—Jackie Slater, L.A. Rams, St. Louis Rams, 1976 through 1995.
Most games played, career
340—George Blanda, Chicago Bears, Baltimore, Houston, Oakland, 1949 through 1975, except 1959.
Most consecutive games played, career
282—Jim Marshall, Cleveland, Minnesota, September 25, 1960 through December 16, 1979.

COACHES

Most years as head coach
40—George Halas, Chicago Bears, 1920 through 1929, 1933 through 1942, 1946 through 1955 and 1958 through 1967.
Most games won as head coach
328—Don Shula, Baltimore, 1963 through 1969; Miami, 1970 through 1995.
Most games lost as head coach
162—Tom Landry, Dallas, 1960 through 1988.

INDIVIDUAL OFFENSE

RUSHING

YARDS

Most yards, career
16,726—Walter Payton, Chicago, 1975 through 1987.
Most yards, season
2,105—Eric Dickerson, Los Angeles Rams, 1984.
Most years leading league in yards
8—Jim Brown, Cleveland, 1957 through 1965, except 1962.
Most consecutive years leading league in yards
5—Jim Brown, Cleveland, 1957 through 1961.
Most years with 1,000 or more yards
10—Walter Payton, Chicago, 1976 through 1986, except 1982.
Most consecutive years with 1,000 or more yards
8—Barry Sanders, Detroit, 1989 through 1996.
Thurman Thomas, Buffalo, 1989 through 1996.
Most yards, game
275—Walter Payton, Chicago vs. Minnesota, November 20, 1977.
Most games with 200 or more yards, career
6—O.J. Simpson, Buffalo, San Francisco, 1969 through 1979.
Most games with 200 or more yards, season
4—Earl Campbell, Houston, 1980.
Most consecutive games with 200 or more yards, season
2—O.J. Simpson, Buffalo, December 9 through 16, 1973.
O.J. Simpson, Buffalo, November 25 through December 5, 1976.
Earl Campbell, Houston, October 19 through 26, 1980.
Most games with 100 or more yards, career
77—Walter Payton, Chicago, 1975 through 1987.
Most games with 100 or more yards, season
12—Eric Dickerson, Los Angeles Rams, 1984.
Barry Foster, Pittsburgh, 1992.
Most consecutive games with 100 or more yards, career
11—Marcus Allen, Los Angeles Raiders, October 28, 1985 through September 14, 1986.
Most consecutive games with 100 or more yards, season
9—Walter Payton, Chicago, October 13 through December 8, 1985.
Marcus Allen, Los Angeles Raiders, October 28 through December 23, 1985.
Longest run from scrimmage
99 yards—Tony Dorsett, Dallas at Minnesota, January 3, 1983 (touchdown).

ATTEMPTS

Most attempts, career
3,838—Walter Payton, Chicago, 1975 through 1987.
Most attempts, season
407—James Wilder, Tampa Bay, 1984.
Most attempts, game
45—Jamie Morris, Washington at Cincinnati, December 17, 1988, overtime.
43—Butch Woolfolk, New York Giants at Philadelphia, November 20, 1983.
James Wilder, Tampa Bay vs. Green Bay, September 30 1984, overtime.
Most years leading league in attempts
6—Jim Brown, Cleveland, 1958 through 1965, except 1960 a 1962.
Most consecutive years leading league in attempts
4—Steve Van Buren, Philadelphia, 1947 through 1950.
Walter Payton, Chicago, 1976 through 1979.

TOUCHDOWNS

Most touchdowns, career
112—Marcus Allen, L.A. Raiders, Kansas City, 1982 through 19
Most touchdowns, season
25—Emmitt Smith, Dallas, 1995.
Most years leading league in touchdowns
5—Jim Brown, Cleveland, 1957 through 1959, 1963, 1965.
Most consecutive years leading league in touchdowns
3—Steve Van Buren, Philadelphia, 1947 through 1949.
Jim Brown, Cleveland, 1957 through 1959.
Abner Haynes, Dallas Texans, 1960 through 1962.
Cookie Gilchrist, Buffalo, 1962 through 1964.
Leroy Kelly, Cleveland, 1966 through 1968.
Most touchdowns, game
6—Ernie Nevers, Chicago Cardinals vs. Chicago Bears, November 28, 1929.
Most consecutive games with one or more touchdowns, care
13—John Riggins, Washington, December 26, 1982 through November 27, 1983.
George Rogers, Washington, November 24, 1985 throu November 2, 1986.
Most consecutive games with one or more touchdowns, seas
12—John Riggins, Washington, September 5 through Novem 27, 1983.

PASSING

PASSER RATING

Highest rating, career (1,500 or more attempts)
96.2—Steve Young, Tampa Bay, San Francisco, 1985 throug 1996.
Highest rating, season (qualifiers)
112.8—Steve Young, San Francisco, 1994.

ATTEMPTS

Most attempts, career
6,904—Dan Marino, Miami, 1983 through 1996.
Most attempts, season
691—Drew Bledsoe, New England, 1994.
Most years leading league in attempts
4—Sammy Baugh, Washington, 1937, 1943, 1947, 1948.
Johnny Unitas, Baltimore, 1957, 1959 through 1961.
George Blanda, Chicago Bears, Houston, 1953, 1963 through 1965.
Dan Marino, Miami, 1984, 1986, 1988, 1992.
Most consecutive years leading league in attempts
3—Johnny Unitas, Baltimore, 1959 through 1961.
George Blanda, Houston, 1963 through 1965.
Most attempts, game
70—Drew Bledsoe, New England vs. Minnesota, November 1 1994 (overtime).
68—George Blanda, Houston vs. Buffalo, November 1, 1964

COMPLETIONS

Most completions, career
6,134—Dan Marino, Miami, 1983 through 1996.
Most completions, season
404—Warren Moon, Houston, 1991.
Most years leading league in completions
6—Sammy Baugh, Washington, 1937, 1943, 1945, 1947, 1948.
Dan Marino, Miami, 1984, 1985, 1986, 1988, 1992.
Most consecutive years leading league in completions
3—George Blanda, Houston, 1963 through 1965.
Dan Marino, Miami, 1984 through 1986.
Most completions, game
45—Drew Bledsoe, New England vs. Minnesota, November 13,
1994 (overtime).
42—Richard Todd, New York Jets vs. San Francisco, September
21, 1980.

YARDS

Most yards, career
51,636—Dan Marino, Miami, 1983 through 1996.
Most yards, season
5,084—Dan Marino, Miami, 1984.
Most years leading league in yards
5—Sonny Jurgensen, Philadelphia, Washington, 1961, 1962,
1966, 1967, 1969.
Dan Marino, Miami, 1984 through 1986, 1988, 1992.
Most consecutive years leading league in yards
4—Dan Fouts, San Diego, 1979 through 1982.
Most years with 3,000 or more yards
11—Dan Marino, Miami, 1984 through 1995, except 1993.
John Elway, Denver, 1985 through 1996, except 1992.
Most yards, game
554—Norm Van Brocklin, Los Angeles at New York Yanks,
September 28, 1951.
Most games with 400 or more yards, career
13—Dan Marino, Miami, 1983 through 1996.
Most games with 400 or more yards, season
4—Dan Marino, Miami, 1984.
Most consecutive games with 400 or more yards, season
3—Dan Fouts, San Diego, December 11 through 20, 1982.
Dan Marino, Miami, December 2 through 9, 1984.
Phil Simms, New York Giants, October 6 through 13, 1985.
Most games with 300 or more yards, career
62—Dan Marino, Miami, 1983 through 1996.
Most games with 300 or more yards, season
9—Dan Marino, Miami, 1984.
Warren Moon, Houston, 1990.
Most consecutive games with 300 or more yards, season
5—Joe Montana, San Francisco, September 19 through December
11, 1982.
Longest pass completion
99 yards—Frank Filchock, Washington vs. Pittsburgh, October
15, 1939 (touchdown).
George Izo, Washington at Cleveland, September 15, 1963
(touchdown).
Karl Sweetan, Detroit at Baltimore, October 16, 1966
(touchdown).
Sonny Jurgensen, Washington at Chicago, September 15,
1968 (touchdown).
Jim Plunkett, Los Angeles Raiders vs. Washington, October
2, 1983 (touchdown).
Ron Jaworski, Philadelphia vs. Atlanta, November 10, 1985
(touchdown).
Stan Humphries, San Diego at Seattle, September 18, 1994
(touchdown).
Brett Favre, Green Bay at Chicago, September 11, 1995
(touchdown).

YARDS PER ATTEMPT

Most yards per attempt, career (1,500 or more attempts)
8.63—Otto Graham, Cleveland, 1950 through 1955 (13,499
yards, 1,565 attempts).
Most yards per attempt, season (qualifiers)
11.17—Tommy O'Connell, Cleveland, 1957 (1,229 yards, 110
attempts).

Most years leading league in yards per attempt
7—Sid Luckman, Chicago Bears, 1939 through 1943, 1946, 1947.
Most consecutive years leading league in yards per attempt
5—Sid Luckman, Chicago Bears, 1939 through 1943.
Most yards per attempt, game (20 or more attempts)
18.58—Sammy Baugh, Washington vs. Boston, October 31,
1948 (446 yards, 24 attempts).

TOUCHDOWNS

Most touchdowns, career
369—Dan Marino, Miami, 1983 through 1996.
Most touchdowns, season
48—Dan Marino, Miami, 1984.
Most years leading league in touchdowns
4—Johnny Unitas, Baltimore, 1957 through 1960.
Len Dawson, Dallas Texans, Kansas City, 1962 through
1966, except 1964.
Most consecutive years leading league in touchdowns
4—Johnny Unitas, Baltimore, 1957 through 1960.
Most touchdowns, game
7—Sid Luckman, Chicago Bears at New York Giants, November
14, 1943.
Adrian Burk, Philadelphia at Washington, October 17, 1954.
George Blanda, Houston vs. New York Titans, November 19,
1961.
Y.A. Tittle, New York Giants vs. Washington, October 28, 1962.
Joe Kapp, Minnesota vs. Baltimore, September 28, 1969.

INTERCEPTIONS

Most interceptions, career
277—George Blanda, Chicago Bears, Baltimore, Houston,
Oakland, 1949 through 1975, except 1959.
Most interceptions, season
42—George Blanda, Houston, 1962.
Most interceptions, game
8—Jim Hardy, Chicago Cardinals vs. Philadelphia, September
24, 1950.
Most attempts with no interceptions, game
70—Drew Bledsoe, New England vs. Minnesota, November 13,
1994 (overtime).
63—Rich Gannon, Minnesota at New England, October 20,
1991 (overtime).
60—Davey O'Brien, Philadelphia at Washington, December 1,
1940.

INTERCEPTION PERCENTAGE

Lowest interception percentage, career (1,500 or more attempts)
2.23—Neil O'Donnell, Pittsburgh, N.Y. Jets, 1991 through 1996
(2,059 attempts, 46 interceptions).
Lowest interception percentage, season (qualifiers)
0.66—Joe Ferguson, Buffalo, 1976 (151 attempts, one interception).
Most years leading league in lowest interception percentage
5—Sammy Baugh, Washington, 1940, 1942, 1944, 1945, 1947.

SACKS (SINCE 1963)

Most times sacked, career
492—Dave Krieg, Seattle, Kansas City, Detroit, Arizona, Chicago,
1980 through 1996.
Most times sacked, season
72—Randall Cunningham, Philadelphia, 1986.
Most times sacked, game
12—Bert Jones, Baltimore vs. St. Louis, October 26, 1980.
Warren Moon, Houston vs. Dallas, September 29, 1985.

RECEIVING

RECEPTIONS

Most receptions, career
1,050—Jerry Rice, San Francisco, 1985 through 1996.
Most receptions, season
123—Herman Moore, Detroit, 1995.
Most years leading league in receptions
8—Don Hutson, Green Bay, 1936 through 1945, except 1938
and 1940.

Most consecutive years leading league in receptions
5—Don Hutson, Green Bay, 1941 through 1945.
Most receptions, game
18—Tom Fears, Los Angeles vs. Green Bay, December 3, 1950.
Most consecutive games with one or more receptions
183—Art Monk, Washington, N.Y. Jets, Philadelphia, January 2, 1983 through December 24, 1995.

YARDS

Most yards, career
16,377—Jerry Rice, San Francisco, 1985 through 1996.
Most yards, season
1,848—Jerry Rice, San Francisco, 1995.
Most years leading league in yards
7—Don Hutson, Green Bay, 1936 through 1944, except 1937 and 1940.
Most consecutive years leading league in yards
4—Don Hutson, Green Bay, 1941 through 1944.
Most years with 1,000 or more yards
11—Jerry Rice, San Francisco, 1986 through 1996.
Most yards, game
336—Willie Anderson, Los Angeles Rams at New Orleans, November 26, 1989 (overtime).
309—Stephone Paige, Kansas City vs. San Diego, December 22, 1985.
Most games with 200 or more yards, career
5—Lance Alworth, San Diego, Dallas, 1962 through 1972.
Most games with 200 or more yards, season
3—Charley Hennigan, Houston, 1961.
Most games with 100 or more yards, career
61—Jerry Rice, San Francisco, 1985 through 1996.
Most games with 100 or more yards, season
11—Michael Irvin, Dallas, 1995.
Most consecutive games with 100 or more yards, season
7—Charley Hennigan, Houston, 1961.
Bill Groman, Houston, 1961.
Michael Irvin, Dallas, 1995.
Longest reception
99 yards—Andy Farkas, Washington vs. Pittsburgh, October 15, 1939 (touchdown).
Bobby Mitchell, Washington at Cleveland, September 15, 1963 (touchdown).
Pat Studstill, Detroit at Baltimore, October 16, 1966 (touchdown).
Gerry Allen, Washington at Chicago, September 15, 1968 (touchdown).
Cliff Branch, Los Angeles Raiders vs. Washington, October 2, 1983 (touchdown).
Mike Quick, Philadelphia vs. Atlanta, November 10, 1985 (touchdown).
Tony Martin, San Diego at Seattle, September 18, 1994 (touchdown).
Robert Brooks, Green Bay at Chicago, September 11, 1995 (touchdown).

TOUCHDOWNS

Most touchdowns, career
154—Jerry Rice, San Francisco, 1985 through 1996.
Most touchdowns, season
22—Jerry Rice, San Francisco, 1987.
Most years leading league in touchdowns
9—Don Hutson, Green Bay, 1935 through 1944, except 1939.
Most consecutive years leading league in touchdowns
5—Don Hutson, Green Bay, 1940 through 1944.
Most touchdowns, game
5—Bob Shaw, Chicago Cardinals vs. Baltimore, October 2, 1950.
Kellen Winslow, San Diego at Oakland, November 22, 1981.
Jerry Rice, San Francisco at Atlanta, October 14, 1990.
Most consecutive games with one or more touchdowns
13—Jerry Rice, San Francisco, December 19, 1986 through December 27, 1987.

COMBINED NET YARDS
(Rushing, receiving, interception returns, punt returns, kickoff returns and fumble returns)

ATTEMPTS

Most attempts, career
4,368—Walter Payton, Chicago, 1975 through 1987.
Most attempts, season
496—James Wilder, Tampa Bay, 1984.
Most attempts, game
48—James Wilder, Tampa Bay at Pittsburgh, October 30, 1983

YARDS

Most yards, career
21,803—Walter Payton, Chicago, 1975 through 1987.
Most yards, season
2,535—Lionel James, San Diego, 1985.
Most years leading league in yards
5—Jim Brown, Cleveland, 1958 through 1961, 1964.
Most consecutive years leading league in yards
4—Jim Brown, Cleveland, 1958 through 1961.
Most yards, game
404—Glyn Milburn, Denver vs. Seattle, December 10, 1995.

SCORING

POINTS

Most points, career
2,002—George Blanda, Chicago Bears, Baltimore, Houston, Oakland, 1949 through 1975, except 1959.
Most points, season
176—Paul Hornung, Green Bay, 1960.
Most years leading league in points
5—Don Hutson, Green Bay, 1940 through 1944.
Gino Cappelletti, Boston, 1961 through 1966, except 1962.
Most consecutive years leading league in points
5—Don Hutson, Green Bay, 1940 through 1944.
Most years with 100 or more points
11—Nick Lowery, Kansas City, 1981 through 1993, except 198 and 1987.
Most points, game
40—Ernie Nevers, Chicago Cardinals vs. Chicago Bears, November 28, 1929.
Most consecutive games with one or more points
206—Morten Andersen, New Orleans, Atlanta, December 11, 1983 through December 22, 1996.

TOUCHDOWNS

Most touchdowns, career
165—Jerry Rice, San Francisco, 1985 through 1996.
Most touchdowns, season
25—Emmitt Smith, Dallas, 1995.
Most years leading league in touchdowns
8—Don Hutson, Green Bay, 1935 through 1938 and 1941 through 1944.
Most consecutive years leading league in touchdowns
4—Don Hutson, Green Bay, 1935 through 1938 and 1941 through 1944.
Most touchdowns, game
6—Ernie Nevers, Chicago Cardinals vs. Chicago Bears, November 28, 1929.
Dub Jones, Cleveland vs. Chicago Bears, November 25, 195
Gale Sayers, Chicago vs. San Francisco, December 12, 1965
Most consecutive games with one or more touchdowns
18—Lenny Moore, Baltimore, October 27, 1963 through September 19, 1965.

EXTRA POINTS

Most extra points attempted, career
959—George Blanda, Chicago Bears, Baltimore, Houston, Oakland, 1949 through 1975, except 1959.
Most extra points made, career
943—George Blanda, Chicago Bears, Baltimore, Houston, Oakland, 1949 through 1975, except 1959.

ost extra points attempted, season
—Uwe von Schamann, Miami, 1984.
ost extra points made, season
—Uwe von Schamann, Miami, 1984.
ost extra points attempted, game
—Charlie Gogolak, Washington vs. New York Giants, November 27, 1966.
ost extra points made, game
—Pat Harder, Chicago Cardinals at New York Giants, October 17, 1948.
Bob Waterfield, Los Angeles vs. Baltimore, October 22, 1950.
Charlie Gogolak, Washington vs. New York Giants, November 27, 1966.

FIELD GOALS AND FIELD-GOAL PERCENTAGE

ost field goals attempted, career
8—George Blanda, Chicago Bears, Baltimore, Houston, Oakland, 1949 through 1975, except 1959.
ost field goals made, career
3—Nick Lowery, New England, Kansas City, N.Y. Jets, 1978 through 1996, except 1979.
ost field goals attempted, season
—Bruce Gossett, Los Angeles, 1966.
Curt Knight, Washington, 1971.
ost field goals made, season
—John Kasay, Carolina, 1996.
ost field goals attempted, game
—Jim Bakken, St. Louis at Pittsburgh, September 24, 1967.
ost field goals made, game
—Jim Bakken, St. Louis at Pittsburgh, September 24, 1967.
Rich Karlis, Minnesota vs. Los Angeles Rams, November 5, 1989 (overtime).
Chris Boniol, Dallas vs. Green Bay, November 18, 1996.
ost field goals made, one quarter
—Garo Yepremian, Detroit vs. Minnesota, November 13, 1966, second quarter.
Curt Knight, Washington at New York Giants, November 15, 1970, second quarter.
Roger Ruzek, Dallas vs. New York Giants, November 2, 1987, fourth quarter.
ost consecutive games with one or more field goals made, career
—Fred Cox, Minnesota, November 17, 1968 through December 5, 1970.
ost consecutive field goals made, career
—Fuad Reveiz, Minnesota, October 10, 1994 through September 17, 1995.
ost field goals of 50 or more yards, career
—Morten Andersen, New Orleans, Atlanta, 1982 through 1996.
ost field goals of 50 or more yards, season
—Morten Andersen, Atlanta, 1995.
ost field goals of 50 or more yards, game
—Morten Andersen, Atlanta vs. New Orleans, December 10, 1995.
ngest field goal made
yards—Tom Dempsey, New Orleans vs. Detroit, November 8, 1970.
ghest field-goal percentage, career (100 or more made)
.25—Doug Pelfrey, Cincinnati, 1993 through 1996 (128 attempted, 104 made).
ghest field-goal percentage, season (qualifiers)
0.00—Tony Zendejas, Los Angeles Rams, 1991 (17 attempted, 17 made).

SAFETIES

ost safeties, career
—Ted Hendricks, Baltimore, Green Bay, Oakland, Los Angeles Raiders, 1969 through 1983.
Doug English, Detroit, 1975 through 1985, except 1980.
ost safeties, season
—Held by many players.
ost safeties, game
—Fred Dryer, Los Angeles vs. Green Bay, October 21, 1973.

PUNTING

Most punts, career
1,154—Dave Jennings, New York Giants, New York Jets, 1974 through 1987.
Most punts, season
114—Bob Parsons, Chicago, 1981.
Most seasons leading league in punting
4—Sammy Baugh, Washington, 1940 through 1943.
Jerrel Wilson, Kansas City, 1965, 1968, 1972, 1973.
Most consecutive seasons leading league in punting
4—Sammy Baugh, Washington, 1940 through 1943.
Most punts, game
15— John Teltschik, Philadelphia at New York Giants, December 6, 1987 (overtime).
14—Dick Nesbitt, Chicago Cardinals at Chicago Bears, November 30, 1933.
Keith Molesworth, Chicago Bears vs. Green Bay, December 10, 1933.
Sammy Baugh, Washington vs. Philadelphia, November 5, 1939.
Carl Kinscherf, New York Giants at Detroit, November 7, 1943.
George Taliaferro, New York Yanks vs. Los Angeles, September 28, 1951.
Longest punt
98 yards—Steve O'Neal, New York Jets at Denver, September 21, 1969.

FUMBLES

Most fumbles, career
150—Dave Krieg, Seattle, Kansas City, Detroit, Arizona, Chicago, 1980 through 1996.
Most fumbles, season
21—Tony Banks, St. Louis, 1996.
Most fumbles, game
7—Len Dawson, Kansas City vs. San Diego, November 15, 1964.

PUNT RETURNS

Most punt returns, career
301—Tim Brown, L.A. Raiders, Oakland, 1988 through 1996.
Most punt returns, season
70—Danny Reece, Tampa Bay, 1979.
Most years leading league in punt returns
3—Les "Speedy" Duncan, San Diego, Washington, 1965, 1966, 1971.
Rick Upchurch, Denver, 1976, 1978, 1982.
Most punt returns, game
11—Eddie Brown, Washington at Tampa Bay, October 9, 1977.

YARDS

Most yards, career
3,317—Billy "White Shoes" Johnson, Houston, Atlanta, Washington, 1974 through 1988, except 1981.
Most yards, season
875—Desmond Howard, Green Bay, 1996.
Most yards, game
207—LeRoy Irvin, Los Angeles at Atlanta, October 11, 1981.
Longest punt return
103 yards—Robert Bailey, Los Angeles Rams at New Orleans, October 23, 1994 (touchdown).

FAIR CATCHES

Most fair catches, career
102—Willie Wood, Green Bay, 1960 through 1971.
Most fair catches, season
27—Leo Lewis, Minnesota, 1989.
Most fair catches, game
7—Lem Barney, Detroit vs. Chicago, November 21, 1976.
Bobby Morse, Philadelphia vs. Buffalo, December 27, 1987.

TOUCHDOWNS

Most touchdowns, career
8—Jack Christiansen, Detroit, 1951 through 1958.
Rick Upchurch, Denver, 1975 through 1983.

Most touchdowns, season
4—Jack Christiansen, Detroit, 1951.
Rick Upchurch, Denver, 1976.

Most touchdowns, game
2—Jack Christiansen, Detroit vs. Los Angeles, October 14, 1951.
Jack Christiansen, Detroit vs. Green Bay, November 22, 1951.
Dick Christy, New York Titans vs. Denver, September 24, 1961.
Rick Upchurch, Denver vs. Cleveland, September 26, 1976.
LeRoy Irvin, Los Angeles at Atlanta, October 11, 1981.
Vai Sikahema, St. Louis vs. Tampa Bay, December 21, 1986.
Todd Kinchen, Los Angeles Rams vs. Atlanta, December 27, 1992.

KICKOFF RETURNS

Most kickoff returns, career
412—Mel Gray, New Orleans, Detroit, Houston, 1986 through 1996.

Most kickoff returns, season
70—Tyrone Hughes, New Orleans, 1996.

Most years leading league in kickoff returns
3—Abe Woodson, San Francisco, 1959, 1962, 1963.
Tyrone Hughes, New Orleans, 1994 through 1996.

Most kickoff returns, game
9—Noland Smith, Kansas City vs. Oakland, November 23, 1967.
Dino Hall, Cleveland vs. Pittsburgh, October 7, 1979.
Paul Palmer, Kansas City at Seattle, September 20, 1987.
Eric Metcalf, Atlanta at San Francisco, September 29, 1996.
Eric Metcalf, Atlanta at St. Louis, November 10, 1996.

YARDS

Most yards, career
10,057—Mel Gray, New Orleans, Detroit, Houston, 1986 through 1996.

Most yards, season
1,791—Tyrone Hughes, New Orleans, 1996.

Most years leading league in yards
3—Bruce Harper, New York Jets, 1977 through 1979.
Tyrone Hughes, New Orleans, 1994 through 1996.

Most yards, game
304—Tyrone Hughes, New Orleans vs. Los Angeles Rams, October 23, 1994.

Longest kickoff return
106 yards—Al Carmichael, Green Bay vs. Chicago Bears, October 7, 1956 (touchdown).
Noland Smith, Kansas City at Denver, December 17, 1967.
Roy Green, St. Louis at Dallas, October 21, 1979.

TOUCHDOWNS

Most touchdowns, career
6—Ollie Matson, Chicago Cardinals, Los Angeles Rams, Detroit, Philadelphia, 1952 through 1964, except 1953.
Gale Sayers, Chicago, 1965 through 1971.
Travis Williams, Green Bay, Los Angeles, 1967 through 1971.
Mel Gray, New Orleans, Detroit, Houston, 1986 through 1996.

Most touchdowns, season
4—Travis Williams, Green Bay, 1967.
Cecil Turner, Chicago, 1970.

Most touchdowns, game
2—Timmy Brown, Philadelphia vs. Dallas, November 6, 1966.
Travis Williams, Green Bay vs. Cleveland, November 12, 1967.
Ron Brown, Los Angeles Rams vs. Green Bay, November 24, 1985.
Tyrone Hughes, New Orleans vs. Los Angeles Rams, October 23, 1994.

COMBINED KICK RETURNS

(KICKOFFS AND PUNTS)

Most kick returns, career
645—Mel Gray, New Orleans, Detroit, Houston, 1986 through 1996.

Most kick returns, season
100—Larry Jones, Washington, 1975.
Tyrone Hughes, New Orleans, 1996.

Most kick returns, game
13—Stump Mitchell, St. Louis at Atlanta, October 18, 1981.
Ron Harris, New England at Pittsburgh, December 5, 1993

YARDS

Most yards, career
12,649—Mel Gray, New Orleans, Detroit, Houston, 1986 through 1996.

Most yards, season
1,943—Tyrone Hughes, New Orleans, 1996.

Most yards, game
347—Tyrone Hughes, New Orleans vs. Los Angeles Rams, October 23, 1994.

TOUCHDOWNS

Most touchdowns, career
9—Ollie Matson, Chicago Cardinals, Los Angeles Rams, Detroit, Philadelphia, 1952 through 1966, except 1953.
Mel Gray, New Orleans, Detroit, Houston, 1986 through 1995.

Most touchdowns, season
4—Jack Christiansen, Detroit, 1951.
Emlen Tunnell, New York Giants, 1951.
Gale Sayers, Chicago, 1967.
Travis Williams, Green Bay, 1967.
Cecil Turner, Chicago, 1970.
Billy "White Shoes" Johnson, Houston, 1975.
Rick Upchurch, Denver, 1976.

Most touchdowns, game
2—Held by many players.

INDIVIDUAL DEFENSE

INTERCEPTIONS

Most interceptions, career
81—Paul Krause, Washington, Minnesota, 1964 through 1979.

Most interceptions, season
14—Dick "Night Train" Lane, Los Angeles, 1952.

Most interceptions, game
4—Held by many players.

Most consecutive games with one or more interceptions
8—Tom Morrow, Oakland, 1962 through 1963.

Most yards on interceptions, career
1,282—Emlen Tunnell, New York Giants, Green Bay, 1948 through 1961.

Most yards on interceptions, season
349—Charlie McNeil, San Diego, 1961.

Most yards on interceptions, game
177—Charlie McNeil, San Diego vs. Houston, September 24, 196

Longest interception return
103—Vencie Glenn, San Diego vs. Denver, November 29, 1987
Louis Oliver, Miami vs. Buffalo, October 4, 1992.
(Note: James Willis, 14 yards, and Troy Vincent, 90 yards combined for a 104-yard interception return for Philadelphia vs. Dallas, November 3, 1996.)

TOUCHDOWNS

Most touchdowns, career
9—Ken Houston, Houston, Washington, 1967 through 1980.

Most touchdowns, season
4—Ken Houston, Houston, 1971.
Jim Kearney, Kansas City, 1972.
Eric Allen, Philadelphia, 1993.

Most touchdowns, game
2—Held by many players.

FUMBLES RECOVERED

Most fumbles recovered (own and opponents'), career
53—Warren Moon, Houston, Minnesota, 1984 through 1996.

ost fumbles recovered (own), career
8—Warren Moon, Houston, Minnesota, 1984 through 1996.
ost opponents' fumbles recovered, career
9—Jim Marshall, Cleveland, Minnesota, 1960 through 1979.
ost fumbles recovered (own and opponents'), season
—Don Hultz, Minnesota, 1963.
 Dave Krieg, Seattle, 1989.
ost fumbles recovered (own), season
—Dave Krieg, Seattle, 1989.
ost opponents' fumbles recovered, season
—Don Hultz, Minnesota, 1963.
ost fumbles recovered (own and opponents'), game
—Otto Graham, Cleveland at New York Giants, October 25, 1953.
 Sam Etcheverry, St. Louis at New York Giants, September 17, 1961.
 Roman Gabriel, Los Angeles at San Francisco, October 12, 1969.
 Joe Ferguson, Buffalo vs. Miami, September 18, 1977.
 Randall Cunningham, Philadelphia at Los Angeles Raiders, November 30, 1986 (overtime).
ost fumbles recovered (own), game
—Otto Graham, Cleveland at New York Giants, October 25, 1953.
 Sam Etcheverry, St. Louis at New York Giants, September 17, 1961.
 Roman Gabriel, Los Angeles at San Francisco, October 12, 1969.
 Joe Ferguson, Buffalo vs. Miami, September 18, 1977.
 Randall Cunningham, Philadelphia at Los Angeles Raiders, November 30, 1986 (overtime).
ost opponents' fumbles recovered, game
—Held by many players.
ongest fumble return
04 yards—Jack Tatum, Oakland at Green Bay, September 24, 1972 (touchdown).

TOUCHDOWNS

ost touchdowns (own and opponents' recovered), career
—Bill Thompson, Denver, 1969 through 1981.
 Jessie Tuggle, Atlanta, 1987 through 1992.
ost touchdowns (own recovered), career
—Held by many players.
ost touchdowns (opponents' recovered), career
—Jessie Tuggle, Atlanta, 1987 through 1992.
ost touchdowns, season
—Held by many players.
ost touchdowns, game
—Fred "Dippy" Evans, Chicago Bears vs. Washington, November 28, 1948.

SACKS (SINCE 1982)

ost sacks, career
65.5—Reggie White, Philadelphia, Green Bay, 1985 through 1996.
ost sacks, season
2—Mark Gastineau, New York Jets, 1984.
ost sacks, game
—Derrick Thomas, Kansas City vs. Seattle, November 11, 1990.

TEAM MISCELLANEOUS
CHAMPIONSHIPS

ost league championships won
2—Green Bay, 1929, 1930, 1931, 1936, 1939, 1944, 1961, 1962, 1965, 1966, 1967, 1996.
ost consecutive league championships won
—Green Bay, 1929 through 1931.
 Green Bay, 1965 through 1967.
ost first-place finishes during regular season (since 1933)
8—Cleveland Browns, 1950 through 1955, 1957, 1964, 1965, 1967, 1968, 1969, 1971, 1980, 1985, 1986, 1987, 1989.

Most consecutive first-place finishes during regular season (since 1933)
7—Los Angeles, 1973 through 1979.

GAMES WON

Most games won, season
15—San Francisco, 1984.
 Chicago, 1985.
Most consecutive games won, season
14—Miami, September 17 through December 16, 1972.
Most consecutive games won from start of season
14—Miami, September 17 through December 16, 1972 (entire season).
Most consecutive games won at end of season
14—Miami, September 17 through December 16, 1972 (entire season).
Most consecutive undefeated games, season
14—Miami, September 17 through December 16, 1972 (entire season).
Most consecutive games won
17—Chicago Bears, November 26, 1933 through December 2, 1934.
Most consecutive undefeated games
25—Canton, 1921 through 1923 (won 22, tied three).
Most consecutive home games won
27—Miami, October 17, 1971 through December 15, 1974.
Most consecutive undefeated home games
30—Green Bay, 1928 through 1933 (won 27, tied three).
Most consecutive road games won
18—San Francisco, November 27, 1988 through December 30, 1990.
Most consecutive undefeated road games
18—San Francisco, November 27, 1988 through December 30, 1990 (won 18).

GAMES LOST

Most games lost, season
15—New Orleans, 1980.
 Dallas, 1989.
 New England, 1990.
 Indianapolis, 1991.
 New York Jets, 1996.
Most consecutive games lost
26—Tampa Bay, September 12, 1976 through December 4, 1977.
Most consecutive winless games
26—Tampa Bay, September 12, 1976 through December 4, 1977 (lost 26).
Most consecutive games lost, season
14—Tampa Bay, September 12 through December 12, 1976.
 New Orleans, September 7 through December 7, 1980.
 Baltimore, September 13 through December 13, 1981.
 New England, September 23 through December 30, 1990.
Most consecutive games lost from start of season
14—Tampa Bay, September 12 through December 12, 1976 (entire season).
 New Orleans, September 7 through December 7, 1980.
Most consecutive games lost at end of season
14—Tampa Bay, September 12 through December 12, 1976 (entire season).
 New England, September 23 through December 30, 1990.
Most consecutive winless games, season
14—Tampa Bay, September 12 through December 12, 1976 (lost 14; entire season).
 New Orleans, September 7 through December 7, 1980 (lost 14).
 Baltimore, September 13 through December 13, 1981 (lost 14).
 New England, September 23 through December 30, 1990 (lost 14).

Most consecutive home games lost
14—Dallas, October 9, 1988 through December 24, 1989.
Most consecutive winless home games
14—Dallas, October 9, 1988 through December 24, 1989 (lost 14).
Most consecutive road games lost
23—Houston, September 27, 1981 through November 4, 1984.
Most consecutive winless road games
23—Houston, September 27, 1981 through November 4, 1984 (lost 23).

TIE GAMES

Most tie games, season
6—Chicago Bears, 1932.
Most consecutive tie games
3—Chicago Bears, September 25 through October 9, 1932.

TEAM OFFENSE
RUSHING

Most years leading league in rushing
16—Chicago Bears, 1932, 1934, 1935, 1939, 1940, 1941, 1942, 1951, 1955, 1956, 1968, 1977, 1983, 1984, 1985, 1986.
Most consecutive years leading league in rushing
4—Chicago Bears, 1939 through 1942.
  Chicago Bears, 1983 through 1986.

ATTEMPTS

Most attempts, season
681—Oakland, 1977.
Most attempts, game
72—Chicago Bears vs. Brooklyn, October 20, 1935.
Most attempts by both teams, game
108—Chicago Cardinals 70, Green Bay 38, December 5, 1948.
Fewest attempts, game
6—Chicago Cardinals at Boston, October 29, 1933.
Fewest attempts by both teams, game
35—New Orleans 20, Seattle 15, September 1, 1991.

YARDS

Most yards, season
3,165—New England, 1978.
Fewest yards, season
298—Philadelphia, 1940.
Most yards, game
426—Detroit vs. Pittsburgh, November 4, 1934.
Most yards by both teams, game
595—Los Angeles 371, New York Yanks 224, November 18, 1951.
Fewest yards, game
-53—Detroit at Chicago Cardinals, October 17, 1943.
Fewest yards by both teams, game
-15—Detroit -53, Chicago Cardinals 38, October 17, 1943.

TOUCHDOWNS

Most touchdowns, season
36—Green Bay, 1962.
Fewest touchdowns, season
1—Brooklyn, 1934.
Most touchdowns, game
7—Los Angeles vs. Atlanta, December 4, 1976.
Most touchdowns by both teams, game
8—Los Angeles 6, New York Yanks 2, November 18, 1951.
  Chicago Bears 5, Green Bay 3, November 6, 1955.
  Cleveland 6, Los Angeles 2, November 24, 1957.

PASSING
ATTEMPTS

Most attempts, season
709—Minnesota, 1981.
Fewest attempts, season
102—Cincinnati, 1933.

Most attempts, game
70—New England vs. Minnesota, November 13, 1994 (overtime)
68—Houston at Buffalo, November 1, 1964.
Most attempts by both teams, game
112—New England 70, Minnesota 42, November 13, 1994 (overtime).
104—Miami 55, New York Jets 49, October 18, 1987 (overtime)
102—San Francisco 57, Atlanta 45, October 6, 1985.
Fewest attempts, game
0—Green Bay vs. Portsmouth, October 8, 1933.
  Detroit at Cleveland, September 10, 1937.
  Pittsburgh vs. Brooklyn, November 16, 1941.
  Pittsburgh vs. Los Angeles, November 13, 1949.
  Cleveland vs. Philadelphia, December 3, 1950.
Fewest attempts by both teams, game
4—Detroit 3, Chicago Cardinals 1, November 3, 1935.
  Cleveland 4, Detroit 0, September 10, 1937.

COMPLETIONS

Most completions, season
432—San Francisco, 1995.
Fewest completions, season
25—Cincinnati, 1933.
Most completions, game
45—New England vs. Minnesota, November 13, 1994 (overtime)
42—New York Jets vs. San Francisco, September 21, 1980.
Most completions by both teams, game
71—New England 45, Minnesota 26, November 13, 1994 (overtime).
68—San Francisco 37, Atlanta 31, October 6, 1985.
Fewest completions, game
0—Held by many teams. Last team: Buffalo vs. New York Jets, September 29, 1974.
Fewest completions by both teams, game
1—Philadelphia 1, Chicago Cardinals 0, November 8, 1936.
  Cleveland 1, Detroit 0, September 10, 1937.
  Detroit 1, Chicago Cardinals 0, September 15, 1940.
  Pittsburgh 1, Brooklyn 0, November 29, 1942.

YARDS

Most yards, season
5,018—Miami, 1984.
Most years leading league in yards
10—San Diego, 1965, 1968, 1971, 1978 through 1983, 1985.
Most consecutive years leading league in yards
6—San Diego, 1978 through 1983.
Fewest yards, season
302—Chicago Cardinals, 1934.
Most yards, game
554—Los Angeles at New York Yanks, September 28, 1951.
Most yards by both teams, game
884—New York Jets 449, Miami 435, September 21, 1986 (overtime).
883—San Diego 486, Cincinnati 397, December 20, 1982.
Fewest yards, game
-53—Denver at Oakland, September 10, 1967.
Fewest yards by both teams, game
-11—Green Bay -10, Dallas -1, October 24, 1965.

TOUCHDOWNS

Most touchdowns, season
49—Miami, 1984.
Fewest touchdowns, season
0—Cincinnati, 1933.
  Pittsburgh, 1945.
Most touchdowns, game
7—Chicago Bears at New York Giants, November 14, 1943.
  Philadelphia at Washington, October 17, 1954.
  Houston vs. New York Titans, November 19, 1961.
  Houston vs. New York Titans, October 14, 1962.
  New York Giants vs. Washington, October 28, 1962.
  Minnesota vs. Baltimore, September 28, 1969.
  San Diego at Oakland, November 22, 1981.

Most touchdowns by both teams, game
2—New Orleans 6, St. Louis 6, November 2, 1969.

INTERCEPTIONS

Most interceptions, season
8—Houston, 1962.
Fewest interceptions, season
—Cleveland, 1960.
Green Bay, 1966.
Kansas City, 1990.
New York Giants, 1990.
Most interceptions, game
—Detroit vs. Green Bay, October 24, 1943.
Pittsburgh vs. Philadelphia, December 12, 1965.
Most interceptions by both teams, game
3—Denver 8, Houston 5, December 2, 1962.

SACKS

Most sacks allowed, season
04—Philadelphia, 1986.
Most years leading league in fewest sacks allowed
0—Miami, 1973 and 1982 through 1990.
Most consecutive years leading league in fewest sacks allowed
—Miami, 1982 through 1990.
Fewest sacks allowed, season
—Miami, 1988.
Most sacks allowed, game
2—Pittsburgh at Dallas, November 20, 1966.
Baltimore vs. St. Louis, October 26, 1980.
Detroit vs. Chicago, December 16, 1984.
Houston vs. Dallas, September 29, 1985.
Most sacks allowed by both teams, game
8—Green Bay 10, San Diego 8, September 24, 1978.

SCORING

POINTS

Most points, season
41—Washington, 1983.
Most points, game
2—Washington vs. New York Giants, November 27, 1966.
Most points by both teams, game
13—Washington 72, New York Giants 41, November 27, 1966.
Fewest points by both teams, game
—Occurred many times. Last time: New York Giants 0, Detroit 0, November 7, 1943.
Most points in a shutout victory
4—Philadelphia vs. Cincinnati, November 6, 1934.
Fewest points in a shutout victory
—Green Bay at Chicago Bears, October 16, 1932.
Chicago Bears at Green Bay, September 18, 1938.
Most points in first half of game
9—Green Bay vs. Tampa Bay, October 2, 1983.
Most points in first half of game by both teams
0—Houston 35, Oakland 35, December 22, 1963.
Most points in second half of game
9—Chicago Bears at Philadelphia, November 30, 1941.
Most points in second half of game by both teams
5—Washington 38, New York Giants 27, November 27, 1966.
Most points in one quarter
1—Green Bay vs. Detroit, October 7, 1945, second quarter.
Los Angeles vs. Detroit, October 29, 1950, third quarter.
Most points in one quarter by both teams
9—Oakland 28, Houston 21, December 22, 1963, second quarter.
Most points in first quarter
5—Green Bay vs. Cleveland, November 12, 1967.
Most points in first quarter by both teams
2—Green Bay 35, Cleveland 7, November 12, 1967.
Most points in second quarter
1—Green Bay vs. Detroit, October 7, 1945.

Most points in second quarter by both teams
49—Oakland 28, Houston 21, December 22, 1963.
Most points in third quarter
41—Los Angeles vs. Detroit, October 29, 1950.
Most points in third quarter by both teams
48—Los Angeles 41, Detroit 7, October 29, 1950.
Most points in fourth quarter
31—Oakland vs. Denver, December 17, 1960.
Oakland vs. San Diego, December 8, 1963.
Atlanta at Green Bay, September 13, 1981.
Most points in fourth quarter by both teams
42—Chicago Cardinals 28, Philadelphia 14, December 7, 1947.
Green Bay 28, Chicago Bears 14, November 6, 1955.
New York Jets 28, Boston 14, October 27, 1968.
Pittsburgh 21, Cleveland 21, October 18, 1969.
Most consecutive games without being shut out
306—San Francisco, October 16, 1977 through December 23, 1996.

TIMES SHUT OUT

Most times shut out, season
8—Frankford, 1927 (lost six, tied two).
Brooklyn, 1931 (lost eight).
Most consecutive times shut out
8—Rochester, 1922 through 1924 (lost eight).

TOUCHDOWNS

Most touchdowns, season
70—Miami, 1984.
Most years leading league in touchdowns
13—Chicago Bears, 1932, 1934, 1935, 1939, 1941, 1942, 1943, 1944, 1946, 1947, 1948, 1956, 1965.
Most consecutive years leading league in touchdowns
4—Chicago Bears, 1941 through 1944.
Los Angeles, 1949 through 1952.
Most touchdowns, game
10—Philadelphia vs. Cincinnati, November 6, 1934.
Los Angeles vs. Baltimore, October 22, 1950.
Washington vs. New York Giants, November 27, 1966.
Most touchdowns by both teams, game
16—Washington 10, New York Giants 6, November 27, 1966.
Most consecutive games with one or more touchdowns
166—Cleveland, 1957 through 1969.

EXTRA POINTS

Most extra points, season
66—Miami, 1984.
Fewest extra points, season
2—Chicago Cardinals, 1933.
Most extra points, game
10—Los Angeles vs. Baltimore, October 22, 1950.
Most extra points by both teams, game
14—Chicago Cardinals 9, New York Giants 5, October 17, 1948.
Houston 7, Oakland 7, December 22, 1963.
Washington 9, New York Giants 5, November 27, 1966.

FIELD GOALS

Most field goals attempted, season
49—Los Angeles, 1966.
Washington, 1971.
Most field goals made, season
37—Carolina, 1996.
Most field goals attempted, game
9—St. Louis at Pittsburgh, September 24, 1967.
Most field goals made, game
7—St. Louis at Pittsburgh, September 24, 1967.
Minnesota vs. Los Angeles Rams, November 5, 1989 (overtime).
Most field goals attempted by both teams, game
11—St. Louis 6, Pittsburgh 5, November 13, 1966.
Washington 6, Chicago 5, November 14, 1971.
Green Bay 6, Detroit 5, September 29, 1974.
Washington 6, New York Giants 5, November 14, 1976.

Most field goals made by both teams, game
8—Cleveland 4, St. Louis 4, September 20, 1964.
  Chicago 5, Philadelphia 3, October 20, 1968.
  Washington 5, Chicago 3, November 14, 1971.
  Kansas City 5, Buffalo 3, December 19, 1971.
  Detroit 4, Green Bay 4, September 29, 1974.
  Cleveland 5, Denver 3, October 19, 1975.
  New England 4, San Diego 4, November 9, 1975.
  San Francisco 6, New Orleans 2, October 16, 1983.
  Seattle 5, Los Angeles Raiders 3, December 18, 1988.
Most consecutive games with one or more field goals made
31—Minnesota, November 17, 1968 through December 5, 1970.

SAFETIES
Most safeties, season
4—Cleveland, 1927.
  Detroit, 1962.
  Seattle, 1993.
Most safeties, game
3—Los Angeles Rams vs. New York Giants, September 30, 1984.
Most safeties by both teams, game
3—Los Angeles Rams 3, New York Giants 0, September 30, 1984.

FIRST DOWNS
Most first downs, season
387—Miami, 1984.
Most first downs, game
39—New York Jets vs. Miami, November 27, 1988.
  Washington at Detroit, November 4, 1990 (overtime).
Most first downs by both teams, game
62—San Diego 32, Seattle 30, September 15, 1985.

PUNTING
Most punts, season
114—Chicago, 1981.
Fewest punts, season
23—San Diego, 1982.
Most punts, game
17—Chicago Bears vs. Green Bay, October 22, 1933.
  Cincinnati vs. Pittsburgh, October 22, 1933.
Most punts by both teams, game
31—Chicago Bears 17, Green Bay 14, October 22, 1933.
  Cincinnati 17, Pittsburgh 14, October 22, 1933.
Fewest punts, game
0—Held by many teams.
Fewest punts by both teams, game
0—Buffalo 0, San Francisco 0, September 13, 1992.

FUMBLES
Most fumbles, season
56—Chicago Bears, 1938.
  San Francisco, 1978.
Fewest fumbles, season
8—Cleveland, 1959.
Most fumbles, game
10—Philadelphia/Pittsburgh vs. New York, October 9, 1943.
  Detroit at Minnesota, November 12, 1967.
  Kansas City vs. Houston, October 12, 1969.
  San Francisco at Detroit, December 17, 1978.
Most fumbles by both teams, game
14—Washington 8, Pittsburgh 6, November 14, 1937.
  Chicago Bears 7, Cleveland 7, November 24, 1940.
  St. Louis 8, New York Giants 6, September 17, 1961.
  Kansas City 10, Houston 4, October 12, 1969.

LOST
Most fumbles lost, season
36—Chicago Cardinals, 1959.

Fewest fumbles lost, season
3—Philadelphia, 1938.
  Minnesota, 1980.
Most fumbles lost, game
8—St. Louis at Washington, October 25, 1976.
  Cleveland at Pittsburgh, December 23, 1990.

RECOVERED
Most fumbles recovered (own and opponents'), season
58—Minnesota, 1963.
Fewest fumbles recovered (own and opponents'), season
9—San Francisco, 1982.
Most fumbles recovered (own and opponents'), game
10—Denver vs. Buffalo, December 13, 1964.
  Pittsburgh vs. Houston, December 9, 1973.
  Washington vs. St. Louis, October 25, 1976.
Most fumbles recovered (own), season
37—Chicago Bears, 1938.
Fewest fumbles recovered (own), season
2—Washington, 1958.

TOUCHDOWNS
Most touchdowns on fumbles recovered (own and opponents'), season
5—Chicago Bears, 1942.
  Los Angeles, 1952.
  San Francisco, 1965.
  Oakland, 1978.
Most touchdowns on own fumbles recovered, season
2—Held by many teams. Last team: Miami, 1996.
Most touchdowns on fumbles recovered (own and opponents'), game
2—Held by many teams.
Most touchdowns on fumbles recovered (own and opponents'), game
3—Detroit 2, Minnesota 1, December 9, 1962.
  Green Bay 2, Dallas 1, November 29, 1964.
  Oakland 2, Buffalo 1, December 24, 1967.
Most touchdowns on own fumbles recovered, game
1—Held by many teams.
Most touchdowns on opponents' fumbles recovered by both teams, game
3—Green Bay 2, Dallas 1, November 29, 1964.
  Oakland 2, Buffalo 1, December 24, 1967.

TURNOVERS
Most turnovers, season
63—San Francisco, 1978.
Fewest turnovers, season
12—Kansas City, 1982.
Most turnovers, game
12—Detroit vs. Chicago Bears, November 22, 1942.
  Chicago Cardinals vs. Philadelphia, September 24, 1950.
  Pittsburgh vs. Philadelphia, December 12, 1965.
Most turnovers by both teams, game
17—Detroit 12, Chicago Bears 5, November 22, 1942.
  Boston 9, Philadelphia 8, December 8, 1946.

PUNT RETURNS
Most punt returns, season
71—Pittsburgh, 1976.
  Tampa Bay, 1979.
  Los Angeles Raiders, 1985.
Fewest punt returns, season
12—Baltimore, 1981.
  San Diego, 1982.
Most punt returns, game
12—Philadelphia at Cleveland, December 3, 1950.
Most punt returns by both teams, game
17—Philadelphia 12, Cleveland 5, December 3, 1950.

YARDS

Most yards, season
785—Los Angeles Raiders, 1985.
Fewest yards, season
27—St. Louis, 1965.
Most yards, game
231—Detroit vs. San Francisco, October 6, 1963.
Most yards by both teams, game
282—Los Angeles 219, Atlanta 63, October 11, 1981.

TOUCHDOWNS

Most touchdowns, season
5—Chicago Cardinals, 1959.
Most touchdowns, game
2—Held by many teams. Last team: Cleveland vs. Pittsburgh, October 24, 1993.
Most touchdowns by both teams, game
2—Occurred many times. Last time: Cleveland 2, Pittsburgh 0, October 24, 1993.

KICKOFF RETURNS

Most kickoff returns, season
38—New Orleans, 1980.
Fewest kickoff returns, season
17—New York Giants, 1944.
Most kickoff returns, game
12—New York Giants at Washington, November 27, 1966.
Most kickoff returns by both teams, game
19—New York Giants 12, Washington 7, November 27, 1966.

YARDS

Most yards, season
1,973—New Orleans, 1980.
Fewest yards, season
282—New York Giants, 1940.
Most yards, game
362—Detroit at Los Angeles, October 29, 1950.
Most yards by both teams, game
560—Detroit 362, Los Angeles 198, October 29, 1950.

TOUCHDOWNS

Most touchdowns, season
4—Green Bay, 1967.
  Chicago, 1970.
  Detroit, 1994.
Most touchdowns, game
2—Chicago Bears at Green Bay, September 22, 1940.
  Chicago Bears vs. Green Bay, November 9, 1952.
  Philadelphia vs. Dallas, November 6, 1966.
  Green Bay vs. Cleveland, November 12, 1967.
  Los Angeles Rams vs. Green Bay, November 24, 1985.
  New Orleans vs. Los Angeles Rams, October 23, 1994.
Most touchdowns by both teams, game (each team scoring)
2—Occurred many times. Last time: Houston 1, Pittsburgh 1, December 4, 1988.

PENALTIES

Most penalties, season
156—L.A. Raiders, 1994.
Fewest penalties, season
19—Detroit, 1937.
Most penalties, game
22—Brooklyn at Green Bay, September 17, 1944.
  Chicago Bears at Philadelphia, November 26, 1944.
Most penalties by both teams, game
37—Cleveland 21, Chicago Bears 16, November 25, 1951.
Fewest penalties, game
0—Held by many teams. Last team: San Francisco vs. Philadelphia, November 29, 1992.
Fewest penalties by both teams, game
0—Brooklyn 0, Pittsburgh 0, October 28, 1934.
  Brooklyn 0, Boston 0, September 28, 1936.
  Cleveland 0, Chicago Bears 0, October 9, 1938.
  Pittsburgh 0, Philadelphia 0, November 10, 1940.

YARDS PENALIZED

Most yards penalized, season
1,274—Oakland, 1969.
Fewest yards penalized, season
139—Detroit, 1937.
Most yards penalized, game
209—Cleveland vs. Chicago Bears, November 25, 1951.
Most yards penalized by both teams, game
374—Cleveland 209, Chicago Bears 165, November 25, 1951.
Fewest yards penalized, game
0—Held by many teams. Last team: San Francisco vs. Philadelphia, November 29, 1992.
Fewest yards penalized by both teams, game
0—Brooklyn 0, Pittsburgh 0, October 28, 1934.
  Brooklyn 0, Boston 0, September 28, 1936.
  Cleveland 0, Chicago Bears 0, October 9, 1938.
  Pittsburgh 0, Philadelphia 0, November 10, 1940.

TEAM DEFENSE

RUSHING

YARDS ALLOWED

Most yards allowed, season
3,228—Buffalo, 1978.
Fewest yards allowed, season
519—Chicago Bears, 1942.

TOUCHDOWNS ALLOWED

Most touchdowns allowed, season
36—Oakland, 1961.
Fewest touchdowns allowed, season
2—Detroit, 1934.
  Dallas, 1968.
  Minnesota, 1971.

PASSING

YARDS ALLOWED

Most yards allowed, season
4,751—Atlanta, 1995.
Fewest yards allowed, season
545—Philadelphia, 1934.

TOUCHDOWNS ALLOWED

Most touchdowns allowed, season
40—Denver, 1963.
Fewest touchdowns allowed, season
1—Portsmouth, 1932.
  Philadelphia, 1934.

YARDS ALLOWED

(RUSHING AND PASSING)

Most yards allowed rushing and passing, season
6,793—Baltimore, 1981.
Fewest yards allowed rushing and passing, season
1,539—Chicago Cardinals, 1934.

SCORING

POINTS ALLOWED

Most points allowed, season
533—Baltimore, 1981.
Fewest points allowed, season (since 1932)
44—Chicago Bears, 1932.

SHUTOUTS

Most shutouts, season
10—Pottsville, 1926 (won nine, tied one).
  New York Giants, 1927 (won nine, tied one).

Most consecutive shutouts
13—Akron, 1920 through 1921 (won 10, tied three).

TOUCHDOWNS ALLOWED

Most touchdowns allowed, season
68—Baltimore, 1981.
Fewest touchdowns allowed, season (since 1932)
6—Chicago Bears, 1932.
Brooklyn, 1933.

FIRST DOWNS ALLOWED

Most first downs allowed, season
406—Baltimore, 1981.
Fewest first downs allowed, season
77—Detroit, 1935.
Most first downs allowed by rushing, season
179—Detroit, 1985.
Fewest first downs allowed by rushing, season
35—Chicago Bears, 1942.
Most first downs allowed by passing, season
230—Atlanta, 1995.
Fewest first downs allowed by passing, season
33—Chicago Bears, 1943.
Most first downs allowed by penalties, season
48—Houston, 1985.
Fewest first downs allowed by penalties, season
1—Boston, 1944.

INTERCEPTIONS

Most interceptions, season
49—San Diego, 1961.
Fewest interceptions, season
3—Houston, 1982.
Most interceptions, game
9—Green Bay at Detroit, October 24, 1943.
Philadelphia at Pittsburgh, December 12, 1965.
Most yards returning interceptions, season
929—San Diego, 1961.
Fewest yards returning interceptions, season
5—Los Angeles, 1959.
Most yards returning interceptions, game
325—Seattle vs. Kansas City, November 4, 1984.
Most touchdowns returning interceptions, season
9—San Diego, 1961.
Most touchdowns returning interceptions, game
4—Seattle vs. Kansas City, November 4, 1984.
Most touchdowns returning interceptions by both teams, game
4—Philadelphia 3, Pittsburgh 1, December 12, 1965.
Seattle 4, Kansas City 0, November 4, 1984.

FUMBLES

Most opponents' fumbles forced, season
50—Minnesota, 1963.
San Francisco, 1978.
Fewest opponents' fumbles forced, season
11—Cleveland, 1956.
Baltimore, 1982.

RECOVERED

Most opponents' fumbles recovered, season
31—Minnesota, 1963.
Fewest opponents' fumbles recovered, season
3—Los Angeles, 1974.
Most opponents' fumbles recovered, game
8—Washington vs. St. Louis, October 25, 1976.
Pittsburgh vs. Cleveland, December 23, 1990.

TOUCHDOWNS

Most touchdowns on opponents' fumbles recovered, season
4—Held by many teams. Last team: Atlanta, 1991.
Most touchdowns on opponents' fumbles recovered, game
2—Held by many teams. Last team: Cincinnati at Seattle,
September 6, 1992.

TURNOVERS

Most opponents' turnovers, season
66—San Diego, 1961.
Fewest opponents' turnovers, season
11—Baltimore, 1982.
Most opponents' turnovers, game
12—Chicago Bears at Detroit, November 22, 1942.
Philadelphia at Chicago Cardinals, September 24, 1950.
Philadelphia at Pittsburgh, December 12, 1965.

SACKS

Most sacks, season
72—Chicago, 1984.
Fewest sacks, season
11—Baltimore, 1982.
Most sacks, game
12—Dallas at Pittsburgh, November 20, 1966.
St. Louis at Baltimore, October 26, 1980.
Chicago at Detroit, December 16, 1984.
Dallas at Houston, September 29, 1985.

PUNTS RETURNED

Most punts returned by opponents, season
71—Tampa Bay, 1976.
Tampa Bay, 1977.
Fewest punts returned by opponents, season
7—Washington, 1962.
San Diego, 1982.
Most yards allowed on punts returned by opponents, season
932—Green Bay, 1949.
Fewest yards allowed on punts returned by opponents, season
22—Green Bay, 1967.
Most touchdowns allowed on punts returned by opponents, season
4—New York, 1959.
Atlanta, 1992.

KICKOFFS RETURNED

Most kickoffs returned by opponents, season
91—Washington, 1983.
Fewest kickoffs returned by opponents, season
10—Brooklyn, 1943.
Most yards allowed on kickoffs returned by opponents, season
2,045—Kansas City, 1966.
Fewest yards allowed on kickoffs returned by opponents, season
225—Brooklyn, 1943.
Most touchdowns allowed on kickoffs returned by opponents, season
3—Minnesota, 1963.
Dallas, 1966.
Minnesota, 1970.
Detroit, 1980.
Pittsburgh, 1986.

STATISTICAL LEADERS

CAREER MILESTONES

TOP 20 RUSHERS

Player	League	Years	Att.	Yds.	Avg.	Long	TD
Walter Payton	NFL	13	3838	16726	4.4	76	110
Eric Dickerson	NFL	11	2996	13259	4.4	85	90
Tony Dorsett	NFL	12	2936	12739	4.3	99	77
Jim Brown	NFL	9	2359	12312	5.2	80	106
Franco Harris	NFL	13	2949	12120	4.1	75	91
Marcus Allen*	NFL	15	2898	11738	4.1	61	112
Barry Sanders*	NFL	8	2384	11725	4.9	85	84
John Riggins	NFL	14	2916	11352	3.9	66	104
O.J. Simpson	AFL-NFL	11	2404	11236	4.7	94	61
Thurman Thomas*	NFL	9	2566	10762	4.2	80	62
Ottis Anderson	NFL	14	2562	10273	4.0	76	81
Emmitt Smith*	NFL	7	2334	10160	4.4	75	108
Joe Perry	AAFC-NFL	16	1929	9723	5.0	78	71
Earl Campbell	NFL	8	2187	9407	4.3	81	74
Jim Taylor	NFL	10	1941	8597	4.4	84	83
Herschel Walker*	NFL	11	1948	8205	4.2	91	61
Roger Craig	NFL	11	1991	8189	4.1	71	56
Gerald Riggs	NFL	10	1989	8188	4.1	58	69
Larry Csonka	AFL-NFL	11	1891	8081	4.3	54	64
Freeman McNeil	NFL	12	1798	8074	4.5	69	38

*Active through 1996 season.

TOP 20 PASSERS

Player	League	Years	Att.	Comp.	Yds.	TD	Int.	Rating Pts.
Steve Young*	NFL	12	3192	2059	25479	174	85	96.2
Joe Montana	NFL	15	5391	3409	40551	273	139	92.3
Brett Favre*	NFL	6	2693	1667	18724	147	79	88.6
Dan Marino*	NFL	14	6904	4134	51636	369	209	88.3
Otto Graham	AAFC-NFL	10	2626	1464	23584	174	135	86.6
Jim Kelly*	NFL	11	4779	2874	35467	237	175	84.4
Roger Staubach	NFL	11	2958	1685	22700	153	109	83.4
Troy Aikman*	NFL	8	3178	2000	22733	110	98	83.0
Neil Lomax	NFL	8	3153	1817	22771	136	90	82.7
Sonny Jurgensen	NFL	18	4262	2433	32224	255	189	82.625
Len Dawson	NFL-AFL	19	3741	2136	28711	239	183	82.555
Jeff Hostetler*	NFL	11	2194	1278	15531	89	61	82.1
Ken Anderson	NFL	16	4475	2654	32838	197	160	81.9
Bernie Kosar*	NFL	12	3365	1994	23301	124	87	81.8
Danny White	NFL	13	2950	1761	21959	155	132	81.7
Dave Krieg*	NFL	17	5288	3092	37946	261	199	81.5
Warren Moon*	NFL	13	6000	3514	43787	254	208	81.0
Neil O'Donnell*	NFL	7	2059	1179	14014	72	46	80.507
Scott Mitchell*	NFL	6	1507	853	10516	71	49	80.484
Bart Starr	NFL	16	3149	1808	24718	152	138	80.465

*Active through 1996 season.

TOP 20 RECEIVERS

Player	League	Years	No.	Yds.	Avg.	Long	TD
Jerry Rice*	NFL	12	1050	16377	15.6	96	154
Art Monk	NFL	16	940	12721	13.5	79	68
Steve Largent	NFL	14	819	13089	16.0	74	100
Henry Ellard*	NFL	14	775	13177	17.0	81	61
Andre Reed*	NFL	12	766	10884	14.2	83	75
James Lofton	NFL	16	764	14004	18.3	80	75
Charlie Joiner	AFL-NFL	18	750	12146	16.2	87	65
Gary Clark	NFL	11	699	10856	15.5	84	65
Cris Carter*	NFL	10	667	8367	12.5	80	76
Ozzie Newsome	NFL	13	662	7980	12.1	74	47
Irving Fryar*	NFL	13	650	10111	15.6	80	69
Charley Taylor	NFL	13	649	9110	14.0	88	79
Drew Hill	NFL	15	634	9831	15.5	81	60
Don Maynard	NFL-AFL	15	633	11834	18.7	87	88
Raymond Berry	NFL	13	631	9275	14.7	70	68

Player	League	Years	No.	Yds.	Avg.	Long	TD
Sterling Sharpe	NFL	7	595	8134	13.7	79	65
Michael Irvin*	NFL	9	591	9500	16.1	87	52
Harold Carmichael	NFL	14	590	8985	15.2	85	79
Fred Biletnikoff	AFL-NFL	14	589	8974	15.2	82	76
Bill Brooks*	NFL	11	583	8001	13.7	84	46

*Active through 1996 season.

TOP 20 SCORERS

Player	League	Years	TD	XP Made	FG Made	Total
George Blanda	NFL-AFL	26	9	943	335	2002
Nick Lowery*	NFL	18	0	562	383	1711
Jan Stenerud	AFL-NFL	19	0	580	373	1699
Lou Groza	AAFC-NFL	21	1	810	264	1608
Gary Anderson*	NFL	15	0	488	356	1556
Morten Andersen*	NFL	15	0	472	355	1537
Eddie Murray	NFL	16	0	498	325	1473
Pat Leahy	NFL	18	0	558	304	1470
Norm Johnson*	NFL	15	0	552	300	1452
Jim Turner	AFL-NFL	16	1	521	304	1439
Matt Bahr	NFL	17	0	522	300	1422
Mark Moseley	NFL	16	0	482	300	1382
Jim Bakken	NFL	17	0	534	282	1380
Fred Cox	NFL	15	0	519	282	1365
Jim Breech	NFL	14	0	517	243	1246
Chris Bahr	NFL	14	0	490	241	1213
Kevin Butler*	NFL	12	0	404	257	1175
Gino Cappelletti	AFL-NFL	11	42	350	†176	†1130
Ray Wersching	NFL	15	0	456	222	1122
Al Del Greco*	NFL	13	0	403	236	1111

*Active through 1996 season.
†Includes four two-point conversions.

YEAR BY YEAR

AFC

RUSHING
(Based on most net yards)

	Net Yds.	Att.	TD
1960—Abner Haynes, Dallas	875	156	9
1961—Billy Cannon, Houston	948	200	6
1962—Cookie Gilchrist, Buffalo	1096	214	13
1963—Clem Daniels, Oakland	1099	215	3
1964—Cookie Gilchrist, Buffalo	981	230	6
1965—Paul Lowe, San Diego	1121	222	7
1966—Jim Nance, Boston	1458	299	11
1967—Jim Nance, Boston	1216	269	7
1968—Paul Robinson, Cincinnati	1023	238	8
1969—Dick Post, San Diego	873	182	6
1970—Floyd Little, Denver	901	209	3
1971—Floyd Little, Denver	1133	284	6
1972—O.J. Simpson, Buffalo	1251	292	6
1973—O.J. Simpson, Buffalo	2003	332	12
1974—Otis Armstrong, Denver	1407	263	9
1975—O.J. Simpson, Buffalo	1817	329	16
1976—O.J. Simpson, Buffalo	1503	290	8
1977—Mark van Eeghen, Oakland	1273	324	7
1978—Earl Campbell, Houston	1450	302	13
1979—Earl Campbell, Houston	1697	368	19
1980—Earl Campbell, Houston	1934	373	13
1981—Earl Campbell, Houston	1376	361	10
1982—Freeman McNeil, N.Y. Jets	786	151	6
1983—Curt Warner, Seattle	1449	335	13
1984—Earnest Jackson, San Diego	1179	296	8
1985—Marcus Allen, L.A. Raiders	1759	380	11
1986—Curt Warner, Seattle	1481	319	13
1987—Eric Dickerson, Indianapolis	1288	283	6
1988—Eric Dickerson, Indianapolis	1659	388	14
1989—Christian Okoye, Kansas City	1480	370	12
1990—Thurman Thomas, Buffalo	1297	271	11
1991—Thurman Thomas, Buffalo	1407	288	7
1992—Barry Foster, Pittsburgh	1690	390	11
1993—Thurman Thomas, Buffalo	1315	355	6
1994—Chris Warren, Seattle	1545	333	9
1995—Curtis Martin, New England	1487	368	14
1996—Terrell Davis, Denver	1538	345	13

PASSING
(Based on highest passer rating among qualifiers*)

	Att.	Com.	Yds.	TD	Int.	Rat.
1960— Jack Kemp, Chargers	406	211	3018	20	25	67.1
1961— George Blanda, Hou.	362	187	3330	36	22	91.3
1962— Len Dawson, Dal.	310	189	2759	29	17	98.3
1963— Tobin Rote, S.D.	286	170	2510	20	17	86.7
1964— Len Dawson, K.C.	354	199	2879	30	18	89.9
1965— John Hadl, S.D.	348	174	2798	20	21	71.3
1966— Len Dawson, K.C.	284	159	2527	26	10	101.7
1967— Daryle Lamonica, Oak.	425	220	3228	30	20	80.8
1968— Len Dawson, K.C.	224	131	2109	17	9	98.6
1969— Greg Cook, Cin.	197	106	1854	15	11	88.3
1970— Daryle Lamonica, Oak.	356	179	2516	22	15	76.5
1971— Bob Griese, Mia.	263	145	2089	19	9	90.9
1972— Earl Morrall, Mia.	150	83	1360	11	7	91.0
1973— Ken Stabler, Oak.	260	163	1997	14	10	88.5
1974— Ken Anderson, Cin.	328	213	2667	18	10	95.9
1975— Ken Anderson, Cin.	377	228	3169	21	11	94.1
1976— Ken Stabler, Oak.	291	194	2737	27	17	103.7
1977— Bob Griese, Mia.	307	180	2252	22	13	88.0
1978— Terry Bradshaw, Pit.	368	207	2915	28	20	84.8
1979— Dan Fouts, S.D.	530	332	4082	24	24	82.6
1980— Brian Sipe, Cle.	554	337	4132	30	14	91.4
1981— Ken Anderson, Cin.	479	300	3754	29	10	98.5
1982— Ken Anderson, Cin.	309	218	2495	12	9	95.5
1983— Dan Marino, Mia.	296	173	2210	20	6	96.0
1984— Dan Marino, Mia.	564	362	5084	48	17	108.9

	Att.	Com.	Yds.	TD	Int.	Rat.
85— Ken O'Brien, NYJ	488	297	3888	25	8	96.2
86— Dan Marino, Mia.	623	378	4746	44	23	92.5
87— Bernie Kosar, Cle.	389	241	3033	22	9	95.4
88— Boomer Esiason, Cin.	388	223	3572	28	14	97.4
89— Boomer Esiason, Cin.	455	258	3525	28	11	92.1
90— Jim Kelly, Buf.	346	219	2829	24	9	101.2
91— Jim Kelly, Buf.	474	304	3844	33	17	97.6
92— Warren Moon, Hou.	346	224	2521	18	12	89.3
93— John Elway, Den.	551	348	4030	25	10	92.8
94— Dan Marino, Mia.	615	385	4453	30	17	89.2
95— Jim Harbaugh, Ind.	314	200	2575	17	5	100.7
96— John Elway, Den.	466	287	3328	26	14	89.2

This chart includes passer rating points for all leaders, although the new rating system was not used for determining leading quarterbacks prior to 1973. The old system was less equitable, yet similar to the new in that the rating was based on percentage of completions, touchdown passes, percentage of interceptions and average gain in yards.

RECEIVING
(Based on most receptions)

	No.	Yds.	TD
60—Lionel Taylor, Denver	92	1235	12
61—Lionel Taylor, Denver	100	1176	4
62—Lionel Taylor, Denver	77	908	4
63—Lionel Taylor, Denver	78	1101	10
64—Charley Hennigan, Houston	101	1546	8
65—Lionel Taylor, Denver	85	1131	6
66—Lance Alworth, San Diego	73	1383	13
67—George Sauer, N.Y. Jets	75	1189	6
68—Lance Alworth, San Diego	68	1312	10
69—Lance Alworth, San Diego	64	1003	4
70—Marlin Briscoe, Buffalo	57	1036	8
71—Fred Biletnikoff, Oakland	61	929	9
72—Fred Biletnikoff, Oakland	58	802	7
73—Fred Willis, Houston	57	371	1
74—Lydell Mitchell, Baltimore	72	544	2
75—Reggie Rucker, Cleveland	60	770	3
Lydell Mitchell, Baltimore	60	544	4
76—MacArthur Lane, Kansas City	66	686	1
77—Lydell Mitchell, Baltimore	71	620	4
78—Steve Largent, Seattle	71	1168	8
79—Joe Washington, Baltimore	82	750	3
80—Kellen Winslow, San Diego	89	1290	9
81—Kellen Winslow, San Diego	88	1075	10
82—Kellen Winslow, San Diego	54	721	6
83—Todd Christensen, L.A. Raiders	92	1247	12
84—Ozzie Newsome, Cleveland	89	1001	5
85—Lionel James, San Diego	86	1027	6
86—Todd Christensen, L.A. Raiders	95	1153	8
87—Al Toon, N.Y. Jets	68	976	5
88—Al Toon, N.Y. Jets	93	1067	5
89—Andre Reed, Buffalo	88	1312	9
90—Haywood Jeffires, Houston	74	1048	8
Drew Hill, Houston	74	1019	5
91—Haywood Jeffires, Houston	100	1181	7
92—Haywood Jeffires, Houston	90	913	9
93—Reggie Langhorne, Indianapolis	85	1038	3
94—Ben Coates, New England	96	1174	7
95—Carl Pickens, Cincinnati	99	1234	17
96—Carl Pickens, Cincinnati	100	1180	12

SCORING
(Based on most total points)

	TD	PAT	FG	Tot.
60— Gene Mingo, Denver	6	33	18	123
61—Gino Cappelletti, Boston	8	48	17	147
62—Gene Mingo, Denver	4	32	27	137
63—Gino Cappelletti, Boston	2	35	22	113
64—Gino Cappelletti, Boston	7	36	25	155
65—Gino Cappelletti, Boston	9	27	17	132
66—Gino Cappelletti, Boston	6	35	16	119
67—George Blanda, Oakland	0	56	20	116
68—Jim Turner, N.Y. Jets	0	43	34	145
69—Jim Turner, N.Y. Jets	0	33	32	129
70—Jan Stenerud, Kansas City	0	26	30	116
1971—Garo Yepremian, Miami	0	33	28	117
1972—Bobby Howfield, N.Y. Jets	0	40	27	121
1973—Roy Gerela, Pittsburgh	0	36	29	123
1974—Roy Gerela, Pittsburgh	0	33	20	93
1975—O.J. Simpson, Buffalo	23	0	0	138
1976—Toni Linhart, Baltimore	0	49	20	109
1977—Errol Mann, Oakland	0	39	20	99
1978—Pat Leahy, N.Y. Jets	0	41	22	107
1979—John Smith, New England	0	46	23	115
1980—John Smith, New England	0	51	26	129
1981—Jim Breech, Cincinnati	0	49	22	115
Nick Lowery, Kansas City	0	37	26	115
1982—Marcus Allen, L.A. Raiders	14	0	0	84
1983—Gary Anderson, Pittsburgh	0	38	27	119
1984—Gary Anderson, Pittsburgh	0	45	24	117
1985—Gary Anderson, Pittsburgh	0	40	33	139
1986—Tony Franklin, New England	0	44	32	140
1987—Jim Breech, Cincinnati	0	25	24	97
1988—Scott Norwood, Buffalo	0	33	32	129
1989—David Treadwell, Denver	0	39	27	120
1990—Nick Lowery, Kansas City	0	37	34	139
1991—Pete Stoyanovich, Miami	0	28	31	121
1992—Pete Stoyanovich, Miami	0	34	30	124
1993—Jeff Jaeger, L.A. Raiders	0	27	35	132
1994—John Carney, San Diego	0	33	34	135
1995—Norm Johnson, Pittsburgh	0	39	34	141
1996—Cary Blanchard, Indianapolis	0	27	36	135

FIELD GOALS

	No.
1960— Gene Mingo, Denver	18
1961— Gino Cappelletti, Boston	17
1962— Gene Mingo, Denver	27
1963— Gino Cappelletti, Boston	22
1964— Gino Cappelletti, Boston	25
1965— Pete Gogolak, Buffalo	28
1966— Mike Mercer, Oakland-Kansas City	21
1967— Jan Stenerud, Kansas City	21
1968— Jim Turner, N.Y. Jets	34
1969— Jim Turner, N.Y. Jets	32
1970— Jan Stenerud, Kansas City	30
1971— Garo Yepremian, Miami	28
1972— Roy Gerela, Pittsburgh	28
1973— Roy Gerela, Pittsburgh	29
1974— Roy Gerela, Pittsburgh	20
1975— Jan Stenerud, Kansas City	22
1976— Jan Stenerud, Kansas City	21
1977— Errol Mann, Oakland	20
1978— Pat Leahy, N.Y. Jets	22
1979— John Smith, New England	23
1980— John Smith, New England	26
Fred Steinfort, Denver	26
1981— Nick Lowery, Kansas City	26
1982— Nick Lowery, Kansas City	19
1983— Raul Allegre, Baltimore	30
1984— Gary Anderson, Pittsburgh	24
Matt Bahr, Cleveland	24
1985— Gary Anderson, Pittsburgh	33
1986— Tony Franklin, New England	32
1987— Dean Biasucci, Indianapolis	24
Jim Breech, Cincinnati	24
1988— Scott Norwood, Buffalo	32
1989— David Treadwell, Denver	27
1990— Nick Lowery, Kansas City	34
1991— Pete Stoyanovich, Miami	31
1992— Pete Stoyanovich, Miami	30
1993— Jeff Jaeger, L.A. Raiders	35
1994— John Carney, San Diego	34
1995— Norm Johnson, Pittsburgh	34
1996— Cary Blanchard, Indianapolis	36

INTERCEPTIONS

	No.	Yds.
1960— Austin Gonsoulin, Denver	11	98
1961— Bill Atkins, Buffalo	10	158

		No.	Yds.
1962—	Lee Riley, N.Y. Jets	11	122
1963—	Fred Glick, Houston	12	180
1964—	Dainard Paulson, N.Y. Jets	12	157
1965—	W.K. Hicks, Houston	9	156
1966—	Johnny Robinson, Kansas City	10	136
	Bobby Hunt, Kansas City	10	113
1967—	Miller Farr, Houston	10	264
	Tom Janik, Buffalo	10	222
	Dick Westmoreland, Miami	10	127
1968—	Dave Grayson, Oakland	10	195
1969—	Emmitt Thomas, Kansas City	9	146
1970—	Johnny Robinson, Kansas City	10	155
1971—	Ken Houston, Houston	9	220
1972—	Mike Sensibaugh, Kansas City	8	65
1973—	Dick Anderson, Miami	8	136
	Mike Wagner, Pittsburgh	8	134
1974—	Emmitt Thomas, Kansas City	12	214
1975—	Mel Blount, Pittsburgh	11	121
1976—	Ken Riley, Cincinnati	9	141
1977—	Lyle Blackwood, Baltimore	10	163
1978—	Thom Darden, Cleveland	10	200
1979—	Mike Reinfeldt, Houston	12	205
1980—	Lester Hayes, Oakland	13	273
1981—	John Harris, Seattle	10	155
1982—	Ken Riley, Cincinnati	5	88
	Bobby Jackson, N.Y. Jets	5	84
	Dwayne Woodruff, Pittsburgh	5	53
	Donnie Shell, Pittsburgh	5	27
1983—	Ken Riley, Cincinnati	8	89
	Vann McElroy, Los Angeles	8	68
1984—	Kenny Easley, Seattle	10	126
1985—	Eugene Daniel, Indianapolis	8	53
	Albert Lewis, Kansas City	8	59
1986—	Deron Cherry, Kansas City	9	150
1987—	Mike Prior, Indianapolis	6	57
	Mark Kelso, Buffalo	6	25
	Keith Bostic, Houston	6	-14
1988—	Erik McMillan, N.Y. Jets	8	168
1989—	Felix Wright, Cleveland	9	91
1990—	Richard Johnson, Houston	8	100
1991—	Ronnie Lott, L.A. Raiders	8	52
1992—	Henry Jones, Buffalo	8	263
1993—	Nate Odomes, Buffalo	9	65
	Eugene Robinson, Seattle	9	80
1994—	Eric Turner, Cleveland	9	199
1995—	Willie Williams, Pittsburgh	7	122
1996—	Tyrone Braxton, Denver	9	128

PUNTING
(Based on highest average yardage per punt by qualifiers)

		No.	Avg.
1960—	Paul Maguire, L.A. Chargers	43	40.5
1961—	Bill Atkins, Buffalo	85	44.5
1962—	Jim Fraser, Denver	55	44.3
1963—	Jim Fraser, Denver	81	44.4
1964—	Jim Fraser, Denver	73	44.2
1965—	Jerrel Wilson, Kansas City	69	45.4
1966—	Bob Scarpitto, Denver	76	45.8
1967—	Bob Scarpitto, Denver	105	44.9
1968—	Jerrel Wilson, Kansas City	63	45.1
1969—	Dennis Partee, San Diego	71	44.6
1970—	Dave Lewis, Cincinnati	79	46.2
1971—	Dave Lewis, Cincinnati	72	44.8
1972—	Jerrel Wilson, Kansas City	66	44.8
1973—	Jerrel Wilson, Kansas City	80	45.5
1974—	Ray Guy, Oakland	74	42.2
1975—	Ray Guy, Oakland	68	43.8
1976—	Marv Bateman, Buffalo	86	42.8
1977—	Ray Guy, Oakland	59	43.4
1978—	Pat McInally, Cincinnati	91	43.1
1979—	Bob Grupp, Kansas City	89	43.6
1980—	Luke Prestridge, Denver	70	43.9
1981—	Pat McInally, Cincinnati	72	45.4
1982—	Luke Prestridge, Denver	45	45.0
1983—	Rohn Stark, Baltimore	91	45.3
1984—	Jim Arnold, Kansas City	98	44.9

		No.	Av
1985—	Rohn Stark, Indianapolis	78	45
1986—	Rohn Stark, Indianapolis	76	45
1987—	Ralf Mojsiejenko, San Diego	67	42
1988—	Harry Newsome, Pittsburgh	65	45
1989—	Greg Montgomery, Houston	56	43
1990—	Mike Horan, Denver	58	44
1991—	Reggie Roby, Miami	54	45
1992—	Greg Montgomery, Houston	53	46
1993—	Greg Montgomery, Houston	54	45
1994—	Jeff Gossett, L.A. Raiders	77	43
1995—	Rick Tuten, Seattle	83	45
1996—	John Kidd, Miami	78	46

PUNT RETURNS
(Based on most total yards)

		No.	Yds.	Av
1960—	Abner Haynes, Dallas	14	215	15
1961—	Dick Christy, N.Y. Jets	18	383	21
1962—	Dick Christy, N.Y. Jets	15	250	16
1963—	Claude Gibson, Oakland	26	307	11
1964—	Bobby Jancik, Houston	12	220	18
1965—	Leslie Duncan, San Diego	30	464	15
1966—	Leslie Duncan, San Diego	18	238	13
1967—	Floyd Little, Denver	16	270	16
1968—	Noland Smith, Kansas City	18	270	15
1969—	Bill Thompson, Denver	25	288	11
1970—	Ed Podolak, Kansas City	23	311	13
1971—	Leroy Kelly, Cleveland	30	292	9
1972—	Chris Farasopolous, N.Y. Jets	17	179	10
1973—	Ron Smith, San Diego	27	352	15
1974—	Lemar Parrish, Cincinnati	18	338	18
1975—	Billy Johnson, Houston	40	612	18
1976—	Rick Upchurch, Denver	39	536	13
1977—	Billy Johnson, Houston	30	539	15
1978—	Rick Upchurch, Denver	36	493	13
1979—	Tony Nathan, Miami	28	306	10
1980—	J.T. Smith, Kansas City	40	581	14
1981—	James Brooks, San Diego	22	290	13
1982—	Rick Upchurch, Denver	15	242	16
1983—	Kirk Springs, N.Y. Jets	23	287	12
1984—	Mike Martin, Cincinnati	24	376	15
1985—	Irving Fryar, New England	37	520	14
1986—	Bobby Joe Edmonds, Seattle	34	419	12
1987—	Bobby Joe Edmonds, Seattle	20	251	12
1988—	Jojo Townsell, N.Y. Jets	35	409	11
1989—	Clarence Verdin, Indianapolis	23	296	12
1990—	Clarence Verdin, Indianapolis	31	396	12
1991—	Rod Woodson, Pittsburgh	28	320	11
1992—	Rod Woodson, Pittsburgh	32	364	11
1993—	Tim Brown, L.A. Raiders	40	465	11
1994—	Tim Brown, L.A. Raiders	40	487	12
1995—	Tamarick Vanover, Kansas City	51	540	10
1996—	David Meggett, New England	52	588	11

KICKOFF RETURNS
(Based on most total yards)

		No.	Yds.	Av
1960—	Ken Hall, Houston	19	594	31
1961—	Dave Grayson, Dallas	16	453	28
1962—	Bobby Jancik, Houston	24	726	30
1963—	Bobby Jancik, Houston	45	1317	29
1964—	Bo Roberson, Oakland	36	975	27
1965—	Abner Haynes, Denver	34	901	26
1966—	Goldie Sellers, Denver	19	541	28
1967—	Zeke Moore, Houston	14	405	28
1968—	George Atkinson, Oakland	32	802	25
1969—	Bill Thompson, Denver	19	594	31
1970—	Jim Duncan, Baltimore	20	707	35
1971—	Mercury Morris, Miami	15	423	28
1972—	Bruce Laird, Baltimore	29	843	29
1973—	Wallace Francis, Buffalo	23	687	29
1974—	Greg Pruitt, Cleveland	22	606	27
1975—	Harold Hart, Oakland	17	518	30
1976—	Duriel Harris, Miami	17	559	32
1977—	Raymond Clayborn, New England	20	869	31
1978—	Keith Wright, Cleveland	30	789	26

	No.	Yds.	Avg.
79— Larry Brunson, Oakland................	17	441	25.9
80— Horace Ivory, New England	36	992	27.6
81— Carl Roaches, Houston.................	28	769	27.5
82— Mike Mosley, Buffalo....................	18	487	27.1
83— Fulton Walker, Miami...................	36	962	26.7
84— Bobby Humphrey, N.Y. Jets..........	22	675	30.7
85— Glen Young, Cleveland.................	35	898	25.7
86— Lupe Sanchez, Pittsburgh	25	591	23.6
87— Paul Palmer, Kansas City.............	38	923	24.3
88— Tim Brown, L.A. Raiders	41	1098	26.8
89— Rod Woodson, Pittsburgh.............	36	982	27.3
90— Kevin Clark, Denver	20	505	25.3
91— Nate Lewis, San Diego	23	578	25.1
92— Jon Vaughn, New England	20	564	28.2
93— Clarence Verdin, Indianapolis	50	1050	21.0
94— Andre Coleman, San Diego	49	1293	26.4
95— Andre Coleman, San Diego	62	1411	22.8
96— Mel Gray, Houston......................	50	1224	24.5

SACKS

	No.
1982— Jesse Baker, Houston.............................	7.5
1983— Mark Gastineau, N.Y. Jets	19.0
1984— Mark Gastineau, N.Y. Jets	22.0
1985— Andre Tippett, New England.................	16.5
1986— Sean Jones, L.A. Raiders	15.5
1987— Andre Tippett, New England.................	12.5
1988— Greg Townsend, L.A. Raiders................	11.5
1989— Lee Williams, San Diego	14.0
1990— Derrick Thomas, Kansas City	20.0
1991— William Fuller, Houston........................	15.0
1992— Leslie O'Neal, San Diego	17.0
1993— Neil Smith, Kansas City........................	15.0
1994— Kevin Greene, Pittsburgh	14.0
1995— Bryce Paup, Buffalo	17.5
1996— Michael McCrary, Seattle	13.5
Bruce Smith, Buffalo	13.5

NFC

RUSHING
(Based on most net yards)

	Net Yds.	Att.	TD
60— Jim Brown, Cleveland	1257	215	9
61— Jim Brown, Cleveland	1408	305	8
62— Jim Taylor, Green Bay	1474	272	19
63— Jim Brown, Cleveland	1863	291	12
64— Jim Brown, Cleveland	1446	280	7
65— Jim Brown, Cleveland	1544	289	17
66— Gale Sayers, Chicago	1231	229	8
67— Leroy Kelly, Cleveland	1205	235	11
68— Leroy Kelly, Cleveland	1239	248	16
69— Gale Sayers, Chicago	1032	236	8
70— Larry Brown, Washington	1125	237	5
71— John Brockington, Green Bay	1105	216	4
72— Larry Brown, Washington	1216	285	8
73— John Brockington, Green Bay	1144	265	3
74— Lawrence McCutcheon, L.A. Rams..	1109	236	3
75— Jim Otis, St. Louis	1076	269	5
76— Walter Payton, Chicago...............	1390	311	13
77— Walter Payton, Chicago...............	1852	339	14
78— Walter Payton, Chicago...............	1395	333	11
79— Walter Payton, Chicago...............	1610	369	14
80— Walter Payton, Chicago...............	1460	317	6
81— George Rogers, New Orleans	1674	378	13
82— Tony Dorsett, Dallas	745	177	5
83— Eric Dickerson, L.A. Rams	1808	390	18
84— Eric Dickerson, L.A. Rams	2105	379	14
85— Gerald Riggs, Atlanta	1719	397	10
86— Eric Dickerson, L.A. Rams	1821	404	11
87— Charles White, L.A. Rams	1374	324	11
88— Herschel Walker, Dallas..............	1514	361	5
89— Barry Sanders, Detroit	1470	280	14
90— Barry Sanders, Detroit	1304	255	13
91— Emmitt Smith, Dallas	1563	365	12
92— Emmitt Smith, Dallas	1713	373	18
93— Emmitt Smith, Dallas	1486	283	9
94— Barry Sanders, Detroit	1883	331	7
95— Emmitt Smith, Dallas	1773	377	25
96— Barry Sanders, Detroit	1553	307	11

PASSING
(Based on highest passer rating among qualifiers*)

	Att.	Com.	Yds.	TD	Int.	Rat.
60— Milt Plum, Cle...............	250	151	2297	21	5	110.4
61— Milt Plum, Cle...............	302	177	2416	18	10	90.3
62— Bart Starr, G.B.	285	178	2438	12	9	90.7
63— Y.A. Tittle, NYG.............	367	221	3145	36	14	104.8
64— Bart Starr, G.B.	272	163	2144	15	4	97.1
65— Rudy Bukich, Chi.	312	176	2641	20	9	93.7
66— Bart Starr, G.B.	251	156	2257	14	3	105.0
67— Sonny Jurgensen, Was..	508	288	3747	31	16	87.3
68— Earl Morrall, Bal.	317	182	2909	26	17	93.2
69— Sonny Jurgensen, Was..	442	274	3102	22	15	85.4

	Att.	Com.	Yds.	TD	Int.	Rat.
1970— John Brodie, S.F.	378	223	2941	24	10	93.8
1971— Roger Staubach, Dal....	211	126	1882	15	4	104.8
1972— Norm Snead, NYG........	325	196	2307	17	12	84.0
1973— Roger Staubach, Dal.....	286	179	2428	23	15	94.6
1974— Sonny Jurgensen, Was..	167	107	1185	11	5	94.6
1975— Fran Tarkenton, Min....	425	273	2994	25	13	91.7
1976— James Harris, L.A.	158	91	1460	8	6	89.8
1977— Roger Staubach, Dal.....	361	210	2620	18	9	87.1
1978— Roger Staubach, Dal.....	413	231	3190	25	16	84.9
1979— Roger Staubach, Dal.....	461	267	3586	27	11	92.4
1980— Ron Jaworski, Phi........	451	257	3529	27	12	90.0
1981— Joe Montana, S.F.	488	311	3565	19	12	88.4
1982— Joe Theismann, Was.....	252	161	2033	13	9	91.3
1983— Steve Bartkowski, Atl. ...	432	274	3167	22	5	97.6
1984— Joe Montana, S.F.	432	279	3630	28	10	102.9
1985— Joe Montana, S.F.	494	303	3653	27	13	91.3
1986— Tommy Kramer, Min.	372	208	3000	24	10	92.6
1987— Joe Montana, S.F.	398	266	3054	31	13	102.1
1988— Wade Wilson, Min........	332	204	2746	15	9	91.5
1989— Joe Montana, S.F.	386	271	3521	26	8	112.4
1990— Phil Simms, NYG	311	184	2284	15	4	92.7
1991— Steve Young, S.F.	279	180	2517	17	8	101.8
1992— Steve Young, S.F.	402	268	3465	25	7	107.0
1993— Steve Young, S.F.	462	314	4023	29	16	101.5
1994— Steve Young, S.F.	461	324	3969	35	10	112.8
1995— Brett Favre, G.B.	570	359	4413	38	13	99.5
1996— Steve Young, S.F.	316	214	2410	14	6	97.2

*This chart includes passer rating points for all leaders, although the same rating system was not used for determining leading quarterbacks prior to 1973. The old system was less equitable, yet similar to the new in that the rating was based on percentage of completions, touchdown passes, percentage of interceptions and average gain in yards.

RECEIVING
(Based on most receptions)

	No.	Yds.	TD
1960—Raymond Berry, Baltimore............	74	1298	10
1961—Jim Phillips, L.A. Rams................	78	1092	5
1962—Bobby Mitchell, Washington	72	1384	11
1963—Bobby Joe Conrad, St. Louis	73	967	10
1964—Johnny Morris, Chicago...............	93	1200	10
1965—Dave Parks, San Francisco...........	80	1344	12
1966—Charley Taylor, Washington.........	72	1119	12
1967—Charley Taylor, Washington.........	70	990	9
1968—Clifton McNeil, San Francisco	71	994	7
1969—Dan Abramowicz, New Orleans.....	73	1015	7
1970—Dick Gordon, Chicago.................	71	1026	13
1971—Bob Tucker, N.Y. Giants	59	791	4
1972—Harold Jackson, Philadelphia........	62	1048	4
1973—Harold Carmichael, Philadelphia ...	67	1116	9
1974—Charles Young, Philadelphia.........	63	696	3
1975—Chuck Foreman, Minnesota	73	691	9
1976—Drew Pearson, Dallas..................	58	806	6
1977—Ahmad Rashad, Minnesota	51	681	2

	No.	Yds.	TD
1978—Rickey Young, Minnesota	88	704	5
1979—Ahmad Rashad, Minnesota	80	1156	9
1980—Earl Cooper, San Francisco	83	567	4
1981—Dwight Clark, San Francisco	85	1105	4
1982—Dwight Clark, San Francisco	60	913	5
1983—Roy Green, St. Louis	78	1227	14
Charlie Brown, Washington	78	1225	8
Earnest Gray, N.Y. Giants	78	1139	5
1984—Art Monk, Washington	106	1372	7
1985—Roger Craig, San Francisco	92	1016	6
1986—Jerry Rice, San Francisco	86	1570	15
1987—J.T. Smith, St. Louis	91	1117	8
1988—Henry Ellard, L.A. Rams	86	1414	10
1989—Sterling Sharpe, Green Bay	90	1423	12
1990—Jerry Rice, San Francisco	100	1502	13
1991—Michael Irvin, Dallas	93	1523	8
1992—Sterling Sharpe, Green Bay	108	1461	13
1993—Sterling Sharpe, Green Bay	112	1274	11
1994—Cris Carter, Minnesota	122	1256	7
1995—Herman Moore, Detroit	123	1686	14
1996—Jerry Rice, San Francisco	108	1254	8

SCORING
(Based on most total points)

	TD	PAT	FG	Tot.
1960— Paul Hornung, Green Bay	15	41	15	176
1961— Paul Hornung, Green Bay	10	41	15	146
1962— Jim Taylor, Green Bay	19	0	0	114
1963— Don Chandler, N.Y. Giants	0	52	18	106
1964— Lenny Moore, Baltimore	20	0	0	120
1965— Gale Sayers, Chicago	22	0	0	132
1966— Bruce Gossett, L.A. Rams	0	29	28	113
1967— Jim Bakken, St. Louis	0	36	27	117
1968— Leroy Kelly, Cleveland	20	0	0	120
1969— Fred Cox, Minnesota	0	43	26	121
1970— Fred Cox, Minnesota	0	35	30	125
1971— Curt Knight, Washington	0	27	29	114
1972— Chester Marcol, Green Bay	0	29	33	128
1973— David Ray, L.A. Rams	0	40	30	130
1974— Chester Marcol, Green Bay	0	19	25	94
1975— Chuck Foreman, Minnesota	22	0	0	132
1976— Mark Moseley, Washington	0	31	22	97
1977— Walter Payton, Chicago	16	0	0	96
1978— Frank Corral, L.A. Rams	0	31	29	118
1979— Mark Moseley, Washington	0	39	25	114
1980— Ed Murray, Detroit	0	35	27	116
1981— Ed Murray, Detroit	0	46	25	121
Rafael Septien, Dallas	0	40	27	121
1982— Wendell Tyler, L.A. Rams	13	0	0	78
1983— Mark Moseley, Washington	0	62	33	161
1984— Ray Wersching, S.F.	0	56	25	131
1985— Kevin Butler, Chicago	0	51	31	144
1986— Kevin Butler, Chicago	0	36	28	120
1987— Jerry Rice, San Francisco	23	0	0	138
1988— Mike Cofer, San Francisco	0	40	27	121
1989— Mike Cofer, San Francisco	0	49	29	136
1990— Chip Lohmiller, Washington	0	41	30	131
1991— Chip Lohmiller, Washington	0	56	31	149
1992— Morten Andersen, New Orleans	0	33	29	120
Chip Lohmiller, Washington	0	30	30	120
1993— Jason Hanson, Detroit	0	28	34	130
1994— Fuad Reveiz, Minnesota	0	30	34	132
1995— Emmitt Smith, Dallas	25	0	0	150
1996— John Kasay, Carolina	0	34	37	145

FIELD GOALS

	No.
1960— Tommy Davis, San Francisco	19
1961— Steve Myhra, Baltimore	21
1962— Lou Michaels, Pittsburgh	26
1963— Jim Martin, Baltimore	24
1964— Jim Bakken, St. Louis	25
1965— Fred Cox, Minnesota	23
1966— Bruce Gossett, L.A. Rams	28
1967— Jim Bakken, St. Louis	27
1968— Mac Percival, Chicago	25

	N
1969— Fred Cox, Minnesota	
1970— Fred Cox, Minnesota	
1971— Curt Knight, Washington	
1972— Chester Marcol, Green Bay	
1973— David Ray, L.A. Rams	
1974— Chester Marcol, Green Bay	
1975— Toni Fritsch, Dallas	
1976— Mark Moseley, Washington	
1977— Mark Moseley, Washington	
1978— Frank Corral, L.A. Rams	
1979— Mark Moseley, Washington	
1980— Eddie Murray, Detroit	
1981— Rafael Septien, Dallas	
1982— Mark Moseley, Washington	
1983— Ali Haji-Sheikh, N.Y. Giants	
1984— Paul McFadden, Philadelphia	
1985— Morten Andersen, New Orleans	
Kevin Butler, Chicago	
1986— Kevin Butler, Chicago	
1987— Morten Andersen, New Orleans	
1988— Mike Cofer, San Francisco	
1989— Rich Karlis, Minnesota	
1990— Chip Lohmiller, Washington	
1991— Chip Lohmiller, Washington	
1992— Chip Lohmiller, Washington	
1993— Jason Hanson, Detroit	
1994— Fuad Reveiz, Minnesota	
1995— Morten Andersen, Atlanta	
1996— John Kasay, Carolina	

INTERCEPTIONS

	No.	Yd
1960— Dave Baker, San Francisco	10	
Jerry Norton, St. Louis	10	
1961— Dick Lynch, N.Y. Giants	9	
1962— Willie Wood, Green Bay	9	13
1963— Dick Lynch, N.Y. Giants	9	25
Rosie Taylor, Chicago	9	1
1964— Paul Krause, Washington	12	1
1965— Bobby Boyd, Baltimore	9	
1966— Larry Wilson, St. Louis	10	1
1967— Lem Barney, Detroit	10	23
Dave Whitsell, New Orleans	10	17
1968— Willie Williams, N.Y. Giants	10	1
1969— Mel Renfro, Dallas	10	1
1970— Dick Le Beau, Detroit	9	
1971— Bill Bradley, Philadelphia	11	2
1972— Bill Bradley, Philadelphia	9	
1973— Bob Bryant, Minnesota	7	1
1974— Ray Brown, Atlanta	8	1
1975— Paul Krause, Minnesota	10	20
1976— Monte Jackson, L.A. Rams	10	1
1977— Rolland Lawrence, Atlanta	7	1
1978— Ken Stone, St. Louis	9	13
Willie Buchanon, Green Bay	9	
1979— Lemar Parrish, Washington	9	
1980— Nolan Cromwell, L.A. Rams	8	1
1981— Everson Walls, Dallas	11	1
1982— Everson Walls, Dallas	7	
1983— Mark Murphy, Washington	9	12
1984— Tom Flynn, Green Bay	9	1
1985— Everson Walls, Dallas	9	
1986— Ronnie Lott, San Francisco	10	13
1987— Barry Wilburn, Washington	9	1
1988— Scott Case, Atlanta	10	
1989— Eric Allen, Philadelphia	8	
1990— Mark Carrier, Chicago	10	
1991— Ray Crockett, Detroit	6	1
Tim McKyer, Atlanta	6	1
Deion Sanders, Atlanta	6	1
Aeneas Williams, Phoenix	6	1
1992— Aubray McMillian, Minnesota	8	15
1993— Deion Sanders, Atlanta	7	
1994— Aeneas Williams, Arizona	9	
1995— Orlando Thomas, Minnesota	9	1
1996— Keith Lyle, St. Louis	9	1

PUNTING
(Based on highest average yardage per punt by qualifiers)

		No.	Avg.
60—	Jerry Norton, St. Louis	39	45.6
61—	Yale Lary, Detroit	52	48.4
62—	Tommy Davis, San Francisco	48	45.8
63—	Yale Lary, Detroit	35	48.9
64—	Bobby Walden, Minnesota	72	46.4
65—	Gary Collins, Cleveland	65	46.7
66—	David Lee, Baltimore	49	45.6
67—	Billy Lothridge, Atlanta	87	43.7
68—	Billy Lothridge, Atlanta	75	44.3
69—	David Lee, Baltimore	50	45.3
70—	Julian Fagan, New Orleans	77	42.5
71—	Tom McNeill, Philadelphia	73	42.0
72—	Dave Chapple, L.A. Rams	53	44.2
73—	Tom Wittum, San Francisco	79	43.7
74—	Tom Blanchard, New Orleans	88	42.1
75—	Herman Weaver, Detroit	80	42.0
76—	John James, Atlanta	101	42.1
77—	Tom Blanchard, New Orleans	82	42.4
78—	Tom Skladany, Detroit	86	42.5
79—	Dave Jennings, N.Y. Giants	104	42.7
80—	Dave Jennings, N.Y. Giants	94	44.8
81—	Tom Skladany, Detroit	64	43.5
82—	Carl Birdsong, St. Louis	54	43.8
83—	Frank Garcia, Tampa Bay	95	42.2
84—	Brian Hansen, New Orleans	69	43.8
85—	Rick Donnelly, Atlanta	59	43.6
86—	Sean Landeta, N.Y. Giants	79	44.8
87—	Rick Donnelly, Atlanta	61	44.0
88—	Jim Arnold, Detroit	97	42.4
89—	Rich Camarillo, Phoenix	76	43.4
90—	Sean Landeta, N.Y. Giants	75	44.1
91—	Harry Newsome, Minnesota	68	45.5
92—	Harry Newsome, Minnesota	72	45.0
93—	Jim Arnold, Detroit	72	44.5
94—	Sean Landeta, L.A. Rams	78	44.8
95—	Sean Landeta, St. Louis	83	44.3
96—	Matt Turk, Washington	75	45.1

PUNT RETURNS
(Based on most total yards)

		No.	Yds.	Avg.
60—	Abe Woodson, San Francisco	13	174	13.4
61—	Willie Wood, Green Bay	14	225	16.1
62—	Pat Studstill, Detroit	29	457	15.8
63—	Dick James, Washington	16	214	13.4
64—	Tommy Watkins, Detroit	16	238	14.9
65—	Leroy Kelly, Cleveland	17	265	15.6
66—	Johnny Roland, St. Louis	20	221	11.1
67—	Ben Davis, Cleveland	18	229	12.7
68—	Bob Hayes, Dallas	15	312	20.8
69—	Alvin Haymond, L.A. Rams	33	435	13.2
70—	Bruce Taylor, San Francisco	43	516	12.0
71—	Les Duncan, Washington	22	233	10.6
72—	Ken Ellis, Green Bay	14	215	15.4
73—	Bruce Taylor, San Francisco	15	207	13.8
74—	Dick Jauron, Detroit	17	286	16.8
75—	Terry Metcalf, St. Louis	23	285	12.4
76—	Eddie Brown, Washington	48	646	13.5
77—	Larry Marshall, Philadelphia	46	489	10.6
78—	Jackie Wallace, L.A. Rams	52	618	11.9
79—	John Sciarra, Philadelphia	16	182	11.4
80—	Kenny Johnson, Atlanta	23	281	12.2
81—	LeRoy Irvin, L.A. Rams	46	615	13.4
82—	Billy Johnson, Atlanta	24	273	11.4
83—	Henry Ellard, L.A. Rams	16	217	13.6
84—	Henry Ellard, L.A. Rams	30	403	13.4
85—	Henry Ellard, L.A. Rams	37	501	13.5
86—	Vai Sikahema, St. Louis	43	522	12.1
87—	Mel Gray, New Orleans	24	352	14.7
88—	John Taylor, San Francisco	44	556	12.6

		No.	Yds.	Avg.
1989—	Walter Stanley, Detroit	36	496	13.8
1990—	Johnny Bailey, Chicago	36	399	11.1
1991—	Mel Gray, Detroit	25	385	15.4
1992—	Johnny Bailey, Phoenix	20	263	13.2
1993—	Tyrone Hughes, New Orleans	37	503	13.6
1994—	Brian Mitchell, Washington	32	452	14.1
1995—	Eric Guliford, Carolina	43	475	11.0
1996—	Desmond Howard, Green Bay	58	875	15.1

KICKOFF RETURNS
(Based on most total yards)

		No.	Yds.	Avg.
1960—	Tom Moore, Green Bay	12	397	33.1
1961—	Dick Bass, L.A. Rams	23	698	30.3
1962—	Abe Woodson, San Francisco	37	1157	31.3
1963—	Abe Woodson, San Francisco	29	935	32.3
1964—	Clarence Childs, N.Y. Giants	34	987	29.0
1965—	Tommy Watkins, Detroit	17	584	34.4
1966—	Gale Sayers, Chicago	23	718	31.2
1967—	Travis Williams, Green Bay	18	739	41.1
1968—	Preston Pearson, Baltimore	15	527	35.1
1969—	Bobby Williams, Detroit	17	563	33.1
1970—	Cecil Turner, Chicago	23	752	32.7
1971—	Travis Williams, L.A. Rams	25	743	29.7
1972—	Ron Smith, Chicago	30	924	30.8
1973—	Carl Garrett, Chicago	16	486	30.4
1974—	Terry Metcalf, St. Louis	20	623	31.2
1975—	Walter Payton, Chicago	14	444	31.7
1976—	Cullen Bryant, L.A. Rams	16	459	28.7
1977—	Wilbert Montgomery, Phila.	23	619	26.9
1978—	Steve Odom, Green Bay	25	677	27.1
1979—	Jimmy Edwards, Minnesota	44	1103	25.1
1980—	Rich Mauti, New Orleans	31	798	27.6
1981—	Mike Nelms, Washington	37	1099	29.7
1982—	Alvin Hall, Detroit	16	426	26.6
1983—	Darrin Nelson, Minnesota	18	445	24.7
1984—	Barry Redden, L.A. Rams	23	530	23.0
1985—	Ron Brown, L.A. Rams	28	918	32.8
1986—	Dennis Gentry, Chicago	20	576	28.8
1987—	Sylvester Stamps, Atlanta	24	660	27.5
1988—	Donnie Elder, Tampa Bay	34	772	22.7
1989—	Mel Gray, Detroit	24	640	26.7
1990—	Dave Meggett, N.Y. Giants	21	492	23.4
1991—	Mel Gray, Detroit	36	929	25.8
1992—	Deion Sanders, Atlanta	40	1067	26.7
1993—	Tony Smith, Atlanta	38	948	24.9
1994—	Tyrone Hughes, New Orleans	63	1556	24.7
1995—	Tyrone Hughes, New Orleans	66	1617	24.5
1996—	Tyrone Hughes, New Orleans	70	1791	25.6

SACKS

		No.
1982—	Doug Martin, Minnesota	11.5
1983—	Fred Dean, San Francisco	17.5
1984—	Richard Dent, Chicago	17.5
1985—	Richard Dent, Chicago	17.0
1986—	Lawrence Taylor, N.Y. Giants	20.5
1987—	Reggie White, Philadelphia	21.0
1988—	Reggie White, Philadelphia	18.0
1989—	Chris Doleman, Minnesota	21.0
1990—	Charles Haley, San Francisco	16.0
1991—	Pat Swilling, New Orleans	17.0
1992—	Clyde Simmons, Philadelphia	19.0
1993—	Renaldo Turnbull, New Orleans	13.0
	Reggie White, Green Bay	13.0
1994—	Ken Harvey, Washington	13.5
	John Randle, Minnesota	13.5
1995—	William Fuller, Philadelphia	13.0
	Wayne Martin, New Orleans	13.0
1996—	Kevin Greene, Carolina	14.5

COACHING RECORDS

COACHES WITH 100 CAREER VICTORIES

(Ranked according to career wins)

	Yrs.	REGULAR SEASON				POSTSEASON			CAREER			
		Won	Lost	Tied	Pct.	Won	Lost	Pct.	Won	Lost	Tied	P
Don Shula	33	328	156	6	.676	19	17	.528	347	173	6	.6
George Halas	40	318	148	31	.671	6	3	.667	324	151	31	.6
Tom Landry	29	250	162	6	.605	20	16	.556	270	178	6	.6
Curly Lambeau	33	226	132	22	.624	3	2	.600	229	134	22	.6
Chuck Noll	23	193	148	1	.566	16	8	.667	209	156	1	.5
Chuck Knox	22	186	147	1	.558	7	11	.389	193	158	1	.5
Paul Brown	21	166	100	6	.621	4	9	.308	170	109	6	.6
Bud Grant	18	158	96	5	.620	10	13	.435	168	109	5	.6
Steve Owen	23	151	100	17	.595	3	8	.273	154	108	17	.5
*Dan Reeves	16	141	106	1	.571	8	7	.533	149	113	1	.5
*Marv Levy	16	137	102	0	.573	11	8	.579	148	110	0	.5
Joe Gibbs	12	124	60	0	.674	16	5	.762	140	65	0	.6
Hank Stram	17	131	97	10	.571	5	3	.625	136	100	10	.5
Weeb Ewbank	20	130	129	7	.502	4	1	.800	134	130	7	.5
*Marty Schottenheimer	13	125	73	1	.631	5	10	.333	130	83	1	.6
Sid Gillman	18	122	99	7	.550	1	5	.167	123	104	7	.5
George Allen	12	116	47	5	.705	4	7	.364	120	54	5	.6
*Bill Parcells	12	109	81	1	.573	10	5	.667	119	86	1	.5
Don Coryell	14	111	83	1	.572	3	6	.333	114	89	1	.5
Mike Ditka	11	106	62	0	.631	6	6	.500	112	68	0	.6
John Madden	10	103	32	7	.750	9	7	.563	112	39	7	.7
*George Seifert	8	98	30	0	.766	10	5	.667	108	35	0	.7
Buddy Parker	15	104	75	9	.577	3	2	.600	107	77	9	.5
Vince Lombardi	10	96	34	6	.728	8	2	.800	104	36	6	.7
Bill Walsh	10	92	59	1	.609	10	4	.714	102	63	1	.6

*Active NFL coaches in 1996.

ACTIVE COACHES CAREER RECORDS

(Ranked according to career NFL percentages)

	Yrs.	REGULAR SEASON				POSTSEASON			CAREER			
		Won	Lost	Tied	Pct.	Won	Lost	Pct.	Won	Lost	Tied	P
Barry Switzer	3	34	14	0	.708	5	2	.714	39	16	0	.7
Mike Holmgren	5	51	29	0	.638	7	3	.700	58	32	0	.6
Bill Cowher	5	53	27	0	.663	4	5	.444	57	32	0	.6
Mike Ditka	11	106	62	0	.631	6	6	.500	112	68	0	.6
Marty Schottenheimer	13	125	73	1	.631	5	10	.333	130	83	1	.6
Ray Rhodes	2	20	12	0	.625	1	2	.333	21	14	0	.6
Dom Capers	2	19	13	0	.594	1	1	.500	20	14	0	.5
Bobby Ross	5	47	33	0	.588	3	3	.500	50	36	0	.5
Bill Parcells	12	109	81	1	.573	10	5	.667	119	86	1	.5
Marv Levy	16	137	102	0	.573	11	8	.579	148	110	0	.5
Dan Reeves	16	141	106	1	.571	8	7	.533	149	113	1	.5
CFL totals	5	43	31	4	.577	7	3	.700	50	34	4	.5
USFL totals	1	5	13	0	.278	0	0	.000	5	13	0	.2
Jimmy Johnson	6	52	44	0	.542	7	1	.875	59	45	0	.5
Dennis Green	5	47	33	0	.588	0	4	.000	47	37	0	.5
Mike Shanahan	4	29	23	0	.558	0	1	.000	29	24	0	.5
Dick Vermeil	7	54	47	0	.535	3	4	.429	57	51	0	.5
Dave Wannstedt	4	32	32	0	.500	1	1	.500	33	33	0	.5
Ted Marchibroda	10	75	79	0	.487	2	4	.333	77	83	0	.4
Dennis Erickson	2	15	17	0	.469	0	0	.000	15	17	0	.4
Bruce Coslet	5	33	40	0	.452	0	1	.000	33	41	0	.4
Vince Tobin	1	7	9	0	.438	0	0	.000	7	9	0	.4
Tom Coughlin	2	13	19	0	.406	2	1	.667	15	20	0	.4
Jeff Fisher	3	16	22	0	.421	0	0	.000	16	22	0	.4
Lindy Infante	5	33	47	0	.413	0	1	.000	33	48	0	.4
Norv Turner	3	18	30	0	.375	0	0	.000	18	30	0	.3
Pete Carroll	1	6	10	0	.375	0	0	.000	6	10	0	.3
Tony Dungy	1	6	10	0	.375	0	0	.000	6	10	0	.3
Joe Bugel	4	20	44	0	.313	0	0	.000	20	44	0	.3
Jim Fassel	0	0	0	0	.000	0	0	.000	0	0	0	.0
Kevin Gilbride	0	0	0	0	.000	0	0	.000	0	0	0	.0
Steve Mariucci	0	0	0	0	.000	0	0	.000	0	0	0	.0

HISTORY *Coaching records*

HALL OF FAME

ROSTER OF MEMBERS
FOUR NEW INDUCTEES IN 1997

Mike Haynes, Wellington Mara, Don Shula and Mike Webster were inducted into Pro Football's Hall of Fame in 97, expanding the list of former stars honored at Canton, Ohio, to 189.

me	Elec. year	College	Pos.	NFL teams
derley, Herb	1980	Michigan State	CB	Green Bay Packers, 1961-69; Dallas Cowboys, 1970-72
vorth, Lance	1978	Arkansas	WR	San Diego Chargers, 1962-70; Dallas Cowboys, 1971-72.
ins, Doug	1982	Tennessee	DE	Cleveland Browns, 1953-54; Chicago Bears, 1955-66; New Orleans Saints, 1967-69
dgro, Morris (Red)	1981	Southern California	E	New York Yankees, 1926; New York Giants, 1930-35
rney, Lem	1992	Jackson State	CB	Detroit Lions, 1967-77
ttles, Cliff	1968	W. Virginia Wesleyan	HB/QB	Boston Braves, Boston Redskins, Washington Redskins, 1932-37; coach, Brooklyn Dodgers, 1946-47
ugh, Sammy	1963	Texas Christian	QB	Washington Redskins, 1937-52; coach, New York Titans, 1960-61; Houston Oilers, 1964
dnarik, Chuck	1967	Pennsylvania	C/LB	Philadelphia Eagles, 1949-62
l, Bert	1963	Pennsylvania	*	NFL Commissioner, 1946-59
l, Bobby	1983	Minnesota	LB	Kansas City Chiefs, 1963-74
rry, Raymond	1973	Southern Methodist	E	Baltimore Colts, 1955-67; coach, New England Patriots, 1984-89
dwill, Charles W.	1967	Loyola	*	Owner, Chicago Cardinals, 1933-47
etnikoff, Fred	1988	Florida State	WR	Oakland Raiders, 1965-78
anda, George	1981	Kentucky	QB/PK	Chicago Bears, 1949-58; Baltimore Colts, 1950; Houston Oilers, 1960-66; Oakland Raiders, 1967-73
unt, Mel	1989	Southern	CB	Pittsburgh Steelers, 1970-83
adshaw, Terry	1989	Louisiana Tech	QB	Pittsburgh Steelers, 1970-83
own, Jim	1971	Syracuse	FB	Cleveland Browns, 1957-65
own, Paul	1967	Miami of Ohio	*	Coach, Cleveland Browns, 1946-62; Cincinnati Bengals, 1968-75
own, Roosevelt	1975	Morgan State	T	New York Giants, 1953-66
own, Willie	1984	Grambling	DB	Denver Broncos, 1963-66; Oakland Raiders, 1967-78
chanan, Buck	1990	Grambling	DT	Kansas City Chiefs, 1963-75
tkus, Dick	1979	Illinois	LB	Chicago Bears, 1965-73
mpbell, Earl	1991	Texas	RB	Houston Oilers, 1978-84; New Orleans Saints, 1984-85
nadeo, Tony	1974	Gonzaga	HB	Green Bay Packers, 1941-44, 46-52
rr, Joe	1963			NFL President, 1921-39
amberlin, Guy	1965	Nebraska	E/WB*	Player/coach, Canton Bulldogs, Cleveland, Frankford Yellowjackets, Chicago Bears, Chicago Cardinals, 1919-28
ristiansen, Jack	1970	Colorado A&M	DB	Detroit Lions, 1951-58; coach, San Francisco 49ers, 1963-67
rk, Dutch	1963	Colorado College	QB	Portsmouth Spartans, Detroit Lions, 1931-38
nnor, George	1975	Notre Dame	T/LB	Chicago Bears, 1948-55
nzelman, Jimmy	1964	Washington (Mo.)	HB*	Coach/executive, Decatur, Rock Island, Milwaukee, Detroit, Providence, Chicago Cardinals, 1920-48
eekmur, Lou	1996	William & Mary	T/G	Detroit Lions, 1950-59
onka, Larry	1987	Syracuse	RB	Miami Dolphins, 1968-74, 79; New York Giants, 1976-78
vis, Al	1992	Syracuse	*	Coach/general manager/president, Oakland-Los Angeles Raiders, 1963-present
vis, Willie	1981	Grambling	DE	Cleveland Browns, 1958-59; Green Bay Packers, 1960-69
wson, Len	1987	Purdue	QB	Pittsburgh Steelers, 1957-58; Cleveland Browns, 1960-61; Dallas Texans, 1962; Kansas City Chiefs, 1963-75
erdorf, Dan	1996	Michigan	T/C	St. Louis Cardinals, 1971-83
tka, Mike	1988	Pittsburgh	TE	Chicago Bears, 1961-66; Philadelphia Eagles, 1967-68; Dallas Cowboys, 1969-72; coach, Chicago Bears, 1982-92; New Orleans Saints, 1997-present
novan, Art	1968	Boston College	DT	Baltimore Colts, New York Yanks, Dallas Texans, 1950-61
rsett, Tony	1994	Pittsburgh	RB	Dallas Cowboys, 1977-87; Denver Broncos, 1988
scoll, Paddy	1965	Northwestern	TB/HB/QB	Player/coach, Chicago Cardinals, Chicago Bears, 1919-31, 41-68
dley, Bill	1966	Virginia	HB	Pittsburgh Steelers, Detroit Lions, Washington Redskins, 1942-53
wards, Turk	1969	Washington State	T	Boston Braves, Boston Redskins, Washington Redskins, 1932-40
bank, Weeb	1978	Miami of Ohio	*	Coach, Baltimore Colts, 1954-62; New York Jets, 1963-73
rs, Tom	1970	Santa Clara	E	Los Angeles Rams, 1948-56; coach, New Orleans Saints, 1967-70
ks, Jim	1995	Tulsa	QB*	Pittsburgh Steelers, 1949-55; administrator, Minnesota Vikings, 1964-73; Chicago Bears, 1974-86; New Orleans Saints, 1987-93
herty, Ray	1976	Gonzaga	E*	Player/coach, Los Angeles Wildcats, New York Yankees, AFL; New York Giants, Boston Redskins, Washington Redskins, New York Yankees, AAFC; Chicago Hornets, 1926-49

Name	Elec. year	College	Pos.	NFL teams
Ford, Len	1976	Michigan	E	Los Angeles Dons, Cleveland Browns, 1948-58
Fortmann, Danny	1965	Colgate	G	Chicago Bears, 1936-43
Fouts, Dan	1993	Oregon	QB	San Diego Chargers, 1973-87
Gatski, Frank	1985	Marshall	C	Cleveland Browns, 1946-56; Detroit Lions, 1957
George, Bill	1974	Wake Forest	LB	Chicago Bears, Los Angeles Rams, 1952-66
Gibbs, Joe	1996	San Diego State	*	Washington Redskins, 1981-92
Gifford, Frank	1977	Southern California	HB/E	New York Giants, 1952-60, 62-64
Gillman, Sid	1983	Ohio State	E*	Cleveland Rams, 1936; coach, Los Angeles Rams, 1955-59; L Angeles Chargers, 1960; San Diego Chargers, 1961-69, 71; Houston Oilers, 1973-74
Graham, Otto	1965	Northwestern	QB	Cleveland Browns, 1946-55; coach, Washington Redskins, 1966-
Grange, Red	1963	Illinois	HB	Chicago Bears, 1925, 29-34; New York Yankees, 1926-27
Grant, Bud	1994	Minnesota	WR*	Philadelphia Eagles, 1951-52; coach, Minnesota Vikings, 1967-83, 1985
Greene, Joe	1987	North Texas State	DT	Pittsburgh Steelers, 1969-81
Gregg, Forrest	1977	Southern Methodist	T	Green Bay Packers, Dallas Cowboys, 1956, 58-71; coach, Cleveland Browns, 1975-77; Cincinnati Bengals, 1980-83; Gre Bay Packers, 1984-87
Griese, Bob	1990	Purdue	QB	Miami Dolphins, 1967-80
Groza, Lou	1974	Ohio State	T/PK	Cleveland Browns, 1946-59, 61-67
Guyon, Joe	1966	Carlisle, Georgia Tech	HB	Canton Bulldogs, Cleveland Indians, Oorang Indians, Rock Isla Independents, Kansas City Cowboys, New York Giants, 1918-2
Halas, George	1963	Illinois	E*	Player/coach/ founder, Chicago Bears, 1920-83
Ham, Jack	1988	Penn State	LB	Pittsburgh Steelers, 1971-82
Hannah, John	1991	Alabama	G	New England Patriots, 1973-85
Harris, Franco	1990	Penn State	RB	Pittsburgh Steelers, 1972-83; Seattle Seahawks, 1984
Haynes, Mike	1997	Arizona State	CB	New England Patriots, 1976-82; Los Angeles Raiders, 1983-89
Healey, Ed	1964	Dartmouth	T	Rock Island, Chicago Bears, 1920-27
Hein, Mel	1963	Washington State	C	New York Giants, 1931-45
Hendricks, Ted	1990	Miami, Fla.	LB	Baltimore Colts, 1969-73; Green Bay Packers, 1974; Oakland/ Los Angeles Raiders, 1975-83
Henry, Wilbur	1963	Wash'ton & Jefferson	T	Canton Bulldogs, Akron Indians, New York Giants, Pottsville Maroons, Pittsburgh Steelers, 1920-30
Herber, Arnie	1966	Regis	HB	Green Bay Packers, New York Giants, 1930-45
Hewitt, Bill	1971	Michigan	E	Chicago Bears, 1932-36; Philadelphia Eagles, 1937-39; Philadelphia/Pittsburgh, 1943
Hinkle, Clarke	1964	Bucknell	FB	Green Bay Packers, 1932-41
Hirsch, Elroy (Crazylegs)	1968	Wisconsin	E/HB	Chicago Rockets, Los Angeles Rams, 1946-57
Hornung, Paul	1986	Notre Dame	RB	Green Bay Packers, 1957-62, 64-66
Houston, Ken	1986	Prairie View	DB	Houston Oilers, 1967-72; Washington Redskins, 1973-80
Hubbard, Cal	1963	Centenary, Geneva	T/E	New York Giants, Green Bay Packers, Pittsburgh Steelers, 1927-3
Huff, Sam	1982	West Virginia	LB	New York Giants, 1956-63; Washington Redskins, 1964-67, 6
Hunt, Lamar	1972	Southern Methodist	*	Founder, American Football League, 1959; president, Dallas Texal 1960-62; Kansas City Chiefs, 1963-present
Hutson, Don	1963	Alabama	E	Green Bay Packers, 1935-45
Johnson, Jimmy	1994	UCLA	DB	San Francisco 49ers, 1961-76
Johnson, John Henry	1987	Arizona State	FB	San Francisco 49ers, 1954-56; Detroit Lions, 1957-59; Pittsburg Steelers, 1960-65; Houston Oilers, 1966
Joiner, Charlie	1966	Grambling	WR	Houston Oilers, 1969-72; Cincinnati Bengals, 1972-75; San Dieg Chargers, 1976-86
Jones, Deacon	1980	South Carolina State	DE	Los Angeles Rams, 1961-71; San Diego Chargers, 1972-73; Washington Redskins, 1974
Jones, Stan	1991	Maryland	G/DT	Chicago Bears, 1954-65; Washington Redskins, 1966
Jordan, Henry	1995	Virginia	DT	Cleveland Browns, 1957-58; Green Bay Packers, 1959-69
Jurgensen, Sonny	1983	Duke	QB	Philadelphia Eagles, 1957-63; Washington Redskins, 1964-74
Kelly, Leroy	1994	Morgan State	RB	Cleveland Browns, 1964-73
Kiesling, Walter	1966	St. Thomas	G/T*	Player/coach, Duluth Eskimos, Pottsville Maroons, Boston Brave Chicago Cardinals, Chicago Bears, Green Bay Packers, Pittsburgh Steelers, 1926-56
Kinard, Frank (Bruiser)	1971	Mississippi	T	Brooklyn Dodgers, 1938-45; New York Yankees, 1946-47
Lambeau, Curly	1963	Notre Dame	TB/FB/E*	Founder/player/coach, Green Bay Packers, 1919-49
Lambert, Jack	1990	Kent State	LB	Pittsburgh Steelers, 1974-84
Landry, Tom	1990	Texas	*	Coach, Dallas Cowboys, 1960-88
Lane, Dick (Night Train)	1974	Scottsbluff J.C.	DB	Los Angeles Rams, Chicago Cardinals, Detroit Lions, 1952-65
Langer, Jim	1987	South Dakota State	C	Miami Dolphins, 1970-79; Minnesota Vikings, 1980-81
Lanier, Willie	1986	Morgan State	LB	Kansas City Chiefs, 1967-77
Largent, Steve	1995	Tulsa	WR	Seattle Seahawks, 1976-89
Lary, Yale	1979	Texas A&M	DB	Detroit Lions, 1952-53, 56-64
Lavelli, Dante	1975	Ohio State	E	Cleveland Browns, 1946-56

ne	Elec. year	College	Pos.	NFL teams
ne, Bobby	1967	Texas	QB	Chicago Bears, New York Bulldogs, Detroit Lions, Pittsburgh Steelers, 1948-62
mans, Tuffy	1978	George Washington	FB	New York Giants, 1936-43
y, Bob	1980	Texas Christian	DT	Dallas Cowboys, 1961-74
e, Larry	1993	Bethune Cookman	G	San Diego Chargers, 1967-68; Miami Dolphins, 1969-80
nbardi, Vince	1971	Fordham	*	Coach, Green Bay Packers, 1959-67; Washington Redskins, 1969
kman, Sid	1965	Columbia	QB	Chicago Bears, 1939-50
nan, Roy (Link)	1964		T	Canton Bulldogs, Cleveland, Chicago Bears, 1922-34
ckey, John	1992	Syracuse	TE	Baltimore Colts, 1963-71; San Diego Chargers, 1972
ra, Tim	1963		*	Founder, New York Giants, 1925-65
ra, Wellington	1997	Fordham	*	President, New York Giants, 1965-present
rchetti, Gino	1972	San Francisco	DE	Dallas Texans, 1952; Baltimore Colts, 1953-66
rshall, George Preston	1963		*	Founder, Washington Redskins, 1932-65
tson, Ollie	1972	San Francisco	HB	Chicago Cardinals, 1952, 54-58; Los Angeles Rams, 1959-62; Detroit Lions, 1963; Philadelphia Eagles, 1964-66
ynard, Don	1987	Texas Western College	WR	New York Giants, 1958; New York Jets, 1960-72; St. Louis Cardinals, 1973
Afee, George	1966	Duke	HB	Chicago Bears, 1940-41, 45-50
Cormack, Mike	1984	Kansas	T	New York Yanks, 1951; Cleveland Browns, 1954-62
Elhenny, Hugh	1970	Washington	HB	San Francisco 49ers, Minnesota Vikings, New York Giants, Detroit Lions, 1952-64
Nally, Johnny Blood	1963	St. John's	HB	Milwaukee Badgers, Duluth Eskimos, Pottsville Maroons, Green Bay Packers, Pittsburgh Steelers, 1925-39
halske, August (Mike)	1964	Penn State	G	New York Yankees, Green Bay Packers, 1927-37
ner, Wayne	1968	Notre Dame	E	Boston Redskins, Washington Redskins, 1936-41, 45
chell, Bobby	1983	Illinois	RB/FL/WR	Cleveland Browns, 1958-61; Washington Redskins, 1962-68
, Ron	1979	Southern California	T	Los Angeles Chargers, 1960; San Diego Chargers, 1961-69; Oakland Raiders, 1971
ore, Lenny	1975	Penn State	HB	Baltimore Colts, 1956-67
tley, Marion	1968	Nevada	FB/LB	Cleveland Browns, Pittsburgh Steelers, 1946-55
sso, George	1982	Milliken	G/DT	Chicago Bears, 1933-44
urski, Bronko	1963	Minnesota	FB/T	Chicago Bears, 1930-37, 43
nath, Joe	1985	Alabama	QB	New York Jets, 1965-76; Los Angeles Rams, 1977
le, Earle (Greasy)	1969	W. Virginia Wesleyan	*	Coach, Philadelphia Eagles, 1941-50
vers, Ernie	1963	Stanford	FB	Duluth Eskimos, Chicago Cardinals, 1926-37
schke, Ray	1978	Illinois	LB	Green Bay Packers, 1958-72
l, Chuck	1993	Dayton	*	Coach, Pittsburgh Steelers, 1969-91
nellini, Leo	1969	Minnesota	DT	San Francisco 49ers, 1953-63
en, Merlin	1982	Utah State	DT	Los Angeles Rams, 1962-76
o, Jim	1980	Miami, Fla.	C	Oaklland Raiders, 1960-74
en, Steve	1966	Phillips	T/G	Player/coach, Kansas City Cowboys, New York Giants, 1924-53
ge, Alan	1988	Notre Dame	DT	Minnesota Vikings, 1967-78; Chicago Bears, 1978-81
ker, Clarence (Ace)	1972	Duke	HB	Brooklyn Dodgers, 1937-41; Boston Yanks, 1945; New York Yankees, 1946
ker, Jim	1973	Ohio State	G	Baltimore Colts, 1957-67
ton, Walter	1993	Jackson State	RB	Chicago Bears, 1975-87
ry, Joe	1969	Compton J.C.	FB	San Francisco 49ers, Baltimore Colts, 1948-63
os, Pete	1970	Indiana	E	Philadelphia Eagles, 1947-55
y, Hugh (Shorty)	1966	Illinois	*	NFL technical adviser and supervisor of officials, 1938-56
ves, Daniel F.	1967	Georgetown	*	Founder, Los Angeles Rams, 1941-71
afro	1996	Oregon	DB	Dallas Cowboys, 1964-77
gins, John	1992	Kansas	FB	New York Jets, 1971-75; Washington Redskins, 1976-85
go, Jim	1981	Syracuse	C	Green Bay Packers, 1953-63; Philadelphia Eagles, 1964-67
bustelli, Andy	1971	Arnold	DE	Los Angeles Rams, 1951-55; New York Giants, 1956-64
oney, Arthur J.	1964	Georgetown	*	Founder, Pittsburgh Steelers, 1933-82
elle, Pete	1985	San Francisco	*	NFL Commissioner, 1960-89
Clair, Bob	1990	Tulsa	T	San Francisco 49ers, 1953-63
ers, Gale	1977	Kansas	RB	Chicago Bears, 1965-71
midt, Joe	1973	Pittsburgh	LB	Detroit Lions, 1953-65; coach, Detroit Lions, 1967-72
ramm, Tex	1991	Texas	*	President/general manager, Dallas Cowboys, 1960-88
mon, Lee Roy	1995	Oklahoma	DE	Tampa Bay Buccaneers, 1976-84
ll, Art	1989	Md.-Eastern Shore	T	Oakland-Los Angeles Raiders, 1968-82; coach, Los Angeles Raiders, 1989-94
la, Don	1997	John Carroll	DB	Cleveland Browns, 1951-52; Baltimore Colts, 1953-56; Washington Redskins, 1957; coach, Baltimore Colts, 1963-69, Miami Dolphins, 1970-95
pson, O.J.	1985	Southern California	RB	Buffalo Bills, 1969-77; San Francisco 49ers, 1978
ith, Jackie	1994	N'western Louisiana	TE	St. Louis Cardinals, 1963-77; Dallas Cowboys, 1978
r, Bart	1977	Alabama	QB	Green Bay Packers, 1956-71; coach, Green Bay Packers, 1975-83
ubach, Roger	1985	Navy	QB	Dallas Cowboys, 1969-79

Name	Elec. year	College	Pos.	NFL teams
Stautner, Ernie	1969	West Virginia	DT	Pittsburgh Steelers, 1950-63
Stenerud, Jan	1991	Montana State	PK	Kansas City Chiefs, 1967-79; Green Bay Packers, 1980-83; Minnesota Vikings, 1984-85
Strong, Ken	1967	New York U.	HB/PK	Staten Island Stapletons, New York Yankees, New York Giants 1929-39, 44-47
Stydahar, Joe	1967	West Virginia	T	Chicago Bears, 1936-42, 45-46
Tarkenton, Fran	1986	Georgia	QB	Minnesota Vikings, 1961-66, 72-78; New York Giants, 1967-7
Taylor, Charley	1984	Arizona State	WR	Washington Redskins, 1964-75, 77
Taylor, Jim	1976	Louisiana State	FB	Green Bay Packers, 1958-66; New Orleans Saints, 1967
Thorpe, Jim	1963	Carlisle	HB	Canton Bulldogs, Oorang Indians, Cleveland Indians, Toledo Maroons, Rock Island Independents, New York Giants, 1915-26, 2
Tittle, Y.A.	1971	Louisiana State	QB	Baltimore Colts, 1948-50; San Francisco 49ers, 1951-60; New York Giants, 1961-64
Trafton, George	1964	Notre Dame	C	Chicago Bears, 1920-32
Trippi, Charlie	1968	Georgia	HB	Chicago Cardinals, 1947-55
Tunnell, Emlen	1967	Iowa	DB	New York Giants, Green Bay Packers, 1948-61
Turner, Clyde (Bulldog)	1966	Hardin-Simmons	C/LB	Chicago Bears, 1940-52; coach, New York Titans, 1962
Unitas, John	1979	Louisville	QB	Baltimore Colts, 1956-72; San Diego Chargers, 1973
Upshaw, Gene	1987	Texas A&I	G	Oakland Raiders, 1967-81
Van Brocklin, Norm	1971	Oregon	QB	Los Angeles Rams, 1949-57; Philadelphia Eagles, 1958-60; coach, Minnesota Vikings, 1961-66; Atlanta Falcons, 1968-74
Van Buren, Steve	1965	Louisiana State	HB	Philadelphia Eagles, 1944-51
Walker, Doak	1986	Southern Methodist	RB	Detroit Lions, 1950-55
Walsh, Bill	1993	San Jose State	*	Coach, San Francisco 49ers, 1979-88
Warfield, Paul	1983	Ohio State	WR	Cleveland Browns, 1964-69, 76-77; Miami Dolphins, 1970-74
Waterfield, Bob	1965	UCLA	QB	Cleveland Rams, Los Angeles Rams, 1945-52; coach, Los Angeles Rams, 1960-62
Webster, Mike	1997	Wisconsin	C-G	Pittsburgh Steelers, 1974-88; Kansas City Chiefs, 1989-90
Weinmeister, Arnie	1984	Washington	T	New York Yankees, 1948-49; New York Giants, 1950-53
White, Randy	1994	Maryland	DT	Dallas Cowboys, 1975-88
Willis, Bill	1977	Ohio State	G	Cleveland Browns, 1946-53
Wilson, Larry	1978	Utah	DB	St. Louis Cardinals, 1960-72
Winslow, Kellen	1995	Missouri	TE	San Diego Chargers, 1979-87
Wojciechowicz, Alex	1968	Fordham	C/LB	Detroit Lions, Philadelphia Eagles, 1938-50
Wood, Willie	1989	Southern California	S	Green Bay Packers, 1960-71

*Hall of Fame member was selected for contributions other than as a player.
Abbreviations of positions: C—Center, CB—Cornerback, DB—Defensive back, DE—Defensive end, DT—Defensive tackle, E—Er
FB—Fullback, FL—Flanker, G—Guard, HB—Halfback, LB—Linebacker, PK—Placekicker, QB—Quarterback, RB—Running back, S
Safety, T—Tackle, TB—Tailback, TE—Tight end.

PLAYER OF THE YEAR

4—Lou Groza, OT/K, Cleveland
5—Otto Graham, QB, Cleveland
6—Frank Gifford, HB, N.Y. Giants
7—Jim Brown, RB, Cleveland
8—Jim Brown, RB, Cleveland
9—Johnny Unitas, QB, Baltimore
0—Norm Van Brocklin, QB, Philadelphia
1—Paul Hornung, HB, Green Bay
2—Y.A. Tittle, QB, N.Y. Giants
3—Y.A. Tittle, QB, N.Y. Giants
4—Johnny Unitas, QB, Baltimore
5—Jim Brown, RB, Cleveland
6—Bart Starr, QB, Green Bay
7—Johnny Unitas, QB, Baltimore
8—Earl Morrall, QB, Baltimore
9—Roman Gabriel, QB, L.A. Rams
0—NFC: John Brodie, QB, San Francisco
   AFC: George Blanda, QB/PK, Oakland
1—NFC: Roger Staubach, QB, Dallas
   AFC: Bob Griese, QB, Miami
2—NFC: Larry Brown, RB, Washington
   AFC: Earl Morrall, QB, Miami
3—NFC: John Hadl, QB, L.A. Rams
   AFC: O.J. Simpson, RB, Buffalo
4—NFC: Chuck Foreman, RB, Minnesota
   AFC: Ken Stabler, QB, Oakland
5—NFC: Fran Tarkenton, QB, Minnesota
   AFC: O.J. Simpson, RB, Buffalo
6—NFC: Walter Payton, RB, Chicago
   AFC: Ken Stabler, QB, Oakland

1977—NFC: Walter Payton, RB, Chicago
   AFC: Craig Morton, QB, Denver
1978—NFC: Archie Manning, QB, New Orleans
   AFC: Earl Campbell, RB, Houston
1979—NFC: Ottis Anderson, RB, St. Louis
   AFC: Dan Fouts, QB, San Diego
1980—Brian Sipe, QB, Cleveland
1981—Ken Anderson, QB, Cincinnati
1982—Mark Moseley, PK, Washington
1983—Eric Dickerson, RB, L.A. Rams
1984—Dan Marino, QB, Miami
1985—Marcus Allen, RB, L.A. Raiders
1986—Lawrence Taylor, LB, N.Y. Giants
1987—Jerry Rice, WR, San Francisco
1988—Boomer Esiason, QB, Cincinnati
1989—Joe Montana, QB, San Francisco
1990—Jerry Rice, WR, San Francisco
1991—Thurman Thomas, RB, Buffalo
1992—Steve Young, QB, San Francisco
1993—Emmitt Smith, RB, Dallas
1994—Steve Young, QB, San Francisco
1995—Brett Favre, QB, Green Bay
1996—Brett Favre, QB, Green Bay
NOTE: From 1970-79, a player was selected as Player of the Year for both the NFC and AFC. In 1980 The Sporting News reinstated the selection of one player as Player of the Year for the entire NFL.

ROOKIE OF THE YEAR

5—Alan Ameche, FB, Baltimore
6—J.C. Caroline, HB, Chicago
7—Jim Brown, FB, Cleveland
8—Bobby Mitchell, HB, Cleveland
9—Nick Pietrosante, FB, Detroit
0—Gail Cogdill, E, Detroit
1—Mike Ditka, E, Chicago
2—Ronnie Bull, HB, Chicago
3—Paul Flatley, WR, Minnesota
4—Charley Taylor, HB, Washington
5—Gale Sayers, RB, Chicago
6—Tommy Nobis, LB, Atlanta
7—Mel Farr, RB, Detroit
8—Earl McCullouch, WR, Detroit
9—Calvin Hill, RB, Dallas
0—NFC: Bruce Taylor, CB, San Francisco
   AFC: Dennis Shaw, QB, Buffalo
1—NFC: John Brockington, RB, Green Bay
   AFC: Jim Plunkett, QB, New England
2—NFC: Chester Marcol, PK, Green Bay
   AFC: Franco Harris, RB, Pittsburgh
3—NFC: Chuck Foreman, RB, Minnesota
   AFC: Boobie Clark, RB, Cincinnati
4—NFC: Wilbur Jackson, RB, San Francisco
   AFC: Don Woods, RB, San Diego
5—NFC: Steve Bartkowski, QB, Atlanta
   AFC: Robert Brazile, LB, Houston

1976—NFC: Sammy White, WR, Minnesota
   AFC: Mike Haynes, CB, New England
1977—NFC: Tony Dorsett, RB, Dallas
   AFC: A.J. Duhe, DT, Miami
1978—NFC: Al Baker, DE, Detroit
   AFC: Earl Campbell, RB, Houston
1979—NFC: Ottis Anderson, RB, St. Louis
   AFC: Jerry Butler, WR, Buffalo
1980—Billy Sims, RB, Detroit
1981—George Rogers, RB, New Orleans
1982—Marcus Allen, RB, L.A. Raiders
1983—Dan Marino, QB, Miami
1984—Louis Lipps, WR, Pittsburgh
1985—Eddie Brown, WR, Cincinnati
1986—Rueben Mayes, RB, New Orleans
1987—Robert Awalt, TE, St. Louis
1988—Keith Jackson, TE, Philadelphia
1989—Barry Sanders, RB, Detroit
1990—Richmond Webb, T, Miami
1991—Mike Croel, LB, Denver
1992—Santana Dotson, DL, Tampa Bay
1993—Jerome Bettis, RB, L.A. Rams
1994—Marshall Faulk, RB, Indianapolis
1995—Curtis Martin, RB, New England
1996—Eddie George, RB, Houston
NOTE: In 1980, The Sporting News began selecting one rookie as Rookie of the Year for the entire NFL.

NFL COACH OF THE YEAR

7—Jimmy Conzelman, Chi. Cardinals
8—Earle (Greasy) Neale, Philadelphia
9—Paul Brown, Cleveland (AAFC)
0—Steve Owen, N.Y. Giants
1—Paul Brown, Cleveland
2—J. Hampton Pool, L.A. Rams

1953—Paul Brown, Cleveland
1954—None
1955—Joe Kuharich, Washington
1956—Jim Lee Howell, N.Y. Giants
1957—None
1958—None

1959—None
1960—None
1961—Vince Lombardi, Green Bay
1962—None
1963—George Halas, Chicago
1964—Don Shula, Baltimore
1965—George Halas, Chicago
1966—Tom Landry, Dallas
1967—George Allen, L.A. Rams
1968—Don Shula, Baltimore
1969—Bud Grant, Minnesota
1970—Don Shula, Miami
1971—George Allen, Washington
1972—Don Shula, Miami
1973—Chuck Knox, L.A. Rams
1974—Don Coryell, St. Louis
1975—Ted Marchibroda, Baltimore
1976—Chuck Fairbanks, New England
1977—Red Miller, Denver

1978—Jack Patera, Seattle
1979—Dick Vermeil, Philadelphia
1980—Chuck Knox, Buffalo
1981—Bill Walsh, San Francisco
1982—Joe Gibbs, Washington
1983—Joe Gibbs, Washington
1984—Chuck Knox, Seattle
1985—Mike Ditka, Chicago
1986—Bill Parcells, N.Y. Giants
1987—Jim Mora, New Orleans
1988—Marv Levy, Buffalo
1989—Lindy Infante, Green Bay
1990—George Seifert, San Francisco
1991—Joe Gibbs, Washington
1992—Bill Cowher, Pittsburgh
1993—Dan Reeves, N.Y. Giants
1994—George Seifert, San Francisco
1995—Ray Rhodes, Philadelphia
1996—Dom Capers, Carolina

NFL EXECUTIVE OF THE YEAR

1955—Dan Reeves, L.A. Rams
1956—George Halas, Chicago
1972—Dan Rooney, Pittsburgh
1973—Jim Finks, Minnesota
1974—Art Rooney, Pittsburgh
1975—Joe Thomas, Baltimore
1976—Al Davis, Oakland
1977—Tex Schramm, Dallas
1978—John Thompson, Seattle
1979—John Sanders, San Diego
1980—Eddie LeBaron, Atlanta
1981—Paul Brown, Cincinnati
1982—Bobby Beathard, Washington
1983—Bobby Beathard, Washington
1984—George Young, N.Y. Giants

1985—Mike McCaskey, Chicago
1986—George Young, N.Y. Giants
1987—Jim Finks, New Orleans
1988—Bill Polian, Buffalo
1989—John McVay, San Francisco
1990—George Young, N.Y. Giants
1991—Bill Polian, Buffalo
1992—Ron Wolf, Green Bay
1993—George Young, N.Y. Giants
1994—Carmen Policy, San Francisco
1995—Bill Polian, Carolina
1996—Bill Polian, Carolina
NOTE: The Executive of the Year Award was not given from 1957-71.

1996 NFL ALL-PRO TEAM

OFFENSE

WR—Herman Moore, Detroit
    Jerry Rice, San Francisco
TE—Shannon Sharpe, Denver
T—Willie Roaf, New Orleans
    Gary Zimmerman, Denver
C—Dermontti Dawson, Pittsburgh
G—Larry Allen, Dallas
    Randall McDaniel, Minnesota
QB—Brett Favre, Green Bay
RB—Terrell Davis, Denver
    Barry Sanders, Detroit

DEFENSE

DE—Alfred Williams, Denver
    Bruce Smith, Buffalo
DT—Bryant Young, San Francisco
    John Randle, Minnesota
LB—Chad Brown, Pittsburgh
    Lamar Lathon, Carolina
    Junior Seau, San Diego
CB—Dale Carter, Kansas City
    Deion Sanders, Dallas
S—LeRoy Butler, Green Bay
    Darren Woodson, Dallas

SPECIALISTS

PR—Desmond Howard, Green Bay
KR—Michael Bates, Carolina
  K—Cary Blanchard, Indianapolis
  P—Chris Gardocki, Indianapolis

ARIZONA CARDINALS
YEAR-BY-YEAR RECORDS

Year	W	L	T	Pct.	PF	PA	Finish	W	L	Highest round	Coach
920*	6	2	2	.750	...	...	T4th				Paddy Driscoll
921*	3	3	2	.500	...	...	T8th				Paddy Driscoll
922*	8	3	0	.727	...	...	3rd				Paddy Driscoll
923*	8	4	0	.667	...	...	6th				Arnold Horween
924*	5	4	1	.556	...	...	8th				Arnold Horween
925*	11	2	1	.846	...	...	1st				Norman Barry
926*	5	6	1	.455	...	...	10th				Norman Barry
927*	3	7	1	.300	...	...	9th				Guy Chamberlin
928*	1	5	0	.167	...	...	9th				Fred Gillies
29*	6	6	1	.500	...	...	T4th				Dewey Scanlon
30*	5	6	2	.455	...	...	T7th				Ernie Nevers
31*	5	4	0	.556	...	...	4th				LeRoy Andrews, Ernie Nevers
32*	2	6	2	.250	...	...	7th				Jack Chevigny
33*	1	9	1	.100	52	101	5th/Western Div.	—	—		Paul Schissler
34*	5	6	0	.455	80	84	4th/Western Div.	—	—		Paul Schissler
35*	6	4	2	.600	99	97	T3rd/Western Div.	—	—		Milan Creighton
36*	3	8	1	.273	74	143	4th/Western Div.	—	—		Milan Creighton
37*	5	5	1	.500	135	165	4th/Western Div.	—	—		Milan Creighton
38*	2	9	0	.182	111	168	5th/Western Div.	—	—		Milan Creighton
39*	1	10	0	.091	84	254	5th/Western Div.	—	—		Ernie Nevers
40*	2	7	2	.222	139	222	5th/Western Div.	—	—		Jimmy Conzelman
41*	3	7	1	.300	127	197	4th/Western Div.	—	—		Jimmy Conzelman
42*	3	8	0	.273	98	209	4th/Western Div.	—	—		Jimmy Conzelman
43*	0	10	0	.000	95	238	4th/Western Div.	—	—		Phil Handler
44†	0	10	0	.000	108	328	5th/Western Div.	—	—		Phil Handler-Walt Kiesling
45*	1	9	0	.100	98	228	5th/Western Div.	—	—		Phil Handler
46*	6	5	0	.545	260	198	T3rd/Western Div.	—	—		Jimmy Conzelman
47*	9	3	0	.750	306	231	1st/Western Div.	1	0	NFL champ	Jimmy Conzelman
48*	11	1	0	.917	395	226	1st/Western Div.	0	1	NFL championship game	Jimmy Conzelman
49*	6	5	1	.545	360	301	3rd/Western Div.	—	—		Phil Handler-Buddy Parker
50*	5	7	0	.417	233	287	5th/American Conf.	—	—		Curly Lambeau
51*	3	9	0	.250	210	287	6th/American Conf.	—	—		Curly Lambeau, Phil Handler-Cecil Isbell
52*	4	8	0	.333	172	221	T5th/American Conf.	—	—		Joe Kuharich
53*	1	10	1	.091	190	337	6th/Eastern Conf.	—	—		Joe Stydahar
54*	2	10	0	.167	183	347	6th/Eastern Conf.	—	—		Joe Stydahar
55*	4	7	1	.364	224	252	T4th/Eastern Conf.	—	—		Ray Richards
56*	7	5	0	.583	240	182	2nd/Eastern Conf.	—	—		Ray Richards
57*	3	9	0	.250	200	299	6th/Eastern Conf.	—	—		Ray Richards
58*	2	9	1	.182	261	356	T5th/Eastern Conf.	—	—		Pop Ivy
59*	2	10	0	.167	234	324	6th/Eastern Conf.	—	—		Pop Ivy
60‡	6	5	1	.545	288	230	4th/Eastern Conf.	—	—		Pop Ivy
61‡	7	7	0	.500	279	267	4th/Eastern Conf.	—	—		Pop Ivy
62‡	4	9	1	.308	287	361	6th/Eastern Conf.	—	—		Wally Lemm
63‡	9	5	0	.643	341	283	3rd/Eastern Conf.	—	—		Wally Lemm
64‡	9	3	2	.750	357	331	2nd/Eastern Conf.	—	—		Wally Lemm
65‡	5	9	0	.357	296	309	T5th/Eastern Conf.	—	—		Wally Lemm
66‡	8	5	1	.615	264	265	4th/Eastern Conf.	—	—		Charley Winner
67‡	6	7	1	.462	333	356	3rd/Century Div.	—	—		Charley Winner
68‡	9	4	1	.692	325	289	2nd/Century Div.	—	—		Charley Winner
69‡	4	9	1	.308	314	389	3rd/Century Div.	—	—		Charley Winner
70‡	8	5	1	.615	325	228	3rd/NFC Eastern Div.	—	—		Charley Winner
71‡	4	9	1	.308	231	279	4th/NFC Eastern Div.	—	—		Bob Hollway
72‡	4	9	1	.308	193	303	4th/NFC Eastern Div.	—	—		Bob Hollway
73‡	4	9	1	.308	286	365	4th/NFC Eastern Div.	—	—		Don Coryell
74‡	10	4	0	.714	285	218	1st/NFC Eastern Div.	0	1	NFC div. playoff game	Don Coryell
75‡	11	3	0	.786	356	276	1st/NFC Eastern Div.	0	1	NFC div. playoff game	Don Coryell
76‡	10	4	0	.714	309	267	3rd/NFC Eastern Div.	—	—		Don Coryell
77‡	7	7	0	.500	272	287	3rd/NFC Eastern Div.	—	—		Don Coryell
78‡	6	10	0	.375	248	296	T4th/NFC Eastern Div.	—	—		Bud Wilkinson
79‡	5	11	0	.313	307	358	5th/NFC Eastern Div.	—	—		Bud Wilkinson, Larry Wilson
30‡	5	11	0	.313	299	350	4th/NFC Eastern Div.	—	—		Jim Hanifan
31‡	7	9	0	.438	315	408	5th/NFC Eastern Div.	—	—		Jim Hanifan
32‡	5	4	0	.556	135	170	T4th/NFC	0	1	NFC first-round pl. game	Jim Hanifan

		REGULAR SEASON						PLAYOFFS		
Year	W	L	T	Pct.	PF	PA	Finish	W	L Highest round	Coach
1983‡	8	7	1	.531	374	428	3rd/NFC Eastern Div.	—	—	Jim Hanifan
1984‡	9	7	0	.563	423	345	T3rd/NFC Eastern Div.	—	—	Jim Hanifan
1985‡	5	11	0	.313	278	414	5th/NFC Eastern Div.	—	—	Jim Hanifan
1986‡	4	11	1	.281	218	351	5th/NFC Eastern Div.	—	—	Gene Stallings
1987‡	7	8	0	.467	362	368	T2nd/NFC Eastern Div.	—	—	Gene Stallings
1988§	7	9	0	.438	344	398	T3rd/NFC Eastern Div.	—	—	Gene Stallings
1989§	5	11	0	.313	258	377	4th/NFC Eastern Div.	—	—	G. Stallings, Hank Kuhlman
1990§	5	11	0	.313	268	396	5th/NFC Eastern Div.	—	—	Joe Bugel
1991§	4	12	0	.250	196	344	5th/NFC Eastern Div.	—	—	Joe Bugel
1992§	4	12	0	.250	243	332	5th/NFC Eastern Div.	—	—	Joe Bugel
1993§	7	9	0	.438	326	269	4th/NFC Eastern Div.	—	—	Joe Bugel
1994	8	8	0	.500	235	267	3rd/NFC Eastern Div.	—	—	Buddy Ryan
1995	4	12	0	.250	275	422	5th/NFC Eastern Div.	—	—	Buddy Ryan
1996	7	9	0	.438	300	397	4th/NFC Eastern Div.	—	—	Vince Tobin

*Chicago Cardinals.
†Card-Pitt, a combined squad of Chicago Cardinals and Pittsburgh Steelers.
‡St. Louis Cardinals.
§Phoenix Cardinals.

FIRST-ROUND DRAFT PICKS

1936—Jim Lawrence, B, Texas Christian
1937—Ray Buivid, B, Marquette
1938—Jack Robbins, B, Arkansas
1939—Charles Aldrich, C, Texas Christian*
1940—George Cafego, B, Tennessee*
1941—John Kimbrough, B, Texas A&M
1942—Steve Lach, B, Duke
1943—Glenn Dobbs, B, Tulsa
1944—Pat Harder, B, Wisconsin*
1945—Charley Trippi, B, Georgia*
1946—Dub Jones, B, Louisiana State
1947—DeWitt (Tex) Coulter, T, Army
1948—Jim Spavital, B, Oklahoma A&M
1949—Bill Fischer, G, Notre Dame
1950—None
1951—Jerry Groom, C, Notre Dame
1952—Ollie Matson, B, San Francisco
1953—Johnny Olszewski, QB, California
1954—Lamar McHan, B, Arkansas
1955—Max Boydston, E, Oklahoma
1956—Joe Childress, B, Auburn
1957—Jerry Tubbs, C, Oklahoma
1958—King Hill, B, Rice*
1959—Billy Stacy, B, Mississippi State
1960—George Izo, QB, Notre Dame
1961—Ken Rice, T, Auburn
1962—Fate Echols, DT, Northwestern
    Irv Goode, C, Kentucky
1963—Jerry Stovall, DB, Louisiana State
    Don Brumm, E, Purdue
1964—Ken Kortas, DT, Louisville
1965—Joe Namath, QB, Alabama
1966—Carl McAdams, LB, Oklahoma
1967—Dave Williams, WR, Washington

1968—MacArthur Lane, RB, Utah State
1969—Roger Wehrli, DB, Missouri
1970—Larry Stegent, RB, Texas A&M
1971—Norm Thompson, DB, Utah
1972—Bobby Moore, RB, Oregon
1973—Dave Butz, DT, Purdue
1974—J.V. Cain, TE, Colorado
1975—Tim Gray, DB, Texas A&M
1976—Mike Dawson, DT, Arizona
1977—Steve Pisarkiewicz, QB, Missouri
1978—Steve Little, K, Arkansas
    Ken Greene, DB, Washington St.
1979—Ottis Anderson, RB, Miami (Fla.)
1980—Curtis Greer, DE, Michigan
1981—E.J. Junior, LB, Alabama
1982—Luis Sharpe, T, UCLA
1983—Leonard Smith, DB, McNeese State
1984—Clyde Duncan, WR, Tennessee
1985—Freddie Joe Nunn, LB, Mississippi
1986—Anthony Bell, LB, Michigan St.
1987—Kelly Stouffer, QB, Colorado St.
1988—Ken Harvey, LB, California
1989—Eric Hill, LB, Louisiana State
    Joe Wolf, G, Boston College
1990—None
1991—Eric Swann, DL, None
1992—None
1993—Garrison Hearst, RB, Georgia
    Ernest Dye, T, South Carolina
1994—Jamir Miller, LB, UCLA
1995—None
1996—Simeon Rice, DE, Illinois
1997—Tom Knight, DB, Iowa
    *First player chosen in draft.

FRANCHISE RECORDS

Most rushing yards, career
7,999—Ottis Anderson
Most rushing yards, season
1,605—Ottis Anderson, 1979
Most rushing yards, game
214—LeShon Johnson at N.O., Sept. 22, 1996
Most rushing touchdowns, season
14—John David Crow, 1962
Most passing attempts, season
560—Neil Lomax, 1984

Most passing attempts, game
61—Neil Lomax at S.D., Sept. 20, 1987
Most passes completed, season
345—Neil Lomax, 1984
Most passes completed, game
37—Neil Lomax at Was., Dec. 16, 1984
    Kent Graham vs. St.L., Sept. 29, 1996 (OT)
Most passing yards, career
34,639—Jim Hart

Most passing yards, season
4,614—Neil Lomax, 1984
Most passing yards, game
522—Boomer Esiason at Was., Nov. 10 1996 (OT)
468—Neil Lomax at Was., Dec. 16, 198▮
Most touchdown passes, season
28—Charley Johnson, 1963
    Neil Lomax, 1984
Most pass receptions, career
522—Roy Green

– 346 –

ost pass receptions, season
1—Larry Centers, 1995
ost pass receptions, game
—Sonny Randle at NYG, Nov. 4, 1962
ost receiving yards, career
497—Roy Green
ost receiving yards, season
555—Roy Green, 1984

Most receiving yards, game
256—Sonny Randle vs. NYG, Nov. 4, 1962
Most receiving touchdowns, season
16—Sonny Randle, 1960
Most touchdowns, career
66—Roy Green
Most field goals, season
30—Greg Davis, 1995

Longest field goal
55 yards—Greg Davis at Sea., Dec. 19,
 1993
 Greg Davis at Det., Sept. 17, 1995
Most interceptions, career
52—Larry Wilson
Most interceptions, season
12—Bob Nussbaumer, 1949

SERIES RECORDS

izona vs.: Atlanta 12-6; Buffalo 3-3; Carolina 0-1; Chicago 25-54-6; Cincinnati 2-3;
allas 22-46-1; Denver 0-4-1; Detroit 15-28-3; Green Bay 21-41-4; Houston 4-2;
dianapolis 6-6; Jacksonville 0-0; Kansas City 1-4-1; Miami 0-7; Minnesota 8-6; New
gland 6-3; New Orleans 11-9; N.Y. Giants 37-70-2; N.Y. Jets 2-2; Oakland 1-2;
iladelphia 46-48-5; Pittsburgh 22-29-3; St. Louis 13-16-2; San Diego 1-6; San
ancisco 9-10; Seattle 5-0; Tampa Bay 7-6; Washington 39-59-1.
OTE: Includes records for entire franchise, from 1920 to present.

RETIRED UNIFORM NUMBERS

No.	Player
8	Larry Wilson
77	Stan Mauldin
88	J.V. Cain
99	Marshall Goldberg

ATLANTA FALCONS
YEAR-BY-YEAR RECORDS

							REGULAR SEASON			PLAYOFFS		
ar	W	L	T	Pct.	PF	PA	Finish	W	L	Highest round	Coach
66	3	11	0	.214	204	437	7th/Eastern Conf.	—	—		Norb Hecker
67	1	12	1	.077	175	422	4th/Coastal Div.	—	—		Norb Hecker
68	2	12	0	.143	170	389	4th/Coastal Div.	—	—		N. Hecker, N. Van Brocklin
69	6	8	0	.429	276	268	3rd/Coastal Div.	—	—		Norm Van Brocklin
70	4	8	2	.333	206	261	3rd/NFC Western Div.	—	—		Norm Van Brocklin
71	7	6	1	.538	274	277	3rd/NFC Western Div.	—	—		Norm Van Brocklin
72	7	7	0	.500	269	274	2nd/NFC Western Div.	—	—		Norm Van Brocklin
73	9	5	0	.643	318	224	2nd/NFC Western Div.	—	—		Norm Van Brocklin
74	3	11	0	.214	111	271	4th/NFC Western Div.	—	—		N. Van Brocklin, M. Campbell
75	4	10	0	.286	240	289	3rd/NFC Western Div.	—	—		Marion Campbell
76	4	10	0	.286	172	312	T3rd/NFC Western Div.	—	—		M. Campbell, Pat Peppler
77	7	7	0	.500	179	129	2nd/NFC Western Div.	—	—		Leeman Bennett
78	9	7	0	.563	240	290	2nd/NFC Western Div.	1	1	NFC div. playoff game	Leeman Bennett
79	6	10	0	.375	300	388	3rd/NFC Western Div.	—	—		Leeman Bennett
80	12	4	0	.750	405	272	1st/NFC Western Div.	0	1	NFC div. playoff game	Leeman Bennett
81	7	9	0	.438	426	355	2nd/NFC Western Div.	—	—		Leeman Bennett
82	5	4	0	.556	183	199	T4th/NFC	0	1	NFC first-round pl. game	Leeman Bennett
83	7	9	0	.438	370	389	4th/NFC Western Div.	—	—		Dan Henning
84	4	12	0	.250	281	382	4th/NFC Western Div.	—	—		Dan Henning
85	4	12	0	.250	282	452	4th/NFC Western Div.	—	—		Dan Henning
86	7	8	1	.469	280	280	3rd/NFC Western Div.	—	—		Dan Henning
87	3	12	0	.200	205	436	4th/NFC Western Div.	—	—		Marion Campbell
88	5	11	0	.313	244	315	4th/NFC Western Div.	—	—		Marion Campbell
89	3	13	0	.188	279	437	4th/NFC Western Div.	—	—		M. Campbell, Jim Hanifan
90	5	11	0	.313	348	365	T3rd/NFC Western Div.	—	—		Jerry Glanville
91	10	6	0	.625	361	338	2nd/NFC Western Div.	1	1	NFC div. playoff game	Jerry Glanville
92	6	10	0	.375	327	414	T3rd/NFC Western Div.	—	—		Jerry Glanville
93	6	10	0	.375	316	385	3rd/NFC Western Div.	—	—		Jerry Glanville
94	7	9	0	.438	313	389	T2nd/NFC Western Div.	—	—		June Jones
95	9	7	0	.563	362	349	2nd/NFC Western Div.	0	1	NFC wild-card game	June Jones
96	3	13	0	.188	309	465	T4th/NFC Western Div.	—	—		June Jones

FIRST-ROUND DRAFT PICKS

66—Tommy Nobis, LB, Texas*
 Randy Johnson, QB, Texas A&I
67—None
68—Claude Humphrey, DE, Tennessee State
69—George Kunz, T, Notre Dame
70—John Small, LB, Citadel
71—Joe Profit, RB, Northeast Louisiana State
72—Clarence Ellis, DB, Notre Dame
73—None
74—None
75—Steve Bartkowski, QB, California*
76—Bubba Bean, RB, Texas A&M
77—Warren Bryant, T, Kentucky
 Wilson Faumuina, DT, San Jose State

1978—Mike Kenn, T, Michigan
1979—Don Smith, DE, Miami (Fla.)
1980—Junior Miller, TE, Nebraska
1981—Bobby Butler, DB, Florida State
1982—Gerald Riggs, RB, Arizona State
1983—Mike Pitts, DE, Alabama
1984—Rick Bryan, DT, Oklahoma
1985—Bill Fralic, T, Pittsburgh
1986—Tony Casillas, DT, Oklahoma
 Tim Green, LB, Syracuse
1987—Chris Miller, QB, Oregon
1988—Aundray Bruce, LB, Auburn*
1989—Deion Sanders, DB, Florida State
 Shawn Collins, WR, Northern Arizona

1990—Steve Broussard, RB, Washington State
1991—Bruce Pickens, CB, Nebraska
    Mike Pritchard, WR, Colorado
1992—Bob Whitfield, T, Stanford
    Tony Smith, RB, Southern Mississippi
1993—Lincoln Kennedy, T, Washington

1994—None
1995—Devin Bush, DB, Florida State
1996—None
1997—Michael Booker, DB, Nebraska
  *First player chosen in draft.

FRANCHISE RECORDS

Most rushing yards, career
6,631—Gerald Riggs
Most rushing yards, season
1,719—Gerald Riggs, 1985
Most rushing yards, game
202—Gerald Riggs at N.O., Sept. 2, 1984
Most rushing touchdowns, season
13—Gerald Riggs, 1984
Most passing attempts, season
557—Jeff George, 1995
Most passing attempts, game
66—Chris Miller vs. Det., Dec. 24, 1989
Most passes completed, season
336—Jeff George, 1995
Most passes completed, game
37—Chris Miller vs. Det., Dec. 24, 1989
Most passing yards, career
23,468—Steve Bartkowski
Most passing yards, season
4,143—Jeff George, 1995

Most passing yards, game
416—Steve Bartkowski vs. Pit., Nov. 15, 1981
Most touchdown passes, season
31—Steve Bartkowski, 1980
Most pass receptions, career
423—Andre Rison
Most pass receptions, season
111—Terance Mathis, 1994
Most pass receptions, game
15—William Andrews vs. Pit., Nov. 15, 1981
Most receiving yards, career
6,257—Alfred Jenkins
Most receiving yards, season
1,358—Alfred Jenkins, 1981
Most receiving yards, game
193—Alfred Jackson vs. S.F., Dec. 2, 1984
    Andre Rison at Det., Sept. 4, 1994

Most receiving touchdowns, season
15—Andre Rison, 1993
Most touchdowns, career
56—Andre Rison
Most field goals, season
31—Morten Andersen, 1995
Longest field goal
59 yards—Morten Andersen vs. S.F., Dec. 24, 1995
Most interceptions, career
39—Rolland Lawrence
Most interceptions, season
10—Scott Case, 1988
Most sacks, career
62.5—Claude Humphrey
Most sacks, season
16—Joel Williams, 1980

SERIES RECORDS

Atlanta vs.: Arizona 6-12; Buffalo 3-4; Carolina 2-2; Chicago 9-9; Cincinnati 2-7; Dallas 6-11; Denver 3-5; Detroit 6-19; Green Bay 9-10; Houston 5-4; Indianapolis 0-10; Jacksonville 0-1; Kansas City 0-4; Miami 1-6; Minnesota 6-13; New England 5-3; New Orleans 31-24; N.Y. Giants 6-6; N.Y. Jets 4-3; Oakland 3-5; Philadelphia 7-9-1; Pittsburgh 1-10; St. Louis 19-39-2; San Diego 4-1; San Francisco 22-37-1; Seattle 1-4; Tampa Bay 8-6; Washington 4-13-1.

RETIRED UNIFORM NUMBERS

No.	Player
10	Steve Bartkowski
31	William Andrews
57	Jeff Van Note
60	Tommy Nobis

BALTIMORE RAVENS

YEAR-BY-YEAR RECORDS

			REGULAR SEASON						PLAYOFFS		
Year	W	L	T	Pct.	PF	PA	Finish	W	L	Highest round	Coach
1996	4	12	0	.250	371	441	5th/Central Div.	—	—		Ted Marchibroda

FIRST-ROUND DRAFT PICKS

1996—Jonathan Ogden, T, UCLA
    Ray Lewis, LB, Miami (Fla.)

1997—Peter Boulware, DE, Florida State
  *First player chosen in draft.

FRANCHISE RECORDS

Most rushing yards, career
737—Bam Morris
Most rushing yards, season
737—Bam Morris, 1996
Most rushing yards, game
149—Earnest Byner vs. N.O., Sept. 29, 1996
Most rushing touchdowns, season
4—Earnest Byner, 1996
    Bam Morris, 1996
Most passing attempts, season
549—Vinny Testaverde, 1996
Most passing attempts, game
51—Vinny Testaverde vs. St.L., Oct. 27, 1996 (OT)

50—Vinny Testaverde vs. Jac., Nov. 24, 1996 (OT)
45—Vinny Testaverde vs. N.E., Oct. 6, 1996
    Vinny Testaverde at Den., Oct. 20, 1996
Most passes completed, season
325—Vinny Testaverde, 1996
Most passes completed, game
31—Vinny Testaverde vs. St.L., Oct. 27, 1996 (OT)
    Vinny Testaverde vs. Jac., Nov. 24, 1996 (OT)
29—Vinny Testaverde vs. N.E., Oct. 6, 1996

Most passing yards, career
4,177—Vinny Testaverde
Most passing yards, season
4,177—Vinny Testaverde, 1996
Most passing yards, game
429—Vinny Testaverde vs. St.L., Oct. 27, 1996 (OT)
366—Vinny Testaverde vs. Jac., Nov. 24, 1996 (OT)
353—Vinny Testaverde vs. N.E., Oct. 6, 1996
Most touchdown passes, season
33—Vinny Testaverde, 1996
Most pass receptions, career
76—Michael Jackson

ost pass receptions, season
6—Michael Jackson, 1996
ost pass receptions, game
—Michael Jackson vs. Jac., Nov. 24,
1996 (OT)
Brian Kinchen vs. Jac., Nov. 24,
1996 (OT)
—Michael Jackson vs. N.E., Oct. 6, 1996
ost receiving yards, career
,201—Michael Jackson
ost receiving yards, season
,201—Michael Jackson, 1996

Most receiving yards, game
198—Derrick Alexander vs. Pit., Dec. 1,
1996
Most receiving touchdowns, season
14—Michael Jackson, 1996
Most touchdowns, career
14—Michael Jackson
Most field goals, season
19—Matt Stover, 1996
Longest field goal
50 yards—Matt Stover vs. St.L., Oct. 27,
1996

Most interceptions, career
5—Antonio Langham
Eric Turner
Most interceptions, season
5—Antonio Langham, 1996
Eric Turner, 1996
Most sacks, career
4.5—Mike Caldwell
Most sacks, season
4.5—Mike Caldwell, 1996

SERIES RECORDS

altimore vs.: Carolina 0-1; Cincinnati 0-2; Denver 0-1; Houston 0-2; Indianapolis 0-1; cksonville 0-2; New England 0-1; New Orleans 1-0; Oakland 1-0; Pittsburgh 1-1; St. uis 1-0; San Francisco 0-1.

RETIRED UNIFORM NUMBERS

No. Player
None

BUFFALO BILLS
YEAR-BY-YEAR RECORDS

| | | | REGULAR SEASON | | | | | | PLAYOFFS | | |
ear	W	L	T	Pct.	PF	PA	Finish	W	L	Highest round	Coach
960*	5	8	1	.385	296	303	3rd/Eastern Div.	—	—		Buster Ramsey
961*	6	8	0	.429	294	342	4th/Eastern Div.	—	—		Buster Ramsey
962*	7	6	1	.538	309	272	3rd/Eastern Div.	—	—		Lou Saban
963*	7	6	1	.538	304	291	2nd/Eastern Div.	0	1	E. Div. championship game	Lou Saban
964*	12	2	0	.857	400	242	1st/Eastern Div.	1	0	AFL champ	Lou Saban
965*	10	3	1	.769	313	226	1st/Eastern Div.	1	0	AFL champ	Lou Saban
966*	9	4	1	.692	358	255	1st/Eastern Div.	0	1	AFL championship game	Joe Collier
967*	4	10	0	.286	237	285	T3rd/Eastern Div.	—	—		Joe Collier
968*	1	12	1	.077	199	367	5th/Eastern Div.	—	—		Joe Collier, Harvey Johnson
969*	4	10	0	.286	230	359	T3rd/Eastern Div.	—	—		John Rauch
970	3	10	1	.231	204	337	4th/AFC Eastern Div.	—	—		John Rauch
971	1	13	0	.071	184	394	5th/AFC Eastern Div.	—	—		Harvey Johnson
972	4	9	1	.321	257	377	4th/AFC Eastern Div.	—	—		Lou Saban
973	9	5	0	.643	259	230	2nd/AFC Eastern Div.	—	—		Lou Saban
974	9	5	0	.643	264	244	2nd/AFC Eastern Div.	0	1	AFC div. playoff game	Lou Saban
975	8	6	0	.571	420	355	3rd/AFC Eastern Div.	—	—		Lou Saban
976	2	12	0	.143	245	363	5th/AFC Eastern Div.	—	—		Lou Saban, Jim Ringo
977	3	11	0	.214	160	313	T4th/AFC Eastern Div.	—	—		Jim Ringo
978	5	11	0	.313	302	354	T4th/AFC Eastern Div.	—	—		Chuck Knox
979	7	9	0	.438	268	279	4th/AFC Eastern Div.	—	—		Chuck Knox
980	11	5	0	.688	320	260	1st/AFC Eastern Div.	0	1	AFC div. playoff game	Chuck Knox
981	10	6	0	.625	311	276	3rd/AFC Eastern Div.	1	1	AFC div. playoff game	Chuck Knox
982	4	5	0	.444	150	154	T8th/AFC	—	—		Chuck Knox
983	8	8	0	.500	283	351	T2nd/AFC Eastern Div.	—	—		Kay Stephenson
984	2	14	0	.125	250	454	5th/AFC Eastern Div.	—	—		Kay Stephenson
985	2	14	0	.125	200	381	5th/AFC Eastern Div.	—	—		Hank Bullough
986	4	12	0	.250	287	348	4th/AFC Eastern Div.	—	—		Hank Bullough, Marv Levy
987	7	8	0	.467	270	305	4th/AFC Eastern Div.	—	—		Marv Levy
988	12	4	0	.750	329	237	1st/AFC Eastern Div.	1	1	AFC championship game	Marv Levy
989	9	7	0	.563	409	317	1st/AFC Eastern Div.	0	1	AFC div. playoff game	Marv Levy
990	13	3	0	.813	428	263	1st/AFC Eastern Div.	2	1	Super Bowl	Marv Levy
991	13	3	0	.813	458	318	1st/AFC Eastern Div.	2	1	Super Bowl	Marv Levy
992	11	5	0	.688	381	283	2nd/AFC Eastern Div.	3	1	Super Bowl	Marv Levy
993	12	4	0	.750	329	242	1st/AFC Eastern Div.	2	1	Super Bowl	Marv Levy
994	7	9	0	.438	340	356	4th/AFC Eastern Div.	—	—		Marv Levy
995	10	6	0	.625	350	335	1st/AFC Eastern Div.	1	1	AFC div. playoff game	Marv Levy
996	10	6	0	.625	319	266	2nd/AFC Eastern Div.	0	1	AFC wild-card night	Marv Levy

*American Football League.

FIRST-ROUND DRAFT PICKS

60—Richie Lucas, QB, Penn State
61—Ken Rice, T, Auburn* (AFL)
62—Ernie Davis, RB, Syracuse
63—Dave Behrman, C, Michigan State
64—Carl Eller, DE, Minnesota

1965—Jim Davidson, T, Ohio State
1966—Mike Dennis, RB, Mississippi
1967—John Pitts, DB, Arizona State
1968—Haven Moses, WR, San Diego St.
1969—O.J. Simpson, RB, Southern California*

1970—Al Cowlings, DE, Southern California
1971—J.D. Hill, WR, Arizona State
1972—Walt Patulski, DE, Notre Dame*
1973—Paul Seymour, T, Michigan
   Joe DeLamielleure, G, Michigan State
1974—Reuben Gant, TE, Oklahoma State
1975—Tom Ruud, LB, Nebraska
1976—Mario Clark, DB, Oregon
1977—Phil Dokes, DT, Oklahoma State
1978—Terry Miller, RB, Oklahoma State
1979—Tom Cousineau, LB, Ohio State*
   Jerry Butler, WR, Clemson
1980—Jim Ritcher, C, North Carolina State
1981—Booker Moore, RB, Penn State
1982—Perry Tuttle, WR, Clemson
1983—Tony Hunter, TE, Notre Dame
   Jim Kelly, QB, Miami (Fla.)

1984—Greg Bell, RB, Notre Dame
1985—Bruce Smith, DT, Virginia Tech*
   Derrick Burroughs, DB, Memphis State
1986—Ronnie Harmon, RB, Iowa
   Will Wolford, T, Vanderbilt
1987—Shane Conlan, LB, Penn State
1988—None
1989—None
1990—James Williams, DB, Fresno State
1991—Henry Jones, S, Illinois
1992—John Fina, T, Arizona
1993—Thomas Smith, DB, North Carolina
1994—Jeff Burris, DB, Notre Dame
1995—Ruben Brown, G, Pittsburgh
1996—Eric Moulds, WR, Mississippi State
1997—Antowain Smith, RB, Houston
*First player chosen in draft.

FRANCHISE RECORDS

Most rushing yards, career
10,762—Thurman Thomas
Most rushing yards, season
2,003—O.J. Simpson, 1973
Most rushing yards, game
273—O.J. Simpson at Det., Nov. 25, 1976
Most rushing touchdowns, season
16—O.J. Simpson, 1975
Most passing attempts, season
508—Joe Ferguson, 1983
Most passing attempts, game
55—Joe Ferguson at Mia., Oct. 9, 1983
Most passes completed, season
304—Jim Kelly, 1991
Most passes completed, game
38—Joe Ferguson at Mia., Oct. 9, 1983
Most passing yards, career
35,467—Jim Kelly

Most passing yards, season
3,844—Jim Kelly, 1991
Most passing yards, game
419—Joe Ferguson at Mia., Oct. 9, 1983
Most touchdown passes, season
33—Jim Kelly, 1991
Most pass receptions, career
766—Andre Reed
Most pass receptions, season
90—Andre Reed, 1994
Most pass receptions, game
15—Andre Reed vs. G.B., Nov. 20, 1994
Most receiving yards, career
10,884—Andre Reed
Most receiving yards, season
1,312—Andre Reed, 1989
Most receiving yards, game
255—Jerry Butler vs. NYJ, Sept. 23, 1979

Most receiving touchdowns, season
11—Bill Brooks, 1995
Most touchdowns, career
82—Thurman Thomas
Most field goals, season
32—Scott Norwood, 1988
Longest field goal
59 yards—Steve Christie vs. Mia., Sept. 26, 1993
Most interceptions, career
40—George Byrd
Most interceptions, season
10—Billy Atkins, 1961
   Tom Janik, 1967
Most sacks, career
140—Bruce Smith
Most sacks, season
19—Bruce Smith, 1990

SERIES RECORDS

Buffalo vs.: Arizona 3-3; Atlanta 4-3; Carolina 1-0; Chicago 2-4; Cincinnati 8-10; Dallas 3-3; Denver 17-11-1; Detroit 1-3-1; Green Bay 5-1; Houston 13-21; Indianapolis 29-23-1; Jacksonville 0-0; Kansas City 17-13-1; Miami 21-40-1; Minnesota 2-5; New England 35-38-1; New Orleans 3-2; N.Y. Giants 5-2; N.Y. Jets 42-31; Oakland 14-15; Philadelphia 4-4; Pittsburgh 7-8; St. Louis 4-3; San Diego 7-16-2; San Francisco 3-3; Seattle 2-4; Tampa Bay 2-4; Washington 4-4.

RETIRED UNIFORM NUMBERS

No.	Player
None	

CAROLINA PANTHERS
YEAR-BY-YEAR RECORDS

	REGULAR SEASON							PLAYOFFS			
Year	W	L	T	Pct.	PF	PA	Finish	W	L	Highest round	Coach
1995	7	9	0	.438	289	325	T3rd/NFC Western Div.	—	—		Dom Capers
1996	12	4	0	.750	367	218	1st/NFC Western Div.	1	1	NFC championship game	Dom Capers

FIRST-ROUND DRAFT PICKS

1995—Kerry Collins, QB, Penn State
   Tyrone Poole, DB, Fort Valley (Ga.) St.
   Blake Brockermeyer, T, Texas

1996—Tim Biakabutuka, RB, Michigan
1997—Rae Carruth, WR, Colorado

FRANCHISE RECORDS

Most rushing yards, career
1,230—Anthony Johnson
Most rushing yards, season
1,120—Anthony Johnson, 1996

Most rushing yards, game
126—Anthony Johnson vs. St.L., Oct. 13, 1996

Most rushing touchdowns, season
6—Anthony Johnson, 1996
Most passing attempts, season
433—Kerry Collins, 1995

Most passing attempts, game	**Most pass receptions, career**	**Most touchdowns, career**
46—Kerry Collins at N.O., Nov. 26, 1995	124—Mark Carrier	10—Wesley Walls
Most passes completed, season	**Most pass receptions, season**	**Most field goals, season**
214—Kerry Collins, 1995	66—Mark Carrier, 1995	37—John Kasay, 1996
Most passes completed, game	**Most pass receptions, game**	**Longest field goal**
26—Kerry Collins vs. Bal., Dec. 15, 1996	9—Willie Green at Atl., Nov. 3, 1996	53 yards—John Kasay vs. Atl., Sept. 1,
Most passing yards, career	**Most receiving yards, career**	1996
5,171—Kerry Collins	1,810—Mark Carrier	**Most interceptions, career**
Most passing yards, season	**Most receiving yards, season**	7—Brett Maxie
2,717—Kerry Collins, 1995	1,002—Mark Carrier, 1995	**Most interceptions, season**
Most passing yards, game	**Most receiving yards, game**	6—Brett Maxie, 1995
335—Kerry Collins at N.O., Nov. 26,	157—Willie Green at St.L., Nov. 12, 1995	**Most sacks, career**
1995	Willie Green at S.F., Dec. 8, 1996	21.5—Lamar Lathon
Most touchdown passes, season	**Most receiving touchdowns, season**	**Most sacks, season**
14—Kerry Collins, 1995, 1996	10—Wesley Walls, 1996	14.5—Kevin Greene, 1996

SERIES RECORDS

Carolina vs.: Arizona 1-0; Atlanta 2-2; Buffalo 0-1; Baltimore 1-0; Chicago 0-1; Cincinnati 0-0; Dallas 0-0; Denver 0-0; Detroit 0-0; Green Bay 0-0; Houston 1-0; Indianapolis 1-0; Jacksonville 0-1; Kansas City 0-0; Miami 0-0; Minnesota 0-1; New England 1-0; New Orleans 3-1; N.Y. Giants 1-0; N.Y. Jets 1-0; Oakland 0-0; Philadelphia 1-1; Pittsburgh 1-0; St. Louis 2-2; San Diego 0-0; San Francisco 3-1; Seattle 0-0; Tampa Bay 1-1; Washington 0-1.

RETIRED UNIFORM NUMBERS

No.	Player
None	

CHICAGO BEARS
YEAR-BY-YEAR RECORDS

		REGULAR SEASON						PLAYOFFS			
Year	W	L	T	Pct.	PF	PA	Finish	W	L	Highest round	Coach
1920*	10	1	2	.909	...	...	2nd				George Halas
1921†	9	1	1	.900	...	...	1st				George Halas
1922	9	3	0	.750	...	...	2nd				George Halas
1923	9	2	1	.818	...	...	2nd				George Halas
1924	6	1	4	.857	...	...	2nd				George Halas
1925	9	5	3	.643	...	...	7th				George Halas
1926	12	1	3	.923	...	...	2nd				George Halas
1927	9	3	2	.750	...	...	3rd				George Halas
1928	7	5	1	.583	...	...	5th				George Halas
1929	4	9	2	.308	...	...	9th				George Halas
1930	9	4	1	.692	...	...	3rd				Ralph Jones
1931	8	5	0	.615	...	...	3rd				Ralph Jones
1932	7	1	6	.875	...	...	1st				Ralph Jones
1933	10	2	1	.833	133	82	1st/Western Div.	1	0	NFL champ	George Halas
1934	13	0	0	1.000	286	86	1st/Western Div.	0	1	NFL championship game	George Halas
1935	6	4	2	.600	192	106	T3rd/Western Div.	—	—		George Halas
1936	9	3	0	.750	222	94	2nd/Western Div.	—	—		George Halas
1937	9	1	1	.900	201	100	1st/Western Div.	0	1	NFL championship game	George Halas
1938	6	5	0	.545	194	148	3rd/Western Div.	—	—		George Halas
1939	8	3	0	.727	298	157	2nd/Western Div.	—	—		George Halas
1940	8	3	0	.727	238	152	1st/Western Div.	1	0	NFL champ	George Halas
1941	10	1	0	.909	396	147	1st/Western Div.	2	0	NFL champ	George Halas
1942	11	0	0	1.000	376	84	1st/Western Div.	0	1	NFL championship game	George Halas, Hunk Anderson-Luke Johnsos
1943	8	1	1	.889	303	157	1st/Western Div.	1	0	NFL champ	H. Anderson-Luke Johnsos
1944	6	3	1	.667	258	172	T2nd/Western Div.	—	—		H. Anderson-Luke Johnsos
1945	3	7	0	.300	192	235	4th/Western Div.	—	—		H. Anderson-Luke Johnsos
1946	8	2	1	.800	289	193	1st/Western Div.	1	0	NFL champ	George Halas
1947	8	4	0	.667	363	241	2nd/Western Div.	—	—		George Halas
1948	10	2	0	.833	375	151	2nd/Western Div.	—	—		George Halas
1949	9	3	0	.750	332	218	2nd/Western Div.	—	—		George Halas
1950	9	3	0	.750	279	207	2nd/National Conf.	0	1	Nat. Conf. champ. game	George Halas
1951	7	5	0	.583	286	282	4th/National Conf.	—	—		George Halas
1952	5	7	0	.417	245	326	5th/National Conf.	—	—		George Halas
1953	3	8	1	.273	218	262	T4th/Western Conf.	—	—		George Halas
1954	8	4	0	.667	301	279	2nd/Western Conf.	—	—		George Halas
1955	8	4	0	.667	294	251	2nd/Western Conf.	—	—		George Halas
1956	9	2	1	.818	363	246	1st/Western Conf.	0	1	NFL championship game	Paddy Driscoll
1957	5	7	0	.417	203	211	5th/Western Conf.	—	—		Paddy Driscoll
1958	8	4	0	.667	298	230	T2nd/Western Conf.	—	—		George Halas

HISTORY Team by team

Year	W	L	T	Pct.	PF	PA	Finish	W	L	Highest round	Coach
				REGULAR SEASON						**PLAYOFFS**	
1959	8	4	0	.667	252	196	2nd/Western Conf.	—	—		George Halas
1960	5	6	1	.455	194	299	5th/Western Conf.	—	—		George Halas
1961	8	6	0	.571	326	302	T3rd/Western Conf.	—	—		George Halas
1962	9	5	0	.643	321	287	3rd/Western Conf.	—	—		George Halas
1963	11	1	2	.917	301	144	1st/Western Conf.	1	0	NFL champ	George Halas
1964	5	9	0	.357	260	379	6th/Western Conf.	—	—		George Halas
1965	9	5	0	.643	409	275	3rd/Western Conf.	—	—		George Halas
1966	5	7	2	.417	234	272	5th/Western Conf.	—	—		George Halas
1967	7	6	1	.538	239	218	2nd/Central Div.	—	—		George Halas
1968	7	7	0	.500	250	333	2nd/Central Div.	—	—		Jim Dooley
1969	1	13	0	.071	210	339	4th/Central Div.	—	—		Jim Dooley
1970	6	8	0	.429	256	261	T3rd/NFC Central Div.	—	—		Jim Dooley
1971	6	8	0	.429	185	276	3rd/NFC Central Div.	—	—		Jim Dooley
1972	4	9	1	.321	225	275	4th/NFC Central Div.	—	—		Abe Gibron
1973	3	11	0	.214	195	334	4th/NFC Central Div.	—	—		Abe Gibron
1974	4	10	0	.286	152	279	4th/NFC Central Div.	—	—		Abe Gibron
1975	4	10	0	.286	191	379	T3rd/NFC Central Div.	—	—		Jack Pardee
1976	7	7	0	.500	253	216	2nd/NFC Central Div.	—	—		Jack Pardee
1977	9	5	0	.643	255	253	2nd/NFC Central Div.	0	1	NFC div. playoff game	Jack Pardee
1978	7	9	0	.438	253	274	T3rd/NFC Central Div.	—	—		Neill Armstrong
1979	10	6	0	.625	306	249	2nd/NFC Central Div.	0	1	AFC wild-card game	Neill Armstrong
1980	7	9	0	.438	304	264	3rd/NFC Central Div.	—	—		Neill Armstrong
1981	6	10	0	.375	253	324	5th/NFC Central Div.	—	—		Neill Armstrong
1982	3	6	0	.333	141	174	T11th/NFC	—	—		Mike Ditka
1983	8	8	0	.500	311	301	T2nd/NFC Central Div.	—	—		Mike Ditka
1984	10	6	0	.625	325	248	1st/NFC Central Div.	1	1	NFC championship game	Mike Ditka
1985	15	1	0	.938	456	198	1st/NFC Central Div.	3	0	Super Bowl champ	Mike Ditka
1986	14	2	0	.875	352	187	1st/NFC Central Div.	0	1	NFC div. playoff game	Mike Ditka
1987	11	4	0	.733	356	282	1st/NFC Central Div.	0	1	NFC div. playoff game	Mike Ditka
1988	12	4	0	.750	312	215	1st/NFC Central Div.	1	1	NFC championship game	Mike Ditka
1989	6	10	0	.375	358	377	4th/NFC Central Div.	—	—		Mike Ditka
1990	11	5	0	.688	348	280	1st/NFC Central Div.	1	1	NFC div. playoff game	Mike Ditka
1991	11	5	0	.688	299	269	2nd/NFC Central Div.	0	1	NFC wild-card game	Mike Ditka
1992	5	11	0	.313	295	361	T3rd/NFC Central Div.	—	—		Mike Ditka
1993	7	9	0	.438	234	230	4th/NFC Central Div.	—	—		Dave Wannstedt
1994	9	7	0	.563	271	307	T2nd/NFC Central Div.	1	1	NFC div. playoff game	Dave Wannstedt
1995	9	7	0	.563	392	360	3rd/NFC Central Div.	—	—		Dave Wannstedt
1996	7	9	0	.438	283	305	3rd/NFC Central Div.	—	—		Dave Wannstedt

*Decatur Staleys.
†Chicago Staleys.

FIRST-ROUND DRAFT PICKS

1936—Joe Stydahar, T, West Virginia
1937—Les McDonald, E, Nebraska
1938—Joe Gray, B, Oregon State
1939—Sid Luckman, B, Columbia
    Bill Osmanski, B, Holy Cross
1940—C. Turner, C, Hardin-Simmons
1941—Tom Harmon, B, Michigan*
    Norm Standlee, B, Stanford
    Don Scott, B, Ohio State
1942—Frankie Albert, B, Stanford
1943—Bob Steuber, B, Missouri
1944—Ray Evans, B, Kansas
1945—Don Lund, B, Michigan
1946—Johnny Lujack, QB, Notre Dame
1947—Bob Fenimore, B, Oklahoma A&M*
1948—Bobby Layne, QB, Texas
    Max Baumgardner, E, Texas
1949—Dick Harris, C, Texas
1950—Chuck Hunsinger, B, Florida
1951—Bob Williams, B, Notre Dame
    Billy Stone, B, Bradley
    Gene Schroeder, E, Virginia
1952—Jim Dooley, B, Miami
1953—Billy Anderson, B, Compton (Ca.) J.C.
1954—Stan Wallace, B, Illinois
1955—Ron Drzewiecki, B, Marquette
1956—Menan (Tex) Schriewer, E, Texas
1957—Earl Leggett, DT, Louisiana State

1958—Chuck Howley, LB, West Virginia
1959—Don Clark, B, Ohio State
1960—Roger Davis, G, Syracuse
1961—Mike Ditka, E, Pittsburgh
1962—Ron Bull, RB, Baylor
1963—Dave Behrman, C, Michigan State
1964—Dick Evey, DT, Tennessee
1965—Dick Butkus, LB, Illinois
1965—Gale Sayers, RB, Kansas
    Steve DeLong, DE, Tennessee
1966—George Rice, DT, Louisiana State
1967—Loyd Phillips, DE, Arkansas
1968—Mike Hull, RB, Southern California
1969—Rufus Mayes, T, Ohio State
1970—None
1971—Joe Moore, RB, Missouri
1972—Lionel Antoine, T, Southern Illinois
    Craig Clemons, DB, Iowa
1973—Wally Chambers, DE, Eastern Kentucky
1974—Waymond Bryant, LB, Tennessee State
    Dave Gallagher, DE, Michigan
1975—Walter Payton, RB, Jackson State
1976—Dennis Lick, T, Wisconsin
1977—Ted Albrecht, T, California
1978—None
1979—Dan Hampton, DT, Arkansas
    Al Harris, DE, Arizona State
1980—Otis Wilson, LB, Louisville

981—Keith Van Horne, T, Southern California
982—Jim McMahon, QB, Brigham Young
983—Jimbo Covert, T, Pittsburgh
   Willie Gault, WR, Tennessee
984—Wilber Marshall, LB, Florida
985—William Perry, DT, Clemson
986—Neal Anderson, RB, Florida
987—Jim Harbaugh, QB, Michigan
988—Brad Muster, RB, Stanford
   Wendell Davis, WR, Louisiana State
989—Donnell Woolford, DB, Clemson
   Trace Armstrong, DE, Florida

1990—Mark Carrier, DB, Southern California
1991—Stan Thomas, T, Texas
1992—Alonzo Spellman, DE, Ohio State
1993—Curtis Conway, WR, Southern California
1994—John Thierry, LB, Alcorn State
1995—Rashaan Salaam, RB, Colorado
1996—Walt Harris, DB, Mississippi State
1997—None
*First player chosen in draft.

FRANCHISE RECORDS

ost rushing yards, career
,726—Walter Payton
ost rushing yards, season
852—Walter Payton, 1977
ost rushing yards, game
'5—Walter Payton vs. Min., Nov. 20, 1977
ost rushing touchdowns, season
—Gale Sayers, 1965
   Walter Payton, 1977
   Walter Payton, 1979
ost passing attempts, season
2—Erik Kramer, 1995
ost passing attempts, game
—Bill Wade at Was., Oct. 25, 1964
ost passes completed, season
5—Erik Kramer, 1995
ost passes completed, game
—Bill Wade at Was., Oct. 25, 1964
ost passing yards, career
,686—Sid Luckman

Most passing yards, season
3,838—Erik Kramer, 1995
Most passing yards, game
468—Johnny Lujack vs. Chi. Cards, Dec. 11, 1949
Most touchdown passes, season
29—Erik Kramer, 1995
Most pass receptions, career
492—Walter Payton
Most pass receptions, season
93—Johnny Morris, 1964
Most pass receptions, game
14—Jim Keane at NYG, Oct. 23, 1949
Most receiving yards, career
5,059—Johnny Morris
Most receiving yards, season
1,301—Jeff Graham, 1995
Most receiving yards, game
214—Harlon Hill at S.F., Oct. 31, 1954
Most receiving touchdowns, season
13—Ken Kavanaugh, 1947
   Dick Gordon, 1970

Most touchdowns, career
125—Walter Payton
Most field goals, season
31—Kevin Butler, 1985
Longest field goal
55 yards—Bob Thomas at L.A. Rams, Nov. 23, 1975
   Kevin Butler vs. Min., Oct. 25, 1993
   Kevin Butler at T.B., Dec. 12, 1993
Most interceptions, career
38—Gary Fencik
Most interceptions, season
10—Mark Carrier, 1990
Most sacks, career
124.5—Richard Dent
Most sacks, season
17.5—Richard Dent, 1984

SERIES RECORDS

icago vs.: Arizona 54-25-6; Atlanta 9-9; Buffalo 4-2; Carolina 1-0; Cincinnati 2-4; llas 7-8; Denver 5-6; Detroit 71-51-3; Green Bay 82-65-6; Houston 3-4; Indianapolis -21; Jacksonville 1-0; Kansas City 4-3; Miami 2-5; Minnesota 32-37-2; New England 4; New Orleans 10-6; N.Y. Giants 25-16-2; N.Y. Jets 4-1; Oakland 4-5; Philadelphia 25- 1; Pittsburgh 19-5-1; St. Louis 35-25-3; San Diego 3-4; San Francisco 25-25-1; Seattle 4; Tampa Bay 29-9; Washington 14-12.
TE: Includes records as Decatur Staleys in 1920 and Chicago Staleys in 1921.

RETIRED UNIFORM NUMBERS

No.	Player
3	Bronko Nagurski
5	George McAfee
7	George Halas
28	Willie Galimore
34	Walter Payton
40	Gale Sayers
41	Brian Piccolo
42	Sid Luckman
51	Dick Butkus
56	Bill Hewitt
61	Bill George
66	Bulldog Turner
77	Red Grange

CINCINNATI BENGALS
YEAR-BY-YEAR RECORDS

			REGULAR SEASON						PLAYOFFS	
ar	W	L	T	Pct.	PF	PA	Finish	W	L	Highest round	Coach
68*	3	11	0	.214	215	329	5th/Western Div.	—	—		Paul Brown
69*	4	9	1	.308	280	367	5th/Western Div.	—	—		Paul Brown
'0	8	6	0	.571	312	255	1st/AFC Central Div.	0	1	AFC div. playoff game	Paul Brown
'1	4	10	0	.286	284	265	4th/AFC Central Div.	—	—		Paul Brown
'2	8	6	0	.571	299	229	3rd/AFC Central Div.	—	—		Paul Brown
'3	10	4	0	.714	286	231	1st/AFC Central Div.	0	1	AFC div. playoff game	Paul Brown
'4	7	7	0	.500	283	259	T2nd/AFC Central Div.	—	—		Paul Brown
'5	11	3	0	.786	340	246	2nd/AFC Central Div.	0	1	AFC div. playoff game	Paul Brown
'6	10	4	0	.714	335	210	2nd/AFC Central Div.	—	—		Bill Johnson
'7	8	6	0	.571	238	235	T2nd/AFC Central Div.	—	—		Bill Johnson

							REGULAR SEASON			PLAYOFFS	
Year	W	L	T	Pct.	PF	PA	Finish	W	L	Highest round	Coach
1978	4	12	0	.250	252	284	4th/AFC Central Div.	—	—		Bill Johnson, Homer Ric
1979	4	12	0	.250	337	421	4th/AFC Central Div.	—	—		Homer Rice
1980	6	10	0	.375	244	312	4th/AFC Central Div.	—	—		Forrest Gregg
1981	12	4	0	.750	421	304	1st/AFC Central Div.	2	1	Super Bowl	Forrest Gregg
1982	7	2	0	.778	232	177	T2nd/AFC	0	1	AFC first-round pl. game	Forrest Gregg
1983	7	9	0	.438	346	302	3rd/AFC Central Div.	—	—		Forrest Gregg
1984	8	8	0	.500	339	339	2nd/AFC Central Div.	—	—		Sam Wyche
1985	7	9	0	.438	441	437	T2nd/AFC Central Div.	—	—		Sam Wyche
1986	10	6	0	.625	409	394	2nd/AFC Central Div.	—	—		Sam Wyche
1987	4	11	0	.267	285	370	4th/AFC Central Div.	—	—		Sam Wyche
1988	12	4	0	.750	448	329	1st/AFC Central Div.	2	1	Super Bowl	Sam Wyche
1989	8	8	0	.500	404	285	4th/AFC Central Div.	—	—		Sam Wyche
1990	9	7	0	.563	360	352	1st/AFC Central Div.	1	1	AFC div. playoff game	Sam Wyche
1991	3	13	0	.188	263	435	4th/AFC Central Div.	—	—		Sam Wyche
1992	5	11	0	.313	274	364	4th/AFC Central Div.	—	—		David Shula
1993	3	13	0	.188	187	319	4th/AFC Central Div.	—	—		David Shula
1994	3	13	0	.188	276	406	3rd/AFC Central Div.	—	—		David Shula
1995	7	9	0	.438	349	374	T2nd/AFC Central Div.	—	—		David Shula
1996	8	8	0	.500	372	369	T3rd/AFC Central Div.	—	—		David Shula, Bruce Cos

*American Football League.

FIRST-ROUND DRAFT PICKS

1968—Bob Johnson, C, Tennessee
1969—Greg Cook, QB, Cincinnati
1970—Mike Reid, DT, Penn State
1971—Vernon Holland, T, Tennessee State
1972—Sherman White, DE, California
1973—Issac Curtis, WR, San Diego State
1974—Bill Kollar, DT, Montana State
1975—Glenn Cameron, LB, Florida
1976—Billy Brooks, WR, Oklahoma
    Archie Griffin, RB, Ohio State
1977—Eddie Edwards, DT, Miami (Fla.)
    Wilson Whitley, DT, Houston
    Mike Cobb, TE, Michigan State
1978—Ross Browner, DE, Notre Dame
    Blair Bush, C, Washington
1979—Jack Thompson, QB, Washington State
    Charles Alexander, RB, Louisiana State
1980—Anthony Munoz, T, Southern California
1981—David Verser, WR, Kansas
1982—Glen Collins, DE, Mississippi State
1983—Dave Rimington, C, Nebraska

1984—Ricky Hunley, LB, Arizona
    Pete Koch, DE, Maryland
    Brian Blados, T, North Carolina
1985—Eddie Brown, WR, Miami (Fla.)
    Emanuel King, LB, Alabama
1986—Joe Kelly, LB, Washington
    Tim McGee, WR, Tennessee
1987—Jason Buck, DT, Brigham Young
1988—Rickey Dixon, S, Oklahoma
1989—None
1990—James Francis, LB, Baylor
1991—Alfred Williams, LB, Colorado
1992—David Klingler, QB, Houston
    Darryl Williams, DB, Miami (Fla.)
1993—John Copeland, DE, Alabama
1994—Dan Wilkinson, DT, Ohio State*
1995—Ki-Jana Carter, RB, Penn State*
1996—Willie Anderson, T, Auburn
1997—Reinard Wilson, LB, Florida State
    *First player chosen in draft.

FRANCHISE RECORDS

Most rushing yards, career
6,447—James Brooks
Most rushing yards, season
1,239—James Brooks, 1989
Most rushing yards, game
201—James Brooks vs. Hou., Dec. 23, 1990
Most rushing touchdowns, season
15—Ickey Woods, 1988
Most passing attempts, season
567—Jeff Blake, 1995
Most passing attempts, game
56—Ken Anderson at S.D., Dec. 20, 1982
Most passes completed, season
326—Jeff Blake, 1995
Most passes completed, game
40—Ken Anderson at S.D., Dec. 20, 1982
Most passing yards, career
32,838—Ken Anderson

Most passing yards, season
3,959—Boomer Esiason, 1986
Most passing yards, game
490—Boomer Esiason at L.A. Rams, Oct. 7, 1990
Most touchdown passes, season
29—Ken Anderson, 1981
Most pass receptions, career
420—Isaac Curtis
Most pass receptions, season
100—Carl Pickens, 1996
Most pass receptions, game
12—James Brooks at Min., Dec. 25, 1989
    Carl Pickens vs. Pit., Nov. 10, 1996
Most receiving yards, career
7,106—Isaac Curtis
Most receiving yards, season
1,273—Eddie Brown, 1988

Most receiving yards, game
216—Eddie Brown vs. Pit., Nov. 16, 198
Most receiving touchdowns, season
17—Carl Pickens, 1995
Most touchdowns, career
70—Pete Johnson
Most field goals, season
29—Doug Pelfrey, 1995
Longest field goal
55 yards—Chris Bahr vs. Hou., Sept. 2 1979
Most interceptions, career
65—Ken Riley
Most interceptions, season
9—Ken Riley, 1976
Most sacks, career
84.5—Eddie Edwards
Most sacks, season
21.5—Coy Bacon, 1976

SERIES RECORDS

Cincinnati vs.: Arizona 3-2; Atlanta 7-2; Buffalo 10-8; Carolina 0-0; Chicago 4-2; Dallas 2-4; Denver 6-12; Detroit 3-3; Green Bay 4-4; Houston 27-28-1; Indianapolis 7-10; Jacksonville 3-1; Kansas City 9-11; Miami 3-12; Minnesota 4-4; New England 7-9; New Orleans 4-5; N.Y. Giants 4-1; N.Y. Jets 6-9; Oakland 7-15; Philadelphia 6-1; Pittsburgh 23-30; St. Louis 5-3; San Diego 8-14; San Francisco 1-7; Seattle 7-7; Tampa Bay 3-2; Washington 2-4.

RETIRED UNIFORM NUMBERS

No.	Player
54	Bob Johnson

DALLAS COWBOYS
YEAR-BY-YEAR RECORDS

Year	W	L	T	Pct.	PF	PA	Finish	W	L	Highest round	Coach
1960	0	11	1	.000	177	369	7th/Western Conf.	—	—		Tom Landry
1961	4	9	1	.308	236	380	6th/Eastern Conf.	—	—		Tom Landry
1962	5	8	1	.385	398	402	5th/Eastern Conf.	—	—		Tom Landry
1963	4	10	0	.286	305	378	5th/Eastern Conf.	—	—		Tom Landry
1964	5	8	1	.385	250	289	5th/Eastern Conf.	—	—		Tom Landry
1965	7	7	0	.500	325	280	T2nd/Eastern Conf.	—	—		Tom Landry
1966	10	3	1	.769	445	239	1st/Eastern Conf.	0	1	NFL championship game	Tom Landry
1967	9	5	0	.643	342	268	1st/Capitol Div.	1	1	NFL championship game	Tom Landry
1968	12	2	0	.857	431	186	1st/Capitol Div.	0	1	E. Conf. championship game	Tom Landry
1969	11	2	1	.846	369	223	1st/Capitol Div.	0	1	E. Conf. championship game	Tom Landry
1970	10	4	0	.714	299	221	1st/NFC Eastern Div.	2	1	Super Bowl	Tom Landry
1971	11	3	0	.786	406	222	1st/NFC Eastern Div.	3	0	Super Bowl champ	Tom Landry
1972	10	4	0	.714	319	240	2nd/NFC Eastern Div.	1	1	NFC championship game	Tom Landry
1973	10	4	0	.714	382	203	1st/NFC Eastern Div.	1	1	NFC championship game	Tom Landry
1974	8	6	0	.571	297	235	3rd/NFC Eastern Div.	—	—		Tom Landry
1975	10	4	0	.714	350	268	2nd/NFC Eastern Div.	2	1	Super Bowl	Tom Landry
1976	11	3	0	.786	296	194	1st/NFC Eastern Div.	0	1	NFC div. playoff game	Tom Landry
1977	12	2	0	.857	345	212	1st/NFC Eastern Div.	3	0	Super Bowl champ	Tom Landry
1978	12	4	0	.750	384	208	1st/NFC Eastern Div.	2	1	Super Bowl	Tom Landry
1979	11	5	0	.688	371	313	1st/NFC Eastern Div.	0	1	NFC div. playoff game	Tom Landry
1980	12	4	0	.750	454	311	2nd/NFC Eastern Div.	2	1	NFC championship game	Tom Landry
1981	12	4	0	.750	367	277	1st/NFC Eastern Div.	1	1	NFC championship game	Tom Landry
1982	6	3	0	.667	226	145	2nd/NFC	2	1	NFC championship game	Tom Landry
1983	12	4	0	.750	479	360	2nd/NFC Eastern Div.	0	1	NFC wild-card game	Tom Landry
1984	9	7	0	.563	308	308	T3rd/NFC Eastern Div.	—	—		Tom Landry
1985	10	6	0	.625	357	333	1st/NFC Eastern Div.	0	1	NFC div. playoff game	Tom Landry
1986	7	9	0	.438	346	337	3rd/NFC Eastern Div.	—	—		Tom Landry
1987	7	8	0	.467	340	348	2nd/NFC Eastern Div.	—	—		Tom Landry
1988	3	13	0	.188	265	381	5th/NFC Eastern Div.	—	—		Tom Landry
1989	1	15	0	.063	204	393	5th/NFC Eastern Div.	—	—		Jimmy Johnson
1990	7	9	0	.438	244	308	4th/NFC Eastern Div.	—	—		Jimmy Johnson
1991	11	5	0	.688	342	310	2nd/NFC Eastern Div.	1	1	NFC div. playoff game	Jimmy Johnson
1992	13	3	0	.813	409	243	1st/NFC Eastern Div.	3	0	Super Bowl champ	Jimmy Johnson
1993	12	4	0	.750	376	229	1st/NFC Eastern Div.	3	0	Super Bowl champ	Jimmy Johnson
1994	12	4	0	.750	414	248	1st/NFC Eastern Div.	1	1	NFC championship game	Barry Switzer
1995	12	4	0	.750	435	291	1st/NFC Eastern Div.	3	0	Super Bowl champ	Barry Switzer
1996	10	6	0	.625	286	250	1st/NFC Eastern Div.	1	1	NFC div. playoff game	Barry Switzer

FIRST-ROUND DRAFT PICKS

1961—Bob Lilly, DT, Texas Christian
1962—None
1963—Lee Roy Jordan, LB, Alabama
1964—Scott Appleton, DT, Texas
1965—Craig Morton, QB, California
1966—John Niland, G, Iowa
1967—None
1968—Dennis Homan, WR, Alabama
1969—Calvin Hill, RB, Yale
1970—Duane Thomas, RB, West Texas State
1971—Tody Smith, DE, Southern California
1972—Bill Thomas, RB, Boston College
1973—Billy Joe DuPree, TE, Michigan State
1974—Ed Jones, DE, Tennessee State*
　　　Charles Young, RB, North Carolina State
1975—Randy White, LB, Maryland
　　　Thomas Henderson, LB, Langston
1976—Aaron Kyle, DB, Wyoming
1977—Tony Dorsett, RB, Pittsburgh

1978—Larry Bethea, DE, Michigan State
1979—Robert Shaw, C, Tennessee
1980—None
1981—Howard Richards, T, Missouri
1982—Rod Hill, DB, Kentucky State
1983—Jim Jeffcoat, DE, Arizona State
1984—Billy Cannon Jr., LB, Texas A&M
1985—Kevin Brooks, DE, Michigan
1986—Mike Sherrard, WR, UCLA
1987—Danny Noonan, DT, Nebraska
1988—Michael Irvin, WR, Miami (Fla.)
1989—Troy Aikman, QB, UCLA*
1990—Emmitt Smith, RB, Florida
1991—Russell Maryland, DL, Miami (Fla.)*
　　　Alvin Harper, WR, Tennessee
　　　Kelvin Pritchett, DT, Mississippi
1992—Kevin Smith, DB, Texas A&M
　　　Robert Jones, LB, East Carolina
1993—None

1994—Shante Carver, DE, Arizona State
1995—None
1996—None

1997—David LaFleur, TE, Louisiana State
*First player chosen in draft.

FRANCHISE RECORDS

Most rushing yards, career
12,036—Tony Dorsett
Most rushing yards, season
1,773—Emmitt Smith, 1995
Most rushing yards, game
237—Emmitt Smith at Phi., Oct. 31, 1993
Most rushing touchdowns, season
25—Emmitt Smith, 1995
Most passing attempts, season
533—Danny White, 1983
Most passing attempts, game
49—Roger Staubach at Phi., Oct. 26, 1975
Gary Hogeboom at S.F., Dec. 22, 1985
Danny White at Was., Oct. 13, 1987
Steve Walsh vs. Pho., Oct. 29, 1989
Most passes completed, season
334—Danny White, 1983
Most passes completed, game
33—Gary Hogeboom at L.A. Rams, Sept. 3, 1984
Troy Aikman at Mia., Oct. 27, 1996

Most passing yards, career
22,733—Troy Aikman
Most passing yards, season
3,980—Danny White, 1983
Most passing yards, game
460—Don Meredith at S.F., Nov. 10, 1963
Most touchdown passes, season
29—Danny White, 1983
Most pass receptions, career
591—Michael Irvin
Most pass receptions, season
111—Michael Irvin, 1995
Most pass receptions, game
13—Lance Rentzel vs. Was., Nov. 19, 1967
Most receiving yards, career
9,500—Michael Irvin
Most receiving yards, season
1,603—Michael Irvin, 1995
Most receiving yards, game
246—Bob Hayes at Was., Nov. 13, 1966

Most receiving touchdowns, season
14—Frank Clarke, 1962
Most touchdowns, career
115—Emmitt Smith
Most field goals, season
28—Eddie Murray, 1993
Longest field goal
54 yards—Toni Fritsch at NYG, Sept. 24 1972
Ken Willis at Cle., Sept. 1, 1991
Most interceptions, career
52—Mel Renfro
Most interceptions, season
11—Everson Walls, 1981
Most sacks, career
113—Harvey Martin
Most sacks, season
20—Harvey Martin, 1977

SERIES RECORDS

Dallas vs.: Arizona 46-22-1; Atlanta 11-6; Buffalo 3-3; Carolina 0-0; Chicago 8-7; Cincinnati 4-2; Denver 4-2; Detroit 7-6; Green Bay 8-9; Houston 5-3; Indianapolis 7-3; Jacksonville 0-0; Kansas City 4-2; Miami 2-6; Minnesota 9-6; New England 7-5; New Orleans 14-3; N.Y. Giants 44-23-2; N.Y. Jets 5-1; Oakland 3-3; Philadelphia 44-28; Pittsburgh 13-11; St. Louis 8-9; San Diego 5-1; San Francisco 7-11-1; Seattle 4-1; Tampa Bay 6-0; Washington 40-30-2.

RETIRED UNIFORM NUMBER

No.	Player
	None

DENVER BRONCOS
YEAR-BY-YEAR RECORDS

		REGULAR SEASON						PLAYOFFS		
Year	W	L	T	Pct.	PF	PA	Finish	W	L	Highest round	Coach
1960*	4	9	1	.308	309	393	4th/Western Div.	—	—		Frank Filchock
1961*	3	11	0	.214	251	432	3rd/Western Div.	—	—		Frank Filchock
1962*	7	7	0	.500	353	334	2nd/Western Div.	—	—		Jack Faulkner
1963*	2	11	1	.154	301	473	4th/Western Div.	—	—		Jack Faulkner
1964*	2	11	1	.154	240	438	4th/Western Div.	—	—		Jack Faulkner, Mac Speedie
1965*	4	10	0	.286	303	392	4th/Western Div.	—	—		Mac Speedie
1966*	4	10	0	.286	196	381	4th/Western Div.	—	—		Mac Speedie, Ray Malava
1967*	3	11	0	.214	256	409	4th/Western Div.	—	—		Lou Saban
1968*	5	9	0	.357	255	404	4th/Western Div.	—	—		Lou Saban
1969*	5	8	1	.385	297	344	4th/Western Div.	—	—		Lou Saban
1970	5	8	1	.385	253	264	4th/AFC Western Div.	—	—		Lou Saban
1971	4	9	1	.308	203	275	4th/AFC Western Div.	—	—		Lou Saban, Jerry Smith
1972	5	9	0	.357	325	350	3rd/AFC Western Div.	—	—		John Ralston
1973	7	5	2	.571	354	296	T2nd/AFC Western Div.	—	—		John Ralston
1974	7	6	1	.536	302	294	2nd/AFC Western Div.	—	—		John Ralston
1975	6	8	0	.429	254	307	2nd/AFC Western Div.	—	—		John Ralston
1976	9	5	0	.643	315	206	2nd/AFC Western Div.	—	—		John Ralston
1977	12	2	0	.857	274	148	1st/AFC Western Div.	2	1	Super Bowl	Red Miller
1978	10	6	0	.625	282	198	1st/AFC Western Div.	0	1	AFC div. playoff game	Red Miller
1979	10	6	0	.625	289	262	2nd/AFC Western Div.	0	1	AFC wild-card game	Red Miller
1980	8	8	0	.500	310	323	T3rd/AFC Western Div.	—	—		Dan Reeves
1981	10	6	0	.625	321	289	2nd/AFC Western Div.	—	—		Dan Reeves
1982	2	7	0	.222	148	226	12th/AFC	—	—		Dan Reeves
1983	9	7	0	.563	302	327	T2nd/AFC Western Div.	0	1	AFC wild-card game	Dan Reeves
1984	13	3	0	.813	353	241	1st/AFC Western Div.	0	1	AFC div. playoff game	Dan Reeves
1985	11	5	0	.688	380	329	2nd/AFC Western Div.	—	—		Dan Reeves
1986	11	5	0	.688	378	327	1st/AFC Western Div.	2	1	Super Bowl	Dan Reeves
1987	10	4	1	.700	379	288	1st/AFC Western Div.	2	1	Super Bowl	Dan Reeves

	REGULAR SEASON							PLAYOFFS			
Year	W	L	T	Pct.	PF	PA	Finish	W	L	Highest round	Coach
1988	8	8	0	.500	327	352	2nd/AFC Western Div.	—	—		Dan Reeves
1989	11	5	0	.688	362	226	1st/AFC Western Div.	2	1	Super Bowl	Dan Reeves
1990	5	11	0	.313	331	374	5th/AFC Western Div.	—	—		Dan Reeves
1991	12	4	0	.750	304	235	1st/AFC Western Div.	1	1	AFC championship game	Dan Reeves
1992	8	8	0	.500	262	329	3rd/AFC Western Div.	—	—		Dan Reeves
1993	9	7	0	.563	373	284	3rd/AFC Western Div.	0	1	AFC wild-card game	Wade Phillips
1994	7	9	0	.438	347	396	4th/AFC Western Div.	—	—		Wade Phillips
1995	8	8	0	.500	388	345	T3rd/AFC Western Div.	—	—		Mike Shanahan
1996	13	3	0	.813	391	275	1st/AFC Western Div.	0	1	AFC div. playoff game	Mike Shanahan

*American Football League.

FIRST-ROUND DRAFT PICKS

1960—Roger Leclerc, C, Trinity (Conn.)
1961—Bob Gaiters, RB, New Mexico State
1962—Merlin Olsen, DT, Utah State
1963—Kermit Alexander, DB, UCLA
1964—Bob Brown, T, Nebraska
1965—None
1966—Jerry Shay, DT, Purdue
1967—Floyd Little, RB, Syracuse
1968—None
1969—None
1970—Bob Anderson, RB, Colorado
1971—Marv Montgomery, T, Southern California
1972—Riley Odoms, TE, Houston
1973—Otis Armstrong, RB, Purdue
1974—Randy Gradishar, LB, Ohio State
1975—Louis Wright, DB, San Jose State
1976—Tom Glassic, G, Virginia
1977—Steve Schindler, G, Boston College
1978—Don Latimer, DT, Miami (Fla.)
1979—Kevin Clark, T, Nebraska

1980—None
1981—Dennis Smith, DB, Southern California
1982—Gerald Willhite, RB, San Jose State
1983—Chris Hinton, G, Northwestern
1984—None
1985—Steve Sewell, RB, Oklahoma
1986—None
1987—Ricky Nattiel, WR, Florida
1988—Ted Gregory, DT, Syracuse
1989—Steve Atwater, DB, Arkansas
1990—None
1991—Mike Croel, LB, Nebraska
1992—Tommy Maddox, QB, UCLA
1993—Dan Williams, DE, Toledo
1994—None
1995—None
1996—John Mobley, LB, Kutztown (Pa.)
1997—Trevor Pryce, DT, Clemson

FRANCHISE RECORDS

Most rushing yards, career
6,323—Floyd Little
Most rushing yards, season
1,538—Terrell Davis, 1996
Most rushing yards, game
194—Terrell Davis vs. Balt., Oct. 20, 1996
Most rushing touchdowns, season
13—Terrell Davis, 1996
Most passing attempts, season
605—John Elway, 1985
Most passing attempts, game
59—John Elway at G.B., Oct. 10, 1993
Most passes completed, season
348—John Elway, 1993
Most passes completed, game
36—John Elway vs. S.D., Sept. 4, 1994
Most passing yards, career
45,034—John Elway
Most passing yards, season
4030—John Elway, 1993

Most passing yards, game
447—Frank Tripucka at Buf., Sept. 15, 1962
Most touchdown passes, season
26—John Elway, 1995, 1996
Most pass receptions, career
543—Lionel Taylor
Most pass receptions, season
100—Lionel Taylor, 1961
Most pass receptions, game
13—Lionel Taylor vs. Oak., Nov. 29, 1964
Robert Anderson vs. Chi., Sept. 30, 1973
Shannon Sharpe vs. S.D., Oct. 6, 1996
Most receiving yards, career
6,872—Lionel Taylor
Most receiving yards, season
1,244—Steve Watson, 1981
Most receiving yards, game
199—Lionel Taylor vs. Buf., Nov. 27, 1960

Most receiving touchdowns, season
13—Steve Watson, 1981
Most touchdowns, career
54—Floyd Little
Most field goals, season
31—Jason Elam, 1995
Longest field goal
57 yards—Fred Steinfort vs. Was., Oct. 13, 1980
Most interceptions, career
44—Steve Foley
Most interceptions, season
11—Goose Gonsoulin, 1960
Most sacks, career
97.5—Simon Fletcher
Most sacks, season
16—Simon Fletcher, 1992

SERIES RECORDS

Denver vs.: Arizona 4-0-1; Atlanta 5-3; Baltimore 1-0; Buffalo 11-17-1; Carolina 0-0; Chicago 6-5; Cincinnati 12-6; Dallas 2-4; Detroit 4-3; Green Bay 4-3-1; Houston 11-20-2; Indianapolis 9-2; Jacksonville 1-0; Kansas City 31-42; Miami 2-5-1; Minnesota 4-5; New England 18-12; New Orleans 4-2; N.Y. Giants 3-3; N.Y. Jets 13-12-1; Oakland 23-32; Philadelphia 2-6; Pittsburgh 10-5-1; San Diego 38-35-1; St. Louis 3-4; San Francisco 4-3; Seattle 24-15; Tampa Bay 3-1; Washington 4-3.

RETIRED UNIFORM NUMBERS

No.	Player
18	Frank Tripucka
44	Floyd Little

DETROIT LIONS
YEAR-BY-YEAR RECORDS

		REGULAR SEASON						PLAYOFFS		
Year	W	L	T	Pct.	PF	PA	Finish	W	L	Highest round	Coach
1930*	5	6	3	.455	...	...	T7th				Tubby Griffen
1931*	11	3	0	.786	...	...	2nd				Potsy Clark
1932*	6	2	4	.750	...	...	3rd				Potsy Clark
1933*	6	5	0	.545	128	87	2nd/Western Div.	—	—		Potsy Clark
1934	10	3	0	.769	238	59	2nd/Western Div.	—	—		Potsy Clark
1935	7	3	2	.700	191	111	1st/Western Div.	1	0	NFL champ	Potsy Clark
1936	8	4	0	.667	235	102	3rd/Western Div.	—	—		Potsy Clark
1937	7	4	0	.636	180	105	T2nd/Western Div.	—	—		Dutch Clark
1938	7	4	0	.636	119	108	2nd/Western Div.	—	—		Dutch Clark
1939	6	5	0	.545	145	150	3rd/Western Div.	—	—		Gus Henderson
1940	5	5	1	.500	138	153	3rd/Western Div.	—	—		Potsy Clark
1941	4	6	1	.400	121	195	3rd/Western Div.	—	—		Bill Edwards
1942	0	11	0	.000	38	263	5th/Western Div.	—	—		Bill Edwards, John Karc
1943	3	6	1	.333	178	218	3rd/Western Div.	—	—		Gus Dorais
1944	6	3	1	.667	216	151	T2nd/Western Div.	—	—		Gus Dorais
1945	7	3	0	.700	195	194	2nd/Western Div.	—	—		Gus Dorais
1946	1	10	0	.091	142	310	2nd/Western Div.	—	—		Gus Dorais
1947	3	9	0	.250	231	305	5th/Western Div.	—	—		Gus Dorais
1948	2	10	0	.167	200	407	5th/Western Div.	—	—		Bo McMillin
1949	4	8	0	.333	237	259	4th/Western Div.	—	—		Bo McMillin
1950	6	6	0	.500	321	285	4th/National Conf.	—	—		Bo McMillin
1951	7	4	1	.636	336	259	T2nd/National Conf.	—	—		Buddy Parker
1952	9	3	0	.750	344	192	1st/National Conf.	2	0	NFL champ	Buddy Parker
1953	10	2	0	.833	271	205	1st/Western Conf.	1	0	NFL champ	Buddy Parker
1954	9	2	1	.818	337	189	1st/Western Conf.	0	1	NFL championship game	Buddy Parker
1955	3	9	0	.250	230	275	6th/Western Conf.	—	—		Buddy Parker
1956	9	3	0	.750	300	188	2nd/Western Conf.	—	—		Buddy Parker
1957	8	4	0	.667	251	231	1st/Western Conf.	2	0	NFL champ	George Wilson
1958	4	7	1	.364	261	276	5th/Western Conf.	—	—		George Wilson
1959	3	8	1	.273	203	275	5th/Western Conf.	—	—		George Wilson
1960	7	5	0	.583	239	212	T2nd/Western Conf.	—	—		George Wilson
1961	8	5	1	.615	270	258	2nd/Western Conf.	—	—		George Wilson
1962	11	3	0	.786	315	177	2nd/Western Conf.	—	—		George Wilson
1963	5	8	1	.385	326	265	T4th/Western Conf.	—	—		George Wilson
1964	7	5	2	.583	280	260	4th/Western Conf.	—	—		George Wilson
1965	6	7	1	.462	257	295	6th/Western Conf.	—	—		Harry Gilmer
1966	4	9	1	.308	206	317	T6th/Western Conf.	—	—		Harry Gilmer
1967	5	7	2	.417	260	259	3rd/Central Div.	—	—		Joe Schmidt
1968	4	8	2	.333	207	241	4th/Central Div.	—	—		Joe Schmidt
1969	9	4	1	.692	259	188	2nd/Central Div.	—	—		Joe Schmidt
1970	10	4	0	.714	347	202	2nd/NFC Central Div.	0	1	NFC div. playoff game	Joe Schmidt
1971	7	6	1	.538	341	286	2nd/NFC Central Div.	—	—		Joe Schmidt
1972	8	5	1	.607	339	290	2nd/NFC Central Div.	—	—		Don McCafferty
1973	6	7	1	.464	271	247	2nd/NFC Central Div.	—	—		Rick Forzano
1974	7	7	0	.500	256	270	2nd/NFC Central Div.	—	—		Rick Forzano
1975	7	7	0	.500	245	262	2nd/NFC Central Div.	—	—		R. Forzano, T. Hudspe
1976	6	8	0	.429	262	220	3rd/NFC Central Div.	—	—		Tommy Hudspeth
1977	6	8	0	.429	183	252	3rd/NFC Central Div.	—	—		Monte Clark
1978	7	9	0	.438	290	300	T3rd/NFC Central Div.	—	—		Monte Clark
1979	2	14	0	.125	219	365	5th/NFC Central Div.	—	—		Monte Clark
1980	9	7	0	.563	334	272	2nd/NFC Central Div.	—	—		Monte Clark
1981	8	8	0	.500	397	322	2nd/NFC Central Div.	—	—		Monte Clark
1982	4	5	0	.444	181	176	T8th/NFC	0	1	NFC first-round pl. game	Monte Clark
1983	9	7	0	.563	347	286	1st/NFC Central Div.	0	1	NFC div. playoff game	Monte Clark
1984	4	11	1	.281	283	408	4th/NFC Central Div.	—	—		Monte Clark
1985	7	9	0	.438	307	366	T3rd/NFC Central Div.	—	—		Darryl Rogers
1986	5	11	0	.313	277	326	3rd/NFC Central Div.	—	—		Darryl Rogers
1987	4	11	0	.267	269	384	T4th/NFC Central Div.	—	—		Darryl Rogers
1988	4	12	0	.250	220	313	T4th/NFC Central Div.	—	—		Darryl Rogers
1989	7	9	0	.438	312	364	3rd/NFC Central Div.	—	—		Wayne Fontes
1990	6	10	0	.375	373	413	T2nd/NFC Central Div.	—	—		Wayne Fontes
1991	12	4	0	.750	339	295	1st/NFC Central Div.	1	1	NFC championship game	Wayne Fontes
1992	5	11	0	.313	273	332	T3rd/NFC Central Div.	—	—		Wayne Fontes
1993	10	6	0	.625	298	292	1st/NFC Central Div.	0	1	NFC wild-card game	Wayne Fontes
1994	9	7	0	.563	357	342	T2nd/NFC Central Div.	0	1	NFC wild-card game	Wayne Fontes
1995	10	6	0	.625	436	336	2nd/NFC Central Div.	0	1	NFC wild-card game	Wayne Fontes
1996	5	11	0	.313	302	368	5th/NFC Central Div.	—	—		Wayne Fontes

*Portsmouth Spartans.

FIRST-ROUND DRAFT PICKS

36—Sid Wagner, G, Michigan State
37—Lloyd Cardwell, B, Nebraska
38—Alex Wojciechowicz, C, Fordham
39—John Pingel, B, Michigan State
40—Doyle Nave, B, Southern California
41—Jim Thomason, B, Texas A&M
42—Bob Westfall, B, Michigan
43—Frank Sinkwich, B, Georgia*
44—Otto Graham, B, Northwestern
45—Frank Szymanski, B, Notre Dame
46—Bill Dellastatious, B, Missouri
47—Glenn Davis, B, Army
48—Y.A. Tittle, B, Louisiana State
49—John Rauch, B, Georgia
50—Leon Hart, E, Notre Dame*
    Joe Watson, C, Rice
51—None
52—None
53—Harley Sewell, G, Texas
54—Dick Chapman, T, Rice
55—Dave Middleton, B, Auburn
56—Howard Cassidy, B, Ohio State
57—Bill Glass, G, Baylor
58—Alex Karras, DT, Iowa
59—Nick Pietrosante, B, Notre Dame
60—John Robinson, DB, Louisiana State
61—None
62—John Hadl, QB, Kansas
63—Daryl Sanders, T, Ohio State
64—Pete Beathard, QB, Southern California
65—Tom Nowatzke, RB, Indiana
66—None
67—Mel Farr, RB, UCLA
68—Greg Landry, QB, Massachusetts
    Earl McCullouch, E, Southern California

1969—None
1970—Steve Owens, RB, Oklahoma
1971—Bob Bell, DT, Cincinnati
1972—Herb Orvis, DE, Colorado
1973—Ernie Price, DE, Texas A&I
1974—Ed O'Neil, LB, Penn State
1975—Lynn Boden, G, South Dakota State
1976—James Hunter, DB, Grambling State
    Lawrence Gaines, FB, Wyoming
1977—None
1978—Luther Bradley, DB, Notre Dame
1979—Keith Dorney, T, Penn State
1980—Billy Sims, RB, Oklahoma*
1981—Mark Nichols, WR, San Jose State
1982—Jimmy Williams, LB, Nebraska
1983—James Jones, RB, Florida
1984—David Lewis, TE, California
1985—Lomas Brown, T, Florida
1986—Chuck Long, QB, Iowa
1987—Reggie Rogers, DE, Washington
1988—Bennie Blades, S, Miami (Fla.)
1989—Barry Sanders, RB, Oklahoma State
1990—Andre Ware, QB, Houston
1991—Herman Moore, WR, Virginia
1992—Robert Porcher, DE, South Carolina State
1993—None
1994—Johnnie Morton, WR, Southern California
1995—Luther Elliss, DT, Utah
1996—Reggie Brown, LB, Texas A&M
    Jeff Hartings, G, Penn State
1997—Bryant Westbrook, DB, Texas
    *First player chosen in draft.

FRANCHISE RECORDS

Most rushing yards, career
?25—Barry Sanders
Most rushing yards, season
?3—Barry Sanders, 1994
Most rushing yards, game
—Barry Sanders vs. T.B., Nov. 13, 1994
Most rushing touchdowns, season
—Barry Sanders, 1991
Most passing attempts, season
—Scott Mitchell, 1995
Most passing attempts, game
—Eric Hipple at L.A. Rams, Oct. 19, 1986
  Scott Mitchell at Was., Oct. 22, 1995
  Scott Mitchell at Atl., Nov. 5, 1995
  Scott Mitchell at Oak., Oct. 13, 1996
Most passes completed, season
—Scott Mitchell, 1995
Most passes completed, game
—Eric Hipple at Cle., Sept. 28, 1986
  Chuck Long vs. G.B., Oct. 25, 1987

Most passing yards, career
15,710—Bobby Layne
Most passing yards, season
4,338—Scott Mitchell, 1995
Most passing yards, game
410—Scott Mitchell vs. Min., Nov. 23, 1995
Most touchdown passes, season
32—Scott Mitchell, 1995
Most pass receptions, career
424—Herman Moore
Most pass receptions, season
123—Herman Moore, 1995
Most pass receptions, game
14—Herman Moore vs. Chi., Dec. 5, 1995
Most receiving yards, career
6,191—Herman Moore
Most receiving yards, season
1,686—Herman Moore, 1995

Most receiving yards, game
302—Cloyce Box vs. Bal., Dec. 3, 1950
Most receiving touchdowns, season
15—Cloyce Box, 1952
Most touchdowns, career
91—Barry Sanders
Most field goals, season
34—Jason Hanson, 1993
Longest field goal
56 yards—Jason Hanson vs. Cle., Oct. 8, 1995
Most interceptions, career
62—Dick LeBeau
Most interceptions, season
12—Don Doll, 1950
    Jack Christiansen, 1953
Most sacks, season
23—Al Baker, 1978

SERIES RECORDS

Detroit vs.: Arizona 28-15-3; Atlanta 19-6; Buffalo 3-1-1; Carolina 0-0; Chicago 51-71-3; Cincinnati 3-3; Dallas 6-7; Denver 3-4; Green Bay 56-65-6; Houston 3-4; Indianapolis 18-?; Jacksonville 1-0; Kansas City 3-5; Miami 2-3; Minnesota 25-44-2; New England 3-?; New Orleans 6-7-1; N.Y. Giants 14-13-1; N.Y. Jets 4-3; Oakland 2-6; Philadelphia 11-?; Pittsburgh 13-12-1; St. Louis 27-32-1; San Diego 3-3; San Francisco 26-28-1; Seattle 3-4; Tampa Bay 21-17; Washington 3-23.
Note: Includes records only from 1934 to present.

RETIRED UNIFORM NUMBERS

No.	Player
7	Dutch Clark
22	Bobby Layne
37	Doak Walker
56	Joe Schmidt
85	Chuck Hughes
88	Charlie Sanders

HISTORY *Team by team*

			REGULAR SEASON				PLAYOFFS			
Year	W	L	T	Pct.	PF	PA	Finish	W	L	Highest round	Coach
1921	3	2	1	.600	...	...	T6th				Curly Lambeau
1922	4	3	3	.571	...	...	T7th				Curly Lambeau
1923	7	2	1	.778	...	...	3rd				Curly Lambeau
1924	7	4	0	.636	...	...	6th				Curly Lambeau
1925	8	5	0	.615	...	...	9th				Curly Lambeau
1926	7	3	3	.700	...	...	5th				Curly Lambeau
1927	7	2	1	.778	...	...	2nd				Curly Lambeau
1928	6	4	3	.600	...	...	4th				Curly Lambeau
1929	12	0	1	1.000	...	...	1st				Curly Lambeau
1930	10	3	1	.769	...	...	1st				Curly Lambeau
1931	12	2	0	.857	...	...	1st				Curly Lambeau
1932	10	3	1	.769	...	...	2nd				Curly Lambeau
1933	5	7	1	.417	170	107	3rd/Western Div.	—	—		Curly Lambeau
1934	7	6	0	.538	156	112	3rd/Western Div.				Curly Lambeau
1935	8	4	0	.667	181	96	2nd/Western Div.	—	—		Curly Lambeau
1936	10	1	1	.909	248	118	1st/Western Div.	1	0	NFL champ	Curly Lambeau
1937	7	4	0	.636	220	122	T2nd/Western Div.	—	—		Curly Lambeau
1938	8	3	0	.727	223	118	1st/Western Div.	0	1	NFL championship game	Curly Lambeau
1939	9	2	0	.818	233	153	1st/Western Div.	1	0	NFL champ	Curly Lambeau
1940	6	4	1	.600	238	155	2nd/Western Div.				Curly Lambeau
1941	10	1	0	.909	258	120	2nd/Western Div.	0	1	W. Div. championship game	Curly Lambeau
1942	8	2	1	.800	300	215	2nd/Western Div.	—	—		Curly Lambeau
1943	7	2	1	.778	264	172	2nd/Western Div.	—	—		Curly Lambeau
1944	8	2	0	.800	238	141	1st/Western Div.	1	0	NFL champ	Curly Lambeau
1945	6	4	0	.600	258	173	3rd/Western Div.	—	—		Curly Lambeau
1946	6	5	0	.545	148	158	T3rd/Western Div.	—	—		Curly Lambeau
1947	6	5	1	.545	274	210	3rd/Western Div.	—	—		Curly Lambeau
1948	3	9	0	.250	154	290	4th/Western Div.	—	—		Curly Lambeau
1949	2	10	0	.167	114	329	5th/Western Div.	—	—		Curly Lambeau
1950	3	9	0	.250	244	406	T5th/National Conf.	—	—		Gene Ronzani
1951	3	9	0	.250	254	375	5th/National Conf.	—	—		Gene Ronzani
1952	6	6	0	.500	295	312	4th/National Conf.	—	—		Gene Ronzani
1953	2	9	1	.182	200	338	6th/National Conf.	—	—		Gene Ronzani, Hugh Devore-Scooter McLe
1954	4	8	0	.333	234	251	5th/Western Conf.	—	—		Lisle Blackbourn
1955	6	6	0	.500	258	276	3rd/Western Conf.	—	—		Lisle Blackbourn
1956	4	8	0	.333	264	342	5th/Western Conf.	—	—		Lisle Blackbourn
1957	3	9	0	.250	218	311	6th/Western Conf.	—	—		Lisle Blackbourn
1958	1	10	1	.091	193	382	6th/Western Conf.	—	—		Scooter McLean
1959	7	5	0	.583	248	246	T3rd/Western Conf.	—	—		Vince Lombardi
1960	8	4	0	.667	332	209	1st/Western Conf.	0	1	NFL championship game	Vince Lombardi
1961	11	3	0	.786	391	223	1st/Western Conf.	1	0	NFL champ	Vince Lombardi
1962	13	1	0	.929	415	148	1st/Western Conf.	1	0	NFL champ	Vince Lombardi
1963	11	2	1	.846	369	206	2nd/Western Conf.	—	—		Vince Lombardi
1964	8	5	1	.615	342	245	T2nd/Western Conf.	—	—		Vince Lombardi
1965	10	3	1	.769	316	224	1st/Western Conf.	2	0	NFL champ	Vince Lombardi
1966	12	2	0	.857	335	163	1st/Western Conf.	2	0	Super Bowl champ	Vince Lombardi
1967	9	4	1	.692	332	209	1st/Central Div.	3	0	Super Bowl champ	Vince Lombardi
1968	6	7	1	.462	281	227	3rd/Central Div.	—	—		Phil Bengtson
1969	8	6	0	.571	269	221	3rd/Central Div.	—	—		Phil Bengtson
1970	6	8	0	.429	196	293	T3rd/NFC Central Div.	—	—		Phil Bengtson
1971	4	8	2	.333	274	298	4th/NFC Central Div.	—	—		Dan Devine
1972	10	4	0	.714	304	226	1st/NFC Central Div.	0	1	NFC div. playoff game	Dan Devine
1973	5	7	2	.429	202	259	3rd/NFC Central Div.	—	—		Dan Devine
1974	6	8	0	.429	210	206	3rd/NFC Central Div.	—	—		Dan Devine
1975	4	10	0	.286	226	285	T3rd/NFC Central Div.	—	—		Bart Starr
1976	5	9	0	.357	218	299	4th/NFC Central Div.	—	—		Bart Starr
1977	4	10	0	.286	134	219	4th/NFC Central Div.	—	—		Bart Starr
1978	8	7	1	.531	249	269	2nd/NFC Central Div.	—	—		Bart Starr
1979	5	11	0	.313	246	316	4th/NFC Central Div.	—	—		Bart Starr
1980	5	10	1	.344	231	371	T4th/NFC Central Div.	—	—		Bart Starr
1981	8	8	0	.500	324	361	3rd/NFC Central Div.	—	—		Bart Starr
1982	5	3	1	.611	226	169	3rd/NFC	1	1	NFC second-round pl. game	Bart Starr
1983	8	8	0	.500	429	439	T2nd/NFC Central Div.	—	—		Bart Starr
1984	8	8	0	.500	390	309	2nd/NFC Central Div.	—	—		Forrest Gregg
1985	8	8	0	.500	337	355	2nd/NFC Central Div.	—	—		Forrest Gregg
1986	4	12	0	.250	254	418	4th/NFC Central Div.	—	—		Forrest Gregg

			REGULAR SEASON					PLAYOFFS			
Year	W	L	T	Pct.	PF	PA	Finish	W	L	Highest round	Coach
1987	5	9	1	.367	255	300	3rd/NFC Central Div.	—	—		Forrest Gregg
1988	4	12	0	.250	240	315	T4th/NFC Central Div.	—	—		Lindy Infante
1989	10	6	0	.625	362	356	2nd/NFC Central Div.	—	—		Lindy Infante
1990	6	10	0	.375	271	347	T2nd/NFC Central Div.	—	—		Lindy Infante
1991	4	12	0	.250	273	313	4th/NFC Central Div.	—	—		Lindy Infante
1992	9	7	0	.563	276	296	2nd/NFC Central Div.	—	—		Mike Holmgren
1993	9	7	0	.563	340	282	T2nd/NFC Central Div.	1	1	NFC div. playoff game	Mike Holmgren
1994	9	7	0	.563	382	287	T2nd/NFC Central Div.	1	1	NFC div. playoff game	Mike Holmgren
1995	11	5	0	.689	404	314	1st/NFC Central Div.	1	1	NFC championship game	Mike Holmgren
1996	13	3	0	.813	456	210	1st/NFC Central Div.	3	0	Super Bowl champ	Mike Holmgren

FIRST-ROUND DRAFT PICKS

1936—Russ Letlow, G, San Francisco
1937—Ed Jankowski, B, Wisconsin
1938—Cecil Isbell, B, Purdue
1939—Larry Buhler, B, Minnesota
1940—Hal Van Every, B, Marquette
1941—George Paskvan, B, Wisconsin
1942—Urban Odson, T, Minnesota
1943—Dick Wildung, T, Minnesota
1944—Merv Pregulman, G, Michigan
1945—Walt Schlinkman, G, Texas Tech
1946—Johnny Strzykalski, B, Marquette
1947—Ernie Case, B, UCLA
1948—Earl Girard, B, Wisconsin
1949—Stan Heath, B, Nevada
1950—Clayton Tonnemaker, G, Minnesota
1951—Bob Gain, T, Kentucky
1952—Babe Parilli, QB, Kentucky
1953—Al Carmichael, B, Southern California
1954—Art Hunter, T, Notre Dame
        Veryl Switzer, B, Kansas State
1955—Tom Bettis, G, Purdue
1956—Jack Losch, B, Miami
1957—Paul Hornung, B, Notre Dame*
        Ron Kramer, E, Michigan
1958—Dan Currie, C, Michigan State
1959—Randy Duncan, B, Iowa*
1960—Tom Moore, RB, Vanderbilt
1961—Herb Adderley, DB, Michigan State
1962—Earl Gros, RB, Louisiana State
1963—Dave Robinson, LB, Penn State
1964—Lloyd Voss, DT, Nebraska
1965—Donny Anderson, RB, Texas Tech
        Larry Elkins, E, Baylor
1966—Jim Grabowski, RB, Illinois
        Gale Gillingham, G, Minnesota
1967—Bob Hyland, C, Boston College
        Don Horn, QB, San Diego State
1968—Fred Carr, LB, Texas-El Paso
        Bill Lueck, G, Arizona

1969—Rich Moore, DT, Villanova
1970—Mike McCoy, DT, Notre Dame
        Rich McGeorge, TE, Elon
1971—John Brockington, RB, Ohio State
1972—Willie Buchanon, DB, San Diego State
        Jerry Tagge, QB, Nebraska
1973—Barry Smith, WR, Florida State
1974—Barty Smith, RB, Richmond
1975—None
1976—Mark Koncar, T, Colorado
1977—Mike Butler, DE, Kansas
        Ezra Johnson, DE, Morris Brown
1978—James Lofton, WR, Stanford
        John Anderson, LB, Michigan
1979—Eddie Lee Ivery, RB, Georgia Tech
1980—Bruce Clark, DT, Penn State
        George Cumby, LB, Oklahoma
1981—Rich Campbell, QB, California
1982—Ron Hallstrom, G, Iowa
1983—Tim Lewis, DB, Pittsburgh
1984—Alphonso Carreker, DT, Florida State
1985—Ken Ruettgers, T, Southern California
1986—None
1987—Brent Fullwood, RB, Auburn
1988—Sterling Sharpe, WR, South Carolina
1989—Tony Mandarich, T, Michigan State
1990—Tony Bennett, LB, Mississippi
        Darrell Thompson, RB, Minnesota
1991—Vincent Clark, DB, Ohio State
1992—Terrell Buckley, DB, Florida State
1993—Wayne Simmons, LB, Clemson
        George Teague, DB, Alabama
1994—Aaron Taylor, T, Notre Dame
1995—Craig Newsome, DB, Arizona State
1996—John Michaels, T, Southern California
1997—Ross Verba, T, Iowa
        *First player chosen in draft.

FRANCHISE RECORDS

Most rushing yards, career
8,207—Jim Taylor

Most rushing yards, season
1,474—Jim Taylor, 1962

Most rushing yards, game
186—Jim Taylor vs. NYG, Dec. 3, 1961

Most rushing touchdowns, season
19—Jim Taylor, 1962

Most passing attempts, season
599—Don Majkowski, 1989

Most passing attempts, game
61—Brett Favre vs. S.F., Oct. 14, 1996 (OT)
61—Don Majkowski at Det., Nov. 12, 1989

Most passes completed, season
363—Brett Favre, 1994

Most passes completed, game
36—Brett Favre at Chi., Dec. 5, 1993

Most passing yards, career
24,718—Bart Starr

Most passing yards, season
4,458—Lynn Dickey, 1983

Most passing yards, game
418—Lynn Dickey at T.B., Oct. 12, 1980

Most touchdown passes, season
39—Brett Favre, 1996

Most pass receptions, career
595—Sterling Sharpe

Most pass receptions, season
112—Sterling Sharpe, 1993

Most pass receptions, game
14—Don Hutson at NYG, Nov. 22, 1942

Most receiving yards, career
9,656—James Lofton

Most receiving yards, season
1,497—Robert Brooks, 1995

Most receiving yards, game
257—Bill Howton vs. L.A. Rams, Oct. 21, 1956

Most receiving touchdowns, season
18—Sterling Sharpe, 1994

Most touchdowns, career
105—Don Hutson

Most field goals, season
33—Chester Marcol, 1972

Longest field goal
54 yards—Chris Jacke at Det., Jan. 2, 1994

Most interceptions, career
52—Bobby Dillon

Most interceptions, season
10—Irv Comp, 1943

Most sacks, career
84—Ezra Johnson

Most sacks, season
20.5—Ezra Johnson, 1978

SERIES RECORDS

Green Bay vs.: Arizona 41-21-4; Atlanta 10-9; Buffalo 1-5; Carolina 0-0; Chicago 65-82-6; Cincinnati 4-4; Dallas 9-8; Denver 3-4-1; Detroit 65-56-6; Houston 3-3; Indianapolis 18-18-1; Jacksonville 1-0; Kansas City 1-5-1; Miami 0-8; Minnesota 34-36-1; New England 2-3; New Orleans 13-4; N.Y. Giants 22-20-2; N.Y. Jets 2-5; Oakland 2-5; Philadelphia 20-8; Pittsburgh 21-11; St. Louis 26-40-1; San Diego 5-1; San Francisco 22-25-1; Seattle 4-3; Tampa Bay 22-13-1; Washington 9-11.

RETIRED UNIFORM NUMBERS

No.	Player
3	Tony Canadeo
14	Don Hutson
15	Bart Starr
66	Ray Nitschke

HOUSTON OILERS
YEAR-BY-YEAR RECORDS

		REGULAR SEASON						PLAYOFFS			
Year	W	L	T	Pct.	PF	PA	Finish	W	L	Highest round	Coach
1960*	10	4	0	.714	379	285	1st/Eastern Div.	1	0	AFL champ	Lou Rymkus
1961*	10	3	1	.769	513	242	1st/Eastern Div.	1	0	AFL champ	Lou Rymkus, Wally Lemm
1962*	11	3	0	.786	387	270	1st/Eastern Div.	0	1	AFL championship game	Pop Ivy
1963*	6	8	0	.429	302	372	3rd/Eastern Div.	—	—		Pop Ivy
1964*	4	10	0	.286	310	355	4th/Eastern Div.	—	—		Sammy Baugh
1965*	4	10	0	.286	298	429	4th/Eastern Div.	—	—		Hugh Taylor
1966*	3	11	0	.214	335	396	T4th/Eastern Div.	—	—		Wally Lemm
1967*	9	4	1	.692	258	199	1st/Eastern Div.	0	1	AFL championship game	Wally Lemm
1968*	7	7	0	.500	303	248	2nd/Eastern Div.	—	—		Wally Lemm
1969*	6	6	2	.500	278	279	2nd/Eastern Div.	0	1	Div. playoff game	Wally Lemm
1970	3	10	1	.231	217	352	4th/AFC Central Div.	—	—		Wally Lemm
1971	4	9	1	.308	251	330	3rd/AFC Central Div.	—	—		Ed Hughes
1972	1	13	0	.071	164	380	4th/AFC Central Div.	—	—		Bill Peterson
1973	1	13	0	.071	199	447	4th/AFC Central Div.	—	—		Bill Peterson, Sid Gillman
1974	7	7	0	.500	236	282	T2nd/AFC Central Div.	—	—		Sid Gillman
1975	10	4	0	.714	293	226	3rd/AFC Central Div.	—	—		Bum Phillips
1976	5	9	0	.357	222	273	4th/AFC Central Div.	—	—		Bum Phillips
1977	8	6	0	.571	299	230	T2nd/AFC Central Div.	—	—		Bum Phillips
1978	10	6	0	.625	283	298	2nd/AFC Central Div.	2	1	AFC championship game	Bum Phillips
1979	11	5	0	.688	362	331	2nd/AFC Central Div.	2	1	AFC championship game	Bum Phillips
1980	11	5	0	.688	295	251	2nd/AFC Central Div.	0	1	AFC wild-card game	Bum Phillips
1981	7	9	0	.438	281	355	3rd/AFC Central Div.	—	—		Ed Biles
1982	1	8	0	.111	136	245	13th/AFC	—	—		Ed Biles
1983	2	14	0	.125	288	460	4th/AFC Central Div.	—	—		Ed Biles, Chuck Studley
1984	3	13	0	.188	240	437	4th/AFC Central Div.	—	—		Hugh Campbell
1985	5	11	0	.313	284	412	4th/AFC Central Div.	—	—		H. Campbell, J. Glanville
1986	5	11	0	.313	274	329	4th/AFC Central Div.	—	—		Jerry Glanville
1987	9	6	0	.600	345	349	2nd/AFC Central Div.	1	1	AFC div. playoff game	Jerry Glanville
1988	10	6	0	.625	424	365	T2nd/AFC Central Div.	1	1	AFC div. playoff game	Jerry Glanville
1989	9	7	0	.563	365	412	T2nd/AFC Central Div.	0	1	AFC wild-card game	Jerry Glanville
1990	9	7	0	.563	405	307	2nd/AFC Central Div.	0	1	AFC wild-card game	Jack Pardee
1991	11	5	0	.688	386	251	1st/AFC Central Div.	1	1	AFC div. playoff game	Jack Pardee
1992	10	6	0	.625	352	258	2nd/AFC Central Div.	0	1	AFC wild-card game	Jack Pardee
1993	12	4	0	.750	368	238	1st/AFC Central Div.	0	1	AFC div. playoff game	Jack Pardee
1994	2	14	0	.125	226	352	4th/AFC Central Div.	—	—		Jack Pardee, Jeff Fisher
1995	7	9	0	.438	348	324	T2nd/AFC Central Div.	—	—		Jeff Fisher
1996	8	8	0	.500	345	319	T3rd/AFC Central Div.	—	—		

*American Football League.

FIRST-ROUND DRAFT PICKS

1960—Billy Cannon, RB, Louisiana State
1961—Mike Ditka, E, Pittsburgh
1962—Ray Jacobs, DT, Howard Payne
1963—Danny Brabham, LB, Arkansas
1964—Scott Appleton, DT, Texas
1965—Lawrence Elkins, WR, Baylor* (AFL)
1966—Tommy Nobis, LB, Texas
1967—George Webster, LB, Michigan State
    Tom Regner, G, Notre Dame
1968—None
1969—Ron Pritchard, LB, Arizona State

1970—Doug Wilkerson, G, North Carolina Central
1971—Dan Pastorini, QB, Santa Clara
1972—Greg Sampson, DE, Stanford
1973—John Matuszak, DE, Tampa*
    George Amundson, RB, Iowa State
1974—None
1975—Robert Brazile, LB, Jackson State
    Don Hardeman, RB, Texas A&I
1976—None
1977—Morris Towns, T, Missouri
1978—Earl Campbell, RB, Texas*

79—None
80—None
81—None
82—Mike Munchak, G, Penn State
83—Bruce Matthews, G, Southern California
84—Dean Steinkuhler, G, Nebraska
85—Ray Childress, DE, Texas A&M
　　Richard Johnson, DB, Wisconsin
86—Jim Everett, QB, Purdue
87—Alonzo Highsmith, FB, Miami (Fla.)
　　Haywood Jeffires, WR, North Carolina State

1988—Lorenzo White, RB, Michigan State
1989—David Williams, T, Florida
1990—Lamar Lathon, LB, Houston
1991—None
1992—None
1993—Brad Hopkins, G, Illinois
1994—Henry Ford, DE, Arkansas
1995—Steve McNair, QB, Alcorn State
1996—Eddie George, RB, Ohio State
1997—Kenny Holmes, DE, Miami (Fla.)
　　*First player chosen in draft.

FRANCHISE RECORDS

ost rushing yards, career
574—Earl Campbell
ost rushing yards, season
934—Earl Campbell, 1980
ost rushing yards, game
6—Billy Cannon at N.Y. Titans, Dec.
　10, 1961
ost rushing touchdowns, season
—Earl Campbell, 1979
ost passing attempts, season
5—Warren Moon, 1991
ost passing attempts, game
—George Blanda at Buf., Nov. 1, 1964
ost passes completed, season
4—Warren Moon, 1991
ost passes completed, game
—Warren Moon vs. Dal., Nov. 10, 1991
ost passing yards, career
,685—Warren Moon

Most passing yards, season
4,690—Warren Moon, 1991
Most passing yards, game
527—Warren Moon at K.C., Dec. 16, 1990
Most touchdown passes, season
36—George Blanda, 1961
Most pass receptions, career
542—Ernest Givins
Most pass receptions, season
101—Charlie Hennigan, 1964
Most pass receptions, game
13—Charlie Hennigan at Boston, Oct.
　13, 1961
　Haywood Jeffires at NYJ, Oct. 13,
　1991
Most receiving yards, career
7,935—Ernest Givins
Most receiving yards, season
1,746—Charlie Hennigan, 1961

Most receiving yards, game
272—Charlie Hennigan at Boston, Oct.
　13, 1961
Most receiving touchdowns, season
17—Bill Groman, 1961
Most touchdowns, career
73—Earl Campbell
Most field goals, season
32—Al Del Greco, 1996
Longest field goal
56 yards—Al Del Greco vs. S.F., Oct. 27,
　1996
Most interceptions, career
45—Jim Norton
Most interceptions, season
12—Freddy Glick, 1963
　Mike Reinfeldt, 1979
Most sacks, season
15.5—Jesse Baker, 1979

SERIES RECORDS

ouston vs.: Arizona 2-4; Atlanta 4-5; Baltimore 2-0; Buffalo 21-13; Carolina 0-1;
icago 4-3; Cincinnati 28-27-1; Dallas 3-5; Denver 20-11-1; Detroit 4-3; Green Bay 3-
Indianapolis 7-7; Jacksonville 2-2; Kansas City 17-24; Miami 11-12; Minnesota 3-4;
w England 14-17-1; New Orleans 4-4-1; N.Y. Giants 0-5; N.Y. Jets 20-12-1; Oakland
-20; Philadelphia 0-6; Pittsburgh 19-34; St. Louis 2-5; San Diego 13-18-1; San
ancisco 3-6; Seattle 4-5; Tampa Bay 4-1; Washington 3-3.

RETIRED UNIFORM NUMBERS

No.	Player
34	Earl Campbell
43	Jim Norton
63	Mike Munchak
65	Elvin Bethea

INDIANAPOLIS COLTS
YEAR-BY-YEAR RECORDS

		REGULAR SEASON							PLAYOFFS			
ar	W	L	T	Pct.	PF	PA	Finish	W	L	Highest round	Coach
53*	3	9	0	.250	182	350	5th/Western Conf.	—	—		Keith Molesworth
54*	3	9	0	.250	131	279	6th/Western Conf.	—	—		Weeb Ewbank
55*	5	6	1	.455	214	239	4th/Western Conf.	—	—		Weeb Ewbank
56*	5	7	0	.417	270	322	4th/Western Conf.	—	—		Weeb Ewbank
57*	7	5	0	.583	303	235	3rd/Western Conf.	—	—		Weeb Ewbank
58*	9	3	0	.750	381	203	1st/Western Conf.	1	0	NFL champ	Weeb Ewbank
59*	9	3	0	.750	374	251	1st/Western Conf.	1	0	NFL champ	Weeb Ewbank
60*	6	6	0	.500	288	234	4th/Western Conf.	—	—		Weeb Ewbank
61*	8	6	0	.571	302	307	T3rd/Western Conf.	—	—		Weeb Ewbank
62*	7	7	0	.500	293	288	4th/Western Conf.	—	—		Weeb Ewbank
63*	8	6	0	.571	316	285	3rd/Western Conf.	—	—		Don Shula
64*	12	2	0	.857	428	225	1st/Western Conf.	0	1	NFL championship game	Don Shula
65*	10	3	1	.769	389	284	2nd/Western Conf.	0	1	W. Conf. champ. game	Don Shula
66*	9	5	0	.643	314	226	2nd/Western Conf.	—	—		Don Shula
67*	11	1	2	.917	394	198	2nd/Coastal Div.	—	—		Don Shula
68*	13	1	0	.929	402	144	1st/Coastal Div.	2	1	Super Bowl	Don Shula
69*	8	5	1	.615	279	268	2nd/Coastal Div.	—	—		Don Shula
70*	11	2	1	.846	321	234	1st/AFC Eastern Div.	3	0	Super Bowl champ	Don McCafferty
71*	10	4	0	.714	313	140	2nd/AFC Eastern Div.	1	1	AFC championship game	Don McCafferty
72*	5	9	0	.357	235	252	3rd/AFC Eastern Div.	—	—		McCafferty, John Sandusky
73*	4	10	0	.286	226	341	T4th/AFC Eastern Div.	—	—		Howard Schnellenberger
74*	2	12	0	.143	190	329	5th/AFC Eastern Div.	—	—		Schnellenberger, Joe Thomas

	REGULAR SEASON						PLAYOFFS			
Year	W	L	T	Pct.	PF	PA	Finish	W	L	Highest round	Coach
1975*	10	4	0	.714	395	269	1st/AFC Eastern Div.	0	1	AFC div. playoff game	Ted Marchibroda
1976*	11	3	0	.786	417	246	1st/AFC Eastern Div.	0	1	AFC div. playoff game	Ted Marchibroda
1977*	10	4	0	.714	295	221	1st/AFC Eastern Div.	0	1	AFC div. playoff game	Ted Marchibroda
1978*	5	11	0	.313	239	421	T4th/AFC Eastern Div.	—	—		Ted Marchibroda
1979*	5	11	0	.313	271	351	5th/AFC Eastern Div.	—	—		Ted Marchibroda
1980*	7	9	0	.438	355	387	4th/AFC Eastern Div.	—	—		Mike McCormack
1981*	2	14	0	.125	259	533	T4th/AFC Eastern Div.	—	—		Mike McCormack
1982*	0	8	1	.056	113	236	14th/AFC	—	—		Frank Kush
1983*	7	9	0	.438	264	354	T4th/AFC Eastern Div.	—	—		Frank Kush
1984	4	12	0	.250	239	414	4th/AFC Eastern Div.	—	—		Frank Kush, Hal Hunter
1985	5	11	0	.313	320	386	4th/AFC Eastern Div.	—	—		Rod Dowhower
1986	3	13	0	.188	229	400	5th/AFC Eastern Div.	—	—		Rod Dowhower, Ron Meyer
1987	9	6	0	.600	300	238	1st/AFC Eastern Div.	0	1	AFC div. playoff game	Ron Meyer
1988	9	7	0	.563	354	315	T2nd/AFC Eastern Div.	—	—		Ron Meyer
1989	8	8	0	.500	298	301	T2nd/AFC Eastern Div.	—	—		Ron Meyer
1990	7	9	0	.438	281	353	3rd/AFC Eastern Div.	—	—		Ron Meyer
1991	1	15	0	.063	143	381	5th/AFC Eastern Div.	—	—		Ron Meyer, Rick Venturi
1992	9	7	0	.563	216	302	3rd/AFC Eastern Div.	—	—		Ted Marchibroda
1993	4	12	0	.250	189	378	5th/AFC Eastern Div.	—	—		Ted Marchibroda
1994	8	8	0	.500	307	320	3rd/AFC Eastern Div.	—	—		Ted Marchibroda
1995	9	7	0	.563	331	316	T2nd/AFC Eastern Div.	2	1	AFC championship game	Ted Marchibroda
1996	9	7	0	.563	317	334	3rd/AFC Eastern Div.	0	1	AFC wild-card game	Lindy Infante

*Baltimore Colts.

FIRST-ROUND DRAFT PICKS

1953—Billy Vessels, B, Oklahoma
1954—Cotton Davidson, B, Baylor
1955—George Shaw, B, Oregon*
　　　Alan Ameche, B, Wisconsin
1956—Lenny Moore, B, Penn State
1957—Jim Parker, T, Ohio State
1958—Lenny Lyles, B, Louisville
1959—Jackie Burkett, C, Auburn
1960—Ron Mix, T, Southern California
1961—Tom Matte, RB, Ohio State
1962—Wendell Harris, DB, Louisiana State
1963—Bob Vogel, T, Ohio State
1964—Marv Woodson, DB, Indiana
1965—Mike Curtis, LB, Duke
1966—Sam Ball, T, Kentucky
1967—Bubba Smith, DT, Michigan State*
　　　Jim Detwiler, RB, Michigan
1968—John Williams, G, Minnesota
1969—Eddie Hinton, WR, Oklahoma
1970—Norm Bulaich, RB, Texas Christian
1971—Don McCauley, RB, North Carolina
　　　Leonard Dunlap, DB, North Texas State
1972—Tom Drougas, T, Oregon
1973—Bert Jones, QB, Louisiana State
　　　Joe Ehrmann, DT, Syracuse
1974—John Dutton, DE, Nebraska
　　　Roger Carr, WR, Louisiana Tech
1975—Ken Huff, G, North Carolina
1976—Ken Novak, DT, Purdue

1977—Randy Burke, WR, Kentucky
1978—Reese McCall, TE, Auburn
1979—Barry Krauss, LB, Alabama
1980—Curtis Dickey, RB, Texas A&M
　　　Derrick Hatchett, DB, Texas
1981—Randy McMillan, RB, Pittsburgh
　　　Donnell Thompson, DT, North Carolina
1982—Johnie Cooks, LB, Mississippi State
　　　Art Schlichter, QB, Ohio State
1983—John Elway, QB, Stanford*
1984—L. Coleman, DB, Vanderbilt
　　　Ron Solt, G, Maryland
1985—Duane Bickett, LB, Southern California
1986—Jon Hand, DT, Alabama
1987—Cornelius Bennett, LB, Alabama
1988—None
1989—Andre Rison, WR, Michigan State
1990—Jeff George, QB, Illinois*
1991—None
1992—Steve Emtman, DE, Washington*
　　　Quentin Coryatt, LB, Texas A&M
1993—Sean Dawkins, WR, California
1994—Marshall Faulk, RB, San Diego State
　　　Trev Alberts, LB, Nebraska
1995—Ellis Johnson, DT, Florida
1996—Marvin Harrison, WR, Syracuse
1997—Tarik Glenn, T, California
*First player chosen in draft.

FRANCHISE RECORDS

Most rushing yards, career
5,487—Lydell Mitchell
Most rushing yards, season
1,659—Eric Dickerson, 1988
Most rushing yards, game
198—Norm Bulaich vs. NYJ, Sept. 19, 1971
Most rushing touchdowns, season
16—Lenny Moore, 1964
Most passing attempts, season
485—Jeff George, 1991

Most passing attempts, game
59—Jeff George at Was., Nov. 7, 1993
Most passes completed, season
292—Jeff George, 1991
Most passes completed, game
37—Jeff George at Was., Nov. 7, 1993
Most passing yards, career
39,768—Johnny Unitas
Most passing yards, season
3,481—Johnny Unitas, 1963

Most passing yards, game
401—Johnny Unitas vs. Atl., Sept. 17, 1967
Most touchdown passes, season
32—Johnny Unitas, 1959
Most pass receptions, career
631—Raymond Berry
Most pass receptions, season
85—Reggie Langhorne, 1993

Most pass receptions, game
13—Lydell Mitchell vs. NYJ, Dec. 15, 1974
    Joe Washington at K.C., Sept. 2, 1979
Most receiving yards, career
9,275—Raymond Berry
Most receiving yards, season
1,298—Raymond Berry, 1960
Most receiving yards, game
224—Raymond Berry at Was., Nov. 10, 1957

Most receiving touchdowns, season
14—Raymond Berry, 1959
Most touchdowns, career
113—Lenny Moore
Most field goals, season
36—Cary Blanchard, 1996
Longest field goal
58 yards—Dan Miller at S.D., Dec. 26, 1982

Most interceptions, career
57—Bob Boyd
Most interceptions, season
11—Tom Keane, 1953
Most sacks, career
56.5—Fred Cook
Most sacks, season
17—John Dutton, 1975

SERIES RECORDS

Indianapolis vs.: Arizona 6-6; Atlanta 10-0; Buffalo 23-29-1; Carolina 0-1; Chicago 21-16; Cincinnati 10-7; Dallas 3-7; Denver 2-9; Detroit 17-18-2; Green Bay 18-18-1; Houston 7-7; Jacksonville 1-0; Kansas City 5-6; Miami 18-36; Minnesota 11-6-1; New England 22-31; New Orleans 3-3; N.Y. Giants 5-5; N.Y. Jets 32-21; Oakland 2-5; Philadelphia 7-6; Pittsburgh 4-12; St. Louis 21-17-2; San Diego 6-10; San Francisco 22-16; Seattle 4-1; Tampa Bay 5-3; Washington 16-9.
NOTE: Includes records as Baltimore Colts from 1953 through 1983.

RETIRED UNIFORM NUMBERS

No.	Player
19	Johnny Unitas
22	Buddy Young
24	Lenny Moore
70	Art Donovan
77	Jim Parker
82	Raymond Berry
89	Gino Marchetti

JACKSONVILLE JAGUARS
YEAR-BY-YEAR RECORDS

	REGULAR SEASON						PLAYOFFS			
Year	W	L	T	Pct.	PF	PA	Finish	W	L	Highest round	Coach
1995	4	12	0	.250	275	404	5th/AFC Central Div.	—	—		Tom Coughlin
1996	9	7	0	.563	325	335	2nd/AFC Central Div.	2	1	AFC championship game	Tom Coughlin

FIRST-ROUND DRAFT PICKS

1995—Tony Boselli, T, Southern California
      James Stewart, RB, Tennessee

1996—Kevin Hardy, LB, Illinois
1997—Renaldo Wynn, DT, Notre Dame

FRANCHISE RECORDS

Most rushing yards, career
1,248—James Stewart
Most rushing yards, season
723—James Stewart, 1996
Most rushing yards, game
112—James Stewart at St.L., Oct. 20, 1996
Most rushing touchdowns, season
—James Stewart, 1996
Most passing attempts, season
557—Mark Brunell, 1996
Most passing attempts, game
52—Mark Brunell at St.L., Oct. 20, 1996
Most passes completed, season
353—Mark Brunell, 1996
Most passes completed, game
37—Mark Brunell at St.L., Oct. 20, 1996
Most passing yards, career
4,535—Mark Brunell
Most passing yards, season
4,367—Mark Brunell, 1996

Most passing yards, game
432—Mark Brunell at N.E., Sept. 22, 1996
Most touchdown passes, season
19—Mark Brunell, 1996
Most pass receptions, career
105—Jimmy Smith
Most pass receptions, season
85—Keenan McCardell, 1996
Most pass receptions, game
16—Keenan McCardell at St.L., Oct. 20, 1996
Most receiving yards, career
1,532—Jimmy Smith
Most receiving yards, season
1,244—Jimmy Smith, 1996
Most receiving yards, game
232—Keenan McCardell at St.L., Oct. 20, 1996
Most receiving touchdowns, season
7—Jimmy Smith, 1996

Most touchdowns, career
13—James Stewart
Most field goals, season
30—Mike Hollis, 1996
Longest field goal
53 yards—Mike Hollis vs. Pit., Oct. 8, 1995
          Mike Hollis vs. Car., Sept. 29, 1996
Most interceptions, career
3—Harry Colon
Most interceptions, season
3—Harry Colon, 1995
Most sacks, career
4—Joel Smeenge
Most sacks, season
7.5—Clyde Simmons, 1996

SERIES RECORDS

Jacksonville vs.: Arizona 0-0; Atlanta 1-0; Baltimore 2-0; Buffalo 0-0; Carolina 1-0; Chicago 0-1; Cincinnati 1-3; Dallas 0-0; Denver 0-1; Detroit 0-1; Green Bay 0-1; Houston 2; Indianapolis 0-1; Kansas City 0-0; Miami 0-0; Minnesota 0-0; New England 0-1; New Orleans 0-1; N.Y. Giants 0-0; N.Y. Jets 1-1; Oakland 0-1; Philadelphia 0-0; Pittsburgh 2; St. Louis 0-1; San Diego 0-0; San Francisco 0-0; Seattle 1-1; Tampa Bay 0-1; Washington 0-0.

RETIRED UNIFORM NUMBERS

No.	Player
	None

KANSAS CITY CHIEFS
YEAR-BY-YEAR RECORDS

		REGULAR SEASON						PLAYOFFS		
Year	W	L	T	Pct.	PF	PA	Finish	W	L	Highest round	Coach
1960*†	8	6	0	.571	362	253	2nd/Western Div.	—	—		Hank Stram
1961*†	6	8	0	.429	334	343	2nd/Western Div.	—	—		Hank Stram
1962*†	11	3	0	.786	389	233	1st/Western Div.	1	0	AFL champ	Hank Stram
1963*	5	7	2	.417	347	263	3rd/Western Div.	—	—		Hank Stram
1964*	7	7	0	.500	366	306	2nd/Western Div.	—	—		Hank Stram
1965*	7	5	2	.583	322	285	3rd/Western Div.	—	—		Hank Stram
1966*	11	2	1	.846	448	276	1st/Western Div.	1	1	Super Bowl	Hank Stram
1967*	9	5	0	.643	408	254	2nd/Western Div.	—	—		Hank Stram
1968*	12	2	0	.857	371	170	2nd/Western Div.	0	1	W. Div. champ. game	Hank Stram
1969*	11	3	0	.786	359	177	2nd/Western Div.	3	0	Super Bowl champ	Hank Stram
1970	7	5	2	.583	272	244	2nd/AFC Western Div.	—	—		Hank Stram
1971	10	3	1	.769	302	208	1st/AFC Western Div.	0	1	AFC div. playoff game	Hank Stram
1972	8	6	0	.571	287	254	2nd/AFC Western Div.	—	—		Hank Stram
1973	7	5	2	.571	231	192	T2nd/AFC Western Div.	—	—		Hank Stram
1974	5	9	0	.357	233	293	T3rd/AFC Western Div.	—	—		Hank Stram
1975	5	9	0	.357	282	341	3rd/AFC Western Div.	—	—		Paul Wiggin
1976	5	9	0	.357	290	376	4th/AFC Western Div.	—	—		Paul Wiggin
1977	2	12	0	.143	225	349	5th/AFC Western Div.	—	—		Paul Wiggin, Tom Bettis
1978	4	12	0	.250	243	327	5th/AFC Western Div.	—	—		Marv Levy
1979	7	9	0	.438	238	262	5th/AFC Western Div.	—	—		Marv Levy
1980	8	8	0	.500	319	336	T3rd/AFC Western Div.	—	—		Marv Levy
1981	9	7	0	.563	343	290	3rd/AFC Western Div.	—	—		Marv Levy
1982	3	6	0	.333	176	184	11th/AFC	—	—		Marv Levy
1983	6	10	0	.375	386	367	T4th/AFC Western Div.	—	—		John Mackovic
1984	8	8	0	.500	314	324	4th/AFC Western Div.	—	—		John Mackovic
1985	6	10	0	.375	317	360	5th/AFC Western Div.	—	—		John Mackovic
1986	10	6	0	.625	358	326	2nd/AFC Western Div.	0	1	AFC wild-card game	John Mackovic
1987	4	11	0	.267	273	388	5th/AFC Western Div.	—	—		Frank Gansz
1988	4	11	1	.281	254	320	5th/AFC Western Div.	—	—		Frank Gansz
1989	8	7	1	.531	318	286	2nd/AFC Western Div.	—	—		Marty Schottenheimer
1990	11	5	0	.688	369	257	2nd/AFC Western Div.	0	1	AFC wild-card game	Marty Schottenheimer
1991	10	6	0	.625	322	252	2nd/AFC Western Div.	1	1	AFC div. playoff game	Marty Schottenheimer
1992	10	6	0	.625	348	282	2nd/AFC Western Div.	0	1	AFC wild-card game	Marty Schottenheimer
1993	11	5	0	.688	328	291	1st/AFC Western Div.	2	1	AFC championship game	Marty Schottenheimer
1994	9	7	0	.563	319	298	2nd/AFC Western Div.	0	1	AFC wild-card game	Marty Schottenheimer
1995	13	3	0	.813	358	241	1st/AFC Western Div.	0	1	AFC div. playoff game	Marty Schottenheimer
1996	9	7	0	.563	297	300	2nd/AFC Western Div.	—	—		Marty Schottenheimer

*American Football League.
†Dallas Texans.

FIRST-ROUND DRAFT PICKS

1960—Don Meredith, QB, Southern Methodist
1961—E.J. Holub, C, Texas Tech
1962—Ronnie Bull, RB, Baylor
1963—Buck Buchanan, DT, Grambling* (AFL)
    Ed Budde, G, Michigan State
1964—Pete Beathard, QB, Southern California
1965—Gale Sayers, RB, Kansas
1966—Aaron Brown, DE, Minnesota
1967—Gene Trosch, DE, Miami
1968—Mo Moorman, G, Texas A&M
    George Daney, G, Texas-El Paso
1969—Jim Marsalis, DB, Tennessee State
1970—Sid Smith, T, Southern California
1971—Elmo Wright, WR, Houston
1972—Jeff Kinney, RB, Nebraska
1973—None
1974—Woody Green, RB, Arizona State
1975—None
1976—Rod Walters, G, Iowa
1977—Gary Green, DB, Baylor
1978—Art Still, DE, Kentucky
1979—Mike Bell, DE, Colorado State
    Steve Fuller, QB, Clemson

1980—Brad Budde, G, Southern California
1981—Willie Scott, TE, South Carolina
1982—Anthony Hancock, WR, Tennessee
1983—Todd Blackledge, QB, Penn State
1984—Bill Maas, DT, Pittsburgh
    John Alt, T, Iowa
1985—Ethan Horton, RB, North Carolina
1986—Brian Jozwiak, T, West Virginia
1987—Paul Palmer, RB, Temple
1988—Neil Smith, DE, Nebraska
1989—Derrick Thomas, LB, Alabama
1990—Percy Snow, LB, Michigan State
1991—Harvey Williams, RB, Louisiana State
1992—Dale Carter, DB, Tennessee
1993—None
1994—Greg Hill, RB, Texas A&M
1995—Trezelle Jenkins, T, Michigan
1996—Jerome Woods, DB, Memphis
1997—Tony Gonzalez, TE, California
    *First player chosen in draft.

FRANCHISE RECORDS

Most rushing yards, career
4,897—Christian Okoye
Most rushing yards, season
1,480—Christian Okoye, 1989
Most rushing yards, game
200—Barry Word vs. Det., Oct. 14, 1990
Most rushing touchdowns, season
13—Abner Haynes, 1962
Most passing attempts, season
603—Bill Kenney, 1983
Most passing attempts, game
55—Joe Montana at S.D., Oct. 9, 1994
Steve Bono at Mia., Dec. 12, 1994
Most passes completed, season
346—Bill Kenney, 1983
Most passes completed, game
37—Joe Montana at S.D., Oct. 9, 1994
Most passing yards, career
28,507—Len Dawson

Most passing yards, season
4,348—Bill Kenney, 1983
Most passing yards, game
435—Len Dawson vs. Den., Nov. 1, 1964
Most touchdown passes, season
30—Len Dawson, 1964
Most pass receptions, career
416—Henry Marshall
Most pass receptions, season
80—Carlos Carson, 1983
Most pass receptions, game
12—Ed Podolak vs. Den., Oct. 7, 1973
Most receiving yards, career
7,306—Otis Taylor
Most receiving yards, season
1,351—Carlos Carson, 1983
Most receiving yards, game
309—Stephone Paige vs. S.D., Dec. 22, 1985

Most receiving touchdowns, season
12—Chris Burford, 1962
Most touchdowns, career
57—Otis Taylor
Most field goals, season
34—Nick Lowery, 1990
Longest field goal
58 yards—Nick Lowery at Was., Sept. 18, 1983
Nick Lowery vs. L.A. Raiders, Sept. 12, 1985
Most interceptions, career
58—Emmitt Thomas
Most interceptions, season
12—Emmitt Thomas, 1974
Most sacks, career
90—Derrick Thomas
Most sacks, season
20—Derrick Thomas, 1990

SERIES RECORDS

Kansas City vs.: Arizona 4-1-1; Atlanta 4-0; Buffalo 13-17-1; Carolina 0-0; Chicago 3-4; Cincinnati 11-9; Dallas 2-4; Denver 42-31; Detroit 5-3; Green Bay 5-1-1; Houston 24-17; Indianapolis 6-5; Jacksonville 0-0; Miami 10-9; Minnesota 3-3; New England 14-7-3; New Orleans 3-3; N.Y. Giants 3-6; N.Y. Jets 14-12-1; Oakland 35-36-2; Philadelphia 1-1; Pittsburgh 5-14; St. Louis 1-4; San Diego 37-35-1; San Francisco 2-4; Seattle 24-12; Tampa Bay 5-2; Washington 4-1.
NOTE: Includes records as Dallas Texans from 1960 through 1962.

RETIRED UNIFORM NUMBERS

No.	Player
3	Jan Stenerud
16	Len Dawson
28	Abner Haynes
33	Stone Johnson
36	Mack Lee Hill
63	Willie Lanier
78	Bobby Bell
86	Buck Buchanan

MIAMI DOLPHINS
YEAR-BY-YEAR RECORDS

Year	W	L	T	Pct.	PF	PA	Finish	W	L	Highest round	Coach
1966*	3	11	0	.214	213	362	T4th/Eastern Div.	—	—		George Wilson
1967*	4	10	0	.286	219	407	T3rd/Eastern Div.	—	—		George Wilson
1968*	5	8	1	.385	276	355	3rd/Eastern Div.	—	—		George Wilson
1969*	3	10	1	.231	233	332	5th/Eastern Div.	—	—		George Wilson
1970	10	4	0	.714	297	228	2nd/AFC Eastern Div.	0	1	AFC div. playoff game	Don Shula
1971	10	3	1	.769	315	174	1st/AFC Eastern Div.	2	1	Super Bowl	Don Shula
1972	14	0	0	1.000	385	171	1st/AFC Eastern Div.	3	0	Super Bowl champ	Don Shula
1973	12	2	0	.857	343	150	1st/AFC Eastern Div.	3	0	Super Bowl champ	Don Shula
1974	11	3	0	.786	327	216	1st/AFC Eastern Div.	0	1	AFC div. playoff game	Don Shula
1975	10	4	0	.714	357	222	2nd/AFC Eastern Div.	—	—		Don Shula
1976	6	8	0	.429	263	264	3rd/AFC Eastern Div.	—	—		Don Shula
1977	10	4	0	.714	313	197	2nd/AFC Eastern Div.	—	—		Don Shula
1978	11	5	0	.688	372	254	2nd/AFC Eastern Div.	0	1	AFC wild-card game	Don Shula
1979	10	6	0	.625	341	257	1st/AFC Eastern Div.	0	1	AFC div. playoff game	Don Shula
1980	8	8	0	.500	266	305	3rd/AFC Eastern Div.	—	—		Don Shula
1981	11	4	1	.719	345	275	1st/AFC Eastern Div.	0	1	AFC div. playoff game	Don Shula
1982	7	2	0	.778	198	131	T2nd/AFC	3	1	Super Bowl	Don Shula
1983	12	4	0	.750	389	250	1st/AFC Eastern Div.	0	1	AFC div. playoff game	Don Shula
1984	14	2	0	.875	513	298	1st/AFC Eastern Div.	2	1	Super Bowl	Don Shula
1985	12	4	0	.750	428	320	1st/AFC Eastern Div.	1	1	AFC championship game	Don Shula
1986	8	8	0	.500	430	405	3rd/AFC Eastern Div.	—	—		Don Shula
1987	8	7	0	.533	362	335	T2nd/AFC Eastern Div.	—	—		Don Shula
1988	6	10	0	.375	319	380	5th/AFC Eastern Div.	—	—		Don Shula
1989	8	8	0	.500	331	379	T2nd/AFC Eastern Div.	—	—		Don Shula
1990	12	4	0	.750	336	242	2nd/AFC Eastern Div.	1	1	AFC div. playoff game	Don Shula
1991	8	8	0	.500	343	349	3rd/AFC Eastern Div.	—	—		Don Shula
1992	11	5	0	.688	340	281	1st/AFC Eastern Div.	1	1	AFC championship game	Don Shula
1993	9	7	0	.563	349	351	2nd/AFC Eastern Div.	—	—		Don Shula
1994	10	6	0	.625	389	327	1st/AFC Eastern Div.	1	1	AFC div. playoff game	Don Shula
1995	9	7	0	.563	398	332	T2nd/AFC Eastern Div.	0	1	AFC wild-card game	Don Shula
1996	8	8	0	.500	279	454	4th/AFC Eastern Div.	—	—		Jimmy Johnson

*American Football League.

FIRST-ROUND DRAFT PICKS

1966—Jim Grabowski, RB, Illinois*
    Rick Norton, QB, Kentucky
1967—Bob Griese, QB, Purdue
1968—Larry Csonka, RB, Syracuse
    Doug Crusan, T, Indiana
1969—Bill Stanfill, DE, Georgia
1970—None
1971—None
1972—Mike Kadish, DT, Notre Dame
1973—None
1974—Don Reese, DE, Jackson State
1975—Darryl Carlton, T, Tampa
1976—Larry Gordon, LB, Arizona State
    Kim Bokamper, LB, San Jose State
1977—A.J. Duhe, DE, Louisiana State
1978—None
1979—Jon Giesler, T, Michigan
1980—Don McNeal, DB, Alabama
1981—David Overstreet, RB, Oklahoma

1982—Roy Foster, G, Southern California
1983—Dan Marino, QB, Pittsburgh
1984—Jackie Shipp, LB, Oklahoma
1985—Lorenzo Hampton, RB, Florida
1986—None
1987—John Bosa, DE, Boston College
1988—Eric Kumerow, DE, Ohio State
1989—Sammie Smith, RB, Florida State
    Louis Oliver, DB, Florida
1990—Richmond Webb, T, Texas A&M
1991—Randal Hill, WR, Miami (Fla.)
1992—Troy Vincent, DB, Wisconsin
    Marco Coleman, LB, Georgia Tech
1993—O.J. McDuffie, WR, Penn State
1994—Tim Bowens, DT, Mississippi
1995—Billy Milner, T, Houston
1996—Daryl Gardener, DT, Baylor
1997—Yatil Green, WR, Miami (Fla.)
*First player chosen in draft.

FRANCHISE RECORDS

Most rushing yards, career
6,737—Larry Csonka
Most rushing yards, season
1,258—Delvin Williams, 1978
Most rushing yards, game
197—Mercury Morris vs. N.E., Sept. 30, 1973
Most rushing touchdowns, season
12—Mercury Morris, 1972
    Don Nottingham, 1975
    Larry Csonka, 1979
Most passing attempts, season
623—Dan Marino, 1986
Most passing attempts, game
60—Dan Marino vs. NYJ, Oct. 23, 1988
Most passes completed, season
385—Dan Marino, 1994
Most passes completed, game
39—Dan Marino at Buf., Nov. 16, 1986

Most passing yards, career
51,636—Dan Marino
Most passing yards, season
5,084—Dan Marino, 1984
Most passing yards, game
521—Dan Marino vs. NYJ, Oct. 23, 1988
Most touchdown passes, season
48—Dan Marino, 1984
Most pass receptions, career
550—Mark Clayton
Most pass receptions, season
86—Mark Clayton, 1988
Most pass receptions, game
12—Jim Jensen at N.E., Nov. 6, 1988
Most receiving yards, career
8,869—Mark Duper
Most receiving yards, season
1,389—Mark Clayton, 1984

Most receiving yards, game
217—Mark Duper vs. NYJ, Nov. 10, 198
Most receiving touchdowns, season
18—Mark Clayton, 1984
Most touchdowns, career
82—Mark Clayton
Most field goals, season
31—Pete Stoyanovich, 1991
Longest field goal
59 yards—Pete Stoyanovich at NYJ, Nov 12, 1989
Most interceptions, career
35—Jake Scott
Most interceptions, season
10—Dick Westmoreland, 1967
Most sacks, career
67.5—Bill Stanfill
Most sacks, season
18.5—Bill Stanfill, 1973

SERIES RECORDS

Miami vs.: Arizona 7-0; Atlanta 6-1; Buffalo 40-21-1; Carolina 0-0; Chicago 5-2; Cincinnati 12-3; Dallas 6-2; Denver 5-2-1; Detroit 3-2; Green Bay 8-0; Houston 12-11; Indianapolis 36-18; Jacksonville 0-0; Kansas City 9-10; Minnesota 4-2; New England 37-23; New Orleans 5-4; N.Y. Giants 1-3; N.Y. Jets 31-28-1; Oakland 5-15-1; Philadelphia 6-3; Pittsburgh 8-7; St. Louis 6-10; San Diego 6-10; San Francisco 4-3; Seattle 4-2; Tampa Bay 4-1; Washington 5-2.

RETIRED UNIFORM NUMBERS

No.	Player
12	Bob Griese

MINNESOTA VIKINGS
YEAR-BY-YEAR RECORDS

	REGULAR SEASON						PLAYOFFS			
Year	W	L	T	Pct.	PF	PA	Finish	W	L	Highest round	Coach
1961	3	11	0	.214	285	407	7th/Western Conf.	—	—		Norm Van Brocklin
1962	2	11	1	.154	254	410	6th/Western Conf.	—	—		Norm Van Brocklin
1963	5	8	1	.385	309	390	T4th/Western Conf.	—	—		Norm Van Brocklin
1964	8	5	1	.615	355	296	T2nd/Western Conf.	—	—		Norm Van Brocklin
1965	7	7	0	.500	383	403	5th/Western Conf.	—	—		Norm Van Brocklin
1966	4	9	1	.308	292	304	T6th/Western Conf.	—	—		Norm Van Brocklin
1967	3	8	3	.273	233	294	4th/Central Div.	—	—		Bud Grant
1968	8	6	0	.571	282	242	1st/Central Div.	0	1	W. Conf. champ. game	Bud Grant
1969	12	2	0	.857	379	133	1st/Central Div.	2	1	Super Bowl	Bud Grant
1970	12	2	0	.857	335	143	1st/NFC Central Div.	0	1	NFC div. playoff game	Bud Grant
1971	11	3	0	.786	245	139	1st/NFC Central Div.	0	1	NFC div. playoff game	Bud Grant

		REGULAR SEASON					PLAYOFFS			
Year	W	L	T	Pct.	PF	PA	Finish	W	L	Highest round	Coach
1972	7	7	0	.500	301	252	3rd/NFC Central Div.	—	—		Bud Grant
1973	12	2	0	.857	296	168	1st/NFC Central Div.	2	1	Super Bowl	Bud Grant
1974	10	4	0	.714	310	195	1st/NFC Central Div.	2	1	Super Bowl	Bud Grant
1975	12	2	0	.857	377	180	1st/NFC Central Div.	0	1	NFC div. playoff game	Bud Grant
1976	11	2	1	.821	305	176	1st/NFC Central Div.	2	1	Super Bowl	Bud Grant
1977	9	5	0	.643	231	227	1st/NFC Central Div.	1	1	NFC championship game	Bud Grant
1978	8	7	1	.531	294	306	1st/NFC Central Div.	0	1	NFC div. playoff game	Bud Grant
1979	7	9	0	.438	259	337	3rd/NFC Central Div.	—	—		Bud Grant
1980	9	7	0	.563	317	308	1st/NFC Central Div.	0	1	NFC div. playoff game	Bud Grant
1981	7	9	0	.438	325	369	4th/NFC Central Div.	—	—		Bud Grant
1982	5	4	0	.556	187	198	T4th/NFC	1	1	NFC second-round pl. game	Bud Grant
1983	8	8	0	.500	316	348	T2nd/NFC Central Div.	—	—		Bud Grant
1984	3	13	0	.188	276	484	5th/NFC Central Div.	—	—		Les Steckel
1985	7	9	0	.438	346	359	T3rd/NFC Central Div.	—	—		Bud Grant
1986	9	7	0	.563	398	273	2nd/NFC Central Div.	—	—		Jerry Burns
1987	8	7	0	.533	336	335	2nd/NFC Central Div.	2	1	NFC championship game	Jerry Burns
1988	11	5	0	.688	406	233	2nd/NFC Central Div.	1	1	NFC div. playoff game	Jerry Burns
1989	10	6	0	.625	351	275	1st/NFC Central Div.	0	1	NFC div. playoff game	Jerry Burns
1990	6	10	0	.375	351	326	T2nd/NFC Central Div.	—	—		Jerry Burns
1991	8	8	0	.500	301	306	3rd/NFC Central Div.	—	—		Jerry Burns
1992	11	5	0	.688	374	249	1st/NFC Central Div.	0	1	NFC wild-card game	Dennis Green
1993	9	7	0	.563	277	290	T2nd/NFC Central Div.	0	1	NFC wild-card game	Dennis Green
1994	10	6	0	.625	356	314	1st/NFC Central Div.	0	1	NFC wild-card game	Dennis Green
1995	8	8	0	.500	412	385	4th/NFC Central Div.	—	—		Dennis Green
1996	9	7	0	.563	298	315	2nd/NFC Central Div.	0	1	NFC wild-card game	Dennis Green

FIRST-ROUND DRAFT PICKS

1961—Tommy Mason, RB, Tulane*
1962—None
1963—Jim Dunaway, T, Mississippi
1964—Carl Eller, DE, Minnesota
1965—Jack Snow, WR, Notre Dame
1966—Jerry Shay, DT, Purdue
1967—Clint Jones, RB, Michigan State
    Gene Washington, WR, Michigan State
    Alan Page, DT, Notre Dame
1968—Ron Yary, T, Southern California*
1969—None
1970—John Ward, DT, Oklahoma State
1971—Leo Hayden, RB, Ohio State
1972—Jeff Siemon, LB, Stanford
1973—Chuck Foreman, RB, Miami (Fla.)
1974—Fred McNeill, LB, UCLA
    Steve Riley, T, Southern California
1975—Mark Mullaney, DE, Colorado State
1976—James White, DT, Oklahoma State
1977—Tommy Kramer, QB, Rice
1978—Randy Holloway, DE, Pittsburgh
1979—Ted Brown, RB, North Carolina State

1980—Doug Martin, DT, Washington
1981—None
1982—Darrin Nelson, RB, Stanford
1983—Joey Browner, DB, Southern California
1984—Keith Millard, DE, Washington State
1985—Chris Doleman, LB, Pittsburgh
1986—Gerald Robinson, DE, Auburn
1987—D.J. Dozier, RB, Penn State
1988—Randall McDaniel, G, Arizona State
1989—None
1990—None
1991—None
1992—None
1993—Robert Smith, RB, Ohio State
1994—DeWayne Washington, CB, North Carolina State
    Todd Steussie, T, California
1995—Derrick Alexander, DE, Florida State
    Korey Stringer, T, Ohio State
1996—Duane Clemons, DE, California
1997—Dwayne Rudd, LB, Alabama
    *First player chosen in draft.

FRANCHISE RECORDS

Most rushing yards, career
5,879—Chuck Foreman
Most rushing yards, season
1,201—Terry Allen, 1992
Most rushing yards, game
200—Chuck Foreman at Phi., Oct. 24, 1976
Most rushing touchdowns, season
13—Chuck Foreman, 1975
    Chuck Foreman, 1976
    Terry Allen, 1992
Most passing attempts, season
606—Warren Moon, 1995
Most passing attempts, game
63—Rich Gannon at N.E., Oct. 20, 1991
Most passes completed, season
377—Warren Moon, 1995

Most passes completed, game
38—Tommy Kramer vs. Cle., Dec. 14, 1980
    Tommy Kramer vs. G.B., Nov. 29, 1981
Most passing yards, career
33,098—Fran Tarkenton
Most passing yards, season
4,264—Warren Moon, 1994
Most passing yards, game
490—Tommy Kramer at Was., Nov. 2, 1986
Most touchdown passes, season
33—Warren Moon, 1995
Most pass receptions, career
578—Cris Carter
Most pass receptions, season
122—Cris Carter, 1994, 1995

Most pass receptions, game
15—Rickey Young at N.E., Dec. 16, 1979
Most receiving yards, career
7,636—Anthony Carter
Most receiving yards, season
1,371—Cris Carter, 1995
Most receiving yards, game
210—Sammy White vs. Det., Nov. 7, 1976
Most receiving touchdowns, season
17—Cris Carter, 1995
Most touchdowns, career
76—Bill Brown
Most field goals, season
46—Fred Cox, 1970

Longest field goal
54 yards—Jan Stenerud vs. Atl., Sept. 16, 1984

Most interceptions, career
53—Paul Krause

Most interceptions, season
10—Paul Krause, 1975

Most sacks, career
130—Carl Eller

Most sacks, season
21—Chris Doleman, 1989

SERIES RECORDS

Minnesota vs.: Arizona 6-8; Atlanta 13-6; Buffalo 5-2; Carolina 1-0; Chicago 37-32-2; Cincinnati 4-4; Dallas 6-9; Denver 5-4; Detroit 44-25-2; Green Bay 36-34-1; Houston 4-3; Indianapolis 6-11-1; Jacksonville 0-0; Kansas City 3-3; Miami 2-4; New England 2-4; New Orleans 13-6; N.Y. Giants 7-5; N.Y. Jets 1-4; Oakland 3-6; Philadelphia 10-6; Pittsburgh 8-4; St. Louis 15-11-2; San Diego 3-4; San Francisco 16-16-1; Seattle 2-4; Tampa Bay 26-12; Washington 4-6.

RETIRED UNIFORM NUMBERS

No.	Player
10	Fran Tarkenton
88	Alan Page

NEW ENGLAND PATRIOTS
YEAR-BY-YEAR RECORDS

		REGULAR SEASON						PLAYOFFS		
Year	W	L	T	Pct.	PF	PA	Finish	W	L	Highest round	Coach
1960*†	5	9	0	.357	286	349	4th/Eastern Div.	—	—		Lou Saban
1961*†	9	4	1	.692	413	313	2nd/Eastern Div.	—	—		Lou Saban, Mike Holovak
1962*†	9	4	1	.692	346	295	2nd/Eastern Div.	—	—		Mike Holovak
1963*†	7	6	1	.538	327	257	1st/Eastern Div.	1	1	AFL championship game	Mike Holovak
1964*†	10	3	1	.769	365	297	2nd/Eastern Div.	—	—		Mike Holovak
1965*†	4	8	2	.333	244	302	3rd/Eastern Div.	—	—		Mike Holovak
1966*†	8	4	2	.667	315	283	2nd/Eastern Div.	—	—		Mike Holovak
1967*†	3	10	1	.231	280	389	5th/Eastern Div.	—	—		Mike Holovak
1968*†	4	10	0	.286	229	406	4th/Eastern Div.	—	—		Mike Holovak
1969*†	4	10	0	.286	266	316	T3rd/Eastern Div.	—	—		Clive Rush
1970†	2	12	0	.143	149	361	5th/AFC Eastern Div.	—	—		Clive Rush, John Mazur
1971	6	8	0	.429	238	325	T3rd/AFC Eastern Div.	—	—		John Mazur
1972	3	11	0	.214	192	446	5th/AFC Eastern Div.	—	—		John Mazur, Phil Bengtson
1973	5	9	0	.357	258	300	3rd/AFC Eastern Div.	—	—		Chuck Fairbanks
1974	7	7	0	.500	348	289	T3rd/AFC Eastern Div.	—	—		Chuck Fairbanks
1975	3	11	0	.214	258	358	T4th/AFC Eastern Div.	—	—		Chuck Fairbanks
1976	11	3	0	.786	376	236	2nd/AFC Eastern Div.	0	1	AFC div. playoff game	Chuck Fairbanks
1977	9	5	0	.643	278	217	3rd/AFC Eastern Div.	—	—		Chuck Fairbanks
1978	11	5	0	.688	358	286	1st/AFC Eastern Div.	0	1	AFC div. playoff game	Chuck Fairbanks, Hank Bullough-Ron Erhardt
1979	9	7	0	.563	411	326	2nd/AFC Eastern Div.	—	—		Ron Erhardt
1980	10	6	0	.625	441	325	2nd/AFC Eastern Div.	—	—		Ron Erhardt
1981	2	14	0	.125	322	370	T4th/AFC Eastern Div.	—	—		Ron Erhardt
1982	5	4	0	.556	143	157	7th/AFC	0	1	AFC first-round pl. game	Ron Meyer
1983	8	8	0	.500	274	289	T2nd/AFC Eastern Div.	—	—		Ron Meyer
1984	9	7	0	.563	362	352	2nd/AFC Eastern Div.	—	—		Ron Meyer, Raymond Berry
1985	11	5	0	.688	362	290	T2nd/AFC Eastern Div.	3	1	Super Bowl	Raymond Berry
1986	11	5	0	.688	412	307	1st/AFC Eastern Div.	0	1	AFC div. playoff game	Raymond Berry
1987	8	7	0	.533	320	293	T2nd/AFC Eastern Div.	—	—		Raymond Berry
1988	9	7	0	.563	250	284	T2nd/AFC Eastern Div.	—	—		Raymond Berry
1989	5	11	0	.313	297	391	4th/AFC Eastern Div.	—	—		Raymond Berry
1990	1	15	0	.063	181	446	5th/AFC Eastern Div.	—	—		Rod Rust
1991	6	10	0	.375	211	305	4th/AFC Eastern Div.	—	—		Dick MacPherson
1992	2	14	0	.125	205	363	5th/AFC Eastern Div.	—	—		Dick MacPherson
1993	5	11	0	.313	238	286	4th/AFC Eastern Div.	—	—		Bill Parcells
1994	10	6	0	.625	351	312	2nd/AFC Eastern Div.	0	1	AFC wild-card game	Bill Parcells
1995	6	10	0	.375	294	377	4th/AFC Eastern Div.	—	—		Bill Parcells
1996	11	5	0	.687	418	313	1st/AFC Eastern Div.	2	1	Super Bowl	Bill Parcells

*American Football League.
†Boston Patriots.

FIRST-ROUND DRAFT PICKS

1960—Ron Burton, RB, Northwestern
1961—Tommy Mason, RB, Tulane
1962—Gary Collins, WR, Maryland
1963—Art Graham, E, Boston College
1964—Jack Concannon, QB, Boston College* (AFL)
1965—Jerry Rush, DE, Michigan State
    Dave McCormick, T, Louisiana State
1966—Karl Singer, T, Purdue
    Willie Townes, T, Tulsa

1967—John Charles, DB, Purdue
1968—Dennis Byrd, DE, North Carolina State
1969—Ron Sellers, WR, Florida State
1970—Phil Olsen, DT, Utah State
1971—Jim Plunkett, QB, Stanford*
1972—None
1973—John Hannah, G, Alabama
    Sam Cunningham, RB, Southern California
    Darryl Stingley, WR, Purdue

1974—None
1975—Russ Francis, TE, Oregon
1976—Mike Haynes, DB, Arizona State
Pete Brock, C, Colorado
Tim Fox, DB, Ohio State
1977—Raymond Clayborn, DB, Texas
Stanley Morgan, WR, Tennessee
1978—Bob Cryder, G, Alabama
1979—Rick Sanford, DB, South Carolina
1980—Roland James, DB, Tennessee
Vagas Ferguson, RB, Notre Dame
1981—Brian Holloway, T, Stanford
1982—Kenneth Sims, DT, Texas*
Lester Williams, DT, Nebraska
1983—Tony Eason, QB, Illinois
1984—Irving Fryar, WR, Nebraska*

1985—Trevor Matich, C, Brigham Young
1986—Reggie Dupard, RB, Southern Methodist
1987—Bruce Armstrong, G, Louisville
1988—J. Stephens, RB, Northwestern Louisiana State
1989—Hart Lee Dykes, WR, Oklahoma State
1990—Chris Singleton, LB, Arizona
Ray Agnew, DL, North Carolina State
1991—Pat Harlow, T, Southern California
Leonard Russell, RB, Arizona State
1992—Eugene Chung, T, Virginia Tech
1993—Drew Bledsoe, QB, Washington State*
1994—Willie McGinest, DE, Southern California
1995—Ty Law, DB, Michigan
1996—Terry Glenn, WR, Ohio State
1997—Chris Canty, DB, Kansas State
*First player chosen in draft.

FRANCHISE RECORDS

Most rushing yards, career
5,453—Sam Cunningham
Most rushing yards, season
1,487—Curtis Martin, 1995
Most rushing yards, game
212—Tony Collins vs. NYJ, Sept. 18, 1983
Most rushing touchdowns, season
14—Curtis Martin, 1995, 1996
Most passing attempts, season
691—Drew Bledsoe, 1994
Most passing attempts, game
70—Drew Bledsoe vs. Min., Nov. 13, 1994 (OT)
60—Drew Bledsoe at Pit., Dec. 16, 1995
Most passes completed, season
400—Drew Bledsoe, 1994
Most passes completed, game
45—Drew Bledsoe vs. Min., Nov. 13, 1994 (OT)
39—Drew Bledsoe at Pit., Dec. 16, 1995

Most passing yards, career
26,886—Steve Grogan
Most passing yards, season
4,555—Drew Bledsoe, 1994
Most passing yards, game
426—Drew Bledsoe vs. Min., Nov. 13, 1994 (OT)
421—Drew Bledsoe at Mia., Sept. 5, 1994
Most touchdown passes, season
31—Babe Parilli, 1964
Most pass receptions, career
534—Stanley Morgan
Most pass receptions, season
96—Ben Coates, 1994
Most pass receptions, game
12—Ben Coates at Ind., Nov. 27, 1994
Most receiving yards, career
10,352—Stanley Morgan
Most receiving yards, season
1,491—Stanley Morgan, 1986

Most receiving yards, game
182—Stanley Morgan vs. Mia., Nov. 8, 1981
Most receiving touchdowns, season
12—Stanley Morgan, 1979
Most touchdowns, career
68—Stanley Morgan
Most field goals, season
32—Tony Franklin, 1986
Longest field goal
55 yards—Matt Bahr at Mia., Nov. 12, 1995
Most interceptions, career
36—Raymond Clayborn
Most interceptions, season
11—Ron Hall, 1964
Most sacks, career
100—Andre Tippett
Most sacks, season
18.5—Andre Tippett, 1984

SERIES RECORDS

New England vs.: Arizona 3-6; Atlanta 3-5; Baltimore 1-0; Buffalo 38-35-1; Carolina 0-1; Chicago 4-2; Cincinnati 9-7; Dallas 0-7; Denver 12-18; Detroit 3-3; Green Bay 3-2; Houston 17-14-1; Indianapolis 7-14; Jacksonville 1-0; Kansas City 7-14-3; Miami 23-37; Minnesota 4-2; New Orleans 5-3; N.Y. Giants 2-3; N.Y. Jets 33-39-1; Oakland 12-13-1; Philadelphia 2-5; Pittsburgh 3-10; St. Louis 3-3; San Diego 15-11-2; San Francisco 1-7; Seattle 6-7; Tampa Bay 3-0; Washington 1-5.
NOTE: Includes records as Boston Patriots from 1960 through 1970.

RETIRED UNIFORM NUMBERS

No.	Player
14	Steve Grogan
20	Gino Cappelletti
57	Steve Nelson
73	John Hannah
79	Jim Hunt
89	Bob Dee

NEW ORLEANS SAINTS
YEAR-BY-YEAR RECORDS

			REGULAR SEASON					PLAYOFFS		
Year	W	L	T	Pct.	PF	PA	Finish	W	L	Highest round	Coach
1967	3	11	0	.214	233	379	4th/Capitol Div.	—	—		Tom Fears
1968	4	9	1	.308	246	327	3rd/Century Div.	—	—		Tom Fears
1969	5	9	0	.357	311	393	3rd/Capitol Div.	—	—		Tom Fears
1970	2	11	1	.154	172	347	4th/NFC Western Div.	—	—		Tom Fears, J.D. Roberts
1971	4	8	2	.333	266	347	4th/NFC Western Div.	—	—		J.D. Roberts
1972	2	11	1	.179	215	361	4th/NFC Western Div.	—	—		J.D. Roberts
1973	5	9	0	.357	163	312	T3rd/NFC Western Div.	—	—		John North
1974	5	9	0	.357	166	263	3rd/NFC Western Div.	—	—		John North
1975	2	12	0	.143	165	360	4th/NFC Western Div.	—	—		John North, Ernie Hefferle
1976	4	10	0	.286	253	346	T3rd/NFC Western Div.	—	—		Hank Stram
1977	3	11	0	.214	232	336	4th/NFC Western Div.	—	—		Hank Stram
1978	7	9	0	.438	281	298	3rd/NFC Western Div.	—	—		Dick Nolan
1979	8	8	0	.500	370	360	2nd/NFC Western Div.	—	—		Dick Nolan
1980	1	15	0	.063	291	487	4th/NFC Western Div.	—	—		Dick Nolan, Dick Stanfel

			REGULAR SEASON						PLAYOFFS		
Year	W	L	T	Pct.	PF	PA	Finish	W	L	Highest round	Coach
1981	4	12	0	.250	207	378	4th/NFC Western Div.	—	—		Bum Phillips
1982	4	5	0	.444	129	160	T8th/NFC	—	—		Bum Phillips
1983	8	8	0	.500	319	337	3rd/NFC Western Div.	—	—		Bum Phillips
1984	7	9	0	.438	298	361	3rd/NFC Western Div.	—	—		Bum Phillips
1985	5	11	0	.313	294	401	3rd/NFC Western Div.	—	—		Bum Phillips, Wade Phillips
1986	7	9	0	.438	288	287	4th/NFC Western Div.	—	—		Jim Mora
1987	12	3	0	.800	422	283	2nd/NFC Western Div.	0	1	NFC wild-card game	Jim Mora
1988	10	6	0	.625	312	283	3rd/NFC Western Div.	—	—		Jim Mora
1989	9	7	0	.563	386	301	3rd/NFC Western Div.	—	—		Jim Mora
1990	8	8	0	.500	274	275	2nd/NFC Western Div.	0	1	NFC wild-card game	Jim Mora
1991	11	5	0	.688	341	211	1st/NFC Western Div.	0	1	NFC wild-card game	Jim Mora
1992	12	4	0	.750	330	202	2nd/NFC Western Div.	0	1	NFC wild-card game	Jim Mora
1993	8	8	0	.500	317	343	2nd/NFC Western Div.	—	—		Jim Mora
1994	7	9	0	.438	348	407	T2nd/NFC Western Div.	—	—		Jim Mora
1995	7	9	0	.438	319	348	T3rd/NFC Western Div.	—	—		Jim Mora
1996	3	13	0	.188	229	339	T4th/NFC Western Div.	—	—		Jim Mora, Rick Venturi

FIRST-ROUND DRAFT PICKS

1967—Les Kelley, RB, Alabama
1968—Kevin Hardy, DE, Notre Dame
1969—John Shinners, G, Xavier (Ohio)
1970—Ken Burrough, WR, Texas Southern
1971—Archie Manning, QB, Mississippi
1972—Royce Smith, G, Georgia
1973—None
1974—Rick Middleton, LB, Ohio State
1975—Larry Burton, WR, Purdue
    Kurt Schumacher, G, Ohio State
1976—Chuck Muncie, RB, California
1977—Joe Campbell, DE, Maryland
1978—Wes Chandler, WR, Florida
1979—Russell Erxleben, P, Texas
1980—Stan Brock, T, Colorado
1981—George Rogers, RB, South Carolina*
1982—Lindsay Scott, WR, Georgia

1983—None
1984—None
1985—Alvin Toles, LB, Tennessee
1986—Jim Dombrowski, T, Virginia
1987—Shawn Knight, DE, Brigham Young
1988—Craig Heyward, RB, Pittsburgh
1989—Wayne Martin, DE, Arkansas
1990—Renaldo Turnbull, DE, West Virginia
1991—None
1992—Vaughn Dunbar, RB, Indiana
1993—Willie Roaf, T, Louisiana Tech
    Irv Smith, TE, Notre Dame
1994—Joe Johnson, DE, Louisville
1995—Mark Fields, LB, Washington State
1996—Alex Molden, DB, Oregon
1997—Chris Naeole, G, Colorado
*First player chosen in draft.

FRANCHISE RECORDS

Most rushing yards, career
4,267—George Rogers
Most rushing yards, season
1,674—George Rogers, 1981
Most rushing yards, game
206—George Rogers vs. St.L., Sept. 4, 1983
Most rushing touchdowns, season
13—George Rogers, 1981
    Dalton Hilliard, 1989
Most passing attempts, season
567—Jim Everett, 1995
Most passing attempts, game
55—Jim Everett at S.F., Sept. 25, 1994
Most passes completed, season
346—Jim Everett, 1994
Most passes completed, game
33—Archie Manning at G.B., Sept. 10, 1978
Most passing yards, career
21,734—Archie Manning

Most passing yards, season
3,970—Jim Everett, 1995
Most passing yards, game
377—Archie Manning at S.F., Dec. 7, 1980
Most touchdown passes, season
26—Jim Everett, 1995
Most pass receptions, career
532—Eric Martin
Most pass receptions, season
85—Eric Martin, 1988
Most pass receptions, game
14—Tony Galbreath at G.B., Sept. 10, 1978
Most receiving yards, career
7,854—Eric Martin
Most receiving yards, season
1,090—Eric Martin, 1989
Most receiving yards, game
205—Wes Chandler vs. Atl., Sept. 2, 1979
Most receiving touchdowns, season
9—Henry Childs, 1977

Most touchdowns, career
53—Dalton Hilliard
Most field goals, season
31—Morten Andersen, 1985
Longest field goal
63 yards—Tom Dempsey vs. Det., Nov. 8, 1970
Most interceptions, career
37—Dave Waymer
Most interceptions, season
10—Dave Whitsell, 1967
Most sacks, career
115—Rickey Jackson
Most sacks, season
17—Pat Swilling, 1991

SERIES RECORDS

New Orleans vs.: Arizona 9-11; Atlanta 24-31; Baltimore 0-1; Buffalo 2-3; Carolina 1-3; Chicago 6-10; Cincinnati 5-4; Dallas 3-14; Denver 2-4; Detroit 7-6-1; Green Bay 4-13; Houston 4-4-1; Indianapolis 3-3; Jacksonville 1-0; Kansas City 3-3; Miami 4-5; Minnesota 6-13; New England 3-5; N.Y. Giants 8-10; N.Y. Jets 4-4; Philadelphia 8-12; Oakland 2-4-1; Pittsburgh 5-6; St. Louis 24-29; San Diego 1-5; San Francisco 15-38-2; Seattle 3-2; Tampa Bay 12-5; Washington 5-12.

RETIRED UNIFORM NUMBERS

No.	Player
31	Jim Taylor
81	Doug Atkins

YEAR-BY-YEAR RECORDS

Year	W	L	T	Pct.	PF	PA	Finish	W	L	Highest round	Coach
			REGULAR SEASON							PLAYOFFS	
1925	8	4	0	.667	122	67	T4th				Bob Folwell
1926	8	4	1	.667	147	51	T6th				Joe Alexander
1927	11	1	1	.917	197	20	1st				Earl Potteiger
1928	4	7	2	.364	79	136	6th				Earl Potteiger
1929	13	1	1	.929	312	86	2nd				LeRoy Andrews
1930	13	4	0	.765	308	98	2nd				LeRoy Andrews, Benny Friedman-Steve Owen
1931	7	6	1	.538	154	100	5th				Steve Owen
1932	4	6	2	.400	93	113	5th				Steve Owen
1933	11	3	0	.786	244	101	1st/Eastern Div.	0	1	NFL championship game	Steve Owen
1934	8	5	0	.615	147	107	1st/Eastern Div.	1	0	NFL champ	Steve Owen
1935	9	3	0	.750	180	96	1st/Eastern Div.	0	1	NFL championship game	Steve Owen
1936	5	6	1	.455	115	163	3rd/Eastern Div.	—	—		Steve Owen
1937	6	3	2	.667	128	109	2nd/Eastern Div.	—	—		Steve Owen
1938	8	2	1	.800	194	79	1st/Eastern Div.	1	0	NFL champ	Steve Owen
1939	9	1	1	.900	168	85	1st/Eastern Div.	0	1	NFL championship game	Steve Owen
1940	6	4	1	.600	131	133	3rd/Eastern Div.	—	—		Steve Owen
1941	8	3	0	.727	238	114	1st/Eastern Div.	0	1	NFL championship game	Steve Owen
1942	5	5	1	.500	155	139	3rd/Eastern Div.				Steve Owen
1943	6	3	1	.667	197	170	2nd/Eastern Div.	0	1	E. Div. champ. game	Steve Owen
1944	8	1	1	.889	206	75	1st/Eastern Div.	0	1	NFL championship game	Steve Owen
1945	3	6	1	.333	179	198	T3rd/Eastern Div.	—	—		Steve Owen
1946	7	3	1	.700	236	162	1st/Eastern Div.	0	1	NFL championship game	Steve Owen
1947	2	8	2	.200	190	309	5th/Eastern Div.	—	—		Steve Owen
1948	4	8	0	.333	297	388	T3rd/Eastern Div.	—	—		Steve Owen
1949	6	6	0	.500	287	298	3rd/Eastern Div.	—	—		Steve Owen
1950	10	2	0	.833	268	150	2nd/American Conf.	0	1	Am. Conf. champ. game	Steve Owen
1951	9	2	1	.818	254	161	2nd/American Conf.	—	—		Steve Owen
1952	7	5	0	.583	234	231	T2nd/American Conf.	—	—		Steve Owen
1953	3	9	0	.250	179	277	5th/Eastern Conf.	—	—		Steve Owen
1954	7	5	0	.583	293	184	3rd/Eastern Conf.	—	—		Jim Lee Howell
1955	6	5	1	.545	267	223	3rd/Eastern Conf.	—	—		Jim Lee Howell
1956	8	3	1	.727	264	197	1st/Eastern Conf.	1	0	NFL champ	Jim Lee Howell
1957	7	5	0	.583	254	211	2nd/Eastern Conf.	—	—		Jim Lee Howell
1958	9	3	0	.750	246	183	1st/Eastern Conf.	1	1	NFL championship game	Jim Lee Howell
1959	10	2	0	.833	284	170	1st/Eastern Conf.	0	1	NFL championship game	Jim Lee Howell
1960	6	4	2	.600	271	261	3rd/Eastern Conf.	—	—		Jim Lee Howell
1961	10	3	1	.769	368	220	1st/Eastern Conf.	0	1	NFL championship game	Allie Sherman
1962	12	2	0	.857	398	283	1st/Eastern Conf.	0	1	NFL championship game	Allie Sherman
1963	11	3	0	.786	448	280	1st/Eastern Conf.	0	1	NFL championship game	Allie Sherman
1964	2	10	2	.167	241	399	7th/Eastern Conf.	—	—		Allie Sherman
1965	7	7	0	.500	270	338	T2nd/Eastern Conf.	—	—		Allie Sherman
1966	1	12	1	.077	263	501	8th/Eastern Conf.	—	—		Allie Sherman
1967	7	7	0	.500	369	379	2nd/Century Div.	—	—		Allie Sherman
1968	7	7	0	.500	294	325	2nd/Capitol Div.	—	—		Allie Sherman
1969	6	8	0	.429	264	298	2nd/Century Div.	—	—		Alex Webster
1970	9	5	0	.643	301	270	2nd/NFC Eastern Div.	—	—		Alex Webster
1971	4	10	0	.286	228	362	5th/NFC Eastern Div.	—	—		Alex Webster
1972	8	6	0	.571	331	247	3rd/NFC Eastern Div.	—	—		Alex Webster
1973	2	11	1	.179	226	362	5th/NFC Eastern Div.	—	—		Alex Webster
1974	2	12	0	.143	195	299	5th/NFC Eastern Div.	—	—		Bill Arnsparger
1975	5	9	0	.357	216	306	4th/NFC Eastern Div.	—	—		Bill Arnsparger
1976	3	11	0	.214	170	250	5th/NFC Eastern Div.	—	—		Bill Arnsparger, John McVay
1977	5	9	0	.357	181	265	T4th/NFC Eastern Div.	—	—		John McVay
1978	6	10	0	.375	264	298	T4th/NFC Eastern Div.	—	—		John McVay
1979	6	10	0	.375	237	323	4th/NFC Eastern Div.	—	—		Ray Perkins
1980	4	12	0	.250	249	425	5th/NFC Eastern Div.	—	—		Ray Perkins
1981	9	7	0	.563	295	257	3rd/NFC Eastern Div.	1	1	NFC div. playoff game	Ray Perkins
1982	4	5	0	.444	164	160	T8th/NFC	—	—		Ray Perkins
1983	3	12	1	.219	267	347	5th/NFC Eastern Div.	—	—		Bill Parcells
1984	9	7	0	.563	299	301	2nd/NFC Eastern Div.	1	1	NFC div. playoff game	Bill Parcells
1985	10	6	0	.625	399	283	2nd/NFC Eastern Div.	1	1	NFC div. playoff game	Bill Parcells
1986	14	2	0	.875	371	236	1st/NFC Eastern Div.	3	0	Super Bowl champ	Bill Parcells
1987	6	9	0	.400	280	312	5th/NFC Eastern Div.	—	—		Bill Parcells
1988	10	6	0	.625	359	304	2nd/NFC Eastern Div.	—	—		Bill Parcells
1989	12	4	0	.750	348	252	1st/NFC Eastern Div.	0	1	NFC div. playoff game	Bill Parcells
1990	13	3	0	.813	335	211	1st/NFC Eastern Div.	3	0	Super Bowl champ	Bill Parcells

Year	W	L	T	Pct.	PF	PA	Finish	W	L	Highest round	Coach
				REGULAR SEASON						**PLAYOFFS**	
1991	8	8	0	.500	281	297	4th/NFC Eastern Div.	—	—		Ray Handley
1992	6	10	0	.375	306	367	4th/NFC Eastern Div.	—	—		Ray Handley
1993	11	5	0	.688	288	205	2nd/NFC Eastern Div.	1	1	NFC div. playoff game	Dan Reeves
1994	9	7	0	.563	279	305	2nd/NFC Eastern Div.	—	—		Dan Reeves
1995	5	11	0	.313	290	340	4th/NFC Eastern Div.	—	—		Dan Reeves
1996	6	10	0	.375	242	297	5th/NFC Eastern Div.	—	—		Dan Reeves

FIRST-ROUND DRAFT PICKS

1936—Art Lewis, T, Ohio
1937—Ed Widseth, T, Minnesota
1938—George Karamatic, B, Gonzaga
1939—Walt Nielson, B, Arizona
1940—Grenville Lansdell, B, Southern California
1941—George Franck, B, Minnesota
1942—Merle Hapes, B, Mississippi
1943—Steve Filipowicz, B, Fordham
1944—Billy Hillenbrand, B, Indiana
1945—Elmer Barbour, B, Wake Forest
1946—George Connor, T, Notre Dame
1947—Vic Schwall, B, Northwestern
1948—Tony Minisi, B, Pennsylvania
1949—Paul Page, B, Southern Methodist
1950—Travis Tidwell, B, Auburn
1951—Kyle Rote, B, Southern Methodist*
　　　Kim Spavital, B, Oklahoma A&M
1952—Frank Gifford, B, Southern California
1953—Bobby Marlow, B, Alabama
1954—None
1955—Joe Heap, B, Notre Dame
1956—Henry Moore, B, Arkansas
1957—None
1958—Phil King, B, Vanderbilt
1959—Lee Grosscup, B, Utah
1960—Lou Cordileone, G, Clemson
1961—None
1962—Jerry Hillebrand, LB, Colorado
1963—None
1964—Joe Don Looney, RB, Oklahoma
1965—T. Frederickson, RB, Auburn*
1966—Francis Peay, T, Missouri
1967—None

1968—None
1969—Fred Dryer, DE, San Diego State
1970—Jim Files, LB, Oklahoma
1971—Rocky Thompson, RB, West Texas State
1972—Eldridge Small, DB, Texas A&I
　　　Larry Jacobson, DT, Nebraska
1973—None
1974—John Hicks, G, Ohio State
1975—None
1976—Troy Archer, DE, Colorado
1977—Gary Jeter, DT, Southern Cal
1978—Gordon King, T, Stanford
1979—Phil Simms, QB, Morehead State
1980—Mark Haynes, DB, Colorado
1981—Lawrence Taylor, LB, North Carolina
1982—Butch Woolfolk, RB, Michigan
1983—Terry Kinard, DB, Clemson
1984—Carl Banks, LB, Michigan State
　　　Bill Roberts, T, Ohio State
1985—George Adams, RB, Kentucky
1986—Eric Dorsey, DT, Notre Dame
1987—Mark Ingram, WR, Michigan State
1988—Eric Moore, T, Indiana
1989—Brian Williams, G, Minnesota
1990—Rodney Hampton, RB, Georgia
1991—Jarrod Bunch, FB, Michigan
1992—Derek Brown, TE, Notre Dame
1993—None
1994—Thomas Lewis, WR, Indiana
1995—Tyrone Wheatley, RB, Michigan
1996—Cedric Jones, DE, Oklahoma
1997—Ike Hilliard, WR, Florida
*First player chosen in draft.

FRANCHISE RECORDS

Most rushing yards, career
6,816—Rodney Hampton
Most rushing yards, season
1,516—Joe Morris, 1986
Most rushing yards, game
218—Gene Roberts vs. Chi. Cardinals,
Nov. 12, 1950
Most rushing touchdowns, season
21—Joe Morris, 1985
Most passing attempts, season
533—Phil Simms, 1984
Most passing attempts, game
62—Phil Simms at Cin., Oct. 13, 1985
Most passes completed, season
286—Phil Simms, 1984
Most passes completed, game
40—Phil Simms at Cin., Oct. 13, 1985
Most passing yards, career
33,462—Phil Simms

Most passing yards, season
4,044—Phil Simms, 1984
Most passing yards, game
513—Phil Simms at Cin., Oct. 13, 1985
Most touchdown passes, season
36—Y.A. Tittle, 1963
Most pass receptions, career
395—Joe Morrison
Most pass receptions, season
78—Earnest Gray, 1983
Most pass receptions, game
12—Mark Bavaro at Cin., Oct. 13, 1985
Most receiving yards, career
5,434—Frank Gifford
Most receiving yards, season
1,209—Homer Jones
Most receiving yards, game
269—Del Shofner vs. Was., Oct. 28, 1962

Most receiving touchdowns, season
13—Homer Jones, 1967
Most touchdowns, career
49—Rodney Hampton
Most field goals, season
35—Ali Haji-Sheikh, 1983
Longest field goal
56 yards—Ali Haji-Sheikh at Det., Nov. 7,
1983
Most interceptions, career
74—Emlen Tunnell
Most interceptions, season
11—Otto Schellbacher, 1951
　　　Jimmy Patton, 1958
Most sacks, career
132.5—Lawrence Taylor
Most sacks, season
20.5—Lawrence Taylor, 1986

SERIES RECORDS

N.Y. Giants vs.: Arizona 71-36-2; Atlanta 6-6; Buffalo 2-5; Carolina 0-1; Chicago 16-25-2; Cincinnati 1-4; Dallas 23-44-2; Denver 3-3; Detroit 13-14-1; Green Bay 20-22-2; Houston 5-0; Indianapolis 5-5; Jacksonville 0-0; Kansas City 6-3; Miami 3-1; Minnesota 5-7; New England 3-2; New Orleans 10-8; N.Y. Jets 4-4; Oakland 2-5; Philadelphia 63-59-2; Pittsburgh 44-28-3; St. Louis 7-19; San Diego 4-3; San Francisco 11-11; Seattle 5-3; Tampa Bay 8-3; Washington 66-50-2.

NEW YORK JETS
YEAR-BY-YEAR RECORDS

	REGULAR SEASON							PLAYOFFS			
Year	W	L	T	Pct.	PF	PA	Finish	W	L	Highest round	Coach
1960*†	7	7	0	.500	382	399	2nd/Eastern Div.	—	—		Sammy Baugh
1961*†	7	7	0	.500	301	390	3rd/Eastern Div.	—	—		Sammy Baugh
1962*†	5	9	0	.357	278	423	4th/Eastern Div.	—	—		Bulldog Turner
1963*	5	8	1	.385	249	399	4th/Eastern Div.	—	—		Weeb Ewbank
1964*	5	8	1	.385	278	315	3rd/Eastern Div.	—	—		Weeb Ewbank
1965*	5	8	1	.385	285	303	2nd/Eastern Div.	—	—		Weeb Ewbank
1966*	6	6	2	.500	322	312	3rd/Eastern Div.	—	—		Weeb Ewbank
1967*	8	5	1	.615	371	329	2nd/Eastern Div.	—	—		Weeb Ewbank
1968*	11	3	0	.786	419	280	1st/Eastern Div.	2	0	Super Bowl champ	Weeb Ewbank
1969*	10	4	0	.714	353	269	1st/Eastern Div.	0	1	Div. playoff game	Weeb Ewbank
1970	4	10	0	.286	255	286	3rd/AFC Eastern Div.	—	—		Weeb Ewbank
1971	6	8	0	.429	212	299	T3rd/AFC Eastern Div.	—	—		Weeb Ewbank
1972	7	7	0	.500	367	324	2nd/AFC Eastern Div.	—	—		Weeb Ewbank
1973	4	10	0	.286	240	306	T4th/AFC Eastern Div.	—	—		Weeb Ewbank
1974	7	7	0	.500	279	300	T3rd/AFC Eastern Div.	—	—		Charley Winner
1975	3	11	0	.214	258	433	T4th/AFC Eastern Div.	—	—		Charley Winner, Ken Shipp
1976	3	11	0	.214	169	383	4th/AFC Eastern Div.	—	—		Lou Holtz, Mike Holovak
1977	3	11	0	.214	191	300	T4th/AFC Eastern Div.	—	—		Walt Michaels
1978	8	8	0	.500	359	364	3rd/AFC Eastern Div.	—	—		Walt Michaels
1979	8	8	0	.500	337	383	3rd/AFC Eastern Div.	—	—		Walt Michaels
1980	4	12	0	.250	302	395	5th/AFC Eastern Div.	—	—		Walt Michaels
1981	10	5	1	.656	355	287	2nd/AFC Eastern Div.	0	1	AFC wild-card game	Walt Michaels
1982	6	3	0	.667	245	166	T4th/AFC	2	1	AFC championship game	Walt Michaels
1983	7	9	0	.438	313	331	4th/AFC Eastern Div.	—	—		Joe Walton
1984	7	9	0	.438	332	364	3rd/AFC Eastern Div.	—	—		Joe Walton
1985	11	5	0	.688	393	264	T2nd/AFC Eastern Div.	0	1	AFC wild-card game	Joe Walton
1986	10	6	0	.625	364	386	2nd/AFC Eastern Div.	1	1	AFC div. playoff game	Joe Walton
1987	6	9	0	.400	334	360	5th/AFC Eastern Div.	—	—		Joe Walton
1988	8	7	1	.531	372	354	4th/AFC Eastern Div.	—	—		Joe Walton
1989	4	12	0	.250	253	411	5th/AFC Eastern Div.	—	—		Joe Walton
1990	6	10	0	.375	295	345	4th/AFC Eastern Div.	—	—		Bruce Coslet
1991	8	8	0	.500	314	293	2nd/AFC Eastern Div.	0	1	AFC wild-card game	Bruce Coslet
1992	4	12	0	.250	220	315	4th/AFC Eastern Div.	—	—		Bruce Coslet
1993	8	8	0	.500	270	247	3rd/AFC Eastern Div.	—	—		Bruce Coslet
1994	6	10	0	.375	264	320	5th/AFC Eastern Div.	—	—		Pete Carroll
1995	3	13	0	.188	233	384	5th/AFC Eastern Div.	—	—		Rich Kotite
1996	1	15	0	.063	279	454	5th/AFC Eastern Div.	—	—		Rich Kotite

*American Football League.
†New York Titans.

FIRST-ROUND DRAFT PICKS

1960—George Izo, QB, Notre Dame
1961—Tom Brown, G, Minnesota
1962—Sandy Stephens, QB, Minnesota
1963—Jerry Stovall, RB, Louisiana State
1964—Matt Snell, RB, Ohio State
1965—Joe Namath, QB, Alabama
    Tom Nowatzke, RB, Indiana
1966—Bill Yearby, DT, Michigan
1967—Paul Seiler, G, Notre Dame
1968—Lee White, RB, Weber State
1969—Dave Foley, T, Ohio State
1970—Steve Tannen, DB, Florida
1971—John Riggins, RB, Kansas

1972—Jerome Barkum, WR, Jackson State
1972—Mike Taylor, LB, Michigan
1973—Burgess Owens, DB, Miami
1974—Carl Barzilauskas, DT, Indiana
1975—None
1976—Richard Todd, QB, Alabama
1977—Marvin Powell, T, Southern California
1978—Chris Ward, T, Ohio State
1979—Marty Lyons, DT, Alabama
1980—Lam Jones, WR, Texas
1981—Freeman McNeil, RB, UCLA
1982—Bob Crable, LB, Notre Dame
1983—Ken O'Brien, QB, California-Davis

...rter, DB, Southern Methodist
...DE, Arkansas
...R, Wisconsin
...ght, T, Iowa
... Vick, FB, Texas A&M
...ve Cadigan, T, Southern California
...eff Lageman, LB, Virginia
—Blair Thomas, RB, Penn State
...1—None

1992—Johnny Mitchell, TE, Nebraska
1993—Marvin Jones, LB, Florida State
1994—Aaron Glenn, DB, Texas A&M
1995—Kyle Brady, TE, Penn State
     Hugh Douglas, DE, Central State (O.)
1996—Keyshawn Johnson, WR, Southern California*
1997—James Farrior, LB, Virginia
*First player chosen in draft.

FRANCHISE RECORDS

Most rushing yards, career
8,074—Freeman McNeil
Most rushing yards, season
1,249—Adrian Murrell, 1996
Most rushing yards, game
199—Adrian Murrell at Ariz., Oct. 27, 1996
Most rushing touchdowns, season
11—Emerson Boozer, 1972
    Johnny Hector, 1987
    Brad Baxter, 1991
Most passing attempts, season
518—Richard Todd, 1983
Most passing attempts, game
62—Joe Namath vs. Bal., Oct. 18, 1970
Most passes completed, season
308—Richard Todd, 1983
Most passes completed, game
42—Richard Todd vs. S.F., Sept. 21, 1980
Most passing yards, career
27,057—Joe Namath

Most passing yards, season
4,007—Joe Namath, 1967
Most passing yards, game
496—Joe Namath at Bal., Sept. 24, 1972
Most touchdown passes, season
26—Al Dorow, 1960
    Joe Namath, 1967
Most pass receptions, career
627—Don Maynard
Most pass receptions, season
93—Al Toon, 1988
Most pass receptions, game
17—Clark Gaines vs. S.F., Sept. 21, 1980
Most receiving yards, career
11,732—Don Maynard
Most receiving yards, season
1,434—Don Maynard, 1967
Most receiving yards, game
228—Don Maynard at Oak., Nov. 17, 1968

Most receiving touchdowns, season
14—Art Powell, 1960
    Don Maynard, 1965
Most touchdowns, career
88—Don Maynard
Most field goals, season
34—Jim Turner, 1968
Longest field goal
55 yards—Pat Leahy vs. Chi., Dec. 14,
    1985
Most interceptions, career
34—Bill Baird
Most interceptions, season
12—Dainard Paulson, 1964
Most sacks, career
107.5—Mark Gastineau
Most sacks, season
22—Mark Gastineau, 1984

SERIES RECORDS

N.Y. Jets vs.: Arizona 2-2; Atlanta 3-4; Buffalo 31-42; Carolina 0-1; Chicago 1-4; Cincinnati 9-6; Dallas 1-5; Denver 12-13-1; Detroit 3-4; Green Bay 5-2; Houston 12-20-1; Indianapolis 21-32; Jacksonville 1-1; Kansas City 12-14-1; Miami 28-31-1; Minnesota 4-1; New England 39-33-1; New Orleans 4-4; N.Y. Giants 4-4; Oakland 9-16-2; Philadelphia 0-6; Pittsburgh 1-12; St. Louis 2-6; San Diego 9-17-1; San Francisco 1-6; Seattle 4-8; Tampa Bay 5-1; Washington 1-5.
NOTE: Includes records as New York Titans from 1960 through 1962.

RETIRED UNIFORM NUMBERS

No.	Player
12	Joe Namath
13	Don Maynard

OAKLAND RAIDERS
YEAR-BY-YEAR RECORDS

		REGULAR SEASON						PLAYOFFS		
Year	W	L	T	Pct.	PF	PA	Finish	W	L	Highest round	Coach
1960*	6	8	0	.429	319	388	3rd/Western Div.	—	—		Eddie Erdelatz
1961*	2	12	0	.143	237	458	4th/Western Div.	—	—		E. Erdelatz, Marty Feldman
1962*	1	13	0	.071	213	370	4th/Western Div.	—	—		M. Feldman, Red Conkright
1963*	10	4	0	.714	363	288	2nd/Western Div.	—	—		Al Davis
1964*	5	7	2	.417	303	350	3rd/Western Div.	—	—		Al Davis
1965*	8	5	1	.615	298	239	2nd/Western Div.	—	—		Al Davis
1966*	8	5	1	.615	315	288	2nd/Western Div.	—	—		John Rauch
1967*	13	1	0	.929	468	233	1st/Western Div.	1	1	Super Bowl	John Rauch
1968*	12	2	0	.857	453	233	1st/Western Div.	1	1	AFL championship game	John Rauch
1969*	12	1	1	.923	377	242	1st/Western Div.	1	1	AFL championship game	John Madden
1970	8	4	2	.667	300	293	1st/AFC Western Div.	1	1	AFC championship game	John Madden
1971	8	4	2	.667	344	278	2nd/AFC Western Div.	—	—		John Madden
1972	10	3	1	.750	365	248	1st/AFC Western Div.	0	1	AFC div. playoff game	John Madden
1973	9	4	1	.679	292	175	1st/AFC Western Div.	1	1	AFC championship game	John Madden
1974	12	2	0	.857	355	228	1st/AFC Western Div.	1	1	AFC championship game	John Madden
1975	11	3	0	.786	375	255	1st/AFC Western Div.	1	1	AFC championship game	John Madden
1976	13	1	0	.929	350	237	1st/AFC Western Div.	3	0	Super Bowl champ	John Madden
1977	11	3	0	.786	351	230	2nd/AFC Western Div.	1	1	AFC championship game	John Madden
1978	9	7	0	.563	311	283	T2nd/AFC Western Div.	—	—		John Madden
1979	9	7	0	.563	365	337	T3rd/AFC Western Div.	—	—		Tom Flores
1980	11	5	0	.688	364	306	2nd/AFC Western Div.	4	0	Super Bowl champ	Tom Flores

				REGULAR SEASON				PLAYOFFS			
Year	W	L	T	Pct.	PF	PA	Finish	W	L	Highest round	Coach
1981	7	9	0	.438	273	343	4th/AFC Western Div.	—	—		Tom Flores
1982†	8	1	0	.889	260	200	1st/AFC	1	1	AFC second-round pl. game	Tom Flores
1983†	12	4	0	.750	442	338	1st/AFC Western Div.	3	0	Super Bowl champ	Tom Flores
1984†	11	5	0	.688	368	278	3rd/AFC Western Div.	0	1	AFC wild-card game	Tom Flores
1985†	12	4	0	.750	354	308	1st/AFC Western Div.	0	1	AFC div. playoff game	Tom Flores
1986†	8	8	0	.500	323	346	4th/AFC Western Div.	—	—		Tom Flores
1987†	5	10	0	.333	301	289	4th/AFC Western Div.	—	—		Tom Flores
1988†	7	9	0	.438	325	369	3rd/AFC Western Div.	—	—		Tom Flores
1989†	8	8	0	.500	315	297	3rd/AFC Western Div.	—	—		Mike Shanahan
1990†	12	4	0	.750	337	268	1st/AFC Western Div.	1	1	AFC championship game	Mike Shanahan, Art Shell
1991†	9	7	0	.563	298	297	3rd/AFC Western Div.	0	1	AFC wild-card game	Art Shell
1992†	7	9	0	.438	249	281	4th/AFC Western Div.	—	—		Art Shell
1993†	10	6	0	.625	306	326	2nd/AFC Western Div.	1	1	AFC div. playoff game	Art Shell
1994†	9	7	0	.563	303	327	3rd/AFC Western Div.	—	—		Art Shell
1995	8	8	0	.500	348	332	T3rd/AFC Western Div.	—	—		Mike White
1996	7	9	0	.438	340	293	T4th/AFC Western Div.	—	—		Mike White

*American Football League.
†Los Angeles Raiders.

FIRST-ROUND DRAFT PICKS

1960—Dale Hackbart, DB, Wisconsin
1961—Joe Rutgens, DT, Illinois
1962—Roman Gabriel, QB, North Carolina State* (AFL)
1963—None
1964—Tony Lorick, RB, Arizona State
1965—Harry Schuh, T, Memphis State
1966—Rodger Bird, DB, Kentucky
1967—Gene Upshaw, G, Texas A&I
1968—Eldridge Dickey, QB, Tenn. State
1969—Art Thoms, DT, Syracuse
1970—Raymond Chester, TE, Morgan State
1971—Jack Tatum, DB, Ohio State
1972—Mike Siani, WR, Villanova
1973—Ray Guy, P, So. Mississippi
1974—Henry Lawrence, T, Florida A&M
1975—Neal Colzie, DB, Ohio State
1976—None
1977—None
1978—None
1979—None
1980—Marc Wilson, QB, Brigham Young

1981—Ted Watts, DB, Texas Tech
      Curt Marsh, G, Washington
1982—Marcus Allen, RB, Southern California
1983—Don Mosebar, T, Southern California
1984—None
1985—Jessie Hester, WR, Florida State
1986—Bob Buczkowski, DT, Pittsburgh
1987—John Clay, T, Missouri
1988—Tim Brown, WR, Notre Dame
      Terry McDaniel, CB, Tennessee
      Scott Davis, DE, Illinois
1989—None
1990—Anthony Smith, DE, Arizona
1991—Todd Marinovich, QB, Southern California
1992—Chester McGlockton, DT, Clemson
1993—Patrick Bates, DB, Texas A&M
1994—Rob Fredrickson, LB, Michigan State
1995—Napoleon Kaufman, RB, Washington
1996—Rickey Dudley, TE, Ohio State
1997—Darrell Russell, DT, Southern California
*First player chosen in draft.

FRANCHISE RECORDS

Most rushing yards, career
,545—Marcus Allen
Most rushing yards, season
,759—Marcus Allen, 1985
Most rushing yards, game
21—Bo Jackson at Sea., Nov. 30, 1987
Most rushing touchdowns, season
—Pete Banaszak, 1975
Most passing attempts, season
8—Ken Stabler, 1979
Most passing attempts, game
—Todd Marinovich vs. Cle., Sept. 20, 1992
Most passes completed, season
4—Ken Stabler, 1979
Most passes completed, game
—Jim Plunkett at K.C., Sept. 12, 1985
Most passing yards, career
078—Ken Stabler

Most passing yards, season
3,615—Ken Stabler, 1979
Most passing yards, game
424—Jeff Hostetler vs. S.D., Oct. 18, 1993
Most touchdown passes, season
34—Daryle Lamonica, 1969
Most pass receptions, career
589—Fred Biletnikoff
Most pass receptions, season
95—Todd Christensen, 1986
Most pass receptions, game
12—Dave Casper at N.E., Oct. 3, 1976
Most receiving yards, career
8,974—Fred Biletnikoff
Most receiving yards, season
1,361—Art Powell, 1964
Most receiving yards, game
247—Art Powell vs. Hou., Dec. 22, 1963

Most receiving touchdowns, season
16—Art Powell, 1964
Most touchdowns, career
95—Marcus Allen
Most field goals, season
35—Jeff Jaeger, 1993
Longest field goal
54 yards—George Fleming vs. Den., Oct. 2, 1961
Most interceptions, career
39—Willie Brown
      Lester Hayes
Most interceptions, season
13—Lester Hayes, 1980
Most sacks, career
107.5—Greg Townsend
Most sacks, season
17.5—Tony Cline, 1970

Oakland vs.: Arizona 2-1; Atlanta 5-3; Baltimore 0-1; Buffalo 15-14; Carolina 0-0; Chicago 5-4; Cincinnati 15-7; Dallas 3-3; Denver 48-23-2; Detroit 6-2; Green Bay 5-2; Houston 20-13; Indianapolis 5-2; Jacksonville 1-0; Kansas City 36-35-2; Miami 15-5-1; Minnesota 6-3; New England 13-12-1; New Orleans 4-2-1; N.Y. Giants 5-2; N.Y. Jets 16-9-2; Philadelphia 3-4; Pittsburgh 7-5; St. Louis 6-2; San Diego 44-28-2; San Francisco 5-3; Seattle 21-17; Tampa Bay 3-1; Washington 6-2.
NOTE: Includes records as Los Angeles Raiders from 1982 through 1994.

No.	Player
None	

PHILADELPHIA EAGLES
YEAR-BY-YEAR RECORDS

			REGULAR SEASON					PLAYOFFS		
Year	W	L	T	Pct.	PF	PA	Finish	W	L	Highest round	Coach

Year	W	L	T	Pct.	PF	PA	Finish	W	L	Highest round	Coach
1933	3	5	1	.375	77	158	4th/Eastern Div.	—	—		Lud Wray
1934	4	7	0	.364	127	85	T3rd/Eastern Div.	—	—		Lud Wray
1935	2	9	0	.182	60	179	5th/Eastern Div.	—	—		Lud Wray
1936	1	11	0	.083	51	206	5th/Eastern Div.	—	—		Bert Bell
1937	2	8	1	.200	86	177	5th/Eastern Div.	—	—		Bert Bell
1938	5	6	0	.455	154	164	4th/Eastern Div.	—	—		Bert Bell
1939	1	9	1	.100	105	200	T4th/Eastern Div.	—	—		Bert Bell
1940	1	10	0	.091	111	211	5th/Eastern Div.	—	—		Bert Bell
1941	2	8	1	.200	119	218	4th/Eastern Div.	—	—		Greasy Neale
1942	2	9	0	.182	134	239	5th/Eastern Div.	—	—		Greasy Neale
1943*	5	4	1	.556	225	230	3rd/Eastern Div.	—	—		Greasy Neale-Walt Kiesling
1944	7	1	2	.875	267	131	2nd/Eastern Div.	—	—		Greasy Neale
1945	7	3	0	.700	272	133	2nd/Eastern Div.	—	—		Greasy Neale
1946	6	5	0	.545	231	220	2nd/Eastern Div.	—	—		Greasy Neale
1947	8	4	0	.667	308	242	1st/Eastern Div.	1	1	NFL championship game	Greasy Neale
1948	9	2	1	.818	376	156	1st/Eastern Div.	1	0	NFL champ	Greasy Neale
1949	11	1	0	.917	364	134	1st/Eastern Div.	1	0	NFL champ	Greasy Neale
1950	6	6	0	.500	254	141	T3rd/American Conf.	—	—		Greasy Neale
1951	4	8	0	.333	234	264	5th/American Conf.	—	—		Bo McMillin, Wayne Millner
1952	7	5	0	.583	252	271	T2nd/American Conf.	—	—		Jim Trimble
1953	7	4	1	.636	352	215	2nd/Eastern Conf.	—	—		Jim Trimble
1954	7	4	1	.636	284	230	2nd/Eastern Conf.	—	—		Jim Trimble
1955	4	7	1	.364	248	231	T4th/Eastern Conf.	—	—		Jim Trimble
1956	3	8	1	.273	143	215	6th/Eastern Conf.	—	—		Hugh Devore
1957	4	8	0	.333	173	230	5th/Eastern Conf.	—	—		Hugh Devore
1958	2	9	1	.182	235	306	T5th/Eastern Conf.	—	—		Buck Shaw
1959	7	5	0	.583	268	278	T2nd/Eastern Conf.	—	—		Buck Shaw
1960	10	2	0	.833	321	246	1st/Eastern Conf.	1	0	NFL champ	Buck Shaw
1961	10	4	0	.714	361	297	2nd/Eastern Conf.	—	—		Nick Skorich
1962	3	10	1	.231	282	356	7th/Eastern Conf.	—	—		Nick Skorich
1963	2	10	2	.167	242	381	7th/Western Conf.	—	—		Nick Skorich
1964	6	8	0	.429	312	313	T3rd/Eastern Conf.	—	—		Joe Kuharich
1965	5	9	0	.357	363	359	T5th/Eastern Conf.	—	—		Joe Kuharich
1966	9	5	0	.643	326	340	T2nd/Eastern Conf.	—	—		Joe Kuharich
1967	6	7	1	.462	351	409	2nd/Capitol Div.	—	—		Joe Kuharich
1968	2	12	0	.143	202	351	4th/Capitol Div.	—	—		Joe Kuharich
1969	4	9	1	.308	279	377	4th/Capitol Div.	—	—		Jerry Williams
1970	3	10	1	.231	241	332	5th/NFC Eastern Div.	—	—		Jerry Williams
1971	6	7	1	.462	221	302	3rd/NFC Eastern Div.	—	—		Jerry Williams, Ed Khayat
1972	2	11	1	.179	145	352	5th/NFC Eastern Div.	—	—		Ed Khayat
1973	5	8	1	.393	310	393	3rd/NFC Eastern Div.	—	—		Mike McCormack
1974	7	7	0	.500	242	217	4th/NFC Eastern Div.	—	—		Mike McCormack
1975	4	10	0	.286	225	302	5th/NFC Eastern Div.	—	—		Mike McCormack
1976	4	10	0	.286	165	286	4th/NFC Eastern Div.	—	—		Dick Vermeil
1977	5	9	0	.357	220	207	T4th/NFC Eastern Div.	—	—		Dick Vermeil
1978	9	7	0	.563	270	250	2nd/NFC Eastern Div.	0	1	NFC wild-card game	Dick Vermeil
1979	11	5	0	.688	339	282	2nd/NFC Eastern Div.	1	1	NFC div. playoff game	Dick Vermeil
1980	12	4	0	.750	384	222	1st/NFC Eastern Div.	2	1	Super Bowl	Dick Vermeil
1981	10	6	0	.625	368	221	2nd/NFC Eastern Div.	0	1	NFC wild-card game	Dick Vermeil
1982	3	6	0	.333	191	195	T11th/NFC	—	—		Dick Vermeil
1983	5	11	0	.313	233	322	4th/NFC Eastern Div.	—	—		Marion Campbell
1984	6	9	1	.406	278	320	5th/NFC Eastern Div.	—	—		Marion Campbell
1985	7	9	0	.438	286	310	4th/NFC Eastern Div.	—	—		M. Campbell, Fred Brum
1986	5	10	1	.344	256	312	4th/NFC Eastern Div.	—	—		Buddy Ryan
1987	7	8	0	.467	337	380	T2nd/NFC Eastern Div.	—	—		Buddy Ryan
1988	10	6	0	.625	379	319	1st/NFC Eastern Div.	0	1	NFC div. playoff game	Buddy Ryan
1989	11	5	0	.688	342	274	2nd/NFC Eastern Div.	0	1	NFC wild-card game	Buddy Ryan

	REGULAR SEASON						PLAYOFFS			
Year	W	L	T	Pct.	PF	PA	Finish	W	L	Highest round	Coach
1990	10	6	0	.625	396	299	T2nd/NFC Eastern Div.	0	1	NFC wild-card game	Buddy Ryan
1991	10	6	0	.625	285	244	3rd/NFC Eastern Div.	—	—		Rich Kotite
1992	11	5	0	.688	354	245	2nd/NFC Eastern Div.	1	1	NFC div. playoff game	Rich Kotite
1993	8	8	0	.500	293	315	3rd/NFC Eastern Div.	—	—		Rich Kotite
1994	7	9	0	.438	308	308	4th/NFC Eastern Div.	—	—		Rich Kotite
1995	10	6	0	.625	318	338	2nd/NFC Eastern Div.	1	1	NFC div. playoff game	Ray Rhodes
1996	10	6	0	.625	363	341	2nd/NFC Eastern Div.	0	1	NFC wild-card game	Ray Rhodes

*Phil-Pitt "Steagles," a combined squad of Philadelphia Eagles and Pittsburgh Steelers.

FIRST-ROUND DRAFT PICKS

1936—Jay Berwanger, B, Chicago*
1937—Sam Francis, B, Nebraska*
1938—John McDonald, B, Nebraska
1939—Davey O'Brien, QB, Texas Christian
1940—Wes McAfee, B, Duke
1941—None
1942—Pete Kmetovic, B, Stanford
1943—Joe Muha, B, Virginia Military
1944—Steve Van Buren, B, Louisiana State
1945—John Yonaker, E, Notre Dame
1946—Leo Riggs, B, Southern California
1947—Neil Armstrong, E, Oklahoma A&M
1948—Clyde Scott, B, Arkansas
1949—Chuck Bednarik, C, Pennsylvania*
        Frank Tripucka, QB, Notre Dame
1950—Bud Grant, E, Minnesota
1951—Ebert Van Buren, B, Louisiana State
        Chet Mutryn, B, Xavier
1952—John Bright, B, Drake
1953—None
1954—Neil Worden, B, Notre Dame
1955—Dick Bielski, B, Maryland
1956—Bob Pellegrini, C, Maryland
1957—Clarence Peaks, B, Michigan State
1958—Walter Kowalczyk, B, Michigan State
1959—None
1960—Ron Burton, B, Northwestern
1961—Art Baker, B, Syracuse
1962—None
1963—Ed Budde, T, Michigan State
1964—Bob Brown, T, Nebraska
1965—None
1966—Randy Beisler, T, Indiana
1967—Harry Jones, RB, Arkansas

1968—Tim Rossovich, DE, Southern California
1969—Leroy Keyes, RB, Purdue
1970—Steve Zabel, E, Oklahoma
1971—Richard Harris, DE, Grambling State
1972—John Reaves, QB, Florida
1973—Jerry Sisemore, T, Texas
        Charle Young, TE, Southern California
1974—None
1975—None
1976—None
1977—None
1978—None
1979—Jerry Robinson, LB, UCLA
1980—Roynell Young, DB, Alcorn State
1981—Leonard Mitchell, DE, Houston
1982—Mike Quick, WR, North Carolina State
1983—Michael Haddix, RB, Mississippi State
1984—Kenny Jackson, WR, Penn State
1985—Kevin Allen, T, Indiana
1986—Keith Byars, RB, Ohio State
1987—Jerome Brown, DT, Miami (Fla.)
1988—Keith Jackson, TE, Oklahoma
1989—None
1990—Ben Smith, DB, Georgia
1991—Antone Davis, T, Tennessee
1992—None
1993—Lester Holmes, T, Jackson State
        Leonard Renfro, DT, Colorado
1994—Bernard Williams, T, Georgia
1995—Mike Mamula, DE, Boston College
1996—Jermane Mayberry, T, Texas A&M-Kingsville
1997—Jon Harris, DE, Virginia
        *First player chosen in draft.

FRANCHISE RECORDS

Most rushing yards, career
,538—Wilbert Montgomery
Most rushing yards, season
,512—Wilbert Montgomery, 1979
Most rushing yards, game
05—Steve Van Buren vs. Pit., Nov. 27, 1949
Most rushing touchdowns, season
5—Steve Van Buren, 1945
Most passing attempts, season
60—Randall Cunningham, 1988
Most passing attempts, game
2—Randall Cunningham at Chi., Oct. 2, 1989
Most passes completed, season
01—Randall Cunningham, 1988
Most passes completed, game
—Randall Cunningham at Was., Sept. 17, 1989
Most passing yards, career
,963—Ron Jaworski

Most passing yards, season
3,808—Randall Cunningham, 1988
Most passing yards, game
447—Randall Cunningham at Was., Sept. 17, 1989
Most touchdown passes, season
32—Sonny Jurgensen, 1961
Most pass receptions, career
589—Harold Carmichael
Most pass receptions, season
88—Irving Fryar, 1996
Most pass receptions, game
14—Don Looney at Was., Dec. 1, 1940
Most receiving yards, career
8,978—Harold Carmichael
Most receiving yards, season
1,409—Mike Quick, 1983
Most receiving yards, game
237—Tommy McDonald vs. NYG, Dec. 10, 1961

Most receiving touchdowns, season
13—Tommy McDonald, 1960
        Tommy McDonald, 1961
        Mike Quick, 1983
Most touchdowns, career
79—Harold Carmichael
Most field goals, season
30—Paul McFadden, 1984
Longest field goal
59 yards—Tony Franklin at Dal., Nov. 12, 1979
Most interceptions, career
34—Bill Bradley
Most interceptions, season
11—Bill Bradley, 1971
Most sacks, career
124—Reggie White
Most sacks, season
21—Reggie White, 1987

SERIES RECORDS

Philadelphia vs.: Arizona 48-46-5; Atlanta 9-7-1; Buffalo 4-4; Carolina 1-0; Chicago 4-25-1; Cincinnati 1-6; Dallas 28-44; Denver 6-2; Detroit 10-11-2; Green Bay 8-20; Houston 6-0; Indianapolis 6-7; Jacksonville 0-0; Kansas City 1-1; Miami 3-6; Minnesota 6-10; New England 5-2; New Orleans 12-8; N.Y. Giants 59-63-2; N.Y. Jets 6-0; Oakland 4-3; Pittsburgh 43-26-3; St. Louis 12-14-1; San Diego 2-4; San Francisco 6-13-1; Seattle 4-2; Tampa Bay 3-2; Washington 53-63-6.
NOTE: Includes records when team combined with Pittsburgh squad and was known as Phil-Pitt in 1943.

RETIRED UNIFORM NUMBERS

No.	Player
15	Steve Van Buren
40	Tom Brookshier
44	Pete Retzlaff
60	Chuck Bednarik
70	Al Wistert
99	Jerome Brown

PITTSBURGH STEELERS
YEAR-BY-YEAR RECORDS

			REGULAR SEASON						PLAYOFFS		
Year	W	L	T	Pct.	PF	PA	Finish	W	L	Highest round	Coach
1933*	3	6	2	.333	67	208	5th/Eastern Div.	—	—		Jap Douds
1934*	2	10	0	.167	51	206	5th/Eastern Div.	—	—		Luby DiMello
1935*	4	8	0	.333	100	209	3rd/Eastern Div.	—	—		Joe Bach
1936*	6	6	0	.500	98	187	2nd/Eastern Div.	—	—		Joe Bach
1937*	4	7	0	.364	122	145	3rd/Eastern Div.	—	—		Johnny Blood
1938*	2	9	0	.182	79	169	5th/Eastern Div.	—	—		Johnny Blood
1939*	1	9	1	.100	114	216	T4th/Eastern Div.	—	—		Johnny Blood-Walt Kiesling
1940*	2	7	2	.222	60	178	4th/Eastern Div.	—	—		Walt Kiesling
1941	1	9	1	.100	103	276	5th/Eastern Div.	—	—		Bert Bell-Buff Donelli-Walt Kiesling
1942	7	4	0	.636	167	119	2nd/Eastern Div.	—	—		Walt Kiesling
1943†	5	4	1	.556	225	230	3rd/Eastern Div.	—	—		Walt Kiesling-Greasy Neale
1944‡	0	10	0	.000	108	328	5th/Western Div.	—	—		Walt Kiesling-Phil Handler
1945	2	8	0	.200	79	220	5th/Eastern Div.	—	—		Jim Leonard
1946	5	5	1	.500	136	117	T3rd/Eastern Div.	—	—		Jock Sutherland
1947	8	4	0	.667	240	259	2nd/Eastern Div.	0	1	E. Div. champ. game	Jock Sutherland
1948	4	8	0	.333	200	243	T3rd/Eastern Div.	—	—		John Michelosen
1949	6	5	1	.545	224	214	2nd/Eastern Div.	—	—		John Michelosen
1950	6	6	0	.500	180	195	T3rd/American Conf.	—	—		John Michelosen
1951	4	7	1	.364	183	235	4th/American Conf.	—	—		John Michelosen
1952	5	7	0	.417	300	273	3rd/American Conf.	—	—		Joe Bach
1953	6	6	0	.500	211	263	4th/Eastern Conf.	—	—		Joe Bach
1954	5	7	0	.417	219	263	4th/Eastern Conf.	—	—		Walt Kiesling
1955	4	8	0	.333	195	285	6th/Eastern Conf.	—	—		Walt Kiesling
1956	5	7	0	.417	217	250	5th/Eastern Conf.	—	—		Walt Kiesling
1957	6	6	0	.500	161	178	3rd/Eastern Conf.	—	—		Buddy Parker
1958	7	4	1	.636	261	230	3rd/Eastern Conf.	—	—		Buddy Parker
1959	6	5	1	.545	257	216	4th/Eastern Conf.	—	—		Buddy Parker
1960	5	6	1	.455	240	275	5th/Eastern Conf.	—	—		Buddy Parker
1961	6	8	0	.429	295	287	5th/Eastern Conf.	—	—		Buddy Parker
1962	9	5	0	.643	312	363	2nd/Eastern Conf.	—	—		Buddy Parker
1963	7	4	3	.636	321	295	4th/Eastern Conf.	—	—		Buddy Parker
1964	5	9	0	.357	253	315	6th/Eastern Conf.	—	—		Buddy Parker
1965	2	12	0	.143	202	397	7th/Eastern Conf.	—	—		Mike Nixon
1966	5	8	1	.385	316	347	6th/Eastern Conf.	—	—		Bill Austin
1967	4	9	1	.308	281	320	4th/Century Div.	—	—		Bill Austin
1968	2	11	1	.154	244	397	4th/Century Div.	—	—		Bill Austin
1969	1	13	0	.071	218	404	4th/Century Div.	—	—		Chuck Noll
1970	5	9	0	.357	210	272	3rd/AFC Central Div.	—	—		Chuck Noll
1971	6	8	0	.429	246	292	2nd/AFC Central Div.	—	—		Chuck Noll
1972	11	3	0	.786	343	175	1st/AFC Central Div.	1	1	AFC championship game	Chuck Noll
1973	10	4	0	.714	347	210	2nd/AFC Central Div.	0	1	AFC div. playoff game	Chuck Noll
1974	10	3	1	.750	305	189	1st/AFC Central Div.	3	0	Super Bowl champ	Chuck Noll
1975	12	2	0	.857	373	162	1st/AFC Central Div.	3	0	Super Bowl champ	Chuck Noll
1976	10	4	0	.714	342	138	1st/AFC Central Div.	1	1	AFC championship game	Chuck Noll
1977	9	5	0	.643	283	243	1st/AFC Central Div.	0	1	AFC div. playoff game	Chuck Noll
1978	14	2	0	.875	356	195	1st/AFC Central Div.	3	0	Super Bowl champ	Chuck Noll
1979	12	4	0	.750	416	262	1st/AFC Central Div.	3	0	Super Bowl champ	Chuck Noll
1980	9	7	0	.563	352	313	3rd/AFC Central Div.	—	—		Chuck Noll
1981	8	8	0	.500	356	297	2nd/AFC Central Div.	—	—		Chuck Noll
1982	6	3	0	.667	204	146	T4th/AFC	0	1	AFC first-round pl. game	Chuck Noll
1983	10	6	0	.625	355	303	1st/AFC Central Div.	0	1	AFC div. playoff game	Chuck Noll
1984	9	7	0	.563	387	310	1st/AFC Central Div.	1	1	AFC championship game	Chuck Noll
1985	7	9	0	.438	379	355	T2nd/AFC Central Div.	—	—		Chuck Noll
1986	6	10	0	.375	307	336	3rd/AFC Central Div.	—	—		Chuck Noll

				REGULAR SEASON				PLAYOFFS			
Year	W	L	T	Pct.	PF	PA	Finish	W	L	Highest round	Coach
1987	8	7	0	.533	285	299	3rd/AFC Central Div.	—	—		Chuck Noll
1988	5	11	0	.313	336	421	4th/AFC Central Div.	—	—		Chuck Noll
1989	9	7	0	.563	265	326	T2nd/AFC Central Div.	1	1	AFC div. playoff game	Chuck Noll
1990	9	7	0	.563	292	240	3rd/AFC Central Div.	—	—		Chuck Noll
1991	7	9	0	.438	292	344	2nd/AFC Central Div.	—	—		Chuck Noll
1992	11	5	0	.688	299	225	1st/AFC Central Div.	0	1	AFC div. playoff game	Bill Cowher
1993	9	7	0	.563	308	281	2nd/AFC Central Div.	0	1	AFC wild-card game	Bill Cowher
1994	12	4	0	.750	316	234	1st/AFC Central Div.	1	1	AFC championship game	Bill Cowher
1995	11	5	0	.689	407	327	1st/AFC Central Div.	2	1	Super Bowl	Bill Cowher
1996	10	6	0	.625	344	257	1st/AFC Central Div.	1	1	AFC div. playoff game	Bill Cowher

*Pittsburgh Pirates.
†Phil-Pitt "Steagles," a combined squad of Philadelphia Eagles and Pittsburgh Steelers.
‡Card-Pitt, a combined squad of Chicago Cardinals and Pittsburgh Steelers.

FIRST-ROUND DRAFT PICKS

1936—Bill Shakespeare, B, Notre Dame
1937—Mike Basrak, C, Duquesne
1938—Byron White, B, Colorado
    Frank Filchock, B, Indiana
1939—None
1940—Kay Eakin, B, Arkansas
1941—Chet Gladchuk, C, Boston College
1942—Bill Dudley, B, Virginia*
1943—Bill Daley, B, Minnesota
1944—Johnny Podesto, B, St. Mary's (Calif.)
1945—Paul Duhart, B, Florida
1946—Doc Blanchard, B, Army
1947—Hub Bechtol, E, Texas
1948—Dan Edwards, E, Georgia
1949—Bobby Gage, B, Clemson
1950—Lynn Chandnois, B, Michigan State
1951—Clarence Avinger, B, Alabama
1952—Ed Modzelewski, B, Maryland
1953—Ted Marchibroda, QB, St. Bonaventure
1954—John Lattner, B, Notre Dame
1955—Frank Varrichione, T, Notre Dame
1956—Gary Glick, B, Colorado State*
    Art Davis, B, Mississippi State
1957—Len Dawson, QB, Purdue
1958—None
1959—None
1960—Jack Spikes, B, Texas Christian
1961—None
1962—Bob Ferguson, RB, Ohio State
1963—None
1964—Paul Martha, RB, Pittsburgh
1965—None
1966—Dick Leftridge, RB, West Virginia

1967—None
1968—Mike Taylor, T, Southern California
1969—Joe Greene, DT, North Texas State
1970—Terry Bradshaw, QB, Louisiana Tech*
1971—Frank Lewis, WR, Grambling State
1972—Franco Harris, RB, Penn State
1973—James Thomas, DB, Florida State
1974—Lynn Swann, WR, Southern California
1975—Dave Brown, DB, Michigan
1976—Bennie Cunningham, TE, Clemson
1977—Robin Cole, LB, New Mexico
1978—Ron Johnson, DB, Eastern Michigan
1979—Greg Hawthorne, RB, Baylor
1980—Mark Malone, QB, Arizona State
1981—Keith Gary, DE, Oklahoma
1982—Walter Abercrombie, RB, Baylor
1983—Gabriel Rivera, DT, Texas Tech
1984—Louis Lipps, WR, Southern Mississippi
1985—Darryl Sims, DT, Wisconsin
1986—John Rienstra, G, Temple
1987—Rod Woodson, DB, Purdue
1988—Aaron Jones, DE, Eastern Kentucky
1989—Tim Worley, RB, Georgia
    Tom Ricketts, T, Pittsburgh
1990—Eric Green, TE, Liberty (Va.)
1991—Huey Richardson, LB, Florida
1992—Leon Searcy, T, Miami (Fla.)
1993—Deon Figures, DB, Colorado
1994—Charles Johnson, WR, Colorado
1995—Mark Bruener, TE, Washington
1996—Jermain Stephens, T, North Carolina A&T
1997—Chad Scott, DB, Maryland
    *First player chosen in draft.

FRANCHISE RECORDS

Most rushing yards, career
1,950—Franco Harris
Most rushing yards, season
,690—Barry Foster, 1992
Most rushing yards, game
18—John Fuqua at Phi., Dec. 20, 1970
Most rushing touchdowns, season
4—Franco Harris, 1976
Most passing attempts, season
36—Neil O'Donnell, 1993
Most passing attempts, game
5—Neil O'Donnell vs. G.B., Dec. 24, 1995
Most passes completed, season
70—Neil O'Donnell, 1993
Most passes completed, game
1—Neil O'Donnell at Chi., Nov. 5, 1995
  (OT)

31—Joe Gilliam at Den., Sept. 22, 1974
  (OT)
30—Terry Bradshaw vs. Cle., Nov. 25, 1979 (OT)
29—Terry Bradshaw vs. Cin., Sept. 19, 1982 (OT)
28—Kent Nix vs. Dal., Oct. 22, 1967
Most passing yards, career
27,989—Terry Bradshaw
Most passing yards, season
3,724—Terry Bradshaw, 1979
Most passing yards, game
409—Bobby Layne vs. Chi. Cardinals, Dec. 13, 1958
Most touchdown passes, season
28—Terry Bradshaw, 1978
Most pass receptions, career
537—John Stallworth

Most pass receptions, season
85—Yancey Thigpen, 1995
Most pass receptions, game
12—J.R. Wilburn vs. Dal., Oct. 22, 1967
Most receiving yards, career
8,723—John Stallworth
Most receiving yards, season
1,395—John Stallworth, 1984
Most receiving yards, game
235—Buddy Dial vs. Cle., Oct. 22, 1961
Most receiving touchdowns, season
12—Buddy Dial, 1961
    Louis Lipps, 1985
Most touchdowns, career
100—Franco Harris
Most field goals, season
34—Norm Johnson, 1995

Longest field goal	Most interceptions, season	Most sacks, season
55 yards—Gary Anderson vs. S.D., Nov. 25, 1984	11—Mel Blount, 1975	15—Mike Merriweather, 1984
Most interceptions, career	**Most sacks, career**	
57—Mel Blount	73.5—L.C. Greenwood	

SERIES RECORDS

Pittsburgh vs.: Arizona 29-21-3; Atlanta 10-1; Baltimore 1-1; Buffalo 8-7; Carolina 0-1; Chicago 5-19-1; Cincinnati 30-23; Dallas 11-13; Denver 5-10-1; Detroit 12-13-1; Green Bay 11-21; Houston 34-19; Indianapolis 12-4; Jacksonville 2-2; Kansas City 14-5; Miami 6-8; Minnesota 4-8; New England 10-3; New Orleans 6-5; N.Y. Giants 28-44-3; N.Y. Jets 13-1; Oakland 5-7; Philadelphia 26-43-3; St. Louis 6-17-2; San Diego 16-5; San Francisco 7-9; Seattle 5-6; Tampa Bay 4-0; Washington 24-39-4.

NOTE: Includes records as Pittsburgh Pirates from 1933 through 1940; also includes records when team combined with Philadelphia squad and was known as Phil-Pitt in 1943 and when team combined with Chicago Cardinals squad and was known as Card-Pitt in 1944.

RETIRED UNIFORM NUMBERS

No.	Player
None	

ST. LOUIS RAMS
YEAR-BY-YEAR RECORDS

	REGULAR SEASON							PLAYOFFS			
Year	W	L	T	Pct.	PF	PA	Finish	W	L	Highest round	Coach
1937*	1	10	0	.091	75	207	5th/Western Div.	—	—		Hugo Bezdek
1938*	4	7	0	.364	131	215	4th/Western Div.	—	—		Hugo Bezdek, Art Lewis
1939*	5	5	1	.500	195	164	4th/Western Div.	—	—		Dutch Clark
1940*	4	6	1	.400	171	191	4th/Western Div.	—	—		Dutch Clark
1941*	2	9	0	.182	116	244	5th/Western Div.	—	—		Dutch Clark
1942*	5	6	0	.455	150	207	3rd/Western Div.	—	—		Dutch Clark
1943*	Rams did not play in 1943.										
1944*	4	6	0	.400	188	224	4th/Western Div.	—	—		Buff Donelli
1945*	9	1	0	.900	244	136	1st/Western Div.	1	0	NFL champ	Adam Walsh
1946†	6	4	1	.600	277	257	2nd/Western Div.	—	—		Adam Walsh
1947†	6	6	0	.500	259	214	4th/Western Div.	—	—		Bob Snyder
1948†	6	5	1	.545	327	269	3rd/Western Div.	—	—		Clark Shaughnessy
1949†	8	2	2	.800	360	239	1st/Western Div.	0	1	NFL championship game	Clark Shaughnessy
1950†	9	3	0	.750	466	309	1st/National Conf.	1	1	NFL championship game	Joe Stydahar
1951†	8	4	0	.667	392	261	1st/National Conf.	1	0	NFL champ	Joe Stydahar
1952†	9	3	0	.750	349	234	2nd/National Conf.	0	1	Nat. Conf. champ. game	Joe Stydahar, Hamp Pool
1953†	8	3	1	.727	366	236	3rd/Western Conf.	—	—		Hamp Pool
1954†	6	5	1	.545	314	285	4th/Western Conf.	—	—		Hamp Pool
1955†	8	3	1	.727	260	231	1st/Western Conf.	0	1	NFL championship game	Sid Gillman
1956†	4	8	0	.333	291	307	6th/Western Conf.	—	—		Sid Gillman
1957†	6	6	0	.500	307	278	4th/Western Conf.	—	—		Sid Gillman
1958†	8	4	0	.667	344	278	T2nd/Western Conf.	—	—		Sid Gillman
1959†	2	10	0	.167	242	315	6th/Western Conf.	—	—		Sid Gillman
1960†	4	7	1	.364	265	297	6th/Western Conf.	—	—		Bob Waterfield
1961†	4	10	0	.286	263	333	6th/Western Conf.	—	—		Bob Waterfield
1962†	1	12	1	.077	220	334	7th/Western Conf.	—	—		B. Waterfield, H. Svare
1963†	5	9	0	.357	210	350	6th/Western Conf.	—	—		Harland Svare
1964†	5	7	2	.417	283	339	5th/Western Conf.	—	—		Harland Svare
1965†	4	10	0	.286	269	328	7th/Western Conf.	—	—		Harland Svare
1966†	8	6	0	.571	289	212	3rd/Western Conf.	—	—		George Allen
1967†	11	1	2	.917	398	196	1st/Coastal Div.	0	1	W. Conf. champ. game	George Allen
1968†	10	3	1	.769	312	200	2nd/Coastal Div.	—	—		George Allen
1969†	11	3	0	.786	320	243	1st/Coastal Div.	0	1	W. Conf. champ. game	George Allen
1970†	9	4	1	.692	325	202	2nd/NFC Western Div.	—	—		George Allen
1971†	8	5	1	.615	313	260	2nd/NFC Western Div.	—	—		Tommy Prothro
1972†	6	7	1	.464	291	286	3rd/NFC Western Div.	—	—		Tommy Prothro
1973†	12	2	0	.857	388	178	1st/NFC Western Div.	0	1	NFC div. playoff game	Chuck Knox
1974†	10	4	0	.714	263	181	1st/NFC Western Div.	1	1	NFC championship game	Chuck Knox
1975†	12	2	0	.857	312	135	1st/NFC Western Div.	1	1	NFC championship game	Chuck Knox
1976†	10	3	1	.750	351	190	1st/NFC Western Div.	1	1	NFC championship game	Chuck Knox
1977†	10	4	0	.714	302	146	1st/NFC Western Div.	0	1	NFC div. playoff game	Chuck Knox
1978†	12	4	0	.750	316	245	1st/NFC Western Div.	1	1	NFC championship game	Ray Malavasi
1979†	9	7	0	.563	323	309	1st/NFC Western Div.	2	1	Super Bowl	Ray Malavasi
1980†	11	5	0	.688	424	289	2nd/NFC Western Div.	0	1	NFC wild-card game	Ray Malavasi
1981†	6	10	0	.375	303	351	3rd/NFC Western Div.	—	—		Ray Malavasi
1982†	2	7	0	.222	200	250	14th/NFC	—	—		Ray Malavasi
1983†	9	7	0	.563	361	344	2nd/NFC Western Div.	1	1	NFC div. playoff game	John Robinson

			REGULAR SEASON						PLAYOFFS		
Year	W	L	T	Pct.	PF	PA	Finish	W	L	Highest round	Coach
1984†	10	6	0	.625	346	316	2nd/NFC Western Div.	0	1	NFC wild-card game	John Robinson
1985†	11	5	0	.688	340	277	1st/NFC Western Div.	1	1	NFC championship game	John Robinson
1986†	10	6	0	.625	309	267	2nd/NFC Western Div.	0	1	NFC wild-card game	John Robinson
1987†	6	9	0	.400	317	361	3rd/NFC Western Div.	—	—		John Robinson
1988†	10	6	0	.625	407	293	2nd/NFC Western Div.	0	1	NFC wild-card game	John Robinson
1989†	11	5	0	.688	426	344	2nd/NFC Western Div.	2	1	NFC championship game	John Robinson
1990†	5	11	0	.313	345	412	T3rd/NFC Western Div.	—	—		John Robinson
1991†	3	13	0	.188	234	390	4th/NFC Western Div.	—	—		John Robinson
1992†	6	10	0	.375	313	383	T3rd/NFC Western Div.	—	—		Chuck Knox
1993†	5	11	0	.313	221	367	4th/NFC Western Div.	—	—		Chuck Knox
1994†	4	12	0	.250	286	365	4th/NFC Western Div.	—	—		Chuck Knox
1995	7	9	0	.438	309	418	T3rd/NFC Western Div.	—	—		Rich Brooks
1996	6	10	0	.375	303	409	3rd/NFC Western Div.	—	—		Rich Brooks

*Cleveland Rams.
†Los Angeles Rams.

FIRST-ROUND DRAFT PICKS

1937—Johnny Drake, B, Purdue
1938—Corbett Davis, B, Indiana*
1939—Parker Hall, B, Mississippi
1940—Ollie Cordill, B, Rice
1941—Rudy Mucha, C, Washington
1942—Jack Wilson, B, Baylor
1943—Mike Holovak, B, Boston College
1944—Tony Butkovich, B, Illinois
1945—Elroy Hirsch, B, Wisconsin
1946—Emil Sitko, B, Notre Dame
1947—Herman Wedemeyer, B, St. Mary's (Cal.)
1948—None
1949—Bobby Thomason, B, Virginia Military
1950—Ralph Pasquariello, B, Villanova
    Stan West, G, Oklahoma
1951—Bud McFadin, G, Texas
1952—Bill Wade, B, Vanderbilt*
    Bob Carey, E, Michigan State
1953—Donn Moomaw, C, UCLA
    Ed Barker, E, Washington State
1954—Ed Beatty, C, Cincinnati
1955—Larry Morris, C, Georgia Tech
1956—Joe Marconi, B, West Virginia
    Charlie Horton, B, Vanderbilt
1957—Jon Arnett, B, Southern California
    Del Shofner, B, Baylor
1958—Lou Michaels, T, Kentucky
    Jim Phillips, E, Auburn
1959—Dick Bass, B, Pacific
    Paul Dickson, G, Baylor
1960—Billy Cannon, RB, Louisiana State*
1961—Marlin McKeever, LB, Southern California
1962—Roman Gabriel, QB, North Carolina State
    Merlin Olsen, DT, Utah State
1963—Terry Baker, QB, Oregon State*
    Rufus Guthrie, G, Georgia Tech
1964—Bill Munson, QB, Utah State
1965—Clancy Williams, DB, Washington State
1966—Tom Mack, G, Michigan
1967—None

1968—None
1969—Larry Smith, RB, Florida
    Jim Seymour, E, Notre Dame
    Bob Klein, TE, Southern California
1970—Jack Reynolds, LB, Tennessee
1971—Isiah Robertson, LB, Southern
    Jack Youngblood, DE, Florida
1972—None
1973—None
1974—John Cappelletti, RB, Penn State
1975—Mike Fanning, DT, Notre Dame
    Dennis Harrah, G, Miami (Fla.)
    Doug France, T, Ohio State
1976—Kevin McLain, LB, Colorado State
1977—Bob Brudzinski, LB, Ohio State
1978—Elvis Peacock, RB, Oklahoma
1979—George Andrews, LB, Nebraska
    Kent Hill, G, Georgia Tech
1980—Johnnie Johnson, DB, Texas
1981—Mel Owens, LB, Michigan
1982—Barry Redden, RB, Richmond
1983—Eric Dickerson, RB, Southern Methodist
1984—None
1985—Jerry Gray, DB, Texas
1986—Mike Schad, T, Queens College (Ont.)
1987—None
1988—Gaston Green, RB, UCLA
    Aaron Cox, WR, Arizona State
1989—Bill Hawkins, DE, Miami (Fla.)
    Cleveland Gary, RB, Miami (Fla.)
1990—Bern Brostek, C, Washington
1991—Todd Lyght, CB, Notre Dame
1992—Sean Gilbert, DE, Pittsburgh
1993—Jerome Bettis, RB, Notre Dame
1994—Wayne Gandy, T, Auburn
1995—Kevin Carter, DE, Florida
1996—Lawrence Phillips, RB, Nebraska
    Eddie Kennison, WR, Louisiana State
1997—Orlando Pace, T, Ohio State*
    *First player chosen in draft.

FRANCHISE RECORDS

Most rushing yards, career
7,245—Eric Dickerson
Most rushing yards, season
2,105—Eric Dickerson, 1984
Most rushing yards, game
247—Willie Ellison vs. N.O., Dec. 5, 1971
Most rushing touchdowns, season
—Eric Dickerson, 1983

Most passing attempts, season
554—Jim Everett, 1990
Most passing attempts, game
55—Mark Rypien vs. Buf., Dec. 10, 1995
Most passes completed, season
308—Jim Everett, 1988
Most passes completed, game
35—Dieter Brock vs. S.F., Oct. 27, 1985

Most passing yards, career
23,758—Jim Everett
Most passing yards, season
4,310—Jim Everett, 1989
Most passing yards, game
554—Norm Van Brocklin at N.Y. Yanks,
    Sept. 28, 1951

Most touchdown passes, season
31—Jim Everett, 1988
Most pass receptions, career
593—Henry Ellard
Most pass receptions, season
119—Isaac Bruce, 1995
Most pass receptions, game
18—Tom Fears vs. G.B., Dec. 3, 1950
Most receiving yards, career
9,761—Henry Ellard
Most receiving yards, season
1,781—Isaac Bruce, 1995

Most receiving yards, game
336—Willie Anderson at N.O., Nov. 26, 1989
Most receiving touchdowns, season
17—Elroy Hirsch, 1951
Most touchdowns, career
58—Eric Dickerson
Most field goals, season
30—David Ray, 1973
Longest field goal
54 yards—Tony Zendejas vs. Pit., Sept. 12, 1993

Most interceptions, career
46—Ed Meador
Most interceptions, season
14—Night Train Lane, 1952
Most sacks, career
151.5—Deacon Jones
Most sacks, season
22—Deacon Jones, 1964
　　　Deacon Jones, 1968

SERIES RECORDS

St. Louis vs.: Arizona 16-13-2; Atlanta 39-19-2; Baltimore 0-1; Buffalo 3-4; Carolina 2-2; Chicago 25-35-3; Cincinnati 3-5; Dallas 9-8; Denver 4-3; Detroit 32-27-1; Green Bay 40-26-1; Houston 5-2; Indianapolis 17-21-2; Jacksonville 1-0; Kansas City 4-1; Miami 1-6; Minnesota 11-15-2; New England 3-3; New Orleans 29-23; N.Y. Giants 19-7; N.Y. Jets 6-2; Oakland 2-6; Philadelphia 14-12-1; Pittsburgh 17-6-2; San Diego 3-3; San Francisco 47-43-2; Seattle 4-1; Tampa Bay 8-3; Washington 6-16-1.
NOTE: Includes records as Los Angeles Rams from 1946 through 1994.

RETIRED UNIFORM NUMBERS

No.	Player
7	Bob Waterfield
74	Merlin Olsen

SAN DIEGO CHARGERS
YEAR-BY-YEAR RECORDS

Year	W	L	T	Pct.	PF	PA	Finish	W	L	Highest round	Coach
							REGULAR SEASON			**PLAYOFFS**	
1960*†	10	4	0	.714	373	336	1st/Western Div.	0	1	AFL championship game	Sid Gillman
1961*	12	2	0	.857	396	219	1st/Western Div.	0	1	AFL championship game	Sid Gillman
1962*	4	10	0	.286	314	392	3rd/Western Div.	—	—		Sid Gillman
1963*	11	3	0	.786	399	256	1st/Western Div.	1	0	AFL champ	Sid Gillman
1964*	8	5	1	.615	341	300	1st/Western Div.	0	1	AFL championship game	Sid Gillman
1965*	9	2	3	.818	340	227	1st/Western Div.	0	1	AFL championship game	Sid Gillman
1966*	7	6	1	.538	335	284	3rd/Western Div.	—	—		Sid Gillman
1967*	8	5	1	.615	360	352	3rd/Western Div.	—	—		Sid Gillman
1968*	9	5	0	.643	382	310	3rd/Western Div.	—	—		Sid Gillman
1969*	8	6	0	.571	288	276	3rd/Western Div.	—	—		Sid Gillman, Charlie Walle
1970	5	6	3	.455	282	278	3rd/AFC Western Div.	—	—		Charlie Waller
1971	6	8	0	.429	311	341	3rd/AFC Western Div.	—	—		Harland Svare
1972	4	9	1	.308	264	344	4th/AFC Western Div.	—	—		Harland Svare
1973	2	11	1	.179	188	386	4th/AFC Western Div.	—	—		Harland Svare, Ron Walle
1974	5	9	0	.357	212	285	T3rd/AFC Western Div.	—	—		Tommy Prothro
1975	2	12	0	.143	189	345	4th/AFC Western Div.	—	—		Tommy Prothro
1976	6	8	0	.429	248	285	3rd/AFC Western Div.	—	—		Tommy Prothro
1977	7	7	0	.500	222	205	3rd/AFC Western Div.	—	—		Tommy Prothro
1978	9	7	0	.563	355	309	T2nd/AFC Western Div.	—	—		Tommy Prothro, Don Cory
1979	12	4	0	.750	411	246	1st/AFC Western Div.	0	1	AFC div. playoff game	Don Coryell
1980	11	5	0	.688	418	327	1st/AFC Western Div.	1	1	AFC championship game	Don Coryell
1981	10	6	0	.625	478	390	1st/AFC Western Div.	1	1	AFC championship game	Don Coryell
1982	6	3	0	.667	288	221	T4th/AFC	1	1	AFC second-round pl. game	Don Coryell
1983	6	10	0	.375	358	462	T4th/AFC Western Div.	—	—		Don Coryell
1984	7	9	0	.438	394	413	5th/AFC Western Div.	—	—		Don Coryell
1985	8	8	0	.500	467	435	T3rd/AFC Western Div.	—	—		Don Coryell
1986	4	12	0	.250	335	396	5th/AFC Western Div.	—	—		Don Coryell, Al Saunder
1987	8	7	0	.533	253	317	3rd/AFC Western Div.	—	—		Al Saunders
1988	6	10	0	.375	231	332	4th/AFC Western Div.	—	—		Al Saunders
1989	6	10	0	.375	266	290	5th/AFC Western Div.	—	—		Dan Henning
1990	6	10	0	.375	315	281	4th/AFC Western Div.	—	—		Dan Henning
1991	4	12	0	.250	274	342	5th/AFC Western Div.	—	—		Dan Henning
1992	11	5	0	.688	335	241	1st/AFC Western Div.	1	1	AFC div. playoff game	Bobby Ross
1993	8	8	0	.500	322	290	4th/AFC Western Div.	—	—		Bobby Ross
1994	11	5	0	.688	381	306	1st/AFC Western Div.	2	1	Super Bowl	Bobby Ross
1995	9	7	0	.563	321	323	2nd/AFC Western Div.	0	1	AFC wild-card game	Bobby Ross
1996	8	8	0	.500	310	376	3rd/AFC Western Div.	—	—		Bobby Ross

*American Football League.
†Los Angeles Chargers.

FIRST-ROUND DRAFT PICKS

1960—Monty Stickles, E, Notre Dame
1961—Earl Faison, E, Indiana
1962—Bob Ferguson, RB, Ohio State
1963—Walt Sweeney, E, Syracuse
1964—Ted Davis, E, Georgia Tech
1965—Steve DeLong, DE, Tennessee
1966—Don Davis, T, Los Angeles State
1967—Ron Billingsley, DT, Wyoming
1968—Russ Washington, T, Missouri
　　　Jim Hill, DB, Texas A&I
1969—Marty Domres, QB, Columbia
　　　Bob Babich, LB, Miami of Ohio
1970—Walker Gillette, WR, Richmond
1971—Leon Burns, RB, Long Beach State
1972—None
1973—Johnny Rodgers, WR, Nebraska
1974—Bo Matthews, RB, Colorado
　　　Don Goode, LB, Kansas
1975—Gary Johnson, DT, Grambling State
　　　Mike Williams, DB, Louisiana State
1976—Joe Washington, RB, Oklahoma
1977—Bob Rush, C, Memphis State
1978—John Jefferson, WR, Arizona State

1979—Kellen Winslow, TE, Missouri
1980—None
1981—James Brooks, RB, Auburn
1982—None
1983—Billy Ray Smith, LB, Arkansas
　　　Gary Anderson, WR, Arkansas
　　　Gill Byrd, DB, San Jose State
1984—Mossy Cade, DB, Texas
1985—Jim Lachey, G, Ohio State
1986—Leslie O'Neal, DE, Oklahoma State
　　　Jim FitzPatrick, T, Southern California
1987—Rod Bernstine, TE, Texas A&M
1988—Anthony Miller, WR, Tennessee
1989—Burt Grossman, DE, Pittsburgh
1990—Junior Seau, LB, Southern California
1991—Stanley Richard, DB, Texas
1992—Chris Mims, DT, Tennessee
1993—Darrien Gordon, DB, Stanford
1994—None
1995—None
1996—None
1997—None

HISTORY Team by team

FRANCHISE RECORDS

Most rushing yards, career
4,963—Paul Lowe

Most rushing yards, season
1,350—Natrone Means, 1994

Most rushing yards, game
217—Gary Anderson vs. K.C., Dec. 18, 1988

Most rushing touchdowns, season
19—Chuck Muncie, 1981

Most passing attempts, season
609—Dan Fouts, 1981

Most passing attempts, game
48—Mark Herrmann at K.C., Dec. 22, 1985

Most passes completed, season
360—Dan Fouts, 1981

Most passes completed, game
37—Dan Fouts vs. Mia., Nov. 18, 1984
　　　(OT)
　　　Mark Herrmann at K.C., Dec. 22, 1985

Most passing yards, career
43,040—Dan Fouts

Most passing yards, season
4,802—Dan Fouts, 1981

Most passing yards, game
444—Dan Fouts vs. NYG, Oct. 19, 1980
　　　Dan Fouts at S.F., Dec. 11, 1982

Most touchdown passes, season
33—Dan Fouts, 1981

Most pass receptions, career
586—Charlie Joiner

Most pass receptions, season
90—Tony Martin, 1995

Most pass receptions, game
15—Kellen Winslow at G.B., Oct. 7, 1984

Most receiving yards, career
9,585—Lance Alworth

Most receiving yards, season
1,602—Lance Alworth, 1965

Most receiving yards, game
260—Wes Chandler vs. Cin., Dec. 20, 1982

Most receiving touchdowns, season
14—Lance Alworth, 1965
　　　Tony Martin, 1996

Most touchdowns, career
83—Lance Alworth

Most field goals, season
34—John Carney, 1994

Longest field goal
54 yards—John Carney vs. Sea., Nov. 10, 1991

Most interceptions, career
42—Gill Byrd

Most interceptions, season
9—Charlie McNeil, 1961

Most sacks, career
105.5—Leslie O'Neal

Most sacks, season
17.5—Gary Johnson, 1980

SERIES RECORDS

San Diego vs.: Arizona 6-1; Atlanta 1-4; Buffalo 16-7-2; Carolina 0-0; Chicago 4-3; Cincinnati 14-8; Dallas 1-5; Denver 35-38-1; Detroit 3-3; Green Bay 1-5; Houston 18-13-1; Indianapolis 10-6; Jacksonville 0-0; Kansas City 35-37-1; Miami 10-6; Minnesota 4-3; New England 11-15-2; New Orleans 5-1; N.Y. Giants 3-4; N.Y. Jets 17-9-1; Oakland 28-41-2; Philadelphia 4-2; Pittsburgh 5-16; St. Louis 3-3; San Francisco 3-4; Seattle 20-16; Tampa Bay 6-1; Washington 0-5.
NOTE: Includes records as Los Angeles Chargers in 1960.

RETIRED UNIFORM NUMBERS

No.	Player
14	Dan Fouts

SAN FRANCISCO 49ERS
YEAR-BY-YEAR RECORDS

| | | | REGULAR SEASON | | | | | PLAYOFFS | | |
Year	W	L	T	Pct.	PF	PA	Finish	W	L	Highest round	Coach
46*	9	5	0	.643	307	189	2nd/Western Div.	—	—		Buck Shaw
47*	8	4	2	.667	327	264	2nd/Western Div.	—	—		Buck Shaw
48*	12	2	0	.857	495	248	2nd/Western Div.	—	—		Buck Shaw
49*	9	3	0	.750	416	227	2nd	—	—		Buck Shaw
50	3	9	0	.250	213	300	T5th/National Conf.	—	—		Buck Shaw

	REGULAR SEASON							PLAYOFFS			
Year	W	L	T	Pct.	PF	PA	Finish	W	L	Highest round	Coach
1951	7	4	1	.636	255	205	T2nd/National Conf.	—	—		Buck Shaw
1952	7	5	0	.583	285	221	3rd/National Conf.	—	—		Buck Shaw
1953	9	3	0	.750	372	237	2nd/Western Conf.	—	—		Buck Shaw
1954	7	4	1	.636	313	251	3rd/Western Conf.	—	—		Buck Shaw
1955	4	8	0	.333	216	298	5th/Western Conf.	—	—		Red Strader
1956	5	6	1	.455	233	284	3rd/Western Conf.	—	—		Frankie Albert
1957	8	4	0	.667	260	264	2nd/Western Conf.	0	1	W. Conf. champ. game	Frankie Albert
1958	6	6	0	.500	257	324	4th/Western Conf.	—	—		Frankie Albert
1959	7	5	0	.583	255	237	T3rd/Western Conf.	—	—		Red Hickey
1960	7	5	0	.583	208	205	T2nd/Western Conf.	—	—		Red Hickey
1961	7	6	1	.538	346	272	5th/Western Conf.	—	—		Red Hickey
1962	6	8	0	.429	282	331	5th/Western Conf.	—	—		Red Hickey
1963	2	12	0	.143	198	391	7th/Western Conf.	—	—		R. Hickey, J. Christiansen
1964	4	10	0	.286	236	330	7th/Western Conf.	—	—		Jack Christiansen
1965	7	6	1	.538	421	402	4th/Western Conf.	—	—		Jack Christiansen
1966	6	6	2	.500	320	325	4th/Western Conf.	—	—		Jack Christiansen
1967	7	7	0	.500	273	337	3rd/Coastal Div.	—	—		Jack Christiansen
1968	7	6	1	.538	303	310	3rd/Coastal Div.	—	—		Dick Nolan
1969	4	8	2	.333	277	319	4th/Coastal Div.	—	—		Dick Nolan
1970	10	3	1	.769	352	267	1st/NFC Western Div.	1	1	NFC championship game	Dick Nolan
1971	9	5	0	.643	300	216	1st/NFC Western Div.	1	1	NFC championship game	Dick Nolan
1972	8	5	1	.607	353	249	1st/NFC Western Div.	0	1	NFC div. playoff game	Dick Nolan
1973	5	9	0	.357	262	319	T3rd/NFC Western Div.	—	—		Dick Nolan
1974	6	8	0	.429	226	236	2nd/NFC Western Div.	—	—		Dick Nolan
1975	5	9	0	.357	255	286	2nd/NFC Western Div.	—	—		Dick Nolan
1976	8	6	0	.571	270	190	2nd/NFC Western Div.	—	—		Monte Clark
1977	5	9	0	.357	220	260	3rd/NFC Western Div.	—	—		Ken Meyer
1978	2	14	0	.125	219	350	4th/NFC Western Div.	—	—		Pete McCulley, Fred O'Connor
1979	2	14	0	.125	308	416	4th/NFC Western Div.	—	—		Bill Walsh
1980	6	10	0	.375	320	415	3rd/NFC Western Div.	—	—		Bill Walsh
1981	13	3	0	.813	357	250	1st/NFC Western Div.	3	0	Super Bowl champ	Bill Walsh
1982	3	6	0	.333	209	206	T11th/NFC	—	—		Bill Walsh
1983	10	6	0	.625	432	293	1st/NFC Western Div.	1	1	NFC championship game	Bill Walsh
1984	15	1	0	.938	475	227	1st/NFC Western Div.	3	0	Super Bowl champ	Bill Walsh
1985	10	6	0	.625	411	263	2nd/NFC Western Div.	0	1	NFC wild-card game	Bill Walsh
1986	10	5	1	.656	374	247	1st/NFC Western Div.	0	1	NFC div. playoff game	Bill Walsh
1987	13	2	0	.867	459	253	1st/NFC Western Div.	0	1	NFC div. playoff game	Bill Walsh
1988	10	6	0	.625	369	294	1st/NFC Western Div.	3	0	Super Bowl champ	Bill Walsh
1989	14	2	0	.875	442	253	1st/NFC Western Div.	3	0	Super Bowl champ	George Seifert
1990	14	2	0	.875	353	239	1st/NFC Western Div.	1	1	NFC championship game	George Seifert
1991	10	6	0	.625	393	239	3rd/NFC Western Div.	—	—		George Seifert
1992	14	2	0	.875	431	236	1st/NFC Western Div.	1	1	NFC championship game	George Seifert
1993	10	6	0	.625	473	295	1st/NFC Western Div.	1	1	NFC championship game	George Seifert
1994	13	3	0	.813	505	296	1st/NFC Western Div.	3	0	Super Bowl champ	George Seifert
1995	11	5	0	.688	457	258	1st/NFC Western Div.	0	1	NFC div. playoff game	George Seifert
1996	12	4	0	.750	398	257	2nd/NFC Western Div.	1	1	NFC div. playoff game	George Seifert

*All-America Football Conference.

FIRST-ROUND DRAFT PICKS

1950—Leo Nomellini, T, Minnesota
1951—Y.A. Tittle, QB, Louisiana State
1952—Hugh McElhenny, RB, Washington
1953—Harry Babcock, E, Georgia*
    Tom Stolhandske, E, Texas
1954—Bernie Faloney, QB, Maryland
1955—Dick Moegel, HB, Rice
1956—Earl Morrall QB, Michigan State
1957—John Brodie, QB, Stanford
1958—Jim Pace, RB, Michigan
    Charles Krueger, T, Texas A&M
1959—Dave Baker, RB, Oklahoma
    Dan James, C, Ohio State
1960—Monty Stickles, E, Notre Dame
1961—Jim Johnson, RB, UCLA
    Bernie Casey, RB, Bowling Green State
    Billy Kilmer, QB, UCLA
1962—Lance Alworth, RB, Arkansas
1963—Kermit Alexander, RB, UCLA
1964—Dave Parks, E, Texas Tech*

1965—Ken Willard, RB, North Carolina
    George Donnelly, DB, Illinois
1966—Stan Hindman, DE, Mississippi
1967—Steve Spurrier, QB, Florida
    Cas Banaszek, LB, Northwestern
1968—Forrest Blue, C, Auburn
1969—Ted Kwalick, TE, Penn State
    Gene Washington, WR, Stanford
1970—Cedrick Hardman, DE, North Texas State
    Bruce Taylor, DB, Boston University
1971—Tim Anderson, DB, Ohio State
1972—Terry Beasley, WR, Auburn
1973—Mike Holmes, DB, Tex. Southern
1974—Wilbur Jackson, RB, Alabama
    Bill Sandifer, DT, UCLA
1975—Jimmy Webb, DT, Mississippi State
1976—None
1977—None
1978—Ken McAfee, TE, Notre Dame
    Dan Bunz, LB, Long Beach State

1979—None
1980—Earl Cooper, RB, Rice
    Jim Stuckey, DE, Clemson
1981—Ronnie Lott, DB, Southern California
1982—None
1983—None
1984—Todd Shell, LB, Brigham Young
1985—Jerry Rice, WR, Mississippi Valley State
1986—None
1987—Harris Barton, T, North Carolina
    Terrence Flager, RB, Clemson
1988—None

1989—Keith DeLong, LB, Tennessee
1990—Dexter Carter, RB, Florida State
1991—Ted Washington, DL, Louisville
1992—Dana Hall, DB, Washington
1993—Dana Stubblefield, DT, Kansas
    Todd Kelly, DE, Tennessee
1994—Bryant Young, DT, Notre Dame
    William Floyd, RB, Florida State
1995—J.J. Stokes, WR, UCLA
1996—None
1997—Jim Druckenmiller, QB, Virginia Tech
*First player chosen in draft.

FRANCHISE RECORDS

Most rushing yards, career
7,344—Joe Perry
Most rushing yards, season
1,502—Roger Craig, 1988
Most rushing yards, game
194—Delvin Williams at St.L., Dec. 31, 1976
Most rushing touchdowns, season
10—Joe Perry, 1953
    J.D. Smith, 1959
    Billy Kilmer, 1961
    Ricky Watters, 1993
    Derek Loville, 1995
Most passing attempts, season
578—Steve DeBerg, 1979
Most passing attempts, game
60—Joe Montana at Was., Nov. 17, 1986
Most passes completed, season
347—Steve DeBerg, 1979
Most passes completed, game
37—Joe Montana at Atl., Nov. 6, 1985

Most passing yards, career
35,142—Joe Montana
Most passing yards, season
4,023—Steve Young, 1993
Most passing yards, game
476—Joe Montana at Atl., Oct. 14, 1990
Most touchdown passes, season
35—Steve Young, 1994
Most pass receptions, career
1,050—Jerry Rice
Most pass receptions, season
122—Jerry Rice, 1995
Most pass receptions, game
16—Jerry Rice at L.A. Rams, Nov. 20, 1994
Most receiving yards, career
16,377—Jerry Rice
Most receiving yards, season
1,848—Jerry Rice, 1995
Most receiving yards, game
289—Jerry Rice vs. Min., Dec. 18, 1995

Most receiving touchdowns, season
22—Jerry Rice, 1987
Most touchdowns, career
165—Jerry Rice
Most field goals, season
30—Jeff Wilkins, 1996
Longest field goal
56 yards—Mike Cofer at Atl., Oct. 14, 1990
Most interceptions, career
51—Ronnie Lott
Most interceptions, season
10—Dave Baker, 1960
    Ronnie Lott, 1986
Most sacks, career
111.5—Cedrick Hardman
Most sacks, season
18—Cedrick Hardman

SERIES RECORDS

an Francisco vs.: Arizona 10-9; Atlanta 37-22-1; Baltimore 1-0; Buffalo 3-3; Carolina 1-; Chicago 25-25-1; Cincinnati 7-1; Dallas 11-7-1; Denver 3-4; Detroit 28-26-1; Green ay 25-22-1; Houston 6-3; Indianapolis 16-22; Jacksonville 0-0; Kansas City 4-2; Miami -4; Minnesota 16-16-1; New England 7-1; New Orleans 38-15-2; N.Y. Giants 11-11; N.Y. ts 6-1; Oakland 3-5; Philadelphia 13-6-1; Pittsburgh 9-7; St. Louis 43-47-2; San Diego -3; Seattle 4-1; Tampa Bay 12-1; Washington 11-6-1.
OTE: Includes records only from 1950 to present.

RETIRED UNIFORM NUMBERS

No.	Player
12	John Brodie
34	Joe Perry
37	Jimmy Johnson
39	Hugh McElhenny
70	Charlie Krueger
73	Leo Nomellini
87	Dwight Clark

SEATTLE SEAHAWKS
YEAR-BY-YEAR RECORDS

				REGULAR SEASON					PLAYOFFS		
ar	W	L	T	Pct.	PF	PA	Finish	W	L	Highest round	Coach
76	2	12	0	.143	229	429	5th/NFC Western Div.	—	—		Jack Patera
77	5	9	0	.357	282	373	4th/AFC Western Div.	—	—		Jack Patera
78	9	7	0	.563	345	358	T2nd/AFC Western Div.	—	—		Jack Patera
79	9	7	0	.563	378	372	T3rd	—	—		Jack Patera
80	4	12	0	.250	291	408	5th/AFC Western Div.	—	—		Jack Patera
81	6	10	0	.375	322	388	5th/AFC Western Div.	—	—		Jack Patera
82	4	5	0	.444	127	147	T8th/AFC	—	—		J. Patera, Mike McCormack
83	9	7	0	.562	403	397	T2nd/AFC Western Div.	2	1	AFC championship game	Chuck Knox
84	12	4	0	.750	418	282	2nd/AFC Western Div.	1	1	AFC div. playoff game	Chuck Knox
85	8	8	0	.500	349	303	T3rd/AFC Western Div.	—	—		Chuck Knox
86	10	6	0	.625	366	293	T2nd/AFC Western Div.	—	—		Chuck Knox
87	9	6	0	.600	371	314	2nd/AFC Western Div.	0	1	AFC wild-card game	Chuck Knox
88	9	7	0	.563	339	329	1st/AFC Western Div.	0	1	AFC div. playoff game	Chuck Knox
89	7	9	0	.438	241	327	4th/AFC Western Div.	—	—		Chuck Knox
90	9	7	0	.563	306	286	3rd/AFC Western Div.	—	—		Chuck Knox
91	7	9	0	.438	276	261	4th/AFC Western Div.	—	—		Chuck Knox
92	2	14	0	.125	140	312	5th/AFC Western Div.	—	—		Tom Flores

		REGULAR SEASON						PLAYOFFS			
Year	W	L	T	Pct.	PF	PA	Finish	W	L	Highest round	Coach
1993	6	10	0	.375	280	314	5th/AFC Western Div.	—	—		Tom Flores
1994	6	10	0	.375	287	323	5th/AFC Western Div.	—	—		Tom Flores
1995	8	8	0	.500	363	366	T3rd/AFC Western Div.	—	—		Dennis Erickson
1996	7	9	0	.438	317	376	T4th/AFC Western Div.	—	—		Dennis Erickson

FIRST-ROUND DRAFT PICKS

1976—Steve Niehaus, DT, Notre Dame
1977—Steve August, G, Tulsa
1978—Keith Simpson, DB, Memphis State
1979—Manu Tuiasosopo, DT, UCLA
1980—Jacob Green, DE, Texas A&M
1981—Kenny Easley, DB, UCLA
1982—Jeff Bryant, DE, Clemson
1983—Curt Warner, RB, Penn State
1984—Terry Taylor, DB, Southern Illinois
1985—None
1986—John L. Williams, RB, Florida
1987—Tony Woods, LB, Pittsburgh

1988—None
1989—Andy Heck, T, Notre Dame
1990—Cortez Kennedy, DT, Miami (Fla.)
1991—Dan McGwire, QB, San Diego State
1992—Ray Roberts, T, Virginia
1993—Rick Mirer, QB, Notre Dame
1994—Sam Adams, DE, Texas A&M
1995—Joey Galloway, WR, Ohio State
1996—Pete Kendall, T, Boston College
1997—Shawn Springs, CB, Ohio State
　　　Walter Jones, T, Florida State

FRANCHISE RECORDS

Most rushing yards, career
6,705—Curt Warner
Most rushing yards, season
1,545—Chris Warren, 1994
Most rushing yards, game
207—Curt Warner vs. K.C., Nov. 27, 1983 (OT)
192—Curt Warner vs. Den., Dec. 20, 1986
Most rushing touchdowns, season
15—Chris Warren, 1995
Most passing attempts, season
532—Dave Krieg, 1985
Most passing attempts, game
51—Dave Krieg vs. Atl., Oct. 13, 1985
Most passes completed, season
286—Dave Krieg, 1989
Most passes completed, game
33—Dave Krieg vs. Atl., Oct. 13, 1985
Most passing yards, career
26,132—Dave Krieg

Most passing yards, season
3,671—Dave Krieg, 1984
Most passing yards, game
418—Dave Krieg vs. Den., Nov. 20, 1983
Most touchdown passes, season
32—Dave Krieg, 1984
Most pass receptions, career
819—Steve Largent
Most pass receptions, season
81—Brian Blades, 1994
Most pass receptions, game
15—Steve Largent vs. Det., Oct. 18, 1987
Most receiving yards, career
13,089—Steve Largent
Most receiving yards, season
1,287—Steve Largent, 1985
Most receiving yards, game
261—Steve Largent vs. Det., Oct. 18, 1987
Most receiving touchdowns, season
13—Daryl Turner, 1985

Most touchdowns, career
101—Steve Largent
Most field goals, season
28—Todd Peterson, 1996
Longest field goal
55 yards—John Kasay vs. K.C., Jan. 2, 1994
Most interceptions, career
50—Dave Brown
Most interceptions, season
10—John Harris, 1981
　　　Kenny Easley, 1984
Most sacks, career
116.0—Jacob Green
Most sacks, season
16.0—Jacob Green, 1983

SERIES RECORDS

Seattle vs.: Arizona 0-5; Atlanta 4-1; Buffalo 4-2; Carolina 0-0; Chicago 4-2; Cincinnati 7-7; Dallas 1-4; Denver 15-24; Detroit 4-3; Green Bay 3-4; Houston 5-4; Indianapolis 1-4; Jacksonville 1-1; Kansas City 12-24; Miami 2-4; Minnesota 4-2; New England 7-6; New Orleans 2-3; N.Y. Giants 3-5; N.Y. Jets 8-4; Oakland 17-21; Philadelphia 2-4; Pittsburgh 6-5; St. Louis 1-4; San Diego 16-20; San Francisco 1-4; Tampa Bay 4-0; Washington 3-5.

RETIRED UNIFORM NUMBERS

No.	Player
80	Steve Largent

TAMPA BAY BUCCANEERS
YEAR-BY-YEAR RECORDS

		REGULAR SEASON						PLAYOFFS			
Year	W	L	T	Pct.	PF	PA	Finish	W	L	Highest round	Coach
1976	0	14	0	.000	125	412	5th/AFC Western Div.	—	—		John McKay
1977	2	12	0	.143	103	223	5th/NFC Central Div.	—	—		John McKay
1978	5	11	0	.313	241	259	5th/NFC Central Div.	—	—		John McKay
1979	10	6	0	.625	273	237	1st/NFC Central Div.	1	1	NFC championship game	John McKay
1980	5	10	1	.344	271	341	T4th/NFC Central Div.	—	—		John McKay
1981	9	7	0	.563	315	268	1st/NFC Central Div.	0	1	NFC div. playoff game	John McKay
1982	5	4	0	.556	158	178	T4th/NFC	0	1	NFC first-round pl. game	John McKay
1983	2	14	0	.125	241	380	5th/NFC Central Div.	—	—		John McKay
1984	6	10	0	.375	335	380	3rd/NFC Central Div.	—	—		John McKay
1985	2	14	0	.125	294	448	5th/NFC Central Div.	—	—		Leeman Bennett

Year	W	L	T	Pct.	PF	PA	Finish	W	L	Highest round	Coach
				REGULAR SEASON						PLAYOFFS	
1986	2	14	0	.125	239	473	5th/NFC Central Div.	—	—		Leeman Bennett
1987	4	11	0	.267	286	360	T4th/NFC Central Div.	—	—		Ray Perkins
1988	5	11	0	.313	261	350	3rd/NFC Central Div.	—	—		Ray Perkins
1989	5	11	0	.313	320	419	5th/NFC Central Div.	—	—		Ray Perkins
1990	6	10	0	.375	264	367	T2nd/NFC Central Div.	—	—		R. Perkins, R. Williamson
1991	3	13	0	.188	199	365	5th/NFC Central Div.	—	—		Richard Williamson
1992	5	11	0	.313	267	365	T3rd/NFC Central Div.	—	—		Sam Wyche
1993	5	11	0	.313	237	376	5th/NFC Central Div.	—	—		Sam Wyche
1994	6	10	0	.375	251	351	5th/NFC Central Div.	—	—		Sam Wyche
1995	7	9	0	.438	238	335	5th/NFC Central Div.	—	—		Sam Wyche
1996	6	10	0	.375	221	293	4th/NFC Central Div.	—	—		Tony Dungy

FIRST-ROUND DRAFT PICKS

1976—Lee Roy Selmon, DE, Oklahoma*
1977—Ricky Bell, RB, Southern California*
1978—Doug Williams, QB, Grambling State
1979—None
1980—Ray Snell, T, Wisconsin
1981—Hugh Green, LB, Pittsburgh
1982—Sean Farrell, G, Penn State
1983—None
1984—None
1985—Ron Holmes, DE, Washington
1986—Bo Jackson, RB, Auburn*
　　　 Rod Jones, DB, Southern Methodist
1987—Vinny Testaverde, QB, Miami (Fla.)*
1988—Paul Gruber, T, Wisconsin

1989—Broderick Thomas, LB, Nebraska
1990—Keith McCants, LB, Alabama
1991—Charles McRae, T, Tennessee
1992—None
1993—Eric Curry, DE, Alabama
1994—Trent Dilfer, QB, Fresno State
1995—Warren Sapp, DT, Miami (Fla.)
　　　 Derrick Brooks, LB, Florida State
1996—Regan Upshaw, DE, California
　　　 Marcus Jones, DT, North Carolina
1997—Warrick Dunn, RB, Florida State
　　　 Reidel Anthony, WR, Florida
*First player chosen in draft.

FRANCHISE RECORDS

Most rushing yards, career
5,957—James Wilder
Most rushing yards, season
1,544—James Wilder, 1984
Most rushing yards, game
219—James Wilder at Min., Nov. 6, 1983
Most rushing touchdowns, season
13—James Wilder, 1984
Most passing attempts, season
521—Doug Williams, 1980
Most passing attempts, game
55—Doug Williams vs. Cle., Sept. 28, 1980
Most passes completed, season
308—Steve DeBerg, 1984
Most passes completed, game
40—Vinny Testaverde at Hou., Dec. 10, 1989
Most passing yards, career
14,820—Vinny Testaverde

Most passing yards, season
3,563—Doug Williams, 1981
Most passing yards, game
486—Doug Williams at Min., Nov. 16, 1980
Most touchdown passes, season
20—Doug Williams, 1980
　　　 Vinny Testaverde, 1989
Most pass receptions, career
430—James Wilder
Most pass receptions, season
86—Mark Carrier, 1989
Most pass receptions, game
13—James Wilder vs. Min., Sept. 15, 1985
Most receiving yards, career
5,018—Mark Carrier
Most receiving yards, season
1,422—Mark Carrier, 1989
Most receiving yards, game
212—Mark Carrier at N.O., Dec. 6, 1987

Most receiving touchdowns, season
9—Kevin House, 1981
　　　 Bruce Hill, 1988
　　　 Mark Carrier, 1989
Most touchdowns, career
46—James Wilder
Most field goals, season
25—Michael Husted, 1996
Longest field goal
57 yards—Michael Husted at L.A. Raiders, Dec. 19, 1993
Most interceptions, career
29—Cedric Brown
Most interceptions, season
9—Cedric Brown, 1981
Most sacks, career
78.5—Lee Roy Selmon
Most sacks, season
13—Lee Roy Selmon, 1977

SERIES RECORDS

Tampa Bay vs.: Arizona 6-7; Atlanta 6-8; Buffalo 4-2; Carolina 1-1; Chicago 9-29; Cincinnati 2-3; Dallas 0-6; Denver 1-3; Detroit 17-21; Green Bay 13-22-1; Houston 1-4; Indianapolis 3-5; Jacksonville 1-0; Kansas City 2-5; Miami 1-4; Minnesota 12-26; New England 0-3; New Orleans 5-12; N.Y. Giants 3-8; N.Y. Jets 1-5; Oakland 1-3; Philadelphia 5; Pittsburgh 0-4; St. Louis 3-8; San Diego 1-6; San Francisco 1-12; Seattle 0-4; Washington 4-4.

RETIRED UNIFORM NUMBERS

No.	Player
63	Lee Roy Selmon

WASHINGTON REDSKINS
YEAR-BY-YEAR RECORDS

Year	W	L	T	Pct.	PF	PA	Finish	W	L	Highest round	Coach
				REGULAR SEASON						PLAYOFFS	
1932*	4	4	2	.500	55	79	4th				Lud Wray
1933†	5	5	2	.500	103	97	3rd/Eastern Div.	—	—		Lone Star Dietz
1934†	6	6	0	.500	107	94	2nd/Eastern Div.	—	—		Lone Star Dietz

			REGULAR SEASON						PLAYOFFS	
Year	W	L	T	Pct.	PF	PA	Finish	W	L	Highest round	Coach
1935†	2	8	1	.200	65	123	4th/Eastern Div.	—	—		Eddie Casey
1936†	7	5	0	.583	149	110	1st/Eastern Div.	0	1	NFL championship game	Ray Flaherty
1937	8	3	0	.727	195	120	1st/Eastern Div.	1	0	NFL champ	Ray Flaherty
1938	6	3	2	.667	148	154	2nd/Eastern Div.	—	—		Ray Flaherty
1939	8	2	1	.800	242	94	2nd/Eastern Div.	—	—		Ray Flaherty
1940	9	2	0	.818	245	142	1st/Eastern Div.	0	1	NFL championship game	Ray Flaherty
1941	6	5	0	.545	176	174	3rd/Eastern Div.	—	—		Ray Flaherty
1942	10	1	0	.909	227	102	1st/Eastern Div.	1	0	NFL champ	Ray Flaherty
1943	6	3	1	.667	229	137	1st/Eastern Div.	1	1	NFL championship game	Dutch Bergman
1944	6	3	1	.667	169	180	3rd/Eastern Div.	—	—		Dudley DeGroot
1945	8	2	0	.800	209	121	1st/Eastern Div.	0	1	NFL championship game	Dudley DeGroot
1946	5	5	1	.500	171	191	T3rd/Eastern Div.	—	—		Turk Edwards
1947	4	8	0	.333	295	367	4th/Eastern Div.	—	—		Turk Edwards
1948	7	5	0	.583	291	287	2nd/Eastern Div.	—	—		Turk Edwards
1949	4	7	1	.364	268	339	4th/Eastern Div.	—	—		John Whelchel, Herman Ball
1950	3	9	0	.250	232	326	6th/American Conf.	—	—		Herman Ball
1951	5	7	0	.417	183	296	3rd/American Conf.	—	—		Herman Ball, Dick Todd
1952	4	8	0	.333	240	287	T5th/American Conf.	—	—		Curly Lambeau
1953	6	5	1	.545	208	215	3rd/Eastern Conf.	—	—		Curly Lambeau
1954	3	9	0	.250	207	432	5th/Eastern Conf.	—	—		Joe Kuharich
1955	8	4	0	.667	246	222	2nd/Eastern Conf.	—	—		Joe Kuharich
1956	6	6	0	.500	183	225	3rd/Eastern Conf.	—	—		Joe Kuharich
1957	5	6	1	.455	251	230	4th/Eastern Conf.	—	—		Joe Kuharich
1958	4	7	1	.364	214	268	4th/Eastern Conf.	—	—		Joe Kuharich
1959	3	9	0	.250	185	350	5th/Eastern Conf.	—	—		Mike Nixon
1960	1	9	2	.100	178	309	6th/Eastern Conf.	—	—		Mike Nixon
1961	1	12	1	.077	174	392	7th/Eastern Conf.	—	—		Bill McPeak
1962	5	7	2	.417	305	376	4th/Eastern Conf.	—	—		Bill McPeak
1963	3	11	0	.214	279	398	6th/Eastern Conf.	—	—		Bill McPeak
1964	6	8	0	.429	307	305	T3rd/Eastern Conf.	—	—		Bill McPeak
1965	6	8	0	.429	257	301	4th/Eastern Conf.	—	—		Bill McPeak
1966	7	7	0	.500	351	355	5th/Eastern Conf.	—	—		Otto Graham
1967	5	6	3	.455	347	353	3rd/Capitol Div.	—	—		Otto Graham
1968	5	9	0	.357	249	358	3rd/Capitol Div.	—	—		Otto Graham
1969	7	5	2	.583	307	319	2nd/Capitol Div.	—	—		Vince Lombardi
1970	6	8	0	.429	297	314	4th/NFC Eastern Div.	—	—		Bill Austin
1971	9	4	1	.692	276	190	2nd/NFC Eastern Div.	0	1	NFC div. playoff game	George Allen
1972	11	3	0	.786	336	218	1st/NFC Eastern Div.	2	1	Super Bowl	George Allen
1973	10	4	0	.714	325	198	2nd/NFC Eastern Div.	0	1	NFC div. playoff game	George Allen
1974	10	4	0	.714	320	196	2nd/NFC Eastern Div.	0	1	NFC div. playoff game	George Allen
1975	8	6	0	.571	325	276	3rd/NFC Eastern Div.	—	—		George Allen
1976	10	4	0	.714	291	217	2nd/NFC Eastern Div.	0	1	NFC div. playoff game	George Allen
1977	9	5	0	.643	196	189	2nd/NFC Eastern Div.	—	—		George Allen
1978	8	8	0	.500	273	283	3rd/NFC Eastern Div.	—	—		Jack Pardee
1979	10	6	0	.625	348	295	3rd/NFC Eastern Div.	—	—		Jack Pardee
1980	6	10	0	.375	261	293	3rd/NFC Eastern Div.	—	—		Jack Pardee
1981	8	8	0	.500	347	349	4th/NFC Eastern Div.	—	—		Joe Gibbs
1982	8	1	0	.889	190	128	1st/NFC	4	0	Super Bowl champ	Joe Gibbs
1983	14	2	0	.875	541	332	1st/NFC East	2	1	Super Bowl	Joe Gibbs
1984	11	5	0	.688	426	310	1st/NFC East	0	1	NFC div. playoff game	Joe Gibbs
1985	10	6	0	.625	297	312	3rd/NFC Eastern Div.	—	—		Joe Gibbs
1986	12	4	0	.750	368	296	2nd/NFC Eastern Div.	2	1	NFC championship game	Joe Gibbs
1987	11	4	0	.733	379	285	1st/NFC Eastern Div.	3	0	Super Bowl champ	Joe Gibbs
1988	7	9	0	.438	345	387	T3rd/NFC Eastern Div.	—	—		Joe Gibbs
1989	10	6	0	.625	386	308	3rd/NFC Eastern Div.	—	—		Joe Gibbs
1990	10	6	0	.625	381	301	T2nd/NFC Eastern Div.	1	1	NFC div. playoff game	Joe Gibbs
1991	14	2	0	.875	485	224	1st/NFC Eastern Div.	3	0	Super Bowl champ	Joe Gibbs
1992	9	7	0	.563	300	255	3rd/NFC Eastern Div.	1	1	NFC div. playoff game	Joe Gibbs
1993	4	12	0	.250	230	345	5th/NFC Eastern Div.	—	—		Richie Petitbon
1994	3	13	0	.188	320	412	5th/NFC Eastern Div.	—	—		Norv Turner
1995	6	10	0	.375	326	359	3rd/NFC Eastern Div.	—	—		Norv Turner
1996	9	7	0	.563	364	312	3rd/NFC Eastern Div.	—	—		Norv Turner

*Boston Braves.
†Boston Redskins.

FIRST-ROUND DRAFT PICKS

1936—Riley Smith, QB, Alabama
1937—Sammy Baugh, QB, Texas Christian
1938—Andy Farkas, B, Detroit
1939—I.B. Hale, T, Texas Christian
1940—Ed Boell, B, New York University
1941—Forrest Evashevski, B, Michigan

2—Orban Sanders, B, Texas
3—Jack Jenkins, B, Missouri
4—Mike Micka, B, Colgate
5—Jim Hardy, B, Southern California
6—Cal Rossi, B, UCLA
7—Cal Rossi, B, UCLA
8—Harry Gilmer, QB, Alabama*
9—Rob Goode, RB, Texas A&M
0—George Thomas, RB, Oklahoma
1—Leon Heath, RB, Oklahoma
2—Larry Isbell, QB, Baylor
3—Jack Scarbath, QB, Maryland
4—Steve Meilinger, TE, Kentucky
5—Ralph Guglielmi, QB, Notre Dame
6—Ed Vereb, RB, Maryland
7—Don Bosseler, RB, Miami (Fla.)
8—None
9—Don Allard, QB, Boston College
0—Richie Lucas, QB, Penn State
1—Joe Rutgens, T, Illinois
  Norm Snead, QB, Wake Forest
2—Ernie Davis, RB, Syracuse*
  Leroy Jackson, RB, Illinois Central
3—Pat Richter, TE, Wisconsin
4—Charley Taylor, RB, Arizona State
5—None
6—Charlie Gogolak, K, Princeton
7—Ray McDonald, RB, Idaho
8—Jim Smith, DB, Oregon
9—None

1970—None
1971—None
1972—None
1973—None
1974—None
1975—None
1976—None
1977—None
1978—None
1979—None
1980—Art Monk, WR, Syracuse
1981—Mark May, T, Pittsburgh
1982—None
1983—Darrell Green, DB, Texas A&I
1984—None
1985—None
1986—None
1987—None
1988—None
1989—None
1990—None
1991—Bobby Wilson, DT, Michigan State
1992—Desmond Howard, WR, Michigan
1993—Tom Carter, DB, Notre Dame
1994—Heath Shuler, QB, Tennessee
1995—Michael Westbrook, WR, Colorado
1996—Andre Johnson, T, Penn State
1997—Kenard Lang, DE, Miami (Fla.)
*First player chosen in draft.

FRANCHISE RECORDS

t rushing yards, career
2—John Riggins

t rushing yards, season
3—Terry Allen, 1996

t rushing yards, game
—Gerald Riggs vs. Phi., Sept. 17, 1989

t rushing touchdowns, season
-John Riggins, 1983

t passing attempts, season
—Jay Schroeder, 1986

t passing attempts, game
-Jay Schroeder vs. S.F., Dec. 1, 1985

t passes completed, season
—Joe Theismann, 1981

t passes completed, game
-Sonny Jurgensen at Cle., Nov. 26, 1967
John Friesz at NYG, Sept. 18, 1994

t passing yards, career
06—Joe Theismann

Most passing yards, season
4,109—Jay Schroeder, 1986

Most passing yards, game
446—Sammy Baugh vs. N.Y. Yanks, Oct. 31, 1948

Most touchdown passes, season
31—Sonny Jurgensen, 1967

Most pass receptions, career
888—Art Monk

Most pass receptions, season
106—Art Monk, 1984

Most pass receptions, game
13—Art Monk vs. Cin., Dec. 15, 1985
Kelvin Bryant vs. NYG, Dec. 7, 1986
Art Monk at Det., Nov. 4, 1990

Most receiving yards, career
13,026—Art Monk

Most receiving yards, season
1,436—Bobby Mitchell, 1963

Most receiving yards, game
255—Anthony Allen vs. St.L., Oct. 4, 1987

Most receiving touchdowns, season
12—Hugh Taylor, 1952
Charley Taylor, 1966
Jerry Smith, 1967
Ricky Sanders, 1988

Most touchdowns, career
90—Charley Taylor

Most field goals, season
33—Mark Moseley, 1983

Longest field goal
57 yards—Steve Cox vs. Sea., Sept. 28, 1986

Most interceptions, career
43—Darrell Green

Most interceptions, season
13—Dan Sandifer, 1948

Most sacks, career
97.5—Dexter Manley

Most sacks, season
18.0—Dexter Manley, 1986

SERIES RECORDS

hington vs.: Arizona 59-39-1; Atlanta 13-4-1; Buffalo 4-4; Carolina 1-0; Chicago 12-
Cincinnati 4-2; Dallas 30-40-2; Denver 3-4; Detroit 23-3; Green Bay 11-9; Houston
Indianapolis 9-16; Jacksonville 0-0; Kansas City 1-4; Miami 2-5; Minnesota 6-4;
England 5-1; New Orleans 12-5; N.Y. Giants 50-66-2; N.Y. Jets 5-1; Oakland 2-6;
delphia 63-53-6; Pittsburgh 39-24-4; St. Louis 16-6-1; San Diego 5-0; San
cisco 6-11-1; Seattle 5-3; Tampa Bay 4-4.
E: Includes records only from 1937 to present.

RETIRED UNIFORM NUMBERS

No.	Player
33	Sammy Baugh